PHILIP'S

STREET ATLAS Somerset

Bath, Bridgwater, Frome, Taunton, Weston-super-Mare, Yeovil

www.philips-maps.co.uk

First published in 2002 by Philip's
a division of Octopus Publishing Group Ltd
www.octopusbooks.co.uk
Carmelite House
50 Victoria Embankment
London EC4Y 0DZ
An Hachette UK Company
www.hachette.co.uk

Third edition 2012
Third impression 2015

SOMCA

ISBN 978-1-84907-247-2 (spiral)

Printed in China

Contents

III **Key to map symbols**

IV **Key to map pages**

VI **Route planning**

X Major administrative and Postcode boundaries

1 **Street maps** at 3½ inches to 1 mile

122 **Street maps** at 1¾ inches to 1 mile

200 **Street maps** at 3½ inches to 1 mile

226 **Street maps** of Bristol and Bath city centres at 7 inches to 1 mile

229 **Index** of towns, villages, streets, hospitals, industrial estates, railway stations, schools, shopping centres, universities and places of interest

Key to map symbols

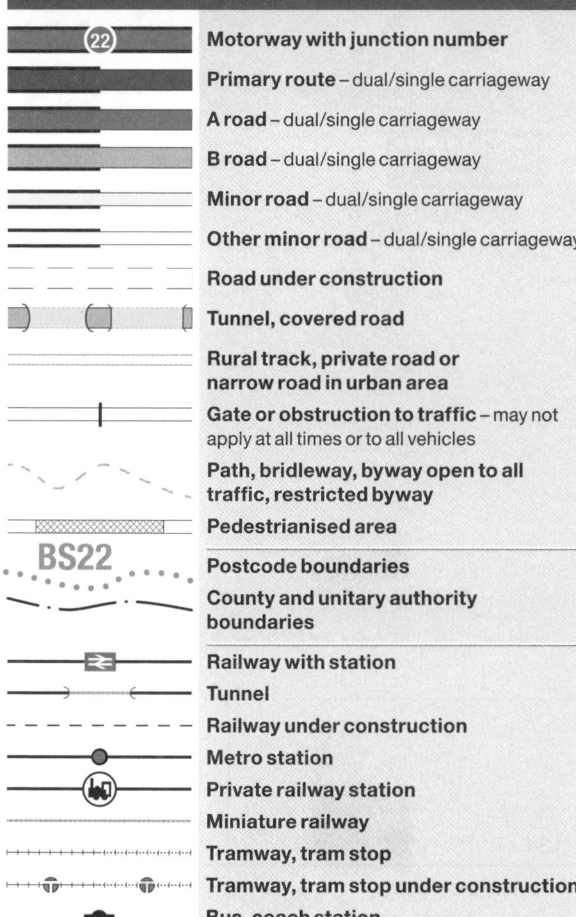

- Motorway with junction number
- **Primary route** – dual/single carriageway
- **A road** – dual/single carriageway
- **B road** – dual/single carriageway
- **Minor road** – dual/single carriageway
- **Other minor road** – dual/single carriageway
- **Road under construction**
- **Tunnel, covered road**
- **Rural track, private road or narrow road in urban area**
- **Gate or obstruction to traffic** – may not apply at all times or to all vehicles
- **Path, bridleway, byway open to all traffic, restricted byway**
- **Pedestrianised area**
- **Postcode boundaries**
- **County and unitary authority boundaries**
- **Railway with station**
- **Tunnel**
- **Railway under construction**
- **Metro station**
- **Private railway station**
- **Miniature railway**
- **Tramway, tram stop**
- **Tramway, tram stop under construction**
- **Bus, coach station**

- **Ambulance station**
- **Coastguard station**
- **Fire station**
- **Police station**
- **Accident and Emergency entrance to hospital**
- **Hospital**
- **Place of worship**
- **Information centre** – open all year
- **Shopping centre, parking**
- P&R PO **Park and Ride, Post Office**
- **Camping site, caravan site**
- **Golf course, picnic site**
- Church ROMAN FORT **Non-Roman antiquity, Roman antiquity**
- Univ **Important buildings, schools, colleges, universities and hospitals**
- **Woods, built-up area**
- River Medway **Water name**
- **River, weir**
- **Stream**
- **Canal, lock, tunnel**
- **Water**
- **Tidal water**
- 58 87 246 **Adjoining page indicators and overlap bands** – the colour of the arrow and band indicates the scale of the adjoining or overlapping page (see scales below)

The dark grey border on the inside edge of some pages indicates that the mapping does not continue onto the adjacent page

The small numbers around the edges of the maps identify the 1-kilometre National Grid lines

Enlarged maps only

- **Railway or bus station building**
- **Place of interest**
- **Parkland**

Acad	**Academy**	Meml	**Memorial**
Allot Gdns	**Allotments**	Mon	**Monument**
Cemy	**Cemetery**	Mus	**Museum**
C Ctr	**Civic centre**	Obsy	**Observatory**
CH	**Club house**	Pal	**Royal palace**
Coll	**College**	PH	**Public house**
Crem	**Crematorium**	Recn Gd	**Recreation ground**
Ent	**Enterprise**	Resr	**Reservoir**
Ex H	**Exhibition hall**	Ret Pk	**Retail park**
Ind Est	**Industrial Estate**	Sch	**School**
IRB Sta	**Inshore rescue boat station**	Sh Ctr	**Shopping centre**
Inst	**Institute**	TH	**Town hall / house**
Ct	**Law court**	Trad Est	**Trading estate**
L Ctr	**Leisure centre**	Univ	**University**
LC	**Level crossing**	W Twr	**Water tower**
Liby	**Library**	Wks	**Works**
Mkt	**Market**	YH	**Youth hostel**

The map scale on the pages numbered in green is 1¾ inches to 1 mile
2.76 cm to 1 km • 1:36206

0 ½ mile 1 mile 1½ miles **2 miles**
0 500m 1 km 1½ km **2km**

The map scale on the pages numbered in blue is 3½ inches to 1 mile
5.52 cm to 1 km • 1:18103

0 ¼ mile ½ mile ¾ mile **1 mile**
0 250m 500m 750m **1km**

The map scale on the pages numbered in red is 7 inches to 1 mile
11.04 cm to 1 km • 1:9051

0 220yds 440yds 660yds **½ mile**
0 125m 250m 375m **500m**

Key to map pages

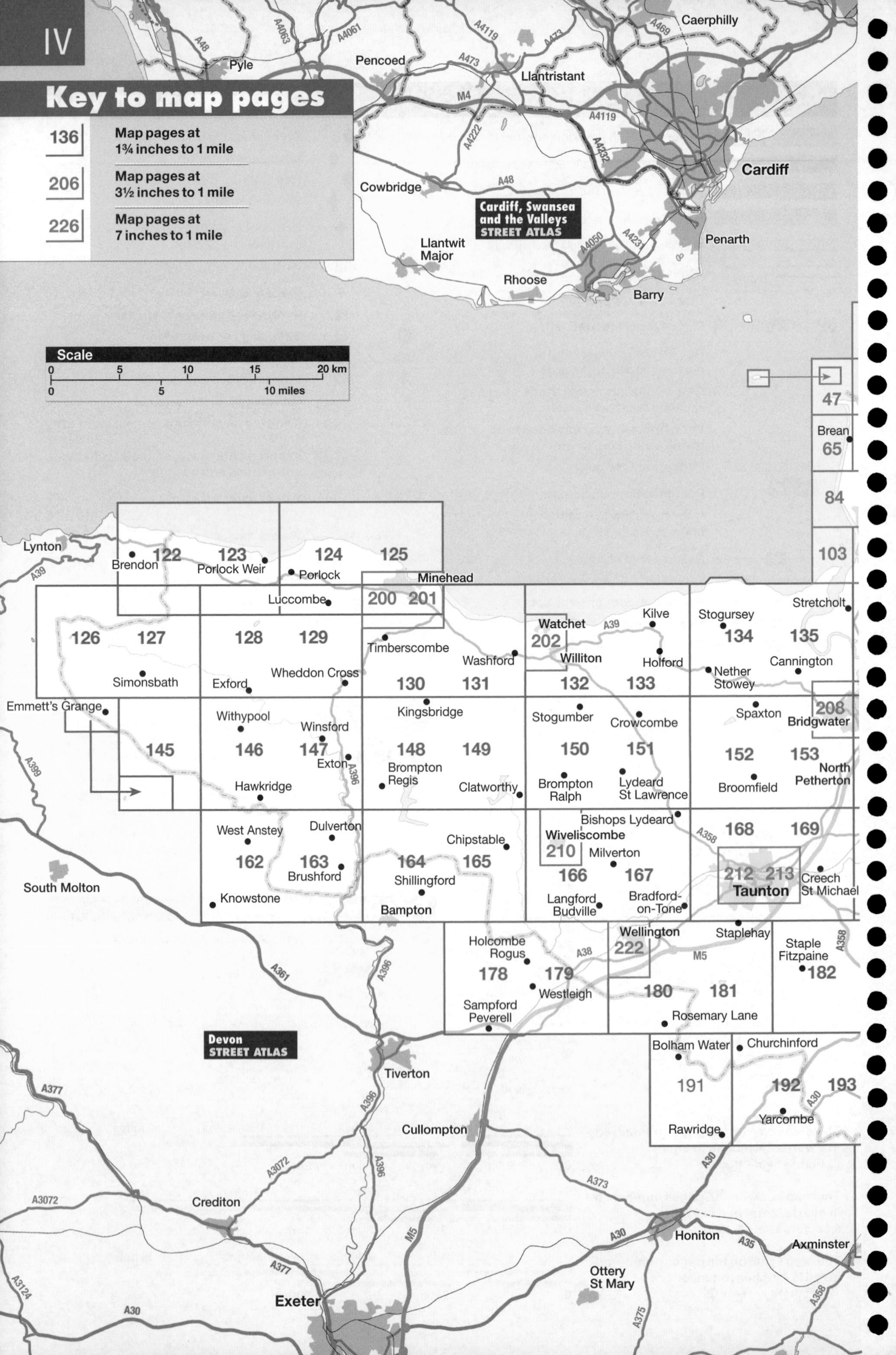

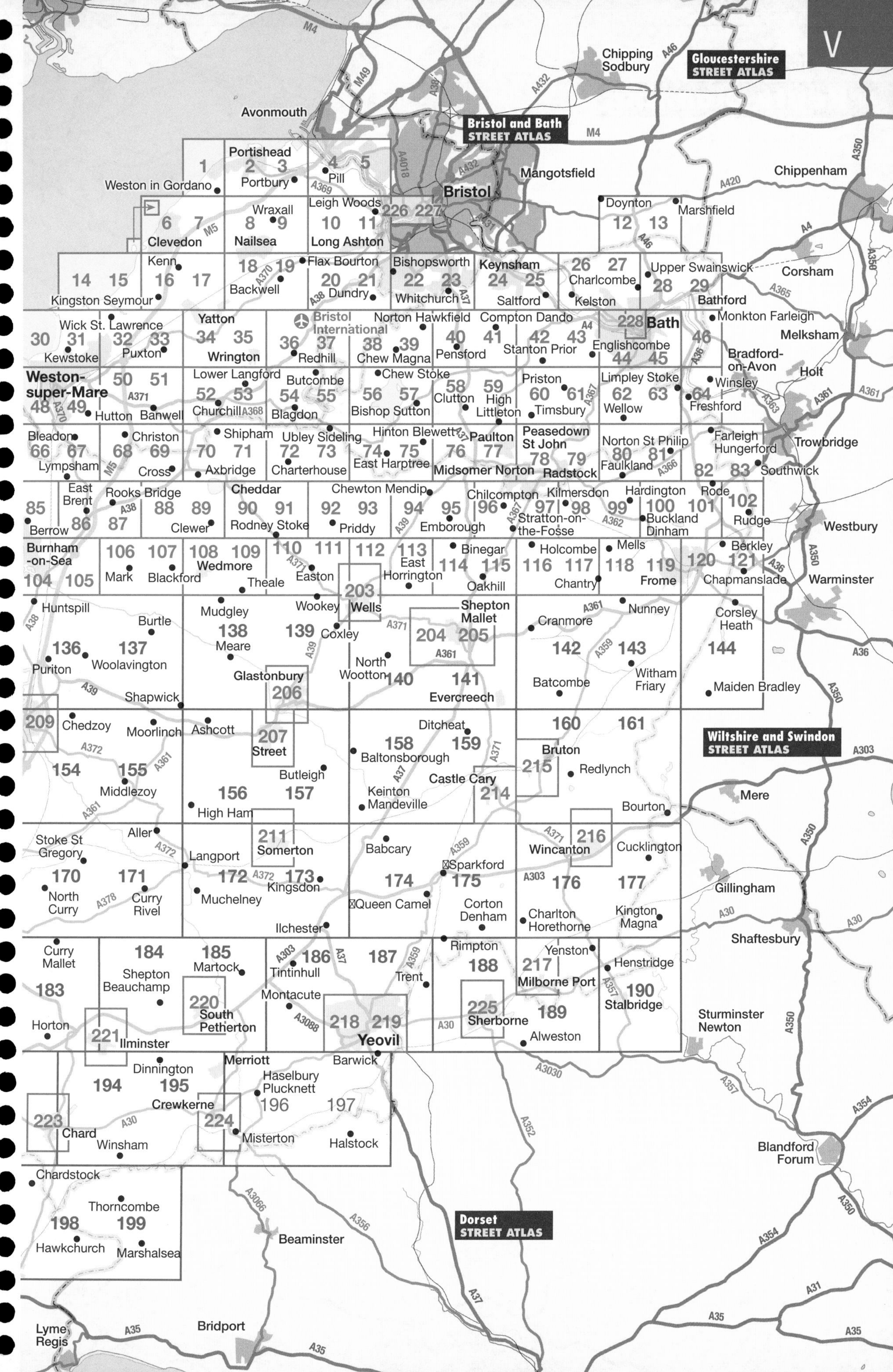
Chipping Sodbury
Gloucestershire STREET ATLAS
Avonmouth
Bristol and Bath STREET ATLAS
M4
Mangotsfield
Chippenham
Portishead
1
2 3
4 5
Weston in Gordano
Portbury
Pill
Bristol
6 7
Clevedon
8 9
Wraxall
Nailsea
Leigh Woods
10 11
Long Ashton
226 227
Doynton
12 13
Marshfield
Corsham
14 15
Kingston Seymour
Kenn
16 17
18 19
Backwell
Flax Bourton
20 21
Dundry
Bishopsworth
22 23
Whitchurch
Keynsham
24 25
Saltford
26 27
Charlcombe
Kelston
Upper Swainswick
28 29
Bathford
Wick St. Lawrence
30 31
Kewstoke
32 33
Puxton
Yatton
34 35
Wrington
Bristol International
36 37
Redhill
Norton Hawkfield
38 39
Chew Magna
40 41
Pensford
Compton Dando
42 43
Stanton Prior
228 Bath
Englishcombe
44 45
46
Monkton Farleigh
Melksham
Bradford-on-Avon
Holt
Weston-super-Mare
48 49
50 51
Hutton
Banwell
Lower Langford
52 53
Churchill
Butcombe
54 55
Blagdon
Chew Stoke
56 57
Bishop Sutton
58 59
Clutton
High Littleton
Priston
60 61
Timsbury
Limpley Stoke
62 63
Wellow
64
Freshford
Winsley
Trowbridge
Bleadon
66 67
Lympsham
Christon
68 69
Cross
Shipham
70 71
Axbridge
Ubley Sideling
72 73
Charterhouse
Hinton Blewett
74 75
East Harptree
Paulton
76 77
Midsomer Norton
Peasedown St John
78 79
Radstock
Norton St Philip
80 81
Faulkland
Farleigh Hungerford
82 83
Southwick
85
Berrow
East Brent
86 87
Rooks Bridge
88 89
Clewer
Cheddar
90 91
Rodney Stoke
Chewton Mendip
92 93
Priddy
94 95
Emborough
Chilcompton
96
97 98
Stratton-on-the-Fosse
Kilmersdon
99
Hardington
100 101
Buckland Dinham
Rode
102
Rudge
Westbury
Burnham-on-Sea
104 105
106 107
Mark
Blackford
108 109
Wedmore
Theale
110 111
Easton
112
113
East Horrington
203
Wells
Binegar
114 115
Oakhill
Holcombe
116 117
Chantry
Mells
118 119
Frome
120 121
Berkley
Chapmanslade
Warminster
Huntspill
Burtle
136
Puriton
137
Woolavington
Mudgley
138
Meare
Wookey
139
Coxley
North Wootton
140
Shepton Mallet
204 205
141
Evercreech
Cranmore
142
Batcombe
Nunney
143
Witham Friary
Corsley Heath
144
Maiden Bradley
Glastonbury
206
Shapwick
209
Chedzoy
Moorlinch
Ashcott
207
Street
Ditcheat
158 159
Baltonsborough
Castle Cary
214
Keinton Mandeville
160 161
Bruton
215
Redlynch
Bourton
Wiltshire and Swindon STREET ATLAS
154
155
Middlezoy
156
High Ham
Butleigh
157
Mere
Stoke St Gregory
Aller
170
North Curry
171
Curry Rivel
Langport
211
Somerton
172 173
Kingsdon
Muchelney
Babcary
174
Sparkford
175
Queen Camel
Corton Denham
216
Wincanton
176
Charlton Horethorne
Cucklington
177
Kington Magna
Gillingham
Shaftesbury
Ilchester
Curry Mallet
183
Horton
184
Shepton Beauchamp
185
Martock
220
South Petherton
221
Ilminster
186
Tintinhull
Montacute
187
Trent
218 219
Yeovil
Rimpton
188
225
Sherborne
Yenston
217
Milborne Port
189
Alweston
Henstridge
190
Stalbridge
Sturminster Newton
Dinnington
194 195
Crewkerne
Merriott
Haselbury Plucknett
196 197
Barwick
223
Chard
Winsham
224
Misterton
Halstock
Blandford Forum
Chardstock
Thorncombe
198 199
Hawkchurch
Marshalsea
Beaminster
Dorset STREET ATLAS
Lyme Regis
Bridport
M4
M49
M5
A38
A37
A39
A303
A30
A35
A350
A361
A36
A4
A46
A420
A432
A4018
A369
A371
A372
A378
A359
A3088
A3066
A356
A352
A357
A354
A3030
A365
A363
A366
A362
A367
A368
A370
A31

Route planning

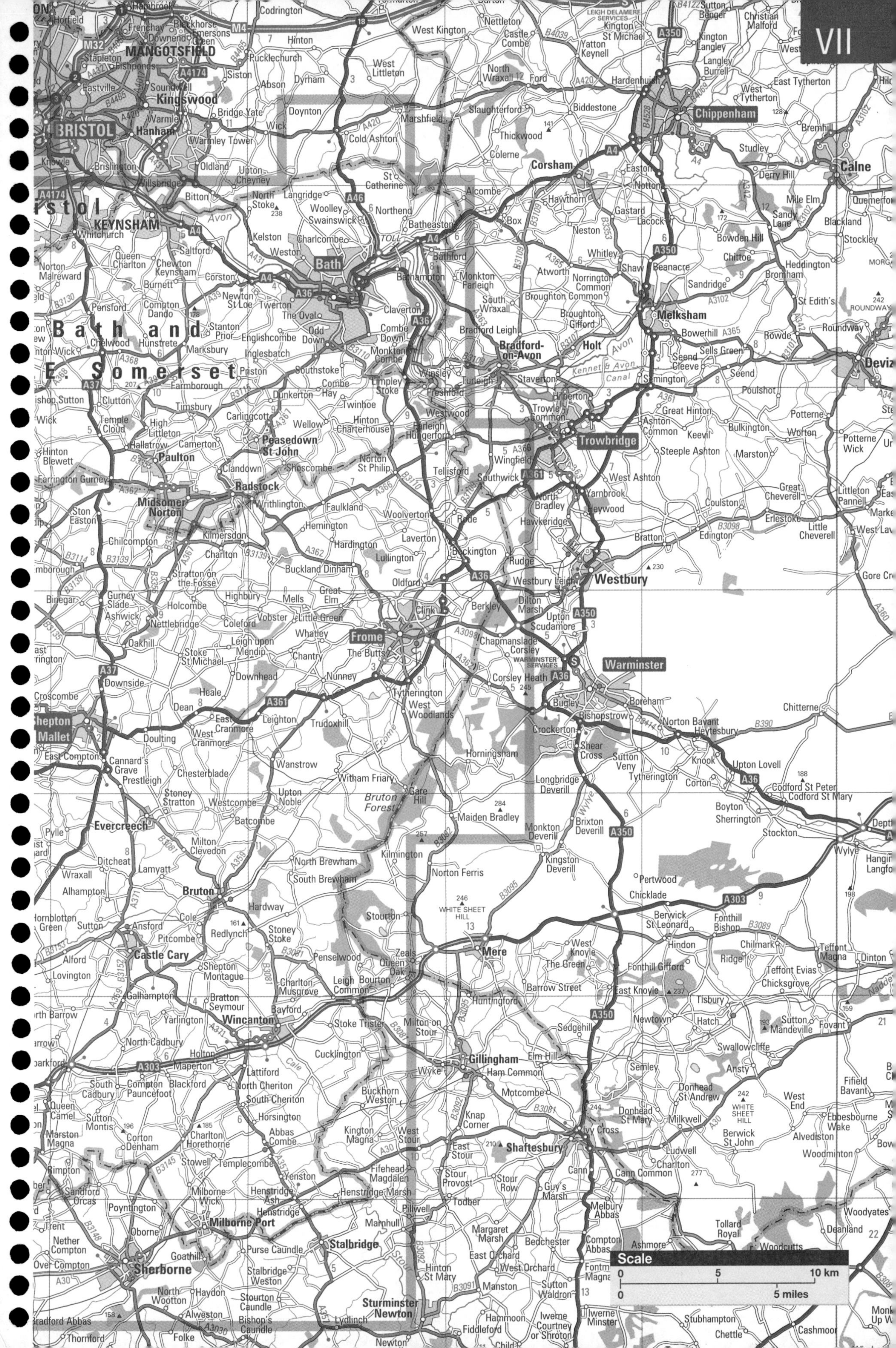
BRISTOL
MANGOTSFIELD
Kingswood
Hanham
KEYNSHAM
Bristol
Bath and
E. Somerset
Bath
Chippenham
Calne
Corsham
Melksham
Bradford-on-Avon
Trowbridge
Westbury
Warminster
Frome
Radstock
Midsomer Norton
Paulton
Peasedown St John
Shepton Mallet
Evercreech
Bruton
Castle Cary
Wincanton
Mere
Gillingham
Shaftesbury
Sherborne
Milborne Port
Stalbridge
Sturminster Newton
Devizes
Holt
Keevil
Heytesbury
Bruton Forest
Kennet & Avon Canal
Avon
Frome
Stour
M4
M32
A4
A36
A46
A37
A303
A350
A361
A362
A30
LEIGH DELAMERE SERVICES
WARMINSTER SERVICES
WHITE SHEET HILL
Scale
0
5
10 km
5 miles

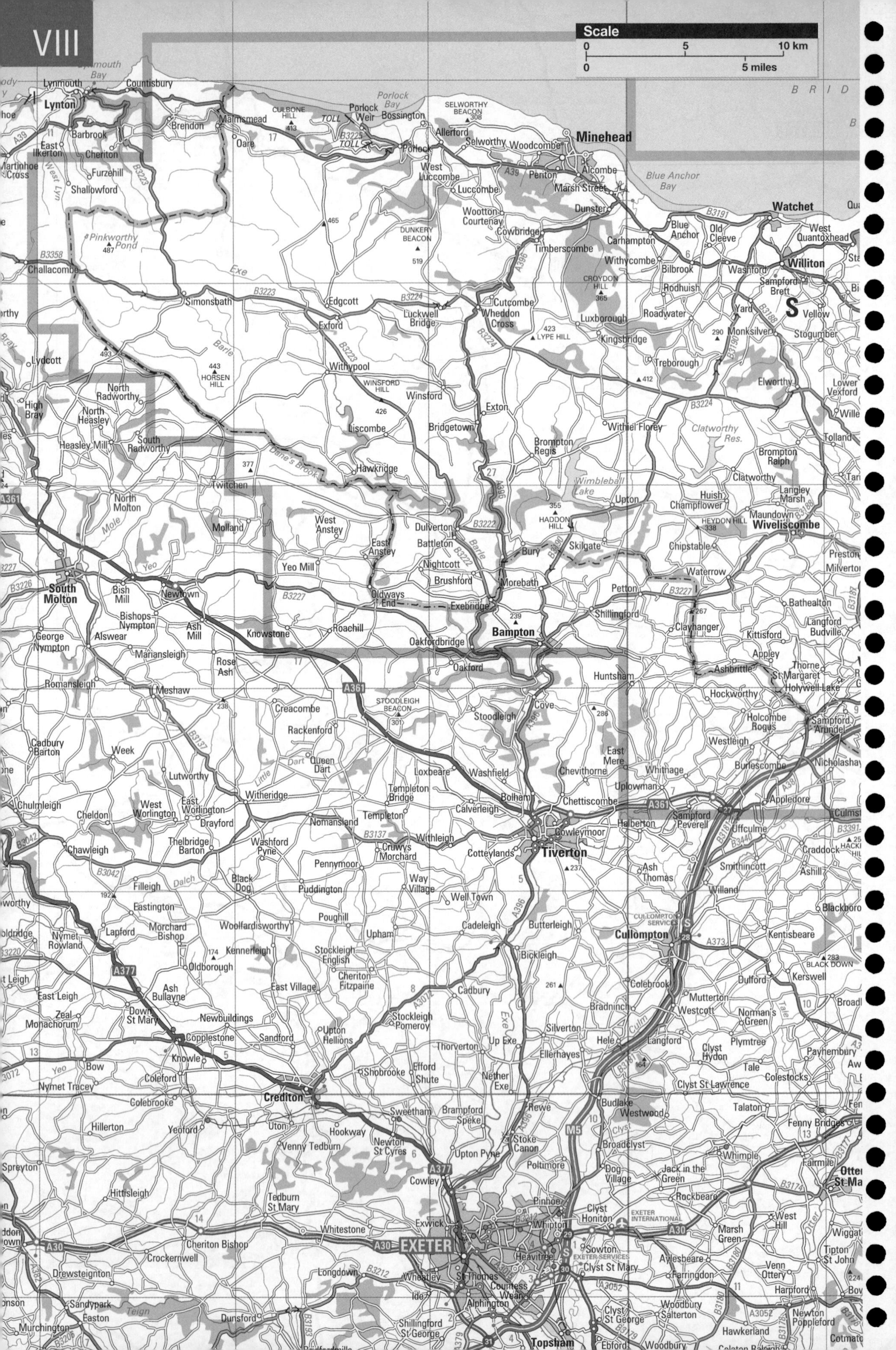

Scale
0
5
10 km
0
5 miles
Lynmouth Bay
Lynmouth
Countisbury
Lynton
Barbrook
East Ilkerton
Cheriton
Furzehill
Shallowford
Martinhoe Cross
West Lyn
Brendon
Malmsmead
Oare
CULBONE HILL
413
TOLL
Porlock Weir
Porlock Bay
Bossington
Porlock
SELWORTHY BEACON
308
Allerford
Selworthy
Woodcombe
Minehead
West Luccombe
Luccombe
Periton
Alcombe
Marsh Street
Dunster
Blue Anchor Bay
Watchet
West Quantoxhead
Wootton Courtenay
Cowbridge
Timberscombe
Carhampton
Blue Anchor
Old Cleeve
Withycombe
Bilbrook
Washford
Williton
Rodhuish
Sampford Brett
DUNKERY BEACON
519
465
CROYDON HILL
365
Pinkworthy Pond
487
B3358
Challacombe
Exe
Simonsbath
B3223
Edgcott
B3224
Exford
Luckwell Bridge
Cutcombe
Wheddon Cross
Luxborough
Roadwater
Yard
Vellow
Monksilver
Stogumber
423
LYPE HILL
Kingsbridge
Treborough
290
B3190
B3188
Lydcott
493
Barle
443
HORSEN HILL
Withypool
WINSFORD HILL
426
Winsford
Exton
412
Elworthy
Lower Vexford
High Bray
North Radworthy
North Heasley
Heasley Mill
South Radworthy
Liscombe
Bridgetown
Withiel Florey
Clatworthy Res.
Brompton Regis
Brompton Ralph
Tolland
Hawkridge
377
Dane's Brook
Twitchen
Wimbleball Lake
Clatworthy
Langley Marsh
Huish Champflower
Maundown
HEYDON HILL
338
Wiveliscombe
Upton
355
HADDON HILL
A361
North Molton
Molland
Mole
West Anstey
East Anstey
Dulverton
Battleton
B3222
Bury
Skilgate
Chipstable
Preston
Milverton
South Molton
Bish Mill
Newtown
Yeo
Yeo Mill
Nightcott
Brushford
Morebath
Waterrow
Petton
B3227
B3226
Oldways End
Exebridge
Shillingford
Bathealton
Langford Budville
239
Bampton
267
Clayhanger
Kittisford
Bishops Nympton
George Nympton
Alswear
Ash Mill
Knowstone
Roachill
Oakfordbridge
Mariansleigh
Rose Ash
Oakford
Huntsham
Appley
Ashbrittle
Thorne St Margaret
Holywell Lake
Romansleigh
Meshaw
238
Creacombe
STOODLEIGH BEACON
301
Stoodleigh
Cove
A396
286
Hockworthy
Holcombe Rogus
Sampford Arundel
Rackenford
Westleigh
Cadbury Barton
Week
B3137
Dart
Queen Dart
Loxbeare
Washfield
East Mere
Burlescombe
Nicholashayne
Lutworthy
Little Dart
Templeton Bridge
Chevithorne
Whitnage
Uplowman
Chulmleigh
West Worlington
East Worlington
Witheridge
Bolham
Chettiscombe
Appledore
Cheldon
Drayford
Nomansland
Templeton
Calverleigh
Sampford Peverell
Halberton
Culmstock
Thelbridge Barton
Washford Pyne
Cruwys Morchard
Withleigh
Cowleymoor
Uffculme
B3391
Chawleigh
B3042
Pennymoor
Cotteylands
Tiverton
237
B3440
Craddock
Ash Thomas
Smithincott
Ashill
Filleigh
Dalch
Black Dog
Puddington
Way Village
Willand
192
Eastington
Well Town
Blackborough
Nymet Rowland
Lapford
Morchard Bishop
Woolfardisworthy
Poughill
Upham
Cadeleigh
Butterleigh
CULLOMPTON SERVICES
Cullompton
A373
Kentisbeare
174
Kennerleigh
Stockleigh English
Bickleigh
283
BLACK DOWN
A377
Oldborough
Cheriton Fitzpaine
Kerswell
East Leigh
Ash Bullayne
East Village
Cadbury
261
Colebrook
Dulford
Zeal Monachorum
Down St Mary
Newbuildings
Stockleigh Pomeroy
Bradninch
Mutterton
Westcott
Norman's Green
Broadhembury
Copplestone
Sandford
Upton Hellions
Silverton
Culm
Langford
Plymtree
Knowle
Thorverton
Up Exe
Hele
Clyst Hydon
Payhembury
Bow
Coleford
Shobrooke
Efford
Shute
Ellerhayes
164
Tale
Colestocks
Nymet Tracey
Nether Exe
Clyst St Lawrence
Crediton
Colebrooke
Rewe
Budlake
Westwood
Talaton
Hillerton
Yeoford
Uton
Sweetham
Brampford Speke
Fenny Bridges
Hookway
Newton St Cyres
Stoke Canon
M5
Clyst
Broadclyst
Whimple
Spreyton
Venny Tedburn
Upton Pyne
Poltimore
Fairmile
Ottery St Mary
Cowley
Dog Village
Jack in the Green
Hittisleigh
Tedburn St Mary
Pinhoe
Rockbeare
Clyst Honiton
EXETER INTERNATIONAL
West Hill
Exwick
Whipton
Whitestone
A30
EXETER
Marsh Green
Wiggaton
Cheriton Bishop
Heavitree
Sowton
EXETER SERVICES
Clyst St Mary
Aylesbeare
Tipton St John
Crockernwell
Drewsteignton
Longdown
B3212
Wheatley
St Thomas
Countess Wear
A3052
Farringdon
Venn Ottery
B3180
Ide
Alphington
Harpford
Sandypark
Easton
Teign
Dunsford
Clyst St George
Woodbury Salterton
Newton Poppleford
Murchington
Shillingford St George
Topsham
Hawkerland
Ebford
Woodbury
Cotmaton

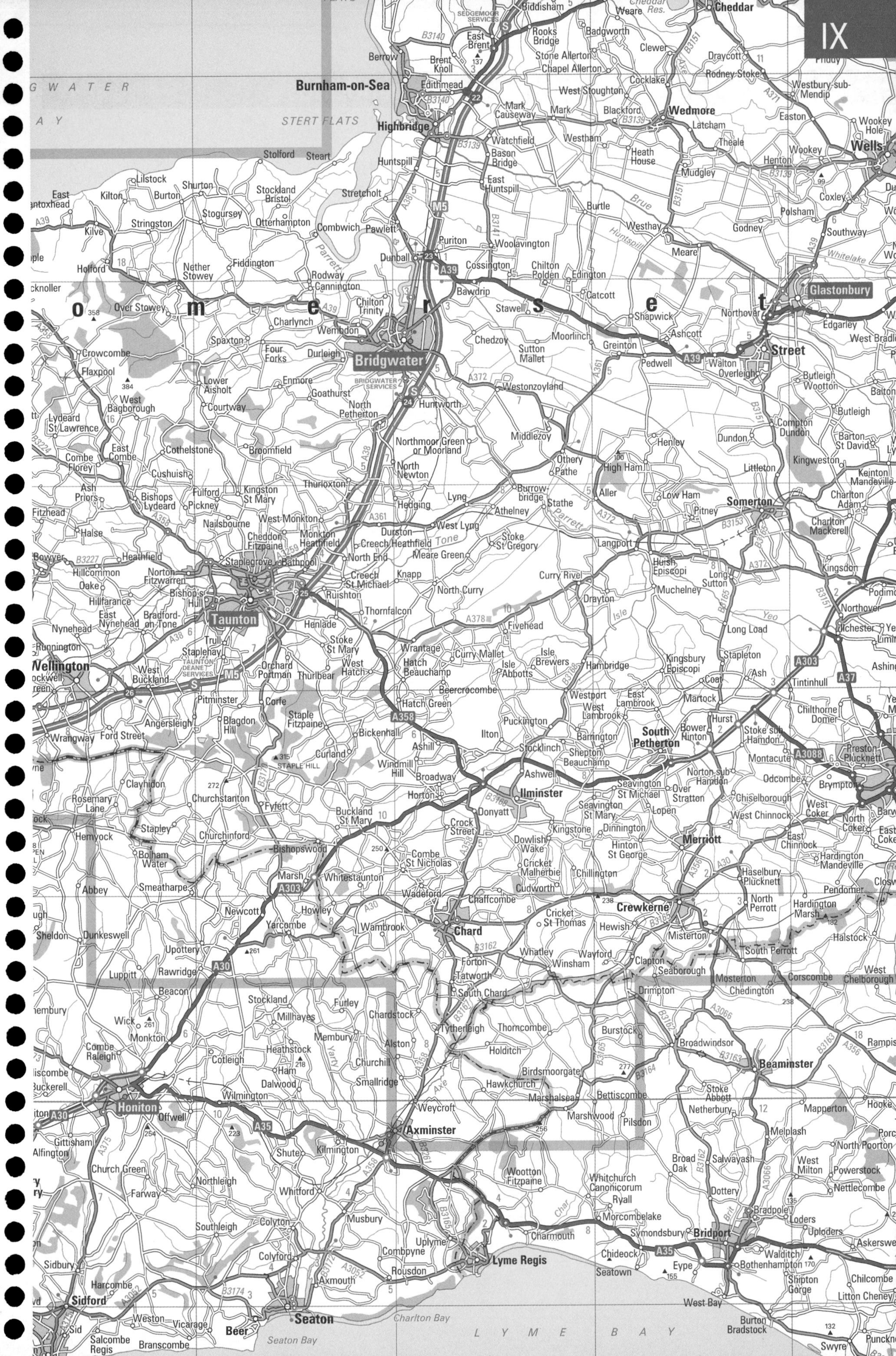

Biddisham
SEDGEMOOR SERVICES
Weare
Cheddar Res.
Cheddar
B3140
East Brent
Rooks Bridge
Badgworth
Clewer
B3151
Berrow
Brent Knoll
137
Stone Allerton
Chapel Allerton
Draycott
Rodney Stoke
Priddy
Burnham-on-Sea
Edithmead
West Stoughton
Cocklake
Westbury-sub-Mendip
A371
G W A T E R
B3140
22
Mark Causeway
Mark
Blackford
B3139
Wedmore
Easton
A Y
STERT FLATS
Highbridge
Latcham
Wookey Hole
Watchfield
Westham
Theale
B3139
Bason Bridge
Heath House
Wookey
Wells
Stolford
Steart
Huntspill
Henton
B3139
Mudgley
East Huntspill
99
Lilstock
Shurton
Stockland Bristol
Stretcholt
M5
East Quantoxhead
Kilton
Burton
A38
Coxley
Burtle
Brue
Polsham
Stogursey
Otterhampton
Stringston
A39
Kilve
Combwich
Pawlett
Westhay
Huntspill
Godney
Southway
Puriton
B3141
Woolavington
Meare
Whitelake
Holford
18
Nether Stowey
Fiddington
Dunball
23
Cossington
Chilton Polden
Edington
Rodway
A39
Cannington
Catcott
Glastonbury
Stocknoller
Chilton Trinity
Bawdrip
Stawell
Shapwick
Northover
Edgarley
358
Over Stowey
A39
Charlynch
Wembdon
Ashcott
West Bradley
A358
Spaxton
Chedzoy
Moorlinch
Greinton
Crowcombe
Four Forks
Durleigh
Bridgwater
Sutton Mallet
A361
Pedwell
A39
Walton
Street
Overleigh
Flaxpool
384
Lower Aisholt
Enmore
BRIDGWATER SERVICES
A372
Westonzoyland
Butleigh Wootton
Baltonsborough
West Bagborough
Courtway
Goathurst
North Petherton
24
Huntworth
B3151
Butleigh
Lydeard St Lawrence
16
Middlezoy
Compton Dundon
Dundon
Henley
Barton St David
Cothelstone
Broomfield
Northmoor Green or Moorland
Othery
Pathe
High Ham
100
Kingweston
B3224
Combe Florey
East Combe
North Newton
Littleton
Keinton Mandeville
Cushuish
Thurloxton
Aller
Low Ham
Ash Priors
Bishops Lydeard
Fulford
Pickney
Kingston St Mary
Lyng
Burrow-bridge
Stathe
Somerton
Charlton Adam
Fitzhead
Hedging
Athelney
Pitney
A358
Nailsbourne
West Monkton
A361
West Lyng
Parrett
A372
B3153
Charlton Mackerell
Halse
Cheddon Fitzpaine
Monkton Heathfield
Durston
Creech Heathfield
Tone
Stoke St Gregory
Langport
A3259
Bowyer
B3227
Heathfield
Staplegrove
Bathpool
North End
Meare Green
Huish Episcopi
A372
B3165
Hillcommon
Norton Fitzwarren
Creech St Michael
Knapp
Curry Rivel
Long Sutton
Kingsdon
Oake
Bishop's Hull
25
Ruishton
North Curry
Muchelney
B3151
Podimore
Hillfarance
Taunton
Drayton
Isle
Northover
East Nynehead
Bradford-on-Tone
Thornfalcon
10
Nynehead
A38
Henlade
A378
Fivehead
Yeo
Long Load
Ilchester
Runnington
Trull
Stoke St Mary
Wrantage
Curry Mallet
Isle Brewers
Kingsbury Episcopi
Stapleton
Wellington
Staplehay
TAUNTON DEANE SERVICES
Orchard Portman
West Hatch
Hatch Beauchamp
Isle Abbotts
Hambridge
Ash
A303
Ashington
West Buckland
M5
Thurlbear
Beercrocombe
Coat
Tintinhull
A37
26
Pitminster
Corfe
Westport
East Lambrook
Martock
Hatch Green
West Lambrook
Hurst
Chilthorne Domer
Angersleigh
Blagdon Hill
Staple Fitzpaine
A358
Puckington
South Petherton
Bower Hinton
Stoke sub Hamdon
Wrangway
Ford Street
Bickenhall
Ilton
Barrington
Ashill
Stocklinch
Preston Plucknett
315
STAPLE HILL
Curland
Windmill Hill
Shepton Beauchamp
Montacute
A3088
Clayhidon
272
Broadway
Ashwell
Norton sub Hamdon
Odcombe
B3170
Seavington St Michael
Over Stratton
Brympton
Rosemary Lane
Churchstanton
Fyfett
Horton
Ilminster
Hemyock
Buckland St Mary
Crock Street
B3168
Donyatt
Seavington St Mary
Lopen
Chiselborough
West Coker
Stapley
Churchinford
Kingstone
Dinnington
West Chinnock
North Coker
East Coker
Bolham Water
Bishopswood
250
Combe St Nicholas
A358
Dowlish Wake
Hinton St George
Merriott
East Chinnock
Hardington Mandeville
Abbey
Smeatharpe
Marsh
Whitestaunton
Cricket Malherbie
Chillington
A356
A30
Haselbury Plucknett
A303
Wadeford
Cudworth
Pendomer
Closworth
Newcott
Howley
A30
Chaffcombe
238
Crewkerne
North Perrott
Harding Marsh
Yarcombe
Wambrook
Chard
Cricket St Thomas
Hewish
B3165
Misterton
182
Sheldon
Dunkeswell
Upottery
261
B3162
Whatley
Wayford
South Perrott
Halstock
A30
Forton
Winsham
Clapton
Seaborough
Luppitt
Rawridge
Tatworth
Mosterton
Corscombe
West Chelborough
Beacon
South Chard
Drimpton
Chedington
238
Stockland
Furley
A3066
Millhayes
Chardstock
B3162
Wick
261
Tytherleigh
Thorncombe
Burstock
18
Rampisham
Membury
Broadwindsor
B3163
A356
Combe Raleigh
Monkton
Heathstock
Alston
Holditch
B3165
Beaminster
Cotleigh
218
Ham
Churchill
277
B3163
Birdsmoorgate
B3164
Dalwood
Smallridge
Hawkchurch
Bettiscombe
Stoke Abbott
Honiton
Wilmington
Axe
Marshalsea
Offwell
Weycroft
Netherbury
Mapperton
Hooke
A30
10
Marshwood
12
223
A35
Axminster
Pilsdon
256
Melplash
254
Gittisham
Alfington
A375
Shute
Kilmington
B3261
Broad Oak
Salwayash
North Poorton
Church Green
Wootton Fitzpaine
Whitchurch Canonicorum
A3066
West Milton
Powerstock
Northleigh
Ryall
Dottery
Farway
Whitford
Nettlecombe
135
Char
Bradpole
Southleigh
Colyton
Musbury
B3165
Morcombelake
Loders
Uplyme
Charmouth
Symondsbury
Bridport
Uploders
Sidbury
Colyford
Combpyne
Lyme Regis
Chideock
A35
Eype
Askerswell
Walditch
Bothenhampton
170
B3172
A3052
Rousdon
Seatown
155
Shipton Gorge
Harcombe
Axmouth
Chilcombe
Sidford
A3052
B3174
Litton Cheney
West Bay
Charlton Bay
Burton Bradstock
132
Weston
Vicarage
Seaton
L Y M E B A Y
Beer
Seaton Bay
Salcombe Regis
Branscombe
Swyre
Puncknowle

Major administrative and Postcode boundaries

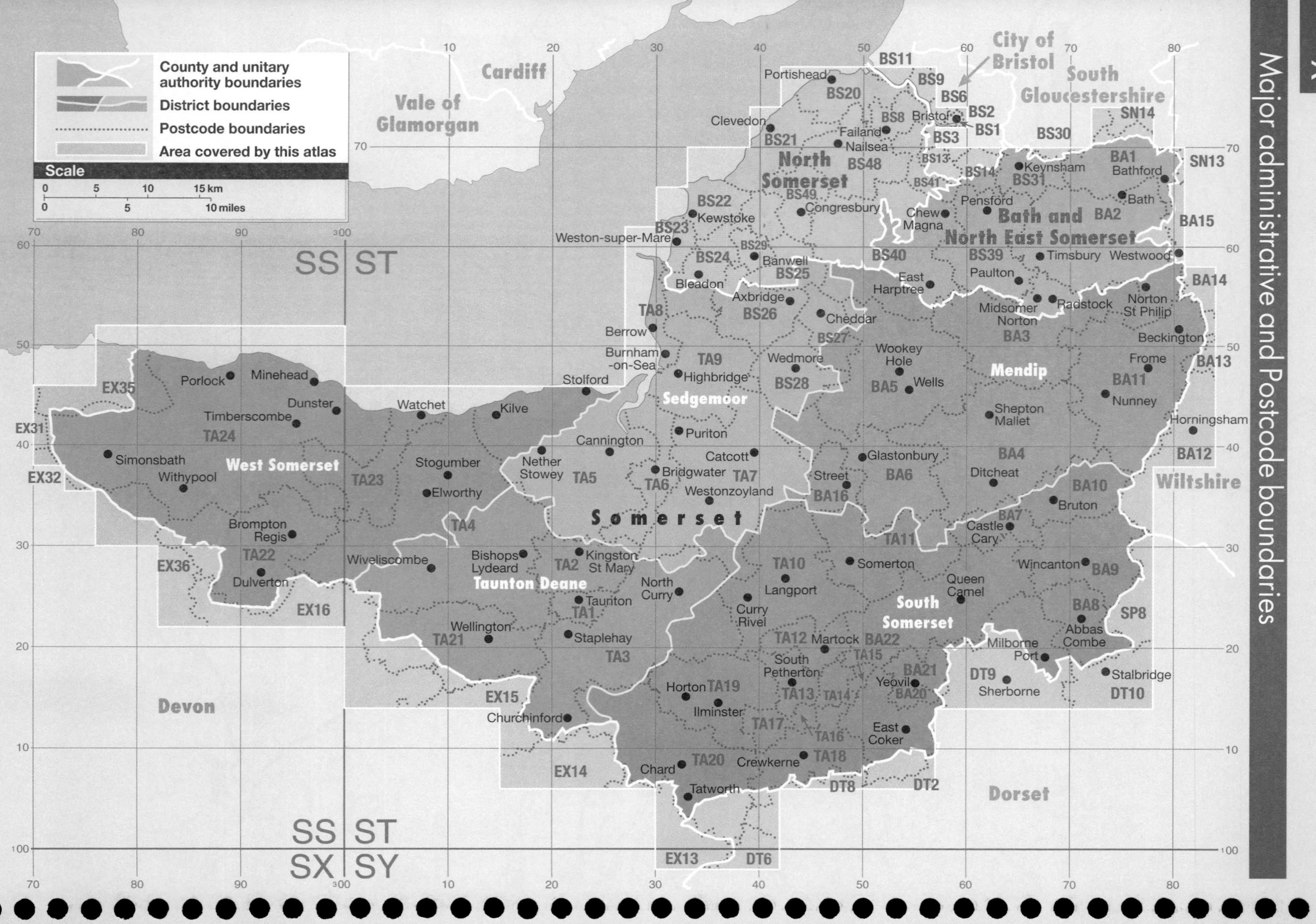

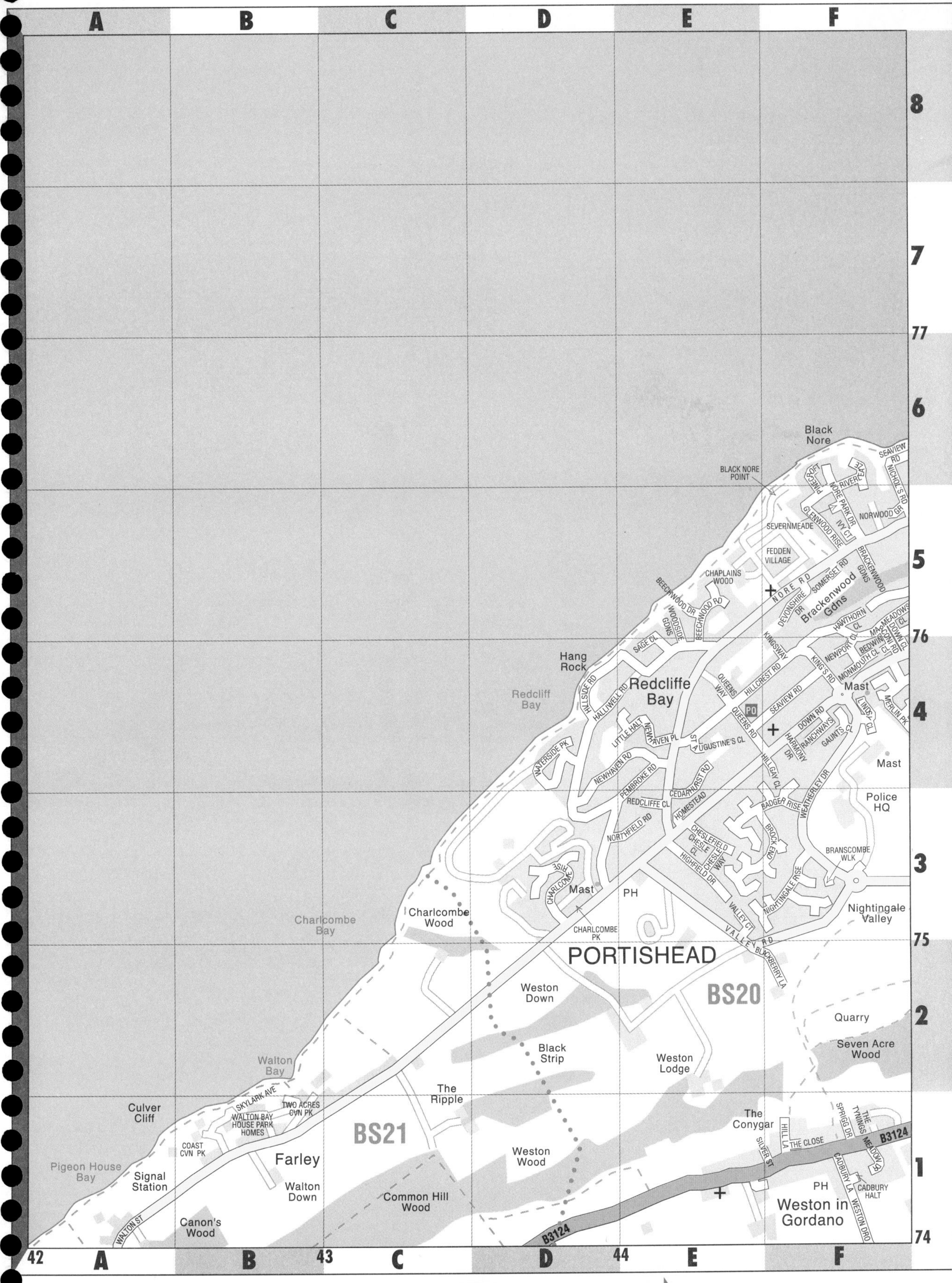
2
A
B
C
D
E
F
8
7
77
6
5
76
4
3
75
2
1
74
42
43
44
Black Nore
BLACK NORE POINT
SEAVIEW RD
NICHOLS RD
PINECROFT
RIVERLEAZE
MORE PARK DR
IVY CT
GLENWOOD RISE
NORWOOD GR
SEVERNMEADE
FEDDEN VILLAGE
CHAPLAINS WOOD
BRACKENWOOD GDNS
SOMERSET RD
NORE RD
DEVONSHIRE DR
Brackenwood Gdns
BEECHWOOD DR
BEECHWOOD RD
WOODSIDE GDNS
HAWTHORN CL
MEADOWS
BEDWIN CL
NEWPORT CL
MONMOUTH CL
KINGSWAY
KING'S RD
SAGE CL
Hang Rock
Redcliff Bay
HILLSIDE RD
HALLIWELL RD
Redcliffe Bay
QUEENS WAY
HILLCREST RD
Mast
LINDSAY CL
MERLIN PK
PO
SEAVIEW RD
QUEENS RD
DOWN RD
RANCHWAYS
GAUNTS CL
HARMONY DR
LITTLE HALT
NEWHAVEN PL
ST AUGUSTINE'S CL
WATERSIDE PK
NEWHAVEN RD
PEMBROKE RD
CEDARHURST RD
HILLGAY CL
Mast
Police HQ
REDCLIFFE CL
HOMESTEAD
BADGER RISE
WEATHERLEY DR
NORTHFIELD RD
CHESLEFIELD
CHESLE CL
CHESLE WAY
HIGHFIELD DR
BROCKEND
BRANSCOMBE WLK
NIGHTINGALE RISE
CHARLCOMBE RISE
Mast
PH
VALLEY CT
Nightingale Valley
Charlcombe Bay
Charlcombe Wood
CHARLCOMBE PK
VALLEY RD
BLACKBERRY LA
PORTISHEAD
Weston Down
BS20
Quarry
Seven Acre Wood
Black Strip
Walton Bay
Weston Lodge
Culver Cliff
SKYLARK AVE
TWO ACRES CVN PK
WALTON BAY HOUSE PARK HOMES
The Ripple
The Conygar
SPRIGG DR
THE TYNINGS
HILL LA
THE CLOSE
MEADOW DR
B3124
COAST CVN PK
BS21
Farley
Weston Wood
SILVER ST
Pigeon House Bay
Signal Station
Walton Down
Common Hill Wood
PH
CADBURY LA
CADBURY HALT
Weston in Gordano
WESTON DRO
WALTON ST
Canon's Wood
B3124
7
2

1

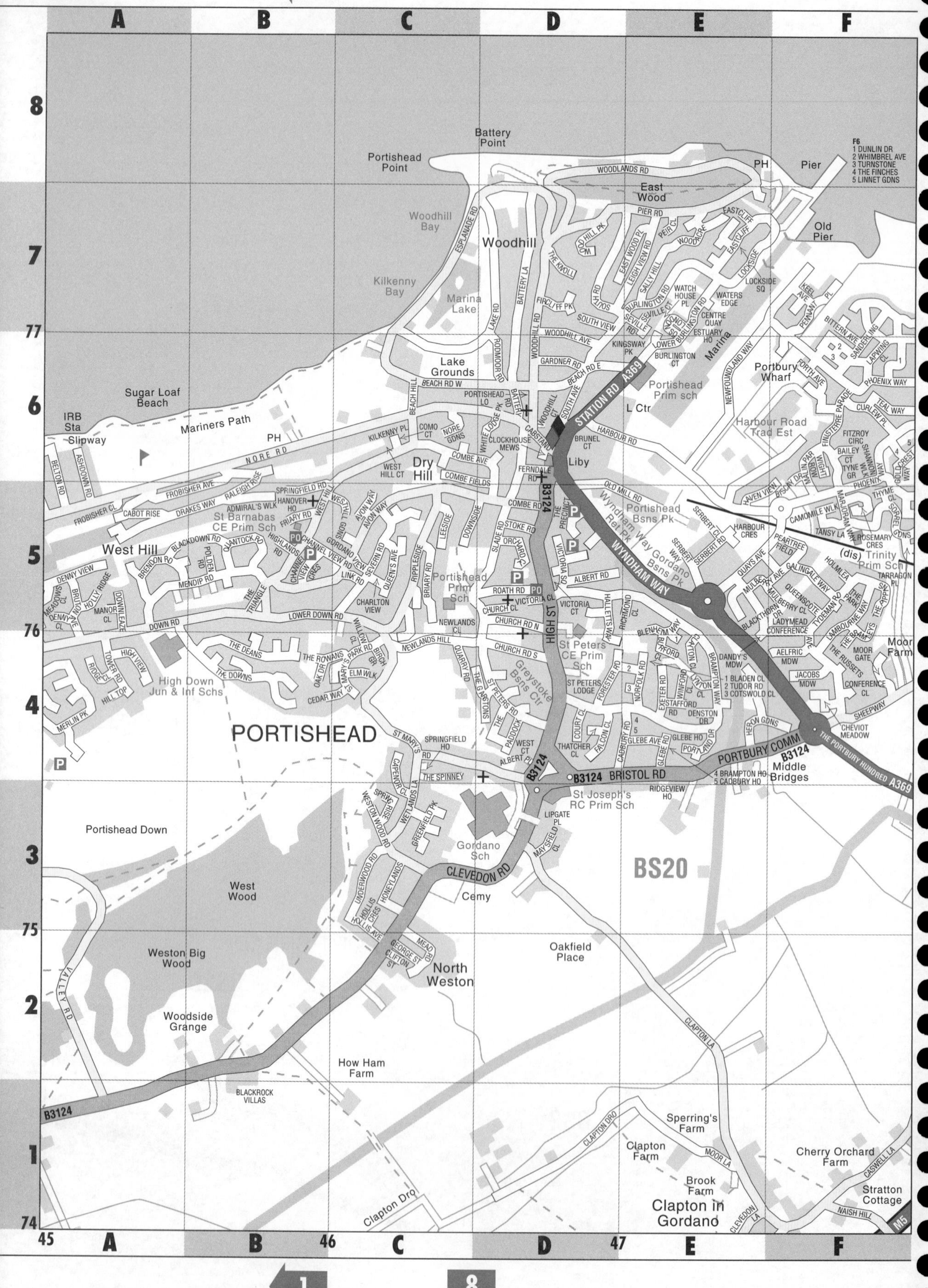
PORTISHEAD
Portishead Point
Battery Point
Woodhill Bay
Kilkenny Bay
Woodhill
Marina Lake
East Wood
Old Pier
Pier
Lake Grounds
Sugar Loaf Beach
IRB Sta Slipway
Mariners Path
Dry Hill
West Hill
St Barnabas CE Prim Sch
Portishead Prim Sch
Portishead Prim sch
L Ctr
Liby
Portbury Wharf
Harbour Road Trad Est
Portishead Bsns Pk
Wyndham Way Ret Pk
Gordano Bsns Pk
Trinity Prim Sch
Moor Farm
St Peters CE Prim Sch
Greystoke Bsns Ctr
High Down Jun & Inf Schs
St Joseph's RC Prim Sch
Middle Bridges
Portishead Down
Gordano Sch
Cemy
West Wood
BS20
Weston Big Wood
Oakfield Place
North Weston
Woodside Grange
How Ham Farm
Blackrock Villas
Sperring's Farm
Clapton Farm
Brook Farm
Cherry Orchard Farm
Stratton Cottage
Clapton in Gordano
F6
1 DUNLIN DR
2 WHIMBREL AVE
3 TURNSTONE
4 THE FINCHES
5 LINNET GDNS
STATION RD A369
WYNDHAM WAY
HIGH ST B3124
B3124 BRISTOL RD
PORTBURY COMM B3124
THE PORTBURY HUNDRED A369
CLEVEDON RD
B3124
M5
1 BLADEN CL
2 TUDOR RD
3 COTSWOLD CL
4 BRAMPTON HO
5 CADBURY HO
A B C D E F
8 7 77 6 5 76 4 3 75 2 1 74
45 46 47

1
8

4

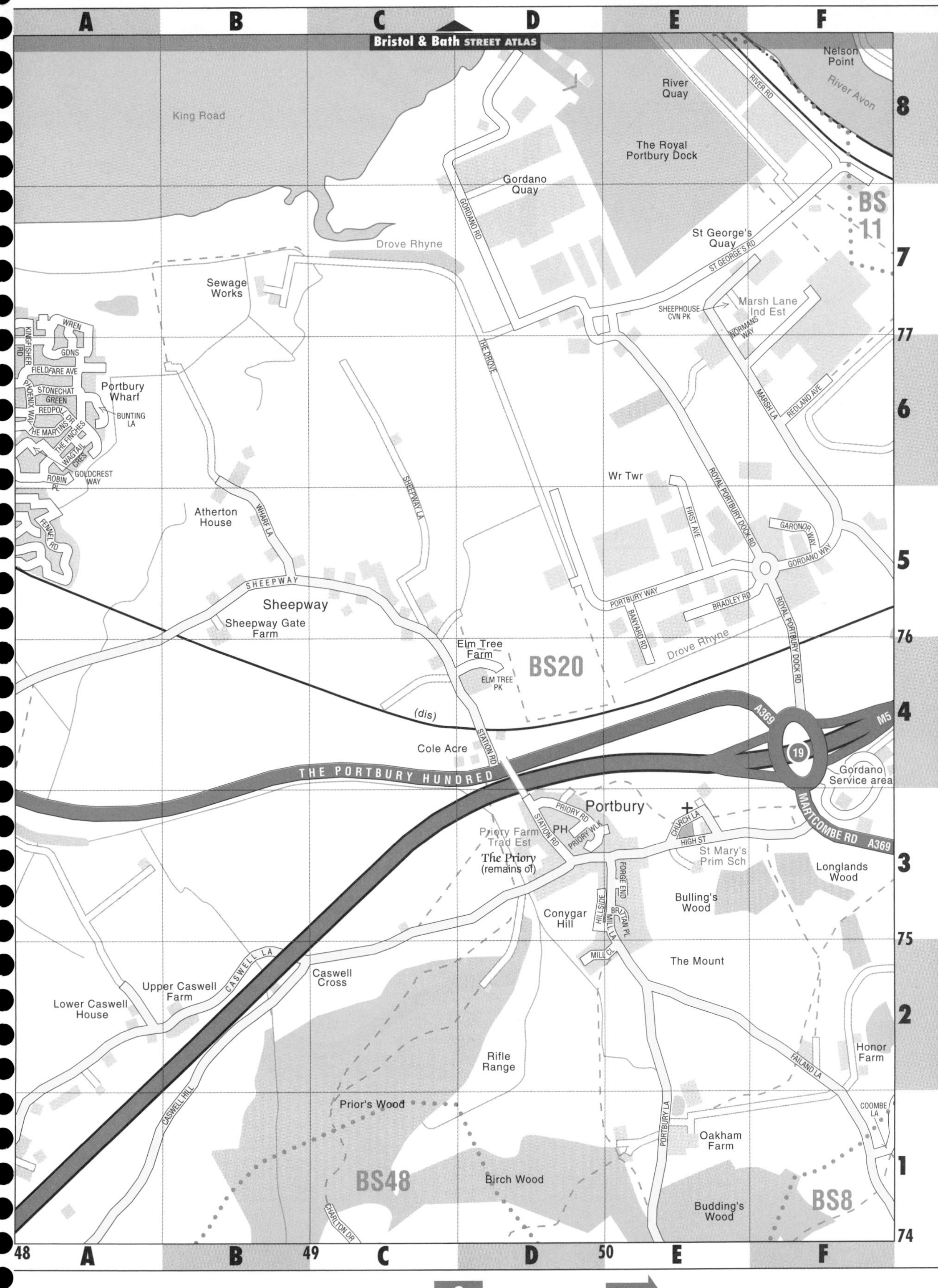
A
B
C
D
E
F
Bristol & Bath STREET ATLAS
Nelson Point
River Avon
River Quay
King Road
The Royal Portbury Dock
RIVER RD
8
Gordano Quay
GORDANO RD
BS 11
St George's Quay
ST GEORGE'S RD
Drove Rhyne
7
Sewage Works
SHEEPHOUSE CVN PK
Marsh Lane Ind Est
NORMANS WAY
WREN GDNS
KINGFISHER RD
FIELDFARE AVE
77
Portbury Wharf
STONECHAT GREEN
PHOENIX WAY
REDPOLL DR
BUNTING LA
THE MARTINS
THE FINCHES
WAGTAIL CRES
GOLDCREST WAY
ROBIN PL
THE DROVE
MARSH LA
REDLAND AVE
6
SHEEPWAY LA
Wr Twr
ROYAL PORTBURY DOCK RD
FIRST AVE
Atherton House
WHARF LA
FENNEL RD
GARONOR WAY
GORDANO WAY
5
SHEEPWAY
Sheepway
Sheepway Gate Farm
PORTBURY WAY
BANYARD RD
BRADLEY RD
Drove Rhyne
76
Elm Tree Farm
ELM TREE PK
BS20
(dis)
A369
M5
4
Cole Acre
STATION RD
19
THE PORTBURY HUNDRED
Gordano Service area
Portbury
PRIORY RD
PH
PRIORY WLK
CHURCH LA
HIGH ST
MARTCOMBE RD
A369
Priory Farm Trad Est
The Priory (remains of)
St Mary's Prim Sch
Longlands Wood
3
FORGE END
Conygar Hill
HILLSIDE
BRITTAN PL
MILL LA
Bulling's Wood
75
MILL CL
The Mount
CASWELL LA
Caswell Cross
Upper Caswell Farm
Lower Caswell House
2
Rifle Range
FAILAND LA
Honor Farm
CASWELL HILL
Prior's Wood
COOMBE LA
PORTBURY LA
Oakham Farm
1
BS48
Birch Wood
Budding's Wood
BS8
CHARLTON DR
74
48
49
50

9

4

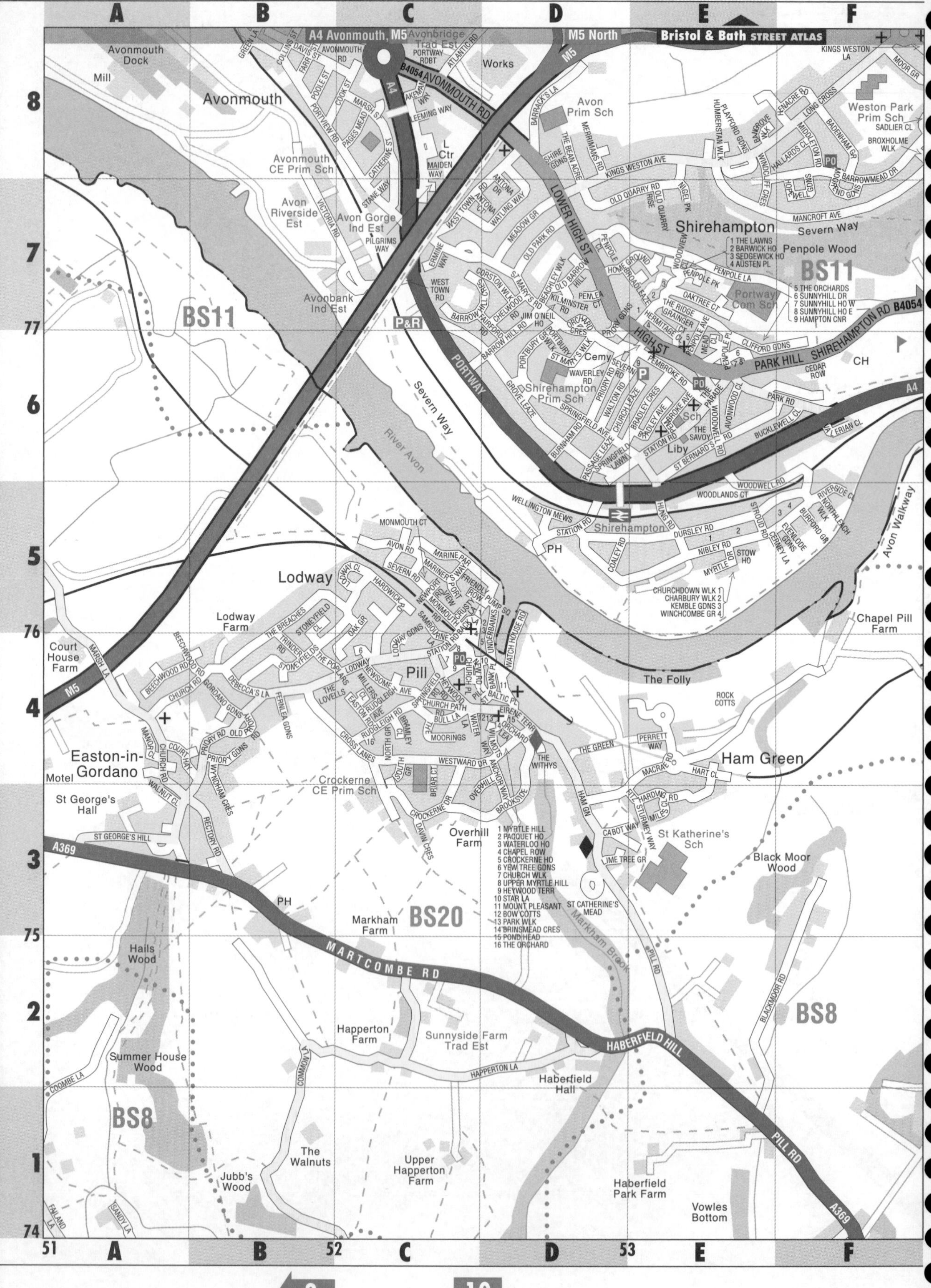
3
A4 Avonmouth, M5
M5 North
Bristol & Bath STREET ATLAS
Avonmouth Dock
Mill
Avonmouth
Avonmouth CE Prim Sch
Avon Riverside Est
Avon Gorge Ind Est
Avonbank Ind Est
BS11
Avonbridge Trad Est
Works
Avon Prim Sch
Weston Park Prim Sch
Shirehampton
Severn Way
Penpole Wood
1 THE LAWNS
2 BARWICK HO
3 SEDGEWICK HO
4 AUSTEN PL
5 THE ORCHARDS
6 SUNNYHILL DR
7 SUNNYHILL HO W
8 SUNNYHILL HO E
9 HAMPTON CNR
Portway Com Sch
LOWER HIGH ST
HIGH ST
PARK HILL
SHIREHAMPTON RD B4054
PORTWAY
Shirehampton Prim Sch
Cemy
Liby
Sch
CH
Severn Way
River Avon
Shirehampton
Avon Walkway
Lodway
Lodway Farm
Court House Farm
Pill
M5
Easton-in-Gordano
Motel
St George's Hall
Crockerne CE Prim Sch
Overhill Farm
Chapel Pill Farm
The Folly
Ham Green
St Katherine's Sch
Black Moor Wood
CHURCHDOWN WLK 1
CHARBURY WLK 2
KEMBLE GDNS 3
WINCHCOMBE GR 4
1 MYRTLE HILL
2 PACQUET HO
3 WATERLOO HO
4 CHAPEL ROW
5 CROCKERNE HO
6 YEW TREE GDNS
7 CHURCH WLK
8 UPPER MYRTLE HILL
9 HEYWOOD TERR
10 STAR LA
11 MOUNT PLEASANT
12 BOW COTTS
13 PARK WLK
14 BRINSMEAD CRES
15 POND HEAD
16 THE ORCHARD
A369
MARTCOMBE RD
BS20
Markham Farm
Markham Brook
PH
Hails Wood
Summer House Wood
Happerton Farm
Sunnyside Farm Trad Est
Haberfield Hall
HABERFIELD HILL
PILL RD
BS8
The Walnuts
Upper Happerton Farm
Jubb's Wood
Haberfield Park Farm
Vowles Bottom
51
52
53
74
75
76
77
3
10

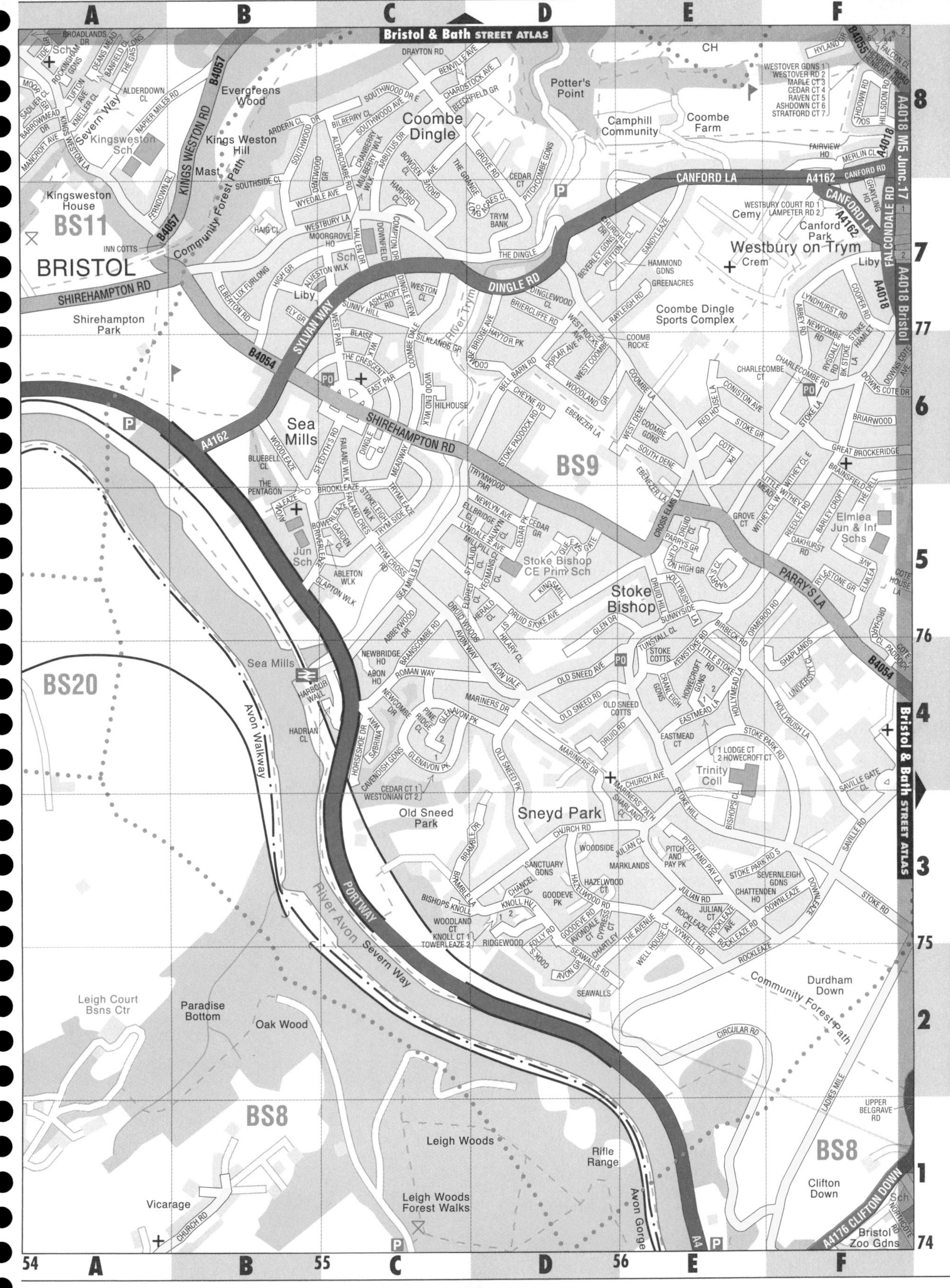
Bristol & Bath STREET ATLAS
Coombe Dingle
Kings Weston Hill
Evergreens Wood
Potter's Point
Camphill Community
Coombe Farm
BS11
BRISTOL
Kingsweston House
Shirehampton Park
Westbury on Trym
Coombe Dingle Sports Complex
Sea Mills
BS9
Stoke Bishop
BS20
Sneyd Park
Old Sneed Park
Trinity Coll
Durdham Down
River Avon
Avon Walkway
Severn Way
Leigh Court Bsns Ctr
Paradise Bottom
Oak Wood
BS8
Leigh Woods
Rifle Range
Leigh Woods Forest Walks
Avon Gorge
Vicarage
Clifton Down
Bristol Zoo Gdns
SHIREHAMPTON RD
DINGLE RD
CANFORD LA
SYLVAN WAY
PORTWAY
PARRY'S LA
KINGS WESTON RD
A4162
B4054
B4057
A4018
A4176 CLIFTON DOWN
Community Forest Path

11

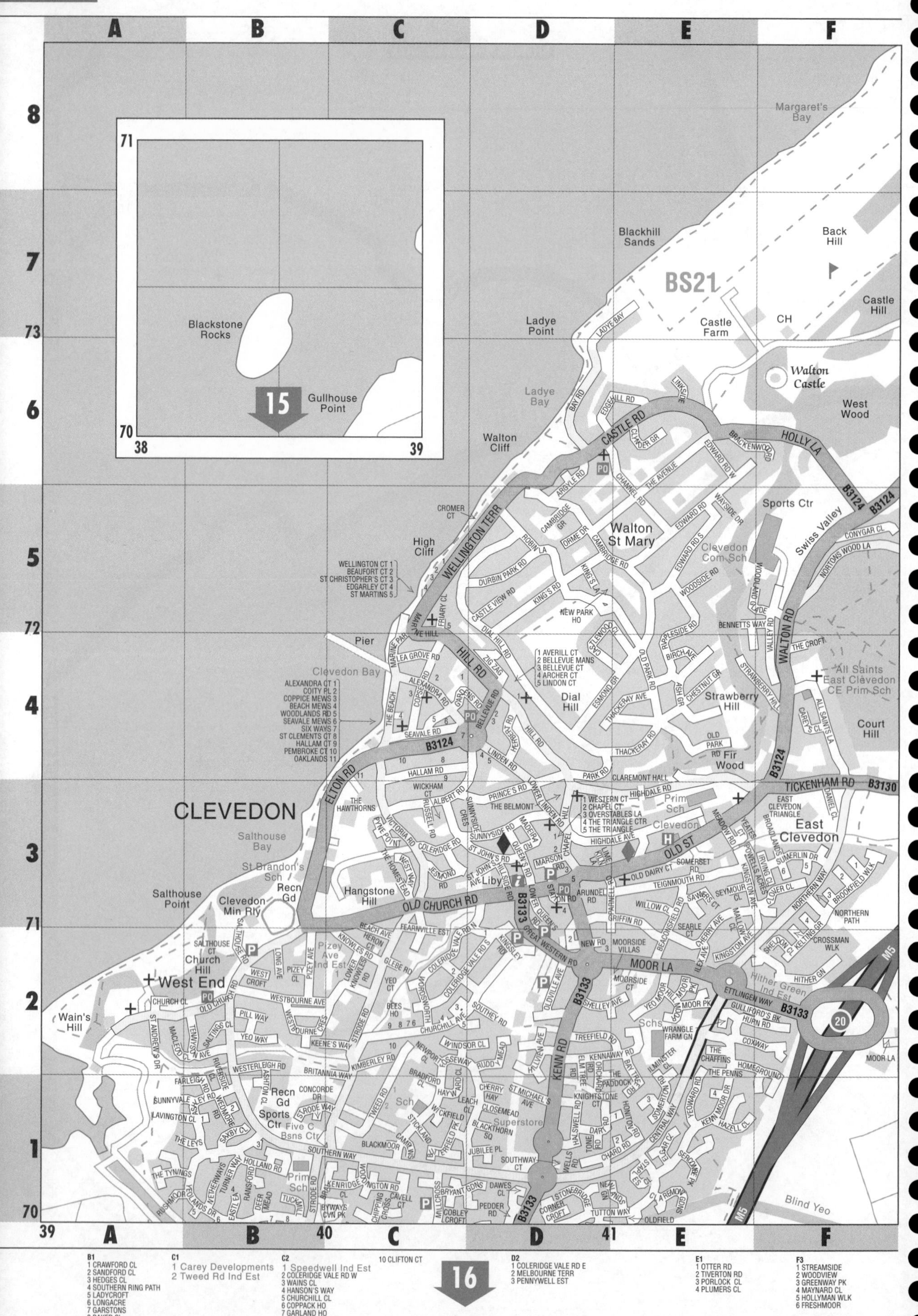

B1
1 CRAWFORD CL
2 SANDFORD CL
3 HEDGES CL
4 SOUTHERN RING PATH
5 LADYCROFT
6 LONGACRE
7 GARSTONS
8 BAKER CL

C1
1 Carey Developments
2 Tweed Rd Ind Est

C2
1 Speedwell Ind Est
2 COLERIDGE VALE RD W
3 WAINS CL
4 HANSON'S WAY
5 CHURCHILL CL
6 COPPACK HO
7 GARLAND HO
8 SHOPLAND HO
9 BRIDGE HO
10 CLIFTON CT

16

D2
1 COLERIDGE VALE RD E
2 MELBOURNE TERR
3 PENNYWELL EST

E1
1 OTTER RD
2 TIVERTON RD
3 PORLOCK CL
4 PLUMERS CL

F3
1 STREAMSIDE
2 WOODVIEW
3 GREENWAY PK
4 MAYNARD CL
5 HOLLYMAN WLK
6 FRESHMOOR

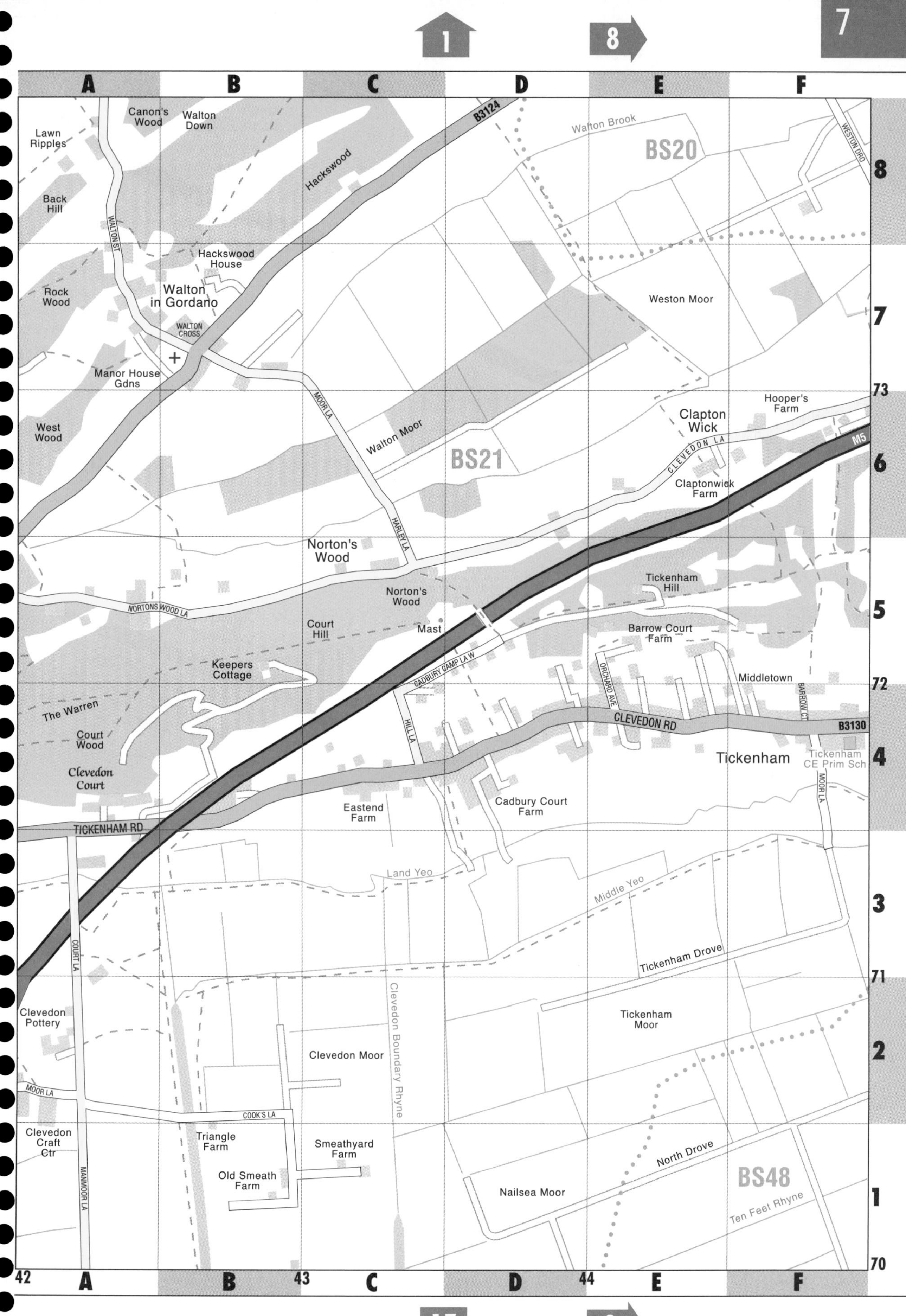
1
8
A
B
C
D
E
F
Lawn Ripples
Canon's Wood
Walton Down
Hackswood
B3124
Walton Brook
BS20
WESTON DRO
8
Back Hill
WALTON ST
Hackswood House
Walton in Gordano
Rock Wood
WALTON CROSS
Weston Moor
7
Manor House Gdns
73
MOOR LA
Hooper's Farm
Clapton Wick
West Wood
Walton Moor
BS21
CLEVEDON LA
M5
6
Claptonwick Farm
HARLEY LA
Norton's Wood
Tickenham Hill
NORTONS WOOD LA
Norton's Wood
5
Court Hill
Mast
Barrow Court Farm
Keepers Cottage
CADBURY CAMP LA W
ORCHARD AVE
Middletown
72
The Warren
BARROW CT
CLEVEDON RD
B3130
HILL LA
Court Wood
Tickenham
Tickenham CE Prim Sch
4
Clevedon Court
MOOR LA
Eastend Farm
Cadbury Court Farm
TICKENHAM RD
Land Yeo
Middle Yeo
3
COURT LA
Tickenham Drove
71
Clevedon Pottery
Clevedon Boundary Rhyne
Tickenham Moor
Clevedon Moor
2
MOOR LA
COOK'S LA
Clevedon Craft Ctr
Triangle Farm
Smeathyard Farm
North Drove
Old Smeath Farm
MANMOOR LA
Nailsea Moor
BS48
1
Ten Feet Rhyne
70
42
A
B
43
C
D
44
E
F
17
8

7
2

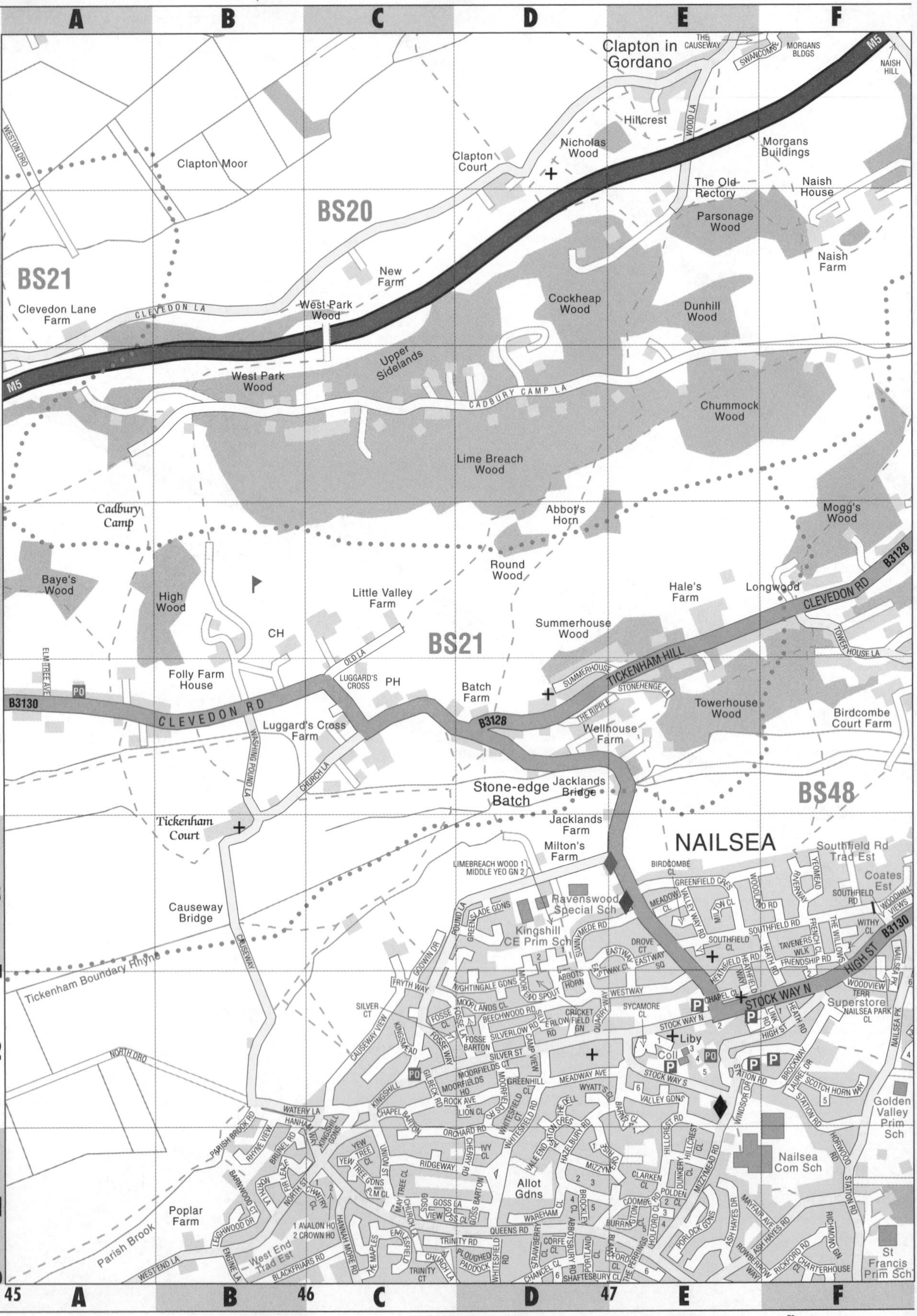

A B C D E F

8
7
73
6
5
72
4
3
71
2
1
70

Clapton in Gordano
THE CAUSEWAY
SWANCOMBE
MORGANS BLDGS
M5
NAISH HILL
Hillcrest
WOOD LA
WESTON DRO
Clapton Moor
Nicholas Wood
Clapton Court
Morgans Buildings
The Old Rectory
Naish House
BS20
Parsonage Wood
BS21
New Farm
Naish Farm
Clevedon Lane Farm
CLEVEDON LA
West Park Wood
Cockheap Wood
Dunhill Wood
Upper Sidelands
West Park Wood
CADBURY CAMP LA
Chummock Wood
Lime Breach Wood
Cadbury Camp
Abbot's Horn
Mogg's Wood
Round Wood
B3128
Baye's Wood
High Wood
Little Valley Farm
Hale's Farm
Longwood
CLEVEDON RD
CH
BS21
Summerhouse Wood
TOWER HOUSE LA
ELM TREE AVE
PO
Folly Farm House
OLD LA
LUGGARD'S CROSS
PH
Batch Farm
SUMMERHOUSE
TICKENHAM HILL
STONEHENGE LA
B3130
CLEVEDON RD
Luggard's Cross Farm
B3128
THE RIPPLE
Wellhouse Farm
Towerhouse Wood
Birdcombe Court Farm
WASHING POUND LA
CHURCH LA
Stone-edge Batch
Jacklands Bridge
BS48
Tickenham Court
Jacklands Farm
NAILSEA
Milton's Farm
Southfield Rd Trad Est
LIMEBREACH WOOD 1
MIDDLE YEO GN 2
BIRDCOMBE CL
Coates Est
Causeway Bridge
Ravenswood Special Sch
Kingshill CE Prim Sch
CAUSEWAY
Tickenham Boundary Rhyne
Superstore
STOCK WAY N
HIGH ST
NAILSEA PARK CL
SILVER CT
Liby
Coll
NORTH DRO
Golden Valley Prim Sch
Nailsea Com Sch
Allot Gdns
Poplar Farm
Parish Brook
West End Trad Est
WEST END LA
BLACKFRIARS RD
1 AVALON HO
2 CROWN HO
St Francis Prim Sch

45 A B 46 C D 47 E F

7
18

D1
1 MIZZYMEAD CL
2 BEAUFORT GDNS
3 AMBERLEY GDNS
4 CLAREMONT GDNS
5 DOWNLAND CL
6 DORCHESTER CL

E1
1 FARMHOUSE CT
2 BRENDON GDNS
3 MENDIP CL
4 SELWORTHY GDNS
5 DUNSTER GDNS
6 BIDDISHAM CL

E2
1 CHRIST CHURCH CL
2 CLEVEDON WLK
3 SOMERSET SQ
4 COLLIERS WLK
5 CROWN GLASS PL
6 VALLEY CL
7 FARMHOUSE CL

F2
1 HOBBS CT
2 FRIENDSHIP GR
3 SCOTS PINE AVE
4 HAWTHORN WAY
5 SCOTCH HORN CL
6 BLACKTHORN WAY

3
10

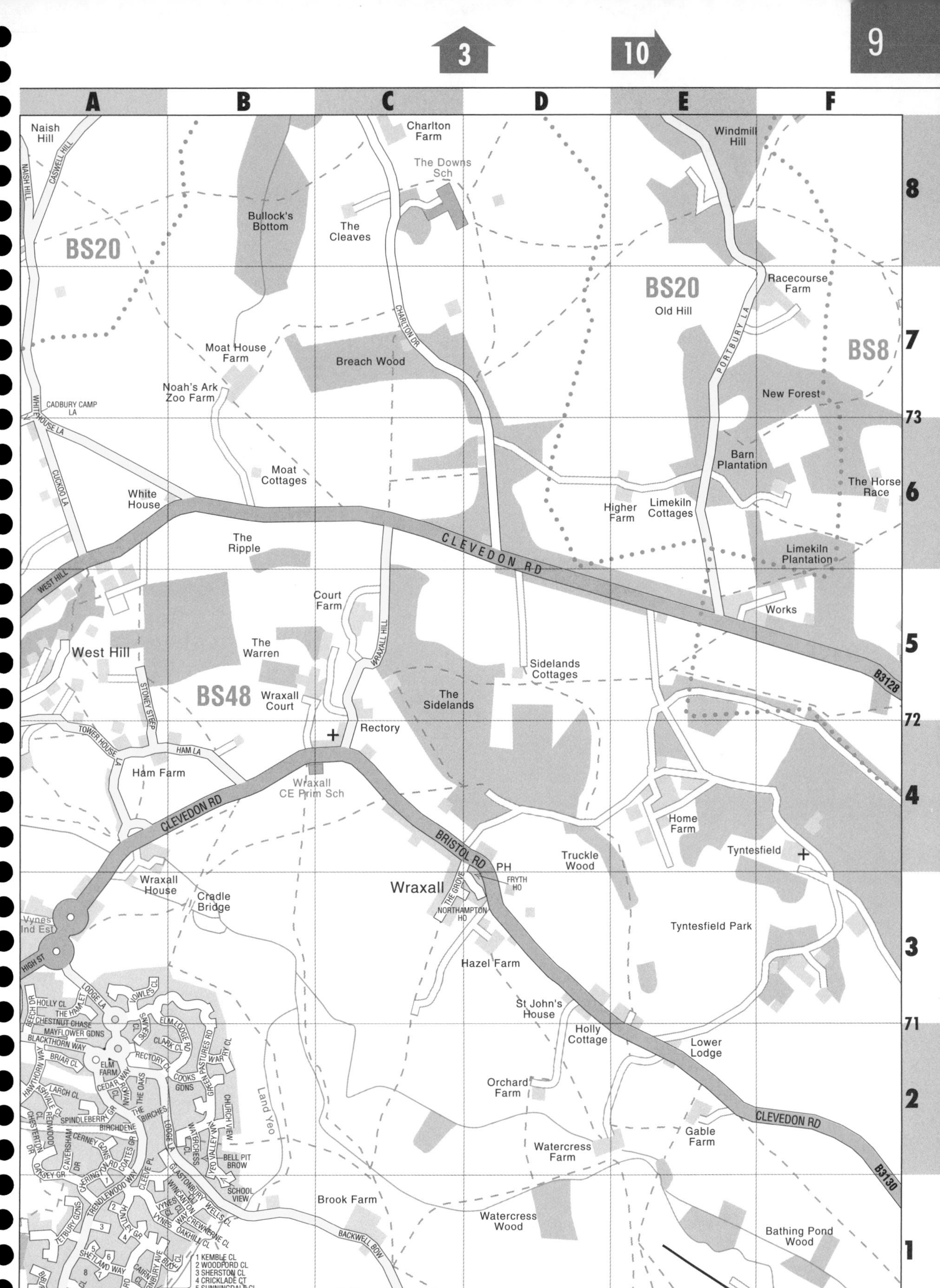
A
B
C
D
E
F
8
7
73
6
5
72
4
3
71
2
1
70
48
49
50
Naish Hill
NAISH HILL
CASWELL HILL
BS20
Bullock's Bottom
Charlton Farm
The Downs Sch
The Cleaves
Windmill Hill
Racecourse Farm
BS20
Old Hill
PORTBURY LA
BS8
CHARLTON DR
Moat House Farm
Breach Wood
Noah's Ark Zoo Farm
CADBURY CAMP LA
WHITEHOUSE LA
New Forest
Barn Plantation
CUCKOO LA
Moat Cottages
White House
Higher Farm
Limekiln Cottages
The Horse Race
The Ripple
CLEVEDON RD
Limekiln Plantation
WEST HILL
Court Farm
Works
West Hill
The Warren
WRAXALL HILL
Sidelands Cottages
BS48
STONEY STEEP
Wraxall Court
The Sidelands
B3128
TOWER HOUSE LA
Rectory
HAM LA
Ham Farm
Wraxall CE Prim Sch
CLEVEDON RD
Home Farm
BRISTOL RD
Truckle Wood
Tyntesfield
PH
FRYTH HO
Wraxall House
Cradle Bridge
Wraxall
THE GROVE
NORTHAMPTON HO
Vynes Ind Est
Tyntesfield Park
HIGH ST
Hazel Farm
LODGE LA
St John's House
Holly Cottage
Lower Lodge
Orchard Farm
Land Yeo
CLEVEDON RD
Gable Farm
Watercress Farm
B3130
BELL PIT BROW
SCHOOL VIEW
Brook Farm
Watercress Wood
Bathing Pond Wood
BACKWELL BOW
BACKWELL COMM
East End
1 KEMBLE CL
2 WOODFORD CL
3 SHERSTON CL
4 CRICKLADE CT
5 SUNNINGDALE CL
6 GLENEAGLES CL
7 ST ANDREWS CL
8 NOWHERE LA
9 CHELVEY RISE
HOLLY CL
THE HAMLET
CHESTNUT CHASE
MAYFLOWER GDNS
BLACKTHORN WAY
BRIAR CL
ELM FARM
HAWTHORN WAY
LARCH CL
CEDAR WAY
ROWAN
THE OAKS
ELM LODGE RD
CLARK CL
RECTORY CL
COOKS GDNS
GREEN PASTURES RD
WARRY CL
CHURCH VIEW
SPINDLEBERRY
BIRCHDENE
THE BIRCHES
CERNEY GDNS
COATES GR
CAVERSHAM DR
REDWOOD CL
CHESTERTON DR
OAKSEY GR
CHERINGTON RD
CLEEVE PL
WATERCRESS CL
LYEO VALLEY WAY
GLASTONBURY WAY
WINCANTON CL
WELLS CL
CREWKERNE CL
OAKHILL CL
TRENDLEWOOD WAY
TETBURY GDNS
HUNTLEY GR
SHETLAND WAY
CAIRN CL
TURNBURY AVE
BIBURY CL
ST AGNES CL
ST IVES CL
TRURO RD
HELSTON RD
FALMOUTH CL
BIRDLIP CL

19
10

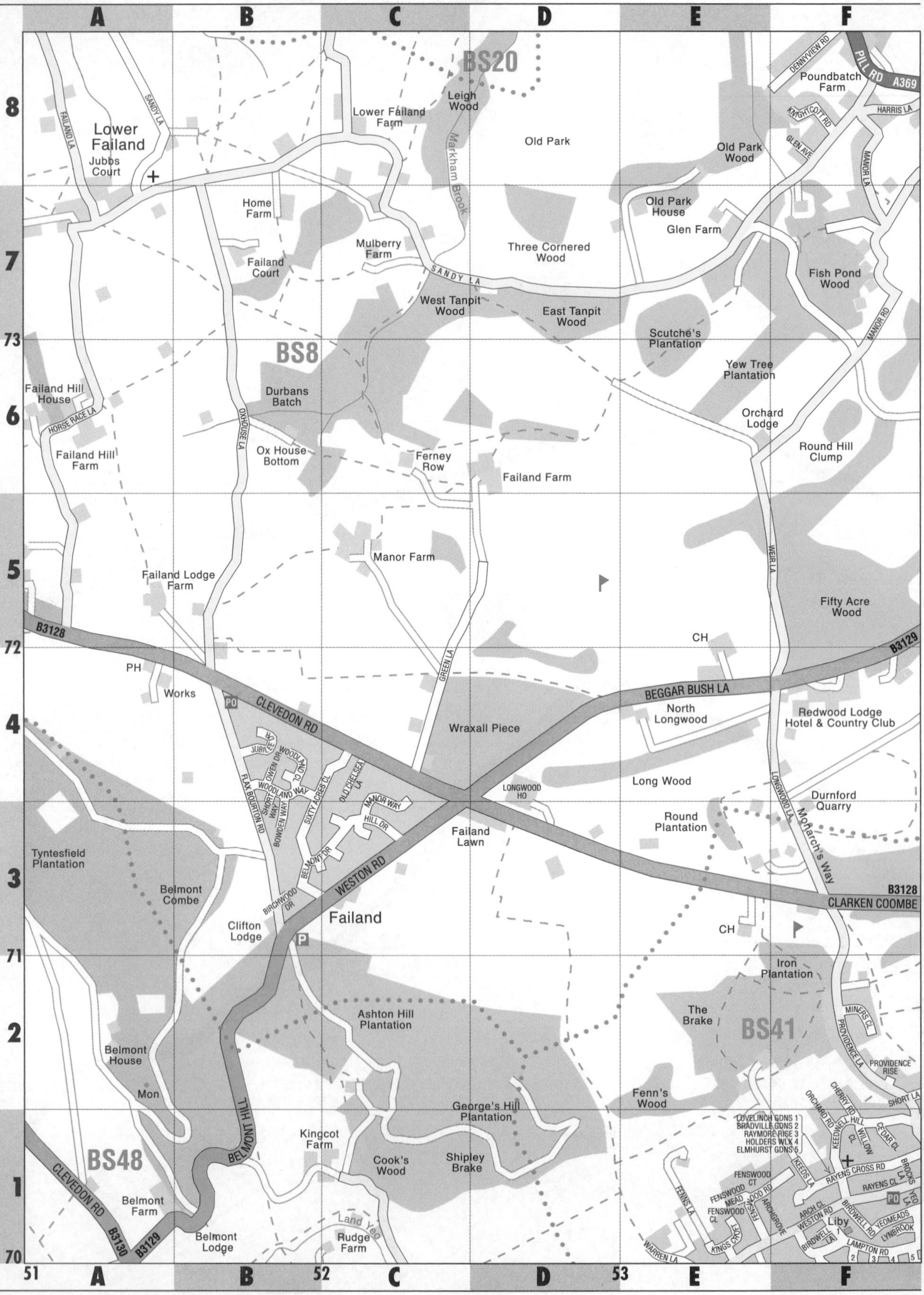

A B C D E F
8 7 73 6 5 72 4 3 71 2 1 70
51 52 53
BS20
BS8
BS41
BS48
Lower Failand
Jubbs Court
Lower Failand Farm
Leigh Wood
Markham Brook
Old Park
Old Park Wood
Poundbatch Farm
PILL RD
A369
DENNYVIEW RD
KNIGHTCOTT RD
HARRIS LA
GLEN AVE
MANOR LA
Home Farm
Mulberry Farm
Failand Court
SANDY LA
Three Cornered Wood
Old Park House
Glen Farm
Fish Pond Wood
West Tanpit Wood
East Tanpit Wood
Scutche's Plantation
Yew Tree Plantation
MANOR RD
FAILAND LA
Failand Hill House
HORSE RACE LA
Failand Hill Farm
Durbans Batch
OXHOUSE LA
Ox House Bottom
Ferney Row
Failand Farm
Orchard Lodge
Round Hill Clump
Manor Farm
Failand Lodge Farm
WEIR LA
Fifty Acre Wood
B3128
PH
Works
CH
B3129
PO
CLEVEDON RD
GREEN LA
Wraxall Piece
BEGGAR BUSH LA
North Longwood
Redwood Lodge Hotel & Country Club
JUBILEE RD
OWEN DR
WOODLAND CL
WOODLAND WAY
SHORT WAY
BOWDEN WAY
SIXTY ACRES CL
OLD CHELSEA LA
MANOR WAY
HILL DR
FLAX BOURTON RD
BELMONT DR
LONGWOOD HO
Long Wood
Durnford Quarry
LONGWOOD LA
Monarch's Way
Failand Lawn
Round Plantation
Tyntesfield Plantation
Belmont Combe
WESTON RD
B3128
CLARKEN COOMBE
BIRCHWOOD DR
Clifton Lodge
Failand
P
CH
Iron Plantation
Ashton Hill Plantation
The Brake
MINERS CL
PROVIDENCE LA
PROVIDENCE RISE
SHORT LA
Belmont House
Mon
Fenn's Wood
George's Hill Plantation
CHERRY RD
ORCHARD RD
KEEDWELL HILL
CL
WILLOW
CEDAR CL
BELMONT HILL
Kingcot Farm
Cook's Wood
Shipley Brake
LOVELINCH GDNS 1
BRADVILLE GDNS 2
RAYMORE RISE 3
HOLDERS WLK 4
ELMHURST GDNS 5
KEEDS LA
RAYENS CROSS RD
BROOKS LA
RAYENS CL
YEO LA
FENSWOOD CT
FENSWOOD MEAD
FENSWOOD CL
FENSWOOD RD
ARCHGROVE
ARCH CL
WESTON RD
BIRDWELL RD
YEOMEADS
LYNBROOK
FENNS LA
Liby
CLEVEDON RD
Belmont Farm
B3130
B3129
Land Yeo
Rudge Farm
Belmont Lodge
WARREN LA
KINGS CROFT
BIRDWELL LA
LAMPTON RD
1 2 3 4 5

F5
1 BRISTOL GATE
2 FARADAY RD
3 DOWRY PL
4 LITTLE CAROLINE PL
5 GRANVILLE CHAPEL
6 HUMPHRY DAVY WAY

F5
7 GRENVILLE PL
8 ASHMEAD WAY
9 CUMBERLAND RD
10 BRUNSWICK PL

F6
1 HABERFIELD HO
2 DAWES CT
3 CLEVE CT
4 BROWNE CT
5 ADAMS CT
6 CUMBERLAND PL
7 CARRICK HO
8 SOUTH GREEN ST
9 ALBERMARLE ROW
10 HOPECHAPEL HILL
11 NORTH GREEN ST
12 HINTON LA
13 WINDSOR CT

F6
14 VICTORIA TERR
15 THE POLYGON
16 GLENDALE
17 PRINCE'S BLDGS
18 WELLINGTON TERR
19 OXFORD PL

F7
1 CLIFTON CL
2 HARLEY MEWS
3 HARLEY CT
4 HARLEY PL
5 CLIFTON DOWN RD
6 GLOUCESTER ROW
7 BEAUFORT BLDGS
8 GLOUCESTER ST
9 WATERLOO ST
10 BEAUFORT MEWS

5

226

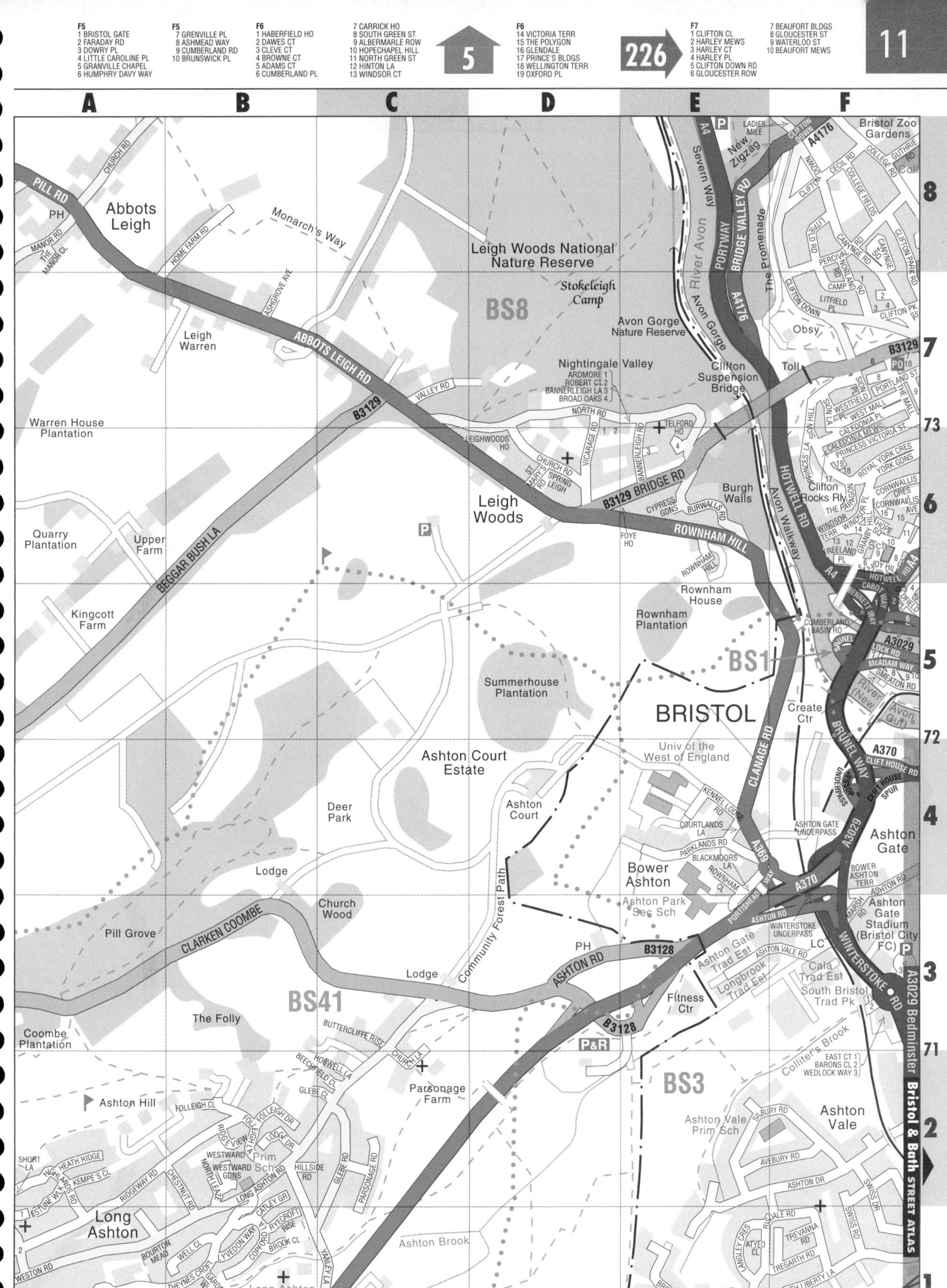

21

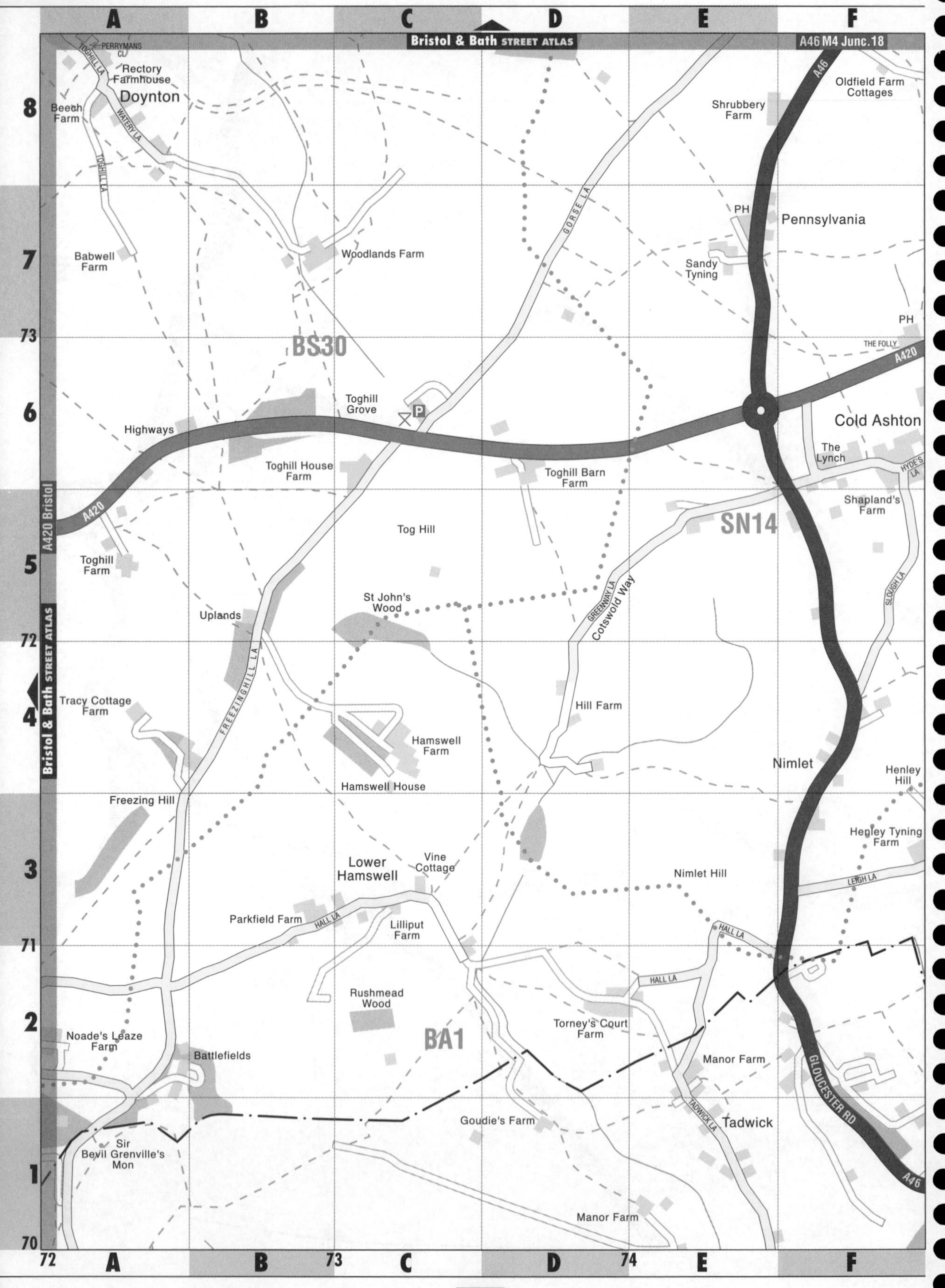
A
B
C
D
E
F
Bristol & Bath STREET ATLAS
A46 M4 Junc.18
Rectory Farmhouse
Doynton
Beech Farm
Babwell Farm
Woodlands Farm
Shrubbery Farm
Oldfield Farm Cottages
Pennsylvania
PH
Sandy Tyning
BS30
PH
THE FOLLY
A420
Toghill Grove
Highways
Cold Ashton
The Lynch
Toghill House Farm
Toghill Barn Farm
Shapland's Farm
SN14
A420 Bristol
Tog Hill
Toghill Farm
St John's Wood
Uplands
Cotswold Way
GREENWAY LA
GORSE LA
FREEZINGHILL LA
SLOUGH LA
HYDE'S LA
Tracy Cottage Farm
Hill Farm
Hamswell Farm
Hamswell House
Nimlet
Henley Hill
Freezing Hill
Henley Tyning Farm
Lower Hamswell
Vine Cottage
Nimlet Hill
LEIGH LA
Parkfield Farm
HALL LA
Lilliput Farm
Rushmead Wood
Torney's Court Farm
Noade's Leaze Farm
BA1
Battlefields
Manor Farm
GLOUCESTER RD
Goudie's Farm
TADWICK LA
Tadwick
Sir Bevil Grenville's Mon
A46
Manor Farm
8
7
73
6
5
72
4
3
71
2
1
70
72
73
74

27

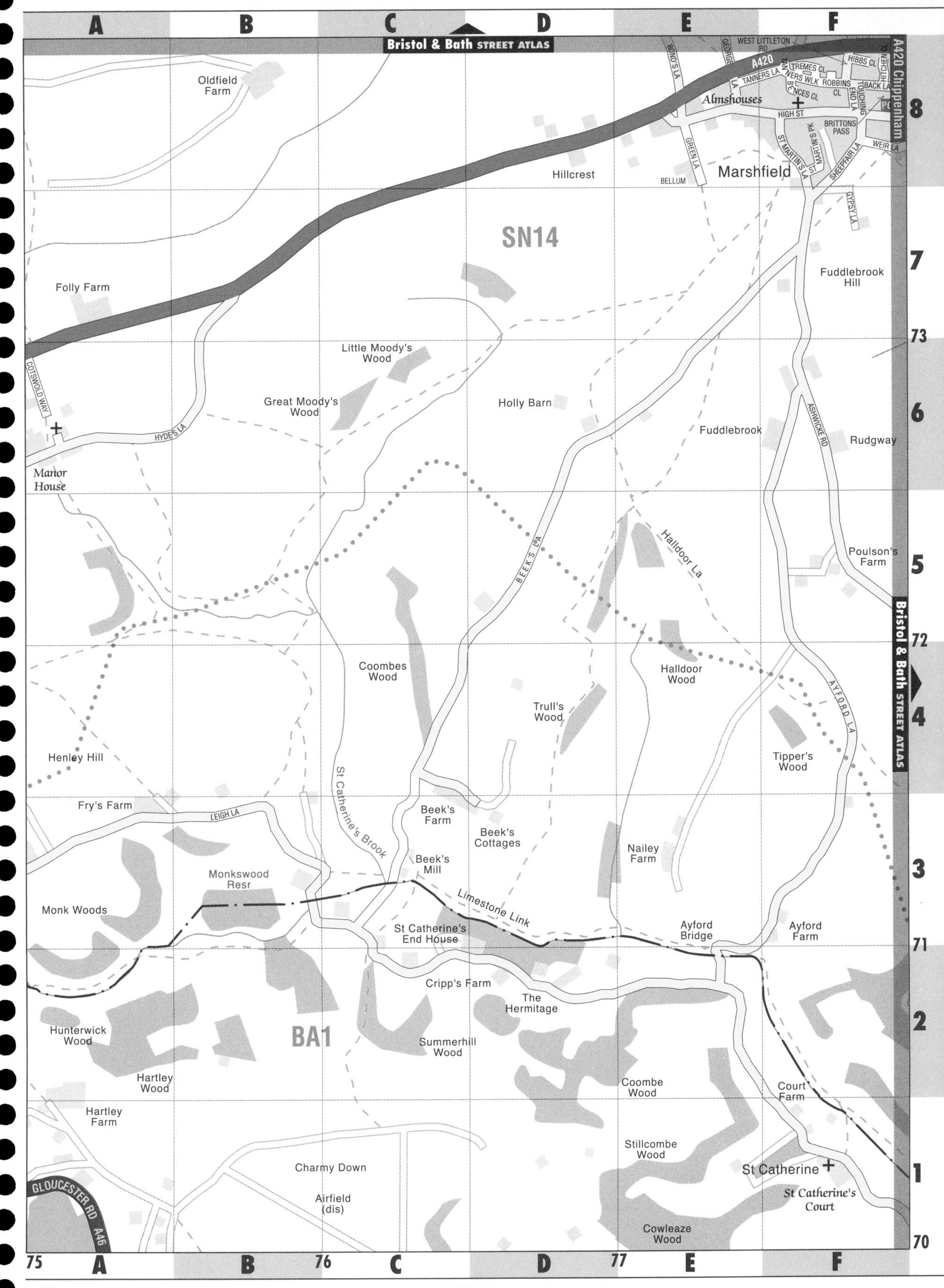

Bristol & Bath STREET ATLAS
A420 Chippenham
Oldfield Farm
Folly Farm
A420
Almshouses
Marshfield
Hillcrest
BELLUM
SN14
Fuddlebrook Hill
Little Moody's Wood
Great Moody's Wood
Holly Barn
Fuddlebrook
Rudgway
COTSWOLD WAY
HYDE'S LA
Manor House
BEEK'S LA
Halldoor La
Poulson's Farm
ASHWICKE RD
Coombes Wood
Halldoor Wood
Trull's Wood
AYFORD LA
Tipper's Wood
Henley Hill
St Catherine's Brook
Fry's Farm
LEIGH LA
Beek's Farm
Beek's Cottages
Nailey Farm
Beek's Mill
Monkswood Resr
Limestone Link
Monk Woods
St Catherine's End House
Ayford Bridge
Ayford Farm
Cripp's Farm
The Hermitage
Hunterwick Wood
BA1
Summerhill Wood
Hartley Wood
Coombe Wood
Court Farm
Hartley Farm
Stillcombe Wood
Charmy Down
St Catherine
Airfield (dis)
St Catherine's Court
GLOUCESTER RD A46
Cowleaze Wood

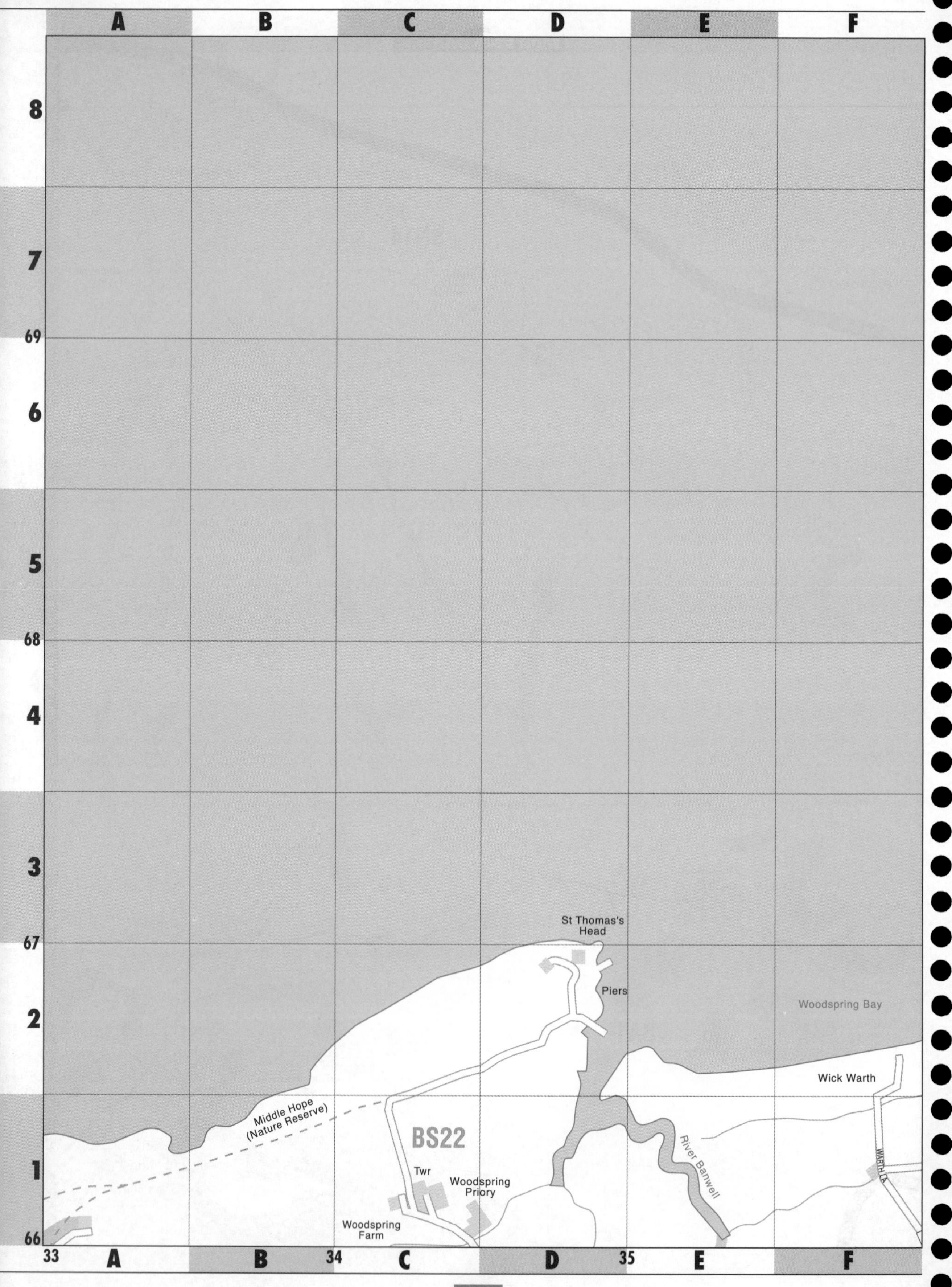
A
B
C
D
E
F
8
7
69
6
5
68
4
3
67
2
1
66
33
34
35
St Thomas's Head
Piers
Woodspring Bay
Wick Warth
Middle Hope (Nature Reserve)
BS22
Twr
Woodspring Priory
Woodspring Farm
River Banwell
WARTH LA

31

16

A B C D E F

8

Dowlais Ditch

7

69

Kingston Pill

6

Seawall Farm

Hook's Ear

Treble House Farm

5

BACK LA

Sewage Works

68

4

Channel View Farm

BS21

MIDDLE LA

MIDDLE LA

Broadstone Rhyne

3

Broadstone Farm

BROADSTONE LA

Wharf Farm

67

HAM LA

New House Farm

Ham Farm

BS22

2

Pool Farm

Ham Rhyne

Sewage Works

1

Mendip View Farm

Yeo Bank Farm

YEO BANK LA

Mill Leaze Rhyne

MIDDY LA

BS22

66

36 A B 37 C D 38 E F

32

16

6

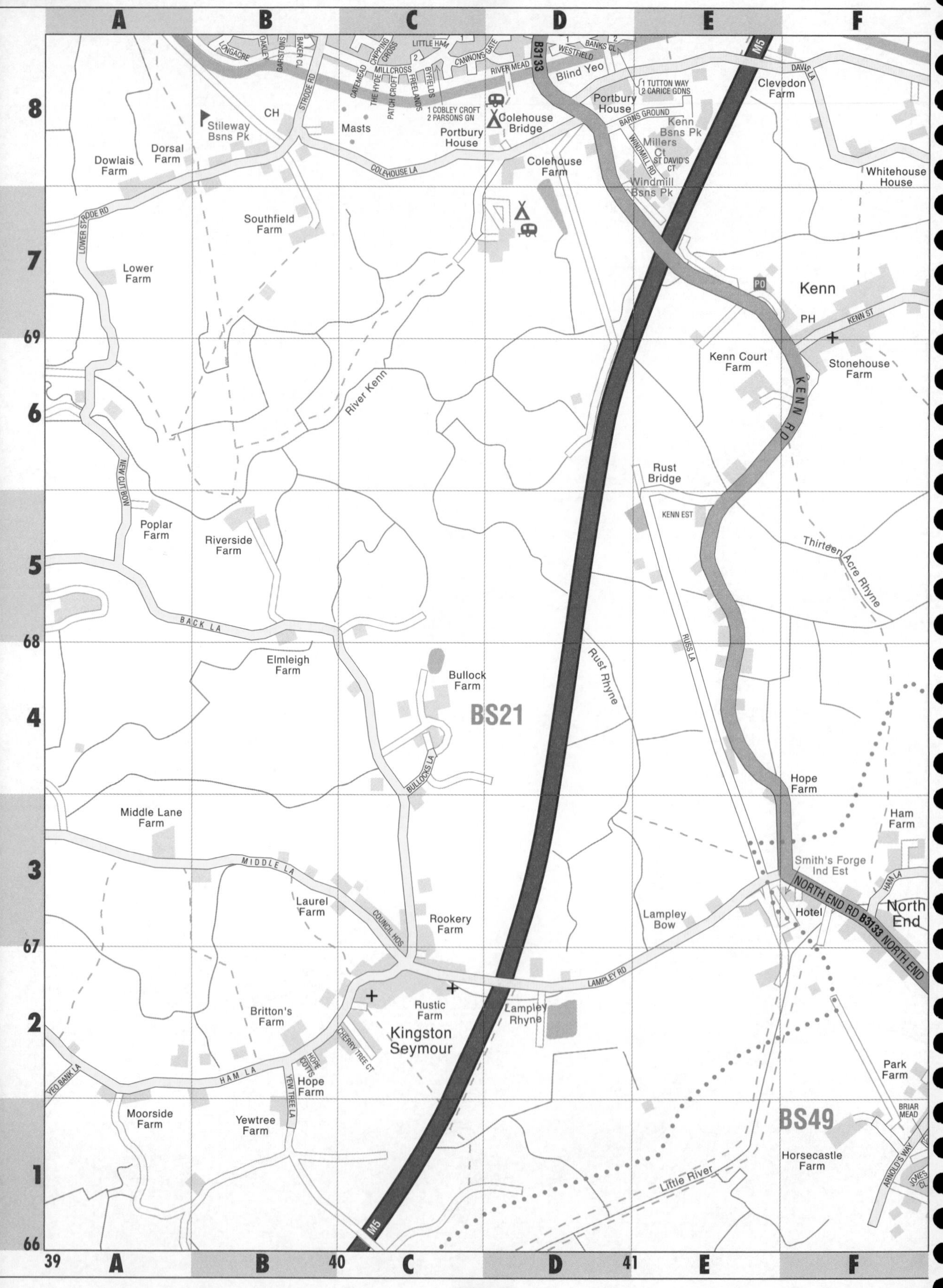
A
B
C
D
E
F
8
7
69
6
5
68
4
3
67
2
1
66
39
40
41
Dowlais Farm
Dorsal Farm
Stileway Bsns Pk
CH
Masts
Portbury House
Colehouse Bridge
Colehouse Farm
Portbury House
Kenn Bsns Pk
Millers Ct
Windmill Bsns Pk
Clevedon Farm
Whitehouse House
Blind Yeo
Southfield Farm
Lower Farm
Kenn
PH
Kenn Court Farm
Stonehouse Farm
River Kenn
Rust Bridge
KENN EST
Thirteen Acre Rhyne
Poplar Farm
Riverside Farm
BACK LA
Elmleigh Farm
Bullock Farm
BS21
Rust Rhyne
RUSS LA
Hope Farm
Middle Lane Farm
MIDDLE LA
Ham Farm
Smith's Forge Ind Est
Laurel Farm
Rookery Farm
Lampley Bow
Hotel
North End
NORTH END RD
B3133 NORTH END
LAMPLEY RD
Britton's Farm
Rustic Farm
Kingston Seymour
Lampley Rhyne
HAM LA
Hope Farm
Moorside Farm
Yewtree Farm
BS49
Park Farm
Horsecastle Farm
Little River
M5
B3133
KENN RD
LOWER STRODE RD
NEW CUT BOW
STRODE RD
COLEHOUSE LA
BULLOCKS LA
COUNCIL HOS
CHERRY TREE CT
YEW TREE LA
YEO BANK LA
KENN ST
HAM LA
BRIAR MEAD
ARNOLD'S WAY
JONES CL
DAVIS LA
1 TUTTON WAY
2 CARICE GDNS
BARNS GROUND
WINDMILL RD
ST DAVID'S CT
BANKS CL
WESTFIELD
RIVER MEAD
CANNONS GATE
LITTLE HAM
1 COBLEY CROFT
2 PARSONS GN
LONGACRE
OAKLEY
BAKER CL
MILLCROSS
CHIPPING CROSS
THE HYDE
CATEMEAD
PATCH CROFT
FREELANDS
BYFIELDS

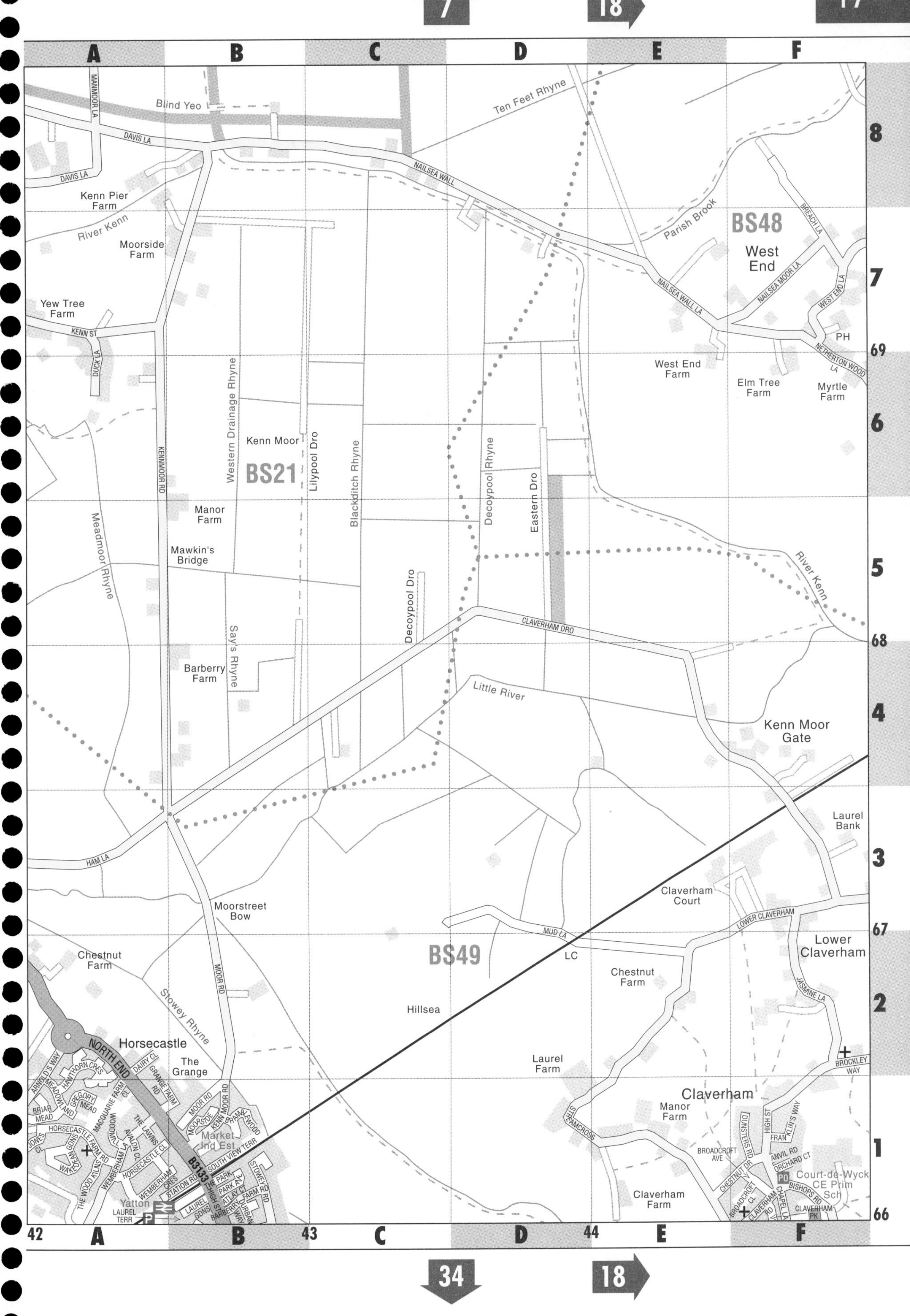
7
18
A
B
C
D
E
F
8
7
69
6
5
68
4
3
67
2
1
66
42
43
44
MANMOOR LA
Blind Yeo
DAVIS LA
DAVIS LA
Ten Feet Rhyne
NAILSEA WALL
Kenn Pier
Farm
River Kenn
Moorside
Farm
Yew Tree
Farm
KENN ST
DUCK LA
Parish Brook
BS48
West
End
BREACH LA
NAILSEA WALL LA
NAILSEA MOOR LA
WEST END LA
PH
NETHERTON WOOD LA
West End
Farm
Elm Tree
Farm
Myrtle
Farm
Western Drainage Rhyne
Kenn Moor
BS21
Lilypool Dro
Blackditch Rhyne
Decoypool Rhyne
Eastern Dro
KENNMOOR RD
Manor
Farm
Mawkin's
Bridge
Meadmoor Rhyne
Decoypool Dro
River Kenn
CLAVERHAM DRO
Say's Rhyne
Barberry
Farm
Little River
Kenn Moor
Gate
Laurel
Bank
HAM LA
Claverham
Court
LOWER CLAVERHAM
Moorstreet
Bow
MUD LA
LC
Lower
Claverham
Chestnut
Farm
BS49
Chestnut
Farm
JASMINE LA
MOOR RD
Stowey Rhyne
Hillsea
Horsecastle
NORTH END
The
Grange
Laurel
Farm
BROCKLEY
WAY
Claverham
Manor
Farm
Market
Ind Est
B3133
SOUTH VIEW TERR
Yatton
LAUREL
TERR
Claverham
Farm
BROADCROFT
AVE
PO
Court-de-Wyck
CE Prim
Sch
CLAVERHAM
PK
34
18

A B C D E F

NAILSEA
BLACKFRIARS RD
KINGSTON WAY
HANNAH MORE RD
KINGSTON RD
KINGSTON DR
THE CHIMES
THE BRAMBLEYS
NEWTON GN
ENGINE LA
ST MARY'S PK
WORCESTER GDNS
BLAKENEY GR
ST MARY'S GR
ALLINGTON GDNS
RUSSETT GR
FERN GR
THE UPLANDS
CHURCH LA
OLD CHURCH RD
WHITEOAK WAY
SHAFTESBURY CL
HASLANDS
MORGANS HILL CL
ILMINSTER CL
HARPTREE CL
Hannah More Inf Sch
Grove Jun Sch
1 WHITESFIELD RD
2 CHANCEL CL
3 STRAWBERRY GDNS
4 DORCHESTER CL
BECKET'S LA
SEDGEMOOR CL
AXBRIDGE CL
BROOM FARM CL
WALNUT CL
WEDMORE RD
QUEENS RD
FOUR ACRES CL
CHARD CL
FARLERS END
THE PERRINGS
WOOKEY CL
SHIPHAM CL
CHEDDAR CL
STATION RD
AVENING CL
TRENDLEWOOD WAY
BUCKLANDS BATCH
BUCKLANDS DR
BUCKLANDS LA
BUCKLANDS END
BUCKLANDS GR
White Oak House
1 LANGPORT GDNS
2 CHURCH HAYES DR
3 CHURCH HAYES CL
4 DINDER CL
5 ASH HAYES RD
6 LITTLE MEADOW END
7 RICKFORD RD
8 BRUTON
Coombe Farm
WEST END LA
West End
Nursebatch Farm
Young Wood Farm
Coombe Grange
P
Nailsea and Backwell
STATION CL
THE BRIARS
MOORFIELD RD
YOUNGWOOD LA
Bizley Farm
Backwell
MOOR LA
LONG-THORN
LUNTY MEAD
GARSTONS CL
Baytree Farm
South Common Farm
NETHERTON WOOD LA
Netherton Wood
Nailsea Ford
Chelvey
CHELVEY RD
Grove Farm
West Town
THE GREEN
WEST TOWN RD
Nailsea Court
BS48
Burnt House Farm
Midgell Farm
Brickyard Wood
A370
KELLWAYS
CHELVEY LA
BROCKLEY LA
Brockley Elm Farm
Brockley Elm
Manor Farm
CHELVEY BATCH
LOWER CLAVERHAM
BROCKLEY WAY
Brockley Court
Brockley Hall
Tap's Combe
Grove Farm
Claverham Green Farm
BS49
LITTLEWOOD LA
ST NICHOLAS WAY
Brockley
MAIN RD
Yorkhouse Cave
BROCKLEY COMBE RD
Brockley Combe
Brockley Wood
MEETINGHOUSE LA
PO
Cleeve House Farm
Cleeve Hill

8
7
69
6
5
68
4
3
67
2
1
66

45 A B 46 C D 47 E F

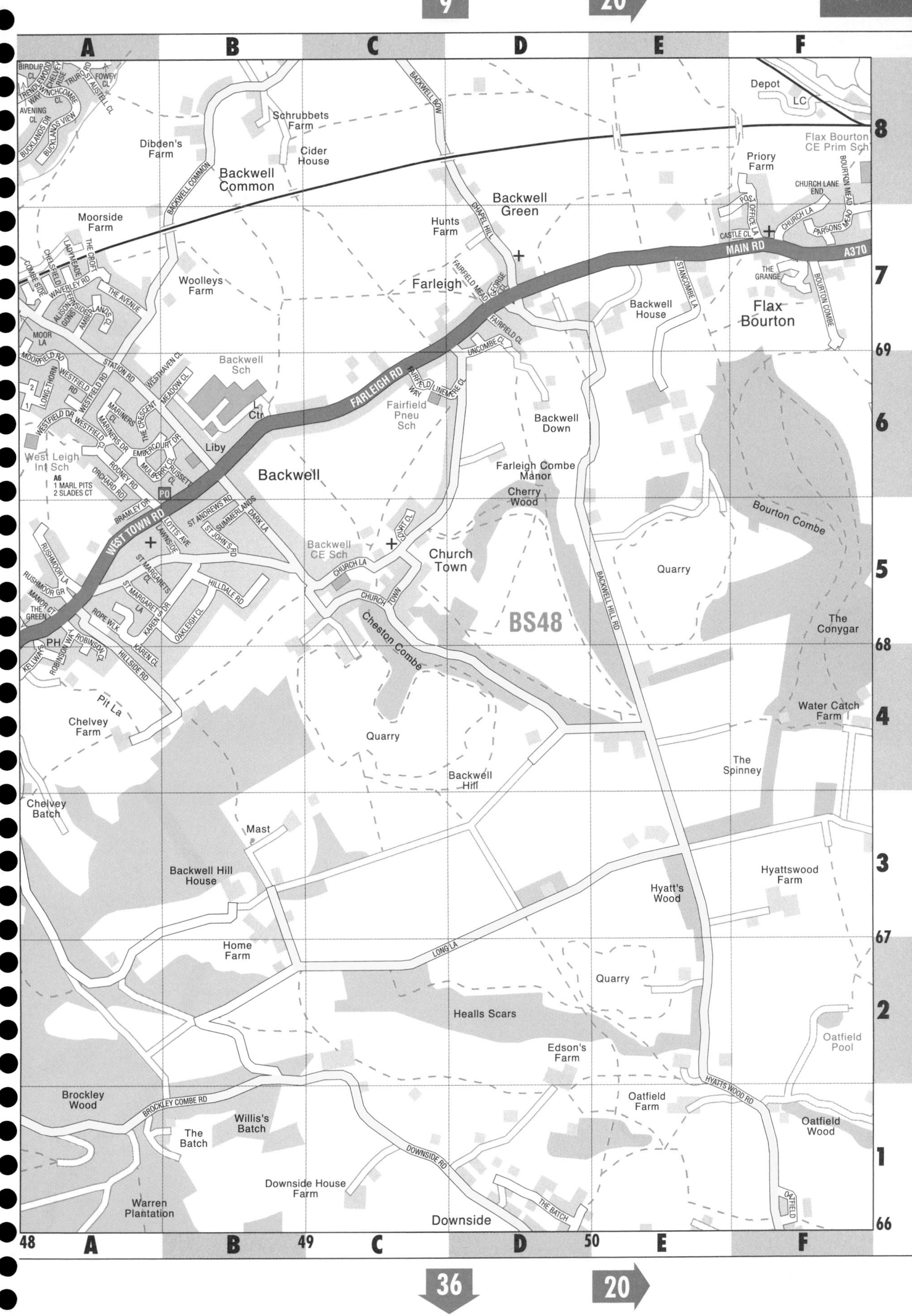

9
20
A
B
C
D
E
F
Depot
LC
Flax Bourton CE Prim Sch
Priory Farm
Schrubbets Farm
Cider House
Dibden's Farm
Backwell Common
Moorside Farm
Hunts Farm
Backwell Green
Church Lane End
Main Rd
A370
Farleigh
Woolleys Farm
Backwell House
Flax Bourton
The Grange
Backwell Sch
L Ctr
Farleigh Rd
Fairfield Pneu Sch
Backwell Down
West Leigh Inf Sch
Liby
Backwell
Farleigh Combe Manor
Cherry Wood
Bourton Combe
PO
West Town Rd
Backwell CE Sch
Church Town
Quarry
BS48
The Conygar
PH
Cheston Combe
Chelvey Farm
Pit La
Water Catch Farm
Quarry
Backwell Hill
The Spinney
Chelvey Batch
Mast
Backwell Hill House
Hyatt's Wood
Hyattswood Farm
Home Farm
Long La
Quarry
Healls Scars
Edson's Farm
Oatfield Pool
Brockley Wood
Brockley Combe Rd
Willis's Batch
The Batch
Oatfield Farm
Hyatts Wood Rd
Oatfield Wood
Downside Rd
Downside House Farm
Warren Plantation
Downside
The Batch
Backwell Hill Rd
A6
1 Marl Pits
2 Slades Ct
48
49
50
66
67
68
69
1
2
3
4
5
6
7
8
36
20

19
10

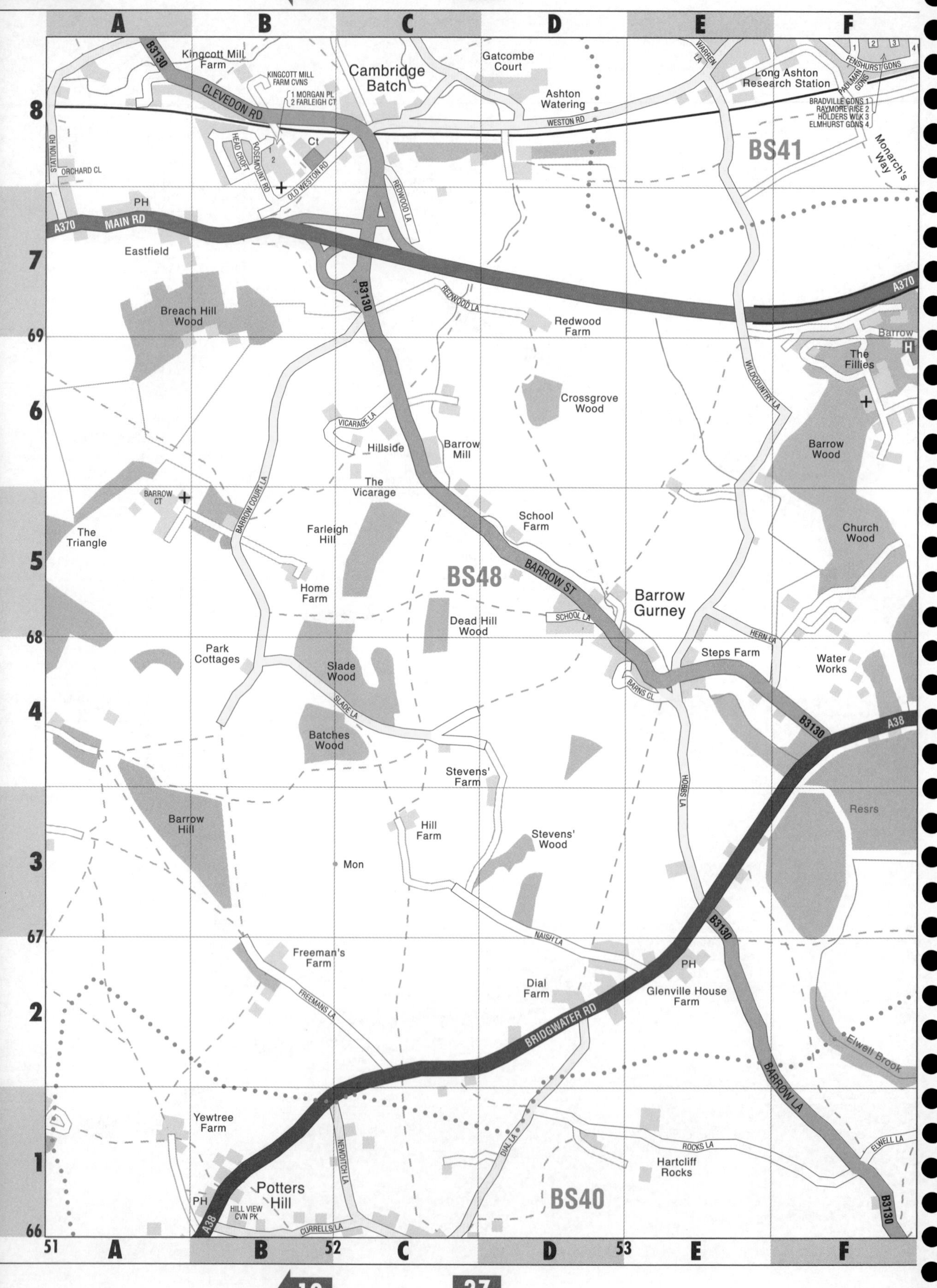
A B C D E F
8
7
69
6
5
68
4
3
67
2
1
66
51
52
53
Kingcott Mill Farm
KINGCOTT MILL FARM CVNS
1 MORGAN PL
2 FARLEIGH CT
Cambridge Batch
Gatcombe Court
Ashton Watering
Long Ashton Research Station
FENSHURST GDNS
PAULMAN GDNS
BRADVILLE GDNS 1
RAYMORE RISE 2
HOLDERS WLK 3
ELMHURST GDNS 4
Monarch's Way
BS41
B3130
CLEVEDON RD
WESTON RD
WARREN LA
STATION RD
ORCHARD CL
HEAD CROFT
ROSEMOUNT RD
OLD WESTON RD
Ct
REDWOOD LA
PH
A370
MAIN RD
Eastfield
Breach Hill Wood
Redwood Farm
Barrow
The Fillies
Crossgrove Wood
WILDCOUNTRY LA
VICARAGE LA
Hillside
Barrow Mill
Barrow Wood
The Vicarage
BARROW CT
BARROW COURT LA
The Triangle
Farleigh Hill
School Farm
Church Wood
BS48
BARROW ST
Home Farm
Barrow Gurney
Dead Hill Wood
SCHOOL LA
HERN LA
Park Cottages
Slade Wood
Steps Farm
Water Works
BARNS CL
SLADE LA
Batches Wood
A38
Stevens' Farm
Resrs
Barrow Hill
Hill Farm
HOBBS LA
Stevens' Wood
Mon
NAISH LA
Freeman's Farm
Dial Farm
Glenville House Farm
FREEMANS LA
BRIDGWATER RD
Elwell Brook
BARROW LA
Yewtree Farm
NEWDITCH LA
DIAL LA
ROCKS LA
Hartcliff Rocks
ELWELL LA
Potters Hill
HILL VIEW CVN PK
CURRELLS LA
BS40

19
37

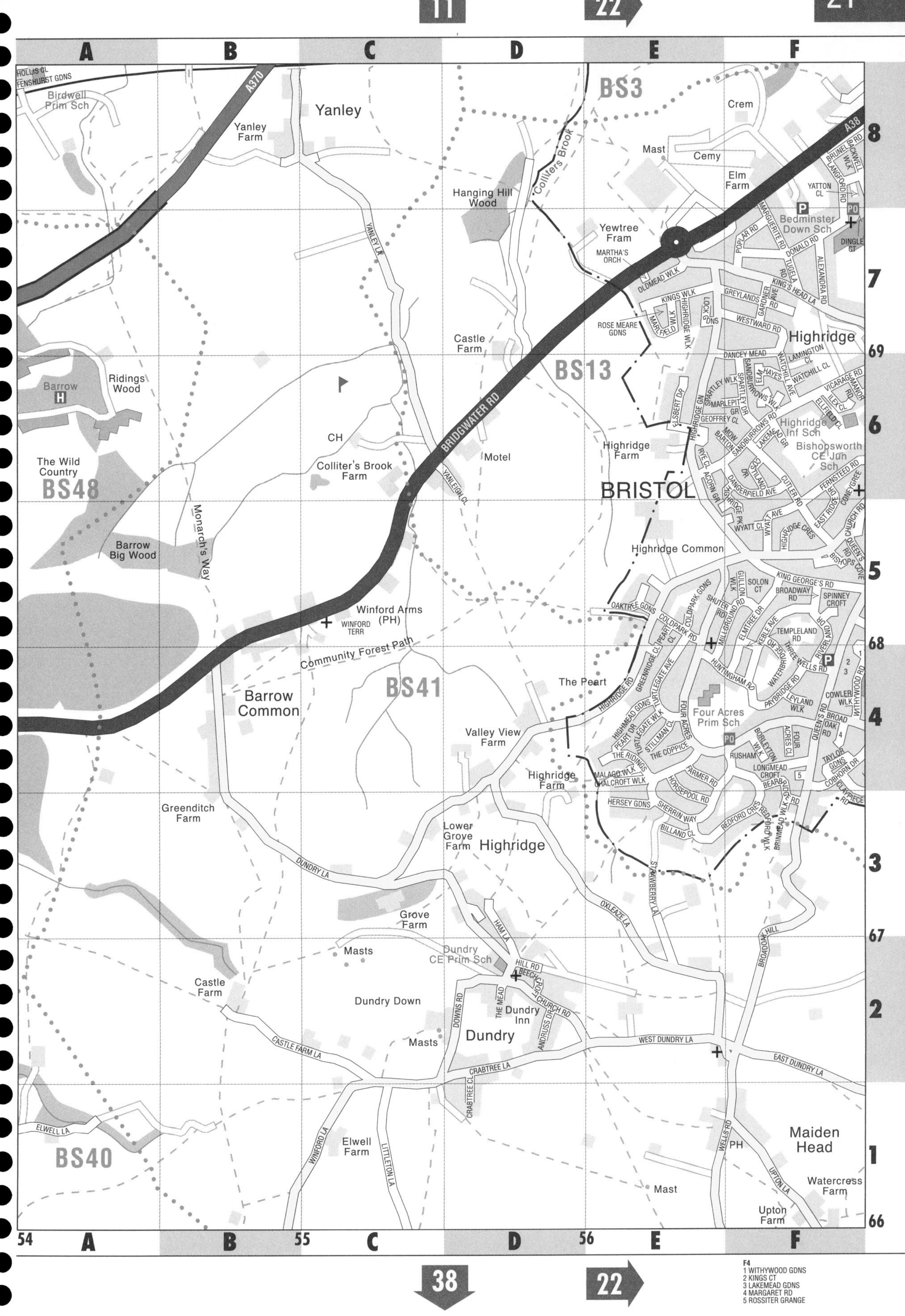

F4
1 WITHYWOOD GDNS
2 KINGS CT
3 LAKEMEAD GDNS
4 MARGARET RD
5 ROSSITER GRANGE

21

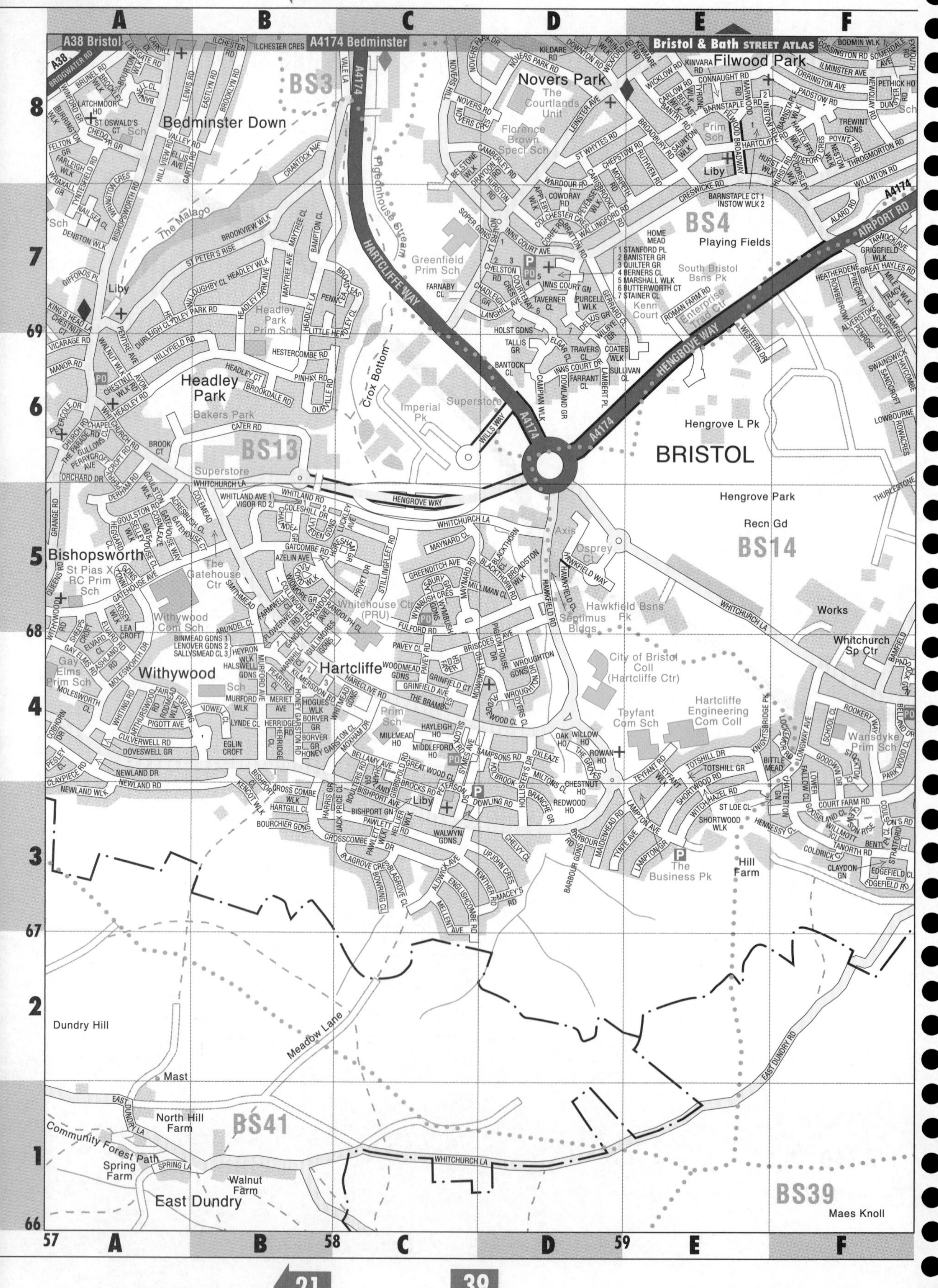
A
B
C
D
E
F
A38 Bristol
A4174 Bedminster
Bristol & Bath STREET ATLAS
8
7
69
6
5
68
4
3
67
2
1
66
57
58
59
BS3
BS4
BS13
BS14
BS41
BS39
Bedminster Down
Novers Park
Filwood Park
The Courtlands Unit
Florence Brown Specl Sch
Greenfield Prim Sch
Headley Park
Headley Park Prim Sch
Bakers Park
Crox Bottom
Imperial Pk
Superstore
Hengrove L Pk
BRISTOL
Hengrove Park
Recn Gd
Playing Fields
South Bristol Bsns Pk
Enterprise Trad Ctr
Kenn Court
Bishopsworth
St Pias X RC Prim Sch
The Gatehouse Ctr
Withywood Com Sch
Withywood
Gay Elms Prim Sch
Hartcliffe
Whitehouse Ctr (PRU)
Axis
Osprey Ct
Hawkfield Bsns Pk
Septimus Bldgs
City of Bristol Coll (Hartcliffe Ctr)
Hartcliffe Engineering Com Coll
Teyfant Com Sch
Works
Whitchurch Sp Ctr
Wansdyke Prim Sch
The Business Pk
Hill Farm
Dundry Hill
Meadow Lane
Mast
North Hill Farm
Community Forest Path
Spring Farm
Walnut Farm
East Dundry
Maes Knoll
HARTCLIFFE WAY
HENGROVE WAY
AIRPORT RD
WHITCHURCH LA
EAST DUNDRY RD
The Malago
Pigeonhouse Stream
A4174

21

39

24

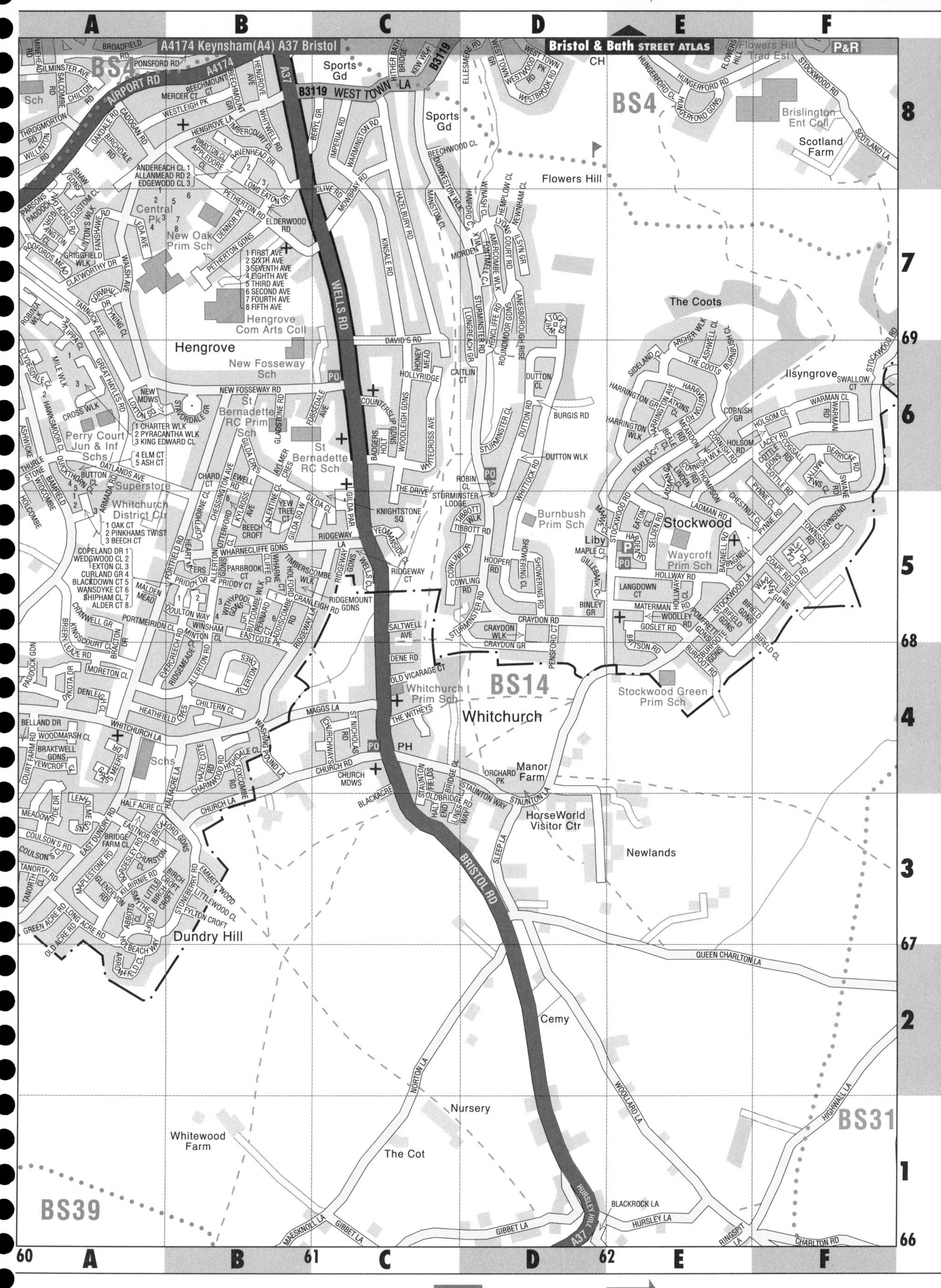

A4174 Keynsham(A4) A37 Bristol
Bristol & Bath STREET ATLAS
P&R
A B C D E F
8 7 6 5 4 3 2 1
69 68 67 66
60 61 62
BS4
BS14
BS31
BS39
AIRPORT RD
A4174
A37
B3119
WEST TOWN LA
WELLS RD
BRISTOL RD
HURSLEY HILL
Sports Gd
Flowers Hill Trad Est
Brislington Ent Coll
Scotland Farm
SCOTLAND LA
Flowers Hill
CH
Central Pk
New Oak Prim Sch
Hengrove Com Arts Coll
Hengrove
New Fosseway Sch
NEW FOSSEWAY RD
St Bernadette RC Prim Sch
St Bernadette RC Sch
Perry Court Jun & Inf Schs
Superstore
Whitchurch District Ctr
The Coots
Ilsyngrove
Stockwood
Burnbush Prim Sch
Waycroft Prim Sch
Stockwood Green Prim Sch
Liby
Whitchurch
Whitchurch Prim Sch
Manor Farm
HorseWorld Visitor Ctr
Newlands
Schs
Dundry Hill
QUEEN CHARLTON LA
Cemy
NORTON LA
WOOLLARD LA
Nursery
The Cot
Whitewood Farm
HIGHWALL LA
BLACKROCK LA
HURSLEY LA
GIBBET LA
MAESKNOLL LA
RINGSPIT LA
CHARLTON RD
STOCKWOOD RD
WHITCHURCH LA
CHURCH RD
STAUNTON LA
SLEEP LA
MAGGS LA
CRAYDON RD
HOLLWAY RD
PO
PH

40

24

23

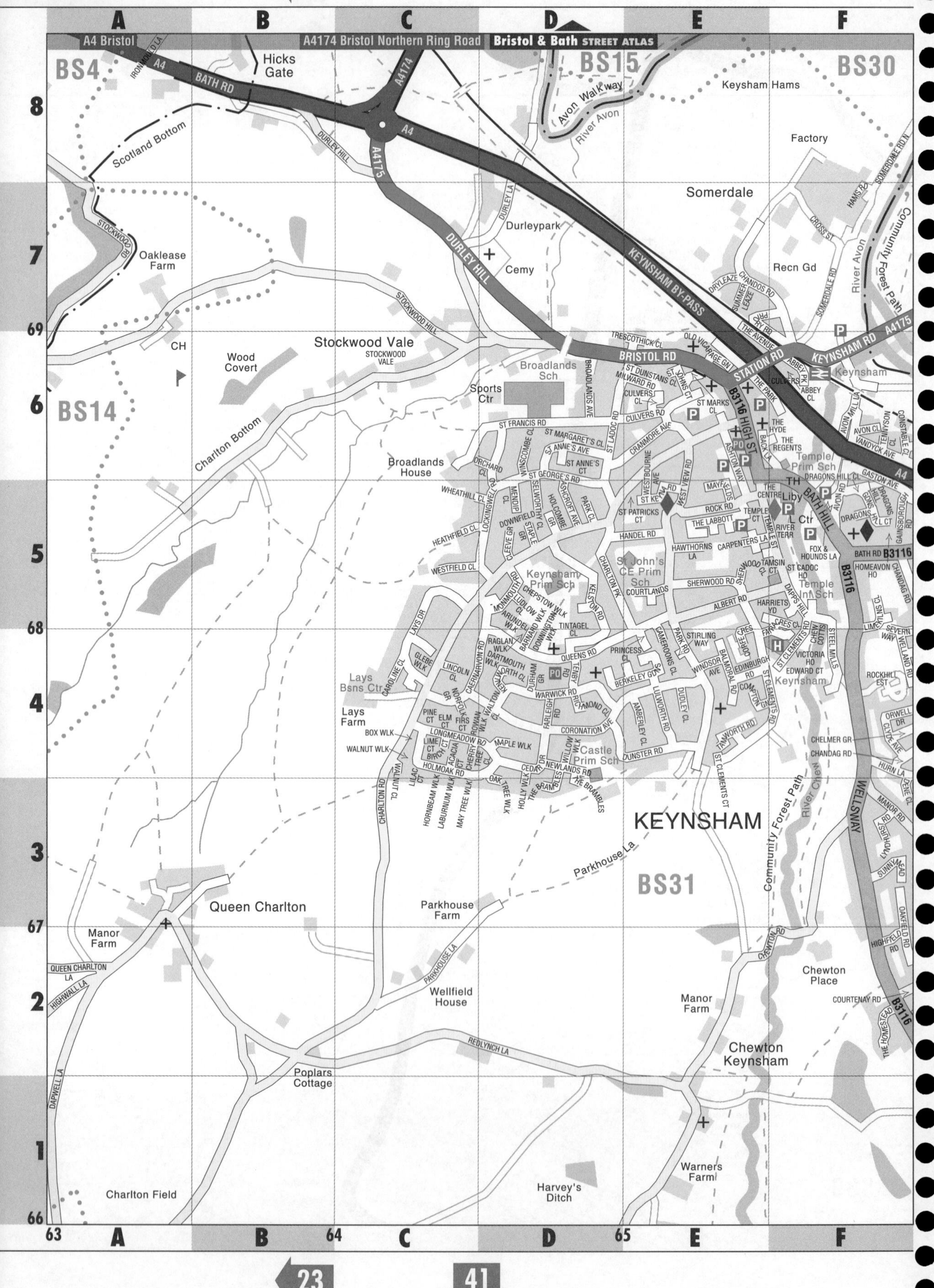
A
B
C
D
E
F
A4 Bristol
A4174 Bristol Northern Ring Road
Bristol & Bath STREET ATLAS
BS4
BS15
BS30
BS14
BS31
8
7
69
6
5
68
4
3
67
2
1
66
63
64
65
Hicks Gate
IRONMOULD LA
BATH RD
A4
A4174
A4175
DURLEY HILL
Scotland Bottom
Avon Walkway
River Avon
Keysham Hams
Factory
Somerdale
Stockwood Rd
Oaklease Farm
Durleypark
Cemy
KEYNSHAM BY-PASS
Recn Gd
STOCKWOOD HILL
Stockwood Vale
STOCKWOOD VALE
CH
Wood Covert
Broadlands Sch
Sports Ctr
BRISTOL RD
STATION RD
KEYNSHAM RD
A4175
Keynsham
Charlton Bottom
Broadlands House
ST FRANCIS RD
B3116 HIGH ST
BATH HILL
Temple Prim Sch
Liby
L Ctr
BATH RD B3116
St John's CE Prim Sch
Keynsham Prim Sch
Temple Inf Sch
Lays Bsns Ctr
Lays Farm
Castle Prim Sch
KEYNSHAM
Community Forest Path
River Chew
WELLSWAY
B3116
Parkhouse La
Queen Charlton
Parkhouse Farm
Manor Farm
QUEEN CHARLTON LA
HIGHWALL LA
PARKHOUSE LA
Wellfield House
CHARLTON RD
Chewton Place
Manor Farm
CHEWTON RD
REDLYNCH LA
Chewton Keynsham
Poplars Cottage
DAPWELL LA
Warners Farm
Harvey's Ditch
Charlton Field

23

41

26

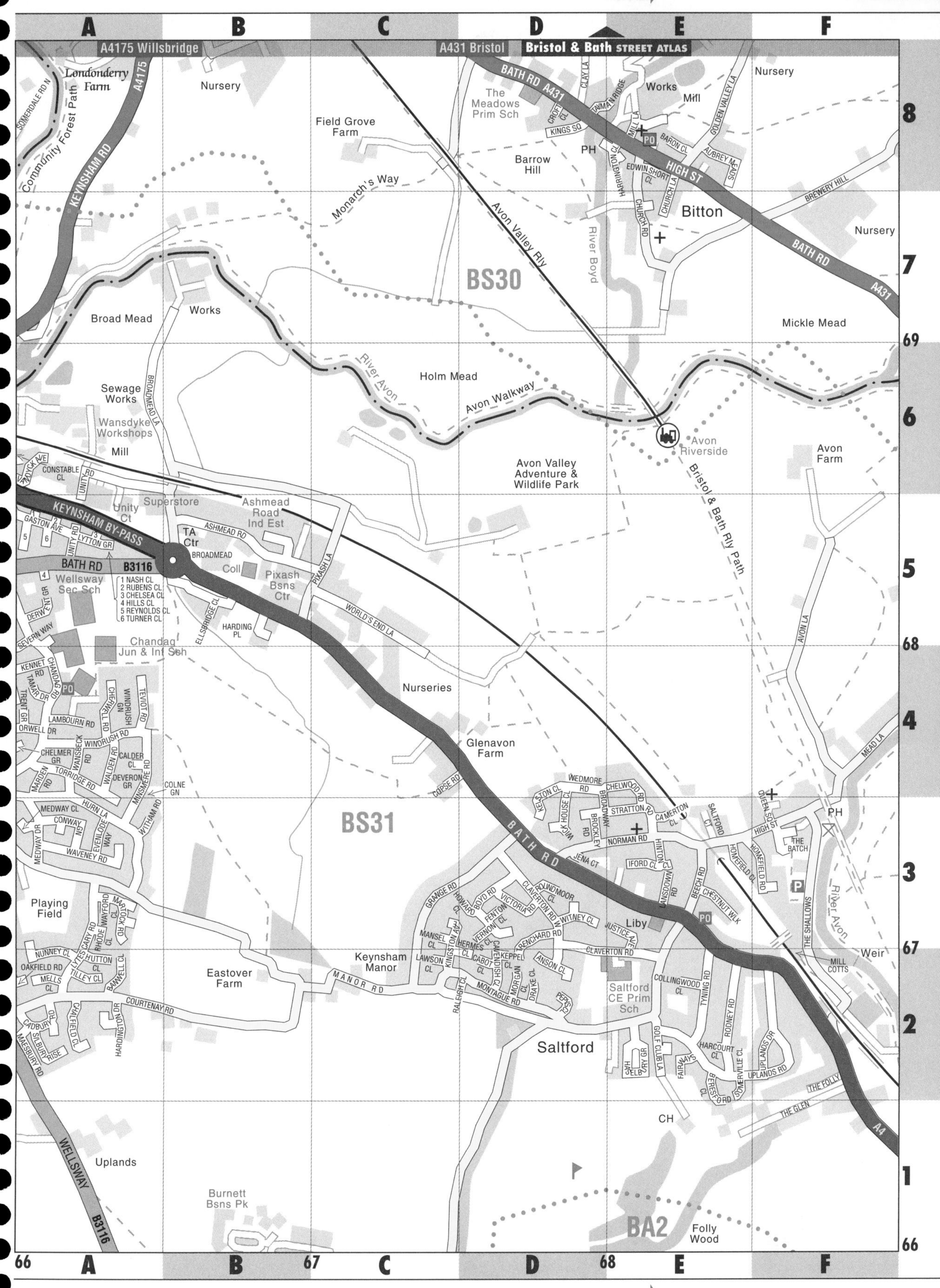

A4175 Willsbridge
A431 Bristol
Bristol & Bath STREET ATLAS
Londonderry Farm
Community Forest Path
KEYNSHAM RD
A4175
Nursery
Field Grove Farm
Monarch's Way
The Meadows Prim Sch
BATH RD A431
Barrow Hill
Works
Mill
Nursery
HIGH ST
Bitton
BREWERY HILL
Nursery
BATH RD
Avon Valley Rly
River Boyd
BS30
Broad Mead
Works
Mickle Mead
River Avon
Holm Mead
Avon Walkway
Sewage Works
Wansdyke Workshops
Mill
Avon Riverside
Avon Valley Adventure & Wildlife Park
Avon Farm
Bristol & Bath Rly Path
KEYNSHAM BY-PASS
Unity Ct
Superstore
Ashmead Road Ind Est
TA Ctr
BATH RD B3116
Wellsway Sec Sch
Coll
Pixash Bsns Ctr
1 NASH CL
2 RUBENS CL
3 CHELSEA CL
4 HILLS CL
5 REYNOLDS CL
6 TURNER CL
WORLD'S END LA
Chandag Jun & Inf Sch
AVON LA
Nurseries
Glenavon Farm
MEAD LA
BS31
BATH RD
PH
THE BATCH
River Avon
THE SHALLOWS
Weir
MILL COTTS
Playing Field
Keynsham Manor
MANOR RD
Liby
Eastover Farm
Saltford CE Prim Sch
Saltford
CH
THE FOLLY
THE GLEN
A4
Uplands
WELLSWAY
B3116
Burnett Bsns Pk
BA2
Folly Wood
A B C D E F
1 2 3 4 5 6 7 8
66 67 68 69

25

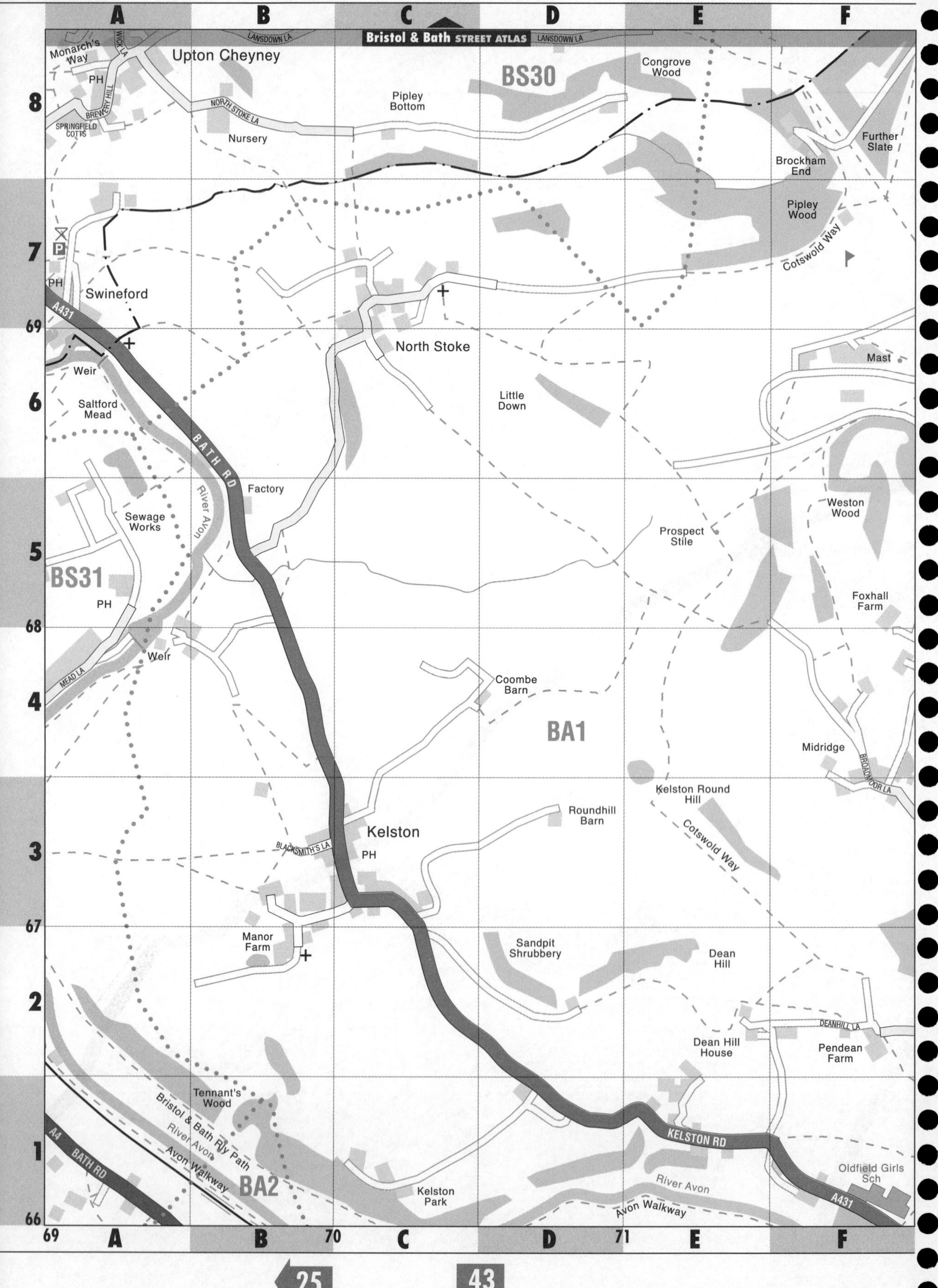

A B C D E F
Bristol & Bath STREET ATLAS
8 7 6 5 4 3 2 1
69 68 67 66
69 70 71
LANSDOWN LA
Monarch's Way
Upton Cheyney
PH
WICK LA
BREWERY HILL
SPRINGFIELD COTTS
NORTH STOKE LA
Nursery
Pipley Bottom
BS30
Congrove Wood
Further Slate
Brockham End
Pipley Wood
Cotswold Way
PH
Swineford
A431
North Stoke
Weir
Mast
Saltford Mead
Little Down
BATH RD
Factory
River Avon
Sewage Works
Weston Wood
Prospect Stile
BS31
PH
Foxhall Farm
Weir
MEAD LA
Coombe Barn
BA1
Midridge
BROADMOOR LA
Kelston Round Hill
Roundhill Barn
Kelston
BLACKSMITH'S LA
PH
Cotswold Way
Manor Farm
Sandpit Shrubbery
Dean Hill
DEANHILL LA
Dean Hill House
Pendean Farm
Tennant's Wood
Bristol & Bath Rly Path
River Avon
Avon Walkway
KELSTON RD
A4
BATH RD
BA2
Kelston Park
River Avon
Oldfield Girls Sch
A431
Avon Walkway

25

43

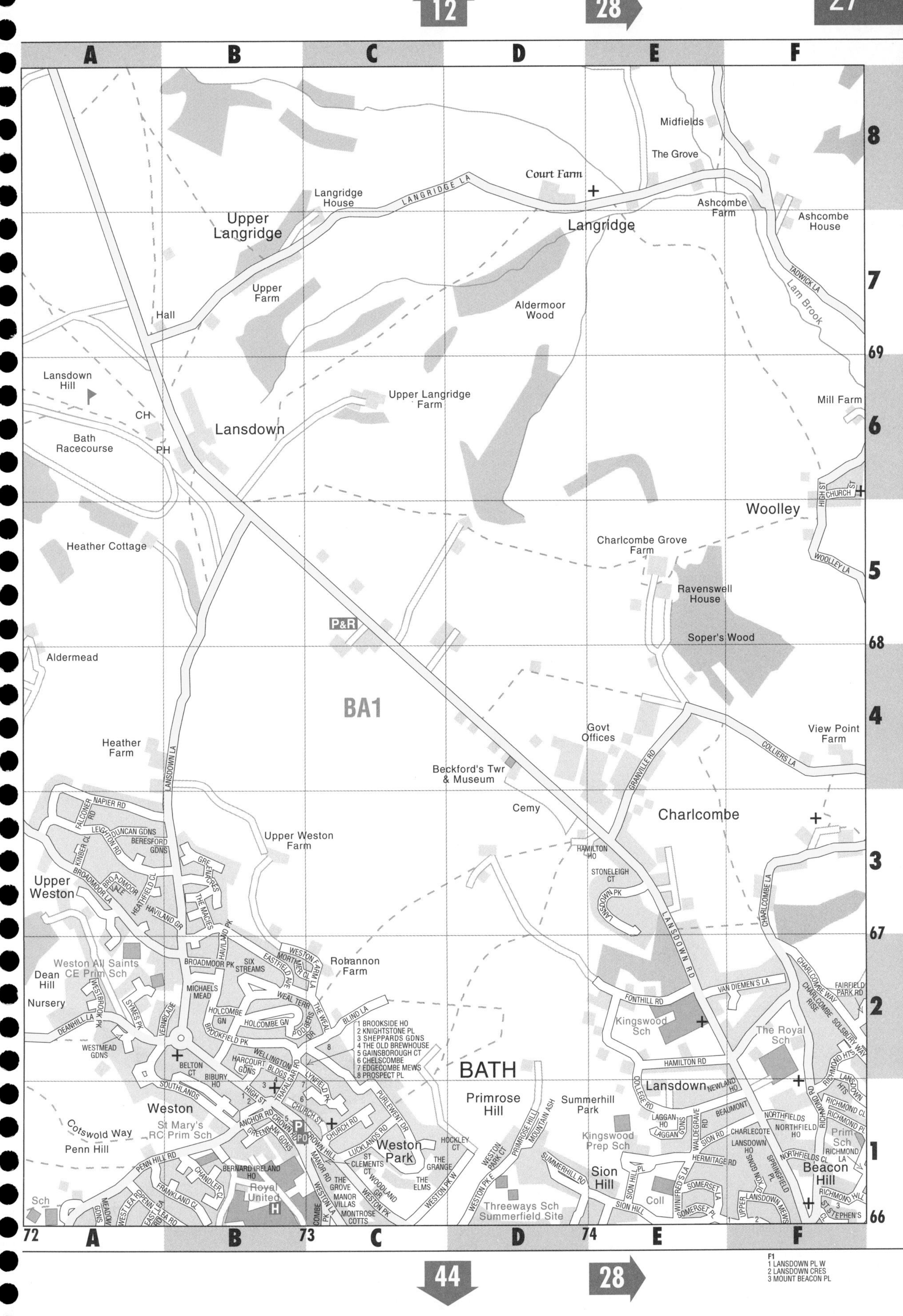

F1
1 LANSDOWN PL W
2 LANSDOWN CRES
3 MOUNT BEACON PL

27
13

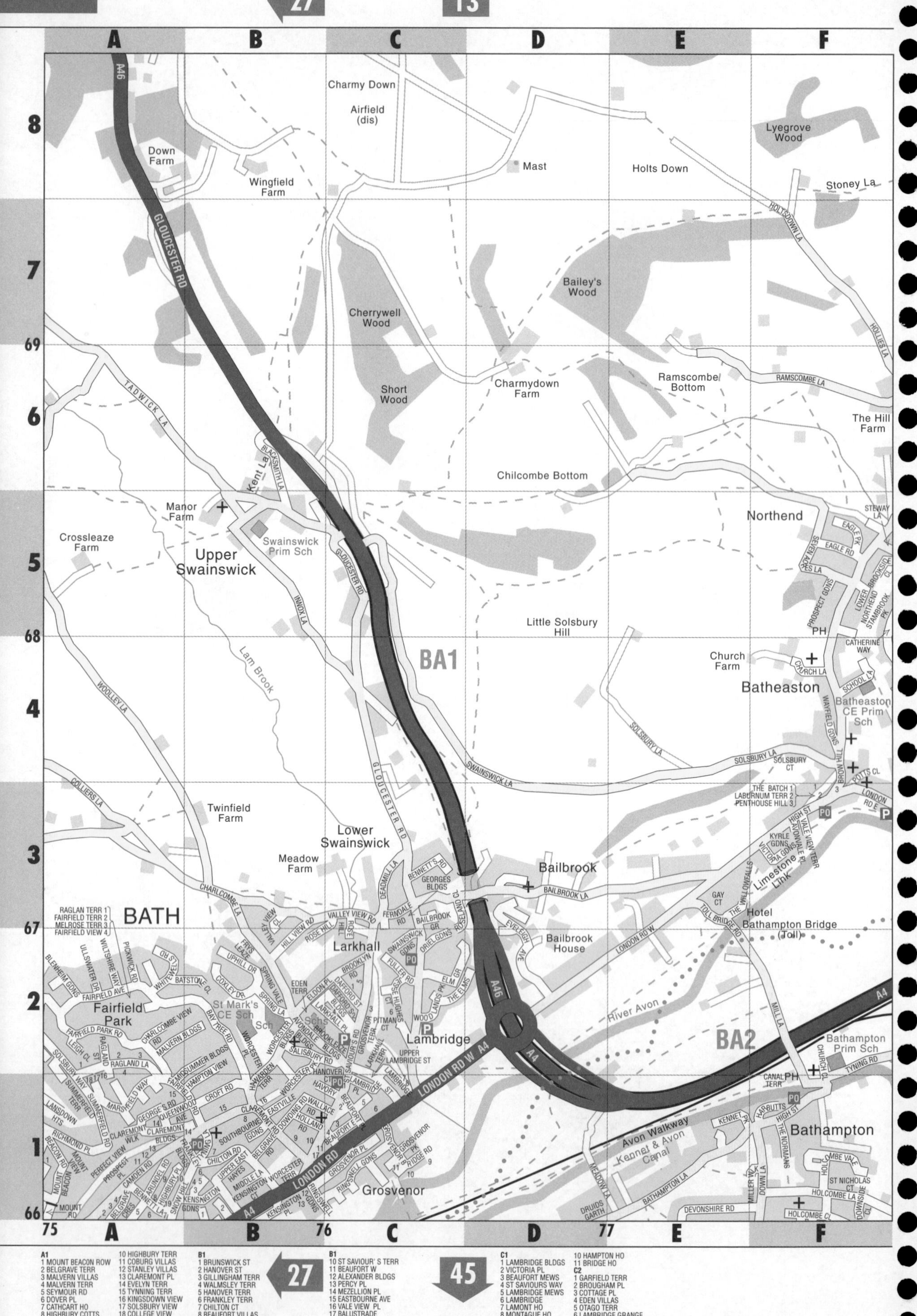

A1
1 MOUNT BEACON ROW
2 BELGRAVE TERR
3 MALVERN VILLAS
4 MALVERN TERR
5 SEYMOUR RD
6 DOVER PL
7 CATHCART HO
8 HIGHBURY COTTS
9 HIGHBURY VILLAS
10 HIGHBURY TERR
11 COBURG VILLAS
12 STANLEY VILLAS
13 CLAREMONT PL
14 EVELYN TERR
15 TYNNING TERR
16 KINGSDOWN VIEW
17 SOLSBURY VIEW
18 COLLEGE VIEW
19 INCHALLOCH

B1
1 BRUNSWICK ST
2 HANOVER ST
3 GILLINGHAM TERR
4 WALMSLEY TERR
5 HANOVER TERR
6 FRANKLEY TERR
7 CHILTON CT
8 BEAUFORT VILLAS
9 GROSVENOR VILLAS

27

B1
10 ST SAVIOUR' S TERR
11 BEAUFORT W
12 ALEXANDER BLDGS
13 PERCY PL
14 MEZELLION PL
15 EASTBOURNE AVE
16 VALE VIEW PL
17 BALUSTRADE

45

C1
1 LAMBRIDGE BLDGS
2 VICTORIA PL
3 BEAUFORT MEWS
4 ST SAVIOURS WAY
5 LAMBRIDGE MEWS
6 LAMBRIDGE
7 LAMONT HO
8 MONTAGUE HO
9 EASTON HO
10 HAMPTON HO
11 BRIDGE HO

C2
1 GARFIELD TERR
2 BROUGHAM PL
3 COTTAGE PL
4 EDEN VILLAS
5 OTAGO TERR
6 LAMBRIDGE GRANGE

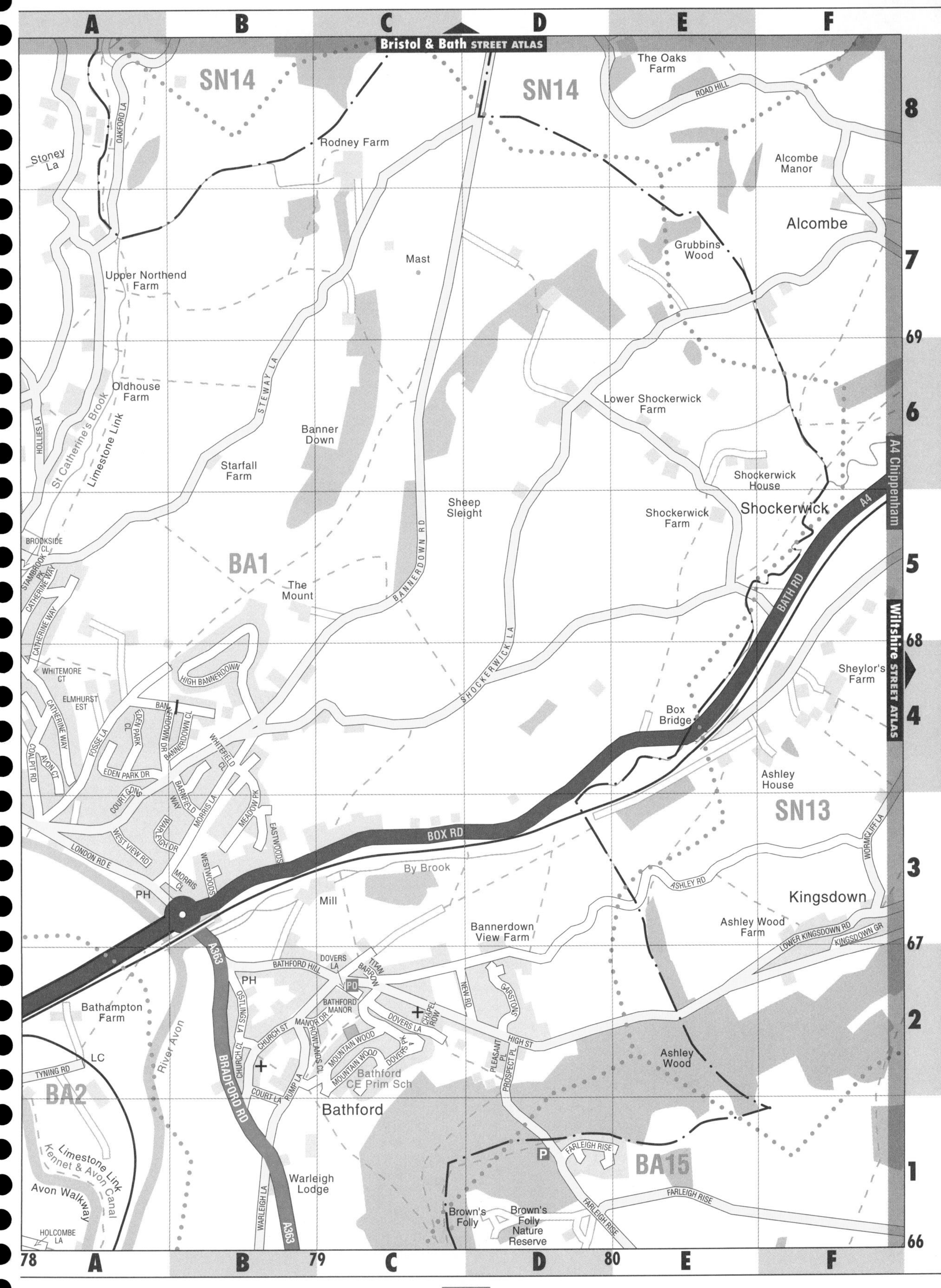
Bristol & Bath STREET ATLAS
SN14
SN14
The Oaks Farm
Road Hill
Stoney La
Oakford La
Rodney Farm
Alcombe Manor
Alcombe
Grubbins Wood
Mast
Upper Northend Farm
Lower Shockerwick Farm
Oldhouse Farm
Steway La
Banner Down
Hollies La
St Catherine's Brook
Limestone Link
Starfall Farm
Shockerwick House
A4 Chippenham
Sheep Sleight
Shockerwick Farm
Shockerwick
Brookside Cl
Stambrook Pk
BA1
The Mount
Bannerdown Rd
Bath Rd
Catherine Way
Wiltshire STREET ATLAS
Whitemore Ct
High Bannerdown
Sheylor's Farm
Elmhurst Est
Shockerwick La
Box Bridge
Fosse La
Eden Park Cl
Bannerdown Dr
Bannerdown Cl
Whitefield Cl
Coalpit Rd
Avon Ct
Eden Park Dr
Ashley House
Court Gdns
Barnfield Way
Morris La
Meadow Pk
SN13
West View Rd
Warleigh Dr
Eastwoods
Womcliff La
London Rd E
Box Rd
Morris Cl
Westwoods
By Brook
Ashley Rd
PH
Mill
Kingsdown
Bannerdown View Farm
Ashley Wood Farm
Lower Kingsdown Rd
Kingsdown Gr
A363
Bathford Hill
Dovers La
Titan Barrow
PH
PO
New Rd
Garstons
Bathampton Farm
Ostlings La
Bathford Manor
Chapel Row
Manor Dr
Dovers La
Church St
Rowlands Cl
Mountain Wood
High St
Dovers Pk
Pleasant Pl
Prospect Pl
LC
Ashley Wood
River Avon
Tyning Rd
Bradford Rd
Church Cl
Pump La
Bathford CE Prim Sch
BA2
Court La
Bathford
Farleigh Rise
P
Limestone Link
Kennet & Avon Canal
BA15
Warleigh Lodge
Avon Walkway
Farleigh Rise
Warleigh La
Brown's Folly
Brown's Folly Nature Reserve
Holcombe La
A363
A B C D E F
8 7 69 6 5 68 4 3 67 2 1 66
78 79 80

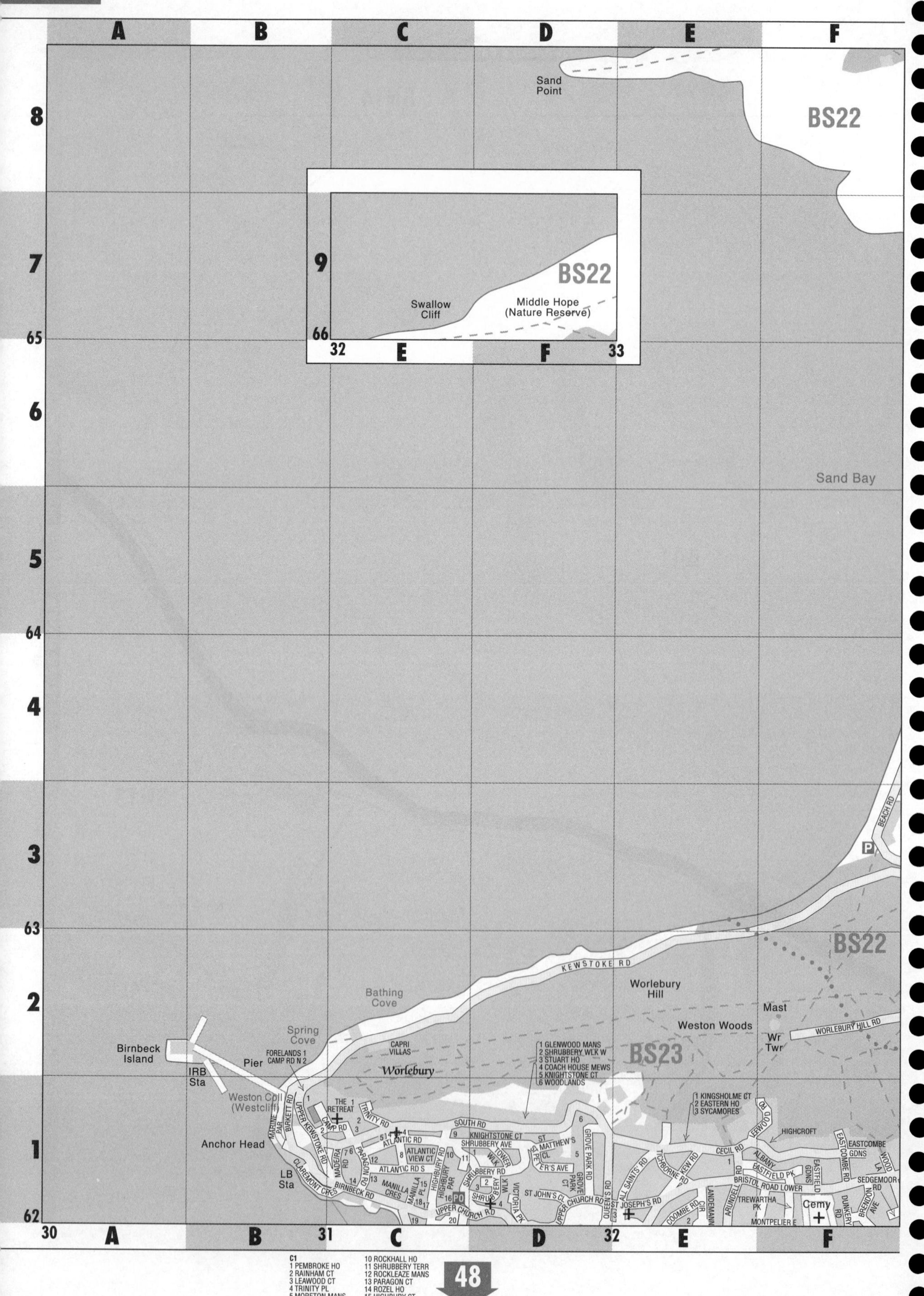

C1
1 PEMBROKE HO
2 RAINHAM CT
3 LEAWOOD CT
4 TRINITY PL
5 MORETON MANS
6 GOSFORD MANS
7 FRANKFORD MANS
8 HAMILTON RD
9 MAPLE CT
10 ROCKHALL HO
11 SHRUBBERY TERR
12 ROCKLEAZE MANS
13 PARAGON CT
14 ROZEL HO
15 HIGHBURY CT
16 VILLA ROSA
17 BADMINTON CT
18 CAIRO CT
19 GLENTWORTH CT
20 RAGLAN PL

48

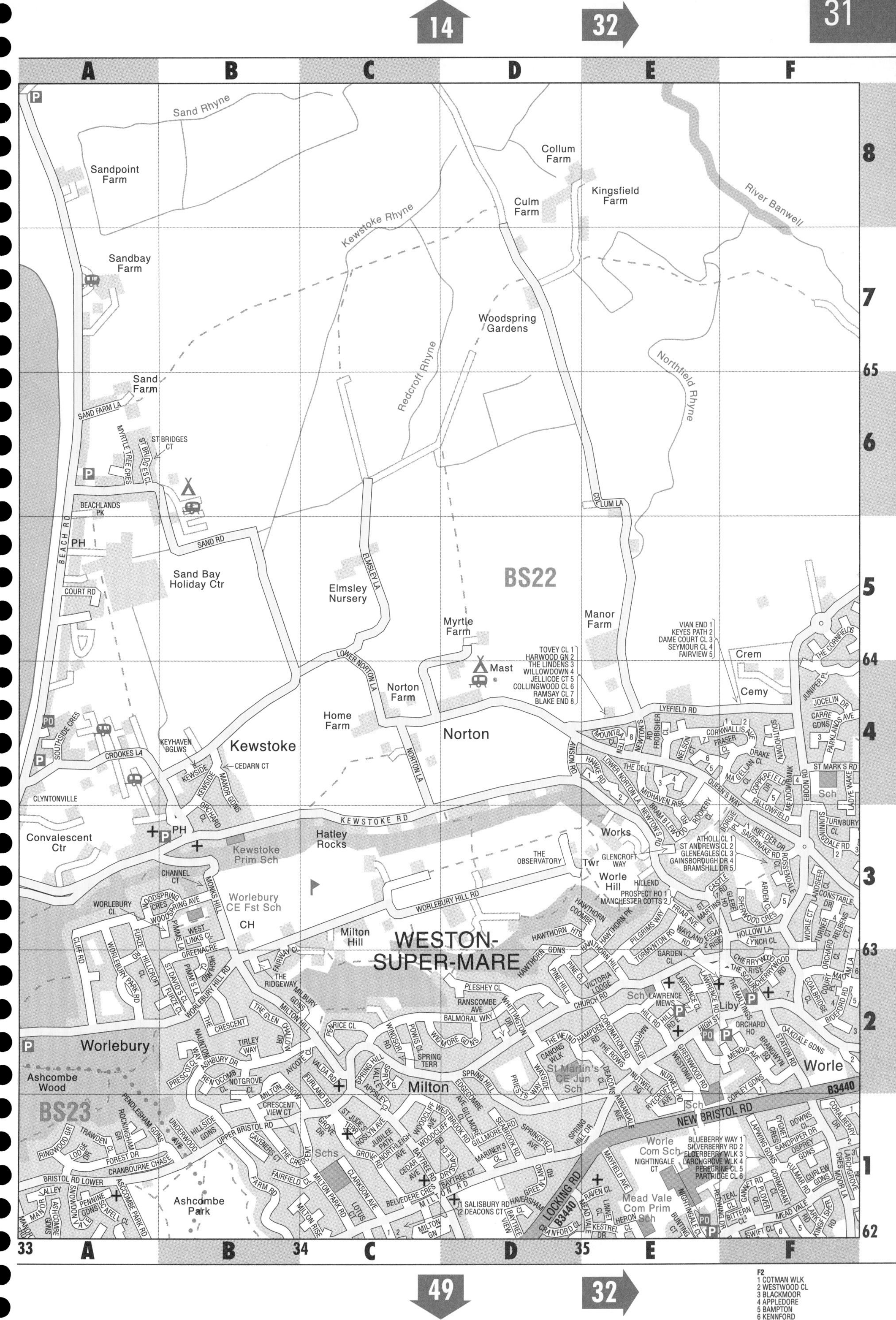

F2
1 COTMAN WLK
2 WESTWOOD CL
3 BLACKMOOR
4 APPLEDORE
5 BAMPTON
6 KENNFORD
7 KNIGHTSTONE PL

31
15

A2
1 KENNFORD
2 ST CLEMENTS CT
3 KINGSWEAR
4 BAMPTON
5 CREDITON
6 FENITON
7 INSTOW
8 IVYBRIDGE
9 HONITON
10 EXBOURNE
11 COLYTON
12 DALWOOD
13 DOWLAND
14 HARTLAND
15 EBDEN LO

B4
1 WELLARD CL
2 TYLER GN
3 TREMLETT MEWS
4 GARNER CT
5 WAINWRIGHT CL
6 EMLYN CL
7 THE SAFFRONS

31
50

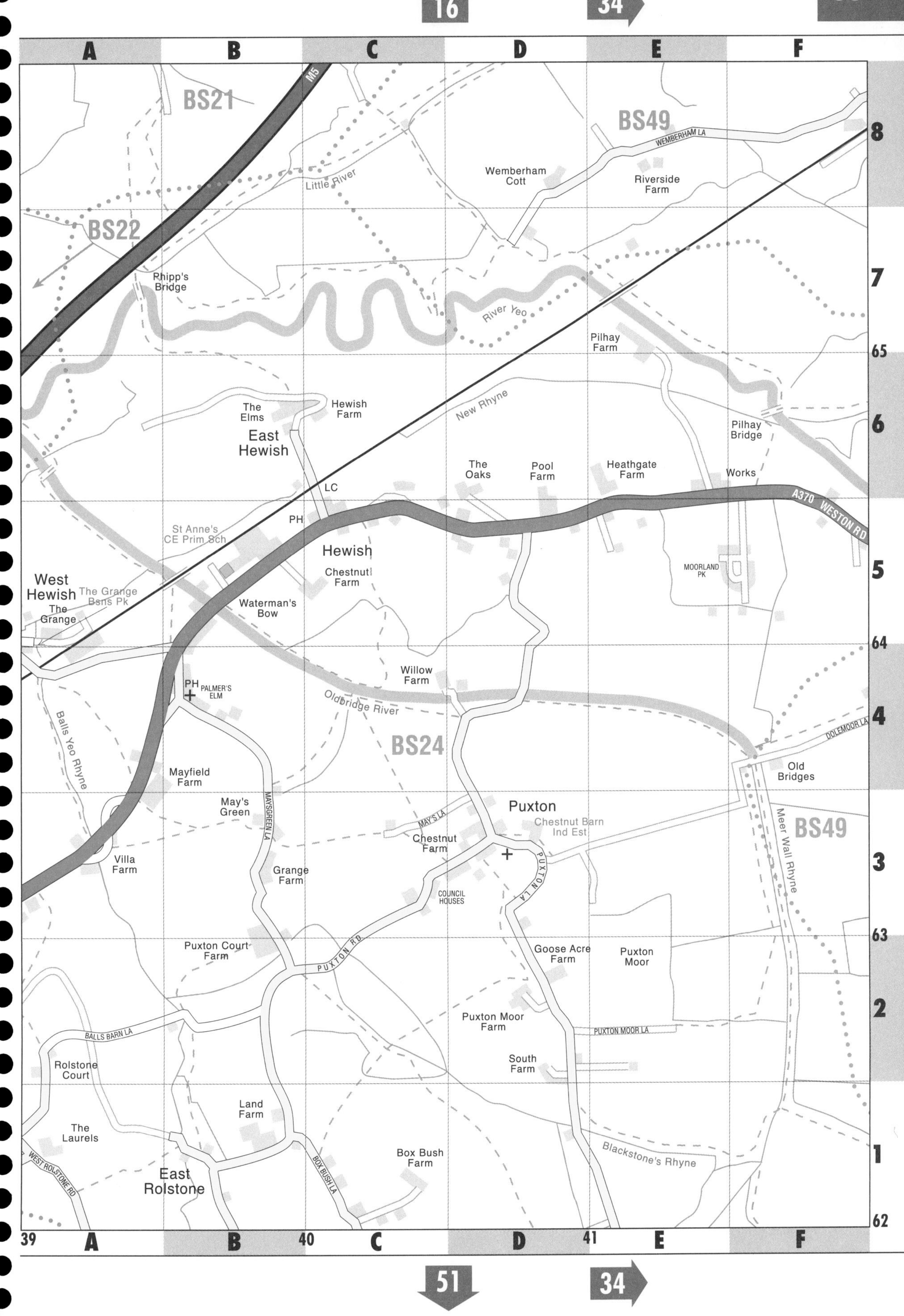
16
34
A B C D E F
BS21
M5
BS49
WEMBERHAM LA
8
Wemberham Cott
Riverside Farm
Little River
BS22
Rhipp's Bridge
7
River Yeo
Pilhay Farm
65
The Elms
Hewish Farm
New Rhyne
East Hewish
6
Pilhay Bridge
The Oaks
Pool Farm
Heathgate Farm
Works
LC
PH
A370 WESTON RD
St Anne's CE Prim Sch
Hewish
Chestnut Farm
MOORLAND PK
5
West Hewish
The Grange Bsns Pk
The Grange
Waterman's Bow
64
Willow Farm
PH
PALMER'S ELM
Oldbridge River
Balls Yeo Rhyne
BS24
4
DOLEMOOR LA
Old Bridges
Mayfield Farm
May's Green
MAYSGREEN LA
Puxton
MAY'S LA
Chestnut Barn Ind Est
BS49
Chestnut Farm
Meer Wall Rhyne
Villa Farm
Grange Farm
PUXTON LA
3
COUNCIL HOUSES
63
Puxton Court Farm
PUXTON RD
Goose Acre Farm
Puxton Moor
2
Puxton Moor Farm
BALLS BARN LA
PUXTON MOOR LA
Rolstone Court
South Farm
Land Farm
The Laurels
1
Blackstone's Rhyne
WEST ROLSTONE RD
BOX BUSH LA
Box Bush Farm
East Rolstone
62
39 A B 40 C D 41 E F
51
34

33
17

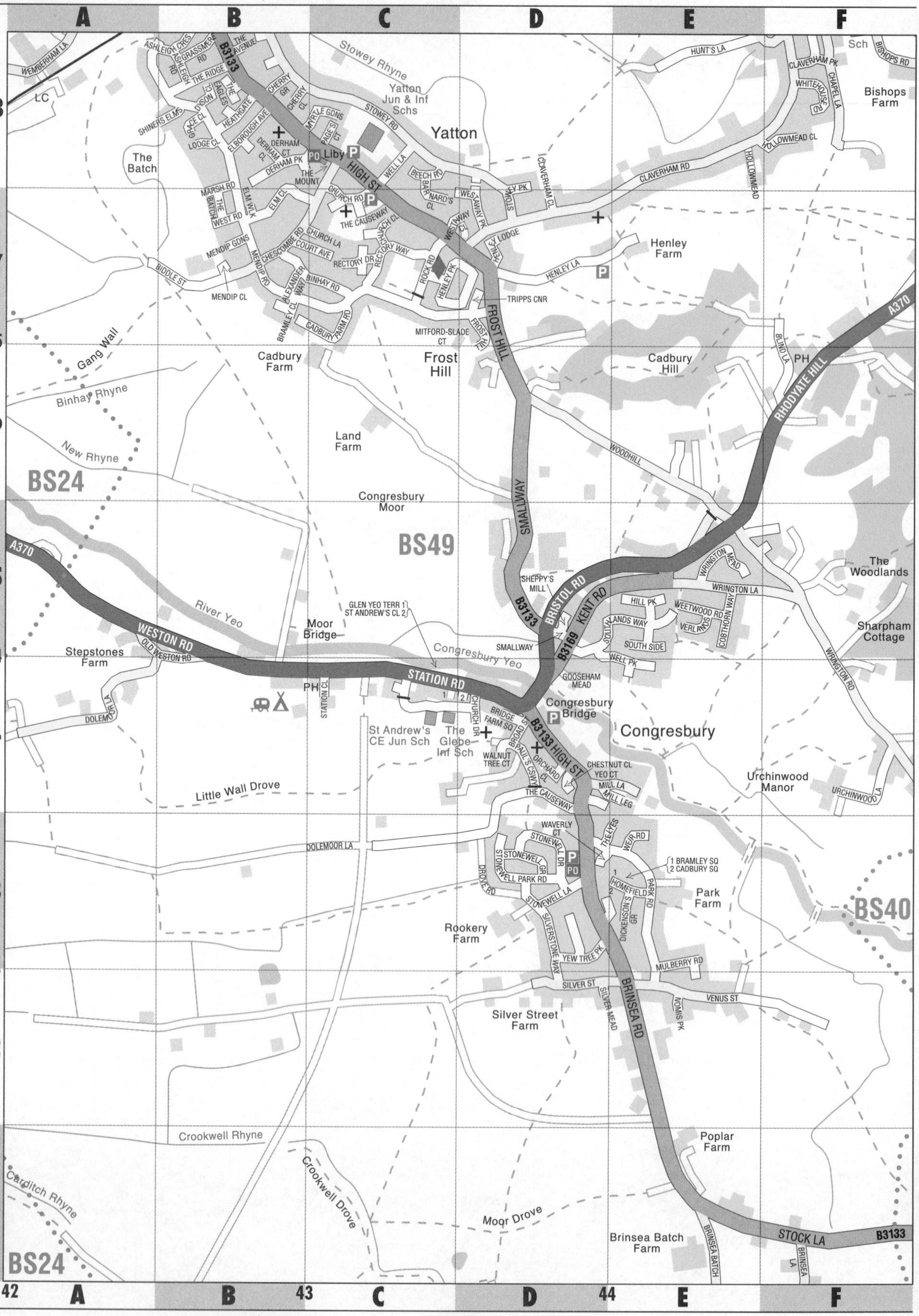

A B C D E F

8
7
65
6
5
64
4
3
63
2
1
62

Yatton
Yatton Jun & Inf Schs
Stowey Rhyne
The Batch
Liby
PO
The Mount
Cadbury Farm
Frost Hill
Tripps Cnr
Mitford-Slade Ct
Henley Farm
Cadbury Hill
Bishops Farm
Sch
PH
LC
Gang Wall
Binhay Rhyne
New Rhyne
BS24
Land Farm
Congresbury Moor
BS49
River Yeo
Moor Bridge
Stepstones Farm
PH
Congresbury Yeo
Glen Yeo Terr 1
St Andrew's Cl 2
Sheppy's Mill
Smallway
Gooseham Mead
Congresbury Bridge
Congresbury
St Andrew's CE Jun Sch
The Glebe Inf Sch
Walnut Tree Ct
The Woodlands
Sharpham Cottage
Urchinwood Manor
Little Wall Drove
Dolemoor La
Waverly Ct
1 Bramley Sq
2 Cadbury Sq
Park Farm
BS40
Rookery Farm
Silver Street Farm
Crookwell Rhyne
Crookwell Drove
Carditch Rhyne
Moor Drove
Poplar Farm
Brinsea Batch Farm
BS24

B3133
A370
B3169
High St
Station Rd
Weston Rd
Old Weston Rd
Frost Hill
Smallway
Bristol Rd
Kent Rd
Rhodyate Hill
Woodhill
Wrington La
Wrington Rd
Wrington Mead
Hill Pk
Weetwood Rd
Verlands
Cobthorn Way
Southlands Way
South Side
Well Pk
Claverham Rd
Claverham Cl
Claverham Pk
Hollowmead
Hollowmead Cl
Hunt's La
Bishops Rd
Whitehouse Rd
Chapel La
Henley La
Henley Lodge
Henley Pk
Rock Rd
Stowey Pk
Stowey Rd
Westaway Pk
Westaway Cl
Beech Rd
Barnard's Cl
Well La
Church Rd
The Causeway
Church La
Church Cl
Rectory Dr
Rectory Way
Court Ave
Chescombe Rd
Binhay Rd
Cadbury Farm Rd
Bramley Cl
Alexander Way
Mendip Rd
Mendip Gdns
Mendip Cl
Biddle St
West Rd
The Batch
Marsh Rd
Elm Wlk
Elm Cl
Elborough Ave
Derham Ct
Derham Cl
Derham Pk
Heathgate
Lodge Cl
Grace Cl
Dyson Cl
Shiners Elms
The Eagles
The Ridge
Ashleigh Rd
Ashleigh Cres
Grassmere Rd
The Avenue
Cherry Gr
Cherry Cl
Myrtle Gdns
Page's Ct
Wemberham La
Station Cl
Church Dr
Bridge Farm Sq
Broad St
Paul's Cswy
Orchard Cl
Chestnut Cl
Yeo Ct
Mill La
Mill Leg
The Causeway
The Leys
Weir Rd
Stonewell Dr
Stonewell Gr
Stonewell Park Rd
Stonewell La
Drove Rd
Silverstone Way
Yew Tree Pk
Homefield Rd
Dickenson's Gr
Park Rd
Mulberry Rd
Silver St
Silver Mead
Venus St
Nomis Pk
Brinsea Rd
Brinsea Batch
Brinsea La
Stock La
Urchinwood La
Blind La

42 A B 43 C D 44 E F

33
52

18
36

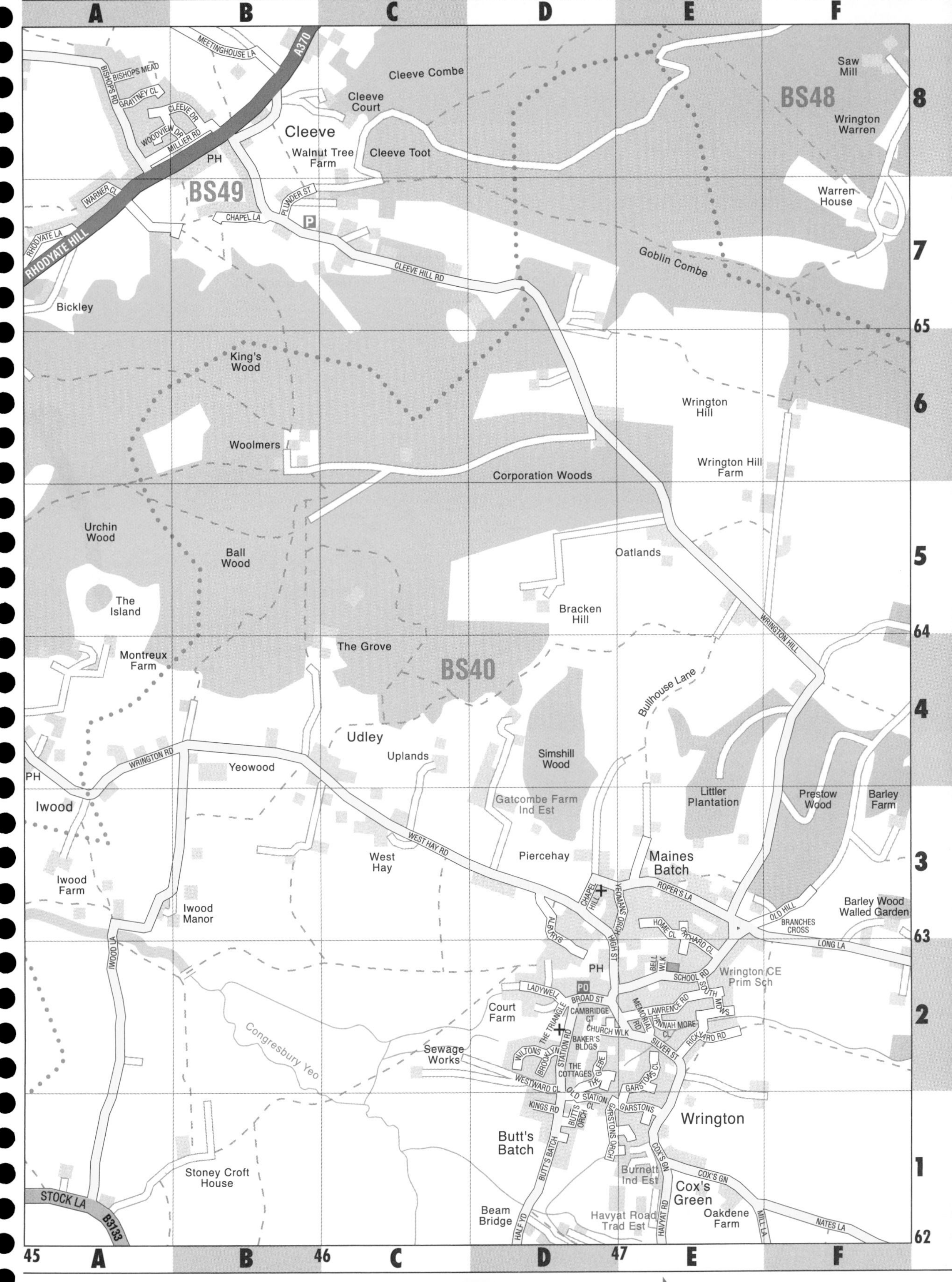
A
B
C
D
E
F
8
7
65
6
5
64
4
3
63
2
1
62
45
46
47
A370
MEETINGHOUSE LA
BISHOPS MEAD
BISHOPS RD
GRAITNEY CL
CLEEVE DR
WOODVIEW DR
MILLIER RD
Cleeve Combe
Cleeve Court
Cleeve
Walnut Tree Farm
Cleeve Toot
PH
BS49
WARNER CL
PLUNDER ST
CHAPEL LA
RHODYATE LA
RHODYATE HILL
CLEEVE HILL RD
BS48
Saw Mill
Wrington Warren
Warren House
Goblin Combe
Bickley
King's Wood
Woolmers
Wrington Hill
Wrington Hill Farm
Corporation Woods
Urchin Wood
Ball Wood
Oatlands
The Island
Bracken Hill
WRINGTON HILL
Montreux Farm
The Grove
BS40
Bullhouse Lane
Udley
Uplands
Simshill Wood
WRINGTON RD
Yeowood
PH
Iwood
Gatcombe Farm Ind Est
Littler Plantation
Prestow Wood
Barley Farm
WEST HAY RD
West Hay
Piercehay
Maines Batch
Iwood Farm
Iwood Manor
CHAPEL HILL
YEOMANS ORCH
ROPER'S LA
Barley Wood Walled Garden
OLD HILL
BRANCHES CROSS
LONG LA
ALBURYS
HOME CL
ORCHARD CL
HIGH ST
IWOOD LA
PH
BELL WLK
SCHOOL RD
Wrington CE Prim Sch
PO
LADYWELL
BROAD ST
SOUTH MEAD
Court Farm
CAMBRIDGE CT
MEMORIAL RD
LAWRENCE RD
HANNAH MORE CL
Congresbury Yeo
THE TRIANGLE
CHURCH WLK
BAKER'S BLDGS
SILVER ST
RICKYARD RD
Sewage Works
WILTONS
BROOKLYN
STATION RD
THE COTTAGES
THE GLEBE
GARSTONS CL
WESTWARD CL
OLD STATION CL
GARSTONS
KINGS RD
BUTTS ORCH
GARSTONS ORCH
Wrington
Butt's Batch
COX'S GN
BUTT'S BATCH
Stoney Croft House
Burnett Ind Est
COX'S GN
Cox's Green
STOCK LA
B3133
Beam Bridge
HALF YD
Havyat Road Trad Est
HAVYAT RD
Oakdene Farm
MILL LA
NATES LA

53
36

35
19
A
B
C
D
E
F
8
7
65
6
5
64
4
3
63
2
1
62
48
49
50
Downside Farm
Lulsgate Farm
Cook's Farm
Stone Farm
DOWNSIDE RD
HYATTS WOOD RD
NORTH SIDE RD
CH
BS48
COOKS BRIDLE PATH
Wrington Warren
North Hill
Bristol International Airport
WINTERS LA
Cornerpool Farm
A38
Spying Copse
Goblin Combe Farm
Broadfield Farm
High Wood
Cornerpool Cottage
Pine Farm
Hailstones Farm
NEW RD
ASHFORD RD
Meeting House Farm
Cottage Farm
ROW OF ASHES LA
BS40
Water Catches
Little Horts Wood
Redhill
Worship's Farm
Burnt House Farm
REDCROFT
Tucker's Grove
REDACRE
CHURCH RD
CHURCH CT
Horts Wood
Whitley Coppice
THE POUND
CHANCELLOR'S POUND
PH
Chancellor's Farm
Scars Wood
Scars Farm
LONG LA
Bottenham Coppice
RED HILL
Redhill House
LYE HOLE LA
Lye Hole
PUMP LA
UNDER LA
Lye Cross
Lyehole Farm
PIGEON LA
LYE CROSS RD
Pigeon House Farm
SUTTON LA
CRIBB'S LA
Lye Cross Farm
A38
35
54

20
38

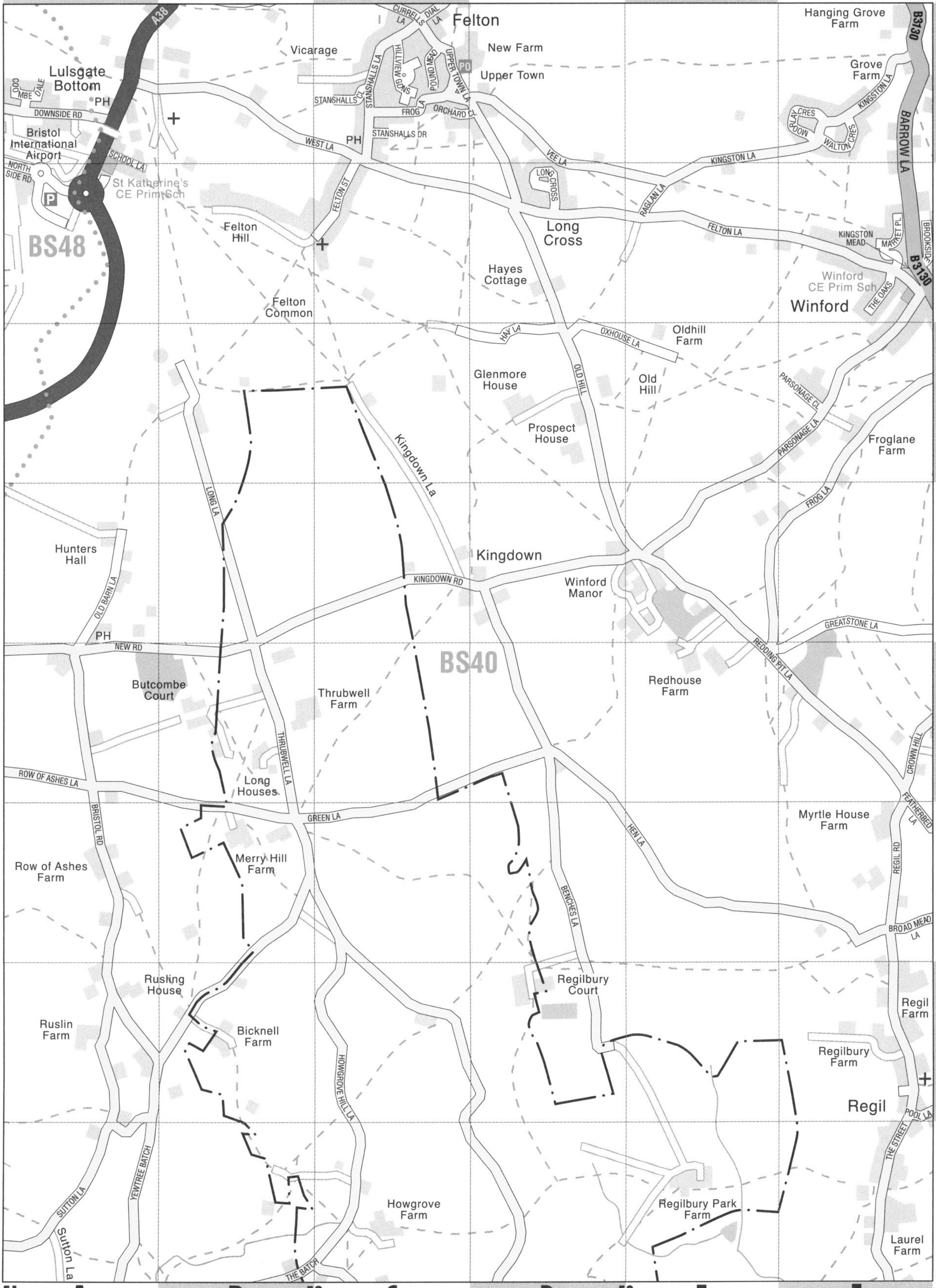

A B C D E F

Felton
New Farm
Upper Town
Vicarage
Lulsgate Bottom
PH
Bristol International Airport
St Katherine's CE Prim Sch
BS48
Felton Hill
Felton Common
Long Cross
Hayes Cottage
Hanging Grove Farm
Grove Farm
Winford CE Prim Sch
Winford
Oldhill Farm
Old Hill
Glenmore House
Prospect House
Froglane Farm
Kingdown La
Kingdown
Winford Manor
Hunters Hall
PH
Butcombe Court
Thrubwell Farm
BS40
Redhouse Farm
Long Houses
Myrtle House Farm
Row of Ashes Farm
Merry Hill Farm
Rusling House
Ruslin Farm
Bicknell Farm
Regilbury Court
Regil Farm
Regilbury Farm
Regil
Howgrove Farm
Regilbury Park Farm
Laurel Farm
Sutton La

A38
DOWNSIDE RD
NORTH SIDE RD
SCHOOL LA
WEST LA
CURRELLS LA
DIAL LA
STANSHALLS CL
STANSHALLS LA
HILLVIEW GDNS
POUND MEAD
UPPER TOWN LA
FROG LA
ORCHARD CL
STANSHALLS DR
FELTON ST
VEE LA
LONG CROSS
RAGLAN LA
KINGSTON LA
FELTON LA
MOOR CRES
WALTON CRES
KINGSTON MEAD
MARKET PL
BROOKSIDE
THE OAKS
B3130
BARROW LA
HAY LA
OXHOUSE LA
OLD HILL
PARSONAGE CL
PARSONAGE LA
LONG LA
FROG LA
KINGDOWN RD
OLD BARN LA
NEW RD
GREATSTONE LA
REDDING PIT LA
CROWN HILL
THRUBWELL LA
ROW OF ASHES LA
GREEN LA
BRISTOL RD
HEN LA
FEATHERBED LA
REGIL RD
BENCHES LA
BROAD MEAD LA
HOWGROVE HILL LA
POOL LA
THE STREET
SUTTON LA
YEWTREE BATCH
THE BATCH

8 7 65 6 5 64 4 3 63 2 1 62
51 52 53

55
38

37
21

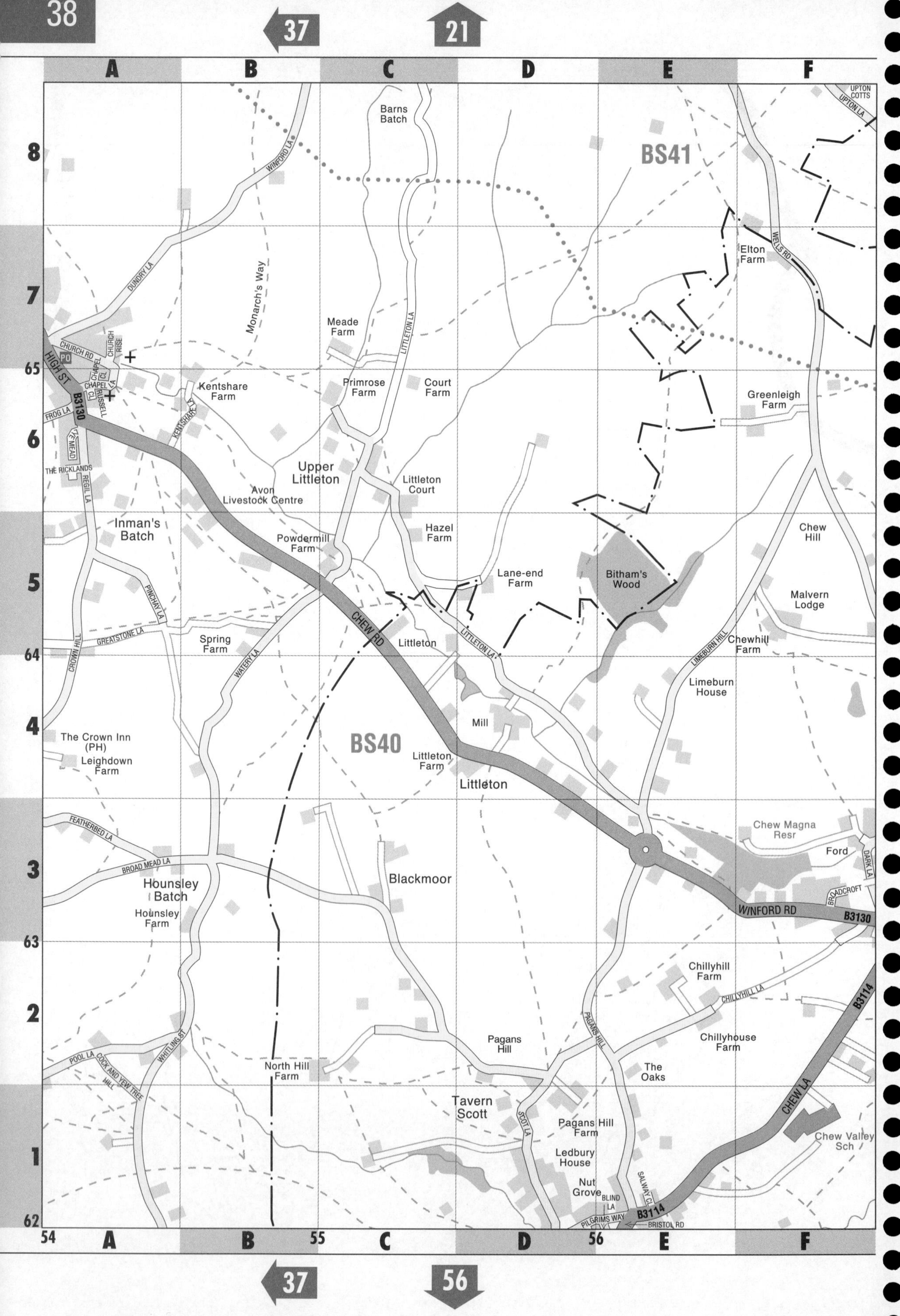
A
B
C
D
E
F
8
7
65
6
5
64
4
3
63
2
1
62
54
55
56
BS41
BS40
Barns Batch
UPTON COTTS
UPTON LA
WINFORD LA
DUNDRY LA
Monarch's Way
Meade Farm
LITTLETON LA
Elton Farm
WELLS RD
CHURCH RD
CHURCH RISE
PO
HIGH ST
CHAPEL CL
CHAPEL LA
RUSSELL
B3130
FROG LA
Kentshare Farm
KENTSHARE LA
Primrose Farm
Court Farm
Greenleigh Farm
YE MEAD
THE RICKLANDS
REGIL LA
Upper Littleton
Avon Livestock Centre
Littleton Court
Chew Hill
Inman's Batch
Powdermill Farm
Hazel Farm
Lane-end Farm
Bitham's Wood
Malvern Lodge
PINCHAY LA
CHEW RD
GREATSTONE LA
Spring Farm
Littleton
LITTLETON LA
Chewhill Farm
CROWN HILL
WATERY LA
LIMEBURN HILL
Limeburn House
Mill
The Crown Inn (PH)
Leighdown Farm
Littleton Farm
Littleton
FEATHERBED LA
Chew Magna Resr
Ford
DARK LA
BROAD MEAD LA
Hounsley Batch
Hounsley Farm
Blackmoor
BROADCROFT
WINFORD RD
B3130
Chillyhill Farm
CHILLYHILL LA
B3114
PAGANS HILL
Pagans Hill
Chillyhouse Farm
POOL LA
COCK AND YEW TREE HILL
WHITLING ST
North Hill Farm
The Oaks
CHEW LA
Tavern Scott
SCOT LA
Pagans Hill Farm
Chew Valley Sch
Ledbury House
Nut Grove
BLIND LA
SALWAY CL
PILGRIMS WAY
B3114
BRISTOL RD
A
B
C
D
E
F

37
56

22
40

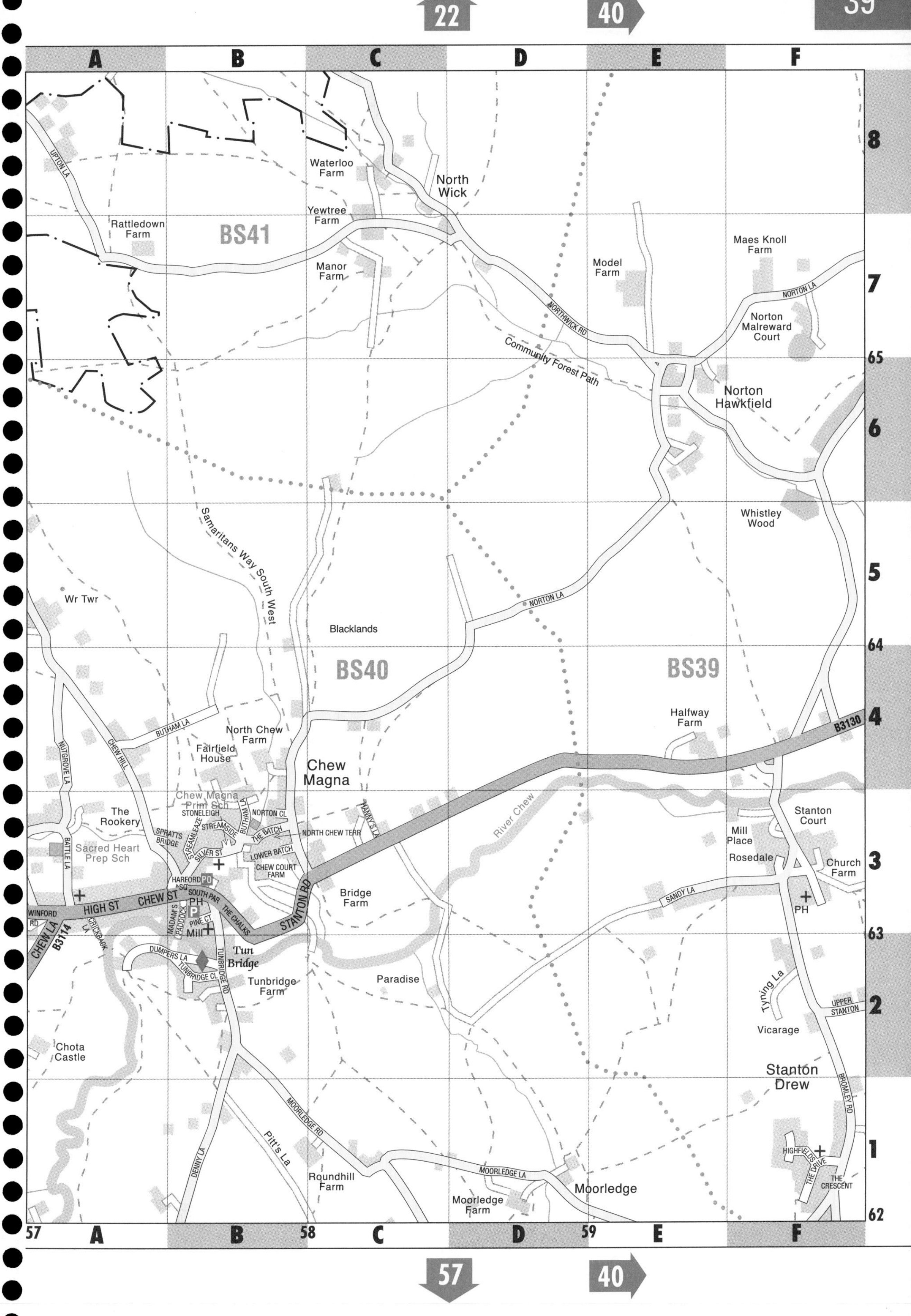
A
B
C
D
E
F
Waterloo Farm
North Wick
Yewtree Farm
Rattledown Farm
BS41
Manor Farm
Model Farm
Maes Knoll Farm
Norton Malreward Court
NORTON LA
NORTHWICK RD
Community Forest Path
Norton Hawkfield
UPTON LA
Whistley Wood
Samaritans Way South West
Wr Twr
Blacklands
NORTON LA
BS40
BS39
Halfway Farm
B3130
BUTHAM LA
North Chew Farm
Fairfield House
Chew Magna
CHEW HILL
NUTGROVE LA
Chew Magna Prim Sch
The Rookery
STONELEIGH
STREAMSIDE
NORTON CL
BUTHAM LA
HANNY'S LA
THE BATCH
NORTH CHEW TERR
River Chew
Stanton Court
Mill Place
Rosedale
Church Farm
SPRATTS BRIDGE
STREAMLEAZE
SILVER ST
LOWER BATCH
CHEW COURT FARM
Sacred Heart Prep Sch
BATTLE LA
HARFORD SQ
PO
SOUTH PAR
PH
P
THE CHALKS
STANTON RD
Bridge Farm
SANDY LA
PH
WINFORD RD
HIGH ST
CHEW ST
MADAM'S PADDOCK
PINE CT
Mill
CRICKBACK LA
CHEW LA
B3114
DUMPERS LA
TUNBRIDGE CL
TUNBRIDGE RD
Tun Bridge
Tunbridge Farm
Paradise
Tyning La
UPPER STANTON
Vicarage
Chota Castle
Stanton Drew
BROMLEY RD
MOORLEDGE RD
Pitt's La
DENNY LA
Roundhill Farm
MOORLEDGE LA
Moorledge
Moorledge Farm
HIGHFIELDS
THE DRIVE
THE CRESCENT
8
7
65
6
5
64
4
3
63
2
1
62
57
58
59

57
40

39
23

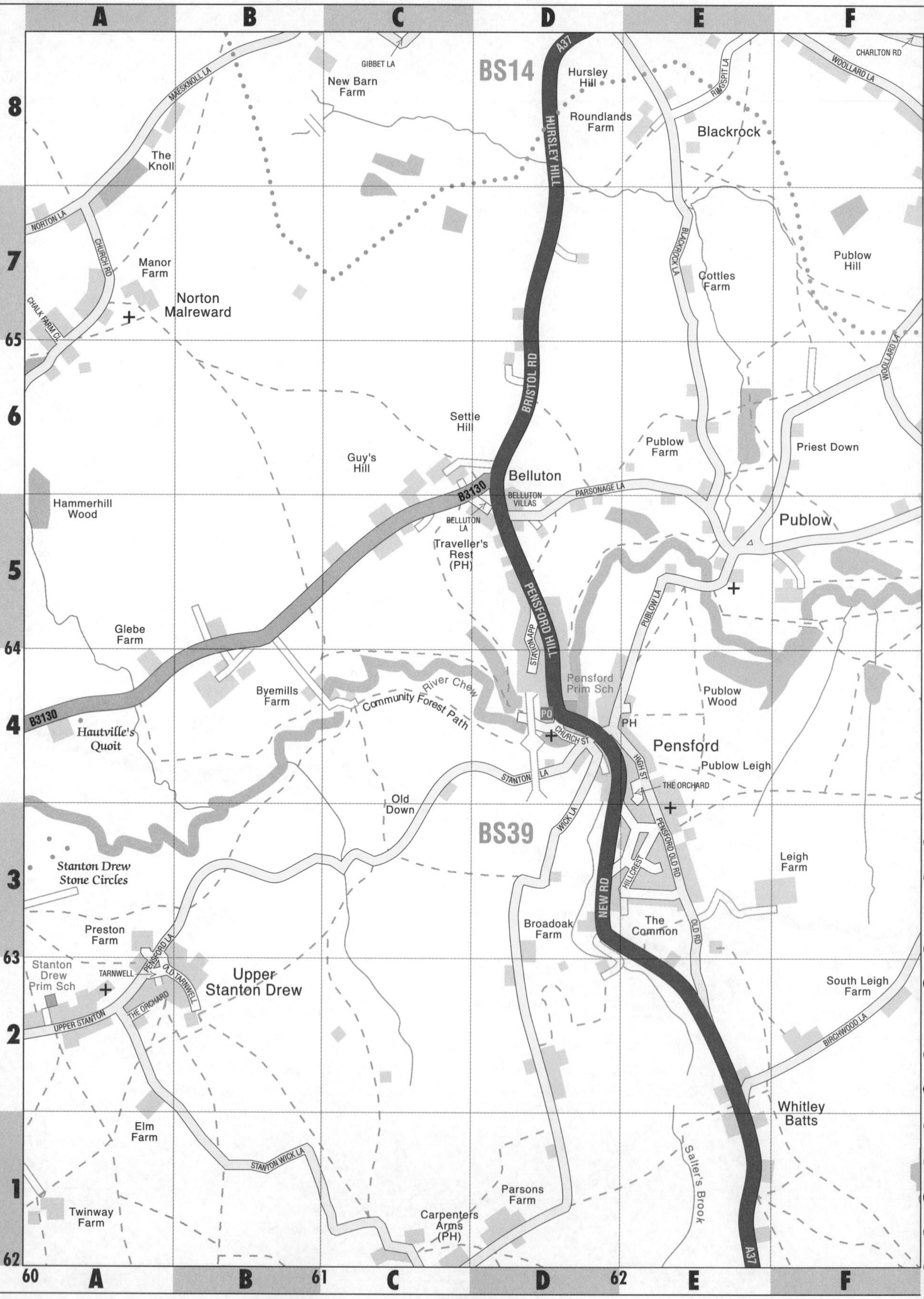

A B C D E F

BS14
BS39

A37
HURSLEY HILL
BRISTOL RD
PENSFORD HILL
NEW RD
B3130
MAESKNOLL LA
NORTON LA
CHURCH RD
CHALK FARM CL
GIBBET LA
WOOLLARD LA
CHARLTON RD
RIMSPIT LA
BLACKROCK LA
PARSONAGE LA
BELLUTON VILLAS
BELLUTON LA
STATION APP
CHURCH ST
PUBLOW LA
HIGH ST
THE ORCHARD
STANTON LA
WICK LA
HILLCREST
PENSFORD OLD RD
OLD RD
BIRCHWOOD LA
PENSFORD LA
TARNWELL
OLD TARNWELL
THE ORCHARD
UPPER STANTON
STANTON WICK LA

New Barn Farm
Hursley Hill
Roundlands Farm
Blackrock
The Knoll
Manor Farm
Norton Malreward
Publow Hill
Cottles Farm
Settle Hill
Guy's Hill
Belluton
Publow Farm
Priest Down
Hammerhill Wood
Traveller's Rest (PH)
Publow
Glebe Farm
Byemills Farm
River Chew
Community Forest Path
Pensford Prim Sch
PO
PH
Publow Wood
Pensford
Publow Leigh
Hautville's Quoit
Old Down
Stanton Drew Stone Circles
Leigh Farm
Preston Farm
Broadoak Farm
The Common
Stanton Drew Prim Sch
Upper Stanton Drew
South Leigh Farm
Whitley Batts
Elm Farm
Salter's Brook
Parsons Farm
Twinway Farm
Carpenters Arms (PH)

8 7 65 6 5 64 4 3 63 2 1 62
60 61 62

39
58

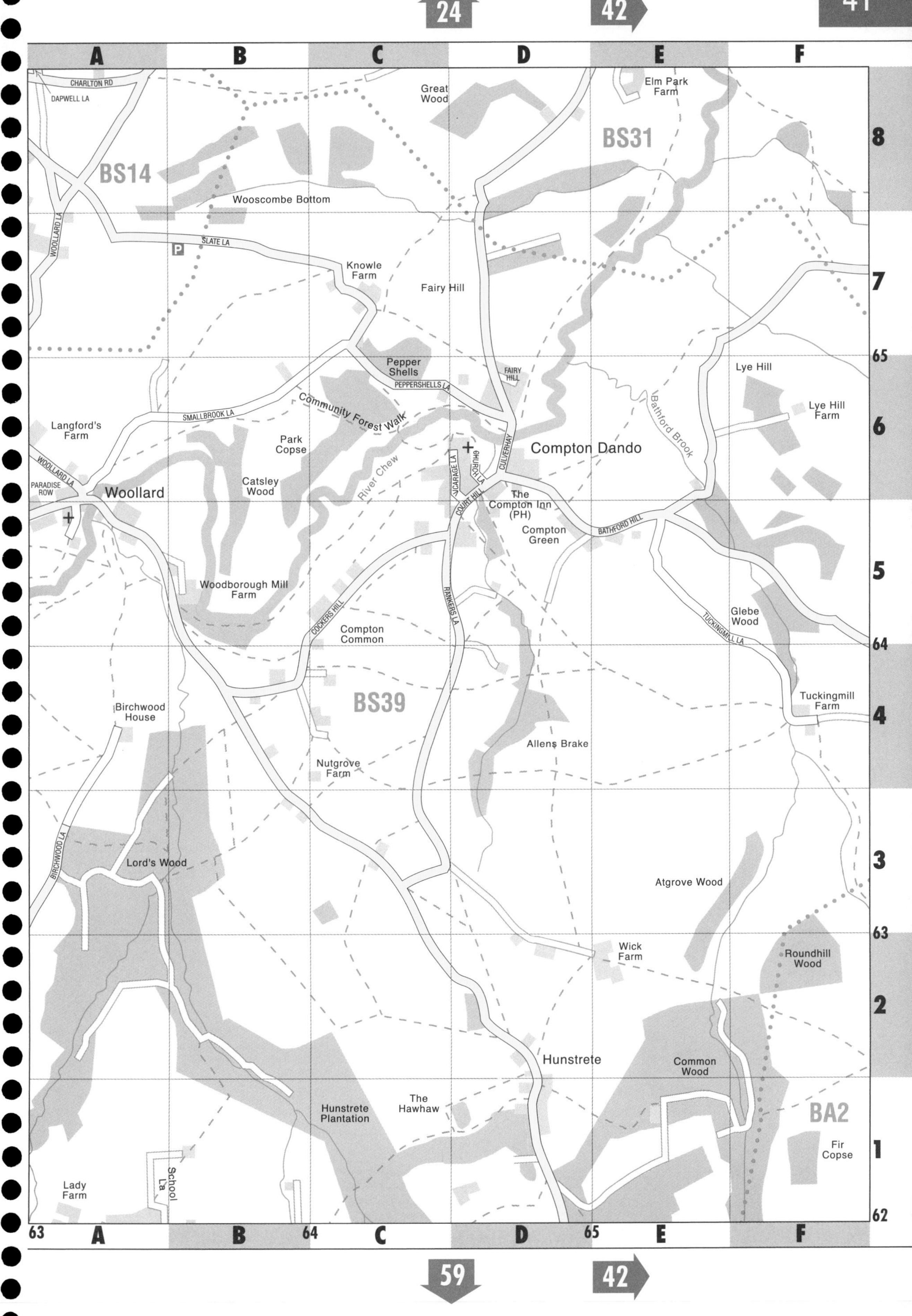
24
42
A
B
C
D
E
F
CHARLTON RD
DAPWELL LA
Great Wood
Elm Park Farm
BS31
8
BS14
Wooscombe Bottom
WOOLLARD LA
SLATE LA
P
Knowle Farm
Fairy Hill
7
Pepper Shells
FAIRY HILL
PEPPERSHELLS LA
65
Lye Hill
Lye Hill Farm
Langford's Farm
SMALLBROOK LA
Community Forest Walk
Park Copse
Bathford Brook
6
Compton Dando
CULVERHAY
CHURCH LA
VICARAGE LA
River Chew
Catsley Wood
WOOLLARD LA
PARADISE ROW
Woollard
COURT HILL
The Compton Inn (PH)
Compton Green
BATHFORD HILL
5
Woodborough Mill Farm
RANKERS LA
COCKERS HILL
Compton Common
Glebe Wood
TUCKINGMILL LA
64
BS39
Tuckingmill Farm
Birchwood House
4
Allens Brake
Nutgrove Farm
BIRCHWOOD LA
Lord's Wood
3
Atgrove Wood
63
Wick Farm
Roundhill Wood
2
Hunstrete
Common Wood
Hunstrete Plantation
The Hawhaw
BA2
1
Fir Copse
School La
Lady Farm
62
63
64
65
59
42

41
25

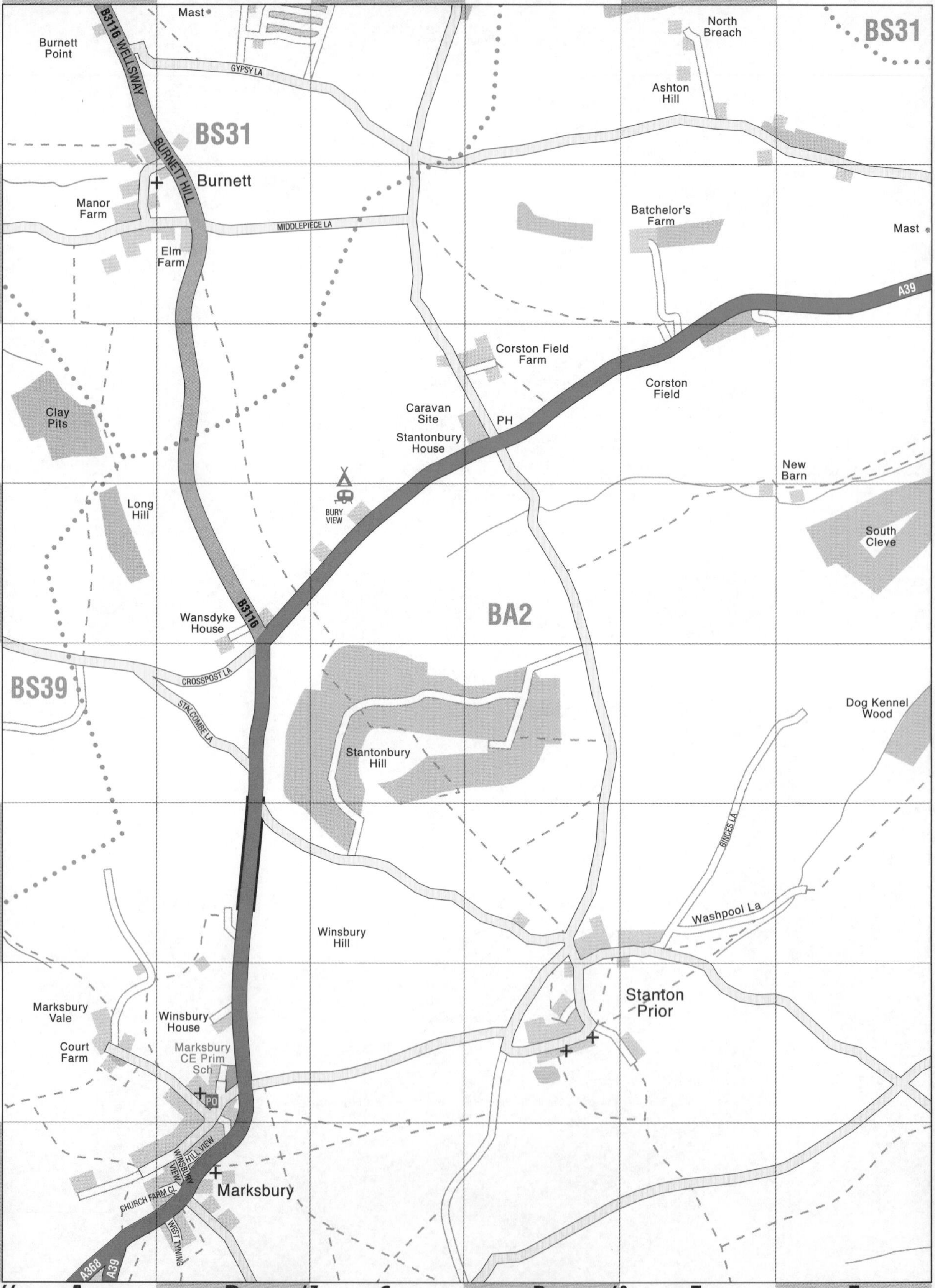

A B C D E F

8 7 65 6 5 64 4 3 63 2 1 62

Mast
Burnett Point
B3116 WELLSWAY
GYPSY LA
North Breach
BS31
Ashton Hill
BS31
BURNETT HILL
Burnett
Manor Farm
MIDDLEPIECE LA
Batchelor's Farm
Mast
Elm Farm
A39
Corston Field Farm
Clay Pits
Caravan Site
PH
Corston Field
Stantonbury House
New Barn
Long Hill
BURY VIEW
South Cleve
BA2
Wansdyke House
B3116
CROSSPOST LA
BS39
STALCOMBE LA
Dog Kennel Wood
Stantonbury Hill
BINCES LA
Washpool La
Winsbury Hill
Stanton Prior
Marksbury Vale
Winsbury House
Court Farm
Marksbury CE Prim Sch
PO
HILL VIEW
WINSBURY VIEW
CHURCH FARM CL
Marksbury
WIST TYNING
A368
A39

66 A B 67 C D 68 E F

41
60

26
44

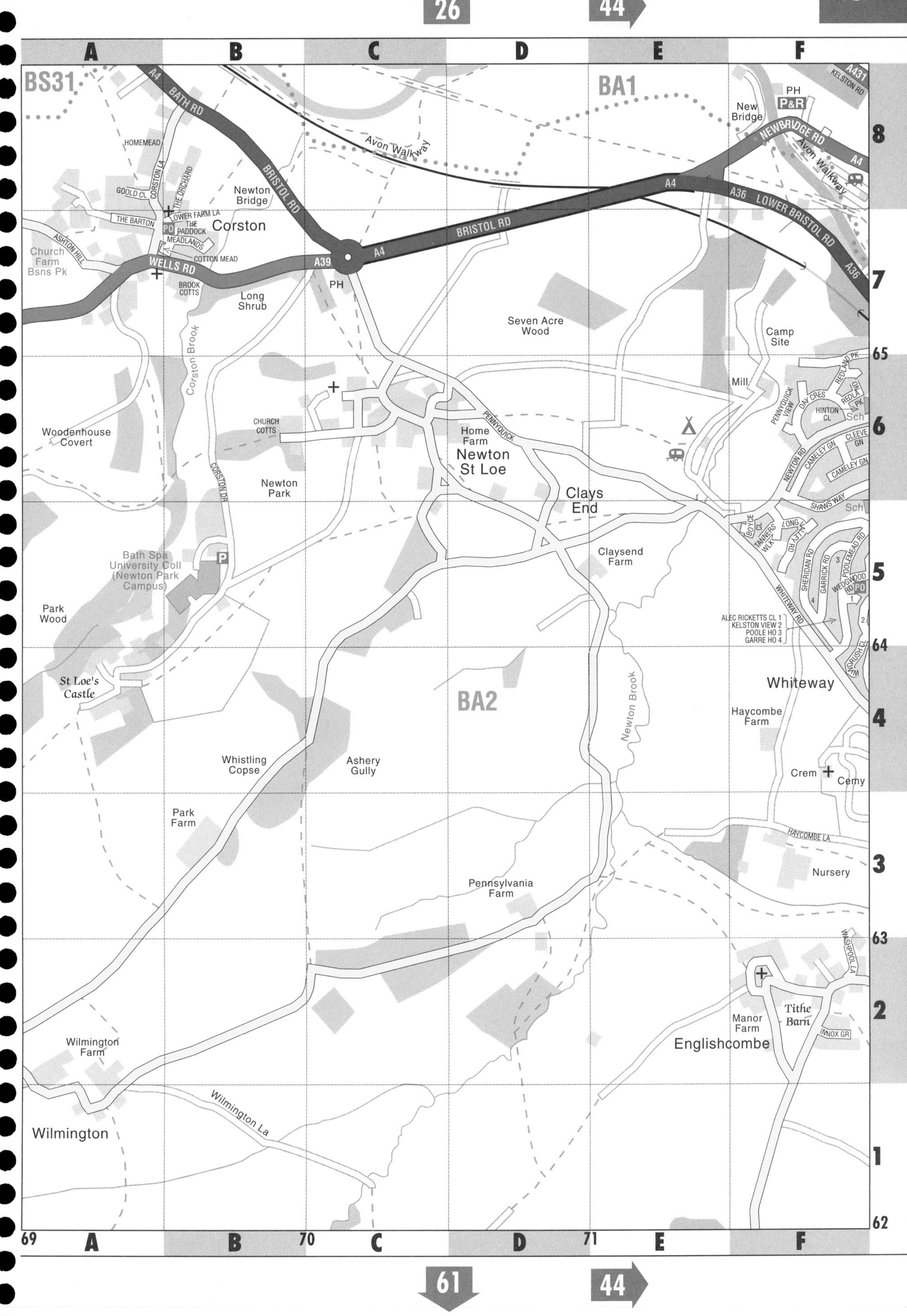
BS31
BA1
BA2
A4
BATH RD
BRISTOL RD
A39
WELLS RD
Avon Walkway
NEWBRIDGE RD
LOWER BRISTOL RD
A36
A431
KELSTON RD
PH
P&R
New Bridge
HOMEMEAD
GOOLD CL
CORSTON LA
THE ORCHARD
THE BARTON
LOWER FARM LA
THE PADDOCK
MEADLANDS
COTTON MEAD
BROOK COTTS
ASHTON HILL
Church Farm Bsns Pk
Corston
Newton Bridge
Long Shrub
Seven Acre Wood
Camp Site
Mill
Corston Brook
CORSTON DR
Woodenhouse Covert
CHURCH COTTS
PENNYQUICK
Home Farm
Newton St Loe
Newton Park
Clays End
Claysend Farm
Bath Spa University Coll (Newton Park Campus)
Park Wood
St Loe's Castle
PENNYQUICK VIEW
DAY CRES
REDLAND PK
REDLAND PK
HINTON CL
Sch
NEWTON RD
CAMELEY GN
CLEEVE GN
SHAWS WAY
BOYCE CL
TANNERS WLK
LONG VALLEY RD
SHERIDAN RD
GARRICK RD
POOLEMEAD RD
WEDGWOOD RD
WHITEWAY RD
ALEC RICKETTS CL 1
KELSTON VIEW 2
POOLE HO 3
GARRE HO 4
Whiteway
Haycombe Farm
Newton Brook
Crem
Cemy
Whistling Copse
Ashery Gully
Park Farm
HAYCOMBE LA
Nursery
Pennsylvania Farm
WASHPOOL LA
Tithe Barn
Manor Farm
Englishcombe
INNOX GR
Wilmington Farm
Wilmington
Wilmington La
A B C D E F
8 7 6 5 4 3 2 1
65 64 63 62
69 70 71

61
44

B6
1 THE PARADE
2 TWERTON FARM CL
3 MILL LA
4 WATERLOO BLDGS
5 ORCHARD TERR
6 ALBANY CT
7 Locksbrook Trad Est
8 Locksbrook Ct

B7
1 ROSSLYN CL
2 HORSTMANN CL
3 WARWICK RD

43

C7
1 ASHLEY TERR
2 SHAFTESBURY AVE
3 WINDSOR VILLAS
4 WINDSOR CT
5 WINDSOR PL

27

D5
1 TRIANGLE VILLAS
2 TRIANGLE CT
3 CRANDALE RD
4 ARLINGTON RD
5 WINCHESTER RD
6 BELVOIR RD
7 SHAFTESBURY MEWS

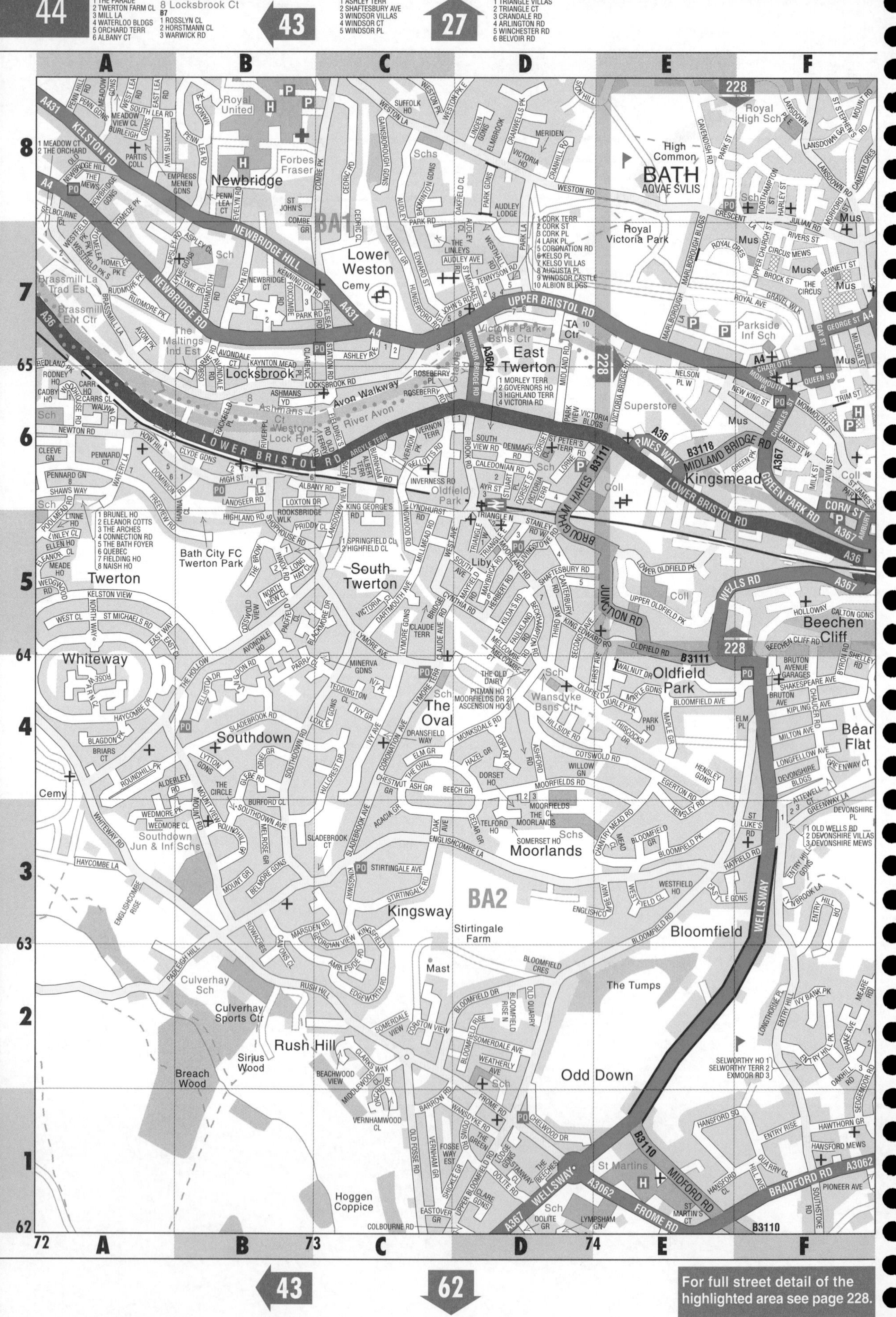

43
62

For full street detail of the highlighted area see page 228.

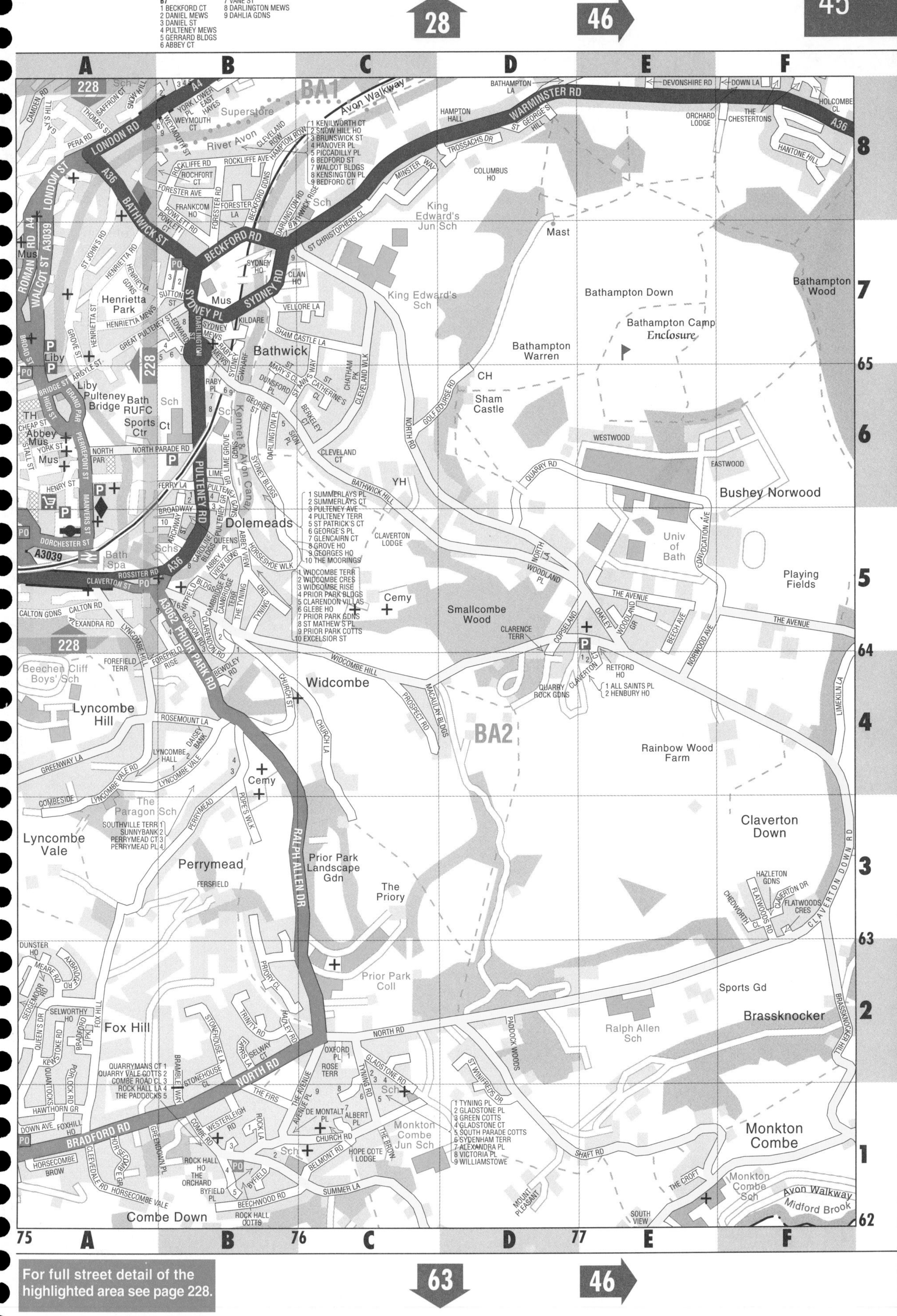

For full street detail of the highlighted area see page 228.

45
29

A
B
C
D
E
F
8
7
65
6
5
64
4
3
63
2
1
62
78
79
80
Holcombe Farm
A36
Warleigh Lodge Farm
A363
BRADFORD RD
Bathford Hill
LINK LA
Manor Ho
PH
Monkton Farleigh
PO
Church Farm
Butt's La
BROAD STONES
SALLY IN THE WOOD
Manor Deer Farm
Hengrove Wood
Manor Farm
Warleigh
Home Wood
BA1
WARLEIGH LA
Claverton Pumping Sta
LC
WARMINSTER RD
BA2
American Mus in Britain
Claverton Manor
Claverton
Dry Arch
PINCKNEY GN
Willocks Wood
HAYESWOOD FARM
CLAVERTON HILL
Avon Walkway
Kennet & Avon Canal
River Avon
Sheephouse Farm
Warleigh Hill
Farleigh Wick
PH
A363
BA15
Vineyards Farm
Inwoods
Claverton Wood
Bassett Farm
Limestone Link
Inwood
Warleigh Wood
Sweeps Coppice
Dundas Aqueduct
Rose's Wood
BRASSKNOCKER HILL
PH
B3108
LOWER STOKE
Mast
Conkwell Farm
Conkwell
BLACKBERRY LA
Conkwell Wood
Parsonage Farm
Haugh Farm
Haugh Potticks Farm
Hartley
Wiltshire STREET ATLAS
A363 Bradford-on-Avon

45
64

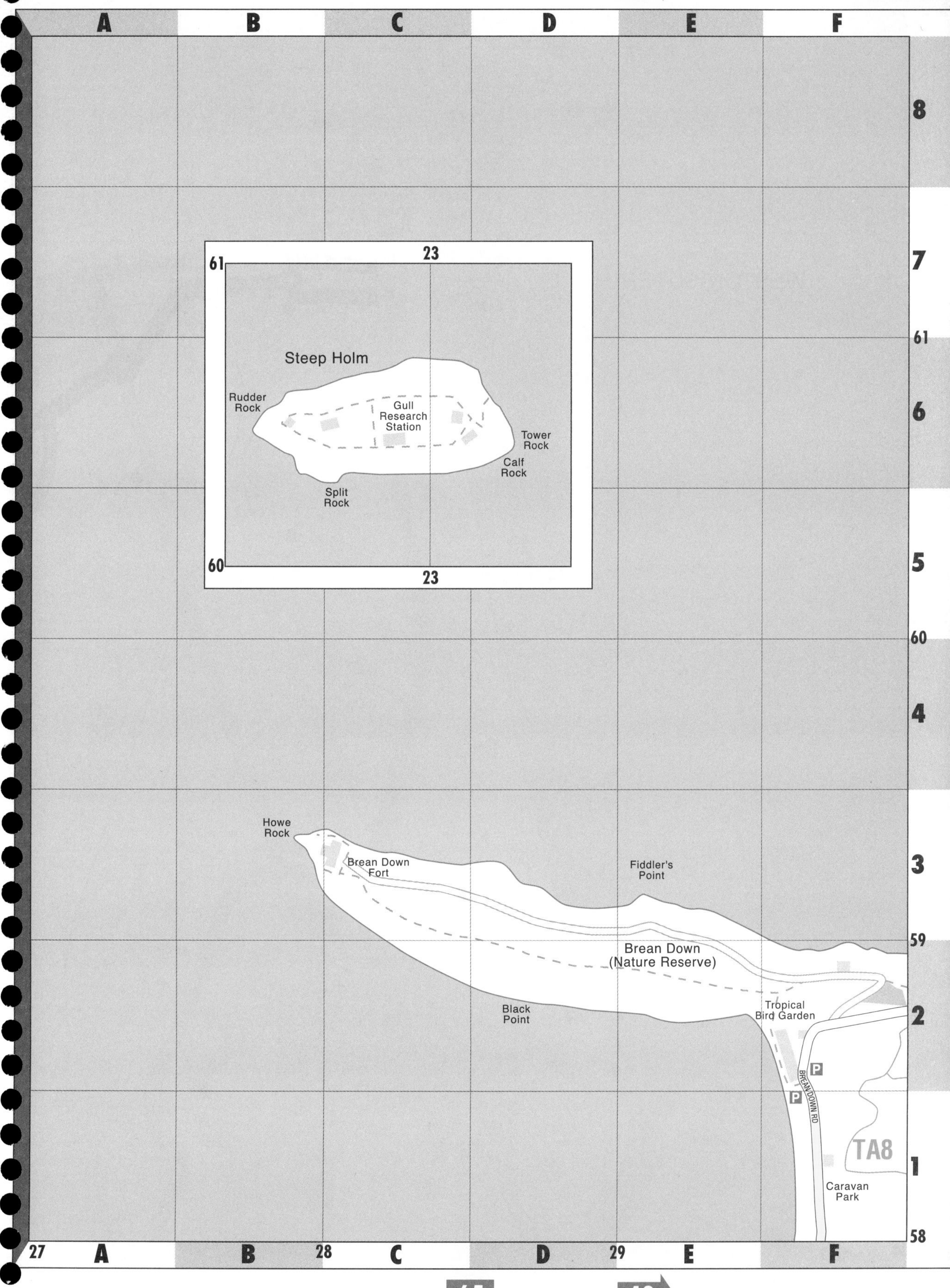
48
A
B
C
D
E
F
8
7
61
6
5
60
4
3
59
2
1
58
23
61
60
23
Steep Holm
Rudder Rock
Gull Research Station
Tower Rock
Calf Rock
Split Rock
Howe Rock
Brean Down Fort
Fiddler's Point
Brean Down (Nature Reserve)
Black Point
Tropical Bird Garden
BREAN DOWN RD
P
P
TA8
Caravan Park
27
28
29
65
48

47 ← 30 ↑

E7
1 ORCHARD PL
2 NORTH LA
3 CROSS ST
4 ALFRED CT
5 ALEXANDER MEWS
6 THE MART
7 FRANCIS FOX RD
8 STATION LODGE
9 HILDESHIEM CT
10 THE CENTRE
11 WALLISCOTE GROVE RD

E8
1 EDINBURGH PL
2 LANDEMANN PATH
3 LONGTON GROVE RD
4 WORTHY PL
5 WORTHY LA
6 KING'S LA
7 PALMER ROW
8 JASMINE CT
9 PROSPECT PL
10 SAFFRON HO
11 HENRY BUTT HO
12 CHRIST CHURCH PATH S
13 HANS PRICE HO
14 MEADOW VILLAS
15 BURLINGTON ST
16 POPLAR PL
17 PAYNES HO
18 HANS PRICE CL

WESTON-SUPER-MARE

Weston Bay

Knightstone

Grand Pier

SeaQuarium

Model Yacht Pond

Weston Miniature Rly

Clarence Park

BS23

Uphill

Black Rock

Brean Down Farm

Slimeridge Farm

Marina

Windmill

West Mendip Way

River Axe

Ferry (P)

TA8

Weston General

BS24

1 MADEIRA CT
2 UPPER CHURCH RD
3 GREENFIELD PL

PARK VILLAS 1
LOVERS' WLK 2
OLD POST OFFICE LA 3
CONNAUGHT PL 4
WESTON LODGE 5
KNIGHTSTONE HO 6
ST MARGARET'S TERR 7
Jill Dando Meml Gdn 8

SALISBURY TERR 1
WELLINGTON PL 2
RICHMOND ST 3
GLOUCESTER ST 4
UNION PL 5
OXFORD PL 6
UNION ST 7
DOLPHIN SQ 8
BIRKBECK CT 9
EDDINGTON CT 10

FERN LODGE 1
BEACH CT 2
CHANDOS CT 3

ETONHURST 4
CLIFFORD HO 5
ROYSTON LODGE 6

HEATHGATES 1
ROYAL CT 2
ROYAL SANDS 3

1 RAYNESWOOD
2 LANSDOWN CT
3 BYRON CT
4 CHELWOOD

1 ELLENBOROUGH CT
2 KNIGHTSTONE GN
3 ELLENBOROUGH CRES
4 PITMAN RD

DEVONSHIRE CT 1
RENNISON CT 2

BURRINGTON CL 1
BROCKLEY CL 2

← 47 ↓ 66

E5
1 SILVERCOMBE
2 WOODFORD CT
3 RALEIGH CT
4 KNIGHTSTONE PK
5 PARK CT
6 WINGARD CT
7 BERROW LODGE

F4
1 ST ANDREW'S PAR
2 BAILDON CT
3 MARLOWE HO
4 KEATS HO
5 ALEXANDER HO
6 TAVERNERS CL

F5
1 SANDRINGHAM RD
2 SANDRINGHAM CT
3 DOUGLAS CT

F7
1 ASHCOMBE CT
2 STANLEY RD
3 SIMONS MEWS
4 ASHCOMBE PL
5 WYVERN MEWS

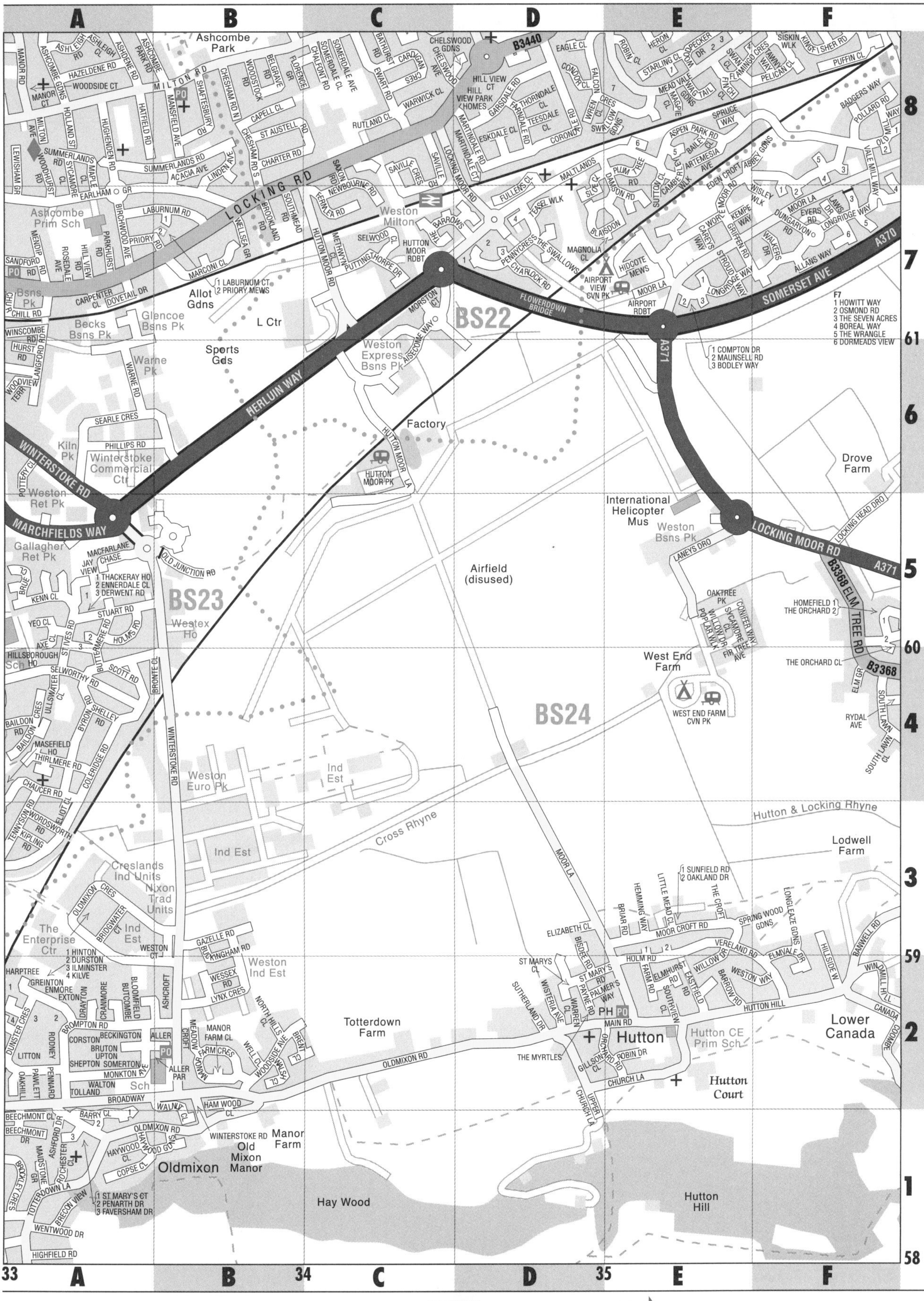

31
50

D7
1 TEMPLARS CT
2 CLOVER CT
3 CHARLOCK CL
4 CAMPION CL

E8
1 MERLIN CL
2 KITE WLK
3 HARRIER PATH
4 THRUSH CL
5 LOMBARDY CL
6 GREENGAGE CL
7 MALLARD WLK

F8
1 SWEETGRASS RD
2 CASTLE VIEW
3 TRELISSICK GDNS
4 MONTACUTE CIR
5 THE INCLOSURES

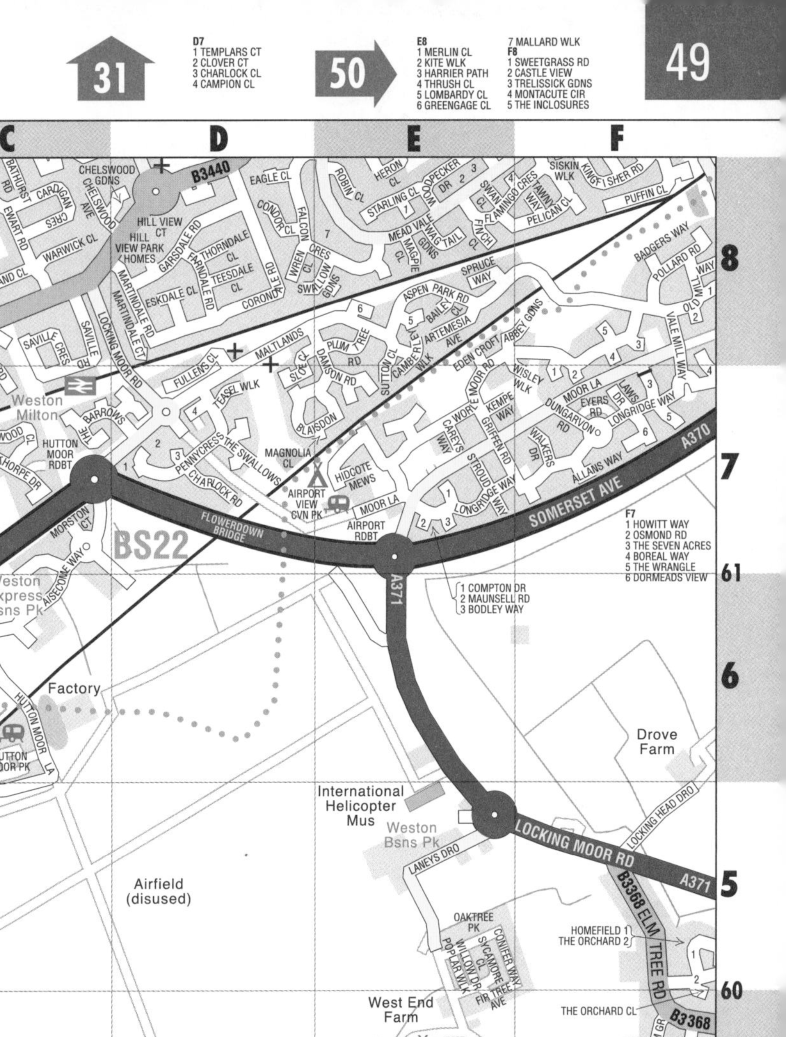

67
50

49
32

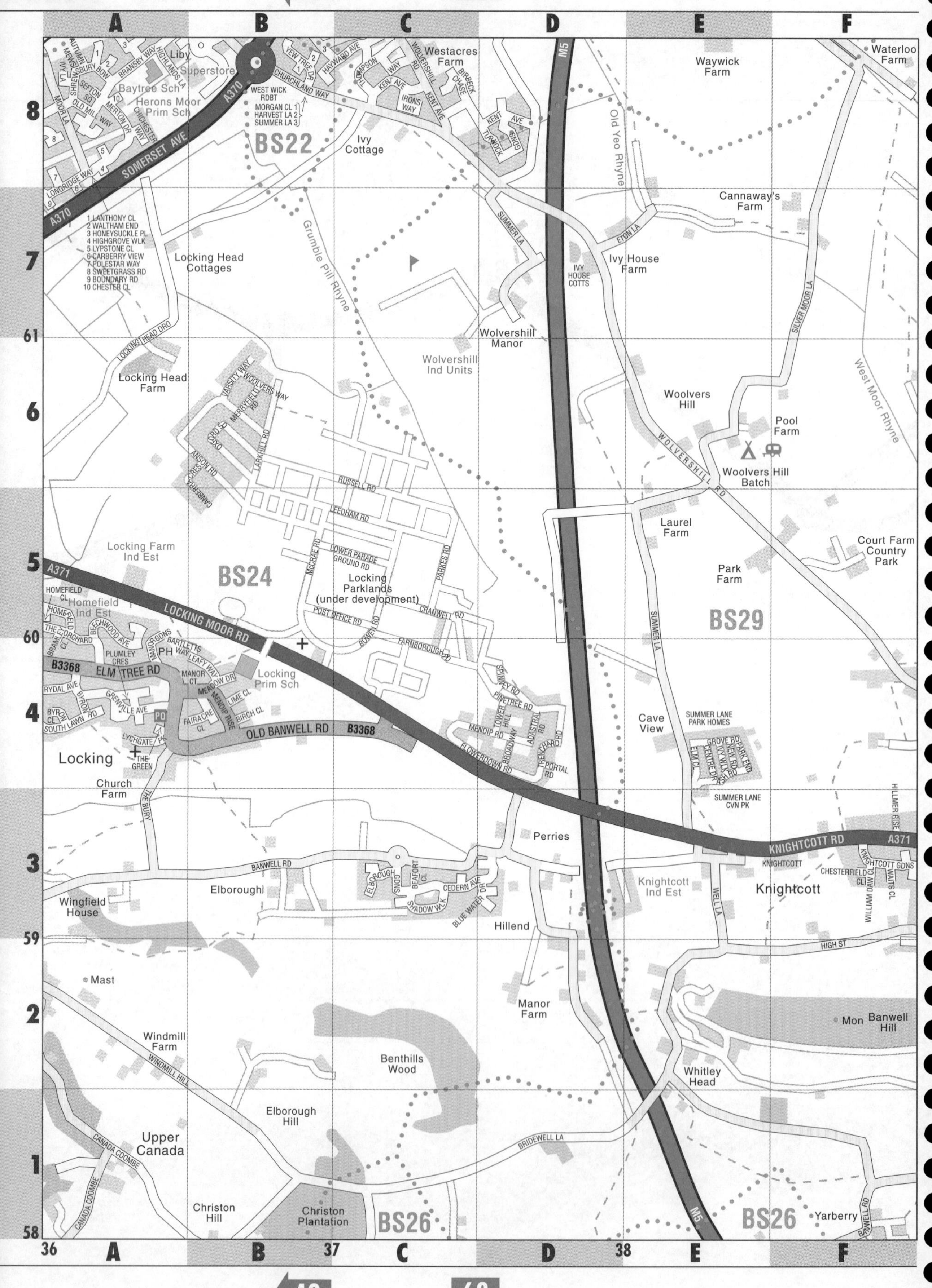
BS22
BS24
BS29
BS26
Westacres Farm
Waywick Farm
Waterloo Farm
Ivy Cottage
Cannaway's Farm
Ivy House Farm
Locking Head Cottages
Locking Head Farm
Wolvershill Manor
Wolvershill Ind Units
Woolvers Hill
Pool Farm
Woolvers Hill Batch
Laurel Farm
Court Farm Country Park
Park Farm
Locking Farm Ind Est
Locking Parklands (under development)
Homefield Ind Est
Locking Prim Sch
Locking
Church Farm
Cave View
Perries
Knightcott Ind Est
Knightcott
Elborough
Wingfield House
Hillend
Manor Farm
Mast
Windmill Farm
Benthills Wood
Mon Banwell Hill
Whitley Head
Elborough Hill
Upper Canada
Christon Hill
Christon Plantation
Yarberry
Liby Superstore
Baytree Sch
Herons Moor Prim Sch
SOMERSET AVE
LOCKING MOOR RD
OLD BANWELL RD
KNIGHTCOTT RD
BANWELL RD
WOLVERSHILL RD
SUMMER LA
SILVER MOOR LA
BRIDEWELL LA
WINDMILL HILL
CANADA COOMBE
HIGH ST
ELM TREE RD
Grumble Pill Rhyne
Old Yeo Rhyne
West Moor Rhyne
SUMMER LANE PARK HOMES
SUMMER LANE CVN PK
1 LANTHONY CL
2 WALTHAM END
3 HONEYSUCKLE PL
4 HIGHGROVE WLK
5 LYPSTONE CL
6 CARBERRY VIEW
7 POLESTAR WAY
8 SWEETGRASS RD
9 BOUNDARY RD
10 CHESTER CL
WEST WICK RDBT
MORGAN CL 1
HARVEST LA 2
SUMMER LA 3

49
68

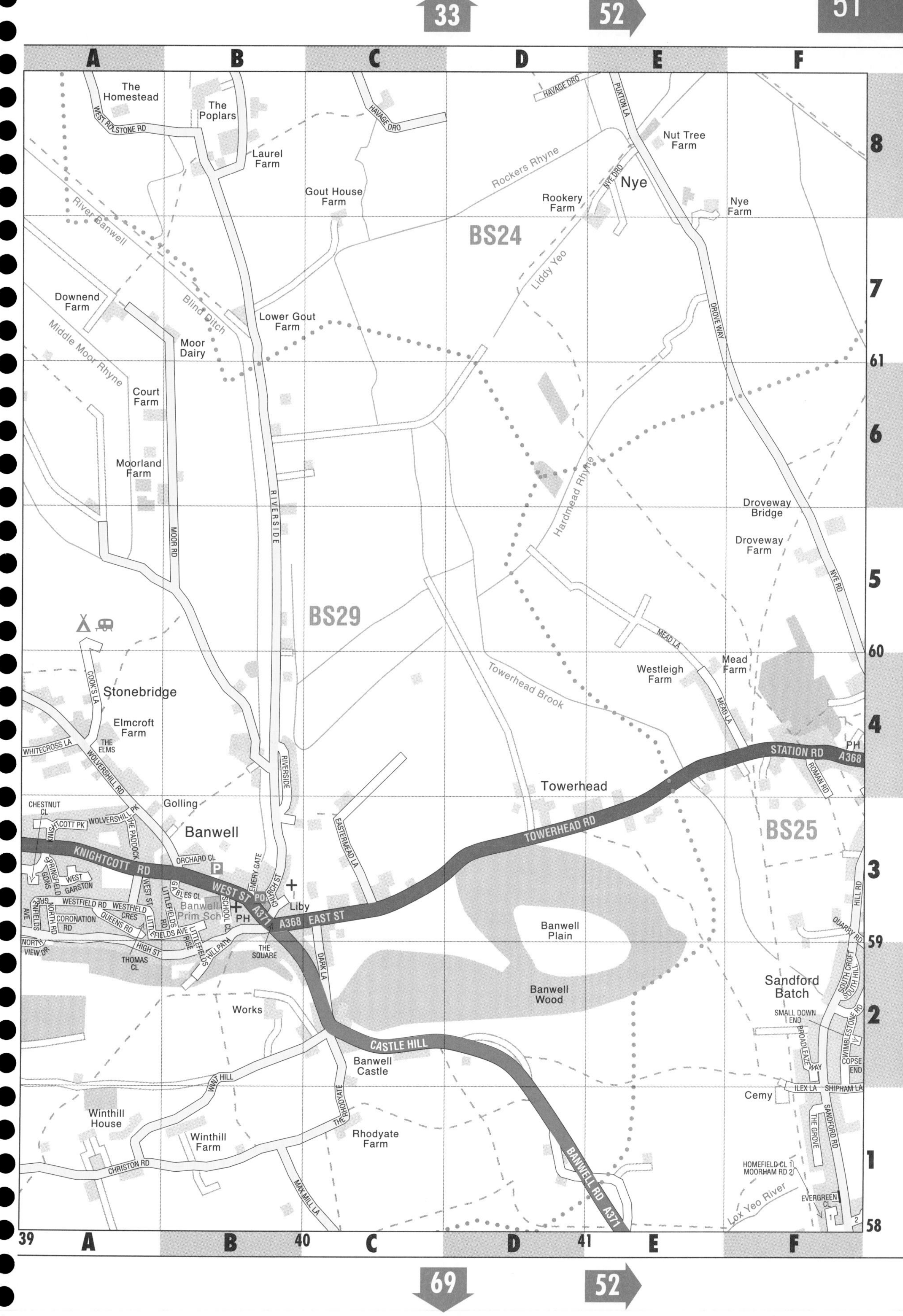
33
52
The Homestead
The Poplars
West Rolstone Rd
Laurel Farm
Havage Dro
Puxton La
Nut Tree Farm
Rockers Rhyne
Nye Dro
Nye
Rookery Farm
Nye Farm
Gout House Farm
River Banwell
BS24
Liddy Yeo
Downend Farm
Blind Ditch
Lower Gout Farm
Drove Way
Middle Moor Rhyne
Moor Dairy
Court Farm
Moorland Farm
Hardmead Rhyne
Riverside
Moor Rd
Droveway Bridge
Droveway Farm
BS29
Nye Rd
Mead La
Cook's La
Towerhead Brook
Westleigh Farm
Mead Farm
Stonebridge
Elmcroft Farm
Whitecross La
The Elms
Wolvershill Rd
Station Rd
A368
PH
Roman Rd
Towerhead
Golling
Chestnut Cl
Knightcott Pk
Wolvershill Pk
The Paddock
Banwell
Eastermead La
Towerhead Rd
BS25
Knightcott Rd
Orchard Cl
Springfield Gdns
West Garston
Emery Gate
Church St
West St
Gables Cl
PO
Liby
Westfield Rd
Westfield Cres
Banwell Prim Sch
School Cl
A371
A368
East St
Hill Rd
Coronation Rd
North Rd
Queens Rd
Littlefields Ave
Littlefields Rd
Littlefields Rise
Quarry Rd
North View Dr
High St
Hill Path
The Square
Dark La
Banwell Plain
Thomas Cl
Sandford Batch
South Croft
South Hill
Banwell Wood
Works
Small Down End
Wimblestone Rd
Broadleaze Way
Castle Hill
Banwell Castle
Copse End
Wint Hill
Ilex La
Shipham La
Cemy
Winthill House
The Rhodyate
Rhodyate Farm
Winthill Farm
The Grove
Sandford Rd
Christon Rd
Banwell Rd
Homefield Cl
Moorham Rd
Max Mill La
Lox Yeo River
Evergreen Cl
A
B
C
D
E
F
8
7
61
6
5
60
4
3
59
2
1
58
39
40
41
69
52

51 34

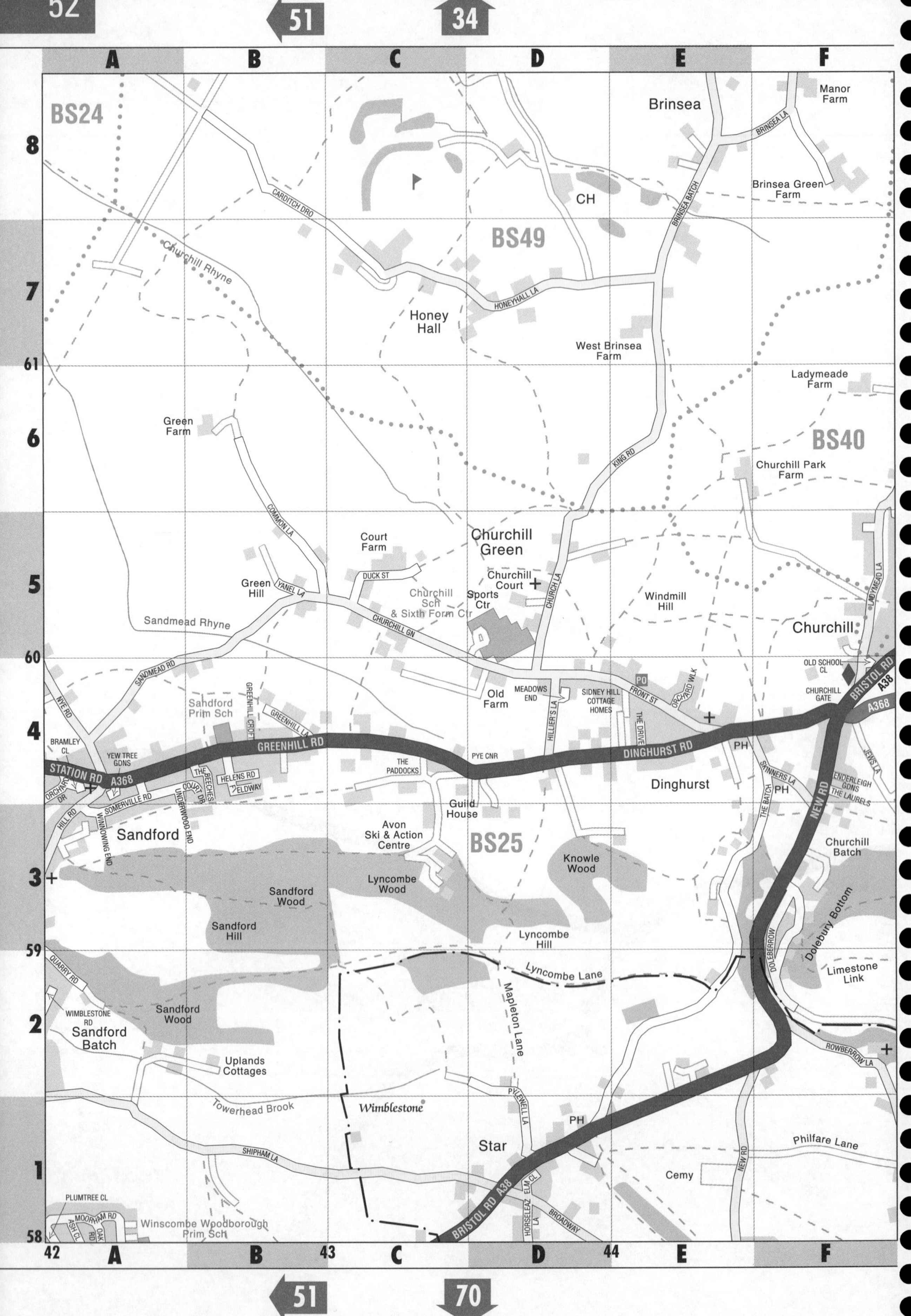

A B C D E F
8 7 61 6 5 60 4 3 59 2 1 58
42 43 44
BS24
BS49
BS40
BS25
Brinsea
Manor Farm
Brinsea Green Farm
CH
CARDITCH DRO
BRINSEA BATCH
BRINSEA LA
Churchill Rhyne
HONEYHALL LA
Honey Hall
West Brinsea Farm
Ladymeade Farm
Green Farm
Churchill Park Farm
KING RD
COMMON LA
Court Farm
Churchill Green
Green Hill
YANEL LA
DUCK ST
Churchill Court
Churchill Sch & Sixth Form Ctr
Sports Ctr
CHURCH LA
Windmill Hill
LADYMEAD LA
Churchill
Sandmead Rhyne
CHURCHILL GN
SANDMEAD RD
NYE RD
OLD SCHOOL CL
BRISTOL RD
A38
A368
Sandford Prim Sch
GREENHILL CROFT
GREENHILL LA
Old Farm
MEADOWS END
SIDNEY HILL COTTAGE HOMES
PO
FRONT ST
ORCHARD WLK
CHURCHILL GATE
BRAMLEY CL
YEW TREE GDNS
GREENHILL RD
HILLIER'S LA
THE DRIVE
DINGHURST RD
PH
STATION RD
THE BEECHES
HELENS RD
ELDWAY
THE PADDOCKS
PYE CNR
Dinghurst
SKINNERS LA
JEWS LA
ENDERLEIGH GDNS
THE LAURELS
ORCHARD DR
SOMERVILLE RD
COURT DR
UNDERWOOD END
HILL RD
WINNOWING END
Sandford
Guild House
Avon Ski & Action Centre
THE BATCH
NEW RD
Churchill Batch
Knowle Wood
Lyncombe Wood
Sandford Wood
Sandford Hill
Dolebury Bottom
Lyncombe Hill
DOLEBERROW
Limestone Link
QUARRY RD
Lyncombe Lane
Mapleton Lane
WIMBLESTONE RD
Sandford Batch
Uplands Cottages
ROWBERROW LA
Towerhead Brook
PYLEWELL LA
Wimblestone
Star
Philfare Lane
SHIPHAM LA
ELM CL
Cemy
PLUMTREE CL
MOORHAM RD
ASH CL
OAK RD
Winscombe Woodborough Prim Sch
HORSELEAZ LA
BROADWAY

51 70

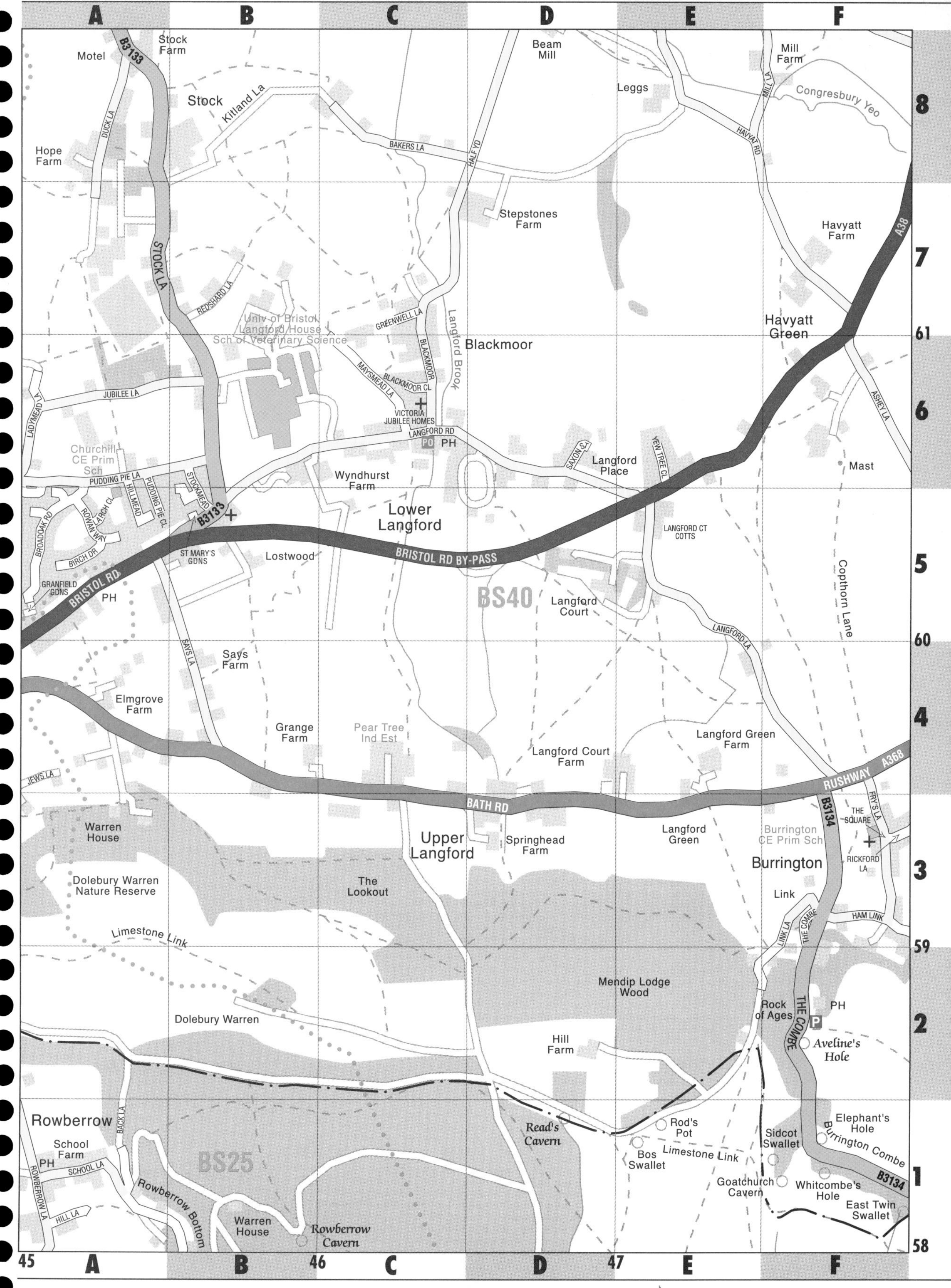

35
54
A
B
C
D
E
F
Motel
Stock Farm
B3133
Beam Mill
Mill Farm
Leggs
Stock
Kitland La
Congresbury Yeo
Hope Farm
DUCK LA
BAKERS LA
HALF YD
HAVYAT RD
MILL LA
8
Stepstones Farm
Havyatt Farm
STOCK LA
A38
7
REDSHARD LA
Univ of Bristol Langford House Sch of Veterinary Science
GREENWELL LA
Langford Brook
Havyatt Green
61
Blackmoor
BLACKMOOR
MAYSMEAD LA
BLACKMOOR CL
JUBILEE LA
LADYMEAD LA
VICTORIA JUBILEE HOMES
ASHEY LA
6
LANGFORD RD
PO
PH
Churchill CE Prim Sch
SAXON ST
Langford Place
YEW TREE CL
Mast
PUDDING PIE LA
Wyndhurst Farm
HILLMEAD
PUDDING PIE CL
STOCKMEAD
Lower Langford
B3133
BROADOAK RD
ROWAN WAY
BIRCH CL
LANGFORD CT COTTS
BIRCH DR
ST MARY'S GDNS
Lostwood
BRISTOL RD BY-PASS
5
GRANFIELD GDNS
BRISTOL RD
PH
BS40
Langford Court
Copthorn Lane
LANGFORD LA
60
SAYS LA
Says Farm
Elmgrove Farm
4
Grange Farm
Pear Tree Ind Est
Langford Green Farm
Langford Court Farm
JEWS LA
RUSHWAY
A368
BATH RD
B3134
THE SQUARE
FRY'S LA
Warren House
Upper Langford
Springhead Farm
Langford Green
Burrington CE Prim Sch
Burrington
RICKFORD LA
3
Dolebury Warren Nature Reserve
The Lookout
Link
HAM LINK
Limestone Link
LINK LA
THE COMBE
59
Mendip Lodge Wood
Rock of Ages
PH
Dolebury Warren
THE COMBE
P
2
Aveline's Hole
Hill Farm
Elephant's Hole
Rowberrow
Read's Cavern
Rod's Pot
Burrington Combe
BACK LA
Bos Swallet
Limestone Link
Sidcot Swallet
School Farm
PH
SCHOOL LA
BS25
B3134
1
Goatchurch Cavern
Whitcombe's Hole
Rowberrow Bottom
ROWBERROW LA
HILL LA
East Twin Swallet
Warren House
Rowberrow Cavern
58
45
A
B
46
C
D
47
E
F
71
54

53
36

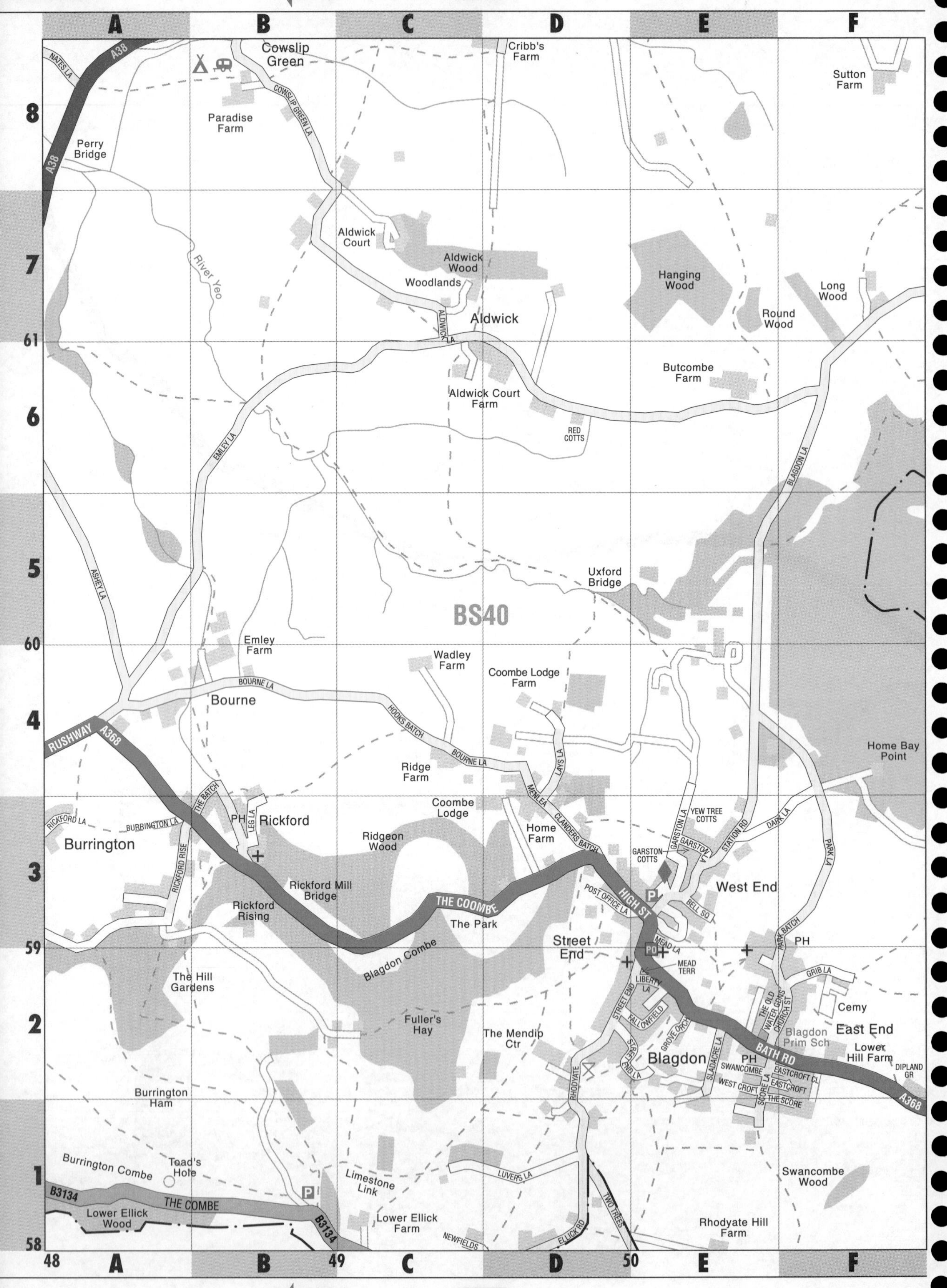
A
B
C
D
E
F
8
7
61
6
5
60
4
3
59
2
1
58
48
49
50
Cowslip Green
Cribb's Farm
Sutton Farm
NATES LA
A38
COWSLIP GREEN LA
Paradise Farm
Perry Bridge
River Yeo
Aldwick Court
Aldwick Wood
Woodlands
Aldwick
ALDWICK LA
Hanging Wood
Long Wood
Round Wood
Butcombe Farm
Aldwick Court Farm
RED COTTS
EMLEY LA
BLAGDON LA
ASHEY LA
Uxford Bridge
BS40
Emley Farm
Wadley Farm
Coombe Lodge Farm
BOURNE LA
Bourne
HOOKS BATCH
RUSHWAY
A368
LAYS LA
Home Bay Point
Ridge Farm
MENLEA
THE BATCH
LEG LA
PH
Rickford
Coombe Lodge
Home Farm
CLANDERS BATCH
GARSTON LA
YEW TREE COTTS
STATION RD
DARK LA
RICKFORD LA
BURRINGTON LA
Burrington
Ridgeon Wood
GARSTON COTTS
PARK LA
RICKFORD RISE
Rickford Mill Bridge
THE COOMBE
POST OFFICE LA
HIGH ST
West End
Rickford Rising
The Park
BELL SQ
Street End
MEAD LA
PARK BATCH
PO
MEAD TERR
LIBERTY LA
GRIB LA
The Hill Gardens
Blagdon Combe
STREET END
FALLOWFIELD
THE OLD WATER GDNS
CHURCH ST
Cemy
Fuller's Hay
GROVE ORCH
Blagdon Prim Sch
East End
The Mendip Ctr
SLADACRE LA
BATH RD
Lower Hill Farm
RHODYATE
STREET END LA
Blagdon
SWANCOMBE
EASTCROFT CL
DIPLAND GR
WEST CROFT
SCORE LA
EASTCROFT
THE SCORE
Burrington Ham
Toad's Hole
Burrington Combe
Limestone Link
LUVERS LA
Swancombe Wood
B3134
THE COMBE
Lower Ellick Wood
P
TWO TREES
ELLICK RD
Lower Ellick Farm
NEWFIELDS
Rhodyate Hill Farm

53
72

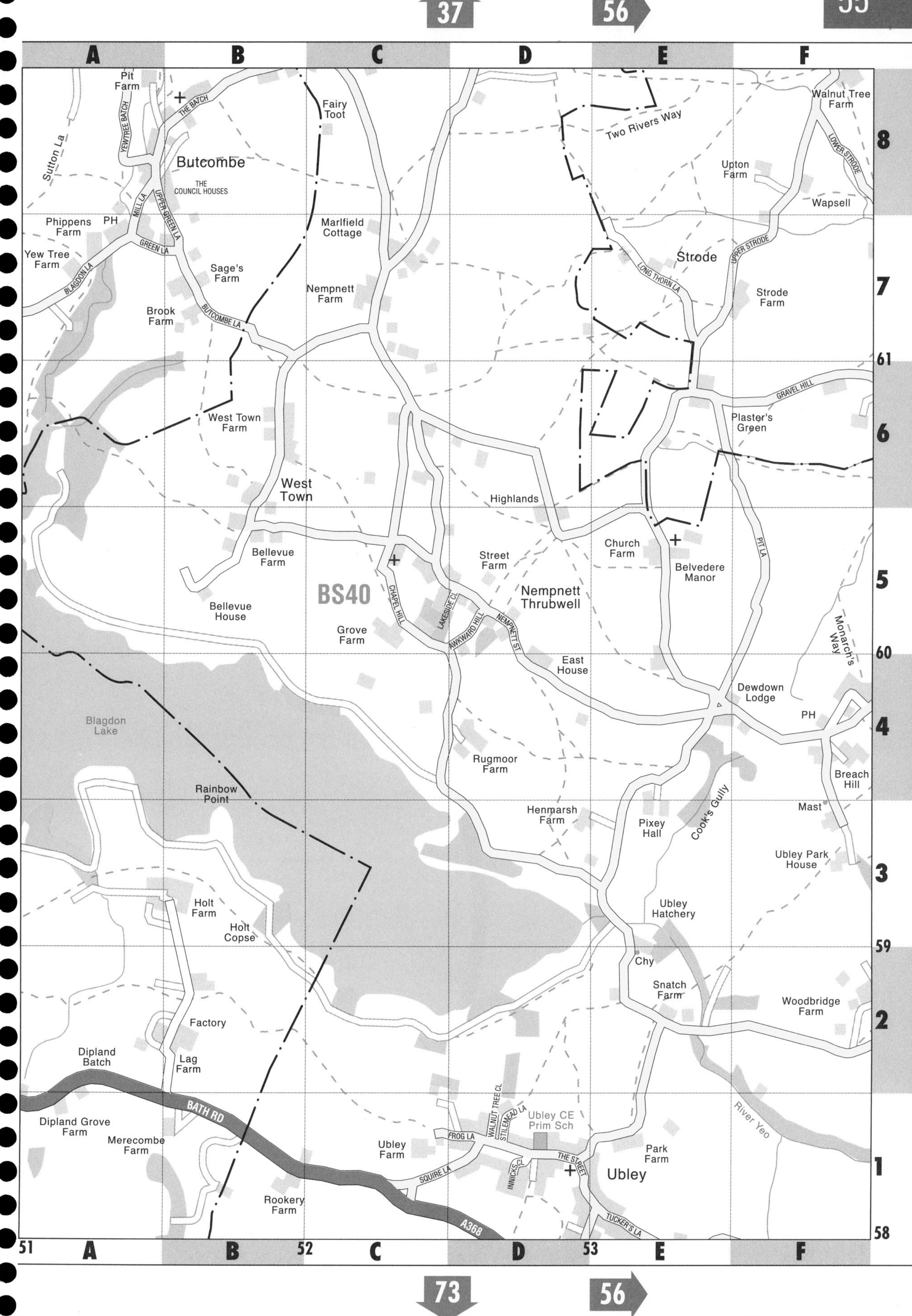
37
56
A
B
C
D
E
F
Pit Farm
THE BATCH
YEWTREE BATCH
Fairy Toot
Two Rivers Way
Walnut Tree Farm
Sutton La
Butcombe
THE COUNCIL HOUSES
MILL LA
UPPER GREEN LA
Upton Farm
LOWER STRODE
Wapsell
Phippens Farm
PH
Marlfield Cottage
Yew Tree Farm
GREEN LA
BLAGDON LA
Sage's Farm
Strode
LONG THORN LA
UPPER STRODE
Nempnett Farm
Strode Farm
Brook Farm
BUTCOMBE LA
West Town Farm
GRAVEL HILL
Plaster's Green
West Town
Highlands
Bellevue Farm
Church Farm
Belvedere Manor
Street Farm
PIT LA
BS40
Nempnett Thrubwell
Bellevue House
CHAPEL HILL
LAKESIDE CL
AWKWARD HILL
NEMPNETT ST
Monarch's Way
Grove Farm
East House
Dewdown Lodge
Blagdon Lake
PH
Rugmoor Farm
Breach Hill
Rainbow Point
Henmarsh Farm
Pixey Hall
Cook's Gully
Mast
Ubley Park House
Holt Farm
Ubley Hatchery
Holt Copse
Chy
Snatch Farm
Woodbridge Farm
Factory
Dipland Batch
Lag Farm
BATH RD
River Yeo
Dipland Grove Farm
WALNUT TREE CL
STILEMEAD LA
Ubley CE Prim Sch
Merecombe Farm
Ubley Farm
FROG LA
INNICKS CL
THE STREET
Park Farm
SQUIRE LA
Ubley
Rookery Farm
A368
TUCKER'S LA
8
7
61
6
5
60
4
3
59
2
1
58
51
52
53
73
56

55
38

A B C D E F

8 7 61 6 5 60 4 3 59 2 1 58

The Knoll
Lower Strode
Whitling St
Lower Strode Farm
Lower Strode
Manor Farm
Gravel Hill
Shoreditch
Church Farm
Scot La
PH
Church La
Pilgrims Way
The Cedars
Blind La
B3114
Bristol Rd
Webbs Mead
The Street
Mill La
Chew Stoke CE Prim Sch
Home Orch
School La
Quarry Hay
Chapel Cl
Bilbie Cl
Bilbie Rd
Bushy Thorn Rd
Works
PO
Chapel La
Wally Court Rd
Walley La
Chew Stoke
Wallis Farm
Scornfield La
Stoke Hill House
Fairseat Workshops
Stoke Hill
Woodford Hill
Perry House Farm
Rose Cottage
Woodford Lodge
Breach Hill La
Monarch's Way
Stoke Villice
Obelisk
Rookery Farm
BS40
Manor Farm
Caple La
Kingshill La
Breach Hill Common
Breach Hill
Nunnery Copse
Herons Green Farm
Herons Green
P
Herons Green Bay
Chew Valley Lake
Moreton Point
Moreton La
Monarch's Way
Moat Farm
Bickfield Farm
Villice La
Bickfield La
Newclose La
Stratford La
River Yeo
Summerlea Farm
Oldbarn La
B3114
A368

54 A B 55 C D 56 E F

55
74

39
58

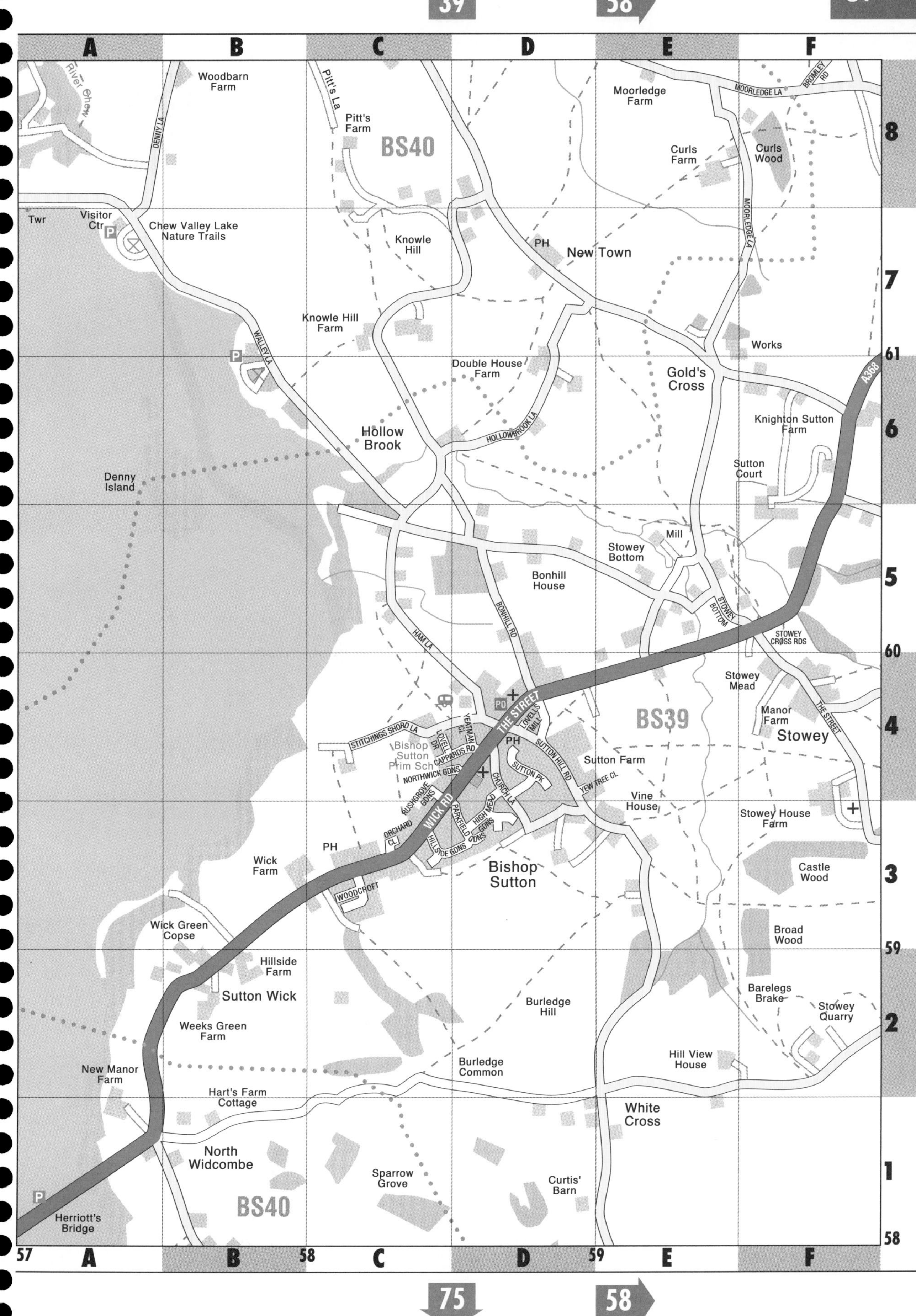
A
B
C
D
E
F
8
7
6
5
4
3
2
1
61
60
59
58
57
Woodbarn Farm
River Chew
DENNY LA
Pitt's La
Pitt's Farm
BS40
Moorledge Farm
MOORLEDGE LA
BROMLEY RD
Curls Farm
Curls Wood
Twr
Visitor Ctr
Chew Valley Lake Nature Trails
Knowle Hill
PH
New Town
MOORLEDGE LA
Knowle Hill Farm
VALLEY LA
Works
Double House Farm
Gold's Cross
A368
Hollow Brook
HOLLOWBROOK LA
Knighton Sutton Farm
Denny Island
Sutton Court
Mill
Stowey Bottom
Bonhill House
BONHILL RD
HAM LA
STOWEY BOTTOM
STOWEY CROSS RDS
Stowey Mead
PO
THE STREET
BS39
Manor Farm
Stowey
THE STREET
STITCHINGS SHORD LA
LOVELL DR
YEATMAN CL
LOVELLS MILL
Bishop Sutton Prim Sch
CAPPARDS RD
PH
SUTTON HILL RD
Sutton Farm
NORTHWICK GDNS
SUTTON PK
RUSHGROVE GDNS
CHURCH LA
YEW TREE CL
Vine House
Stowey House Farm
WICK RD
PARKFIELD GDNS
HIGH MEAD GDNS
ORCHARD CL
HILLSIDE GDNS
PH
Wick Farm
Bishop Sutton
Castle Wood
WOODCROFT
Wick Green Copse
Broad Wood
Hillside Farm
Sutton Wick
Burledge Hill
Barelegs Brake
Stowey Quarry
Weeks Green Farm
New Manor Farm
Burledge Common
Hill View House
Hart's Farm Cottage
White Cross
North Widcombe
Sparrow Grove
Curtis' Barn
P
Herriott's Bridge
BS40

75
58

57
40

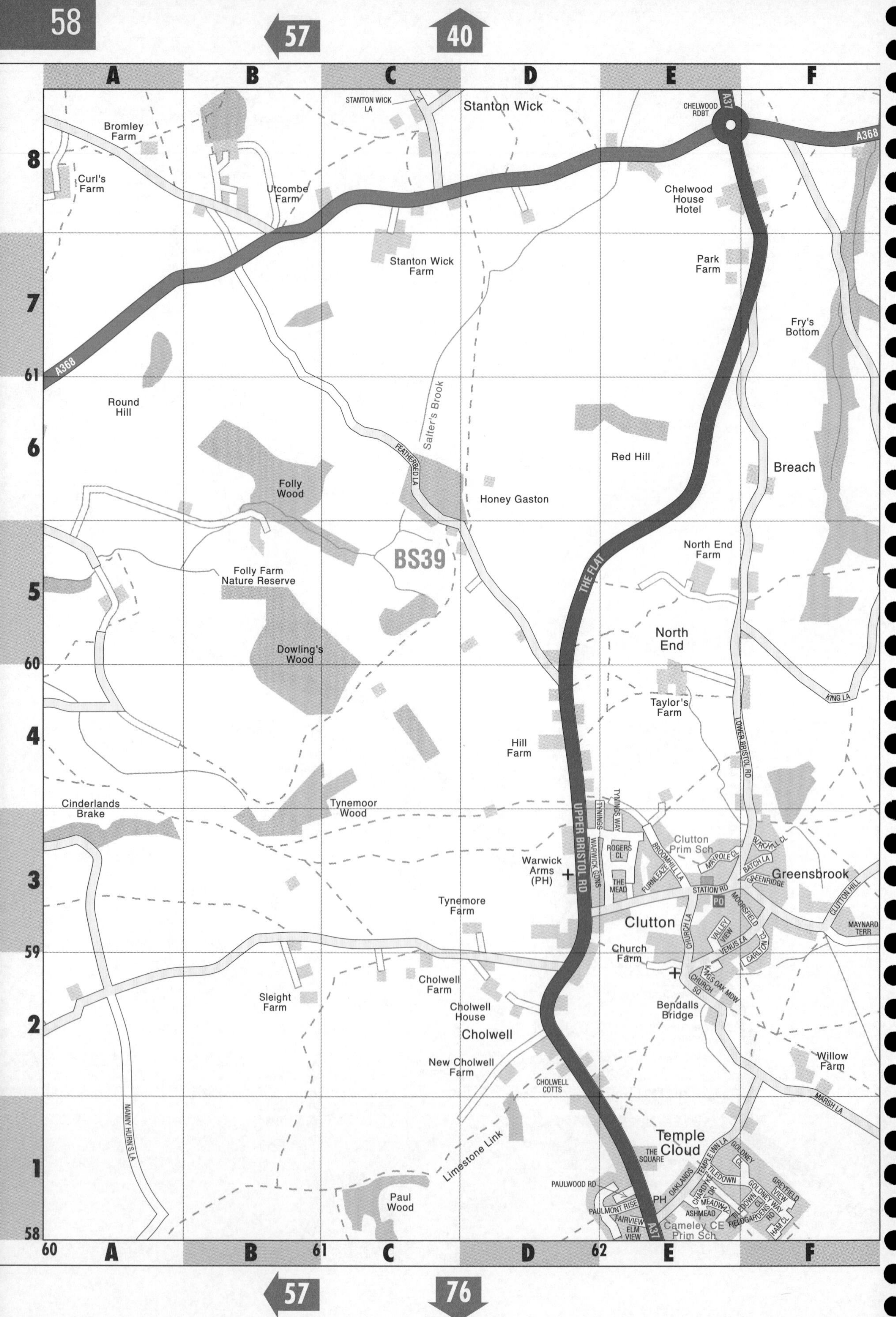
A
B
C
D
E
F
8
7
61
6
5
60
4
3
59
2
1
58
60
61
62
Stanton Wick
STANTON WICK LA
CHELWOOD RDBT
A37
A368
Bromley Farm
Curl's Farm
Utcombe Farm
Chelwood House Hotel
Stanton Wick Farm
Park Farm
Fry's Bottom
Round Hill
Salter's Brook
FEATHERBED LA
Red Hill
Breach
Folly Wood
Honey Gaston
BS39
North End Farm
Folly Farm Nature Reserve
THE FLAT
North End
Dowling's Wood
KING LA
Taylor's Farm
LOWER BRISTOL RD
Hill Farm
Cinderlands Brake
Tynemoor Wood
UPPER BRISTOL RD
TYNINGS
TYNINGS WAY
ROGERS CL
WARWICK GDNS
Clutton Prim Sch
BROOMHILL LA
Warwick Arms (PH)
THE MEAD
FURNLEAZE
MAYPOLE CL
BIRCH HILL CL
BATCH LA
GREENRIDGE
Greensbrook
CLUTTON HILL
STATION RD
PO
MOORSFIELD
Tynemore Farm
Clutton
CHURCH LA
VALLEY VIEW
VENUS LA
CARLTON CT
MAYNARD TERR
Church Farm
KINGS OAK MDW
CHURCH SQ
Cholwell Farm
Sleight Farm
Cholwell House
Bendalls Bridge
Cholwell
Willow Farm
New Cholwell Farm
CHOLWELL COTTS
MARSH LA
NANNY HURN'S LA
Limestone Link
Temple Cloud
THE SQUARE
TEMPLE INN LA
GOLDNEY CL
TILEDOWN
OAKLANDS
CHARDYKE DR
GREYFIELD VIEW
GOLDNEY WAY
PAULWOOD RD
PH
MEADWAY
TILEDOWN CL
FIELDGARDENS RD
Paul Wood
PAULMONT RISE
ASHMEAD
HAM CL
FAIRVIEW
ELM VIEW
Cameley CE Prim Sch

57
76

41
60

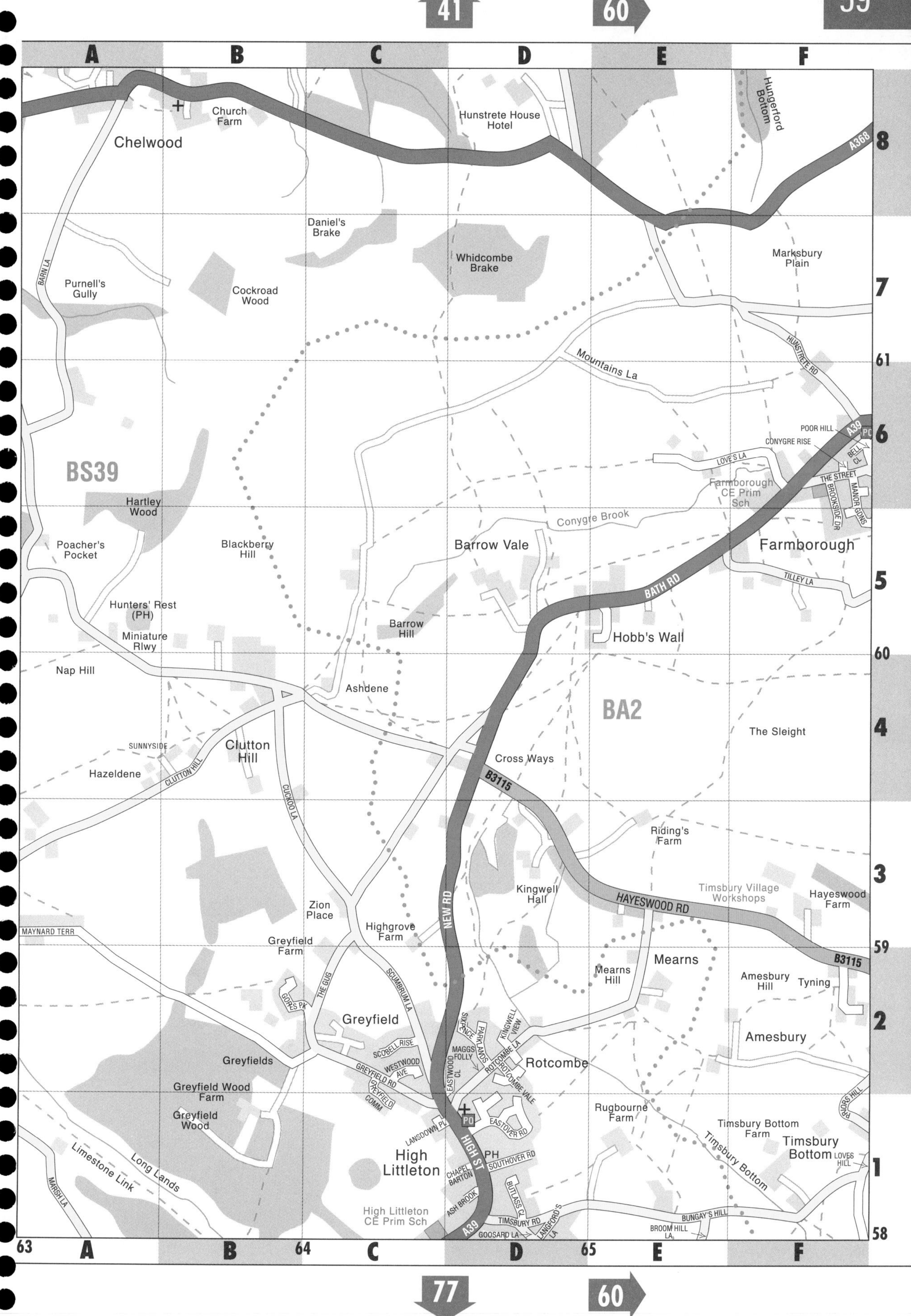
Chelwood
Church Farm
Hunstrete House Hotel
Hungerford Bottom
A368
Daniel's Brake
Whidcombe Brake
Marksbury Plain
Purnell's Gully
Cockroad Wood
BARN LA
Mountains La
HUNSTRETE RD
POOR HILL
CONYGRE RISE
A39
PO
BELL CL
LOVE'S LA
THE STREET
Farmborough CE Prim Sch
BROOKSIDE DR
MANOR GDNS
BS39
Hartley Wood
Conygre Brook
Poacher's Pocket
Blackberry Hill
Barrow Vale
Farmborough
BATH RD
TILLEY LA
Hunters' Rest (PH)
Barrow Hill
Hobb's Wall
Miniature Rlwy
Nap Hill
Ashdene
BA2
SUNNYSIDE
Clutton Hill
The Sleight
Hazeldene
CLUTTON HILL
Cross Ways
B3115
CUCKOO LA
Riding's Farm
Kingwell Hall
Timsbury Village Workshops
Hayeswood Farm
HAYESWOOD RD
Zion Place
NEW RD
MAYNARD TERR
Highgrove Farm
Greyfield Farm
B3115
Mearns
Mearns Hill
Amesbury Hill
Tyning
THE GUG
SCUMBRUM LA
GORES PK
Greyfield
KINGWELL VIEW
PARKLANDS
SIXPENCE
MAGGS FOLLY
Amesbury
Greyfields
SCOBELL RISE
ROTCOMBE LA
Rotcombe
WESTWOOD AVE
EASTWOOD CL
ROTCOMBE VALE
GREYFIELD RD
Greyfield Wood Farm
GREYFIELD COMM
Rugbourne Farm
Greyfield Wood
LANSDOWN PL
EASTOVER RD
Timsbury Bottom Farm
PO
PALMERS HILL
Timsbury Bottom
HIGH ST
PH
Timsbury Bottom
LOVES HILL
Limestone Link
Long Lands
High Littleton
SOUTHOVER RD
CHAPEL BARTON
MARSH LA
ASH BROOK
BUTLASS CL
LANGFORD'S LA
High Littleton CE Prim Sch
TIMSBURY RD
BUNGAY'S HILL
A39
GOOSARD LA
BROOM HILL LA
A B C D E F
8 7 61 6 5 60 4 3 59 2 1 58
63 64 65

77
60

59 42

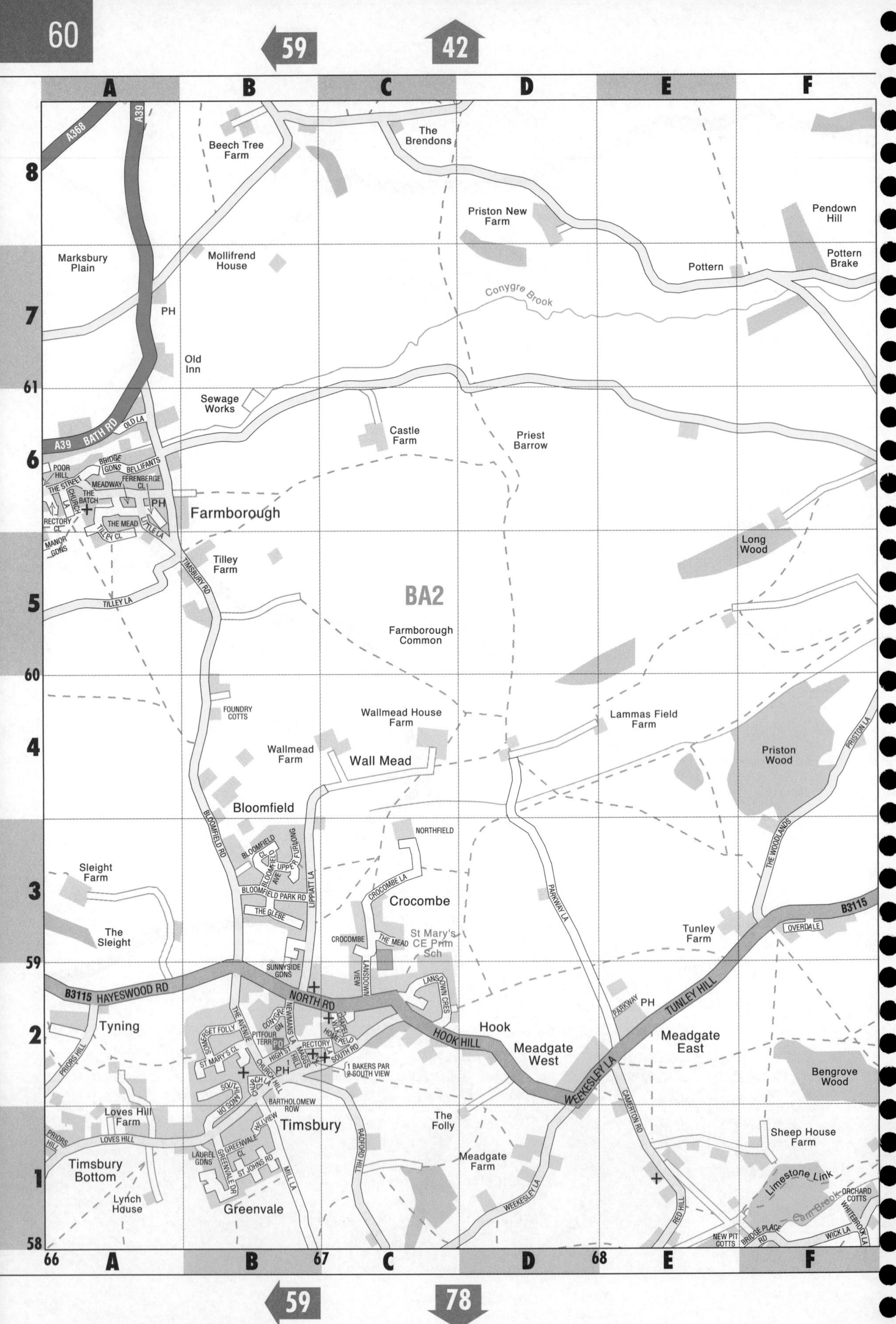

A B C D E F
8 7 61 6 5 60 4 3 59 2 1 58
66 67 68
A368
A39
Beech Tree Farm
The Brendons
Priston New Farm
Pendown Hill
Marksbury Plain
Mollifrend House
Pottern
Pottern Brake
Conygre Brook
PH
Old Inn
Sewage Works
Castle Farm
Priest Barrow
A39 BATH RD
OLD LA
POOR HILL
BRIDGE GDNS
BELLIFANTS
THE STREET
CHURCH LA
MEADWAY
FERENBERGE CL
THE BATCH
PH
Farmborough
RECTORY CL
THE MEAD
LITTLE LA
TILLEY CL
MANOR GDNS
Tilley Farm
Long Wood
TIMSBURY RD
TILLEY LA
BA2
Farmborough Common
FOUNDRY COTTS
Wallmead House Farm
Lammas Field Farm
Wallmead Farm
Wall Mead
Priston Wood
PRISTON LA
Bloomfield
NORTHFIELD
BLOOMFIELD RD
BLOOMFIELD CL
BLOOMFIELD AVE
UPPER FURLONG
LIPPIATT LA
Sleight Farm
BLOOMFIELD PARK RD
CROCOMBE LA
Crocombe
PARKWAY LA
THE WOODLANDS
THE GLEBE
B3115
The Sleight
CROCOMBE
THE MEAD
St Mary's CE Prim Sch
Tunley Farm
OVERDALE
SUNNYSIDE GDNS
LANSDOWN VIEW
LANSDOWN CRES
B3115 HAYESWOOD RD
NORTH RD
PARKWAY
PH
TUNLEY HILL
Tyning
THE AVENUE
SOMERSET FOLLY
CONYGRE GN
NEWMANS LA
CHAPEL FIELD
HOMEFIELD
Hook
HOOK HILL
Meadgate West
Meadgate East
PRIORS HILL
PITFOUR TERR
PO
RECTORY LA
ST MARY'S CL
HIGH ST
MAGGS HILL
SOUTH RD
1 BAKERS PAR
2 SOUTH VIEW
PH
WEEKESLEY LA
CHURCH HILL
SOUTHLANDS DR
Bengrove Wood
BARTHOLOMEW ROW
CAMERTON RD
Loves Hill Farm
HILLVIEW
Timsbury
The Folly
PRIORS HILL
LOVES HILL
GREENVALE CL
RADFORD HILL
Sheep House Farm
Timsbury Bottom
LAUREL GDNS
ST JOHNS RD
Meadgate Farm
GREENVALE DR
ST JOHNS RD
MILL LA
Limestone Link
ORCHARD COTTS
Lynch House
Greenvale
WEEKESLEY LA
RED HILL
Cam Brook
WHITEBROOK LA
NEW PIT COTTS
BRIDGE PLACE RD
WICK LA

59 78

43
62

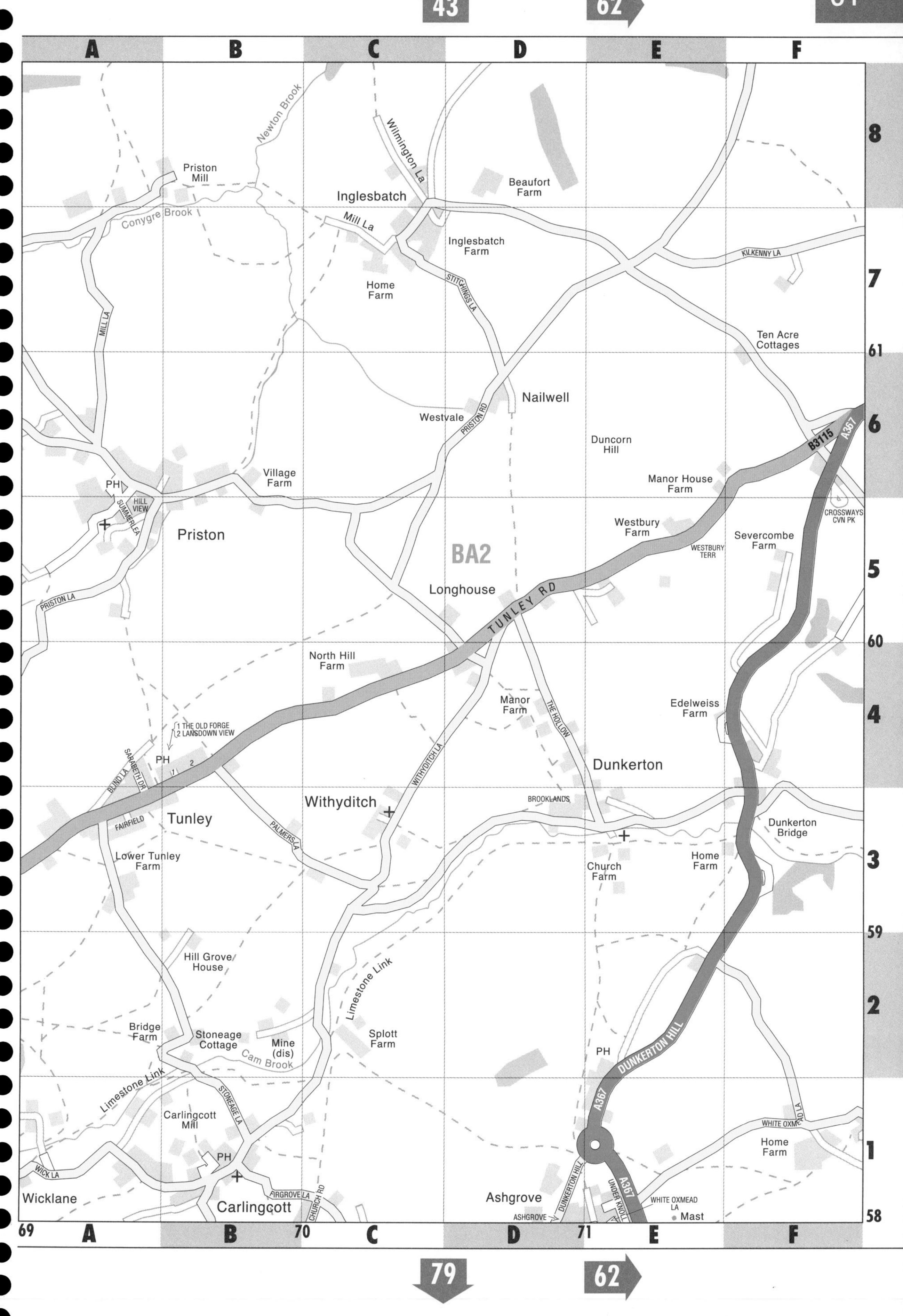
A
B
C
D
E
F
Priston Mill
Newton Brook
Wilmington La
Beaufort Farm
Inglesbatch
Conygre Brook
Mill La
Inglesbatch Farm
KILKENNY LA
Home Farm
STITCHINGS LA
MILL LA
Ten Acre Cottages
Nailwell
Westvale
PRISTON RD
Duncorn Hill
B3115
A367
Manor House Farm
Village Farm
PH
HILL VIEW
SUMMER LA
CROSSWAYS CVN PK
Priston
Westbury Farm
Severcombe Farm
BA2
WESTBURY TERR
Longhouse
PRISTON LA
TUNLEY RD
North Hill Farm
Manor Farm
Edelweiss Farm
THE HOLLOW
1 THE OLD FORGE
2 LANSDOWN VIEW
PH
SARABETH DR
BLIND LA
Dunkerton
Withyditch
WITHYDITCH LA
BROOKLANDS
FAIRFIELD
Tunley
Dunkerton Bridge
PALMERS LA
Lower Tunley Farm
Church Farm
Home Farm
Hill Grove House
Limestone Link
Bridge Farm
Stoneage Cottage
Mine (dis)
Splott Farm
PH
Cam Brook
DUNKERTON HILL
Limestone Link
STONEAGE LA
A367
Carlingcott Mill
WHITE OXMEAD LA
Home Farm
PH
WICK LA
DUNKERTON HILL
A367
UNDER KNOLL
ARGROVE LA
CHURCH RD
Wicklane
Ashgrove
WHITE OXMEAD LA
Carlingcott
ASHGROVE
Mast
8
7
61
6
5
60
4
3
59
2
1
58
69
70
71

79
62

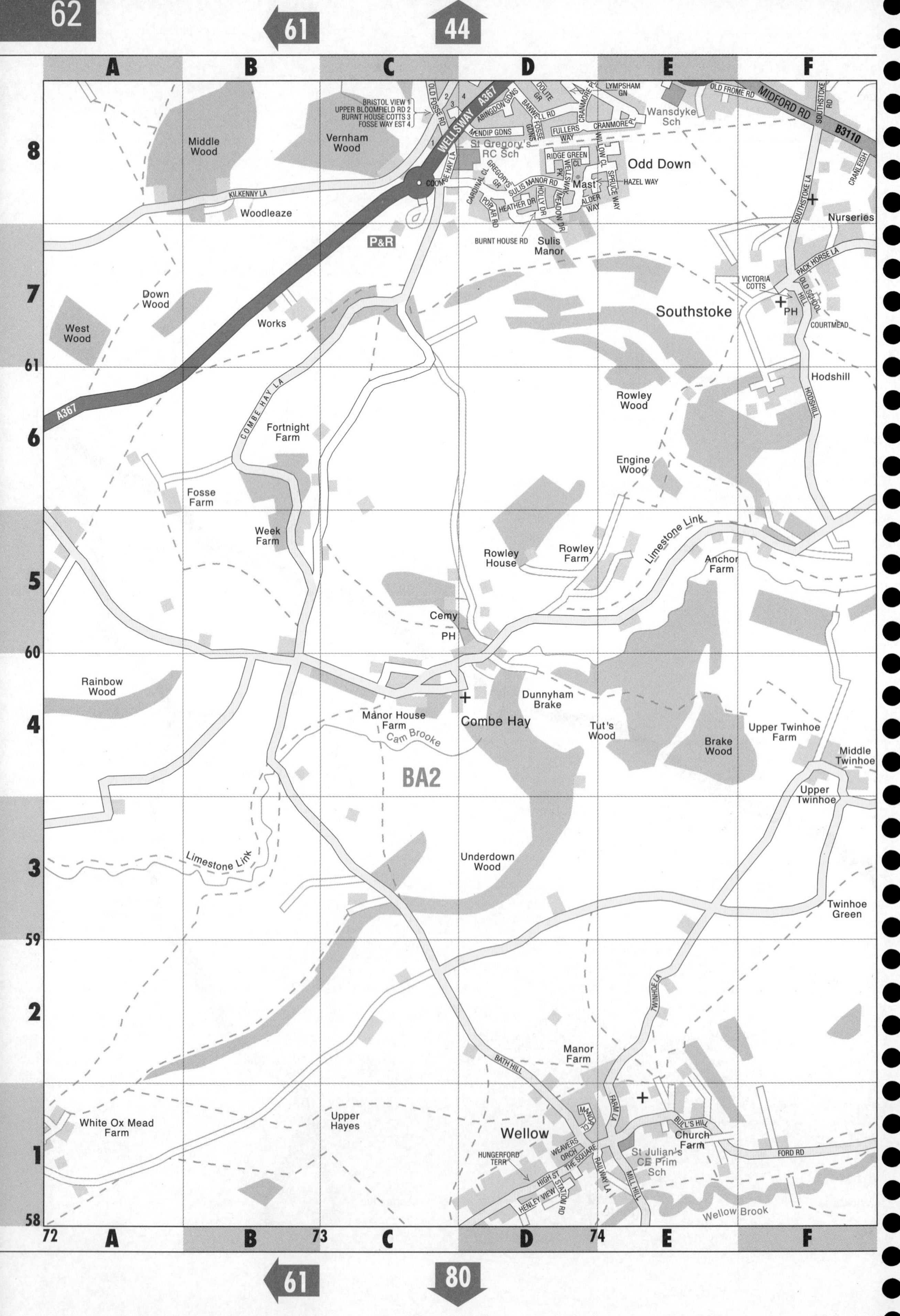

61
44
A
B
C
D
E
F
8
7
61
6
5
60
4
3
59
2
1
58
72
73
74
Middle Wood
Vernham Wood
BRISTOL VIEW 1
UPPER BLOOMFIELD RD 2
BURNT HOUSE COTTS 3
FOSSE WAY EST 4
OLD FOSSE RD
WELLSWAY
A367
ABINGDON GDNS
MENDIP GDNS
BANWELL RD
DOLITE GR
LYMPSHAM GN
CRANMORE PL
CRANMORE
FULLERS WAY
Wansdyke Sch
OLD FROME RD
MIDFORD RD
B3110
SOUTHSTOKE RD
St Gregory's RC Sch
RIDGE GREEN CL
Odd Down
Mast
HAZEL WAY
SPRUCE WAY
ALDER WAY
WILLOW CL
SULIS MANOR RD
HEATHER DR
HOLLY DR
MEADOW DR
CARDINAL CL
GREGORYS GR
POPLAR RD
COOMBE HAY LA
KILKENNY LA
Woodleaze
P&R
BURNT HOUSE RD
Sulis Manor
CRANLEIGH
SOUTHSTOKE LA
Nurseries
PACK HORSE LA
VICTORIA COTTS
OLD SCHOOL HILL
PH
COURTMEAD
Southstoke
Down Wood
West Wood
Works
Hodshill
HODSHILL
Rowley Wood
A367
COMBE HAY LA
Fortnight Farm
Engine Wood
Fosse Farm
Week Farm
Limestone Link
Rowley House
Rowley Farm
Anchor Farm
Cemy
PH
Rainbow Wood
Dunnyham Brake
Manor House Farm
Combe Hay
Cam Brooke
Tut's Wood
Brake Wood
Upper Twinhoe Farm
Middle Twinhoe
BA2
Upper Twinhoe
Limestone Link
Underdown Wood
Twinhoe Green
TWINHOE LA
Manor Farm
BATH HILL
FARM LA
White Ox Mead Farm
Upper Hayes
Wellow
MANOR CL
BULL'S HILL
Church Farm
FORD RD
HUNGERFORD TERR
WEAVERS ORCH
THE SQUARE
St Julian's CE Prim Sch
HIGH ST
STATION RD
RAILWAY LA
MILL HILL
HENLEY VIEW
Wellow Brook
61
80

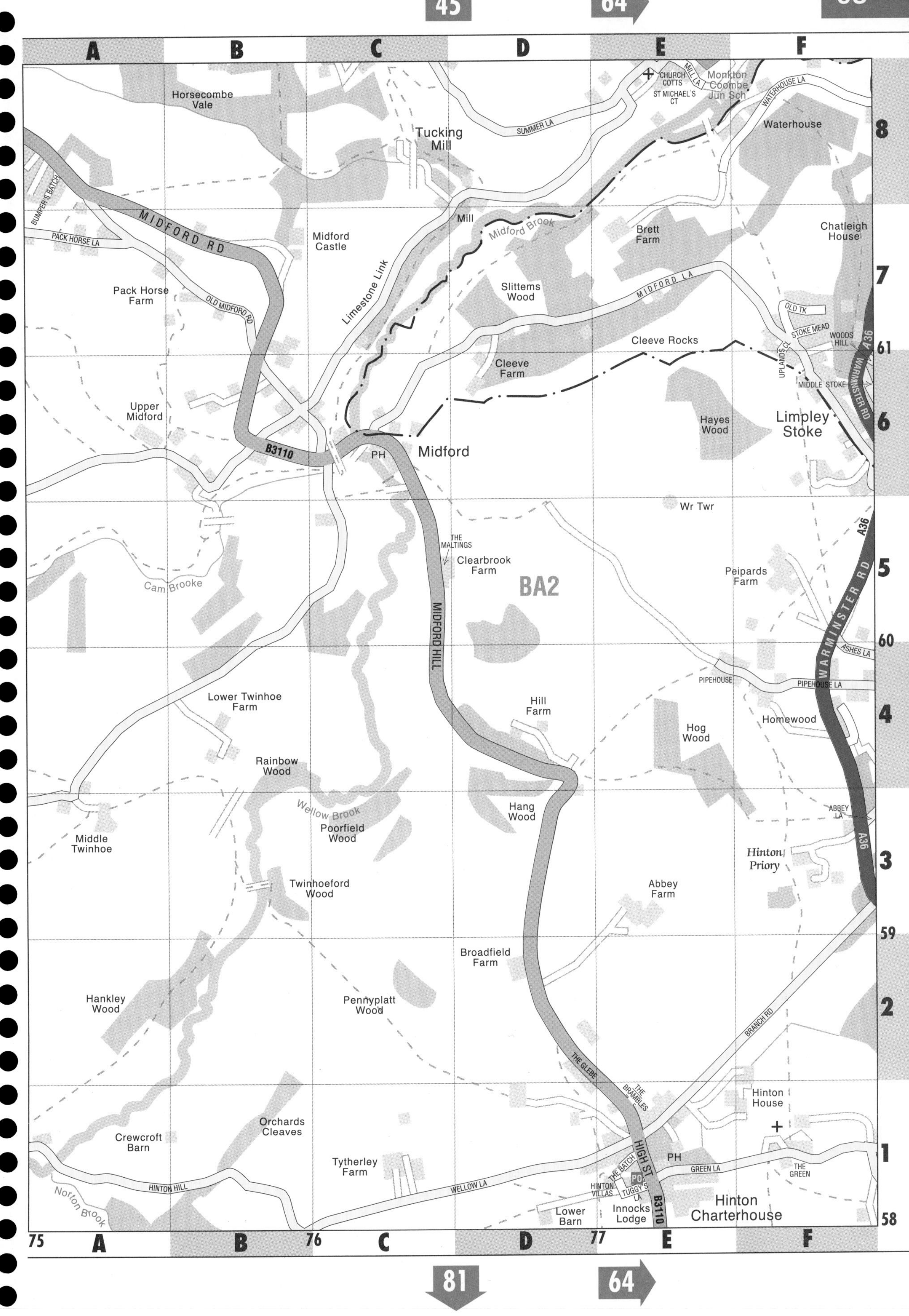
45
64
81
64
A
B
C
D
E
F
8
7
61
6
5
60
4
3
59
2
1
58
75
76
77
Horsecombe Vale
Tucking Mill
SUMMER LA
CHURCH COTTS
MILL LA
Monkton Coombe Jun Sch
ST MICHAEL'S CT
WATERHOUSE LA
Waterhouse
BUMPER'S BATCH
PACK HORSE LA
MIDFORD RD
Midford Castle
Mill
Midford Brook
Brett Farm
Chatleigh House
Pack Horse Farm
OLD MIDFORD RD
Limestone Link
Slittems Wood
MIDFORD LA
OLD TK
STOKE MEAD
WOODS HILL
A36
Cleeve Rocks
UPLANDS CL
Cleeve Farm
MIDDLE STOKE
WARMINSTER RD
Upper Midford
Hayes Wood
Limpley Stoke
B3110
PH
Midford
Wr Twr
THE MALTINGS
Clearbrook Farm
BA2
Peipards Farm
Cam Brooke
MIDFORD HILL
ASHES LA
PIPEHOUSE
PIPEHOUSE LA
Lower Twinhoe Farm
Hill Farm
Homewood
Hog Wood
Rainbow Wood
Wellow Brook
Hang Wood
ABBEY LA
Middle Twinhoe
Poorfield Wood
Hinton Priory
Twinhoeford Wood
Abbey Farm
Broadfield Farm
Hankley Wood
Pennyplatt Wood
BRANCH RD
THE GLEBE
THE BRAMBLES
Hinton House
Orchards Cleaves
Crewcroft Barn
HIGH ST
PH
GREEN LA
THE GREEN
Tytherley Farm
THE BATCH
PO
TUGGY'S LA
HINTON HILL
WELLOW LA
HINTON VILLAS
Norton Brook
Lower Barn
Innocks Lodge
Hinton Charterhouse

63
46

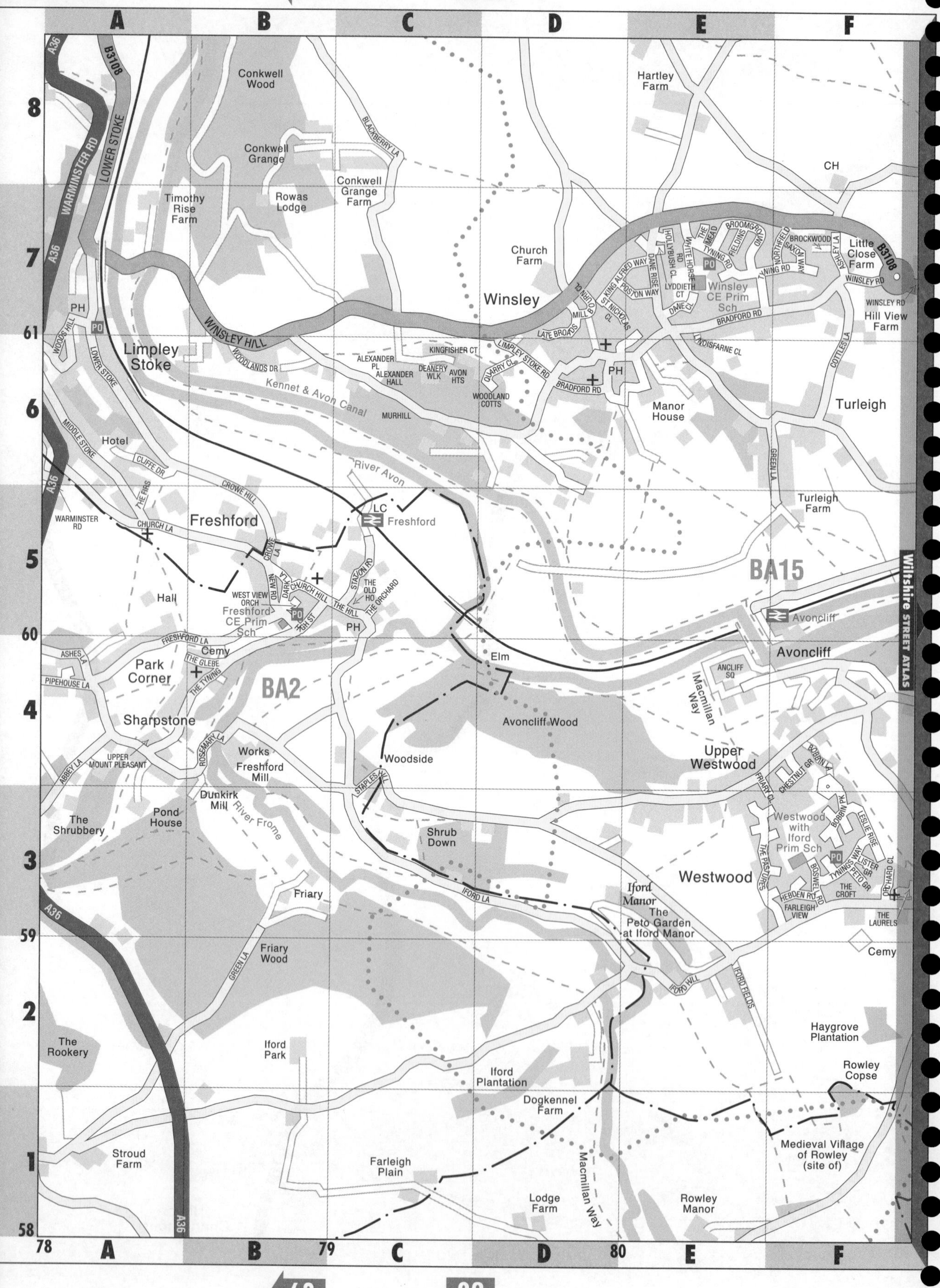
A
B
C
D
E
F
8
7
61
6
5
60
4
3
59
2
1
58
78
79
80
A36
B3108
Conkwell Wood
Conkwell Grange
Rowas Lodge
Conkwell Grange Farm
BLACKBERRY LA
Hartley Farm
CH
WARMINSTER RD
LOWER STOKE
Timothy Rise Farm
Church Farm
Winsley
WINSLEY HILL
Little Close Farm
WINSLEY RD
Hill View Farm
Winsley CE Prim Sch
BRADFORD RD
LINDISFARNE CL
PH
PO
Limpley Stoke
WOODLANDS DR
Kennet & Avon Canal
KINGFISHER CT
ALEXANDER PL
ALEXANDER HALL
DEANERY WLK
AVON HTS
QUARRY CL
LIMPLEY STOKE RD
WOODLAND COTTS
MURHILL
Manor House
Turleigh
COTTLES LA
GREEN LA
Turleigh Farm
MIDDLE STOKE
Hotel
CLIFFE DR
CROWE HILL
River Avon
LC
Freshford
WARMINSTER RD
CHURCH LA
THE FIRS
BA15
Avoncliff
Wiltshire STREET ATLAS
Hall
WEST VIEW ORCH
Freshford CE Prim Sch
HIGH ST
THE HILL
THE ORCHARD
STATION RD
FRESHFORD LA
Cemy
ASHES LA
PIPEHOUSE LA
Park Corner
THE GLEBE
THE TYNING
BA2
Elm
ANCLIFF SQ
Macmillan Way
Sharpstone
ROSEMARY LA
Avoncliff Wood
Upper Westwood
UPPER MOUNT PLEASANT
ABBEY LA
Works
Freshford Mill
Woodside
STAPLES HILL
Dunkirk Mill
River Frome
The Shrubbery
Pond House
Shrub Down
Westwood with Iford Prim Sch
Westwood
Friary
IFORD LA
Iford Manor
The Peto Garden at Iford Manor
FARLEIGH VIEW
THE LAURELS
Friary Wood
GREEN LA
IFORD HILL
IFORD FIELDS
The Rookery
Iford Park
Haygrove Plantation
Rowley Copse
Iford Plantation
Dogkennel Farm
Stroud Farm
Farleigh Plain
Medieval Village of Rowley (site of)
Lodge Farm
Rowley Manor

63
82

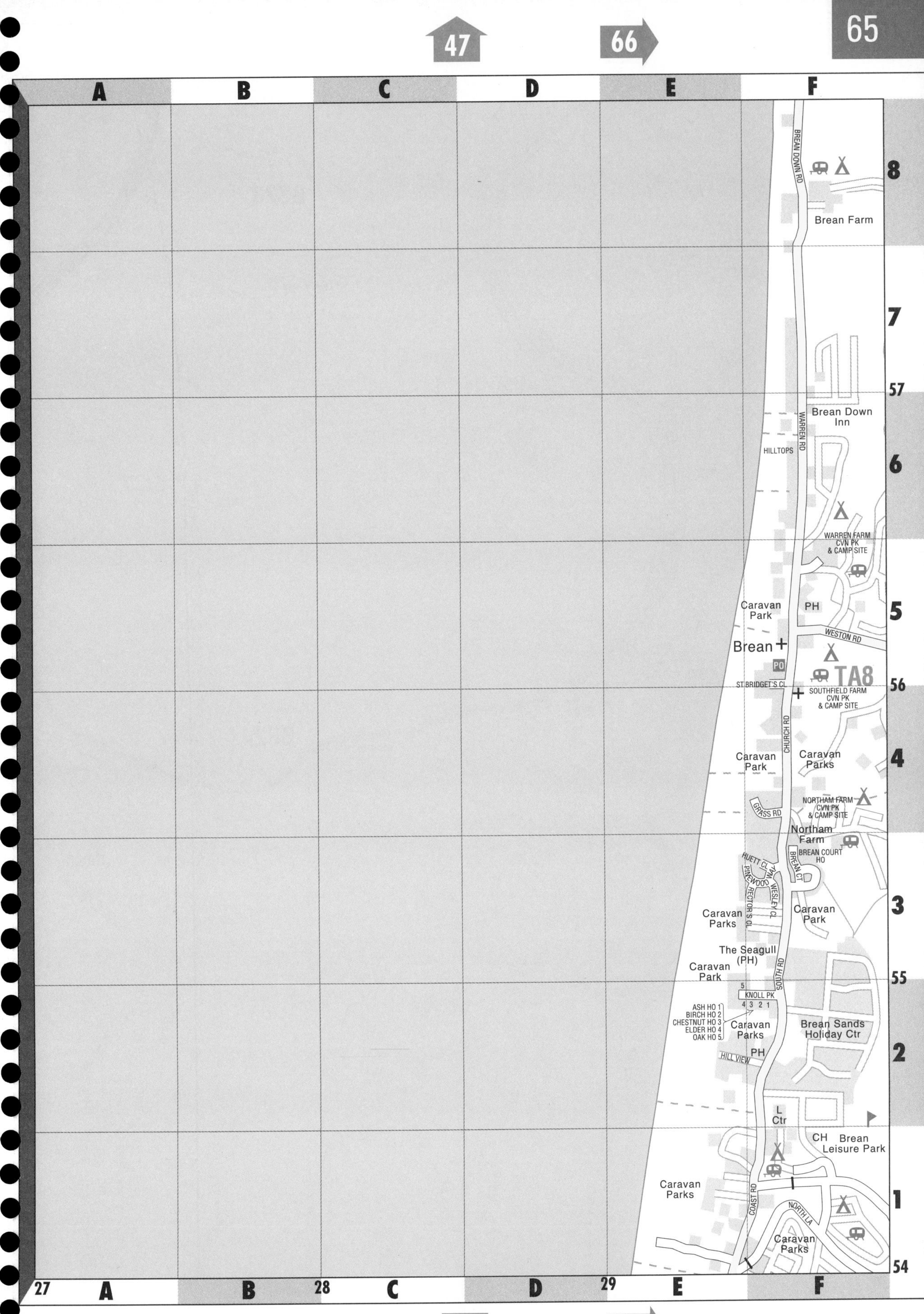
47
66
A
B
C
D
E
F
BREAN DOWN RD
Brean Farm
Brean Down Inn
WARREN RD
HILLTOPS
WARREN FARM CVN PK & CAMP SITE
Caravan Park
PH
WESTON RD
Brean
PO
TA8
ST BRIDGET'S CL
SOUTHFIELD FARM CVN PK & CAMP SITE
CHURCH RD
Caravan Park
Caravan Parks
NORTHAM FARM CVN PK & CAMP SITE
GRASS RD
Northam Farm
BREAN COURT HO
BREAN CT
HUETT CL
PINEWOOD
RECTOR'S CL
WESLEY CL
Caravan Parks
Caravan Park
The Seagull (PH)
Caravan Park
SOUTH RD
KNOLL PK
ASH HO 1
BIRCH HO 2
CHESTNUT HO 3
ELDER HO 4
OAK HO 5
Caravan Parks
Brean Sands Holiday Ctr
PH
HILL VIEW
L Ctr
CH
Brean Leisure Park
Caravan Parks
COAST RD
NORTH LA
Caravan Parks
8
7
57
6
5
56
4
3
55
2
1
54
27
28
29
84
66

65
48

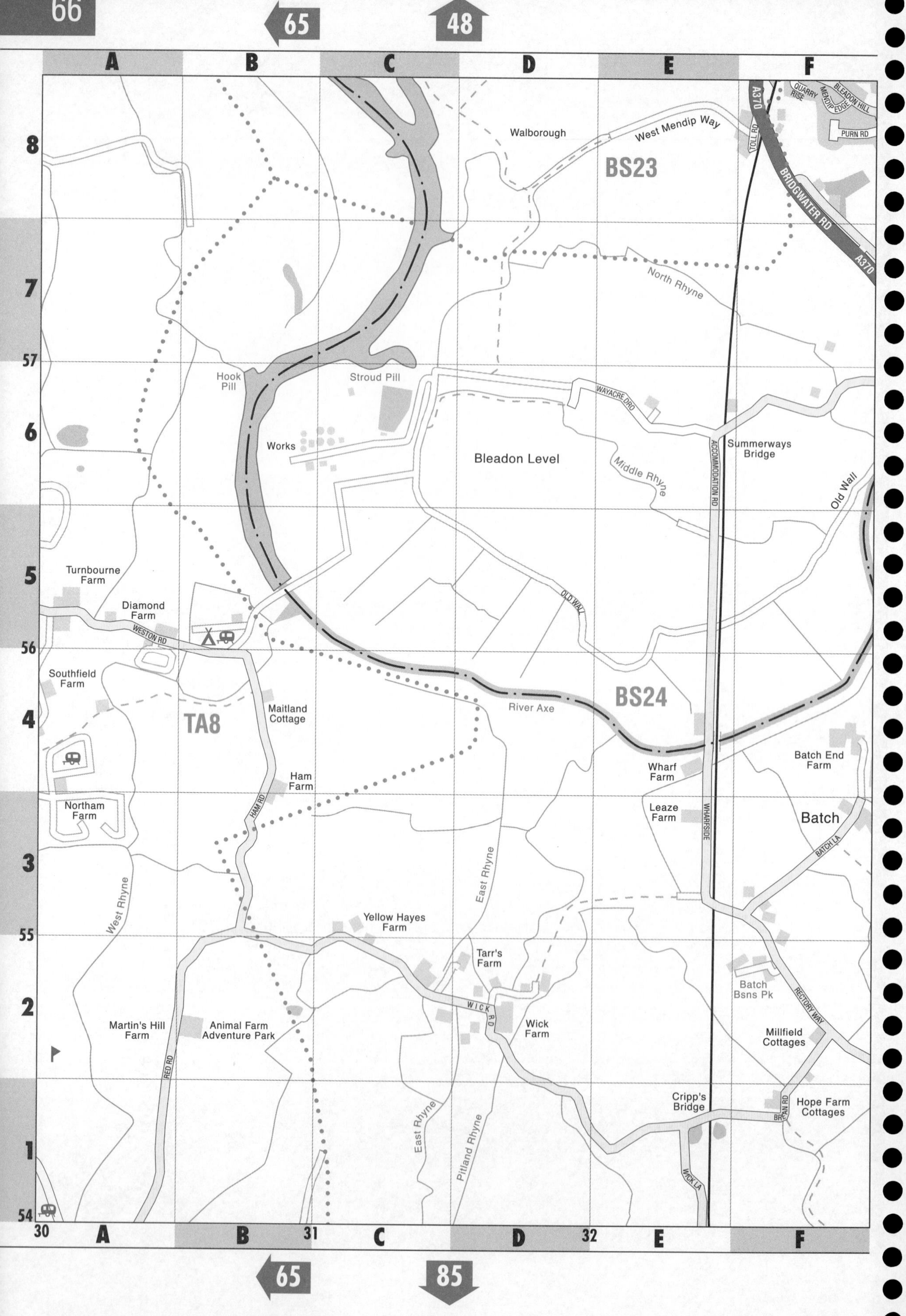
A
B
C
D
E
F
8
7
57
6
5
56
4
3
55
2
1
54
30
31
32
Walborough
West Mendip Way
BS23
A370
TOLL RD
QUARRY RISE
MENDIP EDGE
BLEADON HILL
PURN RD
BRIDGWATER RD
North Rhyne
Hook Pill
Stroud Pill
WAYACRE DRO
Works
Bleadon Level
ACCOMMODATION RD
Summerways Bridge
Middle Rhyne
Old Wall
Turnbourne Farm
Diamond Farm
WESTON RD
OLD WALL
Southfield Farm
Maitland Cottage
River Axe
BS24
TA8
Wharf Farm
Batch End Farm
Ham Farm
Northam Farm
HAM RD
Leaze Farm
WHARFSIDE
Batch
BATCH LA
East Rhyne
West Rhyne
Yellow Hayes Farm
Tarr's Farm
Batch Bsns Pk
WICK RD
RECTORY WAY
Martin's Hill Farm
Animal Farm Adventure Park
Wick Farm
Millfield Cottages
RED RD
Cripp's Bridge
Hope Farm Cottages
BREAN RD
East Rhyne
Pitland Rhyne
WICK LA

65
85

49
68

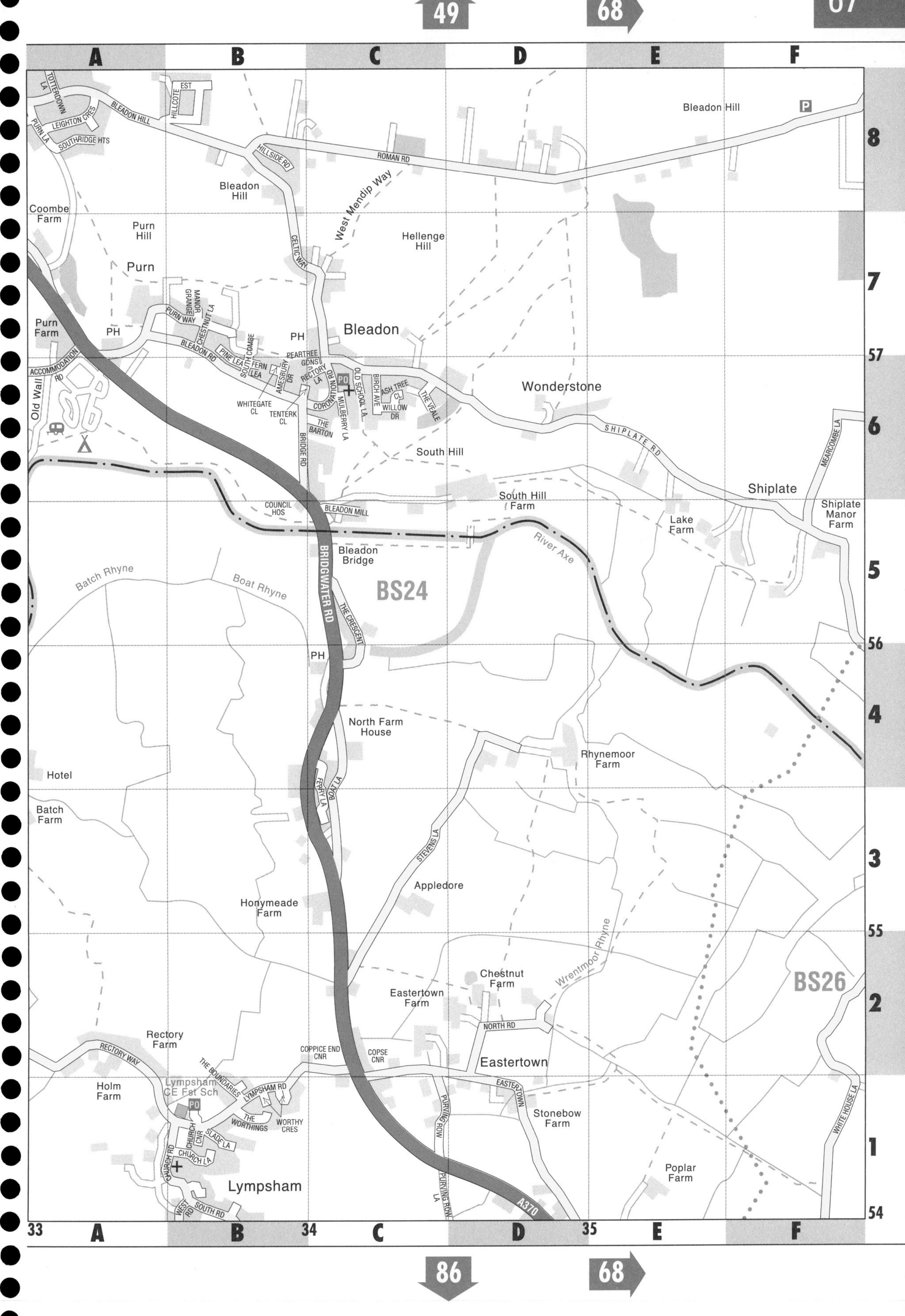
A
B
C
D
E
F
Bleadon Hill
Coombe Farm
Purn Hill
Purn
Purn Farm
PH
Bleadon Hill
West Mendip Way
Hellenge Hill
Bleadon
Wonderstone
South Hill
Shiplate
Shiplate Manor Farm
Lake Farm
South Hill Farm
Bleadon Bridge
BS24
River Axe
Batch Rhyne
Boat Rhyne
Old Wall
North Farm House
Rhynemoor Farm
Hotel
Batch Farm
Appledore
Honymeade Farm
Chestnut Farm
Eastertown Farm
Wrentmoor Rhyne
BS26
Rectory Farm
Eastertown
Holm Farm
Lympsham CE Fst Sch
Stonebow Farm
Poplar Farm
Lympsham
ROMAN RD
BLEADON HILL
LEIGHTON CRES
SOUTHRIDGE HTS
TOTTERDOWN LA
PURN LA
HILLCOTE EST
HILLSIDE RD
CELTIC WAY
BLEADON RD
PURN WAY
ACCOMMODATION RD
SHIPLATE RD
MEARCOMBE LA
BRIDGE RD
BLEADON MILL
COUNCIL HOS
BRIDGWATER RD
THE CRESCENT
FERRY LA
BOAT LA
STEVENS LA
NORTH RD
EASTERTOWN
PURVING ROW
PURVING ROW LA
WHITE HOUSE LA
RECTORY WAY
COPPICE END CNR
COPSE CNR
LYMPSHAM RD
THE BOUNDARIES
THE WORTHINGS
WORTHY CRES
SLADE LA
CHURCH CNR
CHURCH LA
CHURCH RD
WEST RD
SOUTH RD
A370
PO
8
7
57
6
5
56
4
3
55
2
1
54
33
34
35

86
68

67
50

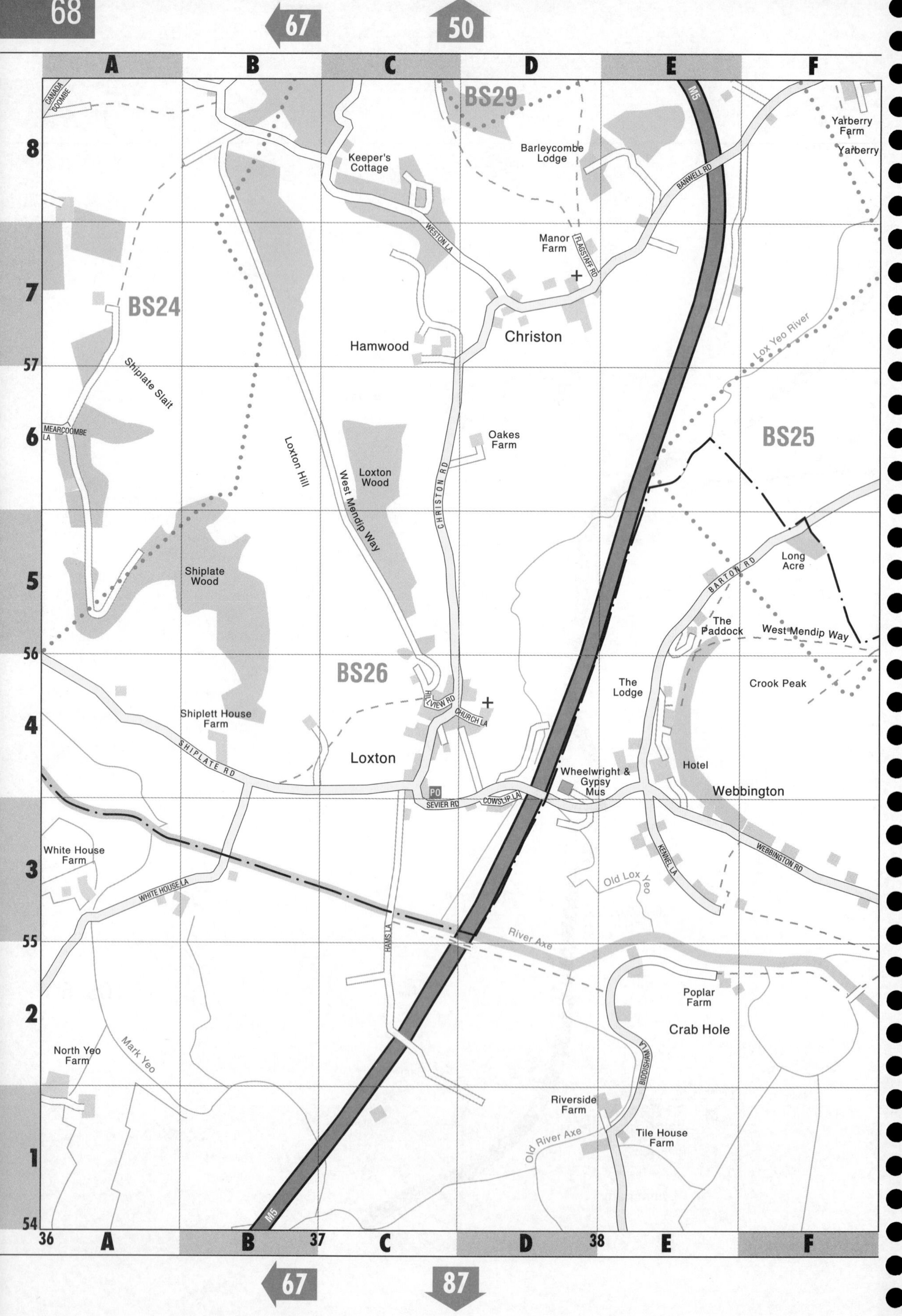
A
B
C
D
E
F
8
7
57
6
5
56
4
3
55
2
1
54
36
37
38
CANADA COOMBE
BS29
M5
Yarberry Farm
Yarberry
Keeper's Cottage
Barleycombe Lodge
BANWELL RD
WESTON LA
Manor Farm
FLAGSTAFF RD
BS24
Christon
Hamwood
Lox Yeo River
Shiplate Slait
MEARCOOMBE LA
Oakes Farm
BS25
Loxton Hill
West Mendip Way
Loxton Wood
CHRISTON RD
Long Acre
BARTON RD
Shiplate Wood
The Paddock
West Mendip Way
BS26
The Lodge
Crook Peak
HILLVIEW RD
CHURCH LA
Shiplett House Farm
SHIPLATE RD
Loxton
Hotel
Wheelwright & Gypsy Mus
PO
Webbington
SEVIER RD
COWSLIP LA
White House Farm
KENNEL LA
WEBBINGTON RD
Old Lox Yeo
WHITE HOUSE LA
HAMS LA
River Axe
Poplar Farm
Crab Hole
North Yeo Farm
Mark Yeo
BIDDISHAM LA
Riverside Farm
Old River Axe
Tile House Farm
M5

67
87

51
70

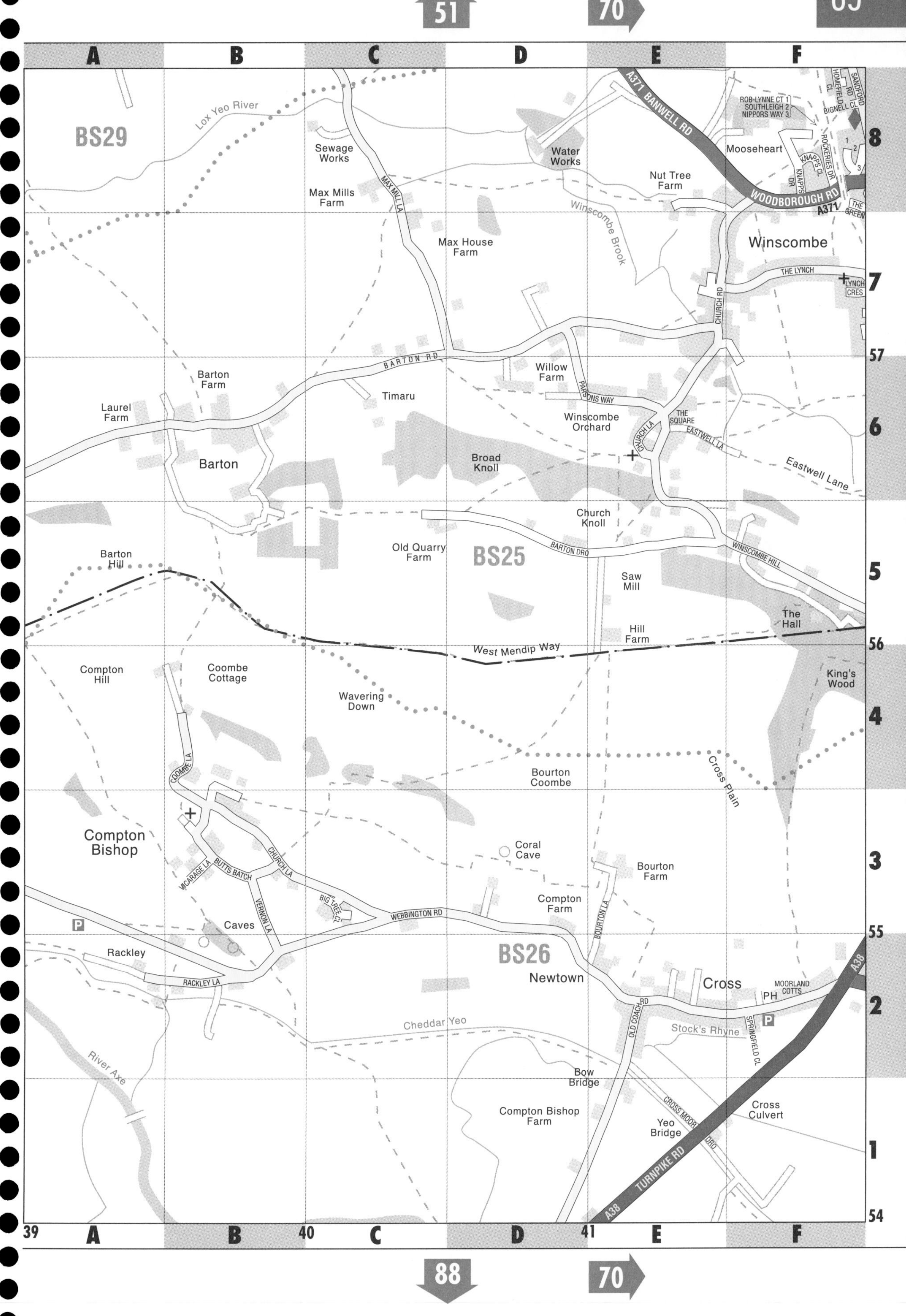
BS29
Lox Yeo River
Sewage Works
Max Mills Farm
MAX MILL LA
Water Works
A371 BANWELL RD
Nut Tree Farm
Mooseheart
ROB-LYNNE CT 1
SOUTHLEIGH 2
NIPPORS WAY 3
HOMEFIELD CL
SANDFORD RD
BIGNELL CL
ROCKERIES DR
KNAPPS CL
KNAPPS DR
WOODBOROUGH RD
A371
THE GREEN
Winscombe Brook
Max House Farm
Winscombe
THE LYNCH
LYNCH CRES
CHURCH RD
BARTON RD
Barton Farm
Laurel Farm
Timaru
Willow Farm
PARSONS WAY
Winscombe Orchard
THE SQUARE
EASTWELL LA
CHURCH LA
Eastwell Lane
Barton
Broad Knoll
Church Knoll
Barton Hill
Old Quarry Farm
BS25
BARTON DRO
WINSCOMBE HILL
Saw Mill
The Hall
Hill Farm
West Mendip Way
Compton Hill
Coombe Cottage
Wavering Down
King's Wood
COOMBE LA
Bourton Coombe
Cross Plain
Compton Bishop
Coral Cave
Bourton Farm
CHURCH LA
BUTTS BATCH
VICARAGE LA
BIG TREE CL
VERNON LA
WEBBINGTON RD
Compton Farm
BOURTON LA
P
Caves
Rackley
RACKLEY LA
BS26
Newtown
Cross
MOORLAND COTTS
PH
A38
OLD COACH RD
Cheddar Yeo
Stock's Rhyne
SPRINGFIELD CL
P
River Axe
Bow Bridge
Compton Bishop Farm
CROSS MOOR DRO
Yeo Bridge
Cross Culvert
TURNPIKE RD
A38
A B C D E F
8 7 57 6 5 56 4 3 55 2 1 54
39 40 41

88
70

69
52

A B C D E F

8
7
57
6
5
56
4
3
55
2
1
54

Winscombe Woodborough Prim Sch
Paddington House
Queensmead Court
Woodborough
Winterhead
Winterhead Farm
Sidcot
The Hall Sch
Sidcot Sch
Playing Field
Oakridge Farm
Sidcot Hill Farm
Gatcombe
Hotel
Hale Coombe
West Mendip Way
Eastwell La
BS25
Winterhead Hill Farm
Winterhead Hill
Cuck Hill
Shipham CE Fst Sch
Shipham
Hotel
Lillypool Cheese & Cider Farm
Callow Hill
Hale Coppice
Shute Shelve Farm
Callow Drove
Works
Callow Rock Quarry
Mast
Fry's Hill
Rose Wood
Shute Shelve Hill
Axbridge Hill
Cheddar Wood
BS26
BS27
Manor Farm
St Michael's Cheshire Home
Cemy
Hillside
Townsend Farm
Axbridge
Axbridge CE Fst Sch
Sewage Works
Middle Rhyne
Boat Yard
Yacht Club
Cheddar Resr
Bloomfield Farm
Allot Gdns
Ellenge Stream

1 MENDIP LODGE
2 WOODBOROUGH CT
3 APPLE TREE DR
4 DUNSTER CT

1 ALLENS LA
2 COURT LA
3 NORTH DOWN CL

1 PENDLE CL

1 MEADOW ST
2 THE SQUARE
3 CHURCH LA
4 THE BUNGALOWS

A38, A371, BRISTOL RD, BRIDGWATER RD, SIDCOT LA, CROSS LA, CHEDDAR RD, AXBRIDGE RD, SHIPHAM RD, WINSCOMBE DRO, WINSCOMBE HILL, WINSCOMBE DR, LONGBOTTOM, BROADWAY, THE AVENUE, HORSELEAZE LA, HILLYFIELDS, HILLYFIELDS WAY, WOODBOROUGH RD, WOODBOROUGH DR, FOUNTAIN LA, NEWCOMBE LA, OAKRIDGE CL, OAKRIDGE LA, FULLERS LA, SOUTHLEAZE, YADLEY LA, YADLEY CL, LYNCHMEAD, YADLEY WAY, THE VINERY, WOODBOROUGH CRES, THE CHESTNUTS, ASHLEY CL, THE GREEN, SANDFORD RD, WOODDENE, PLUMTREE CL, HOMESTEAD WAY, ASH CL, OAK RD, MOORHAM RD, WELL CL, BRIMRIDGE RD, BRAE RISE, BRAE RD, RISEDALE RD, BELMONT RD, SEWELL HO, SOUTHMEAD, OBSERVATORY FIELD, SIDCOT DR, CUCK HILL, TEMPLARS WAY, THE SQUARE, THE TERRACE, THE DRUMHEAD WAY, THE MEAD, KENMEADE CL, SYCAMORE CL, COMRADE AVE, THE DRIVE, TURNPIKE RD, NEW RD, BEECH DR, BEECH CL, BEECH RD, NORTH DOWN LA, FAIR HILL, HOLLOW RD, HIND PITTS, FOLLY LA, TOP RD, GLOVERS FIELD, BARN POOL, DEERLEAP, LIPPIATT LA, ROWBERROW LA, WAVERING DOWN RISE, RECURIUM LODGE, FENNEL LA, WEST ST, COMPTON LA, STARRS CL, COURT HO, ST JOHNS CT, HOULGATE WAY, HORN'S LA, HIGH ST, BACK LA, PH, Mus, ST MARY'S ST, STATION RD, CHESTNUT AVE, MENDIP CL, MARRON CL, HIPPISLEY DR, STRAWBERRY FIELD, FARTHING COMBE, WOODLANDS, WOOD LA, CHEDDAR RD, BARNABAS CL, PARSONAGE LA, BLACK LA, JUBILEE RD, PARKFIELD RD, ORCHARD, FURLONG PL, PENN CT, PENN WAY, OLD CHURCH RD, KNIGHTSTONE CL, OLD CHURCH RD, MOORLAND ST, MOOR GN, WALNUT CL, MILL STREAM CL, WALL GN, BAILIFFS CL, CROSS MOOR RD, CROSS MOOR DR, BAILIFFS' WALL, AXBRIDGE MOOR DRO, PORTMEADE DRO, PROWSE'S LA, BROADWAY ACRES, UPPER NEW RD, PO, P, Liby

42 A B 43 C D 44 E F

69
89

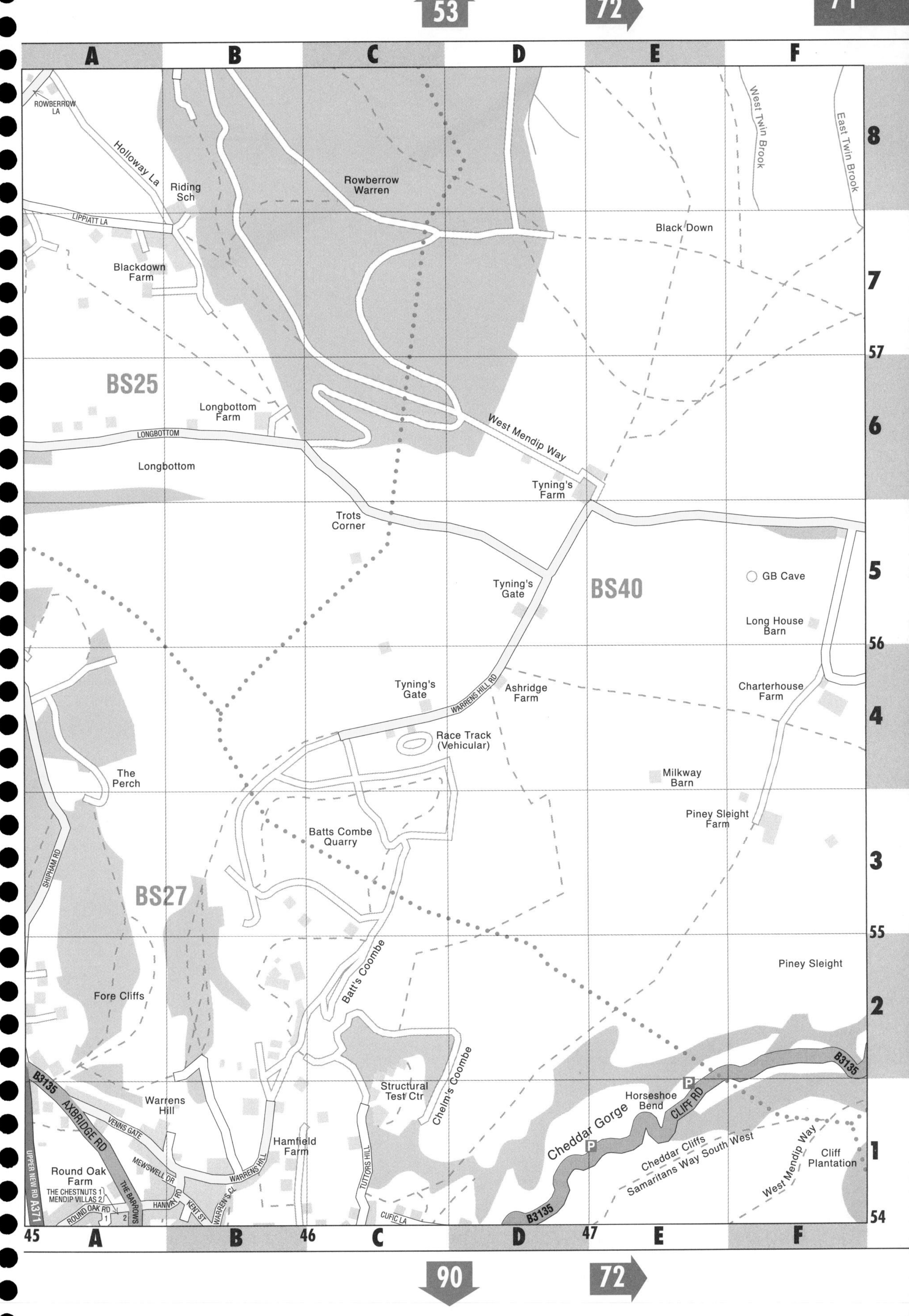
53
72
A
B
C
D
E
F
8
7
57
6
5
56
4
3
55
2
1
54
45
46
47
90
ROWBERROW LA
Holloway La
Riding Sch
Rowberrow Warren
LIPPIATT LA
Blackdown Farm
Black Down
West Twin Brook
East Twin Brook
BS25
Longbottom Farm
LONGBOTTOM
Longbottom
West Mendip Way
Tyning's Farm
Trots Corner
Tyning's Gate
BS40
GB Cave
Long House Barn
Tyning's Gate
WARRENS HILL RD
Ashridge Farm
Charterhouse Farm
Race Track (Vehicular)
The Perch
Milkway Barn
Piney Sleight Farm
Batts Combe Quarry
SHIPHAM RD
BS27
Piney Sleight
Batt's Coombe
Fore Cliffs
B3135
Structural Test Ctr
Chelm's Coombe
Horseshoe Bend
CLIFF RD
Warrens Hill
AXBRIDGE RD
VENNS GATE
Cheddar Gorge
Hamfield Farm
Cheddar Cliffs
Samaritans Way South West
West Mendip Way
Cliff Plantation
MEWSWELL DR
WARRENS HILL
Round Oak Farm
THE CHESTNUTS
MENDIP VILLAS
THE BARROWS
HANNAY RD
KENT ST
WARREN'S CL
TUTTORS HILL
ROUND OAK RD
CUFIC LA
UPPER NEW RD
A371

71
54

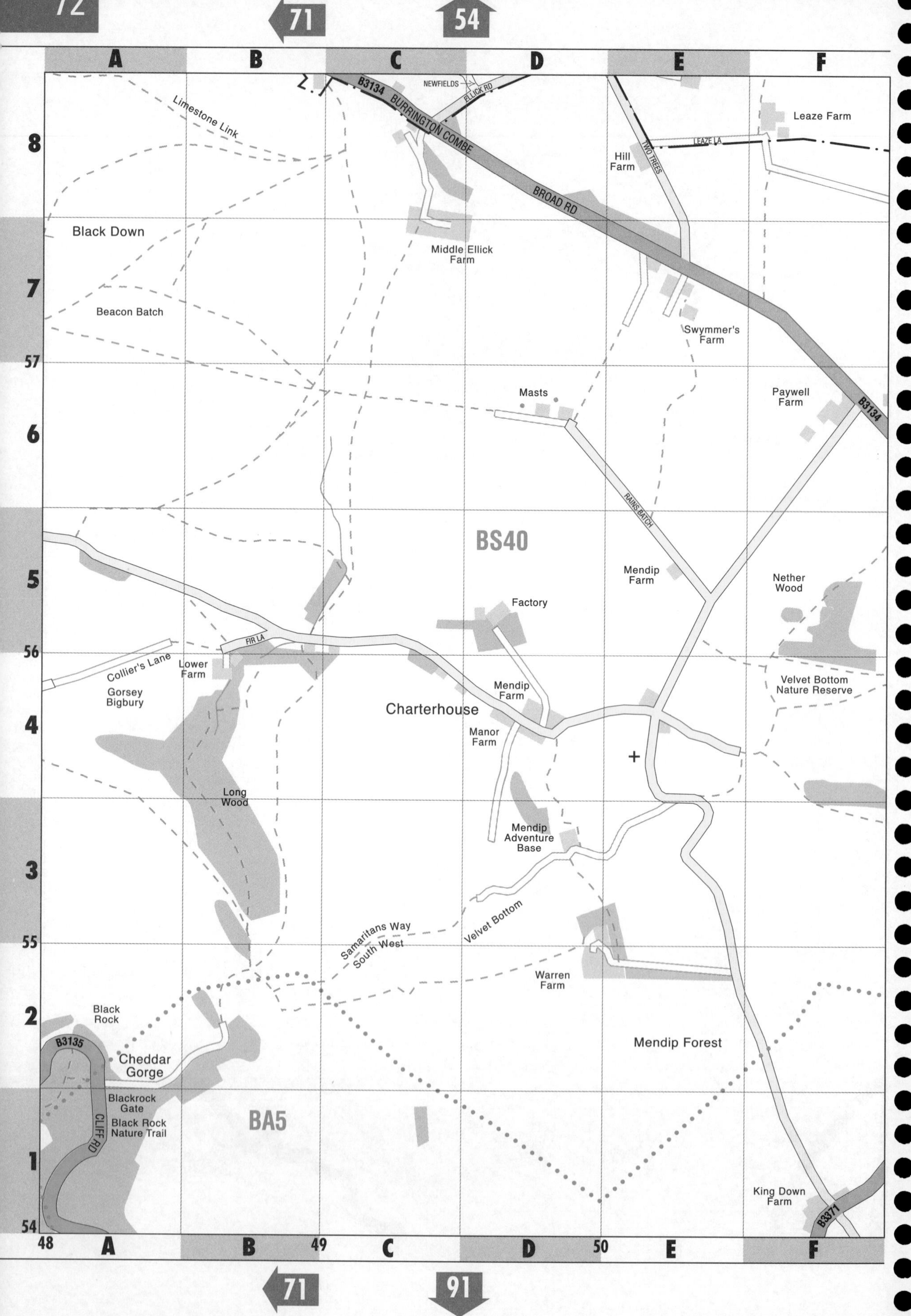
A
B
C
D
E
F
8
7
57
6
5
56
4
3
55
2
1
54
48
49
50
B3134
NEWFIELDS
ELLICK RD
BURRINGTON COMBE
Limestone Link
Leaze Farm
LEAZE LA
Hill
Farm
TWO TREES
BROAD RD
Black Down
Middle Ellick
Farm
Beacon Batch
Swymmer's
Farm
Masts
Paywell
Farm
B3134
RAINS BATCH
BS40
Mendip
Farm
Nether
Wood
Factory
FIR LA
Collier's Lane
Lower
Farm
Gorsey
Bigbury
Mendip
Farm
Charterhouse
Manor
Farm
Velvet Bottom
Nature Reserve
Long
Wood
Mendip
Adventure
Base
Samaritans Way
South West
Velvet Bottom
Warren
Farm
Black
Rock
B3135
Cheddar
Gorge
Mendip Forest
Blackrock
Gate
Black Rock
Nature Trail
CLIFF RD
BA5
King Down
Farm
B3371

71
91

55
74

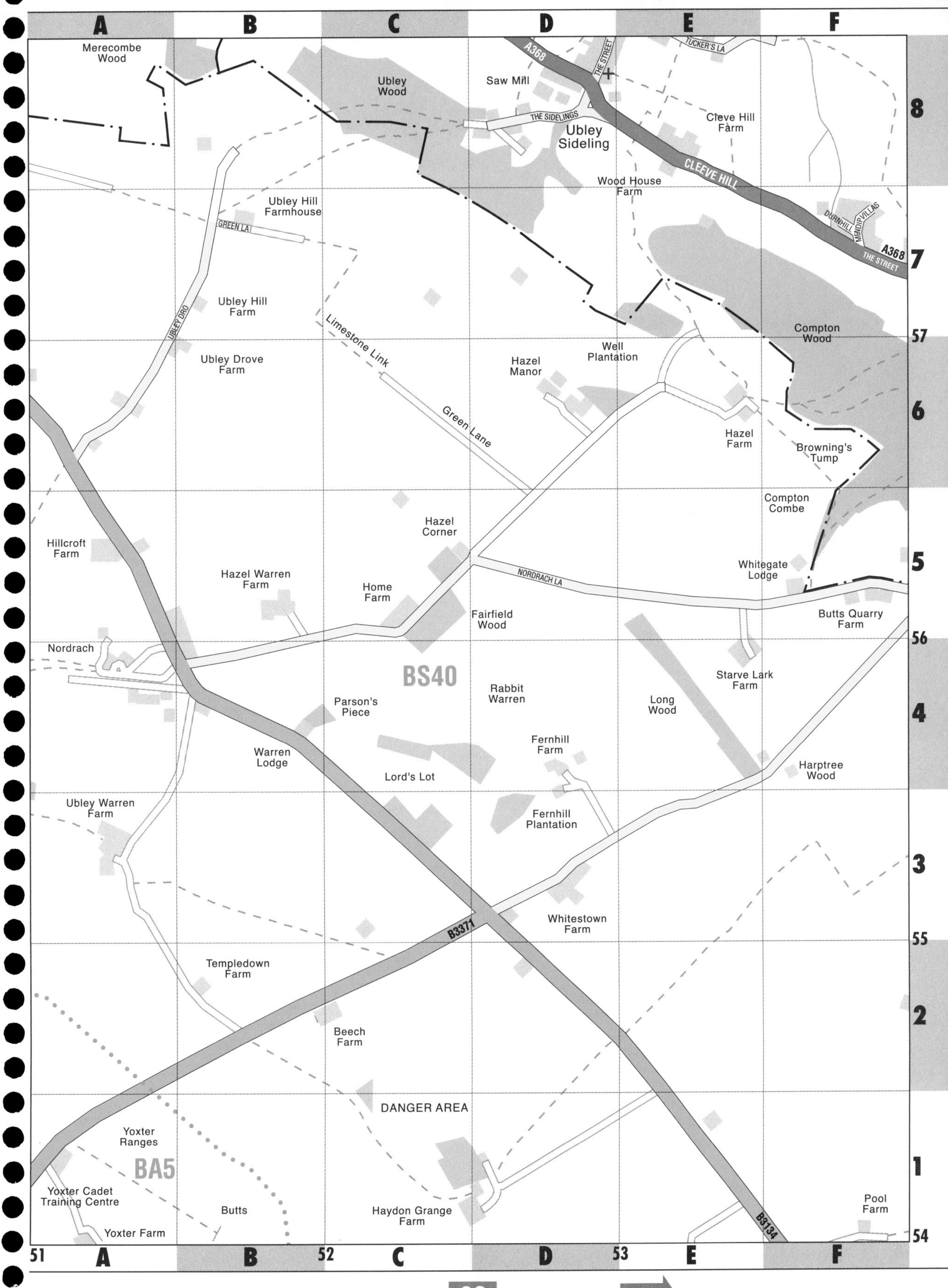
A
B
C
D
E
F
Merecombe Wood
Ubley Wood
Saw Mill
A368
THE STREET
TUCKER'S LA
THE SIDELINGS
Ubley Sideling
Cleve Hill Farm
CLEEVE HILL
Wood House Farm
Ubley Hill Farmhouse
GREEN LA
DURNHILL
MENDIP VILLAS
A368
THE STREET
Ubley Hill Farm
UBLEY DRO
Limestone Link
Compton Wood
Well Plantation
Hazel Manor
Ubley Drove Farm
Green Lane
Hazel Farm
Browning's Tump
Compton Combe
Hazel Corner
Hillcroft Farm
Hazel Warren Farm
Home Farm
NORDRACH LA
Whitegate Lodge
Fairfield Wood
Butts Quarry Farm
Nordrach
BS40
Starve Lark Farm
Parson's Piece
Rabbit Warren
Long Wood
Warren Lodge
Fernhill Farm
Harptree Wood
Lord's Lot
Ubley Warren Farm
Fernhill Plantation
B3371
Whitestown Farm
Templedown Farm
Beech Farm
DANGER AREA
Yoxter Ranges
BA5
Yoxter Cadet Training Centre
Butts
Haydon Grange Farm
Pool Farm
Yoxter Farm
B3134
8
7
57
6
5
56
4
3
55
2
1
54
51
52
53

92
74

73
56

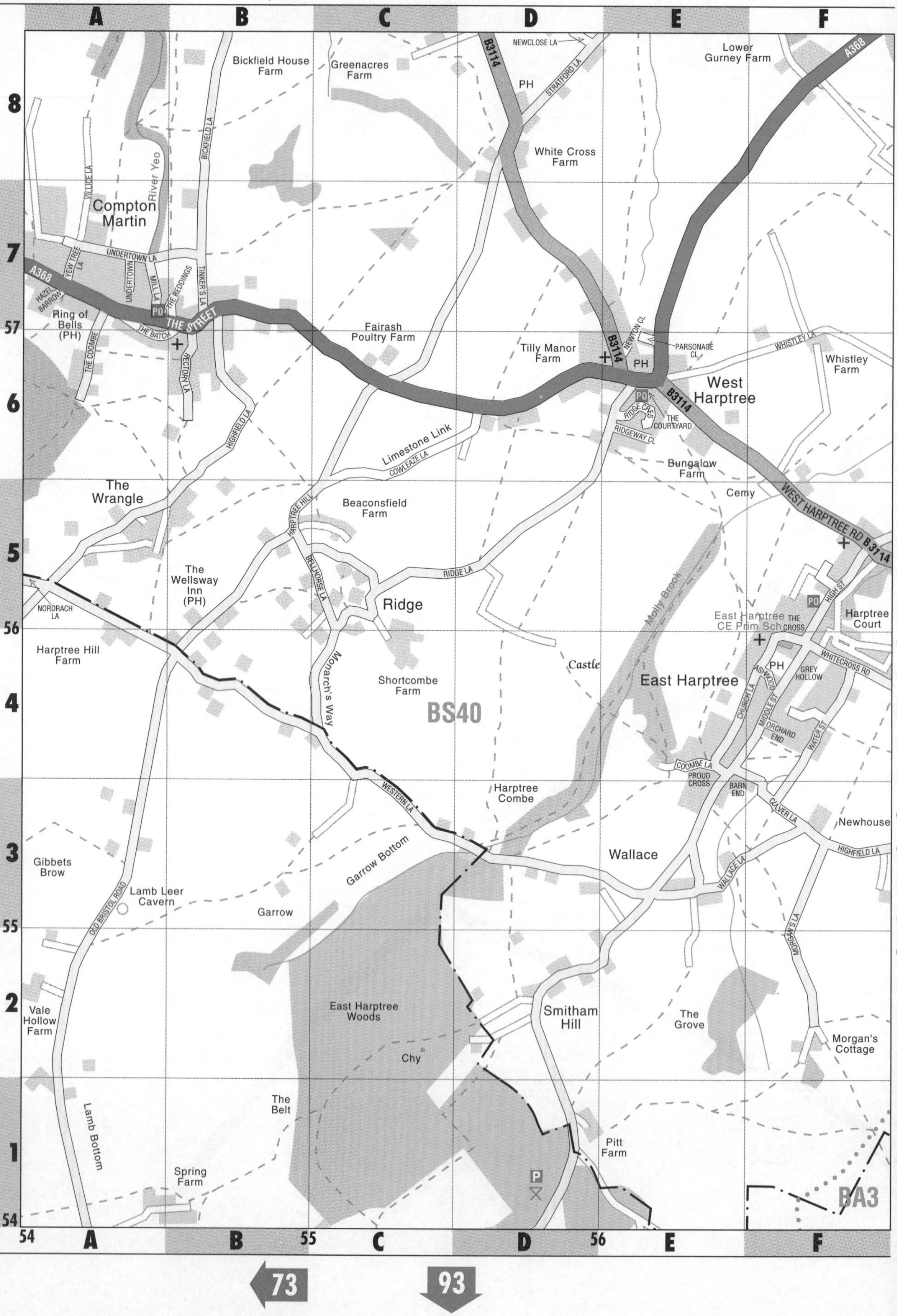

A B C D E F
8 7 57 6 5 56 4 3 55 2 1 54
Bickfield House Farm
Greenacres Farm
NEWCLOSE LA
B3114
PH
STRATFORD LA
Lower Gurney Farm
A368
BICKFIELD LA
River Yeo
VILLICE LA
Compton Martin
White Cross Farm
UNDERTOWN LA
YEW TREE LA
A368
HAZEL BARROW
UNDERTOWN
MILL LA
THE REDDINGS
TINKER'S LA
PO
Ring of Bells (PH)
THE BATCH
THE STREET
THE COOMBE
RECTORY LA
Fairash Poultry Farm
Tilly Manor Farm
B3114
NEWTON CL
PARSONAGE CL
PH
WHISTLEY LA
Whistley Farm
West Harptree
PO
RIDGE CRES
THE COURTYARD
RIDGEWAY CL
B3114
HIGHFIELD LA
Limestone Link
COWLEAZE LA
Bungalow Farm
The Wrangle
HARPTREE HILL
Beaconsfield Farm
Cemy
WEST HARPTREE RD
B3114
The Wellsway Inn (PH)
BELLHORSE LA
RIDGE LA
Molly Brook
NORDRACH LA
Ridge
PO
HIGH ST
East Harptree CE Prim Sch
THE CROSS
Harptree Court
Harptree Hill Farm
Monarch's Way
Castle
PH
ASHWOOD
GREY HOLLOW
WHITECROSS RD
Shortcombe Farm
East Harptree
CHURCH LA
MIDDLE ST
BS40
ORCHARD END
WATER ST
COOMBE LA
PROUD CROSS
BARN END
Harptree Combe
WESTERN LA
CLAVER LA
Newhouse
Gibbets Brow
Garrow Bottom
Wallace
HIGHFIELD LA
Lamb Leer Cavern
OLD BRISTOL ROAD
WALLACE LA
Garrow
MORGAN'S LA
Vale Hollow Farm
East Harptree Woods
Smitham Hill
The Grove
Morgan's Cottage
Chy
Lamb Bottom
The Belt
Pitt Farm
Spring Farm
P
BA3
54 A B 55 C D 56 E F

73
93

57
76

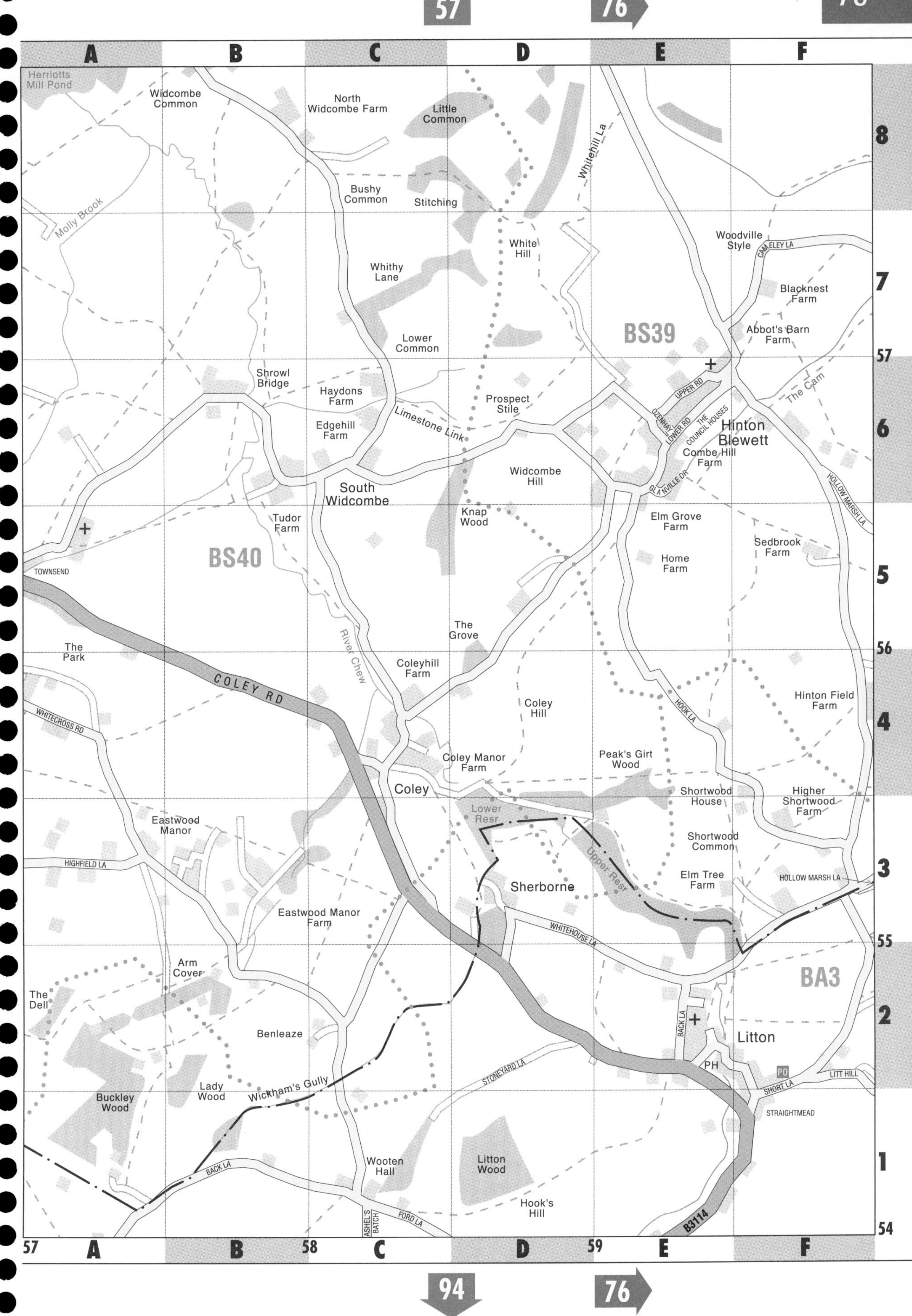
A
B
C
D
E
F
Herriotts
Mill Pond
Widcombe
Common
North
Widcombe Farm
Little
Common
Whitehill La
Molly Brook
Bushy
Common
Stitching
White
Hill
Woodville
Style
CAMELEY LA
Whithy
Lane
Blacknest
Farm
BS39
Abbot's Barn
Farm
Lower
Common
Shrowl
Bridge
Haydons
Farm
Prospect
Stile
UPPER RD
OZENHAY
LOWER RD
THE COUNCIL HOUSES
The Cam
Edgehill
Farm
Limestone Link
Hinton
Blewett
Combe Hill
Farm
Widcombe
Hill
HOLLOW MARSH LA
South
Widcombe
GLANVILLE DR
Tudor
Farm
Knap
Wood
Elm Grove
Farm
Sedbrook
Farm
BS40
Home
Farm
TOWNSEND
The
Grove
River Chew
The
Park
Coleyhill
Farm
COLEY RD
Coley
Hill
Hinton Field
Farm
WHITECROSS RD
HOOK LA
Coley Manor
Farm
Peak's Girt
Wood
Coley
Shortwood
House
Higher
Shortwood
Farm
Lower
Resr
Eastwood
Manor
Shortwood
Common
Upper Resr
HIGHFIELD LA
Elm Tree
Farm
HOLLOW MARSH LA
Sherborne
Eastwood Manor
Farm
WHITEHOUSE LA
Arm
Cover
BA3
The
Dell
BACK LA
Litton
Benleaze
PH
PO
STONEYARD LA
LITT HILL
Lady
Wood
SHORT LA
Buckley
Wood
Wickham's Gully
STRAIGHTMEAD
Wooten
Hall
Litton
Wood
BACK LA
Hook's
Hill
ASHEL'S BATCH
FORD LA
B3114
8
7
57
6
5
56
4
3
55
2
1
54
57
58
59

94
76

75
58

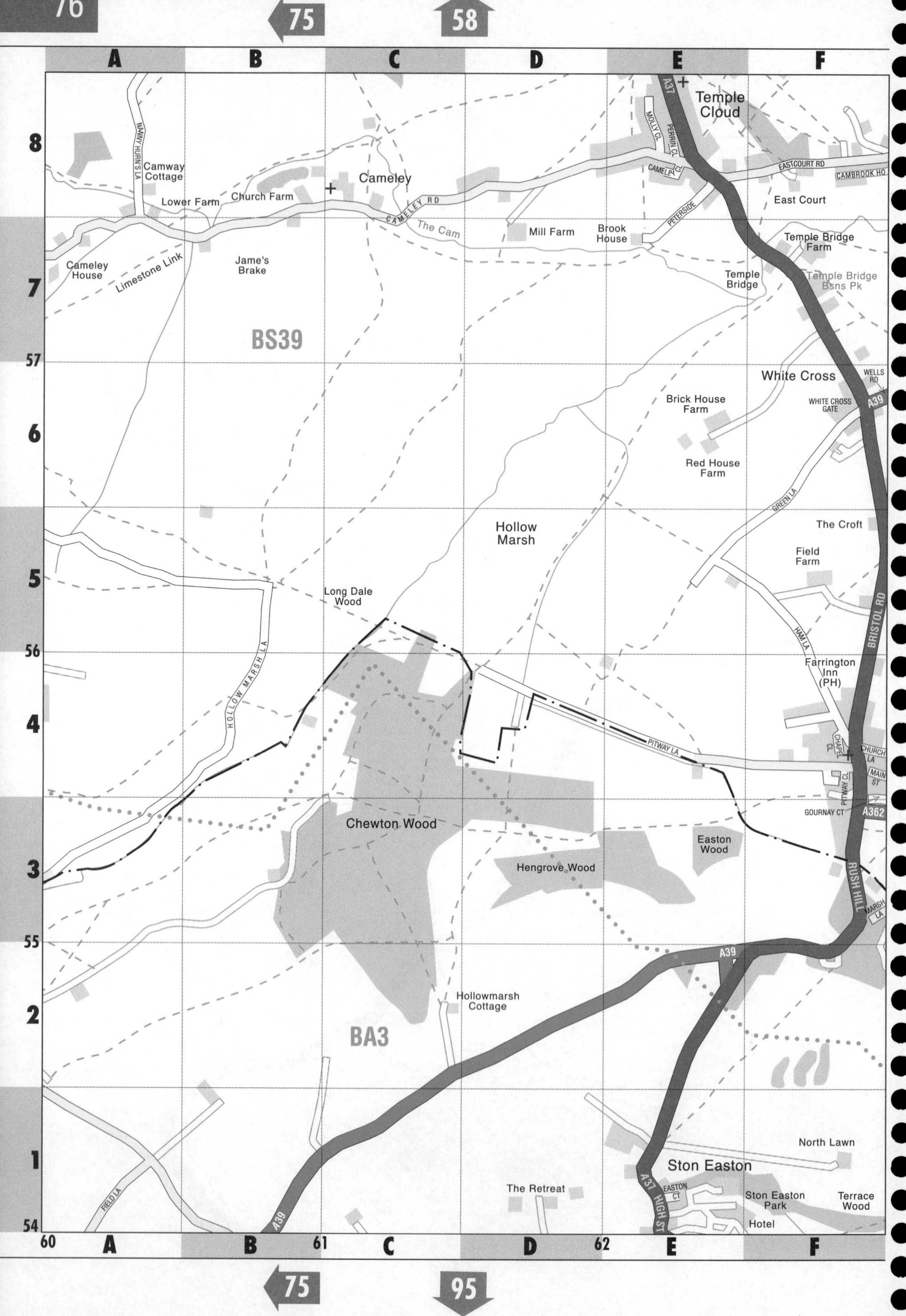
A
B
C
D
E
F
Temple Cloud
A37
MOLLY CL
PERRIN CL
EASTCOURT RD
CAMBROOK HO
CAMELEY CL
Camway Cottage
NANNY HURN'S LA
Cameley
Lower Farm
Church Farm
CAMELEY RD
The Cam
East Court
Mill Farm
Brook House
PETERSIDE
Temple Bridge Farm
Cameley House
James's Brake
Limestone Link
Temple Bridge
Temple Bridge Bsns Pk
BS39
White Cross
WELLS RD
WHITE CROSS GATE
A39
Brick House Farm
Red House Farm
GREEN LA
The Croft
Hollow Marsh
Field Farm
Long Dale Wood
BRISTOL RD
HAM LA
Farrington Inn (PH)
HOLLOW MARSH LA
PITWAY LA
CHAPEL CL
CHURCH LA
MAIN ST
PITWAY CL
GOURNAY CT
A362
Chewton Wood
Easton Wood
Hengrove Wood
RUSH HILL
MARSH LA
A39
Hollowmarsh Cottage
BA3
North Lawn
Ston Easton
The Retreat
A37
EASTON CT
HIGH ST
Ston Easton Park
Hotel
Terrace Wood
FIELD LA
A39
8
7
57
6
5
56
4
3
55
2
1
54
60
61
62

75
95

59
78

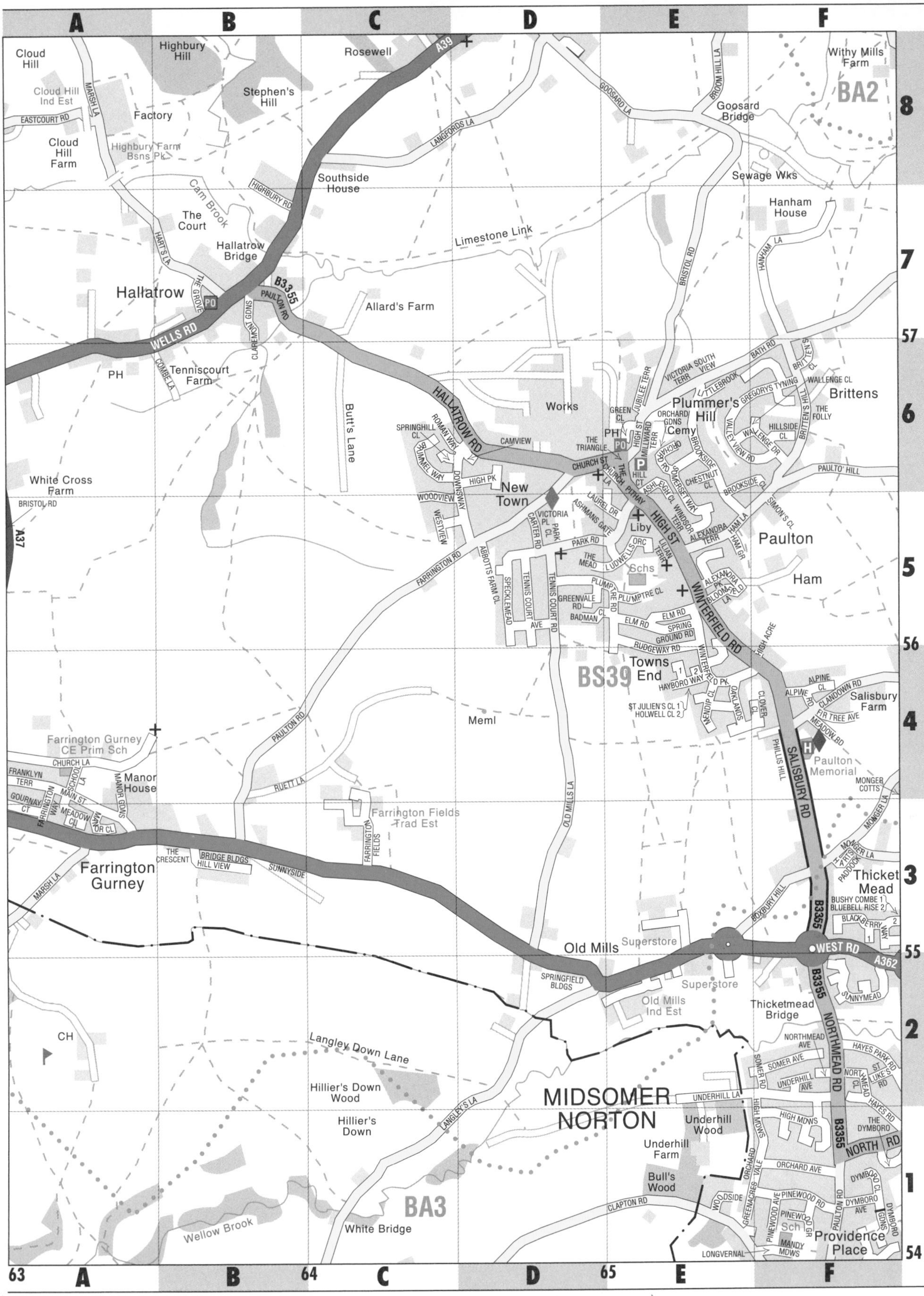

A B C D E F
8 7 6 5 4 3 2 1
57 56 55 54
63 64 65
Cloud Hill
Cloud Hill Ind Est
EASTCOURT RD
Cloud Hill Farm
MARSH LA
Highbury Hill
Factory
Highbury Farm Bsns Pk
Stephen's Hill
Rosewell
A39
LANGFORDS LA
Southside House
HIGHBURY RD
Cam Brook
The Court
Hallatrow Bridge
HARTS LA
THE GROVE
PO
Hallatrow
B3355
PAULTON RD
CLAREMONT GDNS
WELLS RD
COMBE LA
Tenniscourt Farm
PH
Allard's Farm
Limestone Link
Butt's Lane
GOOSARD LA
BROOM HILL LA
Goosard Bridge
Withy Mills Farm
BA2
Sewage Wks
Hanham House
HANHAM LA
BRISTOL RD
BATH RD
VICTORIA SOUTH TERR
VIEW
JUBILEE TERR
LITTLEBROOK
Plummer's Hill
GREGORYS TYNING
WALLENGE CL
Brittens
THE FOLLY
BRITTEN'S HILL
HILLSIDE CL
WALLENGE DR
VALLEY VIEW RD
Works
GREEN CL
PH
PO
ORCHARD GDNS
Cemy
MILLWARD TERR
HIGH ST
THE TRIANGLE
P
HILL CT
BROOKSIDE
CHESTNUT CL
BROOKSIDE CL
PAULTO' HILL
SIMON'S CL
HALLATROW RD
SPRINGHILL CL
ROMAN WAY
BRUMMEL WAY
CAMVIEW
CHURCH ST
THE PITHAY
CHURCH LA
HIGH PK
DOWNSWAY
New Town
WOODVIEW
WESTVIEW
White Cross Farm
BRISTOL RD
A37
VICTORIA PL CL
PARK CL
CARTER RD
ASHMANS GATE
LAUREL DR
ASHLEIGH CL
SOMERSET WAY
WINDSOR TERR
Liby
HIGH ST
ALEXANDRA TERR
HAM LA
HAM GR
Paulton
Ham
FARRINGTON RD
ABBOTTS FARM CL
PARK RD
THE MEAD
LUDWELLS ORC
Schs
LILLIAN TERR
WINTERFIELD RD
ALEXANDRA PK
BLOOMFIELD LA
SPECKLEMEAD
TENNIS COURT AVE
TENNIS COURT RD
GREENVALE RD
PLUMPTRE RD
PLUMPTRE CL
BADMAN CL
ELM RD
SPRING GROUND RD
BUDGEWAY RD
HIGH ACRE
Towns End
BS39
HAYBORO WAY
WINTERFIELD PK
MENDIP CL
OAKLANDS
CLOVER CL
ST JULIEN'S CL 1
HOLWELL CL 2
ALPINE CL
ALPINE RD
CLANDOWN RD
Salisbury Farm
FIR TREE AVE
MEADOW RD
H
Paulton Memorial
PHILLIS HILL
SALISBURY RD
MONGER COTTS
MONGER LA
Meml
PAULTON RD
RUETT LA
Farrington Gurney CE Prim Sch
CHURCH LA
FRANKLYN TERR
SCHOOL LA
GOURNAY CT
FARRINGTON WAY
MAIN ST
MEADOW CL
MANOR CL
Manor House
MANOR GDNS
Farrington Fields Trad Est
FARRINGTON FIELDS
OLD MILLS LA
THE CRESCENT
BRIDGE BLDGS
HILL VIEW
SUNNYSIDE
Farrington Gurney
MARSH LA
MONGER LA
FRYS PADDOCK
Thicket Mead
BUSHY COMBE 1
BLUEBELL RISE 2
BLACKBERRY WAY
ROXBURY HILL
B3355
Superstore
Old Mills
WEST RD
A362
SPRINGFIELD BLDGS
Superstore
Old Mills Ind Est
SUNNYMEAD
B3355
Thicketmead Bridge
NORTHMEAD AVE
NORTHMEAD RD
HAYES PARK RD
SOMER AVE
SOMER RD
UNDERHILL AVE
NORTHMEAD CL
ST LUKE'S RD
HAYES RD
CH
Langley Down Lane
Hillier's Down Wood
Hillier's Down
LANGLEY'S LA
MIDSOMER NORTON
UNDERHILL LA
Underhill Wood
HIGH MDWS
HIGH MDWS
THE DYMBORO
B3355
NORTH RD
Underhill Farm
ORCHARD
ORCHARD AVE
DYMBORO CL
Bull's Wood
CLAPTON RD
WOODSIDE
GREENACRES
VALE
PINEWOOD AVE
PINEWOOD RD
PINEWOOD GR
PAULTON RD
DYMBORO AVE
DYMBORO GDNS
Sch
MANDY MDWS
Providence Place
LONGVERNAL
BA3
Wellow Brook
White Bridge

96
78

77
60

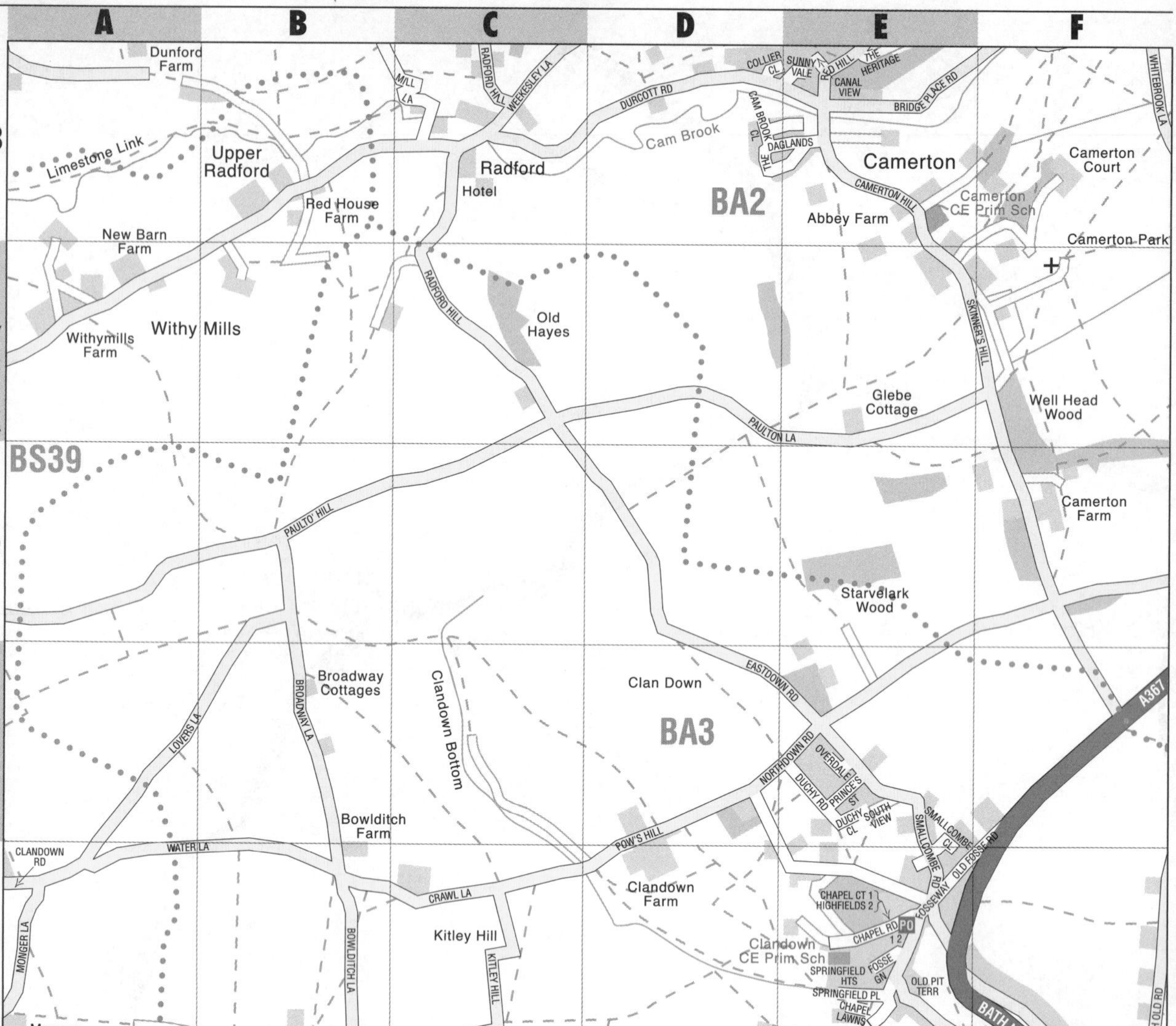

A B C D E F

8 7 57 6 5 56 4 3 55 2 1 54

Dunford Farm
Upper Radford
Limestone Link
Red House Farm
Radford
Hotel
Cam Brook
Camerton
BA2
Abbey Farm
Camerton CE Prim Sch
Camerton Court
Camerton Park
New Barn Farm
Withymills Farm
Withy Mills
Old Hayes
Glebe Cottage
Well Head Wood
BS39
Camerton Farm
Starvelark Wood
Broadway Cottages
Clandown Bottom
Clan Down
BA3
Bowlditch Farm
Clandown Farm
Kitley Hill
Clandown CE Prim Sch
Monger
Clandown
Welton Hill
MIDSOMER NORTON
Greenhill
Belle Vue
Manor Farm
Welton Hollow
Works
Welton
Hayes Park
Welton Prim Sch
Wheeler's Hill
Midsomer Ent Pk
Midsomer Norton Prim Sch
Sp Ctr
River Somer
Norton Radstock Coll
RADSTOCK
West Hill Gardens
Waterside
Mus
Liby
Sch
Cemy
Schs
TH

66 67 68

A B C D E F

77
97

61 80

A B C D E F

Lower Peasedown
Ashgrove
White Ox Mead La
White Ox Mead Knoll
A367
Knightstone Cl
Camvale
Church Rd
Hillside
Firgrove La
Keel's Hill
Ashgrove Ct
Gordon Rd
Eckweek La
North Mews
Under Knoll
Eckweek Rd
Peasedown St John
Ford Rd
Axford Way
Filer Cl
Eckweek Gdns
Cemy
Old Forge Way
Chapel Field
Glenview Ho
Bloomfield Terr
New Bldgs
Church Rd
Vicarage Gdns
Hillcrest
Idwal Cl
Highfield Rd
Greenlands Rd
Lincott View
Fosseway Cl
Huddox Hill
Naishes Ave
Westbury View
Whitebrook La
Bath Rd
PO
Bloomfield Cotts
Belle Vue Cl
French Cl
Orchard Way
Morgan Way
Falkland View
Camerton Park
Whitebrook Farm
Stowborough Cotts
Peasedown St John Prim Sch
Sunnyside View
Fairfield Terr
Frenchfield Rd
Worcester Way
Bourne Farm
Double Hill Farm
Camerton Wood
PH
Red Post
St John's Cl
Albert Ave
Frederick Ave
Braysdown La
Springfield
Sunset Cl
Tyning Rd
Laxton Way
Blenheim Cl
Russet Way
Pippin Cl
Bramley
Roman Way
Wellow Rd
Double Hill
Red Post Ct
Home Farm Cl
Wellow Mead
Tyning Rd
Wellow Tyning
Foxcote Ave
Wellow La
Braysdown Cl
Wansdyke Workshops

Hang Hill
BA2
Braysdown La
Shoscombe Farm
Shoscombe
Applecroft
White Hill
Wood Lea
Rag Hill
Montague Rd
Barn Hill
Gullen
Woodborough House
PH
Bath Old Rd
Green St
Shoscombe CE Prim Sch
St Julian's Rd
Hamilton Terr
Single Hill
Shoscombe Vale
Lower Wood
Sewage Works
Railway Terr
Paglinch Farm
Round Hill
Woodborough Farm
Foxcote Mill (dis)
Ludlow's Farm
Wellow Brook
Foxcote
Woodborough Hill Cotts
Woodborough La
Foxcote Farm
Tyning
Springfield Cres
Colliers Rise
Walnut Bldgs
James Cl
1 Shaftesbury Terr
2 Gordon Bldgs
Lower Whitelands
Whitelands Hill
Northfield
Woodborough Rd
Stoneable Rd
Tyning Hill
Sewage Works
Morley Terr
Plovers Rise
Lower Writhlington
Bath Old Rd
Abbey View
Stanley Terr
Daneacre Rd
Mill
The Retreat
Waldegrave Terr
Chichester Pl
Larchwood Ct
Mill Road Ind Est
Church Hill
Waterloo Rd
Pine Ct
Pines Way
Mill Rd
Holly Bank
P
Riverside Cotts
1 Hanover Ct
2 Writhlington Ct
3 Manor Park Cl
Gallanthill Farm
Magdalene Rd
St Marys Rise
Combe Farm House
Frome Old Rd
Mount Pleasant
Maple Rise
Copse Rd
Longley Wood
Carlingford Terr
Carlingford Terrace Rd
Vale View Terr
Manor Pk
Manor Farm
Southfield
Queen's Rd
Seward Terr
Manor Rd
BA3
Gallanthill Barn
St Nicholas' CE Prim Sch
Southfield
Hawthorn Rd
Lillington Rd
Sycamore Rd
North View
Frome Rd
Writhlington
Green Parlour
Northfield
Trng Ctr
PO
St Mary's CE Prim Sch
Meadow View
(dis)
Highfield Cl
Lillington Cl
Old Rd
Green Parlour Farm
Kilmersdon Rd
Writhlington Sch
Fox Hills
Mells La
Knobsbury La
Green Parlor Rd
A362
Castlemead Wood
Haywood Wood

8 7 57 6 5 56 4 3 55 2 1 54

69 A B 70 C D 71 E F

98 80

79
62

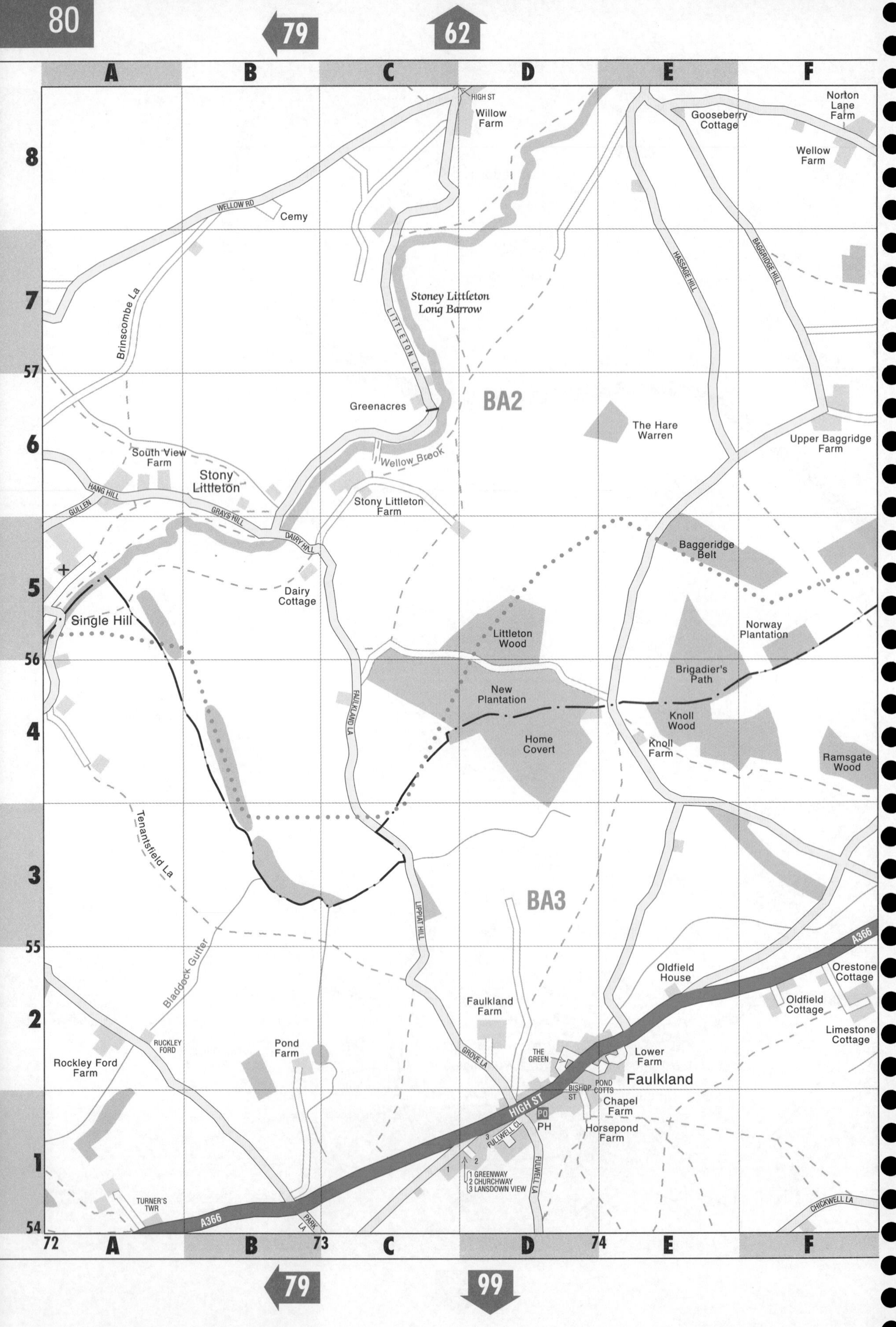
A
B
C
D
E
F
8
7
57
6
5
56
4
3
55
2
1
54
72
73
74
HIGH ST
Willow Farm
Norton Lane Farm
Gooseberry Cottage
Wellow Farm
WELLOW RD
Cemy
HASSAGE HILL
BAGGRIDGE HILL
Brinscombe La
Stoney Littleton Long Barrow
LITTLETON LA
Greenacres
BA2
The Hare Warren
Upper Baggridge Farm
South View Farm
Stony Littleton
Wellow Brook
HANG HILL
GULLEN
GRAYS HILL
DAIRY HILL
Stony Littleton Farm
Baggeridge Belt
Dairy Cottage
Single Hill
Littleton Wood
Norway Plantation
Brigadier's Path
New Plantation
FAULKLAND LA
Knoll Wood
Home Covert
Knoll Farm
Ramsgate Wood
Tenantsfield La
LIPPIAT HILL
BA3
A366
Bladdock Gutter
Oldfield House
Orestone Cottage
Oldfield Cottage
Faulkland Farm
Limestone Cottage
RUCKLEY FORD
Rockley Ford Farm
Pond Farm
GROVE LA
THE GREEN
Lower Farm
Faulkland
BISHOP ST
POND COTTS
Chapel Farm
HIGH ST
PO
PH
Horsepond Farm
FULLWELL CL
1 GREENWAY
2 CHURCHWAY
3 LANSDOWN VIEW
FULWELL LA
TURNER'S TWR
PARK LA
CHICKWELL LA

79
99

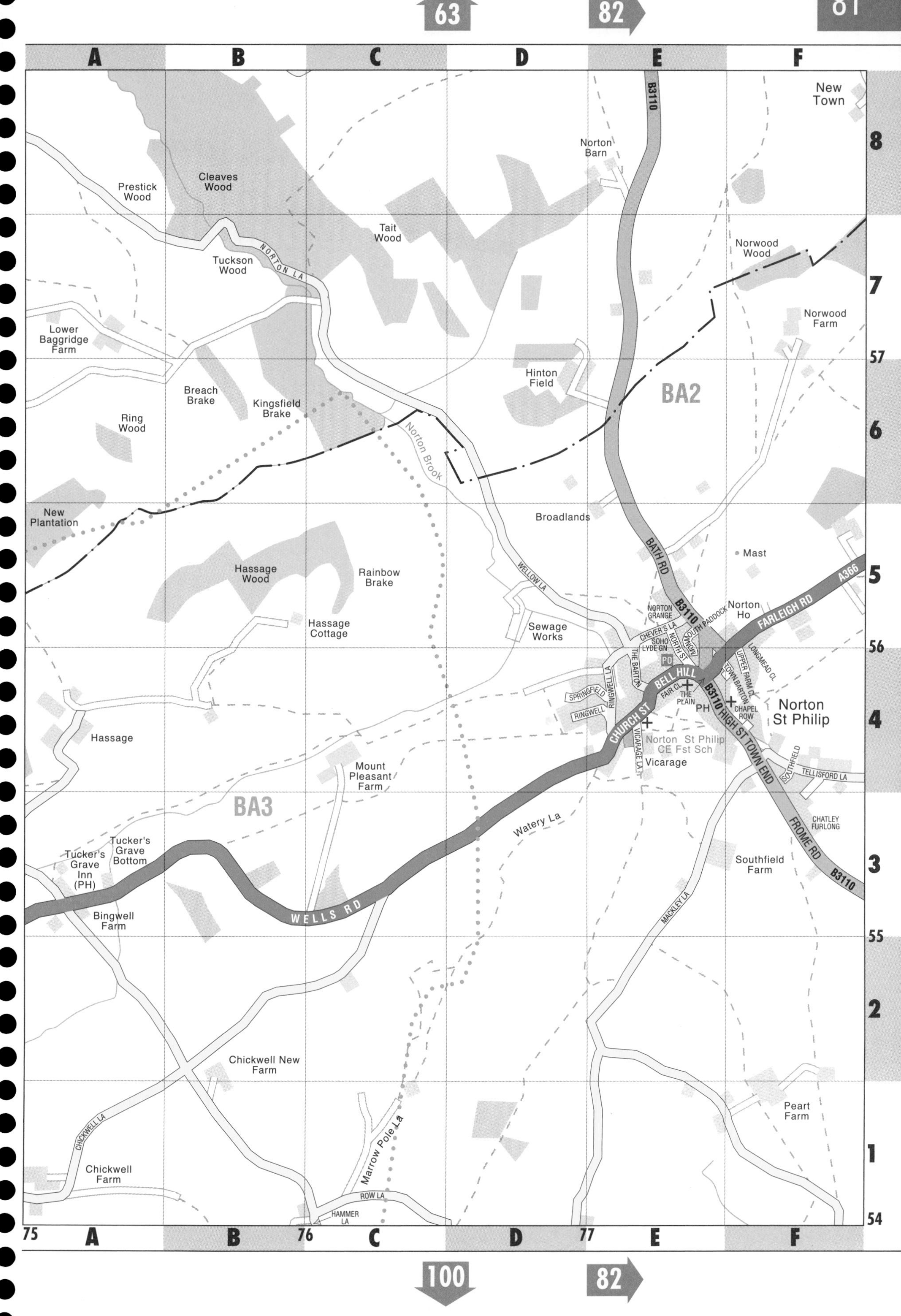
63
82
A
B
C
D
E
F
New Town
Norton Barn
B3110
Prestick Wood
Cleaves Wood
Tait Wood
Tuckson Wood
NORTON LA
Norwood Wood
Norwood Farm
Lower Baggridge Farm
Hinton Field
BA2
Breach Brake
Kingsfield Brake
Ring Wood
Norton Brook
New Plantation
Broadlands
BATH RD
Mast
Hassage Wood
Rainbow Brake
WELLOW LA
FARLEIGH RD
A366
Norton Ho
Hassage Cottage
Sewage Works
NORTON GRANGE
CHEVER'S LA
SOHO
LYDE GN
NORTH ST
SOUTH PADDOCK
LONGMEAD CL
UPPER FARM CL
TOWN BARTON
THE BARTON
RINGWELL LA
PO
BELL HILL
FAIR CL
THE PLAIN
PH
CHAPEL ROW
SPRINGFIELD
RINGWELL
Norton St Philip
Hassage
CHURCH ST
HIGH ST
TOWN END
Norton St Philip CE Fst Sch
VICARAGE LA
Vicarage
SOUTHFIELD
TELLISFORD LA
Mount Pleasant Farm
BA3
CHATLEY FURLONG
FROME RD
Watery La
Tucker's Grave Bottom
Tucker's Grave Inn (PH)
Southfield Farm
WELLS RD
Bingwell Farm
MACKLEY LA
Chickwell New Farm
Peart Farm
CHICKWELL LA
Marrow Pole La
Chickwell Farm
ROW LA
HAMMER LA
8
7
57
6
5
56
4
3
55
2
1
54
75
76
77
100
82

A B C D E F

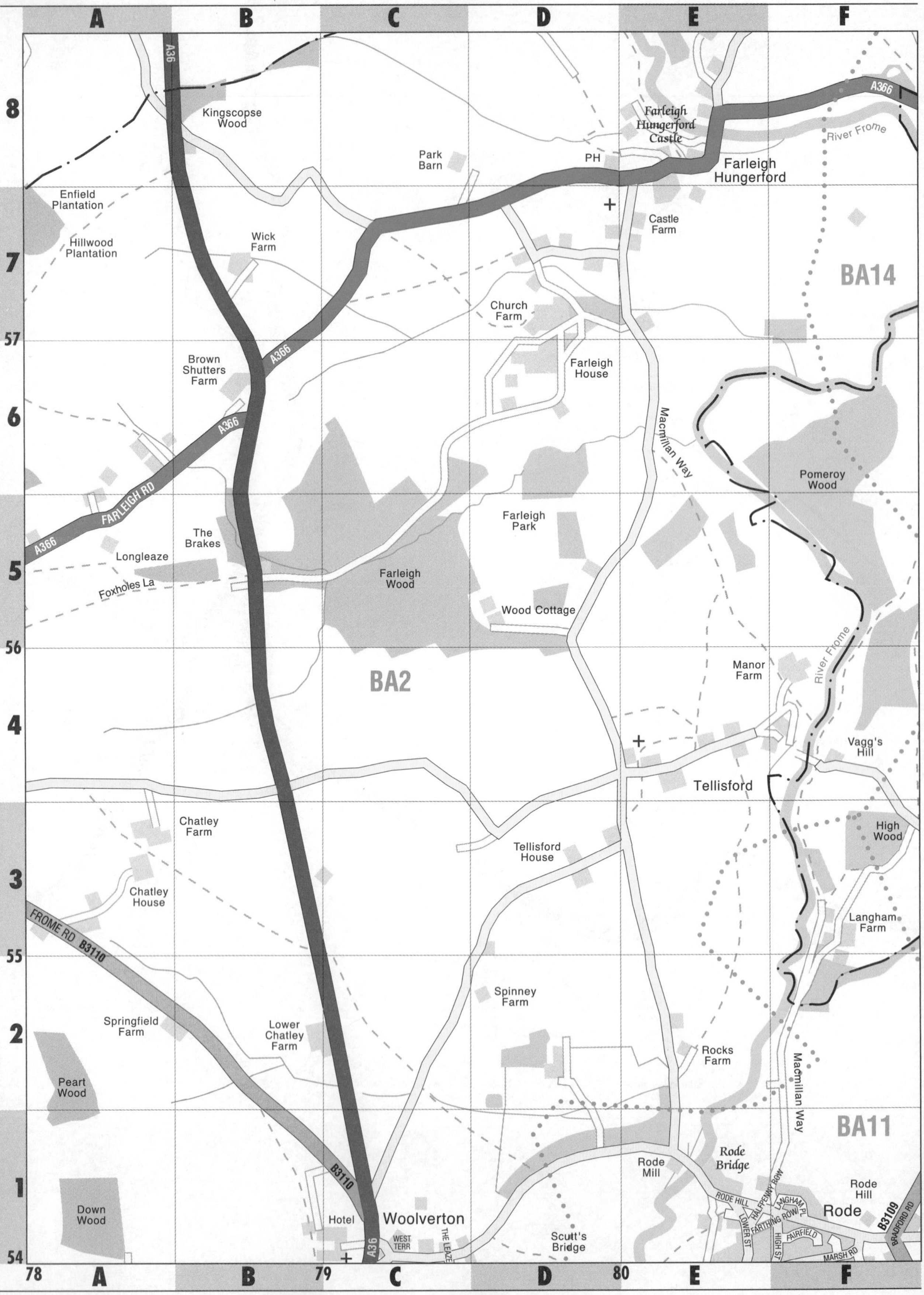

8
Kingscopse Wood
Farleigh Hungerford Castle
Park Barn
PH
Farleigh Hungerford
River Frome
A366
A36
Enfield Plantation
Castle Farm
Hillwood Plantation
Wick Farm
7
BA14
Church Farm
57
Brown Shutters Farm
Farleigh House
6
Macmillan Way
Pomeroy Wood
FARLEIGH RD
The Brakes
Farleigh Park
Longleaze
5
Foxholes La
Farleigh Wood
Wood Cottage
56
BA2
Manor Farm
River Frome
4
Vagg's Hill
Tellisford
Chatley Farm
High Wood
Tellisford House
3
Chatley House
Langham Farm
FROME RD B3110
55
Spinney Farm
Springfield Farm
Lower Chatley Farm
2
Rocks Farm
Peart Wood
Macmillan Way
BA11
Rode Bridge
Rode Mill
Rode Hill
1
B3110
Down Wood
Hotel
Woolverton
Rode
RODE HILL
HALFPENNY ROW
LANGHAM PL
FARTHING ROW
LOWER ST
HIGH ST
FAIRFIELD
MARSH RD
B3109
BRADFORD RD
WEST TERR
THE LEAZE
Scutt's Bridge
54

78 A B 79 C D 80 E F

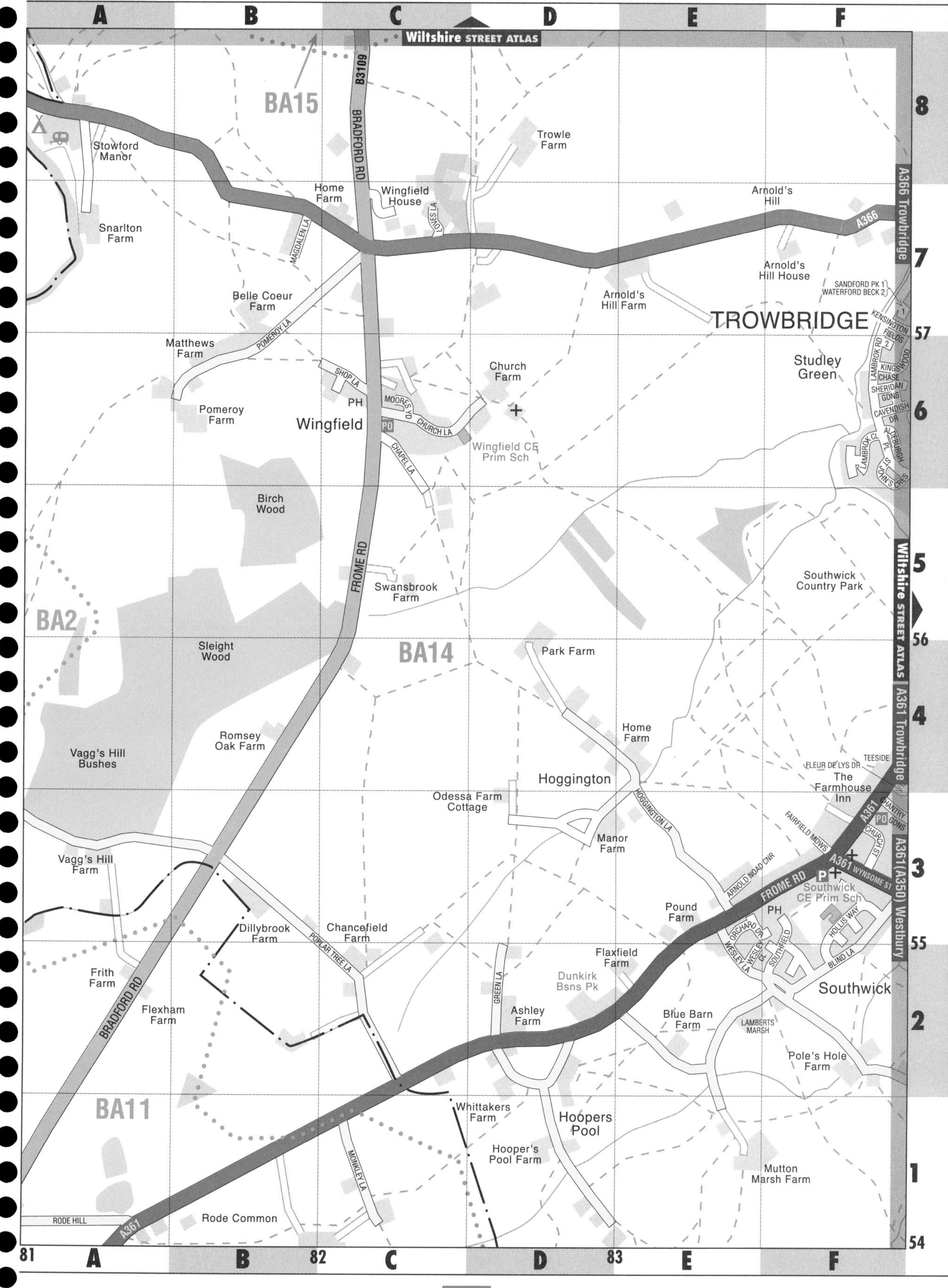
Wiltshire STREET ATLAS
BA15
B3109
BRADFORD RD
Stowford Manor
Trowle Farm
Home Farm
Wingfield House
Snarlton Farm
MAGDALEN LA
LOVES LA
Arnold's Hill
A366
A366 Trowbridge
Arnold's Hill House
Belle Coeur Farm
Arnold's Hill Farm
SANDFORD PK 1
WATERFORD BECK 2
TROWBRIDGE
KENSINGTON FIELDS
Matthews Farm
POMEROY LA
SHOP LA
Church Farm
Studley Green
LAMBROK RD
KINGS CHASE
KINGSWOOD
SHERIDAN GDNS
PH
MOORES YD
Pomeroy Farm
Wingfield
CHURCH LA
PO
CAVENDISH DR
ALDEBURGH PL
Wingfield CE Prim Sch
CHAPEL LA
LAMBROK CL
JOHN'S CRES
Birch Wood
FROME RD
Swansbrook Farm
Southwick Country Park
BA2
Sleight Wood
BA14
Park Farm
Home Farm
Romsey Oak Farm
Vagg's Hill Bushes
Hoggington
TEESIDE
FLEUR DE LYS DR
The Farmhouse Inn
Odessa Farm Cottage
HOGGINGTON LA
CHANTRY GDNS
A361
A361 Trowbridge
Manor Farm
FAIRFIELD MDWS
CHURCH ST
Vagg's Hill Farm
ARNOLD NOAD CNR
A361
WYNSOME ST
FROME RD
P
Southwick CE Prim Sch
A361(A350) Westbury
Pound Farm
PH
Dillybrook Farm
Chancefield Farm
POPLAR TREE LA
ORCHARD DR
WESLEY CL
WESLEY LA
SOUTHFIELD
HOLLIS WAY
BLIND LA
Flaxfield Farm
Frith Farm
Dunkirk Bsns Pk
Southwick
BRADFORD RD
Flexham Farm
GREEN LA
Ashley Farm
Blue Barn Farm
LAMBERTS MARSH
Pole's Hole Farm
Whittakers Farm
BA11
Hoopers Pool
Hooper's Pool Farm
MONKLEY LA
Mutton Marsh Farm
RODE HILL
A361
Rode Common
Wiltshire STREET ATLAS
A B C D E F
8 7 57 6 5 56 4 3 55 2 1 54
81 82 83

65

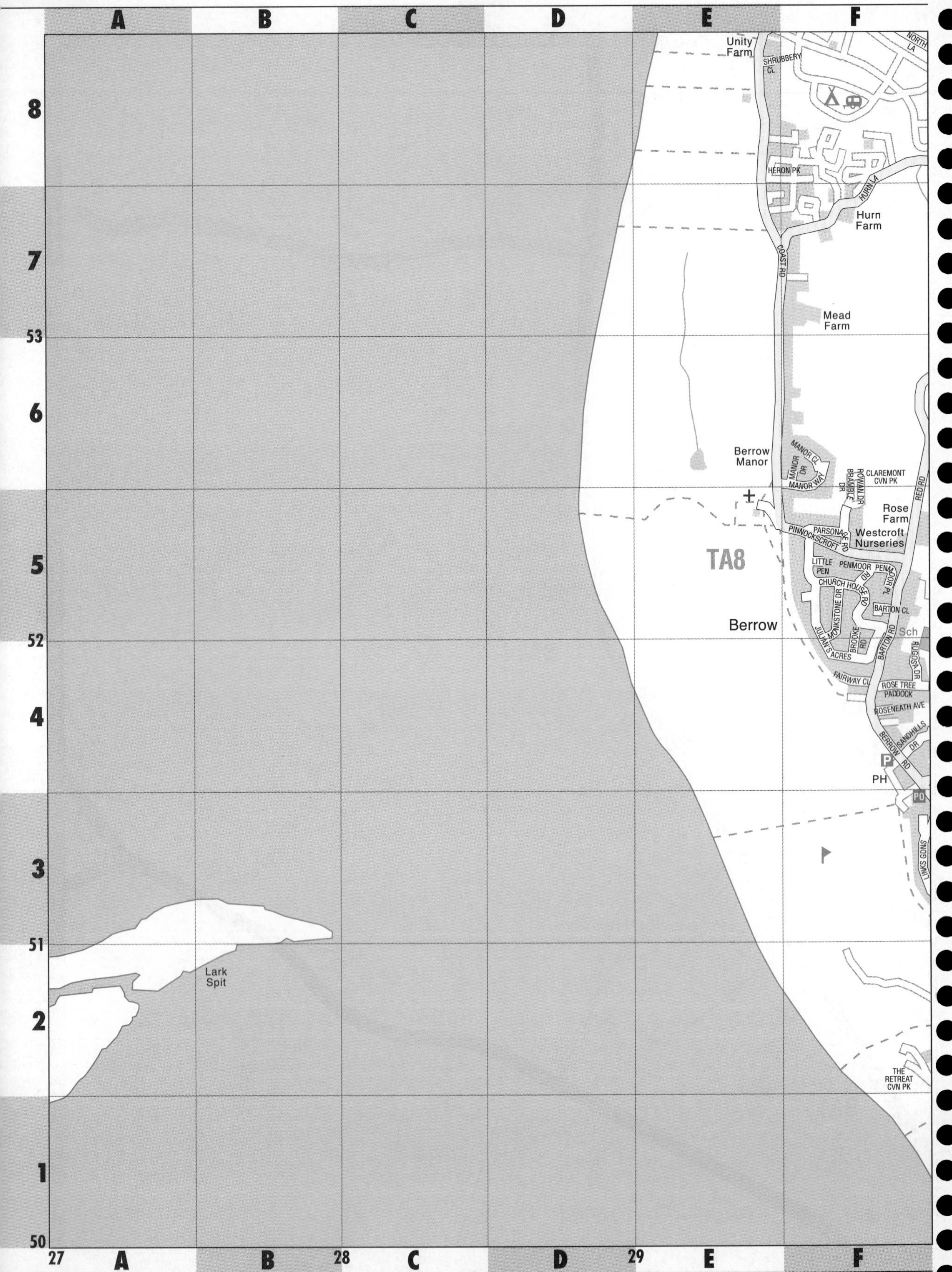
A
B
C
D
E
F
8
7
53
6
5
52
4
3
51
2
1
50
27
28
29
Unity Farm
SHRUBBERY CL
NORTH LA
HERON PK
HURN LA
Hurn Farm
COAST RD
Mead Farm
Berrow Manor
MANOR CL
MANOR DR
MANOR WAY
BRAMBLE DR
ROWAN DR
CLAREMONT CVN PK
RED RD
Rose Farm
PARSONAGE RD
PINNOCKSCROFT
Westcroft Nurseries
TA8
LITTLE PEN
PENMOOR
PENMOOR PL
CHURCH HOUSE RD
MONKSTONE DR
BARTON CL
Berrow
Sch
JULIAN'S ACRES
BROOKE RD
BARTON RD
RUGOSA DR
FAIRWAY CL
ROSE TREE PADDOCK
ROSENEATH AVE
SANDHILLS DR
BERROW RD
PH
PO
LINKS GDNS
Lark Spit
THE RETREAT CVN PK

103

66
86

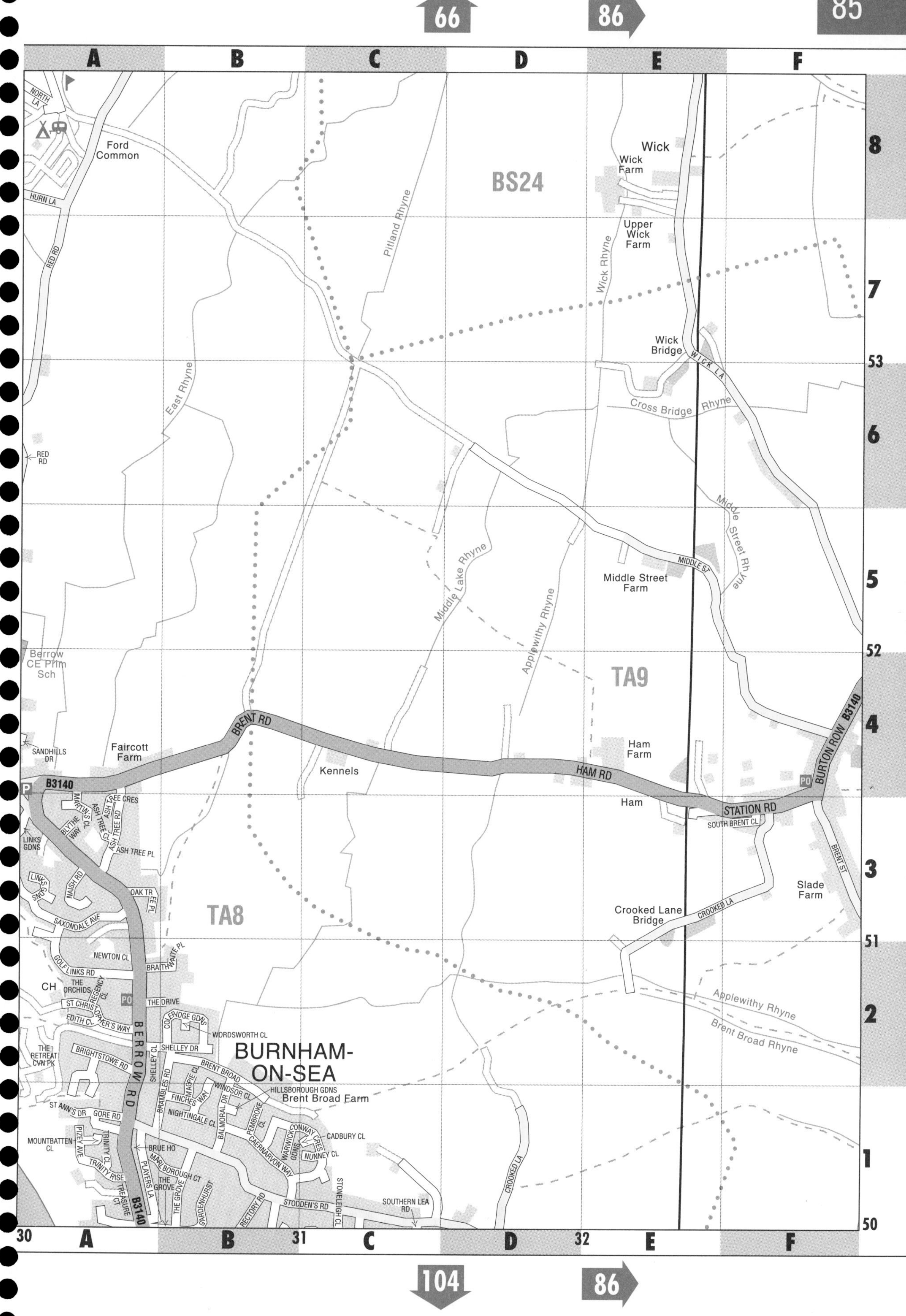
A
B
C
D
E
F
8
7
53
6
5
52
4
3
51
2
1
50
30
31
32
NORTH LA
Ford Common
HURN LA
RED RD
Wick
Wick Farm
BS24
Upper Wick Farm
Pitland Rhyne
Wick Rhyne
Wick Bridge
WICK LA
East Rhyne
Cross Bridge Rhyne
RED RD
Middle Street Rhyne
MIDDLE ST
Middle Street Farm
Middle Lake Rhyne
Applewithy Rhyne
Berrow CE Prim Sch
TA9
BRENT RD
BURTON ROW B3140
SANDHILLS DR
Faircott Farm
Kennels
Ham Farm
HAM RD
Ham
STATION RD
SOUTH BRENT CL
B3140
MARTIN'S CL
ASH TREE CRES
BLYTHE WAY
ASH TREE CL
ASH TREE RD
ASH TREE PL
LINKS GDNS
LINKS GDNS
NASH RD
OAK TREE PL
BRENT ST
Slade Farm
TA8
SAXONDALE AVE
Crooked Lane Bridge
CROOKED LA
NEWTON CL
BRAITHWAITE PL
GOLF LINKS RD
CH
THE ORCHIDS
REGENCY CL
PO
THE DRIVE
ST CHRISTOPHER'S WAY
EDITH CL
COLERIDGE GDNS
Applewithy Rhyne
Brent Broad Rhyne
WORDSWORTH CL
THE RETREAT CVN PK
BRIGHTSTOWE RD
BERROW RD
SHELLEY CL
SHELLEY DR
BURNHAM-ON-SEA
BRENT BROAD
MAGPIE CL
BRAMBLES RD
WINDSOR CL
HILLSBOROUGH GDNS
Brent Broad Farm
FINCHES WAY
ST ANN'S DR
GORE RD
NIGHTINGALE CL
BALMORAL DR
PEMBROKE CL
CONWAY CRES
CADBURY CL
MOUNTBATTEN CL
PIZEY AVE
TRINITY CL
BRUE HO
WARWICK GDNS
CAERNARVON WAY
NUNNEY CL
TRINITY RISE
MARLBOROUGH CT
THE GROVE
THE GROVE
STONELEIGH CL
CROOKED LA
TREASURE CT
PLAYERS LA
GARDENHURST
RECTORY RD
STODDEN'S RD
SOUTHERN LEA RD
B3140

104
86

A B C D E F
8 7 53 6 5 52 4 3 51 2 1 50
33 34 35
SOUTH CL
SOUTH RD
PURVING ROW LA
A370
BRIDGWATER RD
EASTERTOWN
BS26
WHITE HOUSE LA
Blue Coat Farm
Lower Farm
Dulhorn Farm
Brent House Farm
Edingworth
EDINGWORTH RD
DELHORN LA
BS24
Manor Farm
Rookery Farm
WEST RD
Burton Row Rhyne
Groves Rhyne
Delhorn Rhyne
WESTON RD
M5
Sedgemoor Services
STROWLAND LA
STROWLANDS
Motel
Burton Row Farm
East Brent
BS26
BURTON ROW
RED HOUSE RD
JOHNSON CL
POPHAM CL
Manor Farm
Brocks Pill Rhyne
North Grove Farm
BRENT RD
ASH TREES
THE MEAD
MANOR CL
EAST DR
PROSPECT CL
Prospect Farm
A38
Shrub Farm
WICK LA
B3140
CHURCH RD
THE OLD RECTORY
WICKHAM WAY
BRENT RD
ORCHARD CL
OLD BRISTOL RD
East Brent CE Fst Sch
BRIDGWATER RD
Mill Batch Farm Ind Est
JARVIS LA
HILL LA
Elm Tree House
Chapel Farm
TA9
Manor Farm
The Red Cow (PH)
Shipton's Copse
Brent Knoll
BRISTOL RD
Stone
Brent House
Lake House
LAUREL AVE
CHURCH LA
P
THE WILLOWS
CEDAR CL
South Common Farm
CHURCH LANE CNR
Brent Knoll CE Prim Sch
MANOR RIDE
COOMBE SIDE
EAST RIDE
BRENT CL
BRENT ST
Brent Knoll
Battleborough Grange
Smithfield Farm
Battleborough
BATTLEBOROUGH LA
PO
PORTLAND PL
VOLE RD

68
88

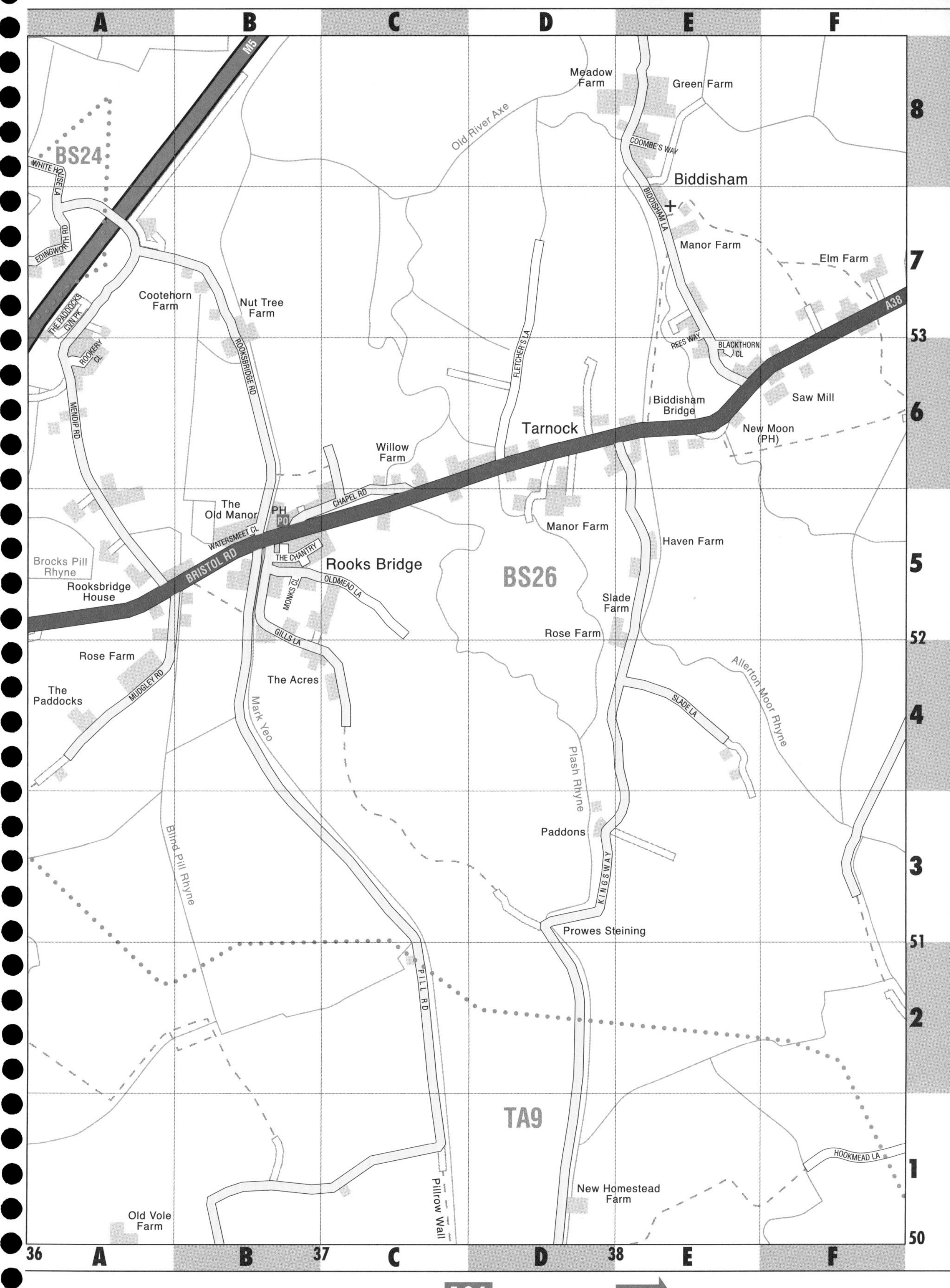
A
B
C
D
E
F
8
7
53
6
5
52
4
3
51
2
1
50
36
37
38
M5
BS24
WHITE HOUSE LA
EDINGWORTH RD
THE PADDOCKS CVN PK
ROOKERY CL
MENDIP RD
Cootehorn Farm
Nut Tree Farm
ROOKSBRIDGE RD
Old River Axe
Meadow Farm
Green Farm
COOMBE'S WAY
Biddisham
BIDDISHAM LA
Manor Farm
Elm Farm
A38
REES WAY
BLACKTHORN CL
FLETCHER'S LA
Saw Mill
Biddisham Bridge
New Moon (PH)
Tarnock
Willow Farm
CHAPEL RD
The Old Manor
PH
PO
WATERSMEET CL
BRISTOL RD
THE CHANTRY
Rooks Bridge
Manor Farm
Haven Farm
BS26
Brocks Pill Rhyne
Rooksbridge House
MONKS CL
OLDMEAD LA
Slade Farm
Rose Farm
GILLS LA
Rose Farm
The Paddocks
MUDGLEY RD
The Acres
Mark Yeo
SLADE LA
Allerton Moor Rhyne
Plash Rhyne
Paddons
Blind Pill Rhyne
KINGSWAY
Prowes Steining
PILL RD
TA9
HOOKMEAD LA
Pillrow Wall
New Homestead Farm
Old Vole Farm

106
88

87 69

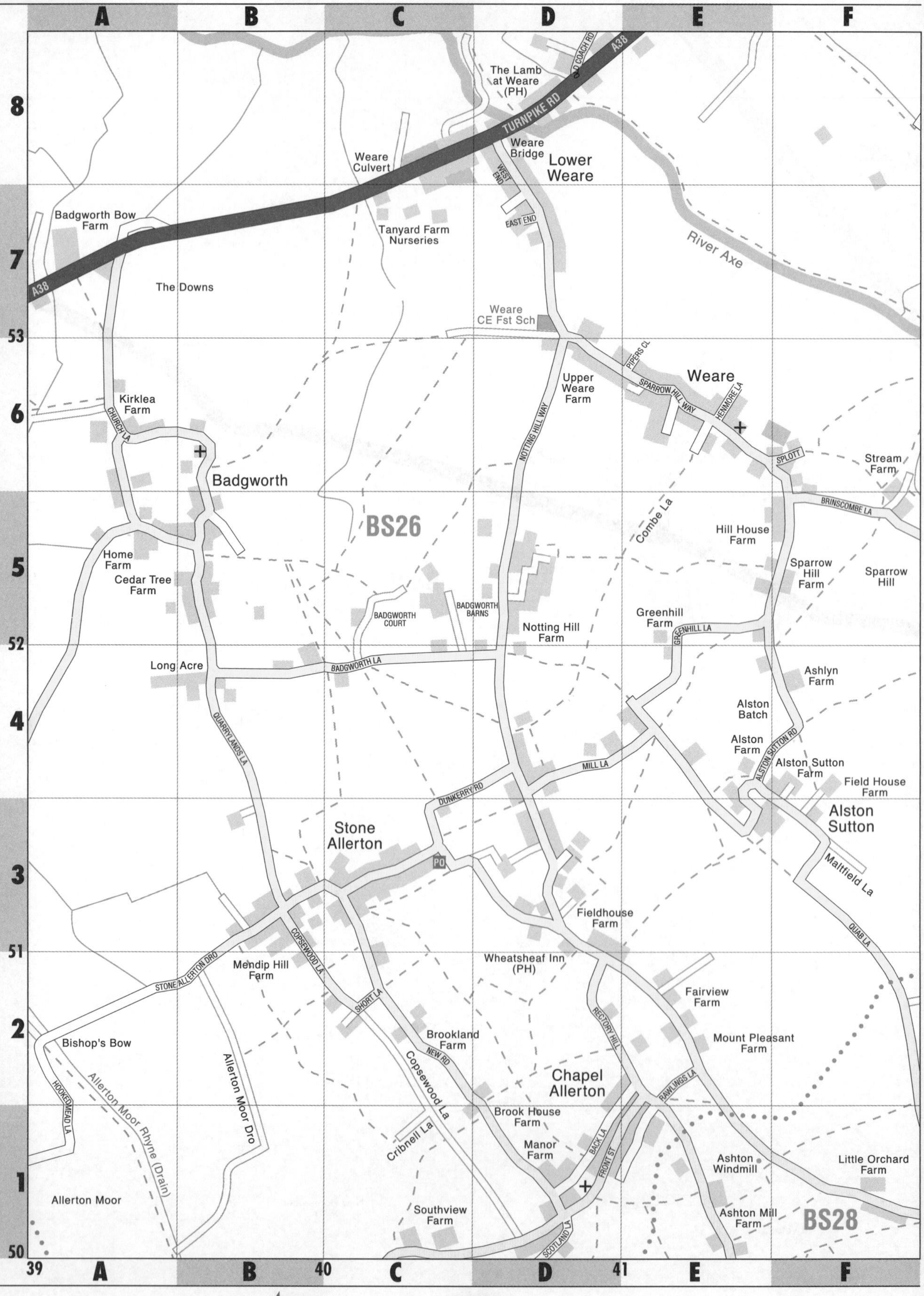

A B C D E F

The Lamb at Weare (PH)
OLD COACH RD
A38
TURNPIKE RD
Weare Culvert
Weare Bridge
Lower Weare
WEST END
EAST END
Badgworth Bow Farm
Tanyard Farm Nurseries
River Axe
The Downs
Weare CE Fst Sch
PIPERS CL
Upper Weare Farm
Weare
SPARROW HILL WAY
HENMORE LA
Kirklea Farm
CHURCH LA
NOTTING HILL WAY
SPLOTT
Stream Farm
Badgworth
BS26
Combe La
BRINSCOMBE LA
Hill House Farm
Home Farm
Cedar Tree Farm
Sparrow Hill Farm
Sparrow Hill
BADGWORTH COURT
BADGWORTH BARNS
Notting Hill Farm
Greenhill Farm
GREENHILL LA
Long Acre
BADGWORTH LA
Ashlyn Farm
Alston Batch
QUARRYLANDS LA
Alston Farm
ALSTON SUTTON RD
Alston Sutton Farm
Field House Farm
MILL LA
DUNKERRY RD
Alston Sutton
Stone Allerton
PO
Maltfield La
Fieldhouse Farm
COPSEWOOD LA
QUAB LA
Wheatsheaf Inn (PH)
STONE ALLERTON DRO
Mendip Hill Farm
Fairview Farm
SHORT LA
Brookland Farm
Mount Pleasant Farm
Bishop's Bow
NEW RD
RECTORY HILL
Allerton Moor Dro
Copsewood La
Chapel Allerton
RAWLINGS LA
Allerton Moor Rhyne (Drain)
Brook House Farm
HOOKEDMEAD LA
Cribnell La
Manor Farm
BACK LA
FRONT ST
Ashton Windmill
Little Orchard Farm
Allerton Moor
Southview Farm
Ashton Mill Farm
BS28
SCOTLAND LA

8 7 53 6 5 52 4 3 51 2 1 50

39 A B 40 C D 41 E F

70
90

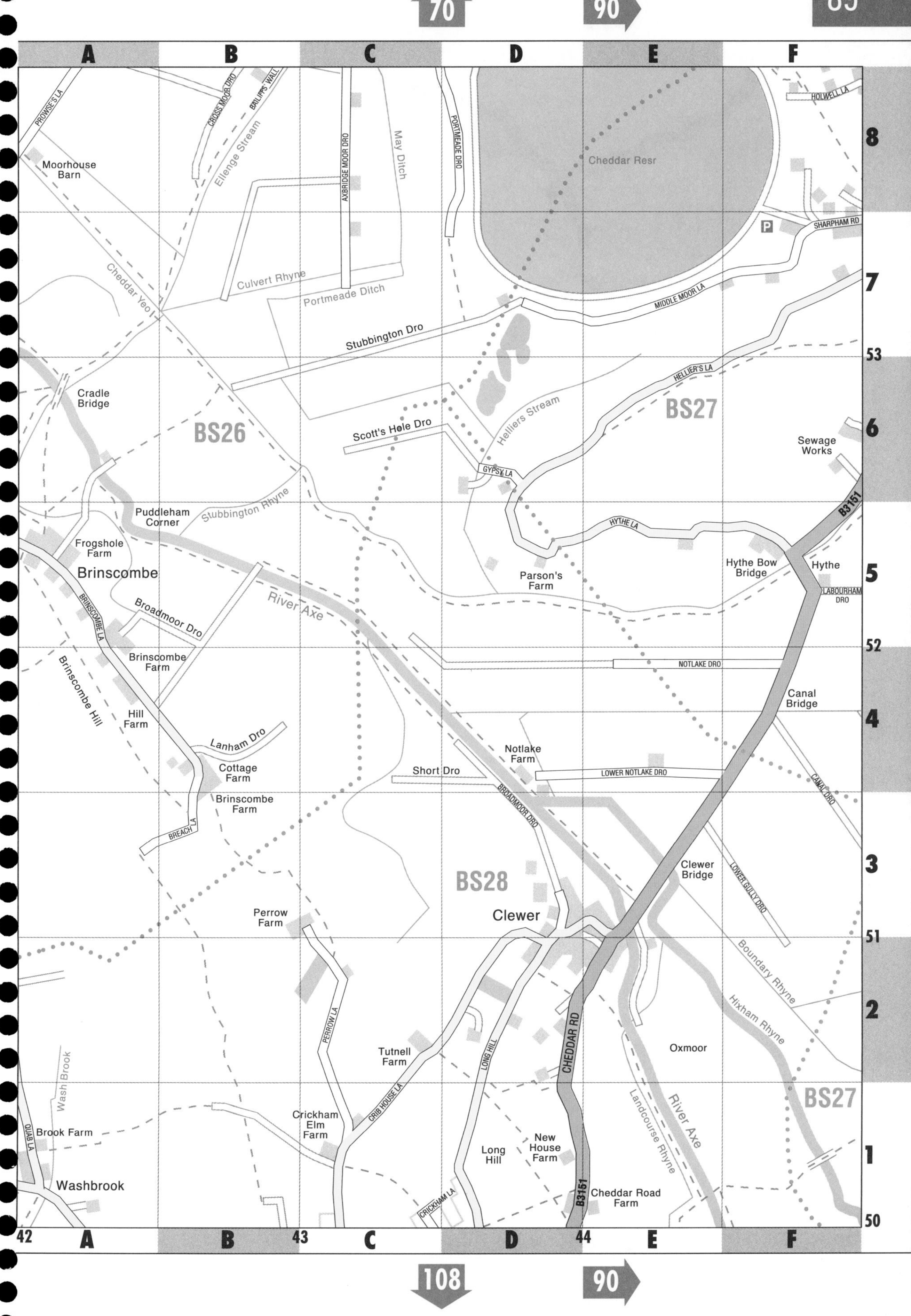
A
B
C
D
E
F
PROWSE'S LA
CROSS MOOR DRO
BAILIFFS' WALL
AXBRIDGE MOOR DRO
May Ditch
PORTMEADE DRO
Cheddar Resr
HOLWELL LA
8
Moorhouse Barn
Ellenge Stream
SHARPHAM RD
Culvert Rhyne
Portmeade Ditch
Cheddar Yeo
7
MIDDLE MOOR LA
Stubbington Dro
53
HELLIER'S LA
Cradle Bridge
BS27
BS26
Helliers Stream
Scott's Hole Dro
6
Sewage Works
GYPSY LA
Puddleham Corner
Stubbington Rhyne
B3151
HYTHE LA
Frogshole Farm
Brinscombe
Parson's Farm
Hythe Bow Bridge
Hythe
5
LABOURHAM DRO
BRINSCOMBE LA
Broadmoor Dro
River Axe
52
NOTLAKE DRO
Brinscombe Farm
Brinscombe Hill
Canal Bridge
Hill Farm
4
Lanham Dro
Notlake Farm
Cottage Farm
Short Dro
LOWER NOTLAKE DRO
CANAL DRO
Brinscombe Farm
BROADMOOR DRO
BREACH LA
3
Clewer Bridge
LOWER GULLY DRO
BS28
Perrow Farm
Clewer
51
Boundary Rhyne
2
Hixham Rhyne
PERROW LA
CHEDDAR RD
Tutnell Farm
LONG HILL
Oxmoor
Wash Brook
BS27
Crickham Elm Farm
CRIB HOUSE LA
Landcourse Rhyne
River Axe
QUAB LA
Brook Farm
New House Farm
Long Hill
1
Washbrook
B3151
Cheddar Road Farm
CRICKHAM LA
50
42
43
44

108
90

89
71

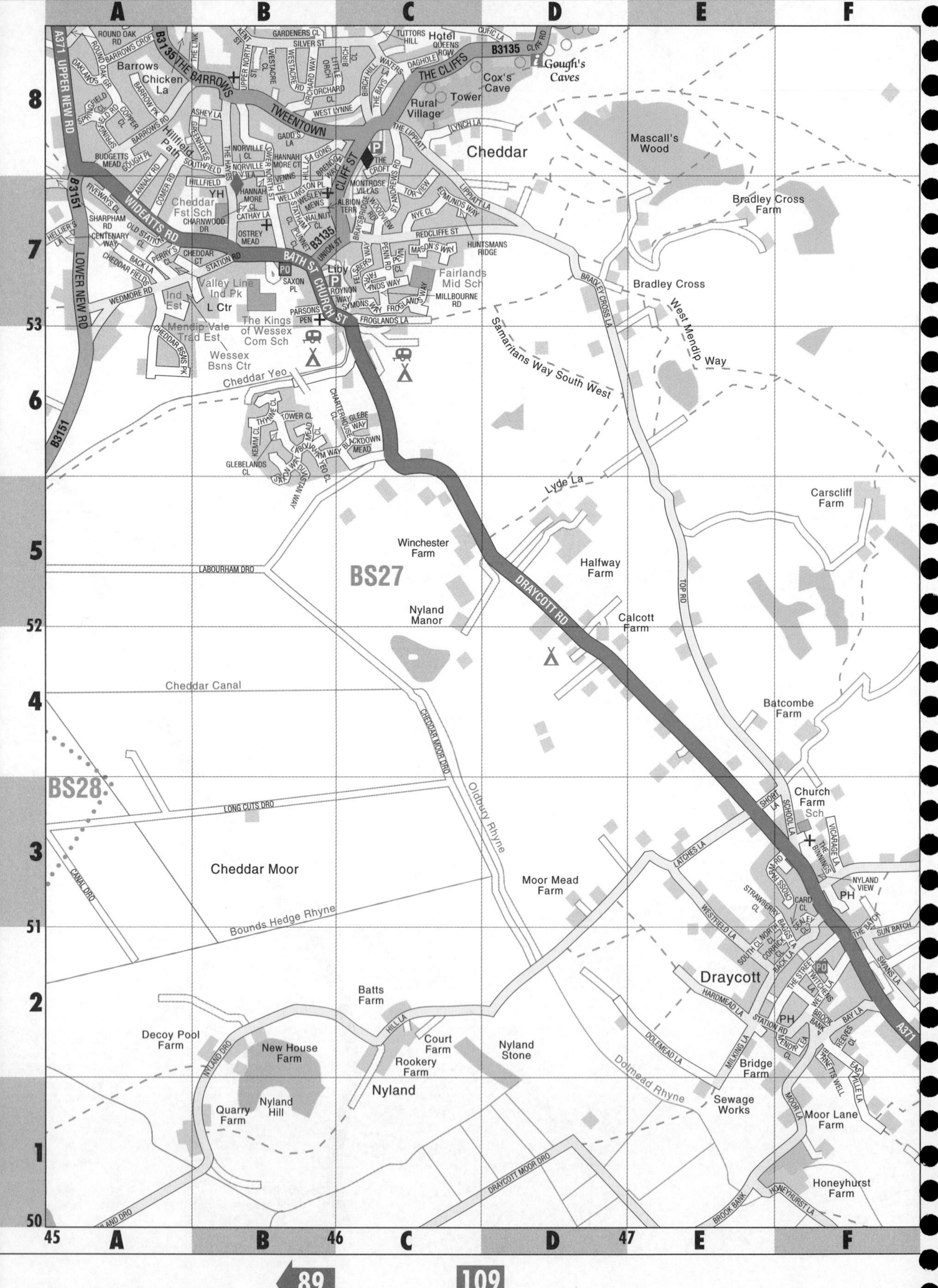
Cheddar
Gough's Caves
Cox's Cave
Rural Village
Tower
Mascall's Wood
Barrows
Chicken La
Hillfield Path
Bradley Cross Farm
Bradley Cross
West Mendip Way
Samaritans Way South West
Fairlands Mid Sch
Valley Line Ind Pk
L Ctr
Mendip Vale Trad Est
Wessex Bsns Ctr
The Kings of Wessex Com Sch
Cheddar Yeo
Lyde La
Carscliff Farm
Winchester Farm
Halfway Farm
BS27
Nyland Manor
Calcott Farm
DRAYCOTT RD
Cheddar Canal
Batcombe Farm
BS28
Church Farm
Cheddar Moor
Moor Mead Farm
Oldbury Rhyne
Bounds Hedge Rhyne
Draycott
Batts Farm
Decoy Pool Farm
New House Farm
Court Farm
Rookery Farm
Nyland Stone
Nyland
Nyland Hill
Quarry Farm
Bridge Farm
Sewage Works
Dolmead Rhyne
Moor Lane Farm
Honeyhurst Farm
A371 UPPER NEW RD
LOWER NEW RD
B3151
B3135
WIDEATTS RD
BATH ST
CHURCH ST
CLIFF ST
THE CLIFFS
TWEENTOWN
THE BARROWS
TOP RD
BRADLEY CROSS LA
LABOURHAM DRO
LONG CUTS DRO
CANAL DRO
CHEDDAR MOOR DRO
NYLAND DRO
DRAYCOTT MOOR DRO
HILL LA
LATCHES LA
WESTFIELD LA
HARDMEAD LA
DOLEMEAD LA
MOOR LA
BROOK BANK
HONEYHURST LA
REDCLIFFE ST
FROGLANDS LA
A371

89
109

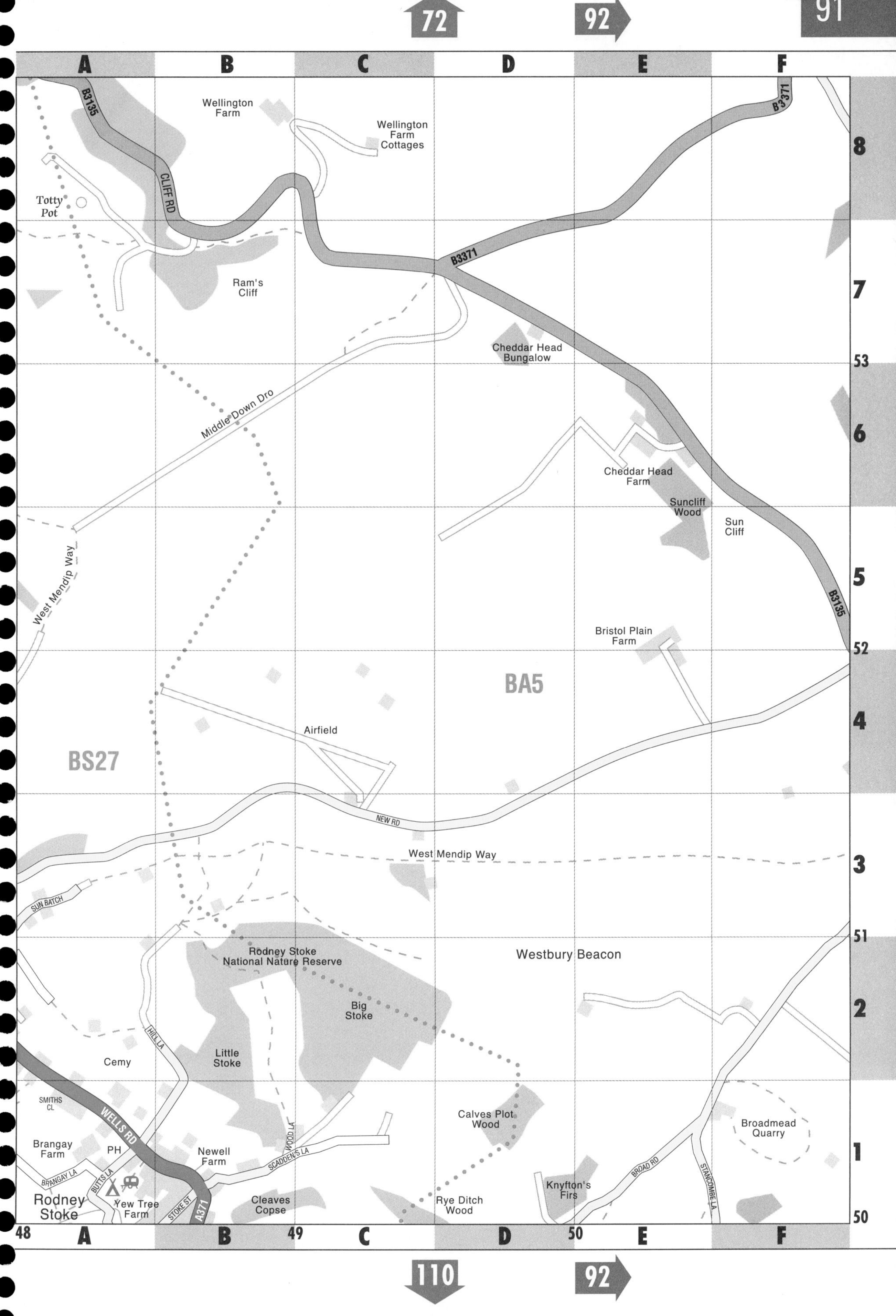
72
92
A
B
C
D
E
F
B3135
Wellington Farm
Wellington Farm Cottages
CLIFF RD
Totty Pot
B3371
Ram's Cliff
Cheddar Head Bungalow
Middle Down Dro
Cheddar Head Farm
Suncliff Wood
Sun Cliff
West Mendip Way
Bristol Plain Farm
BA5
Airfield
BS27
NEW RD
West Mendip Way
SUN BATCH
Rodney Stoke National Nature Reserve
Westbury Beacon
Big Stoke
HILL LA
Little Stoke
Cemy
SMITHS CL
WELLS RD
Calves Plot Wood
Broadmead Quarry
Brangay Farm
PH
Newell Farm
WOOD LA
SCADDEN'S LA
BROAD RD
STANCOMBE LA
BRANGAY LA
BUTTS LA
Rodney Stoke
Yew Tree Farm
STOKE ST
A371
Cleaves Copse
Rye Ditch Wood
Knyfton's Firs
8
7
53
6
5
52
4
3
51
2
1
50
48
49
50
110
92

91
73

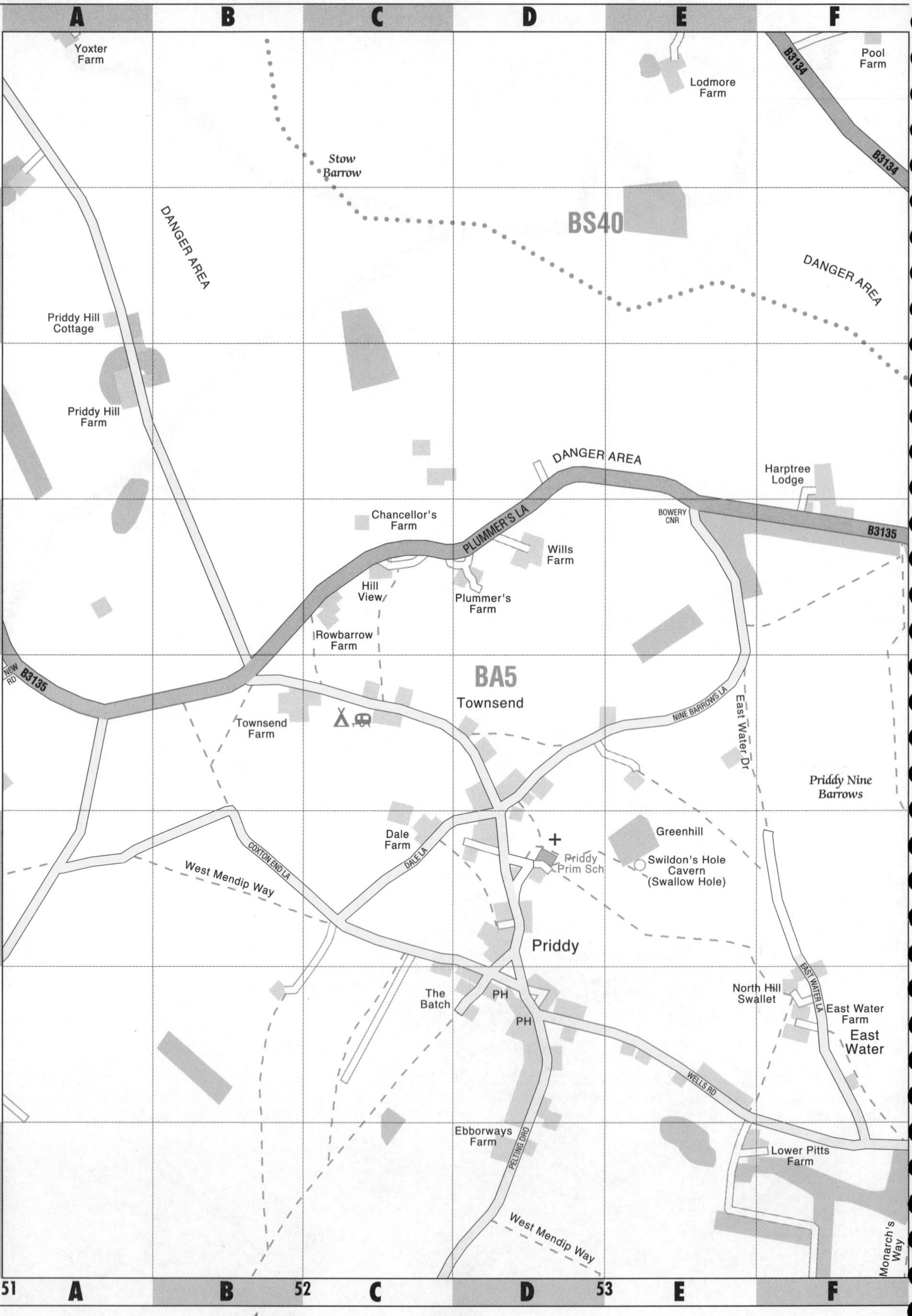

A B C D E F
8 7 53 6 5 52 4 3 51 2 1 50
Yoxter Farm
Lodmore Farm
Pool Farm
B3134
Stow Barrow
BS40
DANGER AREA
DANGER AREA
Priddy Hill Cottage
Priddy Hill Farm
DANGER AREA
Harptree Lodge
Chancellor's Farm
PLUMMER'S LA
BOWERY CNR
B3135
Wills Farm
Hill View
Plummer's Farm
Rowbarrow Farm
NEW RD
B3135
BA5
Townsend
Townsend Farm
NINE BARROWS LA
East Water Dr
Priddy Nine Barrows
Dale Farm
DALE LA
COXTON END LA
Greenhill
Priddy Prim Sch
Swildon's Hole Cavern (Swallow Hole)
West Mendip Way
Priddy
The Batch
PH
PH
North Hill Swallet
EAST WATER LA
East Water Farm
East Water
WELLS RD
Ebborways Farm
PELTING DRO
Lower Pitts Farm
West Mendip Way
Monarch's Way
51 A B 52 C D 53 E F

91
111

74
94

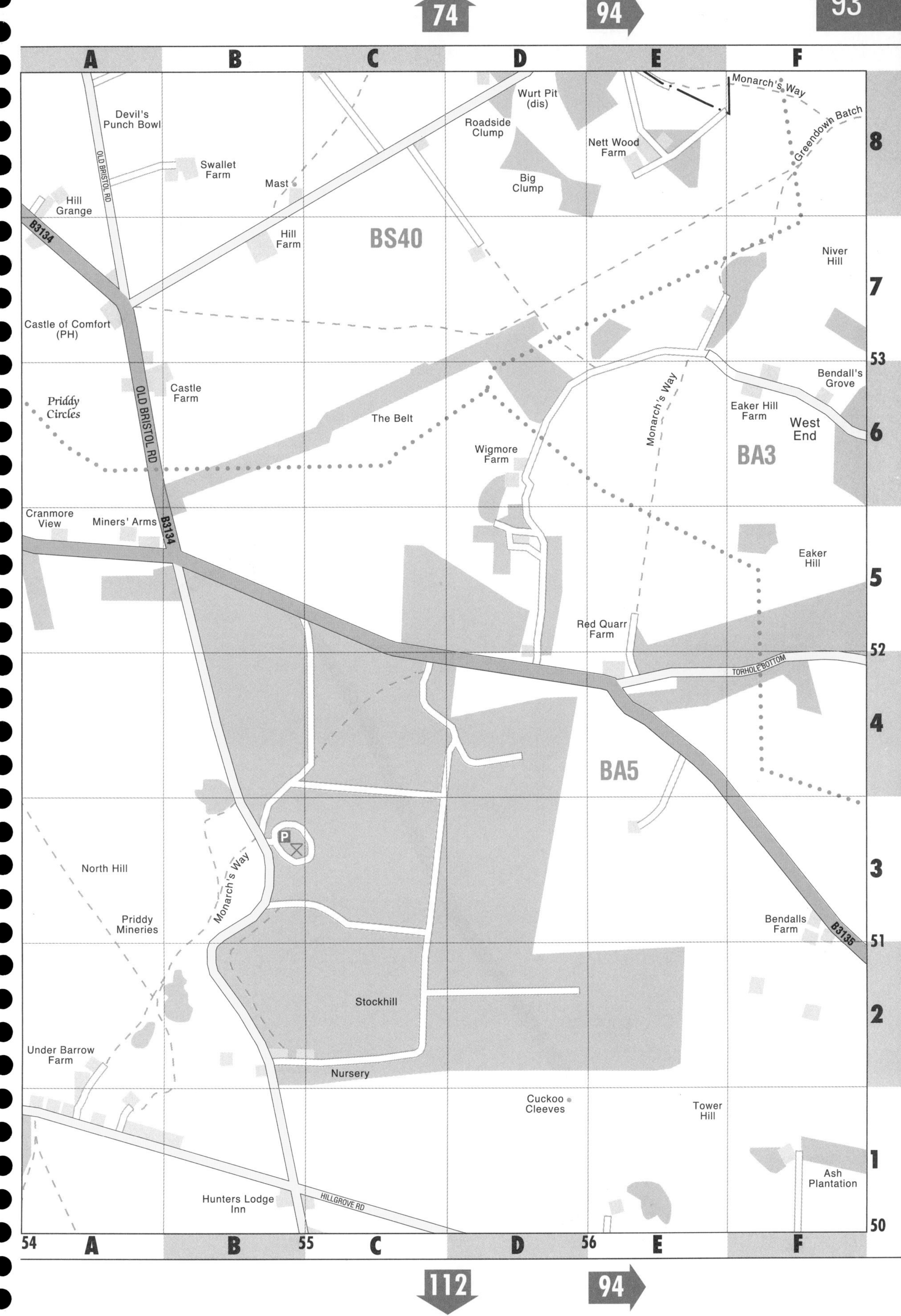
A
B
C
D
E
F
8
7
6
5
4
3
2
1
53
52
51
50
54
55
56
Devil's Punch Bowl
OLD BRISTOL RD
Swallet Farm
Mast
Hill Grange
Hill Farm
B3134
Castle of Comfort (PH)
Wurt Pit (dis)
Roadside Clump
Nett Wood Farm
Big Clump
Monarch's Way
Greendown Batch
BS40
Niver Hill
Priddy Circles
Castle Farm
The Belt
Wigmore Farm
Eaker Hill Farm
Bendall's Grove
West End
BA3
Cranmore View
Miners' Arms
Eaker Hill
Red Quarr Farm
TORHOLE BOTTOM
BA5
North Hill
Priddy Mineries
Bendalls Farm
B3135
Stockhill
Under Barrow Farm
Nursery
Cuckoo Cleeves
Tower Hill
Ash Plantation
Hunters Lodge Inn
HILLGROVE RD

112
94

93
75

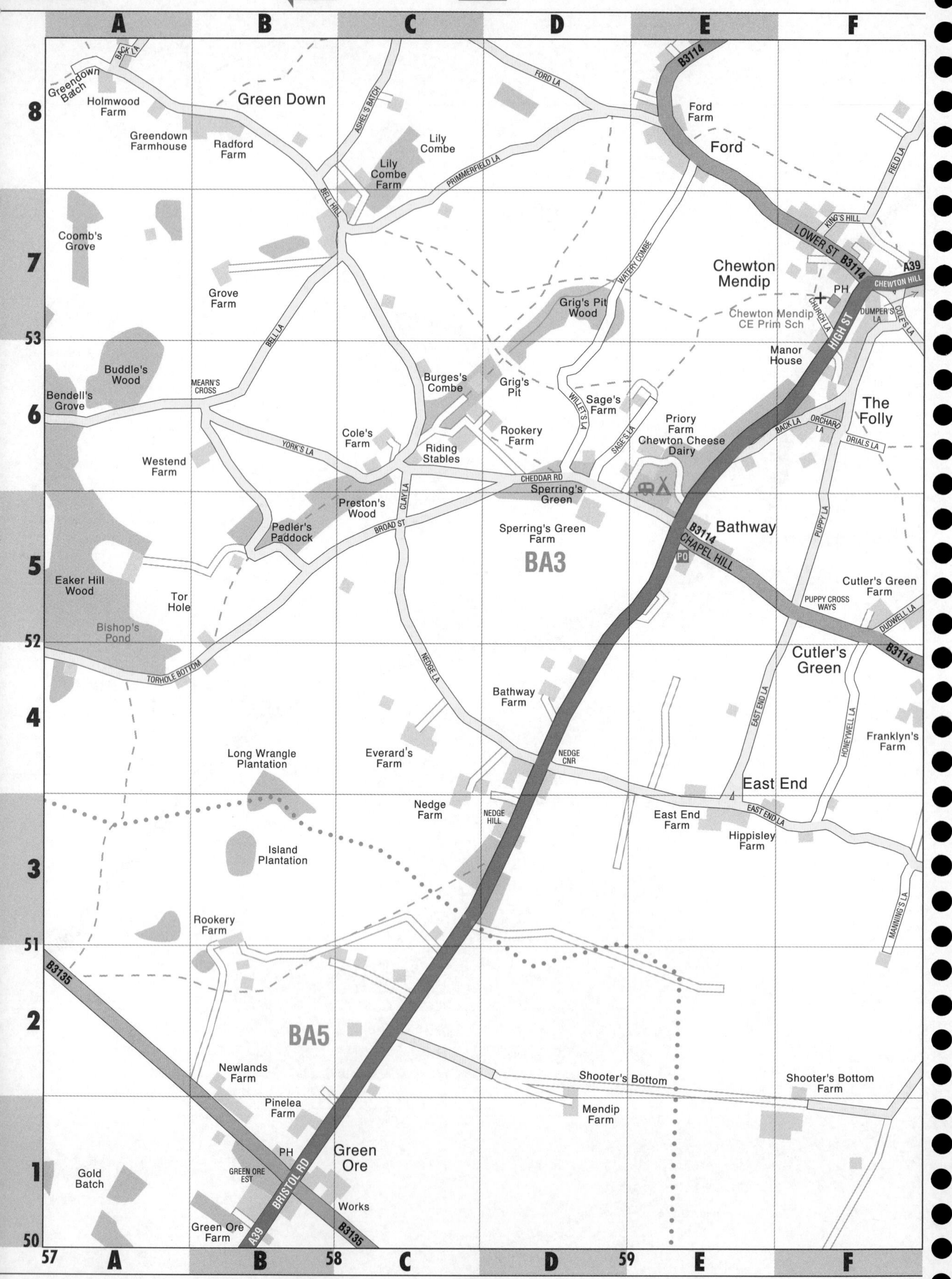
A
B
C
D
E
F
8
7
53
6
5
52
4
3
51
2
1
50
57
58
59
Green Down
Greendown Batch
Holmwood Farm
Greendown Farmhouse
Radford Farm
Lily Combe
Lily Combe Farm
Ford Farm
Ford
Coomb's Grove
Grove Farm
Chewton Mendip
PH
Chewton Mendip CE Prim Sch
Grig's Pit Wood
Buddle's Wood
Bendell's Grove
Burges's Combe
Grig's Pit
Sage's Farm
Manor House
The Folly
Priory Farm
Chewton Cheese Dairy
Rookery Farm
Cole's Farm
Riding Stables
Westend Farm
Sperring's Green
Preston's Wood
Pedler's Paddock
Bathway
Sperring's Green Farm
BA3
PO
Eaker Hill Wood
Tor Hole
Bishop's Pond
Cutler's Green Farm
Cutler's Green
Bathway Farm
Franklyn's Farm
Long Wrangle Plantation
Everard's Farm
East End
Nedge Farm
East End Farm
Hippisley Farm
Island Plantation
Rookery Farm
BA5
Newlands Farm
Shooter's Bottom
Shooter's Bottom Farm
Pinelea Farm
Mendip Farm
PH
Green Ore
Gold Batch
Works
Green Ore Farm
BACK LA
ASHEL'S BATCH
FORD LA
B3114
FIELD LA
PRIMMERFIELD LA
BELL HILL
KING'S HILL
LOWER ST
A39
CHEWTON HILL
WATERY COMBE
CHURCH LA
DUMPER'S LA
COLES LA
HIGH ST
BELL LA
MEARN'S CROSS
WILLET'S LA
SAGE'S LA
BACK LA
ORCHARD LA
DRIALS LA
YORK'S LA
CHEDDAR RD
CLAY LA
BROAD ST
CHAPEL HILL
PUPPY LA
PUPPY CROSS WAYS
DUDWELL LA
TORHOLE BOTTOM
NEDGE LA
EAST END LA
HONEYWELL LA
NEDGE CNR
NEDGE HILL
EAST END LA
MANNING'S LA
B3135
BRISTOL RD
GREEN ORE EST

93
113

76
96

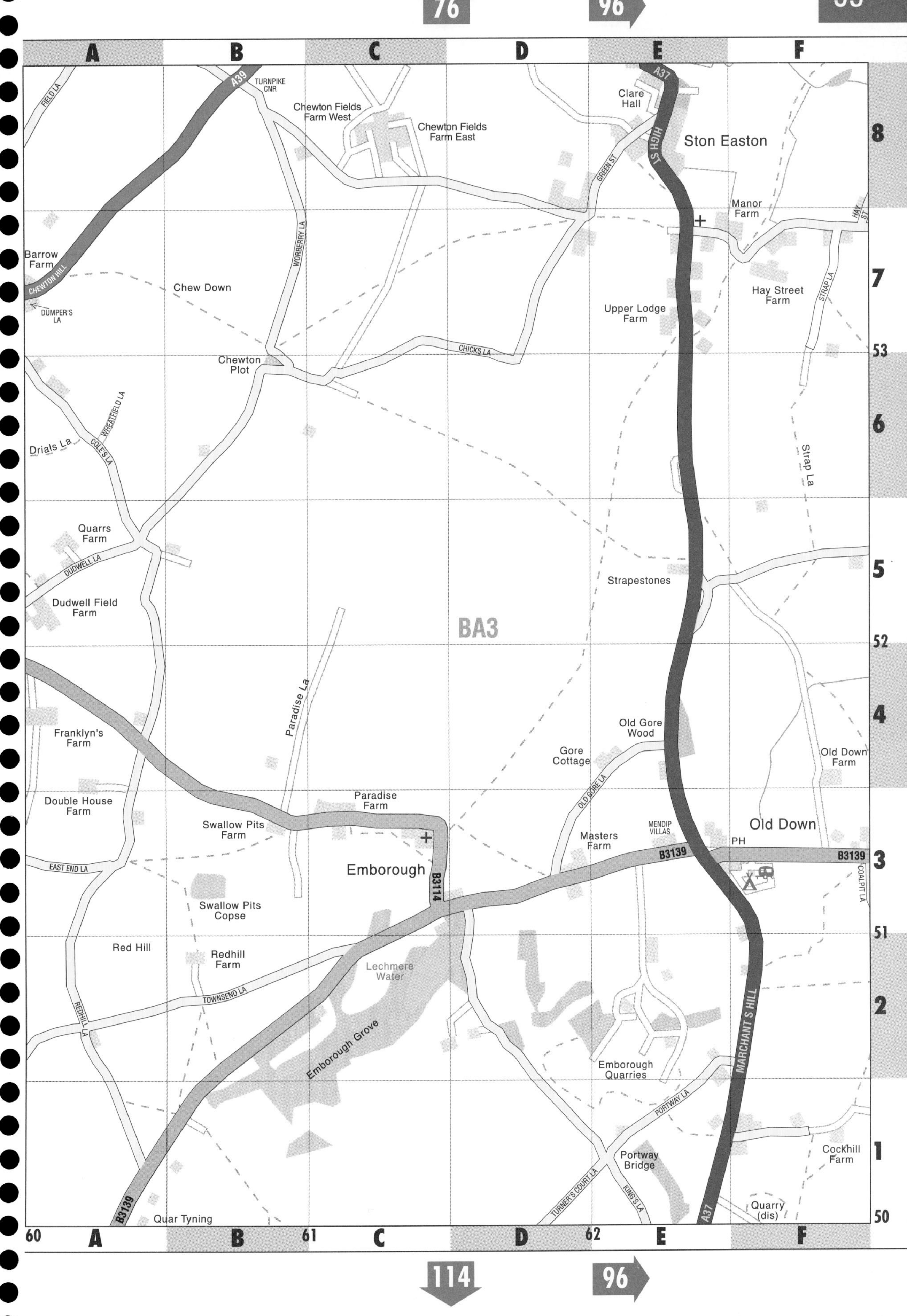
A
B
C
D
E
F
8
7
53
6
5
52
4
3
51
2
1
50
60
61
62
FIELD LA
A39
TURNPIKE CNR
Chewton Fields Farm West
Chewton Fields Farm East
Clare Hall
A37
HIGH ST
Ston Easton
GREEN ST
Manor Farm
HAY ST
Barrow Farm
CHEWTON HILL
DUMPER'S LA
Chew Down
WORBERRY LA
Hay Street Farm
STRAP LA
Upper Lodge Farm
CHICKS LA
Chewton Plot
WHEATFIELD LA
Drials La
COLES LA
Strap La
Quarrs Farm
DUDWELL LA
Strapestones
Dudwell Field Farm
BA3
Paradise La
Old Gore Wood
Franklyn's Farm
Gore Cottage
Old Down Farm
OLD GORE LA
Double House Farm
Paradise Farm
Swallow Pits Farm
Masters Farm
MENDIP VILLAS
Old Down
PH
B3139
EAST END LA
Emborough
B3114
COALPIT LA
Swallow Pits Copse
Red Hill
Redhill Farm
Lechmere Water
TOWNSEND LA
REDHILL LA
MARCHANT'S HILL
Emborough Grove
Emborough Quarries
PORTWAY LA
Portway Bridge
Cockhill Farm
TURNER'S COURT LA
KING'S LA
Quarry (dis)
Quar Tyning

114
96

95 77

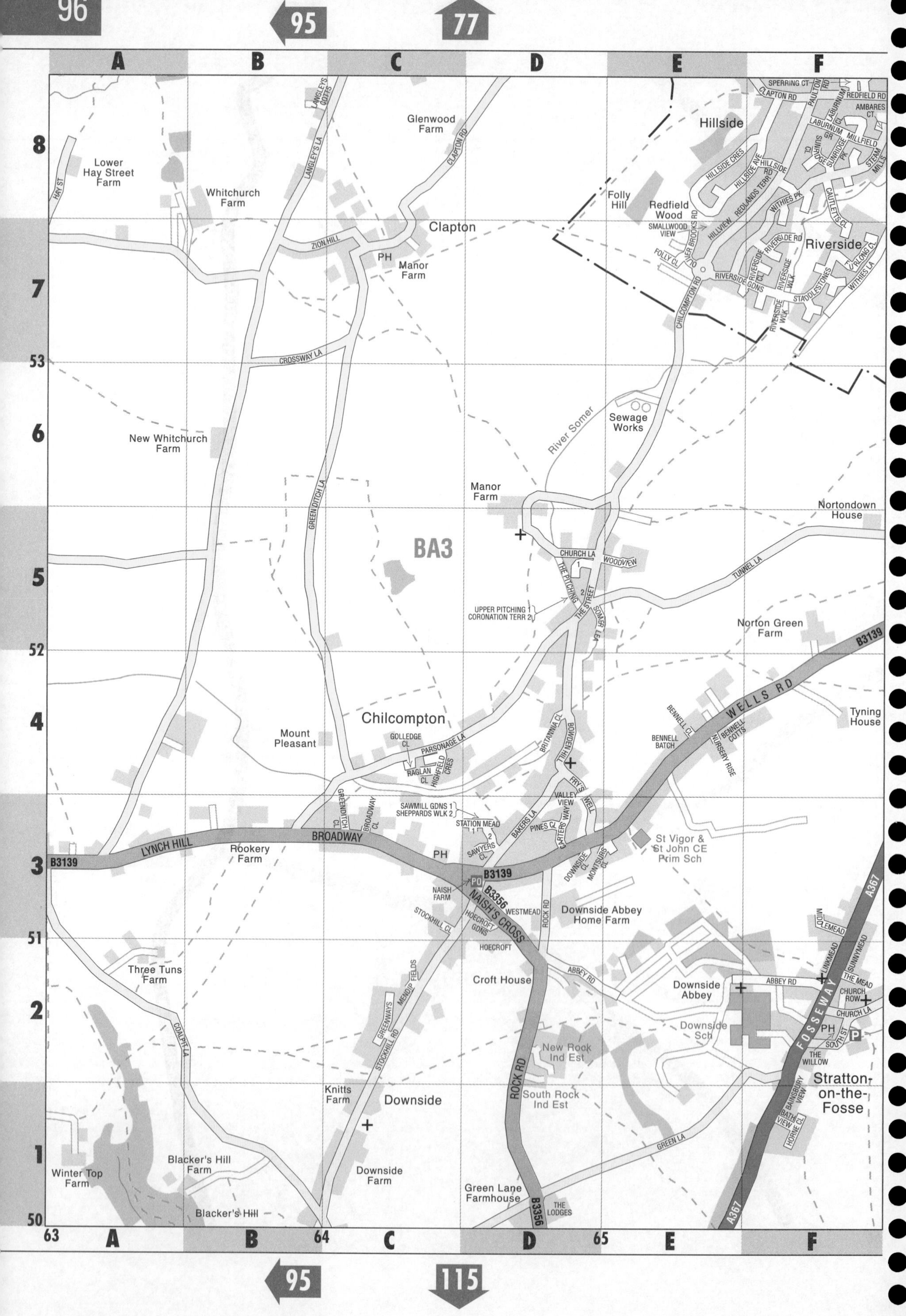
A
B
C
D
E
F
8
7
53
6
5
52
4
3
51
2
1
50
63
64
65
Lower Hay Street Farm
Whitchurch Farm
Glenwood Farm
Hillside
Folly Hill
Redfield Wood
Clapton
Manor Farm
Riverside
New Whitchurch Farm
Sewage Works
River Somer
Manor Farm
Nortondown House
BA3
Norton Green Farm
Tyning House
Chilcompton
Mount Pleasant
Rookery Farm
St Vigor & St John CE Prim Sch
Downside Abbey Home Farm
Croft House
Three Tuns Farm
Downside Abbey
Downside Sch
New Rock Ind Est
South Rock Ind Est
Stratton-on-the-Fosse
Knitts Farm
Downside
Downside Farm
Blacker's Hill Farm
Winter Top Farm
Blacker's Hill
Green Lane Farmhouse
THE LODGES
LYNCH HILL
BROADWAY
B3139
WELLS RD
B3356
NAISH'S CROSS
ROCK RD
A367
FOSSEWAY
UPPER PITCHING 1
CORONATION TERR 2
SAWMILL GDNS 1
SHEPPARDS WLK 2
CHURCH LA
TUNNEL LA
GREEN LA
COALPIT LA
STOCKHILL RD
CROSSWAY LA
GREEN DITCH LA
LANGLEY'S LA
CLAPTON RD
CHILCOMPTON RD
ZION HILL
HAY ST
PH
PO

95 115

78
98

A B C D E F

Somervale Sch
1 REDFIELD GR
2 REDFIELD RD
3 ST CHAD'S GN
STEAM MILLS
B3355
IVY WLK
FERN CL
CHAUCER RD
POETS CNR
KINGSLEY RD
TANNER CL
Fosse Way Sch
ELM TERR
WELLS RD
A367
PH
Westfield
Factory
WATERSIDE RD
LINCOMBE RD
WATERSIDE WAY
THE LEAZE
LARCH CT
WATERFORD PK
BRIAR CL
LINDEN CL
REDWOOD CL
GROVE WOOD RD
GROVE WOOD RD
DOWN VIEW
HAYDON GATE
HAYDON HILL
Haydon Ind Est
Haydon
RADSTOCK
PO
PARK WAY
WITHIES LA
Midsomer Norton South
Midsomer Norton Railway Ctr
Somerset & Dorset Joint Rly
ROBIN CL
NIGHTINGALE WAY
CHAFFINCH DR
KINGFISHER DR
WOODPECKER AVE
LARK CL
LINNET WAY
BLACKBIRD WAY
SWALLOW CL
LONGFELLOW RD
COWDYNNE CL
OLD PIT RD
ST PETER'S RD
COBBLERS WAY
UPPER COURT
FOURTH AVE
Westfield Prim Sch
LYNDHURST RD
CHARLTON RD
LYNTON RD
HAZEL TERR
HAZEL GR
FOSSEWAY
FIRST AVE
LYNWOOD CL
Norton Hill Sch
THE TIMBERS
Westfield Ind & Trad Est
THIRD AVE
SECOND AVE
Tyning Farm
KILMERSDON RD
SILVER ST
Norton Hill
CHARLTON PK
GANGE END
CHARLTON PK
BOUNDARY CL
CHARLTON PK
Sch
Waterside House
The Grange
FOSSEWAY S
FOSSEFIELD RD
Hotel
CH
CHARLTON LA
Waterside Farm
MIDSOMER NORTON
WATERSIDE LA
The Firs
Redhouse Farm
BA3
Charlton Park
WHITE POST
PH
Whitfield Cottages
Redhouse Farm
Norton Hall
TUNNEL LA
BEAUCHAMPS DR
B3139
The Old Red House Farm
Waterlea
The Lodge
B3139
WELLS RD
Norton Down
Charlton
FOSSEWAY
B3355
Manor Farm
Killings Knap Farm
Killing's Knap
Snail's Bottom
Walton Wood
Charmborough Farm Rural Bsns Pk
Charmborough Farm
WATERY LA
Little Wood
Hackmead Farm
Loocombe Wood
Southmead Farm
CHARLTON RD
Loocombe Pond
Sewage Works
CHURCH LA
Holcombe Wood
Moore's Farm
BA11
BURROWS LA
Lipyeate House
DARK LA
Holcombe
Little Field Farm
Holcombe Pond
Brick House Farm
Lipyeate
Lipyeate Farm
SILVER ST
BREWERY LA
STRATTON RD
PITCOT LA
Glasses Farm
ANCHOR RD
UPPER MERRYFIELD

8 7 53 6 5 52 4 3 51 2 1 50

66 A B 67 C D 68 E F

116
98

97
79

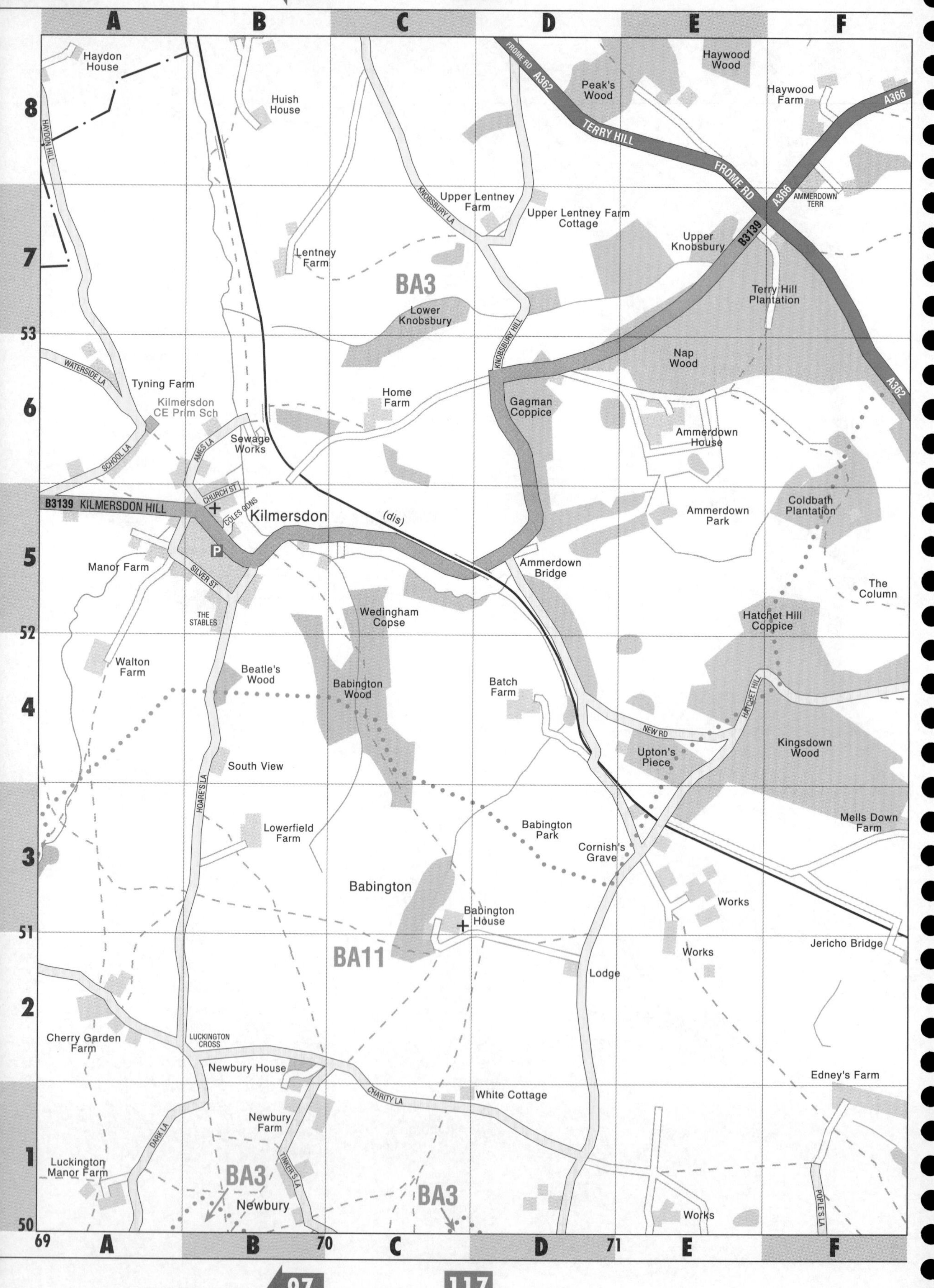
A
B
C
D
E
F
8
7
53
6
5
52
4
3
51
2
1
50
69
70
71
Haydon House
Huish House
Haywood Wood
Peak's Wood
Haywood Farm
FROME RD
A362
TERRY HILL
FROME RD
A366
AMMERDOWN TERR
HAYDON HILL
Upper Lentney Farm
Upper Lentney Farm Cottage
KNOBSBURY LA
Upper Knobsbury
B3139
Lentney Farm
BA3
Lower Knobsbury
Terry Hill Plantation
KNOBSBURY HILL
Nap Wood
WATERSIDE LA
Tyning Farm
Home Farm
Kilmersdon CE Prim Sch
Gagman Coppice
Ammerdown House
Sewage Works
AMES LA
SCHOOL LA
CHURCH ST
B3139 KILMERSDON HILL
COLES GDNS
Kilmersdon
(dis)
Ammerdown Park
Coldbath Plantation
P
Manor Farm
SILVER ST
Ammerdown Bridge
The Column
THE STABLES
Wedingham Copse
Hatchet Hill Coppice
Walton Farm
Beatle's Wood
Babington Wood
Batch Farm
HATCHET HILL
NEW RD
Kingsdown Wood
South View
Upton's Piece
HOARE'S LA
Lowerfield Farm
Babington Park
Cornish's Grave
Mells Down Farm
Babington
Works
Babington House
Jericho Bridge
BA11
Works
Lodge
Cherry Garden Farm
LUCKINGTON CROSS
Newbury House
Edney's Farm
CHARITY LA
White Cottage
Newbury Farm
DARK LA
TINKER'S LA
Luckington Manor Farm
BA3
BA3
Newbury
Works
POPLE'S LA

97
117

80
100

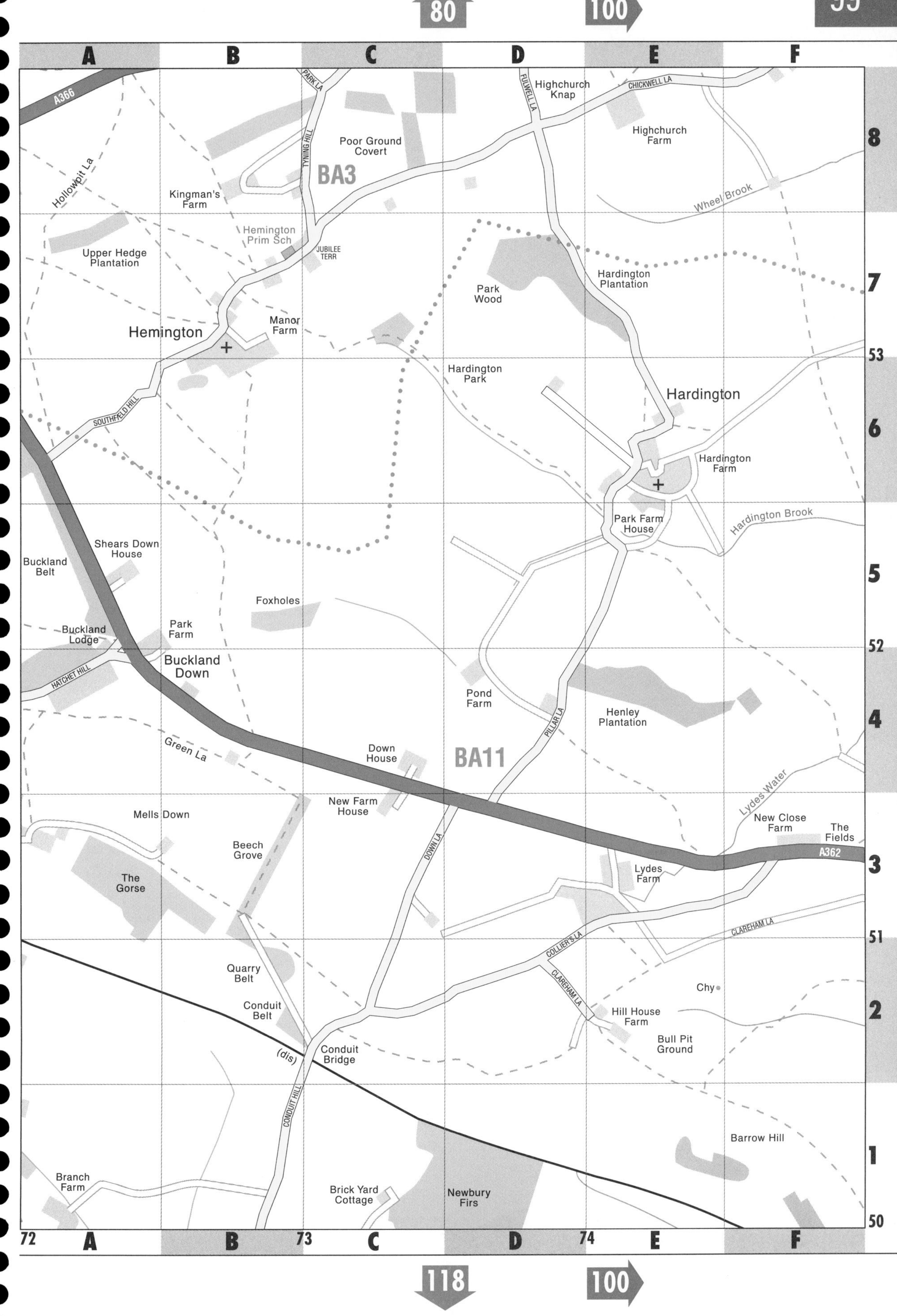

118
100

99
81

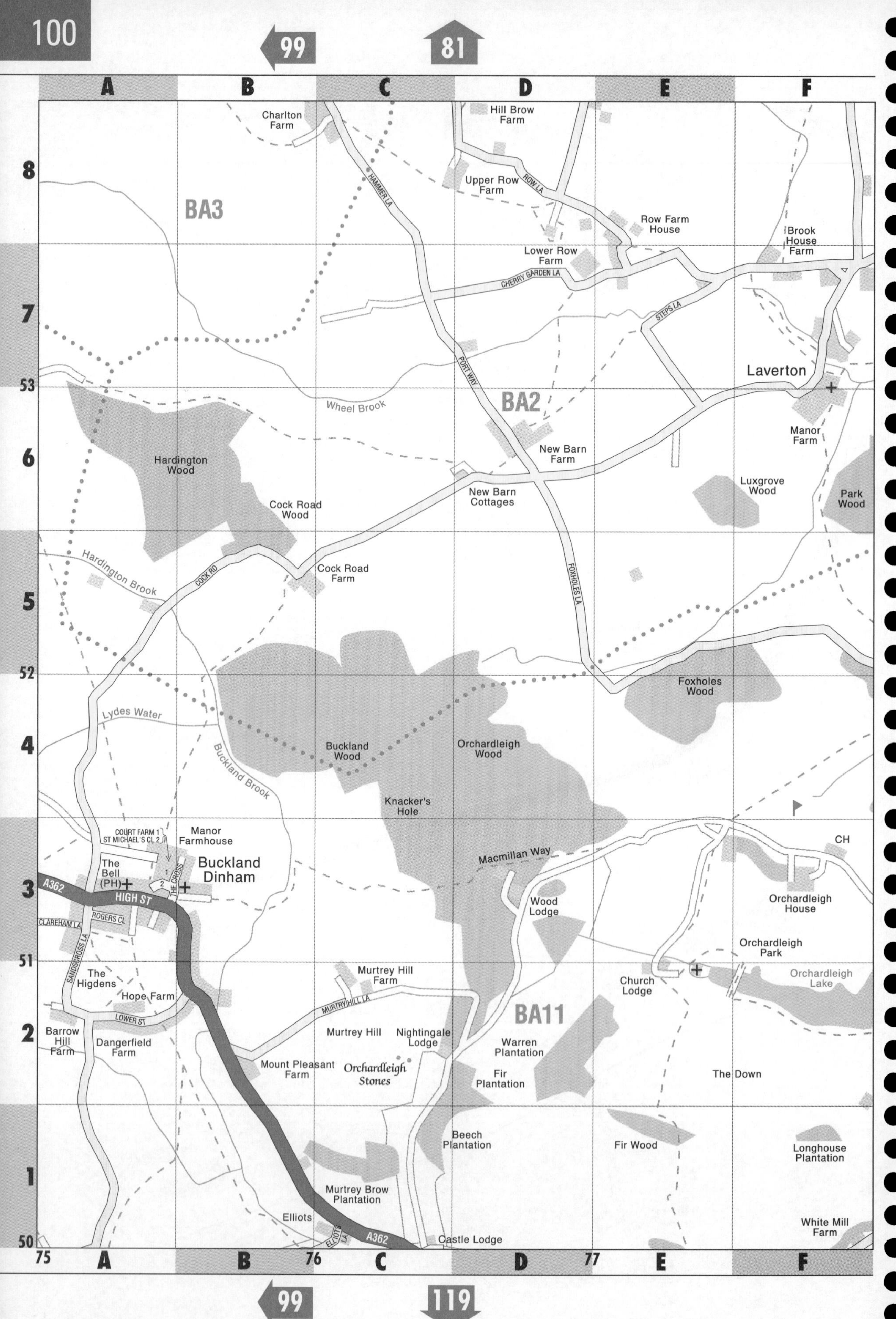
A
B
C
D
E
F
8
7
53
6
5
52
4
3
51
2
1
50
75
76
77
Charlton Farm
Hill Brow Farm
Upper Row Farm
ROW LA
HAMMER LA
BA3
Row Farm House
Brook House Farm
Lower Row Farm
CHERRY GARDEN LA
STEPS LA
PORT WAY
Laverton
BA2
Wheel Brook
Manor Farm
Hardington Wood
New Barn Farm
Luxgrove Wood
Park Wood
New Barn Cottages
Cock Road Wood
Hardington Brook
Cock Road Farm
COCK RD
FOXHOLES LA
Foxholes Wood
Lydes Water
Buckland Wood
Orchardleigh Wood
Buckland Brook
Knacker's Hole
COURT FARM 1
ST MICHAEL'S CL 2
Manor Farmhouse
CH
Buckland Dinham
Macmillan Way
The Bell (PH)
A362
HIGH ST
THE CROSS
Wood Lodge
Orchardleigh House
ROGERS CL
CLAREHAM LA
SANDSCROSS LA
Orchardleigh Park
The Higdens
Murtrey Hill Farm
Church Lodge
Orchardleigh Lake
Hope Farm
MURTRY HILL LA
LOWER ST
BA11
Barrow Hill Farm
Dangerfield Farm
Murtrey Hill
Nightingale Lodge
Warren Plantation
Mount Pleasant Farm
Orchardleigh Stones
Fir Plantation
The Down
Beech Plantation
Fir Wood
Longhouse Plantation
Murtrey Brow Plantation
Elliots
ELLIOTS LA
White Mill Farm
Castle Lodge

99
119

82
102

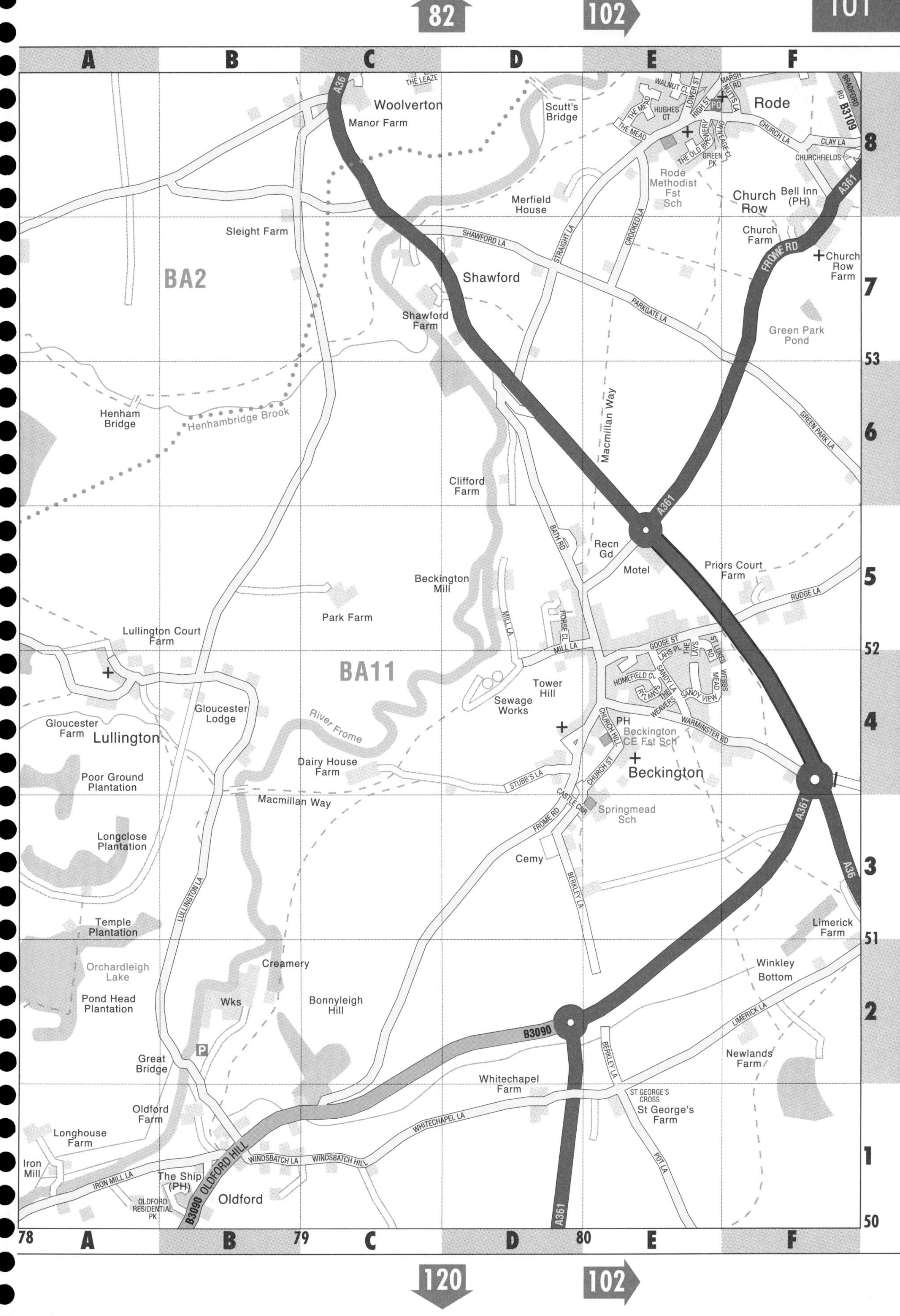

120
102

101
83

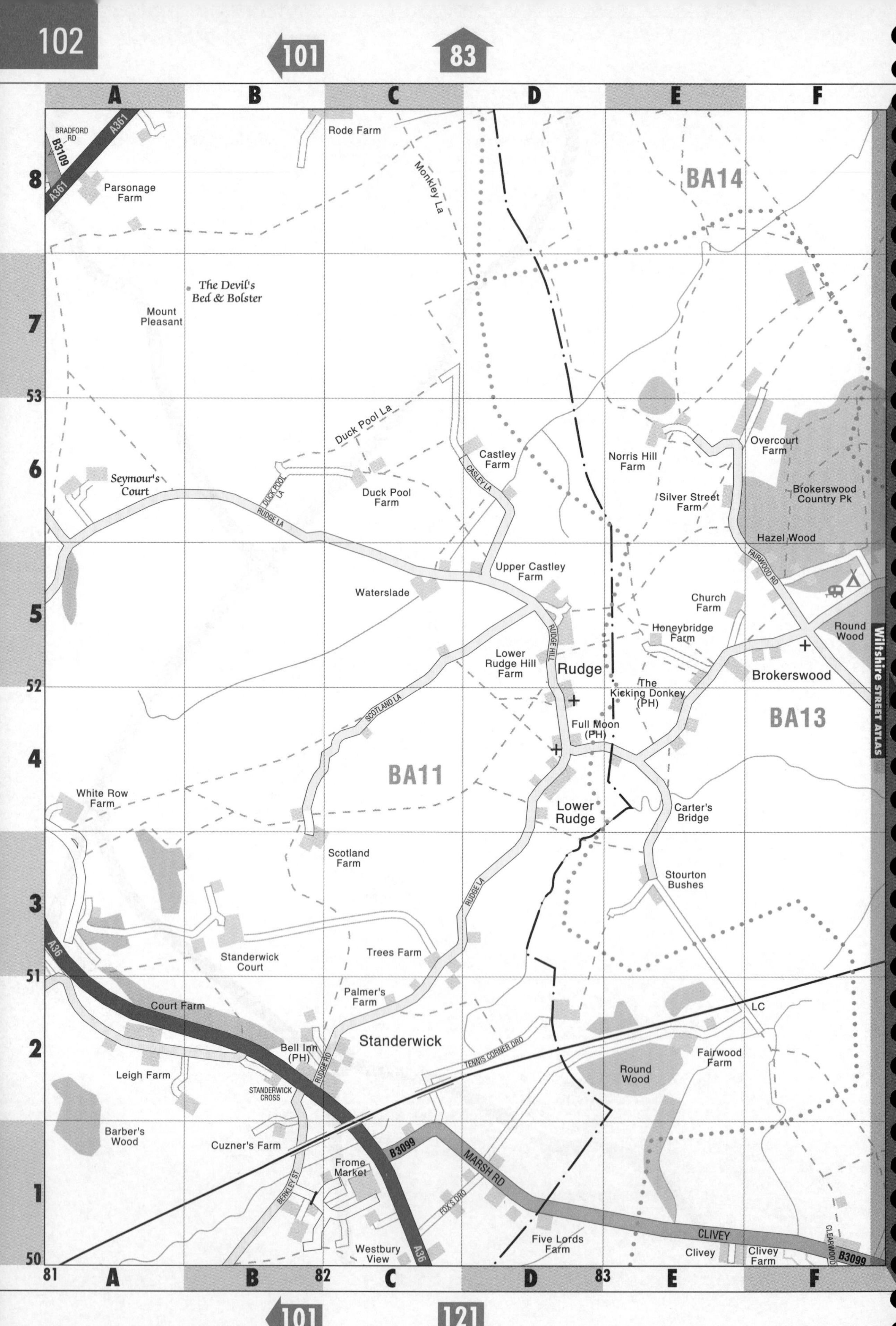

101
121

84
104

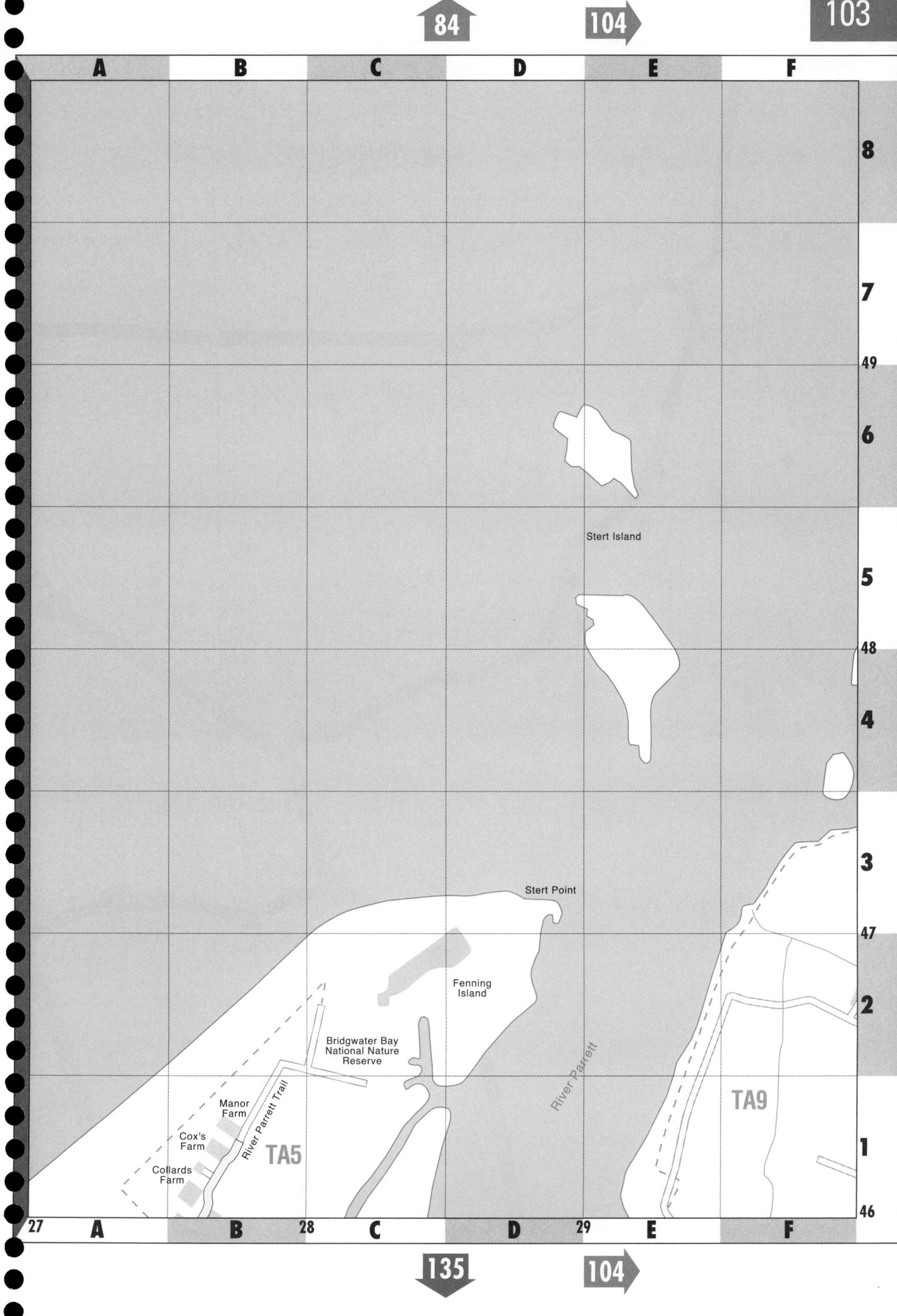

135
104

103
85

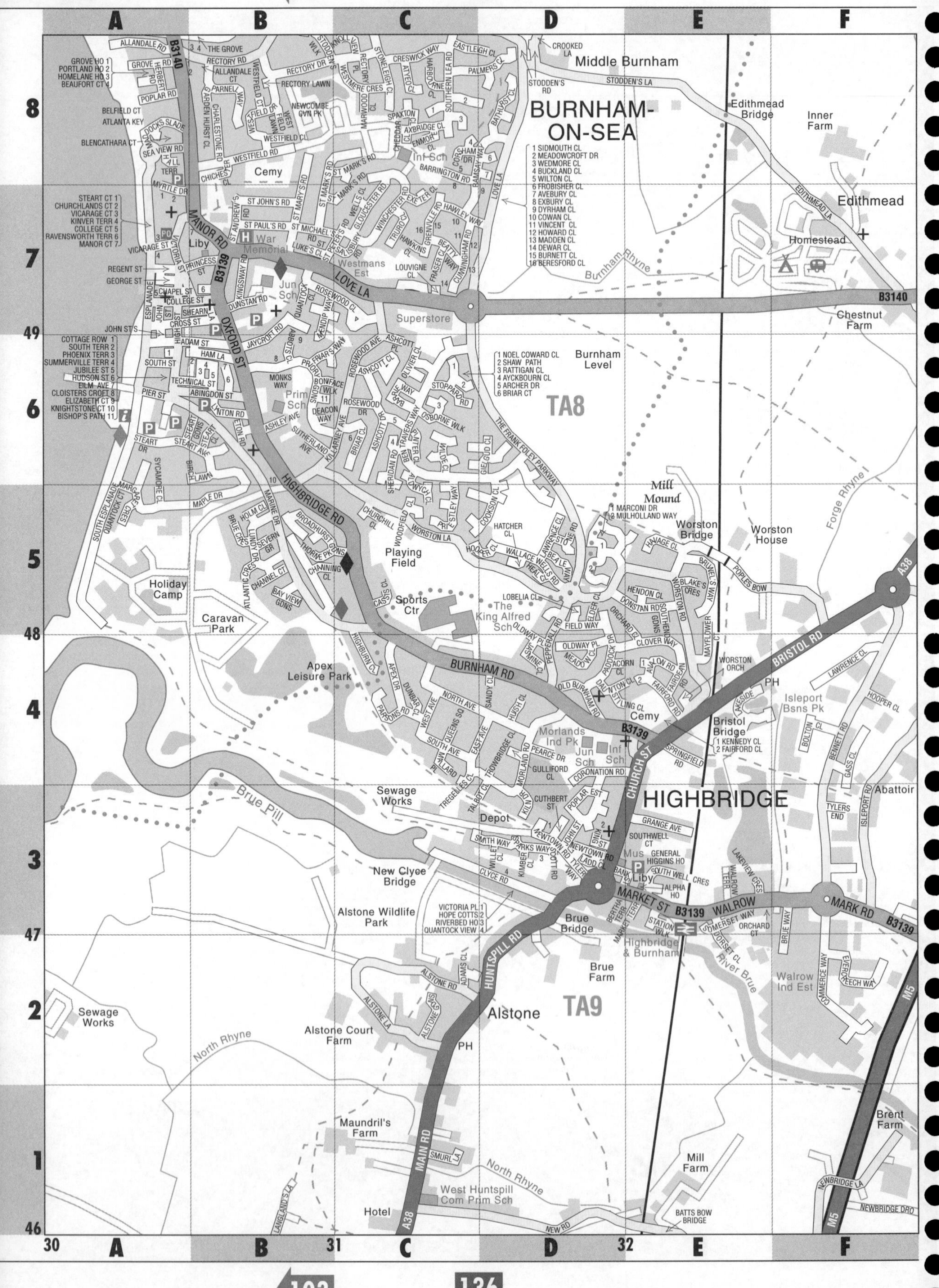

103
136

86
106

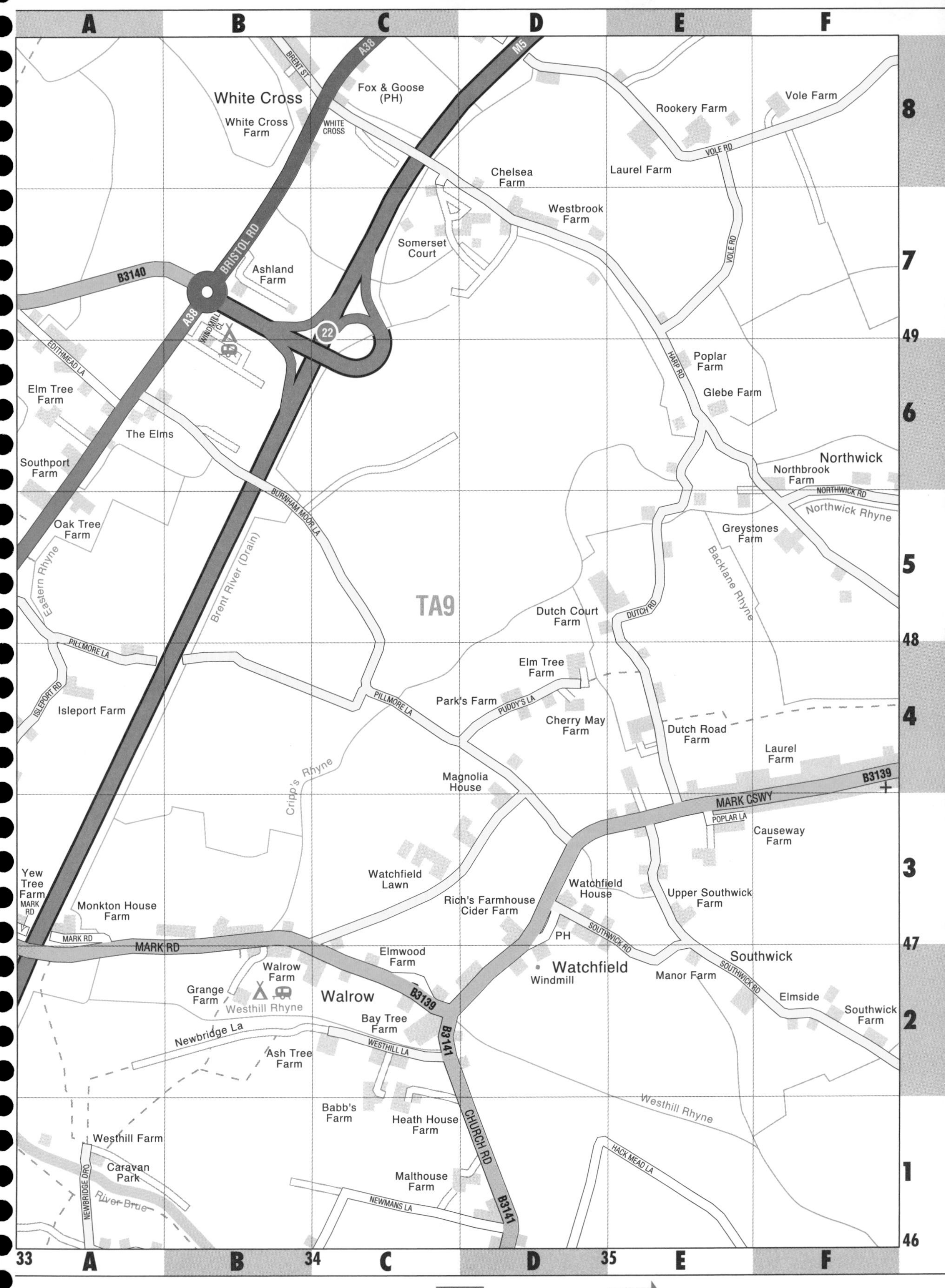

136
106

105
87

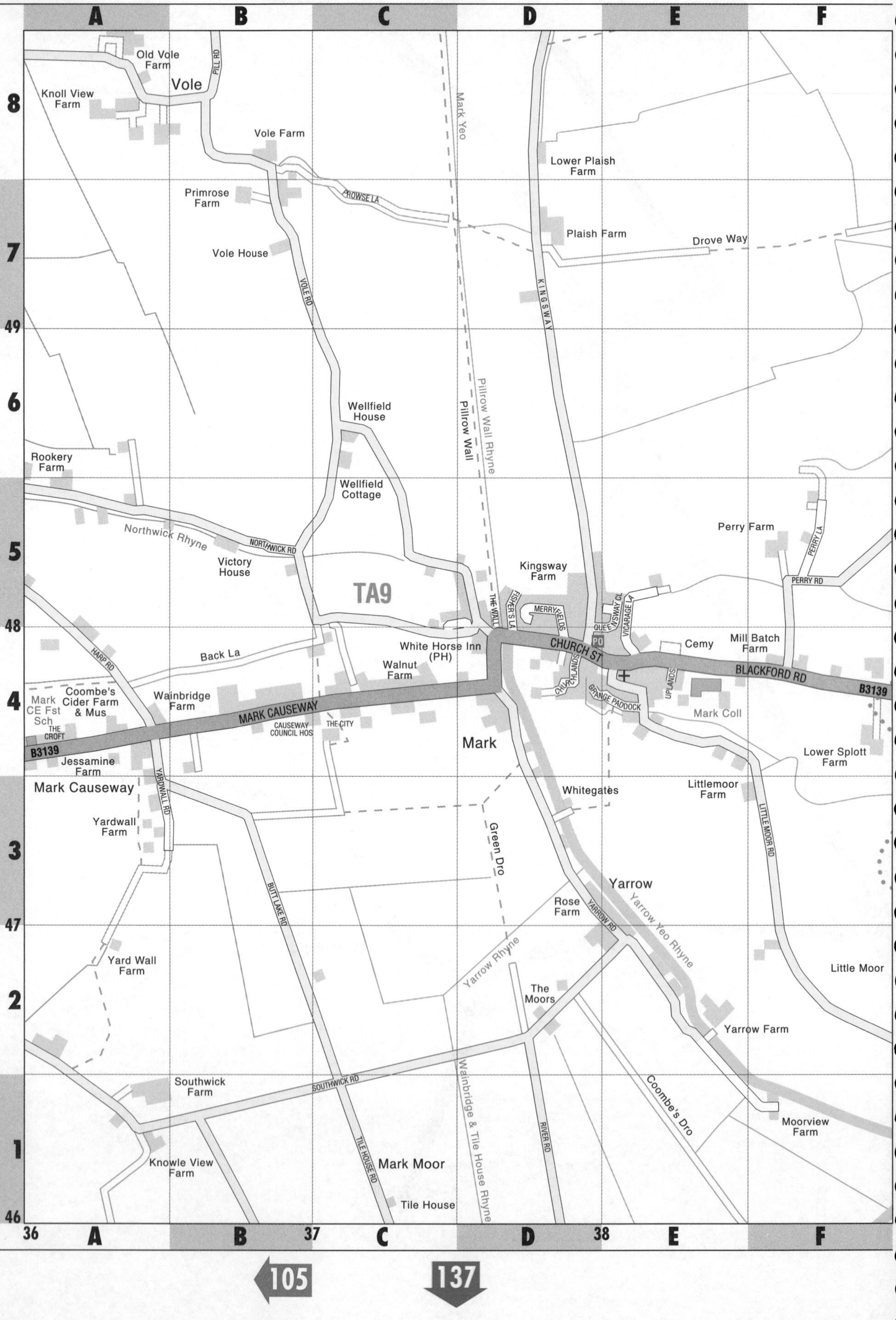

105
137

88
108

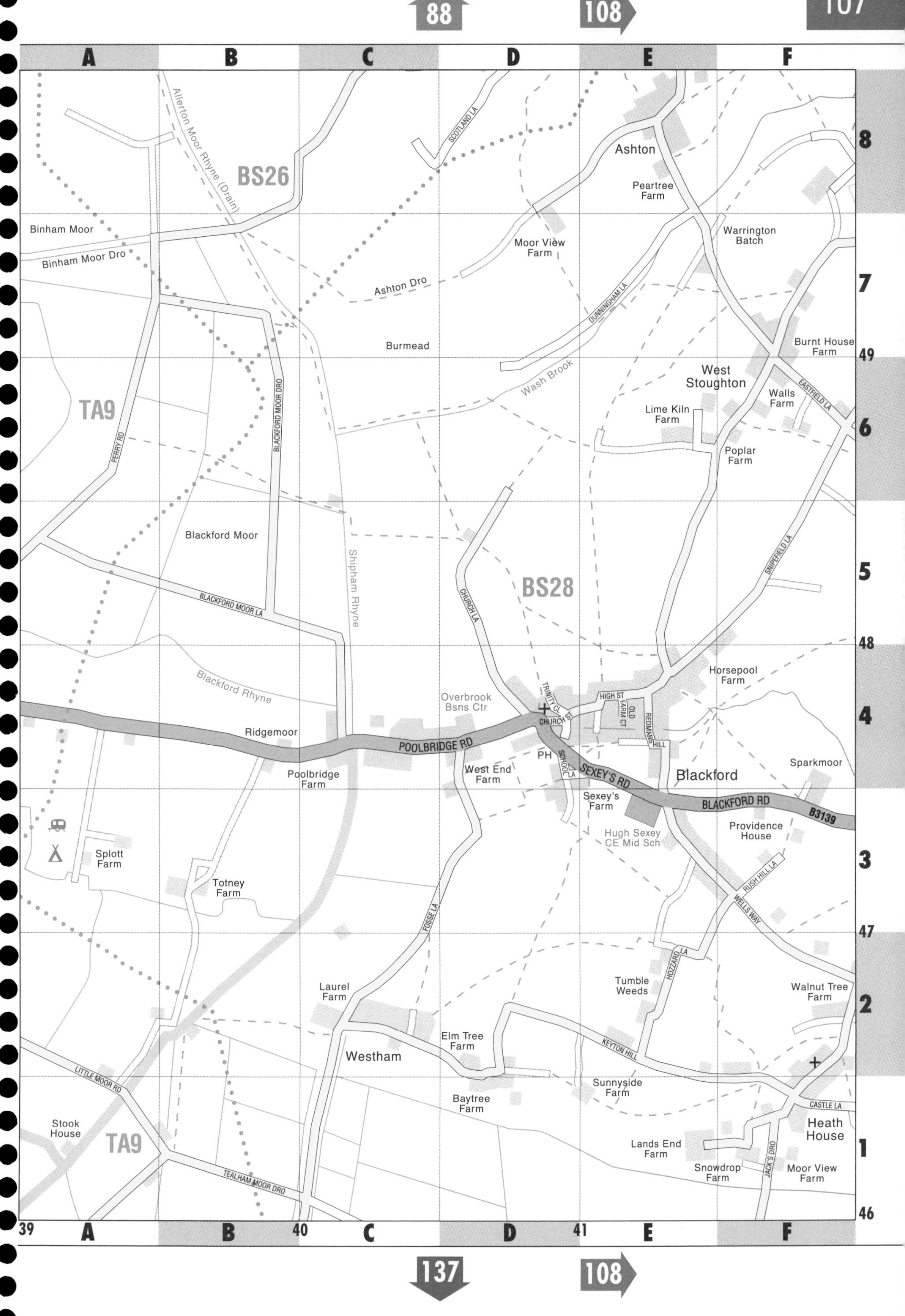

137
108

107
89

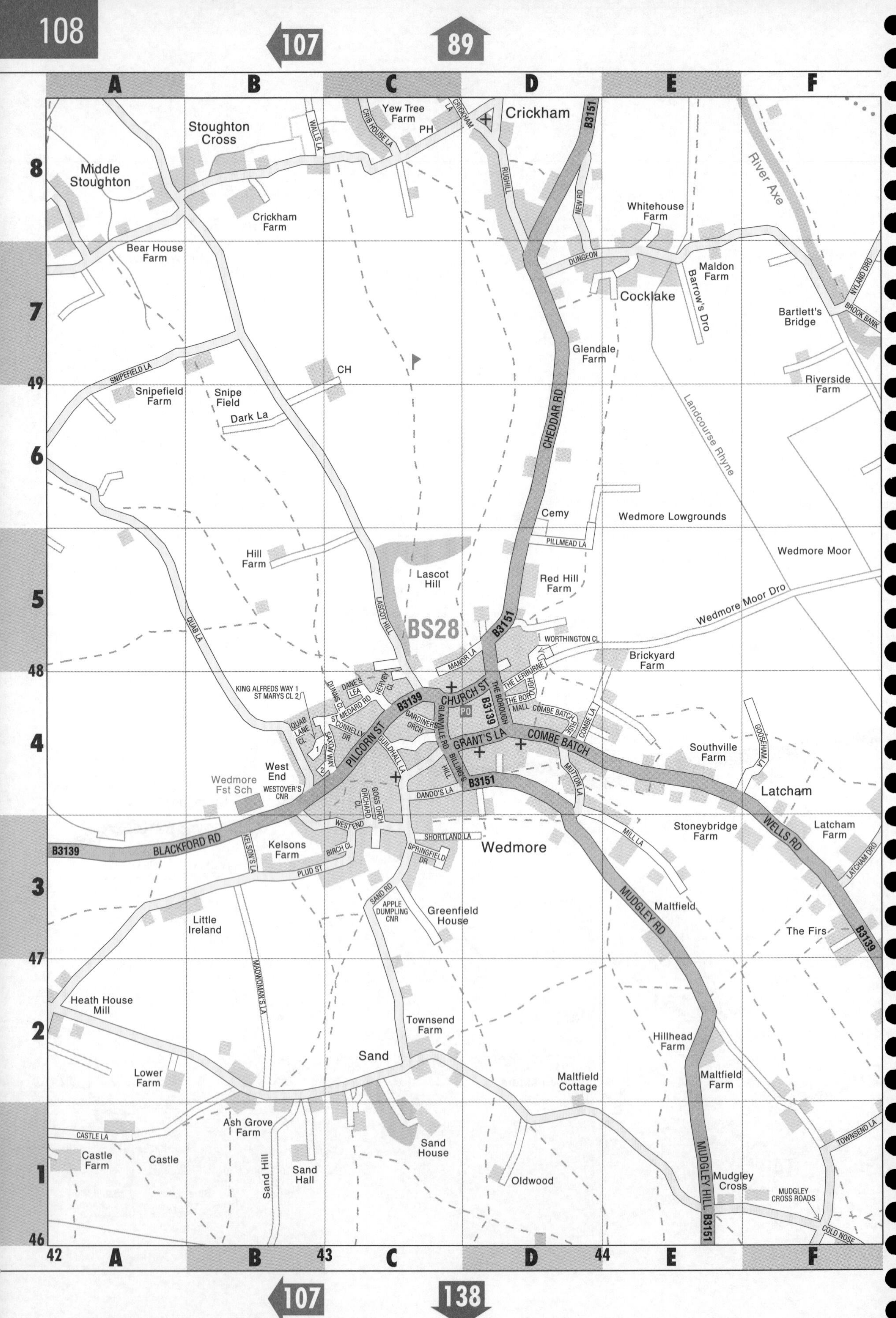

107
138

90
110

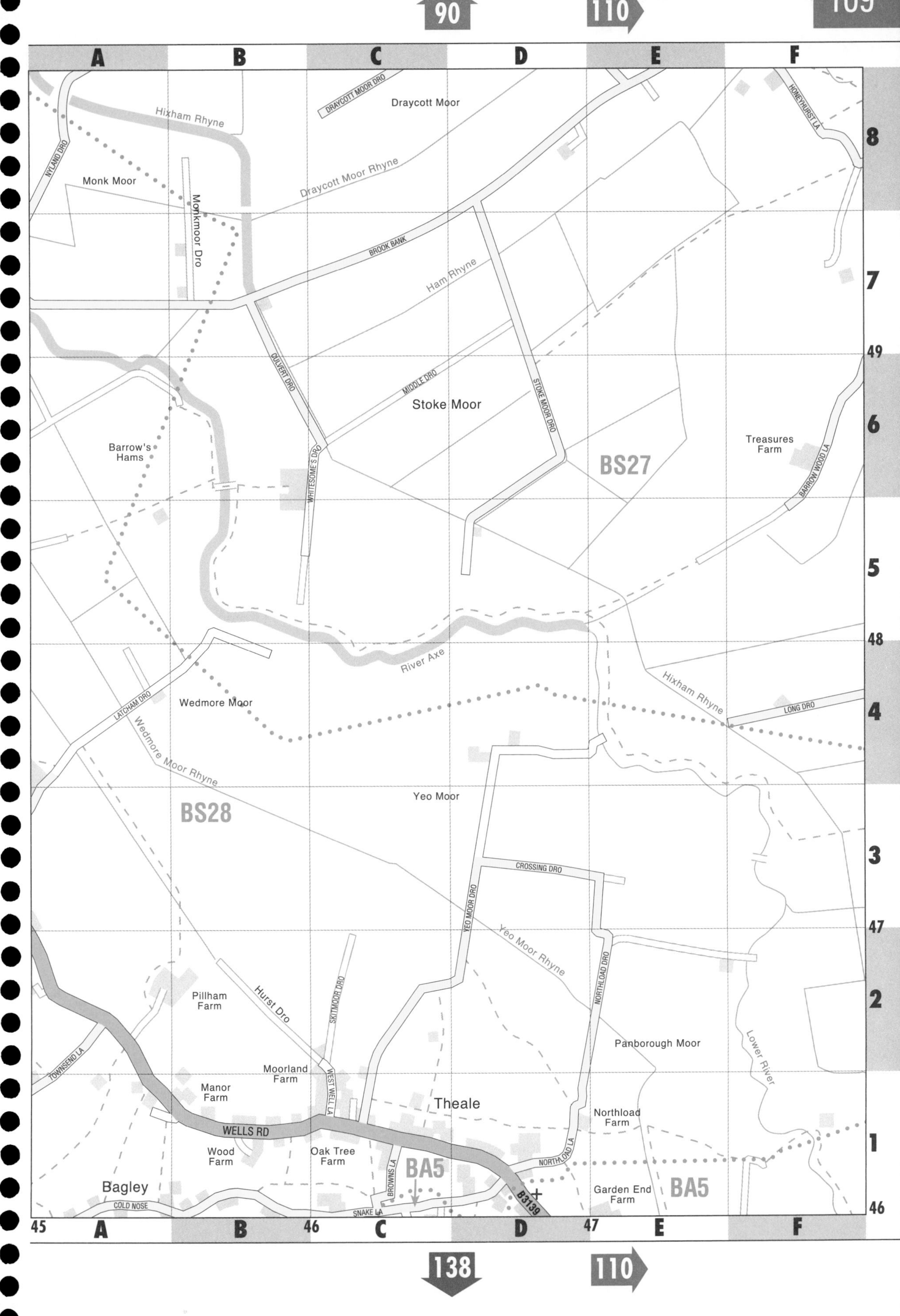

138
110

109
91

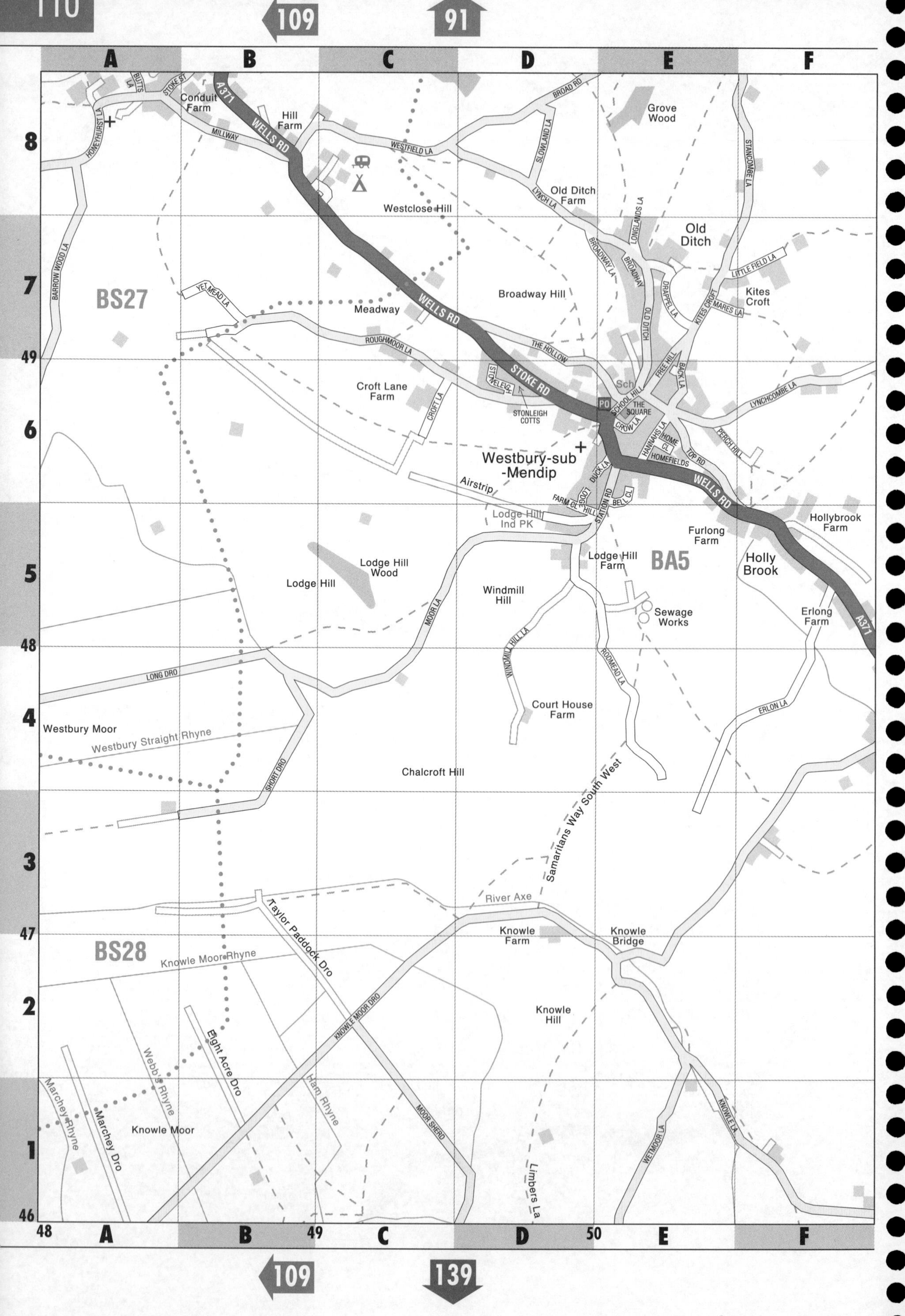

109
139

92
112

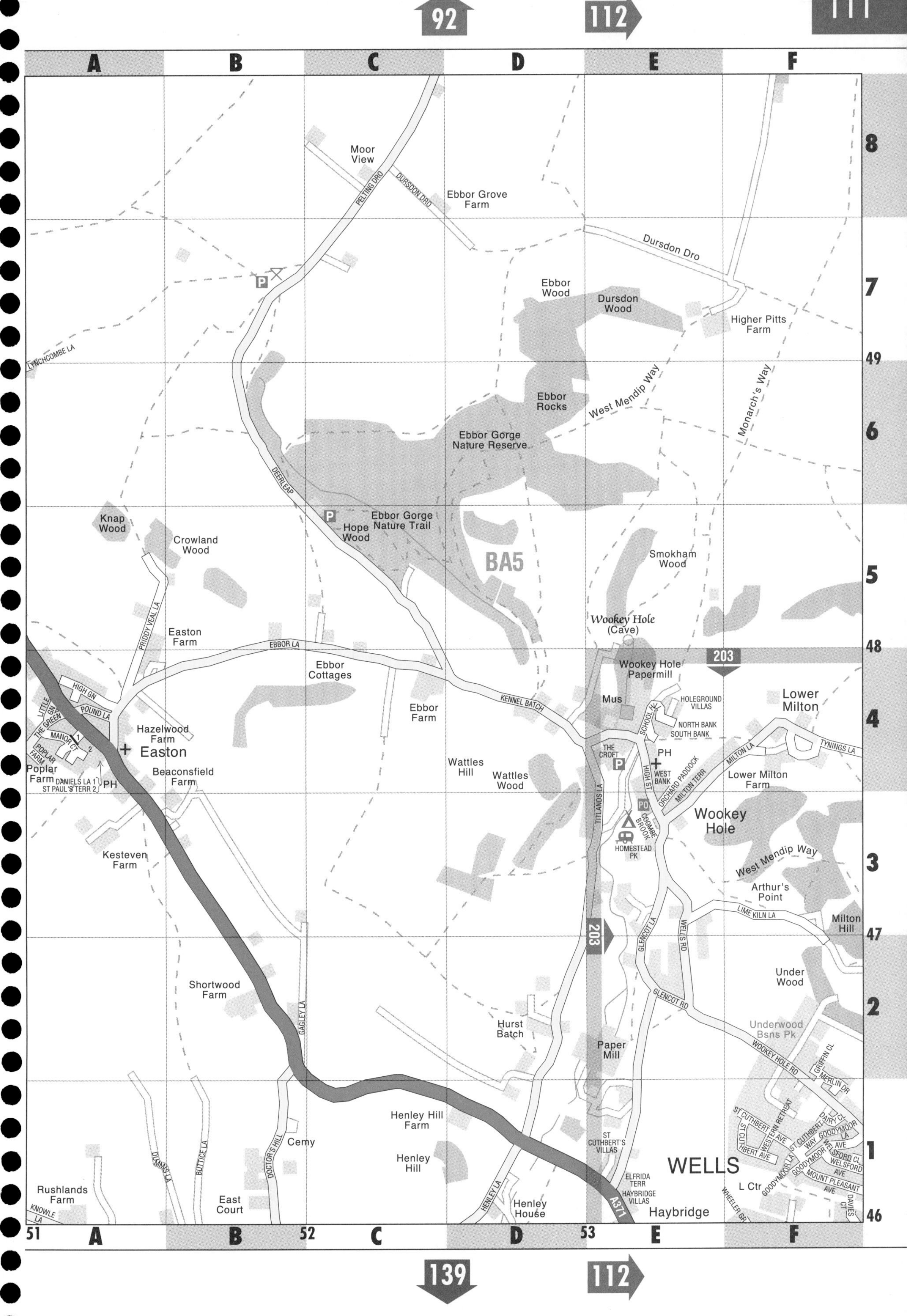

139
112

111
93

111
140

94
114

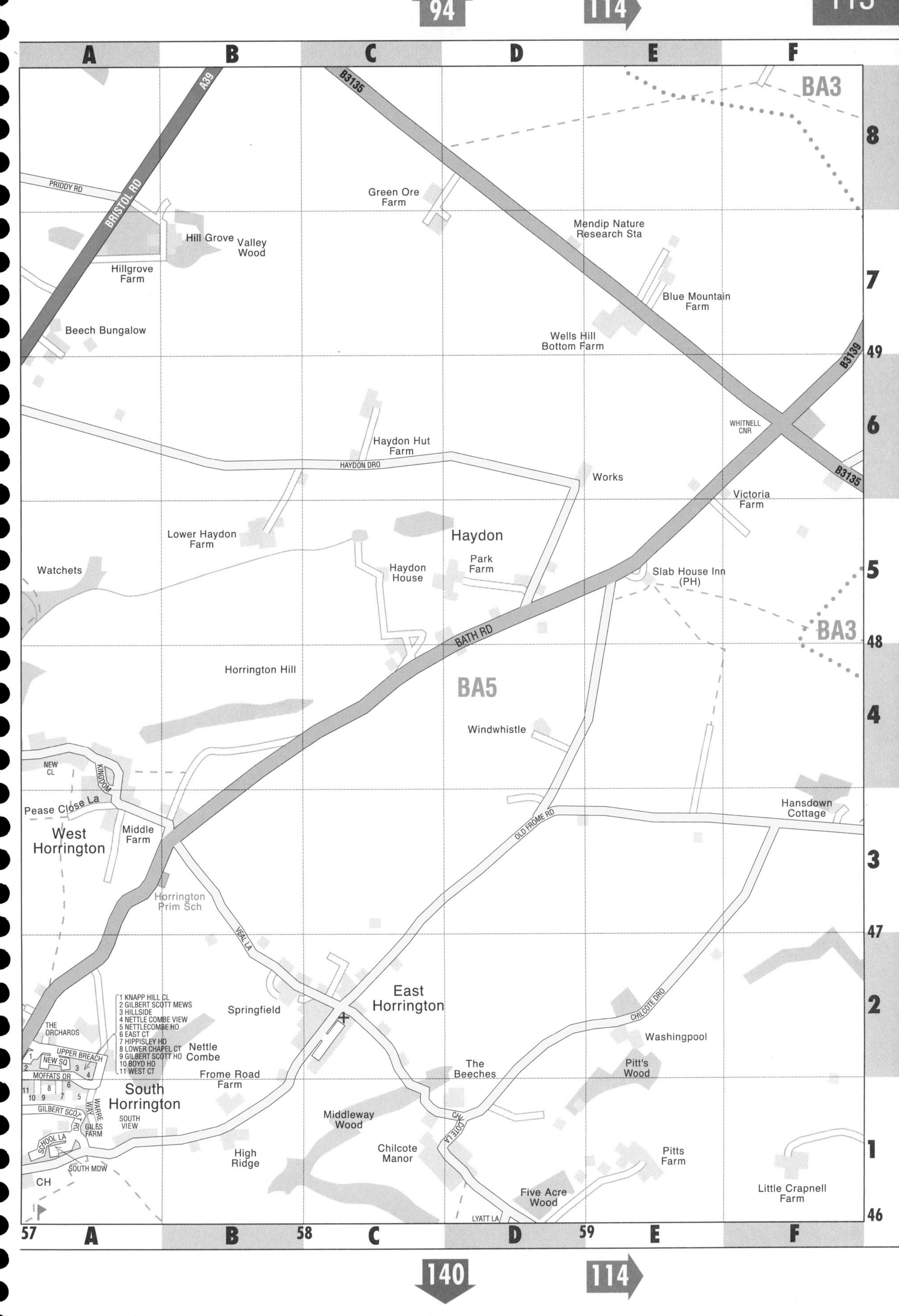

140
114

113
95

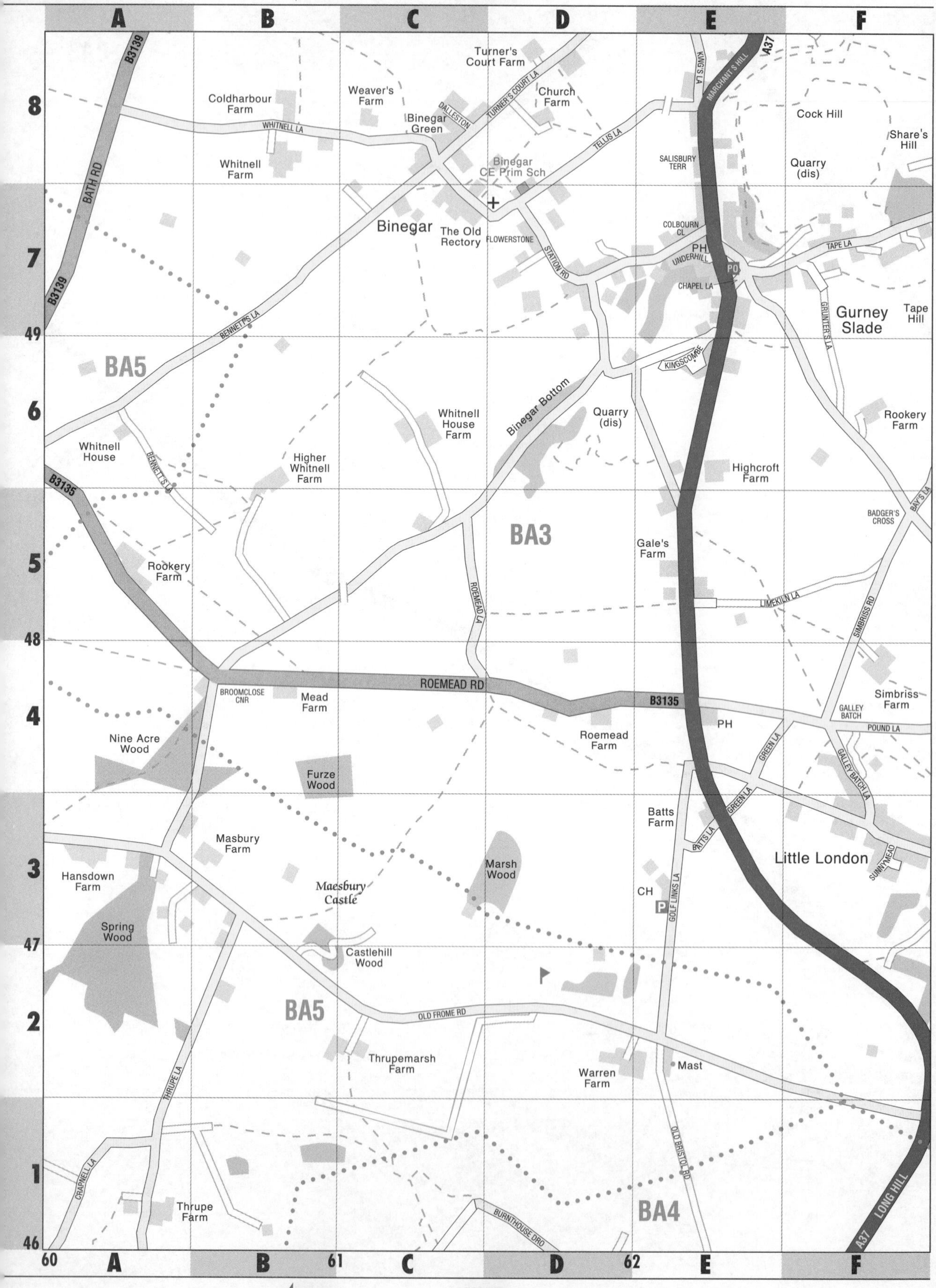

A B C D E F

8
7
49
6
5
48
4
3
47
2
1
46

Turner's Court Farm
Coldharbour Farm
Weaver's Farm
Church Farm
Cock Hill
Binegar Green
Whitnell Farm
Binegar CE Prim Sch
Share's Hill
Quarry (dis)
Binegar
The Old Rectory
Gurney Slade
Tape Hill
BA5
Whitnell House Farm
Quarry (dis)
Rookery Farm
Whitnell House
Higher Whitnell Farm
Highcroft Farm
BA3
Gale's Farm
Rookery Farm
Simbriss Farm
Mead Farm
Roemead Farm
PH
Nine Acre Wood
Furze Wood
Batts Farm
Masbury Farm
Little London
Hansdown Farm
Marsh Wood
Maesbury Castle
CH
Spring Wood
Castlehill Wood
BA5
Thrupemarsh Farm
Warren Farm
Mast
Thrupe Farm
BA4

B3139
BATH RD
WHITNELL LA
DALLESTON
TURNER'S COURT LA
KING'S LA
MARCHANT'S HILL
A37
TELLIS LA
SALISBURY TERR
FLOWERSTONE
STATION RD
COLBOURN CL
PH
UNDERHILL
PO
CHAPEL LA
TAPE LA
GRUNTER'S LA
BENNETT'S LA
KINGSCOMBE
Binegar Bottom
B3135
BAY'S LA
BADGER'S CROSS
ROEMEAD LA
LIMEKILN LA
SIMBRISS RD
BROOMCLOSE CNR
ROEMEAD RD
B3135
GALLEY BATCH
POUND LA
GREEN LA
GALLEY BATCH LA
BATTS LA
SUNNYMEAD
GOLF LINKS LA
P
OLD FROME RD
THRUPE LA
OLD BRISTOL RD
CRAPNELL LA
BURNTHOUSE DRO
LONG HILL
A37

60 61 62

113
141

96
116

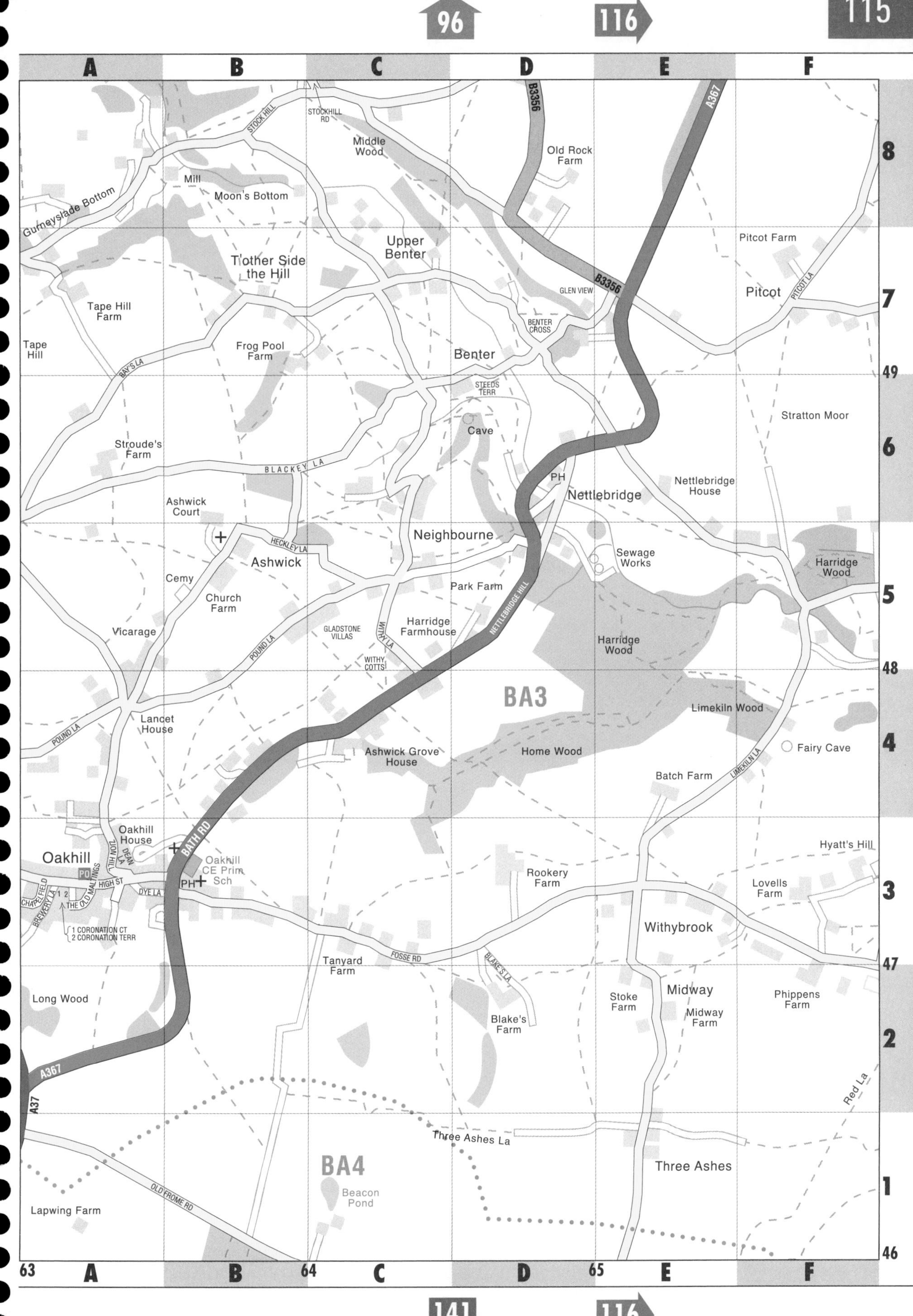

141
116

115 97

A B C D E F

8 7 49 6 5 48 4 3 47 2 1 46

Pitcot La, Barlake Farm, The Ring o' Roses (PH), Stratton Rd, Croft Rd, Charlton Rd, The Mead, Brewery La, Holcombe Manor, Manor Farm, Chapel La, Kingsway, 1 Old Manor Est, 2 Scotts Cl, Holcombe, Kingsmead Cl, Boundary Cl, Longleat La, Longleat Rd, PO, Holcombe Hill, James Cl, Tyning Cotts, Top Wood, Stones Paddock, Woodlands La, Barlake House, Spring Farm, Edford Hill, Edford, Edford Green, Wks, Edford Wood, Duke of Cumberland (PH), Sewage Works, Ham, Ham Hill, Ham Bridge, Ham Farm, Marsh La, Dunsford's Farm, Green La, Moons Hill Farm, Hurdlestone Wood, BA3, Giddy La, Stoke Bottom Farm, Folly Wood, Combe Wood, Frog La, Moons Hill, Rector La, Stoke Lane Slocker Hole, Coalpit La, Stoke St Michael Prim Sch, Moonshill Cotts 1, Steeple View 2, Millennium Cl 3, Tower Cl 4, Moonshill Rd, St Michaels Cl, Tower Hill, Mill La, Portman's Hill, Sweetleaze, Stoke Cres, Field Cl, Moonshill Cl, Stoke Hill, Church St, The Mead, Mead Cl, Susanna's Cross, Cook's Farm, Somer's Farm, Burnt House La, Dark La, Stoke St Michael, Red La, Mendip Rd, East End, Susanna's La, Burge's Hill, Burge's La, Fental La, Mendip Farm, Long Cross Bottom, Moons Hill Quarry, Yellow Marsh Farm, BA4, Kilmersdon Common, Flint House, Common La, Beck's La, Kilmersdon Common Farm, Springer's Hill, Bullock's Hill, Mells Stream, Whitehole Farm, Whitehole Hill, Leigh Wood, Manor House Farm, Chivers Farm, Goldsborough Farm, Grove Shute Farm, Tadhill La, Old Wells Rd, Oakhill Ct, Town's End, Pitten St, Stock's La, Blacker's La, Rope Wlk, Upper Merrifield, Ropewalk Farm, Rush Ash La, Fairfield, Highfield, Highfield View, Merry-Field, Farley Dell, Anchor Rd, Anchor Cl, Coal Barton, Bishop Henderson CE Prim Sch, Mendip Vale, Beacon View, Crossways, Highbury Cotts, Harris Vale, Mendip View, P, Highbury St, Careys Mead, Preachers Vale, Douglas Yates Ct, Lawrence Rd, Church St, Lydford Farm, Roman Way, Coleford, Church La, Wesley Villas 1, Barton Villas 2, Rock Terr 3, Rose & Crown Cotts, The Green, Hippys Farm, High St, Packsaddle Bridge, Manor Farm, Sparks Farm, Leigh St, Park Hayes, Leigh upon Mendip, Tadhill, Tadhill Farm, Tadhill House Farm, Luxton's La, BA4

66 A B 67 C D 68 E F

115 142

98
118

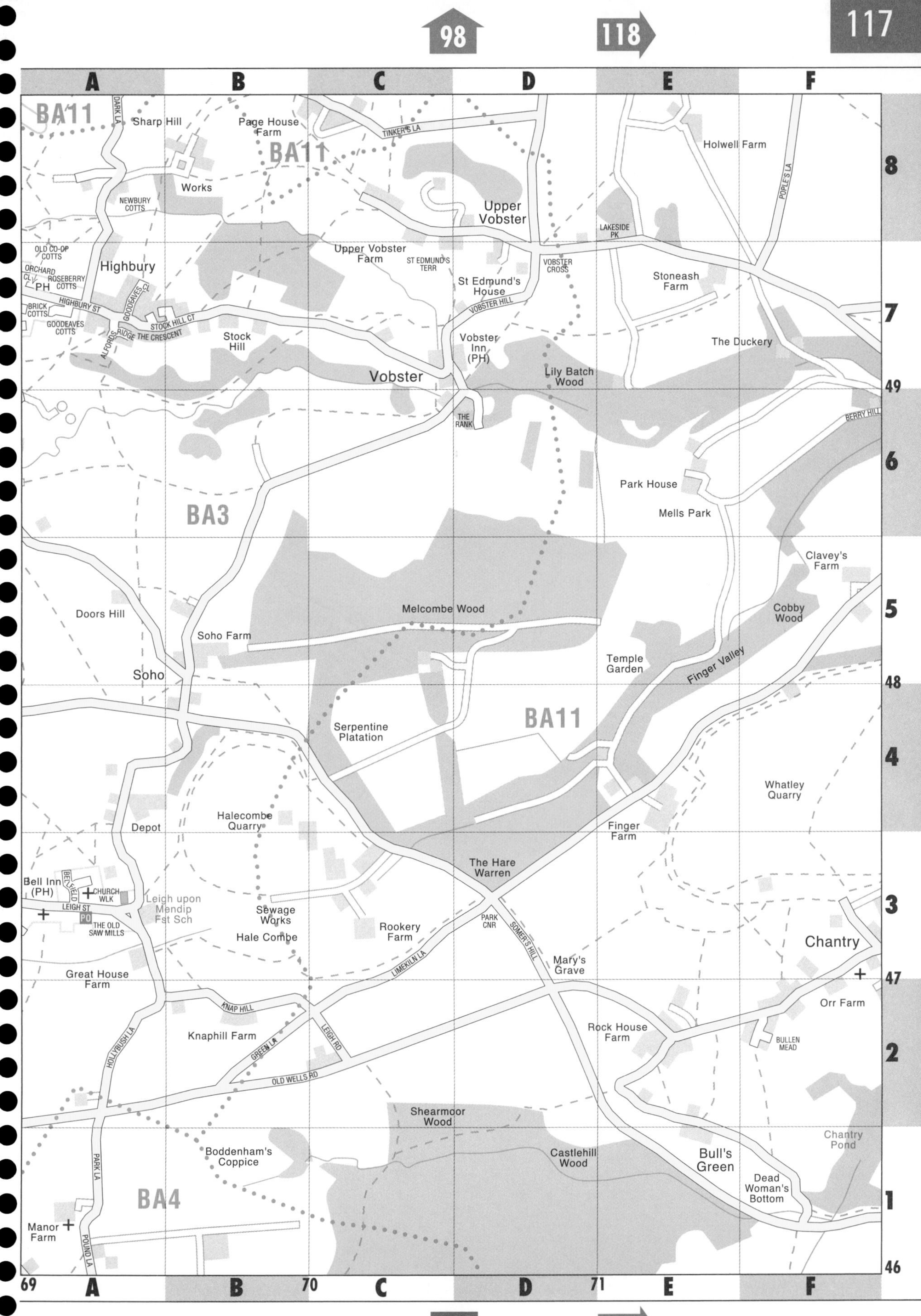

142
118

117
99

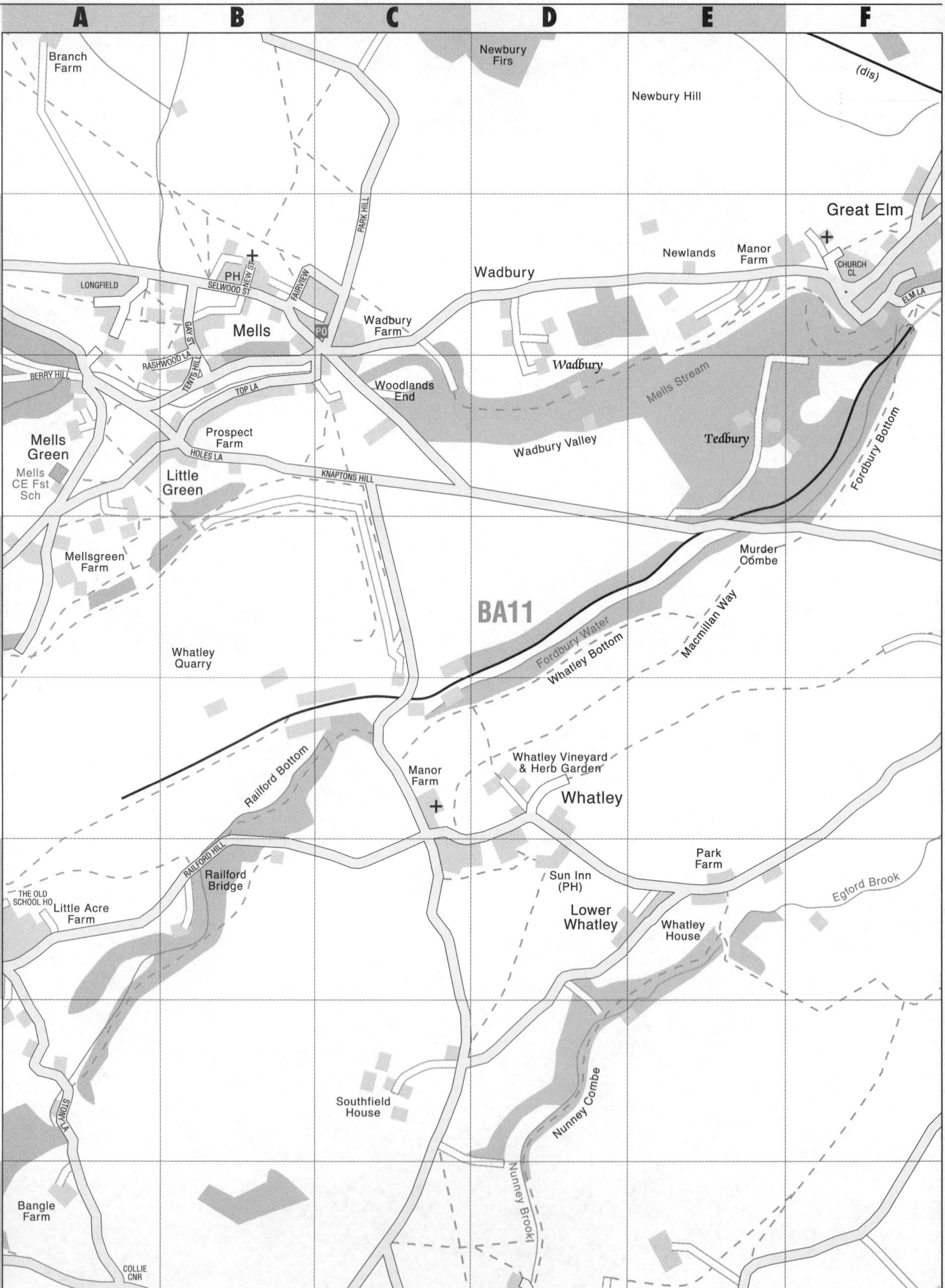

117
143

100
120

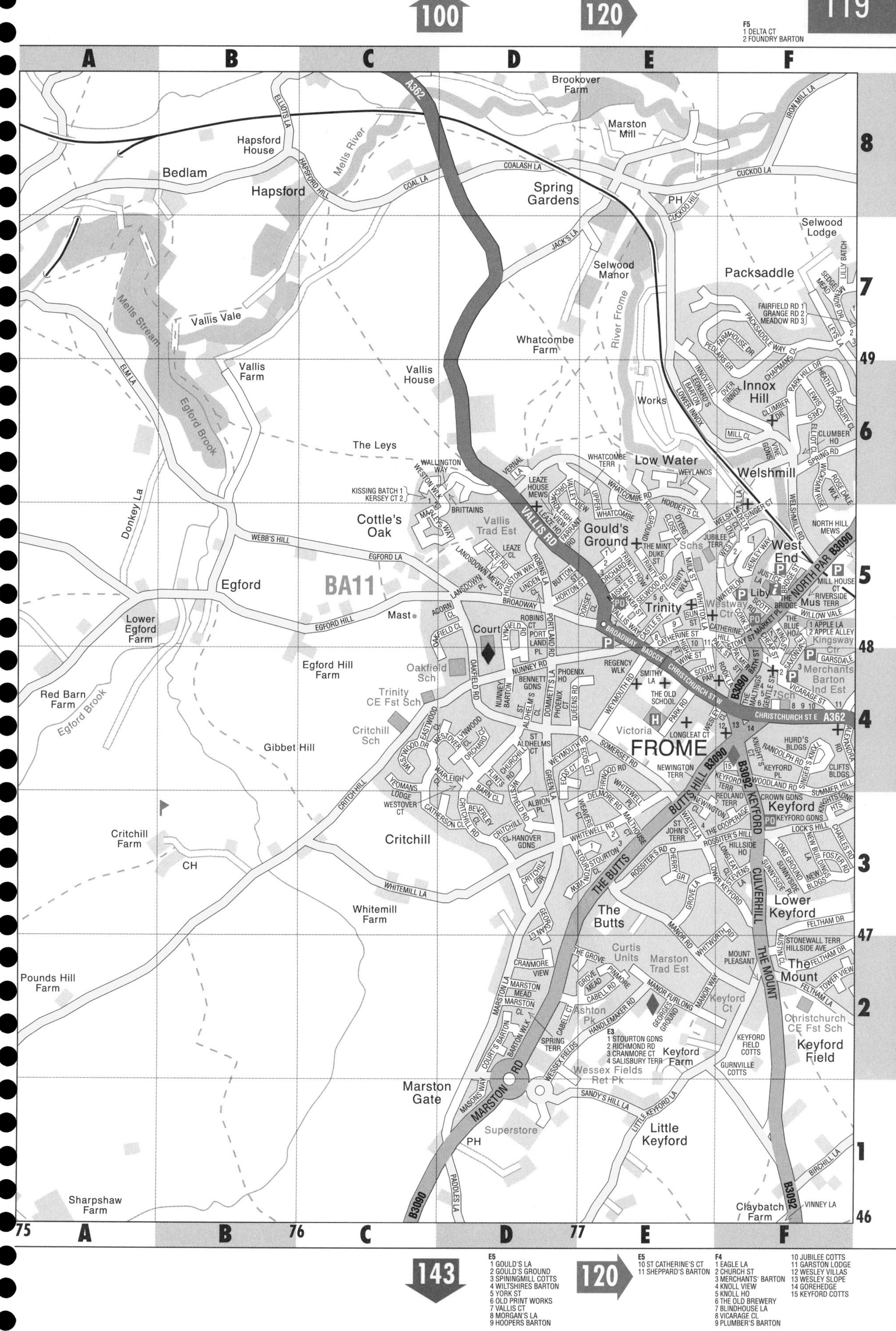

143
120

119
101

A B C D E F

8
7
49
6
5
48
4
3
47
2
1
46

78 A B 79 C D 80 E F

119
144

102

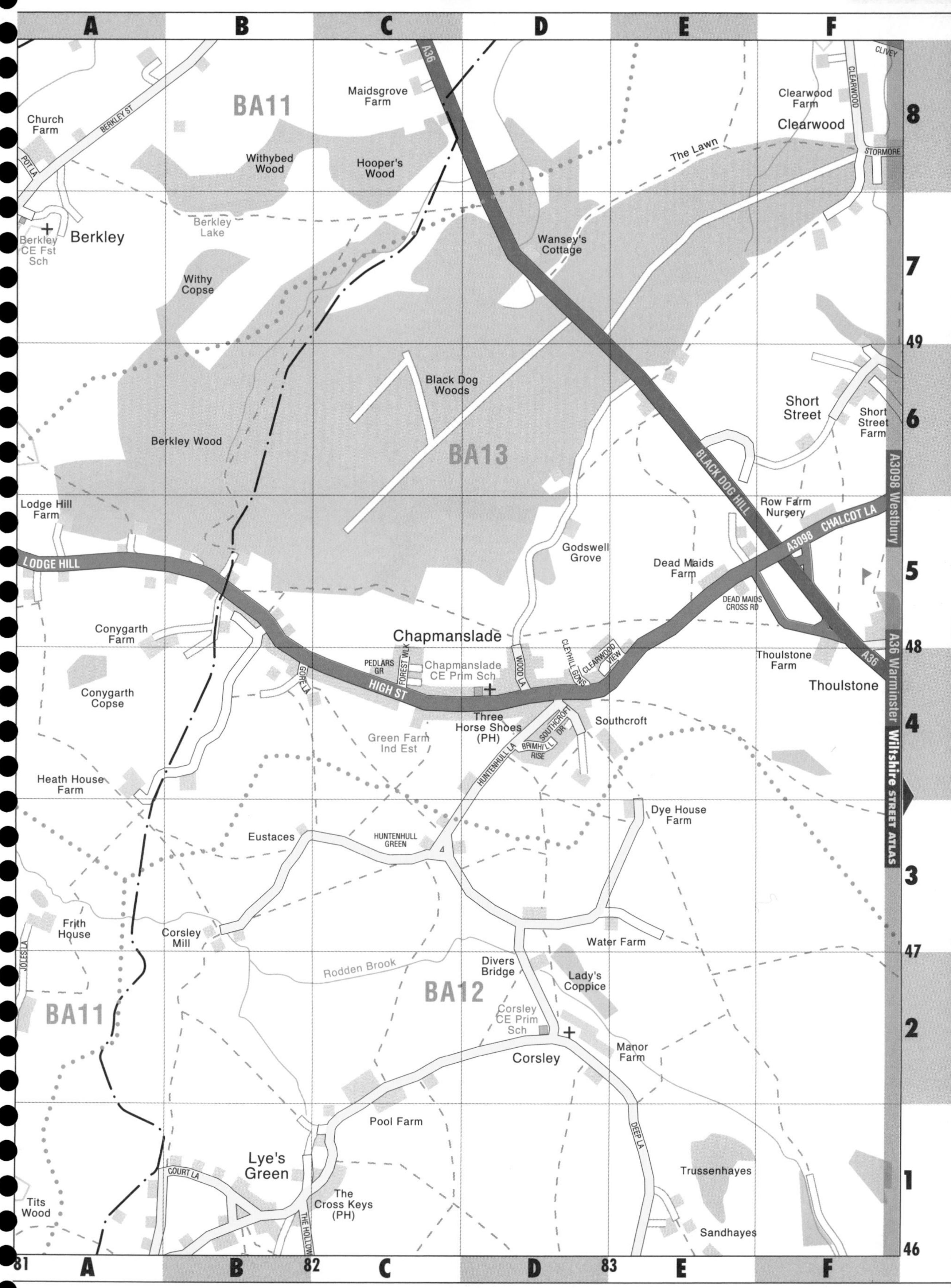
BA11
Maidsgrove Farm
Church Farm
Withybed Wood
Hooper's Wood
Clearwood Farm
Clearwood
The Lawn
Berkley
Berkley CE Fst Sch
Berkley Lake
Withy Copse
Wansey's Cottage
Black Dog Woods
BA13
Berkley Wood
Short Street
Short Street Farm
Lodge Hill Farm
LODGE HILL
Godswell Grove
Dead Maids Farm
Row Farm Nursery
BLACK DOG HILL
A3098 CHALCOT LA
DEAD MAIDS CROSS RD
Conygarth Farm
Chapmanslade
Chapmanslade CE Prim Sch
HIGH ST
Thoulstone Farm
Thoulstone
Conygarth Copse
Three Horse Shoes (PH)
Southcroft
Green Farm Ind Est
Heath House Farm
Dye House Farm
Eustaces
HUNTENHULL GREEN
Frith House
Corsley Mill
Water Farm
Rodden Brook
Divers Bridge
Lady's Coppice
BA12
BA11
Corsley CE Prim Sch
Corsley
Manor Farm
Pool Farm
Lye's Green
COURT LA
The Cross Keys (PH)
Trussenhayes
Tits Wood
Sandhayes
DEEP LA
THE HOLLOW
A3098 Westbury
A36 Warminster
Wiltshire STREET ATLAS

144

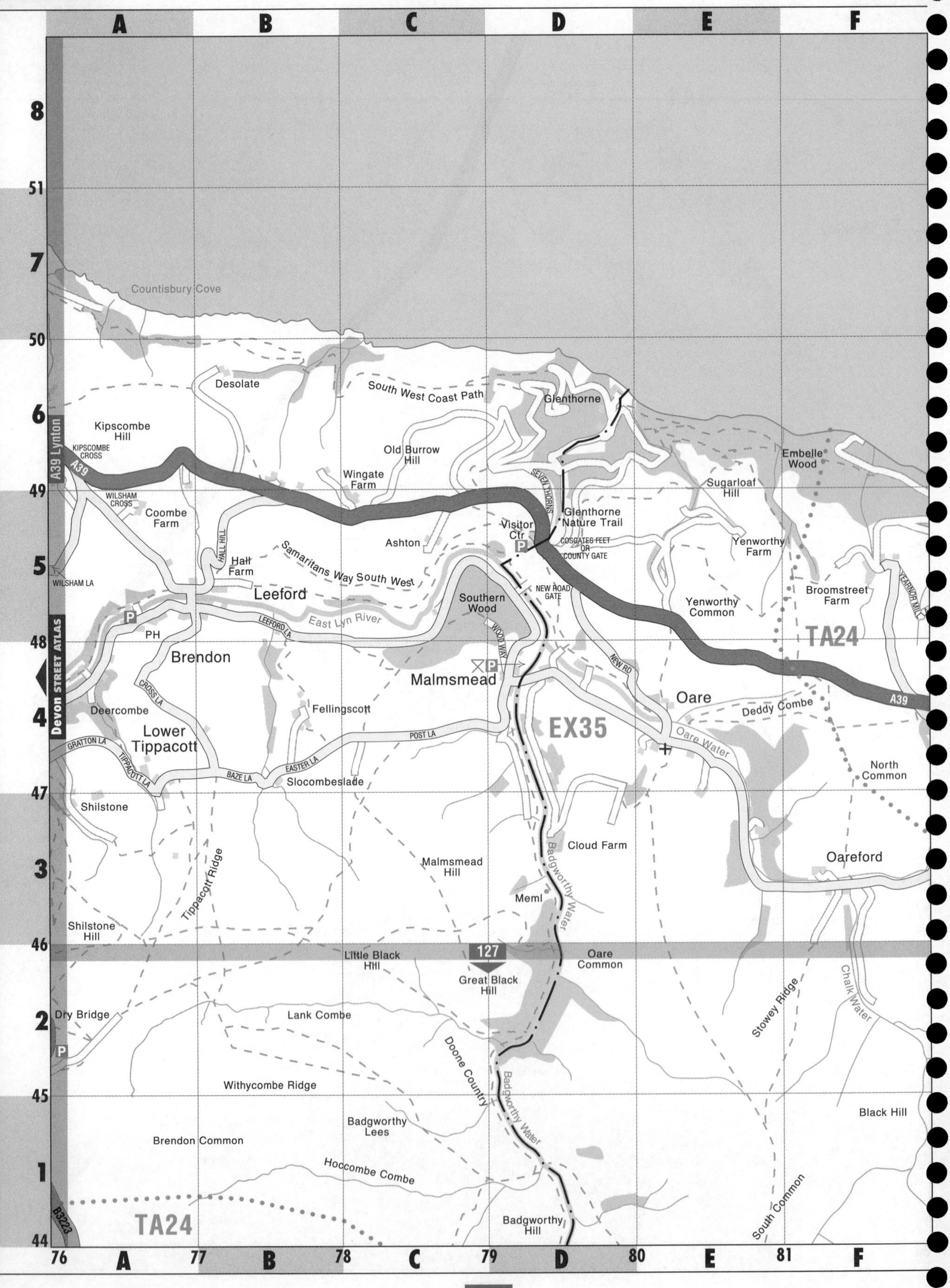
Scale: 1¾ inches to 1 mile
0 ¼ ½ mile
0 250m 500m 750m 1 km
A B C D E F
8
51
7
50
6
49
5
48
4
47
3
46
2
45
1
44
76 77 78 79 80 81
Countisbury Cove
Desolate
South West Coast Path
Glenthorne
Kipscombe Hill
KIPSCOMBE CROSS
A39 Lynton
A39
Old Burrow Hill
Wingate Farm
Embelle Wood
Sugarloaf Hill
WILSHAM CROSS
Coombe Farm
SEVEN THORNS
Glenthorne Nature Trail
Visitor Ctr
Ashton
COSGATES FEET OR COUNTY GATE
Yenworthy Farm
HALL HILL
Hall Farm
Samaritans Way South West
WILSHAM LA
NEW ROAD GATE
Southern Wood
Yenworthy Common
Broomstreet Farm
YEARNOR MILL
Leeford
LEEFORD LA
East Lyn River
WOOD WAY
TA24
PH
Brendon
NEW RD
Malmsmead
Devon STREET ATLAS
CROSS LA
Oare
Deddy Combe
A39
Deercombe
Fellingscott
EX35
Lower Tippacott
GRATTON LA
TIPPACOTT LA
POST LA
Oare Water
North Common
BAZE LA
EASTER LA
Slocombeslade
Shilstone
Cloud Farm
Malmsmead Hill
Badgworthy Water
Oareford
Tippacott Ridge
Meml
Shilstone Hill
Little Black Hill
127
Oare Common
Great Black Hill
Stowey Ridge
Chalk Water
Dry Bridge
Lank Combe
Doone Country
Withycombe Ridge
Badgworthy Water
Black Hill
Badgworthy Lees
Brendon Common
Hoccombe Combe
South Common
B3223
TA24
Badgworthy Hill

127

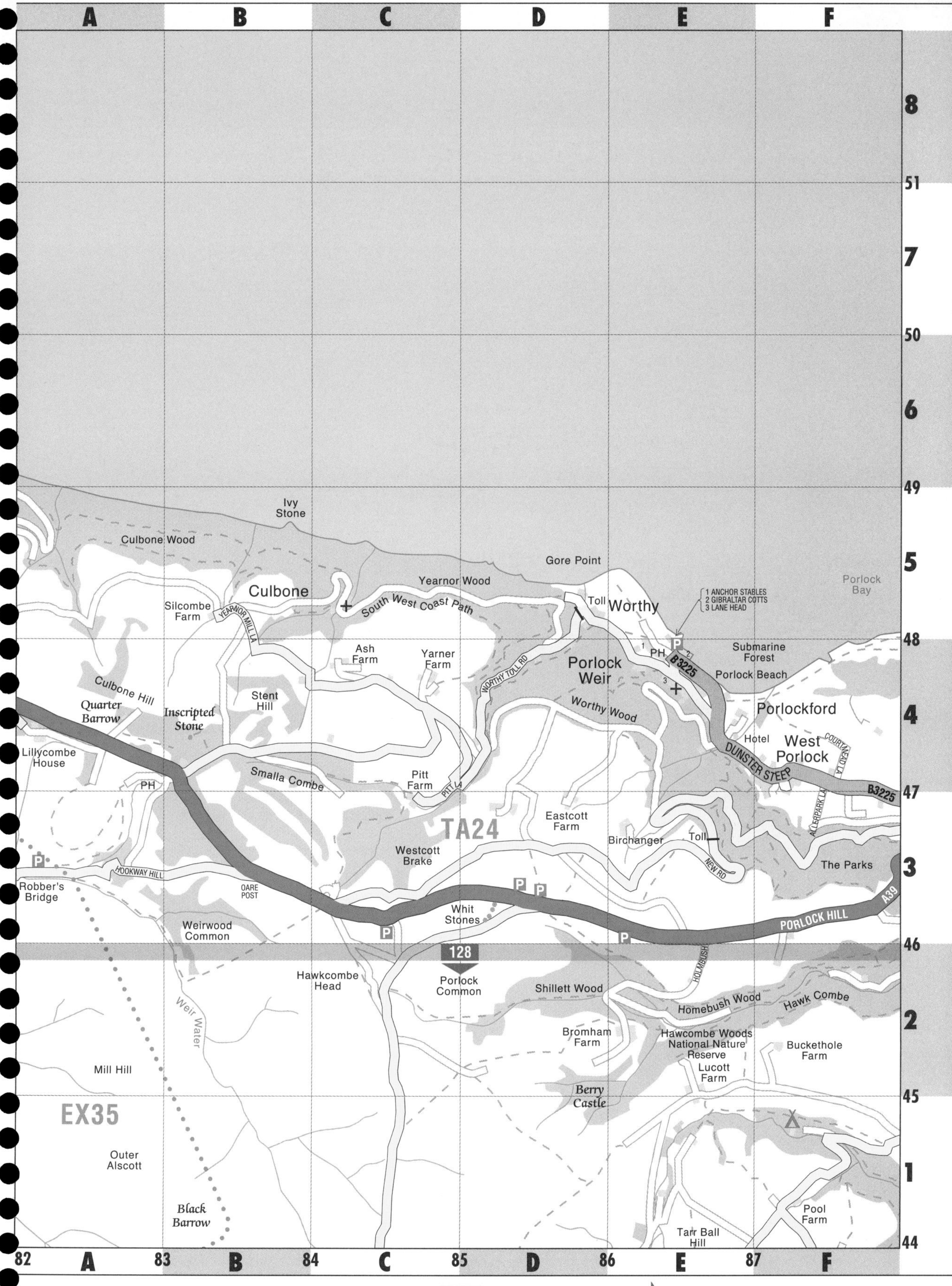
Scale: 1¾ inches to 1 mile
0 ¼ ½ mile
0 250m 500m 750m 1 km
124
Ivy Stone
Culbone Wood
Gore Point
Culbone
Yearnor Wood
Porlock Bay
Silcombe Farm
YEARNOR MILL LA
South West Coast Path
Toll
Worthy
1 ANCHOR STABLES
2 GIBRALTAR COTTS
3 LANE HEAD
Ash Farm
Yarner Farm
WORTHY TOLL RD
Porlock Weir
PH
B3225
Submarine Forest
Porlock Beach
Culbone Hill
Quarter Barrow
Inscripted Stone
Stent Hill
Worthy Wood
Porlockford
Lillycombe House
Hotel
West Porlock
COURTMEAD LA
DUNSTER STEEP
PH
Smalla Combe
Pitt Farm
PITT LA
B3225
ALLERPARK LA
TA24
Eastcott Farm
Birchanger
Toll
Westcott Brake
NEW RD
The Parks
Robber's Bridge
HOOKWAY HILL
OARE POST
A39
Whit Stones
PORLOCK HILL
Weirwood Common
128
HOLMBUSH
Hawkcombe Head
Porlock Common
Shillett Wood
Homebush Wood
Hawk Combe
Weir Water
Bromham Farm
Hawcombe Woods National Nature Reserve
Buckethole Farm
Mill Hill
Lucott Farm
Berry Castle
EX35
Outer Alscott
Black Barrow
Pool Farm
Tarr Ball Hill
A B C D E F
8 51 7 50 6 49 5 48 4 47 3 46 2 45 1 44
82 83 84 85 86 87

128
124

123

Scale: 1¾ inches to 1 mile

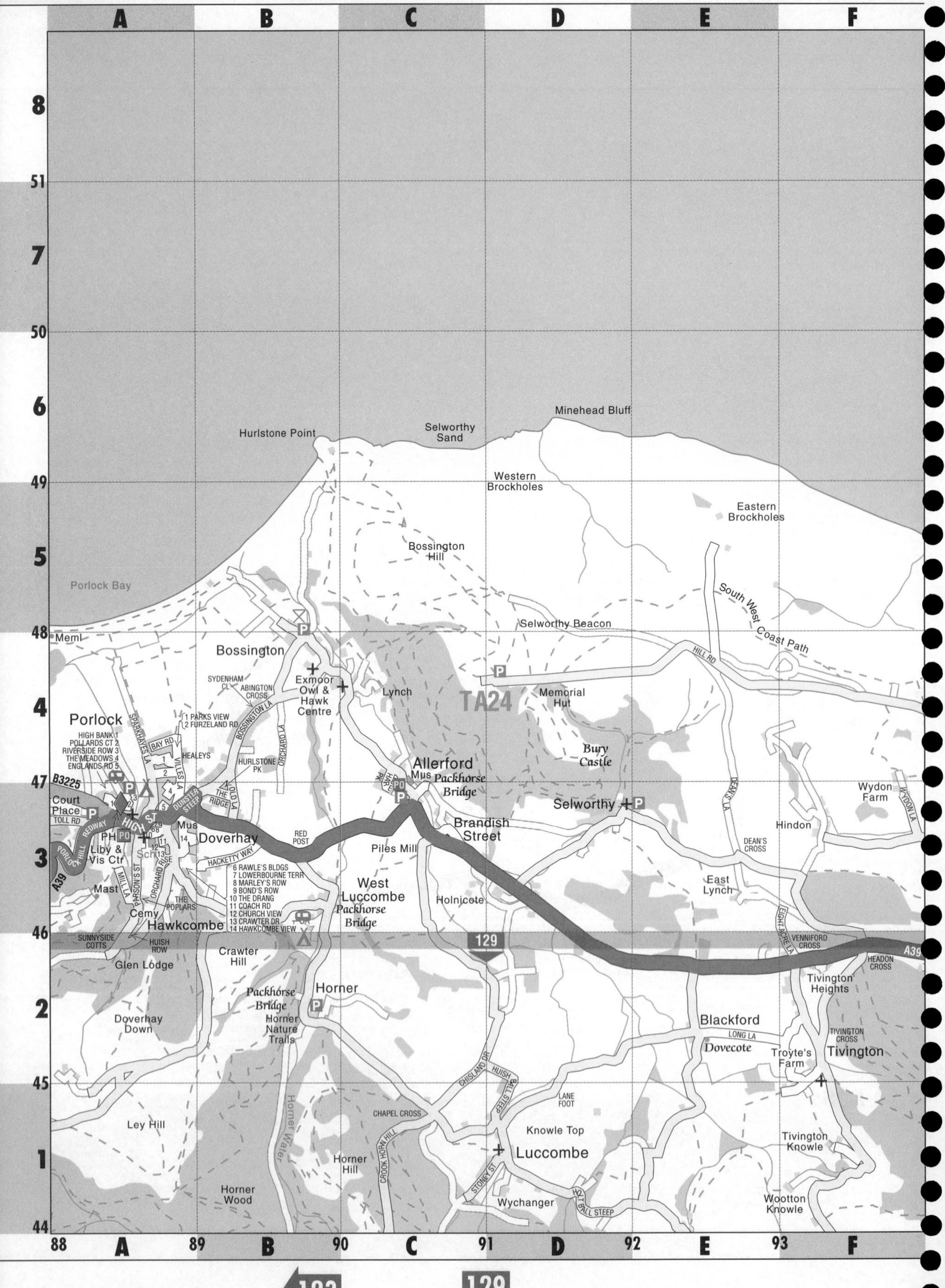

123

129

Scale: 1¾ inches to 1 mile
0 ¼ ½ mile
0 250m 500m 750m 1 km

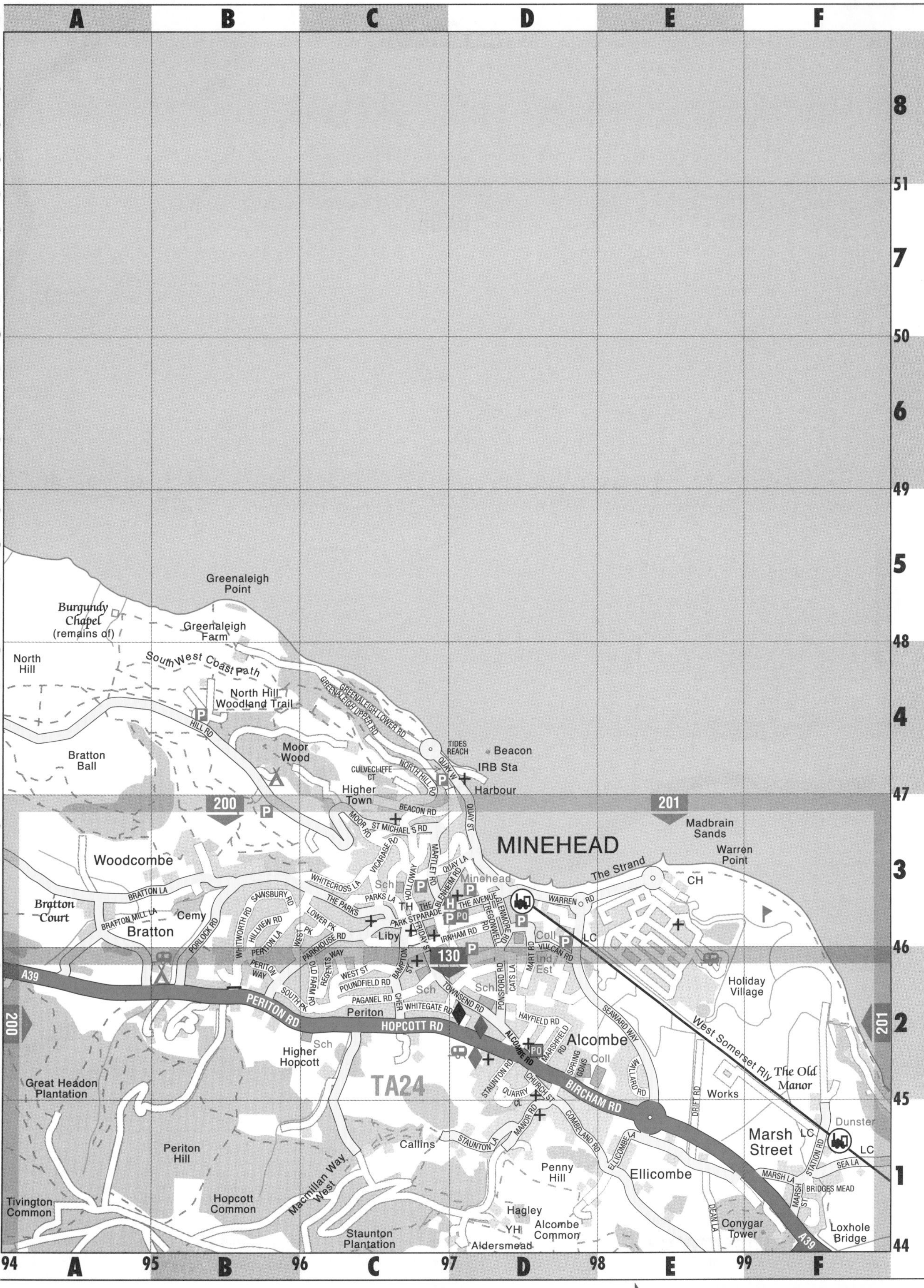
A B C D E F
8
51
7
50
6
49
5
48
4
47
3
46
2
45
1
44
94 95 96 97 98 99
Greenaleigh Point
Burgundy Chapel (remains of)
Greenaleigh Farm
North Hill
South West Coast Path
North Hill Woodland Trail
Bratton Ball
Moor Wood
TIDES REACH
Beacon
IRB Sta
Harbour
Higher Town
200
201
Madbrain Sands
Warren Point
MINEHEAD
The Strand
Woodcombe
Bratton Court
Bratton
Cemy
Minehead
CH
Liby
TH
Sch
Coll
Ind Est
LC
Holiday Village
130
Periton
Higher Hopcott
Alcombe
West Somerset Rly
The Old Manor
Great Headon Plantation
TA24
Works
Dunster
Marsh Street
Periton Hill
Callins
Penny Hill
Ellicombe
Tivington Common
Hopcott Common
Macmillan Way West
Hagley
YH
Alcombe Common
Conygar Tower
Loxhole Bridge
Staunton Plantation
Aldersmead
A39
PERITON RD
HOPCOTT RD
BIRCHAM RD
HILL RD
BRATTON LA
BRATTON MILL LA
PORLOCK RD
WHITECROSS LA
THE PARKS
PARKS LA
WARREN RD
THE AVENUE
SEAWARD WAY
MARSH LA
SEA LA
BRIDGES MEAD
STATION RD
DRIFT RD
DEAN LA
ELLICOMBE LA
COMBELAND RD
STAUNTON LA
MANOR RD
CHURCH ST
QUARRY CL
STAUNTON RD
ALCOMBE RD
MARSHFIELD RD
SPRING GDNS
HAYFIELD RD
MALLARD RD
TOWNSEND RD
WHITEGATE RD
PAGANEL RD
POUNDFIELD RD
WEST ST
OLD FARM RD
REGENTS WAY
PARKHOUSE RD
LOWER PK
WEST PK
SOUTH PK
PERITON WAY
PERITON LA
HILLVIEW RD
WHITWORTH RD
SAINSBURY RD
VICARAGE RD
MOOR RD
ST MICHAEL'S RD
BEACON RD
CULVECLIFFE CT
NORTH HILL RD
QUAY W
QUAY ST
QUAY LA
MARTLET RD
HOLLOWAY
BLENHEIM RD
GLENMORE RD
TREGONWELL RD
IRNHAM RD
PARK ST
THE PARADE
FRIDAY ST
BAMPTON ST
CHER
PONSFORD RD
CATS LA
MART RD
VULCAN RD
GREENALEIGH LOWER RD
GREENALEIGH UPPER RD

130
131
For full street detail of the highlighted areas see pages 200 and 201.

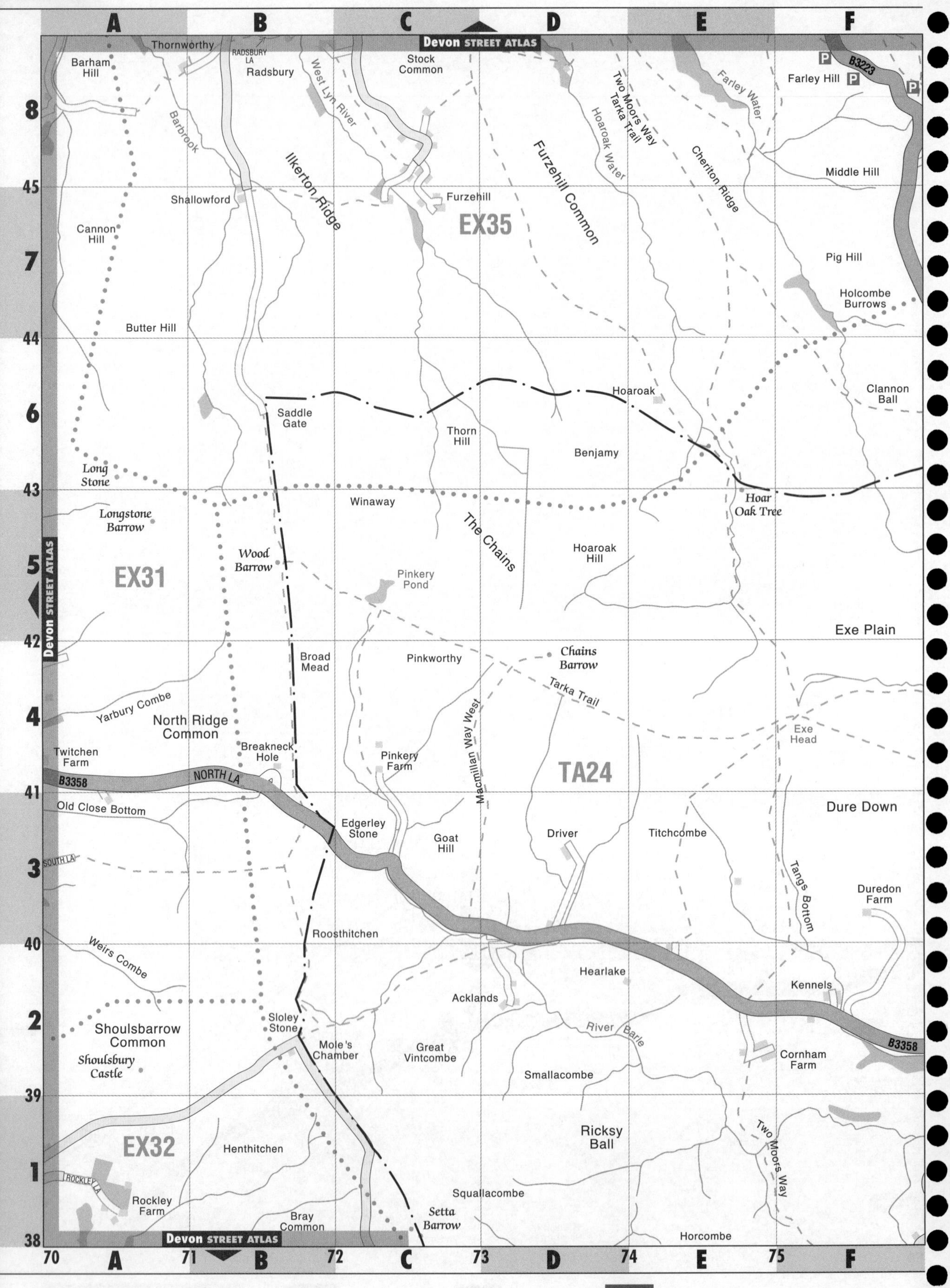
Scale: 1¾ inches to 1 mile
0 ¼ ½ mile
0 250m 500m 750m 1 km
Devon STREET ATLAS
Thornworthy
Barham Hill
Radsbury
Stock Common
West Lyn River
Two Moors Way Tarka Trail
Farley Water
Farley Hill
B3223
Barbrook
Hoaroak Water
Furzehill Common
Cheriton Ridge
Ilkerton Ridge
Middle Hill
Shallowford
Furzehill
EX35
Cannon Hill
Pig Hill
Holcombe Burrows
Butter Hill
Clannon Ball
Hoaroak
Saddle Gate
Thorn Hill
Benjamy
Long Stone
Hoar Oak Tree
Winaway
Longstone Barrow
The Chains
Wood Barrow
Hoaroak Hill
EX31
Pinkery Pond
Exe Plain
Broad Mead
Pinkworthy
Chains Barrow
Tarka Trail
Yarbury Combe
North Ridge Common
Exe Head
Twitchen Farm
Breakneck Hole
Pinkery Farm
Macmillan Way West
TA24
B3358
NORTH LA
Old Close Bottom
Edgerley Stone
Dure Down
Goat Hill
Driver
Titchcombe
SOUTH LA
Tangs Bottom
Duredon Farm
Roosthitchen
Weirs Combe
Hearlake
Kennels
Acklands
Shoulsbarrow Common
Sloley Stone
River Barle
Mole's Chamber
Great Vintcombe
Cornham Farm
Shoulsbury Castle
Smallacombe
Ricksy Ball
Two Moors Way
EX32
Henthitchen
ROCKLEY LA
Rockley Farm
Squallacombe
Bray Common
Setta Barrow
Horcombe
Devon STREET ATLAS
A B C D E F
70 71 72 73 74 75
8 45 7 44 6 43 5 42 4 41 3 40 2 39 1 38

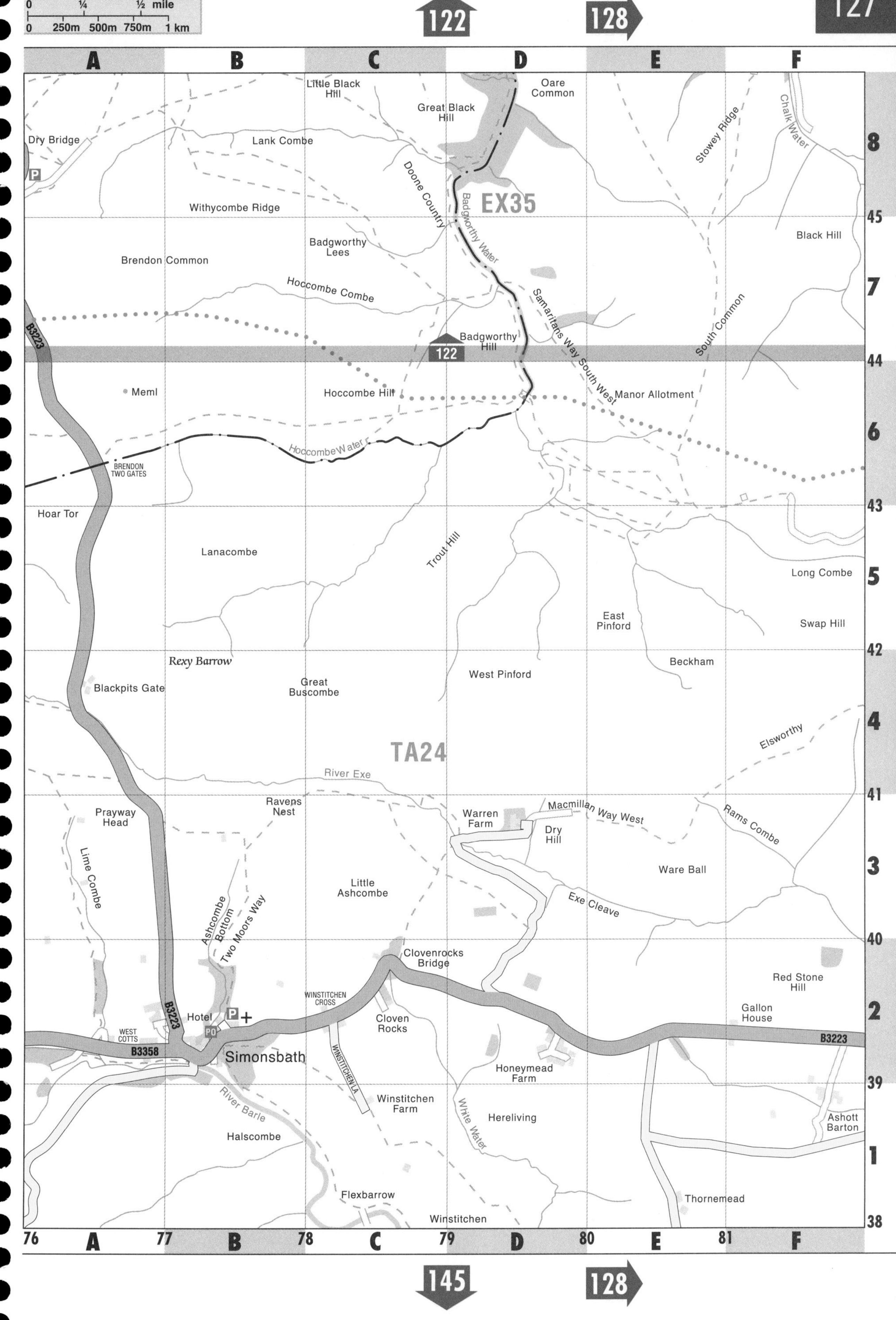
Scale: 1¾ inches to 1 mile
0 ¼ ½ mile
0 250m 500m 750m 1 km
122
128
A B C D E F
Little Black Hill
Oare Common
Great Black Hill
Dry Bridge
Lank Combe
Stowey Ridge
Chalk Water
Doone Country
EX35
Badgworthy Water
Withycombe Ridge
Black Hill
Badgworthy Lees
Brendon Common
Hoccombe Combe
Samaritans Way South West
South Common
B3223
Badgworthy Hill
Meml
Hoccombe Hill
Manor Allotment
Hoccombe Water
BRENDON TWO GATES
Hoar Tor
Lanacombe
Trout Hill
Long Combe
East Pinford
Swap Hill
Rexy Barrow
Beckham
West Pinford
Blackpits Gate
Great Buscombe
Elsworthy
TA24
River Exe
Prayway Head
Ravens Nest
Warren Farm
Macmillan Way West
Dry Hill
Rams Combe
Lime Combe
Little Ashcombe
Ware Ball
Ashcombe Bottom
Two Moors Way
Exe Cleave
Clovenrocks Bridge
Red Stone Hill
WINSTITCHEN CROSS
Gallon House
Hotel
Cloven Rocks
WEST COTTS
PO
B3358
Simonsbath
Honeymead Farm
WINSTITCHEN LA
River Barle
Winstitchen Farm
White Water
Hereliving
Ashott Barton
Halscombe
Flexbarrow
Thornemead
Winstitchen
8 45 7 44 6 43 5 42 4 41 3 40 2 39 1 38
76 77 78 79 80 81
145

127

Scale: 1¾ inches to 1 mile

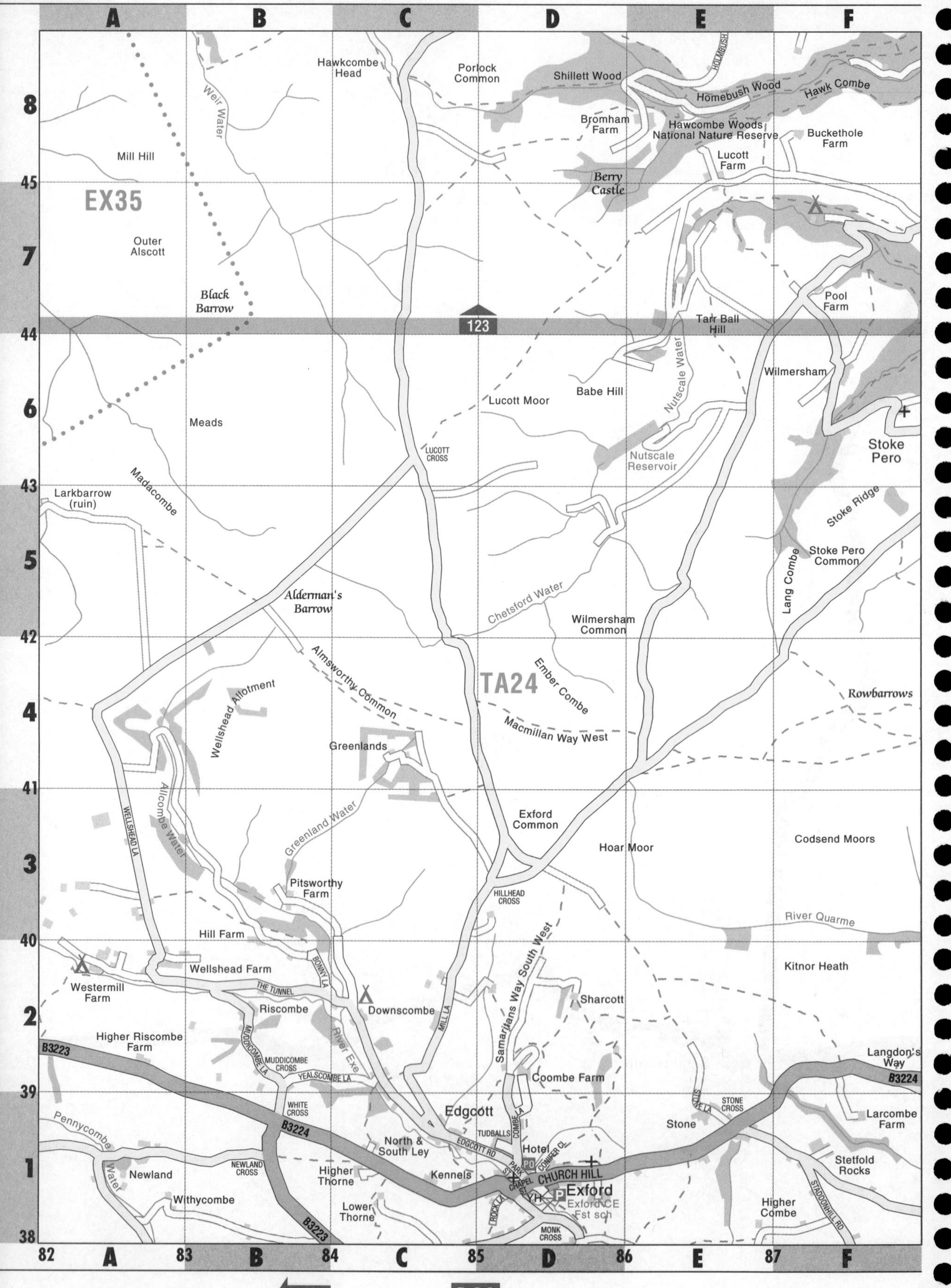

127

146

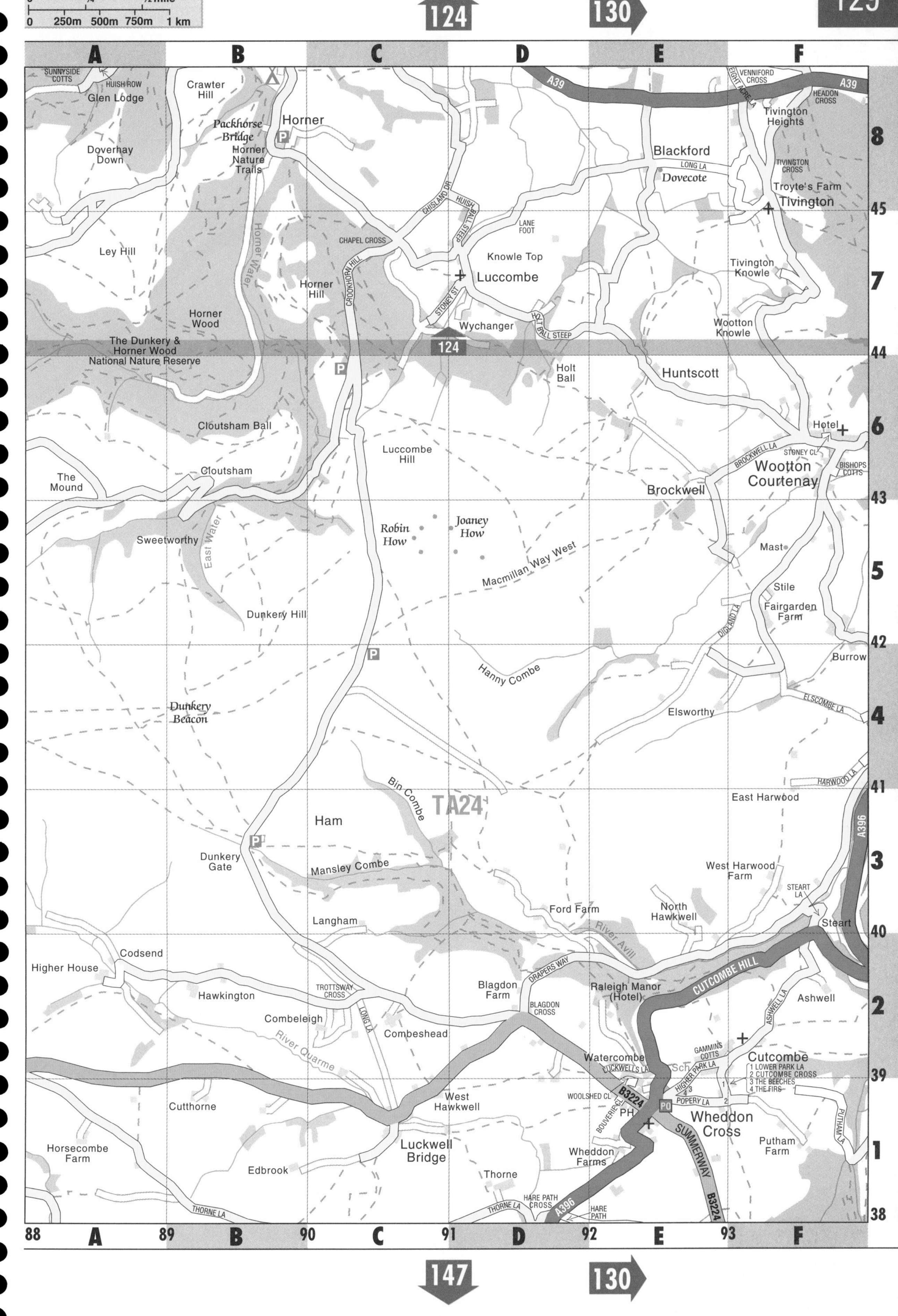
Scale: 1¾ inches to 1 mile
0 ¼ ½ mile
0 250m 500m 750m 1 km
124
130
A B C D E F
Sunnyside Cotts
Huish Row
Glen Lodge
Crawter Hill
Packhorse Bridge
Horner
Horner Nature Trails
Doverhay Down
Ley Hill
Horner Water
Horner Hill
Horner Wood
The Dunkery & Horner Wood National Nature Reserve
Chapel Cross
Crookhorn Hill
Chisland Dr
Huish Ball Steep
Luccombe
Knowle Top
Lane Foot
Stoney St
Wychanger
Holt Ball Steep
A39
Venniford Cross
Eight Acre La
Headon Cross
Tivington Heights
Blackford
Long La
Dovecote
Tivington Cross
Troyte's Farm
Tivington
Tivington Knowle
Wootton Knowle
Holt Ball
Huntscott
Hotel
Brockwell La
Stoney Cl
Wootton Courtenay
Bishops Cotts
Brockwell
Cloutsham Ball
Luccombe Hill
The Mound
Cloutsham
Sweetworthy
East Water
Robin How
Joaney How
Macmillan Way West
Mast
Stile
Fairgarden Farm
Dunkery Hill
Digland La
Burrow
Hanny Combe
Elscombe La
Dunkery Beacon
Elsworthy
Harwood La
Bin Combe
TA24
East Harwood
Ham
A396
Dunkery Gate
Mansley Combe
West Harwood Farm
Steart La
Langham
Ford Farm
North Hawkwell
Steart
River Avill
Cutcombe Hill
Codsend
Higher House
Drapers Way
Raleigh Manor (Hotel)
Trottsway Cross
Blagdon Farm
Ashwell
Hawkington
Blagdon Cross
Ashwell La
Combeleigh
Long La
Combeshead
Gammins Cotts
River Quarme
Watercombe
Luckwells La
Sch
Higher Park La
Cutcombe
1 Lower Park La
2 Cutcombe Cross
3 The Beeches
4 The Firs
Woolshed Cl
B3224
Popery La
PO
West Hawkwell
Cutthorne
Bouverie Cl
PH
Wheddon Cross
Putham La
Summerway
Horsecombe Farm
Luckwell Bridge
Putham Farm
Wheddon Farms
Edbrook
Thorne
Thorne La
Hare Path Cross
Hare Path
88 89 90 91 92 93
45 44 43 42 41 40 39 38
8 7 6 5 4 3 2 1
147

129
125

Scale: 1¾ inches to 1 mile
0 ¼ ½ mile
0 250m 500m 750m 1 km

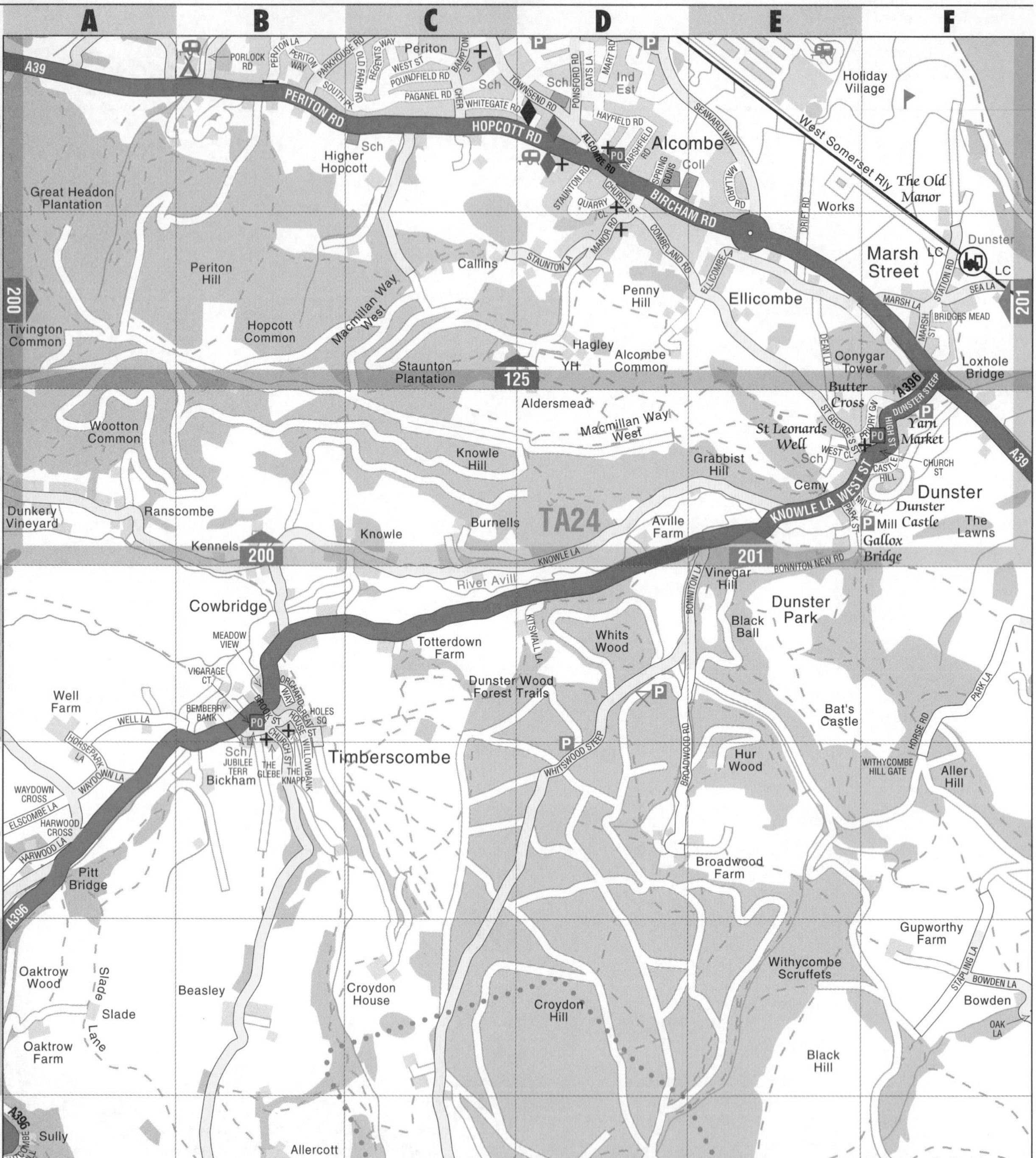

A B C D E F

8
45
7
44
6
43
5
42
4
41
3
40
2
39
1
38

A39
PORLOCK RD
PERITON LA
PERITON WAY
PARKHOUSE RD
OLD FARM RD
REGENTS WAY
Periton
WEST ST
POUNDFIELD RD
BAMPTON ST
PAGANEL RD
SOUTH PK
CHER
WHITEGATE RD
TOWNSEND RD
Sch
PONSFORD RD
CATS LA
MARY RD
Ind Est
HAYFIELD RD
SEAWARD WAY
Holiday Village
PERITON RD
HOPCOTT RD
Higher Hopcott
ALCOMBE RD
MARSHFIELD RD
Alcombe
Coll
SPRING GDNS
STAUNTON RD
QUARRY CL
CHURCH ST
BIRCHAM RD
WALLARD RD
West Somerset Rly
The Old Manor
DRIFT RD
Works
Great Headon Plantation
Periton Hill
Callins
STAUNTON LA
MANOR RD
COMBELAND RD
ELLICOMBE LA
Marsh Street
LC
Dunster
STATION RD
SEA LA
Ellicombe
MARSH LA
MARSH ST
BRIDGES MEAD
Penny Hill
Tivington Common
Hopcott Common
Macmillan Way West
Hagley
YH
Alcombe Common
DEAN LA
Conygar Tower
Loxhole Bridge
Staunton Plantation
Butter Cross
A396
DUNSTER STEEP
Aldersmead
Wootton Common
Macmillan Way West
St Leonards Well
ST GEORGE'S ST
PRIORY GN
HIGH ST
Yarn Market
PO
Knowle Hill
Grabbist Hill
WEST CL
CASTLE HILL
CHURCH ST
Sch
Cemy
Dunster
Dunkery Vineyard
Ranscombe
MILL LA
Dunster Castle
Knowle
Burnells
TA24
Aville Farm
KNOWLE LA
WEST ST
PARK ST
Mill
The Lawns
Kennels
Gallox Bridge
KNOWLE LA
BONNITON NEW RD
River Avill
Vinegar Hill
BONNITON LA
Cowbridge
KITSWALL LA
Dunster Park
Black Ball
Whits Wood
MEADOW VIEW
Totterdown Farm
VICARAGE CT
ORCHARD WAY
GREAT HOUSE ST
Dunster Wood Forest Trails
PARK LA
Well Farm
BEMBERRY BANK
HOLES SQ
BROADWOOD RD
Bat's Castle
WELL LA
BROOK ST
CHURCH ST
WILLOWBANK
HORSE RD
HORSEPARK LA
Sch
JUBILEE TERR
THE GLEBE
THE KNAPP
Timberscombe
WHITSWOOD STEEP
Hur Wood
WITHYCOMBE HILL GATE
Aller Hill
WAYDOWN CROSS
WAYDOWN LA
Bickham
ELSCOMBE LA
HARWOOD CROSS
HARWOOD LA
Broadwood Farm
Pitt Bridge
A396
Gupworthy Farm
Oaktrow Wood
Slade Lane
Beasley
Withycombe Scruffets
STAPLING LA
BOWDEN LA
Croydon House
Croydon Hill
Slade
Bowden
OAK LA
Oaktrow Farm
Black Hill
A396
Sully
CUTCOMBE HILL
Allercott
Well
Rodhuish Common
Stowey Farm
TA23
PUTHAM LA
Kersham
KERSHAM LA
COUPLE CROSS
Monkham Hill
Nurcott Farm
Old Stowey
BEECH TREE
Churchtown
Slowley Farm
Kersham Hill
WESTCOTT CROSS
PERLEY LA
Luxborough
STOUT'S WAY LA
Slowley Wood
STOUT'S WAY LA

200
201
125
200
201

94 A 95 B 96 C 97 D 98 E 99 F

For full street detail of the highlighted areas see pages 200 and 201.

129
148

132

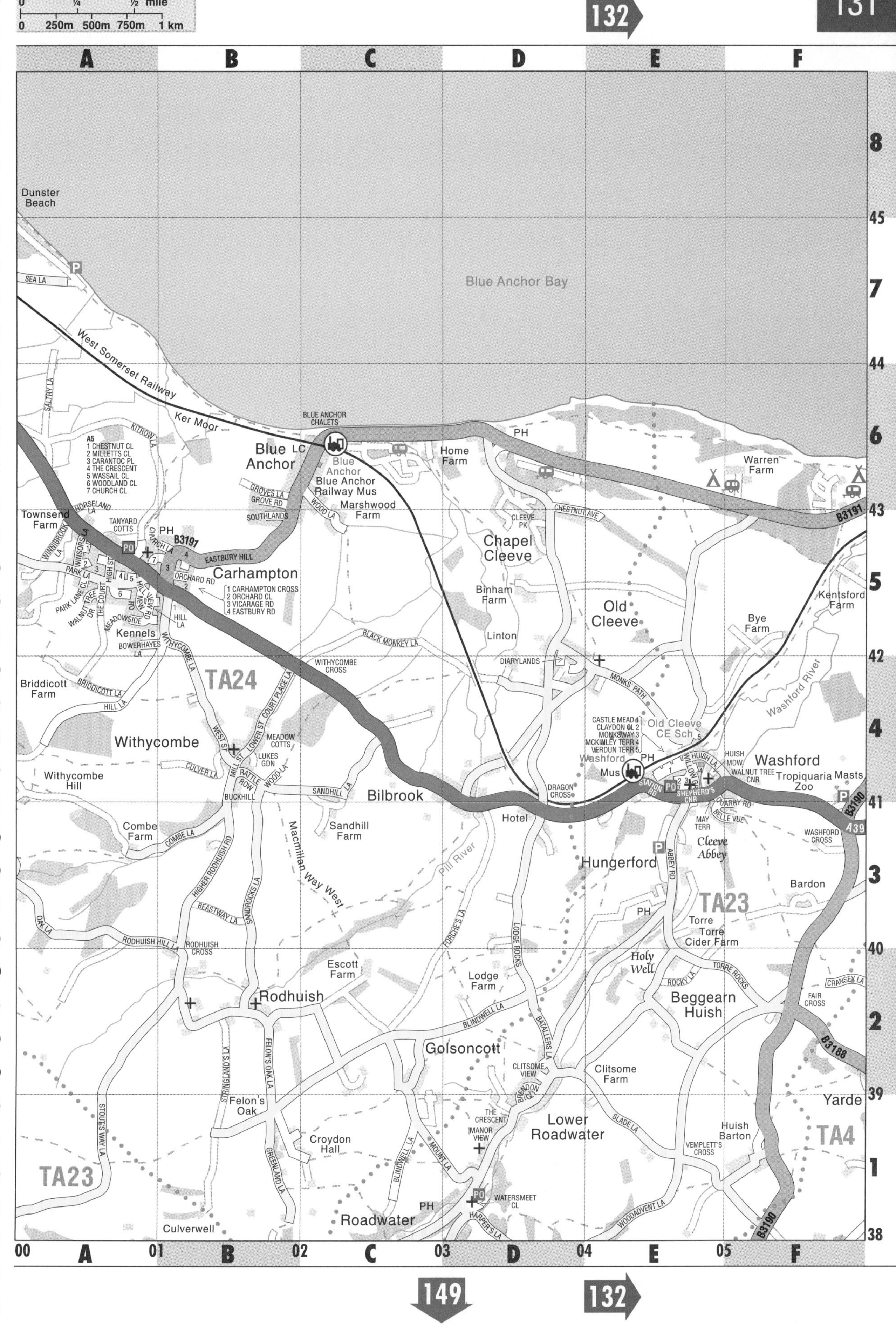
Scale: 1¾ inches to 1 mile
0 ¼ ½ mile
0 250m 500m 750m 1 km
A B C D E F
Dunster Beach
SEA LA
Blue Anchor Bay
West Somerset Railway
Ker Moor
SALTRY LA
KITROW LA
A5
1 CHESTNUT CL
2 MILLETTS CL
3 CARANTOC PL
4 THE CRESCENT
5 WASSAIL CL
6 WOODLAND CL
7 CHURCH CL
BLUE ANCHOR CHALETS
Blue Anchor
Blue Anchor Railway Mus
Home Farm
PH
Warren Farm
GROVES LA
GROVE RD
SOUTHLANDS
WOOD LA
Marshwood Farm
CLEEVE PK
CHESTNUT AVE
B3191
Townsend Farm
HORSELAND LA
TANYARD COTTS
WINNIBROOK LA
WINSORS LA
CHURCH LA
EASTBURY HILL
Carhampton
ORCHARD RD
1 CARHAMPTON CROSS
2 ORCHARD CL
3 VICARAGE RD
4 EASTBURY RD
PARK LA
PARK LANE CL
WALNUT TREE DR
THE COURT
HIGH ST
HILL VIEW RD
MEADOWSIDE
HILL LA
Kennels
BOWERHAYES LA
Chapel Cleeve
Binham Farm
Old Cleeve
Kentsford Farm
Bye Farm
Linton
BLACK MONKEY LA
DIARYLANDS
MONKS' PATH
WITHYCOMBE CROSS
WITHYCOMBE LA
TA24
Briddicott Farm
BRIDDICOTT LA
HILL LA
Washford River
CASTLE MEAD 1
CLAYDON CL 2
MONKSWAY 3
MCKINLEY TERR 4
VERDUN TERR 5
Old Cleeve CE Sch
Withycombe
WEST ST
LOWER ST
COURT PLACE LA
MEADOW COTTS
LUKES GDN
CULVER LA
MILL ST
RATTLE ROW
WOOD LA
BUCKHILL
SANDHILL LA
Bilbrook
Washford
Mus
HUISH LA
HUISH MDW
WALNUT TREE CNR
Tropiquaria Zoo
Masts
STATION RD
SHEPHERD'S CNR
QUARRY RD
BELLE VUE
DRAGON CROSS
Withycombe Hill
Hotel
MAY TERR
B3190
A39
Combe Farm
COMBE LA
Sandhill Farm
Macmillan Way West
Pill River
Cleeve Abbey
WASHFORD CROSS
HIGHER RODHUISH RD
SANDROCKS LA
Hungerford
ABBEY RD
Bardon
TA23
OAK LA
BEASTWAY LA
FORCHE'S LA
LODGE ROCKS
PH
Torre
Torre Cider Farm
RODHUISH HILL LA
RODHUISH CROSS
Escott Farm
Holy Well
TORRE ROCKS
CRANSEY LA
FAIR CROSS
Lodge Farm
ROCKY LA
Beggearn Huish
Rodhuish
BLINDWELL LA
BATALLERS LA
B3188
STRINGLAND'S LA
FELON'S OAK LA
Golsoncott
CLITSOME VIEW
Clitsome Farm
BRENDON CL
Felon's Oak
THE CRESCENT
MANOR VIEW
Lower Roadwater
SLADE LA
Yarde
STOUTS WAY LA
Croydon Hall
Huish Barton
VEMPLETT'S CROSS
TA4
BLINDWELL LA
MOUNT LA
GREENLAND LA
TA23
PH
WATERSMEET CL
WOODADVENT LA
Roadwater
HARPER'S LA
Culverwell
8
45
7
44
6
43
5
42
4
41
3
40
2
39
1
38
00 01 02 03 04 05

149
132

131

Scale: 1¾ inches to 1 mile
0 ¼ ½ mile
0 250m 500m 750m 1 km

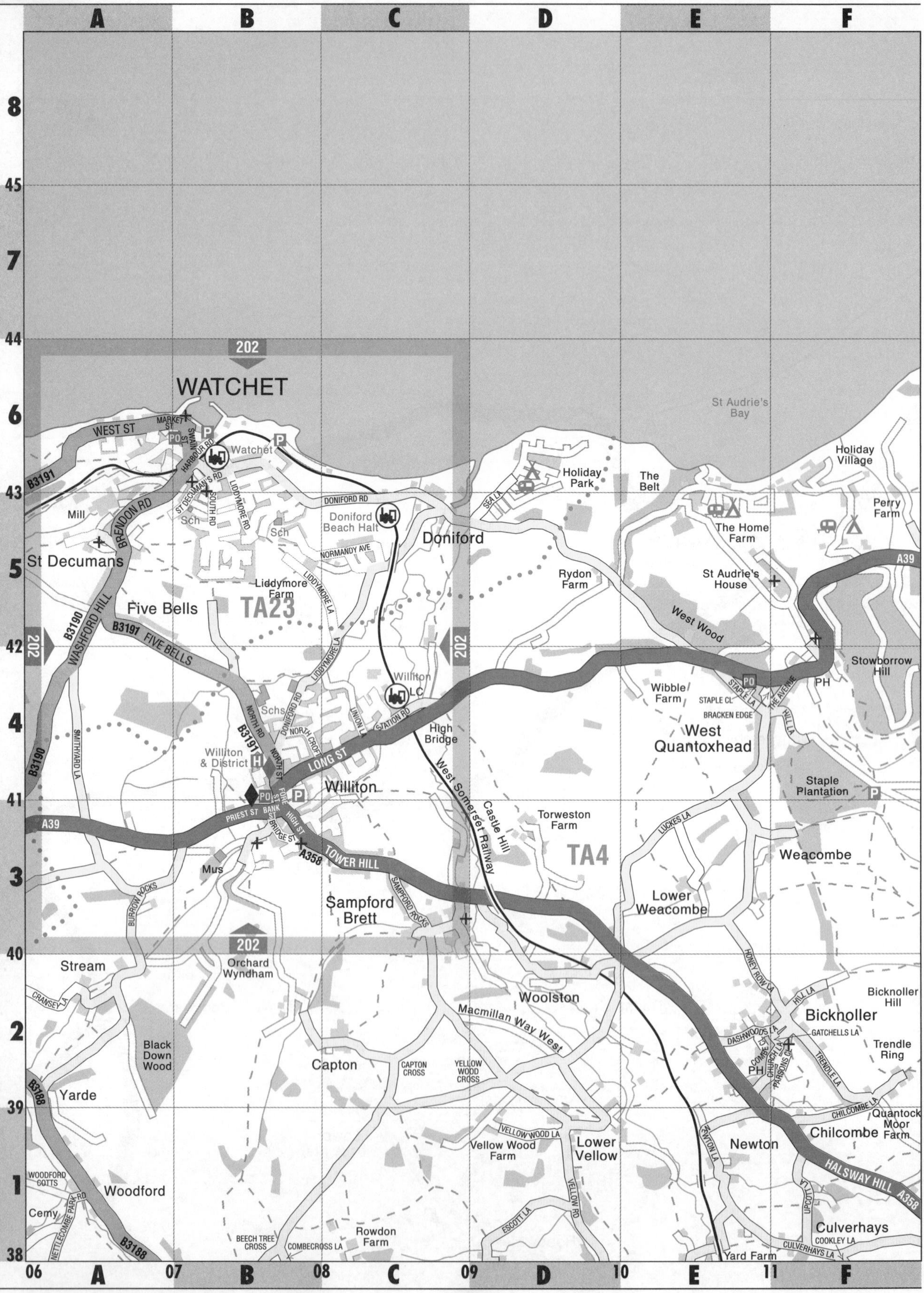

A B C D E F

06 A 07 B 08 C 09 D 10 E 11 F

For full street detail of the highlighted area see page 202.

131

150

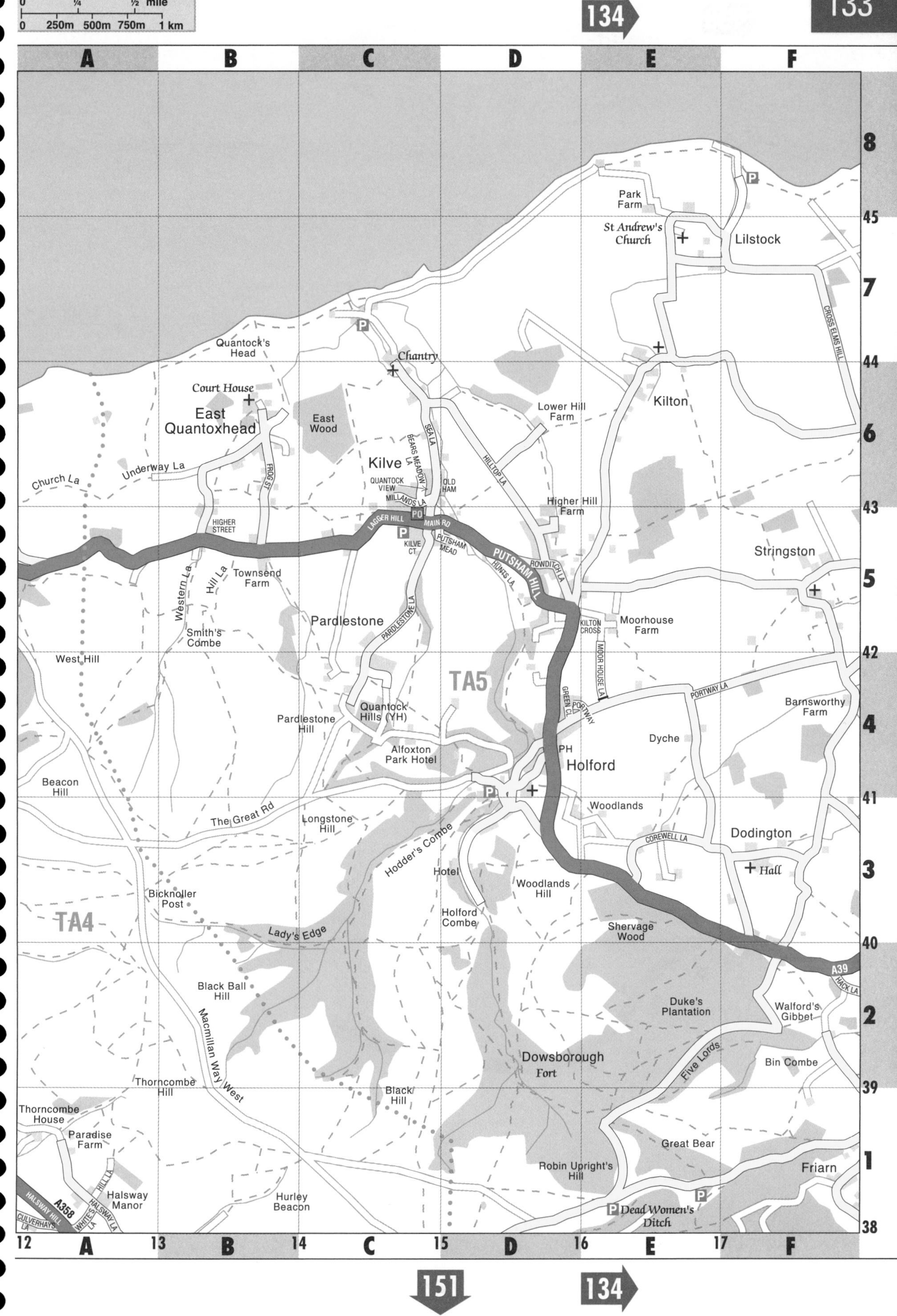
Scale: 1¾ inches to 1 mile
134
East Quantoxhead
Kilve
Pardlestone
Holford
Kilton
Lilstock
Stringston
Dodington
Friarn
Dowsborough
Fort
TA5
TA4
A39
A358
Macmillan Way West
151
134

133

Scale: 1¾ inches to 1 mile

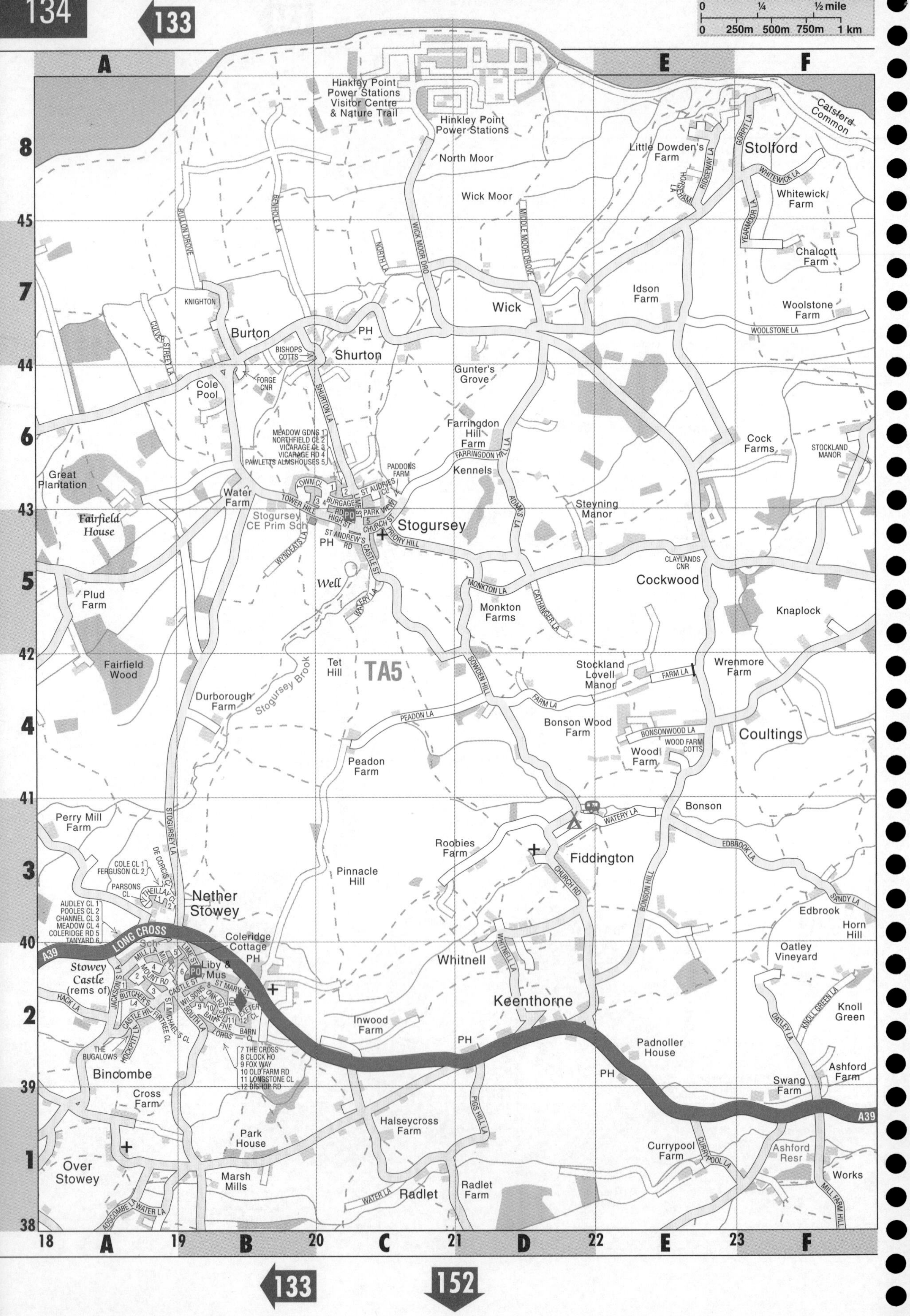

133
152

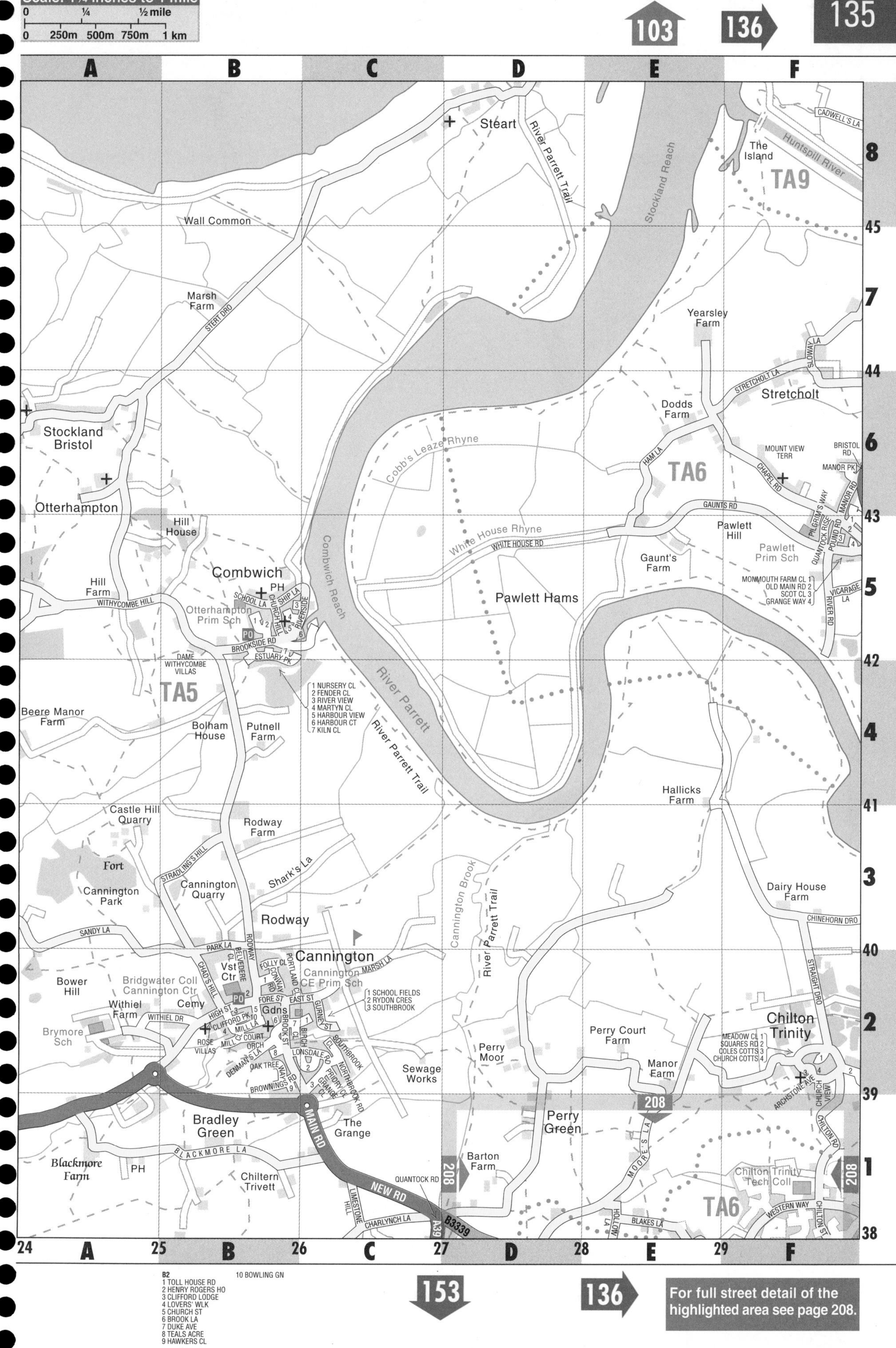

B2
1 TOLL HOUSE RD
2 HENRY ROGERS HO
3 CLIFFORD LODGE
4 LOVERS' WLK
5 CHURCH ST
6 BROOK LA
7 DUKE AVE
8 TEALS ACRE
9 HAWKERS CL
10 BOWLING GN

153

136

For full street detail of the highlighted area see page 208.

Scale: 1¾ inches to 1 mile

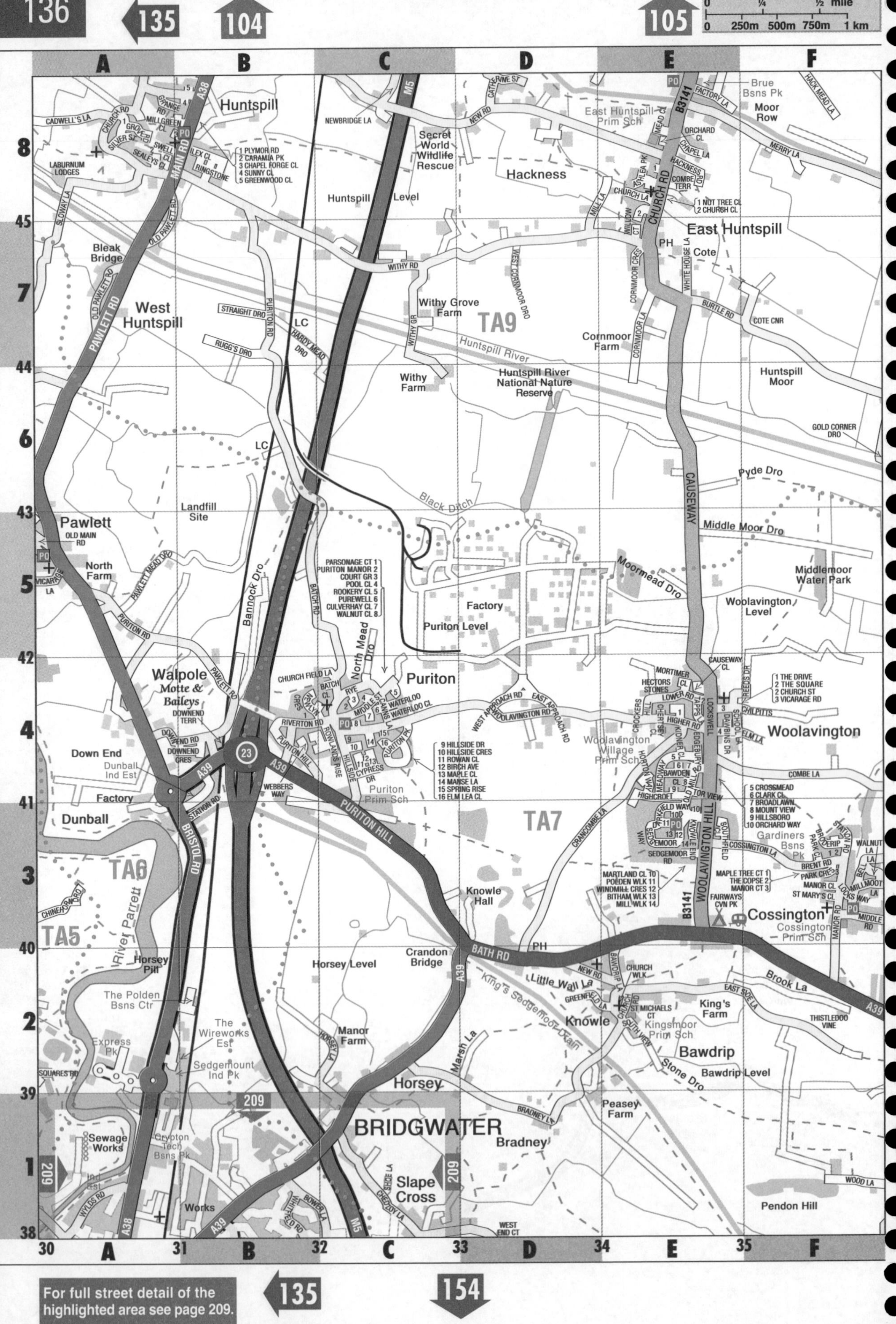

For full street detail of the highlighted area see page 209.

106 107 138

Scale: 1¾ inches to 1 mile
0 ¼ ½ mile
0 250m 500m 750m 1 km

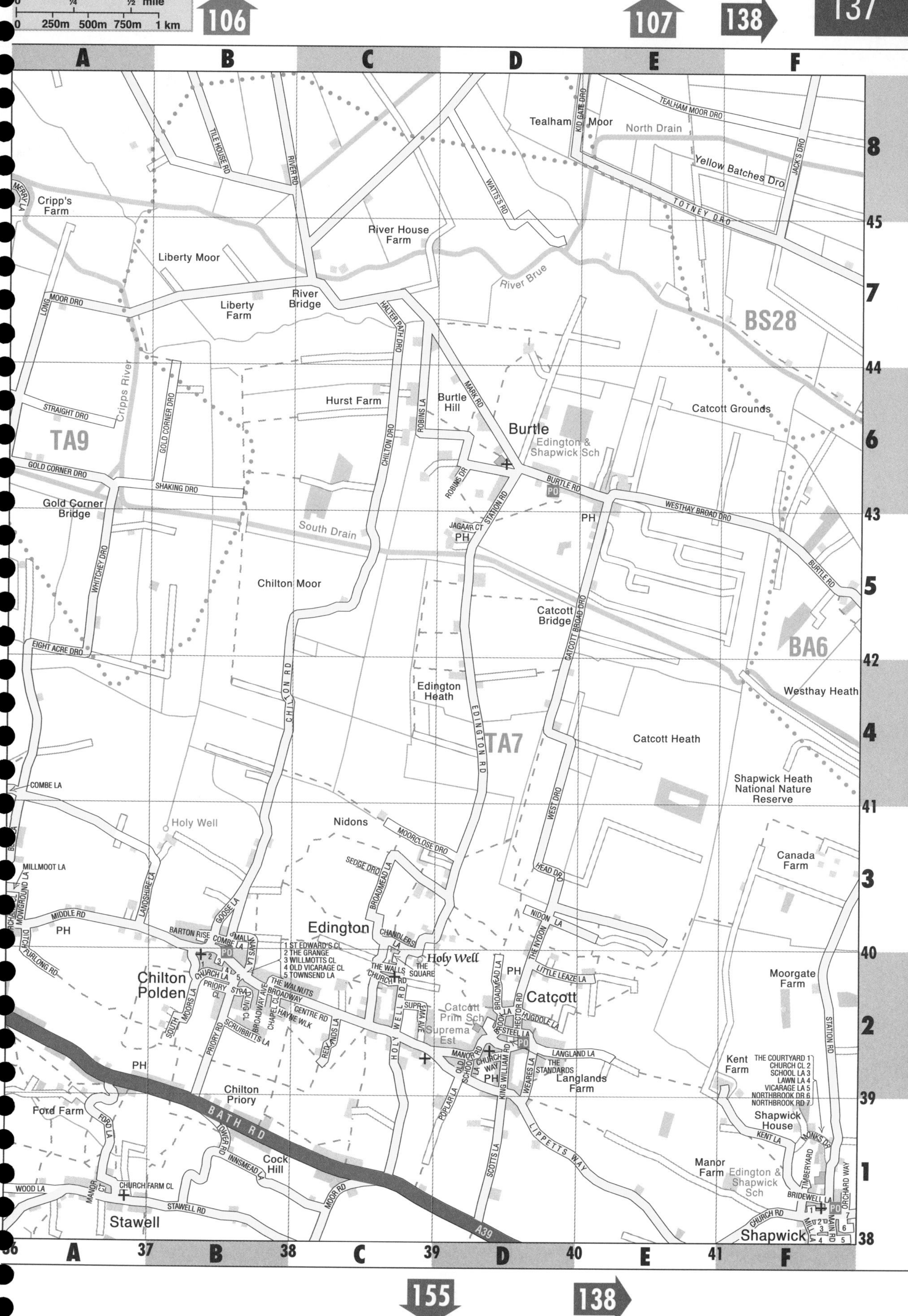

155 138

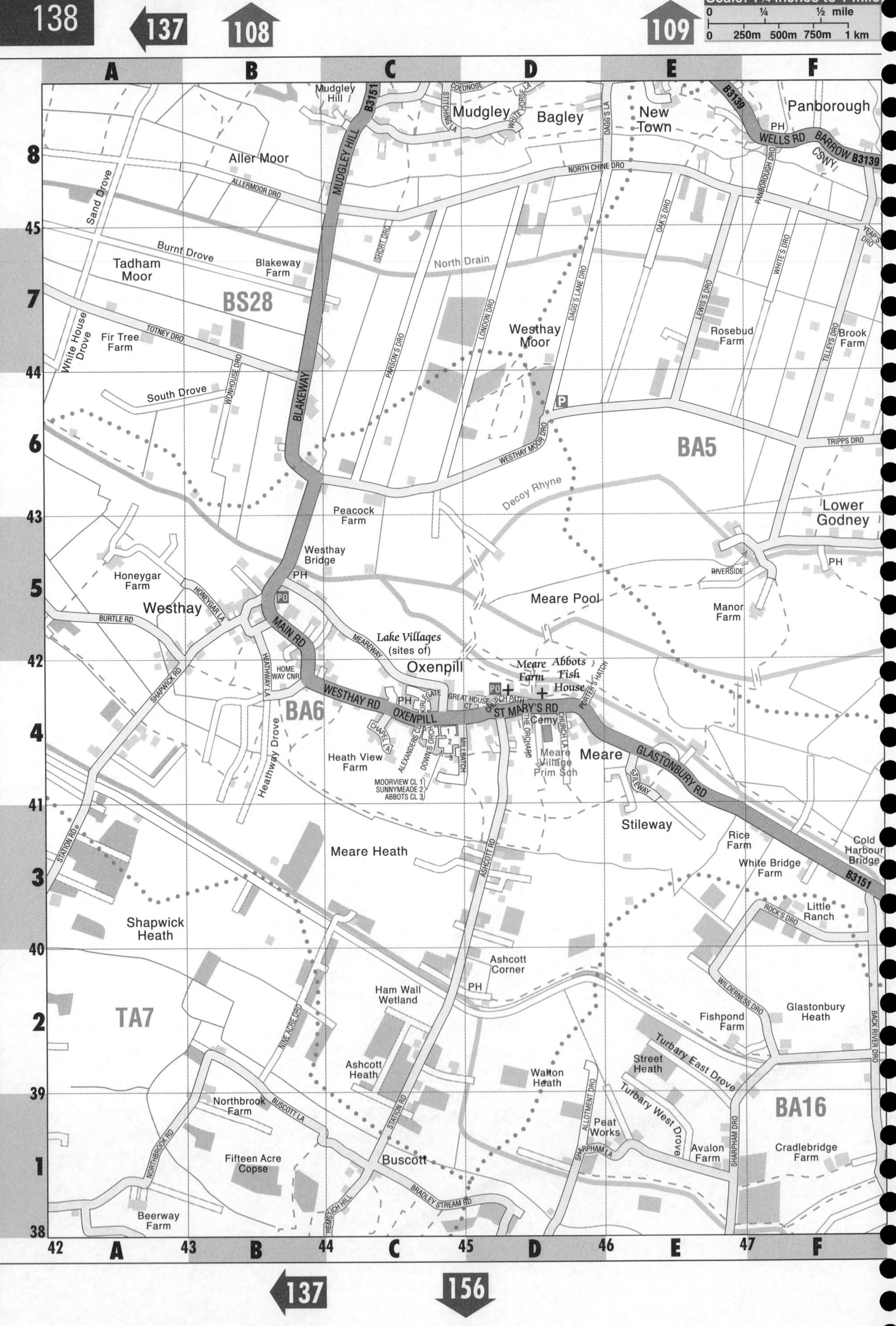
137
108
109
Scale: 1¾ inches to 1 mile
0
¼
½ mile
0
250m
500m
750m
1 km
A
B
C
D
E
F
8
45
7
44
6
43
5
42
4
41
3
40
2
39
1
38
42
43
44
45
46
47
Mudgley Hill
B3151
COXDNOSE
STITCHING LA
Mudgley
WHITE HORSE LA
Bagley
DAGG'S LA
New Town
B3139
Panborough
PH
WELLS RD
BARROW CSWY
B3139
Aller Moor
MUDGLEY HILL
NORTH CHINE DRO
ALLERMOOR DRO
PANBOROUGH DRO
Sand Drove
OAK'S DRO
YEAP'S DRO
SHORT DRO
WHITE'S DRO
Burnt Drove
Tadham Moor
Blakeway Farm
North Drain
DAGG'S LANE DRO
LEWIS'S DRO
BS28
LONDON DRO
PARSON'S DRO
Westhay Moor
Rosebud Farm
TILLEYS DRO
Brook Farm
White House Drove
Fir Tree Farm
TOTNEY DRO
WONHOUSE DRO
BLAKEWAY
P
South Drove
WESTHAY MOOR DRO
BA5
TRIPPS DRO
Decoy Rhyne
Peacock Farm
Lower Godney
Westhay Bridge
PH
RIVERSIDE
Honeygar Farm
PH
Westhay
HONEYGAR LA
PO
Meare Pool
Manor Farm
BURTLE RD
MAIN RD
MEAREWAY
Lake Villages (sites of)
Oxenpill
Meare Farm
Abbots Fish House
PORTER'S HATCH
HEATHWAY LA
HOME WAY CNR
SHAPWICK RD
WESTHAY RD
PH
KIRLEGATE
GREAT HOUSE CT
PO
CHURCH PATH
ST MARY'S RD
BA6
OXENPILL
THE ORCHARD
Cemy
CHURCH LA
CHAPEL LA
ALEXANDERS CL
DOWN'S ORCH
MILLBATCH
Meare Village Prim Sch
Meare
GLASTONBURY RD
STILEWAY
Heathway Drove
Heath View Farm
MOORVIEW CL 1
SUNNYMEADE 2
ABBOTS CL 3
Stileway
STATION RD
Meare Heath
ASHCOTT RD
Rice Farm
White Bridge Farm
Cold Harbour Bridge
B3151
Shapwick Heath
ROCK'S DRO
Little Ranch
Ashcott Corner
TA7
Ham Wall Wetland
PH
WILDERNESS DRO
Glastonbury Heath
BACK RIVER DRO
NINE ACRE DRO
Fishpond Farm
Turbary East Drove
Street Heath
Ashcott Heath
Walton Heath
Turbary West Drove
Northbrook Farm
BUSCOTT LA
STATION RD
ALLOTMENT DRO
Peat Works
BA16
SHARPHAM DRO
NORTHBROOK RD
SHARPHAM LA
Avalon Farm
Cradlebridge Farm
Fifteen Acre Copse
Buscott
BRADLEY STREAM RD
HEMSTICH HILL
Beerway Farm
137
156

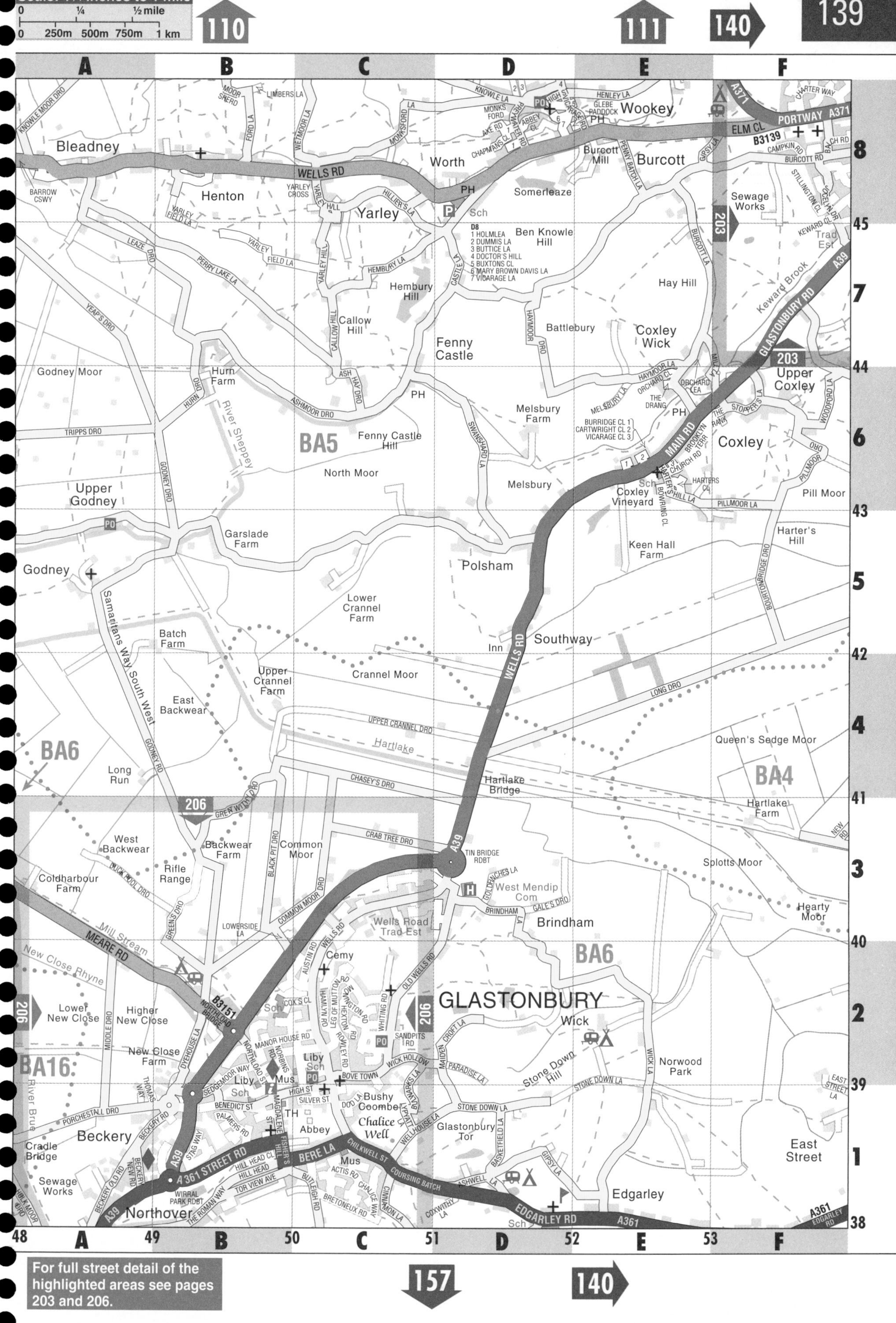

For full street detail of the highlighted areas see pages 203 and 206.

139 112 113

Scale: 1¾ inches to 1 mile
0 ¼ ½ mile
0 250m 500m 750m 1 km

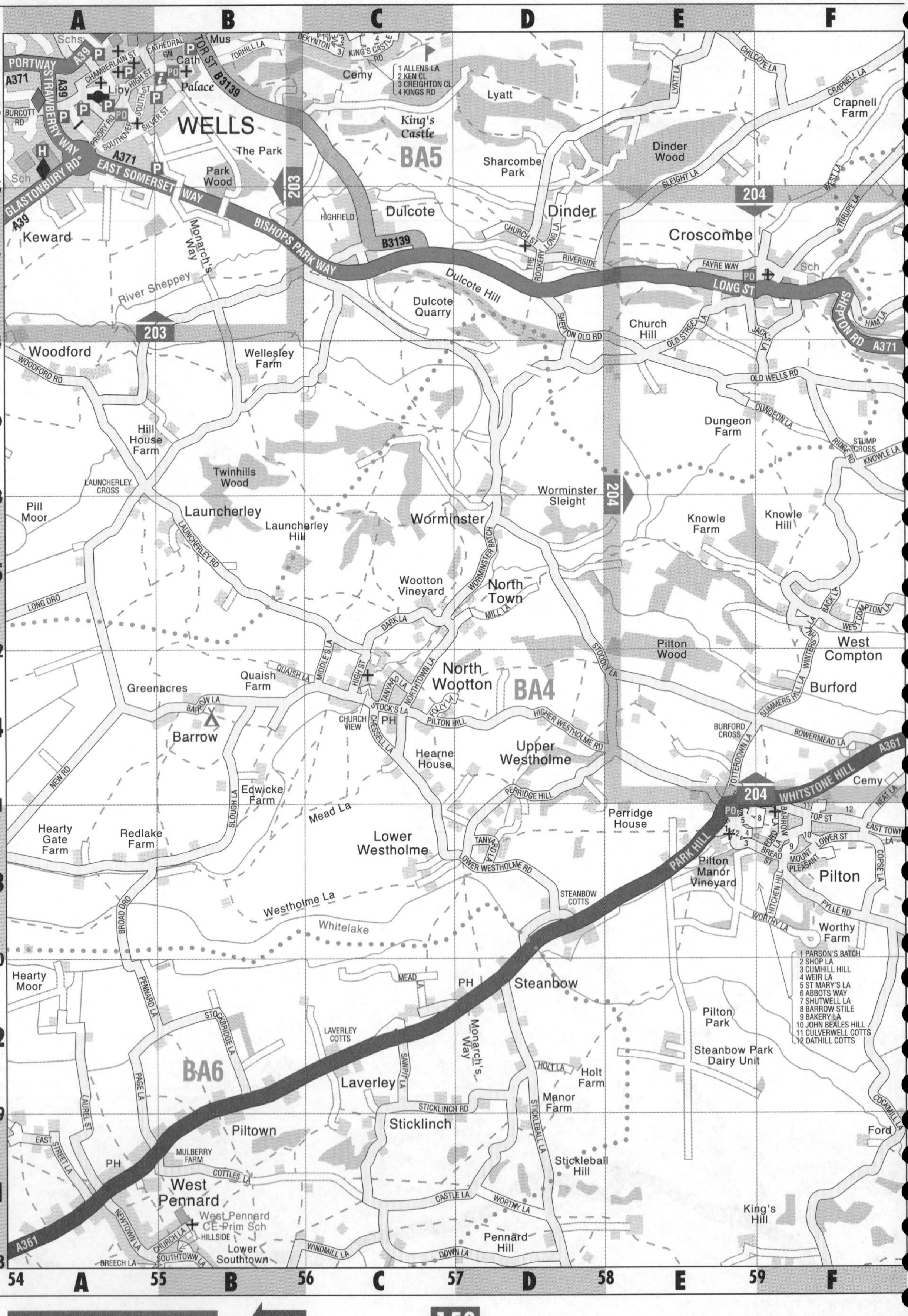

For full street detail of the highlighted area see pages 203 and 204.

139 158

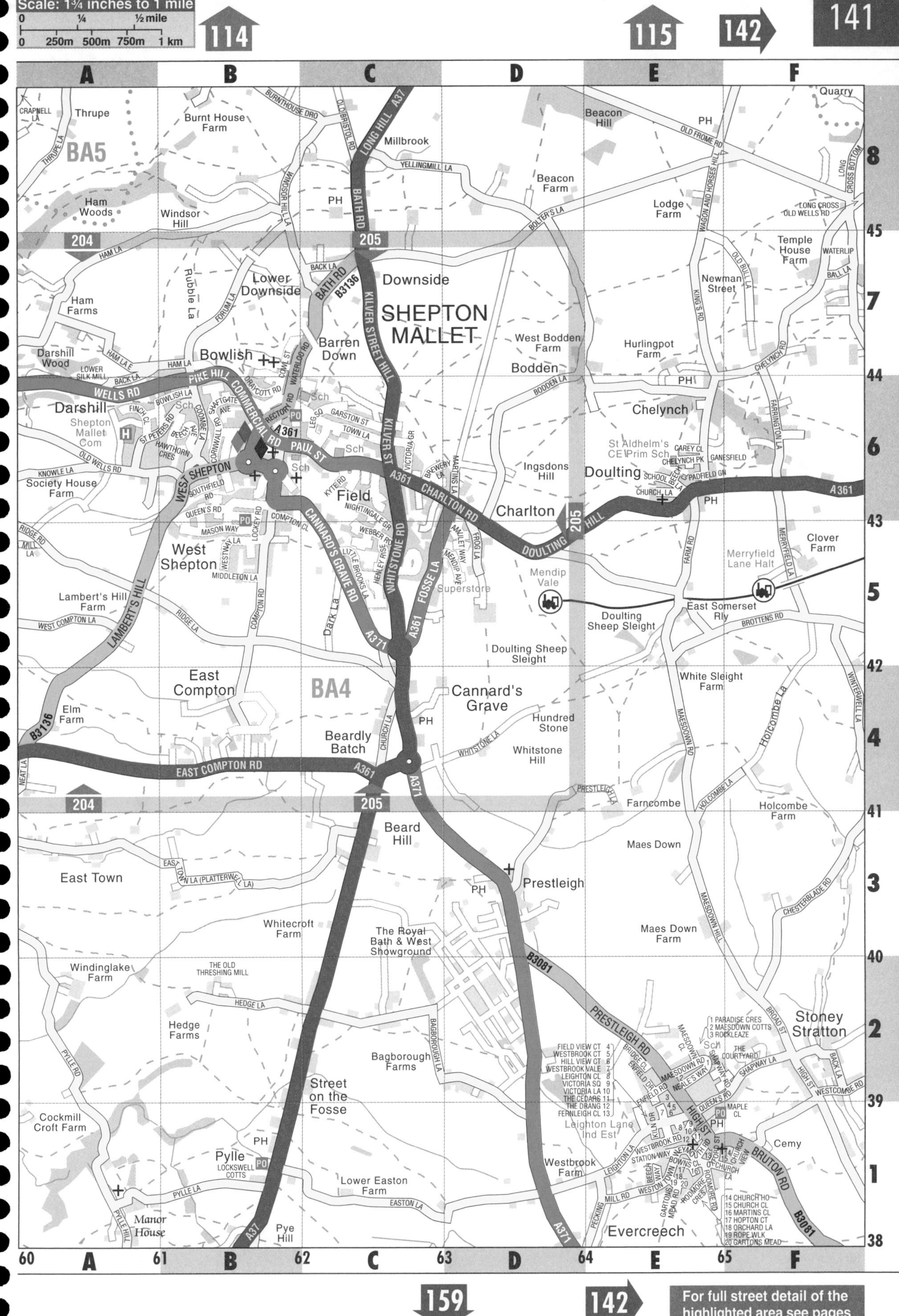

For full street detail of the highlighted area see pages 204 and 205.

Scale: 1¾ inches to 1 mile
0 ¼ ½ mile
0 250m 500m 750m 1 km

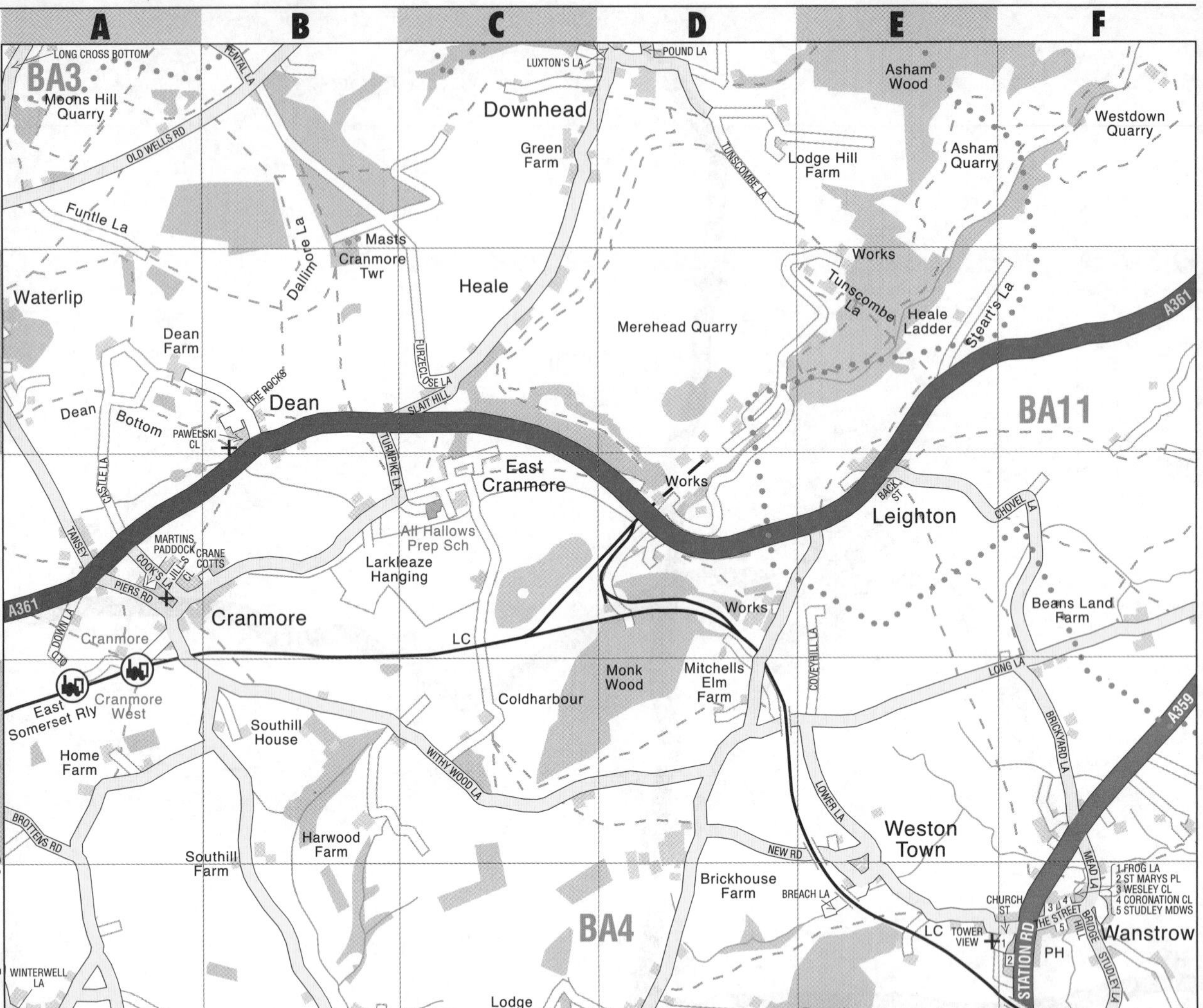

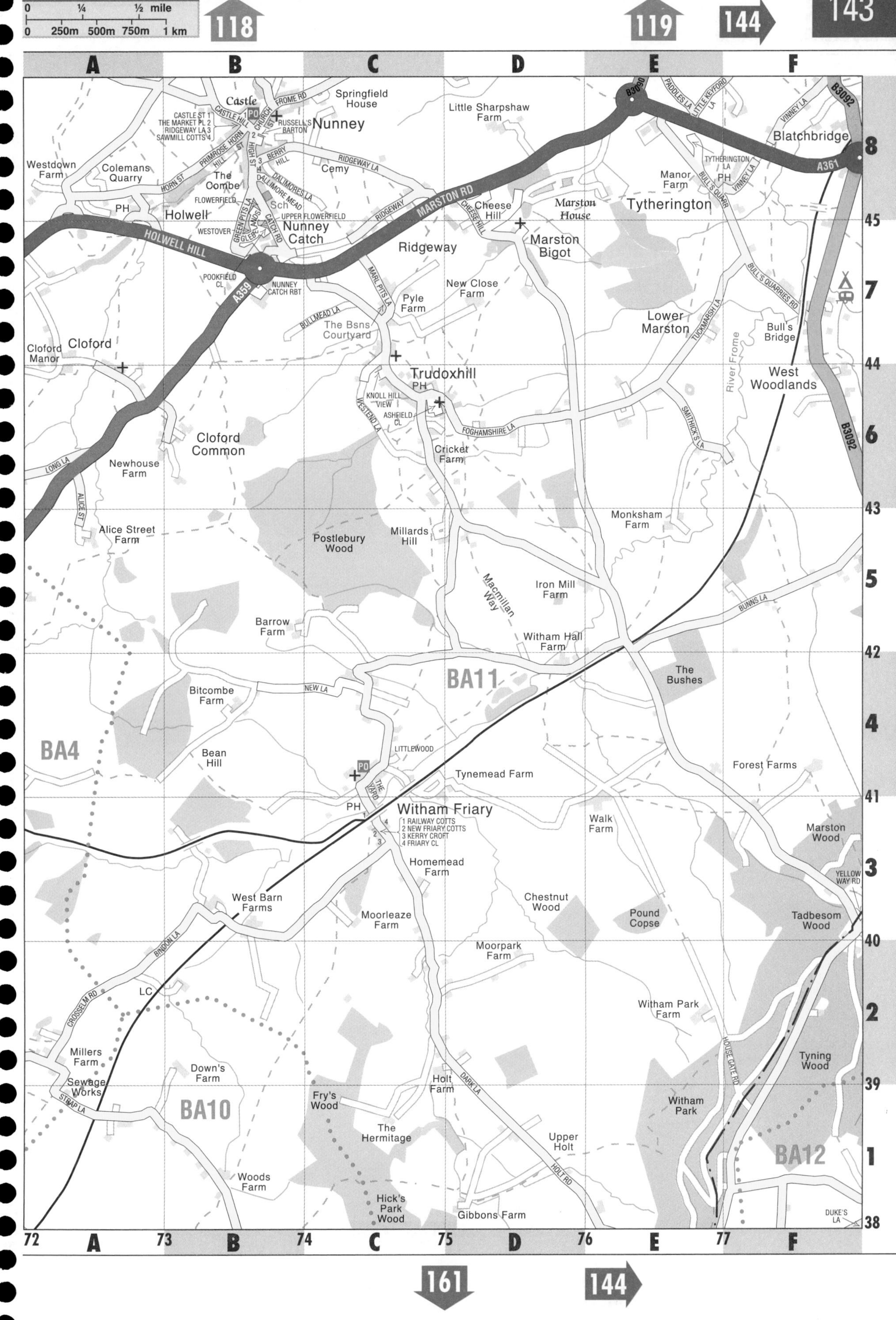
Scale: 1¾ inches to 1 mile
0 ¼ ½ mile
0 250m 500m 750m 1 km
118
119
144
A B C D E F
Castle
Springfield House
Little Sharpshaw Farm
Nunney
Blatchbridge
Westdown Farm
Colemans Quarry
The Combe
Cemy
Manor Farm
Holwell
PH
Cheese Hill
Marston House
Tytherington
Nunney Catch
Ridgeway
Marston Bigot
HOLWELL HILL
MARSTON RD
A359
A361
B3090
B3092
New Close Farm
Pyle Farm
Lower Marston
Bull's Bridge
The Bsns Courtyard
Cloford Manor
Cloford
Trudoxhill
West Woodlands
River Frome
Cloford Common
Cricket Farm
FOGHAMSHIRE LA
Newhouse Farm
Monksham Farm
Alice Street Farm
Postlebury Wood
Millards Hill
Macmillan Way
Iron Mill Farm
Barrow Farm
Witham Hall Farm
BA11
The Bushes
Bitcombe Farm
NEW LA
BUNNS LA
BA4
Bean Hill
Tynemead Farm
Forest Farms
Witham Friary
1 RAILWAY COTTS
2 NEW FRIARY COTTS
3 KERRY CROFT
4 FRIARY CL
Walk Farm
Marston Wood
Homemead Farm
West Barn Farms
Chestnut Wood
Pound Copse
Tadbesom Wood
Moorleaze Farm
Moorpark Farm
Witham Park Farm
LC
Millers Farm
Down's Farm
Tyning Wood
Sewage Works
Holt Farm
Witham Park
Fry's Wood
BA10
The Hermitage
Upper Holt
BA12
Woods Farm
Hick's Park Wood
Gibbons Farm
DARK LA
HOLT RD
72 73 74 75 76 77
38 39 1 2 40 3 41 4 42 5 43 6 44 7 45 8

Scale: 1¾ inches to 1 mile

0 ¼ ½ mile

0 250m 500m 750m 1 km

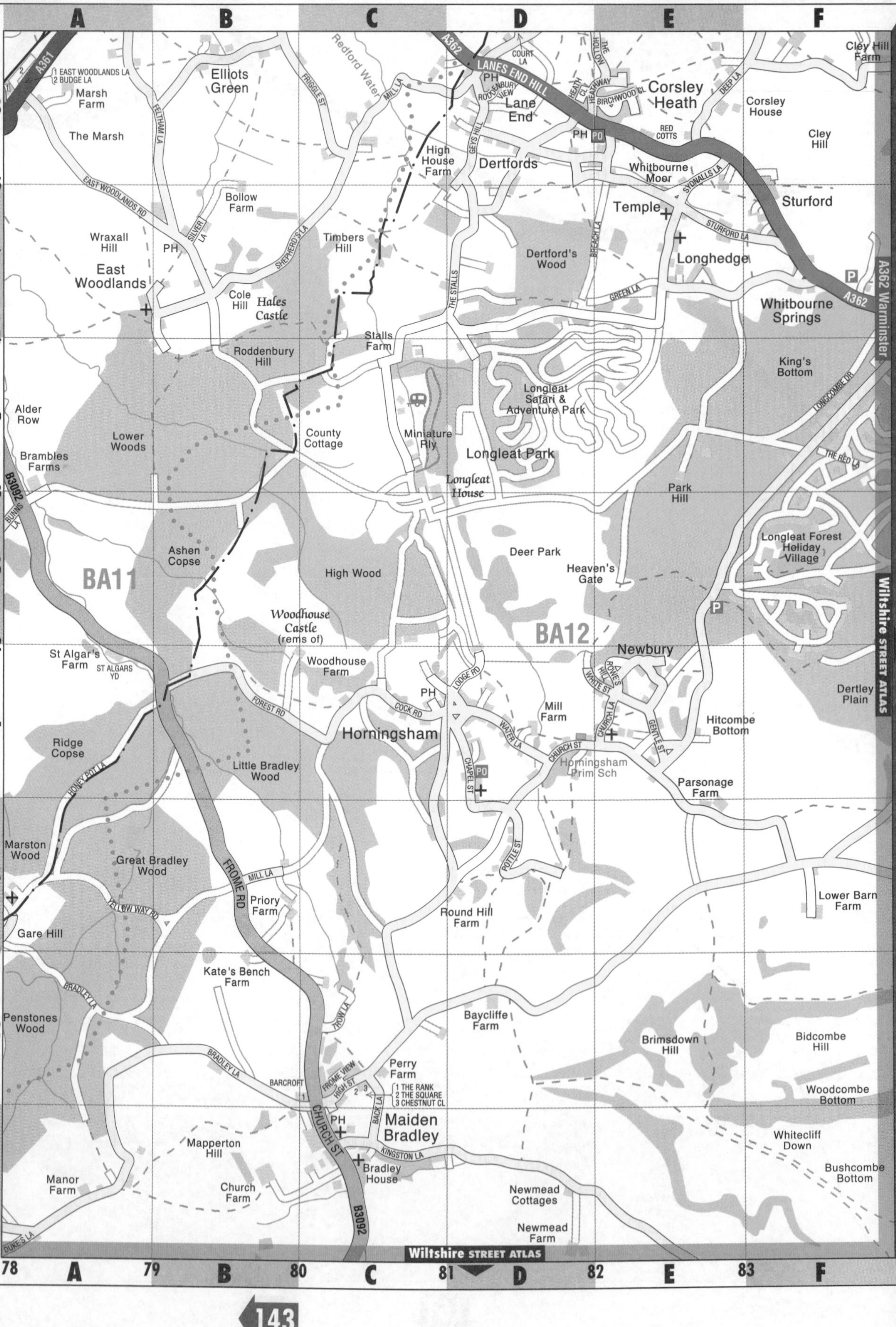

A B C D E F

Elliots Green
Marsh Farm
The Marsh
Redford Water
Lane End
Corsley Heath
Cley Hill Farm
Corsley House
Cley Hill
High House Farm
Dertfords
Whitbourne Moor
Bollow Farm
Temple
Sturford
Wraxall Hill
Timbers Hill
Longhedge
East Woodlands
Dertford's Wood
Cole Hill
Hales Castle
Whitbourne Springs
Roddenbury Hill
Stalls Farm
King's Bottom
Alder Row
Lower Woods
County Cottage
Miniature Rly
Longleat Safari & Adventure Park
Longleat Park
Brambles Farms
Longleat House
Park Hill
Ashen Copse
High Wood
Deer Park
Heaven's Gate
Longleat Forest Holiday Village
BA11
Woodhouse Castle (rems of)
BA12
St Algar's Farm
Woodhouse Farm
Newbury
Dertley Plain
Ridge Copse
Horningsham
Mill Farm
Hitcombe Bottom
Little Bradley Wood
Horningsham Prim Sch
Parsonage Farm
Marston Wood
Great Bradley Wood
Priory Farm
Round Hill Farm
Lower Barn Farm
Gare Hill
Kate's Bench Farm
Baycliffe Farm
Penstones Wood
Brimsdown Hill
Bidcombe Hill
Perry Farm
Woodcombe Bottom
Maiden Bradley
Mapperton Hill
Whitecliff Down
Bradley House
Bushcombe Bottom
Manor Farm
Church Farm
Newmead Cottages
Newmead Farm

A361, A362, B3092, LANES END HILL, COURT LA, MILL LA, FRIGGLE ST, FELTHAM LA, EAST WOODLANDS RD, SILVER LA, SHEPHERD'S LA, GEYS HILL, RODDENBURY VIEW, HEATH CL, HEATHWAY, THE HOLLOW, BIRCHWOOD CL, RED COTTS, DEEP LA, SYDNALLS LA, STURFORD LA, BREACH LA, GREEN LA, THE STALLS, LONGCOMBE DR, THE BED LA, BUNNS LA, FOREST RD, LODGE RD, COCK RD, WATER LA, CHAPEL ST, CHURCH ST, CHURCH LA, WHITE ST, ROWE'S HILL, GENTLE ST, POTTLE ST, HONEY POT LA, MILL LA, FROME RD, YELLOW WAY RD, BRADLEY LA, TROW LA, FROME VIEW, HIGH ST, BARCROFT, BACK LA, KINGSTON LA, DUKE'S LA, ST ALGARS YD

1 EAST WOODLANDS LA
2 BUDGE LA

1 THE RANK
2 THE SQUARE
3 CHESTNUT CL

PH PO P

A362 Warminster

8 45 7 44 6 43 5 42 4 41 3 40 2 39 1 38

78 A 79 B 80 C 81 D 82 E 83 F

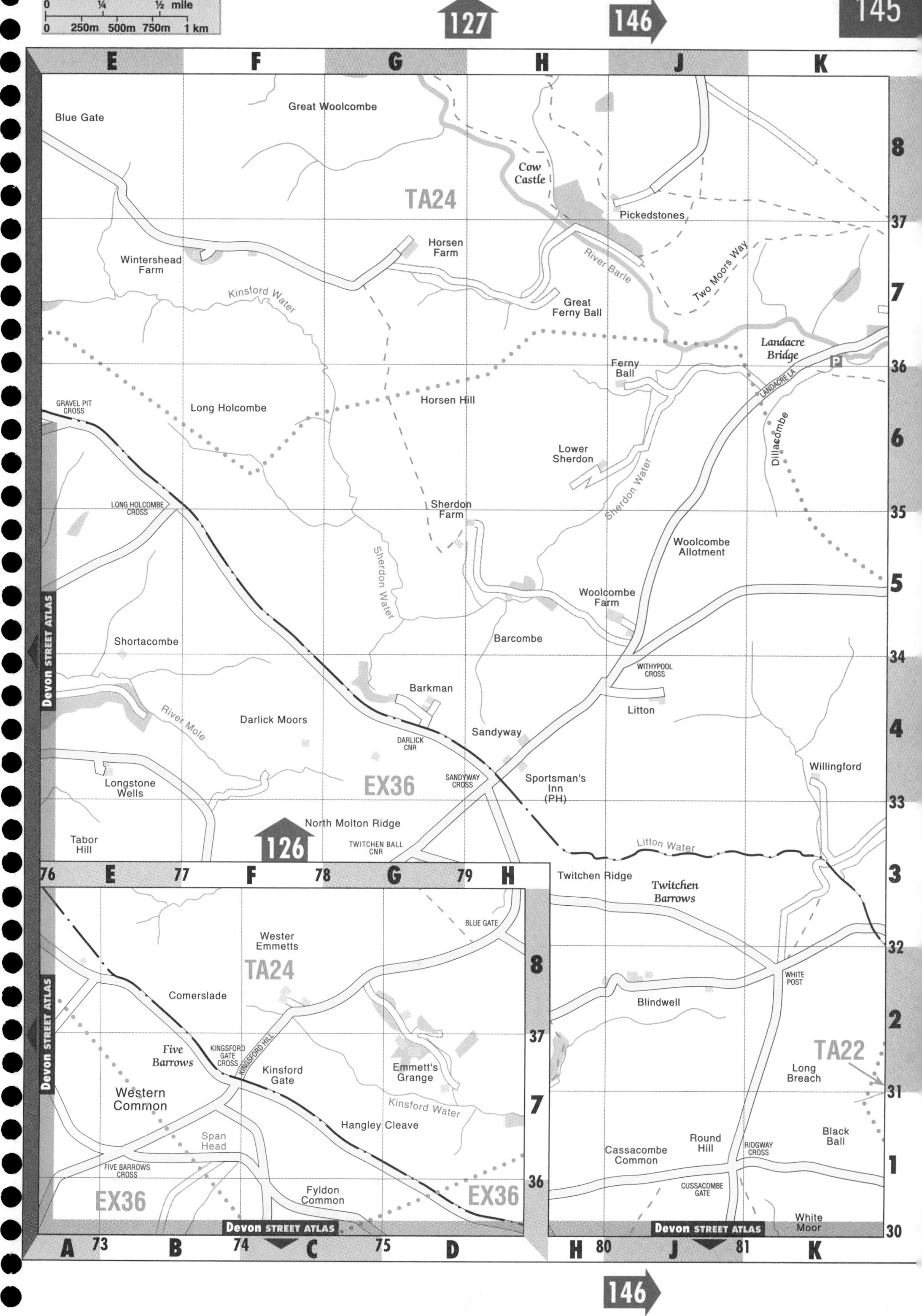
Scale: 1¾ inches to 1 mile
0 ¼ ½ mile
0 250m 500m 750m 1 km
127
146
E F G H J K
Blue Gate
Great Woolcombe
Cow Castle
TA24
Pickedstones
Horsen Farm
Wintershead Farm
River Barle
Two Moors Way
Great Ferny Ball
Kinsford Water
Landacre Bridge
Ferny Ball
LANDACRE LA
GRAVEL PIT CROSS
Long Holcombe
Horsen Hill
Dillacombe
Lower Sherdon
LONG HOLCOMBE CROSS
Sherdon Farm
Sherdon Water
Woolcombe Allotment
Woolcombe Farm
Shortacombe
Barcombe
WITHYPOOL CROSS
Barkman
Litton
River Mole
Darlick Moors
Sandyway
DARLICK CNR
Willingford
Longstone Wells
SANDYWAY CROSS
Sportsman's Inn (PH)
EX36
North Molton Ridge
Tabor Hill
126
TWITCHEN BALL CNR
Litton Water
Twitchen Ridge
Twitchen Barrows
WHITE POST
Blindwell
TA22
Long Breach
Black Ball
Cassacombe Common
Round Hill
RIDGWAY CROSS
CUSSACOMBE GATE
White Moor
Devon STREET ATLAS
76 E 77 F 78 G 79 H
BLUE GATE
Wester Emmetts
TA24
Comerslade
Five Barrows
KINGSFORD GATE CROSS
KINGSFORD HILL
Kinsford Gate
Emmett's Grange
Western Common
Kinsford Water
Hangley Cleave
Span Head
FIVE BARROWS CROSS
EX36
Fyldon Common
EX36
A 73 B 74 C 75 D
H 80 J 81 K
8 37 7 36 6 35 5 34 4 33 3 32 2 31 1 30
146

145
128

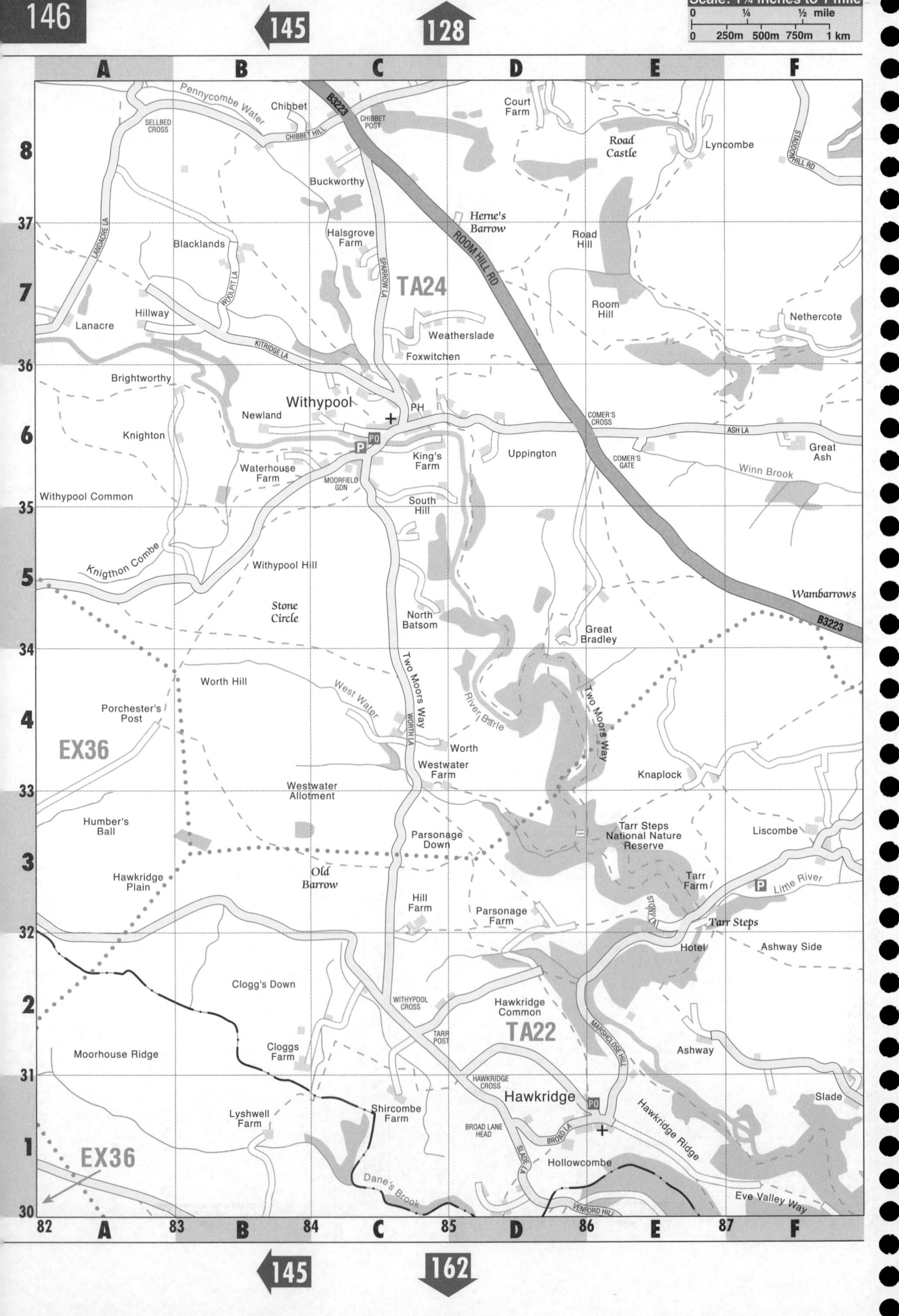

145
162

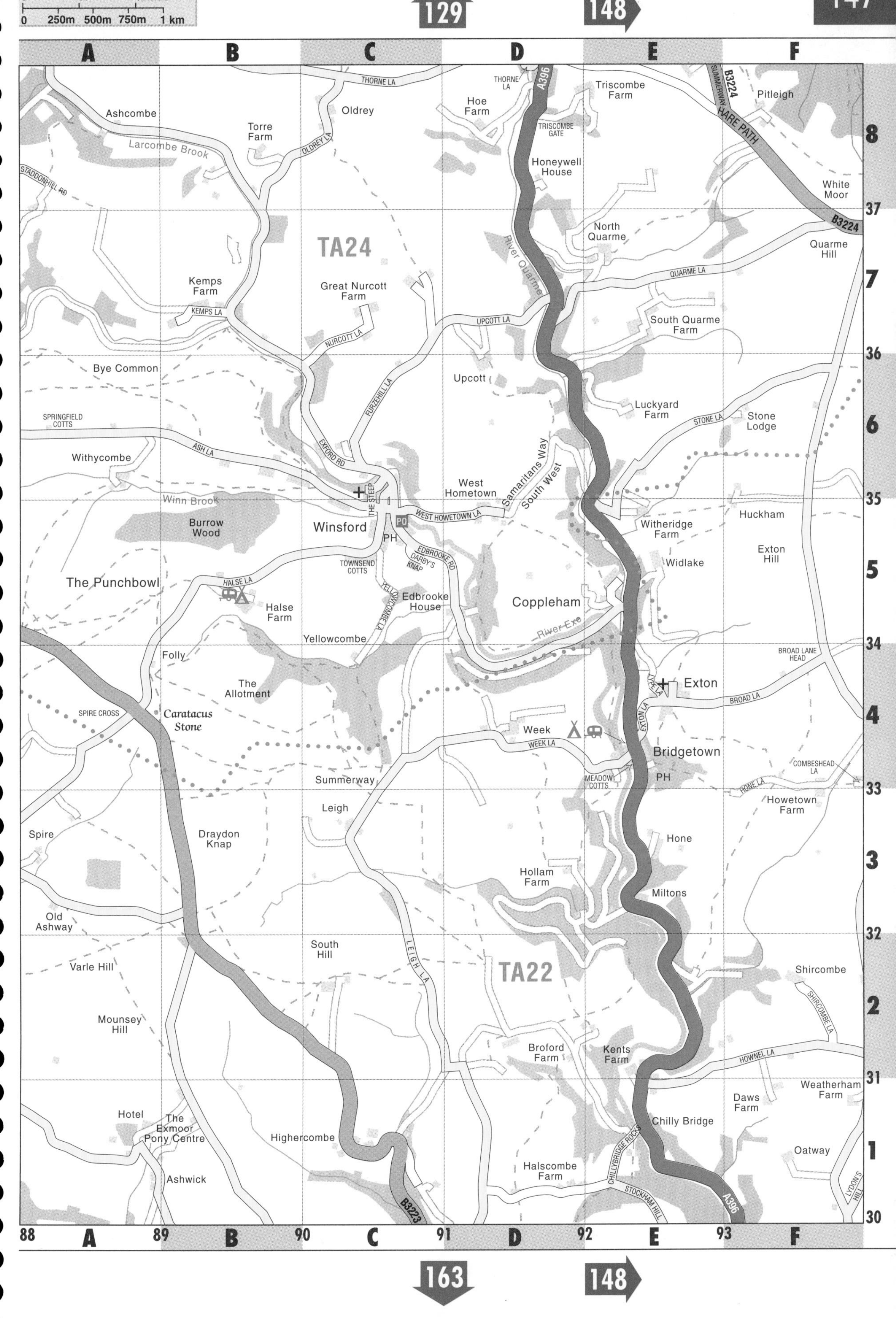
Scale: 1¾ inches to 1 mile
0 ¼ ½ mile
0 250m 500m 750m 1 km
129
148
A
B
C
D
E
F
THORNE LA
THORNE LA
A396
Triscombe Farm
B3224
SUMMERWAY HARE PATH
Pitleigh
Ashcombe
Oldrey
Hoe Farm
Torre Farm
TRISCOMBE GATE
Larcombe Brook
OLDREY LA
8
Honeywell House
STADDONHILL RD
White Moor
37
B3224
North Quarme
TA24
River Quarme
Quarme Hill
Kemps Farm
Great Nurcott Farm
QUARME LA
7
KEMPS LA
UPCOTT LA
South Quarme Farm
NURCOTT LA
Bye Common
36
Upcott
FURZEHILL LA
Luckyard Farm
SPRINGFIELD COTTS
STONE LA
Stone Lodge
6
ASH LA
Withycombe
EXFORD RD
West Hometown
Samaritans Way South West
Winn Brook
THE STEEP
35
WEST HOWETOWN LA
Huckham
Burrow Wood
PO
Winsford
Witheridge Farm
PH
EDBROOKE RD
Exton Hill
TOWNSEND COTTS
DARBY'S KNAP
Widlake
5
The Punchbowl
HALSE LA
YELLOWCOMBE LA
Edbrooke House
Coppleham
Halse Farm
River Exe
Yellowcombe
34
BROAD LANE HEAD
Folly
Exton
The Allotment
EXTON LA
BROAD LA
SPIRE CROSS
Caratacus Stone
4
Week
WEEK LA
Bridgetown
COMBESHEAD LA
MEADOW COTTS
PH
Summerway
33
HONE LA
Leigh
Howetown Farm
Spire
Draydon Knap
Hone
3
Hollam Farm
Miltons
Old Ashway
32
South Hill
LEIGH LA
Varle Hill
TA22
Shircombe
SHIRCOMBE LA
Mounsey Hill
2
Broford Farm
Kents Farm
HOWNEL LA
31
Weatherham Farm
Hotel
The Exmoor Pony Centre
Daws Farm
Chilly Bridge
CHILLYBRIDGE ROCKS
Highercombe
Oatway
1
Ashwick
Halscombe Farm
STOCKHAM HILL
LYDON'S HILL
B3223
A396
30
88
A
89
B
90
C
91
D
92
E
93
F
163
148

147
130

Scale: 1¾ inches to 1 mile

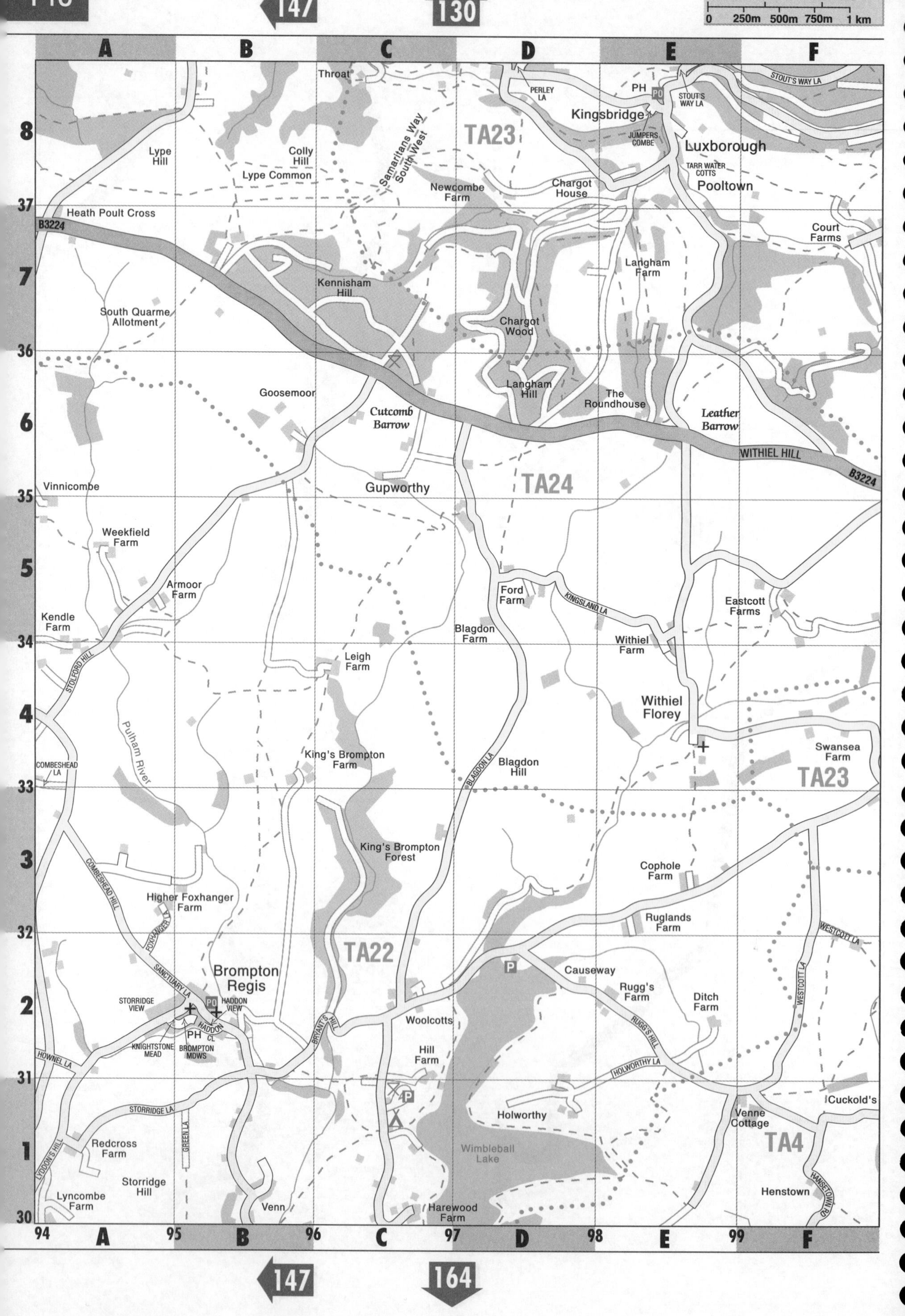

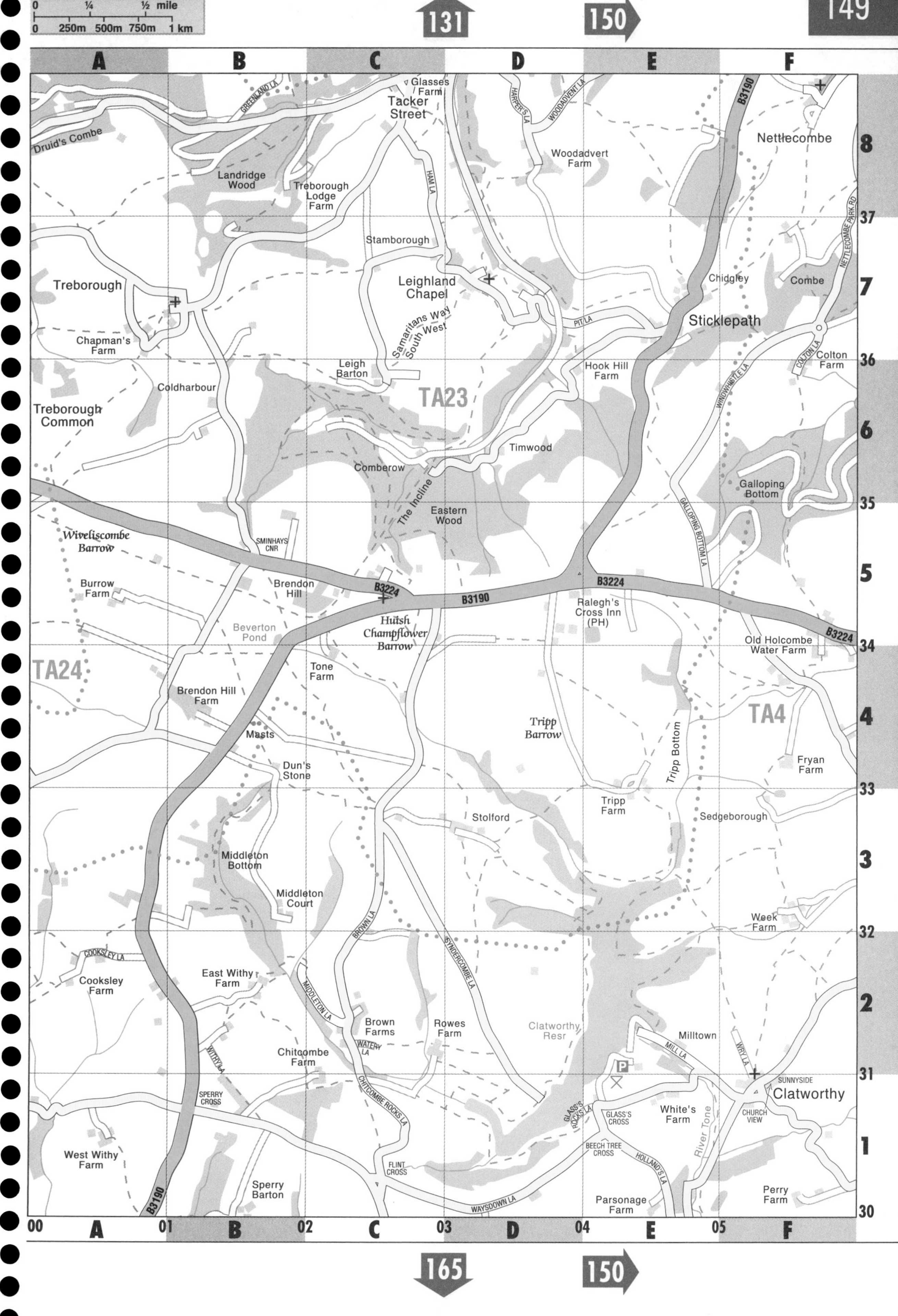
Scale: 1¾ inches to 1 mile
0 ¼ ½ mile
0 250m 500m 750m 1 km
131
150
Glasses Farm
Tacker Street
Druid's Combe
Landridge Wood
Treborough Lodge Farm
Woodadvert Farm
Nettlecombe
Stamborough
Treborough
Leighland Chapel
Chidgley
Combe
Sticklepath
Samaritans Way South West
Chapman's Farm
Leigh Barton
Hook Hill Farm
Colton Farm
Coldharbour
TA23
Treborough Common
Timwood
Comberow
Galloping Bottom
The Incline
Eastern Wood
Wiveliscombe Barrow
Burrow Farm
Brendon Hill
B3224
B3190
Raleigh's Cross Inn (PH)
Beverton Pond
Hutsh Champflower Barrow
Old Holcombe Water Farm
TA24
Tone Farm
Brendon Hill Farm
Tripp Barrow
TA4
Masts
Dun's Stone
Tripp Bottom
Fryan Farm
Tripp Farm
Stolford
Sedgeborough
Middleton Bottom
Middleton Court
Week Farm
Cooksley Farm
East Withy Farm
Brown Farms
Rowes Farm
Clatworthy Resr
Milltown
Chitcombe Farm
Clatworthy
White's Farm
River Tone
West Withy Farm
Sperry Barton
Parsonage Farm
Perry Farm
00 A 01 B 02 C 03 D 04 E 05 F
165
150

149 132

Scale: 1¾ inches to 1 mile

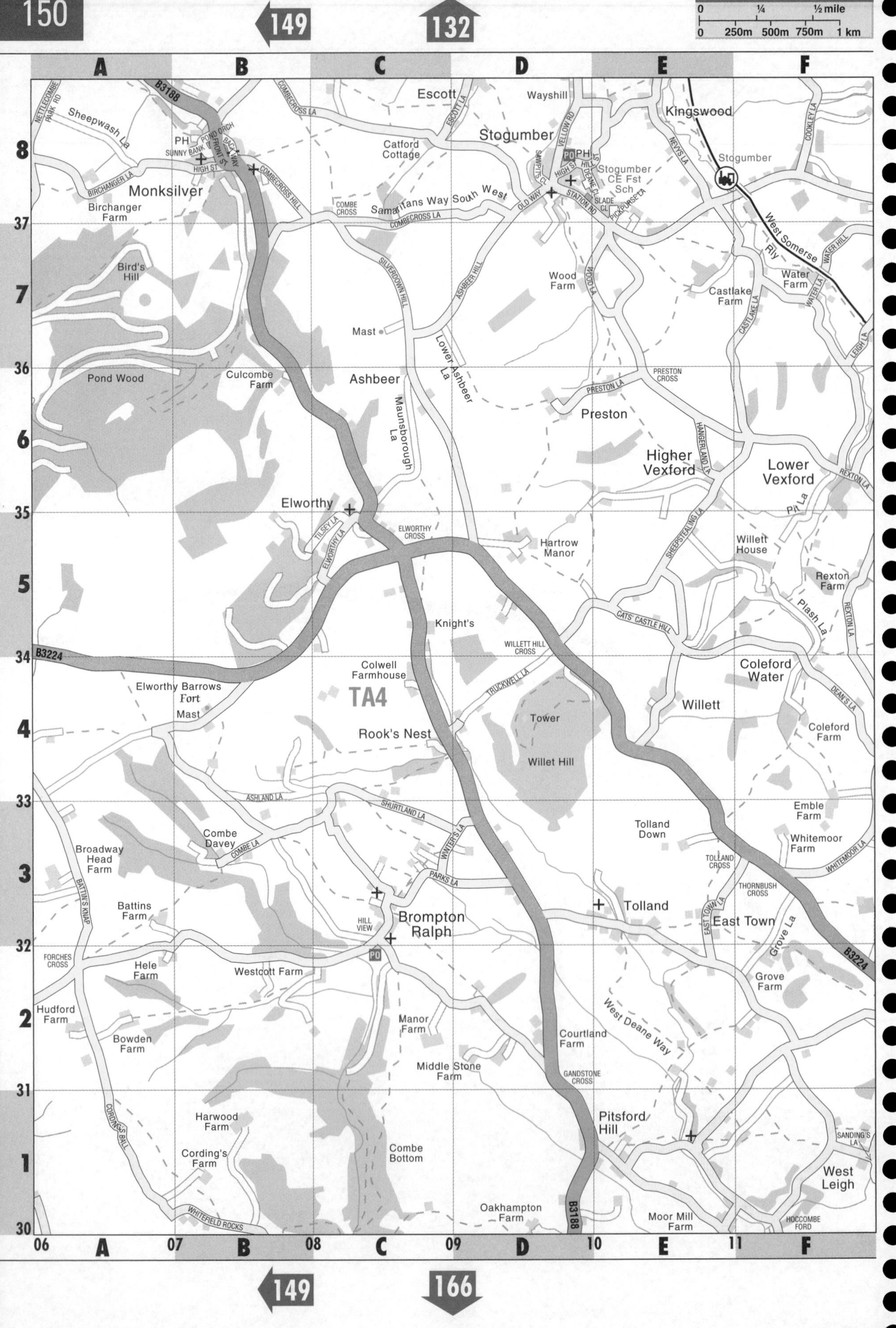

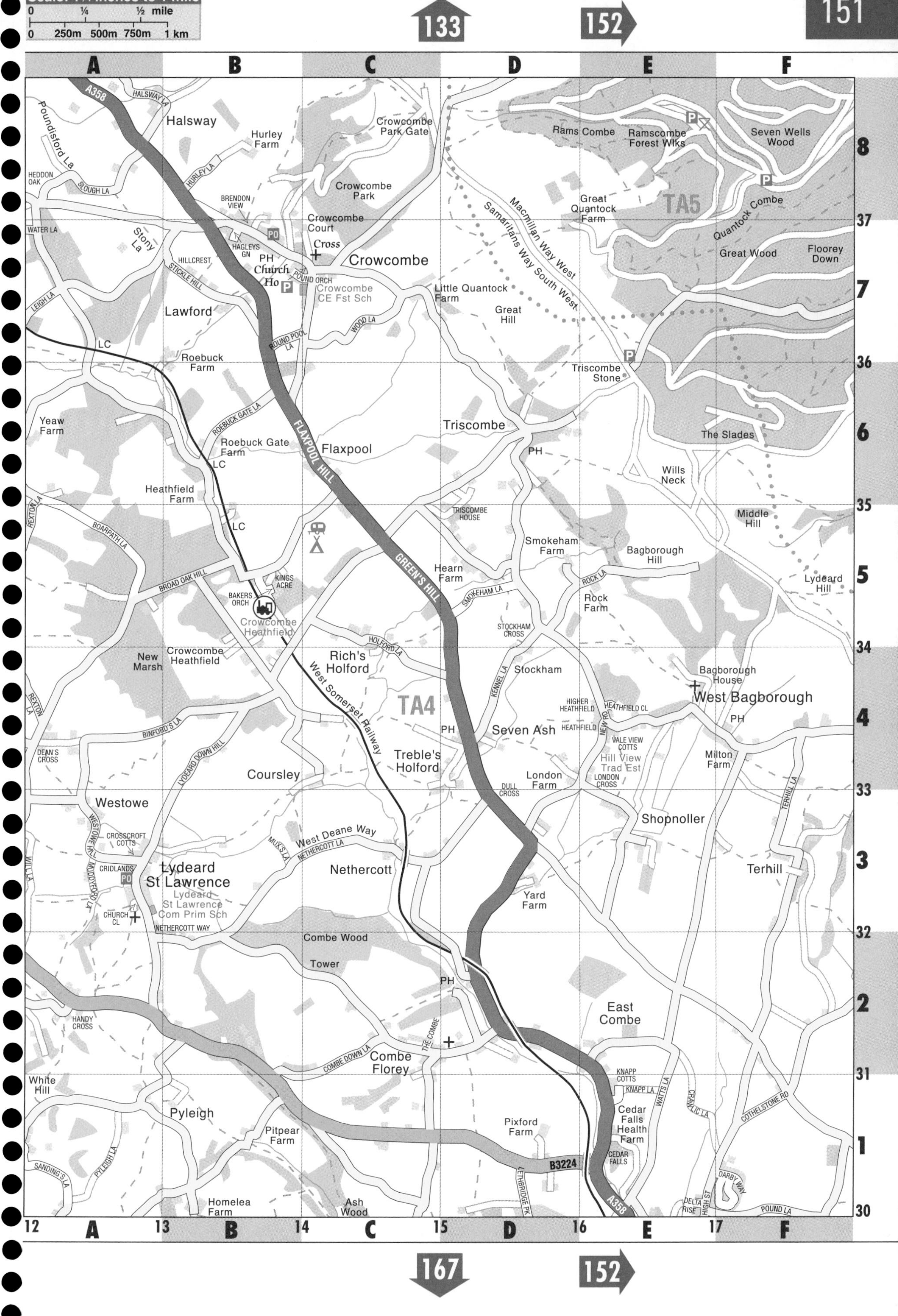
Scale: 1¾ inches to 1 mile
133
152
Halsway
Hurley Farm
Crowcombe Park Gate
Rams Combe
Ramscombe Forest Wlks
Seven Wells Wood
Crowcombe Park
Great Quantock Farm
TA5
Quantock Combe
Crowcombe Court
Cross
Crowcombe
Great Wood
Floorey Down
Church Ho
Crowcombe CE Fst Sch
Little Quantock Farm
Macmillan Way West
Samaritans Way South West
Lawford
Great Hill
Roebuck Farm
Triscombe Stone
Yeaw Farm
Triscombe
The Slades
Roebuck Gate Farm
Flaxpool
FLAXPOOL HILL
Wills Neck
Heathfield Farm
Middle Hill
Smokeham Farm
Bagborough Hill
Hearn Farm
GREEN'S HILL
Rock Farm
Lydeard Hill
Crowcombe Heathfield
New Marsh
Rich's Holford
Stockham
Bagborough House
West Bagborough
West Somerset Railway
TA4
Seven Ash
Hill View Trad Est
Milton Farm
Coursley
Treble's Holford
London Farm
Westowe
Shopnoller
West Deane Way
Lydeard St Lawrence
Nethercott
Terhill
Lydeard St Lawrence Com Prim Sch
Yard Farm
Combe Wood
Tower
East Combe
Combe Florey
White Hill
Pyleigh
Cedar Falls Health Farm
Pitpear Farm
Pixford Farm
B3224
A358
Homelea Farm
Ash Wood
167
152

151
134

Scale: 1¾ inches to 1 mile
0 ¼ ½ mile
0 250m 500m 750m 1 km

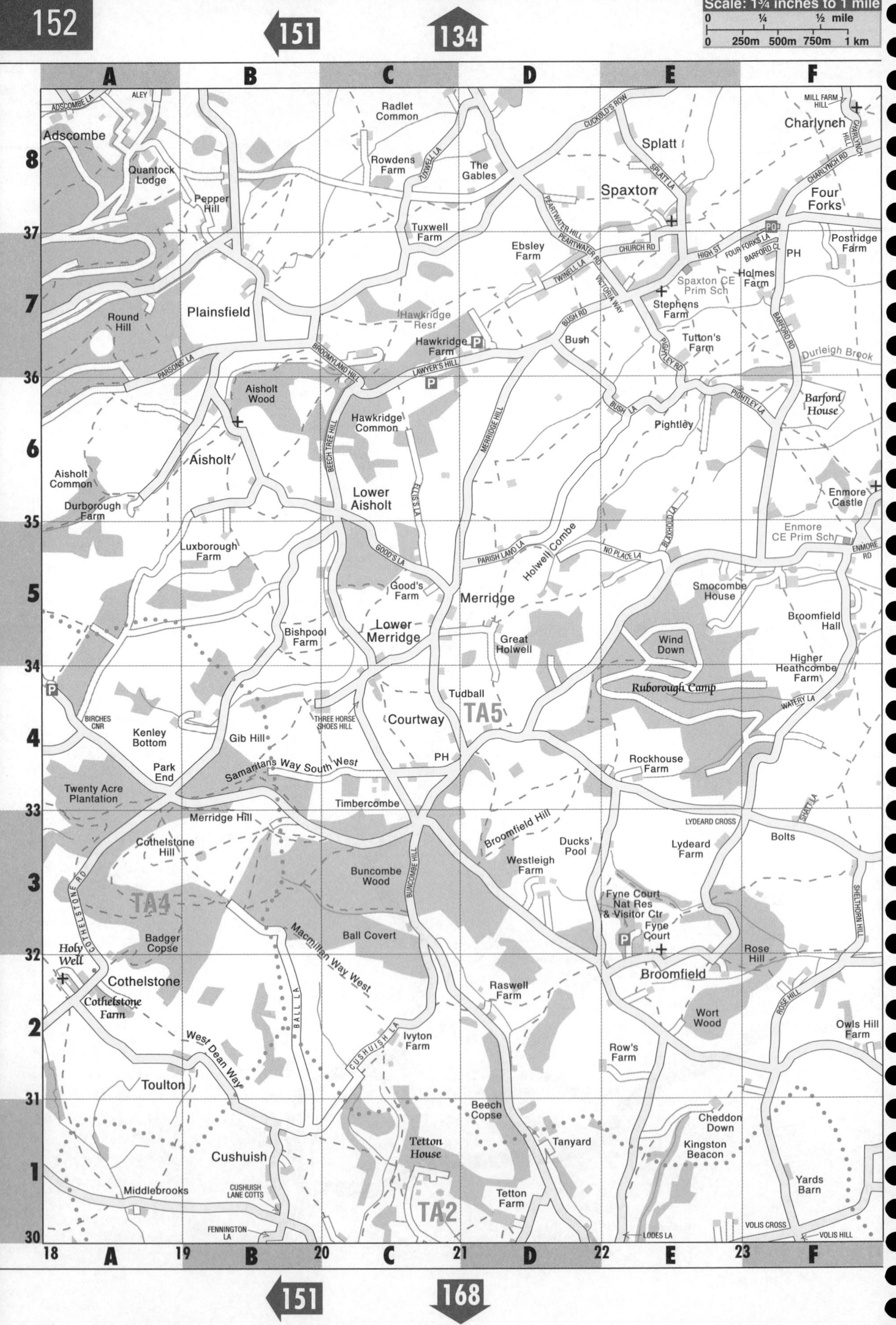

151
168

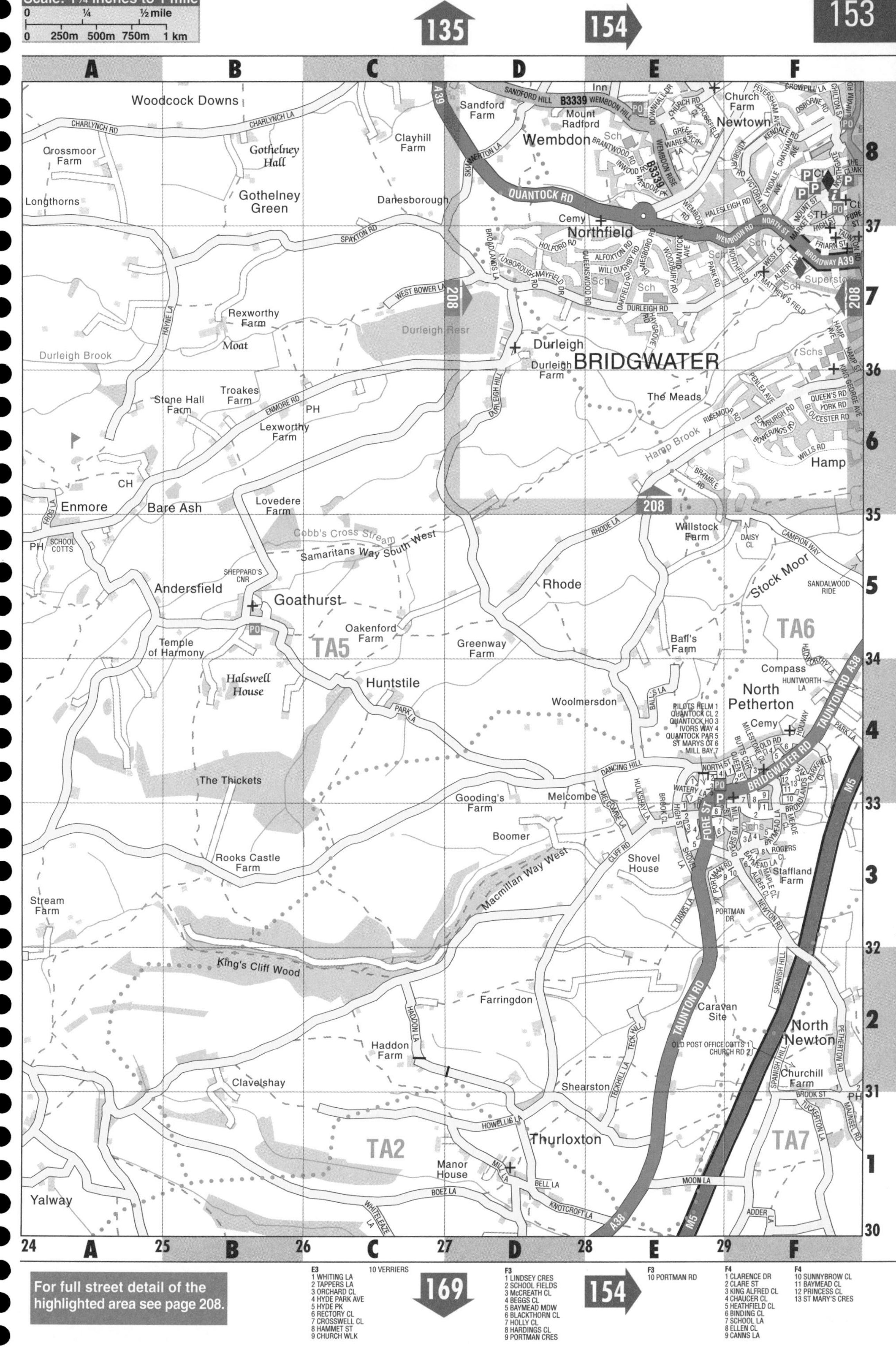
Scale: 1¾ inches to 1 mile
0 ¼ ½ mile
0 250m 500m 750m 1 km
135
154
Woodcock Downs
Crossmoor Farm
Gothelney Hall
Gothelney Green
Clayhill Farm
Danesborough
Longthorns
Sandford Farm
Mount Radford
Wembdon
Inn
Church Farm
Newtown
QUANTOCK RD
Cemy
Northfield
BRIDGWATER
Durleigh
Durleigh Farm
Durleigh Resr
Durleigh Brook
Rexworthy Farm
Moat
Stone Hall Farm
Troakes Farm
Lexworthy Farm
PH
CH
Enmore
Bare Ash
Lovedere Farm
The Meads
Hamp Brook
Hamp
Willstock Farm
Stock Moor
Rhode
Cobb's Cross Stream
Samaritans Way South West
Andersfield
Goathurst
Temple of Harmony
Oakenford Farm
Greenway Farm
TA5
TA6
Ball's Farm
Compass
North Petherton
Halswell House
Huntstile
Woolmersdon
The Thickets
Gooding's Farm
Melcombe
Boomer
Rooks Castle Farm
Shovel House
Stafford Farm
Macmillan Way West
Stream Farm
King's Cliff Wood
Farringdon
Caravan Site
North Newton
Haddon Farm
Clavelshay
Shearston
Churchill Farm
Thurloxton
TA2
TA7
Manor House
Yalway
TAUNTON RD
A38
M5
208
For full street detail of the highlighted area see page 208.
169
154
E3
1 WHITING LA
2 TAPPERS LA
3 ORCHARD CL
4 HYDE PARK AVE
5 HYDE PK
6 RECTORY CL
7 CROSSWELL CL
8 HAMMET ST
9 CHURCH WLK
10 VERRIERS
F3
1 LINDSEY CRES
2 SCHOOL FIELDS
3 McCREATH CL
4 BEGGS CL
5 BAYMEAD MDW
6 BLACKTHORN CL
7 HOLLY CL
8 HARDINGS CL
9 PORTMAN CRES
10 PORTMAN RD
F4
1 CLARENCE DR
2 CLARE ST
3 KING ALFRED CL
4 CHAUCER CL
5 HEATHFIELD CL
6 BINDING CL
7 SCHOOL LA
8 ELLEN CL
9 CANNS LA
10 SUNNYBROW CL
11 BAYMEAD CL
12 PRINCESS CL
13 ST MARY'S CRES

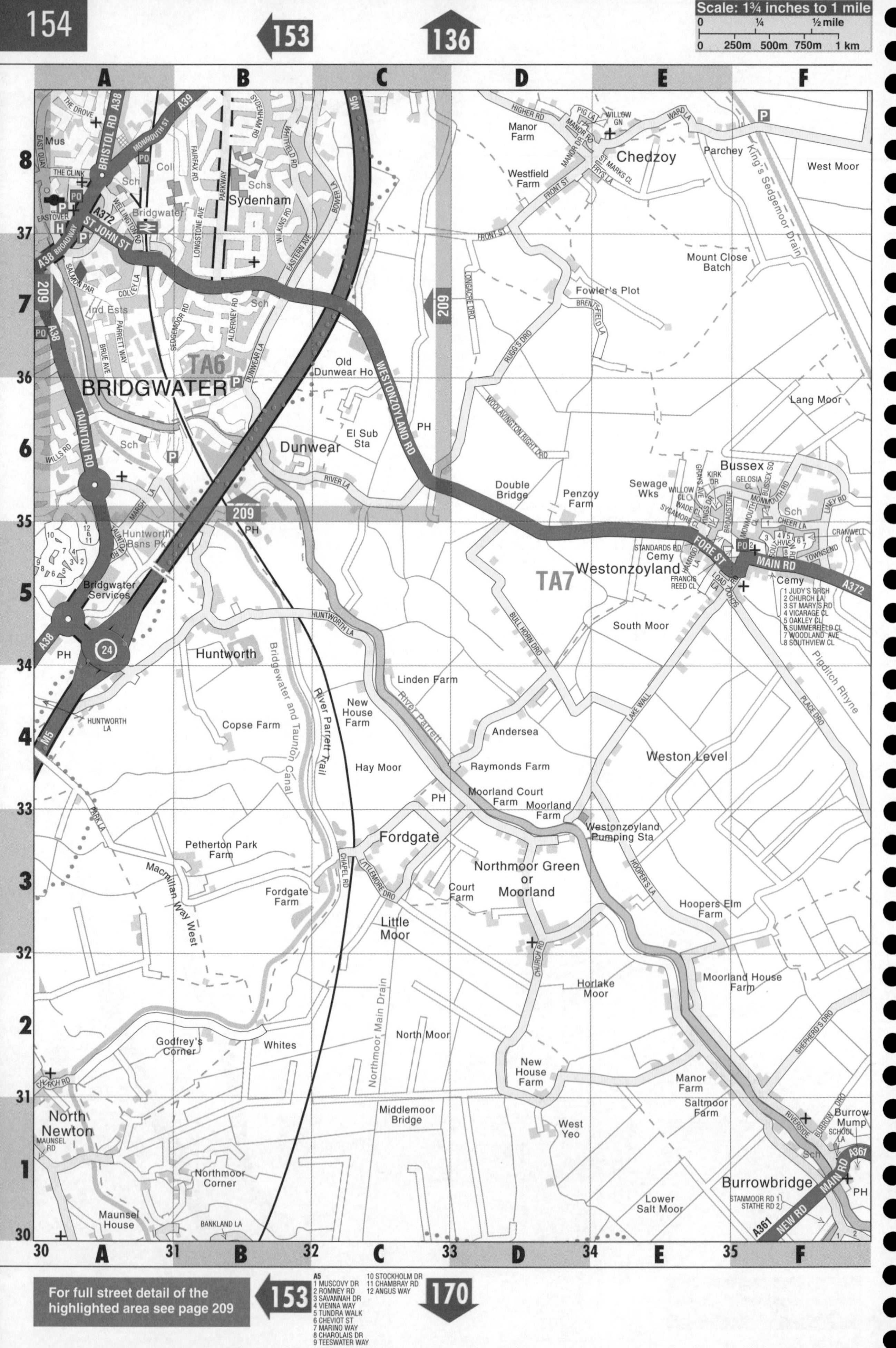

For full street detail of the highlighted area see page 209

153

A5
1 MUSCOVY DR
2 ROMNEY RD
3 SAVANNAH DR
4 VIENNA WALK
5 TUNDRA WALK
6 CHEVIOT ST
7 MARINO WAY
8 CHAROLAIS DR
9 TEESWATER WAY
10 STOCKHOLM DR
11 CHAMBRAY RD
12 ANGUS WAY

170

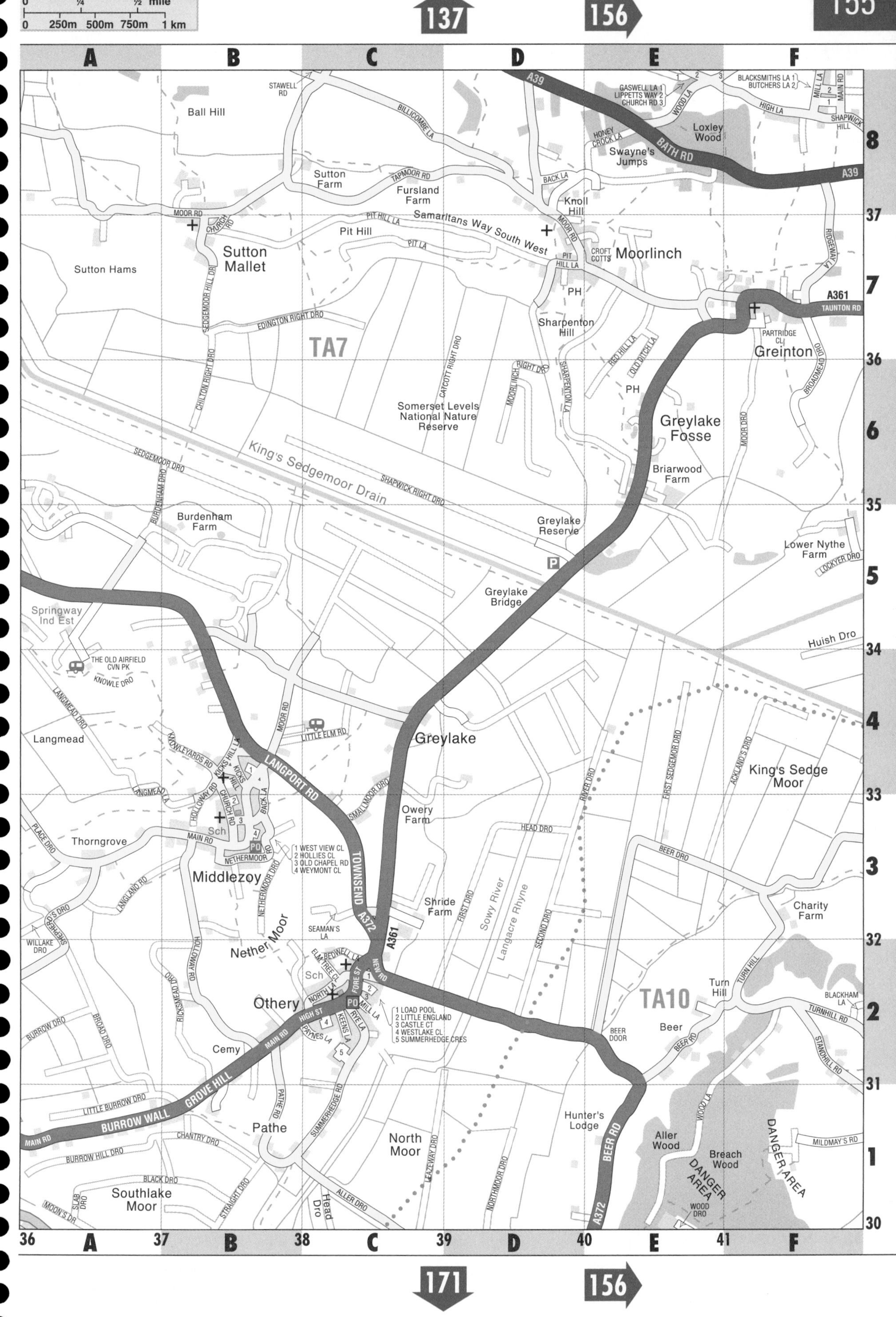
Scale: 1¾ inches to 1 mile
137
156
171
Sutton Mallet
Moorlinch
Greinton
Greylake Fosse
Somerset Levels National Nature Reserve
King's Sedgemoor Drain
Greylake
Middlezoy
Othery
Nether Moor
King's Sedge Moor
TA7
TA10
Beer
Pathe
North Moor
Southlake Moor
Sutton Hams
Langmead
Thorngrove
Springway Ind Est
Burdenham Farm
Greylake Reserve
Greylake Bridge
Owery Farm
Shride Farm
Charity Farm
Turn Hill
Hunter's Lodge
Aller Wood
Breach Wood
DANGER AREA
Loxley Wood
Swayne's Jumps
Knoll Hill
Sharpenton Hill
Briarwood Farm
Lower Nythe Farm
Sutton Farm
Fursland Farm
Pit Hill
Ball Hill
Samaritans Way South West
BATH RD
A39
A361
A372
LANGPORT RD
TOWNSEND
BURROW WALL
GROVE HILL
BEER RD
TAUNTON RD
Sowy River
Langacre Rhyne
Huish Dro
THE OLD AIRFIELD CVN PK
1 WEST VIEW CL
2 HOLLIES CL
3 OLD CHAPEL RD
4 WEYMONT CL
1 LOAD POOL
2 LITTLE ENGLAND
3 CASTLE CT
4 WESTLAKE CL
5 SUMMERHEDGE CRES
GASWELL LA 1
LIPPETTS WAY 2
CHURCH RD 3
BLACKSMITHS LA 1
BUTCHERS LA 2

155
138

Scale: 1¾ inches to 1 mile
0 ¼ ½ mile
0 250m 500m 750m 1 km

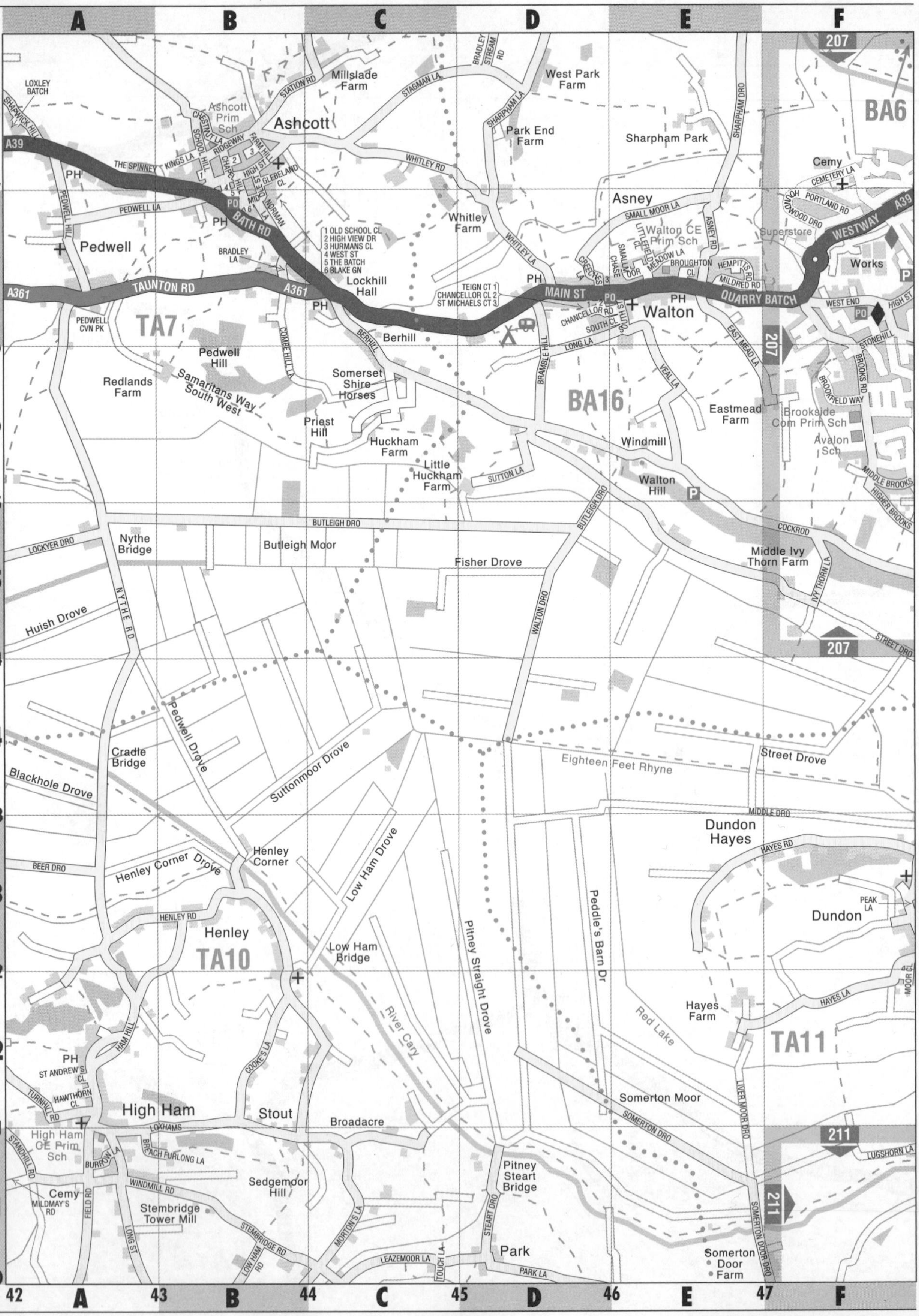

A B C D E F

8 37 7 36 6 35 5 34 4 33 3 32 2 31 1 30

LOXLEY BATCH
SHARPWICK HILL
A39
Ashcott Prim Sch
Ashcott
CHESTNUT LA
SCHOOL HILL
RIDGEWAY
KINGS LA
THE SPINNEY
CHAPEL HILL
HIGH ST
FARM HILL
GLEBELAND CL
NORMAN
MID LA
STATION RD
Millslade Farm
STAGMAN LA
BRADLEY STREAM RD
West Park Farm
SHARPHAM LA
Park End Farm
Sharpham Park
SHARPHAM DRO
WHITLEY RD
PH
PEDWELL HILL
PEDWELL LA
Pedwell
PO
BATH RD
1 OLD SCHOOL CL
2 HIGH VIEW DR
3 HURMANS CL
4 WEST ST
5 THE BATCH
6 BLAKE GN
BRADLEY LA
Whitley Farm
WHITLEY LA
Asney
SMALL MOOR LA
LITTLEFIELD CL
Walton CE Prim Sch
ASNEY RD
MEADOW LA
SMALL MOOR CHASE
BROUGHTON CL
HEMPITTS RD
MILDRED RD
CRECHES LA
A361
TAUNTON RD
Lockhill Hall
TEIGN CT 1
CHANCELLOR CL 2
ST MICHAELS CT 3
MAIN ST
PO
Walton
PH
QUARRY BATCH
PEDWELL CVN PK
TA7
COMBE HILL LA
BERHILL
Berhill
CHANCELLOR RD
SOUTH CL
LONG LA
Pedwell Hill
Redlands Farm
Samaritans Way South West
Somerset Shire Horses
BRAMBLE HILL
BA16
VEAL LA
EAST MEAD LA
Priest Hill
Huckham Farm
Little Huckham Farm
Windmill
Eastmead Farm
SUTTON LA
Walton Hill
P
BUTLEIGH DRO
LOCKYER DRO
Nythe Bridge
Butleigh Moor
Fisher Drove
COCKROD
Middle Ivy Thorn Farm
IVY THORN LA
Huish Drove
NYTHE RD
WALTON DRO
STREET DRO
Pedwell Drove
Cradle Bridge
Blackhole Drove
Suttonmoor Drove
Eighteen Feet Rhyne
Street Drove
MIDDLE DRO
Dundon Hayes
HAYES RD
BEER DRO
Henley Corner
Henley Corner Drove
Low Ham Drove
Pedde's Barn Dr
PEAK LA
Dundon
HENLEY RD
Henley
TA10
Low Ham Bridge
Pitney Straight Drove
Red Lake
Hayes Farm
HAYES LA
MOOR
River Cary
TA11
HAM HILL
PH
ST ANDREW'S CL
HAWTHORN CL
TURNHILL RD
COOKE'S LA
LIVER MOOR DRO
Somerton Moor
SOMERTON DRO
High Ham
Stout
LOXHAMS
Broadacre
High Ham CE Prim Sch
BURROW LA
BREACH FURLONG LA
LUGSHORN LA
STANDHILL RD
Pitney Steart Bridge
Cemy
MILDMAY'S RD
FIELD RD
WINDMILL RD
Sedgemoor Hill
STEART DRO
SOMERTON DOOR DRO
Stembridge Tower Mill
MORTON'S LA
LONG ST
STEMBRIDGE RD
LOW HAM RD
LEAZEMOOR LA
TOUCH LA
Park
PARK LA
Somerton Door Farm

207
BA6
Cemy
CEMETERY LA
PORTLAND RD
WOOD DRO
WESTWAY
A39
Superstore
Works
P
WEST END
HIGH ST
PO
STONEHILL
BROOKS RD
BROOKFIELD WAY
Brookside Com Prim Sch
Avalon Sch
MIDDLE BROOKS
HIGHER BROOKS
207
207
211
211

42 A 43 B 44 C 45 D 46 E 47 F

155
172

For full street detail of the highlighted area see pages 207 and 211.

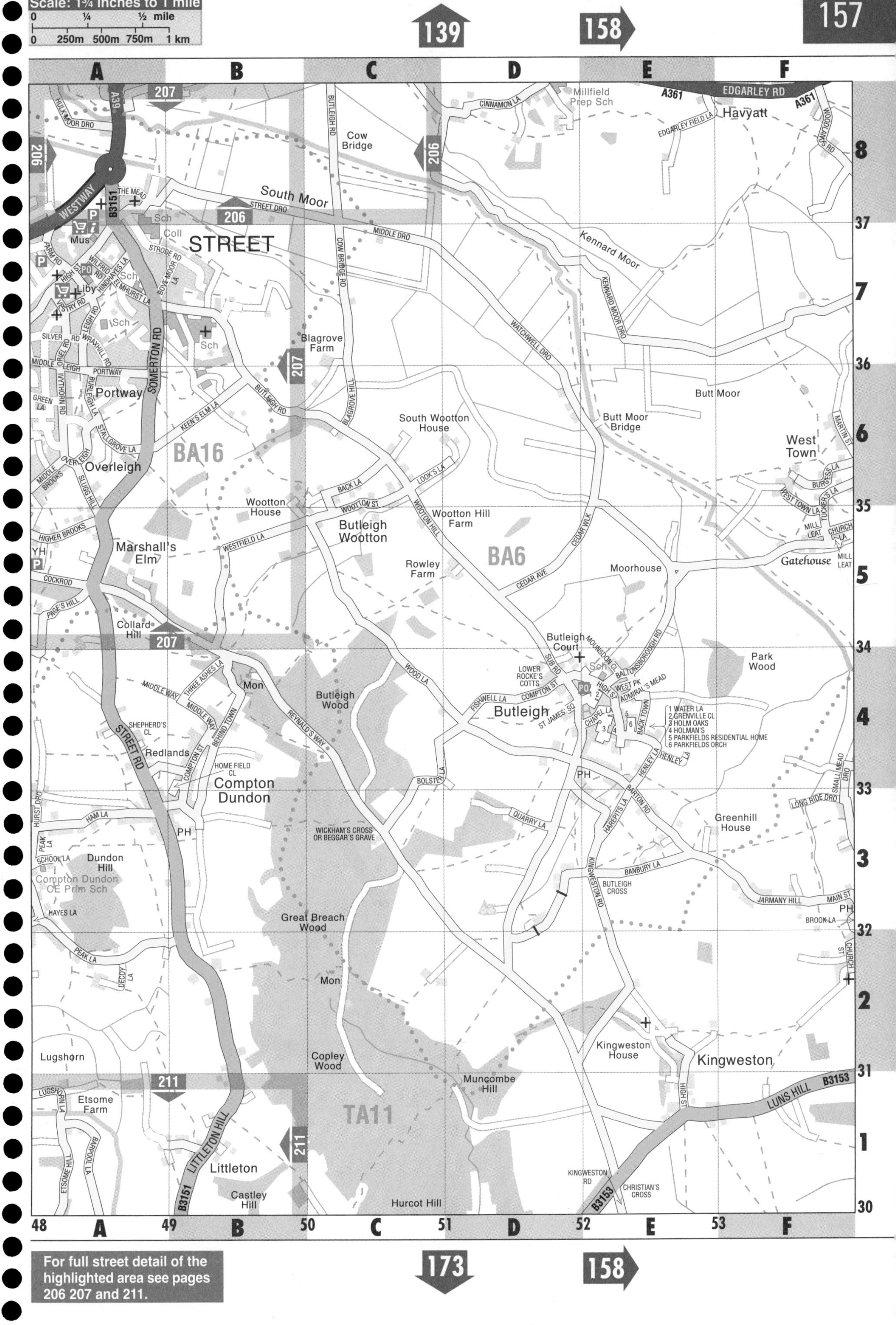
Scale: 1¾ inches to 1 mile
0 ¼ ½ mile
0 250m 500m 750m 1 km
139
158
A B C D E F
8 37 7 36 6 35 5 34 4 33 3 32 2 31 1 30
48 49 50 51 52 53
206
207
211
173
STREET
South Moor
Kennard Moor
Cow Bridge
Millfield Prep Sch
Havyatt
EDGARLEY RD
A361
A39
B3151
WESTWAY
STREET DRO
MIDDLE DRO
WATCHWELL DRO
KENNARD MOOR DRO
Blagrove Farm
Portway
Overleigh
BA16
South Wootton House
Butt Moor Bridge
Butt Moor
West Town
Wootton House
Butleigh Wootton
Wootton Hill Farm
Marshall's Elm
Rowley Farm
BA6
Moorhouse
Gatehouse
Collard Hill
Butleigh Court
Park Wood
Butleigh Wood
Butleigh
Redlands
Compton Dundon
PH
Dundon Hill
Compton Dundon CE Prim Sch
Greenhill House
WICKHAM'S CROSS OR BEGGAR'S GRAVE
Great Breach Wood
Mon
Lugshorn
Copley Wood
Muncombe Hill
Kingweston House
Kingweston
Etsome Farm
TA11
Littleton
Castley Hill
Hurcot Hill
KINGWESTON RD
CHRISTIAN'S CROSS
LUNS HILL
B3153
LITTLETON HILL
STREET RD
SOMERTON RD
1 WATER LA
2 GRENVILLE CL
3 HOLM OAKS
4 HOLMAN'S
5 PARKFIELDS RESIDENTIAL HOME
6 PARKFIELDS ORCH
For full street detail of the highlighted area see pages 206 207 and 211.

157 140

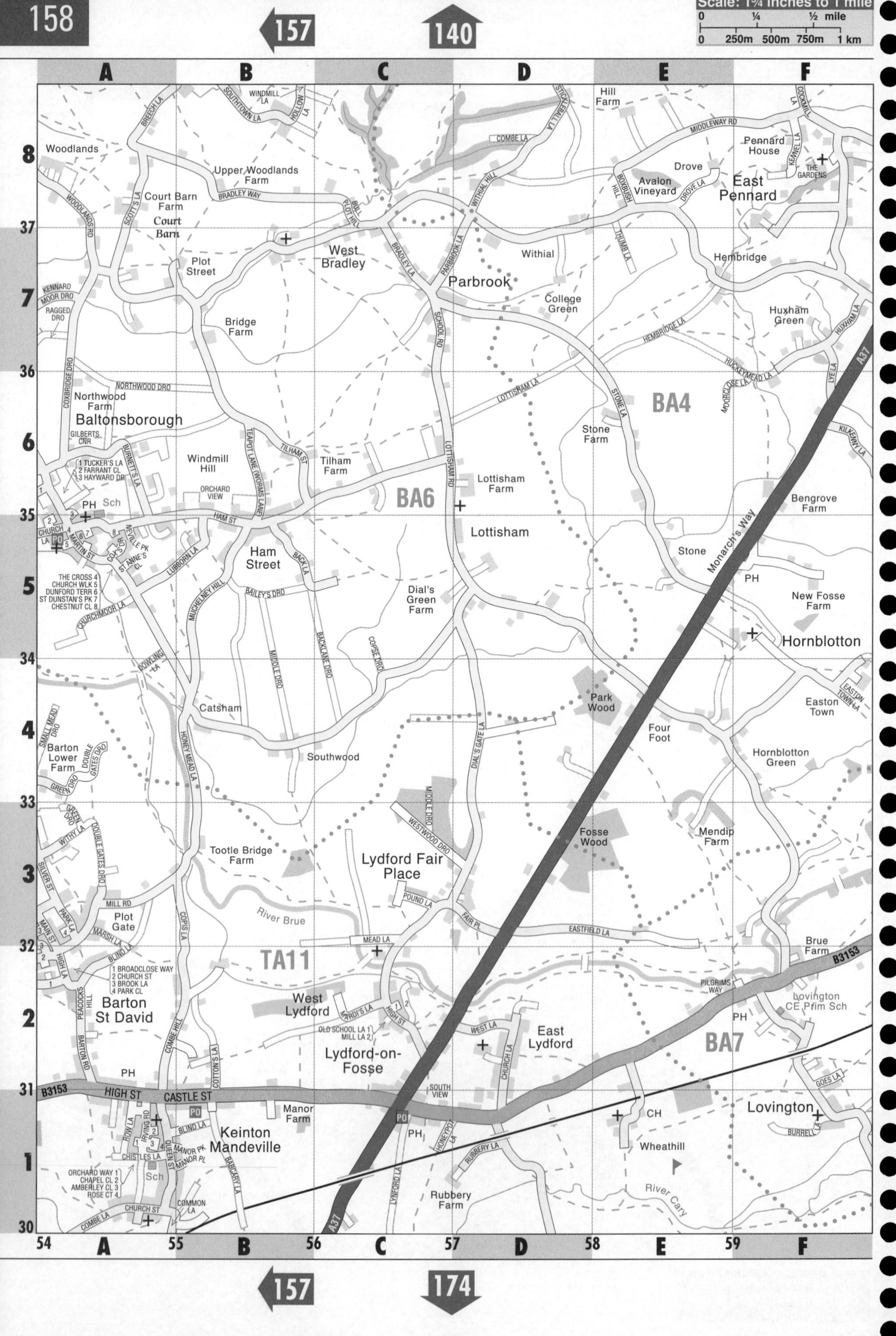

157 174

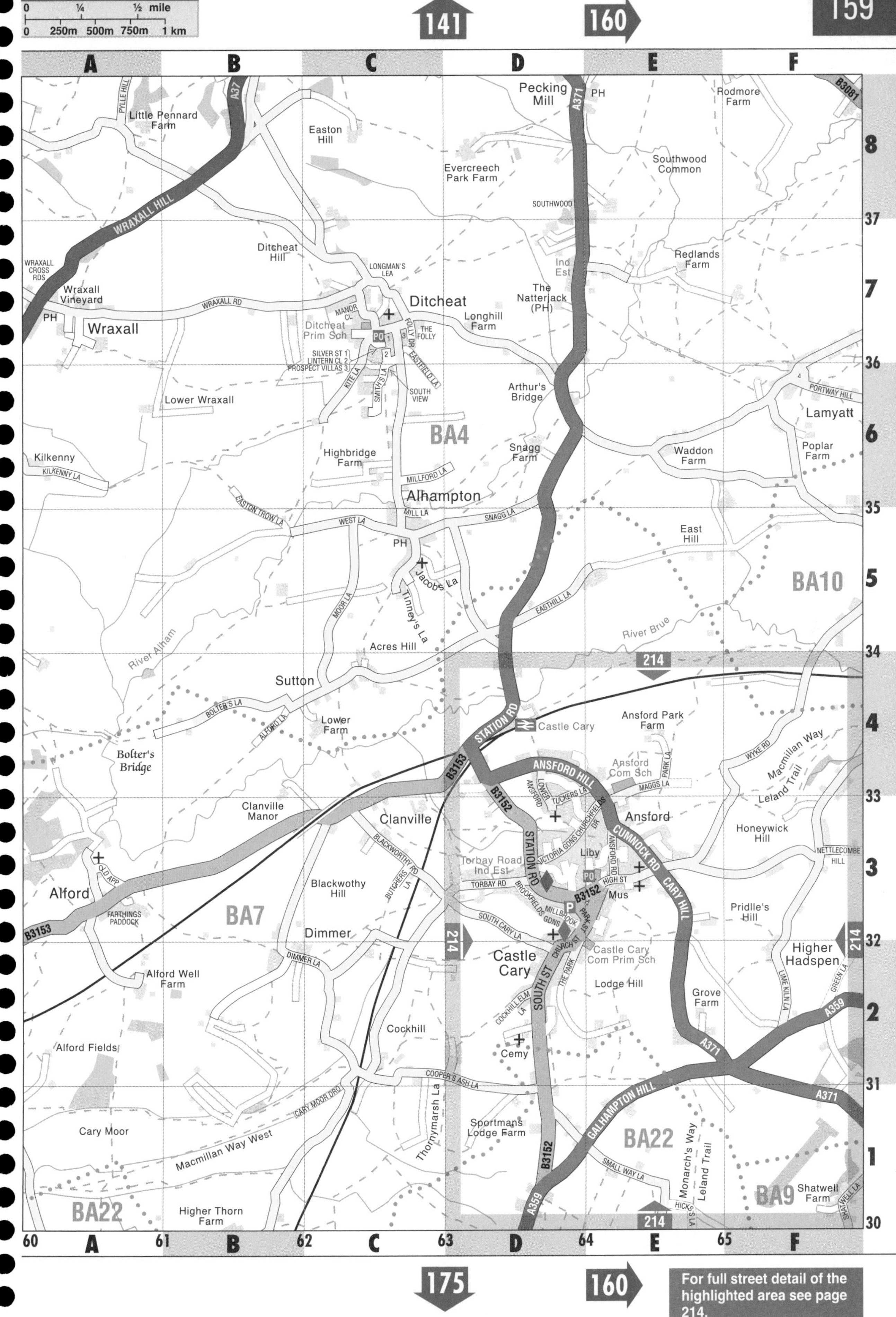

For full street detail of the highlighted area see page 214.

159
142

Scale: 1¾ inches to 1 mile
0 ¼ ½ mile
0 250m 500m 750m 1 km

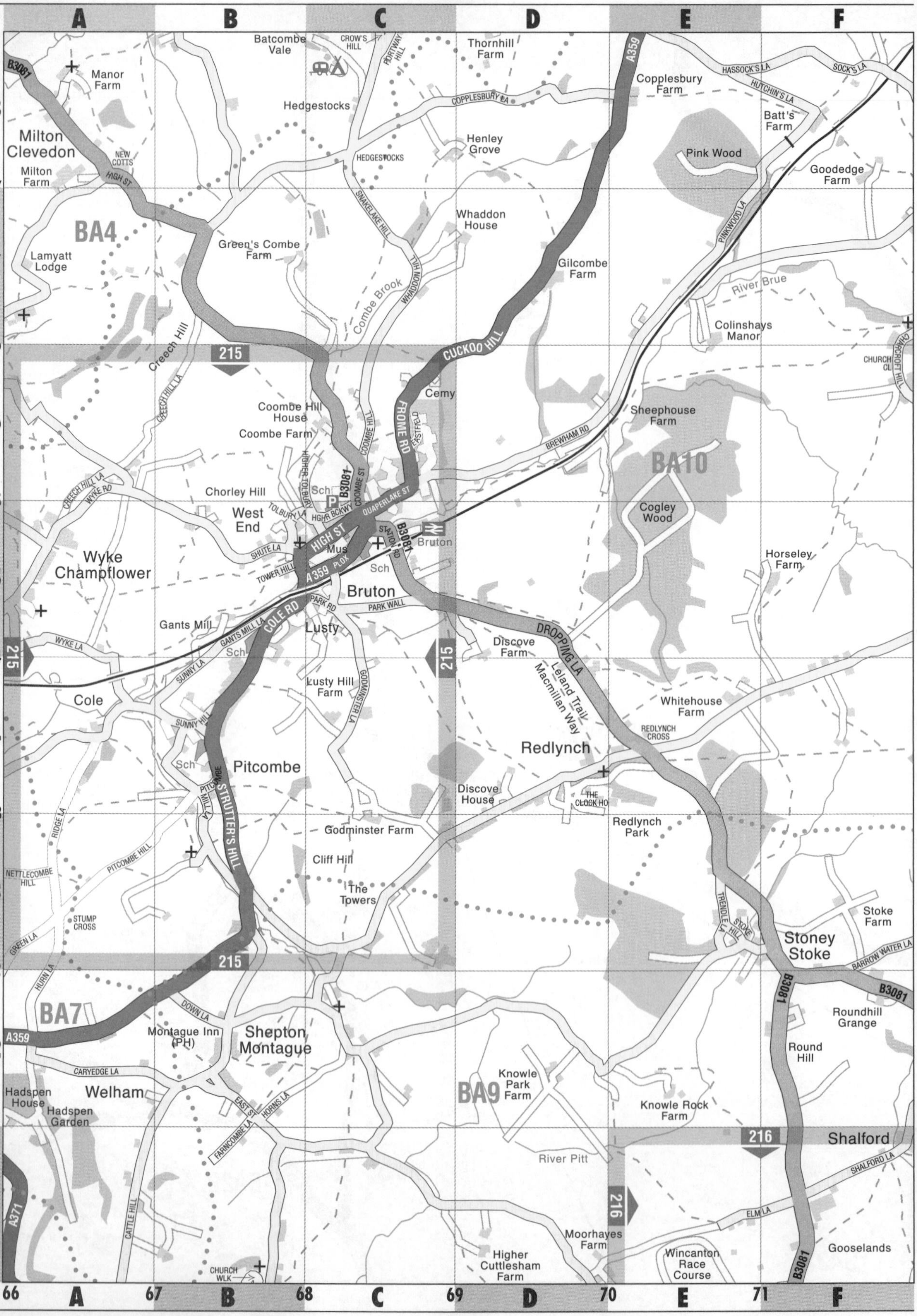

For full street detail of the highlighted area see pages 215 and 216.
159
176

Scale: 1¾ inches to 1 mile
0 ¼ ½ mile
0 250m 500m 750m 1 km

143

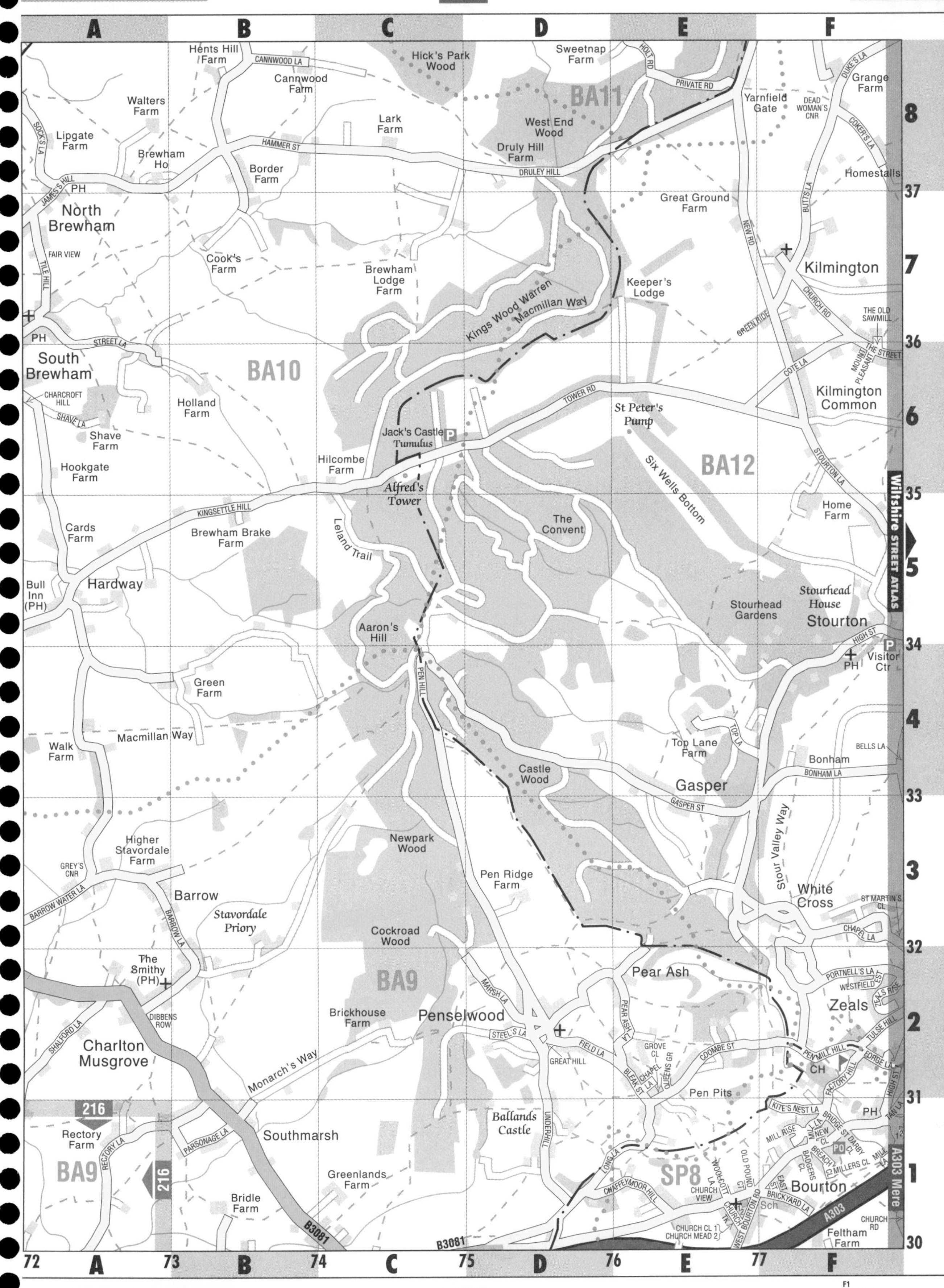

F1
1 SILTON RD
2 THE MEADOWS

For full street detail of the highlighted area see page 216.

177

146

Scale: 1¾ inches to 1 mile

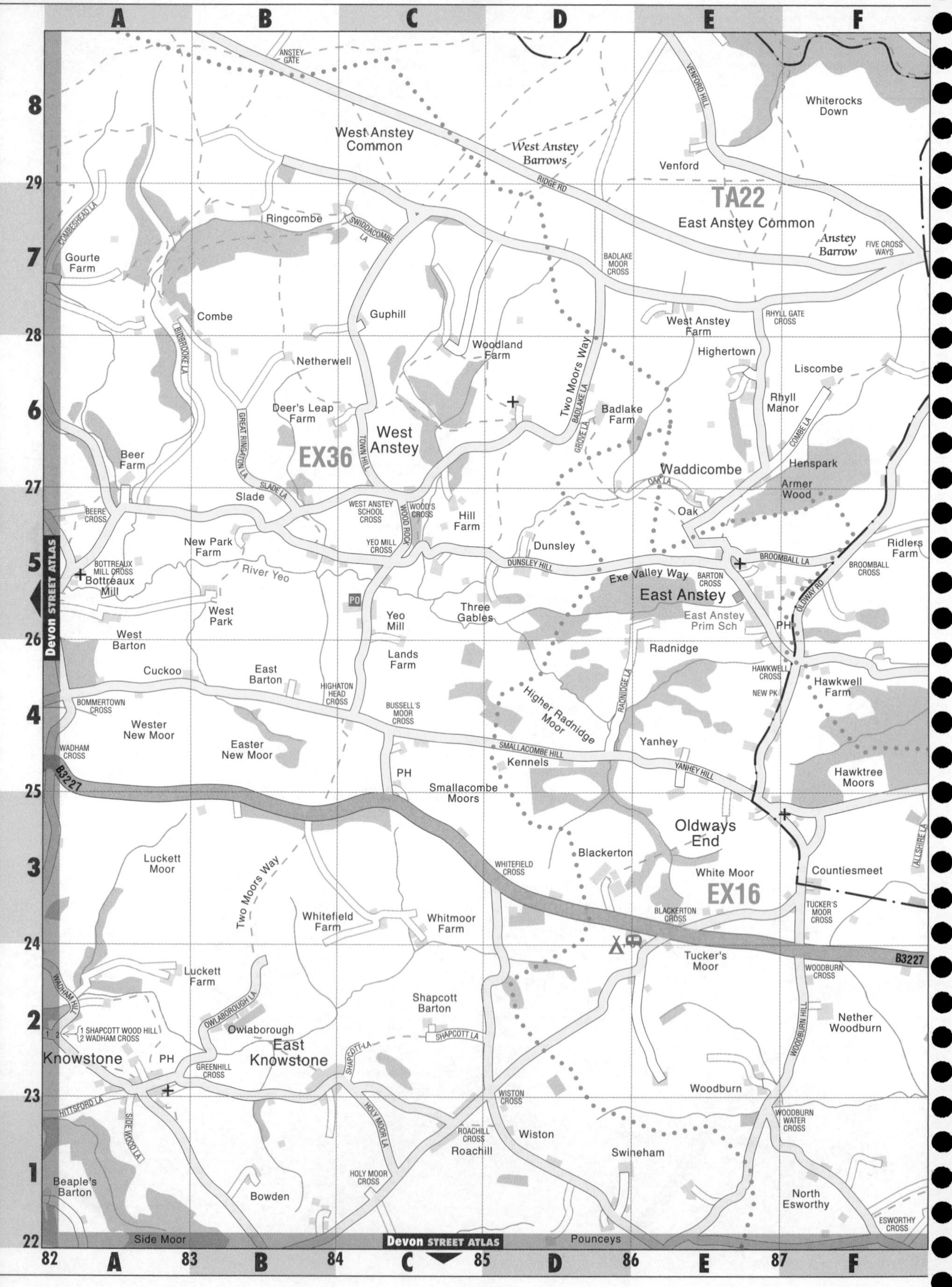

Scale: 1¾ inches to 1 mile

147
164

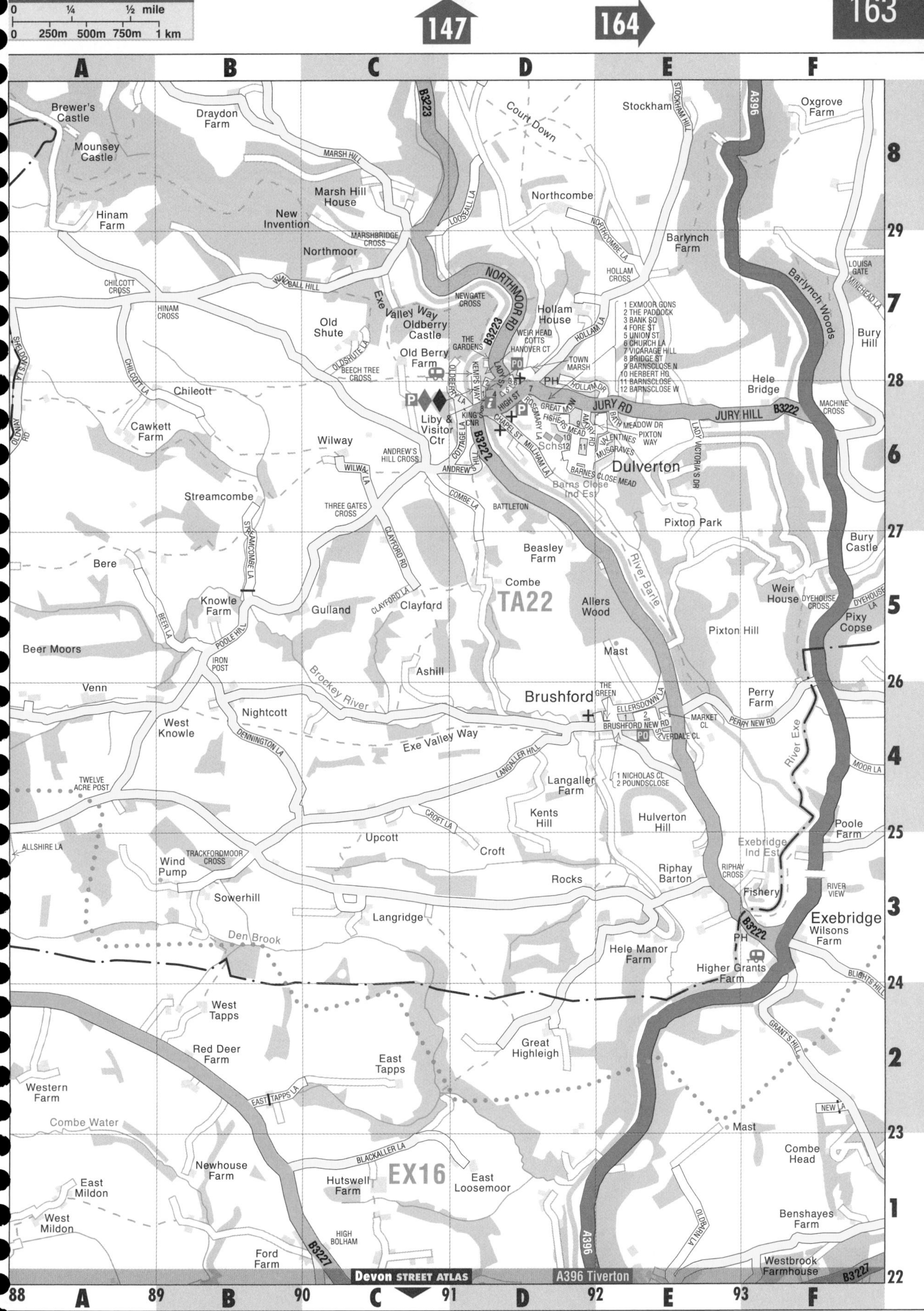

34

163
148

Scale: 1¾ inches to 1 mile
0 ¼ ½ mile
0 250m 500m 750m 1 km

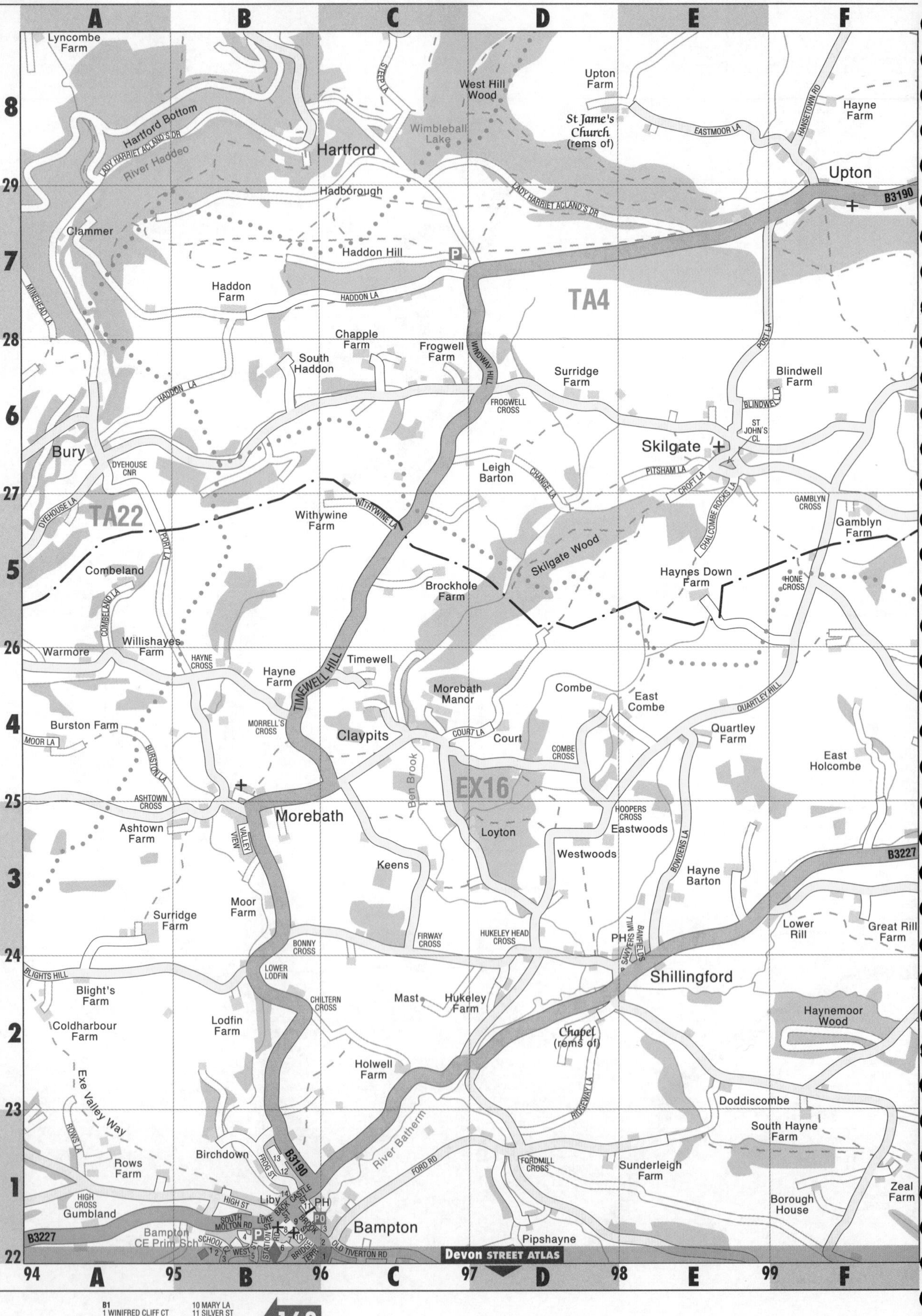

A B C D E F

8
29
7
28
6
27
5
26
4
25
3
24
2
23
1
22

Lyncombe Farm
West Hill Wood
Upton Farm
Hayne Farm
Hartford Bottom
LADY HARRIET ACLAND'S DR
River Haddeo
Wimbleball Lake
Hartford
St Jame's Church (rems of)
EASTMOOR LA
HANSETOWN RD
Upton
B3190
Hadborough
LADY HARRIET ACLAND'S DR
Clammer
Haddon Hill
P
MINEHEAD LA
Haddon Farm
HADDON LA
TA4
Chapple Farm
Frogwell Farm
WINDWAY HILL
POST LA
South Haddon
Surridge Farm
Blindwell Farm
HADDON LA
FROGWELL CROSS
BLINDWELL LA
ST JOHN'S CL
Bury
DYEHOUSE CNR
Leigh Barton
CHANGE LA
Skilgate
PITSHAM LA
CROFT LA
CHALCOMBE ROCKS LA
GAMBLYN CROSS
DYEHOUSE LA
TA22
PORT LA
Withywine Farm
WITHYWINE LA
Gamblyn Farm
Skilgate Wood
Combeland
Brockhole Farm
Haynes Down Farm
HONE CROSS
COMBELAND LA
Warmore
Willishayes Farm
HAYNE CROSS
TIMEWELL HILL
Timewell
Hayne Farm
Morebath Manor
Combe
East Combe
QUARTLEY HILL
Burston Farm
MOORE LA
MORRELL'S CROSS
Claypits
COURT LA
Court
Quartley Farm
BURSTON LA
Ben Brook
COMBE CROSS
East Holcombe
EX16
ASHTOWN CROSS
Morebath
VALLEY VIEW
HOOPERS CROSS
Ashtown Farm
Loyton
Eastwoods
Westwoods
BOWDENS LA
B3227
Keens
Hayne Barton
Moor Farm
Surridge Farm
FIRWAY CROSS
HUKELEY HEAD CROSS
PH
BANFIELDS
SAWYERS MILL
Lower Rill
Great Rill Farm
BONNY CROSS
BLIGHTS HILL
LOWER LODFIN
Shillingford
Blight's Farm
CHILTERN CROSS
Mast
Hukeley Farm
Lodfin Farm
Haynemoor Wood
Coldharbour Farm
Chapel (rems of)
Exe Valley Way
Holwell Farm
RIDGEWAY LA
Doddiscombe
ROWS LA
River Batherm
South Hayne Farm
Birchdown
B3190
FROG ST
FORD RD
FORDMILL CROSS
Sunderleigh Farm
Rows Farm
HIGH CROSS
Gumbland
HIGH ST
Liby
BACK CASTLE ST
PH
PO
Zeal Farm
Borough House
B3227
SOUTH MOLTON RD
LUKE ST
Bampton
Bampton CE Prim Sch
SCHOOL CL
WEST ST
STATION RD
BROOK ST
BRIDGE TERR
OLD TIVERTON RD
Pipshayne

94 A 95 B 96 C 97 D 98 E 99 F

B1
1 WINIFRED CLIFF CT
2 MEADOW VIEW
3 BALLHILL LA
4 MARKET CL
5 LORDS MEADOW LA
6 BARNHAY
7 CHURCH TERR
8 NEWTON SQ
9 FORE ST
10 MARY LA
11 SILVER ST
12 BOURCHIER DR
13 BOURCHIER CL
14 NEWTON CT
C1
1 TIVERTON RD
2 BRITON ST
3 NEW BLDGS

163

Scale: 1¾ inches to 1 mile
0 ¼ ½ mile
0 250m 500m 750m 1 km

149
166

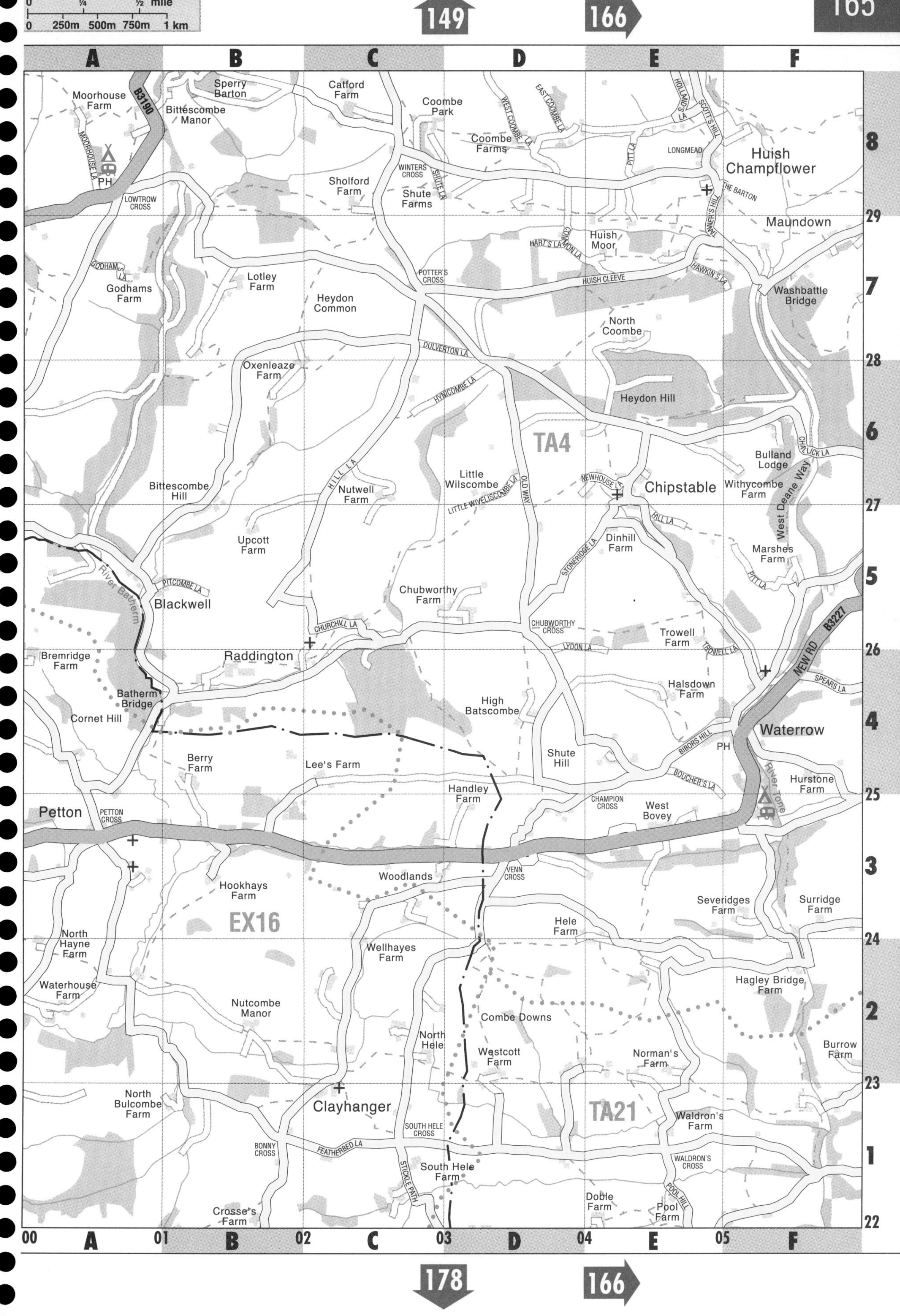

178
166

165
150

Scale: 1¾ inches to 1 mile
0 ¼ ½ mile
0 250m 500m 750m 1 km

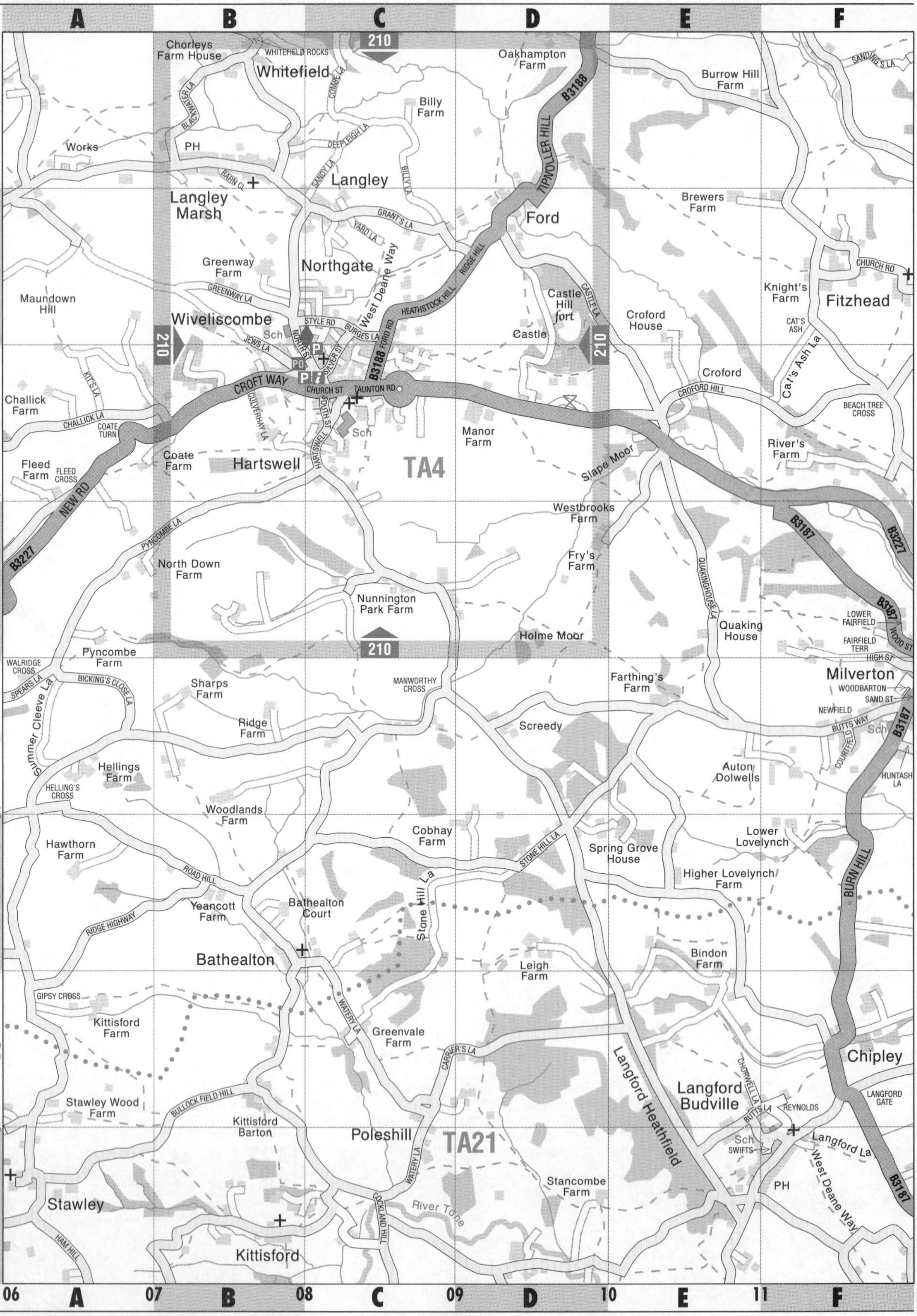

For full street detail of the highlighted area see page 210.
165
179

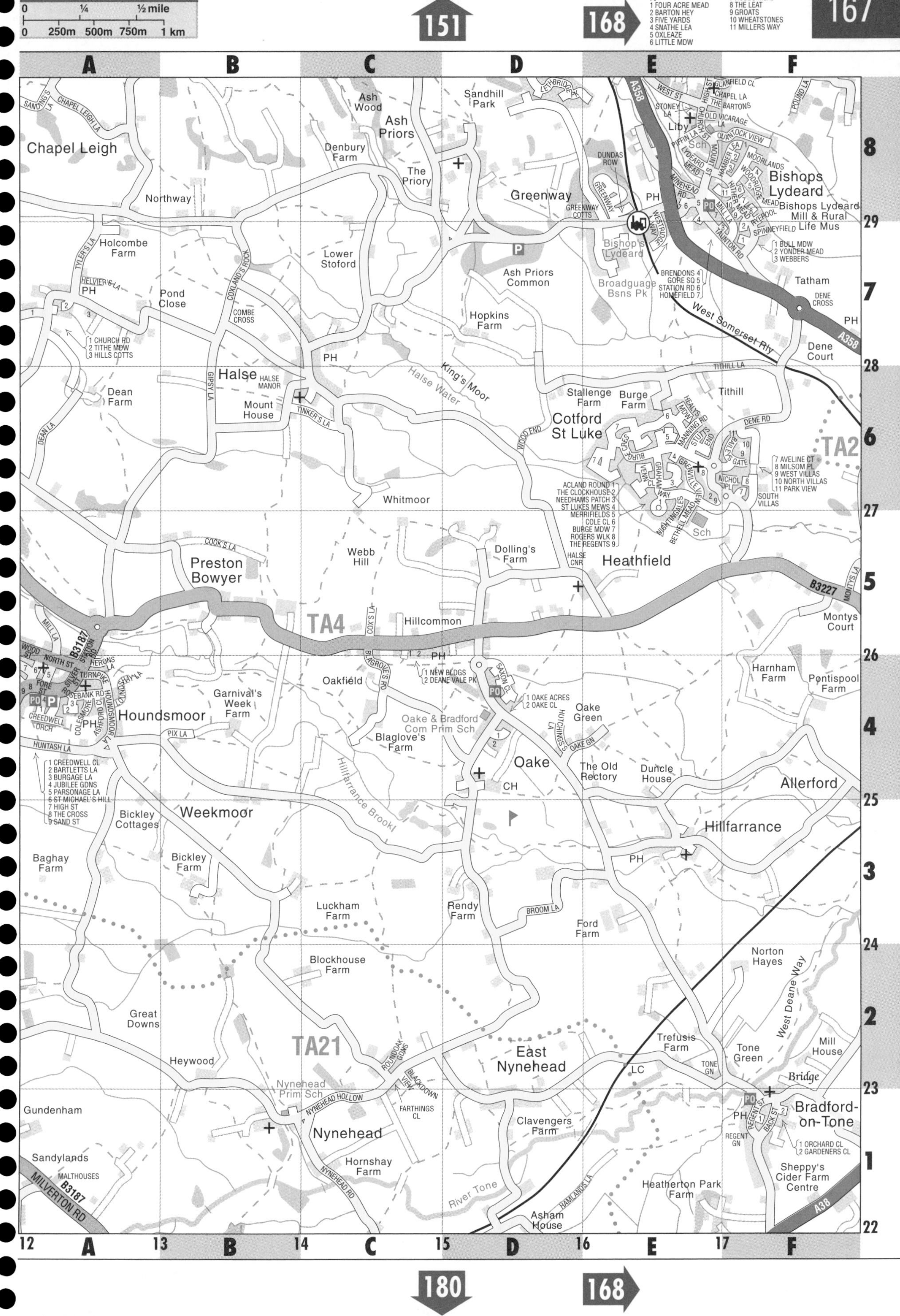

Scale: 1¾ inches to 1 mile
0 ¼ ½ mile
0 250m 500m 750m 1 km
151
168
F8
1 FOUR ACRE MEAD
2 BARTON HEY
3 FIVE YARDS
4 SNATHE LEA
5 OXLEAZE
6 LITTLE MDW
7 HOBBS MEAD
8 THE LEAT
9 GROATS
10 WHEATSTONES
11 MILLERS WAY
Chapel Leigh
Ash Wood
Ash Priors
Sandhill Park
Denbury Farm
The Priory
Greenway
Bishops Lydeard
Bishops Lydeard Mill & Rural Life Mus
Northway
Holcombe Farm
Lower Stoford
Ash Priors Common
Bishop's Lydeard
Broadguage Bsns Pk
Tatham
Pond Close
Hopkins Farm
West Somerset Rly
Dene Court
Halse
Halse Manor
Mount House
Halse Water
King's Moor
Stallenge Farm
Burge Farm
Tithill
Cotford St Luke
Dean Farm
Whitmoor
TA2
Preston Bowyer
Webb Hill
Dolling's Farm
Heathfield
TA4
Hillcommon
Montys Court
Oakfield
Harnham Farm
Pontispool Farm
Houndsmoor
Garnival's Week Farm
Oake & Bradford Com Prim Sch
Blaglove's Farm
Oake Green
Oake
The Old Rectory
Duncle House
Allerford
Weekmoor
Bickley Cottages
Hillfarrance Brook
Hillfarrance
Baghay Farm
Bickley Farm
Luckham Farm
Rendy Farm
Ford Farm
Blockhouse Farm
Norton Hayes
West Deane Way
Great Downs
Heywood
TA21
East Nynehead
Trefusis Farm
Tone Green
Mill House
Bridge
Nynehead Prim Sch
Nynehead
Bradford-on-Tone
Gundenham
Clavengers Farm
Sandylands
Hornshay Farm
River Tone
Heatherton Park Farm
Sheppy's Cider Farm Centre
Asham House
A358
B3227
B3187
A38
MILVERTON RD

Scale: 1¾ inches to 1 mile
0 ¼ ½ mile
0 250m 500m 750m 1 km

VILBERIE CL 8
DABINETT CL 9

PROWSES MDW 1
KINGDOM LA 2
COOPERS MILL 3
CHURCH CL 4
NORTHWOOD CL 5
COPPIN RD 6
YARLINGTON CL 7

SLAPES CL 1
BLACKTHORN GDNS 2
SOUTHFIELD CL 3

POPE CL 1
FIVASH CL 2
STONE CL 3
HEWETT CL 4

1 THE PADDOCK
2 COPLESTONS
3 WILD OAK HO
4 TRULL GREEN DR
5 ORCHARD CL
6 FAIRVIEW TERR
7 GLENCOE TERR
8 SOUTH VIEW TERR

9 EASTBROOK TERR
10 MILL LANE CL
11 CHERRY ORCH
12 WYATTS FIELD
13 SOUTHWELL CL
14 SOUTHWELL
15 HAYGROVE PK

KILLAMS CL 1
KILLAMS LA 2
THE PADDOCK 3
KILLAMS DR 4
KILLAMS CRES 5
FULLANDS CT 6
FULLANDS AVE 7
BILBERRY GR 8
SAFFRON CL 9

For full street detail of the highlighted area see pages 212 and 213.

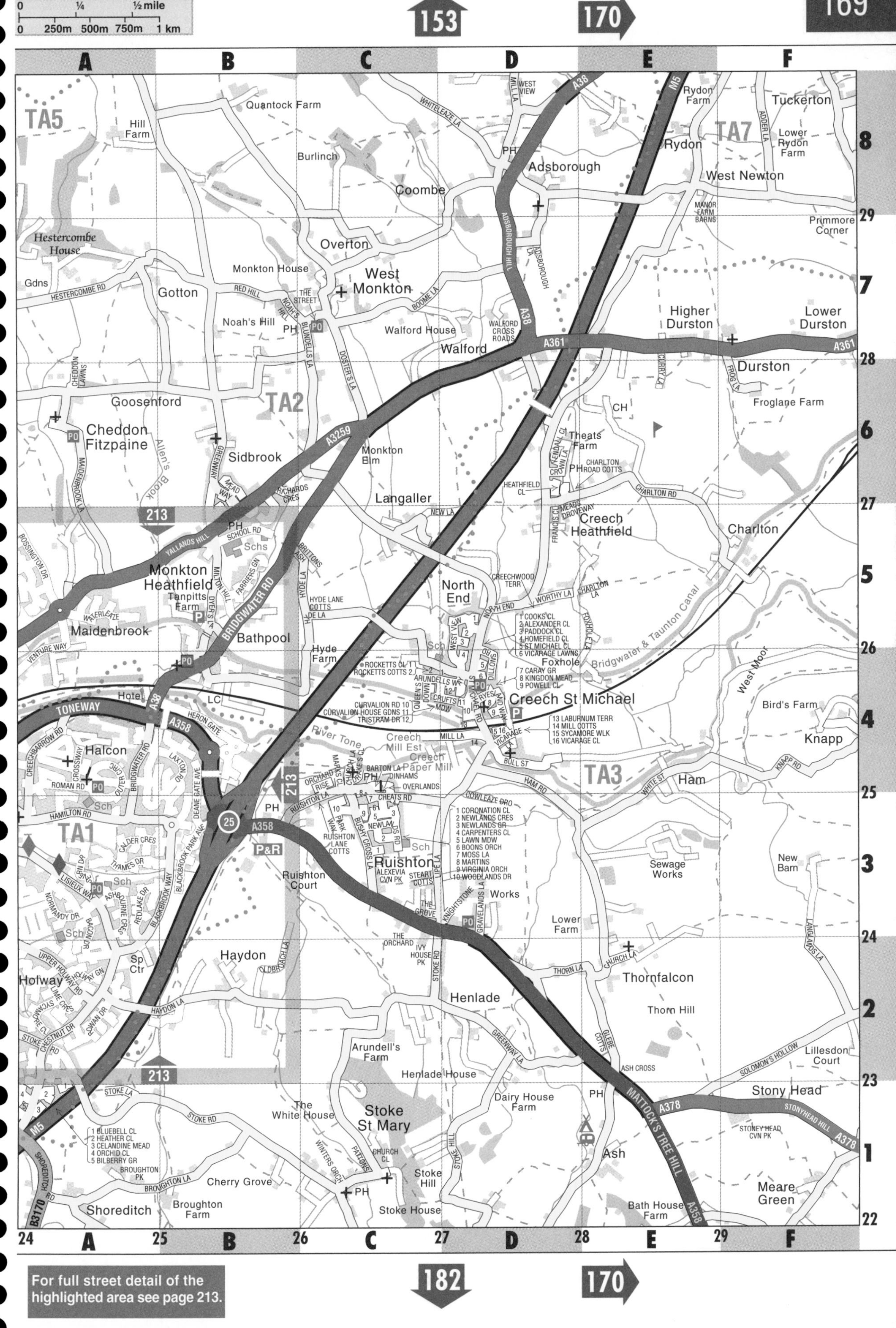

For full street detail of the highlighted area see page 213.

169
154

Scale: 1¾ inches to 1 mile
0 ¼ ½ mile
0 250m 500m 750m 1 km

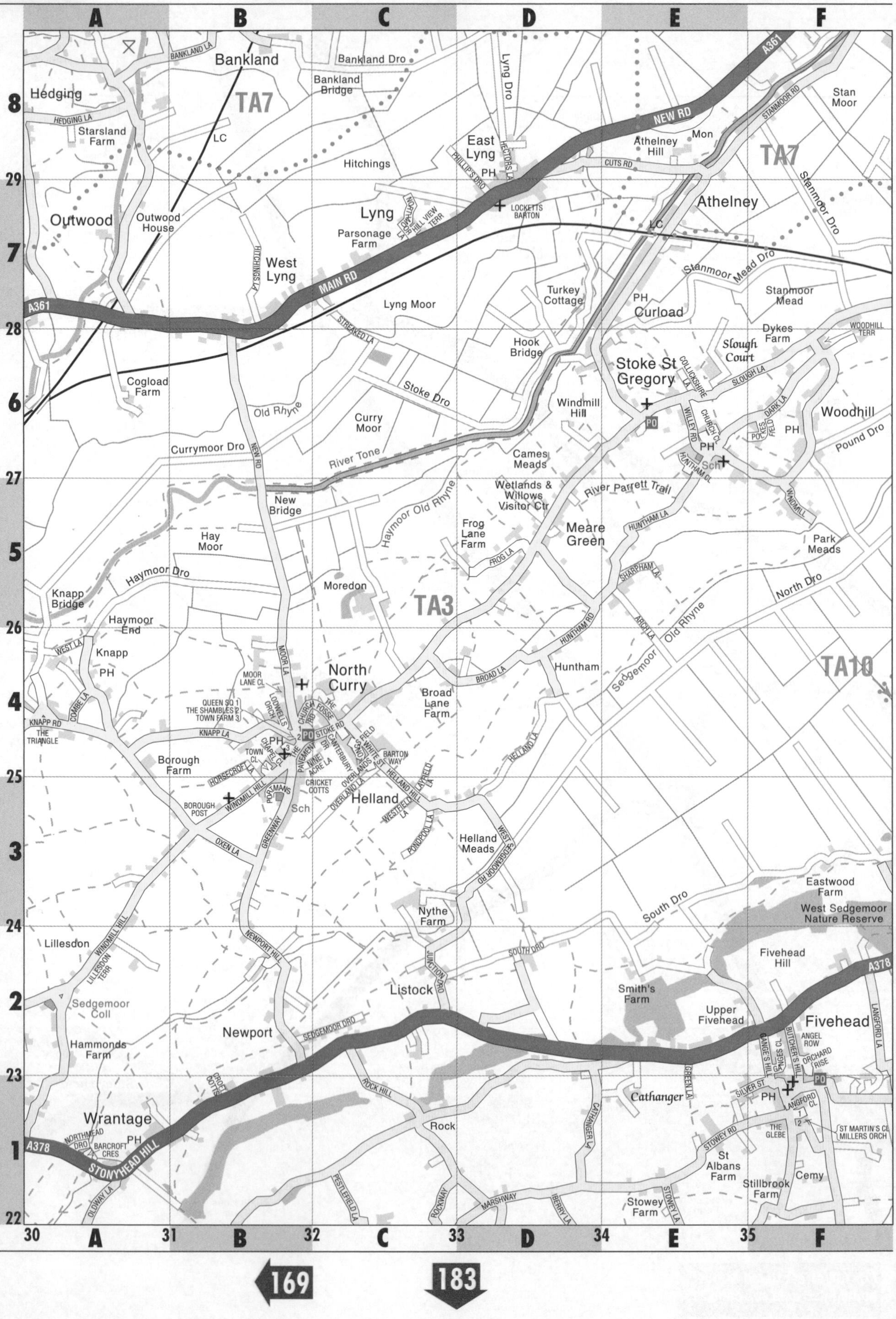

169
183

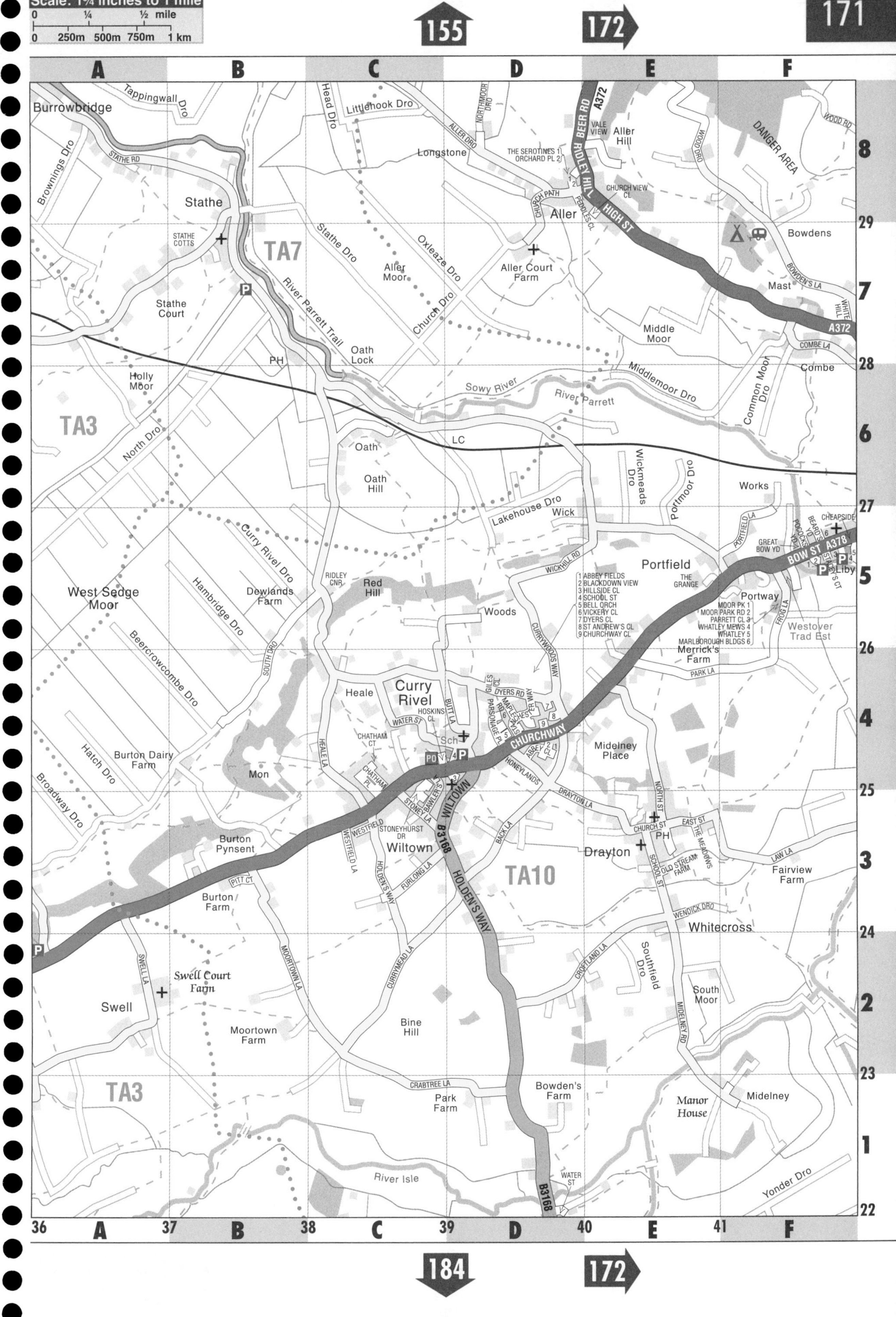
Scale: 1¾ inches to 1 mile
0 ¼ ½ mile
0 250m 500m 750m 1 km
155
172
A
B
C
D
E
F
Burrowbridge
Tappingwall Dro
Head Dro
Littlehook Dro
Northmoor Dro
Aller Dro
Longstone
Brownings Dro
Stathe Rd
Stathe
Stathe Cotts
TA7
Stathe Dro
Oxleaze Dro
Aller Moor
Church Dro
River Parrett Trail
Stathe Court
Oath Lock
PH
Holly Moor
TA3
North Dro
Sowy River
River Parrett
Middlemoor Dro
Middle Moor
LC
Oath
Oath Hill
Lakehouse Dro
Wick
Wickmeads Dro
Portmoor Dro
Works
Curry Rivel Dro
West Sedge Moor
Hambridge Dro
Dewlands Farm
Ridley Cnr
Red Hill
Beercrowcombe Dro
South Dro
Woods
Wickhill Rd
Currywoods Way
1 Abbey Fields
2 Blackdown View
3 Hillside Cl
4 School St
5 Bell Orch
6 Vickery Cl
7 Dyers Cl
8 St Andrew's Cl
9 Churchway Cl
Portfield
The Grange
Portway
Moor Pk 1
Moor Park Rd 2
Parrett Cl 3
Whatley Mews 4
Whatley 5
Marlborough Bldgs 6
Merrick's Farm
Park La
Westover Trad Est
Frog La
Heale
Curry Rivel
Hoskins Cl
Butt La
Giles Cl
Dyers Rd
Parsonage Pl
Maple Mews
Water St
Sch
Chatham Ct
Chatham Pl
Heale La
Churchway
Abbey Cl
Honeylands
Midelney Place
Hatch Dro
Burton Dairy Farm
Mon
Broadway Dro
Stone La
Bowlers St
Wiltown
Drayton La
North St
Church St
East St
The Meadows
Westfield
Stoneyhurst Dr
Westfield La
B3168
Back La
Burton Pynsent
Drayton
PH
School St
Old Stream Farm
Law La
Fairview Farm
Pitt Ct
Burton Farm
Holden's Way
Furlong La
TA10
Wendick Dro
Whitecross
Currymead La
Cropland La
Southfield Dro
Swell La
Swell Court Farm
Swell
Moortown La
Moortown Farm
Bine Hill
South Moor
Midelney Rd
Crabtree La
Park Farm
Bowden's Farm
Midelney
Manor House
River Isle
Water St
Yonder Dro
Beer Rd
A372
Vale View
Aller Hill
Ridley Hill
The Serotines 1
Orchard Pl 2
Church View Cl
Church Path
Peddles Cl
High St
Aller
Aller Court Farm
Wood Dro
Danger Area
Wood Rd
Bowdens
Bowden's La
Mast
White Hill
Combe La
Combe
Common Moor Dro
Portfield La
Cheapside
Beard's Yd
Pococks Yd
Great Bow Yd
Bow St A378
Liby
P
8
29
7
28
6
27
5
26
4
25
3
24
2
23
1
22
36
37
38
39
40
41
184
172

171
156

Scale: 1¾ inches to 1 mile
0 ¼ ½ mile
0 250m 500m 750m 1 km

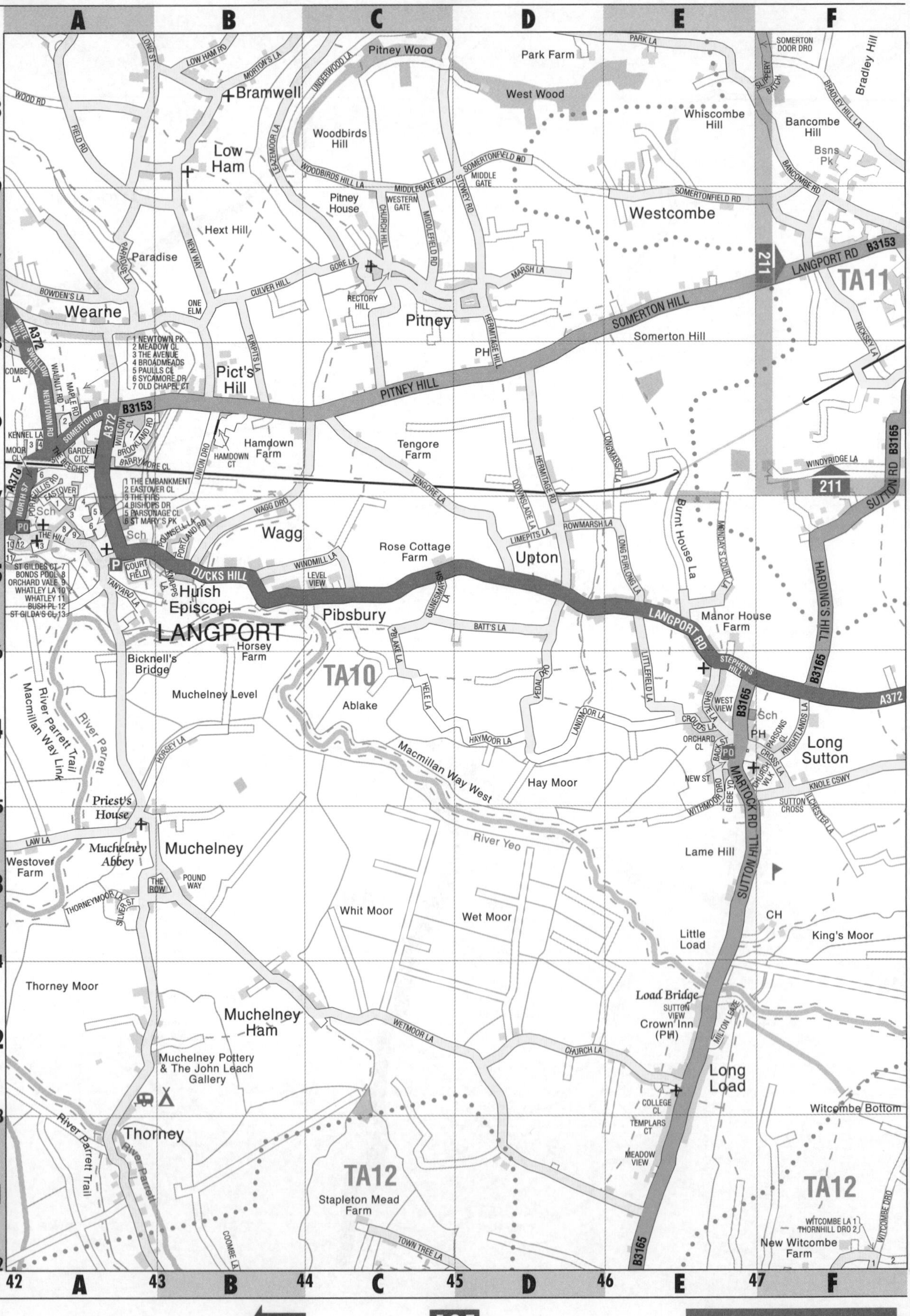

171
185

For full street detail of the highlighted area see page 211.

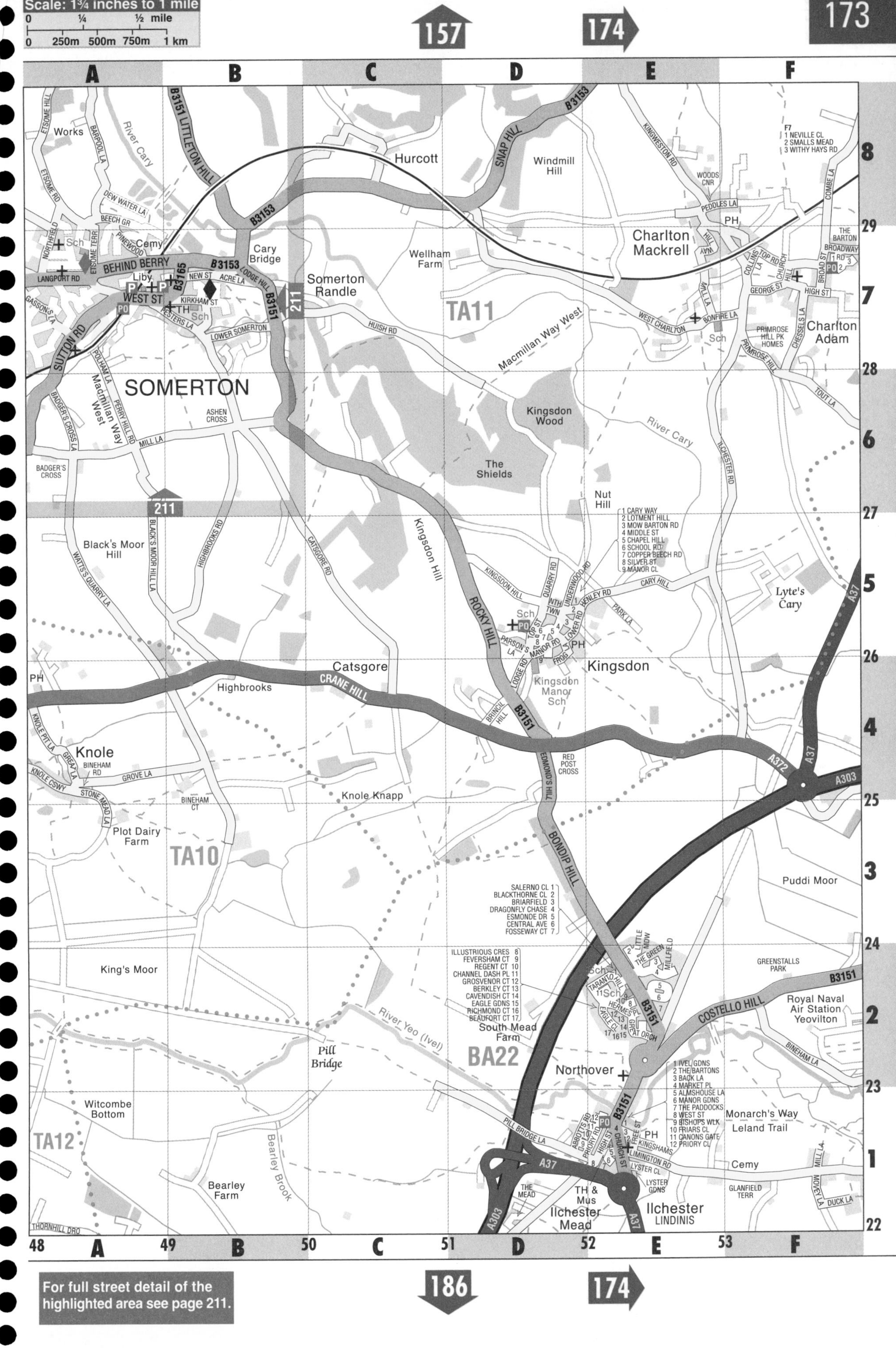
Scale: 1¾ inches to 1 mile
157
174
SOMERTON
Somerton Randle
Hurcott
Windmill Hill
Charlton Mackrell
Charlton Adam
Cary Bridge
Wellham Farm
TA11
Kingsdon Wood
The Shields
Nut Hill
Lyte's Cary
Kingsdon
Catsgore
Highbrooks
Black's Moor Hill
Knole
Knole Knapp
Plot Dairy Farm
TA10
King's Moor
Pill Bridge
South Mead Farm
BA22
Northover
Witcombe Bottom
TA12
Bearley Farm
Ilchester Mead
Ilchester LINDINIS
Puddi Moor
Royal Naval Air Station Yeovilton
Greenstalls Park
Monarch's Way
Leland Trail
Kingsdon Hill
River Cary
River Yeo (Ivel)
Bearley Brook
F7
1 NEVILLE CL
2 SMALLS MEAD
3 WITHY HAYS RD
1 CARY WAY
2 LOTMENT HILL
3 MOW BARTON RD
4 MIDDLE ST
5 CHAPEL HILL
6 SCHOOL RD
7 COPPER BEECH RD
8 SILVER ST
9 MANOR CL
SALERNO CL 1
BLACKTHORNE CL 2
BRIARFIELD 3
DRAGONFLY CHASE 4
ESMONDE DR 5
CENTRAL AVE 6
FOSSEWAY CT 7
ILLUSTRIOUS CRES 8
FEVERSHAM CT 9
REGENT CT 10
CHANNEL DASH PL 11
GROSVENOR CT 12
BERKLEY CT 13
CAVENDISH CT 14
EAGLE GDNS 15
RICHMOND CT 16
BEAUFORT CT 17
1 IVEL GDNS
2 THE BARTONS
3 BACK LA
4 MARKET PL
5 ALMSHOUSE LA
6 MANOR GDNS
7 THE PADDOCKS
8 WEST ST
9 BISHOPS WLK
10 FRIARS CL
11 CANONS GATE
12 PRIORY CL
B3151
B3153
A372
A37
A303
186
174
211

For full street detail of the highlighted area see page 211.

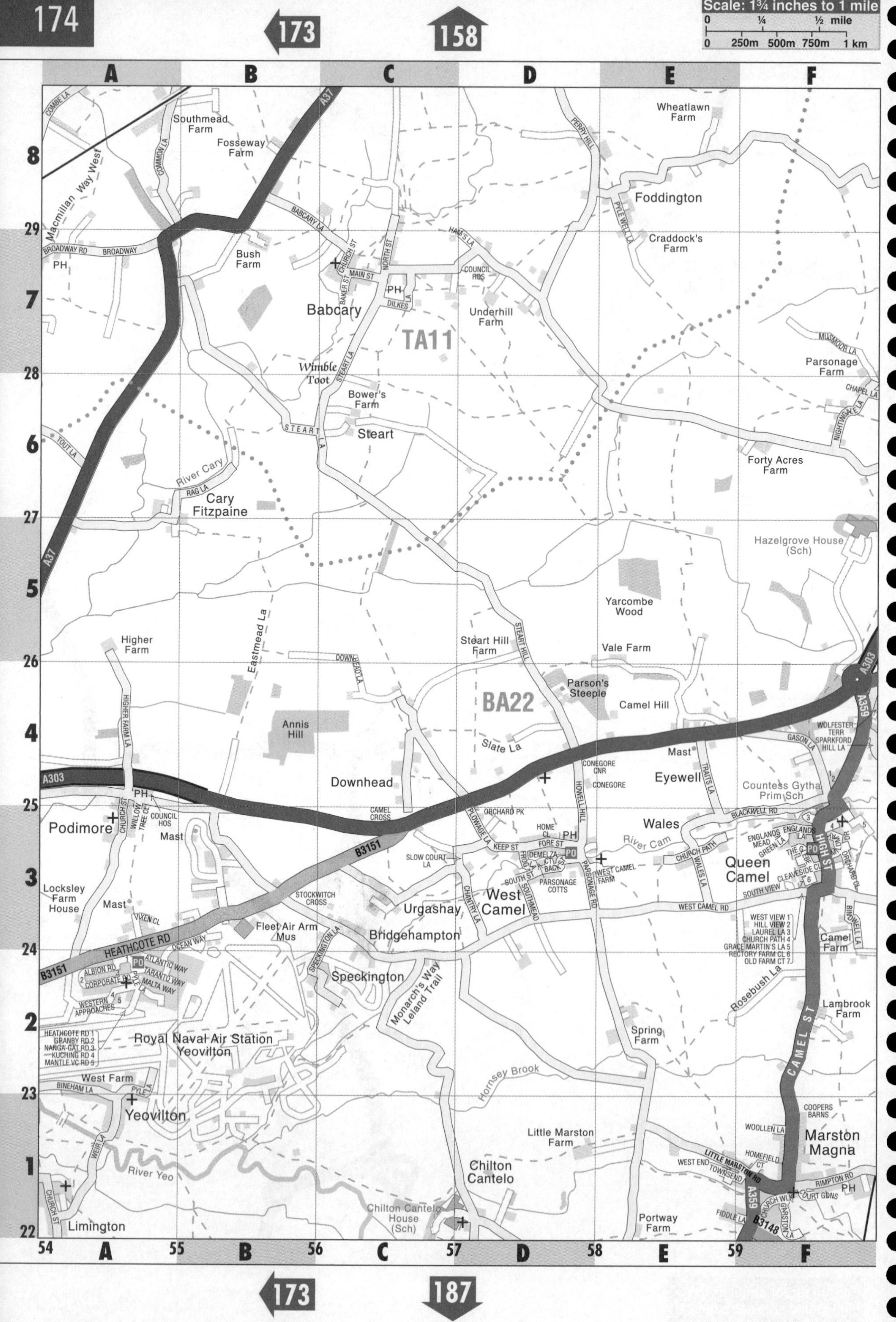
173
158
Scale: 1¾ inches to 1 mile
Southmead Farm
Fosseway Farm
Wheatlawn Farm
Foddington
Craddock's Farm
Bush Farm
Babcary
Underhill Farm
TA11
Wimble Toot
Bower's Farm
Steart
Parsonage Farm
Forty Acres Farm
Cary Fitzpaine
River Cary
Hazelgrove House (Sch)
Yarcombe Wood
Higher Farm
Steart Hill Farm
Vale Farm
Eastmead La
Parson's Steeple
BA22
Camel Hill
Annis Hill
Slate La
Downhead
Mast
Eyewell
Countess Gytha Prim Sch
Podimore
Wales
River Cam
Queen Camel
Locksley Farm House
Urgashay
West Camel
Fleet Air Arm Mus
Bridgehampton
Camel Farm
Speckington
Monarch's Way Leland Trail
Rosebush La
Lambrook Farm
Royal Naval Air Station Yeovilton
Spring Farm
West Farm
Hornsey Brook
Yeovilton
Little Marston Farm
Marston Magna
River Yeo
Chilton Cantelo
Chilton Cantelo House (Sch)
Portway Farm
Limington
173
187

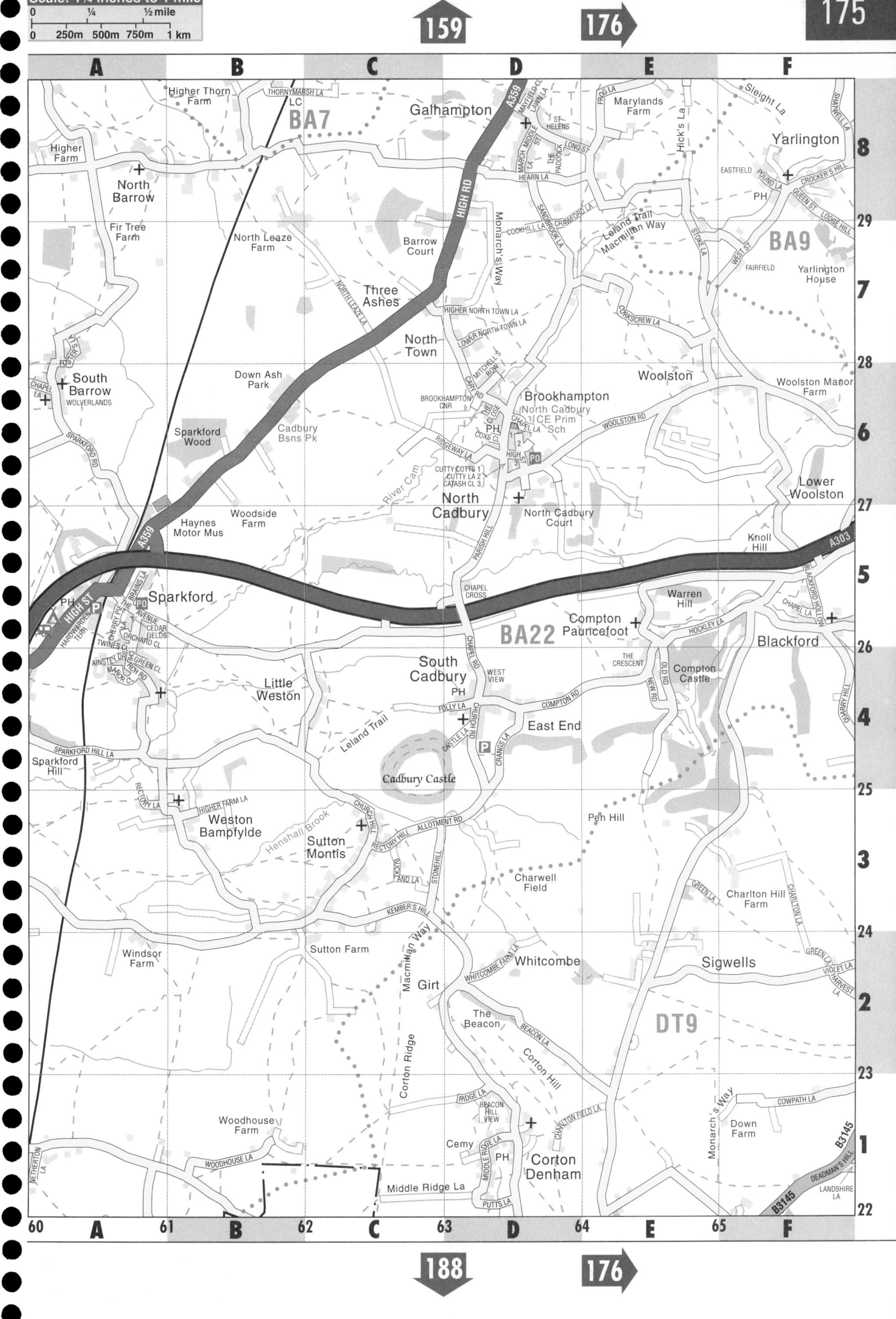
Scale: 1¾ inches to 1 mile
0 ¼ ½ mile
0 250m 500m 750m 1 km
159
176
A B C D E F
Higher Thorn Farm
THORNYMARSH LA
LC
BA7
Galhampton
A359
MAYFIELD CL
LAWN LA
ST HELENS
FROG LA
Marylands Farm
Hick's La
Sleight La
SHANWELL LA
Yarlington
Higher Farm
North Barrow
MARCH LA
MIDDLE ST
THE PADDOCK
LONG ST
HEARN LA
HIGH RD
EASTFIELD
POUND LA
CROCKER'S HILL
PH
QUEEN ST
LODGE HILL
Fir Tree Farm
North Leaze Farm
Barrow Court
Monarch's Way
COCKHILL LA
SANDBROOK LA
CRAWFORD LA
Leland Trail
Macmillan Way
STOKE LA
BA9
WEST ST
FAIRFIELD
Yarlington House
NORTH LEAZE LA
Three Ashes
HIGHER NORTH TOWN LA
CORKSCREW LA
LOWER NORTH TOWN LA
North Town
FOSTER'S LA
MITCHELL'S ROW
CHAPEL LA
South Barrow
WOLVERLANDS
Down Ash Park
CARY RD
BROOKHAMPTON CNR
Brookhampton
North Cadbury CE Prim Sch
Woolston
Woolston Manor Farm
THE CLOSE
CHAPEL LA
WOOLSTON RD
SPARKFORD RD
Sparkford Wood
Cadbury Bsns Pk
PH
COXS CL
RIDGEWAY LA
HIGH ST
PO
River Cam
CUTTY COTTS
CUTTY LA
CATASH CL
North Cadbury
North Cadbury Court
Lower Woolston
Haynes Motor Mus
Woodside Farm
PARISH HILL
Knoll Hill
A303
BRAINS LA
Sparkford
PH
HIGH ST
P
PO
THE AVENUE
CHERRY PIE LA
HARDWARDEN TERR
CEDAR FIELDS
ORCHARD CL
TWINES CL
CHAPEL CROSS
Warren Hill
BLACKFORD HOLLOW
CHAPEL LA
Compton Pauncefoot
BA22
HOCKLEY LA
Blackford
AINSTEY DR
GREEN CL
CHURCH RD
MANOR CL
CHAPEL RD
WEST VIEW
THE CRESCENT
OLD RD
Compton Castle
South Cadbury
PH
NEW RD
QUARRY HILL
Little Weston
FOLLY LA
CHURCH RD
COMPTON RD
East End
Leland Trail
CASTLE LA
CRANGS LA
P
SPARKFORD HILL LA
Sparkford Hill
Cadbury Castle
RECTORY LA
HIGHER FARM LA
Weston Bampfylde
Henshall Brook
CHURCH HILL
Sutton Montis
RECTORY HILL
ALLOTMENT RD
Pen Hill
BUCKLAND LA
STONEHILL
Charwell Field
GREEN LA
Charlton Hill Farm
CHARLTON LA
KEMBER'S HILL
Windsor Farm
Sutton Farm
Macmillan Way
WHITCOMBE FARM LA
Whitcombe
Sigwells
GREEN LA
VIOLET LA
HARVEST LA
Girt
The Beacon
BEACON LA
DT9
Corton Ridge
Corton Hill
RIDGE LA
BEACON HILL VIEW
CHARLTON FIELD LA
Monarch's Way
COWPATH LA
Down Farm
Woodhouse Farm
Cemy
MIDDLE RIDGE LA
PH
Corton Denham
B3145
DEADMAN'S HILL
LANDSHIRE LA
WOODHOUSE LA
NETHERTON LA
Middle Ridge La
PUTTS LA
B3145
8 29 7 28 6 27 5 26 4 25 3 24 2 23 1 22
60 61 62 63 64 65
188
176

175
160

Scale: 1¾ inches to 1 mile
0 ¼ ½ mile
0 250m 500m 750m 1 km

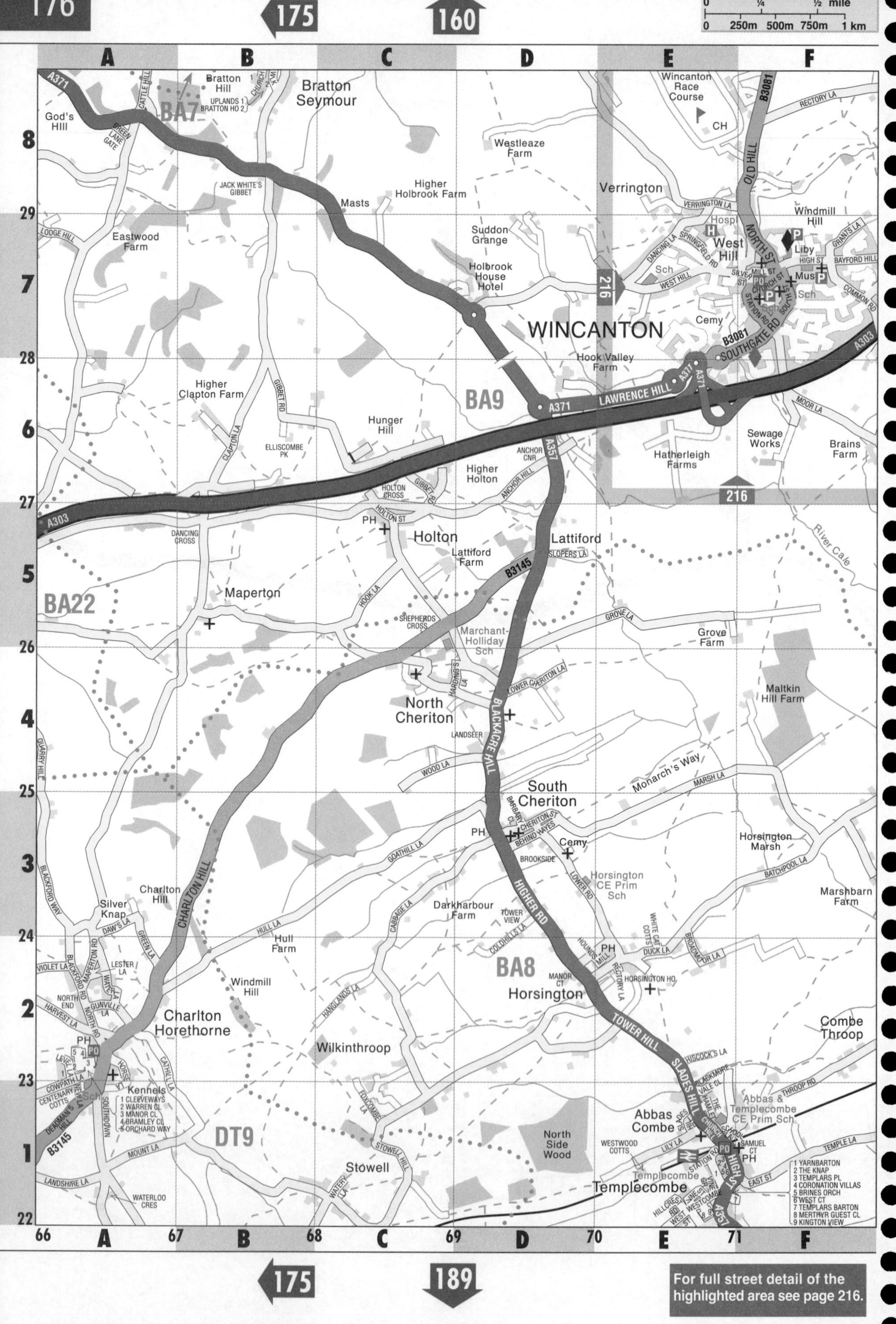

175
189
For full street detail of the highlighted area see page 216.

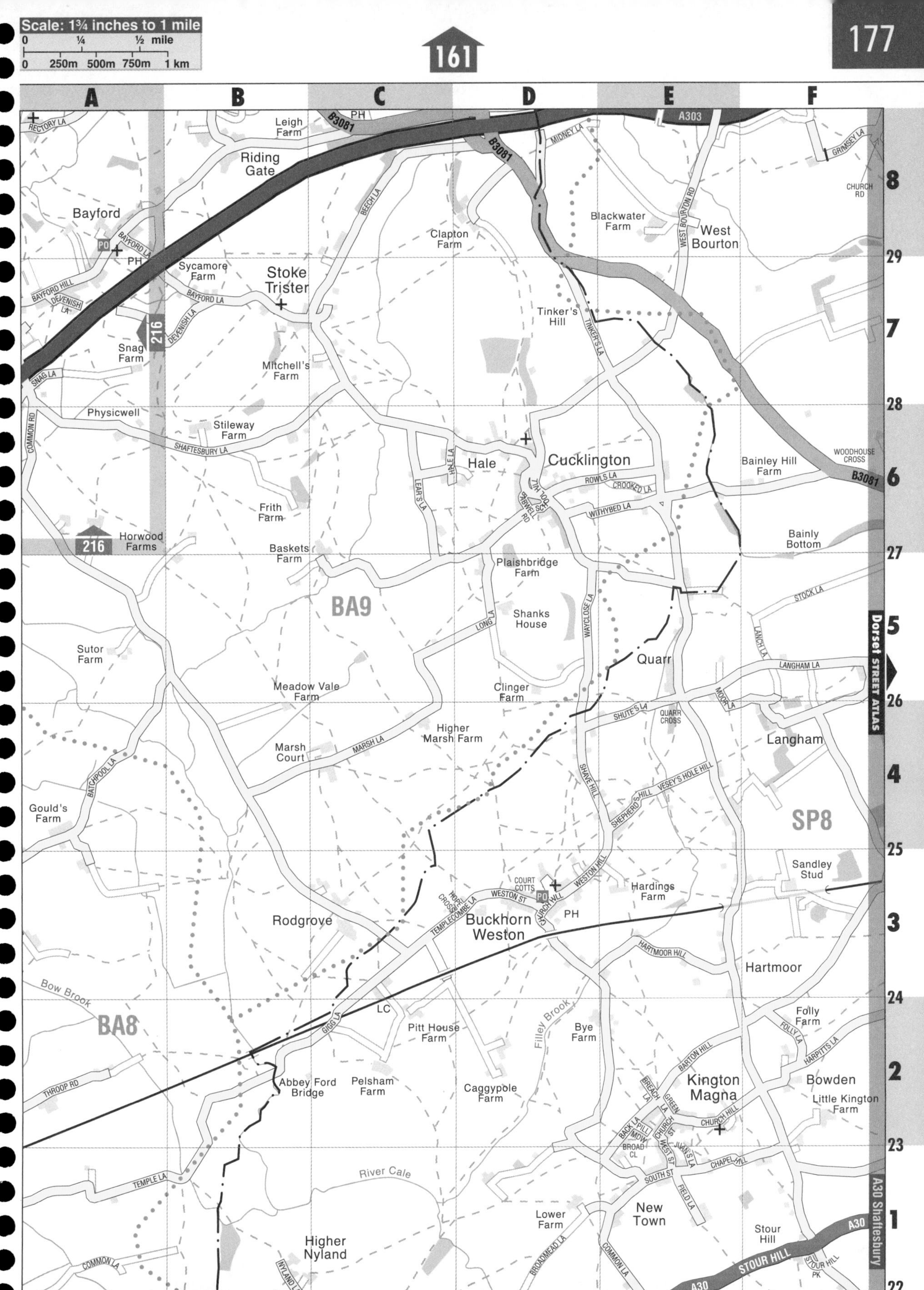

190

For full street detail of the highlighted area see page 216.

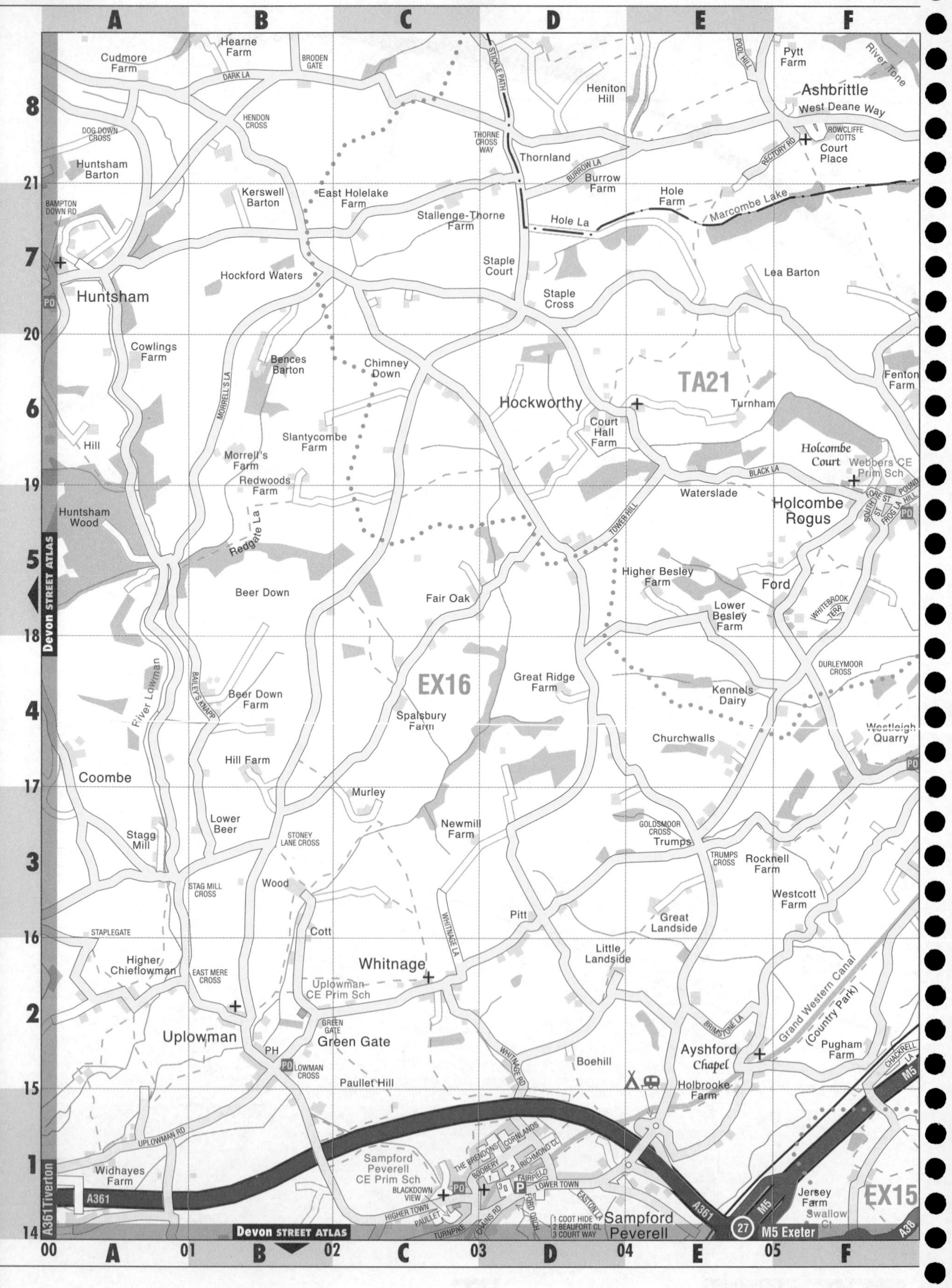
165
Scale: 1¾ inches to 1 mile
A
B
C
D
E
F
Hearne Farm
Cudmore Farm
DARK LA
BRODEN GATE
STICKLE PATH
Heniton Hill
POOL HILL
Pytt Farm
River Tone
Ashbrittle
West Deane Way
DOG DOWN CROSS
HENDON CROSS
THORNE CROSS WAY
Thornland
RECTORY RD
ROWCLIFFE COTTS
Court Place
Huntsham Barton
BURROW LA
Burrow Farm
Kerswell Barton
East Holelake Farm
Hole Farm
BAMPTON DOWN RD
Stallenge-Thorne Farm
Hole La
Marcombe Lake
Staple Court
Hockford Waters
Lea Barton
Huntsham
Staple Cross
Cowlings Farm
Bences Barton
MORRELL'S LA
Chimney Down
TA21
Fenton Farm
Hockworthy
Turnham
Court Hall Farm
Slantycombe Farm
Hill
Morrell's Farm
Holcombe Court
Webbers CE Prim Sch
BLACK LA
Redwoods Farm
Waterslade
Huntsham Wood
Holcombe Rogus
TOWER HILL
Redgate La
Higher Besley Farm
Ford
Beer Down
Fair Oak
Lower Besley Farm
WHITEBROOK TERR
EX16
DURLEYMOOR CROSS
Great Ridge Farm
River Lowman
BAILEY'S KNAPP
Beer Down Farm
Kennels Dairy
Spalsbury Farm
Westleigh Quarry
Churchwalls
Hill Farm
Coombe
Murley
Lower Beer
Newmill Farm
GOLDSMOOR CROSS
Trumps
Stagg Mill
STONEY LANE CROSS
TRUMPS CROSS
Rocknell Farm
STAG MILL CROSS
Wood
Westcott Farm
Pitt
Great Landside
STAPLEGATE
Cott
WHITNAGE LA
Higher Chieflowman
Whitnage
Little Landside
EAST MERE CROSS
Uplowman CE Prim Sch
Grand Western Canal (Country Park)
GREEN GATE
BRIMSTONE LA
Uplowman
Green Gate
Ayshford Chapel
Pugham Farm
PH
WHITNAGE RD
Boehill
CHACKRELL LA
LOWMAN CROSS
Paullet Hill
Holbrooke Farm
M5
UPLOWMAN RD
CORNLANDS
RICHMOND CL
THE BRENDONS
Sampford Peverell CE Prim Sch
BOOBERY
FAIRFIELD
Widhayes Farm
LOWER TOWN
EASTON LA
BLACKDOWN VIEW
Jersey Farm
A361
FORD ORCH
EX15
HIGHER TOWN
PAULLET
CHAINS RD
1 COOT HIDE
2 BEAUFORT CL
3 COURT WAY
Sampford Peverell
Swallow Cl
A38
TURNPIKE
27
M5 Exeter
A361 Tiverton
Devon STREET ATLAS
00
01
02
03
04
05
8
7
6
5
4
3
2
1
21
20
19
18
17
16
15
14

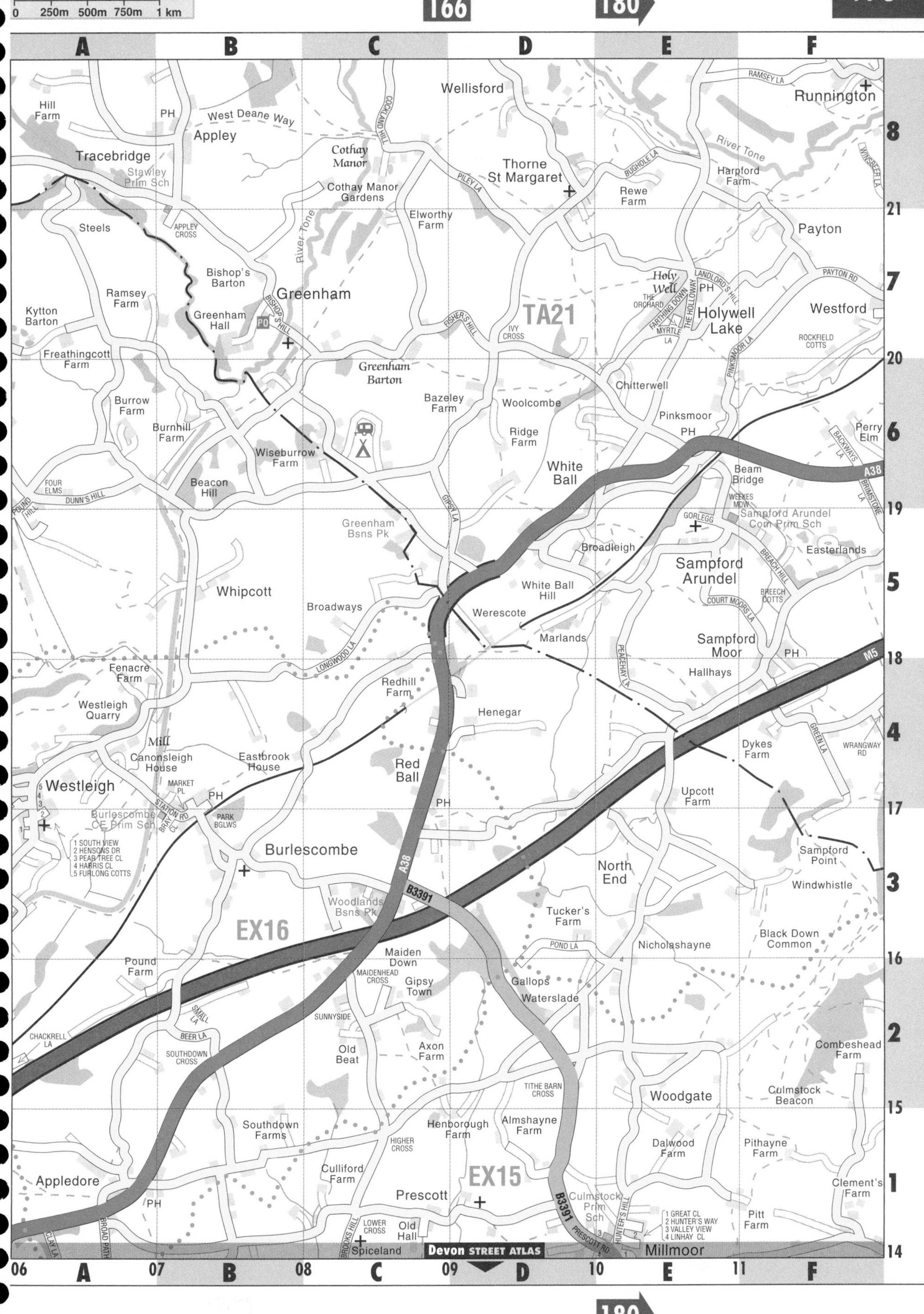
Scale: 1¾ inches to 1 mile
166
180
Wellisford
Runnington
Hill Farm
Appley
West Deane Way
Tracebridge
Stawley Prim Sch
Cothay Manor
Cothay Manor Gardens
Thorne St Margaret
Rewe Farm
Harpford Farm
River Tone
Steels
Elworthy Farm
Payton
Bishop's Barton
Greenham
Ramsey Farm
Kytton Barton
Greenham Hall
TA21
Holywell Lake
Westford
Freathingcott Farm
Greenham Barton
Chitterwell
Burrow Farm
Bazeley Farm
Woolcombe
Pinksmoor
Burnhill Farm
Ridge Farm
Perry Elm
Wiseburrow Farm
White Ball
Beam Bridge
Beacon Hill
Greenham Bsns Pk
Sampford Arundel Com Prim Sch
Broadleigh
Easterlands
Sampford Arundel
Whipcott
White Ball Hill
Broadways
Werescote
Marlands
Sampford Moor
Fenacre Farm
Hallhays
Redhill Farm
Westleigh Quarry
Henegar
Dykes Farm
Canonsleigh House
Eastbrook House
Red Ball
Westleigh
Upcott Farm
Burlescombe CE Prim Sch
Burlescombe
North End
Sampford Point
Windwhistle
Woodlands Bsns Pk
Tucker's Farm
EX16
Black Down Common
Nicholashayne
Pound Farm
Maiden Down
Gipsy Town
Gallops
Waterslade
Old Beat
Axon Farm
Combeshead Farm
Culmstock Beacon
Woodgate
Southdown Farms
Henborough Farm
Almshayne Farm
Dalwood Farm
Pithayne Farm
Appledore
Culliford Farm
EX15
Prescott
Culmstock Prim Sch
Clement's Farm
Pitt Farm
Old Hall
Spiceland
Millmoor
A38
M5
B3391
Devon STREET ATLAS
180

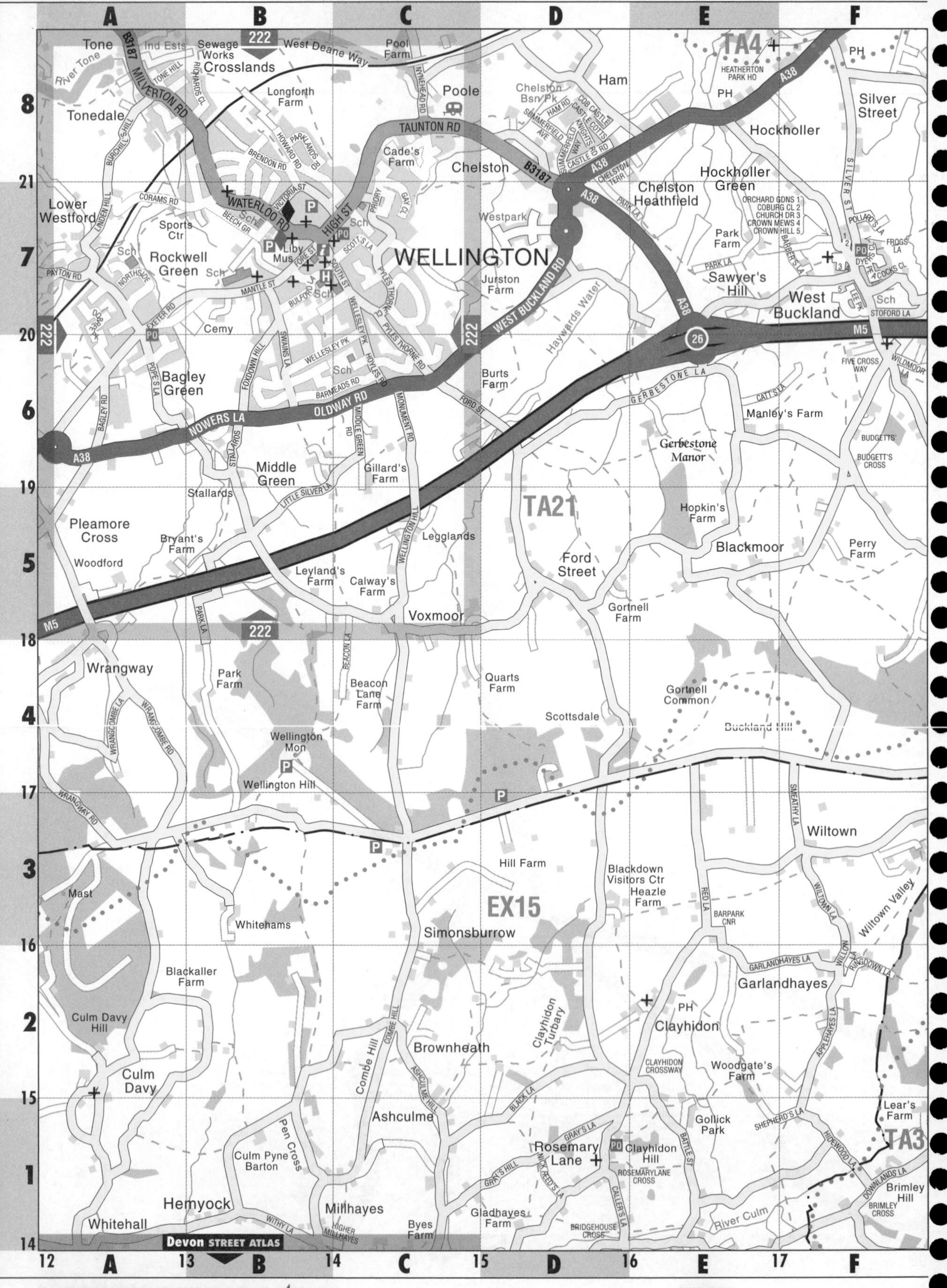
Tone
Ind Ests
Sewage Works
Crosslands
West Deane Way
Pool Farm
TA4
Heatherton Park Ho
Tonedale
Longforth Farm
Poole
Chelston Bsn Pk
Ham
Silver Street
Milverton Rd
Taunton Rd
Hockholler
Cade's Farm
Chelston
Hockholler Green
Lower Westford
Chelston Heathfield
Waterloo Rd
High St
Sports Ctr
Westpark
Park Farm
Rockwell Green
WELLINGTON
Jurston Farm
Sawyer's Hill
West Buckland
Cemy
West Buckland Rd
M5
Bagley Green
Oldway Rd
Nowers La
Burts Farm
Haywards Water
Gerbestone La
Manley's Farm
A38
Gerbestone Manor
Middle Green
Gillard's Farm
Budgett's Cross
Stallards
TA21
Hopkin's Farm
Pleamore Cross
Bryant's Farm
Legglands
Blackmoor
Perry Farm
Woodford
Ford Street
Leyland's Farm
Calway's Farm
Voxmoor
Gortnell Farm
Wrangway
Park Farm
Beacon Lane Farm
Quarts Farm
Gortnell Common
Scottsdale
Buckland Hill
Wellington Mon
Wellington Hill
Wiltown
Hill Farm
Blackdown Visitors Ctr
Heazle Farm
Mast
EX15
Whitehams
Simonsburrow
Wiltown Valley
Blackaller Farm
Garlandhayes
Culm Davy Hill
Clayhidon
Brownheath
Clayhidon Turbary
Woodgate's Farm
Culm Davy
Ashculme
Gollick Park
Lear's Farm
TA3
Culm Pyne Barton
Pen Cross
Rosemary Lane
Clayhidon Hill
Brimley Hill
Hemyock
Millhayes
Gladhayes Farm
River Culm
Whitehall
Byes Farm
Devon STREET ATLAS

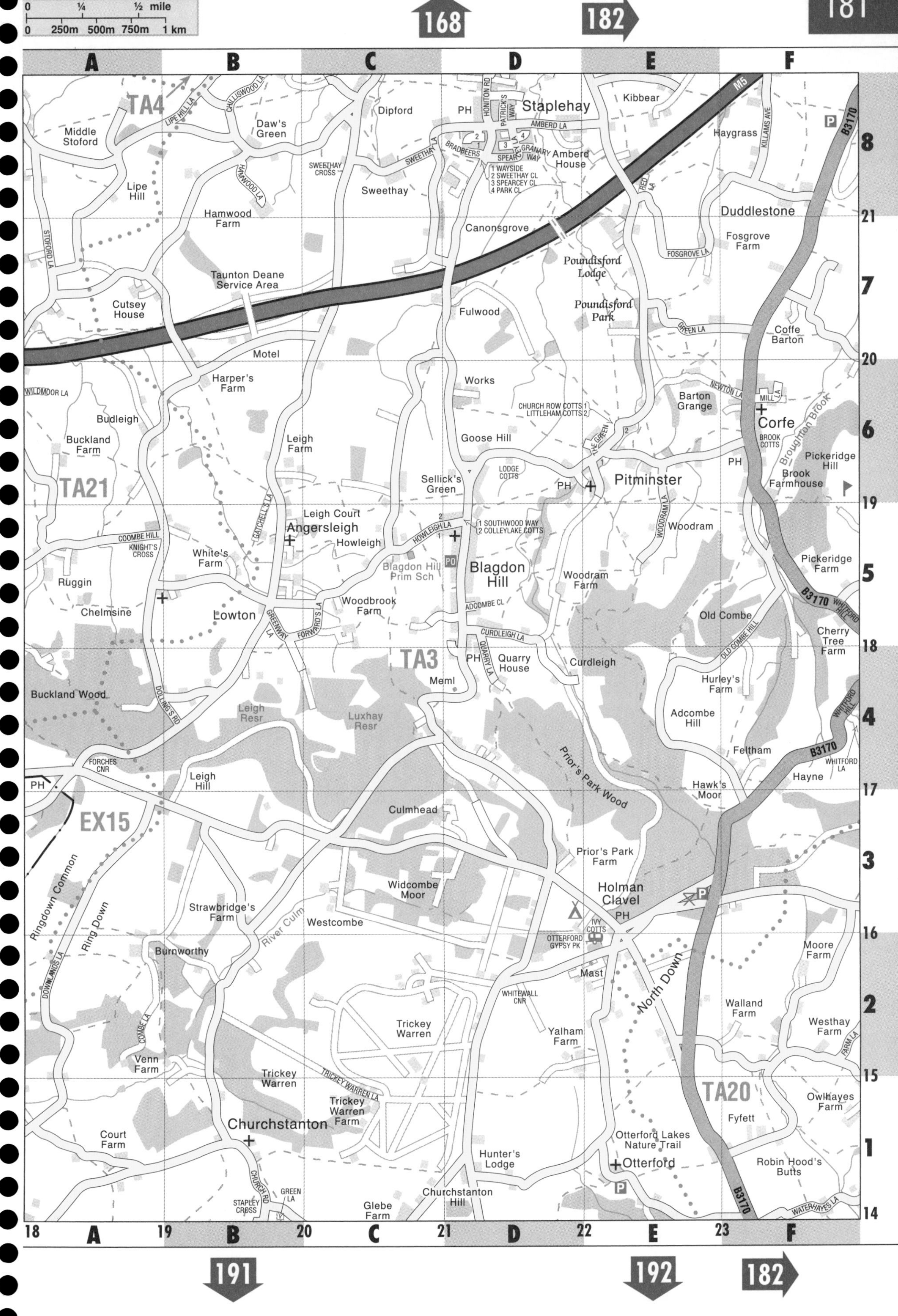
Scale: 1¾ inches to 1 mile
0 ¼ ½ mile
0 250m 500m 750m 1 km
168
182
A B C D E F
TA4
Middle Stoford
Daw's Green
Dipford
PH
Staplehay
Kibbear
Haygrass
M5
B3170
Lipe Hill
Sweethay Cross
Sweethay
Amberd House
1 WAYSIDE
2 SWEETHAY CL
3 SPEARCEY CL
4 PARK CL
Hamwood Farm
Canonsgrove
Duddlestone
Fosgrove Farm
Taunton Deane Service Area
Poundisford Lodge
Cutsey House
Fulwood
Poundisford Park
Coffe Barton
Motel
Harper's Farm
Works
Barton Grange
Budleigh
CHURCH ROW COTTS
LITTLEHAM COTTS
Corfe
Buckland Farm
Leigh Farm
Goose Hill
Pickeridge Hill
TA21
Sellick's Green
LODGE COTTS
PH
Pitminster
Brook Farmhouse
Leigh Court
Angersleigh
Howleigh
1 SOUTHWOOD WAY
2 COLLEYLAKE COTTS
Woodram
White's Farm
Blagdon Hill Prim Sch
Blagdon Hill
Pickeridge Farm
Ruggin
Woodram Farm
Chelmsine
Lowton
Woodbrook Farm
Old Combe
Cherry Tree Farm
TA3
PH
Quarry House
Curdleigh
Buckland Wood
Meml
Hurley's Farm
Leigh Resr
Luxhay Resr
Adcombe Hill
Feltham
Prior's Park Wood
FORCHES CNR
PH
Leigh Hill
Hawk's Moor
Hayne
EX15
Culmhead
Prior's Park Farm
Ringdown Common
Ring Down
Widcombe Moor
Holman Clavel
Strawbridge's Farm
Westcombe
River Culm
PH
IVY COTTS
OTTERFORD GYPSY PK
Burnworthy
Moore Farm
Mast
North Down
WHITEWALL CNR
Walland Farm
Trickey Warren
Yalham Farm
Westhay Farm
Venn Farm
Trickey Warren
Trickey Warren Farm
TA20
Owlhayes Farm
Churchstanton
Fyfett
Court Farm
Otterford Lakes Nature Trail
Hunter's Lodge
Otterford
Robin Hood's Butts
STAPLEY CROSS
GREEN LA
Glebe Farm
Churchstanton Hill
18 19 20 21 22 23
8 21 7 20 6 19 5 18 4 17 3 16 2 15 1 14
191
192
182

181
169

Scale: 1¾ inches to 1 mile
0 ¼ ½ mile
0 250m 500m 750m 1 km

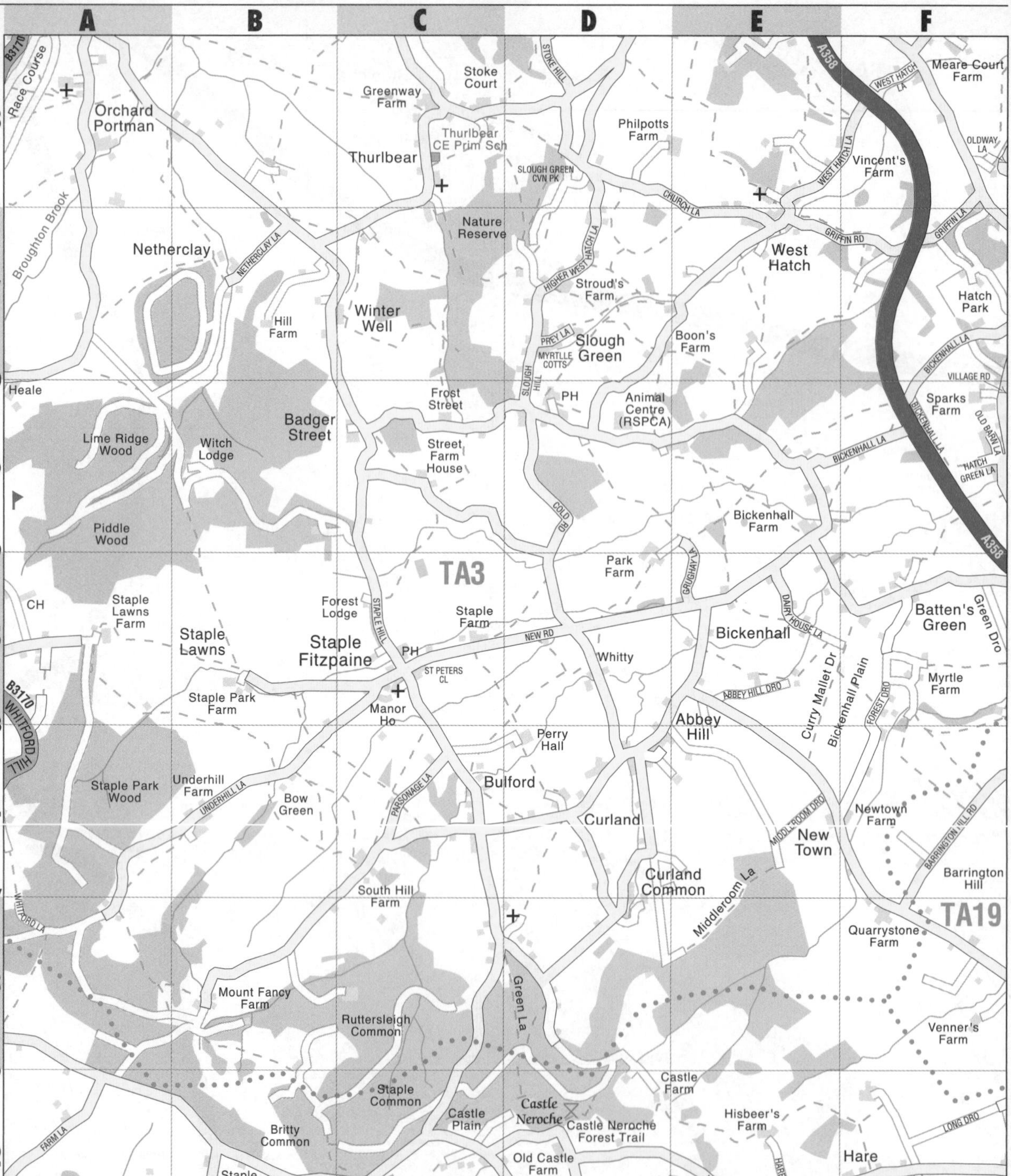
A B C D E F
8 21 7 20 6 19 5 18 4 17 3 16 2 15 1 14
24 25 26 27 28 29
Race Course
B3170
Orchard Portman
Greenway Farm
Stoke Court
STOKE HILL
Meare Court Farm
A358
WEST HATCH LA
Philpotts Farm
Thurlbear CE Prim Sch
Thurlbear
SLOUGH GREEN CVN PK
OLDWAY LA
Vincent's Farm
WEST HATCH LA
Broughton Brook
CHURCH LA
Nature Reserve
GRIFFIN LA
GRIFFIN RD
West Hatch
Netherclay
NETHERCLAY LA
HIGHER WEST HATCH LA
Stroud's Farm
Hatch Park
Hill Farm
Winter Well
PREY LA
Slough Green
MYRTLLE COTTS
Boon's Farm
BICKENHALL LA
VILLAGE RD
Heale
SLOUGH HILL
Frost Street
PH
Animal Centre (RSPCA)
Sparks Farm
Badger Street
Lime Ridge Wood
Witch Lodge
Street Farm House
BICKENHALL LA
OLD BARN LA
HATCH GREEN LA
BICKENHALL LA
COLD RD
Piddle Wood
Bickenhall Farm
TA3
Park Farm
GRUGHAY LA
CH
Staple Lawns Farm
Forest Lodge
STAPLE HILL
Staple Farm
DAIRY HOUSE LA
Batten's Green
Green Dro
Staple Lawns
Staple Fitzpaine
PH
NEW RD
Bickenhall
Whitty
ST PETERS CL
Myrtle Farm
B3170
WHITFORD HILL
Staple Park Farm
Manor Ho
ABBEY HILL DRO
Curry Mallet Dr
Bickenhall Plain
FOREST DRO
Abbey Hill
Perry Hall
Staple Park Wood
Underhill Farm
UNDERHILL LA
Bow Green
PARSONAGE LA
Bulford
Newtown Farm
BARRINGTON HILL RD
Curland
MIDDLEROOM DRO
New Town
Curland Common
Barrington Hill
South Hill Farm
Middleroom La
WHITFORD LA
TA19
Quarrystone Farm
Mount Fancy Farm
Green La
Ruttersleigh Common
Venner's Farm
Castle Farm
Staple Common
Castle Neroche
Castle Plain
Castle Neroche Forest Trail
Hisbeer's Farm
LONG DRO
FARM LA
Britty Common
Old Castle Farm
Hare
Staple Hill Farm
Blackwater
HARE LA
HARE LA
Buckland Farm
TA20
White's Farm
Rydiness Farm
Dommett
RACKLEY LA
Blindmoor
Beehive Farm
Roses Farm
Dingford Farm
River Ding
CHARMOOR LA
Lower Burnt House Farm
HORNSEY LA
Colley Farm
Dommett Moor
FOLLY LA
CHARMOOR DRO
HAMWAY LA
HAMLEY LA
BLIND LA
Birchwood
POUND LA

181
192
193

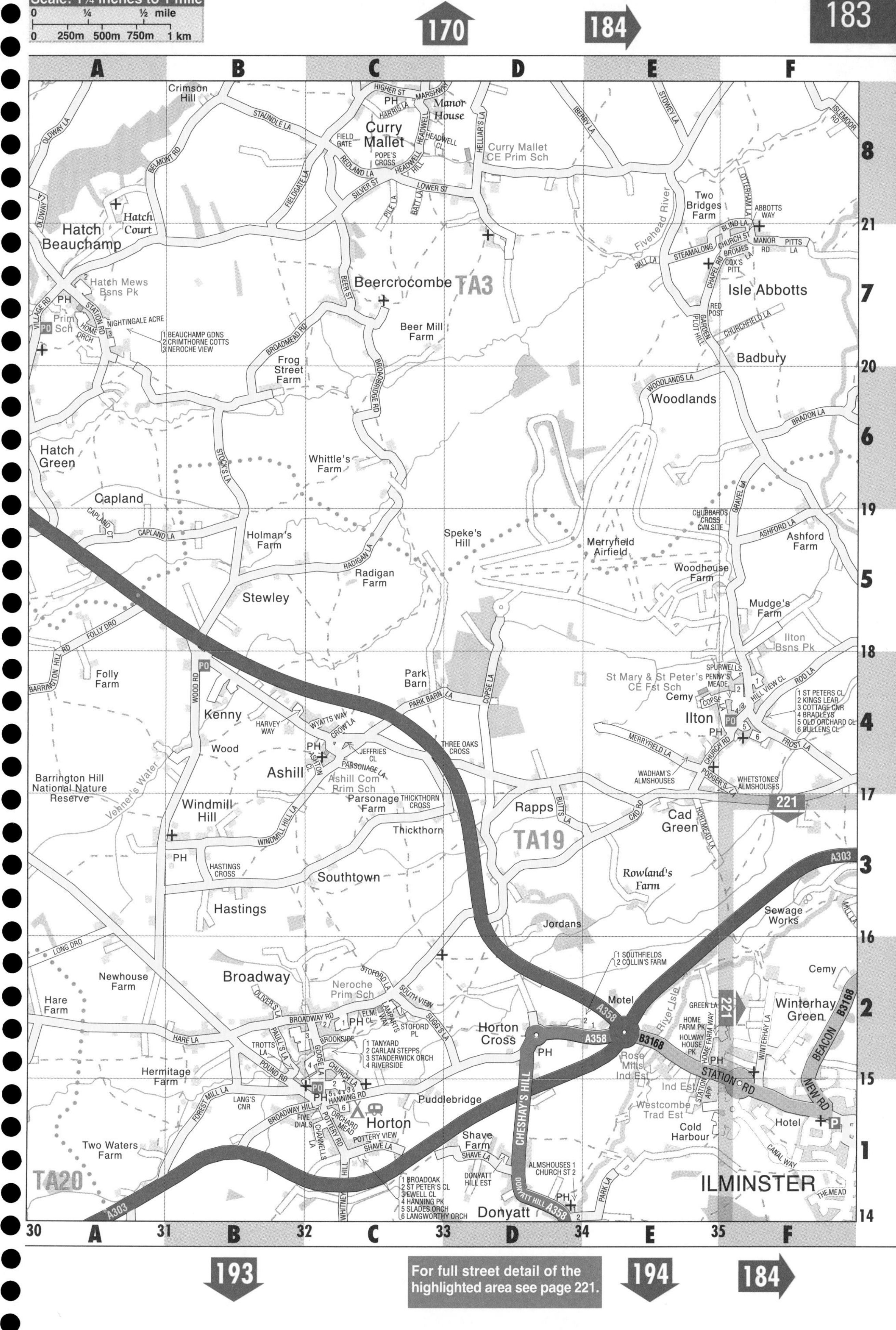
Scale: 1¾ inches to 1 mile
170
184
Crimson Hill
Curry Mallet
Manor House
Curry Mallet CE Prim Sch
Hatch Beauchamp
Hatch Court
Hatch Mews Bsns Pk
Beercrocombe
TA3
Beer Mill Farm
Two Bridges Farm
Isle Abbotts
Badbury
Frog Street Farm
Woodlands
Hatch Green
Whittle's Farm
Capland
Holman's Farm
Speke's Hill
Merryfield Airfield
Ashford Farm
Woodhouse Farm
Radigan Farm
Stewley
Mudge's Farm
Ilton Bsns Pk
Folly Farm
Park Barn
St Mary & St Peter's CE Fst Sch
Cemy
Kenny
Ilton
Wood
Ashill
Ashill Com Prim Sch
Barrington Hill National Nature Reserve
Windmill Hill
Parsonage Farm
Rapps
Cad Green
Thickthorn
TA19
Rowland's Farm
Southtown
Hastings
Jordans
Sewage Works
Broadway
Neroche Prim Sch
Newhouse Farm
Hare Farm
Motel
Winterhay Green
Horton Cross
Rose Mills Ind Est
Hermitage Farm
Horton
Puddlebridge
Westcombe Trad Est
Cold Harbour
Hotel
Two Waters Farm
Shave Farm
ILMINSTER
TA20
Donyatt
A303
A358
B3168
221
193
194
For full street detail of the highlighted area see page 221.
184

183
171

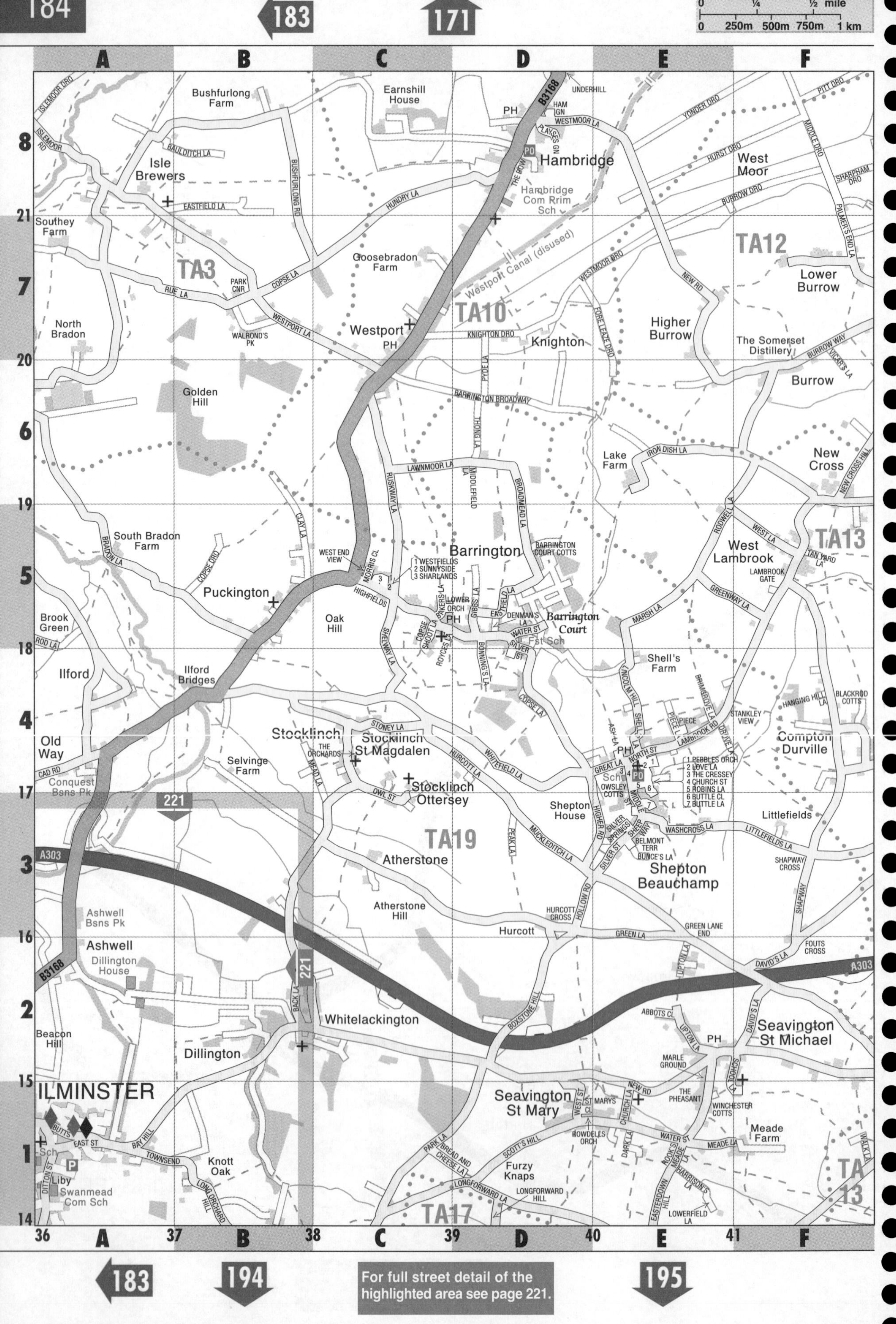

183
194
For full street detail of the highlighted area see page 221.
195

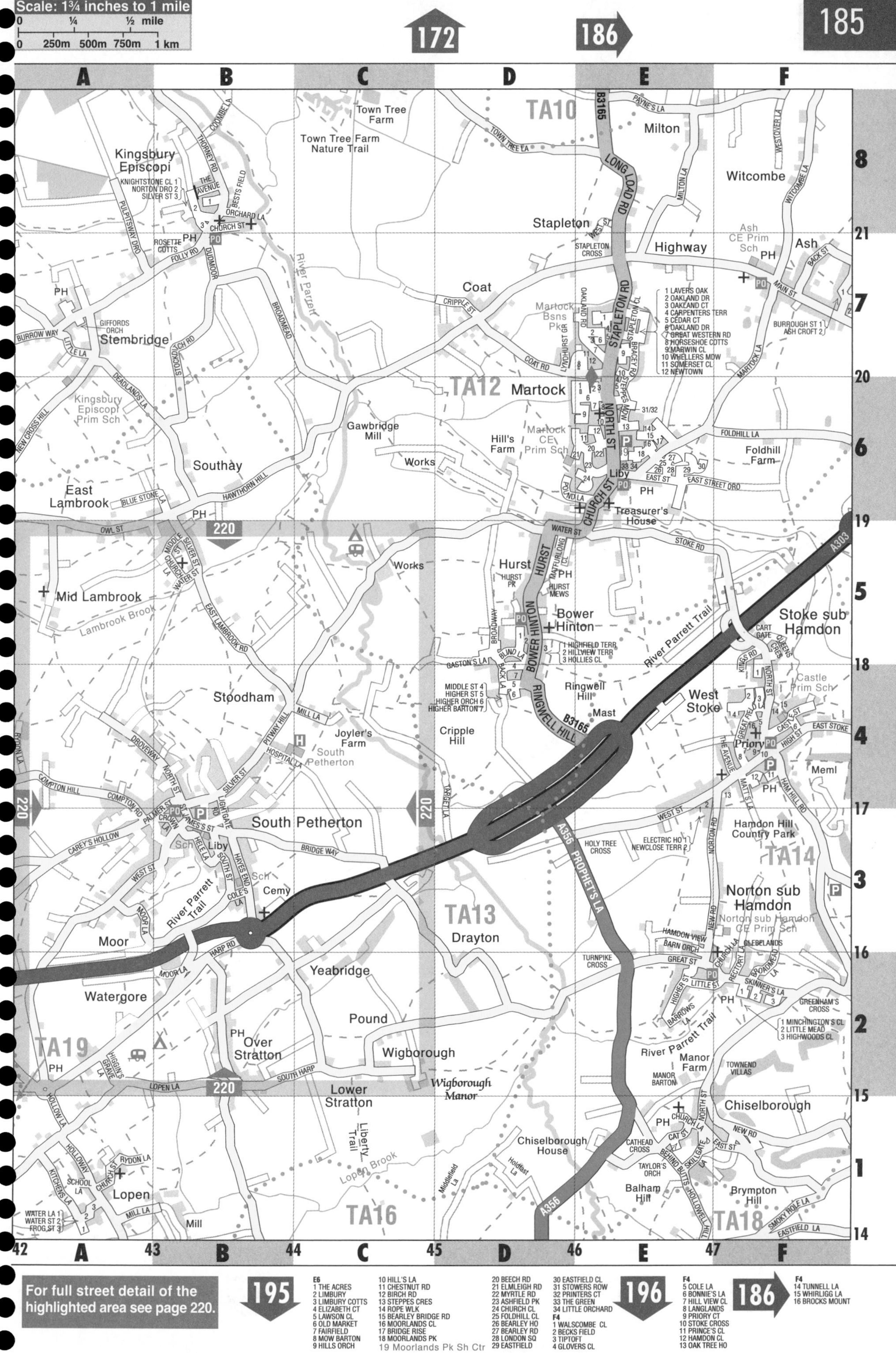

Scale: 1¾ inches to 1 mile
0 ¼ ½ mile
0 250m 500m 750m 1 km
172
186
A B C D E F
TA10
Town Tree Farm
Town Tree Farm Nature Trail
Milton
Witcombe
Kingsbury Episcopi
KNIGHTSTONE CL 1
NORTON DRO 2
SILVER ST 3
THE AVENUE
BESTS FIELD
COOMBE LA
THORNEY RD
ORCHARD LA
CHURCH ST
ROSETTE COTTS
PH
PO
FOLLY RD
DUDMOOR
PULPITSWAY DRO
River Parrett
B3165
LONG LOAD RD
PAYNE'S LA
TOWN TREE LA
MILTON LA
WESTOVER LA
WITCOMBE LA
Stapleton
WEST ST
STAPLETON CROSS
Highway
Ash CE Prim Sch
Ash
BACK ST
MAIN ST
Coat
CRIPPLE ST
BROADMEAD
PH
GIFFORDS ORCH
BURROW WAY
Stembridge
LITTLE LA
STOCKDITCH RD
Martock Bsns Pk
OAKLAND DR
STAPLETON RD
1 LAVERS OAK
2 OAKLAND DR
3 OAKLAND CT
4 CARPENTERS TERR
5 CEDAR CT
6 OAKLAND DR
7 GREAT WESTERN RD
8 HORSESHOE COTTS
9 MARWIN CL
10 WHELLERS MDW
11 SOMERSET CL
12 NEWTOWN
BURROUGH ST 1
ASH CROFT 2
MARTOCK LA
COAT RD
LYNDHURST GR
BRACEY RD
STEPPES MDW
Kingsbury Episcopi Prim Sch
DEADLANDS LA
NEW CROSS HILL
TA12
Martock
NORTH ST
31/32
Gawbridge Mill
Hill's Farm
Martock CE Prim Sch
FOLDHILL LA
Foldhill Farm
Works
Southay
East Lambrook
BLUE STONE LA
HAWTHORN HILL
Liby
EAST ST
EAST STREET DRO
POUND LA
CHURCH ST
Treasurer's House
OWL ST
220
MIDDLE ST
SILVER ST
CHURCH LA
WATER ST
Mid Lambrook
Lambrook Brook
EAST LAMBROOK RD
Works
Hurst
HURST PK
HURST
MAYFURLONG CL
HURST MEWS
STOKE RD
A303
Bower Hinton
BOWER HINTON
BROADWAY
River Parrett Trail
1 HIGHFIELD TERR
2 HILLVIEW TERR
3 HOLLIES CL
Stoke sub Hamdon
CART GATE
QUEENS CRES
KINGS RD
NORTH ST
Castle Prim Sch
GASTON'S LA
BLIND LA
BACK LA
MIDDLE ST 4
HIGHER ST 5
HIGHER ORCH 6
HIGHER BARTON 7
Ringwell Hill
RINGWELL HILL
Mast
West Stoke
EAST STOKE
CASTLE ST
HIGH ST
Stoodham
MILL LA
Joyler's Farm
Cripple Hill
B3165
Priory
THE AVENUE
GREAT ST
DROVEWAY
PITWAY HILL
H
South Petherton
HOSPITAL LA
RYDON LA
COMPTON HILL
COMPTON RD
NORTH ST
SILVER ST
Meml
MATTS LA
HAM HILL RD
PALMER ST
CROWN LA
ST JAMES'S ST
LIGHTGATE RD
South Petherton
TARGETLA
WEST ST
HOLY TREE CROSS
ELECTRIC HO 1
NEWCLOSE TERR 2
NORTON RD
Hamdon Hill Country Park
TA14
CAREY'S HOLLOW
Sch
Liby
HELE LA
SOUTH ST
HAYES END
BRIDGE WAY
A356
PROPHET'S LA
WEST ST
Sch
Cemy
COLE'S LA
River Parrett Trail
NOOR LA
Moor
TA13
Drayton
Norton sub Hamdon
Norton sub Hamdon CE Prim Sch
NEW RD
HAMDON VIEW
BARN ORCH
CHURCH LA
GLEBELANDS
HARP RD
MOOR LA
Yeabridge
TURNPIKE CROSS
GREAT ST
LITTLE ST
RECTORY LA
BROADMEAD LA
SKINNER'S LA
GREENHAM'S CROSS
Watergore
HIGHER ST
BARROWS LA
1 MINCHINGTON'S CL
2 LITTLE MEAD
3 HIGHWOODS CL
Pound
TA19
PH
Over Stratton
Wigborough
River Parrett Trail
Manor Farm
MANOR BARTON
TOWNEND VILLAS
HIGGINS GROVE LA
LOPEN LA
SOUTH HARP
Lower Stratton
Wigborough Manor
Chiselborough
CHURCH LA
NORTH ST
NEW RD
HOLLOW LA
Liberty Trail
Chiselborough House
CAT ST
CATHEAD CROSS
EAST ST
HOLLOWAY
RYDON LA
SCHOOL LA
CHURCH ST
KITCHENS LA
Lopen
Lopen Brook
Middlefield La
Holdfast La
TAYLOR'S ORCH
SKILGATE LA
BEHIND BUTTS
Balham Hill
Brympton Hill
SMOKY HOLE LA
WATER LA 1
WATER ST 2
FROG ST 3
MILL LA
Mill
TA16
A356
HOLLOWELL HILL
TA18
EASTFIELD LA
42 43 44 45 46 47
8 21 7 20 6 19 5 18 4 17 3 16 2 15 1 14
For full street detail of the highlighted area see page 220.
195
196
186
E6
1 THE ACRES
2 LIMBURY
3 LIMBURY COTTS
4 ELIZABETH CT
5 LAWSON CL
6 OLD MARKET
7 FAIRFIELD
8 MOW BARTON
9 HILLS ORCH
10 HILL'S LA
11 CHESTNUT RD
12 BIRCH RD
13 STEPPES CRES
14 ROPE WLK
15 BEARLEY BRIDGE RD
16 MOORLANDS CL
17 BRIDGE RISE
18 MOORLANDS PK
19 Moorlands Pk Sh Ctr
20 BEECH RD
21 ELMLEIGH RD
22 MYRTLE RD
23 ASHFIELD PK
24 CHURCH CL
25 FOLDHILL CL
26 BEARLEY HO
27 BEARLEY RD
28 LONDON SQ
29 EASTFIELD
30 EASTFIELD CL
31 STOWERS ROW
32 PRINTERS CT
33 THE GREEN
34 LITTLE ORCHARD
F4
1 WALSCOMBE CL
2 BECKS FIELD
3 TIPTOFT
4 GLOVERS CL
F4
5 COLE LA
6 BONNIE'S LA
7 HILL VIEW CL
8 LANGLANDS
9 PRIORY CT
10 STOKE CROSS
11 PRINCE'S CL
12 HAMDON CL
13 OAK TREE HO
F4
14 TUNNELL LA
15 WHIRLIGIG LA
16 BROCKS MOUNT

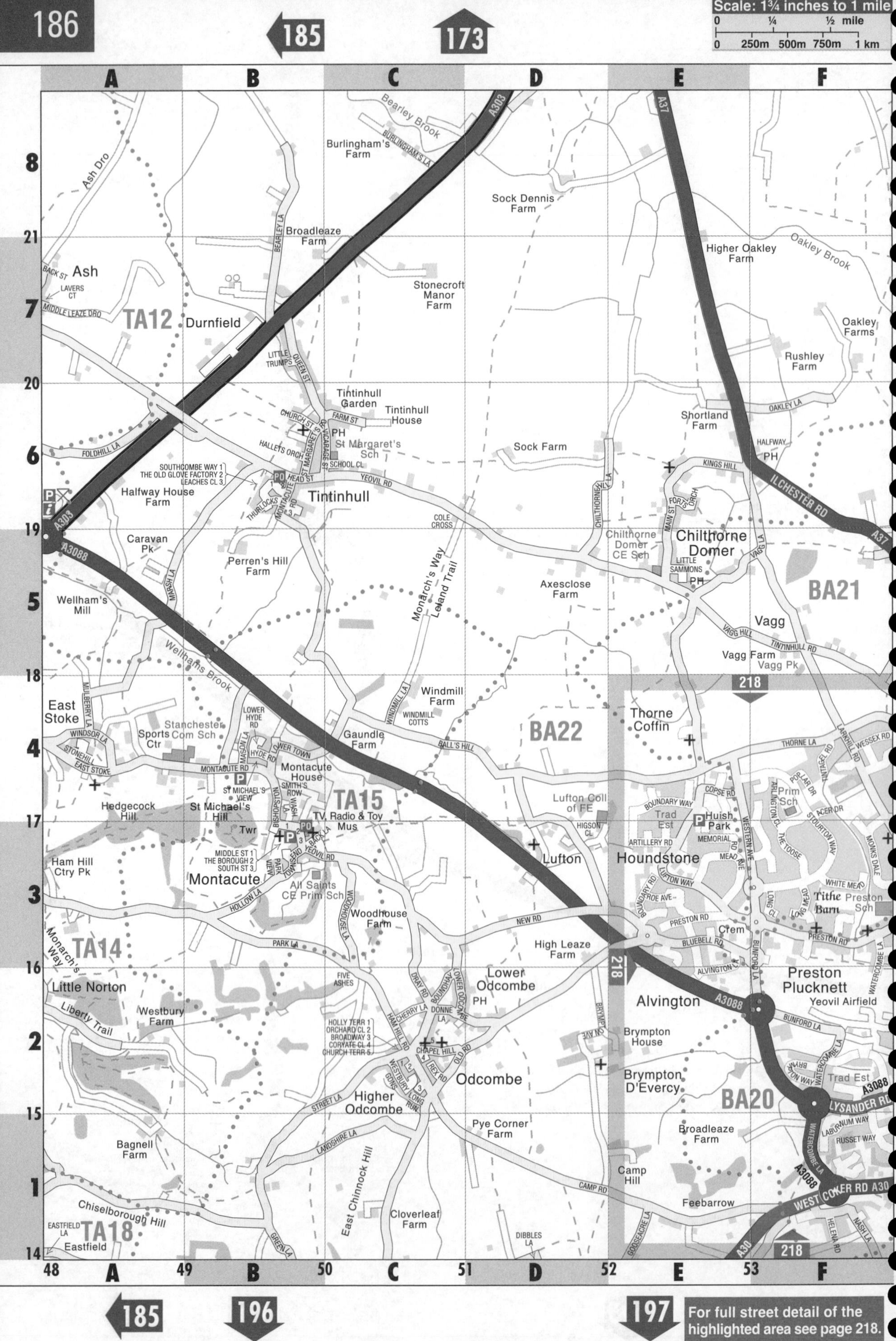

For full street detail of the highlighted area see page 218.

Scale: 1¾ inches to 1 mile

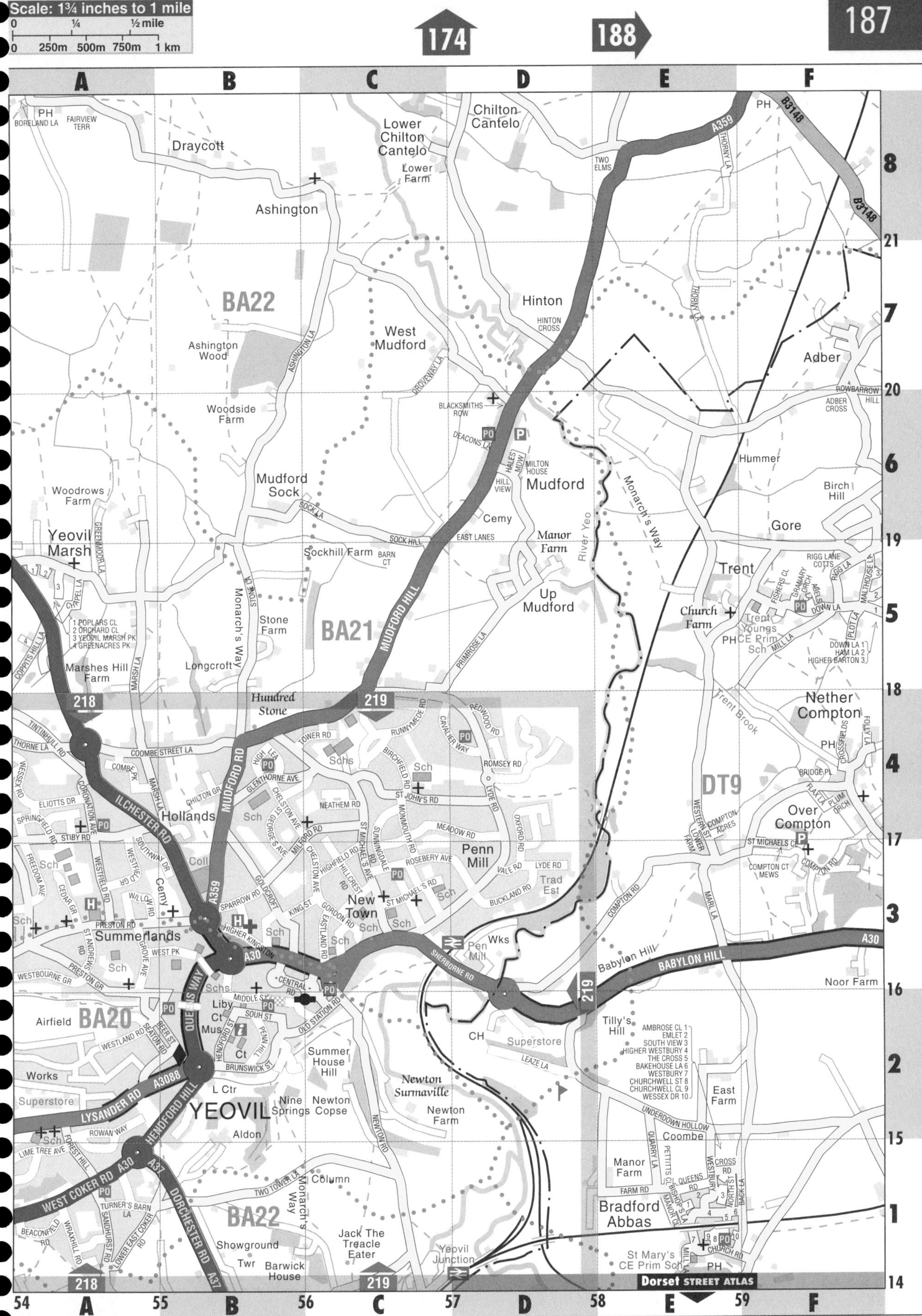

For full street detail of the highlighted area see pages 218 and 219.

187
175

Scale: 1¾ inches to 1 mile
0 ¼ ½ mile
0 250m 500m 750m 1 km

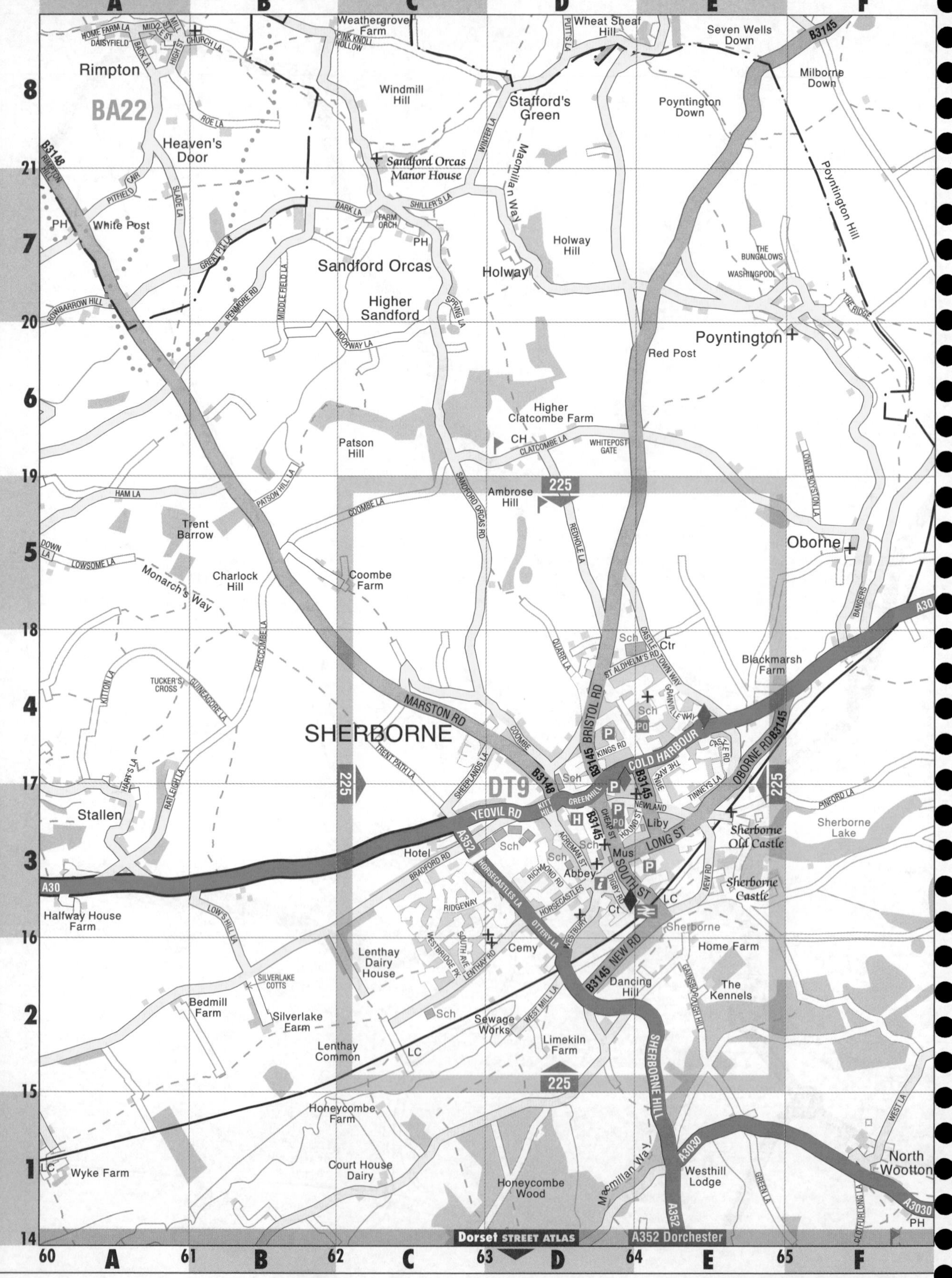

187

For full street detail of the highlighted area see page 225.

Scale: 1¾ inches to 1 mile
0 ¼ ½ mile
0 250m 500m 750m 1 km

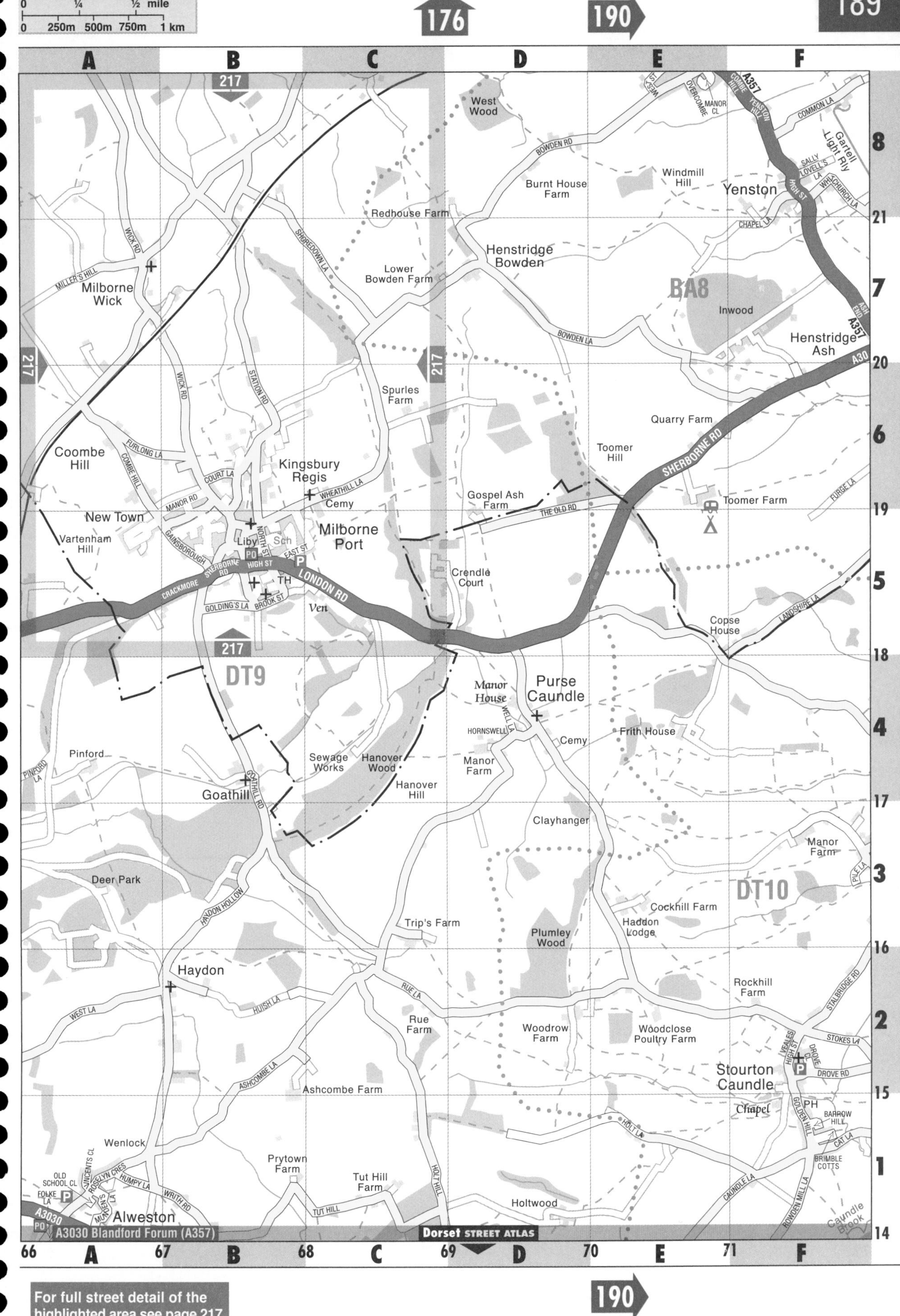

For full street detail of the highlighted area see page 217.

190

A6
1 VIRGINIA CL
2 PLAYFIELD CL
3 BROOKLAND WAY
4 ST NICHOLAS CL
5 POND CL
6 BLACKMOOR LA
7 BROOK LA
8 CHURCH ST
9 THE CROSS
10 TOWNSEND GN
11 BUGLE CT
12 WOODHAYES HO
13 COTTON CNR
14 VICTORIA TERR
15 VICTORIA GDNS
16 ELIZABETH GDNS
17 WINDSOR TERR
18 CHURCH FARM PL
19 WOODHAYES CT

189
177

Scale: 1¾ inches to 1 mile
0 ¼ ½ mile
0 250m 500m 750m 1 km

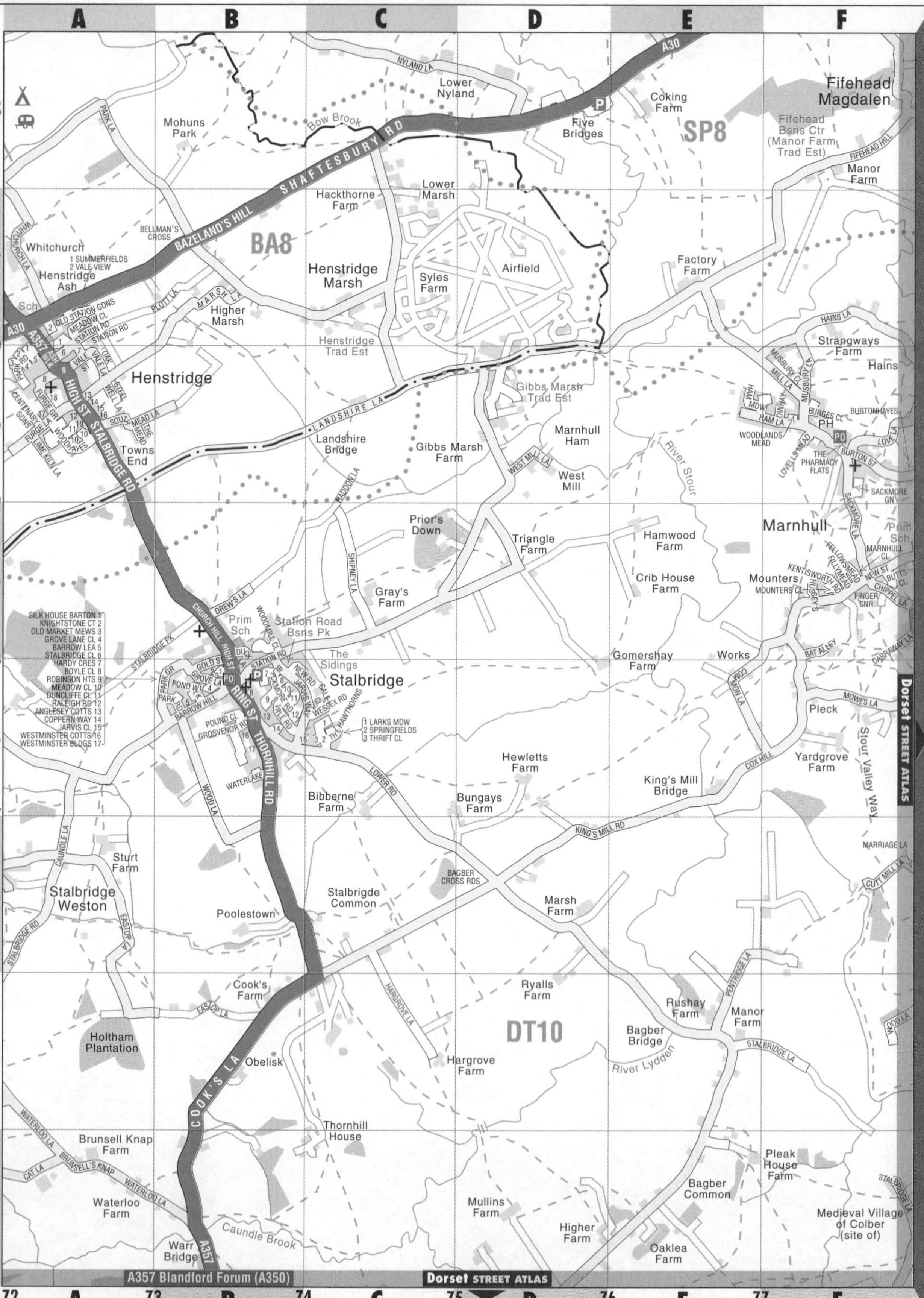

A B C D E F

Lower Nyland
Mohuns Park
Bow Brook
Five Bridges
Coking Farm
SP8
Fifehead Magdalen
Fifehead Bsns Ctr (Manor Farm Trad Est)
Manor Farm
SHAFTESBURY RD
BAZELAND'S HILL
Hackthorne Farm
Lower Marsh
BELLMAN'S CROSS
BA8
Whitchurch
1 SUMMERFIELDS
2 VALE VIEW
Henstridge Ash
Henstridge Marsh
Syles Farm
Airfield
Factory Farm
Higher Marsh
Henstridge Trad Est
Strangways Farm
Hains
Henstridge
Gibbs Marsh Trad Est
LANDSHIRE LA
Landshire Bridge
Gibbs Marsh Farm
Marnhull Ham
West Mill
River Stour
Towns End
HIGH ST
STALBRIDGE RD
Prior's Down
Triangle Farm
Hamwood Farm
Marnhull
Gray's Farm
Crib House Farm
Mounters
SILK HOUSE BARTON 1
KNIGHTSTONE CT 2
OLD MARKET MEWS 3
GROVE LANE CL 4
BARROW LEA 5
STALBRIDGE CL 6
HARDY CRES 7
BOYLE CL 8
ROBINSON HTS 9
MEADOW CL 10
DUNCLIFFE CL 11
RALEIGH RD 12
ANGLESEY COTTS 13
COPPERN WAY 14
JARVIS CL 15
WESTMINSTER COTTS 16
WESTMINSTER BLDGS 17
Prim Sch
Station Road Bsns Pk
The Sidings
Stalbridge
Gomershay Farm
Works
1 LARKS MDW
2 SPRINGFIELDS
3 THRIFT CL
Pleck
Hewletts Farm
King's Mill Bridge
Yardgrove Farm
Stour Valley Way
Bibberne Farm
Bungays Farm
THORNHILL RD
Sturt Farm
BAGBER CROSS RDS
Stalbridge Weston
Poolestown
Stalbrigde Common
Marsh Farm
Cook's Farm
Ryalls Farm
Rushay Farm
Manor Farm
Holtham Plantation
DT10
Bagber Bridge
Obelisk
Hargrove Farm
River Lydden
Brunsell Knap Farm
Thornhill House
Pleak House Farm
Waterloo Farm
Mullins Farm
Bagber Common
Higher Farm
Medieval Village of Colber (site of)
Caundle Brook
Warr Bridge
Oaklea Farm

A357 Blandford Forum (A350)

72 A 73 B 74 C 75 D 76 E 77 F

189

A B C D E F

Dunsgreen Farm
Palmer's Farm
Carlingwark
Grant's Farm
Stapley
Willand
ACOMBE CROSS
DROVE WAY
CHURCH RD
DUNSGREEN LA
BISCOMBE CROSS
ULLYCOMBE LA
RIDGEWOOD CROSS
Biscombe
Churchstanton Prim Sch
Ridgewood Hill
RIDGEWOOD LA
SHACKEL CROSS
Paye Farm
RAINBOW LA
TA3
Bolham Hill
Luddery Hill
Jewell's Farm
Smythes Farm
BROAD ST
Higher Munty
Redlane
SMYTHES CROSS
BAKER'S CROSS
BAKER'S LA
Batten's Farm
Clivehayes Farm
RED LA
Wr Twr
Bolham Water
Baker's Farm
BUTTLE'S CROSS
BROOM'S LA
Lemon's Hill
South Down
Buttle's Farm
BUTTLE'S LA
Bolham River
Fields Farm
Higher Southey Farm
KNACKER'S HOLE LA
Crocker's Farm
Lemon's Hill Farm
Middleton Barton
LAMPARK CT
Lower Southey Farm
EX15
Hole Farm
Southey Moor
Valentine's Farm
SLOUGH LA
Burrow's Farm
Gotleigh Moor
Abbotsford Farm
Smeatharpe
HOLEMORE CROSS
NEWCOT CROSS
Middle Luxton
The Knowle
Cockhayes
Mackham
Moonhayes
MOONHAYES CROSS
Gorwell Farm
WHITEDOWN CROSS
ULLCOMBE LA
Minson's Hill
Riggle's Farm
Chapelhayes
Bywood Copse
Beacon Hill
Cleave Farm
Bywood Farm
RIGGLES CROSS
Fair Oak Farm
Baxter's Farm
EX14
Holmwood Farm
TWISTGATES LA
MATTYS CROSS
Turfhouse
Harvestwood Farm
Gullylane Farm
Hense Moor
Mathayes Farm
Rough Grey Bottom
Upottery Prim Sch
DANES CL
PIPERS PL
OAK TREE CL
MANOR GN
Upottery
Overday Farm
Aller Farm
SANDY'S LA
Southlands Farm
Combeshead
PH
CROSSLAND LA
Braddicksknap Hill
Hillend Farm
Bidwell Farm
Luppitt Common
NEW RD
Calhayes Farm
Budgells Farm
Courtmoor Farm
Old Highwood
Odle Farm
PH
Spurtham Farm
PO
Rawridge
Windsor Farm
Luppitt
POUND LA
VINEY LA
Hartridge
Dolish Farm
Shelf Farm
OTTER VALE CL
Rawridge Farm
A30
A30 Honiton
COTLEIGH CROSSING

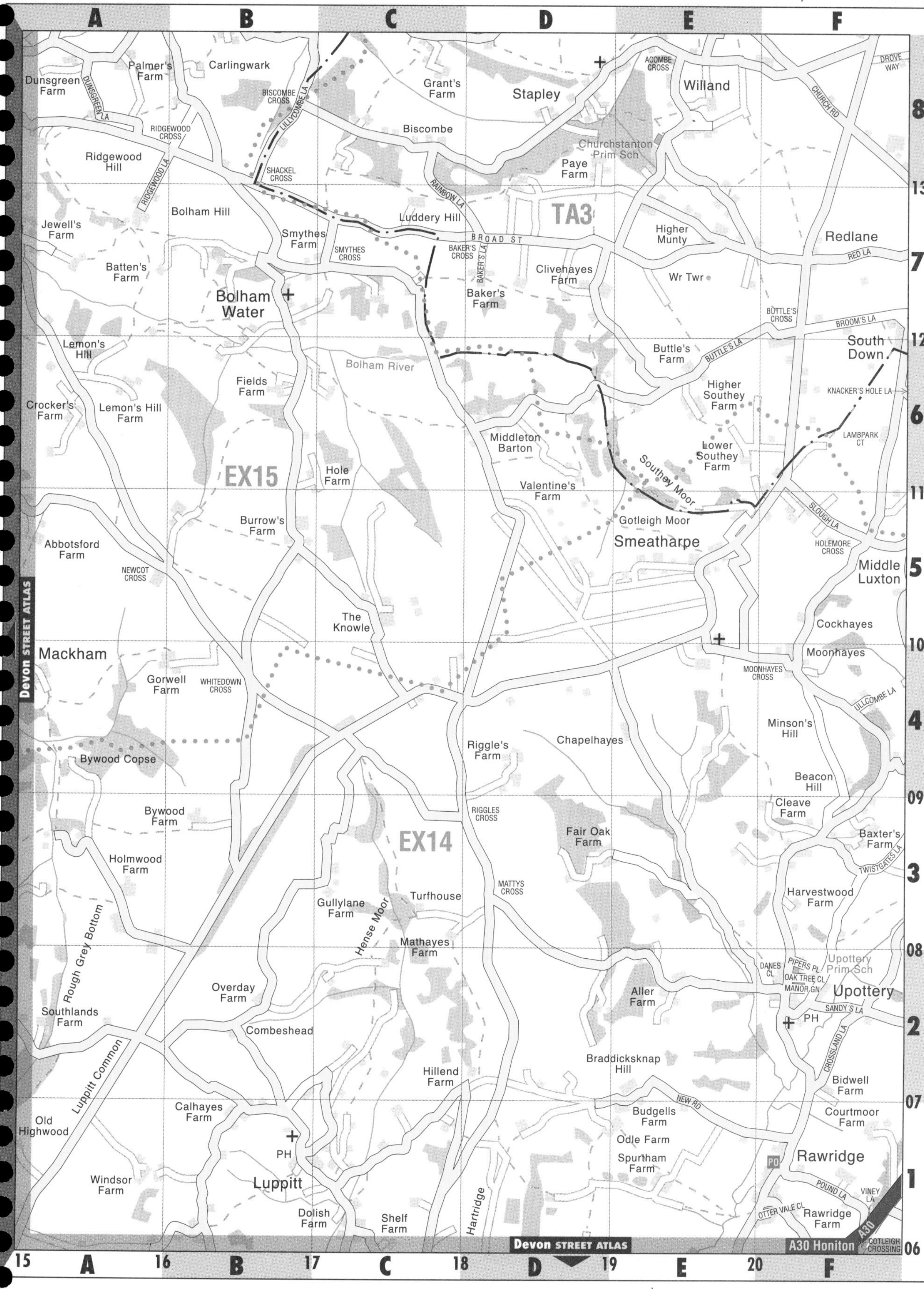

13 8 7 12 6 11 5 10 4 09 3 08 2 07 1 06

15 16 17 18 19 20
A B C D E F

191
181
182

Scale: 1¾ inches to 1 mile

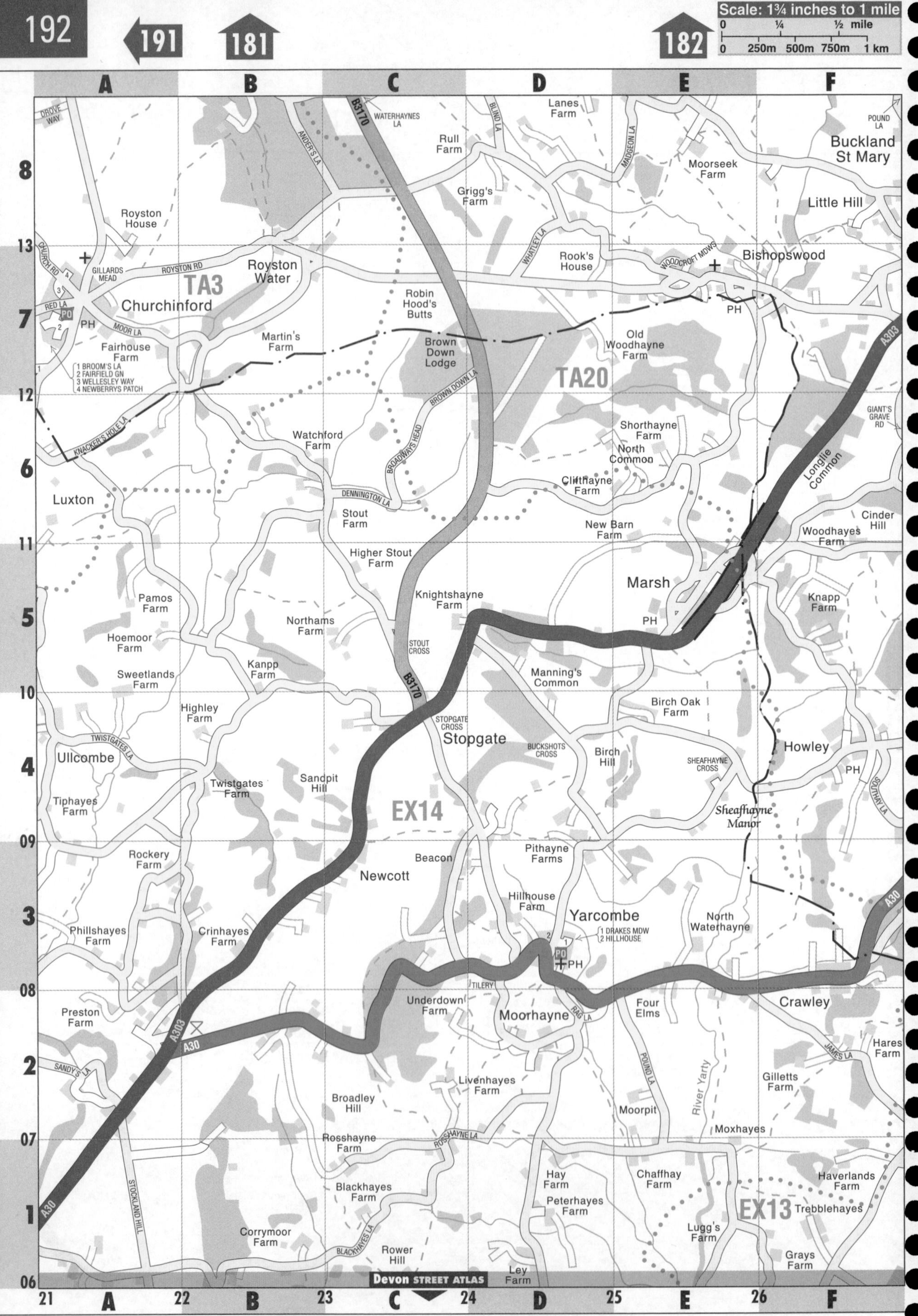

191

Scale: 1¾ inches to 1 mile

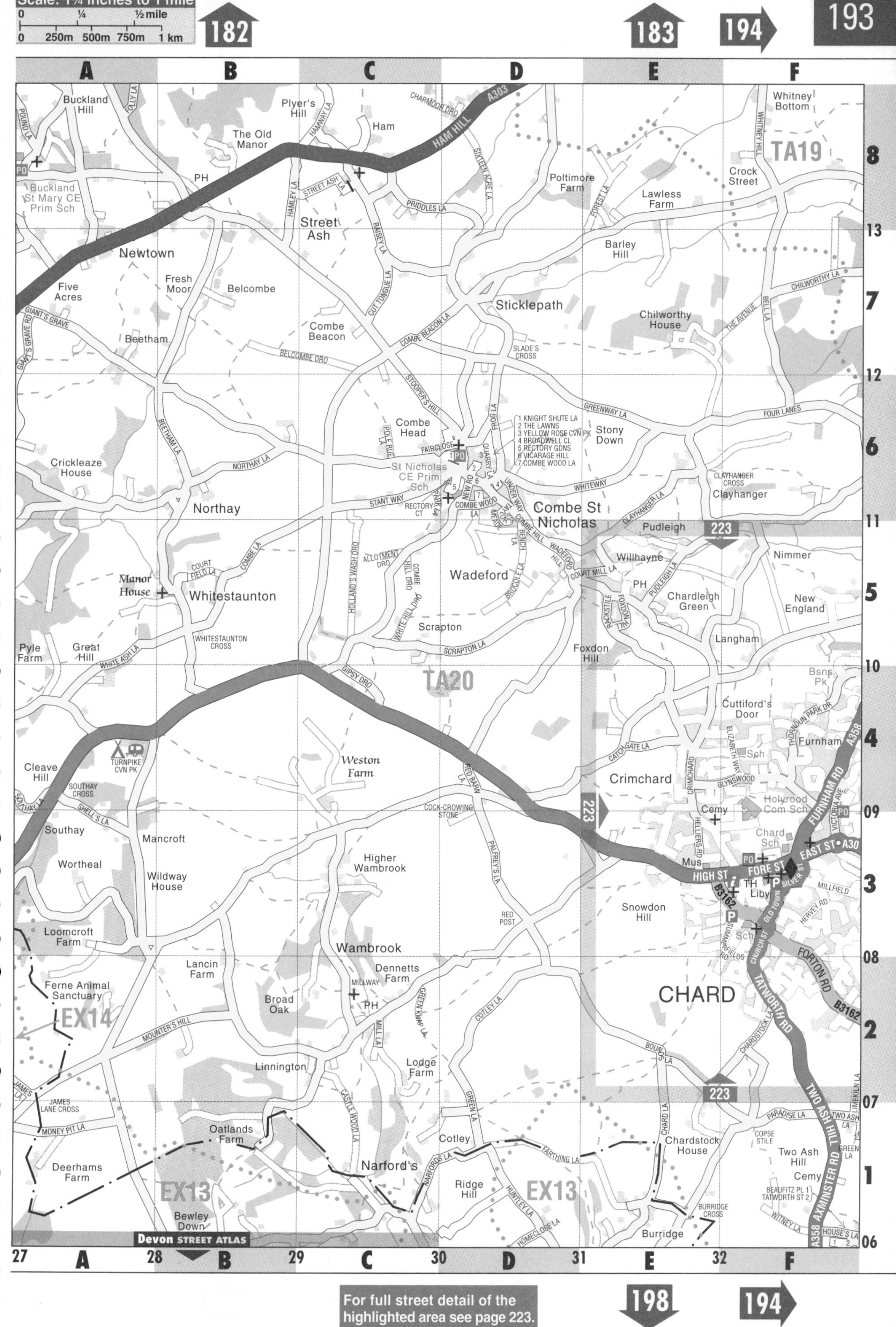

For full street detail of the highlighted area see page 223.

198
194

Scale: 1¾ inches to 1 mile

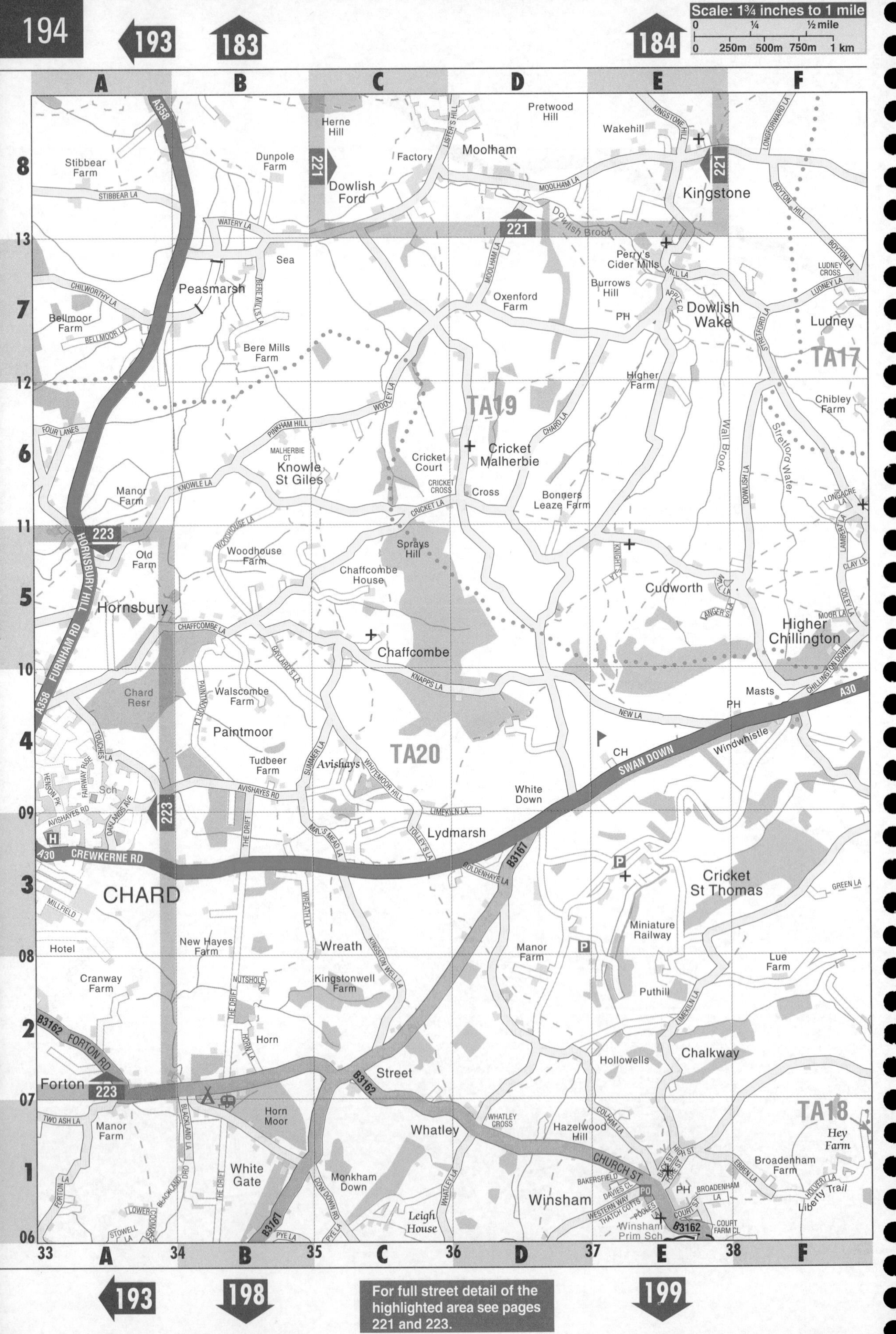

For full street detail of the highlighted area see pages 221 and 223.

Scale: 1¾ inches to 1 mile

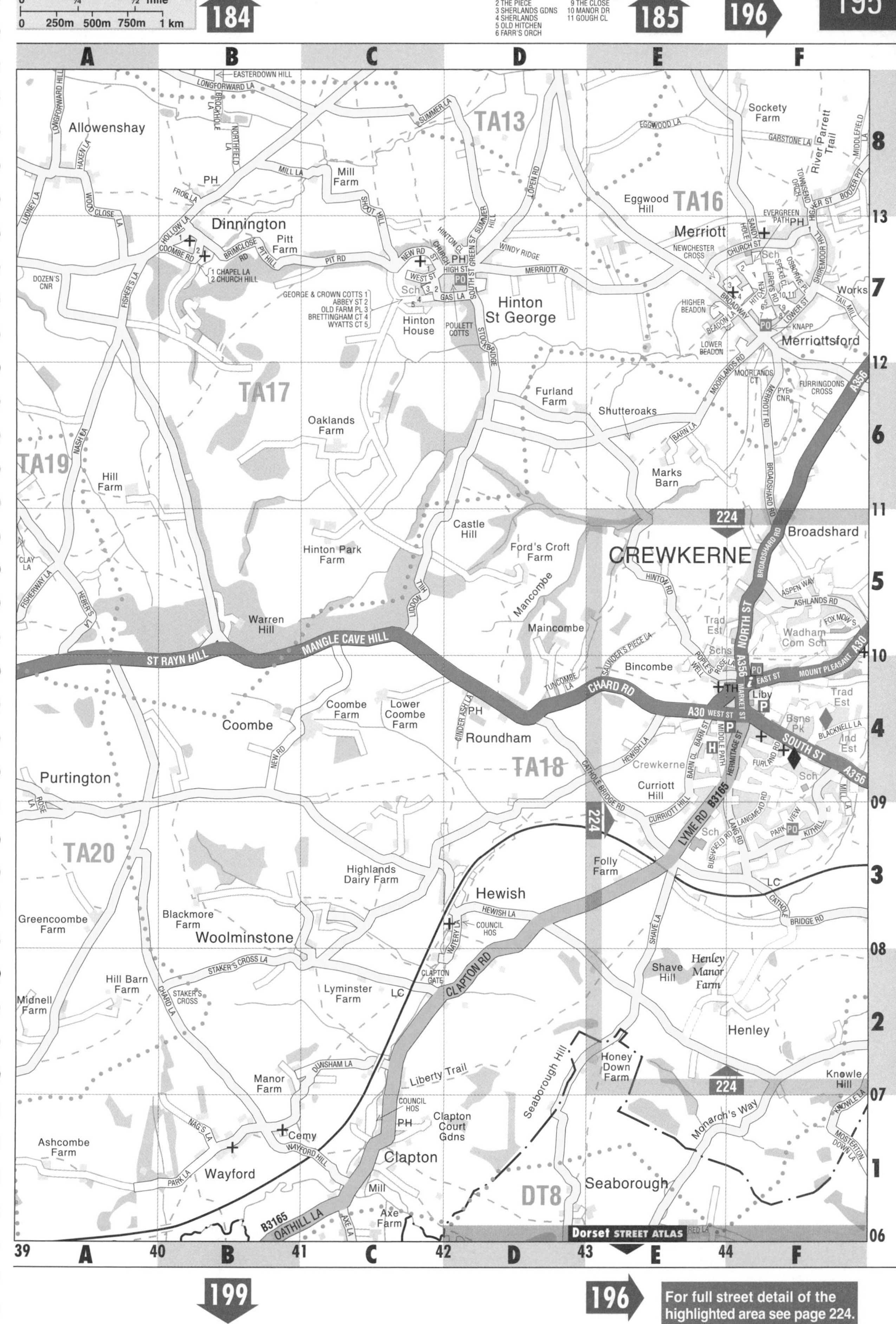

199
196
For full street detail of the highlighted area see page 224.

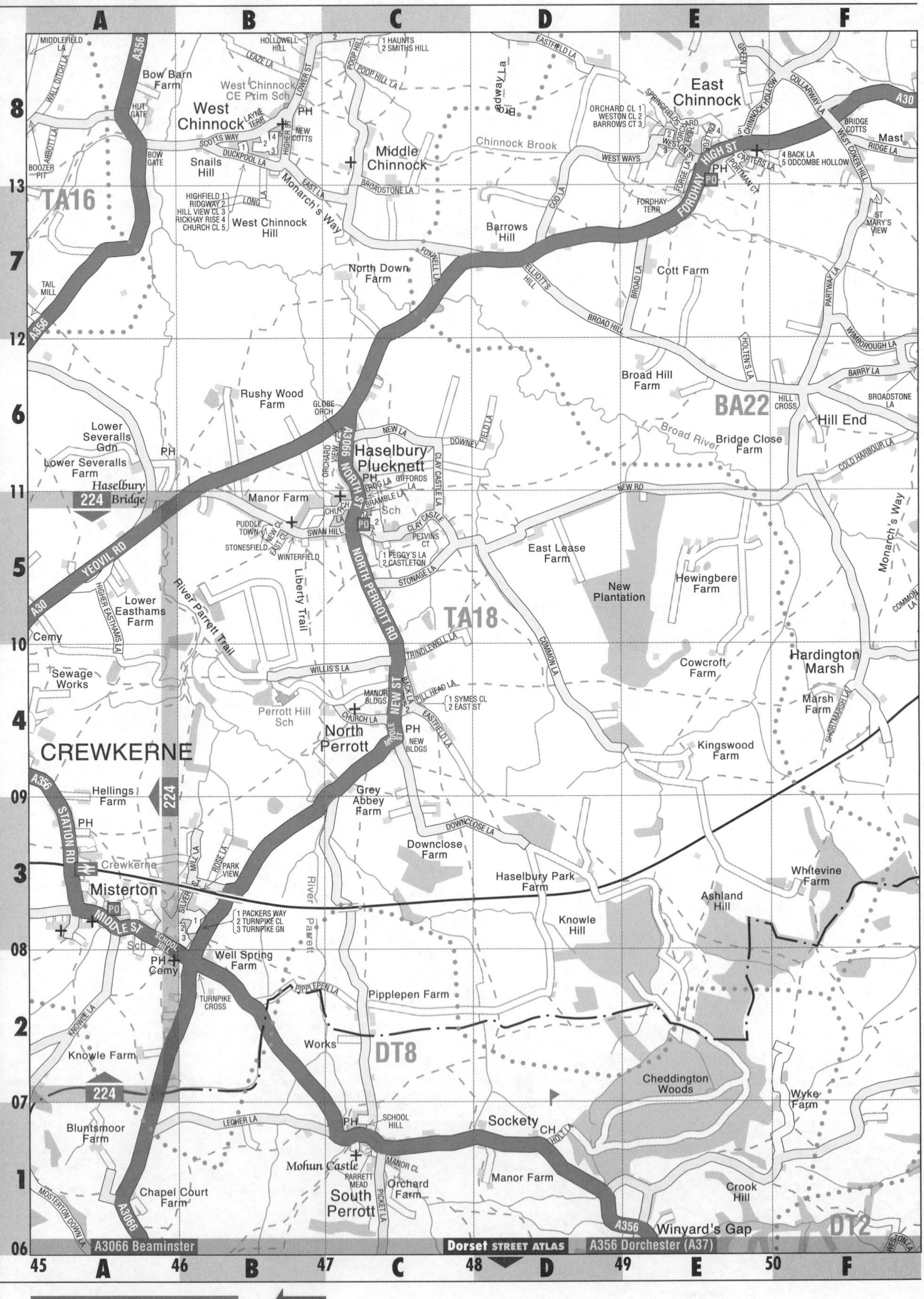

For full street detail of the highlighted area see page 224.
195

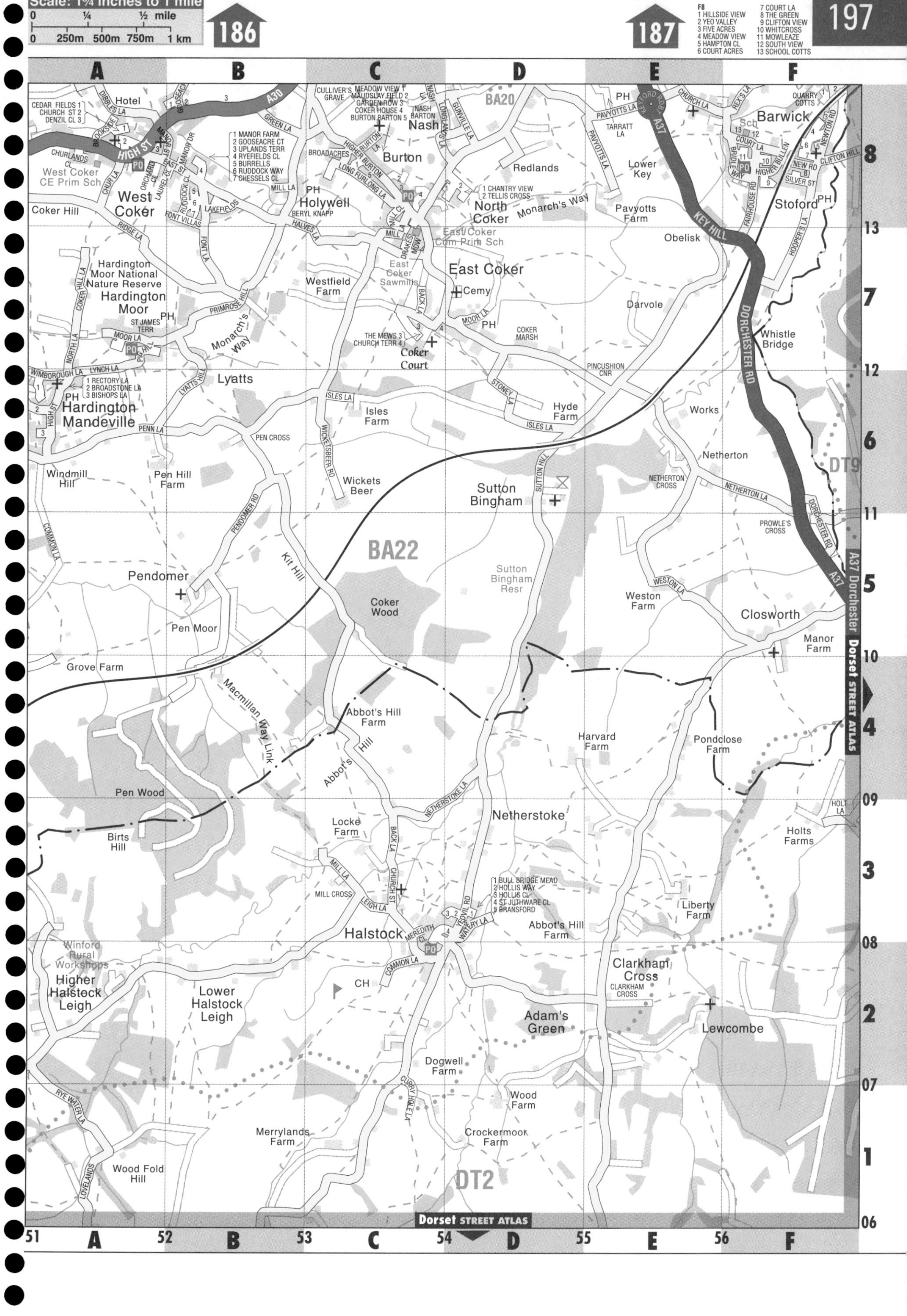
Scale: 1¾ inches to 1 mile
0 ¼ ½ mile
0 250m 500m 750m 1 km
186
187
F8
1 HILLSIDE VIEW
2 YEO VALLEY
3 FIVE ACRES
4 MEADOW VIEW
5 HAMPTON CL
6 COURT ACRES
7 COURT LA
8 THE GREEN
9 CLIFTON VIEW
10 WHITCROSS
11 MOWLEAZE
12 SOUTH VIEW
13 SCHOOL COTTS
A
B
C
D
E
F
Hotel
CEDAR FIELDS 1
CHURCH ST 2
DENZIL CL 3
HIGH ST
A30
West Coker
West Coker CE Prim Sch
Coker Hill
1 MANOR FARM
2 GOOSEACRE CT
3 UPLANDS TERR
4 RYEFIELDS CL
5 BURRELLS
6 RUDDOCK WAY
7 CHESSELS CL
LAKEFIELDS
FONT VILLAS
FONT LA
RIDGE LA
CULLIVER'S GRAVE
MEADOW VIEW 1
MAUDSLAY FIELD 2
GARDEN ROW 3
COKER HOUSE 4
BURTON BARTON 5
NASH BARTON
Nash
Burton
BROADACRES
LONG FURLONG LA
Holywell
BERYL KNAPP
HALVES LA
MILL LA
BA20
Redlands
1 CHANTRY VIEW
2 TELLIS CROSS
North Coker
Monarch's Way
East Coker Com Prim Sch
East Coker Sawmills
East Coker
Cemy
Westfield Farm
THE MEWS 3
CHURCH TERR 4
Coker Court
COKER MARSH
MOOR LA
PH
Hardington Moor National Nature Reserve
Hardington Moor
ST JAMES TERR
PRIMROSE HILL
Monarch's Way
Lyatts
WIMBOROUGH LA
LYNCH LA
1 RECTORY LA
2 BROADSTONE LA
3 BISHOPS LA
Hardington Mandeville
PENN LA
ISLES LA
Isles Farm
PEN CROSS
Windmill Hill
Pen Hill Farm
Wickets Beer
WICKETSBEER RD
PENDOMER RD
COMMON LA
Kit Hill
BA22
Pendomer
Pen Moor
Coker Wood
Grove Farm
Macmillan Way Link
Abbot's Hill Farm
Abbot's Hill
Pen Wood
Birts Hill
Locke Farm
MILL LA
MILL CROSS
BACK LA
CHURCH ST
LEIGH LA
Halstock
MEREDITH CL
COMMON LA
Winford Rural Workshops
Higher Halstock Leigh
Lower Halstock Leigh
CH
RYE WATER LA
LOVELANDS
Wood Fold Hill
Merrylands Farm
CURRY HOLE LA
Dogwell Farm
Wood Farm
Crockermoor Farm
DT2
NETHERSTOKE LA
Netherstoke
1 BULL BRIDGE MEAD
2 HOLLIS WAY
3 HOLLIS CL
4 ST JUTHWARE CL
5 BRANSFORD
YEOVIL RD
WATERY LA
Abbot's Hill Farm
Adam's Green
Clarkham Cross
CLARKHAM CROSS
Lewcombe
Liberty Farm
Harvard Farm
Pondclose Farm
Holts Farms
HOLT LA
Sutton Bingham
SUTTON HILL
Sutton Bingham Resr
STONEY LA
Hyde Farm
ISLES LA
PINCUSHION CNR
PH
PAVYOTTS LA
TARRATT LA
KEYFORD RDB
A37
Lower Key
Pavyotts Farm
KEY HILL
Obelisk
Darvole
Works
Netherton
NETHERTON CROSS
NETHERTON LA
Weston Farm
WESTON LA
Closworth
Manor Farm
CHURCH LA
REX'S LA
QUARRY COTTS
Barwick
Sch
COURT LA
BRIDLE WAY
HIGHER BULLEN
NEW RD
SILVER ST
CLIFTON HILL
NEWTON RD
FAIRHOUSE RD
Stoford
HOOPER'S LA
Whistle Bridge
DORCHESTER RD
PROWLE'S CROSS
DT9
A37 Dorchester
Dorset STREET ATLAS
8
13
7
12
6
11
5
10
4
09
3
08
2
07
1
06
51
52
53
54
55
56

193
194

Scale: 1¾ inches to 1 mile
0 ¼ ½ mile
0 250m 500m 750m 1 km

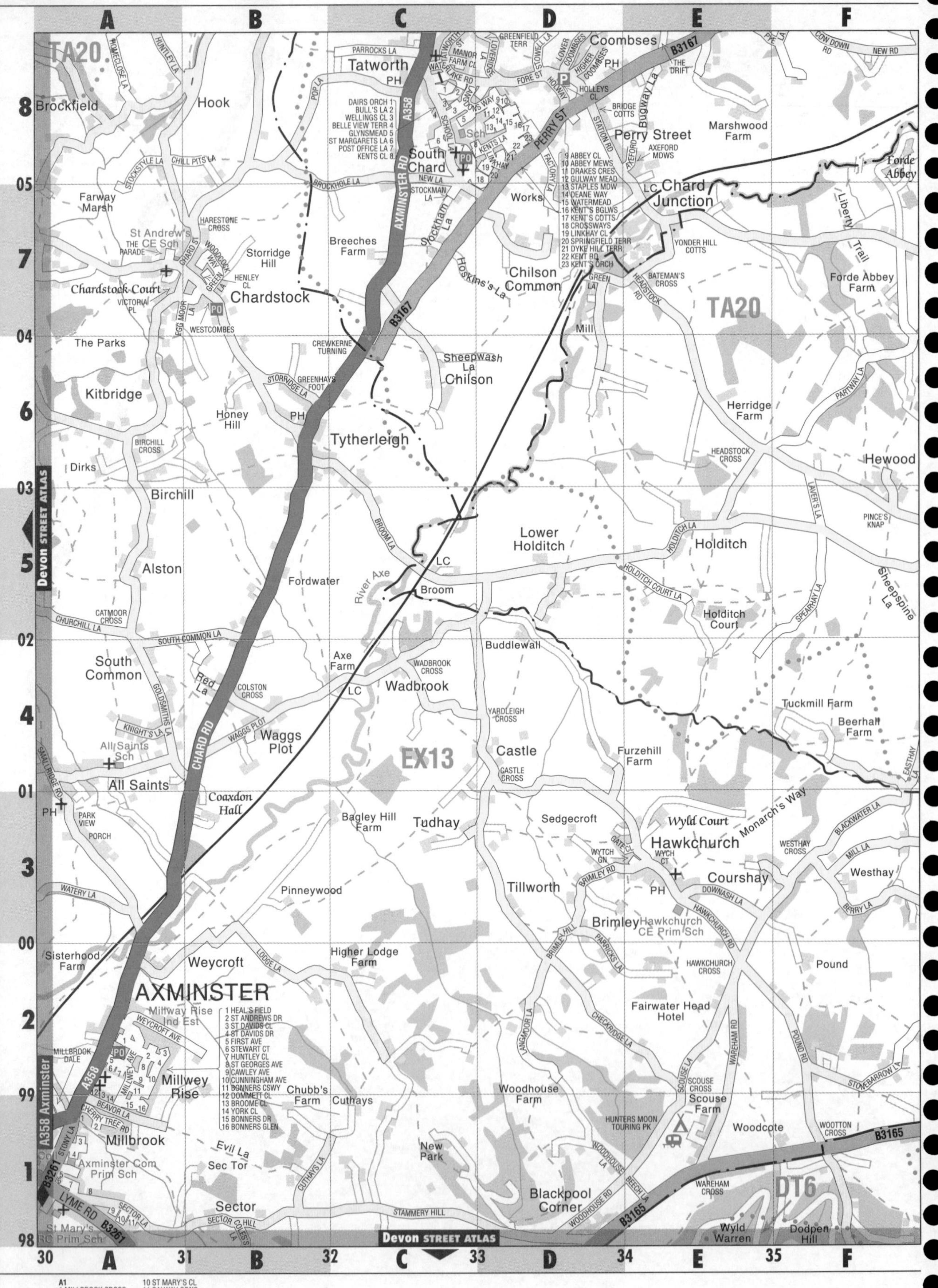

A1
1 MILLBROOK CROSS
2 CATNIP CL
3 JEFFS WAY
4 NEWBERY CL
5 LORETTO GDNS
6 MONKSTONE GDNS
7 CRIDLAKE
8 VALLEY VIEW
9 PRESTOR
10 ST MARY'S CL
11 SALWAY GDNS

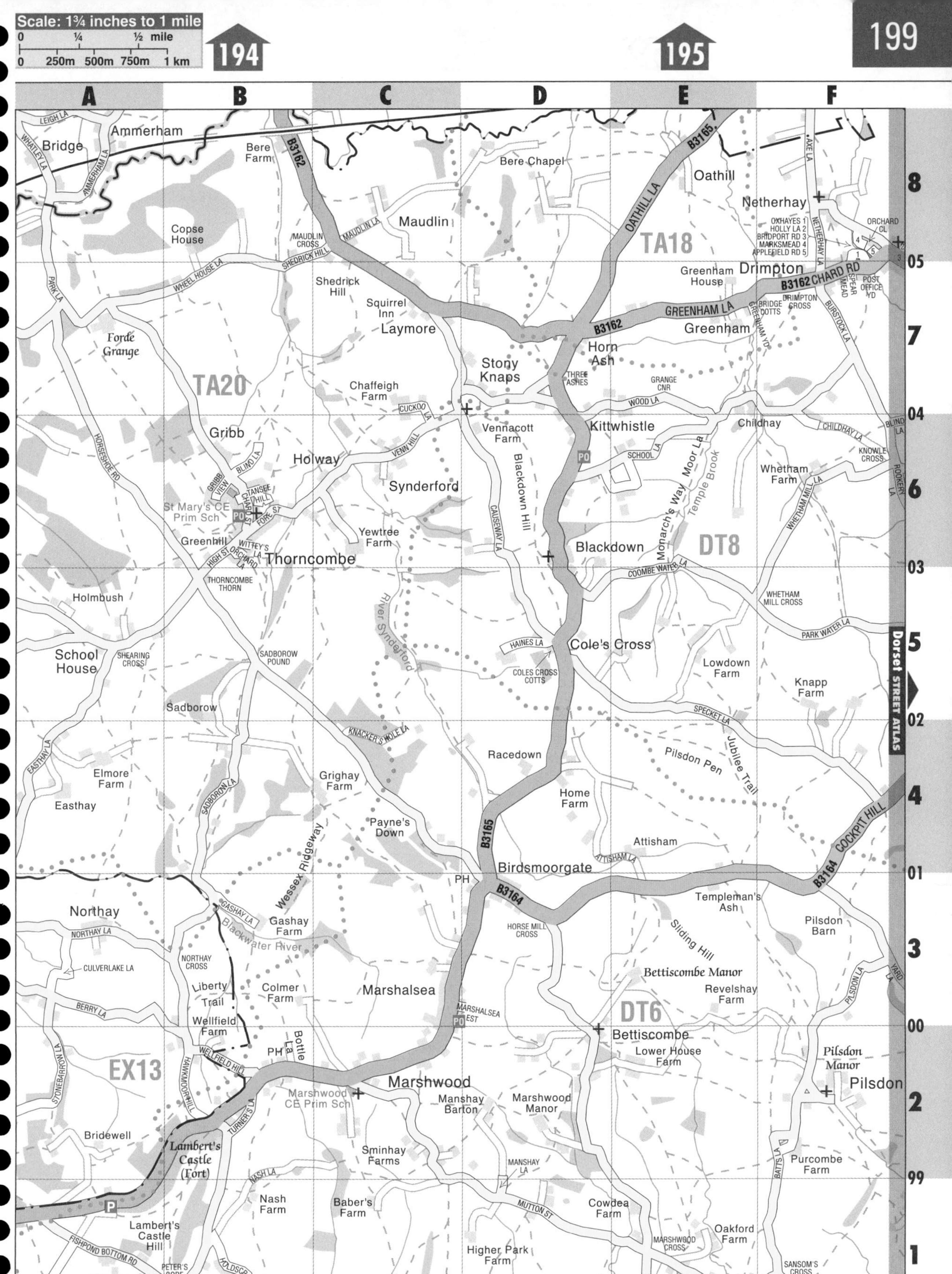
Scale: 1¾ inches to 1 mile
0 ¼ ½ mile
0 250m 500m 750m 1 km
194
195
A
B
C
D
E
F
8
05
7
04
6
03
5
02
4
01
3
00
2
99
1
98
36
37
38
39
40
41
Dorset STREET ATLAS
LEIGH LA
WHATLEY LA
Bridge
Ammerham
AMMERHAM LA
Bere Farm
B3162
Bere Chapel
B3165
Oathill
AXE LA
Netherhay
OATHILL LA
Copse House
MAUDLIN CROSS
MAUDLIN LA
Maudlin
TA18
OXHAYES 1
HOLLY LA 2
BRIDPORT RD 3
MARKSMEAD 4
APPLEFIELD RD 5
NETHERHAY LA
ORCHARD CL
WHEEL HOUSE LA
SHEDRICK HILL
Shedrick Hill
Greenham House
Drimpton
B3162 CHARD RD
SPEAR MEAD
POST OFFICE YD
PARK LA
Squirrel Inn
Laymore
GREENHAM LA
BRIDGE COTTS
DRIMPTON CROSS
GREENHAM YD
BURSTOCK LA
Forde Grange
B3162
Greenham
Horn Ash
Stony Knaps
THREE ASHES
GRANGE CNR
TA20
Chaffeigh Farm
CUCKOO LA
WOOD LA
Vennacott Farm
Kittwhistle
Childhay
CHILDHAY LA
BLIND LA
Gribb
VENN HILL
BLIND LA
Holway
PO
SCHOOL LA
Moor La
Temple Brook
KNOWLE CROSS
Whetham Farm
ROOKERY LA
HORSESHOE RD
GRIBB VIEW
TANSEE HILL
CHARD ST
Synderford
Blackdown Hill
Monarch's Way
WHETHAM MILL LA
St Mary's CE Prim Sch
PO
FORE ST
Yewtree Farm
CAUSEWAY LA
DT8
Greenhill
WITTEY'S LA
HIGH ST
ORCHARD LA
Thorncombe
Blackdown
COOMBE WATER LA
THORNCOMBE THORN
Holmbush
WHETHAM MILL CROSS
River Synderford
PARK WATER LA
HAINES LA
Cole's Cross
School House
SHEARING CROSS
SADBOROW POUND
Lowdown Farm
COLES CROSS COTTS
Knapp Farm
Sadborow
SPECKET LA
KNACKER'S HOLE LA
Racedown
Pilsdon Pen
Jubilee Trail
EASTHAY LA
Elmore Farm
Grighay Farm
SADBOROW LA
Home Farm
Easthay
Payne's Down
Wessex Ridgeway
B3165
Attisham
COCKPIT HILL
ATTISHAM LA
Birdsmoorgate
B3164
PH
B3164
Templeman's Ash
Northay
GASHAY LA
Gashay Farm
Pilsdon Barn
NORTHAY LA
HORSE MILL CROSS
Sliding Hill
Blackwater River
NORTHAY CROSS
CULVERLAKE LA
Bettiscombe Manor
YARD LA
Liberty Trail
Colmer Farm
Marshalsea
Revelshay Farm
PILSDON LA
BERRY LA
MARSHALSEA EST
PO
DT6
Wellfield Farm
Bottle La
Bettiscombe
EX13
PH
Lower House Farm
Pilsdon Manor
Pilsdon
STONEBARROW LA
WELLFIELD HILL
HAWKMOOR HILL
Marshwood
Marshwood CE Prim Sch
Manshay Barton
Marshwood Manor
TURNER'S LA
Bridewell
Lambert's Castle (Fort)
Sminhay Farms
MANSHAY LA
BATTS LA
Purcombe Farm
NASH LA
Nash Farm
Baber's Farm
MUTTON ST
Cowdea Farm
P
Lambert's Castle Hill
Oakford Farm
MARSHWOOD CROSS
FISHPOND BOTTOM RD
Higher Park Farm
SANSOM'S CROSS
PETER'S GORE
HOLDSCROFT LA
TAPHOUSE LA
CHARING CROSS
Fishpond Bottom
ABBOTT'S WOOTTON LA
LONG LA
POORHOUSE LA
SHAVE CROSS

124
125

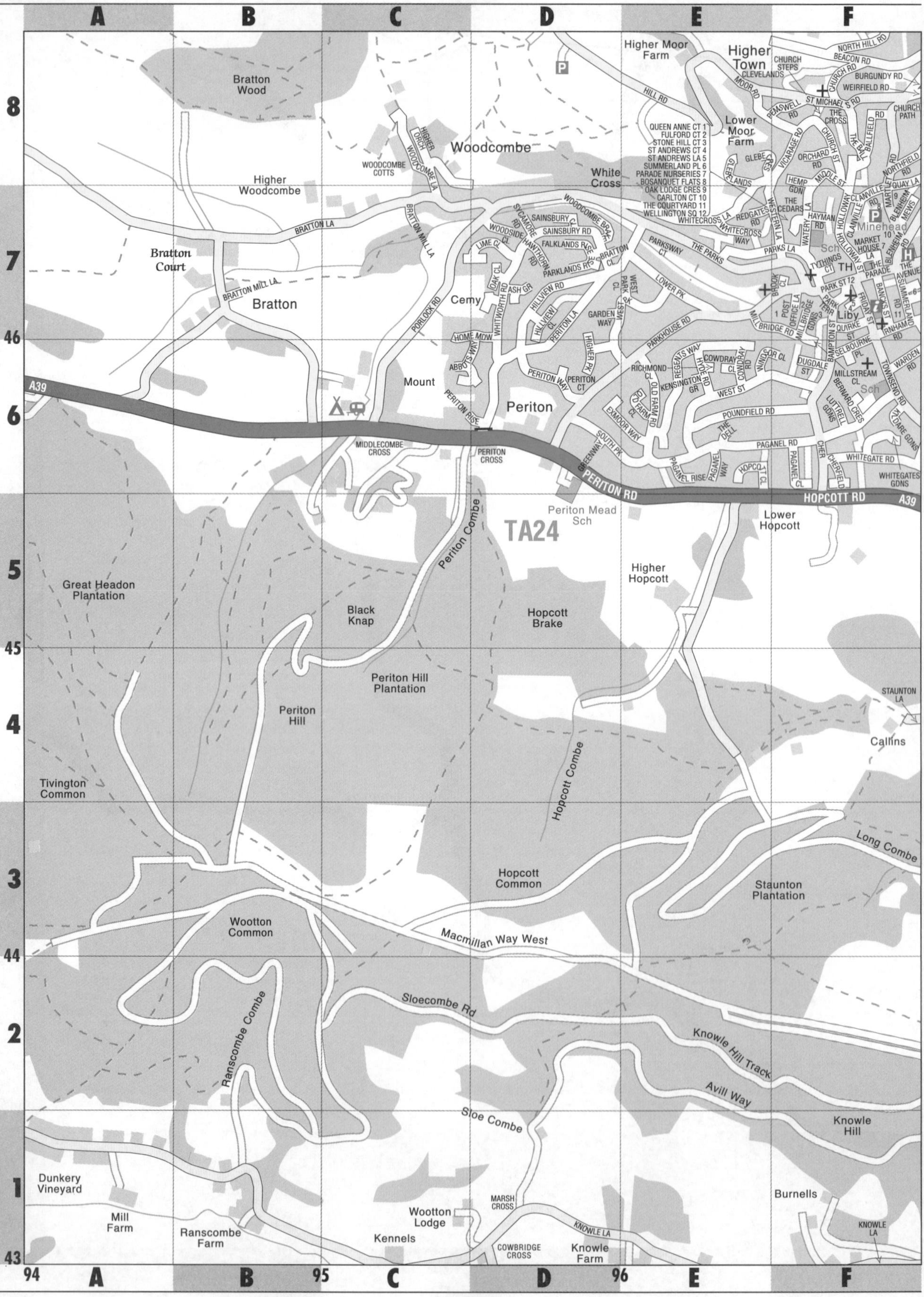

Bratton Wood
Woodcombe
Higher Woodcombe
Bratton Court
Bratton
Higher Moor Farm
Higher Town
Lower Moor Farm
White Cross
QUEEN ANNE CT 1
FULFORD CT 2
STONE HILL CT 3
ST ANDREWS CT 4
ST ANDREWS LA 5
SUMMERLAND PL 6
PARADE NURSERIES 7
BOSANQUET FLATS 8
OAK LODGE CRES 9
CARLTON CT 10
THE COURTYARD 11
WELLINGTON SQ 12
Minehead
Cemy
Mount
Periton
MIDDLECOMBE CROSS
PERITON CROSS
PERITON RD
HOPCOTT RD
A39
Periton Mead Sch
TA24
Lower Hopcott
Higher Hopcott
Great Headon Plantation
Black Knap
Hopcott Brake
Periton Combe
Periton Hill Plantation
Periton Hill
Tivington Common
Hopcott Combe
STAUNTON LA
Callins
Long Combe
Hopcott Common
Staunton Plantation
Wootton Common
Macmillan Way West
Sloecombe Rd
Ransscombe Combe
Knowle Hill Track
Avill Way
Sloe Combe
Knowle Hill
Dunkery Vineyard
Mill Farm
Ranscombe Farm
Kennels
Wootton Lodge
MARSH CROSS
COWBRIDGE CROSS
Knowle Farm
KNOWLE LA
Burnells

129
130

125
131

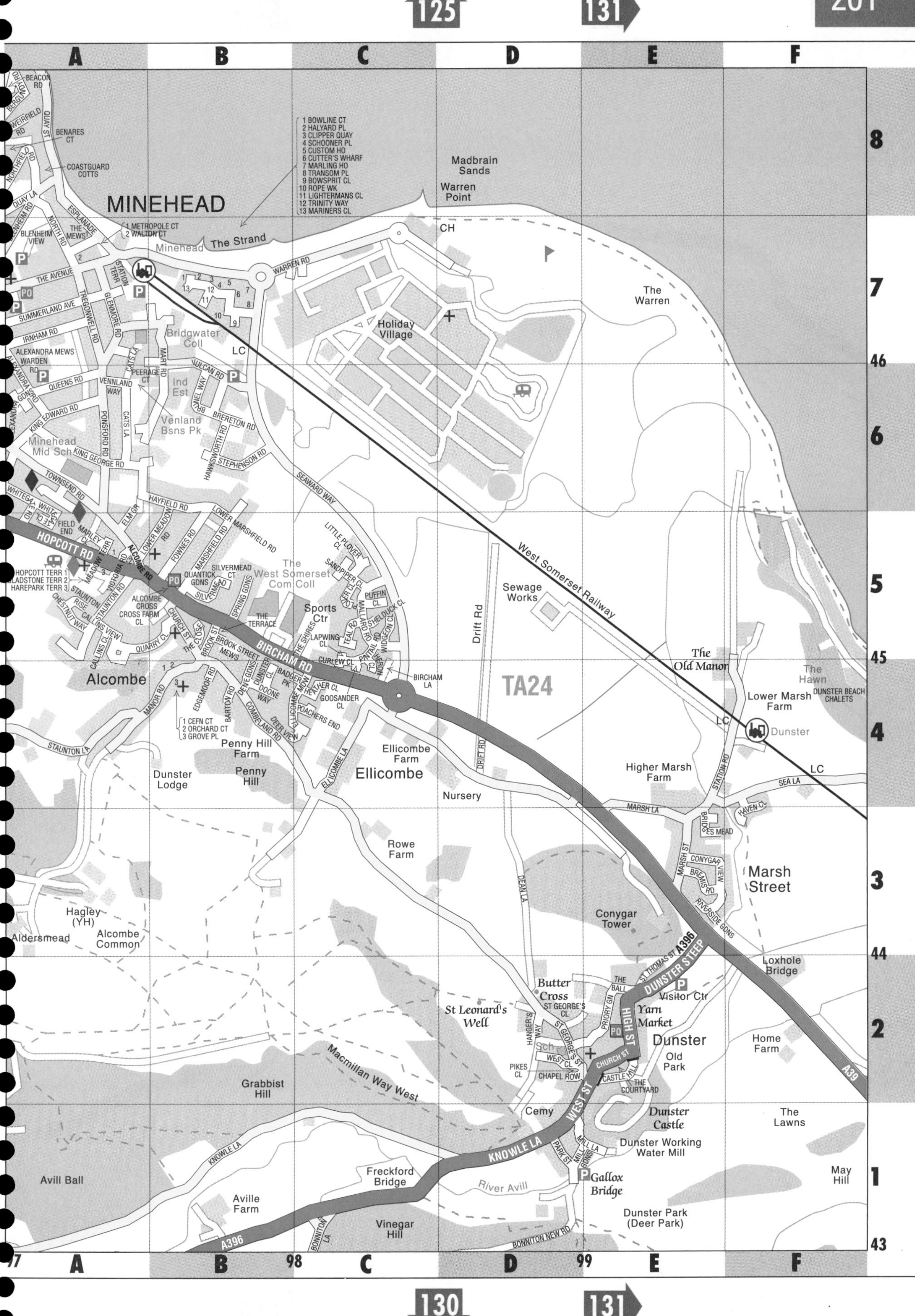

130
131

131 132

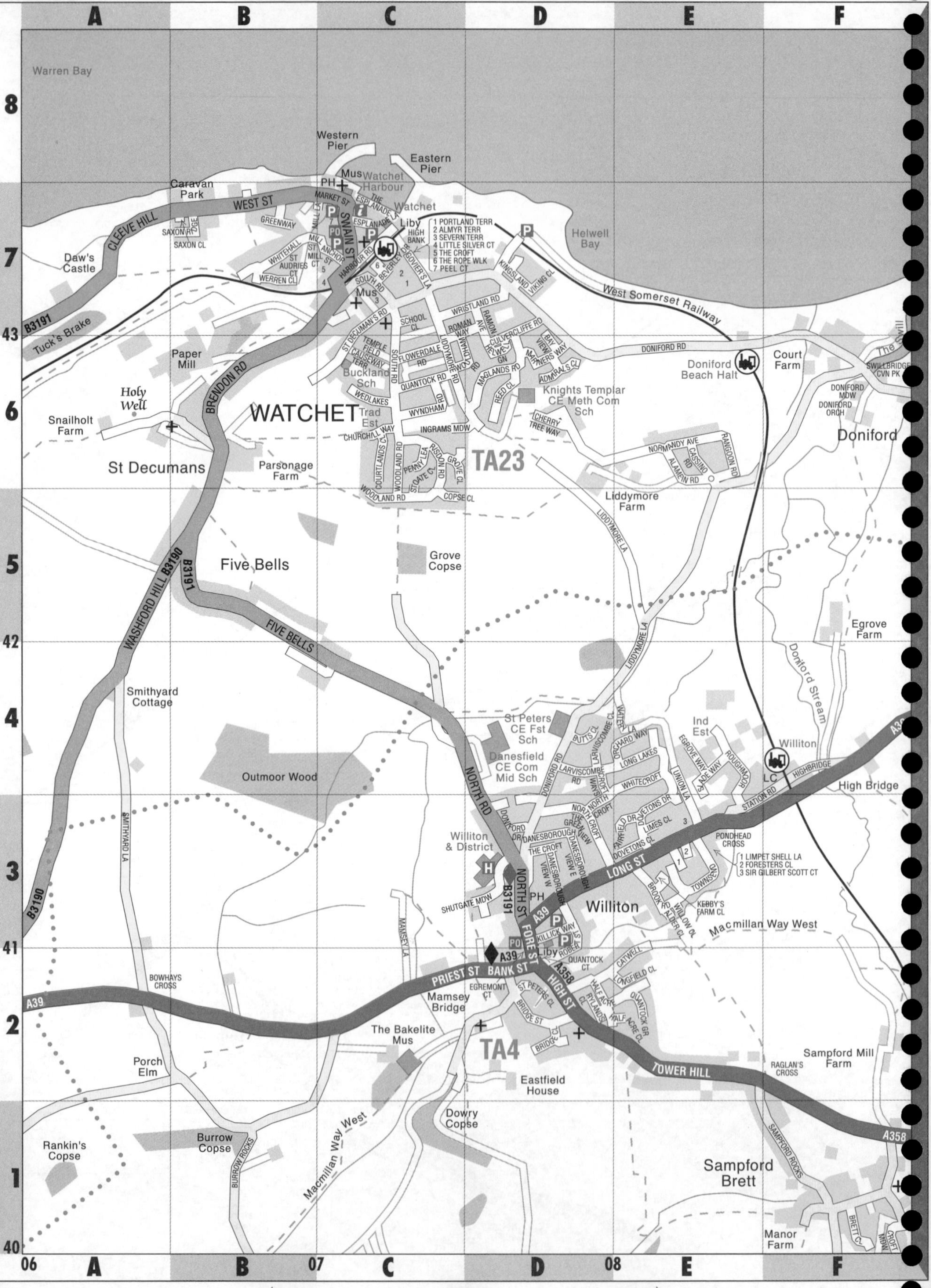

A B C D E F

8 7 43 6 5 42 4 3 41 2 1 40

Warren Bay

Western Pier

Eastern Pier

PH Mus Watchet Harbour

Caravan Park

WEST ST

CLEEVE HILL

SAXON RDGE

SAXON CL

GREENWAY

MARKET ST

SWAIN ST

THE ESPLANADE

ESPLANADE LA

Watchet

Liby

HIGH BANK

1 PORTLAND TERR
2 ALMYR TERR
3 SEVERN TERR
4 LITTLE SILVER CT
5 THE CROFT
6 THE ROPE WLK
7 PEEL CT

Helwell Bay

WHITEHALL

ST AUDRIES CT

WERREN CL

MILL ST

HARBOUR RD

SOUTH RD

BEVERLEY DR

GOVIER'S LA

KINGSLAND

VIKING CL

West Somerset Railway

Daw's Castle

B3191

Tuck's Brake

Mus

WRISTLAND RD

SCHOOL CL

ROMAN WAY

RAMONA

CULVERCLIFFE RD

BAY VIEW

MARINERS WAY

ADMIRALS CL

HELWELL GN

ST DECUMAN'S RD

TEMPLE FIELD

CAUSEWAY TERR

Buckland Sch

FLOWERDALE RD

LIDDYMORE RD

MAGLANDS RD

REED CL

QUANTOCK RD

DONIFORD RD

Doniford Beach Halt

Court Farm

The Swill

SWILLBRIDGE CVN PK

DONIFORD MDW

DONIFORD ORCH

Doniford

Paper Mill

BRENDON RD

Holy Well

Snailholt Farm

WATCHET

WEDLAKES

WYNDHAM

Trad Est

Knights Templar CE Meth Com Sch

CHERRY TREE WAY

INGRAMS MDW

CHURCHILL WAY

COURTLANDS CL

WOODLAND RD

PENNY LEA

STOATE CL

RISDON RD

GROVE CL

COPSE CL

TA23

NORMANDY AVE

CASSINO RD

ALAMEIN RD

RANGOON RD

St Decumans

Parsonage Farm

Liddymore Farm

LIDDYMORE LA

Five Bells

Grove Copse

B3190

WASHFORD HILL

FIVE BELLS

Egrove Farm

Doniford Stream

Smithyard Cottage

St Peters CE Fst Sch

Danesfield CE Com Mid Sch

BUTTS CL

WATERY LA

LARVISCOMBE CL

ORCHARD WAY

LONG LAKES

LARVISCOMBE RD

WAYSIDE

WHITECROFT

UNION LA

EGROVE WAY

GLADE WAY

ROUGHMOOR

Ind Est

Williton

LC

HIGHBRIDGE

High Bridge

A39

Outmoor Wood

NORTH RD

DONIFORD RD

NORTH CROFT

THE GREEN

FAIRFIELD DR

DOVETONS DR

LIMES CL

DOVETONS CL

STATION RD

PONDHEAD CROSS

1 LIMPET SHELL LA
2 FORESTERS CL
3 SIR GILBERT SCOTT CT

SMITHYARD LA

Williton & District

DANESBOROUGH VIEW

THE CROFT

DANESBOROUGH VIEW W

VIEW E

LONG ST

H

NORTH ST

B3191

PH

SHUTGATE MDW

MAMSEY LA

Williton

BROOK ST

ALDER CL

WILLOW CL

KEBBY'S FARM CL

TOWNSEND

Macmillan Way West

FORE ST

KILLICK WAY

ROBERT ST

PO

Liby

A39

BANK ST

PRIEST ST

HIGH ST

A358

QUANTOCK CT

CATWELL

LONGFIELD CL

BOWHAYS CROSS

EGREMONT CT

Mamsey Bridge

ST PETERS CL

BRIDGE ST

HALF ACRE

RYLANDS CL

QUANTOCK GR

ACRE CL

The Bakelite Mus

TA4

Sampford Mill Farm

RAGLAN'S CROSS

TOWER HILL

Porch Elm

Eastfield House

Dowry Copse

A358

Macmillan Way West

Rankin's Copse

Burrow Copse

BURROW ROCKS

Sampford Brett

SAMPFORD ROCKS

Manor Farm

BRETT CL

CROFT MDW

06 A B 07 C D 08 E F

131 132 132

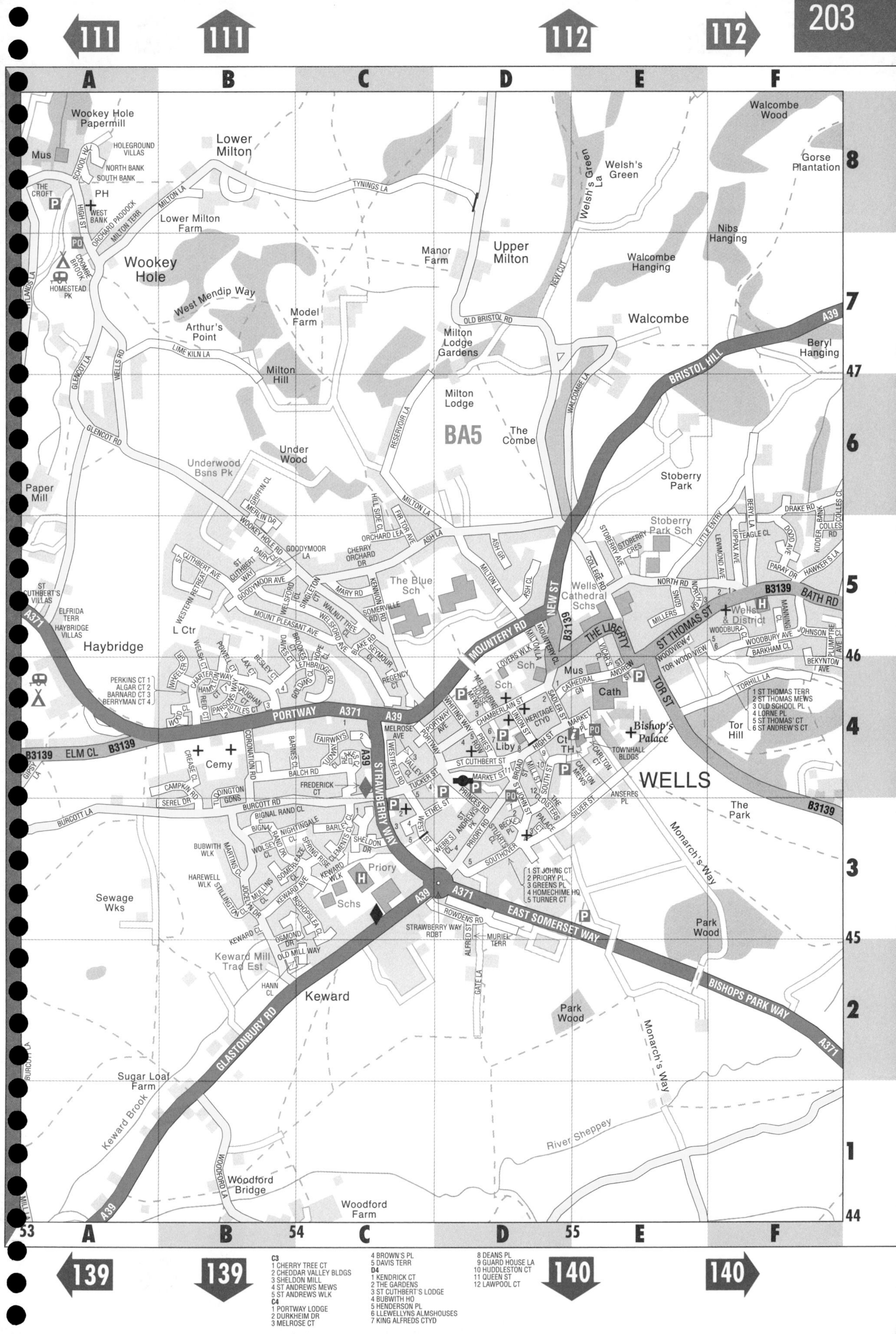
111
111
112
112
A
B
C
D
E
F
8
7
47
6
5
46
4
3
45
2
1
44
53
54
55
139
139
140
140
Wookey Hole Papermill
Mus
HOLEGROUND VILLAS
NORTH BANK
SOUTH BANK
SCHOOL HILL
THE CROFT
PH
WEST BANK
HIGH ST
ORCHARD PADDOCK
MILTON TERR
MILTON LA
Lower Milton
Lower Milton Farm
TYNINGS LA
PO
COMBE BROOK
HOMESTEAD PK
Wookey Hole
West Mendip Way
Manor Farm
Upper Milton
NEW CUT
Welsh's Green La
Welsh's Green
Walcombe Wood
Gorse Plantation
Nibs Hanging
Walcombe Hanging
Walcombe
Beryl Hanging
A39
Model Farm
Arthur's Point
LIME KILN LA
Milton Hill
OLD BRISTOL RD
Milton Lodge Gardens
Milton Lodge
BRISTOL HILL
WALCOMBE LA
GLENCOT LA
WELLS RD
GLENCOT RD
RESERVOIR LA
BA5
The Combe
Under Wood
Underwood Bsns Pk
Paper Mill
Stoberry Park
GRIFFIN CL
MERLIN DR
WOOKEY HOLE RD
HILL SIDE CL
FIR TOR AVE
MILTON LA
ORCHARD LEA
CHERRY ORCHARD DR
ASH LA
ASH GR
GOODYMOOR LA
DAIRY CL
ST CUTHBERT AVE
ST CUTHBERT WAY
GOODYMOOR AVE
WESTERN RETREAT
WELSFORD CL
SINGLETON CT
MARY RD
KENNION RD
The Blue Sch
ASH CL
NEW ST
Wells Cathedral Schs
COLLEGE RD
STOBERRY AVE
STOBERRY CRES
Stoberry Park Sch
LITTLE ENTRY
LEMMOND AVE
KIPPAX AVE
BERYL LA
TEAGLE CL
DODD AVE
KIDDER BANK
DRAKE RD
COLLES CL
COLLES RD
PARAY DR
HAWKER'S LA
NORTH RD
NORTH ST
GUNS
MILLERS
B3139
BATH RD
H
Wells & District
MANNING CL
JOHNSON CL
PLUMPTRE AVE
ST CUTHBERT'S VILLAS
ELFRIDA TERR
HAYBRIDGE VILLAS
A371
Haybridge
L Ctr
MOUNT PLEASANT AVE
WALNUT TREE CL
WELSFORD AVE
SOMERVILLE RD
MOUNTERY RD
MOUNTERY CL
MILTON LA
THE LIBERTY
VICAR'S CL
ST ANDREW ST
ST THOMAS ST
WOODBURY CL
WOODVIEW
TOR WOOD VIEW
WOODBURY AVE
BARKHAM CL
BEKYNTON AVE
WELSH CT
POWELL CT
LAX CT
BESLEY CT
DAVIES CT
BROOKES CT
HOPE CL
LETHBRIDGE RD
BLAKE RD
SEYMOUR CL
REGENCY CT
LOVERS WLK
Sch
Mus
CATHEDRAL GN
Cath
TOR ST
TORHILL LA
1 ST THOMAS TERR
2 ST THOMAS MEWS
3 OLD SCHOOL PL
4 LORNE PL
5 ST THOMAS' CT
6 ST ANDREW'S CT
WHEELER GR
CHARTER WAY
HAMILTON CL
VAUGHAN CT
GOLDING CL
PERKINS CT 1
ALGAR CT 2
BARNARD CT 3
BERRYMAN CT 4
REID CT
PARSONS WAY
STILES CT
WOOD CL
PORTWAY
A371
A39
MELBOURNE HOUSE MEWS
WHITING WAY
CHAMBERLAIN ST
UNION ST
HERITAGE CTYD
SADLER ST
MARKET PL
PO
Bishop's Palace
Tor Hill
B3139
ELM CL
CREASE CL
Cemy
CORONATION RD
BARNES CL
FAIRWAYS
LUDWAY
MELROSE AVE
WESTFIELD RD
PORTWAY AVE
VALLEY CL
PRIEST ROW
Liby
HIGH ST
Ct TH
CARLTON CT
TOWNHALL BLDGS
WELLS
GIPSY LA
CAMPKIN RD
TUDDINGTON GDNS
SEREL DR
BALCH RD
FREDERICK CT
A39
STRAWBERRY WAY
TUCKER ST
ST CUTHBERT ST
MARKET ST
BROAD ST
MILL ST
SOUTH ST
CARLTON MEWS
BURCOTT LA
BURCOTT RD
BIGNAL RAND CL
BIGNAL RAND DR
NIGHTINGALE CL
BARLEY CL
ETHEL ST
PRINCES RD
ST ANDREWS PK
THE CLOISTERS
SILVER ST
ANSERES PL
The Park
B3139
BUBWITH WLK
MARTINS CL
WOLSEY CL
SPRING RISE
CLEMENTS CL
SHELDON DR
WEST ST
WEBB'S CL
PRIORY RD
STUART'S PL
BECKET PL
PALACE CT
Monarch's Way
HAREWELL WLK
STILLINGTON CL
JOCELYN DR
MULLINS CL
SOMERLEAZE CL
KEWARD AVE
KEWARD WLK
Priory
SOUTHOVER
1 ST JOHNS CT
2 PRIORY PL
3 GREENS PL
4 HOMECHIME HO
5 TURNER CT
Sewage Wks
Schs
BISHOPSLEA CL
A371
ROWDENS RD
EAST SOMERSET WAY
STRAWBERRY WAY RDBT
ALFRED ST
MURIEL TERR
Park Wood
KEWARD CL
OSMOND DR
OLD MILL WAY
Keward Mill Trad Est
HANN CL
Keward
GATE LA
BISHOPS PARK WAY
Park Wood
A371
GLASTONBURY RD
BURCOTT LA
Monarch's Way
Sugar Loaf Farm
Keward Brook
River Sheppey
WOODFORD LA
Woodford Bridge
Woodford Farm
A39
MILL LA
C3
1 CHERRY TREE CT
2 CHEDDAR VALLEY BLDGS
3 SHELDON MILL
4 ST ANDREWS MEWS
5 ST ANDREWS WLK
C4
1 PORTWAY LODGE
2 DURKHEIM DR
3 MELROSE CT
4 BROWN'S PL
5 DAVIS TERR
D4
1 KENDRICK CT
2 THE GARDENS
3 ST CUTHBERT'S LODGE
4 BUBWITH HO
5 HENDERSON PL
6 LLEWELLYNS ALMSHOUSES
7 KING ALFREDS CTYD
8 DEANS PL
9 GUARD HOUSE LA
10 HUDDLESTON CT
11 QUEEN ST
12 LAWPOOL CT

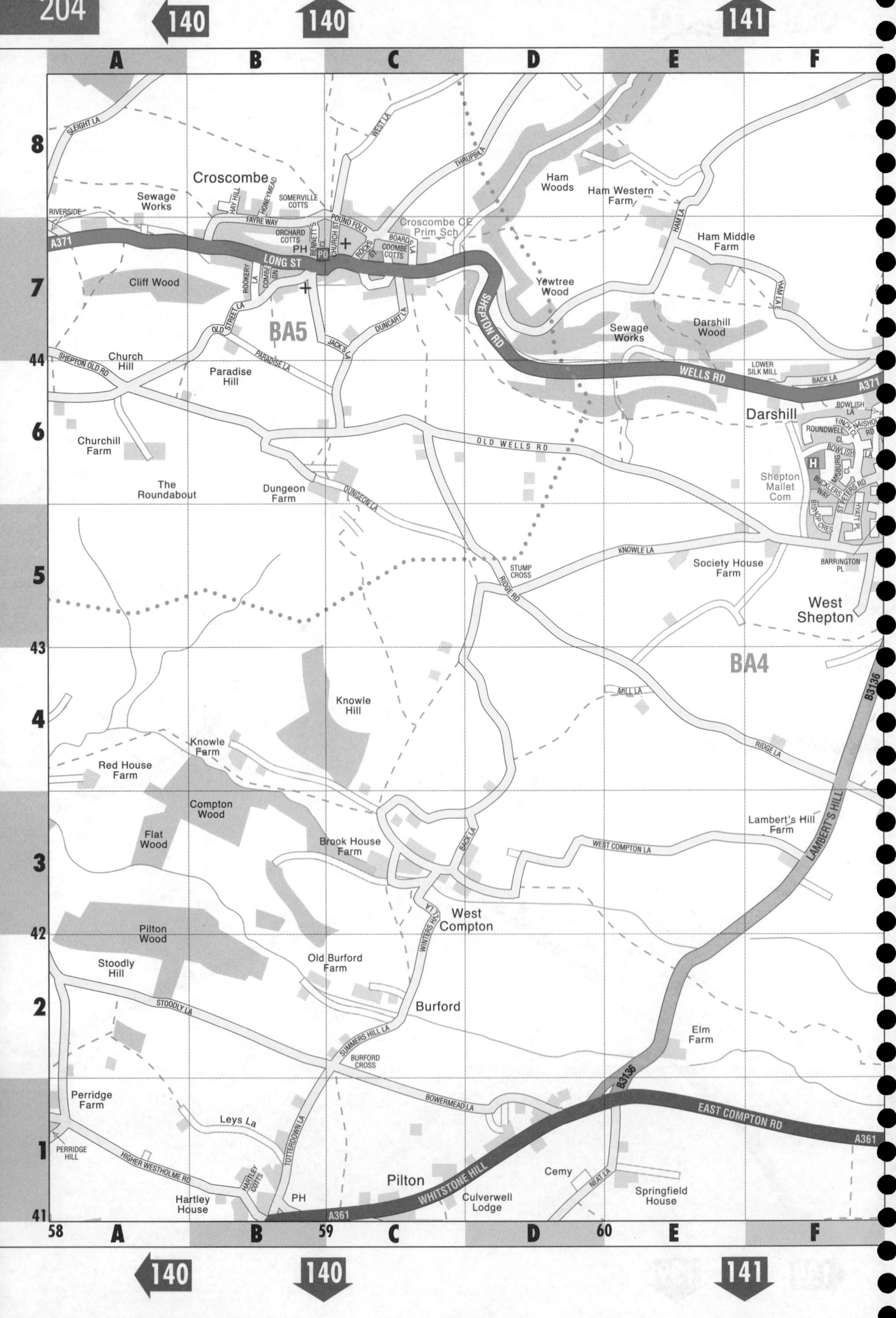
Croscombe
Sewage Works
Ham Woods
Ham Western Farm
Croscombe CE Prim Sch
Ham Middle Farm
Cliff Wood
Yewtree Wood
Sewage Works
Darshill Wood
BA5
Church Hill
Paradise Hill
Darshill
Churchill Farm
Shepton Mallet Com
The Roundabout
Dungeon Farm
Society House Farm
West Shepton
BA4
Knowle Hill
Knowle Farm
Red House Farm
Compton Wood
Flat Wood
Brook House Farm
Lambert's Hill Farm
West Compton
Pilton Wood
Stoodly Hill
Old Burford Farm
Burford
Elm Farm
Perridge Farm
Leys La
Pilton
Cemy
Springfield House
Hartley House
Culverwell Lodge
PH
A371
LONG ST
SHEPTON RD
WELLS RD
OLD WELLS RD
KNOWLE LA
RIDGE RD
STUMP CROSS
MILL LA
RIDGE LA
WEST COMPTON LA
LAMBERT'S HILL
B3136
EAST COMPTON RD
A361
WHITSTONE HILL
STOODLY LA
SUMMERS HILL LA
BURFORD CROSS
BOWERMEAD LA
TOTTERDOWN LA
HIGHER WESTHOLME RD
PERRIDGE HILL
HARTLEY COTTS
NEAT LA
SLEIGHT LA
WEST LA
THRUPP LA
HAM LA
RIVERSIDE
SHEPTON OLD RD
OLD STREET LA
PARADISE LA
JACK'S LA
DUNCART LA
DUNGEON LA
BACK LA
LOWER SILK MILL
BARRINGTON PL

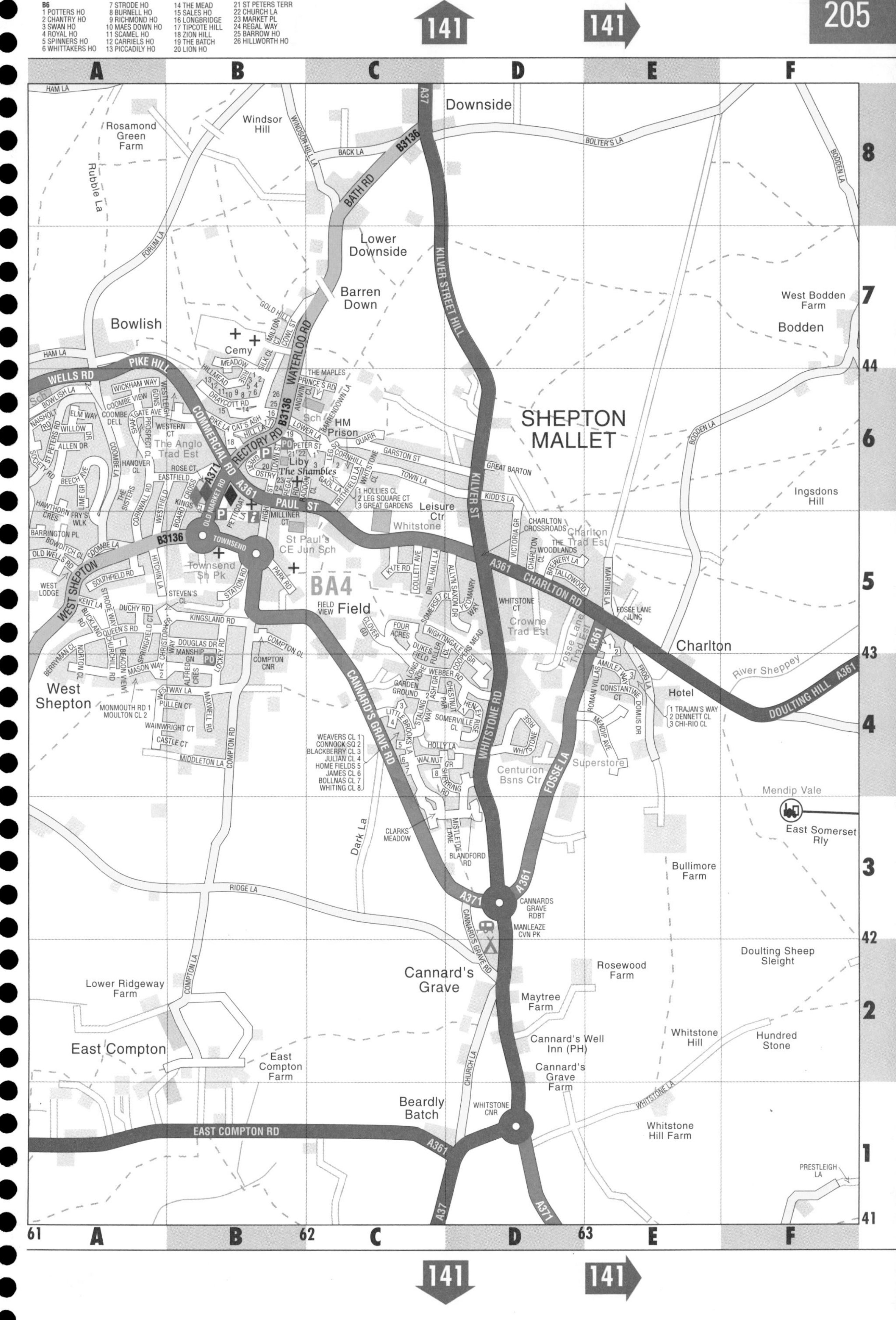
B6
1 POTTERS HO
2 CHANTRY HO
3 SWAN HO
4 ROYAL HO
5 SPINNERS HO
6 WHITTAKERS HO
7 STRODE HO
8 BURNELL HO
9 RICHMOND HO
10 MAES DOWN HO
11 SCAMEL HO
12 CARRIELS HO
13 PICCADILY HO
14 THE MEAD
15 SALES HO
16 LONGBRIDGE
17 TIPCOTE HILL
18 ZION HILL
19 THE BATCH
20 LION HO
21 ST PETERS TERR
22 CHURCH LA
23 MARKET PL
24 REGAL WAY
25 BARROW HO
26 HILLWORTH HO
141
141
A
B
C
D
E
F
8
7
44
6
5
43
4
3
42
2
1
41
61
62
63
HAM LA
Rosamond Green Farm
Rubble La
Windsor Hill
Downside
BACK LA
BOLTER'S LA
BODDEN LA
BATH RD
B3136
A37
Lower Downside
Barren Down
KILVER STREET HILL
FORUM LA
GOLD HILL
Bowlish
Cemy
West Bodden Farm
Bodden
WELLS RD
PIKE HILL
WICKHAM WAY
BOWLISH LA
COOMBE VIEW
COOMBE DELL
ELM WAY
WILLOW DR
ALLEN DR
WESTERN CT
The Anglo Trad Est
HANOVER CL
ROSE CT
EASTFIELD
COMMERCIAL RD
RECTORY RD
WATERLOO RD
THE MAPLES
PRINCE'S RD
HM Prison
Sch
PETER ST
Liby
The Shambles
GARSTON ST
TOWN LA
GREAT BARTON
KIDD'S LA
SHEPTON MALLET
BODDEN LA
Ingsdons Hill
1 HOLLIES CL
2 LEG SQUARE CT
3 GREAT GARDENS
Leisure Ctr
Whitstone
PAUL ST
A361
A371
MILLINER CT
St Paul's CE Jun Sch
TOWNSEND
Townsend Sh Pk
B3136
BARRINGTON PL
OLD WELLS RD
WEST SHEPTON
SOUTHFIELD RD
WEST LODGE
BA4
Field
CHARLTON CROSSROADS
Charlton Trad Est
THE WOODLANDS
CHARLTON RD
KILVER ST
WHITSTONE CT
Crowne Trad Est
Fosse Lane Trad Est
FOSSE LANE JUNC
Charlton
River Sheppey
DOULTING HILL
Hotel
1 TRAJAN'S WAY
2 DENNETT CL
3 CHI-RIO CL
West Shepton
MONMOUTH RD 1
MOULTON CL 2
CASTLE CT
MIDDLETON LA
COMPTON RD
COMPTON CNR
CANNARD'S GRAVE RD
WEAVERS CL 1
CONNOCK SQ 2
BLACKBERRY CL 3
JULIAN CL 4
HOME FIELDS 5
JAMES CL 6
BOLLNAS CL 7
WHITING CL 8
WHITSTONE RD
Centurion Bsns Ctr
Superstore
FOSSE LA
Mendip Vale
East Somerset Rly
Dark La
CLARKS MEADOW
BLANDFORD RD
RIDGE LA
CANNARDS GRAVE RDBT
MANLEAZE CVN PK
Bullimore Farm
Doulting Sheep Sleight
Rosewood Farm
Lower Ridgeway Farm
COMPTON LA
Cannard's Grave
Maytree Farm
Cannard's Well Inn (PH)
Whitstone Hill
Hundred Stone
East Compton
East Compton Farm
Cannard's Grave Farm
Beardly Batch
WHITSTONE CNR
WHITSTONE LA
Whitstone Hill Farm
CHURCH LA
EAST COMPTON RD
A361
A37
A371
PRESTLEIGH LA

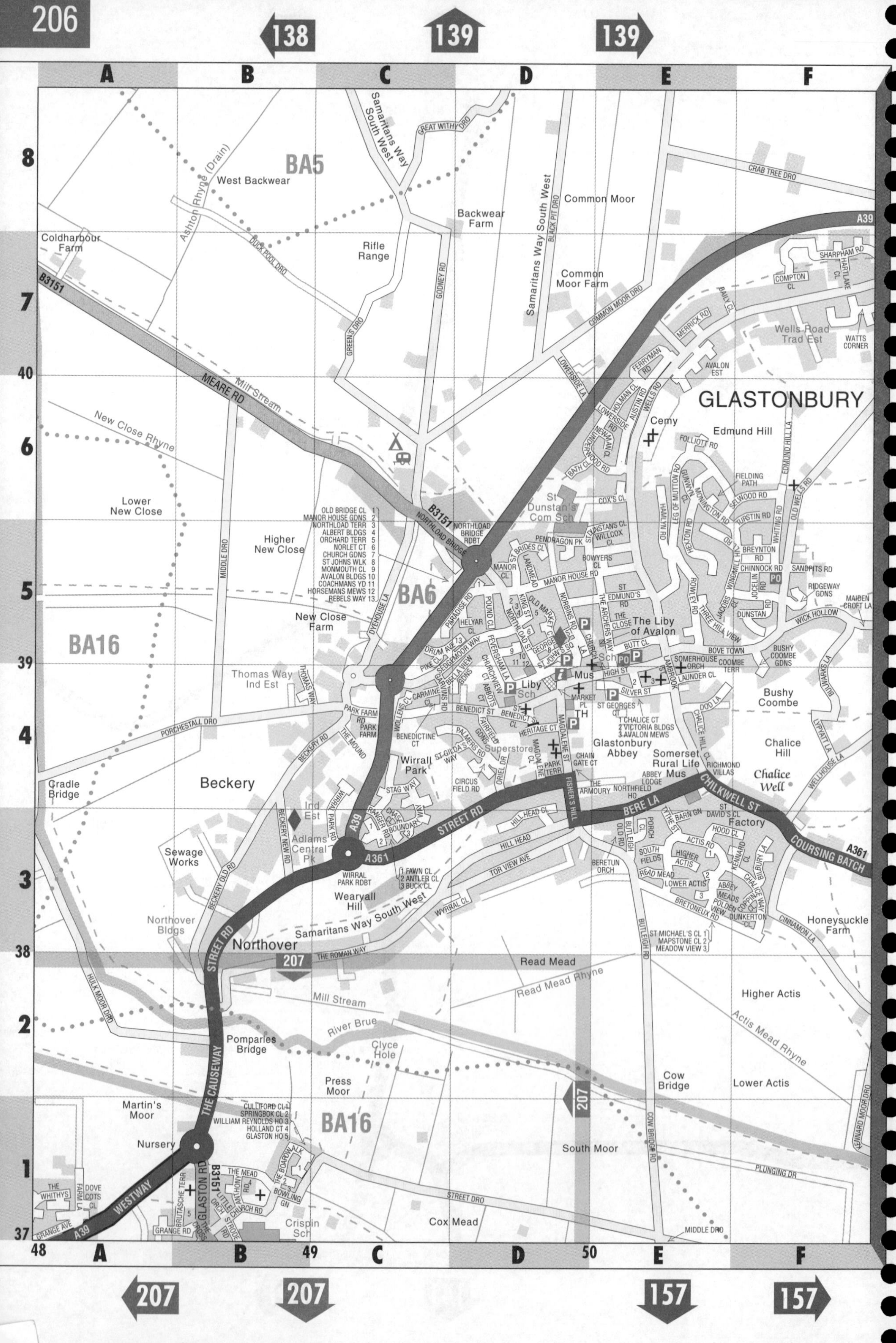
138
139
139
A
B
C
D
E
F
8
7
40
6
5
39
4
3
38
2
1
37
48
49
50
BA5
BA6
BA16
BA16
GLASTONBURY
West Backwear
Ashton Rhyne (Drain)
Samaritans Way South West
GREAT WITHY DRO
Backwear Farm
Common Moor
BLACK PIT DRO
Coldharbour Farm
DUCK POOL DRO
Rifle Range
GODNEY RD
Common Moor Farm
COMMON MOOR DRO
CRAB TREE DRO
A39
SHARPHAM RD
COMPTON CL
HARTLAKE CL
B3151
GREEN'S DRO
BAILY CL
MERRICK RD
Wells Road Trad Est
WATTS CORNER
MEARE RD
Mill Stream
LOWERSIDE LA
FERRYMAN RD
AVALON EST
New Close Rhyne
HOLMAN CL
AUSTIN RD
WELLS RD
Cemy
Edmund Hill
FOLLIOTT RD
Lower New Close
BATH CL
LOWERSIDE RD
UNDERWOOD RD
St Dunstan's Com Sch
COX'S CL
FIELDING PATH
SELWOOD RD
TURSTIN RD
EDMUND HILL LA
OLD WELLS RD
WHITING RD
OLD BRIDGE CL 1
MANOR HOUSE GDNS 2
NORTHLOAD TERR 3
ALBERT BLDGS 4
ORCHARD TERR 5
NORLET CT 6
CHURCH GDNS 7
ST JOHNS WLK 8
MONMOUTH CL 9
AVALON BLDGS 10
COACHMANS YD 11
HORSEMANS MEWS 12
REBELS WAY 13
NORTHLOAD BRIDGE
NORTHLOAD BRIDGE RDBT
Higher New Close
MIDDLE DRO
PENDRAGON PK
ST DUNSTANS CL
WILLCOX CL
BOWYERS CL
MANOR HOUSE RD
ST BRIDES CL
LANDMEAD
MANOR CL
BREYNTON RD
CHINNOCK RD
SANDPITS RD
RIDGEWAY GDNS
MAIDEN CROFT LA
ST EDMUND'S RD
DUNSTAN
WICK HOLLOW
New Close Farm
DYEHOUSE LA
PARADISE RD
POUND CL
HELYAR CL
KING ST
NORTHLOAD ST
OLD MARKET CT
NORBINS RD
THE ARCHERS WAY
THE CLOSE
The Liby of Avalon
BUTT CL
BOVE TOWN
BUSHY COOMBE GDNS
Thomas Way Ind Est
THOMAS WAY
DRUMMOND AVE
SEDGEMOOR WAY
PIKE CL
BELLA VIEW GDNS
FEVERSHAM LA
ST GEORGE'S
ST JOHN'S SQ
CHURCH LA
Sch
Mus
HIGH ST
SOMERHOUSE ORCH
COOMBE TERR
LAUNDER CL
LAMBROOK ST
Liby
Sch
CHURCHVIEW CT
ABBOTS CT
CARMINE CL
GARVINS RD
MARKET PL
TH
SILVER ST
ST GEORGES CT
Bushy Coombe
DOD LA
BULWARKS LA
PARK FARM RD
PARK FARM
WOLLENS CL
BENEDICT ST
ST BENEDICT'S CL
PORCHESTALL DRO
BECKERY RD
THE MOUND
BENEDICTINE CT
HERITAGE CT
1 CHALICE CT
2 VICTORIA BLDGS
3 AVALON MEWS
CHALICE HILL CL
Chalice Hill
LYPYATT LA
PALMERS RD
FAIRFIELD GDNS
MAGDALENE ST
Glastonbury Abbey
Superstore
ST GILDA'S WAY
ORIEL DR
MAGDALENE CL
PARK TERR
Wirrall Park
CHAIN GATE CT
Somerset Rural Life Mus
RICHMOND VILLAS
WELLHOUSE LA
Cradle Bridge
Beckery
CIRCUS FIELD RD
ABBEY LODGE
THE ARMOURY
NORTHFIELD HO
Chalice Well
STAG WAY
FISHER'S HILL
BERE LA
CHILKWELL ST
Ind Est
WIRRAL PARK RD
RANGER RD
CHASE LA
BOUNDARY WAY
STREET RD
HILL HEAD CL
HILL HEAD
BUTLEIGH
OLD RD
PORCH CL
TYTHE ST
BARN GN
ST DAVID'S CL
Factory
HOOD CL
COURSING BATCH
A361
BECKERY NEW RD
Adlams Central Pk
ACTIS RD
SOUTH FIELDS
HIGHER ACTIS
KENNARD CL
BURY LA
Sewage Works
BECKERY OLD RD
WIRRAL PARK RDBT
1 FAWN CL
2 ANTLER CL
3 BUCK CL
TOR VIEW AVE
BERETUN ORCH
READ MEAD
LOWER ACTIS
ABBEY MEADS
POLDEN VIEW
COPPIN CL
CHALICE WAY
DUNKERTON CL
BRETONEUX RD
Wearyall Hill
WYRRAL CL
Samaritans Way South West
CINNAMON LA
Honeysuckle Farm
Northover Bldgs
ST MICHAEL'S CL 1
MAPSTONE CL 2
MEADOW VIEW 3
Northover
STREET RD
THE ROMAN WAY
207
Read Mead
Read Mead Rhyne
HULK MOOR DRO
Mill Stream
Higher Actis
River Brue
Actis Mead Rhyne
Pomparles Bridge
Clyce Hole
Press Moor
Cow Bridge
Lower Actis
THE CAUSEWAY
207
Martin's Moor
CULLIFORD CL 1
SPRINGBOK CL 2
WILLIAM REYNOLDS HO 3
HOLLAND CT 4
GLASTON HO 5
KENNARD MOOR DRO
Nursery
South Moor
COW BRIDGE RD
PLUNGING DR
THE BOARDWALK
THE MEAD
GLASTON RD
B3151
BOWLING GN
THE WHITHYS
FARM LA
DOVE COTS CL
WESTWAY
BRUTASCHE TERR
ANTHONY RD
LITTLE ORCH
CHURCH RD
STREET DRO
GRANGE AVE
GRANGE RD
THE CROSS
STRODE RD
Crispin Sch
Cox Mead
MIDDLE DRO
A39
A
B
C
D
E
F

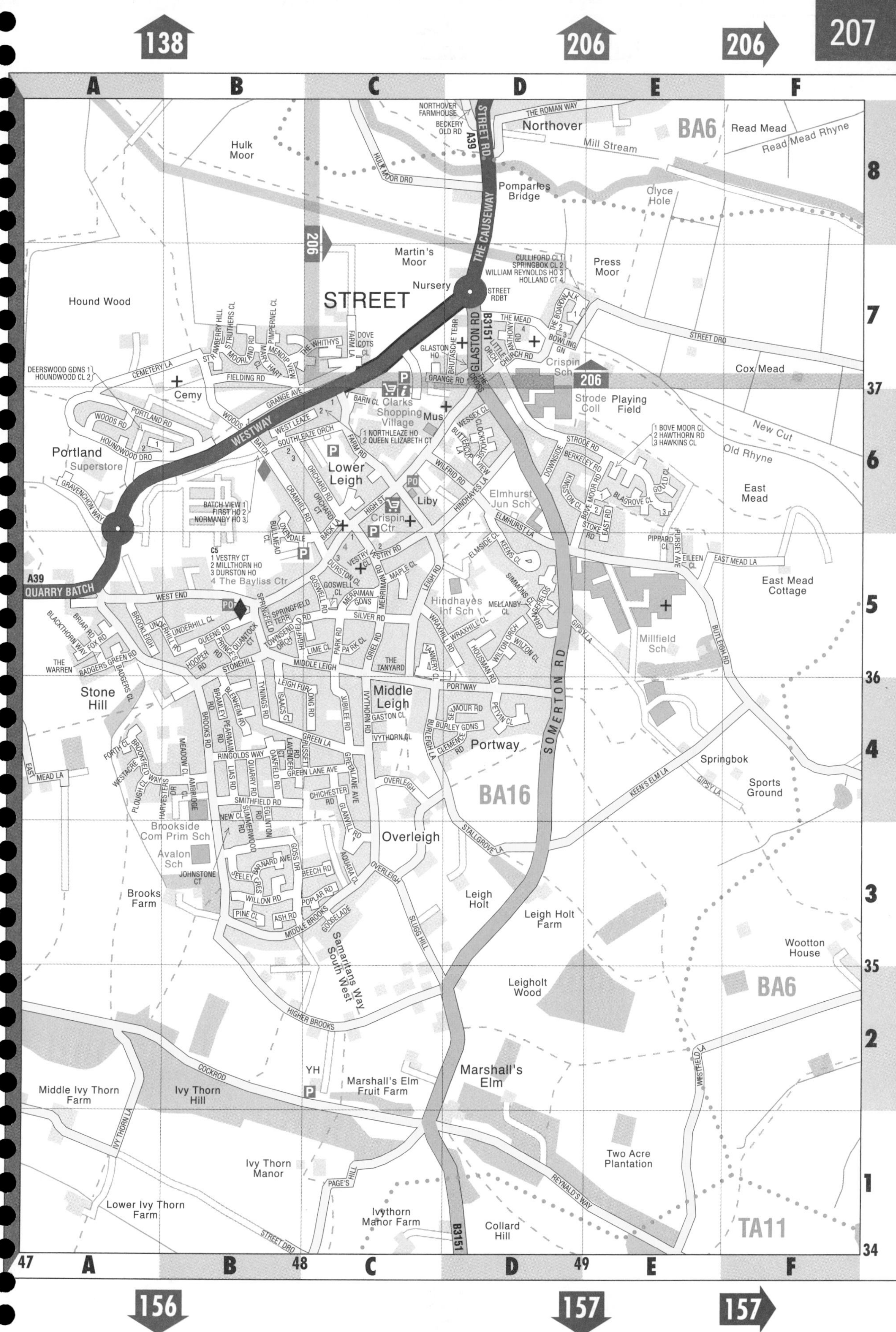
138
206
206
A
B
C
D
E
F
STREET
Northover
BA6
Read Mead
Read Mead Rhyne
Mill Stream
Hulk Moor
Pomparles Bridge
Glyce Hole
Martin's Moor
Press Moor
Hound Wood
Nursery
Cemy
Crispin Sch
Cox Mead
Strode Coll
Playing Field
New Cut
Old Rhyne
Portland
Superstore
Lower Leigh
Clarks Shopping Village
Mus
Liby
Crispin Ctr
Elmhurst Jun Sch
East Mead
East Mead Cottage
Hindhayes Inf Sch
Millfield Sch
Stone Hill
Middle Leigh
Portway
BA16
Springbok
Sports Ground
Brookside Com Prim Sch
Avalon Sch
Overleigh
Brooks Farm
Leigh Holt
Leigh Holt Farm
Wootton House
Samaritans Way South West
Leigholt Wood
BA6
Middle Ivy Thorn Farm
Ivy Thorn Hill
YH
Marshall's Elm Fruit Farm
Marshall's Elm
Ivy Thorn Manor
Two Acre Plantation
Lower Ivy Thorn Farm
Ivythorn Manor Farm
Collard Hill
TA11
SOMERTON RD
WESTWAY
THE CAUSEWAY
QUARRY BATCH
A39
B3151
47
48
49
34
35
36
37
8
7
6
5
4
3
2
1
156
157
157

135
135

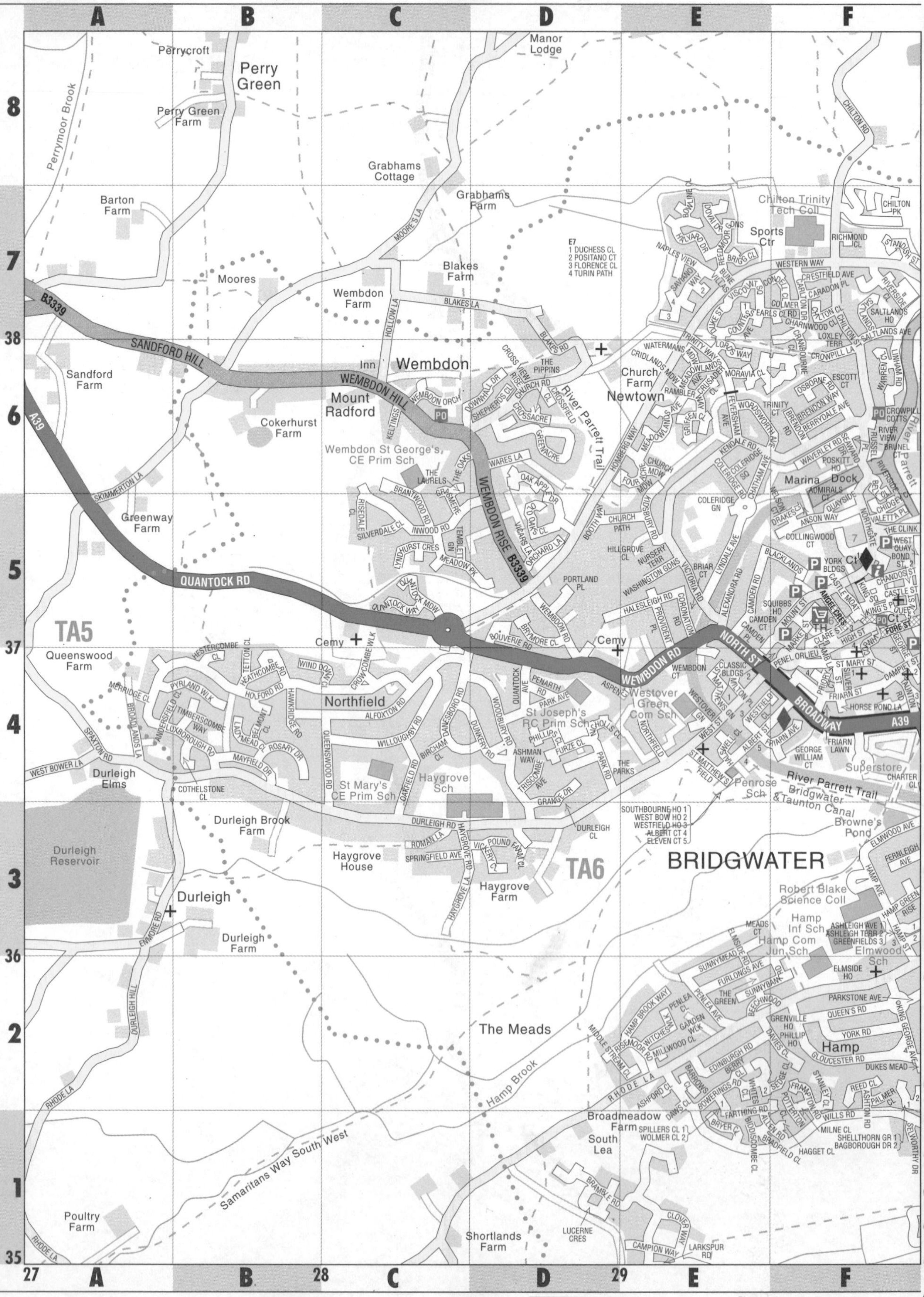

BRIDGWATER

E7
1 DUCHESS CL
2 POSITANO CT
3 FLORENCE CL
4 TURIN PATH

SOUTHBOURNE HO 1
WEST BOW HO 2
WESTFIELD HO 3
ALBERT CT 4
ELEVEN CT 5

153
153

F4
1 ST MARY'S CT
2 BLAKE ST
3 OLD TAUNTON RD
4 GREEN DRAGON CT

F5
1 CHALICE MEWS
2 HOMECASTLE HO
3 THE AVENUE
4 CHURCH PASS
5 COURT ST
6 Angel Place Sh Ctr
7 Bridgwater Ent Ctr
8 MARKET CT

136 136

A B C D E F

8 7 38 6 5 37 4 3 36 2 1 35

TA5 Sewage Works
Crypton Tech Bsns Pk
River Parrett
Ind Est
Kings Down (under dev)
Sydenham Manor Works
Sandringham Cl
Cemy
Superstore Works
Bristol Rd
A38
Bath Rd
M5
A39
1 Severn Cl
2 Cloverton Dr
3 Windsor Dr
4 Ivy Grove Cl
5 Eldergrove Cl
Medway Farm
New Metford Farm
Meads Farm
Temple Farm
Crow La
Bower House Farm
Slape Cross
East Side Farm
Greens Farm
1 Claremont Gr
2 Bower Fields
3 Squibbs Cl
Sandpit Farm
East Bower
1 Bloom Row
2 Sycamore Cl
3 Whitebeam Cl
4 Hornbeam Cl
5 Hazelwood Dr
Transform Ind Est
Mast
Mus
Kings Castle Bsns Est
Castle Field Ind Est
Gallagher Ret Pk
East Quay Mews
Winford Terr
Bath Bridge
Bath Bridge Bsns Pk
1 Branksome Ave
2 Albion Cl
Sydenham
Com Jun Sch
Sedgemoor Manor Inf Sch
East Bridgwater Com Sch
Sp Ctr
1 Raleigh Ho
2 Mountbatten Ho
3 Connaught Ho
4 Windsor Ho
TA6
Bridgwater Ret Pk
Monmouth St
Prim Sch
Eastover
Bridgwater Coll
Bridgwater General
Liby
Broadway
A372 St John St
Eastover Park
Wills Ind Est
Summerway Cottage
Portwall Dro
Bower Farm
TA7
Westonzoyland Rd
Prim Sch
5 Shearwater Cl
6 St Marks Ct
Hamp Ind Est
Blake Ind Est
Colley Lane Ind Est
Old Dunwear House
Wrenmoor Cl 1
Somerset Gdns 2
Cherry Cl 3
Cormorant Cl 4
Follett's Farm
Taunton Rd
River Parrett
1 Kinglake Villas
2 Sandown Cl
3 Beaconsfield Ho
4 Avondale Ho
5 Kingscliffe Terr
6 Buckingham Cl
Somerset Bridge
Half Way Bridge
Hamp Bridge
Merretts Farm
El Sub Sta
Halfway Inn (PH)
Bridgwater & Taunton Canal
River Parrett Trail
Dunwear Ind Est
Upper Dunwear Farm
New Barn Farm
7 Regent Way
8 Arlington Cl
9 Athlone Rd
10 Waterford Cl
11 Shellthorn Gr
Crossways Swing Bridge
Festival Units
Bsns Pk
Somerset Bridge Prim Sch
Nature Reserve
Moorshard Farm
River La
A372

30 A B 31 C D 32 E F

A1
1 BRETON DR
2 TORI GREEN
3 SAXONY PL
4 EMBDEN WALK
5 TOULOUSE RD

B4
1 PARKSIDE CT
2 STEAM PACKET TERR
3 PATHFINDER TERR
4 OXFORD TERR
5 THE MEWS
6 HUGHES CL
7 GRAVES CL
8 MOONRAKER CL

C4
1 NIGHTINGALE CL
2 HERON HO
3 DUNWEAR HO

154 154

166 150 166

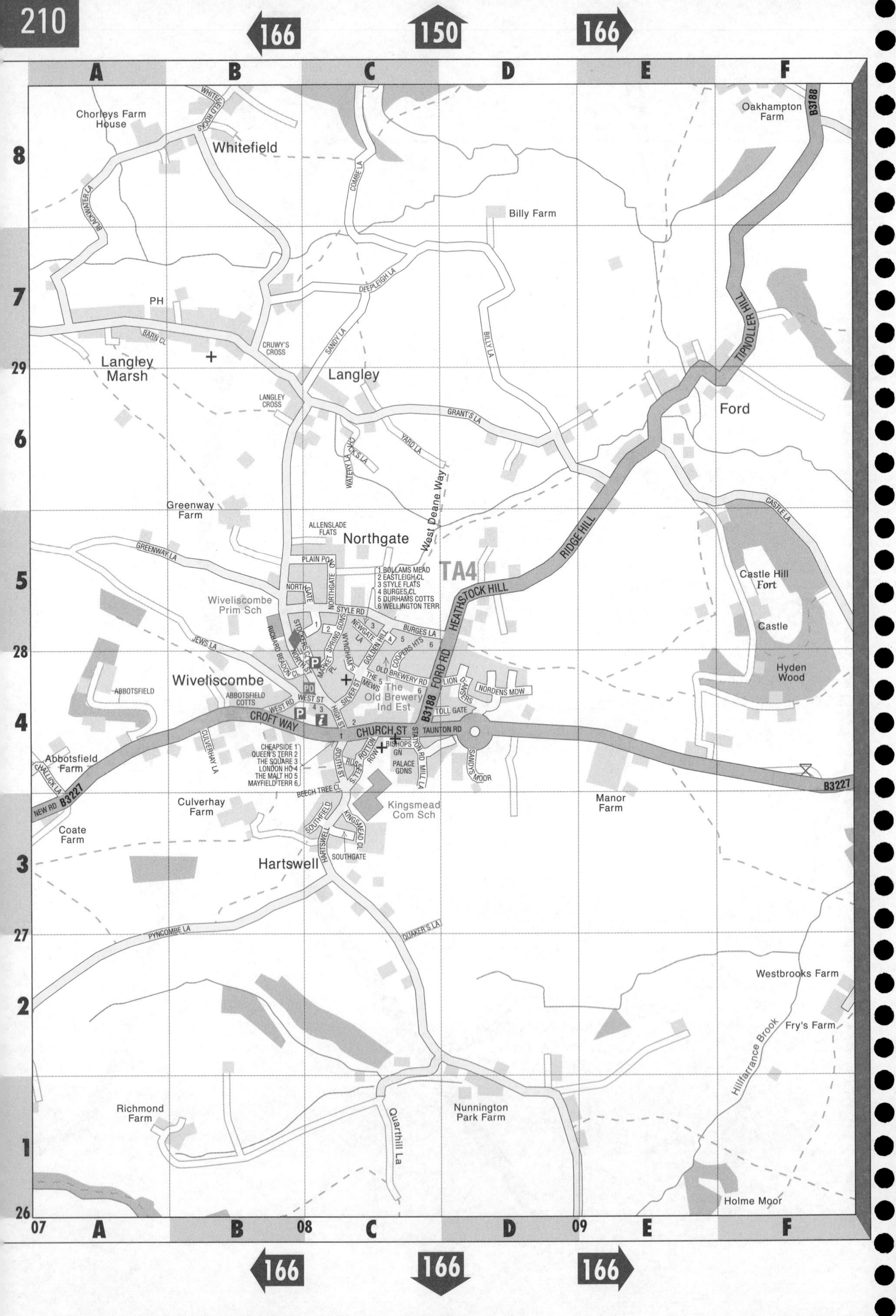

166 166 166

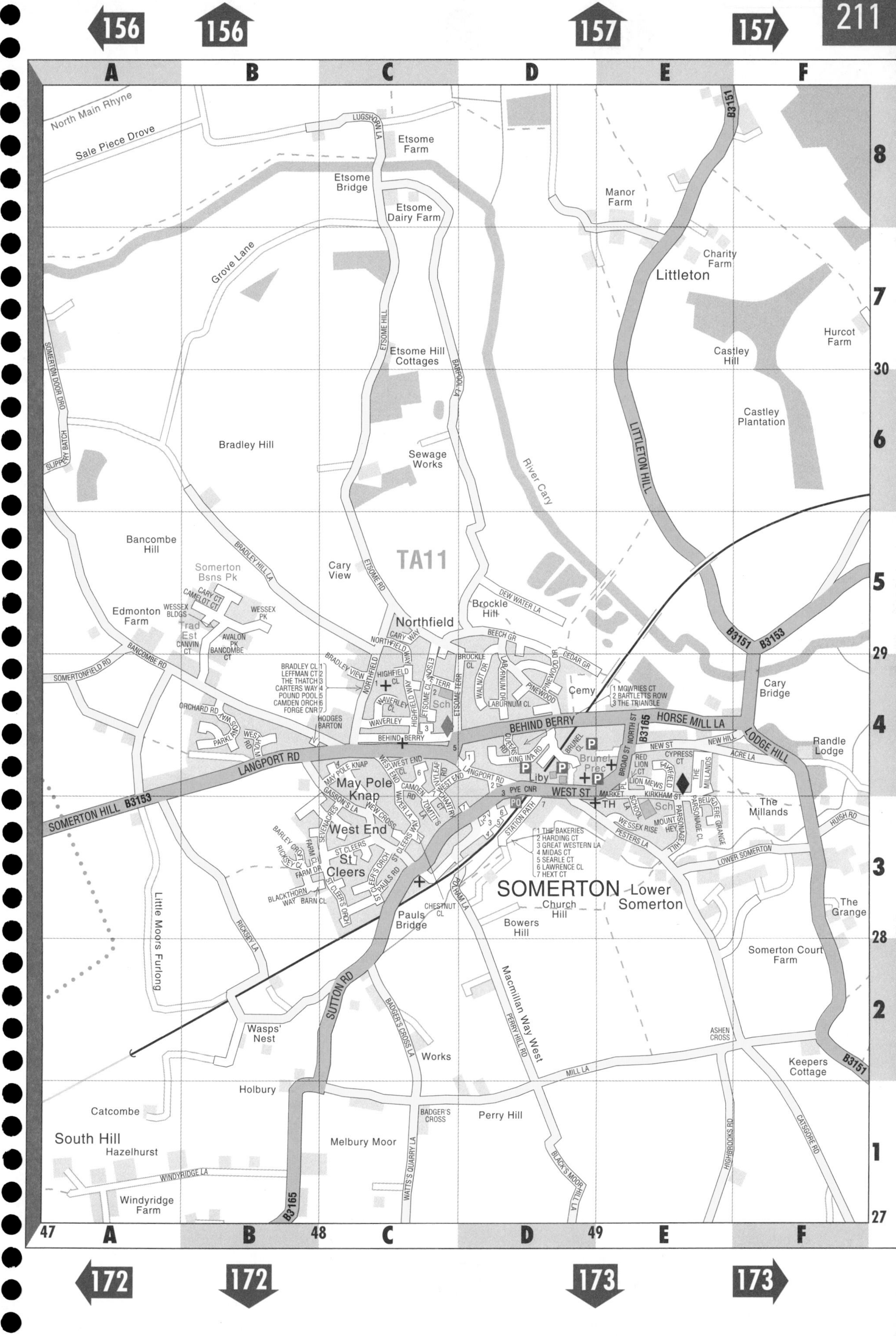
156
157
172
173
SOMERTON
Lower Somerton
TA11
Littleton
Northfield
May Pole Knap
West End
St Cleers
Etsome Farm
Etsome Bridge
Etsome Dairy Farm
Manor Farm
Charity Farm
Castley Hill
Hurcot Farm
Castley Plantation
Etsome Hill Cottages
Bradley Hill
Sewage Works
River Cary
Bancombe Hill
Somerton Bsns Pk
Cary View
Brockle Hill
Edmonton Farm
Cary Bridge
Randle Lodge
The Millands
The Grange
Somerton Court Farm
Church Hill
Bowers Hill
Pauls Bridge
Little Moors Furlong
Wasps' Nest
Works
Keepers Cottage
Holbury
Catcombe
South Hill
Hazelhurst
Perry Hill
Melbury Moor
Windyridge Farm
Badger's Cross
Ashen Cross
North Main Rhyne
Sale Piece Drove
Grove Lane
Littleton Hill
Langport Rd
Somerton Hill
Behind Berry
Horse Mill La
Lodge Hill
West St
Sutton Rd
Macmillan Way West
Mill La
Windyridge La
B3153
B3151
B3165
1 BRADLEY CL
2 LEFFMAN CT
3 THE THATCH
4 CARTERS WAY
5 POUND POOL
6 CAMDEN ORCH
7 FORGE CNR
1 MOWRIES CT
2 BARTLETTS ROW
3 THE TRIANGLE
1 THE BAKERIES
2 HARDING CT
3 GREAT WESTERN LA
4 MIDAS CT
5 SEARLE CT
6 LAWRENCE CL
7 HEXT CT
A
B
C
D
E
F
8
7
30
6
5
29
4
3
28
2
1
27
47
48
49

168 168

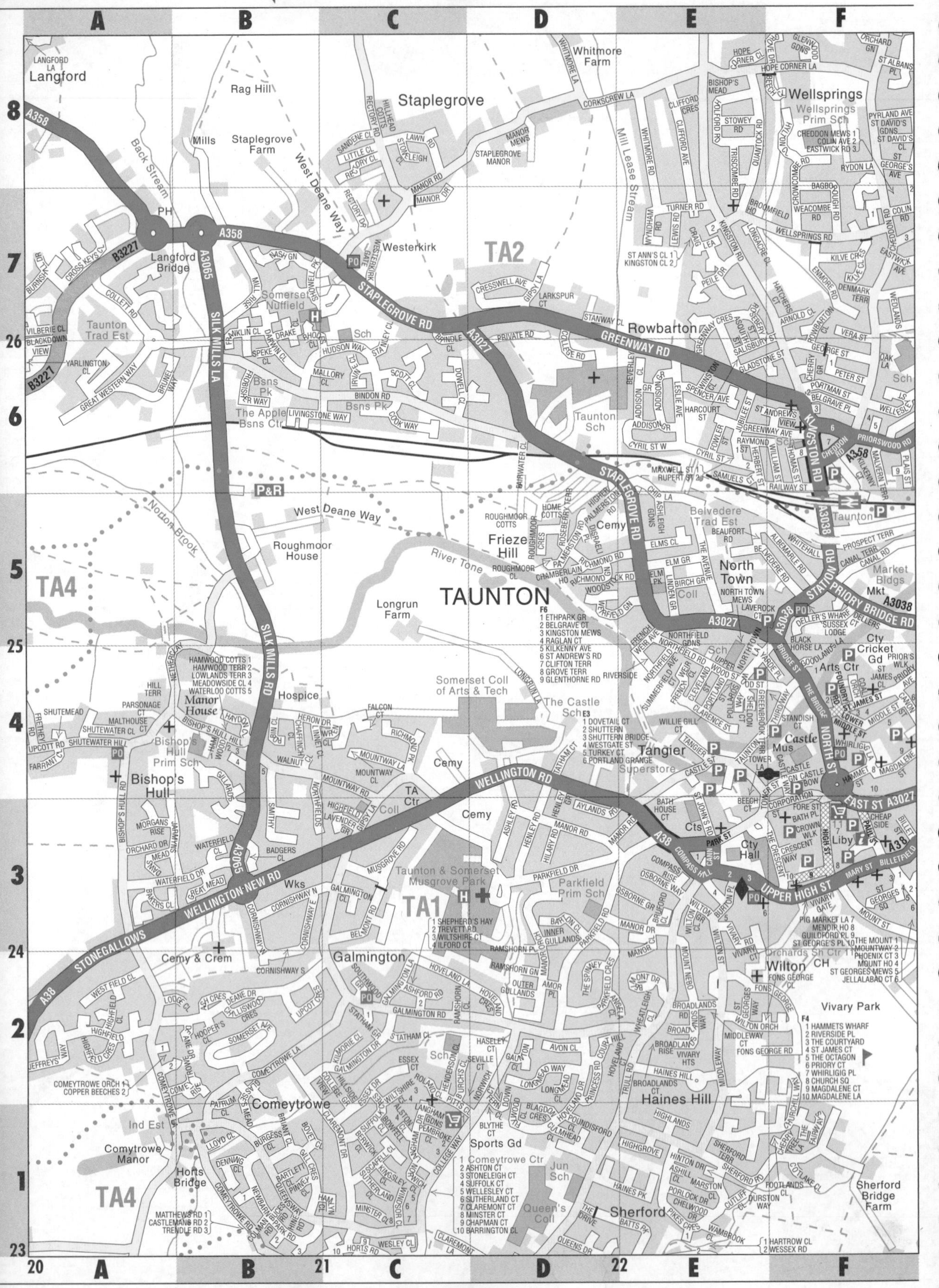

168 168

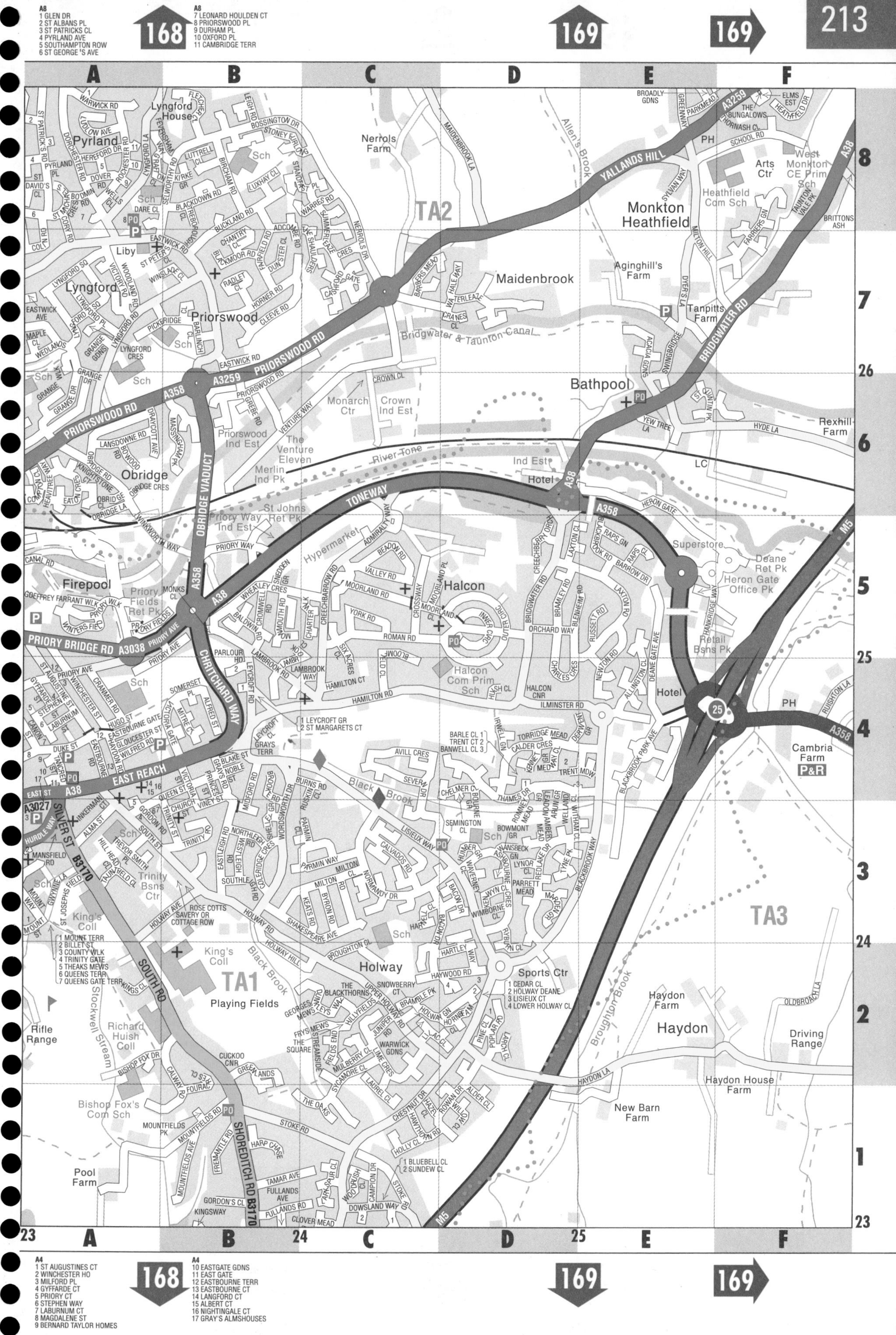
A8
1 GLEN DR
2 ST ALBANS PL
3 ST PATRICKS CL
4 PYRLAND AVE
5 SOUTHAMPTON ROW
6 ST GEORGE'S AVE
A8
7 LEONARD HOULDEN CT
8 PRIORSWOOD PL
9 DURHAM PL
10 OXFORD PL
11 CAMBRIDGE TERR
168
169
169
A
B
C
D
E
F
8
7
26
6
5
25
4
3
24
2
1
23
Lyngford House
Pyrland
Nerrols Farm
TA2
Monkton Heathfield
West Monkton CE Prim Sch
Arts Ctr
Heathfield Com Sch
YALLANDS HILL
Lyngford
Priorswood
Maidenbrook
Aginghill's Farm
Tanpitts Farm
BRIDGWATER RD
Bridgwater & Taunton Canal
PRIORSWOOD RD
Bathpool
Monarch Ctr
Crown Ind Est
Rexhill Farm
Priorswood Ind Est
The Venture Eleven
Merlin Ind Pk
River Tone
Obridge
OBRIDGE VIADUCT
TONEWAY
Ind Est
Hotel
St Johns Ret Pk
Priory Way Ind Est
Hypermarket
Superstore
Deane Ret Pk
Heron Gate Office Pk
Firepool
Priory Fields Ret Pk
Halcon
PRIORY BRIDGE RD
CRITCHARD WAY
Halcon Com Prim Sch
Retail Bsns Pk
Hotel
Cambria Farm
P&R
EAST REACH
Black Brook
SILVER ST
Trinity Bsns Ctr
King's Coll
TA3
Holway
Sports Ctr
TA1
Playing Fields
Rifle Range
Richard Huish Coll
Haydon Farm
Haydon
Driving Range
Broughton Brook
Bishop Fox's Com Sch
Haydon House Farm
New Barn Farm
SHOREDITCH RD
Pool Farm
M5
A4
1 ST AUGUSTINES CT
2 WINCHESTER HO
3 MILFORD PL
4 GYFFARDE CT
5 PRIORY CT
6 STEPHEN WAY
7 LABURNUM CT
8 MAGDALENE ST
9 BERNARD TAYLOR HOMES
A4
10 EASTGATE GDNS
11 EAST GATE
12 EASTBOURNE TERR
13 EASTBOURNE CT
14 LANGFORD CT
15 ALBERT CT
16 NIGHTINGALE CT
17 GRAY'S ALMSHOUSES
168
169
169

159 159 215

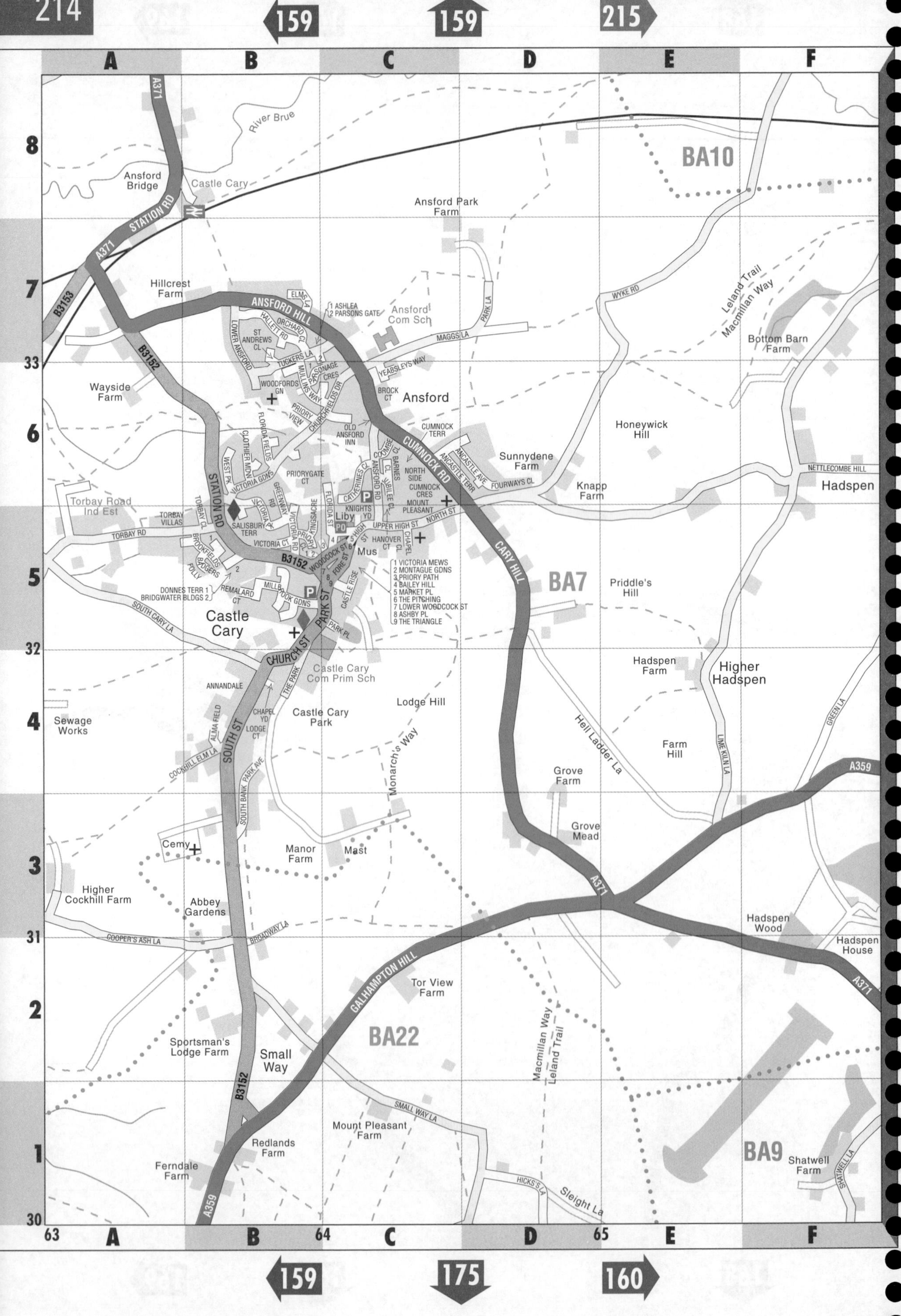

159 175 160

160 160

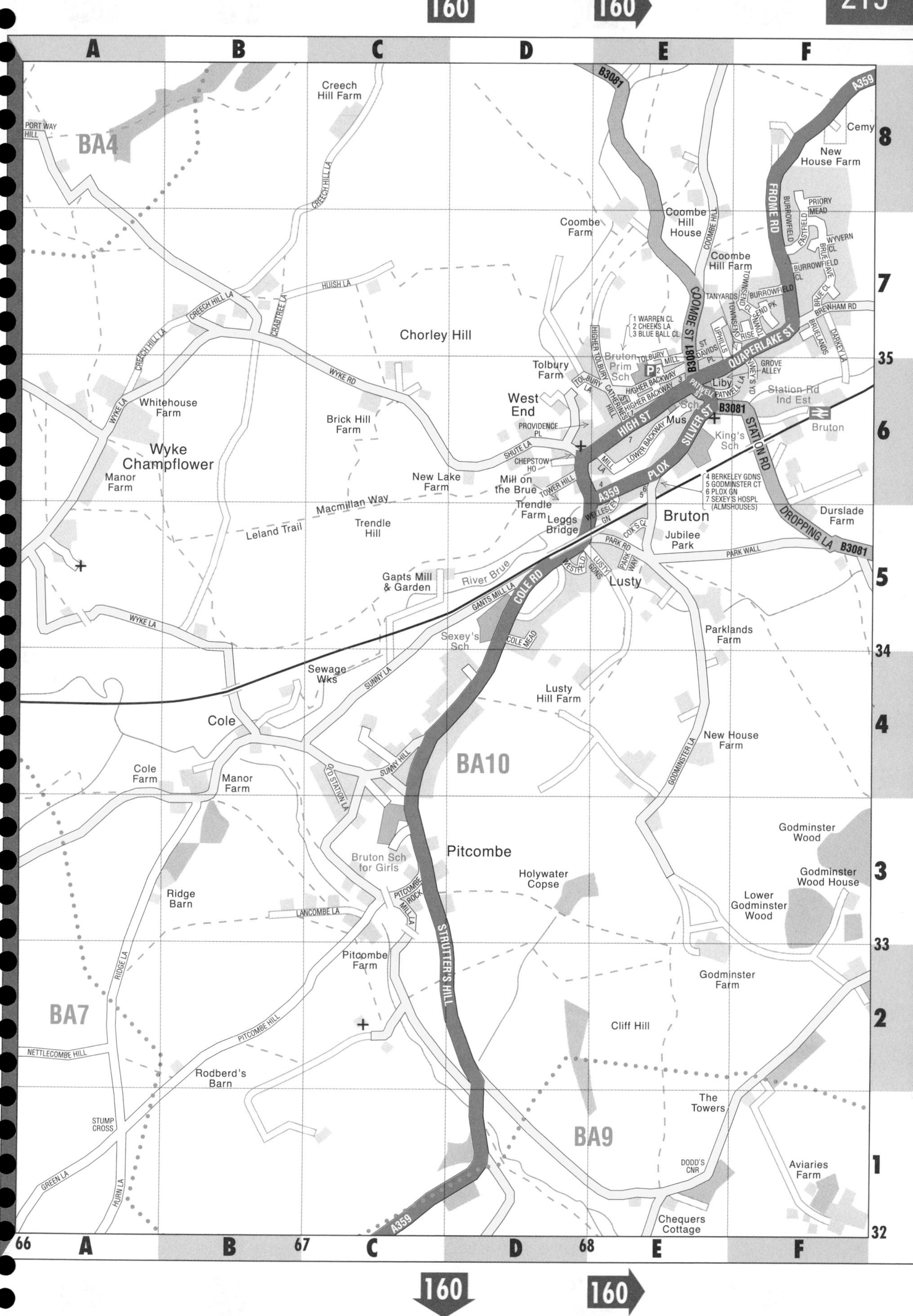

160 160

160 160 161 161

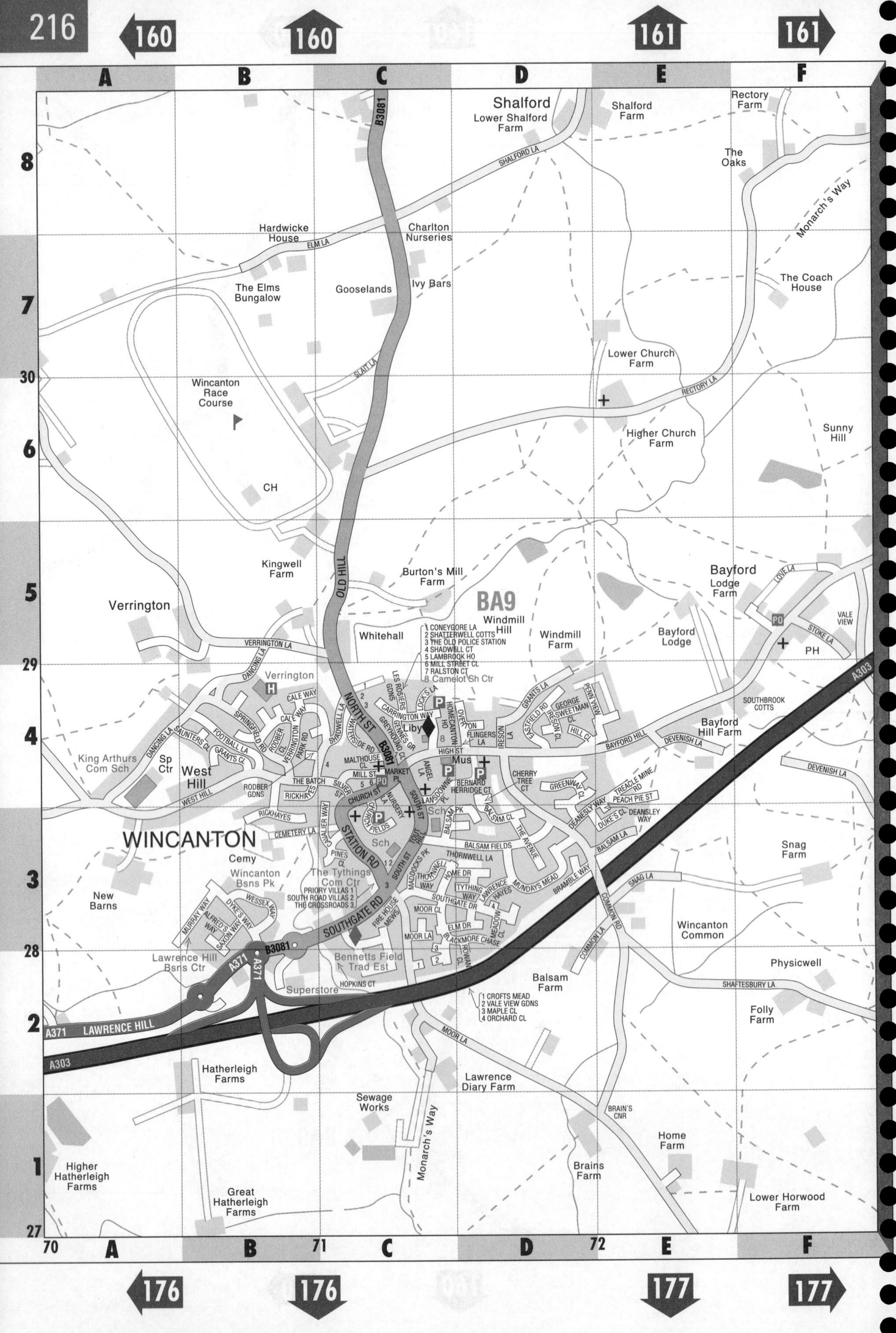

176 176 177 177

188
176
189

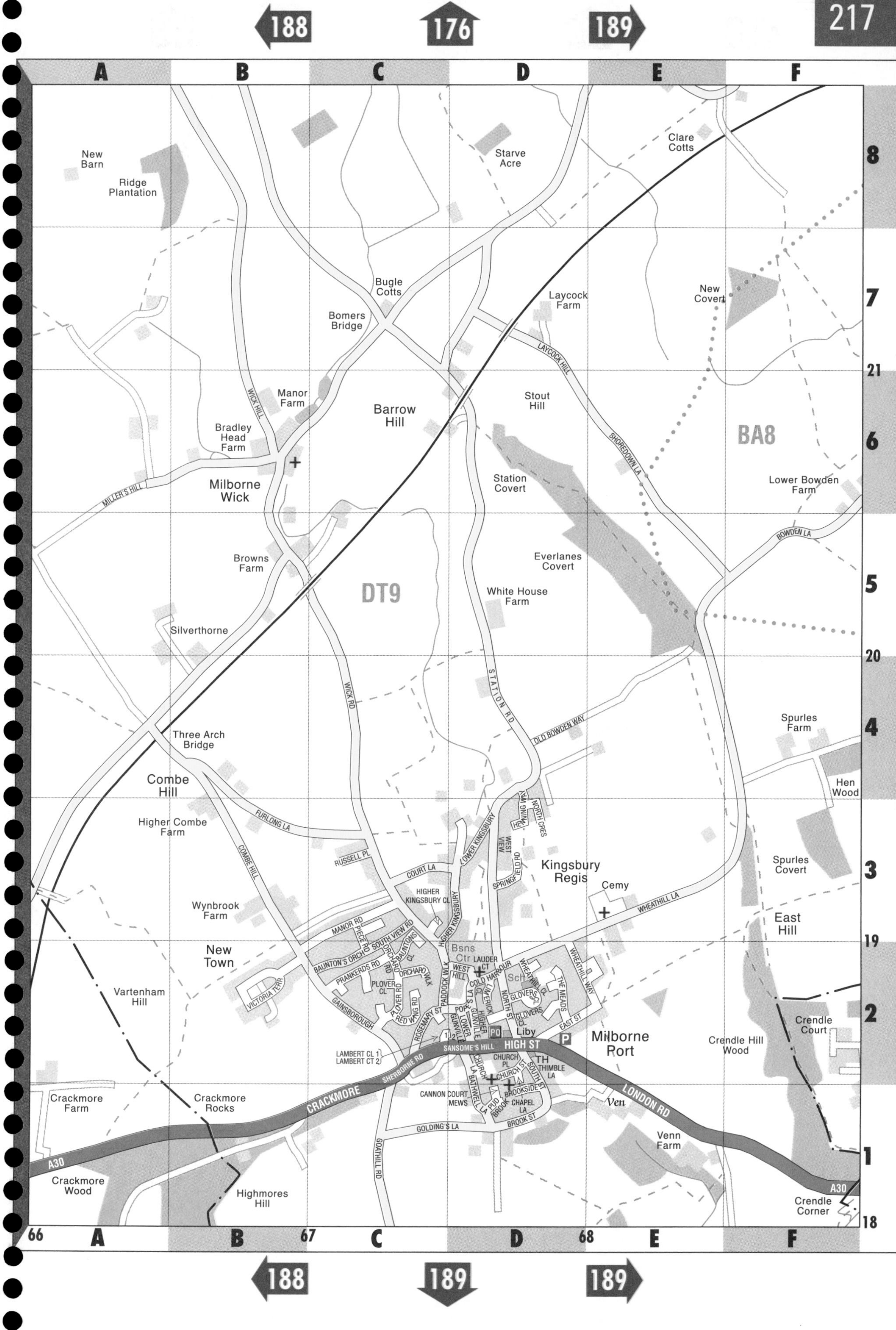

188
189
189

C6
1 KINGSLAND GRANGE
2 HAWKINS WAY
3 TRELLECH CT
4 THE REGENTS
5 GREAT CNR
6 MALMESBURY CT

F7
1 THATCHAM CT
2 THATCHAM CL
3 NEWBERRY TERR
4 LOCKWOOD CT

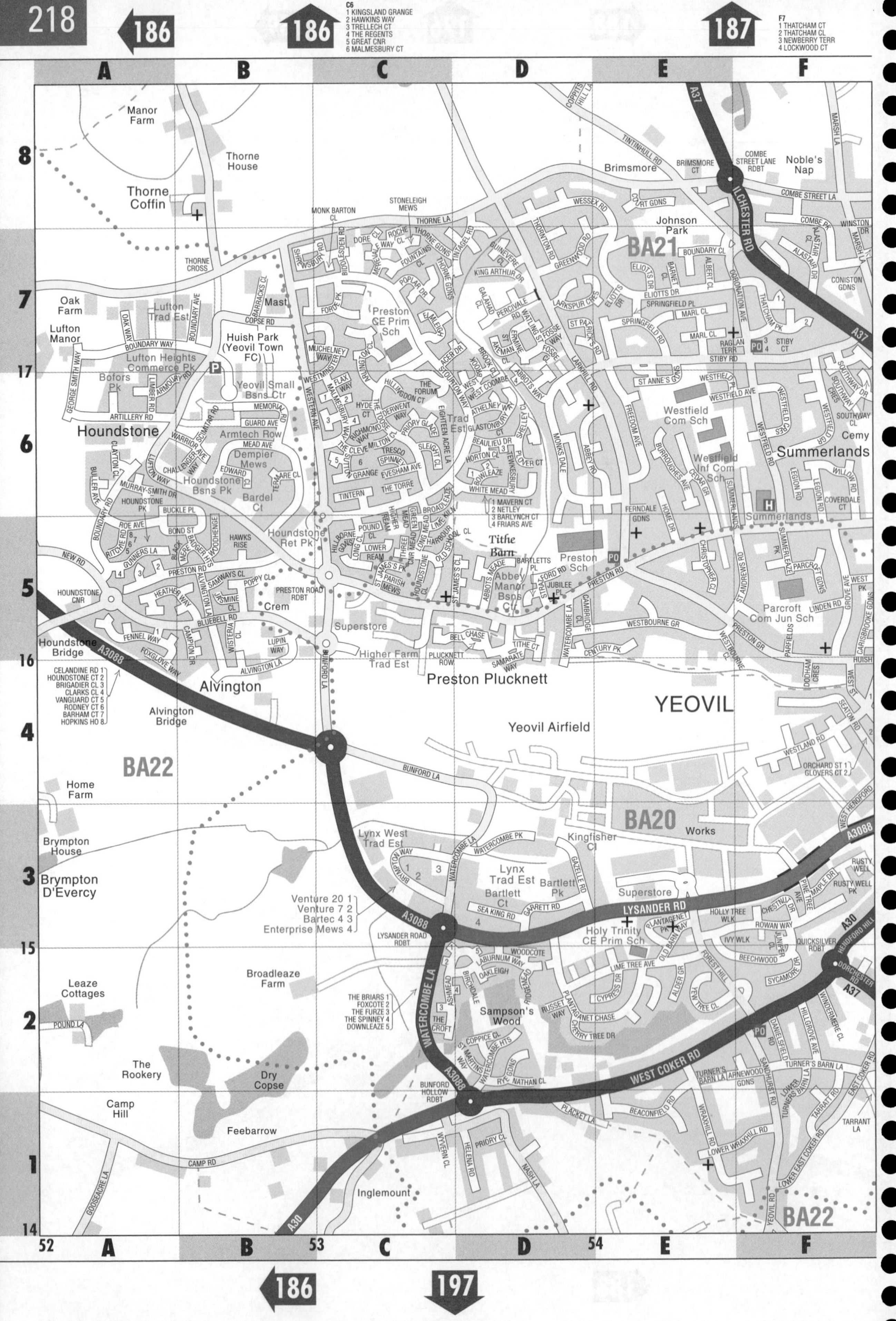

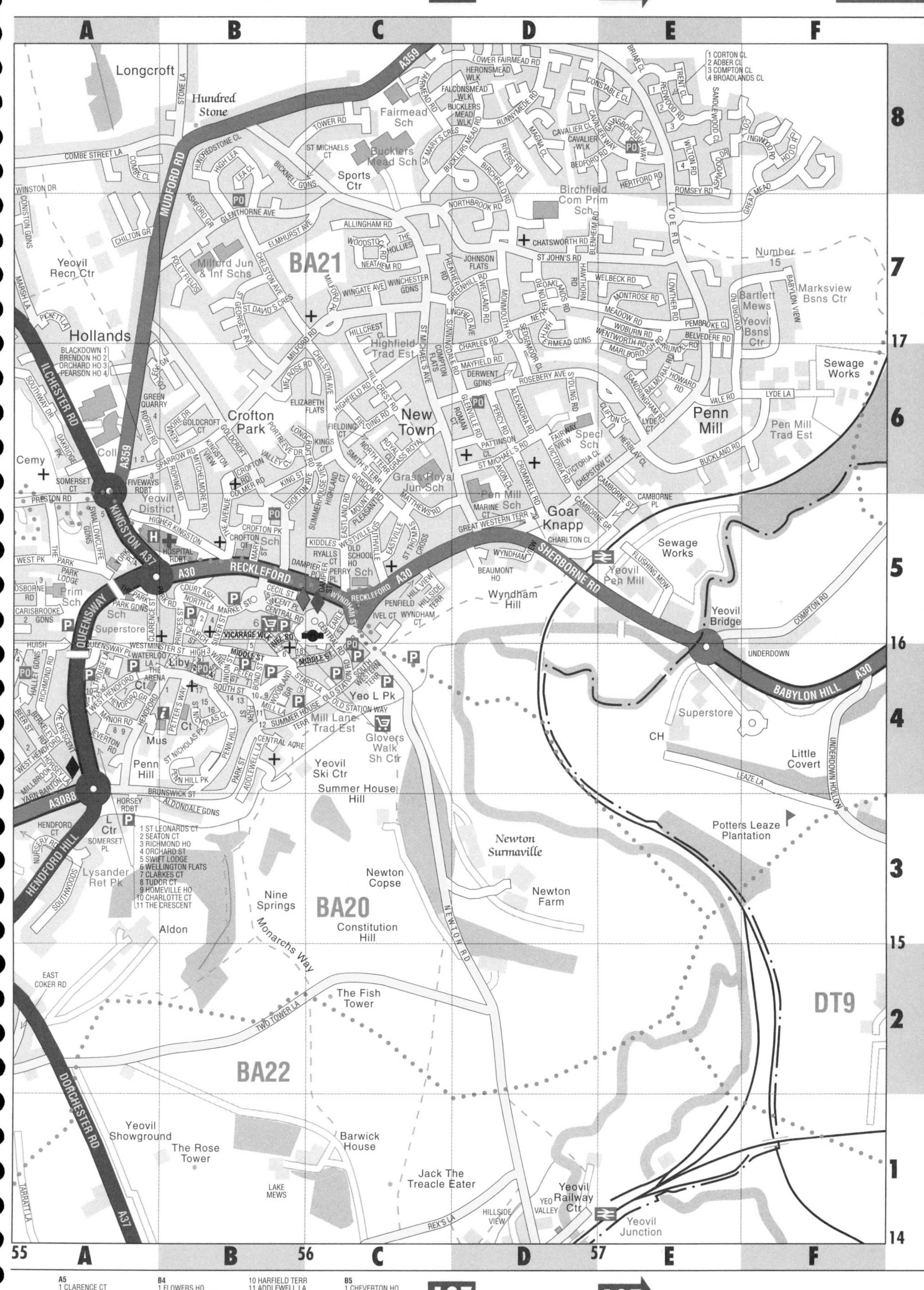

A5
1 CLARENCE CT
2 HUISH GDNS
3 SANDOWN CL
4 YORK LODGE
5 SWALLOWCLIFFE CT

B4
1 FLOWERS HO
2 KING GEORGE ST
3 THE BOROUGH
4 TABERNACLE LA
5 FREDRICK PL
6 VICARAGE ST
7 YEOVIL TRINITY FOYER
8 CLARENCE TERR
9 BROAD OAK
10 HARFIELD TERR
11 ADDLEWELL LA
12 TAUNUSSTEIN WAY
13 TRINITY CT
14 BELMONT HO
15 TOWNRISE
16 MARSH POTTINSON HO
17 PEGASUS CT
18 GLOVERS WLK

B5
1 CHEVERTON HO
2 CHURCH PATH
3 ST JOHNS HO
4 CHURCH TERR
5 VINCENT ST
6 Quedam Sh Ctr

184 185 185

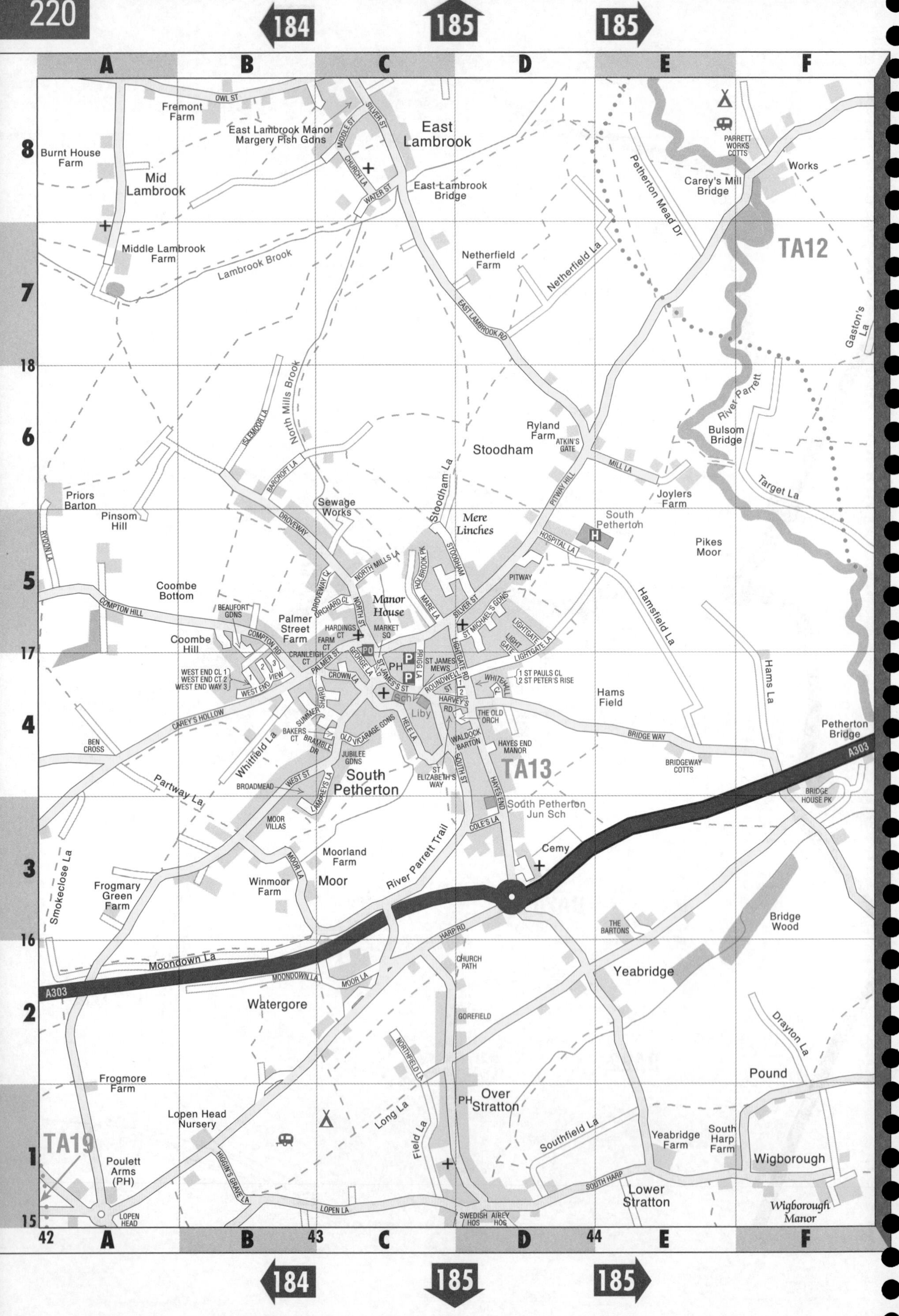

184 185 185

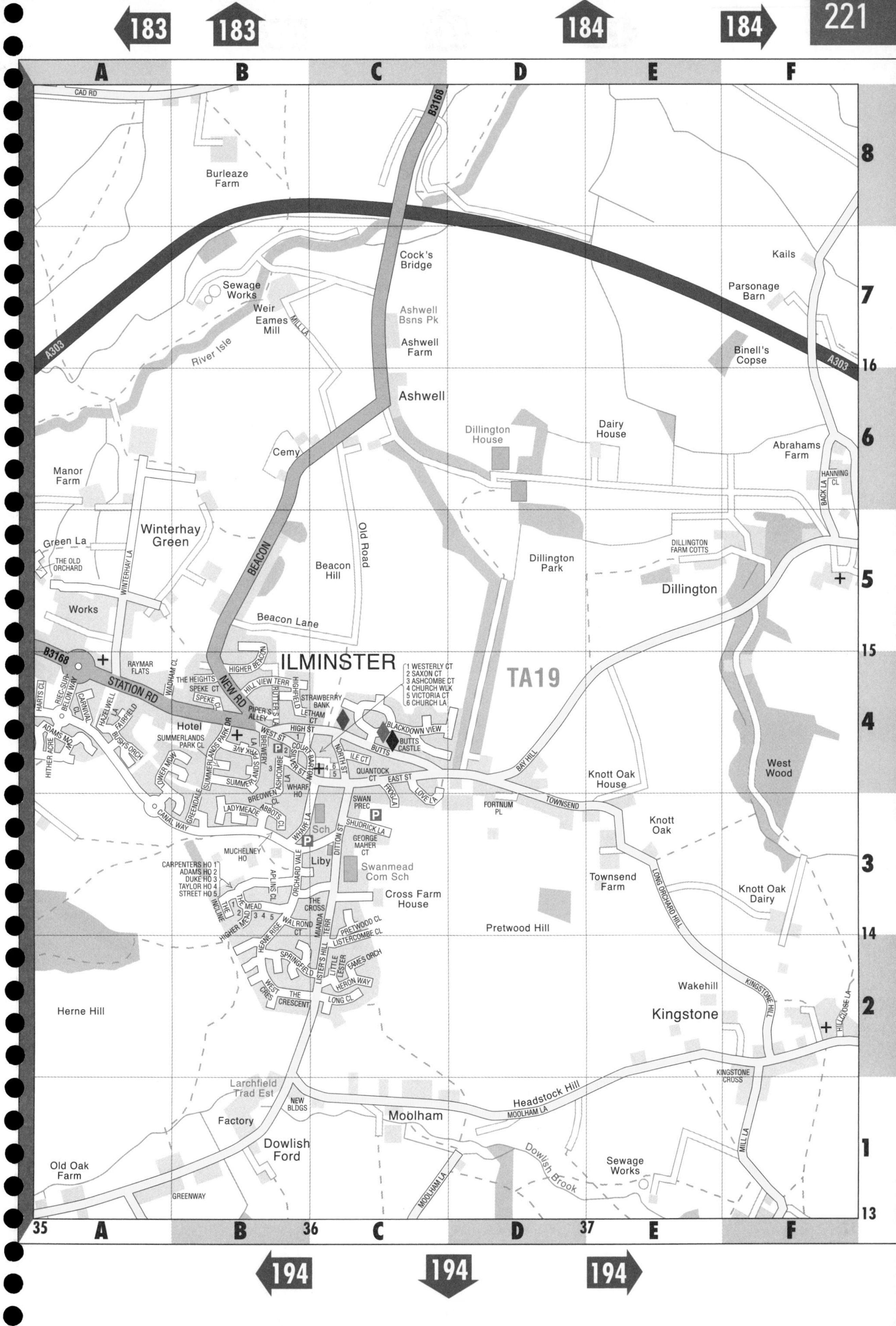

183
183
184
184
A
B
C
D
E
F
8
7
16
6
5
15
4
3
14
2
1
13
35
36
37
Burleaze Farm
Cock's Bridge
Sewage Works
Weir
Eames Mill
Ashwell Bsns Pk
Ashwell Farm
Kails
Parsonage Barn
Binell's Copse
A303
River Isle
Ashwell
Dillington House
Dairy House
Abrahams Farm
Manor Farm
Cemy
Winterhay Green
Green La
Beacon Hill
Old Road
Dillington Park
Dillington
Works
Beacon Lane
ILMINSTER
TA19
B3168
STATION RD
NEW RD
Hotel
West Wood
Knott Oak House
Knott Oak
TOWNSEND
Sch
Liby
Swanmead Com Sch
Cross Farm House
Townsend Farm
Knott Oak Dairy
Pretwood Hill
Herne Hill
Wakehill
Kingstone
Larchfield Trad Est
Factory
Headstock Hill
Moolham
Dowlish Ford
Old Oak Farm
Sewage Works
Dowlish Brook
MOOLHAM LA
GREENWAY
MILL LA
LONG ORCHARD HILL
KINGSTONE HILL
KINGSTONE CROSS
1 WESTERLY CT
2 SAXON CT
3 ASHCOMBE CT
4 CHURCH WLK
5 VICTORIA CT
6 CHURCH LA
CARPENTERS HO 1
ADAMS HO 2
DUKE HO 3
TAYLOR HO 4
STREET HO 5
194
194
194

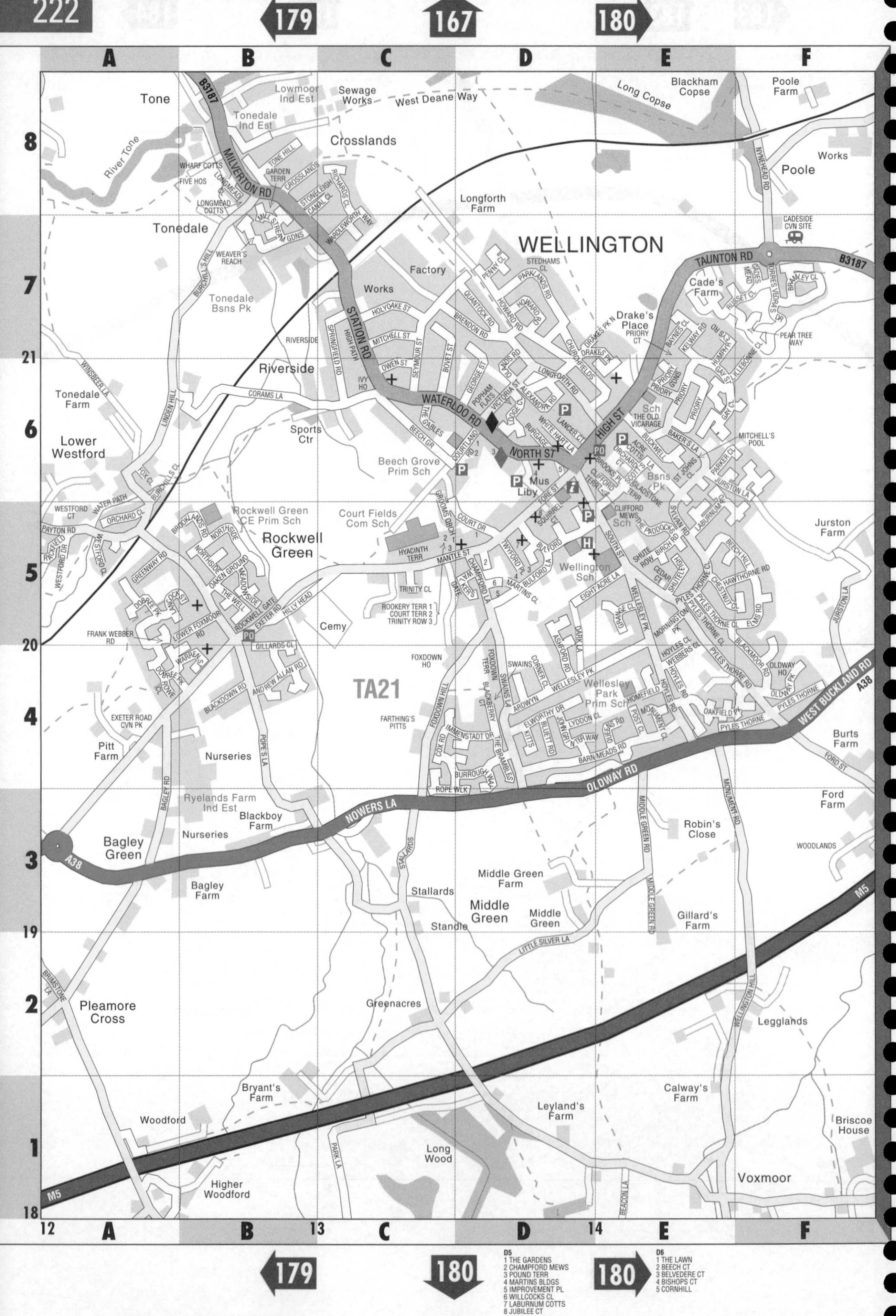

D5
1 THE GARDENS
2 CHAMPFORD MEWS
3 POUND TERR
4 MARTINS BLDGS
5 IMPROVEMENT PL
6 WILLCOCKS CL
7 LABURNUM COTTS
8 JUBILEE CT

D6
1 THE LAWN
2 BEECH CT
3 BELVEDERE CT
4 BISHOPS CT
5 CORNHILL

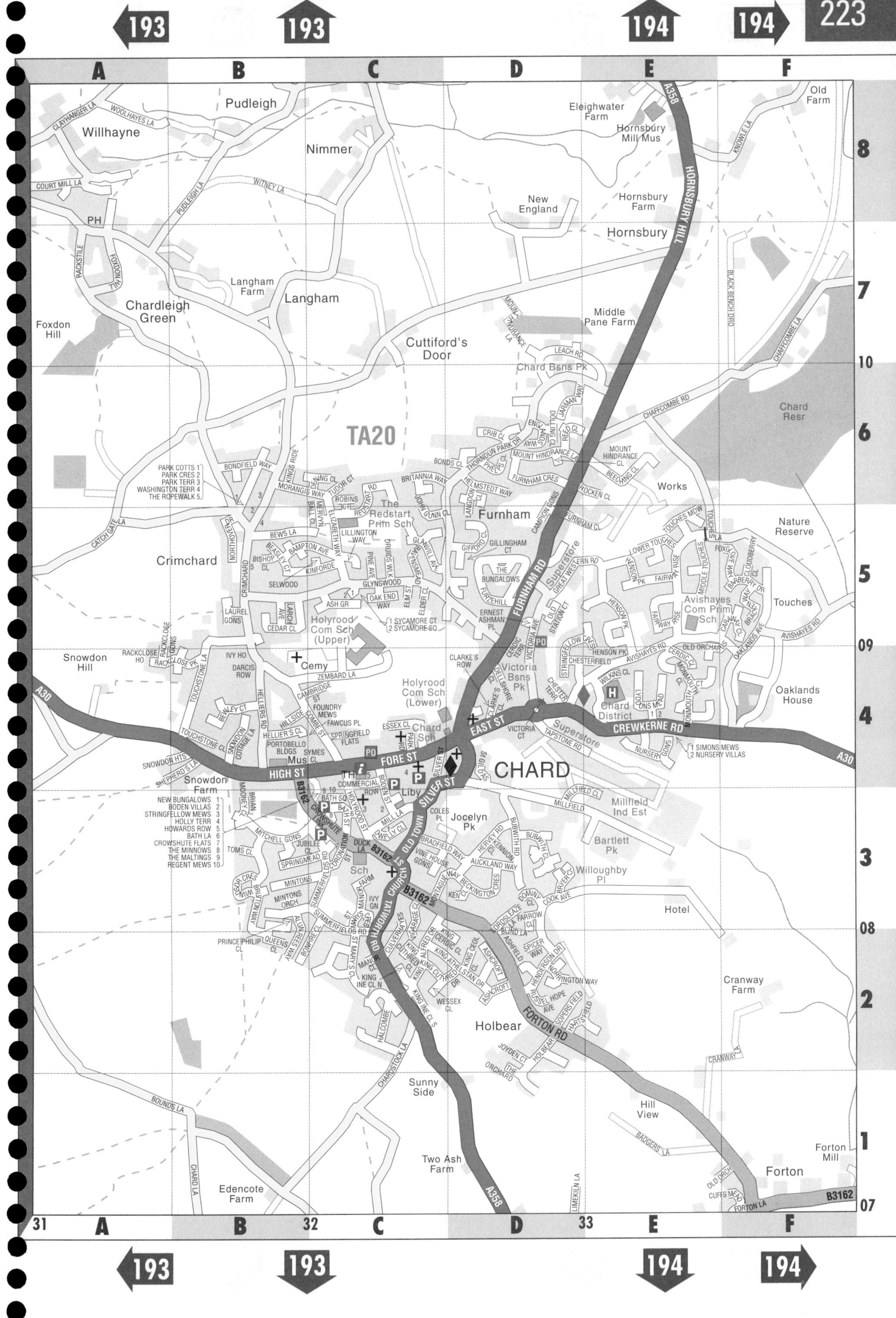
193
193
194
194
A
B
C
D
E
F
8
7
10
6
5
09
4
3
08
2
1
07
31
32
33
Pudleigh
Willhayne
Nimmer
Eleighwater Farm
Hornsbury Mill Mus
Old Farm
New England
Hornsbury Farm
Hornsbury
HORNSBURY HILL
A358
PH
Langham Farm
Langham
Chardleigh Green
Foxdon Hill
Cuttiford's Door
Middle Pane Farm
Chard Bsns Pk
Chard Resr
TA20
Works
Furnham
The Redstart Prim Sch
Nature Reserve
Crimchard
Superstore
Avishayes Com Prim Sch
Touches
Holyrood Com Sch (Upper)
Snowdon Hill
Cemy
Victoria Bsns Pk
Oaklands House
Holyrood Com Sch (Lower)
Chard District
A30
EAST ST
CREWKERNE RD
HIGH ST
FORE ST
CHARD
Chard Sch
Mus
Snowdon Farm
Liby
Jocelyn Pk
Millfield Ind Est
Bartlett Pk
Willoughby Pl
Hotel
Sch
Cranway Farm
Holbear
FORTON RD
Sunny Side
Hill View
Two Ash Farm
Forton Mill
Forton
Edencote Farm
B3162
FURNHAM RD
SILVER ST
OLD TOWN
TATWORTH RD
PARK COTTS 1
PARK CRES 2
PARK TERR 3
WASHINGTON TERR 4
THE ROPEWALK 5
NEW BUNGALOWS 1
BODEN VILLAS 2
STRINGFELLOW MEWS 3
HOLLY TERR 4
HOWARDS ROW 5
BATH LA 6
CROWSHUTE FLATS 7
THE MINNOWS 8
THE MALTINGS 9
REGENT MEWS 10
1 SYCAMORE CT
2 SYCAMORE SQ
1 SIMONS MEWS
2 NURSERY VILLAS

195 195 196 196

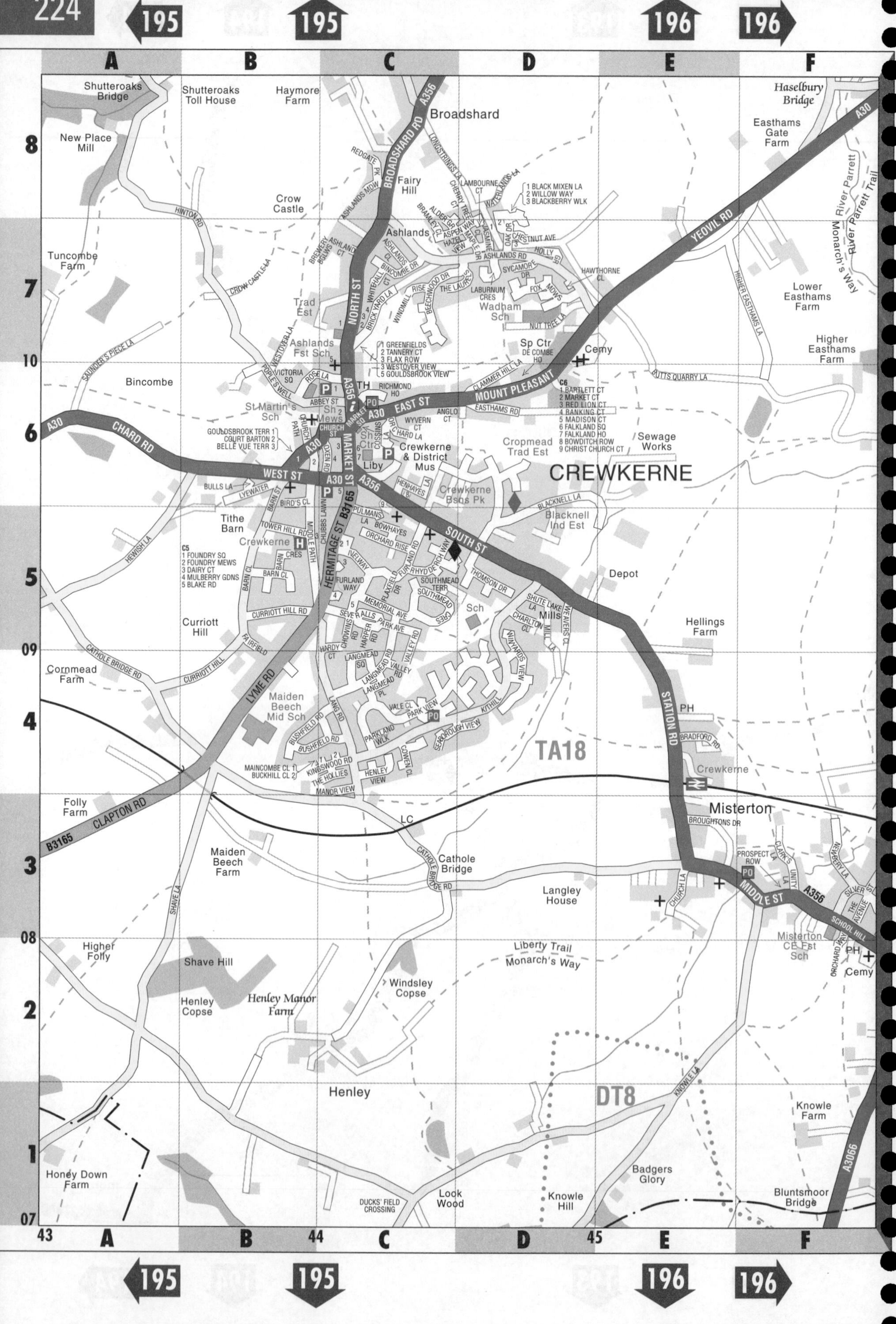

195 195 196 196

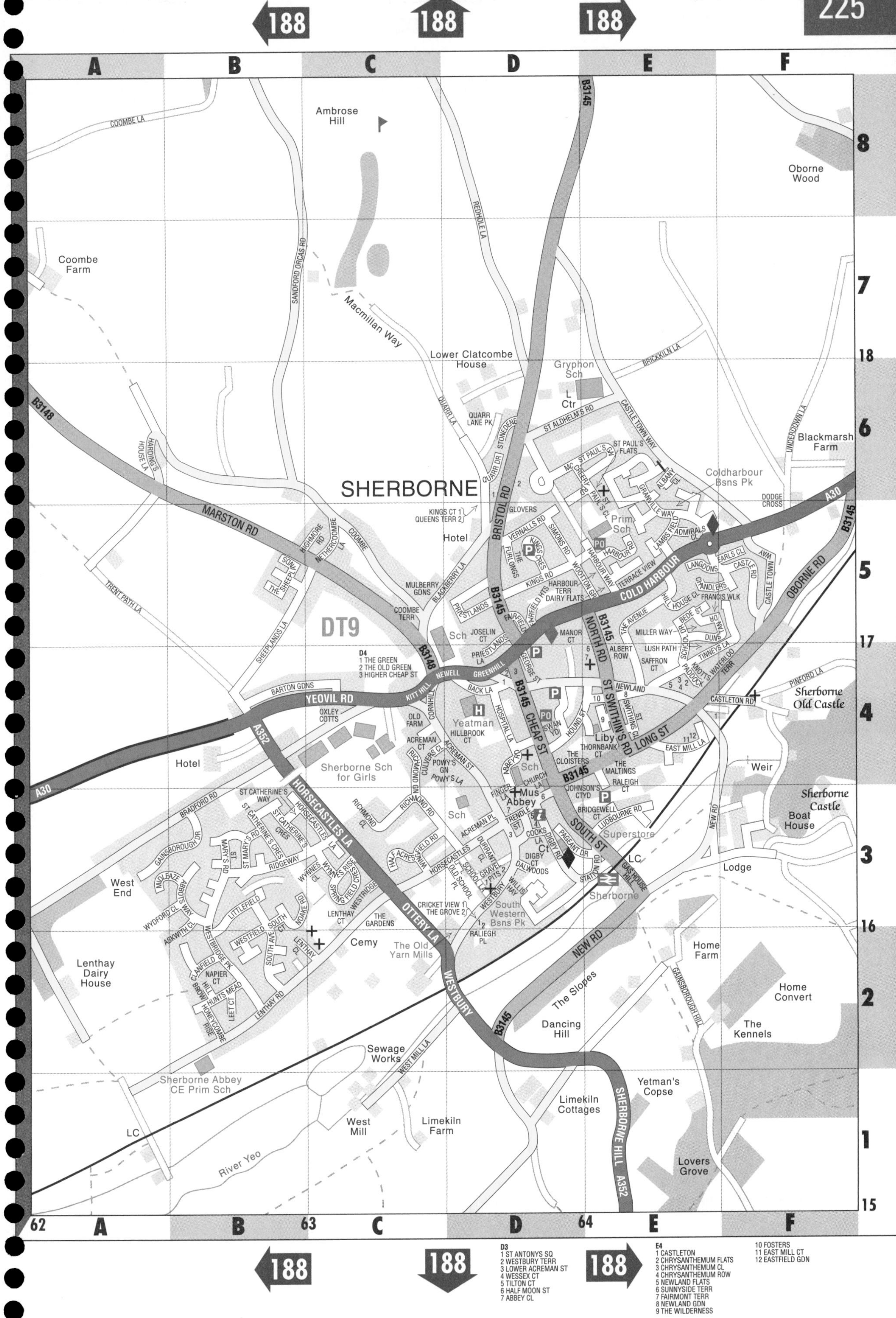
188
188
188
SHERBORNE
DT9
Ambrose Hill
Coombe Farm
Macmillan Way
Lower Clatcombe House
Gryphon Sch
L Ctr
Oborne Wood
Blackmarsh Farm
Coldharbour Bsns Pk
Sherborne Old Castle
Sherborne Castle
Boat House
Weir
Lodge
Hotel
Yeatman
Sherborne Sch for Girls
Sch
Mus
Abbey
Superstore
Sherborne
South Western Bsns Pk
The Old Yarn Mills
Cemy
West End
Lenthay Dairy House
Home Farm
Home Convert
The Kennels
The Slopes
Dancing Hill
Sewage Works
Sherborne Abbey CE Prim Sch
Limekiln Cottages
Yetman's Copse
West Mill
Limekiln Farm
Lovers Grove
River Yeo
LC
A30
B3145
B3148
A352
MARSTON RD
YEOVIL RD
COLD HARBOUR
OBORNE RD
CHEAP ST
SOUTH ST
NORTH RD
LONG ST
NEW RD
HORSECASTLES LA
OTTERY LA
WESTBURY
SHERBORNE HILL
BRISTOL RD
COOMBE LA
SANDFORD ORCAS RD
REDHOLE LA
BRICKKILN LA
UNDERDOWN LA
TRENT PATH LA
SHEEPLANDS LA
WEST MILL LA
GAINSBOROUGH HILL
D4
1 THE GREEN
2 THE OLD GREEN
3 HIGHER CHEAP ST
D3
1 ST ANTONYS SQ
2 WESTBURY TERR
3 LOWER ACREMAN ST
4 WESSEX CT
5 TILTON CT
6 HALF MOON ST
7 ABBEY CL
E4
1 CASTLETON
2 CHRYSANTHEMUM FLATS
3 CHRYSANTHEMUM CL
4 CHRYSANTHEMUM ROW
5 NEWLAND FLATS
6 SUNNYSIDE TERR
7 FAIRMONT TERR
8 NEWLAND GDN
9 THE WILDERNESS
10 FOSTERS
11 EAST MILL CT
12 EASTFIELD GDN
188
188
188

House numbers
1 59 HIGH ST

11

One-way Streets

Scale: 5⅓ inches to 1 mile
0 110 yards 220 yards
0 125 m 250 m

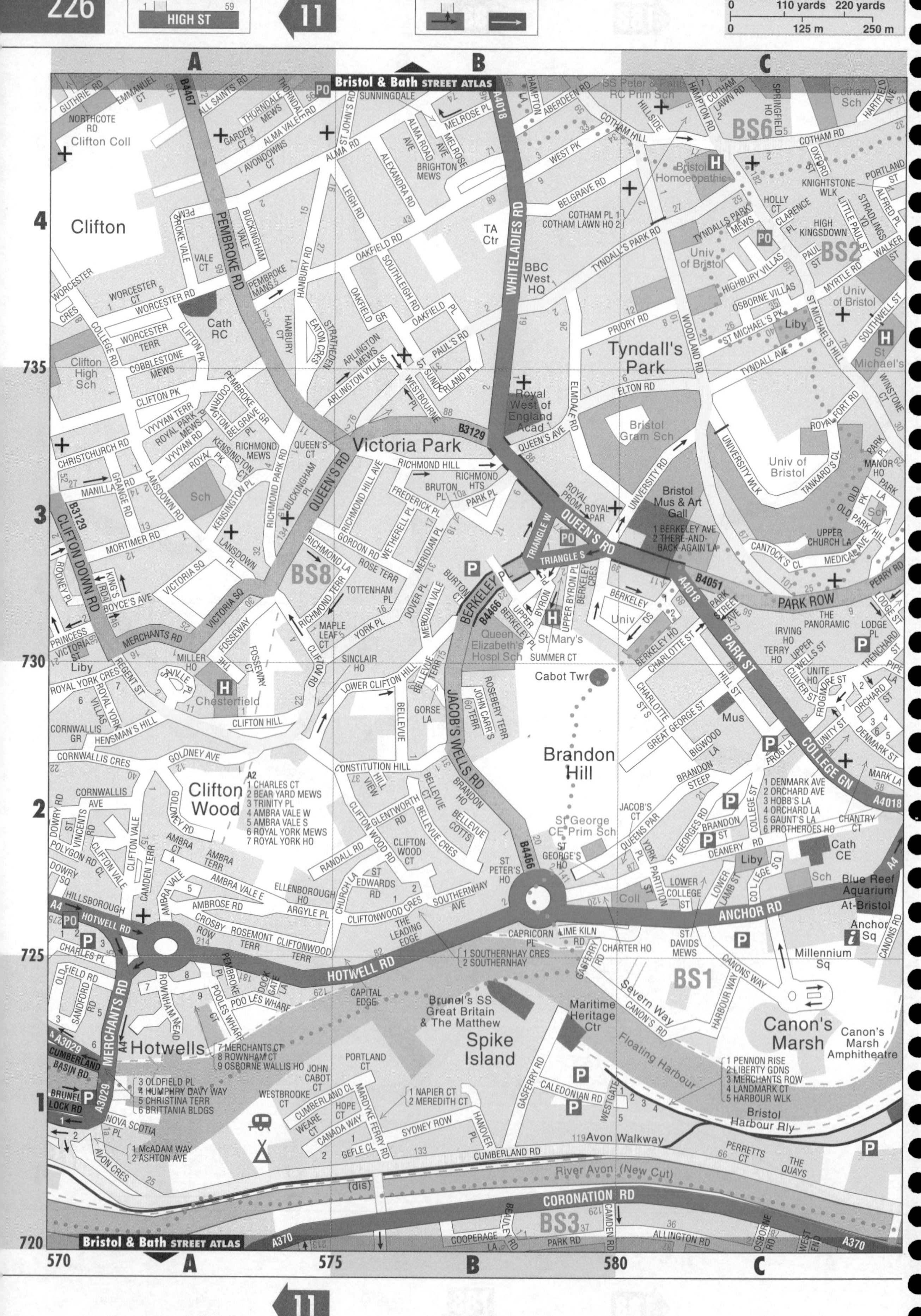

11

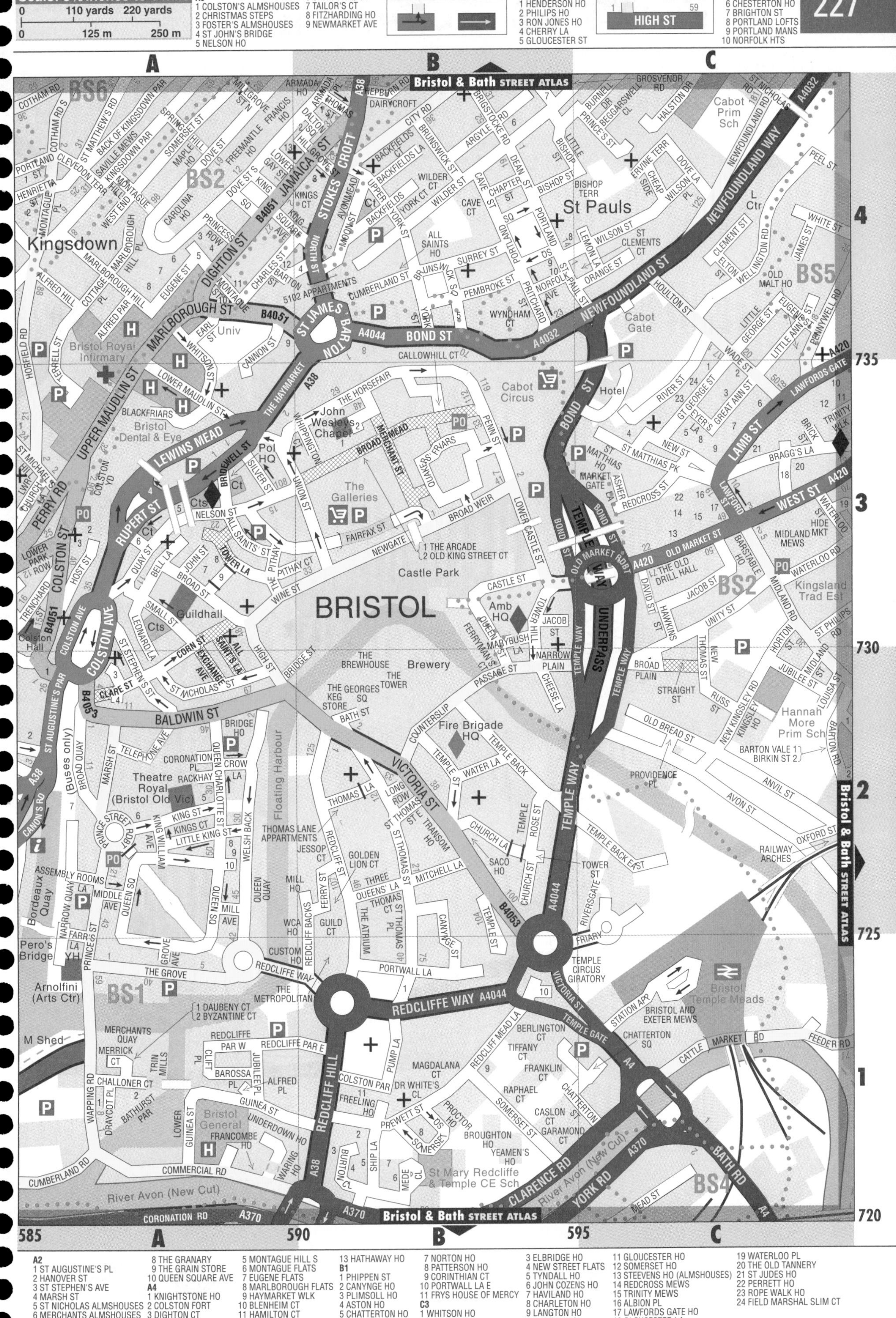
Scale: 5⅓ inches to 1 mile
0 110 yards 220 yards
0 125 m 250 m
A3
1 COLSTON'S ALMSHOUSES
2 CHRISTMAS STEPS
3 FOSTER'S ALMSHOUSES
4 ST JOHN'S BRIDGE
5 NELSON HO
6 CHRISTMAS ST
7 TAILOR'S CT
8 FITZHARDING HO
9 NEWMARKET AVE
One-way streets
B4
1 HENDERSON HO
2 PHILIPS HO
3 RON JONES HO
4 CHERRY LA
5 GLOUCESTER ST
House numbers
1 59
HIGH ST
B4
6 CHESTERTON HO
7 BRIGHTON ST
8 PORTLAND LOFTS
9 PORTLAND MANS
10 NORFOLK HTS
A
B
C
Bristol & Bath STREET ATLAS
BS6
BS2
BS5
BS1
BS4
Kingsdown
St Pauls
BRISTOL
Castle Park
Cabot Circus
The Galleries
Bristol Royal Infirmary
Bristol Dental & Eye
John Wesleys Chapel
Guildhall
Theatre Royal (Bristol Old Vic)
Floating Harbour
Arnolfini (Arts Ctr)
M Shed
Bristol General
St Mary Redcliffe & Temple CE Sch
Bristol Temple Meads
River Avon (New Cut)
Hannah More Prim Sch
Kingsland Trad Est
Cabot Prim Sch
4
735
3
730
2
725
1
720
585
590
595
A2
1 ST AUGUSTINE'S PL
2 HANOVER ST
3 ST STEPHEN'S AVE
4 MARSH ST
5 ST NICHOLAS ALMSHOUSES
6 MERCHANTS ALMSHOUSES
7 KING GEORGE V PL
8 THE GRANARY
9 THE GRAIN STORE
10 QUEEN SQUARE AVE
A4
1 KNIGHTSTONE HO
2 COLSTON FORT
3 DIGHTON CT
4 MONTAGUE CT
5 MONTAGUE HILL S
6 MONTAGUE FLATS
7 EUGENE FLATS
8 MARLBOROUGH FLATS
9 HAYMARKET WLK
10 BLENHEIM CT
11 HAMILTON CT
12 CHERRY CT
13 HATHAWAY HO
B1
1 PHIPPEN ST
2 CANYNGE HO
3 PLIMSOLL HO
4 ASTON HO
5 CHATTERTON HO
6 SPENCER HO
7 NORTON HO
8 PATTERSON HO
9 CORINTHIAN CT
10 PORTWALL LA E
11 FRYS HOUSE OF MERCY
C3
1 WHITSON HO
2 ELTON HO
3 ELBRIDGE HO
4 NEW STREET FLATS
5 TYNDALL HO
6 JOHN COZENS HO
7 HAVILAND HO
8 CHARLETON HO
9 LANGTON HO
10 WESSEX HO
11 GLOUCESTER HO
12 SOMERSET HO
13 STEEVENS HO (ALMSHOUSES)
14 REDCROSS MEWS
15 TRINITY MEWS
16 ALBION PL
17 LAWFORDS GATE HO
18 GLOUCESTER LA
19 WATERLOO PL
20 THE OLD TANNERY
21 ST JUDES HO
22 PERRETT HO
23 ROPE WALK HO
24 FIELD MARSHAL SLIM CT

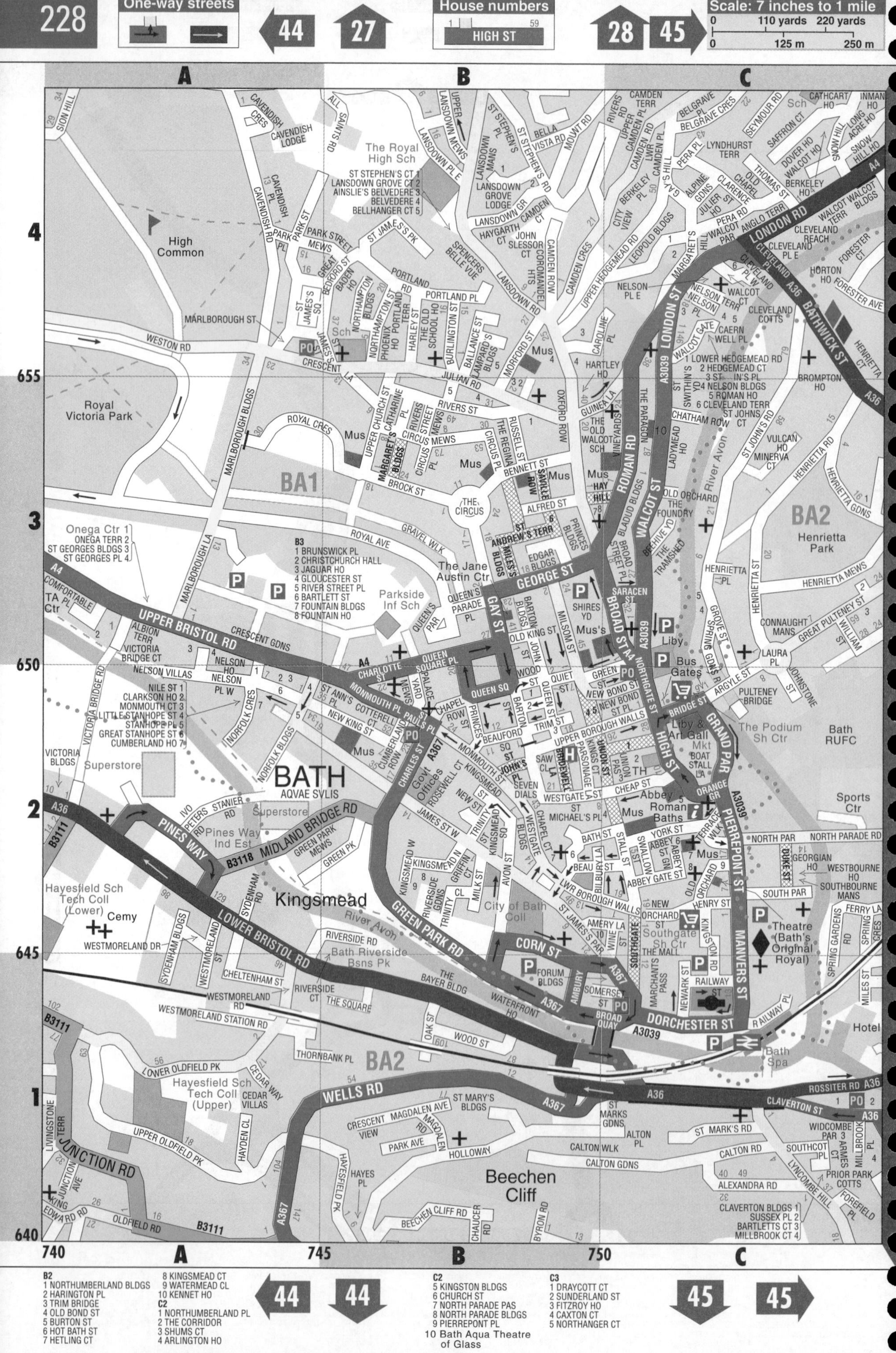
One-way streets
44
27
House numbers
1
59
HIGH ST
28
45
Scale: 7 inches to 1 mile
0
110 yards
220 yards
0
125 m
250 m
A
B
C
4
3
2
1
655
650
645
640
740
745
750
BATH
AQVAE SVLIS
BA1
BA2
BA2
High Common
Royal Victoria Park
The Royal High Sch
ST STEPHEN'S CT 1
LANSDOWN GROVE CT 2
AINSLIE'S BELVEDERE 3
BELVEDERE 4
BELLHANGER CT 5
Onega Ctr 1
ONEGA TERR 2
ST GEORGES BLDGS 3
ST GEORGES PL 4
B3
1 BRUNSWICK PL
2 CHRISTCHURCH HALL
3 JAGUAR HO
4 GLOUCESTER ST
5 RIVER STREET PL
6 BARTLETT ST
7 FOUNTAIN BLDGS
8 FOUNTAIN HO
NILE ST 1
CLARKSON HO 2
MONMOUTH CT 3
LITTLE STANHOPE ST 4
STANHOPE PL 5
GREAT STANHOPE ST 6
CUMBERLAND HO 7
1 LOWER HEDGEMEAD CT
2 HEDGEMEAD CT
3 ST IN'S PL
4 NELSON BLDGS
5 ROMAN HO
6 CLEVELAND TERR
ST JOHNS CT
CLAVERTON BLDGS 1
SUSSEX PL 2
BARTLETTS CT 3
MILLBROOK CT 4
The Jane Austin Ctr
Parkside Inf Sch
The Circus
Kingsmead
Beechen Cliff
Henrietta Park
Bath RUFC
Sports Ctr
The Podium Sh Ctr
Pulteney Bridge
Liby & Art Gall
Abbey
Roman Baths
Southgate Sh Ctr
Theatre (Bath's Original Royal)
Bath Spa
Hotel
City of Bath Coll
Hayesfield Sch Tech Coll (Lower)
Hayesfield Sch Tech Coll (Upper)
Cemy
Superstore
Pines Way Ind Est
Bath Riverside Bsns Pk
River Avon
Govt Offices
Bus Gates
Mkt
UPPER BRISTOL RD
LOWER BRISTOL RD
WELLS RD
LONDON RD
LONDON ST
WALCOT ST
ROMAN RD
BROAD ST
GEORGE ST
GAY ST
MILSOM ST
HIGH ST
GRAND PAR
PIERREPONT ST
MANVERS ST
DORCHESTER ST
CORN ST
GREEN PARK RD
JAMES ST W
MIDLAND BRIDGE RD
PINES WAY
ROYAL CRES
ROYAL AVE
BROCK ST
GRAVEL WALK
QUEEN SQ
CHARLES ST
MONMOUTH ST
WESTGATE ST
NORTH PARADE RD
NORTH PAR
SOUTH PAR
ARGYLE ST
GREAT PULTENEY ST
HENRIETTA RD
BATHWICK ST
CLAVERTON ST
ROSSITER RD
WIDCOMBE PAR
CALTON RD
CALTON GDNS
ALEXANDRA RD
HOLLOWAY
JUNCTION RD
UPPER OLDFIELD PK
LOWER OLDFIELD PK
OLDFIELD RD
WESTMORELAND STATION RD
WESTON RD
MARLBOROUGH BLDGS
MARLBOROUGH LA
VICTORIA BRIDGE RD
LANSDOWN RD
CAMDEN RD
A4
A36
A367
A3039
B3111
B3118
B2
1 NORTHUMBERLAND BLDGS
2 HARINGTON PL
3 TRIM BRIDGE
4 OLD BOND ST
5 BURTON ST
6 HOT BATH ST
7 HETLING CT
8 KINGSMEAD CT
9 WATERMEAD CL
10 KENNET HO
C2
1 NORTHUMBERLAND PL
2 THE CORRIDOR
3 SHUMS CT
4 ARLINGTON HO
C2
5 KINGSTON BLDGS
6 CHURCH ST
7 NORTH PARADE PAS
8 NORTH PARADE BLDGS
9 PIERREPONT PL
10 Bath Aqua Theatre of Glass
C3
1 DRAYCOTT CT
2 SUNDERLAND ST
3 FITZROY HO
4 CAXTON CT
5 NORTHANGER CT
44
44
45
45

Place name May be abbreviated on the map	**Church Rd** [6] Beckenham BR2 .... **53** C6
Location number Present when a number indicates the place's position in a crowded area of mapping	
Locality, town or village Shown when more than one place has the same name	
Postcode district District for the indexed place	
Page and grid square Page number and grid reference for the standard mapping	

Cities, towns and villages are listed in CAPITAL LETTERS

Public and commercial buildings are highlighted in magenta **Places of interest** are highlighted in blue with a star★

Abbreviations used in the index

Acad	Academy
App	Approach
Arc	Arcade
Ave	Avenue
Bglw	Bungalow
Bldg	Building
Bsns, Bus	Business
Bvd	Boulevard
Cath	Cathedral
Cir	Circus
Cl	Close
Cnr	Corner
Coll	College
Com	Community
Comm	Common
Cott	Cottage
Cres	Crescent
Cswy	Causeway
Ct	Court
Ctr	Centre
Ctry	Country
Cty	County
Dr	Drive
Dro	Drove
Ed	Education
Emb	Embankment
Est	Estate
Ex	Exhibition
Gd	Ground
Gdn	Garden
Gn	Green
Gr	Grove
H	Hall
Ho	House
Hospl	Hospital
HQ	Headquarters
Hts	Heights
Ind	Industrial
Inst	Institute
Int	International
Intc	Interchange
Junc	Junction
L	Leisure
La	Lane
Liby	Library
Mdw	Meadow
Meml	Memorial
Mkt	Market
Mus	Museum
Orch	Orchard
Pal	Palace
Par	Parade
Pas	Passage
Pk	Park
Pl	Place
Prec	Precinct
Prom	Promenade
Rd	Road
Recn	Recreation
Ret	Retail
Sh	Shopping
Sq	Square
St	Street
Sta	Station
Terr	Terrace
TH	Town Hall
Univ	University
Wk, Wlk	Walk
Wr	Water
Yd	Yard

Index of towns, villages, streets, hospitals, industrial estates, railway stations, schools, shopping centres, universities and places of interest

5102 Apartments BS1 ... **227** B4

A

ABBAS COMBE **176** E1
Abbas & Templecombe CE Prim Sch BA8 .... **176** E1
Abbey Cl
Curry Rivel TA10 .... **171** D4
Keynsham BS31 .... **24** F6
[7] Sherborne DT9 .... **225** D3
Tatworth TA20 .... **198** D8
Wookey BA5 .... **139** D8
Abbey Ct [6] BA2 .... **45** B7
Abbey Fields TA10 .... **171** D4
Abbey Gate St BA1 .... **228** C2
Abbey Gdns BS22 .... **49** E8
Abbey Gn BA1 .... **228** C2
ABBEY HILL **182** E5
Abbey Hill Dro TA3 .... **182** E5
Abbey La BA3 .... **64** A4
Abbey Lodge BA6 .... **206** E4
Abbey Manor Bsns Ctr BA21 .... **218** D5
Abbey Meads BA6 .... **206** E3
Abbey Mews TA20 .... **198** D8
Abbey Pk BS31 .... **24** F6
Abbey Rd
Bristol BS9 .... **5** F7
Chilcompton BA3 .... **96** D2
Sherborne DT9 .... **225** D4
Stratton-on-t F BA3 .... **96** F2
Washford TA23 .... **131** E3
Yeovil BA21 .... **218** D6
Abbey St
Bath BA1 .... **228** C2
Crewkerne TA18 .... **224** C6
Hinton St George TA17 .... **195** C7
Abbey Trad Est BA21 .... **218** D6
Abbey View
Bath BA2 .... **45** B5
Radstock BA3 .... **79** A3
Abbey View Gdns BA2 .... **45** B5
Abbeywood Dr BS9 .... **5** C5
Abbotsbury Rd BS48 .... **8** D1
Abbots Cl
Bristol BS14 .... **23** A3
Burnham-on-S TA8 .... **104** B6
Ilminster TA19 .... **221** B3
Oxenpill BA6 .... **138** C4
Seavington St Michael TA19 .... **184** E2
Abbot's Cl BS22 .... **32** A3
Abbots Ct BA6 .... **206** D4
Abbotsfield TA4 .... **210** A4
Abbotsfield Cotts TA4 .... **210** B4
Abbots Fish House★ BA6 .... **138** D4
Abbots Horn BS48 .... **8** D2
ABBOTS LEIGH **11** A8
Abbots Leigh Rd BS8 .... **11** C7
Abbots Meade BA21 .... **218** D5
Abbots Way
Minehead TA24 .... **200** C6
Pilton BA4 .... **140** E3
Sherborne DT9 .... **225** B3
Yeovil BA21 .... **218** D6
Abbott La TA16 .... **196** A8
Abbotts Farm Cl BS39 .... **77** D5
Abbotts Rd BA22 .... **173** D1
Abbotts Way TA3 .... **183** F7
Abbott's Wootton La DT6 .... **199** B1
Abels La DT9 .... **187** F5
Aberdeen Rd BS6 .... **226** B4
Abingdon Gdns BA2 .... **62** D8
Abingdon St TA8 .... **104** B6
Abington Cross TA24 .... **124** B4
Ablake La TA10 .... **172** C5
Ableton Wlk BS9 .... **5** C5
Abon Ho BS9 .... **5** C4
Acacia Ave BS23 .... **49** B8
Acacia Ct BS31 .... **24** C4
Acacia Dr BA11 .... **120** C7
Acacia Gdns TA2 .... **213** E7
Acacia Gr BA2 .... **44** C3
Acacia Rd BA3 .... **78** E1
Accommodation Rd BS24 .... **66** E6
Acer Dr BA21 .... **218** C7
Ackland's Dro TA10 .... **155** F4
Acland Round TA4 .... **167** E6
Acombe Cross TA3 .... **191** E8
Aconite Cl BS22 .... **32** B5
Acorn Cl
Frome BA11 .... **119** D5
Highbridge TA9 .... **104** D4
Acorn Gr BS13 .... **21** E6
Acre Cotts TA21 .... **222** E6
Acre La TA11 .... **211** F4
Acreman Ct DT9 .... **225** C4
Acreman Pl DT9 .... **225** D3
Acreman St DT9 .... **225** D4
Acresbush Cl BS13 .... **22** A5
Acres Ct BA22 .... **197** F8
Acres The [1] TA12 .... **185** E6
Actis Rd BA6 .... **206** E3
Adams Cl
Highbridge TA9 .... **104** C2
Peasedown St John BA2 .... **79** D8
Adams Ct [5] BS8 .... **11** F6
ADAM'S GREEN **197** D2
Adams Ho TA19 .... **221** B3
Adam's La TA5 .... **134** D6
Adams Mdw TA19 .... **221** A4
Adam St TA8 .... **104** B6
Adastral Rd BS24 .... **50** D4
ADBER **187** F7
Adber Cl BA21 .... **219** E8
Adber Cross DT9 .... **187** F6
Adcombe Cl TA3 .... **181** D5
Adcombe Rd TA2 .... **213** B8
Adder La TA7 .... **169** F8
ADDERWELL **120** A3
Adderwell BA11 .... **120** A3
Adderwell Cl BA11 .... **120** A3
Addicott Rd BS23 .... **48** E6
Addiscombe Rd
Bristol BS14 .... **23** B5
Weston-Super-Mare BS23 .... **48** E4
Addison Gr TA2 .... **212** E6
Addlewell La [11] BA20 .... **219** B4
Adlams Central Pk BA6 .... **206** B3
Admirals Cl
Sherborne DT9 .... **225** E5
Watchet TA23 .... **202** D6
Admirals Ct TA6 .... **208** F5
Admiral's Mead BA6 .... **157** E4
Admiral's Wlk BS20 .... **2** B5
Admiralty Way TA1 .... **213** C5
ADSBOROUGH **169** D8
Adsborough Hill TA2 .... **169** D7
Adsborough La TA2 .... **169** D7
ADSCOMBE **152** A8
Adscombe Ave TA6 .... **209** C6
Adscombe La TA5 .... **134** A1
Aelfric Mdw BS20 .... **2** F4
Ainslie's Belvedere BA1 .... **228** B4
Ainstey Dr BA22 .... **175** A4
Airey Hos TA13 .... **220** D1
Airport Rd BS14 .... **23** A8
Airport Rdbt BS24 .... **49** E7
Airport View Cvn Pk BS24 .... **49** D7
Aisecome Way BS22 .... **49** C6
AISHOLT **152** B6
Akeman Cl BA21 .... **218** D7
Akeman Way BS11 .... **4** C8
Alamein Rd TA23 .... **202** E6
Alard Rd BS4 .... **22** F7
Alastair Cl BA21 .... **218** F7
Alastair Dr BA21 .... **218** F7
Albany BS23 .... **30** F1
Albany Cl DT9 .... **225** E6
Albany Ct [6] BA1 .... **44** B6
Albany Rd BA2 .... **44** C6
Albemarle Rd TA1 .... **212** F5
Albermarle Row [9] BS8 .... **11** F6
Albert Ave
Peasedown St John BA2 .... **79** C7
Weston-Super-Mare BS23 .... **48** E6
Albert Bldgs BA6 .... **206** D5
Albert Cl BA21 .... **218** E7
Albert Ct
Bridgwater TA6 .... **208** E4
[15] Taunton TA1 .... **213** A4
Weston-Super-Mare BS23 .... **48** E6
Albert Pl
Bath BA2 .... **45** C1
Portishead BS20 .... **2** D4
Albert Quadrant BS23 .... **48** E8
Albert Rd
Clevedon BS21 .... **6** C3
Keynsham BS31 .... **24** E5
Portishead BS20 .... **2** D5
Weston-Super-Mare BS23 .... **48** E6
Albert Row DT9 .... **225** E4
Albert St TA6 .... **208** E4
Albert Terr BA2 .... **44** C6
Albion Bldgs BA1 .... **44** D7
Albion Cl TA6 .... **209** B5
Albion Pl
[16] Bristol BS2 .... **227** C3
Frome BA11 .... **119** D3
Albion Rd BA22 .... **174** A2
Albion Terr
Bath BA1 .... **228** A3
Cheddar BS27 .... **90** B7
Alburys BS40 .... **35** D3
ALCOMBE
Kingsdown **29** F7
Minehead **201** A4
Alcombe Cross TA24 .... **201** B5
Alcombe Rd TA24 .... **201** A5
Aldeburgh Pl BA14 .... **83** F6
Alder Cl
North Petherton TA6 .... **153** F3
Taunton TA1 .... **213** D1
Williton TA4 .... **202** E3
Aldercombe Rd BS9 .... **5** C8
Alder Ct BS14 .... **23** B5
Alderdown Cl BS11 .... **5** A8
Alder Gr
Crewkerne TA18 .... **224** C7
Yeovil BA20 .... **218** E2
Alderley Rd BA2 .... **44** B4
Alderney Rd TA6 .... **209** C3
Alder Terr BA3 .... **78** E2
Alder Way BA2 .... **62** D8
Alder Wlk BA11 .... **120** B7
Aldondale Gdns BA20 .... **219** B3
ALDWICK **54** D7
Aldwick Ave BS13 .... **22** C3
Aldwick La BS40 .... **54** C7
Aldwych Cl TA8 .... **104** C6
Alec Ricketts Cl BA2 .... **43** F5
Alexander Bldgs [12] BA1 .... **28** B1
Alexander Cl TA3 .... **169** D5
Alexander Hall BA3 .... **64** C6
Alexander Ho [5] BS23 .... **48** F4
Alexander Mews [5] BS23 .... **48** E7
Alexander Pl BA3 .... **64** C6
Alexanders Cl BA6 .... **138** C4
Alexander Way BS49 .... **34** B7
Alexandra Ct BS21 .... **6** C4
Alexandra Gdns TA24 .... **201** A6
Alexandra Mews TA24 .... **201** A7
Alexandra Par BS23 .... **48** E7
Alexandra Pk BS39 .... **77** E5
Alexandra Pl BA2 .... **45** C1
Alexandra Rd
Bath BA2 .... **228** C1
Bridgwater TA6 .... **208** E5
Bristol BS8 .... **226** B4
Bristol, Highridge BS13 .... **21** F7
Clevedon BS21 .... **6** C4
Frome BA11 .... **119** F4
Minehead TA24 .... **201** A6
Wellington TA21 .... **222** D6
Yeovil BA21 .... **219** D6
Alexandra Terr BS39 .... **77** E5
Alexevia Cvn Pk TA3 .... **169** C3
Aley TA5 .... **152** A8
ALFORD **159** A3
Alford La BA4, BA7 .... **159** B4
Alfords Ridge BA3 .... **117** A7
Alfoxton Rd TA6 .... **208** C4
Alfred Cres BA4 .... **205** B4
Alfred Ct [4] BS23 .... **48** E7
Alfred Hill BS2 .... **227** A4
Alfred Par BS2 .... **227** A4

Alfred Pl
Bristol BS2 226 C4
BS1 227 A1
Alfred St
Bath BA1 228 B3
Taunton TA1 213 B4
Wells BA5 203 D3
Weston-Super-Mare BS23 48 E8
Alfred's Twr★ BA10 161 C6
Alfred's Way BA9 216 B3
Algar Ct BA5 203 B4
ALHAMPTON 159 C6
Alice St BA11 143 A6
Alison Gdns BS48 19 A7
Allandale Ct TA8 104 B8
Allandale Rd TA8 104 A8
Allanmead Rd BS14 23 B8
Allans Way BS24 49 F7
Allen Dr BA4 205 A6
Allen Rd TA6 208 F1
Allens La
Shipham BS25 70 F8
Wells BA5 112 E1
Allenslade Flats TA4 210 C5
ALLER 171 D8
Aller BS24 49 B2
Aller Dro
Aller TA10 171 D8
Othery TA7 155 C1
ALLERFORD
Porlock 124 C4
Taunton 167 F4
Allermoor Dro BS28 138 B8
Aller Par BS24 49 B2
Allerpark La TA24 123 F3
Allerton Cres BS14 23 B4
Allerton Gdns BS14 23 B5
Allerton Rd
Bridgwater TA6 209 B7
Bristol BS14 23 B4
All Hallows Prep Sch
BA4 142 C6
Allingham Rd BA21 219 C7
Allington Cl TA1 213 E4
Allington Gdns BS48 18 C8
Allington Rd BS3 226 C1
Allotment Dro
Combe St Nicholas TA20 193 C5
Glastonbury BA16 138 D1
Allotment Rd BA22 175 C3
ALLOWENSHAY 195 A8
ALL SAINTS 198 A4
All Saints CE Prim Sch
Dulverton TA22 163 D6
Montacute TA15 186 B3
All Saints CE Sch EX13 198 A4
All Saints East Clevedon CE
Prim Sch BS21 6 F4
All Saints Ho BS2 227 B4
All Saints La BS21 6 F4
All Saints' La BS1 227 A2
All Saints Pl BA2 45 E4
All Saints Rd BA1 228 B4
All Saints' Rd
Bristol BS8 226 A4
Weston-Super-Mare BS23 30 E1
All Saints' St BS1 227 A3
All Saints' Terr TA6 209 B4
Allshire La EX16 162 F3
Allyn Saxon Dr BA4 205 D5
Alma Field BA7 214 B4
Alma Rd BS8 226 B4
Alma Road Ave BS8 226 B4
Alma St
Taunton TA1 213 A3
Weston-Super-Mare BS23 48 E7
Alma Vale Rd BS8 226 A4
Almond Cl BS22 32 A1
Almond Tree Cl TA6 209 D4
Almshouse La BA22 173 E1
Almshouses
Donyatt TA19 183 D1
Marshfield SN14 13 E8
Almyr Terr TA23 202 C7
Alpha Cotts TA2 168 E8
Alpha Ho TA9 104 E3
Alpine Cl BS39 77 F4
Alpine Gdns BA1 228 C4
Alpine Rd BS39 77 F4
ALSTON 198 A5
Alston Cl TA1 212 C1
Alstone Gdns TA9 104 C2
Alstone La TA9 104 C2
Alstone Rd TA9 104 C2
Alstone Wildlife Pk★
TA9 104 C3
ALSTON SUTTON 88 F3
Alston Sutton Rd BS26 88 F4
Alton Pl BA2 228 C1
Alun Rees Way TA20 223 B3
Alverstoke BS14 22 F7
Alveston Wlk BS9 5 B7
ALVINGTON 218 B4
Alvington La BA22 218 B5
ALWESTON 189 A1
Alweston DT9 189 A1
Ambares Ct BA3 96 F8
Amberd La TA3 181 D8
Amberey Rd BS23 48 F5
Amberlands Cl BS48 19 A7
Amberley Cl
Keinton Mandeville TA11 158 A1
Keynsham BS31 24 E4
Amberley Gdns 3 BS48 8 D1
Amber Mead TA1 213 D3
Ambleside Rd BA2 44 C2
Ambra Ct BS8 226 A2
Ambra Terr BS8 226 A2
Ambra Vale BS8 226 A2
Ambra Vale E BS8 226 A2
Ambra Vale S 5 BS8 226 A2
Ambra Vale W 4 BS8 226 A2
Ambridge Cl BA16 207 B4
Ambrose Cl DT9 187 E1
Ambrose Rd BS8 226 A2
Ambury BA1 228 B1
Amercombe Wlk BS14 23 D7
American Mus in Britain★
BA2 46 A5
Amery La BA1 228 C2
AMESBURY 59 F2
Amesbury Dr BS24 67 B6
Ames La BA3 98 B6
Ammerdown Terr BA3 98 F7
AMMERHAM 199 A8
Ammerham La TA20 199 A8
Amor Pl TA1 212 D2
Amory Rd TA22 163 D6
Amulet Way BA4 205 E4
Ancastle Ave BA7 214 D6
Ancastle Terr BA7 214 C6
Anchor Cl BA3 116 E8
Anchor Cnr BA9 176 D6
Anchor Hill BA9 176 D6
Anchor Rd
Bath BA1 27 B1
Bristol BS1 226 C2
Coleford BA3 116 E8
Anchor Sq BS1 226 C2
Anchor St TA23 202 C7
Anchor Stables TA24 123 E4
Anchor Way BS20 4 D4
Ancliff Sq BA15 64 E4
Andereach Cl BS14 23 B8
ANDERSFIELD 153 B5
Andersfield Cl TA6 208 A4
Ander's La TA3 192 B8
Andrew Allan Rd TA21 222 B4
Andrew's Hill TA22 163 D6
Andrew's Hill Cross
TA22 163 C6
Andruss Dr BS41 21 D2
Angela Cl TA1 212 D2
Angel Cres TA6 208 F5
Angel La BA9 216 C4
Angel Place Sh Ctr 6
TA6 208 F5
Angel Row TA3 170 F2
ANGERSLEIGH 181 C5
Anglesey Cotts DT10 190 B4
Anglo Ct TA18 224 C6
Anglo Terr BA1 228 C4
Anglo Trad Est The BA4 205 B6
Angus Way 12 TA6 154 A5
Angwin Cl BA4 205 B6
Animal Farm Adventure
Park★ TA8 66 B2
Annaly Rd BS27 90 A7
Annandale BA7 214 B4
Annandale Ave BS22 31 E1
Anseres Pl BA5 203 E4
ANSFORD 214 C6
Ansford Com Sch BA7 214 C7
Ansford Hill BA7 214 B7
Ansford Rd BA7 214 C6
Anson Cl BS31 25 D2
Anson Rd
Locking BS24 50 B6
Weston-Super-Mare BS22 31 D4
Anson Way TA6 208 F5
Anstey Gate TA22 162 B8
Anthony Rd BA16 207 D7
Antler Cl BA6 206 C3
Antona Ct BS11 4 D7
Antona Dr BS11 4 D7
Anvil Rd BS49 17 F1
Anvil St BS2 227 C2
Apex Dr TA9 104 C4
Aplins Cl TA19 221 B3
Apple Alley BA11 119 F5
Apple Bsns Ctr The TA2 212 B6
Appleby Wlk BS4 22 D7
Apple Cl TA19 194 E7
Applecroft BA2 79 E6
APPLEDORE 179 A1
Appledore 4 BS22 31 F2
Appledore Cl BS14 23 B8
Apple Dumpling Cnr
BS28 108 C3
Applefield Rd DT8 199 F8
Applehayes La EX15 180 F2
Apple La BA11 119 F5
Apple Tree Cl TA6 209 D4
Appletree Ct BS22 32 B2
Apple Tree Dr BS25 70 A8
Appletree Mews BS22 32 B2
APPLEY 179 B8
Appley Cross TA21 179 B7
Appsley Cl BS22 31 C1
Apricot Tree Cl TA6 209 D5
Apsley Rd BA1 44 A7
Aquara Cl BA16 207 C3
Arbutus Dr BS9 5 C8
Arcade The BS1 227 B3
Archbishop Cranmer CE Com
Prim Sch TA1 213 A4
Arch Cl BS41 10 F1
Archer Ct BS21 6 D4
Archer Dr TA8 104 C6
Archers Way The BA6 206 E5
Archer Wlk BS14 23 E6
Arches The BA2 44 A6
Archgrove BS41 10 F1
Arch La TA3 170 E4
Archstone Ave TA5 135 F2
Archway St BA2 45 B5
Arden Cl BS22 31 F3
Ardern Cl BS9 5 B8
Ardmore BS8 11 D7
Ardwyn TA21 222 D4
Arena The BA20 219 A4
Argyle Ave BS23 48 F4
Argyle Pl BS8 226 A2
Argyle Rd
Bristol BS2 227 B4
Clevedon BS21 6 D6
Argyle St BA2 228 C2
Argyle Terr BA2 44 C6
Arlington Cl
Bridgwater TA6 209 A2
Yeovil BA21 218 C7
Arlington Ho 4 BA1 228 C2
Arlington Mans BS8 226 B4
Arlington Rd 4 BA2 44 D5
Arlington Villas BS8 226 B3
Armada Ho BS2 227 A4
Armada Pl BS1 227 B4
Armada Rd BS14 23 A6
Armes Ct BA2 228 C1
Armoury Rd BA22 218 A6
Armoury The BA6 206 D4
Armstrong Rd BA11 120 B5
Armtech Row BA22 218 B6
Arnewood Gdns BA20 218 F2
Arnold Cl TA2 212 F7
Arnold Noad Cnr BA14 83 E3
Arnold's Way BS49 17 A2
Arnolfini (Arts Ctr)★
BS1 227 A1
Arnor Cl BS22 32 A4
Arrowfield Cl BS14 23 A2
Artemesia Ave BS22 49 E8
Arthurswood Rd BS13 22 A4
Artillery Rd BA22 218 A6
Arundel Cl BS13 22 B5
Arundell Ct BS23 48 E8
Arundell Rd BS23 30 E1
Arundells Way TA3 169 D4
Arundel Rd
Bath BA1 28 A1
Clevedon BS21 6 D3
Yeovil BA21 219 E6
Arundel Wlk BS31 24 D5
Arun Gr TA1 213 D4
Ascension Ho BA2 44 D4
ASH
Martock 185 F7
Taunton 169 E1
ASHBEER 150 C6
Ashbeer Hill TA4 150 D7
Ashbourne Cres TA1 213 D3
ASHBRITTLE 178 F8
Ash Brook BS39 59 D1
Ashbrooke House Sch
BS23 48 D6
Ashbury Dr BS22 31 B2
Ashby Pl BA7 214 C5
Ash CE Prim Sch TA12 185 F7
Ash Cl
Bridgwater TA6 209 D4
Wells BA5 203 D5
Weston-Super-Mare BS22 32 D2
Winscombe BS25 52 A1
Ashcombe Ct
Ilminster TA19 221 B4
1 Weston-Super-Mare
BS23 48 F7
Ashcombe Gdns BS23 49 A8
Ashcombe La
Alweston DT9 189 B2
Ilminster TA19 221 B4
Ashcombe Park Rd BS23 31 A1
Ashcombe Pl 4 BS23 48 F7
Ashcombe Prim Sch BS23 49 A7
Ashcombe Rd BS23 48 F7
ASHCOTT 156 B8
Ashcott BS14 22 F7
Ashcott Cl TA8 104 C6
Ashcott Dr TA8 104 C6
Ashcott Pl TA8 104 C6
Ashcott Prim Sch TA7 156 B8
Ashcott Rd BA6 138 D3
Ash Cres TA1 212 B2
Ashcroft
Chard TA20 223 D2
Weston-Super-Mare BS24 49 B2
Ash Croft TA12 185 F7
Ashcroft Ave BS31 24 D5
Ashcroft Rd BS9 5 C7
Ash Cross TA3 169 E2
Ash Ct BS14 23 A6
ASHCULME 180 C1
Ashculme Hill EX15 180 C2
Ashdene Rd BS23 49 A8
Ashdown Ct BS9 5 F8
Ashdown Rd BS20 2 A6
Ashel's Batch BA3 94 C8
Ashen Cross TA11 211 E2
Ash End BA8 189 F7
Asher La BS2 227 C3
Ashes La BA3 64 A4
Ashey La
Burrington BS40 54 A5
Cheddar BS27 90 B8
Ashfield TA20 223 D2
Ashfield Cl BA11 143 C6
Ashfield Pk 23 TA12 185 E6
Ashford Cl
Bridgwater TA6 208 E2
Milverton TA4 167 A4
Ashford Dr BS24 49 A1
Ashford Gr BA21 219 B7
Ashford La TA19 183 F5
Ashford Rd
Bath BA2 44 D4
Redhill BS40 36 E4
Taunton TA1 212 C2
Wellington TA21 222 D4
Ash Gr
Bath BA2 44 C4
Chard TA20 223 C5
Clevedon BS21 6 E4
Minehead TA24 200 D7
Shepton Mallet BA4 205 C4
Wells BA5 203 D5
Weston-Super-Mare BS23 48 E2
ASHGROVE 79 D8
Ashgrove BA2 79 D8
Ashgrove Ave BS8 11 B7
Ashgrove Ct BA2 79 D8
Ash Grove Way TA6 209 D7
Ash Hay Dro BA5 139 C6
Ash Hayes Dr BS48 8 E1
Ash Hayes Rd BS48 8 F1
Ash Ho TA8 65 F2
ASHILL 183 B4
Ashill Cl TA1 212 E1
Ashill Com Prim Sch
TA19 183 C4
ASHINGTON 187 B8
Ashington La BA21 187 B7
Ash La
Shepton Beauchamp
TA19 184 E4
Wells BA5 203 C5
Winsford TA24 147 B6
Ashland Ct TA18 224 C7
Ashland La TA4 150 B4
Ashland Rd BS13 22 A4
Ashlands Cl TA18 224 C7
Ashlands Fst Sch TA18 224 C7
Ashlands Mdw TA18 224 C8
Ashlands Rd TA18 224 D7
Ashlea BA7 214 B6
Ashlea Pk TA9 136 E8
Ashleigh Ave TA6 209 A3
Ashleigh Cl
Paulton BS39 77 E6
Weston-Super-Mare BS23 49 A8
Ashleigh Cres BS49 34 B8
Ashleigh Gdns TA1 212 E5
Ashleigh Rd
Weston-Super-Mare BS23 49 A8
Yatton BS49 34 B8
Ashleigh Terr TA6 209 A3
Ashley Ave
Bath BA1 44 C7
Burnham-on-S TA8 104 B6
Ashley Cl BS25 70 A7
Ashley La BA15 64 F7
Ashley Rd
Bathford BA1 29 E3
Clevedon BS21 6 B1
Taunton TA1 212 D3
Ashley Terr 1 BA1 44 C7
Ashmans Ct BA1 44 B6
Ashmans Gate BS39 77 E5
Ashmans Yd BA1 44 B6
Ashman Way TA6 208 D4
Ashmead
Temple Cloud BS39 58 E1
Yeovil BA20 218 C2
Ashmead Rd BS31 25 B5
Ashmead Road Ind Est
BS31 25 B5
Ashmead Way 8 BS1 11 F5
Ashmoor Dro BA5 139 C6
ASH PRIORS 167 C8
Ash Rd
Banwell BS29 50 E4
Street BA16 207 B3
ASHTON 107 E8
Ashton Ave BS1 226 A1
Ashton Cl
Ashill TA19 183 C4
Clevedon BS21 6 B1
Ashton Court Estate★
BS41 11 C4
Ashton Cres BS48 8 D1
Ashton Ct TA1 212 C1
Ashton Dr BS3 11 F2
ASHTON GATE 11 F4
Ashton Gate Stadium (Bristol
City FC)★ BS3 11 F3
Ashton Gate Trad Est BS3 11 E3
Ashton Gate Underpass
BS3 11 F3
Ashton Hill BA2 43 A7
Ashton Park Sec Sch BS3 11 E3
Ashton Pk BA11 119 E2
Ashton Rd
Bridgwater TA6 208 F2
Bristol, Ashton Gate BS3 11 F4
Bristol, Bower Ashton BS3 11 D3
ASHTON VALE 11 F2
Ashton Vale Prim Sch
BS3 11 F2
Ashton Vale Rd BS3 11 E3
Ashton Vale Trad Est BS3 11 F1
Ashton Way BS31 24 E6
Ashton Windmill★ BS28 88 E1
Ashtown Cross EX16 164 A3
Ash Tree Cl
Bleadon BS24 67 C6
Burnham-on-S TA8 85 A3
Ash Tree Cres TA8 85 A3
Ash Tree Ct BA3 78 E1
Ash Tree Pl TA8 85 A3
Ashtree Rd BA11 120 A6
Ash Tree Rd TA8 85 A3
Ash Trees TA9 86 C5
Ashvale Cl BS48 9 A2
ASHWELL 221 C6
Ashwell Bsns Pk TA19 221 C7
Ashwell Cl BS14 23 E6
Ashwell La
Glastonbury BA6 139 D1
Wheddon Cross TA24 129 F2
ASHWICK 115 B5
Ashwicke BS14 23 A6
Ash Wlk BA8 190 A6
Ashwood BS40 74 F4
Ashwood Dr BA21 219 E8
Askwith Cl DT9 225 B3
ASNEY 156 E7
Asney Rd BA16 156 E7
Aspen Cl BA11 120 B7
Aspen Ct TA6 208 E4
Aspen Park Rd BS22 49 E8
Aspen Way TA18 224 D7
Aspley Cl BA1 44 B7
Asquith St TA2 212 E6
Assembly Rooms La BS1 227 A2
Aston Ho 4 BS1 227 B1
At-Bristol★ BS1 226 C1
Athelney Way BA21 218 D6
ATHERSTONE 184 C3
Athlone Rd TA6 209 A2
Atholl Cl BS22 31 F3
Atkins Cl BS14 23 E6
Atkin's Gate TA13 220 D6
Atlanta Key TA8 104 A8
Atlantic Cres TA8 104 B5
Atlantic Rd
Bristol BS11 4 C8
Weston-Super-Mare BS23 30 C1
Atlantic Rd S BS23 30 C1
Atlantic View Ct BS23 30 C1
Atlantic Way BA22 174 A2
Atlay Ct BS49 17 B1
Atrium The BS1 227 B2
Attewell Ct BA2 44 F4
Attisham La DT6 199 D4
Atyeo Cl
Bristol BS3 11 E1
Burnham-on-S TA8 104 C8
Aubrey Meads BS30 25 E8
Auckland Cl BS23 48 F3
Auckland Way TA20 223 D3
Audley Ave BA1 44 D7
Audley Cl
Bath BA1 44 D7
Nether Stowey TA5 134 A2
Audley Gr BA1 44 C7
Audley Lodge BA1 44 D7
Audley Park Rd BA1 44 C7
Augusta Pl BA1 44 D7
Augustine's Cl BS20 1 E4
Austen Dr BS22 32 B4
Austen Pl BS11 4 E7
Austin Cl BA11 119 F2
Austin Rd BA6 206 E6
Autumn Mews BS24 50 A8
Avalon Bldgs BA6 206 D5
Avalon Cl BS49 17 A1
Avalon Est BA6 206 E7
Avalon Ho BS48 8 C1
Avalon Mews BA6 206 E4
Avalon Pk TA11 211 B5
Avalon Rd
Bridgwater TA6 209 D5
Highbridge TA9 104 E4
Avalon Sch BA16 207 B3
Avalon Vineyard BA4 158 E8
Avebury Cl TA8 104 D8
Avebury Dr TA6 209 D5
Avebury Rd BS3 11 F2
Aveline Ct TA4 167 F6
Avening Cl BS48 19 A8
Avenue Pl BA2 45 B1
Avenue Rd BA11 120 A4
Avenue The
Backwell BS48 19 A7
Bath, Bushey Norwood BA2 45 E5
Bath, Combe Down BA2 45 C1
Bicknoller TA4 132 F4
3 Bridgwater TA6 208 F5
Bristol, Sneyd Park BS9 5 E3
Chard TA20 193 F7
Clevedon BS21 6 E6
Keynsham BS31 24 E6
Kingsbury Episcopi TA12 185 B8
Langport TA10 172 A6
Minehead TA24 201 A7
Misterton TA18 224 F3
Sherborne DT9 225 E5
Sparkford BA22 175 A5
Stoke sub Hamdon TA14 185 F4
Taunton TA1 212 E5
Timsbury BA2 60 B2
Weston-Super-Mare BS22 32 C3
Wincanton BA9 216 D3
Winscombe BS25 70 C8
Yatton BS49 34 B8
Yeovil BA21 219 B5
Averill Ct BS21 6 D4
Avill Cres TA1 213 C4
Avishayes Com Prim Sch
TA20 223 E5
Avishayes Rd TA20 223 E4
Avonbank Ind Est BS11 4 B7
Avonbridge Trad Est BS11 4 C8
Avon Cl
Keynsham BS31 24 F6
Taunton TA1 212 D2
Weston-Super-Mare BS23 48 F2
Yeovil BA21 219 D6

AVONCLIFF 64 F4
Avoncliff Halt BA15 64 F5
Avon Cres BS1 226 A1
Avon Ct BA1 29 A4
Avondale Bldgs BA1 28 B2
Avondale Ct
Bath BA1 44 B7
Bristol, Sneyd Park BS9 5 D3
Avondale Ho
Bath BA2 44 B5
Bridgwater TA6 209 A2
Avondale Rd BA1 44 B6
Avondowns Ct BS8 226 A4
Avon Gorge Ind Est BS11 4 C7
Avon Gorge Nature Reserve★ BS8 11 E7
Avon Gr BS9 5 D2
Avon Hts BA3 64 C6
Avon La BS31 25 F5
Avonleaze BS9 5 B5
Avonmead BS2 227 B4
Avon Mill La BS31 24 F6
AVONMOUTH 4 B8
Avonmouth CE Prim Sch BS11 4 C8
Avonmouth Rd BS11 4 C8
Avon Pk BA1 44 A7
Avon Prim Sch BS11 4 D8
Avon Rd
Bristol BS13 22 A6
Keynsham BS31 24 F5
Pill BS20 4 C5
Avon Riverside Est BS11 4 B7
Avon Riverside Sta★ BS30 25 E6
Avon Ski & Action Centre★ BS25 52 C3
Avon & Somerset Pol HQ BS20 1 F3
Avon St
Bath BA1 228 B2
Bristol BS2 227 C2
Avon Vale BS9 5 D4
Avonvale Pl BA1 28 F3
Avon Valley Adventure & Wildlife Pk★ BS31 25 D6
Avon Valley Rly★ BS30 25 D7
Avon Way
Bristol, Sneyd Park BS9 5 C4
Portishead BS20 2 C5
Avonwood Cl BS11 4 E6
Awkward Hill BS40 55 D5
AXBRIDGE 70 B1
Axbridge CE Fst Sch BS26 70 C1
Axbridge Cl
Burnham-on-S TA8 104 C8
Nailsea BS48 18 E8
Axbridge & District Mus★ BS26 70 C2
Axbridge Moor Dro BS26 70 C1
Axbridge Rd
Bath BA2 45 A2
Cheddar BS27 70 F2
Axe Cl BS23 49 A5
Axeford TA20 198 E8
Axeford Mdws TA20 198 E8
Axe La
Clapton DT8 195 C1
Drimpton DT8 199 F8
Axe Rd
Bridgwater TA6 209 B3
Wookey BA5 139 D8
Axe Valley Com Coll The EX13 198 A1
Axford Way BA2 79 D8
Axis BS14 22 D5
AXMINSTER 198 B2
Axminster Com Prim Sch EX13 198 A1
Axminster Rd TA20 198 C7
Ayckbourn Cl TA8 104 C6
Aycote Cl BS22 31 C2
Ayford La SN14 13 F4
Aylands Rd TA1 212 D3
Aylmer Cres BS14 23 B6
Ayr St BA2 44 D6
AYSHFORD 178 E2
Azalea Rd BS22 32 A5
Azelin Ave BS13 22 B5

B

BABCARY 174 C7
Babcary La BA22 174 B8
Babwell Rd BA9 177 D6
Babylon Hill
Sherborne DT9 188 A3
Yeovil BA21 219 F4
Babylon View BA21 219 F7
Backfields BS2 227 B4
Backfields Ct BS2 227 B4
Backfields La BS2 227 B4
Back La
Axbridge BS26 70 C2
Baltonsborough BA6 158 B5
Batcombe BA4 142 C2
Bradford Abbas DT9 187 F1
Chapel Allerton BS26 88 D1
Cheddar BS27 90 A7
Chewton Mendip BA3 75 B1
Curry Rivel TA10 171 D3
Draycott BS27 90 F2
East Chinnock BA22 196 E8
East Coker BA22 197 C7
Halstock BA22 197 C3
Ilchester BA22 173 E1
Keynsham BS31 24 E6
Back La *continued*
Kingston Seymour BS21 16 A5
Kington Magna SP8 177 E2
Litton BA3 75 E2
Maiden Bradley BA12 144 C2
Marshfield SN14 13 F8
Martock TA12 185 D4
Middlezoy TA7 155 B3
Montacute TA15 186 B3
Moorlinch TA7 155 D8
North Perrott TA18 196 C4
Pill BS20 4 C5
Pilton BA4 204 D3
Rimpton BA22 188 A8
Rowberrow BS25 53 A1
Shepton Mallet, Darshill BA4 204 F6
Shepton Mallet, Downside BA4 205 C8
Sherborne DT9 225 D4
Stoney Stratton BA4 141 F2
Street BA16 207 C6
Street, Butleigh Wootton BA6 157 C6
Westbury-sub-Mendip BA5 110 E6
Whitelackington TA19 221 F6
Backlane Dro BA6 158 C5
Back Of Kingsdown Par BS6 227 A4
Back River Dro BA16 138 F2
Back St
Ash TA12 186 A7
Bampton EX16 164 B1
Bradford On Tone TA4 167 F1
Leighton BA11 142 E6
Long Sutton TA10 172 E4
Martock TA12 185 F7
West Camel BA22 174 D3
Weston-Super-Mare BS23 48 E7
Winsham TA20 194 E1
Back Stoke La BS9 5 F6
Back Town BA6 157 E4
Back Way TA4 150 B8
Backways La TA21 179 F6
BACKWELL 19 B6
Backwell Bow BS48 9 C1
Backwell CE Jun Sch BS48 19 C5
Backwell Comm BS48 19 B8
BACKWELL COMMON 19 B8
BACKWELL GREEN 19 D8
Backwell Hill Rd BS48 19 E5
Backwell Sch BS48 19 B6
Backwell Wlk BS13 21 F8
Bacon Dr TA1 213 D3
BADBURY 183 F7
Badcox BA11 119 E4
Badenham Gr BS11 4 F8
Baden Ho BA1 228 B4
Badger Hts BA22 218 B5
Badger Pk TA24 201 C4
Badger Rise BS20 1 F3
Badgers Cl
Bourton SP8 161 F1
Street BA16 207 A5
Taunton TA1 212 B3
Badger's Cross
Oakhill BA3 114 F5
Somerton TA11 211 C1
Badger's Cross La TA11 211 C2
Badgers Folly BA7 214 B5
Badgers Green Rd BA16 207 A5
Badgers Hill BA11 120 A5
Badgers Holt BS14 23 C6
Badgers' La TA20 223 E1
Badgers The BS22 32 D3
BADGER STREET 182 B6
Badgers Way BS24 49 F8
BADGWORTH 88 B6
Badgworth Barns BS26 88 D5
Badgworth Ct BS26 88 C5
Badgworth La BS26 88 C4
Badlake La EX36 162 D6
Badlake Moor Cross TA22 162 D7
Badman Cl BS39 77 D5
Badminton Ct 17 BS23 30 C1
Badminton Gdns BA1 44 C8
Bagber Cross Rds DT10 190 D3
Bagborough Dr TA6 208 F2
Bagborough La BA4 141 C2
Bagborough Rd TA2 212 F7
Baggridge Hill BA2 80 F7
Baggs La BS27 90 F2
BAGLEY 109 A1
BAGLEY GREEN 222 A3
Bagley Rd TA21 222 A3
Bagnell Cl BS14 23 E5
Bagnell Rd BS14 23 E5
BAILBROOK 28 D3
Bailbrook Gr BA1 28 C3
Bailbrook La BA1 28 D3
Baildon Cres BS23 49 A4
Baildon Ct 2 BS23 48 F4
Baildon Rd BS23 49 A4
Bailey Cl BS22 49 E8
Bailey Ct BS20 2 F6
Bailey Hill BA7 214 C5
Bailey's Dro BA6 158 B5
Baileys Gate TA4 167 F6
Bailey's Knapp EX16 178 B4
Bailey's La BA4 142 B1
Bailey St TA6 209 B5
Bailiffs Cl BS26 70 C1
Bailiffs' Wall BS26 70 B1
Baily Cl BA6 206 E7
Bainsbury View BA3 96 F1
Bakehouse 1 TA16 195 F7
Bakehouse La DT9 187 E1
Bakelite Mus The★ TA4 202 C2
Baker Cl 8 BS21 6 B1
Bakeries The TA11 211 D3
Baker's Bldgs BS40 35 D2
Bakers Cl TA1 212 A3
Baker's Cross TA3 191 D7
Bakers Ct TA13 220 C4
Bakersfield TA20 194 E1
Bakers La
Barrington TA19 184 C5
Chilcompton BA3 96 D3
Lower Langford BS40 53 C8
Baker's La
Churchinford TA3 191 D7
Wellington TA21 222 E6
Bakers Orch TA4 151 B5
Bakers Par BA2 60 B2
Bakers Pk BS13 22 B6
Baker St
Babcary TA11 174 C7
Frome BA11 119 E5
Weston-Super-Mare BS23 48 E8
Bakery La BA4 140 F3
Balch Rd BA5 203 C4
Baldwin Rd TA1 213 B5
Baldwin St BS1 227 A2
Ballance St BA1 228 B4
Ballfield Rd TA24 200 F8
Ballhill La EX16 164 B1
Ball La
Doulting BA4 141 F7
Isle Abbotts TA3 183 E7
Spaxton TA2 & TA5 152 B2
Balls Barn La BS24 33 A2
Ball's Hill BA22, TA15 186 C4
Ball's La TA5 153 E4
Ball The
Dunster TA24 201 E2
Minehead TA24 200 F8
Balmoral Dr TA8 85 B1
Balmoral Ho TA6 209 C4
Balmoral Rd
Keynsham BS31 24 E4
Yeovil BA21 219 E6
Balmoral Way BS22 31 D2
Balsam Cl BA9 216 D3
Balsam Fields BA9 216 D3
Balsam La BA9 216 E3
Balsam Pk BA9 216 C3
Baltic Pl BS20 4 D4
BALTONSBOROUGH 158 A6
Baltonsborough CE Prim Sch BA6 158 A6
Baltonsborough Rd BA6 157 E4
Balustrade 17 BA1 28 B1
Bamfield BS14 23 A6
BAMPTON 164 C1
Bampton 5 BS22 31 F2
Bampton Ave TA20 223 B5
Bampton Cl BS13 22 B7
Bampton Down Rd EX16 178 A7
Bampton Prim Sch EX16 164 B1
Bampton St TA24 200 F6
Banbury La BA6 157 E3
Bancks St TA24 200 F7
Bancombe Ct TA11 211 B5
Bancombe Rd TA11 211 A4
Banfield Cl BS11 5 A8
Bangers DT9 188 F5
Bangrove Wlk BS11 4 E8
Banister Gr BS4 22 D7
Banking Ct 4 TA18 224 C6
Bankland La TA7 154 B1
Bank Pl BS20 4 D4
Banks Cl BS21 16 D8
Bank Sq TA22 163 D6
Bank St
Highbridge TA9 104 D3
Williton TA4 202 D2
Bannerdown Cl BA1 29 B4
Bannerdown Dr BA1 29 A4
Bannerdown Rd BA1 29 C5
Bannerleigh La BS8 11 E6
Bannerleigh Rd BS8 11 E6
Banneson Rd TA5 134 B2
Bantock Cl BS4 22 D6
Bantry Rd BS4 22 E8
BANWELL 51 B3
Banwell Cl
Bristol BS13 22 A8
Keynsham BS31 25 A2
Taunton TA1 213 D4
Banwell Prim Sch BS29 51 B3
Banwell Rd
Banwell BS26, BS29 68 E8
Bath BA2 62 D8
Locking BS24 50 B3
Winscombe BS25, BS29 69 E8
Banyard Rd BS20 3 E5
Barbary Cl BA8 176 D3
Barberry Dr TA20 223 F5
Barberry Farm Rd BS49 17 B1
Barber's La TA21 180 F7
Barbers Mead TA2 213 C7
Barbour Gdns BS13 22 D3
Barbour Rd BS13 22 D3
Barclay St TA6 209 A5
Barcroft BA12 144 B2
Barcroft Cres TA3 170 A1
Barcroft La TA13 220 B6
Bardel Ct BA22 218 B6
BARE ASH 153 B6
Barford Cl TA5 152 F7
Barford Rd TA5 152 F7
Barham Ct BA22 218 A5
Barhams Cl TA6 209 A7
Barkham Cl BA5 203 F5
Barle Cl TA1 213 D4
Barley Cl BA5 203 C3
Barley Croft
Bristol BS9 5 F5
Somerton TA11 211 B3
Barley Cross BS22 32 A5
Barley Wood Walled Garden★ BS40 35 F3
Barlinch Cl TA2 213 B7
Barlynch Ct BA21 218 D6
Barnabas Cl BS26 70 D2
Barnaby Cl BA3 78 B2
Barnard Ave BA16 207 B3
Barnard Ct BA5 203 B4
Barnard's Cl BS49 34 C7
Barnard Wlk BS31 24 D4
Barn Cl
Crewkerne TA18 224 B5
Frome BA11 119 D3
Nether Stowey TA5 134 B2
Somerton TA11 211 B3
Street BA16 207 C6
Wiveliscombe TA4 210 A7
Barn Cres TA18 224 B5
Barn Ct BA21 187 C5
Barn End BS40 74 E3
Barnes Cl
Castle Cary BA7 214 C6
Wells BA5 203 B4
Barnes Close Mead TA22 163 D6
Barnet Cl BA21 218 E7
Barnetts Well BS27 90 F2
Barnfield Way BA1 29 B3
Barn Gn BA6 206 E3
Barnhay 6 EX16 164 B1
Barn Hill BA2 79 F5
Barn La
Clutton BS39 59 A7
Crewkerne TA18 195 E6
Barn Meads Rd TA21 222 E4
Barn Orchard TA14 185 E3
Barn Pool BS25 70 F8
Barns Cl
Barrow Gurney BS48 20 E4
Nailsea BS48 8 E2
Barnsclose TA22 163 D6
Barns Close Ind Est TA22 163 D6
Barnsclose N TA22 163 D6
Barnsclose W TA22 163 D6
Barns Gd BS21 16 E8
Barn St TA18 224 B6
Barnstaple Ct BS4 22 E8
Barnstaple Rd BS4 22 E8
Barnstaple Wlk BS4 22 F8
Barnwood Ct BS48 8 B1
Baron Cl BS30 25 E8
Barons Cl BS3 11 F3
Barossa Pl BS1 227 A1
Barpark Cnr EX15 180 E3
Barpool La TA11 211 D6
BARR 168 B3
Barracks Cl BA22 218 B7
Barrack's La BS11 4 D8
BARREN DOWN 205 C7
Barrendown La BA4 205 C6
Barrie Way TA8 104 C6
BARRINGTON 184 D5
Barrington Broadway TA10 184 D6
Barrington Cl TA1 212 C1
Barrington Court★ TA19 184 D5
Barrington Court Cotts TA19 184 D5
Barrington Hill National Nature Reserve★ TA19 183 A4
Barrington Hill Rd TA19 182 F4
Barrington Pl BA4 204 F5
Barrington Rd TA8 104 C8
BARROW
Wells 140 B4
Wincanton 161 B3
BARROW COMMON 21 B4
Barrow Court La BS19 20 B5
Barrow Cswy BA5 138 F8
Barrow Ct
Barrow Gurney BS48 20 A5
Tickenham BS21 7 F4
Barrow Dr TA1 213 E5
BARROW GURNEY 20 E5
Barrow Hill
Stalbridge DT10 190 B4
Stourton Caundle DT10 189 F1
Barrow Hill Cres BS11 4 C7
Barrow Hill Rd BS11 4 D6
Barrow Ho 25 BA4 205 B6
Barrow Hospital BS48 20 F6
Barrow Hospl BS48 21 A6
Barrow La
Charlton Musgrove BA9 161 B3
North Wootton BA4 140 B4
Pilton BA4 140 F3
Winford BS40 20 F1
Barrow Lea DT10 190 B4
Barrowmead Dr BS11 4 F7
Barrow Pk BS27 90 A8
Barrow Rd
Bath BA2 44 C1
Hutton BS24 49 E2
Barrows Cl TA6 208 E2
Barrows Croft BS27 90 A8
Barrows Ct BA22 196 E8
Barrows La TA14 185 E2
Barrows Rd BS27 90 A8
Barrow St BS48 20 D5
Barrows The
Cheddar BS27 90 A8
Barrows The *continued*
Weston-Super-Mare BS22 49 C7
Barrow Stile BA4 140 F3
BARROW VALE 59 D5
Barrow Water La BA9 161 A3
Barrow Wood La BS27 110 A7
Barry Cl BS24 49 A1
Barry La BA22 196 F6
Barrymore Cl TA10 172 A6
Barstable Ho BS2 227 C3
Bartec 4 BA20 218 C3
Bartholomew Row BA2 60 B2
Bartlett Cl
Frome BA11 120 C6
Taunton TA1 212 B1
Bartlett Ct 1 TA18 224 C6
Bartlett Ct BA20 218 D3
Bartlett Mews BA21 219 F7
Bartlett Pk
Chard TA20 223 E3
Yeovil BA20 218 D3
Bartletts Ct BA2 228 C1
Bartletts La TA4 167 A4
Bartletts Pl BA21 218 D5
Bartletts Row TA11 211 D4
Bartlett St 6 BA1 228 B3
Bartletts Way BS24 50 A4
BARTON 69 B6
Barton Bldgs BA1 228 B3
Barton Cl
Berrow TA8 84 F5
Taunton TA1 212 D3
Barton Cross EX16 162 E5
Barton Dro BS25 69 D5
Barton Gdns DT9 225 B4
Barton Gn TA3 168 D1
Barton Hey 2 TA4 167 F8
Barton Hill SP8 177 E2
Barton La TA3 169 C4
Barton Rd
Barton St David TA11 158 A2
Berrow TA8 84 F4
Bristol BS2 227 C2
Butleigh BA6 157 E3
Minehead TA24 201 B4
Winscombe BS26 69 C6
Barton Rise TA7 137 B3
BARTON ST DAVID 158 A2
Barton St
Bath BA1 228 B2
Bristol BS1 227 A4
Bartons The
Bishops Lydeard TA4 167 E8
Ilchester BA22 173 E1
South Petherton TA13 220 E3
Barton The
Bleadon BS24 67 C6
Charlton Adam TA11 173 F7
Corston BA2 43 A7
Huish Champflower TA4 165 E8
Norton St Philip BA2 81 E4
Barton Vale BS2 227 C2
Barton Villas BA3 116 F6
Barton Way TA3 170 C4
Barton Wlk BA11 119 D2
BARWICK 197 F8
Barwick Ho BS11 4 E7
Barwick & Stoford Com Prim Sch BA22 197 F8
Basketfield La BA6 139 D1
Batallers La TA23 131 D2
Bat Alley DT10 190 F5
BATCH 66 F3
Batch Bsns Pk BS24 66 F2
Batch Cl TA7 136 C4
Batch La
Clutton BS39 58 F3
Lympsham BS24 66 F3
Batchpool La BA8 176 F3
Batch Rd TA7 136 B5
Batch The
Ashcott TA7 156 B7
Backwell BS48 19 D1
Batheaston BA1 28 F3
Burrington BS40 54 B3
Butcombe BS40 55 B8
Chew Magna BS40 39 B3
Churchill BS25 52 F4
Draycott BS27 90 F2
Farmborough BA2 60 A6
Hinton Charterhouse BA2 63 E1
Saltford BS31 25 F3
19 Shepton Mallet BA4 205 B6
Wincanton BA9 216 B4
Yatton BS49 34 B7
Batch View BA16 207 B6
BATCOMBE 142 D1
Bateman's Cross TA20 198 E7
BATH 228 A2
Bath Abbey★ BA1 228 C2
BATHAMPTON 28 F1
Bathampton La BA2 28 E1
Bathampton Prim Sch BA2 28 F2
Bath Aqua Theatre of Glass★ 10 BA1 228 C3
Bath Bridge Bsns Pk TA6 209 B6
Bath City FC Twerton Park BA2 44 B5
Bath Cl BA6 206 D6
BATHEALTON 166 B3
BATHEASTON 28 F4
Batheaston CE Prim Sch BA1 28 F4

BATHFORD 29 C1
Bathford CE Prim Sch BA1 29 C2
Bathford Hill
Bathford BA1 29 B2
Compton Dando BS39 41 E5
Bathford Manor BA1 29 C2
Bath Foyer The BA2 44 A6
Bath Hill
Keynsham BS31 24 F5
Wellow BA2 62 D2
Bath House Ct TA1 212 E3
Bath La TA20 223 C3
Bath Meadow Dr TA22 163 E6
Bath New Rd BA3 78 F4
Bath Old Rd BA3 78 F4
Bath Pl TA1 212 F3
BATHPOOL 213 E6
Bath Postal Mus★ BA1 228 C3
Bath Racecourse★ BA1 27 A6
Bath Rd
Ashcott TA7 156 B7
Bawdrip TA7 136 D2
Beckington BA11 101 D5
Bitton BS30 25 D8
Blagdon BS40 55 B1
Bridgwater TA6 209 C7
Bristol BS2 227 C1
Farmborough BA2 59 E5
Frome BA11 120 A7
Horrington BA3, BA5 113 D5
Kelston BA1, BS30 26 B6
Kingsdown SN13 29 F5
Moorlinch TA7 155 E8
Norton St Philip BA2 81 E5
Oakhill BA3 115 B3
Paulton BS39 77 F6
Peasedown St John BA2 79 C7
Saltford BS31 25 D3
Shepton Mallet BA4 141 C8
Stawell TA7 137 B1
Upper Langford BS40 53 D3
Wells BA5 112 E1
Bath Riverside Bsns Pk BA2 228 B1
Bath's Original Theatre Royal & Masonic Mus★ BA1 228 C2
Bath Spa Sta BA1 228 C1
Bath Spa Univ Coll BA1 27 E1
Bath Spa University Coll (Newton Pk Campus) BA2 43 B5
Bath Sq TA20 223 C3
Bath St
Bath BA1 228 C2
Bristol BS1 227 B2
Chard TA20 223 C3
Cheddar BS27 90 B7
Frome BA11 119 F4
Bathurst Cl TA8 104 D8
Bathurst Par BS1 227 A1
Bathurst Rd BS22 49 C8
Bath View BA3 96 F1
BATHWAY 94 E5
Bathwell La DT9 217 D1
BATHWICK 45 B7
Bathwick Hill BA2 45 C6
Bathwick Rise BA2 45 B7
Bathwick St BA1, BA2 228 C4
Batstone Cl BA1 28 B2
BATTEN'S GREEN 182 F5
Battery La BS20 2 D7
Battery Rd BS20 2 D6
Battin's Knap TA4 150 A3
Batt La TA3 183 C8
BATTLEBOROUGH 86 C1
Battleborough La TA9 86 B1
Battle La BS40 39 A3
Battle St EX15 180 E1
Battleton TA22 163 D6
Batts Bow Bridge TA9 104 E1
Batts La
Oakhill BA3 114 E3
Pilsdon DT6 199 F2
Batt's La TA10 172 D5
Battson Rd BS14 23 E4
Batts Pk TA1 212 E1
Baulditch La TA3 184 B8
Bauntons Cl DT9 217 C2
Baunton's Orch DT9 217 C2
Bawden Cl TA7 136 E4
BAWDRIP 136 E2
Bawdrip La TA7 136 E2
Bawler's La TA10 171 C3
Bayer Bldg The BA2 228 B1
BAYFORD 216 F5
Bayford Hill BA9 216 E4
Bayford La BA9 177 B7
Bayford Rd TA6 209 C6
Bay Hill TA19 221 D4
Bay La BS27 90 F2
Bayliss Ctr The 4 BA16 207 C5
Baymead Cl 11 TA6 153 F4
Baymead La TA6 153 F3
Baymead Mdw 5 TA6 153 F3
Baynes Cl TA21 222 E7
Bay Rd
Clevedon BS21 6 D6
Porlock TA24 124 A4
Bay's La BA3 115 A7
Bays The BS27 90 C8
Baytree Ct BS22 31 D1
Baytree Rd BS22 31 C1
Bay Tree Rd
Bath BA1 28 B2
Bay Tree Rd *continued*
Clevedon BS21 6 E1
Baytree Sch BS24 50 A8
Baytree View BS22 31 D1
Bay Tree View BS22 31 D1
Bay View TA23 202 D6
Bay View Gdns TA8 104 B5
Baze La EX35 122 B4
Bazelands Hill BA8 190 B7
Beach Ave BS21 6 C2
Beach Ct BS23 48 D6
Beach End Rd BS23 48 C2
Beach Hill BS20 2 C6
Beachlands Pk BS22 31 A6
Beachley Wlk BS11 4 D7
Beach Mews BS21 6 C4
Beach Rd
Weston-Super-Mare BS23 48 D6
Weston-Super-Mare, Kewstoke BS22 31 A5
Beach Rd E BS20 2 D6
Beach Rd W BS20 2 C6
Beach The BS21 6 C4
Beach Tree Cross TA4 166 F6
Beachwood View BA2 44 C2
Beacon TA19 221 B5
Beaconfield Ho TA6 209 A2
Beaconfield Rd BA20 218 E1
BEACON HILL 27 F1
Beacon Hill View DT9 175 D1
Beacon La
Corton Denham DT9 175 D2
Wellington TA21 180 C4
Beacon Rd
Bath BA1 28 A1
Minehead TA24 200 F8
Beaconsfield Rd
Clevedon BS21 6 E3
Weston-Super-Mare BS23 48 E7
Beaconsfield Way BA11 120 B7
Beacon View
Coleford BA3 116 E7
Shepton Mallet BA4 205 A4
Beadon La TA16 195 F7
Beadon Rd TA1 213 C5
Beafort Cl BS24 50 C3
Beale Cl BS14 23 E6
Beale Way TA8 104 D5
Bean Acre The BS11 4 D8
Bearbridge Rd BS13 21 F4
BEARD HILL 141 C3
BEARDLY BATCH 205 C1
Beard's Yd TA10 171 F5
BEAR FLAT 44 F4
Bearley Bridge Rd 15 TA12 185 E6
Bearley Ho 26 TA12 185 E6
Bearley La BA22 186 B7
Bearley Rd 27 TA12 185 E6
Bears Meadow La TA5 133 C6
Bear Yard Mews 2 BS8 226 A2
Beasley Ct TA20 223 B5
Beastway La TA24 131 B3
Beatty Way TA8 104 C7
Beauchamp Gdns TA3 183 A7
Beauchamps Dr BA3 97 A5
Beaufitz Pl TA20 193 F1
Beauford Pk TA2 168 B4
Beauford Sq BA1 228 B2
Beaufort Ave BA3 78 A2
Beaufort Bldgs 7 BS8 11 F7
Beaufort Cl EX16 178 D1
Beaufort Ct
Clevedon BS21 6 C5
Ilchester BA22 173 E2
Beaufort E BA1 28 C1
Beaufort Gdns
2 Nailsea BS48 8 D1
South Petherton TA13 220 B5
Beaufort Mews
3 Bath BA1 28 C1
10 Bristol BS8 11 F7
Beaufort Pl BA1 28 C1
Beaufort Rd
Taunton TA1 212 E5
Weston-Super-Mare BS23 48 F7
Beaufort Villas 8 BA1 28 B1
Beaufort W 11 BA1 28 B1
Beauley Rd BS3 226 B1
Beaulieu Dr BA21 218 D6
Beaumont BA1 27 F1
Beaumont Cl BS23 48 F4
Beaumont Ho BA21 219 D5
Beau St BA1 228 B2
Beavor La EX13 198 A1
BECKERY 206 B4
Beckery New Rd BA6 206 B3
Beckery Old Rd BA6 206 B3
Beckery Rd BA6 206 B4
Becket Dr BS22 32 A3
Becket Pl BA5 203 D3
Becket Prim Sch BS22 32 A2
Becket Rd BS22 32 A4
Becket's La BS48 18 E8
Beckford Ct 1 BA2 45 B7
Beckford Gdns
Bath BA2 45 B8
Bristol BS14 23 A3
Beckford Rd BA2 45 B7
Beckford's Twr & Mus★ BA1 27 D4
Beckhampton Rd BA2 44 D5
BECKINGTON 101 E4
Beckington BS24 49 A2
Beckington CE Fst Sch BA11 101 E4
Beckington Cres TA20 223 D3
Becks Bsns Pk BS23 49 A7
Becks Field 2 TA14 185 F4
Beck's La BA3 116 D6
Beckworth Cl TA6 209 C3
Bector La BA3 116 C4
Bede St DT9 225 E5
Bedford Cl TA6 209 C3
Bedford Ct BA1 45 B8
Bedford Rd
Wells BA5 112 E1
Weston-Super-Mare BS23 48 E4
Yeovil BA21 219 D8
Bedford St BA1 45 B8
BEDLAM 119 B8
BEDMINSTER DOWN 22 B8
Bedminster Down Sch BS13 21 F7
Bedwell La TA7 155 C2
Bedwin Cl BS20 1 F4
Beech Ave
Bath BA2 45 E5
Shepton Mallet BA4 205 A6
Beech Cl
Doulting BA4 141 E6
Shipham BS25 70 F8
Taunton TA2 212 F8
Beechcroft BS41 21 D2
Beech Croft BS14 23 B5
Beech Ct
Bristol BS14 23 A5
Frome BA11 120 B7
Taunton TA1 212 E3
2 Wellington TA21 222 D6
Beech Dr
Bridgwater TA6 209 D5
Nailsea BS48 9 A3
Shipham BS25 70 E8
BEECHEN CLIFF 228 B1
Beechen Cliff Boys' Sch BA2 45 A4
Beechen Cliff Rd BA2 228 B1
Beeches The
Bath BA2 44 D1
Langport TA10 172 A6
Sandford BS25 52 B4
Wheddon Cross TA24 129 E1
Beechfield Cl BS41 11 C2
Beechfield Gr BS9 5 C8
Beechfield Inf Sch TA9 104 D4
Beech Gr
Bath BA2 44 D4
Somerton TA11 211 D5
Wellington TA21 222 C6
Beech Grove Prim Sch TA21 222 C6
Beech Hill TA21 222 F5
Beeching Cl TA20 223 E6
Beech La
Axminster EX13 198 E1
Stoke Trister BA9 177 C8
Beechmont Dr BS24 49 A1
Beechmount Cl BS24 48 F1
Beechmount Ct BS14 23 B8
Beechmount Gr BS14 23 B8
Beech Rd
Bridgwater TA6 209 D5
20 Martock TA12 185 E6
Saltford BS31 25 E3
Shipham BS25 70 F8
Street BA16 207 C3
Yatton BS49 34 C8
Beech Terr BA3 78 E1
Beech Tree TA23 130 D1
Beech Tree Cl TA4 210 C4
Beech Tree Cross
Clatworthy TA4 149 E1
Dulverton TA22 163 C7
Monksilver TA4 132 B1
Beech Tree Hill TA5 152 C6
Beech Way BA4 141 E1
Beechwood
Bridgwater TA6 208 E2
Yeovil BA20 218 F2
Beechwood Ave
Frome BA11 120 A5
Locking BS24 50 A5
Beechwood Cl
Bristol BS14 23 C8
Frome BA11 120 A5
Beechwood Dr
Crewkerne TA18 224 C7
Portishead BS20 1 E5
Beechwood Rd
Bath BA2 45 B1
Easton-in-G BS20 4 A4
Nailsea BS48 8 D2
Portishead BS20 1 E5
Beehive Yd BA1 228 C3
Beek's La SN14, BA1 13 D5
Beer Door TA10 155 E2
Beer Dro TA10 155 E3
Beere Cross EX36 162 A5
Beer La
Burlescombe EX16 179 B2
Dulverton TA22 163 B5
Beer Rd TA10 155 E1
Beer St
Curry Mallet TA3 183 C7
Yeovil BA20 219 A4
Bees Ho BS21 6 C2
Beetham La TA20 193 B6
Beggar Bush La BS8 11 B6
Beggarswell Cl BS2 227 C4
Beggs Cl 4 TA6 153 F3
Behind Berry TA11 211 D4
Behind Butts TA14 185 E1
Behind Hayes BA8 176 D3
Behind Town TA11 157 B4
Bekynton Ave BA5 203 F4
Belcombe Dro TA20 193 B7
Belfast Wlk BS4 22 E8
Belfield Ct TA8 104 A8
Belgrave Cres BA1 228 C4
Belgrave Ct 2 TA2 212 F6
Belgrave Pl
Bath BA1 228 C4
Bristol BS8 226 A3
Taunton TA2 212 F6
Belgrave Rd
Bath BA1 28 B1
Bristol BS8 226 B4
Weston-Super-Mare BS22 49 B8
Belgrave Terr 2 BA1 28 A1
Bellamy Ave BS13 22 C4
Belland Dr BS14 22 F4
Bella View Gdns BA6 206 D4
Bella Vista Rd BA1 228 B4
Bell Barn Rd BS9 5 D6
Bell Chase BA20 218 D5
Bell Cl
Bridgwater TA6 208 F6
Farmborough BA2 59 F6
Westbury-sub-Mendip BA5 110 E6
Belle View Terr TA20 198 C8
BELLE VUE 78 B3
Bellevue BS8 226 B2
Belle Vue
Midsomer Norton BA3 78 B3
Washford TA23 131 E3
Belle Vue Cl BA2 79 D7
Bellevue Cotts BS8 226 B2
Bellevue Cres BS8 226 B2
Bellevue Ct
Bristol BS8 226 B2
Clevedon BS21 6 D4
Bellevue Mans BS21 6 D4
Bellevue Rd BS21 6 D4
Bellevue Terr BS8 226 B2
Belle Vue Terr TA18 224 B6
Bellfield BA3 117 A3
Bellhanger Ct BA1 228 B4
Bell Hill
Chewton Mendip BA3 94 B7
Norton St Philip BA2 81 E4
Bellhorse La BS40 74 C5
Bellifants BA2 60 A6
Bell La
Bristol BS1 227 A3
Chard TA19, TA20 193 F7
Chewton Mendip BA3 94 B7
Cossington TA7 137 A3
Thurloxton TA2 153 D1
Bell Language Sch The BA1 44 C8
Bellman's Cross BA8 190 B7
Bellmoor La TA19 194 A7
Bell Orch TA10 171 D4
Bellotts Rd BA2 44 C6
Bell Pit Brow BS48 9 B2
Bell Sq BS40 54 E3
Bellum SN14 13 E8
BELLUTON 40 D6
Belluton La BS39 40 D5
Belluton Villas BS39 40 D5
Bell Wlk BS40 35 E2
Belmont Cl TA6 208 B4
Belmont Dr
Failand BS8 10 B3
Taunton TA1 212 E2
Belmont Hill BS48 10 B1
Belmont Ho 14 BA20 219 B4
Belmont Rd
Bath BA2 45 C1
Hatch Beauchamp TA3 183 A8
Taunton TA1 212 C3
Winscombe BS25 70 A8
Belmont Terr TA19 184 E3
Belmont The BS21 6 D3
Belmore Gdns BA2 44 B3
Belstone Wlk BS4 22 C8
Belton Ct BA1 27 B2
Belton Rd BS20 2 A6
Belvedere BA1 228 B4
Belvedere Cl TA5 135 B2
Belvedere Cres BS22 31 C1
Belvedere Ct 3 TA21 222 D6
Belvedere Grange TA11 211 E3
Belvedere Rd
Taunton TA1 212 F5
Yeovil BA21 219 E7
Belvedere Trad Est TA1 212 E5
Belvoir Rd 6 BA2 44 D5
Bemberry Bank TA24 130 B5
Benares Ct TA24 201 A8
Bences Cl SN14 13 F8
Benches La BS40 37 D3
Bench La TA20 193 D5
Ben Cross TA13 220 A4
Benedictine Ct BA6 206 C4
Benedict St BA6 206 D4
Benhole La TA5 134 B8
Bennell Batch BA3 96 E4
Bennell Cl BA3 96 E4
Bennell Cotts BA3 96 E4
Bennett Gdns BA11 119 D4
Bennett La BA1 28 A1
Bennett Rd TA9 104 F4
Bennett's Cl BA5 204 B7
Bennetts Field Trad Est BA9 216 C2
Bennett's La BA3, BA5 114 B7
Bennett's Rd BA1 28 C3
Bennett St BA1 228 B3
Bennetts Way BS21 6 E5
Bennett Way BS1, BS8 11 F5
BENTER 115 D7
Benter Cross BA3 115 D7
Bentley Cl BS14 22 F3
Bentley Rd BS22 32 B3
Ben Travers Way TA8 104 C6
Benville Ave BS9 5 C8
Bere La BA6 206 E4
Bere Mills La TA19 194 B7
Beresford Cl
Burnham-on-S TA8 104 C7
Saltford BS31 25 E2
Beresford Gdns BA1 27 A3
Beretun Orch BA6 206 E3
Berhill TA7 156 C7
Berkeley Ave
Bristol BS8 226 C3
Midsomer Norton BA3 78 A2
Berkeley Cres
Bristol BS8 226 B3
Weston-Super-Mare BS23 48 C2
Berkeley Ct BA2 45 C6
Berkeley Gdns
Bruton BA10 215 E6
Keynsham BS31 24 E4
Berkeley Ho
Bath BA1 228 C4
Bristol BS1 226 C3
Berkeley Pl
Bath BA1 228 C4
Bristol BS8 226 B3
Berkeley Rd
Street BA16 207 E6
Yeovil BA20 219 A4
Berkeley Sq BS8 226 B3
BERKLEY 121 A7
Berkley Ave BS8 226 B3
Berkley CE Fst Sch BA11 121 A7
Berkley Cross BA11 120 F6
Berkley Ct BA22 173 E2
BERKLEY DOWN 120 C5
Berkley La
Beckington BA11 101 D3
Frome BA11 120 D8
BERKLEY MARSH 120 F7
Berkley Rd BA11 120 B6
Berkley St BA11 121 A8
Berlington Ct BS1 227 B1
Bernard Cres TA24 200 F6
Bernard Herridge Ct BA9 216 D4
Bernard Ireland Ho BA1 27 B1
Bernard Taylor Homes 9 TA1 213 A4
Berners Cl BS4 22 D7
BERROW 84 E5
Berrow CE Prim Sch TA8 84 F4
Berrow Lodge 7 BS23 48 E5
Berrow Rd TA8 85 A2
Berry Cl TA6 208 E2
Berrydale Ave TA6 208 F6
Berry Hill
Mells BA11 118 A6
Nunney BA11 143 B8
Berry La EX13 198 F3
Berryman Cl BA4 205 A5
Berryman Ct BA5 203 B4
Bertha Terr TA9 104 D3
Berwick Cl TA1 212 C1
Beryl Gr BS14 23 C8
Beryl Knapp BA22 197 B8
Beryl La BA5 203 F6
Besley Ct BA5 203 B4
Bests Field TA12 185 B8
Bethell Mead TA4 167 E6
BETTISCOMBE 199 E2
Beverley Cl
Frome BA11 119 D3
Taunton TA2 212 E6
Beverley Dr TA23 202 C7
Beverley Gdns BS9 5 D7
Bewdley Rd BA2 45 B4
Bewley Ct TA20 223 B4
Bews La TA20 223 B5
Bibors Hill TA4 165 E4
Bibury Cl BS48 9 A1
Bibury Ho BA1 27 B2
BICKENHALL 182 E5
Bickenhall La TA3 182 F6
Bickfield La BS40 74 B8
Bicking's Close La TA4 166 A4
Bicknell Gdns BA21 219 B8
BICKNOLLER 132 F2
Bidbrooke La EX36 162 A6
Biddiscombe Cl TA6 208 E1
BIDDISHAM 87 E8
Biddisham Cl 6 BS48 8 E1
Biddisham La BS26 87 E7
Biddlesden Rd BA21 218 C7
Biddle St BS49 34 B7
Bideford Cres BS4 22 F8
Bideford Rd BS22 31 F2
Bifield Cl BS14 23 F5
Bifield Gdns BS14 23 E5
Bifield Rd BS14 23 F5
Bignal Rand Cl BA5 203 B3
Bignal Rand Dr BA5 203 B3
Bignell Cl BS25 69 F8
Big Tree Cl BS26 69 C3
Bigwood La BS1 226 C2
Bilberry Cl BS9 5 C8
Bilberry Gr TA1 168 F1
Bilbie Cl BS40 56 E8
Bilbie Rd
Chew Stoke BS40 56 E8
Weston-Super-Mare BS22 32 B3
BILBROOK 131 C4
Bilbury La
Bath BA1 228 B2
Glastonbury BA6 206 F3

Billand Cl BS13 ... 21 E3
Billetfield TA1 ... 212 F3
Billet St TA1 ... 212 F3
Billicombe La TA7 ... 155 C8
Billing's Hill BS28 ... 108 C4
Billy La TA4 ... 210 D7
Binces La BA2 ... 42 E3
Bince's Lodge La BA3 ... 78 B3
BINCOMBE ... 134 A2
Bincombe Dr TA18 ... 224 C7
Bincombe Rd TA6 ... 209 C4
Binding Cl 6 TA6 ... 153 F4
Bindon La BA11 ... 143 B2
Bindon Rd TA2 ... 212 C6
Bindwell La BA22 ... 174 F3
BINEGAR ... 114 C7
Binegar CE Prim Sch BA3 ... 114 D8
Bineham Ct TA10 ... 173 B4
Bineham La
 Ilchester BA22 ... 173 F2
 Yeovilton BA22 ... 174 A2
Bineham Rd TA10 ... 173 A4
Binford Pl TA6 ... 209 A5
Binford's La TA4 ... 151 A4
Binhay Rd BS49 ... 34 C7
Binley Gr BS14 ... 23 D5
Binmead Gdns BS13 ... 22 B4
Binnings The BS27 ... 90 F3
Birbeck Chase BS24 ... 50 C8
Birbeck Rd BS9 ... 5 E5
Bircham Cl TA6 ... 208 C4
Bircham La TA24 ... 201 C4
Bircham Rd
 Minehead TA24 ... 201 B5
 Taunton TA2 ... 213 B8
Birchanger La TA4 ... 150 A8
Birch Ave
 Bleadon BS24 ... 67 C6
 Clevedon BS21 ... 6 E4
 Puriton TA7 ... 136 C4
Birch Cl
 Bridgwater TA6 ... 209 D5
 Cannington TA5 ... 135 B2
 Cheddar BS27 ... 90 C8
 Locking BS24 ... 50 B4
 Wedmore BS28 ... 108 C3
Birch Croft BS14 ... 23 A3
Birch Ct BS31 ... 24 C4
Birchdale BA20 ... 218 D2
Birchdale Rd BS14 ... 23 A8
Birchdene BS48 ... 9 A2
Birch Dr BS40 ... 53 A5
Birches Cnr TA4 ... 152 A4
Birches The BS48 ... 9 A2
Birchfield Com Prim Sch BA21 ... 219 D7
Birchfield Rd BA21 ... 219 D8
Birch Gr
 Portishead BS20 ... 2 C4
 Taunton TA1 ... 212 E5
Birch Hill BS27 ... 90 C8
Birch Ho TA8 ... 65 F2
BIRCHILL ... 198 A5
Birchill Cross EX13 ... 198 A6
Birchill La BA11 ... 120 A1
Birch Lawn TA8 ... 104 B6
Birch Rd
 12 Martock TA12 ... 185 E6
 Radstock BA3 ... 78 E1
 Wellington TA21 ... 222 E5
Birch Wlk BA11 ... 120 B7
BIRCHWOOD ... 182 A1
Birchwood Ave BS23 ... 49 A7
Birchwood Cl BA12 ... 144 E8
Birchwood Dr BS8 ... 10 B3
Birchwood La BS39 ... 40 F2
Birdcombe Cl BS48 ... 8 E3
Birdlip Cl BS48 ... 9 A1
Bird's Cl TA18 ... 224 B6
BIRDSMOORGATE ... 199 D4
Birdwell La BS41 ... 10 F1
Birdwell Prim Sch BS41 ... 21 A8
Birdwell Rd BS41 ... 10 F1
Birkbeck Ct BS23 ... 48 D7
Birkett Rd BS23 ... 30 B1
Birkin St BS2 ... 227 C2
Birnbeck Rd BS23 ... 30 C1
Biscay Dr BS20 ... 2 F6
Biscombe Cross TA3 ... 191 B8
Bisdee Rd BS24 ... 49 D2
Bishop Ave BS22 ... 32 A3
Bishop Cl TA20 ... 223 B5
Bishop Cres BA4 ... 204 F5
Bishop Fox Dr TA1 ... 213 A2
Bishop Fox's Com Sch TA1 ... 213 A1
Bishop Henderson CE Prim Sch
 Coleford BA3 ... 116 E8
 Taunton TA1 ... 212 C2
Bishop Rd TA5 ... 134 B2
Bishops Cl BS9 ... 5 E3
Bishops Cotts
 Stogursey TA5 ... 134 B7
 Wootton Courtenay TA24 ... 129 F6
Bishops Cove BS13 ... 21 F5
Bishops Ct 4 TA21 ... 222 D6
Bishops Dr TA10 ... 172 A5
Bishops Gn TA4 ... 210 C4
Bishop's Hill TA21 ... 179 B7
BISHOP'S HULL ... 212 A4
Bishop's Hull Hill TA1 ... 212 B4
Bishop's Hull Prim Sch TA1 ... 212 B4
Bishop's Hull Rd TA1 ... 212 A3
Bishops Knoll BS9 ... 5 C3
Bishops La BA22 ... 197 A6
Bishop's La DT9 ... 187 E1
Bishopslea Cl BA5 ... 203 C3
BISHOPS LYDEARD ... 167 F8
Bishops Lydeard CE Prim Sch TA4 ... 167 E8
Bishops Lydeard Mill & Rural Life Mus TA4 ... 167 F8
Bishops Lydeard Mill & Rural Life Mus★ TA4 ... 167 F8
Bishop's Lydeard Sta TA4 ... 167 E7
Bishops Mead BS49 ... 35 A8
Bishop's Mead TA2 ... 212 E8
Bishop's Palace★ BA5 ... 203 E4
Bishops Park Way BA5 ... 203 F2
Bishop's Path TA8 ... 104 B6
Bishops Rd BS49 ... 35 A8
Bishop St
 Bristol BS2 ... 227 B4
 Faulkland BA3 ... 80 D2
Bishopston TA15 ... 186 B4
BISHOP SUTTON ... 57 D3
Bishop Sutton Prim Sch BS39 ... 57 D4
Bishops Wlk BA22 ... 173 D1
BISHOPSWOOD ... 192 E7
BISHOPSWORTH ... 22 A5
Bishopsworth CE Jun Sch BS13 ... 21 F6
Bishopsworth Rd BS13 ... 22 A7
Bishop Terr BS2 ... 227 C4
Bishport Ave BS13 ... 22 C3
Bishport Cl BS13 ... 22 B4
Bishport Gn BS13 ... 22 C3
Bitham Wlk TA7 ... 136 E3
Bittern Ave BS20 ... 2 F7
Bittern Cl BS22 ... 31 F1
Bittlemead BS13 ... 22 F4
BITTON ... 25 E7
Blackacre BS14 ... 23 C4
Blackacre Hill BA8 ... 176 D4
Blackaller La EX16 ... 163 C1
Black Bench Dro TA20 ... 223 F7
Blackberry Cl BA4 ... 205 C4
Blackberry Ct TA21 ... 222 D4
Blackberry Dr BS22 ... 32 A2
Blackberry La
 Portishead BS20 ... 1 F2
 Sherborne DT9 ... 225 D5
 Winsley BA3, BA15 ... 64 C8
Blackberry Way BA3 ... 77 F3
Blackberry Wlk TA18 ... 224 D7
Blackbird Cl BA3 ... 97 B8
Blackbird Way BA11 ... 120 B6
Blackbrook Park Ave TA1 ... 213 E4
Blackbrook Prim Sch TA1 ... 213 D3
Blackbrook Rd TA1 ... 213 E5
Blackbrook Way TA1 ... 213 E3
Black Dog Hill BA13 ... 121 E6
BLACKDOWN ... 199 D6
Blackdown BA21 ... 219 A6
Blackdown Bsns Pk TA21 ... 222 E6
Blackdown Ct BS14 ... 23 B5
Blackdown Mead BS27 ... 90 C6
Blackdown Rd
 Bridgwater TA6 ... 209 D4
 Portishead BS20 ... 2 B5
 Rockwell Green TA21 ... 222 B4
 Taunton TA2 ... 213 B8
Blackdown View
 Curry Rivel TA10 ... 171 D4
 Ilminster TA19 ... 221 C4
 Norton Fitzwarren TA2 ... 168 B5
 Nynehead TA21 ... 167 C2
 Sampford Peverell EX16 ... 178 C1
Blackdown Visitors Ctr★ EX15 ... 180 D3
Black Dro TA7 ... 155 A1
Blacker's La BA3 ... 116 E2
Blackerton Cross EX16 ... 162 E3
Blackey La BA3 ... 115 B6
BLACKFORD
 Minehead ... 129 E8
 Wedmore ... 107 E4
 Wincanton ... 175 F5
Blackford Hollow BA22 ... 175 F5
Blackford Moor Dro BS26, BS28 ... 107 B6
Blackford Moor La TA9, BS28 ... 107 B5
Blackford Rd
 Charlton Horethorne DT9 ... 176 A2
 Mark TA9 ... 106 F4
 Wedmore BS28 ... 108 A3
Blackford Way DT9 ... 176 A3
Blackfriars BS1 ... 227 A3
Blackfriars Rd BS48 ... 8 B1
Blackham La TA10 ... 155 F2
Blackhayes La EX14 ... 192 C1
Black Horse La TA1 ... 212 F5
Black La
 Axbridge BS26 ... 70 E2
 Hemyock EX15 ... 180 D2
 Holcombe Rogus TA21 ... 178 E6
Blackland Dro TA20 ... 194 A1
Blackland La TA20 ... 194 B1
Blacklands TA6 ... 208 F5
Black Mere BA22 ... 218 B5
Black Mixen La TA18 ... 224 C7
Black Monkey La TA24 ... 131 C5
BLACKMOOR
 Chew Stoke ... 38 C3
 Churchill ... 53 D6
 Wellington ... 180 E5
Blackmoor
 Clevedon BS21 ... 6 C1
 Lower Langford BS40 ... 53 C6
 3 Weston-Super-Mare BS22 ... 31 F2
Blackmoor Cl BS40 ... 53 C6
Blackmoor La 6 BA8 ... 190 A6
Blackmoor Rd
 Abbots Leigh BS8 ... 4 E2
 Taunton TA2 ... 213 B7
 Wellington TA21 ... 222 F4
Blackmoors La BS3 ... 11 E4
Blackmore Chase BA9 ... 216 D3
Blackmore Dr BA2 ... 44 C5
Blackmore La TA5 ... 135 B1
Blackmore Rd DT10 ... 190 B4
Blackmore Vale Cl BA8 ... 176 E1
Blacknell Ind Est TA18 ... 224 D5
Blacknell La TA18 ... 224 D6
Black Nore Point BS20 ... 1 F5
Black Pit Dro BA6 ... 206 D8
BLACKPOOL CORNER ... 198 D1
BLACKROCK ... 40 E8
Blackrock La BS39 ... 40 E7
Black Rock Nature Trail★ BA5 ... 72 A1
Blackrock Villas BS20 ... 2 B1
Blackrod Cotts TA13 ... 184 F4
Blacksmith La BA1 ... 28 B6
Blacksmiths La TA7 ... 155 F8
Blacksmith's La BA1 ... 26 B3
Blacksmiths Row BA21 ... 187 D6
Black's Moor Hill La TA11 ... 173 A5
Blackthorn Cl
 Biddisham BS26 ... 87 E6
 Bristol BS13 ... 22 D5
 6 North Petherton TA6 ... 153 F3
Blackthorn Dr BS20 ... 2 E5
Blackthorne Cl BA22 ... 173 E2
Blackthorn Gdns
 Taunton TA2 ... 168 F6
 Weston-Super-Mare BS22 ... 32 A1
Blackthorn Rd BS13 ... 22 D5
Blackthorn Sq BS21 ... 6 D1
Blackthorns The TA1 ... 213 C2
Blackthorn Terr BS22 ... 32 A1
Blackthorn Way
 Nailsea BS48 ... 9 A2
 Somerton TA11 ... 211 B3
 Street BA16 ... 207 A5
BLACKWATER ... 182 C2
Blackwater La
 Axminster EX13 ... 198 F3
 Wiveliscombe TA4 ... 210 A8
BLACKWELL ... 165 B5
Blackwell Rd BA22 ... 174 F3
Blackworthy Rd BA7 ... 159 C3
Bladen Cl BS20 ... 2 E4
Bladud Bldgs BA1 ... 228 C3
BLAGDON ... 54 E2
Blagdon Cl BS24 ... 48 F1
Blagdon Cres TA1 ... 212 D1
Blagdon Cross TA24 ... 129 D2
BLAGDON HILL ... 181 D5
Blagdon Hill Prim Sch TA3 ... 181 C5
Blagdon La
 Blagdon BS40 ... 54 F6
 Brompton Regis TA22, TA24 ... 148 D4
Blagdon Pk BA2 ... 44 A4
Blagdon Prim Sch BS40 ... 54 F2
Blagdon Wlk BA11 ... 120 D7
Blagrove Cl
 Bristol BS13 ... 22 C3
 Street BA16 ... 207 E6
Blagrove Cres BS13 ... 22 C3
Blagrove Hill BA6 ... 157 C6
Blagrove's Rd TA4 ... 167 C4
Blaisdon BS22 ... 49 D7
Blaise Wlk BS9 ... 5 C6
Blake End BS22 ... 31 E4
Blake Gn TA7 ... 156 B7
Blake Ind Est TA6 ... 209 A3
Blake Mus The★ TA6 ... 209 A4
Blakeney Gr BS48 ... 18 C8
Blake Pl TA6 ... 209 A5
Blake Rd
 5 Crewkerne TA18 ... 224 C5
 Wells BA5 ... 203 C5
Blake's Cres TA9 ... 104 E5
Blakes La TA5, TA6 ... 208 C7
Blake's La BA3 ... 115 D2
Blakes Rd TA6 ... 208 D6
Blake St
 2 Bridgwater TA6 ... 208 F4
 Taunton TA1 ... 213 B4
Blakeway BS28 ... 138 B6
Blandford Cl BS48 ... 8 E1
Blandford Rd BA4 ... 205 D3
BLATCHBRIDGE ... 143 F8
Blaxhold La TA5 ... 152 E5
BLEADNEY ... 139 A8
BLEADON ... 67 C7
Bleadon Hill BS23, BS24 ... 67 A8
Bleadon Mill BS24 ... 67 C5
Bleadon Rd BS24 ... 67 B7
Bleak St BA9 ... 161 E2
Blencathara Ct TA8 ... 104 A8
Blenheim Cl
 Peasedown St John BA2 ... 79 D7
 Weston-Super-Mare BS22 ... 32 A2
Blenheim Ct 10 BS1 ... 227 A4
Blenheim Gdns BA1 ... 28 A2
Blenheim Mews TA24 ... 200 F7
Blenheim Rd
 Bridgwater TA6 ... 209 D7
Blenheim Rd *continued*
 Minehead TA24 ... 201 A7
 Street BA16 ... 207 B4
 Taunton TA1 ... 213 D5
 Yeovil BA21 ... 219 D7
Blenheim View TA24 ... 201 A7
Blenheim Way BS20 ... 2 E5
Blights Hill EX16, TA22 ... 163 F3
Blindhouse La 7 BA11 ... 119 F4
Blind La
 Barton St David TA11 ... 158 A2
 Bath BA1 ... 27 C2
 Buckland St Mary TA20 ... 182 A1
 Chard TA20 ... 223 D2
 Chew Stoke BS40 ... 56 E8
 Congresbury BS49 ... 34 F6
 Drimpton DT8 ... 199 F6
 Isle Abbotts TA3 ... 183 F8
 Keinton Mandeville TA11 ... 158 B1
 Martock TA12 ... 185 D5
 Southwick BA14 ... 83 F2
 Thorncombe TA20 ... 199 B6
 Tunley BA2 ... 61 A4
Blindwell La
 Golsoncott TA23, TA24 ... 131 C1
 Skilgate TA4 ... 164 E6
BLOOMFIELD
 Bath ... 44 E3
 Timsbury ... 60 B4
Bloomfield BS24 ... 49 A2
Bloomfield Ave
 Bath BA2 ... 44 E4
 Timsbury BA2 ... 60 B3
Bloomfield Cl
 Taunton TA1 ... 213 C5
 Timsbury BA2 ... 60 B3
Bloomfield Cotts BA2 ... 79 C7
Bloomfield Cres BA2 ... 44 D2
Bloomfield Dr BA2 ... 44 D2
Bloomfield Gr BA2 ... 44 E3
Bloomfield La BS39 ... 77 E5
Bloomfield Park Rd BA2 ... 60 B3
Bloomfield Pk BA2 ... 44 E3
Bloomfield Rd
 Bath BA2 ... 44 E3
 Timsbury BA2 ... 60 B3
Bloomfield Rise BA2 ... 44 D2
Bloomfield Rise N BA2 ... 44 D2
Bloomfield Terr BA2 ... 79 C7
Bloom Row TA6 ... 209 D5
Blossom Cl TA6 ... 209 C5
BLUE ANCHOR ... 131 B6
Blue Anchor Chalets TA24 ... 131 C6
Blue Anchor Railway Mus★ TA24 ... 131 C6
Blue Anchor Sta TA24 ... 131 C6
Blue Ball Cl BA10 ... 215 E6
Bluebell Cl
 Bristol BS9 ... 5 B6
 Taunton TA1 ... 213 C1
Bluebell Rd
 Weston-Super-Mare BS22 ... 32 A6
 Yeovil BA22 ... 218 B5
Bluebell Rise BA3 ... 77 F3
Blueberry Way BS22 ... 31 F1
Blue Gate TA24 ... 145 D8
Blue Ho The BA11 ... 119 F5
Blue Reef Aquarium★ BS1 ... 226 C2
Blue Sch The BA5 ... 203 C5
Blue Stone La TA13 ... 185 B6
Bluett Rd TA21 ... 222 D4
Blue Water Dr BS24 ... 50 D3
Blundells La TA2 ... 169 C7
Blythe Ct TA1 ... 212 D1
Blythe Gdns BS22 ... 32 A3
Blythe Way TA8 ... 85 A3
Board Cross BA4 ... 205 B6
Boards La BA5 ... 204 C7
Boards Rd TA6 ... 209 A6
Boardwalk The BA16 ... 207 D7
Boarpath La TA4 ... 151 A5
Boat La BS24 ... 67 C3
Boat Stall La BA2 ... 228 C2
Bobbin La BA15 ... 64 F4
Bobbin Pk BA15 ... 64 F3
BODDEN ... 205 F7
Bodden La BA4 ... 205 E6
Boden St TA20 ... 223 C3
Boden Villas TA20 ... 223 C3
Bodley Way BS24 ... 49 E7
Bodmin Rd TA2 ... 213 A8
Bodmin Wlk BS4 ... 22 F8
Boez La TA2 ... 153 D1
Bofors Pk BA22 ... 218 A6
BOLHAM WATER ... 191 B7
Bollams Mead TA4 ... 210 C5
Bollnas Cl BA4 ... 205 C4
Bolster La BA6 ... 157 C4
Bolter's La
 Alhampton BA4, BA7 ... 159 B4
 Shepton Mallet BA4 ... 141 D8
Bolton Cl TA9 ... 104 F4
Bommertown Cross EX36 ... 162 A4
Bondfield Way TA20 ... 223 B6
Bondip Hill BA22, TA11 ... 173 D3
Bonds Cl TA20 ... 223 D6
Bond's La SN14 ... 13 E8
Bonds Pool TA10 ... 172 A5
Bond's Row TA24 ... 124 A3
Bond St
 Bridgwater TA6 ... 208 F5
 Bristol BS1 ... 227 B3
 Yeovil BA20 ... 219 B4
 Yeovil, Houndstone BA22 ... 218 B5
Bonfire Cl TA20 ... 223 C2
Bonfire La TA11 ... 173 E7
Bonham La BA12 ... 161 F4
Bonhill Rd BS39 ... 57 D5
Boniface Wlk TA8 ... 104 B6
Bonners Cswy EX13 ... 198 A2
Bonners Dr EX13 ... 198 A1
Bonners Glen EX13 ... 198 A1
Bonnie's La 6 TA14 ... 185 F4
Bonning's La TA19 ... 184 D4
Bonniton La TA24 ... 130 E5
Bonniton New Rd TA24 ... 201 D1
Bonny Cross
 Clayhanger EX16 ... 165 B1
 Morebath EX16 ... 164 B3
Bonny La TA24 ... 128 B2
Bonson Hill TA5 ... 134 E3
Bonsonwood La TA5 ... 134 E4
Boobery EX16 ... 178 D1
Boome La TA2 ... 169 C7
Boons Orch TA3 ... 169 C3
Booth Way TA6 ... 208 D5
Boozer Pit TA16 ... 195 F8
Borden Gate EX16 ... 178 B8
Bordesley Rd BS14 ... 23 A3
Boreal Way 4 BS24 ... 49 F7
Boreland La BA22 ... 187 A8
Borgie Pl BS22 ... 31 F3
Borleyton Wlk BS13 ... 21 F4
Borough Mall The BS28 ... 108 D4
Borough Post TA3 ... 170 B3
Borough The
 Montacute TA15 ... 186 B3
 Wedmore BS28 ... 108 D4
 3 Yeovil BA20 ... 219 B4
Borver Gr BS13 ... 22 B4
Bosanquet Flats TA24 ... 200 F7
BOSSINGTON ... 124 B4
Bossington Dr TA2 ... 213 B8
Bossington La TA24 ... 124 B4
Boswell Rd BA15 ... 64 F3
Botham Cl BS22 ... 32 A4
Bottreaux Mill Cross EX36 ... 162 A5
Boucher's La TA4 ... 165 E4
Boulevard BS23 ... 48 E8
Boulters Rd BS13 ... 22 C4
Boundaries The BS24 ... 67 B1
Boundary Ave
 Frome BA11 ... 120 B5
 Yeovil BA22 ... 218 B7
Boundary Cl
 Holcombe BA3 ... 116 C8
 Midsomer Norton BA3 ... 97 B7
 Weston-Super-Mare BS23 ... 48 E3
 Yeovil BA21 ... 218 E7
Boundary Rd
 Weston-Super-Mare BS24 ... 50 A7
 Yeovil BA22 ... 218 A5
Boundary Way
 Glastonbury BA6 ... 206 C3
 Yeovil BA22 ... 218 A7
Boundhay BA22 ... 186 C2
Bounds La TA20 ... 223 A1
Bourchier Cl 13 EX16 ... 164 B1
Bourchier Dr 12 EX16 ... 164 B1
Bourchier Gdns BS13 ... 22 B3
BOURNE ... 54 B4
Bourne Gr TA1 ... 213 D4
Bourne La
 Blagdon BS40 ... 54 C4
 Burrington BS40 ... 54 B4
Bournville Inf Sch BS23 ... 49 A4
Bournville Jun Sch BS23 ... 48 F5
Bournville Rd BS23 ... 48 F4
BOURTON
 Gillingham ... 161 F1
 Weston-super-Mare ... 32 E6
Bourtonbridge Dro BA5 ... 139 F5
Bourton Combe BS48 ... 19 F7
Bourton La
 Cross BS26 ... 69 E3
 Weston-Super-Mare BS22 ... 32 D4
Bourton Mead
 Flax Bourton BS48 ... 19 F8
 Long Ashton BS41 ... 11 A1
Bourton Wlk BS13 ... 22 A8
Bouverie Cl TA24 ... 129 E1
Bouverie Rd TA6 ... 208 D5
Bove Moor Cl BA16 ... 207 E6
Bove Moor Rd BA16 ... 207 E6
Bovet Cl TA1 ... 212 B1
Bove Town BA6 ... 206 E5
Bovet St TA21 ... 222 C6
Bow Cotts BS20 ... 4 C4
BOWDEN ... 177 F2
Bowden Cl BS9 ... 5 C8
Bowden Hill BA3 ... 96 D4
Bowden La
 Milborne Port BA8 ... 217 F5
 Rodhuish TA24 ... 130 F3
 Yenston BA8 ... 189 D7
Bowden Rd BA8 ... 189 D8
Bowdens La EX16 ... 164 E3
Bowden's La TA10 ... 171 F7
Bowden Way BS8 ... 10 B3
Bowditch Cl BA4 ... 205 A5
Bowditch Row 8 TA18 ... 224 C6
Bowen Rd BS24 ... 50 C5
BOWER ASHTON ... 11 E4
Bower Ashton Terr BS3 ... 11 F4
Bower Ave TA6 ... 209 C6
Bower Fields TA6 ... 209 D6
Bowerhayes La TA24 ... 131 A5
BOWER HINTON ... 185 D5
Bower Hinton TA12 ... 185 D5

Bowerings Rd TA6 208 E2
Bower La TA6 209 E6
Bowerleaze BS9 5 C5
Bower Manor Sh Ctr
TA6 209 D6
Bowermead La BA4 204 C1
Bowery Cnr BA5 92 E5
Bowfell Cl TA1 212 C1
Bow Gate TA18 196 A8
Bowhayes TA18 224 C5
Bowhays Cross TA4 202 A2
Bowlditch La BA3 78 B4
Bowleaze BA21 218 D6
Bowline Cl TA6 208 E7
Bowline Ct TA24 201 B7
Bowling Gn
10 Cannington TA5 135 B2
Street BA16 207 D7
BOWLISH 205 A7
Bowlish Inf Sch BA4 205 A6
Bowlish La BA4 205 A6
Bowmont Gr TA1 213 D3
Bowns Cl BA4 141 E1
Bowood Rd TA2 213 A6
Bowring Cl
Bristol BS13 22 C3
Coxley BA5 139 E6
Bowsprit Cl TA24 201 B7
Bow St TA10 171 F5
Bowyers Cl BA6 206 E5
Boxbury Hill BS39 77 F3
Boxbush Hill BA4 158 E8
Box Bush La BS24 33 C1
Box Rd BA1 29 C3
Boxstone Hill TA19 184 D2
Box Wlk BS31 24 C4
Boyce Cl BA2 43 F5
Boyce's Ave BS8 226 A3
Boyd Ho BA5 113 A1
Boyd Rd BS31 25 D3
Boyle Cl DT10 190 B4
Boyton Hill TA19 194 F8
Boyton La TA19 194 F7
Bracey Rd TA12 185 E7
Bracken Edge TA4 132 E4
Bracken Way TA20 223 F5
Brackenwood Gdns★ BS20 1 F5
Brackenwood Rd BS21 6 E6
Bracton Dr BS14 23 A5
Bradbeers TA3 181 D8
Bradfield Cl TA6 208 E1
Bradfield Way TA20 223 C3
BRADFORD ABBAS 187 E1
Bradford Cl
Clevedon BS21 6 C1
Taunton TA1 168 D1
BRADFORD ON TONE 167 F1
Bradford Pk BA2 45 A2
Bradford Rd
Bath BA2 45 A1
Bathford BA1 29 B2
Misterton TA18 224 E4
Rode BA11, BA14 83 A2
Sherborne DT9 225 B3
Wingfield BA14, BA15 83 C8
Winsley BA15 64 D6
Winsley BA15 64 E7
Bradley Ave BS11 4 E6
Bradley Cl TA11 211 C4
Bradley Cres BS11 4 E6
Bradley Cross La BS27 90 D7
BRADLEY GREEN 135 B1
Bradley Hill La TA11 211 B5
Bradley La
Ashcott TA7 156 B7
Maiden Bradley BA11,
BA12 144 B2
Parbrook BA6 158 C7
Bradley Rd BS20 3 E5
Bradleys TA19 183 F4
Bradley Stream Rd BA16,
TA7 138 C1
Bradley View TA11 211 C4
Bradley Way BA6 158 B8
BRADNEY 136 D1
Bradney La TA7 136 D1
Bradon La
Isle Abbotts TA3 183 F6
Stocklinch TA19 184 A5
Bradville Gdns BS41 20 F8
Brae Rd BS25 70 B8
Brae Rise BS25 70 A8
Bragg's La BS2 227 C3
Braikenridge Cl BS21 6 C1
Brain's Cnr BA9 216 E1
Brainsfield BS9 5 F6
Brains La BA22 175 A5
Braithwaite Pl TA8 85 A2
Braithwaite Way BA11 120 C6
Brakewell Gdns BS14 23 A4
Bramble Dr
Berrow TA8 84 F5
Bristol BS9 5 D3
South Petherton TA13 220 C4
Bramble Hill BA16 156 D6
Bramble La
Bristol BS9 5 C3
Haselbury Plucknett TA18 196 C5
Bramble Pk TA1 213 C2
Bramble Rd TA6 208 D1
Brambles Rd TA8 85 B1
Brambles The
Bristol BS13 22 C4
Hinton Charterhouse BA2 63 E1
Keynsham BS31 24 D3
Brambles The *continued*
Wellington TA21 222 D4
Weston-Super-Mare BS22 32 D2
Bramble Way BA2 45 B1
Bramblewood BS49 17 B1
Bramblewood Rd BS22 31 E3
Bramley Cl
Charlton Horethorne
DT9 176 A2
Crewkerne TA18 224 C7
Locking BS24 50 A5
Peasedown St John BA2 79 D7
Pill BS20 4 C4
Sandford BS25 52 A4
Wellington TA21 222 F7
Yatton BS49 34 B7
Bramley Dr
Backwell BS48 19 A5
Frome BA11 120 C6
Bramley Rd
Street BA16 207 B4
Taunton TA1 213 D5
Bramley Sq BS49 34 E3
Bramleys The
Nailsea BS48 18 B8
Portishead BS20 2 F5
Brampton Ho BS20 2 E4
Brampton Way BS20 2 E4
Bramshill Dr BS22 31 F3
BRAMWELL 172 B8
Branche Gr BS13 22 D3
Branches Cross BS40 35 E3
Branch Rd BA2 63 F2
BRANDISH STREET 124 C3
BRANDON HILL 226 B2
Brandon Ho BS8 226 B2
Brandon St BS1 226 C2
Brandon Steep BS1 226 C2
Brangay La BS27 91 A1
Brangwyn Sq BS22 31 F2
Branksome Ave TA6 209 B5
Bransby Way BS24 50 A8
Branscombe Rd BS9 5 C4
Branscombe Wlk BS20 1 F3
Bransford BA22 197 D3
Brantwood Rd TA6 208 C5
BRASSKNOCKER 45 F2
Brassknocker Hill BA2 45 F2
Brassmill Ent Ctr BA1 44 A7
Brassmill La BA1 44 A7
Brassmill Lane Trad Est
BA1 44 A7
BRATTON 200 B7
Bratton Cl TA24 200 D7
Bratton Ho BA9 176 B8
Bratton La TA24 200 B7
Bratton Mill La
Minehead, Bratton TA24 200 B7
Minehead, Woodcombe
TA24 200 C7
Bratton Rd BS4 22 D7
BRATTON SEYMOUR 176 C8
Bray Cl EX16 179 B3
Braysbridge BS27 90 C7
Braysdown Cl BA2 79 B6
Braysdown La BA2 79 C7
BREACH 58 F6
Breach Cl SP8 161 F1
Breaches The BS20 4 B5
Breach Furlong La TA10 156 A1
Breach Hill TA21 179 F5
Breach Hill La BS40 56 C6
Breach La
Brinscombe BS26 89 B3
Corsley Heath BA12 144 E7
Kington Magna SP8 177 E2
Nailsea BS48 17 F7
Weston Town BA4 142 E4
Bread And Cheese La
TA19 184 C1
Bread St BA4 140 F3
BREAN 65 F5
Brean Court Ho TA8 65 F3
Brean Ct TA8 65 F3
Brean Down Ave BS23 48 E4
Brean Down Rd TA8 47 F1
Brean Leisure Pk★ TA8 65 F1
Brean Rd BS24 66 F1
Brecon View BS24 49 A1
Breech Cotts TA21 179 F5
Breech La BA6 158 A8
Bree Cl BS22 32 A4
Bremis Rd TA24 201 E3
BRENDON 122 A4
Brendon Ave BS23 48 F8
Brendon Cl TA23 131 D2
Brendon Gdns 2 BS48 8 E1
Brendon Ho BA21 219 A6
Brendon Rd
Bridgwater TA6 208 F6
Portishead BS20 2 A5
Watchet TA23 202 B6
Wellington TA21 222 D7
Brendons TA4 167 E8
Brendons The EX16 178 D1
Brendon Two Gates
TA24 127 A6
Brendon View TA4 151 B7
Brendon Way
Bridgwater TA6 208 F6
Cheddar BS27 90 C8
Brent Broad TA8 85 B2
Brent Cl
Brent Knoll TA9 86 B1
Weston-Super-Mare BS24 49 B2
BRENT KNOLL 86 A1
Brent Knoll CE Prim Sch
TA9 86 A2
Brent Rd
Burnham-on-S TA8, TA9 85 B4
Cossington TA7 136 F3
East Brent TA9 86 C5
Brentsfield La TA7 154 E7
Brent St TA9 86 A2
Breowen Cl TA19 221 B3
Brereton Rd TA24 201 B6
Breton Dr 1 TA6 209 A1
Bretoneux Rd BA6 206 E3
Brett Cl TA4 202 F1
Brettingham Ct TA17 195 C7
Brewery Bglws TA18 224 C7
Brewery Hill BS30 25 F7
Brewery La
Holcombe BA3 97 D1
Ilminster TA19 221 B4
Oakhill BA3 115 A3
Shepton Mallet BA4 205 D5
Brewham Rd BA10 160 D6
Brewhouse The BS1 227 B2
Brewhouse Theatre & Arts
Ctr★ TA1 212 F4
Breynton Rd BA6 206 F5
Brian Mooney Cl TA20 223 B3
Briant Cl TA1 212 B1
Briar Cl
Burnham-on-S TA8 104 C6
Frome BA11 120 B7
Nailsea BS48 9 A2
Radstock BA3 97 D8
Yeovil BA21 219 E8
Briar Ct
Bridgwater TA6 208 E5
Burnham-on-S TA8 104 C6
Pill BS20 4 C4
Briarfield BA22 173 E2
Briar Mead BS49 17 A1
Briar Rd
Hutton BS24 49 E3
Street BA16 207 A5
Briars Ct BA2 44 A4
Briars The
Backwell BS48 18 F7
Yeovil BA20 218 C2
Briarwood BS9 5 F6
Briary Rd BS20 2 C5
Brick Cotts BA3 117 A7
Brickkiln La DT9 225 E7
Brick St BS2 227 C3
Brickyard La
Bourton SP8 161 F1
Wanstrow BA4 142 F5
Brick Yard La TA18 224 C7
Briddicott La TA24 131 A4
Bridewell La
Bath BA1 228 B2
Hutton BS24, BS26, BS29 50 D1
Shapwick TA7 137 F1
Bridewell St BS1 227 A3
BRIDGE 199 A8
Bridge Bldgs BS39 77 B3
Bridge Cl
Evercreech BA4 141 E2
Whitchurch BS14 23 C4
Williton TA4 202 D2
Bridge Cotts
Chard Junction TA20 198 D8
Drimpton DT8 199 F7
East Chinnock BA22 196 F8
Bridge Farm Cl BS14 23 A3
Bridge Farm Inf Sch BS14 23 A4
Bridge Farm Jun Sch
BS14 23 A4
Bridge Farm Sq BS49 34 D4
Bridge Gdns BA2 60 A6
BRIDGEHAMPTON 174 C3
Bridge Hill BA4 142 F4
Bridge Ho
11 Bath BA1 28 C1
Bristol BS1 227 A2
9 Clevedon BS21 6 C2
Weston-Super-Mare BS23 48 F6
Bridgehouse Cross EX15 180 D1
Bridge House Pk TA13 220 F4
Bridge Pl DT9 187 F4
Bridge Place Rd BA2 78 E8
Bridge Rd
Bath BA2 44 C5
Bleadon BS24 67 B6
Leigh Woods BS8 11 E6
Weston-Super-Mare BS23 48 F6
Bridge Rise 17 TA12 185 E6
Bridges Mead TA24 201 E3
Bridge St
Bath BA2 228 C2
Bourton SP8 161 F1
Bristol BS1 227 A2
Dulverton TA22 163 D6
Frome BA11 119 F5
Taunton TA1 212 F4
Williton TA4 202 D2
Bridge Terr EX16 164 B1
Bridge The
Frome BA11 119 F5
Taunton TA1 212 F4
BRIDGETOWN 147 E4
Bridge Valley Rd BS8 11 E8
Bridge Way TA13 220 E4
Bridgeway Cotts TA13 220 E4
Bridgewell Ct DT9 225 E3
BRIDGWATER 208 E3
Bridgwater TA6 208 F4
Bridgwater Bay National
Nature Reserve★ TA5 103 C2
Bridgwater Bldgs BA7 214 B5
Bridgwater Coll
Bridgwater TA6 209 B5
Bridgwater Coll *continued*
Minehead TA24 201 A7
Bridgwater Coll Cannington
Ctr TA5 135 B2
Bridgwater Ct BS24 49 A3
Bridgwater Ent Ctr 7
TA6 208 F5
Bridgwater General Hospl
TA6 209 A5
Bridgwater Rd
Dundry BS41, BS13, BS48 21 D6
East Brent TA9 86 D4
Lympsham BS24 67 C5
North Petherton TA6 153 F4
Taunton, Bathpool TA2 213 F7
Taunton TA1 213 D5
Weston-Super-Mare BS23,
BS24 48 F2
Winscombe BS25 70 A5
Bridgwater Ret Pk TA6 209 A5
Bridgwater Sta TA6 209 B4
Bridle Way BA22 197 F8
Bridport Rd DT8 199 F8
Briercliffe Rd BS9 5 D7
Briery Leaze Rd BS14 23 A4
Brigadier Cl BA22 218 A5
Brigg Cl TA6 208 E7
Brighton Mews BS8 226 B4
Brighton Rd BS23 48 E6
Brighton St 7 BS2 227 B4
Brightstowe Rd TA8 85 A2
Brigstocke Rd BS2 227 B4
Brimble Cotts DT10 189 F1
Brimbleworth La BS22 32 C3
Brimclose Rd TA17 195 B7
Brimgrove La TA19 184 E4
Brimhill Rise BA13 121 D4
BRIMLEY 198 D3
Brimley Cross TA3 180 F1
Brimley Hill EX13 198 D2
Brimley Rd EX13 198 D3
Brimridge Rd BS25 70 A8
Brimsmore Ct BA21 218 E8
Brimstone La
Rockwell Green TA21 222 A2
Sampford Arundel TA21 179 F6
Sampford Peverell EX16 178 E2
Brincil Hill TA11 173 D4
BRINDHAM 139 D3
Brindham La BA6 139 D3
Brindle Cl TA2 212 C7
Brines Orch BA8 176 E1
Brinmead Wlk BS13 21 F3
BRINSCOMBE 89 A5
Brinscombe La BS26 89 A5
BRINSEA 52 E8
Brinsea Batch BS49 52 E8
Brinsea La BS49 52 F8
Brinsea Rd BS49 34 E2
Brinsmead Cres BS20 4 D4
Briscoes Ave BS13 22 D4
Brislington Ent Coll BS4 23 F8
BRISTOL 227 B3
Bristol and Exeter Mews
BS1 227 C1
Bristol Cathedral Sch
BS1 226 C2
Bristol Dental Hospl
BS1 227 A3
Bristol Eye Hospl BS1 227 A3
Bristol Gate 1 BS8 11 F5
Bristol General Hospl
BS1 227 A1
Bristol Gram Sch BS8 226 C3
Bristol Harbour Rly★
BS1 226 C1
Bristol Hill BA5 112 E3
Bristol Homeopathic Hospl
BS8 226 C4
Bristol International Airport
BS48 36 E7
Bristol Mus & Art Gall★
BS8 226 C3
Bristol Rd
Bridgwater TA6 209 B7
Chew Stoke BS40 56 E8
Chewton Mendip BA5 113 A8
Churchill BS25 53 A5
Congresbury BS49 34 D5
Farrington Gurney BS39 76 F5
Highbridge TA9 104 F4
Horrington BA5 112 F6
Keynsham BS31 24 E6
Newton St Loe BA2 43 D7
Paulton BS39 77 E7
Pensford BS39 40 D6
Portishead BS20 2 E4
Radstock BA3 78 F3
Redhill BS40 37 A3
Rooks Bridge BS26, TA9 87 B5
Sherborne DT9 225 D5
Walpole TA6 136 B3
Weston-Super-Mare BS22 32 C2
Whitchurch BS14 23 D3
Winscombe BS25 70 C8
Wraxall BS48 9 D4
Bristol Rd By-pass BS40 53 C5
Bristol Rd Lower BS23 30 F1
Bristol Road Lower BS23 30 E1
Bristol Royal Infmy BS2 227 A4
Bristol Temple Meads Sta
BS1 227 C1
Bristol View BA2 62 C8
Bristol Zoo Gdns★ BS8 5 F1
Britannia Cl BA3 96 D4
Britannia Way
Chard TA20 223 C6
Clevedon BS21 6 C1
Briton St 2 EX16 164 C1
Brittains BA11 119 D6
Brittania Bldgs BS8 226 A1
Brittan Pl BS20 3 E3
BRITTENS 77 F6
Britten's Cl BS39 77 F6
Britten's Hill BS39 77 F6
Brittons Ash TA2 213 F8
Brittons Pass SN14 13 F8
Broadacres BA22 197 C8
Broadbridge Rd TA3 183 C6
Broadbury Rd BS4 22 E8
Broad Cl
Kington Magna SP8 177 E1
Wells BA5 112 E1
Broadclose Way TA11 158 A2
Broadcroft BS40 38 F3
Broadcroft Ave BS49 17 F1
Broadcroft Cl BS49 17 F1
Broad Dro
Burrowbridge TA7 155 A2
North Wootton BA4 140 A3
Broadenham La TA20 194 E1
Broadfield Rd BS4 23 A8
Broadguage Bsns Pk
TA4 167 E7
Broadhay BA5 110 E7
Broad Hill BA22 196 D7
Broadhurst Gdns TA8 104 B5
Broad La
East Chinnock BA22 196 E7
Hawkridge TA22 146 D1
North Curry TA3 170 D4
Winsford TA22 147 F4
Broadlands BS21 6 F3
Broadlands Ave
Keynsham BS31 24 D6
North Petherton TA6 153 F4
Broadlands Cl BA21 219 E8
Broadlands Ct TA1 212 E2
Broadlands Dr BS11 5 A8
Broadlands La TA5 208 A4
Broadlands Rd TA1 212 E2
Broadlands Rise TA1 212 E2
Broadlands Sch BS31 24 D6
Broadlands Way TA1 212 E2
Broad Lane Head
Hawkridge TA22 146 D1
Winsford TA22 147 F4
Broadlawn TA7 136 E4
Broadleas BS13 22 C7
Broadleaze
Bristol BS11 4 E7
Yeovil BA21 218 C6
Broadleaze Way BS25 51 F2
Broadly Gdns TA2 213 E8
Broadmead
Bristol BS1 227 B3
Keynsham BS31 25 B5
Kingsbury Episcopi TA12 185 B7
South Petherton TA13 220 B4
Broadmead Dro TA7 155 F6
Broadmead La
Barrington TA19 184 D6
Catcott TA7 137 D2
Edington TA7 137 C3
Keynsham BS31 25 A6
Kington Magna SP8 177 D1
Norton Sub Hamdon TA14 185 F2
Broad Mead La BS40 38 A3
Broadmead Rd TA3 183 B7
Broadmeads TA10 172 A6
Broadmoor Dro BS28 89 D3
Broadmoor La
Bath BA1 27 A3
Horsington BA8 176 E2
Broadmoor Pk BA1 27 B2
Broadmoor Vale BA1 27 A3
Broadoak TA19 183 C1
Broad Oak 9 BA20 219 B4
Broadoak Hill BS41 21 F2
Broad Oak Hill TA4 151 B5
Broadoak Mathematics &
Computing Coll BS23 48 E3
Broadoak Rd
Bridgwater TA6 209 D5
Churchill BS40 53 A5
Weston-Super-Mare BS23 48 D3
Broad Oak Rd BS13 21 F4
Broad Oaks BS8 11 E6
Broad Path EX15 179 A1
Broad Plain BS2 227 C2
Broad Quay
Bath BA1 228 C1
Bristol BS1 227 A2
Broad Rd
Blagdon BS40 72 D8
Rodney Stoke BA5 91 E1
Broadshard Rd TA18 224 C8
Broad St
Bath BA1 228 C3
Bristol BS1 227 A3
Charlton Adam TA11 173 F7
Chewton Mendip BA3 94 C5
Churchinford TA3 191 D7
Congresbury BS49 34 D4
Somerton TA11 211 E4
Stoney Stratton BA4 141 F2
Wells BA5 203 D4
Wrington BS40 35 D2
Broadstone TA7 154 E6
Broadstone La
Hardington Mandeville
BA22 197 A6
Kingston Seymour BS21 15 F3
West Chinnock TA18 196 C7
Broad Stones BA15 46 E7
Broadstone Wlk BS13 22 D5

Broad Street Pl BA1 228 C3
BROADWAY 183 B2
Broadway
Bath BA2 45 B6
Bridgwater TA6 208 F4
Charlton Adam TA11 174 A7
Chilcompton BA3 96 C3
Chilton Polden TA7 137 B2
Frome BA11 119 D5
Locking BS24 50 D4
Merriott TA16 195 F7
Odcombe BA22 186 C2
Saltford BS31 25 D3
Shipham BS25 70 E8
Weston-Super-Mare BS24 49 A2
Broad Way TA12 185 D5
Broadway Acres BS27 70 F1
Broadway Ave TA7 137 B2
Broadway Cl BA3 96 C3
Broadway Hill TA19 183 B1
Broadway La
Castle Cary BA22 214 B3
Midsomer Norton BA3 78 B5
Westbury-sub-Mendip BA5 110 D7
Broadway Rd
Bristol, Bishopsworth BS13 21 F5
Charlton Adam TA11 173 F7
Horton TA19 183 C2
Broadways Head EX14, TA20 192 C6
Broad Weir BS1 227 B3
Broadwell Cl TA20 193 D6
Broadwood Rd TA24 130 D4
Brock Ct BA7 214 C6
Brock End BS20 1 F3
BROCKFIELD 198 A8
Brockhole La
Dinnington TA17 195 B8
Tatworth EX13, TA20 198 B7
Brockle Cl TA11 211 D4
BROCKLEY 18 C2
Brockley Cl
Nailsea BS48 8 D1
Weston-Super-Mare BS24 48 F1
Brockley Combe Rd BS48 19 B1
Brockley Cres BS24 48 F1
Brockley La BS48 18 D4
Brockley Rd BS31 25 D3
Brockley Way BS49 18 B3
Brockley Wlk BS13 22 A8
Brocks La BS41 10 F1
Brocks Mount 16 TA14 185 F4
Brocks Rd BS13 22 C3
Brock St BA1 228 B3
Brockway BS48 8 F2
BROCKWELL 129 E6
Brockwell La TA24 129 F6
Brockwood BA15 64 F7
Brocole La TA20 193 D5
Broderip TA7 136 F3
BROKERSWOOD 102 F5
Brokerswood Country Pk★ BA13 102 F6
Bromes La TA3 183 F7
Bromley Rd BS39 39 F1
Brompton Ho BA2 228 C4
Brompton Mdws TA22 148 B2
BROMPTON RALPH 150 C3
Brompton Rd BS24 49 A2
BROMPTON REGIS 148 B2
Bronte Cl BS23 49 B4
Brook Bank
Draycott BS27 90 F2
Rodney Stoke BS27 109 C7
Brook Cl
Long Ashton BS41 11 B1
Minehead TA24 200 F7
North Petherton TA6 153 E3
Yeovil BA21 218 D7
Brook Cotts
Corfe TA3 181 F6
Corston BA2 43 B7
Brook Ct BS13 22 A6
Brookdale Rd BS13 22 B6
Brooke Rd
Berrow TA8 84 F4
Taunton TA1 213 B4
Brookes Ct BA5 203 C5
Brookfield Pk BA1 27 B2
Brookfields BA7 214 B5
Brookfield Way BA16 207 A4
Brookfield Wlk BS21 6 F3
Brook Gate BS3 11 E1
BROOKHAMPTON 175 D6
Brookhampton Cnr BA22 175 D6
Brook La
Barton St David BA6 157 F3
6 Cannington TA5 135 B2
Catcott TA7 137 D2
7 Henstridge BA8 190 A6
Brookland Rd
Langport TA10 172 A6
Weston-Super-Mare BS22 49 B7
Brooklands
Bridgwater TA6 209 C5
Dunkerton BA2 61 D3
Brooklands Rd TA21 222 B5
Brookland Way 3 BA8 190 A6
Brookleaze BS9 5 C5
Brookleaze Bldgs BA1 28 B2
Brookleigh BA16 207 A5
Brooklyn BS40 35 D2
Brooklyn Rd
Bath BA1 28 C2
Bristol BS13 22 B8
Brooklyn Terr BA5 139 E6
Brook Rd
Bath BA2 44 D6
Williton TA4 202 E3
Brook's Hill EX15 179 C1
Brookside
Broadway TA19 183 C2
Milborne Port DT9 217 D1
Paulton BS39 77 E6
Pill BS20 4 D3
South Cheriton BA8 176 D3
West Coker BA22 197 A8
Brookside Cl
Batheaston BA1 28 F5
Paulton BS39 77 E6
Taunton TA3 168 D1
Brookside Com Prim Sch BA16 207 B4
Brookside Dr BA2 59 F6
Brookside Ho BA1 27 B1
Brookside Rd TA5 135 B5
Brooks Pl TA21 222 E6
Brooks Rd BA16 207 B4
Brook St
Bampton EX16 164 B1
Cannington TA5 135 B2
Milborne Port DT9 217 D1
Minehead TA24 201 B5
North Newton TA7 153 F1
Timberscombe TA24 130 B5
Brook Street Mews TA24 201 B5
Brookview Wlk BS13 22 B7
Broomball Cross TA22 162 F5
Broomball La EX16 162 E5
Broomclose Cnr BA3 114 B4
Broome Cl EX13 198 A1
Broom Farm Cl BS48 18 E8
BROOMFIELD 152 E2
Broomfield Ho TA2 212 E7
Broomground BA15 64 E7
Broomhill La BS39 58 E3
Broom Hill La BS39 77 E8
Broom La
Chardstock EX13 198 C5
Oake TA4 167 D3
Broom's La TA3 191 F7
Broomyland Hill TA5 152 C7
Brottens Rd
Cranmore BA4 142 A5
Doulting BA4 141 F5
Brougham Hayes BA2 44 D6
Brougham Pl 2 BA1 28 C2
Broughton Cl
Taunton TA1 213 C2
Walton BA16 156 E7
Broughton Ho BS1 227 B1
Broughton La TA3 169 B1
Broughton Pk TA3 169 A1
Broughtons Dr TA18 224 E3
Brow Hill BA2 28 F4
Brown Down La TA20 192 C7
Browne Ct 4 BS8 11 F6
BROWNHEATH 180 C2
Brownings Rd TA5 135 B2
Brown La TA4, TA23 149 C3
Brownlow Rd BS23 48 E4
Browns Ct BS23 48 E6
Brown's Folly Nature Reserve BA15 29 D1
Browns La BS28 109 C1
Brown's Pl 4 BA5 203 C4
Brow The
Bath BA2 44 B5
Bath, Combe Down BA2 45 C1
Broxholme Wlk BS11 4 F8
Brue Ave
Bridgwater TA6 209 B3
Bruton BA10 215 F7
Brue Bsns Pk TA9 136 E8
Brue Cl
Bruton BA10 215 F7
Weston-Super-Mare BS23 49 A5
Brue Cres TA8 104 B5
Brue Ho TA8 85 A1
Bruelands BA10 215 F7
Brue Way TA9 104 F3
Bruford Cl TA1 212 E3
Brummel Way BS39 77 C6
Brunel Cl
Somerton TA11 211 D4
Weston-Super-Mare BS24 48 F1
Brunel Ct
Bridgwater TA6 208 F6
Portishead BS20 2 D6
Brunel Ho BA2 44 A6
Brunel Lock Rd BS1 11 F5
Brunel Prec TA11 211 D4
Brunel Rd
Bristol BS13 22 A8
Nailsea BS48 8 B1
Brunel's SS Great Britain & The Matthew★ BS1 226 B1
Brunel's Way TA9 104 E5
Brunel Way
Bristol BS1, BS3 11 F4
Frome BA11 120 C7
Minehead TA24 201 B6
Taunton TA2 212 A6
Brunsell's Knap DT10 190 A1
Brunswick Pl
1 Bath BA1 228 B3
10 Bristol BS1 11 F5
Brunswick Sq BS2 227 B4
Brunswick St
1 Bath BA1 28 B1
Bristol BS2 227 B4
Yeovil BA20 219 A4
BRUSHFORD 163 D4
Brushford New Rd TA22 163 E4
Brutasche Terr BA16 207 D7
BRUTON 215 E5
Bruton BS24 49 A2
Bruton Ave
Bath BA2 44 F4
Portishead BS20 2 A5
Bruton Avenue Garages BA2 44 F4
Bruton Cl BS48 18 E8
Bruton La BA4 142 F2
Bruton Mus★ BA10 215 E6
Bruton Pl BS8 226 B3
Bruton Prim Sch BA10 215 E6
Bruton Rd BA4 141 F1
Bruton Sch for Girls BA10 215 C3
Bruton Sta BA10 215 F6
Brutton Way TA20 223 B3
Bryant Ave BA3 78 D1
Bryant Gdns BS21 6 C1
Bryant's Hill TA22 148 C2
Bryer Cl
Bridgwater TA6 208 E1
Chard TA20 223 D3
Brymore Cl TA6 208 D5
Brymore Sch TA5 135 A2
Brympton Ave BA22 186 D2
BRYMPTON D'EVERCY 218 A3
Brympton Way BA20 218 C3
Bsns Courtyard The BA11 143 C7
Bubwith Cl TA20 223 D3
Bubwith Ho 4 BA5 203 D4
Bubwith Rd TA20 223 D3
Bubwith Wlk BA5 203 B3
Buces Rd TA1 212 B1
Buck Cl BA6 206 C3
Buckhill TA24 131 B4
Buckhill Cl TA18 224 C4
BUCKHORN WESTON 177 D3
Buckingham Cl TA6 209 A2
Buckingham Pl BS8 226 A3
Buckingham Rd BS24 49 B2
Buckingham Vale BS8 226 A4
Buckland Cl TA8 104 C8
BUCKLAND DINHAM 100 A3
BUCKLAND DOWN 99 B4
Buckland Gn BS22 32 A5
Buckland La BA22 175 C3
Buckland Rd
Shepton Mallet BA4 205 A5
Taunton TA2 213 B8
Yeovil BA21 219 E6
BUCKLAND ST MARY 192 F8
Buckland St Mary CE Prim Sch TA20 193 A8
Bucklands Batch BS48 18 F8
Buckland Sch TA23 202 C6
Bucklands Dr BS48 19 A8
Bucklands End BS48 18 F8
Bucklands Gr BS48 18 F8
Bucklands La BS48 18 F8
Bucklands View BS48 19 A8
Buckle Pl BA22 218 B6
Bucklers Mead Rd BA21 219 D8
Bucklers Mead Sch BA21 219 C8
Bucklers Mead Wlk BA21 219 D8
Bucklers Way BA4 204 F6
Bucklewell Cl BS11 4 F6
Buckshots Cross EX14 192 D4
Buckwell TA21 222 E6
Bude Cl BS48 9 B1
Budge La BA11 144 A8
Budgetts TA21 180 F6
Budgett's Cross TA21 180 F6
Bughole La TA21 179 E8
Bugle Ct 11 BA8 190 A6
Building of Bath Mus★ BA1 228 C3
BULFORD 182 C4
Bulford TA21 222 D5
Bulford La TA21 222 D5
Bull Bridge Mead BA22 197 D3
Bullen Mead BA11 117 F2
Bullens Cl TA19 183 F4
Buller Ave BA22 218 A6
Bull Horn Dro TA7 154 D5
Bull La BS20 4 C4
Bull Mdw TA4 167 F7
Bullmead Cl BA16 207 B5
Bullmead La BA11 143 C7
Bullock Field Hill TA21 166 B2
Bullocks La BS21 16 C4
Bullon Drove TA5 134 B7
Bull Plot Hill BA6 158 C8
BULL'S GREEN 117 E1
Bull's Hill BA2 62 E1
Bulls La TA18 224 B6
Bull's La
Tatworth TA20 198 C8
Upton Noble BA4 142 F2
Bull's Quarr BA11 143 E8
Bull's Quarries Rd BA11 143 F7
Bull St TA3 169 D4
Bulwarks La BA6 206 F4
Bumper's Batch BA2 63 A8
Bunce's La TA19 184 E3
Buncombe Hill TA5 152 C3
Bune Villas TA6 208 E7
Bunford Hollow Rdbt BA20 218 D1
Bunford La BA20, BA21 218 C4
Bungalows The
Axbridge BS26 70 C2
Chard TA20 223 D5
Bungalows The *continued*
Monkton Heathfield TA2 213 F8
Nether Stowey TA5 134 A2
Poyntington DT9 188 E7
Bungay's Hill BA2, BS39 59 E1
Bunker Military Mus The★ TA9 104 D3
Bunns La
Horningsham BA11 144 A5
Witham Friary BA11 143 F5
Bunting Ct BS22 31 E1
Bunting La BS20 3 A6
Burchill Cl BS39 58 F3
Burchills Cl TA21 222 A6
Burchill's Hill TA21 222 B7
Burch's Cl TA1 212 C2
BURCOTT 139 E8
Burcott La
Coxley BA5 139 E7
Wells BA5 203 A3
Burcott Mill★ BA5 139 E8
Burcott Rd BA5 203 B3
Burdenham Dro TA7 155 A6
Burfoote Gdns BS14 23 E4
Burfoot Rd BS14 23 E4
BURFORD 204 C2
Burford Cl
Bath BA2 44 B3
Portishead BS20 2 E4
Burford Cross BA4 204 C2
Burford Gr BS11 4 F5
Burgage TA21 222 D6
Burgage La TA4 167 A4
Burgage Rd TA5 134 C6
Burge Cres TA4 167 E6
Burge Mdw TA4 167 E6
Burges Cl
Marnhull DT10 190 F6
Wiveliscombe TA4 210 C5
Burge's Hill BA3 116 B1
Burges La TA4 210 C5
Burge's La BA3 116 B1
Burgess Cl TA1 212 B1
Burgess La BA6 157 F6
Burgis Rd BS14 23 D6
Burgundy Rd TA24 201 A8
BURLANDS 168 C6
Burleigh Gdns BA1 44 A8
Burleigh La BA16 207 C4
BURLESCOMBE 179 B3
Burlescombe CE Prim Sch EX16 179 B3
Burley Gdns BA16 207 D4
Burlingham's La BA22 186 C8
Burlington Ct BS20 2 E6
Burlington Rd
Midsomer Norton BA3 78 C2
Portishead BS20 2 E7
Burlington St
Bath BA1 228 B4
15 Weston-Super-Mare BS23 48 E8
Burnbush Cl BS14 23 E6
Burnbush Prim Sch BS14 23 D5
Burnell Dr BS2 227 C4
Burnell Ho 8 BA4 205 B6
BURNETT 42 B7
Burnett Bsns Pk BS31 25 B1
Burnett Cl TA8 104 C7
Burnett Hill BS31 42 B8
Burnett Ind Est BS40 35 E1
Burnett's La BA6 158 A6
Burnham Cl BS24 48 F1
Burnham Dr BS24 48 F1
Burnham Moor La TA9 105 B5
BURNHAM-ON-SEA 104 D8
Burnham-on-Sea Inf Sch TA8 104 C8
Burnham Rd
Bath BA2 44 C6
Bristol BS11 4 D6
Highbridge TA9 104 D4
Burn Hill TA4, TA21 166 F3
Burnshill Dr TA2 212 A7
Burns Rd TA1 213 C4
Burnt House Cotts BA2 62 C8
Burnthouse Dro BA5 141 B8
Burnt House La BA3 116 C2
Burnt House Rd BA2 62 D8
Burrell La BA7 158 F1
Burrells BA22 197 B8
Burridge Cl BA5 139 E6
Burridge Cross TA20 193 E1
BURRINGTON 53 F3
Burrington Ave BS24 48 F1
Burrington CE Prim Sch BS40 53 F3
Burrington Cl
Nailsea BS48 8 E1
Weston-Super-Mare BS24 48 F1
Burrington Combe BS40 72 C8
Burrington Coombe★ BS40 54 A1
Burrington La BS40 54 A3
Burrington Wlk BS13 22 A8
Burroughes Ave BA21 218 E6
Burrough St TA12 185 F7
Burrough Way TA21 222 D4
BURROW 184 F6
BURROWBRIDGE 154 F1
Burrowbridge CE Sch TA7 154 F1
Burrow Dro
Burrowbridge TA7 154 F1
Hambridge TA12 184 F8
Burrowfield BA10 215 F7
Burrowfield Cl BA10 215 F7
Burrow Hill Dro TA7 155 A1
Burrow La
Ashbrittle TA21 178 D8
High Ham TA10 156 A1
Burrow Mump★ TA7 154 F1
Burrow Rocks TA4 202 B1
Burrows La BA3 97 B1
Burrows The BS22 32 D3
Burrow Wall TA7 155 A1
Burrow Way
Hambridge TA12 184 F7
Kingsbury Episcopi TA12 185 A7
Burstock La DT8 199 F7
Burston La EX16 164 A4
BURTLE 137 D6
Burtle Rd
Burtle TA7 137 D6
East Huntspill TA9 136 E7
Westhay BA6 138 A5
BURTON
Stogursey 134 B7
Yeovil 197 C8
Burton Barton BA22 197 C8
Burton Cl BS1 227 B1
Burton Ct BS8 226 B3
Burtonhayes DT10 190 F6
Burton La BA22 197 C8
Burton Pl TA1 212 E3
Burton Row TA9 86 A5
Burton St
5 Bath BA1 228 B2
Marnhull DT10 190 F6
Burt's Hill BA4 142 F3
Burwalls Rd BS8 11 E6
BURY 164 A6
Bury The BS24 50 A3
Bury View BA2 42 C5
BUSCOTT 138 C1
Buscott La TA7 138 B1
BUSHEY NORWOOD 45 F6
Bushfield Rd TA18 224 B4
Bushfurlong Rd TA3 184 B8
Bush La TA5 152 E6
Bush Pl TA10 172 A5
Bush Rd TA5 152 D7
Bushs Orch TA19 221 A4
Bushy Combe BA3 77 F3
Bushy Coombe Gdns BA6 206 F5
Bushy Cross La TA3 169 C3
Bushy Thorn Rd BS40 56 E8
Business Pk The BS13 22 E3
Bussell's Moor Cross EX36 162 C4
BUSSEX 154 F6
Bussex Sq TA7 154 F6
Butcher's Hill TA3 170 F2
Butchers La
Castle Cary BA7 159 C3
Shapwick TA7 155 F8
Butcher's La TA5 134 A2
BUTCOMBE 55 B8
Butcombe BS24 49 A2
Butcombe La BS40 55 B7
Butcombe Wlk BS14 23 B5
Butham La
Chew Magna BS40 39 A4
Chew Magna BS40 39 B3
Butlass Cl BS39 59 D1
BUTLEIGH 157 D4
Butleigh CE Prim Sch BA6 157 E4
Butleigh Cl TA6 209 D4
Butleigh Cross BA6 157 E3
Butleigh Dro
Ashcott TA7, BA16 156 C5
Walton BA16 156 D6
Butleigh Old Rd BA6 206 E3
Butleigh Rd
Glastonbury BA6 206 E3
Street BA16 207 E5
BUTLEIGH WOTTON 157 C5
Butler's Gdns BA11 120 A4
Butt Cl BA6 206 E5
Buttercliffe Rise BS41 11 C3
Buttercup La BA16 207 D6
Butterfield Pk BS21 6 C1
Buttermere Rd BS23 49 A5
Butterworth Ct BS4 22 D7
Buttice La BA5 111 B1
Butt La TA10 171 D4
Butt Lake Rd TA9 106 B3
Buttle Cl TA19 184 E4
Buttle La TA19 184 E3
Buttle's Cross TA3 191 F7
Buttle's La TA3 191 E6
Button Cl BS14 23 A6
Button St BA11 119 D5
Butts TA19 221 C4
BUTT'S BATCH 35 D1
Butts Batch BS26 69 B3
Butt's Batch BS40 35 D1
Butts Castle TA19 221 C4
Butts Cl
Marnhull DT10 190 F5
Williton TA4 202 D4
Butts Cnr TA6 153 F4
Butts Hill BA11 119 E3
Butts La
Ilton TA19 183 D3
Kilmington BA12 161 F7
Langford Budville TA21 166 F2
Rodney Stoke BS27 91 A1
Butts Orch BS40 35 D1
Butts Quarry La TA18 224 E6
Butts The BA11 119 E3

Butts Way TA4 . . . . 166 F4
Buxtons Cl [5] BA5 . . . . . . 139 D8
Byfield BA2. . . . . 45 B1
Byfield Pl BA2 . . . . 45 B1
Byfields BS21. . . . . 16 C8
Byron Cl BS24 . . . . 50 A4
Byron Ct BS23 . . . . 48 F8
Byron Pl BS8 . . . . 226 B3
Byron Rd
Bath BA2. . . . . 44 F4
Locking BS24. . . . . 50 A4
Taunton TA1 . . . . 213 C3
Weston-Super-Mare BS23. . 49 A4
Byways Cvn Pk BS21 . . . . . . 6 C1
Byzantine Ct BS1 . . . . 227 A1

C

Cabbage La BA8 . . . . 176 C3
Cabell Ct BA11. . . . . 119 D2
Cabell Rd BA11 . . . . 119 E2
Cabot Circus Sh Ctr BS1 227 B3
Cabot Cl BS31 . . . . 25 D2
Cabot Gate BS2. . . . . 227 C4
Cabot Prim Sch BS2 . . . . 227 C4
Cabot Rise BS20 . . . . 2 A5
Cabot Twr★ BS8 . . . . 226 B2
Cabot Way
Bristol BS8. . . . . 11 F5
Pill BS20 . . . . 4 D3
Weston-Super-Mare BS22. . 32 A3
Cabstand BS20. . . . . 2 D6
Cadbury Bsns Pk BA22 . . 175 B6
Cadbury Camp La BS20. . . . 8 D6
Cadbury Camp La W BS21 . 7 C5
Cadbury Castle★ BA22 . . 175 C4
Cadbury Cl TA8 . . . . 85 C1
Cadbury Farm Rd BS49. . . 34 C7
Cadbury Halt BS20. . . . . 1 F1
Cadbury Ho BS20 . . . . 2 E4
Cadbury La BS20. . . . . 1 F1
Cadbury Rd
Keynsham BS31. . . . . 25 A2
Portishead BS20 . . . . 2 E4
Cadbury Sq BS49 . . . . 34 E3
Cadby Ho BA2 . . . . 44 A6
Cadeside Cvn Site TA21 . 222 F7
Cades Mead TA21. . . . . . . 222 F7
CAD GREEN. 183 E3
Cadogan Rd BS14 . . . . 23 A8
Cad Rd
Ilminster TA19 . . . . 221 A8
Ilton TA19 . . . . 183 E3
Cadwell's La TA9 . . . . 136 A8
Caernarvon Rd BS31 . . . . . 24 C4
Caernarvon Way TA8. . . . . 85 B1
Caern Well Pl BA1 . . . . . . 228 C4
Cairn Cl BS48. . . . . 9 A1
Cairo Ct [18] BS23 . . . . 30 C1
Caitlin Ct BS14. . . . . 23 D6
Cala Trad Est BS3 . . . . 11 F3
Calder Cl BS31. . . . . 25 A4
Calder Cres TA1 . . . . 213 D4
Cale Cl DT10. . . . . 190 C4
Caledonia Mews BS8. . . . . 11 F6
Caledonian Rd
Bath BA2 . . . . 44 D6
Bristol BS1. . . . . 226 B1
Caledonia Pl BS8 . . . . 11 F7
Cale Way BA9. . . . . 216 B4
Caller's La EX15 . . . . 180 D1
Callins Cl TA24. . . . . 201 A5
Callins View TA24. . . . . . . 201 A5
Callow Hill BA5. . . . . 139 C7
Callowhill Ct BS1 . . . . 227 B3
Calluna Cl BS22. . . . . 32 A5
Calton Gdns BA2. . . . . 228 C1
Calton Rd BA2 . . . . 228 C1
Calton Wlk BA2. . . . . 228 B1
Calvados Rd TA1. . . . . 213 C3
Calway Rd TA1. . . . . 213 B2
Camberley Rd BS4 . . . . 22 D8
Camberley Wlk BS22 . . . . . 49 E8
Camborne Gr BA21. . . . . . 219 E5
Camborne Pl BA21. . . . . . 219 E5
Camborne St BA21. . . . . . 219 E5
CAMBRIDGE BATCH 20 C8
Cambridge Cl BA20 . . . . . 218 D5
Cambridge Ct BS40 . . . . . . 35 D2
Cambridge Gr BS21. . . . . . . 6 D5
Cambridge Pl
Bath BA2. . . . . 45 B5
Weston-Super-Mare BS23. . 48 D8
Cambridge Rd BS21. . . . . . . 6 D5
Cambridge St TA20 . . . . . 223 C4
Cambridge Terr
Bath BA2. . . . . 45 B5
[11] Taunton TA2 . . . . 213 A8
Cam Brook Cl BA2 . . . . 78 D8
Cambrook Ho BS39 . . . . . . 76 F8
Camden Cres BA1. . . . . . . 228 B4
Camden Ct
Bath BA1 . . . . 228 B4
Bridgwater TA6 . . . . 208 E5
Camden Orch TA11 . . . . . 211 C4
Camden Pl TA6 . . . . 208 E5
Camden Rd
Bath BA1. . . . . 28 A1
Bridgwater TA6 . . . . 208 E5
Bristol BS3. . . . . 226 B1
Somerton TA11 . . . . 211 C4
Camden Row BA1. . . . . . . 228 B4
Camden Terr
Bath BA1 . . . . 228 C4
Camden Terr *continued*
Bristol BS8. . . . . 226 A2
Weston-Super-Mare BS23. . 48 E7
Camel Cross BA22 . . . . . . 174 C3
CAMELEY 76 C8
Cameley CE Prim Sch
BS39. . . . . 58 E1
Cameley Cl BS39. . . . . 76 E8
Cameley Gn BA2. . . . . 43 F6
Cameley La BS39 . . . . 75 F7
Cameley Rd BS39 . . . . 76 C8
Camelot Ct TA11 . . . . 211 B5
Camelot Sh Ctr BA9. . . . . 216 C4
Camel St BA22. . . . . 174 F2
Cameroons Cl BS31 . . . . . . 24 E4
CAMERTON. 78 E8
Camerton CE Prim Sch
BA2. . . . . 78 E8
Camerton Cl BS31. . . . . 25 E3
Camerton Hill BA2 . . . . 78 E8
Camerton Rd BA2. . . . . 60 E1
Camomile Wlk BS20. . . . . . . 2 F5
Campian Wlk BS4. . . . . 22 D6
Campion Cl [4] BS22. . . . . . 49 D7
Campion Dr
Taunton TA1 . . . . 213 C1
Yeovil BA22 . . . . 218 B5
Campion Gdns TA20. . . . . 223 D5
Campion Way TA6 . . . . . . 208 E1
Campkin Rd BA5. . . . . 203 B4
Camplins BS21. . . . . 6 C1
Camp Rd
Bristol BS8. . . . . 11 F7
Weston-Super-Mare BS23. . 30 C1
Yeovil BA22 . . . . 186 D1
Camp Rd N BS23 . . . . 30 B1
Camp View BS48. . . . . 8 D2
Camvale BA2 . . . . 79 B8
Camview BS39. . . . . 77 D6
Canada Coombe BS24. . . . 50 A1
Canada Way BS1. . . . . 226 B1
Canal Cl TA21. . . . . 222 B8
Canal Dro BS27, BS28 . . . . 90 A3
Canal Rd TA1 . . . . 212 F5
Canal Terr
Bathampton BA2 . . . . 28 F1
Taunton TA1 . . . . 212 F5
Canal View TA6. . . . . 209 A4
Canal Way TA19 . . . . 221 A3
Canberra Cres BS24. . . . . . 50 B6
Canberra Rd BS23 . . . . 48 F3
Canford La BS9 . . . . 5 E8
Canford Rd BS9. . . . . 5 F8
CANNARD'S GRAVE 205 D2
Cannard's Grave Rd BA4 205 C4
Cannards Grave Rdbt
BA4 . . . . 205 D3
CANNINGTON 135 C2
Cannington CE Prim Sch
TA5 . . . . 135 C2
Cannington College Gdns★
TA5 . . . . 135 B2
Cannington Countryside Vst
Ctr★ TA5. . . . . 135 B2
Cannon Cl TA6. . . . . 209 B5
Cannon Court Mews
DT9 . . . . 217 D1
Cannons Gate BS21 . . . . . . 16 C8
CANNON'S MARSH 226 C1
Cannon St BS1. . . . . 227 A4
Canns La
[9] North Petherton TA6 . . 153 F4
Puriton TA7 . . . . 136 C4
Cann St TA1 . . . . 212 E3
Cannwood La BA10 . . . . . 161 B8
Canons Cl BA2. . . . . 44 B2
Canons Gate BA22 . . . . . . 173 E1
Canon's Marsh
Amphitheatre★
BS1. . . . . 226 C1
Canons Rd BS1 . . . . 226 C2
Canon's Rd BS1. . . . . 226 C1
Canon St TA1. . . . . 213 A4
Canons Way BS1. . . . . 226 C1
Canons Wlk BS22 . . . . 31 D2
Cantell Gr BS14. . . . . 23 F5
Canterbury Cl BS22 . . . . . . 32 B3
Canterbury Dr TA3 . . . . . . 170 C4
Canterbury Rd BA2. . . . . . . 44 D5
Cantock's Cl BS8. . . . . 226 C3
Canvin Ct TA11 . . . . 211 B5
Canworth Way TA6. . . . . . 209 C3
Canynge Ho [2] BS1 . . . . . 227 B1
Canynge Rd BS8 . . . . 11 F8
Canynge Sq BS8 . . . . 11 F8
Canynge St BS1. . . . . 227 B2
Capell Cl BS22 . . . . 49 B8
Capenor Cl BS20. . . . . 2 C4
Capes Cl TA6 . . . . 209 A5
Capital Edge BS8 . . . . 226 B1
CAPLAND 183 A6
Capland Ct TA3. . . . . 183 A5
Capland La TA3. . . . . 183 A5
Caple La BS40 . . . . 56 B5
Cappards Rd BS39 . . . . 57 D4
Capricorn Pl BS8 . . . . 226 B2
Capri Villas BS23. . . . . 30 C2
CAPTON. 132 C2
Capton TA4. . . . . 132 C2
Capton Cross TA4. . . . . . . 132 C2
Caradon Pl TA6 . . . . 208 F7
Caramia Pk TA9 . . . . 136 A8
Carantoc Pl [3] TA24. . . . . 131 A5
Caraway Cl TA20. . . . . 223 F5
Caray Gr TA3 . . . . 169 D4
Carberry View BS24. . . . . . 50 A8
Card Cl BS27 . . . . 90 F3
Cardigan Cres BS22. . . . . . 49 C8
Cardill Cl BS13. . . . . 22 A8
Cardinal Cl BA2. . . . . 62 D8
Carditch Dro BS49 . . . . 52 B8
Carey Cl BA4 . . . . 141 E6
Carey Developments [1]
BS21. . . . . 6 C1
Carey's Cl BS21. . . . . 6 F4
Carey's Hollow TA13 . . . . 220 B4
Careys Mead BA3 . . . . 116 F7
Careys Way BS24 . . . . 49 E7
CARHAMPTON 131 B5
Carhampton Cross TA24. 131 B5
Carice Gdns BS21. . . . . 16 D8
Carisbrooke Gdns BA20 . 218 F5
Carisbrooke Rd BS4. . . . . . 22 D7
Carlan Stepps TA19 . . . . . 183 C2
CARLINGCOTT 61 B1
Carlingford Terr BA3. . . . . 79 A2
Carlingford Terrace Rd
BA3 . . . . 79 A2
Carlow Rd BS4. . . . . 22 E8
Carlton Cl BS39 . . . . 58 F3
Carlton Ct
Minehead TA24 . . . . 200 F7
Wells BA5 . . . . 203 E4
Carlton Dr TA6. . . . . 208 F7
Carlton Mans BS23. . . . . . . 48 D7
Carlton Mews BA5 . . . . . . 203 E4
Carlton St BS23. . . . . 48 D7
Carmine Cl BA6. . . . . 206 C4
Carnival Cl TA19 . . . . 221 A4
Carolina Ho BS2 . . . . 227 A4
Caroline Bldgs BA2 . . . . . . 45 B5
Caroline Cl BS31. . . . . 24 C4
Caroline Pl BA1. . . . . 228 B4
Carpenter Cl BS23 . . . . 49 A7
Carpenters Cl TA3 . . . . . . 169 C3
Carpenters Ho TA19. . . . . 221 B3
Carpenters La BS31 . . . . . . 24 E5
Carpenters Terr TA12 . . . 185 E7
Carraway La DT10. . . . . . . 190 F5
Carre Gdns BS22. . . . . 31 F4
Carr Ho BA2. . . . . 44 A6
Carrick Ho [7] BS8. . . . . 11 F6
Carriels Ho [12] BA4 . . . . . 205 B6
Carrier's La TA21 . . . . 166 C2
Carrington Way BA9 . . . . 216 C4
Carrs Cl BA2. . . . . 44 A6
Carstons Cl BS48. . . . . 18 F6
Carter Rd BS39 . . . . 77 D5
Carters La BA22. . . . . 196 E8
Carters Way
Chilcompton BA3 . . . . 96 D3
Somerton TA11 . . . . 211 C4
Cart Gate TA14 . . . . 185 F5
Cartwright Cl BA5. . . . . . . 139 E6
Carvers Rd TA6 . . . . 209 A5
Cary Ct TA11. . . . . 211 B5
Caryedge La BA7. . . . . 160 A2
CARY FITZPAINE 174 B6
Cary Hill
Castle Cary BA7. . . . . 214 D5
Kingsdon TA11. . . . . 173 E5
Cary Moor Dro BA7 . . . . . 159 C1
Cary Rd BA22 . . . . 175 D6
Cary Way
Kingsdon TA11. . . . . 173 D5
Somerton TA11 . . . . 211 C5
Cashford Gate TA2. . . . . . 213 C7
Casion Ct BS1 . . . . 227 B1
Casley La BA11 . . . . 102 D6
Cassino Rd TA23. . . . . 202 E6
Cassis Cl TA8 . . . . 104 C5
Castlake La TA4. . . . . 150 F7
CASTLE 198 D4
Castle Batch Prim Sch
BS22. . . . . 32 A5
Castle Bow TA1. . . . . 212 F4
CASTLE CARY. 214 B5
Castle Cary Com Prim Sch
BA7. . . . . 214 C4
Castle Cary Mus★ BA7 . . 214 C5
Castle Cary Sta BA7. . . . . 214 B8
Castle Cl BS48 . . . . 19 F7
Castle Cnr BA11 . . . . 101 D3
Castle Cotts TA21 . . . . 180 D8
Castle Cross EX13. . . . . . . 198 D4
Castle Ct
Othery TA7. . . . . 155 C2
Shepton Mallet BA4. . . . . . 205 A4
Castle Farm La BS41 . . . . . 21 B2
Castle Field Ind Est TA6 . 209 A6
Castlefield La TA4 . . . . . . 168 B1
Castle Gdns BA2. . . . . 44 E3
Castle Gn TA1 . . . . 212 F4
Castle Hill
Banwell BS29. . . . . 51 C2
Dunster TA24 . . . . 201 E2
Nether Stowey TA5 . . . . . . 134 A2
Nunney BA11. . . . . 143 B8
Castle La
Cranmore BA4. . . . . 142 A6
South Cadbury BA22 . . . . . 175 D4
Wedmore BS28 . . . . 108 A1
West Pennard BA6 . . . . . . 140 C1
Wiveliscombe TA4 . . . . . . 210 F6
Yarley BA5. . . . . 139 D7
Castlemans Rd TA1 . . . . . 212 B1
Castle Mead TA23. . . . . . . 131 E4
Castle Moat TA6 . . . . 208 F5
Castle Neroche Forest Trail★
TA20. . . . . 182 D2
Castle Prim Sch BS31. . . . . 24 D4
Castle Rd
Clevedon BS21. . . . . 6 E6
Sherborne DT9 . . . . 225 F5
Wellington TA21. . . . . 180 D8
Weston-Super-Mare BS22. . 31 E3
Castle Rise BA7 . . . . 214 C5
Castle Sch The TA1. . . . . . 212 D4
Castle St
Bampton EX16. . . . . 164 B1
Bridgwater TA6 . . . . 208 F5
Bristol BS1. . . . . 227 B3
Frome BA11. . . . . 119 E5
Keinton Mandeville TA11 . . 158 B1
Nether Stowey TA5 . . . . . . 134 B2
Nunney BA11. . . . . 143 B8
Stogursey TA5 . . . . 134 C5
Stoke sub Hamdon TA14 . . 185 F4
Taunton TA1 . . . . 212 E4
Castleton
Haselbury Plucknett
TA18 . . . . 196 C5
[1] Sherborne DT9 . . . . 225 E4
Castleton Rd DT9 . . . . 225 F4
Castle Town Way DT9 . . . 225 E6
Castle View [2] BS24. . . . . . 49 F8
Castle View Rd BS21 . . . . . . 6 D5
Castle Way TA1 . . . . 212 F4
Castlewood Cl BS21. . . . . . . 6 D4
Castle Wood La EX13,
TA20 . . . . 193 C1
Caswell Hill BS20 . . . . 3 B1
Caswell La BS20 . . . . 3 B2
Catash Cl BA22 . . . . 175 D6
Catch Gate La TA20 . . . . . 223 A5
Catch Rd BA11. . . . . 143 B7
CATCOTT. 137 D2
Catcott Broad Dro TA7 . . 137 D5
Catcott Prim Sch TA7 . . . 137 D2
Catcott Right Dro TA7. . . 155 D6
Catemead BS21. . . . . 16 C8
Cater Rd BS13 . . . . 22 B6
Cathanger La
Fivehead TA3 . . . . 170 D1
Stogursey TA5 . . . . 134 D5
Catharine Pl BA1 . . . . 228 B3
Cathay La BS27 . . . . 90 B7
Cathcart Ho [7] BA1 . . . . . . 28 A1
Cathead Cross TA14. . . . . 185 E1
Cathedral Church of The
Holy & Undivided Trinity★
BS1. . . . . 226 C2
Cathedral Gn BA5. . . . . . . 203 E4
Catherine Hill BA11 . . . . . 119 F5
Catherines Cl BA7 . . . . . . 214 C6
Catherine St
Avonmouth BS11 . . . . 4 C8
East Huntspill TA9 . . . . . . 136 D8
Frome BA11. . . . . 119 E5
Catherine Way BA1 . . . . . . 29 A5
Catherston Cl BA11 . . . . . 119 D3
Cathill La DT9 . . . . 176 A2
Cathole Bridge Rd TA18 . 224 A4
Cat La
Stalbridge DT10. . . . . 190 A1
Stourton Caundle DT10 . . . 189 F1
Catley Gr BS41. . . . . 11 B2
Catmoor Cross EX13 . . . . 198 A5
Catnip Cl [2] EX13 . . . . . . 198 A1
Cat's Ash TA4. . . . . 166 F7
Cat's Ash BA4. . . . . 205 B6
Cats' Castle Hill TA4 . . . . 150 E5
CATSGORE 173 C4
Catsgore Rd TA11. . . . . . . 173 C5
Cats La
Minehead TA24 . . . . 201 A6
Taunton TA2. . . . . 168 F6
Cat St TA14. . . . . 185 E1
Cattle Hill
Bratton Seymour BA9 . . . . 176 A8
Welham BA7 . . . . 160 A1
Cattle Market Rd BS1 . . . 227 C1
Catt's La TA21 . . . . 180 E6
Catwell TA4 . . . . 202 E2
Caulfield Rd BS22. . . . . 32 B4
Caundle La
Stalbridge Weston DT10 . . 190 A3
Stourton Caundle DT10. . . . 189 F1
Causeway
Nailsea BS48. . . . . 8 B3
Woolavington TA7, TA9. . . . 136 E6
Causeway Cl TA7 . . . . 136 E4
Causeway Council Hos
TA9 . . . . 106 B4
Causeway La DT8 . . . . 199 D6
Causeway Terr TA23 . . . . 202 C6
Causeway The
Congresbury BS49. . . . . 34 D4
Nailsea BS20. . . . . 8 F8
Street BA16. . . . . 207 D8
Yatton BS49. . . . . 34 C7
Causeway View BS48. . . . . . 8 C2
Caulletts Cl BA3 . . . . 96 F8
Cavalier Cl BA21 . . . . 219 D8
Cavalier Way
Wincanton BA9 . . . . 216 C3
Yeovil BA21 . . . . 219 E8
Cavalier Wlk BA21 . . . . . . 219 D8
Cave Ct BS2 . . . . 227 B4
Cavell Ct BS21. . . . . 6 C1
Cavendish Cl BS31 . . . . 25 D2
Cavendish Cres BA1. . . . . 228 A4
Cavendish Ct BA22 . . . . . 173 E2
Cavendish Dr BA14. . . . . . . 83 F6
Cavendish Gdns BS9 . . . . . . 5 C4
Cavendish Lodge BA1 . . . 228 A4
Cavendish Pl BA1 . . . . 228 A4
Cavendish Rd BA1 . . . . . . 228 A4
Caveners Ct BS22 . . . . 31 B1
Caversham Dr BS48 . . . . 9 A2
Cave St BS2 . . . . 227 B4
Cawley Ave EX13. . . . . 198 A2
Caxton Ct [4] BA2 . . . . 228 C3
Caxton Rd BA11. . . . . 120 A3
Cecil Rd
Bristol, Clifton BS8 . . . . 11 F8
Weston-Super-Mare BS23. . 30 E1
Cecil St BA20. . . . . 219 B5
Cecil Terr TA6 . . . . 209 B4
Cedar Ave
Butleigh BA6 . . . . 157 D5
Weston-Super-Mare BS22. . 31 C1
Cedar Cl
Brent Knoll TA9 . . . . 86 B2
Bridgwater TA6 . . . . 209 C3
Chard TA20. . . . . 223 B5
Long Ashton BS41 . . . . 10 F1
Taunton TA1 . . . . 213 D2
Cedar Ct
Bristol, Combe Dingle BS9 . . 5 D7
Bristol, Sneyd Park BS9. . . . . 5 C4
Bristol, Westbury on T BS9 . . . 5 F8
Martock TA12. . . . . 185 E7
Wellington TA21. . . . . 222 E5
Cedar Dr BS31 . . . . 24 D4
Cedar Falls TA4. . . . . 151 E1
Cedar Fields
Sparkford BA22. . . . . 175 A5
West Coker BA22 . . . . 197 A8
Cedar Gr
Bath BA2 . . . . 44 D3
Bristol BS9. . . . . 5 D5
Somerton TA11 . . . . 211 D4
Yeovil BA21 . . . . 218 E6
Cedarhurst Rd BS20. . . . . . . 1 E4
Cedarn Ct BS22 . . . . 31 B4
Cedar Pk BS9. . . . . 5 D5
Cedar Row BS11 . . . . 4 F6
Cedars The
Chew Stoke BS40 . . . . 56 D8
Evercreech BA4. . . . . 141 E1
Minehead TA24 . . . . 200 F7
Cedar Terr BA3 . . . . 78 D1
Cedar Villas BA2. . . . . 228 A1
Cedar Way
Bath BA2 . . . . 228 A1
Nailsea BS48. . . . . 9 A2
Portishead BS20 . . . . 2 C4
Cedar Wlk BA6 . . . . 157 E5
Cedern Ave BS24 . . . . 50 C3
Cedric Cl BA1. . . . . 44 C7
Cedric Rd BA1 . . . . 44 C8
Cefn Ct TA24 . . . . 201 B4
Celandine Mead TA1 . . . . 169 A1
Celandine Rd BA22. . . . . . 218 A5
Celtic Way BS24 . . . . 67 B7
Cemetery La
Street BA16. . . . . 207 A7
Wincanton BA9 . . . . 216 B3
Centenary Cotts DT9 . . . . 176 A1
Centenary Gdns BA8 . . . . 190 A6
Centenary Way BS27 . . . . . 90 A7
Central Acre BA20 . . . . . . 219 B4
Central Ave BA22 . . . . 173 E2
Central Pk BS14 . . . . 23 B7
Central Rd BA20 . . . . 219 B5
Central Way BS21. . . . . 6 E1
Centre Dr BS29 . . . . 50 E4
Centre Quay BS20. . . . . 2 E7
Centre Rd TA7. . . . . 137 C2
Centre The
Keynsham BS31. . . . . 24 F5
[10] Weston-Super-Mare
BS23. . . . . 48 E7
Centurion Bsns Ctr BA4 . 205 D4
Century Pk BA20. . . . . 218 E5
Cerdic Cl TA20. . . . . 223 E4
Cerdic Terr TA20. . . . . 223 D4
Cerney Gdns BS48 . . . . 9 A2
Cerney La BS11. . . . . 4 E5
Chackrell La EX16. . . . . . . 178 F2
Chadleigh Gr BS4. . . . . 22 D7
Chad's Hill TA5 . . . . 135 B2
CHAFFCOMBE 194 C5
Chaffcombe La TA20 . . . . 194 B5
Chaffcombe Rd TA20. . . . 223 E6
Chaffeymoor Hill SP8 . . . 161 E1
Chaffinch Ave BA11 . . . . . 120 B6
Chaffinch Cl TA1. . . . . 212 B4
Chaffinch Dr BA3 . . . . 97 B8
Chaffins The BS21 . . . . 6 E2
Chain Gate Ct BA6 . . . . . . 206 D4
Chains Rd EX16. . . . . 178 D1
Chalcombe Rocks La
TA4 . . . . 164 E5
Chalcot La BA13 . . . . 121 F5
Chalcroft Wlk BS13 . . . . . . 21 E4
Chalfield Cl BS31 . . . . 25 A2
Chalfont Rd BS22 . . . . 49 C8
Chalice Ct BA6. . . . . 206 E4
Chalice Hill Cl BA6. . . . . . 206 E4
Chalice Mews [1] TA6 . . . . 208 F5
Chalice Way BA6. . . . . 206 F3
Chalice Well★ BA6. . . . . . 206 F4
Chalk Farm Cl BS39 . . . . . . 40 A7
Chalks The BS40 . . . . 39 B3
CHALKWAY. 194 E2
Challenger Way BA22 . . . 218 B6
Challick La TA4 . . . . 166 A6
Challoner Ct BS1 . . . . 227 A1
Challow Dr BS22. . . . . 31 B2
Chamberlain Ho TA1 . . . . 212 D5
Chamberlain St BA5. . . . . 203 D4
Chamberlin Ave TA6 . . . . 209 C6
Chambray Rd [11] TA6 . . . . 154 A5
Champford La TA21 . . . . . 222 D5
Champford Mews [2]
TA21 . . . . 222 D5
Champion Cross TA4. . . . 165 E3
Champney Rd BA11 . . . . . 120 A7
Chancel Cl
Bristol BS9. . . . . 5 D3

Chancel Cl *continued*
Nailsea BS48 . . . . . 8 D1
Chancellor Cl BA16 . . . . . 156 D7
Chancellor Rd BA16 . . . . . 156 D7
Chancellor's Pound BS40. 36 D3
Chandag Inf Sch BS31 . . . . 25 A4
Chandag Jun Sch BS31 . . . 25 A4
Chandag Rd BS31 . . . . . 25 A4
Chandler Cl BA1 . . . . . 27 B1
Chandlers DT9 . . . . . 225 E5
Chandlers La TA7 . . . . . 137 C3
Chandos Ct BS23 . . . . . 48 D6
Chandos Rd BS31 . . . . . 24 E7
Chandos St TA6 . . . . . 208 F5
Change La TA4 . . . . . 164 D6
Channel Cl TA5 . . . . . 134 A2
Channel Ct
Burnham-on-S TA8 . . . . . 104 B5
Weston-Super-Mare BS22 . . 31 B3
Channel Dash Pl BA22 . . . 173 E2
Channel Hts BS24 . . . . . 48 F1
Channells La TA19 . . . . . 183 C1
Channel Rd BS21 . . . . . 6 E5
Channel View Cres BS20 . . . 2 B5
Channel View Rd BS20 . . . . 2 B5
Channing Cl TA8 . . . . . 104 B5
CHANTRY 117 F3
Chantry Cl
Nailsea BS48 . . . . . 8 C1
Taunton TA2 . . . . . 213 B7
Chantry Ct
Bristol BS1 . . . . . 226 C2
Somerton TA11 . . . . . 211 C3
Chantry Dr BS22 . . . . . 32 A4
Chantry Dro TA7 . . . . . 155 B1
Chantry Gdns BA14 . . . . . 83 F3
Chantry Ho 2 BA4 . . . . . 205 B6
Chantry La BA22 . . . . . 174 D3
Chantry Mead Rd BA2 . . . . 44 E3
Chantry The BS26 . . . . . 87 B5
Chantry View BA22 . . . . . 197 D8
CHAPEL ALLERTON 88 D2
Chapel Barton
High Littleton BS39 . . . . . 59 D1
Nailsea BS48 . . . . . 8 C2
Chapel Cl
Castle Cary BA7 . . . . . 214 C5
Chew Stoke BS40 . . . . . 56 E8
Chilton Polden TA7 . . . . . 137 B2
Farrington Gurney BS39 . . . 76 F4
Keinton Mandeville TA11 . . 158 A1
Nailsea BS48 . . . . . 8 E2
North Curry TA3 . . . . . 170 B4
Winford BS40 . . . . . 38 A6
CHAPEL CLEEVE 131 D5
Chapel Cross
North Cadbury BA22 . . . . . 175 D5
Porlock TA24 . . . . . 129 C7
Chapel Ct
Bath BA1 . . . . . 228 B2
Clandown BA3 . . . . . 78 E4
Clevedon BS21 . . . . . 6 D3
Chapelfield BA3 . . . . . 115 A3
Chapel Field BA2 . . . . . 79 E8
Chapel Forge Cl TA9 . . . . 136 B8
Chapel Hill
Ashcott TA7 . . . . . 156 B8
Backwell BS48 . . . . . 19 D7
Chewton Mendip BA3 . . . . . 94 E5
Clevedon BS21 . . . . . 6 D3
Kingsdon TA11 . . . . . 173 D5
Kington Magna SP8 . . . . . 177 E1
Odcombe BA22 . . . . . 186 C2
Ubley BS40 . . . . . 55 C5
Wrington BS40 . . . . . 35 D3
Chapel La
Bishops Lydeard TA4 . . . . . 167 E8
Butleigh BA6 . . . . . 157 E4
Chew Stoke BS40 . . . . . 56 D8
Claverham BS49 . . . . . 34 F8
Cleeve BS49 . . . . . 35 B7
Dinnington TA17 . . . . . 195 B7
East Huntspill TA9 . . . . . 136 E8
Gurney Slade BA3 . . . . . 114 E7
Holcombe BA3 . . . . . 116 C8
Milborne Port DT9 . . . . . 217 D2
North Cadbury BA22 . . . . . 175 D6
Oxenpill BA6 . . . . . 138 C4
Penselwood BA9 . . . . . 161 E2
South Cadbury BA22 . . . . . 175 F5
Sparkford BA22 . . . . . 175 A6
Winford BS40 . . . . . 38 A6
Wingfield BA14 . . . . . 83 C6
Yenston BA8 . . . . . 189 F7
Yeovil Marsh BA21 . . . . . 187 A5
Zeals BA12 . . . . . 161 F3
Chapel Lawns BA3 . . . . . 78 E4
CHAPEL LEIGH 167 A8
Chapel Leigh La TA4 . . . . 167 A8
Chapel Rd
Bristol, Bishopsworth
BS13 . . . . . 22 A6
Clandown BA3 . . . . . 78 E4
Fordgate TA7 . . . . . 154 C3
Isle Abbotts TA3 . . . . . 183 E7
Pawlett TA6 . . . . . 135 F6
Rooks Bridge BS26 . . . . . 87 C5
South Cadbury BA22 . . . . . 175 D4
Chapel Row
Bath BA1 . . . . . 228 B2
Bathford BA1 . . . . . 29 C2
Dunster TA24 . . . . . 201 D2
Norton St Philip BA2 . . . . . 81 F4
Pill BS20 . . . . . 4 C4
Chapel St
Bridgwater TA6 . . . . . 209 A5
Burnham-on-S TA8 . . . . . 104 A7
Dulverton TA22 . . . . . 163 D6
Chapel St *continued*
Exford TA24 . . . . . 128 D1
Horningsham BA12 . . . . . 144 D4
Upton Noble BA4 . . . . . 142 F2
Chapel Wlk BA2 . . . . . 60 C2
Chapel Yd BA7 . . . . . 214 B4
Chaplains Wood BS20 . . . . . 1 E5
Chapman Ct TA1 . . . . . 212 C1
Chapmans Cl
Frome BA11 . . . . . 119 F6
Wookey BA5 . . . . . 139 D8
CHAPMANSLADE 121 C5
Chapmanslade CE Prim Sch
BA13 . . . . . 121 D4
Chapter St BS2 . . . . . 227 B4
Charbury Wlk BS11 . . . . . 4 E5
Charcroft Hill BA10 . . . . . 160 F6
CHARD 223 D4
Chard Bsns Pk TA20 . . . . . 223 D6
Chard Cl BS48 . . . . . 18 F8
Chard Ct BS14 . . . . . 23 B6
Chard & District Hospl
TA20 . . . . . 223 E4
CHARD JUNCTION 198 E7
Chard La
Chard TA20 . . . . . 223 B1
Drimpton DT8 . . . . . 199 F8
Ilminster TA19 . . . . . 194 D6
Tatworth EX13, TA20 . . . . . 193 E1
Woolminstone TA18, TA20 . 195 B2
CHARDLEIGH GREEN 223 A7
Chard Mus★ TA20 . . . . . 223 B4
Chard Rd
Axminster EX13 . . . . . 198 B4
Clevedon BS21 . . . . . 6 E1
Crewkerne TA18 . . . . . 224 A6
Drimpton DT8 . . . . . 199 F7
Chard Sch TA20 . . . . . 223 C4
Chard St
Chardstock EX13 . . . . . 198 B7
Thorncombe TA20 . . . . . 199 B6
CHARDSTOCK 198 B7
Chardstock Ave BS9 . . . . . 5 D8
Chardstock La TA20 . . . . . 223 C2
Chardyke Dr BS39 . . . . . 58 E1
Charing Cross DT6 . . . . . 199 E1
Charity La BA11 . . . . . 98 C1
CHARLCOMBE 27 E3
Charlcombe La BA1 . . . . . 27 F3
Charlcombe Pk BS20 . . . . . 1 D3
Charlcombe Rise BA1 . . . . 27 F2
Charlcombe View Rd BA1 28 A2
Charlcombe Way BA1 . . . . 27 F2
Charlcome Rise BS20 . . . . . 1 D3
Charlecombe Ct BS9 . . . . . 5 F6
Charlecombe Rd BS9 . . . . . 5 F6
Charlecote BA1 . . . . . 27 F1
Charles Cres TA1 . . . . . 213 D4
Charles Ct 1 BS8 . . . . . 226 A2
Charles Pl BS8 . . . . . 226 A2
Charles Rd
Frome BA11 . . . . . 119 F3
Yeovil BA21 . . . . . 219 D6
Charles St
Bath BA1 . . . . . 228 B2
Bristol BS1 . . . . . 227 A4
Charlestone Rd TA8 . . . . . 104 B8
Charleton Ho 8 BS2 . . . . . 227 C3
Charlock Cl 3 BS22 . . . . . 49 D7
Charlock Rd BS22 . . . . . 49 D7
Charlotte Ct BA20 . . . . . 219 A4
Charlotte St S BS1 . . . . . 226 C2
Charlotte St
Bath BA1 . . . . . 228 B2
Bristol, Brandon Hill BS1 . . 226 C3
CHARLTON
Creech St Michael 169 F5
Radstock 97 E5
Shepton Mallet 205 E5
CHARLTON ADAM 173 F7
Charlton Ave BS23 . . . . . 48 D4
Charlton Cl
Bridgwater TA6 . . . . . 209 C4
Crewkerne TA18 . . . . . 224 D5
Shepton Mallet BA4 . . . . . 205 D5
Yeovil BA21 . . . . . 219 D5
Charlton Crossroads
BA4 . . . . . 205 D5
Charlton Dr BS48 . . . . . 9 C7
Charlton Field La DT9 . . . 175 D1
Charlton Hill DT9, BA8 . . . 176 B3
CHARLTON HORETHORNE 176 B2
Charlton Horethorne CE
Prim Sch DT9 . . . . . 176 A1
Charlton La
Creech St Michael TA3 . . . . 169 E5
Radstock BA3 . . . . . 97 D6
Sparkford DT9 . . . . . 175 F3
CHARLTON MACKRELL . . . 173 E7
Charlton Mackrell CE Prim
Sch TA11 . . . . . 173 E7
CHARLTON MUSGROVE . . 161 A2
Charlton Pk
Keynsham BS31 . . . . . 24 D5
Midsomer Norton BA3 . . . . . 97 B7
Charlton Rd
Creech St Michael TA3 . . . . 169 E6
Holcombe BA3 . . . . . 97 D3
Keynsham BS31, BS14 . . . . . 24 C3
Midsomer Norton BA3 . . . . . 97 B8
Shepton Mallet BA4 . . . . . 205 D5
Weston-Super-Mare BS23 . . 48 D4
Charlton Road Cotts
TA3 . . . . . 169 D6
Charlton Trad Est BA4 . . . 205 E5
Charlton View BS20 . . . . . 2 C5
CHARLYNCH 152 F8
Charlynch Hill TA5 . . . . . 152 F8
Charlynch La TA5 . . . . . 153 B8
Charlynch Rd TA5 . . . . . 153 A8
Charmborough Farm Rural
Bsns Pk BA3 . . . . . 97 D3
Charmoor Dro TA20 . . . . . 182 F1
Charmoor La TA20 . . . . . 182 F1
Charmouth Rd BA1 . . . . . 44 B7
Charnwood Cl TA6 . . . . . 208 F7
Charnwood Dr BS27 . . . . . 90 F3
Charnwood Rd BS14 . . . . . 23 B4
Charolais Dr 8 TA6 . . . . . 154 A5
Charter Cl TA6 . . . . . 209 A4
Charter Ho BS1 . . . . . 226 B2
CHARTERHOUSE 72 C4
Charterhouse Cl
Cheddar BS27 . . . . . 90 C6
Nailsea BS48 . . . . . 8 F1
Charterhouse Dr BA11 . . . 120 C7
Charter Rd BS22 . . . . . 49 B8
Charter Way BA5 . . . . . 203 B4
Charter Wlk
Bristol BS14 . . . . . 23 A6
Taunton TA1 . . . . . 213 C5
Chartley BS9 . . . . . 5 D2
Chase Cl BA6 . . . . . 206 C3
Chasey's Dro BA6 . . . . . 139 C4
Chatham Ave TA6 . . . . . 208 E6
Chatham Ct TA10 . . . . . 171 C4
Chatham Pk BA2 . . . . . 45 C6
Chatham Pl TA10 . . . . . 171 C4
Chatham Row BA1 . . . . . 228 C3
Chatley Furlong BA2 . . . . . 81 F3
Chatsworth Rd BA21 . . . . . 219 D7
Chattenden Ho BS9 . . . . . 5 F3
Chatterton Gn BS14 . . . . . 22 F3
Chatterton Ho 5 BS1 . . . 227 B1
Chatterton Sq BS1 . . . . . 227 C1
Chatterton St BS1 . . . . . 227 C1
Chaucer Cl 4 TA6 . . . . . 153 F4
Chaucer Rd
Bath BA2 . . . . . 44 F4
Midsomer Norton BA3 . . . . . 97 B8
Weston-Super-Mare BS23 . . 49 A4
Chaundey Gr BS13 . . . . . 22 B5
Cheapside
Bristol BS2 . . . . . 227 C4
Langport TA10 . . . . . 171 F5
Taunton TA1 . . . . . 212 F3
Wiveliscombe TA4 . . . . . 210 C4
Cheap St
Bath BA1 . . . . . 228 C2
Frome BA11 . . . . . 119 F5
Sherborne DT9 . . . . . 225 D4
Cheats Rd TA3 . . . . . 169 C3
Checcombe La DT9 . . . . . 188 B4
Checkridge La EX13 . . . . . 198 D2
CHEDDAR 90 D8
Cheddar Bsns Pk BS27 . . . 90 A6
Cheddar Cl
Burnham-on-S TA8 . . . . . 104 C8
Frome BA11 . . . . . 120 C7
Nailsea BS48 . . . . . 18 F8
Cheddar Ct BS27 . . . . . 90 B7
Cheddar Fields BS27 . . . . . 90 A7
Cheddar Fst Sch BS27 . . . . 90 B7
Cheddar Gorge★ BS27 . . . 71 E1
Cheddar Gorge Rural
Village★ BS27 . . . . . 90 C8
Cheddar Gr BS13 . . . . . 22 A8
Cheddar Grove Prim Sch
BS13 . . . . . 22 A8
Cheddar Moor Dro BS27 . . 90 C4
Cheddar Rd
Axbridge BS26 . . . . . 70 E2
Chewton Mendip BA3 . . . . . 94 D6
Clewer BS28 . . . . . 89 D2
Wedmore BS28 . . . . . 108 D6
Cheddar Valley Bldgs 2
BA5 . . . . . 203 C3
CHEDDON FITZPAINE 169 A6
Cheddon Fitzpaine CE Prim
Sch TA2 . . . . . 168 F6
Cheddon Lawns TA2 . . . . 169 A6
Cheddon Mews TA2 . . . . . 212 F7
Cheddon Rd TA2 . . . . . 212 F7
Chedworth Cl BA2 . . . . . 45 F3
CHEDZOY 154 E8
Chedzoy La TA7 . . . . . 209 E7
Cheeks La BA10 . . . . . 215 E6
Cheer La TA7 . . . . . 154 F5
Cheese Hill BA11 . . . . . 143 D8
Cheese La BS2 . . . . . 227 B2
Chelmer Cl TA1 . . . . . 213 D4
Chelmer Gr BS31 . . . . . 24 F4
Chelscombe BA1 . . . . . 27 B1
Chelsea Cl BS31 . . . . . 25 A5
Chelsea Rd BA1 . . . . . 44 C7
Chelsfield BS48 . . . . . 19 A7
CHELSTON 180 D8
Chelston Ave BA21 . . . . . 219 B7
Chelston Bsn Pk TA21 . . . 180 D8
CHELSTON HEATHFIELD 180 E7
Chelston Rd BS4 . . . . . 22 D7
Chelston Terr TA21 . . . . . 180 D8
Chelswood Ave BS22 . . . . 49 C8
Chelswood Gdns BS22 . . . 49 D8
Cheltenham St BA2 . . . . . 228 A1
CHELVEY 18 D5
Chelvey Batch BS48 . . . . . 18 F3
Chelvey La BS48 . . . . . 18 E4
Chelvey Rd BS48 . . . . . 18 D5
Chelvey Rise BS48 . . . . . 9 A1
Chelvy Cl BS13 . . . . . 22 D3
CHELWOOD 59 A8
Chelwood BS23 . . . . . 48 F8
Chelwood Dr
Bath BA2 . . . . . 44 D1
Taunton TA1 . . . . . 212 E1
Chelwood Rd
Bristol BS11 . . . . . 4 D7
Saltford BS31 . . . . . 25 E4
Chelwood Rdbt BS39 . . . . . 58 E8
CHELYNCH 141 E6
Chelynch Pk BA4 . . . . . 141 E6
Chelynch Rd BA4 . . . . . 141 F7
Chepstow Ave TA6 . . . . . 209 A2
Chepstow Ct BA21 . . . . . 219 D6
Chepstow Ho BA10 . . . . . 215 D6
Chepstow Rd BS4 . . . . . 22 D8
Chepstow Wlk BS31 . . . . . 24 D5
Cher TA24 . . . . . 200 F6
Cherfield TA24 . . . . . 200 F6
Cherington Rd BS48 . . . . . 9 A2
Cheriton St BA8 . . . . . 176 D3
Cherry Ave BS21 . . . . . 6 E2
Cherry Cl
Bridgwater TA6 . . . . . 209 C3
Yatton BS49 . . . . . 34 B8
Cherry Ct 12 BS1 . . . . . 227 A4
Cherry Garden La BA2 . . . 100 D7
Cherry Gr
Frome BA11 . . . . . 119 E3
Taunton TA2 . . . . . 212 F6
Yatton BS49 . . . . . 34 B8
Cherry Hay BS21 . . . . . 6 D1
Cherry La
4 Bristol BS1 . . . . . 227 B4
Odcombe BA22 . . . . . 186 C2
Cherry Orch TA3 . . . . . 168 D1
Cherry Orchard Dr BA5 . . 203 C5
Cherry Pie La BA22 . . . . . 175 A5
Cherry Rd
Long Ashton BS41 . . . . . 10 F1
Nailsea BS48 . . . . . 8 D1
Cherry Tree Cl
Keynsham BS31 . . . . . 24 C4
Radstock BA3 . . . . . 78 E1
Cherry Tree Ct
Crewkerne TA18 . . . . . 224 D8
Kingston Seymour BS21 . . . 16 C2
1 Wells BA5 . . . . . 203 C3
Wincanton BA9 . . . . . 216 D4
Cherry Tree Dr BA20 . . . . 218 D2
Cherry Tree La TA1 . . . . . 212 F1
Cherry Tree Rd EX13 . . . . 198 A1
Cherry Tree Way TA23 . . . 202 D6
Cherrywood Rd BS22 . . . . . 31 F2
Cherrywood Rise BS22 . . . . 31 F2
Chertsey Cl TA7 . . . . . 136 E4
Cherwell Rd BS31 . . . . . 25 A4
Chescombe Rd BS49 . . . . . 34 B7
Chesham Rd N BS22 . . . . . 49 B8
Chesham Rd S BS22 . . . . . 49 B8
Cheshay's Hill TA19 . . . . . 183 D1
Chesle Cl BS20 . . . . . 1 E3
Cheslefield BS20 . . . . . 1 E3
Chesle Way BS20 . . . . . 1 E3
Chessell La BA4 . . . . . 140 C4
Chessels Cl BA22 . . . . . 197 B8
Chessels La TA11 . . . . . 173 F7
Chessington Ave BS14 . . . . 23 B5
CHESTERBLADE 142 A4
Chesterblade Rd
Chesterblade BA4 . . . . . 142 A4
Evercreech BA4 . . . . . 141 F3
Chester Cl BS24 . . . . . 50 A8
Chester Cres BS13 . . . . . 22 B8
Chesterfield TA20 . . . . . 223 D4
Chesterfield Cl BS29 . . . . . 50 F3
Chesterfield Ho BA3 . . . . . 78 B1
Chesterfield Hospl BS8 . . 226 A2
Chester Terr TA20 . . . . . 223 D4
Chesterton Dr BS48 . . . . . 9 A2
Chesterton Ho 6 BS2 . . . 227 B4
Chestertons The BA2 . . . . 45 F8
Chestnut Ave
Axbridge BS26 . . . . . 70 C2
Chapel Cleeve TA24 . . . . . 131 D5
Crewkerne TA18 . . . . . 224 D7
Weston-Super-Mare BS22 . . 32 A1
Chestnut Barn Ind Est
BS24 . . . . . 33 D3
Chestnut Chase BS48 . . . . . 9 A3
Chestnut Cl
Baltonsborough BA6 . . . . . 158 A5
Banwell BS29 . . . . . 51 A3
Bridgwater TA6 . . . . . 209 C4
Bristol BS14 . . . . . 23 F5
1 Carhampton TA24 . . . . . 131 A5
Congresbury BS49 . . . . . 34 D4
Frome BA11 . . . . . 120 C7
Maiden Bradley BA12 . . . . . 144 C2
Paulton BS39 . . . . . 77 E6
Radstock BA3 . . . . . 78 E1
Somerton TA11 . . . . . 211 C3
Wellington TA21 . . . . . 222 E5
Chestnut Ct BS13 . . . . . 22 A7
Chestnut Dr
Claverham BS49 . . . . . 17 F1
Taunton TA1 . . . . . 213 C1
Yeovil BA20 . . . . . 218 F3
Chestnut Gr
Bath BA2 . . . . . 44 C4
Clevedon BS21 . . . . . 6 E4
Westwood BA15 . . . . . 64 F4
Chestnut Ho
Brean TA8 . . . . . 65 F2
Bristol BS13 . . . . . 22 D3
Chestnut La
Ashcott TA7 . . . . . 156 B8
Bleadon BS24 . . . . . 67 B7
Chestnut Par BA4 . . . . . 205 D4
Chestnut Rd
Long Ashton BS41 . . . . . 11 B2
11 Martock TA12 . . . . . 185 E6
Chestnuts The
Cheddar BS27 . . . . . 71 A1
Winscombe BS25 . . . . . 70 A7
Chestnut Way TA24 . . . . . 201 A5
Chestnut Wlk
Bristol BS13 . . . . . 22 A6
Saltford BS31 . . . . . 25 E3
Chever's La BA2 . . . . . 81 E5
Cheverton Ho 1 BA21 . . . 219 B5
Cheviot Mdw BS20 . . . . . 2 F4
Cheviot St 6 TA6 . . . . . 154 A5
Chew Cotts BS31 . . . . . 24 F5
Chew Court Farm BS40 . . . 39 B3
Chew Hill BS40 . . . . . 39 A4
Chew La BS40 . . . . . 38 F1
CHEW MAGNA 39 C4
Chew Magna Prim Sch
BS40 . . . . . 39 B3
Chew Rd BS40 . . . . . 38 C5
Chew St BS40 . . . . . 39 A3
CHEW STOKE 56 D8
Chew Stoke CE Prim Sch
BS40 . . . . . 56 D8
Chewton Cheese Dairy★
BA3 . . . . . 94 E6
Chewton Hill BA3 . . . . . 95 A7
CHEWTON KEYNSHAM 24 E2
CHEWTON MENDIP 94 E7
Chewton Mendip CE Prim
Sch BA3 . . . . . 94 F7
Chewton Rd BS31 . . . . . 24 F2
Chew Valley Lake Nature
Trails★ BS39 . . . . . 57 B7
Chew Valley Sch BS40 . . . . 38 F1
Cheyne Rd BS9 . . . . . 5 D6
Chibbet Hill TA24 . . . . . 146 B8
Chibbet Post TA24 . . . . . 146 C8
Chichester Cl TA8 . . . . . 104 B8
Chichester Pl BA3 . . . . . 79 A2
Chichester Rd BA16 . . . . . 207 C4
Chichester Way BS24 . . . . 50 A8
Chicks La BA3 . . . . . 95 D7
Chick's La TA4 . . . . . 210 C6
Chickwell La BA3 . . . . . 81 A1
Chidgey Cl TA6 . . . . . 208 F5
CHILCOMBE 132 F1
Chilcombe La TA4 . . . . . 132 F1
CHILCOMPTON 96 C4
Chilcompton Rd BA3 . . . . . 96 E7
Chilcote Dro BA5 . . . . . 113 E2
Chilcote La BA5 . . . . . 113 D1
Chilcott Cross TA22 . . . . . 163 A7
Chilcott La TA22 . . . . . 163 A7
Childhay La DT8 . . . . . 199 F6
Chilkwell St BA6 . . . . . 206 E4
Chillington Down TA19,
TA20 . . . . . 194 F4
Chilliswood Cres TA1 . . . 212 B2
Chilliswood La
Staplehay TA3 . . . . . 181 B8
Taunton TA3 . . . . . 168 B1
Chill Pits La EX13 . . . . . 198 B8
Chillybridge Rocks TA22 147 E1
Chillyhill La BS40 . . . . . 38 F2
Chilpitts TA7 . . . . . 136 F4
CHILSON 198 C6
CHILSON COMMON 198 D7
Chiltern Cl BS14 . . . . . 23 B4
Chiltern Cross EX16 . . . . . 164 B2
CHILTHORNE DOMER 186 E5
Chilthorne Domer CE Sch
BA22 . . . . . 186 E5
Chilthornehill La BA22 . . 186 D6
CHILTON CANTELO 174 D1
Chilton Cantelo House (Sch)
BA22 . . . . . 174 C1
Chilton Cl TA6 . . . . . 208 F7
Chilton Ct 7 BA1 . . . . . 28 B1
Chilton Dro TA7 . . . . . 137 C6
Chilton Gr BA21 . . . . . 219 A7
Chilton Pk TA6 . . . . . 208 F7
CHILTON POLDEN 137 B2
Chilton Rd
Bath BA1 . . . . . 28 B1
Bridgwater TA5, TA6 . . . . . 208 F8
Bristol BS4 . . . . . 23 A8
Chilton Polden TA7 . . . . . 137 B4
Chilton Right Dro TA7 . . . 155 B6
Chilton St TA6 . . . . . 208 F7
CHILTON TRINITY 135 F2
Chilton Trinity Tech Coll
TA6 . . . . . 208 F7
Chilworthy La TA19, TA20 193 F7
Chimes The BS48 . . . . . 18 C8
Chinehorn Dro TA5 . . . . . 135 F3
Chinnock Hollow BA22 . . . 196 E8
Chinnock Rd BA6 . . . . . 206 F5
Chip La TA1 . . . . . 212 E5
CHIPLEY 166 F2
Chippel La DT10 . . . . . 190 F5
Chipping Cross BS21 . . . . . 16 C8
CHIPSTABLE 165 E6
Chi-Rio Cl BA4 . . . . . 205 E4
CHISELBOROUGH 185 F1
Chisland Dr TA24 . . . . . 129 C8
Chistles La TA11 . . . . . 158 A1
Chitcombe Rocks La
TA4 . . . . . 149 C1
CHOLWELL 58 D2
Cholwell Cotts BS39 . . . . . 58 D2
Chorwell La TA21 . . . . . 166 E2
Chovel La BA11 . . . . . 142 F6

Chowins Rd TA18 . . . . 224 C5
Christchurch CE Fst Sch
BA11. . . . . 119 F2
Christ Church CE Prim Sch
Bristol BS8. . . . . 226 A3
Weston-Super-Mare BS23. . 48 E8
Christ Church Cl 1 BS48 . . .8 E2
Christ Church Ct 9
TA18 . . . . 224 C6
Christchurch Hall 2
BA1 . . . . 228 B3
Christ Church Path S 12
BS23 . . . . 48 E8
Christchurch Rd BS8 . . . . 226 A3
Christchurch St E BA11. . 119 F4
Christchurch St W BA11. 119 E4
Christian Cl BS22 . . . . 32 A3
Christian's Cross BA6 . . . 157 E1
Christina Terr BS8 . . . . . . 226 A1
Christmas St 6 BS1. . . . . 227 A3
Christmas Steps 2 BS1 . 227 A3
CHRISTON. 68 D7
Christon Rd
Banwell BS29. . . . . 51 A1
Loxton BS26. . . . . 68 C6
Christon Terr BS23. . . . . . . 48 F2
Christopher Cl BA20 . . . . 218 E5
Christopher Way BA4 . . . 205 A5
Chritchard Way TA1. . . . . 213 B4
Chrysanthemum Cl 3
DT9 . . . . 225 E4
Chrysanthemum Flats 2
DT9 . . . . 225 E4
Chrysanthemum Row 4
DT9 . . . . 225 E4
Chubbards Cross Cvn Site
TA19 . . . . 183 E5
Chubbs Lawn TA18. . . . . . 224 C5
Chubworthy Cross TA4 . . 165 D5
Church Ave BS9 . . . . .5 E4
Church Cl
Bathampton BA2 . . . . 28 F2
Bathford BA1. . . . . 29 B2
Bourton SP8. . . . . 161 E1
7 Carhampton TA24. . . . . 131 A5
Clevedon BS21. . . . . 6 A2
East Huntspill TA9 . . . . 136 E8
Evercreech BA4. . . . . 141 E1
Great Elm BA11. . . . . 118 F7
Lydeard St Lawrence TA4 . 151 A3
24 Martock TA12 . . . . 185 E6
Norton Fitzwarren TA2. . . . 168 B4
Portishead BS20 . . . . 2 D5
Shapwick TA7. . . . . 137 F1
South Brewham BA10 . . . . 160 F6
Stoke St Gregory TA3. . . . . 170 E6
Stoke St Mary TA3 . . . . 169 C1
West Chinnock TA18 . . . . . 196 B8
Yatton BS49. . . . . 34 C7
Church Cnr BS24. . . . . 67 B1
Church Cotts
Chilton Trinity TA5 . . . . 135 F2
Monkton Combe BA2. . . . . . 63 E8
Newton St Loe BA2 . . . . 43 B6
Church Ct
Midsomer Norton BA3. . . . . 78 A1
Redhill BS40 . . . . 36 D3
Churchdown Wlk BS11 . . . .4 E5
Church Dr
Congresbury BS49. . . . . 34 D4
West Buckland TA21 . . . . . 180 F7
Church Farm Bsns Pk
BA2. . . . . 43 A7
Church Farm Cl
Marksbury BA2 . . . . 42 B1
Stawell TA7 . . . . 137 A1
Church Farm Pl 18 BA8. . 190 A6
Churchfield La TA3 . . . . . 183 F7
Church Field La TA7 . . . . 136 C4
Churchfields
Rode BA11. . . . . 101 F8
Wellington TA21. . . . . 222 D7
Church Fields
Wellington TA21. . . . . 222 E6
Wincanton BA9 . . . . 216 C3
Churchfields Dr BA7 . . . . 214 C6
Church Gdns BA6 . . . . 206 D5
Church Hayes Cl BS48. . . . 18 E8
Church Hayes Dr BS48 . . . 18 E8
Church Hill
Beckington BA11. . . . . 101 E4
Buckhorn Weston SP8. . . . 177 D3
Charlton Adam TA11 . . . . . 173 F7
Combwich TA5 . . . . 135 B5
Dinnington TA17. . . . . 195 B7
Exford TA24 . . . . 128 D1
Freshford BA3. . . . . 64 B5
Kington Magna SP8. . . . . . 177 E2
Pitney TA10 . . . . 172 C7
Radstock BA3 . . . . 79 C3
South Cadbury BA22 . . . . . 175 C3
Stalbridge DT10. . . . . 190 B5
Templecombe BA8. . . . . . . 176 E1
Timsbury BA2 . . . . 60 B2
Church Ho BA4 . . . . 141 F1
Church House Rd TA8. . . . 84 F5
CHURCHILL. 52 F5
Churchill Ave
Clevedon BS21. . . . . 6 C2
Wells BA5 . . . . 112 E1
Churchill Bsns Pk BS23 . . 49 A7
Churchill CE Prim Sch
BS40. . . . . 53 A5
Churchill Cl
Burnham-on-S TA8. . . . . . . 104 C5

Churchill Cl *continued*
5 Clevedon BS21. . . . . 6 C2
Wells BA5 . . . . 112 E1
Churchill Dr BS9. . . . . 5 D7
Churchill Gate BS25. . . . . . 52 F4
Churchill Gn BS25 . . . . 52 C5
CHURCHILL GREEN 52 D5
Churchill La
Axminster EX13. . . . . 198 A5
Chipstable TA4. . . . . 165 C5
Churchill Rd
Frome BA11. . . . . 119 D4
Shepton Mallet BA4. . . . . . 205 A5
Wells BA5 . . . . 112 E1
Weston-Super-Mare BS23. . 49 A7
Churchill Rd E BA5. . . . . . 112 E1
Churchill Sch & Sixth Form
Ctr BS25 . . . . 52 D5
Churchill Way
Taunton TA1. . . . . 212 F1
Watchet TA23. . . . . 202 C6
CHURCHINFORD 192 A7
Church La
Axbridge BS26. . . . . 70 C2
Backwell BS48. . . . . 19 C5
Badgworth BS26 . . . . 88 A6
Baltonsborough BA6 . . . . . 158 A5
Bath BA2 . . . . 45 C4
Batheaston BA1. . . . . 28 F4
Bicknoller TA4 . . . . 132 F2
Bishop Sutton BS39. . . . . . . 57 D4
Bitton BS30 . . . . 25 E7
Blackford BS28 . . . . 107 D5
Brent Knoll TA9 . . . . 86 A2
Bristol BS1. . . . . 227 B2
Bristol, Clifton Wood BS8 . 226 B2
Bristol, Dundry Hill BS14. . . 23 B3
Carhampton TA24. . . . . 131 B5
Chew Stoke BS40 . . . . 56 D8
Chewton Mendip BA3 . . . . . 94 F7
Chilcompton BA3. . . . . 96 D5
Chilton Polden TA7. . . . . . . 137 B2
Churchill BS25. . . . . 52 D5
Clutton BS39 . . . . 58 E3
Coleford BA3. . . . . 116 F7
Compton Bishop BS26. . . . . . 69 B3
Compton Dando BS39 . . . . . 41 D6
Doulting BA4 . . . . 141 E6
Dulverton TA22 . . . . 163 D6
East Coker BA22 . . . . 197 E8
East Harptree BS40. . . . . . . 74 E4
East Huntspill TA9 . . . . 136 E8
East Lambrook TA13 . . . . . 220 C8
Evercreech BA4. . . . . 141 E1
Farmborough BA2 . . . . 60 A6
Farrington Gurney BS39 . . . 77 A4
Flax Bourton BS48. . . . . 19 F7
Glastonbury BA6 . . . . 206 D5
Haselbury Plucknett TA18 . 196 C5
Hatch Beauchamp TA3. . . . 182 E8
Horningsham BA12 . . . . . . 144 E4
Horton TA19. . . . . 183 C2
Hutton BS24 . . . . 49 E2
Ilminster TA19. . . . . 221 C4
Kingston St Mary TA2 . . . . 168 E8
Limpley Stoke BA3. . . . . 64 A5
Long Ashton BS41. . . . . 11 C2
Long Sutton TA10. . . . . 172 D2
Loxton BS26. . . . . 68 D4
Lympsham BS24. . . . . 67 B1
Lynford-on-F TA11 . . . . 158 D2
Meare BA6. . . . . 138 D4
Midsomer Norton BA3. . . . . 78 A1
Milborne Port DT9. . . . . . . 217 D2
Misterton TA18 . . . . 224 E3
Nailsea BS21. . . . . 8 C4
Nailsea BS48. . . . . 8 C1
North Perrott TA18 . . . . . . 196 C4
Norton Sub Hamdon,
Chiselborough TA14 . . . . . 185 E1
Norton Sub Hamdon TA14 . 185 F2
Paulton BS39. . . . . 77 E6
Portbury BS20. . . . . 3 E3
Rimpton BA22 . . . . 188 B8
Rode BA11. . . . . 101 F8
Ruishton TA3 . . . . 169 C4
Ruishton, Thornfalcon TA3 . 169 E2
Seavington St Mary TA19. . 184 E1
22 Shepton Mallet BA4 . . . 205 B6
Shepton Mallet, Cannards Grave
BA4. . . . . 205 D2
Sherborne DT9 . . . . 225 D4
Stratton-on-t F BA3. . . . . . . 96 F2
Timsbury BA2 . . . . 60 B2
Westonzoyland TA7 . . . . . . 154 F5
West Pennard BA6 . . . . . . 140 B1
Wingfield BA14 . . . . 83 C6
Winscombe BS25. . . . . 69 E6
Yatton BS49. . . . . 34 C7
Churchlands TA9 . . . . 106 D4
Churchlands Ct TA8. . . . . 104 A7
Churchland Way BS22. . . . 50 B8
Church Lane Cnr TA9 . . . . 86 A2
Church Lane End BS48 . . . 19 F8
Church Leaze BS11 . . . . 4 D6
Church Mdw TA6 . . . . 208 E6
Church Mdws BS14 . . . . . . 23 C4
Church Mead SP8. . . . . . . 161 E1
Churchmoor La BA6. . . . . 158 A5
Church Pass 4 TA6. . . . . 208 F5
Church Path
Aller TA10 . . . . 171 D8
Bridgwater TA6 . . . . 208 E5
Crewkerne TA18. . . . . 224 B6
Meare BA6. . . . . 138 D4
Minehead TA24 . . . . 200 F8
Queen Camel BA22 . . . . . . 174 F3
South Petherton TA13 . . . . 220 C2

Church Path *continued*
2 Yeovil BA20. . . . . 219 B5
Church Path Rd BS20 . . . . . 4 C4
Church Pl
Milborne Port DT9. . . . . . . 217 D2
Pill BS20 . . . . 4 C4
Church Rd
Abbots Leigh BS8. . . . . 11 A8
Bath, Combe Down BA2. . . . 45 C1
Bath, Weston Park BA1 . . . . 27 C1
Bawdrip TA7. . . . . 136 E2
Bitton BS30 . . . . 25 E7
Bourton SP8. . . . . 177 F8
Bradford Abbas DT9 . . . . . 187 E1
Brean TA8 . . . . 65 F4
Bristol, Bishopsworth BS13. 22 A6
Bristol, Sneyd Park BS9. . . . . 5 D3
Chapel Leigh TA4 . . . . 167 A7
Churchinford TA3. . . . . 191 F8
Churchstanton TA3. . . . . . . 181 B1
Coxley BA5. . . . . 139 E6
Dundry BS41 . . . . 21 D2
East Brent TA9. . . . . 86 C4
Easton-in-G BS20. . . . . 4 A4
Edington TA7 . . . . 137 C2
Fitzhead TA4 . . . . 166 F7
Fordgate TA7 . . . . 154 D3
Huntspill TA9 . . . . 136 A8
Ilton TA19 . . . . 183 E4
Keenthorne TA5 . . . . 134 D3
Kilmington BA12 . . . . 161 F7
Leigh Woods BS8. . . . . 11 D6
Lympsham BS24. . . . . 67 B1
Middlezoy TA7 . . . . 155 B3
Minehead TA24 . . . . 200 F8
North Curry TA3. . . . . 170 B4
North Newton TA7 . . . . 154 A2
Peasedown St John BA2 . . . 79 B8
Pensford BS39. . . . . 40 A7
Redhill BS40 . . . . 36 D3
Shapwick TA7. . . . . 137 F1
South Cadbury BA22 . . . . . 175 D4
Sparkford BA22. . . . . 175 A4
Spaxton TA5. . . . . 152 E7
Street BA16. . . . . 207 D7
Sutton Mallet TA7 . . . . 155 B7
Taunton TA3. . . . . 168 D1
Wembdon TA6 . . . . 208 D6
Weston-Super-Mare BS22. . 31 E2
Whitchurch BS14. . . . . 23 C4
Winford BS40 . . . . 38 A7
Winscombe BS25. . . . . 69 E7
Yatton BS49. . . . . 34 C7
Church Rd N BS20 . . . . 2 D5
Church Rd S BS20. . . . . 2 D4
Church Rise BS40. . . . . 38 A7
CHURCH ROW. 101 F8
Church Row BA3. . . . . 96 F2
Church Row Cotts TA3 . . 181 E6
Church Sq
Clutton BS39 . . . . 58 E2
Midsomer Norton BA3. . . . . 78 A1
8 Taunton TA1 . . . . 212 F4
Church St
Babcary TA11. . . . . 174 C7
Banwell BS29. . . . . 51 B3
Barton St David BA6 . . . . . 157 F2
6 Bath BA1 . . . . 228 C2
Bathford BA1. . . . . 29 B2
Bath, Weston park BA1 . . . . 27 B1
Bath, Widcombe BA2. . . . . . 45 B4
Beckington BA11 . . . . 101 E4
Bishops Lydeard TA4 . . . . . 167 E8
Blackford BS28 . . . . 107 D4
Blagdon BS40 . . . . 54 F2
Bridgwater TA6 . . . . 209 A5
Bristol BS1. . . . . 227 B2
5 Cannington TA5. . . . . . . 135 B2
Castle Cary BA7. . . . . 214 B4
Chard TA20. . . . . 223 C3
Cheddar BS27 . . . . 90 B7
Coleford BA3. . . . . 116 F7
Crewkerne TA18. . . . . 224 C6
Croscombe BA5 . . . . 204 C7
Dinder BA5 . . . . 140 D7
Donyatt TA19 . . . . 183 D1
Drayton TA10. . . . . 171 E3
Dunster TA24 . . . . 201 E2
2 Frome BA11. . . . . 119 F4
Halstock BA22. . . . . 197 C3
8 Henstridge BA8 . . . . 190 A6
Highbridge TA9 . . . . 104 E4
Hinton St George TA17 . . . . 195 C7
Horningsham BA12 . . . . . . 144 D4
Ilchester BA22. . . . . 173 E1
Isle Abbotts TA3 . . . . 183 F7
Keinton Mandeville TA11 . . 158 A1
Kilmersdon BA3. . . . . 98 B5
Kingsbury Episcopi TA12 . . 185 B8
Kington Magna SP8. . . . . . 177 E2
Lopen TA13 . . . . 185 A1
Maiden Bradley BA12 . . . . 144 C1
Mark TA9 . . . . 106 D4
Martock TA12. . . . . 185 E6
Merriott TA16. . . . . 195 F7
Milborne Port DT9. . . . . . . 217 D2
Minehead, Alcombe TA24. . 201 B5
Minehead TA24 . . . . 200 F8
Norton St Philip BA2 . . . . . . 81 E4
Nunney BA11. . . . . 143 B8
Paulton BS39. . . . . 77 D6
Pensford BS39. . . . . 40 D4
Podimore BA22 . . . . 174 A3
Radstock BA3 . . . . 78 F2
Shepton Beauchamp TA19 . 184 E4
Southwick BA14. . . . . 83 F3
Stogursey TA5 . . . . 134 C5
Stoke St Michael BA3 . . . . 116 A2

Church St *continued*
Taunton TA1. . . . . 213 B3
Timberscombe TA24 . . . . . 130 B5
Tintinhull BA22 . . . . 186 B6
Upton Noble BA4. . . . . 142 F2
Wanstrow BA4. . . . . 142 F4
Wedmore BS28 . . . . 108 D4
West Coker BA22 . . . . 197 A8
Wincanton BA9 . . . . 216 C4
Winsham TA20. . . . . 194 E1
Wiveliscombe TA4 . . . . 210 C4
Woolavington TA7 . . . . 136 E4
Woolley BA1 . . . . 27 F6
Yeovil BA20 . . . . 219 B5
Yeovilton BA22. . . . . 174 A1
CHURCHSTANTON. 181 B1
Churchstanton Prim Sch
TA3 . . . . 191 E8
Church Steps TA24. . . . . . 200 F8
Church Terr
7 Bampton EX16 . . . . 164 B1
East Coker BA22 . . . . 197 C7
Odcombe BA22 . . . . 186 C2
4 Yeovil BA20. . . . . 219 B5
Church Tk SP8. . . . . 161 E1
CHURCH TOWN 19 C5
Church Town BS48. . . . . . . 19 C5
Church View
Bourton SP8. . . . . 161 E1
Chilton Trinity TA5 . . . . 135 F2
Clatworthy TA4. . . . . 149 F1
Evercreech BA4. . . . . 141 E1
North Wootton BA4 . . . . . . 140 C4
Porlock TA24 . . . . 124 A3
Wraxall BS48. . . . . 9 B2
Church View Cl TA10. . . . 171 E8
Churchview Ct BA6 . . . . . 206 D4
Churchward Dr BA11. . . . 120 C6
Churchward Rd BS22. . . . . 32 B3
Churchway
Curry Rivel TA10 . . . . 171 D4
Faulkland BA3 . . . . 80 D1
Church Way TA7. . . . . 137 D2
Churchway Cl TA10 . . . . . 171 D4
Churchways BS14. . . . . 23 C4
Churchwell Cl DT9. . . . . . . 187 E1
Churchwell St DT9. . . . . . 187 E1
Church Wlk
Baltonsborough BA6 . . . . . 158 A5
Bawdrip TA7. . . . . 136 E2
Bratton Seymour BA9 . . . . 176 B8
Ilminster TA19. . . . . 221 C4
Leigh u M BA3. . . . . 117 A3
Long Sutton TA10. . . . . 172 F4
Marston Magna BA22 . . . . . 174 F1
9 North Petherton TA6 . . 153 E3
Pill BS20 . . . . 4 C4
Wrington BS40 . . . . 35 D2
Chur La BA22. . . . . 197 A8
Churlands Cl BA22 . . . . . . 197 A8
Churston Cl BS14 . . . . 23 A3
Cinder Ash La TA18 . . . . . 195 D4
Cinnamon La BA6. . . . . . . 206 F3
Circle The BA2. . . . . 44 B3
Circular Rd BS9. . . . . .5 E2
Circus Field Rd BA6. . . . . 206 D4
Circus Mews BA1 . . . . 228 B3
Circus Pl BA1. . . . . 228 B3
Circus The BA1 . . . . 228 B3
City of Bath Coll BA1. . . . . 228 B2
City of Bristol Coll BS1. . 226 C2
City of Bristol Coll (Hartcliffe
Ctr) BS13. . . . . 22 D4
City Rd BS2. . . . . 227 B4
City The TA9. . . . . 106 C4
City View BA1 . . . . 228 C4
Clammer Hill La TA18 . . . 224 D6
Clanage Rd BS3. . . . . 11 E4
Clanders Batch BS40 . . . . . 54 D3
CLANDOWN 78 E4
Clandown CE Prim Sch
BA3. . . . . 78 E4
Clandown Rd BS39. . . . . . . 77 F4
Clanfield DT9. . . . . 225 B2
Clan Ho BA2. . . . . 45 C7
CLANVILLE 159 C3
Clanville TA24 . . . . 200 F7
Clanville Rd TA24 . . . . 200 F7
CLAPTON
Crewkerne. 195 C1
Midsomer Norton 96 C7
Clapton Court Gdns★
TA18 . . . . 195 D1
Clapton Dro BS20. . . . . 2 D1
Clapton Gate TA18 . . . . . . 195 C2
CLAPTON IN GORDANO. 2 E1
Clapton La
Holton BA9. . . . . 176 B6
Portishead BS20 . . . . 2 E2
Clapton Rd
Hewish TA18 . . . . 195 D2
Midsomer Norton BA3. . . . . 77 D1
CLAPTON WICK 7 E6
Clapton Wlk BS9. . . . . 5 C5
Clare Gdns BA2. . . . . 44 D1
Clareham La
Buckland Dinham BA11 . . . . 99 D2
Buckland Dinham BA11 . . . . 99 F3
Claremont Bldgs BA1 . . . . . 28 A1
Claremont Cres BS23. . . . . 30 B1
Claremont Ct TA1. . . . . . . 212 C1
Claremont Cvn Pk TA8 . . . . 84 F6
Claremont Dr TA1. . . . . . . 212 C1
Claremont Gdns
Clevedon BS21. . . . . 6 E1
Hallatrow BS39 . . . . 77 B7
4 Nailsea BS48 . . . . 8 D1
Claremont Gr TA6. . . . . . . 209 D6

Claremont Hall BS21 . . . . . . .6 E4
Claremont La TA1. . . . . . . 212 C1
Claremont Pl 13 BA1 . . . . . 28 A1
Claremont Rd BA1 . . . . 28 B1
Claremont Wlk BA1 . . . . . . 28 A1
Clarence Ct 1 BA20 . . . . 219 A5
Clarence Dr 1 TA6 . . . . . 153 F4
Clarence Grove Rd BS23. . 48 E5
Clarence Pl
Bath BA1 . . . . 44 B6
Bristol BS2. . . . . 226 C4
Clarence Rd BS1. . . . . 227 B1
Clarence Rd E BS23 . . . . . . 48 E5
Clarence Rd N BS23. . . . . . 48 D5
Clarence Rd S BS23 . . . . . . 48 D5
Clarence St
Bath BA1 . . . . 228 C4
Taunton TA1 . . . . 212 E4
Yeovil BA20 . . . . 219 A5
Clarence Terr
Bath BA2 . . . . 45 D5
8 Yeovil BA20. . . . . 219 B4
Clarendon Rd
Bath BA2 . . . . 45 B5
Weston-Super-Mare BS23. . 48 F8
Clarendon Villas BA2. . . . . 45 B5
Clare St
Bridgwater TA6 . . . . 208 F5
Bristol BS1. . . . . 227 A2
2 North Petherton TA6 . . 153 F4
Clark Cl
Woolavington TA7 . . . . 136 E4
Wraxall BS48. . . . . 9 B2
Clarken Cl BS48. . . . . .8 E1
Clarken Coombe BS41. . . . 11 B3
Clarke's Cl TA20 . . . . 223 D4
Clarkes Ct BA20. . . . . 219 A4
Clarke's Row TA20 . . . . . . 223 D4
CLARKHAM CROSS 197 E2
Clarkham Cross BA22 . . . . 197 E2
Clarks Cl BA22. . . . . 218 A5
Clark's La TA18 . . . . 224 F3
Clarks Meadow BA4. . . . . . 205 C3
Clarkson Ave BS22. . . . . . . 31 C1
Clarkson Ho BA1. . . . . 228 A2
Clarks Rd TA6 . . . . 209 C4
Clarks Shopping Village
BA16. . . . . 207 C6
Clarks Way BA2. . . . . 44 C2
Classic Bldgs TA6. . . . . . . 208 F4
Clatcombe La DT9 . . . . . . 188 D6
CLATWORTHY 149 F1
Clatworthy Dr BS14 . . . . . . 23 A7
Clatworthy Resr★ TA4. . . . 149 D2
Claude Ave BA2. . . . . 44 C5
Claude Terr BA2 . . . . 44 C5
CLAVERHAM. 17 E1
Claverham Cl BS49 . . . . 34 D7
Claverham Dro BS49 . . . . . 17 D5
Claverham Pk BS49 . . . . . . 34 F8
Claverham Rd BS49 . . . . . . 34 E8
CLAVERTON 46 B5
Claverton Bldgs BA2 . . . . 228 C1
Claverton Ct BA2 . . . . 45 E4
CLAVERTON DOWN. 45 F3
Claverton Down Rd BA2 . . 45 F3
Claverton Dr BA2 . . . . 45 F3
Claverton Hill BA2 . . . . 46 A4
Claverton Lodge BA2. . . . . 45 C5
Claverton Pumping Sta★
BA2. . . . . 46 C5
Claverton Rd BS31 . . . . 25 E2
Claverton Rd W BS31. . . . . 25 D3
Claverton St BA2. . . . . 228 C1
Clay Castle TA18 . . . . 196 C5
Clay Castle La TA18 . . . . . 196 C6
Claydon Cl TA23 . . . . 131 E4
Claydon Gn BS14. . . . . 22 F3
Clayford La TA22. . . . . 163 C5
Clayford Rd TA22 . . . . 163 C5
CLAYHANGER. 165 C1
Clayhanger Cross TA20. . 193 E6
Clayhanger La
Chard TA20. . . . . 223 A8
Combe St Nicholas TA20 . . 193 E6
CLAYHIDON 180 E2
Clayhidon Crossway
EX15. . . . . 180 E2
Clay La
Barrington TA19. . . . . 184 B5
Bitton BS30 . . . . 25 D8
Chewton Mendip BA3 . . . . . 94 C5
Higher Chillington TA19 . . . 194 F5
Millmoor EX15. . . . . 179 A1
Rode BA11. . . . . 101 F8
Claylands Cnr TA5 . . . . . . 134 E5
Claypiece Rd BS13 . . . . 22 A4
CLAYPITS 164 C4
CLAYS END 43 D6
Clayton Cl
Portishead BS20 . . . . 2 E4
Yeovil BA22 . . . . 218 A6
CLEARWOOD 121 F8
Clearwood BA13 . . . . 121 F8
Clearwood View BA13 . . . 121 E4
Cleaveside Cl BA22. . . . . . 174 F3
CLEEVE 35 B8
Cleeve Abbey★ TA23 . . . . 131 E3
Cleevedale Rd BA2. . . . . . . 45 A1
Cleeve Dr BS49 . . . . 35 B8
Cleeve Gn BA2. . . . . 44 A6
Cleeve Gr BS31 . . . . 24 D5
Cleeve Hill
Ubley BS40 . . . . 73 E8
Watchet TA23. . . . . 202 A7
Cleeve Hill Rd BS40 . . . . . . 35 C7
Cleeve Pk TA24 . . . . 131 D5
Cleeve Pl BS48. . . . . 9 A1

Cleeve Rd TA2 213 B7
Cleeveways DT9 176 A2
Clemence Rd BA16 207 D4
Clements Cl BA5 203 C3
Clement St BS2 227 C4
Cleve Ct 3 BS8 11 F6
CLEVEDON 6 B3
Clevedon Com Sch BS21 6 F5
Clevedon Court★ BS21 7 A4
Clevedon Craft Ctr★ BS21 7 A1
Clevedon Hospl BS21 6 E3
Clevedon La BS21 8 B7
Clevedon Min Rly★ BS21 6 B3
Clevedon Pier★ BS21 6 C4
Clevedon Rd
Flax Bourton BS48 9 F2
Midsomer Norton BA3 78 A2
Nailsea BS21 8 B4
Portishead BS20 2 D3
Weston-Super-Mare BS23 48 E6
Wraxall BS48 9 B4
Wraxall BS48 9 D6
Clevedon Terr BS6 227 A4
Clevedon Wlk 2 BS48 8 E2
Cleveland Cotts BA1 228 C4
Cleveland Ct BA2 45 C6
Cleveland Pl BA1 228 C4
Cleveland Pl E BA1 228 C4
Cleveland Pl W BA1 228 C4
Cleveland Reach BA1 228 C4
Cleveland Row BA1 45 B8
Clevelands TA24 200 F8
Cleveland St TA1 212 E4
Cleveland Terr BA1 228 C4
Cleveland Wlk BA2 45 C6
Cleve The BA21 218 C6
CLEWER 89 D3
Clewson Rise BS14 22 F3
Cleyhill Gdns BA13 121 D4
Cliffe Dr BA3 64 A6
Clifford Ave TA2 212 E8
Clifford Cres TA2 212 E8
Clifford Gdns BS11 4 E6
Clifford Ho BS23 48 D6
Clifford Lodge 3 TA5 135 B2
Clifford Mews TA21 222 E6
Clifford Pk TA5 135 B2
Clifford Terr TA21 222 E6
Cliff Rd
Cheddar BS27 71 E1
North Petherton TA6 153 E3
Weston-Super-Mare BS22 31 A2
Cliff St BS27 90 C8
Cliffs The BS27 90 C8
Clift House Rd BS3 11 F4
Clift House Spur BS3 11 F4
CLIFTON 226 A4
Clifton Ave BS23 48 E5
Clifton Cl
1 Bristol BS8 11 F7
Yeovil BA21 219 E6
Clifton Coll BS8 226 A4
Clifton College Prep Sch
BS8 5 F1
Clifton Ct 10 BS21 6 C2
Clifton Down BS8 11 F7
Clifton Down Rd BS8 226 A3
Clifton High Gr BS9 5 E5
Clifton High Sch BS8 226 A4
Clifton Hill
Barwick BA22 197 F8
Bristol BS8 226 A2
Clifton Park Rd BS8 11 F8
Clifton Pk BS8 226 A3
Clifton Rd
Bristol BS8 226 A2
Weston-Super-Mare BS23 48 E5
Clifton Rocks Railway★
BS8 11 F6
Clifton St BS20 2 C2
Clifton Suspension Bridge★
BS8 11 E7
Clifton Terr 7 TA2 212 F6
Clifton Vale BS8 226 A2
Clifton Vale Cl BS8 226 A2
Clifton View 9 BA22 197 F8
CLIFTON WOOD 226 A2
Cliftonwood Cres BS8 226 B2
Clifton Wood Ct BS8 226 B2
Clifton Wood Rd BS8 226 B2
Cliftonwood Terr BS8 226 A2
Clift Pl BS1 227 A1
Clifts Bldgs BA11 119 F4
CLINK 120 C6
Clink Farm Ct BA11 120 C6
Clink Rd BA11 120 D6
Clink The TA6 209 A5
Clipper Cl TA6 209 C4
Clipper Quay TA24 201 B7
Clitsome View TA23 131 D2
Clive Rd BS14 23 C8
Clivey BA13 102 E1
Clock Ho TA5 134 B2
Clock Ho The BA10 160 D4
Clockhouse Mews BS20 2 D6
Clockhouse The TA4 167 E6
Clockhouse View BA16 207 D6
CLOFORD 143 A7
CLOFORD COMMON 143 B6
Cloisters Croft TA8 104 B6
Cloisters The BA5 203 D3
Cloister The DT9 225 D4
Closemead BS21 6 D1
Close The
Glastonbury BA6 206 E5
9 Merriott TA16 195 F7
Minehead TA24 201 B5
North Cadbury BA22 175 D6
Close The *continued*
Portishead BS20 1 F1
CLOSWORTH 197 F5
Clotfurlong La DT9 188 F1
Clothier Mdw BA7 214 B6
Cloudberry Cl TA20 223 F5
Cloud Hill Ind Est BS39 77 A8
Clovelly Rd BS22 32 A2
Clover Cl
Clevedon BS21 6 F3
Paulton BS39 77 E4
Clover Ct 2 BS22 49 D7
Clover Gd BA4 205 C5
Clover Mead TA1 213 C1
Clover Rd BS22 32 A6
Cloverton Dr TA6 209 D7
Clover Way
Bridgwater TA6 208 E1
Highbridge TA9 104 E4
Clumber Dr BA11 119 F6
Clumber Ho BA11 119 F6
CLUTTON 58 E3
CLUTTON HILL 59 B4
Clutton Hill BS39 59 B4
Clutton Prim Sch BS39 58 E3
Clyce Rd TA9 104 D3
Clyde Ave BS31 24 F4
Clyde Gdns BA2 44 B6
Clydesdale Cl BS14 23 A6
Clynder Gr BS21 6 E6
Clyntonville BS22 31 A4
Coach House Mews BS23 30 D1
Coachmans Yd BA6 206 D5
Coach Rd TA24 124 A3
Coalash La BA11 119 D8
Coal Barton BA3 116 E8
Coalbridge Cl BS22 31 F2
Coaley Rd BS11 4 D5
Coal La BA11 119 C8
Coal Orch TA1 212 F4
Coalpit La
Chilcompton BA3 96 A2
Stoke St Michael BA3 116 B3
Coalpit Rd BA1 29 A4
Coape Rd BS14 23 F5
Coast Cvn Pk BS21 1 B1
Coastguard Cotts TA24 201 A8
Coast Rd TA8 84 F7
COAT 185 D7
Coates Est BS48 8 F3
Coates Gr BS48 9 A2
Coates Wlk BS4 22 D6
Coate Turn TA4 166 A6
Coat Rd TA12 185 D7
Cobblers Way BA3 97 C8
Cobblestone Mews BS8 226 A4
Cob Castle TA21 180 D8
Cobhorn Dr BS13 21 F4
Cobley Croft BS21 16 C8
Cobthorn Way BS49 34 E5
Coburg Cl TA21 180 F7
Coburg Villas 11 BA1 28 A1
Cock And Yew Tree Hill
BS40 38 A2
Cock-Crowing Stone
TA20 193 D4
Cockers Hill BS39 41 C5
Cockhill Elm La BA7 214 B4
Cockhill La BA22 175 D7
COCKLAKE 108 E7
Cockland Hill TA21 166 C1
Cockmill La BA4 140 F1
Cockpit Hill DT6, DT8 199 F4
Cockpit La BA4 142 C2
Cock Rd
Buckland Dinham BA2,
BA11 100 B5
Horningsham BA12 144 C4
Cockrod BA16 207 B2
COCKWOOD 134 E5
Cod La BA22 196 D7
Codrington Pl BS8 226 A3
Cogsall Rd BS14 23 F6
Coity Pl BS21 6 C4
Coker Hill BA22 196 F8
Coker Hill La BA22 197 A7
Coker Ho BA22 197 C8
Coker Marsh BA22 197 D7
Coker Rd BS22 32 B2
Coker's La BA12 161 F8
Colbourn Cl BA3 114 E7
Colbourne Rd BA2 44 D1
Colchester Cres BS4 22 D7
COLD ASHTON 12 F6
Cold Harbour
Milborne Port DT9 217 D2
Sherborne DT9 225 E5
Coldharbour Bsns Pk
DT9 225 E6
Coldharbour La BS23 48 D3
Cold Harbour La BA22 196 F6
Coldhills La BA8 176 D2
Cold Nose BS28 138 D8
Coldpark Gdns BS13 21 E5
Coldpark Rd BS13 21 E5
Cold Rd TA3 182 D6
Coldrick Cl BS14 22 F3
Cole Cl
Cotford St Luke TA4 167 E6
Nether Stowey TA5 134 A3
Cole Cross BA22 186 C6
COLEFORD 116 F7
COLEFORD WATER 150 F4
Colehouse La BS21 16 C8
Cole La 5 TA14 185 F4
Colemead BS13 22 B5
Cole Mead BA10 215 D5
Cole Rd BA10 215 D5
Coleridge Cottage★ TA5 134 B2
Coleridge Cres TA1 213 B3
Coleridge Gdns TA8 85 B2
Coleridge Gn TA6 208 E5
Coleridge Rd
Bridgwater TA6 208 E6
Clevedon BS21 6 C3
Nether Stowey TA5 134 A2
Weston-Super-Mare BS23 49 A4
Coleridge Sq TA6 208 E6
Coleridge Vale Rd E 1
BS21 6 D2
Coleridge Vale Rd N BS21 6 C2
Coleridge Vale Rd S BS21 6 D2
Coleridge Vale Rd W 2
BS21 6 C2
Coles Cotts TA5 135 F2
COLE'S CROSS 199 D5
Coles Cross Cotts DT8 199 D5
Coles Gdns BA3 98 B5
Coleshill Dr BS13 22 B5
Cole's La
Chewton Mendip BA3 95 A6
South Petherton TA13 220 D3
Colesmore TA4 167 A4
Coles Place TA20 223 C3
Coles's La EX13 198 B1
COLEY 75 C4
Coley La TA19 194 F5
Coley Rd BS40 75 B4
Colham La TA20 194 E1
Colin Ave TA2 212 F7
Colin Rd TA2 213 A7
Collarway La BA22 196 F8
College BA22 196 E8
College Cl TA10 172 E2
College Ct TA8 104 A7
College Fields BS8 11 F8
College Gn
Bristol BS1 226 C2
Yeovil BA21 219 B6
College Rd
Bath BA1 27 E1
Bristol, Clifton BS8 11 F8
Taunton TA2 212 D6
Wells BA5 203 E5
College Sq BS1 226 C2
College St
Bristol BS1 226 C2
Burnham-on-S TA8 104 A7
College View
18 Bath BA1 28 A1
Taunton TA1 212 C2
College Way
Bridgwater TA6 209 C6
Taunton TA1 212 C1
Colles Cl BA5 203 F5
Colles Rd BA5 203 F5
Collett Ave BA4 205 C5
Collett Cl BS22 32 C4
Collett Rd TA2 212 A7
Collett Way BA11 120 C7
Colley La TA6 209 B4
Colleylake Cotts TA3 181 C5
Colley Lane Ind Est TA6 209 B3
Collickshire La TA3 170 E6
Collie Cnr BA11 118 A1
Collier Cl BA2 78 D8
Colliers La BA1 27 F4
Collier's La BA11 99 D2
Colliers Rise BA3 79 A3
Colliers Wlk 4 BS48 8 E2
Collingwood Cl
Saltford BS31 25 E2
Weston-Super-Mare BS22 31 E4
Collingwood Ct TA6 208 F5
Collingwood Rd BA21 219 F8
Collin's Farm TA19 183 E2
Collins' La TA11 173 F7
Collinson Rd BS13 22 B5
Collins St BS11 4 B8
Collum La BS22 31 E6
Colman Rd TA1 212 B1
Colmer Rd
Bridgwater TA6 208 F7
Yeovil BA21 219 B6
Colne Gn BS31 25 A4
Colombo Cres BS23 48 E3
Colston Ave BS1 227 A2
Colston Cross EX13 198 B4
Colston Fort 2 BS2 227 A4
Colston Par BS1 227 B1
Colston's Almshouses 1
BS1 227 A3
Colston St BS1 227 A3
Colston Yd BS1 227 A3
Colton La TA4 149 F7
Columbus Ho BA2 45 D8
Colyton 11 BS22 32 A2
Combe Ave BS20 2 C6
Combe Batch BS28 108 D4
Combe Batch Rise BS28 108 D4
Combe Beacon La TA20 193 C7
Combe Cl
Bicknoller TA4 132 E2
Yeovil BA21 219 A8
Combe Cross
Halse TA4 167 B7
Monksilver TA4 150 C8
Shillingford EX16 164 D4
Combecross Hill TA4 150 B8
Combecross La
Monksilver TA4 150 B8
Stogumber TA4 150 C8
COMBE DOWN 45 B1
Combe Down CE Prim Sch
BA2 45 B1
Combe Down La TA4 151 C2
Combe Fields BS20 2 C6
COMBE FLOREY 151 C2
Combe Gn BA5 204 B7
Combe Gr BA1 44 B8
COMBE HAY 62 D4
Combe Hay La BA2 62 B6
COMBE HILL 217 A4
Combe Hill
Barton St David TA11 158 A2
Combe St Nicholas TA20 193 D5
Hemyock EX15 180 C2
Milborne Port DT9 217 B3
Templecombe BA8 176 E1
Yenston BA8 189 F8
Combe Hill Dro TA20 193 C5
Combe Hill La TA7 156 B7
Combe La
Brompton Ralph TA4 150 B3
Charlton Adam TA11 173 F8
Chilton Polden TA7 137 B3
Churchstanton TA3 181 A2
Combe St Nicholas TA20 193 B5
Dulverton TA22 163 D6
East Anstey TA22 162 F6
Exford TA24 128 D1
Hallatrow BS39 77 B6
Langport TA10 171 F7
North Curry TA3 170 A4
Parbrook BA4 158 D8
Rodhuish TA24 131 B3
Wedmore BS28 108 D4
Wiveliscombe TA4 210 C8
Woolavington TA7 136 F4
Combeland La TA22 164 A5
Combeland Rd TA24 201 B4
Combe Pk
Bath BA1 44 C8
Yeovil BA21 218 F8
Combe Rd
Bath BA2 45 B1
Portishead BS20 2 D5
Combe Road Cl BA2 45 B1
COMBE ST NICHOLAS 193 D6
Combeshead Hill TA22 148 A3
Combeshead La
Brompton Regis TA22 148 A4
West Anstey EX36 162 A7
Combeside BA2 45 A3
Combe Side BS48 19 A7
Combe St TA20 223 C4
Combe Street La BA21 219 A8
Combe Street Lane Rdbt
BA21 218 F8
Combe Terr TA9 136 E8
Combe The
Burrington BS40 53 F2
Lydeard St Lawrence TA4 151 C2
COMBE THROOP 176 F2
COMBWICH 135 B5
Comer Rd BS27 90 A7
Comer's Cross TA24 146 E6
Comer's Gate TA24 146 E6
COMEYTROWE 212 B1
Comeytrowe Ctr TA1 212 C1
Comeytrowe La TA1, TA4 212 A2
Comeytrowe Orch TA1 212 A2
Comeytrowe Rd TA1 212 B1
Comeytrowe Rise TA1 212 B2
Comfortable Pl BA1 228 A3
Commerce Pk BA11 120 D8
Commerce Way TA9 104 F2
Commercial Rd
Bristol BS1 227 A1
Shepton Mallet BA4 205 B6
Commercial Row TA20 223 C4
Commercial Way BS22 32 B2
Common La
Charlton Adam TA11 174 A8
Churchill Green BS25 52 B5
Easton-in-G BS20 4 B2
Halstock BA22 197 C2
Hardington Mandeville
BA22 197 A5
Holcombe BA3 116 D7
Huish Champflower TA4 165 D7
Kington Magna SP8 177 E1
Marnhull DT10 190 E4
North Perrott TA18 196 D4
Templecombe BA8 177 A1
Wincanton BA9 216 D3
Yenston BA8 189 F8
Common Moor Dro BA6 206 E7
Common Rd BA9 216 E3
Como Ct BS20 2 C6
Compass Hill TA1 212 E3
Compass Rise TA1 212 E3
Compton Acres DT9 187 E4
COMPTON BISHOP 69 A3
Compton Cl
Glastonbury BA6 206 F7
Shepton Mallet BA4 205 B5
Taunton TA2 213 A6
Yeovil BA21 219 E8
Compton Cnr BA4 205 B5
Compton Ct Mews DT9 187 F3
COMPTON DANDO 41 D6
Compton Dr
Bristol BS9 5 C7
Weston-Super-Mare BS24 49 E7
COMPTON DUNDON 157 B4
Compton Dundon CE Prim
Sch TA11 157 A3
COMPTON DURVILLE 184 F4
Compton Flats BA21 219 C6
Compton Gdns BA11 120 D7
Compton Gn BS31 24 E4
Compton Hill TA13 220 A5
Compton La
Axbridge BS26 70 B1
Shepton Mallet BA4 205 B2
COMPTON MARTIN 74 A7
COMPTON
PAUNCEFOOT 175 E5
Compton Rd
Shepton Mallet BA4 205 B4
South Cadbury BA22 175 D4
South Petherton TA13 220 B5
Yeovil BA21 187 E3
Compton St
Butleigh BA6 157 D4
Compton Dundon TA11 157 B4
Comrade Ave BS25 70 E8
Concorde Dr BS21 6 B1
Condell Cl TA6 208 F7
Condor Cl BS22 49 D8
Conduit Hill BA11 99 B1
Conegore BA22 174 D4
Conegore Cnr BA22 174 D4
Coneygree BS13 21 F6
Conference Ave BS20 2 F5
Conference Cl BS20 2 F4
CONGRESBURY 34 E4
Conies The TA2 168 E8
Conifer Cl TA24 128 D1
Conifer Way BS24 49 E5
Coniston Ave BS9 5 E6
Coniston Cres BS23 48 F4
Coniston Gdns BA21 219 A7
CONKWELL 46 C1
Connaught Ho TA6 209 C5
Connaught Mans BA2 228 C3
Connaught Pl BS23 48 D8
Connaught Rd BS4 22 E8
Connection Rd BA2 44 A6
Connelly Dr BS28 108 C4
Connock Sq BA4 205 C4
Conquest Bsns Pk TA19 184 A4
Constable Cl
Keynsham BS31 24 F6
Yeovil BA21 219 E8
Constable Dr BS22 31 F3
Constantine Ct BA4 205 E4
Constitution Hill BS8 226 B2
Convocation Ave BA2 45 E5
Conway Cres TA8 85 C1
Conway Gn BS31 25 A3
Conway Rd TA5 135 B2
Conygar Cl BS21 6 F5
Conygar View TA24 201 E3
Conygre Gn BA2 60 B2
Conygre Rise BA2 59 F6
Cook Ave TA20 223 D3
Cooke's La TA10 156 B2
Cookley La TA4 150 F8
Cooks Bridle Path BS48 36 D8
Cooks Cl TA3 169 D5
Cook's Folly Rd BS9 5 D3
Cooks Gdns BS48 9 A2
Cooks La DT9 225 D3
Cook's La
Banwell BS29 51 A4
Clevedon BS21 7 B2
Cranmore BA4 142 A6
Milverton TA4 167 B5
Stalbridge DT10 190 B2
Cooksley La TA4 149 A2
Cookson Cl TA8 104 D5
Cook St BS11 4 C8
Cook Way TA2 212 C6
COOMBE
Crewkerne 195 B4
Sampford Peverell 178 A4
Taunton 169 C8
Coombe DT9 225 C5
Coombe Bridge Ave BS9 5 D6
Coombe Brook BA5 203 A7
Coombe Cl BA7 214 C6
Coombe Cotts BA5 204 C7
Coombe Dale
Backwell BS48 37 A8
Bristol BS9 5 C6
Coombe Dell BA4 205 A6
COOMBE DINGLE 5 C8
Coombe Gdns BS9 5 E6
Coombe Hill
Blagdon Hill TA21 181 A5
Bruton BA10 215 E7
Coombe La
Bristol BS9 5 E6
Compton Bishop BS26 69 B4
East Harptree BS40 74 E4
Easton-in-G BS8 4 A2
Kingsbury Episcopi TA12 185 B8
Shepton Mallet BA4 205 A6
Coomb End BA3 78 F3
Coombend Ho BA3 78 F3
Coombe Rd
Dinnington TA17 195 B7
Nailsea BS48 8 E1
Weston-Super-Mare BS23 30 E1
Coombe's Cider Farm &
Mus★ TA9 106 A4
Coombe Side TA9 86 B2
Coombe St
Bruton BA10 215 E7
Penselwood BA9 161 E2
Coombe's Way BS26 87 E8
Coombe Terr
Glastonbury BA6 206 E5
Sherborne DT9 225 C5
Coombe The
Blagdon BS40 54 C3

Coombe The *continued*
Compton Martin BS40 74 A6
Coombe View BA4 205 A6
Coombe Water La DT8 199 E5
Coomb Rocke BS9 5 D6
Cooperage La BS3 226 B1
Cooperage The BA11 119 F3
Cooper Rd BS9 5 F7
Cooper's Ash La BA7, BA22 214 A2
Coopers Barns BA22 174 F1
Coopers Hts TA4 210 C4
Coopers Mead BA4 205 D4
Coopers Mill TA2 168 B4
Coot Hide EX16 178 D1
Coots The BS14 23 E6
Copeland Dr BS14 23 B5
Copford La BS41 11 B1
Copis La TA11 158 B3
Coplestons TA3 168 D1
Copley Gdns BS22 31 F2
Coppack Ho 6 BS21 6 C2
Copper Beeches TA1 212 A2
Copper Beech Rd TA11 173 D5
Copper Cl BS27 90 A8
Copperfield Dr BS22 31 F4
Coppern Way DT10 190 B4
Coppice Cl BA20 218 D2
Coppice End Cnr BS24 67 C2
Coppice Mews BS21 6 C4
Coppice The BS13 21 E4
Coppin Cl BA6 206 F3
Coppin Rd TA2 168 B4
Coppits Hill La
Yeovil BA21 218 D8
Yeovil Marsh BA21 187 A5
COPPLEHAM 147 D5
Copplesbury La BA4, BA10 160 D8
Copse Cl
Watchet TA23 202 C5
Weston-Super-Mare BS24 49 A1
Copse Cnr BS24 67 C2
Copse Dro
Baltonsborough BA6 158 C5
Barrington TA19 184 B5
Copse End BS25 51 F2
Copse La
Ashill TA19 183 D4
Barrington TA19 184 D4
Hambridge TA3 184 B7
Ilton TA19 183 F4
Pilton BA4 140 F3
Copseland BA2 45 D5
Copse Rd
Clevedon BS21 6 C4
Keynsham BS31 25 C4
Yeovil BA22 218 B7
Copse Shoot La TA19 184 C5
Copse Stile TA20 193 F1
Copse The
Bridgwater TA6 209 D5
Cossington TA7 136 F3
Frome BA11 120 B6
Weston-Super-Mare BS22 32 D2
Copsewood La BS26 88 B2
Copthorne Cl BS14 23 B5
Coralberry Dr BS22 31 F1
Corams La TA21 222 B6
Cording's Ball TA4 150 A1
Corewell La TA5 133 E3
CORFE 181 F6
Corfe Cl BS48 8 D1
Corfe Cres BS31 24 E4
Corfe Rd BS4 22 D7
Corinthian Ct 9 BS1 227 B1
Cork Pl BA1 44 D7
Corkscrew La
North Cadbury BA22 175 E7
Staplegrove TA2 212 D8
Cork St
Bath BA1 44 D7
Frome BA11 119 F5
Cork Terr BA1 44 D7
Cormorant Cl
Bridgwater TA6 209 C3
Weston-Super-Mare BS22 31 F1
Cornborough Pl TA6 209 B5
Cornbrash BA11 120 D7
Corner Cl TA21 222 D4
Corner Croft BS21 6 D1
Cornfields The BS22 31 F5
Cornhill
Bridgwater TA6 208 F5
Shepton Mallet BA4 205 C6
Sherborne DT9 225 C4
5 Wellington TA21 222 D6
Cornhill Dr BS14 23 A7
Cornish Gr BS14 23 E6
Cornish Rd BS14 23 E6
Cornishway E TA1 212 B3
Cornishway N TA1 212 B3
Cornishway S TA1 212 B2
Cornishway W TA1 212 B3
Cornish Wlk BS14 23 E6
Cornlands EX16 178 D1
Cornleaze BS13 22 A5
Cornmoor Cres TA9 136 E7
Cornmoor La TA9 136 E7
Corn St
Bath BA1 228 B2
Bristol BS1 227 A3
Cornwallis Ave
Bristol BS8 226 A2
Weston-Super-Mare BS22 31 F4
Cornwallis Cres BS8 11 F6
Cornwallis Gr BS8 226 A2
Cornwall Rd BA4 205 A6
Coromandel Hts BA1 228 B4
Coronation Ave
Bath BA2 44 C4
Keynsham BS31 24 D4
Yeovil BA21 218 F7
Coronation Cl
Ruishton TA3 169 C3
Wanstrow BA4 142 F4
Coronation Ct BA3 115 A3
Coronation Est BS23 48 F3
Coronation Ho TA6 209 C6
Coronation Pl BS1 227 A2
Coronation Rd
Banwell BS29 51 A3
Bath BA1 44 D7
Bleadon BS24 67 C6
Bridgwater TA6 208 E5
Bristol BS3 226 B1
Frome BA11 120 B5
Highbridge TA9 104 D4
Wells BA5 203 B4
Weston-Super-Mare BS22 31 E2
Coronation St TA20 223 C3
Coronation Terr
Chilcompton BA3 96 D5
Oakhill BA3 115 A3
Coronation Villas BA8 176 E1
Corondale Rd BS22 49 D8
Corporate Rd BA22 174 A2
Corporation St TA1 212 F3
Corpus Christi RC Prim Sch BS23 48 D6
Corrick Cl BS27 90 F2
Corridor The 2 BA1 228 C2
Corsham Dr TA8 104 C8
CORSLEY 121 D2
Corsley CE Prim Sch BA12 121 D2
CORSLEY HEATH 144 E8
Corsley Wlk BS4 22 F8
CORSTON 43 B7
Corston BS24 49 A2
Corston Dr BA2 43 B6
Corston La BA2 43 A8
Corston View BA2 44 C2
Corston Wlk BS11 4 D7
Corton Cl BA21 219 E8
CORTON DENHAM 175 D1
Coryate Cl BA22 186 C2
Cory Rd TA2 213 A8
Cosgates Feet or County Gate EX35 122 D5
COSSINGTON 136 F3
Cossington La TA7 136 E3
Cossington Prim Sch TA7 136 F3
Cossington Rd BS4 22 F8
Cossins La TA18 224 C6
Costello Hill BA22 173 F2
Costiland Dr BS13 21 F6
Cote Cnr TA9 136 F7
Cote House La BS9 5 F5
Cote La BA12 161 F6
Cote Paddock BS9 5 F4
Cote Pk BS9 5 E6
COTFORD ST LUKE 167 E6
Cotford St Luke Prim Sch TA4 167 E5
Cotham Hill BS6 226 C4
Cotham Lawn Ho BS6 226 C4
Cotham Lawn Rd BS6 226 C4
Cotham Pl BS6 226 C4
Cotham Rd BS6 226 C4
Cotham Rd S BS6 227 A4
Cotham Sch BS6 226 C4
Cothay Manor Gardens* TA21 179 C8
COTHELSTONE 152 A2
Cothelstone Cl TA6 208 B4
Cothelstone Rd TA4 151 F1
Cotlake Cl TA1 212 F1
Cotlake Rise TA1 168 E1
Cotleigh Crossing EX14 191 F1
Cotley La TA20 193 D2
Cotman Wlk 1 BS22 31 F2
Cotswold Cl BS20 2 E4
Cotswold Rd BA2 44 E4
Cotswold View BA2 44 B5
Cotswold Way SN14 13 A6
Cottage Cnr TA19 183 F4
Cottage La TA22 163 D6
Cottage Pl
3 Bath BA1 28 C2
Bristol BS2 227 A4
Cottage Row TA8 104 A6
Cottages The BS40 35 D2
Cotterell Ct BA1 228 B2
Cottle Gdns BS14 23 F6
Cottle Rd BS14 23 F6
Cottles La
West Pennard BA6 140 B1
Winsley BA15 64 F6
COTTLE'S OAK 119 C5
Cotton Cnr 13 BA8 190 A6
Cotton Mead BA2 43 B7
Cotton's La TA11 158 B2
Coulson Dr BS22 32 B3
Coulson's Cl BS14 23 A3
Coulson's Rd BS14 23 A3
COULTINGS 134 F4
Council Hos
Babcary TA11 174 D7
Bleadon BS24 67 B5
Clapton TA18 195 C1
Hewish TA18 195 D3
Council Hos *continued*
Kingston Seymour BS21 16 C3
Podimore BA22 174 A4
Wick St Lawrence BS22 32 B8
Council Houses BS24 33 C3
Council Houses The
Butcombe BS40 55 B8
Hinton Blewett BS39 75 E6
Counterslip BS1 227 B2
Counterslip Gdns BS14 23 C6
Countess Ave TA6 208 E7
Countess Gytha Prim Sch BA22 174 F3
County Wlk TA1 213 A3
Couple Cross TA24 130 B1
COURSHAY 198 E3
Coursing Batch BA6 206 F3
COURSLEY 151 B4
Court Acres 6 BA22 197 F8
Court Ash BA20 219 B5
Court Ave BS49 34 C7
Court Barton
Crewkerne TA18 224 B6
Ilminster TA19 221 C4
Court Cl
Backwell BS48 19 C5
Portishead BS20 2 D4
Court Cotts SP8 177 D3
Court-de-Wyck CE Prim Sch BS49 17 F1
Court Dr
Sandford BS25 52 B4
Wellington TA21 222 D5
Courtenay Cres BS4 22 D7
Courtenay Rd BS31 25 B2
Courtenay Wlk BS22 32 A3
Court Farm BA11 100 A3
Court Farm Cl TA20 194 E1
Court Farm Country Park* BS29 50 F5
Court Farm Rd BS14 22 F3
Courtfield
Langport TA10 172 A5
Milverton TA4 166 F4
Court Field La TA20 193 B5
Court Fields Com Sch TA21 222 C5
Court Gdns
Batheaston BA1 29 A4
Marston Magna BA22 174 F1
Yeovil BA21 218 E8
Court Gr TA7 136 C4
Court Hay BS20 4 A4
Court Hill
Compton Dando BS39 41 D5
Taunton TA1 212 D2
Court Ho BS26 70 B2
Court La
7 Barwick BA22 197 F8
Bathford BA1 29 B2
Clevedon BS21 7 A3
Lye's Green BA12 121 B1
Milborne Port DT9 217 C3
Morebath EX16 164 D4
Shipham BS25 70 F8
Courtland Rd TA21 222 D6
Courtlands BS31 24 E5
Courtlands TA2 168 B5
Courtlands Cl TA23 202 C6
Courtlands La BS3 11 E4
Courtlands Unit BS4 22 D8
Courtmead BA2 62 F7
Courtmead La TA24 123 F4
Court Mill La TA20 223 A8
Court Moors La TA21 179 E5
Court Orch TA5 135 B2
Court Pl BS22 31 F2
Court Place La TA24 131 B4
Court Rd
Norton Fitzwarren TA2 168 B4
Weston-Super-Mare BS22 31 A5
Court's Barton BA11 119 D2
Court St
5 Bridgwater TA6 208 F5
Winsham TA20 194 E1
Court Terr TA21 222 C5
Court The TA24 131 A5
COURTWAY 152 C4
Court Way EX16 178 D1
Courtway Ave TA6 209 C4
Courtyard The
Dunster TA24 201 E2
Evercreech BA4 141 F2
Minehead TA24 200 F7
Shapwick TA7 137 F1
3 Taunton TA1 212 F4
West Harptree BS40 74 E6
Coverdale Ct BA21 218 F6
Coveyhill La BA4 142 E5
Cowan Cl TA8 104 C7
COWBRIDGE 130 B5
Cowbridge Cross TA24 200 D1
Cow Bridge Rd BA6 157 C7
Cow Down Rd TA20 194 C1
Cowdray Cl TA24 200 E6
Cowdray Rd
Bristol BS4 22 D7
Minehead TA24 200 E6
Cowen Cl TA18 224 C4
Cowleaze Dro TA3 169 D3
Cowleaze La BS40 74 C6
Cowler Wlk BS13 21 F4
Cowling Dr BS14 23 C5
Cowling Rd BS14 23 D5
Cowl St BA4 205 B7
Cowpath La DT9 176 A1
COWSLIP GREEN 54 B8
Cowslip Green La BS40 54 B8
Cowslip La BS26 68 D3
Coxbridge Dro BA6 158 A6
Cox Hill DT10 190 E4
Coxland's Rock TA4 167 B7
COXLEY 139 F6
Coxley Dr BA1 28 B2
Coxley Prim Sch BA5 139 E6
COXLEY WICK 139 E7
Cox Rd TA21 222 C4
Coxs Cl BA22 175 D6
Cox's Cl
Bruton BA10 215 E5
Glastonbury BA6 206 E6
Cox's Dr BA6 158 A5
Cox's Gn BS40 35 E1
COX'S GREEN 35 E1
Cox's La TA4 167 C5
Coxton End La BA5 92 B3
Coxway BS21 6 F2
Coxwithy La BA6 139 D1
Coxwynne Cl BA3 97 C8
Crabtree Cl BS41 21 D1
Crab Tree Dro BA6 206 F8
Crabtree La
Curry Rivel TA10 171 C1
Dundry BS41 21 D2
Wyke Champflower BA10 215 B7
Crackmore DT9 217 C1
Craig Lea TA2 212 E7
Cranberry Wlk BS9 5 C8
Cranbourne Chase BS23 31 A1
Cranbourne Cl TA6 208 F6
Crancombe La TA7 136 D3
Crandale Rd 3 BA2 44 D5
Crane Cotts BA4 142 B6
Crane Hill TA10, TA11 173 C4
Cranes Cl TA2 213 D7
Cranford Cl BS22 31 D1
Crangs La BA22 175 D4
Cranhill Rd
Bath BA1 44 D8
Street BA16 207 B6
Cranleigh BA2 62 F8
Cranleigh Ct TA13 220 B4
Cranleigh Gdns
Bridgwater TA6 209 A4
Bristol BS9 5 E4
Cranleigh Rd BS14 23 B5
Cranmer Rd TA1 213 A4
CRANMORE 142 B6
Cranmore BS24 49 A2
Cranmore Ave BS31 24 E6
Cranmore Ct 3 BA11 119 E3
Cranmore Pl BA2 62 E8
Cranmore Sta* BA4 142 A5
Cranmore View BA11 119 D2
Cranmore West Sta* BA4 142 A5
Cransey La
Washford TA4, TA23 131 F2
Williton TA4 132 A2
Crantock Ave BS13 22 B8
Cranway La TA20 223 F2
Cranwell Cl TA7 154 F5
Cranwell Gr BS14 23 A5
Cranwell Rd BS24 50 C5
Cranwells Pk BA1 44 D8
Crapnell La BA5 140 F8
Crawford Cl 1 BS21 6 B1
Crawford La BA22 175 D7
CRAWLEY 192 F2
Crawlic La TA4 151 E1
Crawl La BA3 78 C4
Crawter Dr TA24 124 A3
Craydon Gr BS14 23 D4
Craydon Rd BS14 23 D5
Craydon Wlk BS14 23 D5
Crease Cl BA5 203 B4
Create Ctr* BS1 11 F5
Crediton 5 BS22 32 A2
Creechbarrow Rd TA1 213 C5
Creechberry Orch TA1 213 D5
Creeches La BA16 156 D7
CREECH HEATHFIELD 169 E5
Creech Hill La BA10 215 B7
Creech Mill Est TA3 169 C4
Creech Paper Mill TA3 169 C4
CREECH ST MICHAEL 169 D4
Creech St Michael CE Prim Sch TA3 169 D4
Creechwood Terr TA3 169 D5
Creedwell Cl TA4 167 A4
Creedwell Orch TA4 167 A4
Creighton Cl BA5 140 C8
Crescent Gdns BA1 228 A3
Crescent La BA1 228 B4
Crescent The
Backwell BS48 19 A6
Bristol, Sea Mills BS9 5 C6
4 Carhampton TA24 131 A5
Coleford BA3 117 A7
Farrington Gurney BS39 77 B3
Golsoncott TA23 131 D1
Ilminster TA19 221 B2
Lympsham BS24 67 C5
South Cadbury BA22 175 E4
Stanton Drew BS39 39 F1
Taunton TA1 212 F3
Weston-Super-Mare BS22 31 B1
Yeovil BA20 219 A4
Crescent View BA2 228 B1
Crescent View Ct BS22 31 B1
Crescent Way TA1 212 F3
Creslands Ind Units BS24 49 A3
Cressey The TA19 184 E4
Cresswell Ave TA2 212 D7
Cresswell Cl BS22 32 A2
Crestfield Ave TA6 208 F7
Creswicke Rd BS4 22 E7
Creswick Way TA8 104 C8
CREWKERNE 224 D6
Crewkerne Bsns Pk TA18 224 D6
Crewkerne Cl BS48 9 B1
Crewkerne & District Mus* TA18 224 C6
Crewkerne Hospl TA18 224 B5
Crewkerne Rd TA20 223 E4
Crewkerne Sta TA18 224 E4
Crewkerne Turning EX13 198 C6
Cribb's La BS40 36 D1
Crib Cl TA20 223 D6
Crib House La BS28 89 C1
Crickback La BS40 39 A3
Cricket Cotts TA3 170 B3
Cricket Cross TA19 194 C6
Cricket Field Gn BS48 8 D2
Cricket La TA19, TA20 194 C6
CRICKET MALHERBIE 194 D6
CRICKET ST THOMAS 194 E3
Cricket St Thomas Miniature Rly* TA20 194 E3
Cricket View DT9 225 D3
CRICKHAM 108 D8
Crickham La BS28 108 D8
Cricklade Ct BS48 9 A1
Cridlake 7 EX13 198 A1
Cridlands Mdw TA6 208 E6
CRIMCHARD 223 B5
Crimchard TA20 223 B5
Crimthorne Cotts TA3 183 A7
Cripple St TA12 185 D7
Crispin Ctr BA16 207 C6
Crispin Sch BA16 207 D7
Critch Hill BA11 119 C3
CRITCHILL 119 C3
Critchill Cl BA11 119 D3
Critchill Gr BA11 119 D3
Critchill Rd BA11 119 D3
Critchill Sch BA11 119 C4
Crockerne CE Prim Sch BS20 4 C4
Crockerne Dr BS20 4 C3
Crockerne Ho BS20 4 D4
Crockers Hill TA7 136 E4
Crocker's Hill BA9 175 F8
CROCOMBE 60 C3
Crocombe BA2 60 C3
Crocombe La BA2 60 C3
Croford Hill TA4 166 E6
Croft Cl BS30 25 D8
Croft Cotts
Moorlinch TA7 155 E7
Wrantage TA3 170 B1
Croft La
Brushford TA22 163 C4
Skilgate TA4 164 E6
Westbury-sub-Mendip BA5 110 C6
Croftland La TA10 171 E2
Croft Mdw TA4 202 F1
Crofton Ave BA21 219 B6
Crofton Ct BA21 219 B5
CROFTON PARK 219 B6
Crofton Pk BA21 219 B5
Crofton Rd BA21 219 B6
Croft Rd
Bath BA1 28 B1
Holcombe BA3 116 C8
Crofts Mead BA9 216 C2
Croft The
Backwell BS48 19 A7
Cheddar BS27 90 C8
Clevedon BS21 6 F4
Hutton BS24 49 E3
Mark TA9 106 A4
Monkton Combe BA2 45 E1
Watchet TA23 202 C7
Westwood BA15 64 F3
Williton TA4 202 D3
Wookey Hole BA5 203 A8
Yeovil BA20 218 C2
Croft Way TA4 210 C4
Croftways TA4 202 D4
Cromer Ct BS21 6 D5
Cromer Rd BS23 48 E5
Cromwell Dr BS22 32 A4
Cromwell Rd
Bridgwater TA6 209 A2
Taunton TA1 213 B5
Yeovil BA21 219 D6
Crooked La
Brent Knoll TA9 85 E3
Burnham-on-S TA8 85 D1
Cucklington SP8 177 E6
Rode BA11 101 E7
Crookes La BS22 31 A4
Crookhorn Hill TA24 129 C7
Cropmead Trad Est TA18 224 D6
Crosby Row BS8 226 A2
CROSCOMBE 204 B8
Croscombe CE Prim Sch BA5 204 C7
Croscombe Gdns BA11 120 D6
CROSS 69 E2
Crossacre TA6 208 D6
Crosscombe Dr BS13 22 C3
Cross Combe Wlk BS13 22 B3
Crosscroft Cotts TA4 151 A3
Crosselm Rd BA4 143 A2
Cross Elms Hill TA5 133 F7
Cross Elms La BS9 5 E5
Cross Farm Cl TA24 201 A5
Cross Farm Rd BS27 90 F3
Crossfield Cl TA6 208 D6

Crossfields DT9 187 F4
Crossing Dro BS28 109 D3
Cross Keys Cl TA2 212 A7
Cross La
Axbridge BS26 70 A2
Brendon EX35 122 A4
Long Sutton TA10 172 F4
Crossland La EX14 191 F2
CROSSLANDS 222 C8
Crosslands TA21 222 B8
Cross Lanes BS20 4 C4
Crossman Wlk BS21 6 F2
Crossmead TA7 136 E4
Cross Moor Dr BS26 70 B1
Cross Moor Dro BS26 69 E1
Cross Moor Rd BS26 70 B1
Crosspost La BA2 42 B4
Cross Rd DT9 187 E1
Crossroads The BA9 216 C3
Cross St
Burnham-on-S TA8 104 A7
Keynsham BS31 24 F7
3 Weston-Super-Mare BS23 48 E7
Cross The
Baltonsborough BA6 158 A5
Bradford Abbas DT9 187 E1
Buckland Dinham BA11 100 A3
East Harptree BS40 74 F4
9 Henstridge BA8 190 A6
Ilminster TA19 221 C3
Milverton TA4 167 A4
Minehead TA24 200 F8
Nether Stowey TA5 134 B2
Street BA16 207 D7
Cross View Rise TA6 208 D6
Crossway TA1 213 C5
Cross Way DT9 187 E1
Crossway La BA3 96 B7
Crossways
Coleford BA3 116 F7
Tatworth TA20 198 D8
Crossways Cvn Pk BA2 61 F5
Crossways Rd TA6 209 B1
Crosswell Cl 7 TA6 153 E3
Cross Wlk BS14 23 A6
Crouds La TA10 172 E4
Crow Castle La TA18 224 B7
CROWCOMBE 151 C7
Crowcombe CE Fst Sch TA4 151 C7
Crowcombe Heathfield Sta★ TA4 151 B5
Crowcombe Rd TA2 212 F8
Crowcombe Wlk TA6 208 C4
Crowe Hill BA3 64 B5
Crowe La BA3 64 B5
Crow La
Ashill TA19 183 C4
Bridgwater TA7 209 E7
Bristol BS1 227 A2
Broadway TA19 194 A8
Slape Cross TA7 209 E6
Westbury-sub-Mendip BA5 110 E6
Crown Cl TA2 213 C6
Crowne Trad Est BA4 205 D5
Crown Gdns BA11 119 F3
Crown Glass Pl 5 BS48 8 E2
Crown Hill
Bath BA1 27 C1
West Buckland TA21 180 F7
Winford BS40 38 A5
Crown Ho BS48 8 C1
Crown Ind Est TA2 213 C6
Crown La
Creech St Michael TA3 169 D6
South Petherton TA13 220 C4
Crown Mews TA21 180 F7
Crown Rd BA1 27 B1
Crown Wlk TA1 212 F3
Crowpill Cotts TA6 208 F6
Crowpill La TA6 208 F6
Crow's Hill BA4 142 C1
Crowshute Flats TA20 223 C3
Crowshute Link TA20 223 C3
Crufts Mdw TA3 169 D4
Crusader Cl TA6 208 E6
Crusty La BS20 4 C5
Cruwy's Cross TA4 210 B7
Crypton Tech Bsns Pk TA6 209 B8
Cuck Hill BS25 70 E7
CUCKLINGTON 177 D6
Cuckold's Row TA5 152 E8
Cuckoo Cnr TA1 213 B2
Cuckoo Hill
Bruton BA10 160 D6
Frome BA11 119 E8
Cuckoo La
Frome BA11 119 F8
High Littleton BS39 59 B3
Thorncombe TA20 199 C7
Wraxall BS48 9 A6
CUDWORTH 194 E5
Cuffs Mead TA20 223 F1
Cufic La BS27 90 C8
CULBONE 123 B5
Culliford Cl BA16 207 D7
Culliver's Grave BA22 197 C8
CULM DAVY 180 A2
Culmhead Cl TA1 212 D1
Culmstock Prim Sch EX15 179 E1
Culvecliffe Ct TA24 125 C4
Culvercliffe Rd TA23 202 D7
Culverhay BS39 41 D6
Culverhay Cl TA7 136 C4
Culverhayes TA20 223 C2
Culverhay La TA4 210 B4
CULVERHAYS 132 F1
Culverhay Sch BA2 44 B2
Culverhays La TA4 132 F1
Culverhill BA11 119 F3
Culver Hill TA10 172 B7
Culver La
Carhampton TA24 131 B4
East Harptree BS40 74 F3
Culverlake La EX13 199 A3
Culvers Cl
Keynsham BS31 24 E6
Sherborne DT9 225 C4
Culvers Rd BS31 24 E6
Culver St BS1 226 C2
Culver Street La TA5 134 A7
Culvert Dro BS27 109 B6
Culverwell Cotts BA4 140 F3
Culverwell Rd BS13 22 A4
Cumberland Basin Rd BS8 11 F5
Cumberland Cl BS1 226 A1
Cumberland Ho BA1 228 A2
Cumberland Pl 6 BS8 11 F6
Cumberland Rd BS1 226 B1
Cumberland Row BA1 228 B2
Cumberland St BS2 227 B4
Cumhill Hill BA4 140 E3
Cumnock Cres BA7 214 C6
Cumnock Rd BA7 214 C6
Cumnock Terr BA7 214 C6
Cunningham Ave EX13 198 A2
Cunningham Rd TA8 104 C7
Curdleigh La TA3 181 D5
CURLAND 182 D4
CURLAND COMMON 182 D4
Curland Gr BS14 23 B5
Curlew Cl TA24 201 C4
Curlew Gdns BS22 31 F1
Curlew Pl BS20 2 F6
CURLOAD 170 E7
Currells La BS40 20 B1
Curriott Hill TA18 224 B4
Curriott Hill Rd TA18 224 B5
Curry Hole La BA22 197 C2
Curry La TA3 169 E6
CURRY MALLET 183 C8
Curry Mallet CE Prim Sch TA3 183 D8
Currymead La TA10 171 C2
Currypool La TA5 134 E1
CURRY RIVEL 171 C4
Curry Rivel CE Prim Sch TA10 171 D4
Currywoods Way TA10 171 D4
Curtis Units BA11 119 E2
Curvalion House Gdns TA3 169 D4
Curvalion Rd TA3 169 D4
CUSHUISH 152 B1
Cushuish La TA2 & TA5 152 C2
Cushuish Lane Cotts TA2 152 B1
Cussacombe Gate EX36 145 J1
Custom Cl BS14 23 A7
Custom Ho
Bristol BS1 227 A1
Minehead TA24 201 B7
CUTCOMBE 129 F2
Cutcombe CE Fst Sch TA24 129 E1
Cutcombe Cross TA24 129 E1
Cutcombe Hill TA24 129 F2
Cuthays La EX13 198 B1
Cuthbert St TA9 104 D3
Cutler Rd BS13 21 F6
CUTLER'S GREEN 94 F4
Cutliff Cl TA1 212 E1
Cuts Rd TA3, TA7 170 E8
Cutter's Wharf TA24 201 B7
CUTTIFORD'S DOOR 223 C7
Cutt Mill La DT10 190 F3
Cut Tongue La TA20 193 C7
Cutty Cotts BA22 175 D6
Cutty La BA22 175 D6
Cygnet Cres BS22 31 F1
Cynthia Rd BA2 44 D5
Cypress Ct
Bristol BS9 5 D3
Somerton TA11 211 E4
Cypress Dr
Puriton TA7 136 C4
Yeovil BA20 218 E2
Cypress Gdns BS8 11 E6
Cypress Terr BA3 78 D1
Cypress Way BA11 120 C7
Cyril St W TA2 212 E6
Cyril St TA2 212 E6

D

Dabinett Cl TA2 168 B5
Dafford's Bldgs BA1 28 C2
Dafford St BA1 28 C2
Dagg's La BS28 138 E8
Dagg's Lane Dro BA5, BS28 138 D7
Daghole BS27 90 C8
Daglands The BA2 78 E8
Dahlia Gdns 9 BA2 45 B7
Dairs Orch TA20 198 C8
Dairy Cl
Horsecastle BS49 17 A2
Wells BA5 203 B5
Dairycroft BS2 227 B4
Dairy Ct 3 TA18 224 C5
Dairy Flats DT9 225 E5
Dairy Hill BA2 80 B5
Dairy House La TA3 182 E5
Dairylands TA24 131 D4
Daisey Bank BA2 45 B4
Daisy Cl TA6 153 F5
Daisyfield BA22 188 A8
Dakota Dr BS14 23 A4
Dale La BA5 92 C3
Daley Cl BS22 32 B3
Dalimores La BA11 143 B8
Dalleston BA3 114 C8
Dallimore Mead BA11 143 B8
Dalton Sq BS2 227 B4
Dalwood 12 BS22 32 A2
Dalwoods DT9 225 D3
Dame Court Cl BS22 31 F4
Dame Withycombe Villas TA5 135 B5
Dampier Pl BA21 219 C5
Dampier St BA21 219 C5
Dampiet St TA6 208 F4
Damson Rd BS22 49 E7
Dancey Mead BS13 21 F6
Dancing Cross BA9 176 B5
Dancing Hill TA6 153 E4
Dancing La BA9 216 A4
DandO's La BS28 108 C4
Dandy's Mdw BS20 2 E4
Daneacre Rd BA3 79 A3
Dane Cl BA15 64 E7
Dane Rise BA15 64 E7
Danesboro Rd TA6 208 C4
Danesborough View TA4 202 D3
Danesborough View E TA4 202 D3
Danesborough View W TA4 202 D3
Danes Cl EX14 191 F2
Danesfield CE Com Mid Sch TA4 202 D4
Dane's Lea BS28 108 C4
Dangerfield Ave BS13 21 F6
Daniel Cl BS21 6 F3
Daniel Mews 2 BA2 45 B7
Danielsfield Rd BA20 218 F2
Daniels La BA5 111 A4
Daniel St 3 BA2 45 B7
Dapps Hill BS31 24 F5
Dapwell La BS14, BS31 24 A1
Darby Cl SP8 161 F1
Darby's Knap TA24 147 C5
Darby Way TA4 151 F1
Darcis Row TA20 223 B4
Dare Cl TA2 213 A8
Darkey La BA10 215 F7
Darkfield Way TA7 136 E3
Dark La
Backwell BS48 19 B5
Banwell BS29 51 C2
Berkley BA11 120 E8
Blagdon BS40 54 E3
Chew Magna BS40 38 F3
Freshford BA3 64 B5
Hockworthy EX16 178 B8
Holcombe BA3 97 C1
Kilmersdon BA11 98 A1
North Wootton BA4 140 C5
Sandford Orcas DT9 188 C7
Seavington St Mary TA19 184 E1
Stoke St Gregory TA3 170 F6
Stoke St Michael BA3 116 C2
Upton Noble BA4 142 F2
Wellington TA21 222 D5
Witham Friary BA11 143 D2
Darlick Cnr EX36 145 G4
Darlington Mews 8 BA2 45 B7
Darlington Pl BA2 45 B6
Darlington Rd BA2 45 B8
Darlington St BA2 45 B7
Darmead BS24 32 B1
DARSHILL 204 F6
Dartmouth Ave BA2 44 C5
Dartmouth Cl BS22 32 A2
Dartmouth Wlk BS31 24 D4
Dart Rd BS21 6 D1
Darwin Cl TA2 212 B6
Dashwoods La TA4 132 E2
Daubeny Ct BS1 227 A1
Daunton Cl TA9 104 D4
David's La TA19 184 F2
David's Rd BS14 23 C6
David St BS2 227 C3
Davies Cl
Bridgwater TA6 208 F2
Winsham TA20 194 E1
Davies Ct BA5 203 B4
Davin Cres BS20 4 C3
Davis La BS21 16 F8
Davis St BS11 4 B8
Davis Terr 5 BA5 203 C4
Dawbins Dr TA7 136 E4
Dawes Cl BS21 6 D1
Dawes Ct 2 BS8 11 F6
Daws Cl TA6 208 E2
Daws La TA6 153 E3
Daw's La DT9 176 A3
Daws Mead TA1 212 A3
Day Cres BA2 43 F6
Deacon Rd TA6 209 C6
DEACONS 168 C7
Deacons Cl BS22 31 E2
Deacons Ct BS22 31 C1
Deacons La BA21 187 D6
Deacon Way TA8 104 B6
Deadlands La TA12, TA13 185 A6
Dead Maids Cross Rd BA13 121 E5
Deadman's Hill DT9 176 A1
Deadmill La BA1 28 C3
Dead Woman's Cnr BA12 161 F8
Deal Cl TA6 209 D5
DEAN 142 B7
Dean Cl
Frome BA11 120 C6
Weston-Super-Mare BS22 32 B3
Deane Cl TA4 150 D8
Deane Dr TA1 212 B2
Deane Gate Ave TA1 213 E5
Deane Ret Pk TA1 213 F5
Deanery Rd BS1 226 C2
Deanery Wlk BA3 64 C6
Deanesly Way BA9 216 D3
Deane Way TA20 198 D8
Deanhill La BA1 27 A2
Dean La
Dunster TA24 201 D3
Milverton TA4 167 A6
Oakhill BA3 115 A3
Dean's Cross TA24 124 E3
Dean's Cross TA4 151 A4
Dean's La
Allerford TA24 124 E3
Brompton Ralph TA4 150 F4
Deansley Way BA9 216 E3
Deans Mead BS11 5 A8
Deans Pl 8 BA5 203 D4
Dean St BS2 227 B4
Deans The BS20 2 B4
Dean Vale Pk TA4 167 C4
Debecca's La BS20 4 B4
De Combe Ho TA18 224 D6
De Corcis Cl TA5 134 A3
Decoy La TA11 157 A2
Deep La BA12 121 E1
Deepleigh La TA4 210 C7
Deerleap
Easton BA5 111 B6
Shipham BS25 70 F8
Deer Mead BS21 6 B1
Deerswood Gdns BA16 207 A6
Deer View TA24 201 C4
Delapre Rd BS23 48 D3
Delhorn La BS24 86 C7
Delius Gr BS4 22 D7
Dellers Ct TA1 212 F5
Deller's Wharf TA1 212 F5
Dellshore Cl TA20 223 D4
Dell The
Bristol, Westbury on T BS9 5 F5
Minehead TA24 200 E6
Nailsea BS48 8 D2
Weston-Super-Mare BS22 31 E4
Delmore Rd BA11 119 E3
Delta Cl BA11 119 F5
Delta Ct 1 BA11 119 F5
Delta Rise TA4 151 E1
Demelza Ct BA22 174 D3
De Montalt Pl BA2 45 B1
Dempier Mews BA22 218 B6
Dene Cl BS31 24 F3
Dene Cross TA4 167 F7
Dene Gdns TA24 201 B4
Dene Rd
Cotford St Luke TA4 167 F6
Whitchurch BS14 23 C4
Dening Cl TA20 223 C6
Denleigh Cl BS14 23 A4
Denman's La TA19 184 D5
Denman's La TA5 135 B2
Denmark Ave BS1 226 C2
Denmark Rd BA2 44 D6
Denmark St BS1 226 C2
Denmark Terr TA2 212 F7
Dennett Cl BA4 205 E4
Denning Cl TA1 212 B1
Denning Ct BS22 32 B4
Dennington La
Churchinford EX14 192 C6
Dulverton TA22 163 B4
Dennor Pk BS14 23 B7
Denny Cl BS20 2 A5
Denny La BS40 39 B1
Denny View BS20 2 A5
Dennyview Rd BS8 10 F8
Denston Dr BS20 2 E4
Denston Wlk BS13 22 A7
Dentwood Gr BS9 5 B8
Denzil Cl BA22 197 A8
Derham Cl BS49 34 B8
Derham Ct BS49 34 B8
Derham Pk BS49 34 B8
Derham Rd BS13 22 A5
Derricke Rd BS14 23 F6
DERTFORDS 144 D8
Dertfords BA12 144 D8
Derwent Gdns BA21 219 D6
Derwent Gr
Keynsham BS31 25 A5
Taunton TA1 213 E4
Derwent Rd BS23 49 A5
Derwent Way BA21 218 C6
Devenish La BA9 216 F4
Deveron Gr BS31 25 A4
Devonia Pk TA4 168 A1
Devonshire Bldgs BA2 44 F4
Devonshire Ct BS23 48 E4
Devonshire Dr BS20 1 F5
Devonshire Mews BA2 44 F3
Devonshire Pl BA2 44 F4
Devonshire Rd
Bathampton BA2 28 E1
Weston-Super-Mare BS23 48 E4
Devonshire St TA6 209 B5
Devonshire Villas BA2 44 F3
Dewar Cl TA8 104 C7
Dew Water La TA11 211 D5
Dial Hill Rd BS21 6 D4
Dial La BS40 20 D1
Dial's Gate La BA6, TA11 158 D4
Diamond Batch BS24 32 B1
Dibbens Row BA9 161 A2
Dibbles La BA22 197 A8
Dickenson Rd BS23 48 E6
Dickenson's Gr BS49 34 E3
Digby Ct DT9 225 D3
Digby Rd DT9 225 D3
Dighton Ct 3 BS2 227 A4
Dighton St BS2 227 A4
Digland La TA24 129 F5
Dilkes La TA11 174 C7
DILLINGTON 221 E5
Dillington Farm Cotts TA19 221 E5
Dillington House TA19 221 D6
Dillons Rd TA3 169 D4
DIMMER 159 C3
Dimmer La BA7 159 B2
DINDER 140 D7
Dinder Cl BS48 18 E8
DINGHURST 52 E4
Dinghurst Rd BS25 52 E4
Dingle Cl BS9 5 C6
Dingle Ct BS13 21 F7
Dingle Rd BS9 5 D7
Dingle The BS9 5 D7
Dingle View BS9 5 C7
Dinglewood Cl BS9 5 D7
Dinhams TA3 169 C4
Dinhay DT10 190 F6
DINNINGTON 195 B7
Dipford Rd TA3 168 D1
Dipland Gr BS40 54 F2
Disraeli Pl TA1 212 D5
DITCHEAT 159 C7
Ditcheat Prim Sch BA4 159 C7
Ditch Furlong Rd TA7 137 A2
Ditton St TA19 221 C3
Dixon Gdns BA1 27 F1
Dobree Pk TA21 222 A4
Dock Gate La BS8 226 A1
Doctor's Hill BA5 111 B1
Dodd Ave BA5 203 F5
Dodd's Cnr BA9 215 E1
Dodge Cross DT9 225 F5
Dodham Cres BA20 218 F4
DODHILL 168 D7
DODINGTON 133 F3
Dod La BA6 206 E4
Dog Down Cross EX16 178 A8
Doleberrow BS25 52 F3
Dolebury Warren Nature Reserve★ BS40 53 A3
Dolemead La BS27 90 E2
DOLEMEADS 45 B5
Dolemoor La
Congresbury BS49 34 A4
Congresbury BS49 34 C3
Dolling Cl TA20 223 D6
Dolling's Rd TA3 181 B4
Dolphin Sq BS23 48 D7
Dominion Rd BA2 44 A6
Dominy Cl TA20 223 D3
DOMMETT 182 D1
Dommett Cl EX13 198 A2
Dommett's La BA11 119 D4
Domus Dr BA4 205 E4
Donald Rd BS13 21 F7
DONIFORD 202 F6
Doniford Beach Halt TA23 202 E6
Doniford Dr TA4 202 D3
Doniford Mdw TA23 202 F6
Doniford Orch TA23 202 F6
Doniford Rd
Watchet TA23 202 E6
Williton TA4 202 D4
Donne La BA22 186 C2
Donnes Terr BA7 214 B5
Donnington Wlk BS31 24 D4
Donstan Rd TA9 104 E5
DONYATT 183 D1
Donyatt Hill TA19 183 D1
Donyatt Hill Est TA19 183 D1
Doone Way TA24 201 B4
Dorchester Cl 6 BS48 8 D1
Dorchester Rd
Barwick BA22 197 F7
East Coker BA22 197 F5
Taunton TA2 213 A8
Yeovil BA22 219 A1
Dorchester St BA1 228 C1
Dore Cl BA21 218 C7
Dormeads View 6 BS24 49 F7
Dorset Cl
Bath BA2 44 D6
Frome BA11 119 E5
Highbridge TA9 104 E2
Dorset Ho BA2 44 D3
Dorset Rd TA6 209 C3
Dorset St BA2 44 D6
Doster's La TA2 169 C6
Double Gates Dro TA11 158 A3
Double Hill BA2 79 F7
Douglas Ct 3 BS23 48 F5
Douglas Dr BA4 205 B5
Douglas Rd BS23 48 F5
Douglas Yates Ct BA3 116 F7
DOULTING 141 E6
Doulting Ct BA11 120 D7

Doulting Hill BA4 205 F4
Doulton Way BS14 23 B5
Dovai Dr TA6 208 E7
Dove Cots Cl BA16 207 C7
Dove La BS2 227 C4
DOVERHAY 124 B3
Dover Ho BA1 228 C4
Dover Pl
6 Bath BA1 28 A1
Bristol BS8 226 B3
Dover Rd TA2 213 A8
Dovers La BA1 29 C2
Dovers Pk BA1 29 C2
Dovery Manor Mus★ TA24 124 A3
Dove St S BS2 227 A4
Dove St BS2 227 A4
Doveswell Gr BS13 22 A4
Dovetail Ct 1 TA1 212 E3
Dovetail Dr BS23 49 A7
Dovetons Cl TA4 202 E3
Dovetons Dr TA4 202 E3
Dowding Rd BA1 28 B1
Dowell Cl TA2 212 C6
Dowland 18 BS22 32 A2
Dowland Gr BS4 22 D6
Dowling La BA6 158 A5
Dowling Rd BS13 22 D3
DOWLISH FORD 221 B1
Dowlish La TA19 194 F5
DOWLISH WAKE 194 E7
Downash La EX13 198 E3
Down Ave BA2 45 A1
Down Cl BS20 1 F4
Downclose La TA18 196 C3
Downend Cres TA6 136 B4
Downend Rd TA6 136 B4
Downend Terr TA6 136 B4
Downey Field La TA18 196 D6
Downfield
Bristol BS9 5 C7
Keynsham BS31 24 D5
Downhall Dr TA6 208 D6
DOWNHEAD
Stoke St Michael 142 C8
Yeovilton 174 C4
Downhead La BA22 174 C5
Down La
Bathampton BA2 28 F1
Buckland Dinham BA11 99 C3
Shepton Montague BA9 160 B2
Sherborne DT9 188 A5
Trent DT9 187 F5
West Pennard BA4, BA6 140 C1
Downland Cl 5 BS48 8 D1
Downlands La EX15, TA3 181 A2
Downleaze
Bristol, Stoke Bishop BS9 5 F3
Portishead BS20 2 A5
Yeovil BA20 218 D2
Downleaze Rd BS9 5 F3
Down Rd BS20 1 F4
Downs Cl BS22 31 F1
Downs Cote Ave BS9 5 F6
Downs Cote Dr BS9 5 F6
DOWNSIDE
Chilcompton 96 C1
Felton 19 D1
Shepton Mallet 205 D8
Downside
Portishead BS20 2 C5
Street BA16 207 D6
Downside Abbey★ BA3 96 E2
Downside Cl
Bathampton BA2 28 F1
Chilcompton BA3 96 D3
Downside Rd
Backwell BS48 36 E8
Weston-Super-Mare BS23 48 F4
Downside Sch BA3 96 E2
Downslade La TA10 172 D5
Down's Orch BA6 138 C4
Downs Rd BS41 21 D2
Downs Sch The BS48 9 C8
Downs The BS20 2 B4
Downsway BS39 77 D6
Downton Rd BS13 22 D8
Down View BA3 97 F8
Dowry Pl 3 BS8 11 F5
Dowry Rd BS8 226 A2
Dowry Sq BS8 226 A2
DOWSLANDS 168 F1
Dowsland Way TA1 213 C1
DOYNTON 12 A8
Dozen's Cnr TA17 195 A7
Dragon Cross TA24 131 D3
Dragonfly Chase BA22 173 E2
Dragons Hill Cl BS31 24 F5
Dragons Hill Ct BS31 24 F5
Dragons Hill Gdns BS31 24 F5
Drake Ave BA2 44 F2
Drake Cl
Saltford BS31 25 D2
Staplegrove TA2 212 B7
Weston-Super-Mare BS22 31 F4
Drake Rd BA5 203 F6
Drakes Cl TA6 208 F5
Drake's Cl TA3 169 C4
Drakes Cres TA20 198 D8
Drakes Mdw
East Coker BA22 197 C7
Yarcombe EX14 192 D3
Drakes Pk TA21 222 D7
Drakes Pk N TA21 222 D7
Drakes Way BS20 2 B5
Drang The
Coxley BA5 139 E6
Evercreech BA4 141 E1
Porlock TA24 124 A3
Dransfield Way BA2 44 C4
Drapers Way TA24 129 D2
Drappel La BA5 110 E7
Draycot Pl BS1 227 A1
DRAYCOTT
Cheddar 90 E2
Yeovil 187 B8
Draycott Ave TA2 213 A6
Draycott Ct 1 BA2 228 C3
Draycott Moor Dro BS27 90 D1
Draycott Rd
Cheddar BS27 90 D5
Shepton Mallet BA4 205 B6
Draycott & Rodney Stoke CE Fst Sch BS27 90 F3
Draydon Rd BS4 22 D8
Dray Rd BA22 186 C2
DRAYTON
Curry Rival 171 E3
Southerton 185 D3
Drayton BS24 49 A2
Drayton Cl BS14 23 B8
Drayton La TA10 171 D3
Drayton Rd BS9 5 C8
Drew's La DT10 190 B5
Drials La BA3 94 F6
Drift Rd TA24 201 D4
Drift The
Chard Junction TA20 198 E8
Chard TA20 194 B3
Drill Hall La BA4 205 C5
DRIMPTON 199 F7
Drimpton Cross DT8 199 F7
Dring The BA3 78 E2
Drive The
Bristol BS14 23 C6
Burnham-on-S TA8 85 A2
Churchill BS25 52 E4
Shipham BS25 70 E8
Stanton Drew BS39 39 F1
Taunton TA1 212 D1
Weston-Super-Mare BS23 48 F8
Woolavington TA7 136 E4
Dropping La BA10 160 D5
Drove Cl DT10 189 F2
Drove Ct BS48 8 E3
Drove La
East Pennard BA4 158 E8
Shepton Beauchamp TA19 184 E4
Drove Rd
Congresbury BS49 34 D3
Stourton Caundle DT10 189 F2
Weston-Super-Mare BS23 48 F5
Drove The
Bridgwater TA6 209 A6
Portbury BS20 3 D6
Droveway TA13 220 B5
Drove Way
Churchinford TA3 191 F8
Sandford BS24, BS25 51 E7
Droveway Cl TA13 220 C5
Droveway La BA21 187 C7
Druid Cl BS9 5 E5
Druid Hill BS9 5 E5
Druid Rd BS9 5 D4
Druids Garth BA2 28 D1
Druid Stoke Ave BS9 5 D5
Druids Wlk TA20 223 C5
Druid Woods BS9 5 C5
Druley Hill BA10 161 D8
Drum Ave BA6 206 C5
Drumhead Way The BS25 70 E8
Dr White's Cl BS1 227 B1
DRY HILL 2 C6
Dryleaze BS31 24 E7
Drysdale Cl BS22 31 D1
Duchess Cl 1 TA6 208 E7
Duchy Cl BA3 78 E5
Duchy Rd
Clandown BA3 78 E5
Shepton Mallet BA4 205 A5
Duck La
Chard TA20 223 C3
Churchill BS40 53 A8
Horsington BA8 176 E2
Ilchester BA22 173 F1
Kenn BS21 17 A6
Stalbridge DT10 190 B5
Westbury-sub-Mendip BA5 110 E6
Duck Pool Dro BA6 206 B7
Duckpool La TA18 196 B8
Duck Pool La BA11 102 B6
Ducks' Field Crossing TA18 224 C1
Ducks Hill TA10 172 B5
Ducks La BS22 32 A8
Duck St BS25 52 C5
DUDDLESTONE 181 F8
Dudley Cl BS31 24 E4
Dudmoor TA12 185 B7
Dudwell La BA3 95 A5
Dugdale St TA24 200 F6
Duke Ave 7 TA5 135 B2
Duke Ho TA19 221 B3
Duke's Cl BA9 216 E3
Dukes Field BA4 205 C5
Duke's La
Horningsham BA12 144 A1
Kilmington BA12 161 F8
Dukes Mead TA6 209 A2
Duke St
Bath BA2 228 C2
Bridgwater TA6 208 E7
Frome BA11 119 E5
Duke St *continued*
Taunton TA1 213 A4
DULCOTE 140 C7
Dull Cross TA4 151 D3
DULVERTON 163 E6
Dulverton La TA4 165 D7
Dulverton Mid & Com Sch TA22 163 D6
Dumfries Pl BS23 48 E5
Dummis La BA5 111 A1
Dumpers La BS40 39 B2
Dumper's La BA3 94 F7
DUNBALL 136 A3
Dunball Ind Est TA6 136 B4
Dunbar Cl TA9 104 C4
Duncan Gdns BA1 27 A3
Duncart La BA5 204 C7
Duncliffe Cl DT10 190 B4
Duncombe Cl TA6 209 D5
Dundas Row TA4 167 E8
DUNDON 156 F3
DUNDON HAYES 156 E3
DUNDRY 21 D2
Dundry CE Prim Sch BS41 21 D2
DUNDRY HILL 23 B3
Dundry La
Dundry BS41 21 C3
Winford BS40 38 A7
Dunedin Way BS22 32 C4
Dunford Terr BA6 158 A5
Dungarvon Rd BS24 49 F7
Dungeon BS28 108 D7
Dungeon La BA5 204 C6
Dunkerry Rd BS26 88 C4
DUNKERTON 61 E4
Dunkerton Cl BA6 206 F3
Dunkerton Hill BA2 61 E2
Dunkerton Rise TA2 168 B5
Dunkery Cl BS48 8 E1
Dunkery & Horner Wood National Nature Reserve The★ TA24 129 A7
Dunkery Rd
Bridgwater TA6 208 D4
Weston-Super-Mare BS23 30 F1
Dunkery Vineyard★ TA24 200 A1
Dunkirk Bsns Pk BA14 83 D2
Dunkleys Way TA1 213 C2
Dunlin Dr 1 BS20 2 F6
Dunningham La BS28 107 E7
Dunns Cl BS28 108 C4
Dunn's Hill TA21 179 A6
Dunsford Pl BA2 45 B6
Dunsgreen La EX15 191 A8
Dunsham La TA18 195 C2
Dunsley Hill EX16, EX36 162 D5
Dunstan Dr DT9 225 E5
Dunstan Rd
Burnham-on-S TA8 104 B7
Glastonbury BA6 206 F5
Dunstan Way BS27 90 B6
DUNSTER 201 E2
Dunster Beach Chalets TA24 201 F4
Dunster Castle★ TA24 201 E1
Dunster Cl
Minehead TA24 201 B4
Taunton TA2 213 B7
Dunster Cres BS24 49 A2
Dunster Ct BS25 70 A8
Dunster Fst Sch TA24 201 D2
Dunster Gdns 5 BS48 8 E1
Dunster Ho BA2 45 A2
Dunster Rd
Bristol BS4 22 F8
Keynsham BS31 24 E4
Dunsters Rd BS49 17 F1
Dunster Sta★ TA24 201 F4
Dunster Steep
Dunster TA24 201 E2
Porlock, Doverhay TA24 124 A3
Porlock, West Porlock TA24 123 F4
Dunster Visitor Ctr★ TA24 201 E2
Dunster Wood Forest Trails★ TA24 130 D5
Dunster Working Water Mill★ TA24 201 E1
DUNWEAR 209 D1
Dunwear Ho 3 TA6 209 C4
Dunwear La TA6 209 D3
Durban Way BS49 17 B1
Durbin Park Rd BS21 6 D5
Durcott Rd BA2 78 D8
Durham Gr BS31 24 D4
Durham Pl 9 TA2 213 A8
Durhams Cotts TA4 210 C5
Durkheim Dr 2 BA5 203 C4
DURLEIGH 208 B3
Durleigh Cl
Bridgwater TA6 208 D3
Bristol BS13 22 A7
Durleigh Hill TA5 208 A2
Durleigh Rd TA6 208 C3
Durley Hill BS31 24 C7
Durley La BS31 24 D7
Durleymoor Cross EX16 178 F4
Durley Pk BA2 44 E4
DURNFIELD 186 B7
Durnhill BS40 73 F7
Durrant Cl DT9 225 D3
Dursdon Dro
Priddy BA5 111 C8
Wells BA5 112 B6
Dursley Rd BS11 4 E5
DURSTON 169 F6
Durston BS24 49 A2
Durston Cl BA16 207 C5
Durston Ho 3 BA16 207 C5
Durston Way TA1 212 E1
Durville Rd BS13 22 B6
Durweston Wlk BS14 23 C8
Dutch Rd TA9 105 E5
Dutton Cl BS14 23 D6
Dutton Rd BS14 23 D6
Dutton Wlk BS14 23 D6
Dwelly Cl TA20 223 C3
Dyehouse Cnr TA22 164 A6
Dyehouse Cross TA22 163 F5
Dyehouse La
Bury TA22 164 A5
Glastonbury BA6 206 C5
Dye La BA3 115 A3
Dyers Cl
Bristol BS13 22 D4
Curry Rivel TA10 171 D4
West Buckland TA21 180 F7
Dyers' Close La BA11 119 E5
Dyers Gn TA6 153 F3
Dyer's La TA2 213 E7
Dyers Rd TA10 171 D4
Dyke Hill Terr TA20 198 D8
Dyke's Way BA9 216 B3
Dymboro Ave BA3 77 F1
Dymboro Cl BA3 77 F1
Dymboro Gdns BA3 77 F1
Dymboro The BA3 77 F1
Dyrham Cl TA8 104 D7
Dyson Cl BS49 34 B8

E

Eagle Cl
Ilchester BA22 173 E2
Weston-Super-Mare BS22 49 D8
Eagle Gdns BA22 173 E2
Eagle La 1 BA11 119 F4
Eagle Pk BA1 28 F5
Eagle Rd BA1 28 F5
Eagles The BS49 34 B8
Eames Orch TA19 221 C2
Earlesfield BS48 8 C1
Earle St BA20 219 C5
Earlham Gr BS23 49 A7
Earls Cl
Bridgwater TA6 208 E7
Sherborne DT9 225 F5
Earl St BS1 227 A4
EAST ANSTEY 162 E5
East Anstey Prim Sch EX16 162 E5
East Approach Rd TA7 136 D4
East Ave TA9 104 C4
Eastbourne Ave 15 BA1 28 B1
Eastbourne Ct 18 TA1 213 A4
Eastbourne Gate TA1 213 A4
Eastbourne Rd TA1 213 A4
Eastbourne Terr 12 TA1 213 A4
EAST BOWER 209 E6
EAST BRENT 86 D5
East Brent CE Fst Sch TA9 86 C4
East Bridgwater Com Sch TA6 209 C5
EASTBROOK 168 E1
Eastbrook Terr TA3 168 D1
Eastbury Hill TA24 131 B5
Eastbury Rd TA24 131 B5
EAST CHINNOCK 196 E8
East Cl
Bath BA2 44 A5
Haselbury Plucknett TA18 196 B5
EAST CLEVEDON 6 F3
East Clevedon Triangle BS21 6 F3
Eastcliff BS20 2 E7
EAST COKER 197 D7
East Coker Com Prim Sch BA22 197 C7
East Coker Rd BA20 218 F2
East Coker Sawmills BA22 197 C7
EAST COMBE 151 E2
Eastcombe Gdns BS23 30 F1
Eastcombe La BA4 142 E2
Eastcombe Rd BS23 30 F1
EAST COMPTON 205 A2
East Compton Rd
Pilton BA4 204 E1
Shepton Mallet BA4 205 B1
East Coombe La TA4 165 D8
Eastcote Pk BS14 23 B5
Eastcourt Rd BS39 76 F8
EAST CRANMORE 142 C6
Eastcroft BS40 54 E2
Eastcroft Cl BS40 54 E2
East Ct BS3 11 F3
East Ct BA5 113 A1
Eastdown Rd BA3 78 D5
East Dr TA9 86 E4
EAST DUNDRY 22 A1
East Dundry La BS41 22 A1
East Dundry Rd BS13, BS14 22 F2
EAST END
Blagdon 54 F2
Chewton Mendip 94 E4
Nailsea 9 A1
South Cadbury 175 D4
Stoke St Michael 116 C2
East End BS26 88 D7
East End La BA3 94 E4
Easterdown Hill
Dinnington TA17 195 B8
Seavington St Mary TA19 184 E1
Easter La EX35 122 B4
Eastermead La BS29 51 C3
Eastern Ave TA6 209 D4
Eastern Ho BS23 30 E1
EASTERTOWN 67 D2
Eastertown BS24 67 D1
Eastfield
Bruton BA10 215 F7
29 Martock TA12 185 E6
Shepton Mallet BA4 205 B6
Yarlington BA9 175 F8
Eastfield Ave BA1 27 B2
Eastfield Cl 30 TA12 185 E6
Eastfield Gdn 12 DT9 225 E4
Eastfield Gdns BS23 30 F1
Eastfield La
Barrington TA19 184 D5
Blackford BS28 107 F6
Ditcheat BA4 159 C7
East Chinnock BA22 196 D8
Hambridge TA3 184 B8
Lydford Fair Place TA11 158 D3
North Perrott TA18 196 C4
Norton Sub Hamdon BA22 185 F1
Eastfield Pk BS23 30 F1
Eastfield Rd
Hutton BS24 49 E2
Wincanton BA9 216 D4
East Gate 11 TA1 213 A4
Eastgate Gdns 10 TA1 213 A4
Easthams Rd TA18 224 D6
EAST HARPTREE 74 E4
East Harptree CE Prim Sch BS40 74 F4
Easthay La TA20 199 A4
EAST HEWISH 33 B6
EASTHILL 120 B4
Easthill BA11 120 B4
Easthill La BA7 159 D5
EAST HUNTSPILL 136 E7
East Huntspill Prim Sch TA9 136 E8
EAST KNOWSTONE 162 B2
East La TA18 196 B7
EAST LAMBROOK 220 C8
East Lambrook Manor Gdns★ TA13 220 C8
East Lambrook Rd TA13 220 D7
Eastland Rd BA21 219 C5
East Lanes BA21 187 D6
Eastlea BS21 6 B1
East Lea Rd BA1 44 A8
Eastleigh Cl
Burnham-on-S TA8 104 C8
Frome BA11 120 A7
Wiveliscombe TA4 210 C5
Eastleigh Rd TA1 213 B3
EAST LYDFORD 158 D2
EAST LYNG 170 D8
Eastlyn Rd BS13 22 B8
East Mead BA3 78 B2
Eastmead Ct BS9 5 E4
Eastmead La BS9 5 E4
East Mead La
Street BA16 207 F5
Walton BA16 156 E6
East Mere Cross EX16 178 B2
East Mill Ct 11 DT9 225 E4
East Mill La DT9 225 E4
Eastmoor La TA4 164 E8
Eastnor Rd BS14 23 A3
EAST NYNEHEAD 167 D2
EASTON 111 A4
Easton Ct BA3 76 E1
Easton Ho 9 BA1 28 C1
EASTON-IN-GORDANO 4 A4
Easton La
Pylle BA4 141 C1
Sampford Peverell EX16 178 D1
Easton Rd BS20 4 C4
Easton Town La BA4 158 F4
Easton Trow La BA4 159 B5
Eastop La DT10 190 A3
EASTOVER 209 B5
Eastover
Bridgwater TA6 209 A5
Langport TA10 172 A6
Eastover Cl TA10 172 A5
Eastover Com Prim Sch TA6 209 B5
Eastover Gr BA2 44 C1
Eastover Rd BS39 59 D1
East Par BS9 5 C6
EAST PENNARD 158 F8
EAST QUANTOXHEAD 133 B6
East Quay TA6 209 A6
East Quay Mews TA6 209 A6
East Rd BA16 207 E6
East Reach TA1 213 A4
East Ride TA9 86 B1
East Ridge Dr BS13 21 F5
EAST ROLSTONE 33 B1
East Side La TA7 136 F2
East Somerset Railway★ BA4 205 F3
East Somerset Way BA5 203 D3
East St
Banwell BS29 51 C3
Bourton SP8 161 F1
Cannington TA5 135 C2
Chard TA20 223 D4
Crewkerne TA18 224 C6
Drayton TA10 171 E3
East Coker BA22 197 B8
Ilminster TA19 221 C4

East St continued
Martock TA12 185 E6
Milborne Port DT9 217 D2
North Perrott TA18 196 C4
Norton Sub Hamdon TA14 185 F1
Shepton Montague BA9 160 B2
Taunton TA1 212 F3
Templecombe BA8 176 F1
EAST STOKE 186 A4
East Stoke TA14 185 F4
EAST STREET 139 F1
East Street Dro TA12 185 E6
East Street La BA6 140 A1
East Tapps La EX16 163 B2
EAST TOWN
Lydeard St Lawrence 150 E3
Shepton Mallet 141 A3
East Town La TA4 150 E3
East Town La (Platterwell La) BA4 141 B3
EAST TWERTON 44 D7
Eastville
Bath BA1 28 B1
Yeovil BA21 219 C5
Eastville La BS27 90 F1
EAST WATER 92 F2
East Water La BA5 92 F2
Eastway BS48 8 E3
East Way BA2 44 A5
Eastway Cl BS48 8 D2
Eastway Sq BS48 8 E3
Eastwell La BS25 69 E6
Eastwick Ave TA2 212 F7
Eastwick Rd TA2 213 B7
Eastwood BA2 45 F6
Eastwood Cl
Bridgwater TA6 209 C4
Frome BA11 119 C4
High Littleton BS39 59 C1
EAST WOODLANDS 144 A7
East Woodlands Rd BA11 144 A7
East Wood Pl BS20 2 E7
Eastwoods BA1 29 B3
Eaton Cl BS14 23 E5
Eaton Cres
Bristol BS8 226 A4
Taunton TA2 213 A6
Ebben La TA20 194 F1
Ebbor Gorge Nature Reserve★ BA5 111 D6
Ebbor Gorge Nature Trail★ BA5 111 C5
Ebbor La BA5 111 B5
Ebden Lo 15 BS22 32 A2
EBDON 32 B6
Ebdon La BS22 32 C5
Ebdon Rd BS22 31 F4
Ebenezer La BS9 5 E5
Eckweek Gdns BA2 79 D8
Eckweek La BA2 79 E8
Eckweek Rd BA2 79 D8
Ecos Ct BA11 119 D4
Edbrooke Rd TA24 147 C5
Edbrook La TA5 134 F3
Eddington Ct BS23 48 D7
Eden Croft BS22 49 E8
Eden Park Cl BA1 29 A4
Eden Park Dr BA1 29 A4
Eden Terr BA1 28 B2
Eden Villas 4 BA1 28 C2
EDFORD 116 C7
Edford Hill BA3 116 C6
Edgar Bldgs BA1 228 B3
EDGARLEY 139 E1
Edgarley Ct BS21 6 C5
Edgarley Field La BA6 157 E8
Edgarley Rd
Glastonbury BA6 139 D1
West Pennard BA6 139 F1
EDGCOTT 128 C1
Edgcott Rd TA24 128 C1
Edgebury TA7 136 E4
Edgecombe Ave BS22 31 D2
Edgecombe Mews BA1 27 B1
Edgefield Cl BS14 22 F3
Edgefield Rd BS14 22 F3
Edgehill Rd BS21 6 D6
Edgemoor Rd TA24 201 B4
Edgewood Cl BS14 23 B8
Edgeworth Rd BA2 44 C2
Edinburgh Pl 1 BS23 48 E8
Edinburgh Rd
Bridgwater TA6 208 E2
Keynsham BS31 24 E4
EDINGTON 137 C3
Edington Rd TA7 137 D4
Edington Right Dro TA7 155 B7
Edington & Shapwick Sch
Burtle TA7 137 D6
Shapwick TA7 137 F1
EDINGWORTH 86 F7
Edingworth Rd BS24 86 F7
Edith Cl TA8 85 A2
EDITHMEAD 104 F7
Edithmead La TA9 105 A6
Edmond's Hill TA11 173 D4
Edmund Hill La BA6 206 F6
Edmunds Way BS27 90 C7
Edward Cl BA22 218 B6
Edward Ct BS31 24 F4
Edward Rd BS21 6 E5
Edward Rd S BS21 6 E5
Edward Rd W BS21 6 E6
Edward St
Bath, Bathwick BA2 45 B7
Bath, Lower Weston BA1 44 C7
Bridgwater TA6 209 B5
Edwin Short Cl BS30 25 E8
Egerton Rd BA2 44 E4
EGFORD 119 B5
Egford Hill BA11 119 C5
Egford La BA11 119 C5
Egg Moor La EX13 198 A7
Eggwood La TA13, TA16 195 E8
Eglin Croft BS13 22 B4
Eglinton Rd BA16 207 B4
Egremont Ct TA4 202 D2
Egrove Way TA4 202 E4
Eight Acre Dro TA7, TA9 137 A5
Eight Acre La
Wellington TA21 222 E5
Wootton Courtenay TA24 129 F8
Eighteen Arce La BA21 218 C6
Eighth Ave BS14 23 A7
Eileen Cl BA16 207 E5
Eirene Terr BS20 4 D4
Elberton Rd BS9 5 B7
Elborough Ave BS49 34 B8
Elborough Gdns BS24 50 C3
Elbridge Ho 3 BS2 227 C3
Elderberry Wlk BS22 31 F1
Elder Cl
Chard TA20 223 C5
Highbridge TA9 104 D5
Eldergrove Cl TA6 209 D7
Elder Ho TA8 65 E2
Elderwood Rd BS14 23 B7
Eldon Pl BA1 28 B2
Eldred Cl BS9 5 D5
Eleanor Cl BA2 44 A5
Eleanor Cotts BA2 44 A6
Electric Ho TA14 185 E3
Eleven Ct TA6 208 E4
Elfrida Terr BA5 203 A5
Elgar Cl
Bristol BS4 22 D6
Clevedon BS21 6 E1
Eliot Cl BS23 49 A3
Eliotts Dr BA21 218 E7
Elizabeth Cl BS24 49 D3
Elizabeth Ct
Burnham-on-S TA8 104 B6
4 Martock TA12 185 E6
Elizabeth Flats BA21 219 C6
Elizabeth Gdns 16 BA8 190 A6
Elizabeth Way
Bridgwater TA6 209 C5
Chard TA20 223 C5
Ellbridge Cl BS9 5 D5
Ellenborough Cres BS23 48 E6
Ellenborough Ct BS23 48 E6
Ellenborough Ho BS8 226 A2
Ellenborough Park Rd BS23 48 E6
Ellenborough Pk N BS23 48 D6
Ellenborough Pk S BS23 48 D6
Ellen Cl 8 TA6 153 F4
Ellen Ho BA2 44 A5
Ellersdown La TA22 163 E4
Ellesmere Rd
Bristol BS4 23 D8
Weston-Super-Mare BS23 48 D2
Ellfield Cl BS13 21 F6
Ellick Rd BS40 54 D1
ELLICOMBE 201 C4
Ellicombe La TA24 201 C4
Ellicombe Mdw TA24 201 C4
Elliot Cl BA11 119 F6
ELLIOTS GREEN 144 B8
Elliots La BA11 119 B8
Elliott's Hill BA22 196 D7
Ellis Ave BS13 22 A8
Elliscombe Pk BA9 176 B6
Ellis Gr TA2 168 B5
Ellis Pk BS22 32 C4
Ellis's La TA5 152 C6
Elliston Dr BA2 44 B4
Ellsbridge Cl BS31 25 B5
Ellsbridge Ho Norton Radstock Coll BS31 25 B5
Ellworthy Ct BA11 120 B4
Elm Ave TA8 104 B6
Elmbrook BA1 44 D8
Elm Cl
Banwell BS29 50 E4
Broadway TA19 183 C2
Nailsea BS48 8 C1
Star BS25 52 D1
Wells BA5 203 A4
Yatton BS49 34 B7
Elm Ct
Bristol BS14 23 A6
Keynsham BS31 24 C4
Elmdale Rd BS8 226 B3
Elm Dr BA9 216 C3
Elm Farm BS48 9 A2
Elm Gr
Bath, Larkhill BA1 28 C2
Bath, The Oval BA2 44 C4
Locking BS24 49 F4
Minehead TA24 201 A5
Taunton TA1 212 E5
Elmgrove Cl TA6 209 D7
Elmham Way BS24 32 B1
Elm Hayes BS13 21 F6
Elmhurst Ave BA21 219 B7
Elmhurst Est BA1 29 A4
Elmhurst Gdns BS41 20 F8
Elmhurst Jun Sch BA16 207 D6
Elmhurst La BA16 207 D6
Elmhurst Rd BS24 49 E2
Elmhyrst Rd BS23 48 F8
Elm La
Great Elm BA11 119 A6
Shalford BA9 216 B7
Elm La continued
Woolavington TA7 136 F4
Elmlea Ave BS9 5 F5
Elm Lea Cl TA7 136 C4
Elmlea Jun & Inf Schs BS9 5 F5
Elmleigh BA21 218 C7
Elm Leigh BA11 120 C6
Elmleigh Rd 21 TA12 185 E6
Elm Lodge Rd BS48 9 B2
Elm Pk TA1 212 E5
Elm Pl BA2 44 F4
Elm Rd BS39 77 E5
Elms Cl TA1 212 E5
Elms Est TA2 213 F8
Elmside Cl BA16 207 D5
Elmside Ho TA6 208 F2
Elmside Rd TA6 208 E2
Elms La BA7 214 B7
Elmsleigh Rd BS23 48 E4
Elmsley La BS22 31 C5
Elms Rd TA21 222 F5
Elm St TA20 223 C5
Elms The
Banwell BS29 51 A4
Bath, Lambridge BA1 28 C2
Bath, Weston Park BA1 27 C1
Elmswood BS23 48 F8
Elm Terr BA3 97 C8
Elm Tree Ave
Nailsea BS21 8 A4
Radstock BA3 78 D1
Elm Tree Cl TA7 155 C2
Elmtree Dr BS13 21 F5
Elm Tree Pk BS20 3 D3
Elm Tree Rd
Clevedon BS21 6 D2
Locking BS24 50 A4
Elmvale Dr BS24 49 F3
Elm View
Midsomer Norton BA3 78 B1
Temple Cloud BS39 58 E1
Elm Way BA4 205 A6
Elm Wlk
Portishead BS20 2 C4
Yatton BS49 34 B7
Elmwood Ave TA6 208 F3
Elmwood Sch TA6 208 F3
Elsbert Dr BS13 21 E6
Elscombe La
Timberscombe TA24 130 A4
Wootton Courtenay TA24 129 F4
Elton Ho 2 BS2 227 C3
Elton Rd
Bristol BS8 226 C3
Clevedon BS21 6 C3
Weston-Super-Mare BS22 32 A4
Elton St BS2 227 C4
Elvard Cl BS13 22 A4
Elvard Rd BS13 22 A4
Elwell La BS40, BS41 21 A1
ELWORTHY 150 C6
Elworthy Cross TA4 150 C5
Elworthy Dr TA21 222 D4
Elworthy La TA4 150 C5
Ely Gr BS9 5 B7
Embankment The TA10 172 A5
Embden Walk 4 TA6 209 A1
Embercourt Dr BS48 19 A6
EMBOROUGH 95 C3
Emery Gate BS29 51 B3
Emlet DT9 187 E1
Emley La BS40 54 B6
Emlyn Cl 6 BS22 32 B4
Emmanuel Ct BS8 226 A4
Empress Wood BS14 23 B3
Empress Menen Gdns BA1 44 A8
Enderleigh Gdns BS25 52 F4
Enfield Dr BA4 141 E2
Enfield Rd BA4 141 E2
Engine La BS48 18 B8
Englands La BA22 174 F3
Englands Mead BA22 174 F3
Englands Rd TA24 124 A3
Englands Way TA20 223 D6
ENGLISHCOMBE 43 F2
Englishcombe La BA2 44 D3
Englishcombe Rd BS13 22 C3
Englishcombe Rise BA2 44 A3
Englishcombe Tithe Barn★ BA2 43 F2
Englishcombe Way BA2 44 E3
ENMORE 153 A6
Enmore BS24 49 A2
Enmore CE Prim Sch TA5 152 F5
Enmore Cl TA8 104 C8
Enmore Rd
Bridgwater TA5 153 B6
Taunton TA2 212 F7
Ennerdale Cl BS23 49 A5
Enterprise Ctr The BS24 49 A3
Enterprise Mews BA20 218 D3
Enterprise Trade Ctr BS4 22 E7
Entry Hill BA2 44 F2
Entry Hill Dr BA2 44 F3
Entry Hill Gdns BA2 44 F3
Entry Hill Pk BA2 44 F2
Entry Rise BA2 44 F1
Erin Wlk BS4 22 D8
Erlon La BA5 110 F4
Ermine St BA21 218 D7
Ermine Way BS11 4 C7
Ernest Ashman Pl TA20 223 D5
Ervine Terr BS2 227 C4
ESCOTT 150 C8
Escott Ct TA6 208 F6
Escott La TA4 132 D1
Esgar Rise BS22 31 E3
Eskdale Cl BS22 49 D8
Esmonde Dr BA22 173 E2
Esmond Gr BS21 6 D4
Esplanade
Burnham-on-S TA8 104 A7
Minehead TA24 201 A7
Esplanade La TA23 202 C7
Esplanade Rd BS20 2 C7
Esplanade The TA23 202 C7
Essex Cl TA20 223 C4
Essex Ct TA1 212 C2
Essex Dr TA1 212 C2
Estuary Ho BS20 2 E7
Estuary Pk TA5 135 B5
Estune Wlk BS41 11 A2
Esworthy Cross EX16 162 F1
Ethel St BA5 203 C3
Ethpark Gr 1 TA2 212 F6
Etonhurst BS23 48 D6
Eton La BS29 50 E7
Eton Rd TA8 104 B6
Etsome Cl TA11 211 C4
Etsome Hill TA11 211 C7
Etsome Rd TA11 211 C5
Etsome Terr TA11 211 C4
Ettlingen Way BS21 6 F2
Eugene Flats 7 BS2 227 A4
Eugene St
Bristol, Kingsdown BS2 227 A4
Bristol, St Pauls BS2, BS5 227 C4
Eveleigh Ave BA1 28 D2
Evelyn Rd BA1 44 B8
Evelyn Terr 14 BA1 28 A1
Evenlode Gdns BS11 4 F5
Evenlode Way BS31 25 A3
EVERCREECH 141 E1
Evercreech CE Prim Sch BA4 141 E2
Evercreech Rd BS14 23 B4
Evercreech Way TA9 104 F2
Everett Cl BA5 112 E1
Evergreen Cl BS25 51 F1
Evergreen Path TA16 195 F7
Everton Rd BA20 219 A4
Evesham Ave BA21 218 C6
Evesham Dr TA6 209 A1
Ewart Rd BS22 49 C8
Ewell Cl TA19 183 C1
Exbourne 10 BS22 32 A2
Exbury Cl TA8 104 C7
Excelsior St BA2 45 B5
Excelsior Terr BA3 78 B1
Exchange Ave BS1 227 A2
EXEBRIDGE 163 F3
Exebridge Ind Est TA22 163 F3
Exeter Cl
Burnham-on-S TA8 104 C7
Nether Stowey TA5 134 B2
Exeter Rd
Portishead BS20 2 E4
Rockwell Green TA21 222 B5
Weston-Super-Mare BS23 48 E5
Exeter Road Cvn Pk TA21 222 A4
EXFORD 128 D1
Exford CE Fst sch TA24 128 D1
Exford Cl BS23 48 F2
Exford Rd TA24 147 C6
Exmoor Gdns TA22 163 D6
Exmoor Owl & Hawk Centre★ TA24 124 B4
Exmoor Pony Centre The★ TA22 147 A1
Exmoor Rd BA2 44 F2
Exmoor Way TA24 200 E6
Exmouth Rd BS4 22 F8
Express Pk TA6 136 A2
EXTON 147 E4
Exton BS24 49 A2
Exton Cl BS14 23 B5
Exton La TA22 147 E4
Eyer's La BS2 227 C3
Eyers Rd BS24 49 F7
EYEWELL 174 E4

F

Faber Gr BS13 22 C4
Factory Hill SP8 161 F2
Factory La
East Huntspill TA9 136 E8
Tatworth TA20 198 D8
FAILAND 10 C3
Failand Cres BS9 5 C5
Failand La
Easton-in-G BS8 4 A1
Portbury BS20 3 F2
Failand Wlk BS9 5 C6
Fairacre Cl BS24 50 B4
Fairacres Cl BS31 24 F5
Fair Cl BA2 81 E4
Fairclose TA20 193 D6
Fair Cross TA23 131 F2
Fairdean Rd TA9 104 E4
Fairfax Cl TA6 209 C6
Fairfax Rd TA6 209 C5
Fairfax St BS1 227 B3
Fairfield
Coleford BA3 116 E8
Crewkerne TA18 224 B5
Ilminster TA19 221 A4
7 Martock TA12 185 E6
Rode BA11 82 F1
Sampford Peverell EX16 178 D1
Sherborne DT9 225 D5
Somerton TA11 211 E4
Fairfield continued
Tunley BA2 61 A3
Yarlington BA9 175 F7
Fairfield Ave BA1 28 A2
Fairfield Cl
Backwell BS48 19 D7
Frome BA11 120 A7
Marshfield SN14 13 F8
Weston-Super-Mare BS22 31 B1
Fairfield Dr TA4 202 E3
Fairfield Gdns BA6 206 D4
Fairfield Gn TA3 192 A7
Fairfield Hts DT9 225 D5
Fairfield Mdws BA14 83 F3
Fairfield Mead BS48 19 D7
FAIRFIELD PARK 28 A2
Fairfield Park Rd BA1 28 A2
Fairfield Pneu Sch BS48 19 C6
Fairfield Rd
Bath BA1 28 B1
Taunton TA2 213 B7
Fairfield Terr
Bath BA1 28 A1
Fitzhead TA4 166 F5
Peasedown St John BA2 79 C7
Fairfield View BA1 28 A2
Fairfield Way BS48 19 C6
Fairford Cl TA9 104 E4
Fairford Rd
Bristol BS11 4 D7
Highbridge TA9 104 E4
Fair Furlong BS13 22 A4
Fair Furlong Prim Sch BS13 22 B4
Fair Hill BS25 70 F8
Fairhouse Rd BA22 197 F8
Fairlands Mid Sch BS27 90 C7
Fairlands Way BS27 90 C7
Fairmead Rd BA21 219 C8
Fairmead Sch BA21 219 C8
Fairmont Terr 7 DT9 225 E4
Fair Pl TA11 158 D3
Fairseat Workshops BS40 56 E7
Fairview
Mells BA11 118 B7
Weston-Super-Mare BS22 31 F4
Fair View BA10 161 A7
Fairview Ho BS9 5 F8
Fairview Terr
Taunton TA3 168 D1
Yeovilton BA22 187 A8
Fairwater Cl TA2 212 D6
Fairway BS4 23 D8
Fairway Cl
Berrow TA8 84 F4
Weston-Super-Mare BS22 31 B2
Fairway Rise TA20 223 E5
Fairways
Saltford BS31 25 E2
Wells BA5 203 C4
Fairways Cvn Pk TA7 136 E3
Fairways The TA1 212 F1
Fairway View BA21 219 D6
Fairwood Rd BA13 102 F5
Fairy Hill BS39 41 D6
Falcon Cl
Bristol, Westbury on T BS9 5 F8
Portishead BS20 2 D4
Falcon Cres BS22 49 D8
Falcon Ct TA1 212 C4
Falcondale Rd BS9 5 F7
Falconer Rd BA1 27 A3
Falconsmead Wlk BA21 219 D8
Falkland Ho 7 TA18 224 C6
Falkland Sq 6 TA18 224 C6
Falklands Rise TA24 200 D7
Fallowfield
Blagdon BS40 54 E2
Weston-Super-Mare BS22 31 F3
Falmouth Cl BS48 9 A1
Fanshawe Rd BS14 23 A7
Faraday Rd 2 BS8 11 F5
FARLEIGH 19 D7
Farleigh Ct BS48 20 B8
FARLEIGH HUNGERFORD 82 E8
Farleigh Hungerford Castle★ BA2 82 E8
Farleigh Rd
Backwell BS48 19 C6
Clevedon BS21 6 B1
Keynsham BS31 24 D4
Norton St Philip BA2 81 F5
Farleigh Rise BA15 29 E1
Farleigh View BA15 64 F3
FARLEIGH WICK 46 E4
Farleigh Wlk BS13 22 A8
Farler's End BS48 18 F8
FARLEY 1 B1
Farley Cl BA11 120 C6
Farley Dell BA3 116 E8
FARMBOROUGH 60 B6
Farmborough CE Prim Sch BA2 59 F6
Farm Cl
Somerton TA11 211 B3
Westbury-sub-Mendip BA5 110 D6
Weston-Super-Mare BS22 32 C4
Farm Ct TA13 220 C5
Farm Dr TA11 211 B3
Farmer Rd BS13 21 E4
Farm Hill TA7 156 B8
Farmhouse Cl 7 BS48 8 E2
Farmhouse Ct 1 BS48 8 E1
Farmhouse Dr BA11 119 F7

Farm La
Buckland St Mary TA20 182 A2
Coultings TA5 134 E4
Stogursey TA5 134 D4
Street BA16 207 C7
Wellow BA2 62 E1
Farm Orch DT9 188 C7
Farm Rd
Bradford Abbas DT9 187 E1
Doulting BA4 141 E5
Hutton BS24 49 E2
Street BA16 207 C6
Weston-Super-Mare BS22 31 B1
Farm St BA22 186 C6
Farm View TA2 168 F6
Farmwell Cl BS13 22 B5
Farnaby Cl BS4 22 C7
Farnborough Rd BS24 50 C4
Farncombe La BA9 160 B1
Farndale Rd BS22 49 D8
Farrant Cl
Baltonsborough BA6 158 A5
Bristol BS4 22 D6
Taunton TA1 212 A4
Farrant Rd BA11 119 D5
Farriers Gn TA2 213 F7
Farringdon Hill La TA5 134 D6
Farrington Fields BS39 77 C3
Farrington Fields Trad Est BS39 77 C3
FARRINGTON GURNEY 77 A3
Farrington Gurney CE Prim Sch BS39 77 A4
Farrington La BA4 141 F6
Farrington Rd BS39 77 C5
Farrington Way BS39 77 A3
Farrow Cl TA20 223 D3
Farrs La BA2 45 B2
Farr's La BS1 227 A2
Farr's Orch 6 TA16 195 F7
Farr St BS11 4 B8
Farthing Combe BS26 70 D2
Farthing Down TA21 179 E7
Farthing La EX13 193 D1
Farthing Rd TA6 208 E1
Farthing Row BA11 82 E1
Farthings Cl TA21 167 C2
Farthings Paddock BA7 159 A3
Farthing's Pitts TA21 222 C4
Fashion Mus★ BA1 228 B3
FAULKLAND 80 E2
Faulkland La BA2, BA3 80 C4
Faulkland Rd BA2 44 D5
Faulkland View BA2 79 E7
Faversham Dr BS24 49 A1
Fawcus Pl TA20 223 C4
Fawn Cl BA6 206 C3
Fayre Way BA5 204 B7
Fearnville Est BS21 6 C2
Featherbed La
Chew Stoke BS40 38 A3
Clayhanger EX16 165 C1
Clutton BS39 58 C6
Fedden Village BS21 1 F5
Feeder Rd BS2 227 C1
Fellowsmead DT10 190 F5
Felon's Oak La TA24 131 B2
Felsberg Way BS27 90 C7
Feltham Dr BA11 120 A3
Feltham La BA11 144 B8
FELTON 37 C8
Felton Gr BS13 22 A8
Felton La BS40 37 E7
Felton St BS40 37 C7
Fender Cl TA5 135 B5
Feniton 6 BS22 32 A2
Fennel La BS26 70 B2
Fennel Rd BS20 3 A5
Fennel Way BA22 218 A5
Fenners BS22 32 B4
FENNINGTON 168 B8
Fennington La TA2 168 B8
Fenns La BS41 10 E1
FENNY CASTLE 139 D7
Fenshurst Gdns BS41 20 F8
Fenswood Cl BS41 10 F1
Fenswood Ct BS41 10 E1
Fenswood Mead BS41 10 E1
Fenswood Rd BS41 10 E1
Fental La BA3 116 C1
Fenton Cl BS31 25 D3
Ferenberge Cl BA2 60 A6
Ferguson Cl TA5 134 A3
Fermoy BA11 120 B6
Fern Cl BA3 78 B1
Ferndale Dr TA1 168 D1
Ferndale Gdns BA21 218 E6
Ferndale Rd
Bath BA1 28 C3
Portishead BS20 2 D6
Ferndown Cl
Bristol BS11 5 A7
Taunton TA1 212 D1
Ferne Animal Sanctuary★ TA20 193 A2
Fern Gr BS48 18 C8
Fern Lea BS24 67 B6
Fernlea Gdns BS20 4 B4
Fernlea Rd BS22 49 C7
Fernleigh Ave TA6 209 A3
Fernleigh Cl BA4 141 E1
Fern Lodge BS23 48 D6
Fernside BS48 19 A7
Fernsteed Rd BS13 21 F6
Ferry Ct BA2 45 B6
Ferry La
Bath BA2 45 B6
Lympsham BS24 67 C3
Ferryman Rd BA6 206 E7
Ferryman's Ct BS2 227 B2
Ferry St BS1 227 B2
Fersfield BA2 45 B3
Festival Units TA6 209 B1
Feversham Ave TA6 208 E6
Feversham Ct BA22 173 E2
Feversham La BA6 206 D5
Feversham Way TA2 213 A8
FIDDINGTON 134 D3
Fiddle La BA22 174 F1
FIELD 205 C5
Field Cl BA3 116 A3
Field End
Axminster EX13 198 A1
Minehead TA24 201 A5
Fielders The BS22 32 B4
Fieldfare Ave BS20 3 A6
Fieldgardens Rd BS39 58 F1
Field Gate TA3 183 C8
Fieldgate La TA3 183 B8
Fielding Ct BA21 219 C6
Fielding Ho BA2 44 A6
Fielding Path BA6 206 E6
Fielding Rd
Street BA16 207 B7
Yeovil BA21 219 C6
Fielding's Rd BA2 44 C6
Fieldins BA15 64 E7
Field La
Chewton Mendip BA3 94 F8
Kington Magna SP8 177 E1
Penselwood BA9 161 D2
Field Marshal Slim Ct 24 BS2 227 C3
Field Rd TA10 156 A1
Fields End TA1 213 C2
Fields The BS22 32 D2
Field View BA4 205 C5
Field View Cl BA4 141 E1
Fieldway BS25 52 B4
Field Way TA9 104 D5
Fifehead Bsns Ctr (Manor Farm Trad Est) BA8 190 F8
Fifehead Hill BA8 190 F8
FIFEHEAD MAGDALEN 190 F8
Fifth Ave BS14 23 B7
Filer Cl BA2 79 D8
Fillymead DT10 190 F5
Filwood Broadway BS4 22 E8
FILWOOD PARK 22 E8
Finch Cl
Shepton Mallet BA4 204 F6
Weston-Super-Mare BS22 49 E8
Finches The
4 Portishead BS20 2 F6
Portishead BS20 3 A6
Finches Way TA8 85 B1
Finger Cnr DT10 190 F5
Finger La DT9 225 D3
Finisterre Parade BS20 2 F6
Finmere Gdns BS22 32 A4
Fircliff Pk BS20 2 D7
Fire House Mews BA9 216 C3
FIREPOOL 213 A5
Firgrove La BA2 61 B1
Fir La BS40 72 B5
Fir Leaze BS48 8 B1
Firs Ct BS31 24 C4
First Ave
Axminster EX13 198 A2
Bath BA2 44 E4
Bristol BS14 23 A7
Portbury BS20 3 E5
Radstock BA3 97 C8
First Dro TA7 155 D3
Firs The
Bath BA2 45 B1
Langport TA10 172 A5
Limpley Stoke BA3 64 A5
Wheddon Cross TA24 129 E1
First Ho BA16 207 B6
First Sedgemoor Dro TA10 155 E4
Fir Tor Ave BA5 203 C5
Fir Tree Ave
Paulton BS39 77 F4
Weston-Super-Mare BS24 49 E4
Firtree Cl TA5 134 A2
Fir Tree Cl TA6 209 D4
Firway Cross EX16 164 C3
Firwood Rd BA11 119 E4
Fishers Brook BA11 120 A5
Fishers Cl DT9 187 F5
Fisher's Hill
Glastonbury BA6 206 D4
Holywell Lake TA21 179 D7
Fisher's La
Dinnington TA17 195 A7
Mark TA9 106 D5
Fishers Mead TA22 163 D6
Fisherway La TA19 195 A5
FISHPOND BOTTOM 199 A1
Fishpond Bottom Rd DT6 199 A1
Fishwell La BA6 157 D4
Fitzharding Ho 8 BS1 227 A3
Fitzharding Rd BS20 4 E3
FITZHEAD 166 F7
FITZROY 168 A6
Fitzroy Circ BS20 2 F6
Fitzroy Ho 3 BA2 228 C3
Fivash Cl TA1 168 D1
Five Acres 3 BA22 197 F8
Five Arches Cl BA3 78 D2
Five Ashes BA22 186 C2
Five Barrows Cross EX36 145 B7
FIVE BELLS 202 B5
Five Bells TA23 202 B5
Five C Bsns Ctr BS21 6 B1
Five Cross Way TA21 180 F6
Five Cross Ways TA22 162 F7
Five Dials TA19 183 C1
FIVEHEAD 170 F2
Five Hos TA21 222 B8
Five Lords TA5 134 B2
Fiveways Cl BS27 90 A7
Fiveways Rdbt BA21 219 A6
Fiveways Specl Sch BA21 219 D6
Five Yards 3 TA4 167 F8
Flagstaff Rd BS26 68 D7
Flamingo Cres BS22 49 E8
Flat The BS39 58 D5
Flatwoods Cres BA2 45 F3
Flatwoods Rd BA2 45 F3
FLAX BOURTON 19 F7
Flax Bourton CE Prim Sch BS48 19 F8
Flax Bourton Rd BS8 10 B3
Flaxfield Dr TA18 224 C5
Flax La DT9 187 F4
FLAXPOOL 151 C6
Flaxpool Hill TA4 151 C6
Flax Row TA18 224 C7
Flax Way BA21 218 C6
Fleed Cross TA4 166 A6
Fleet Air Arm Mus★ BA22 174 B3
Fletcher Cl TA2 213 B8
Fletcher's La BS26 87 D6
Fleur De Lys Dr BA14 83 F4
Flingers La BA9 216 D4
Flint Cross TA4 149 C1
Flints Cl BA11 119 D4
Florence Brown Specl Sch BS4 22 D8
Florence Cl 3 TA6 208 E7
Florence Gr BS22 49 B8
Florida Fields BA7 214 B6
Florida St BA7 214 C5
Florida Terr BA3 78 C2
Flowerdale Rd TA23 202 C6
Flowerdown Bridge BS22 49 D7
Flowerdown Rd BS24 50 D4
Flowerfield BA11 143 B8
Flowers Hill BS4 23 E8
Flowers Ho 1 BA20 219 B4
Flowerstone BA3 114 D7
Flowerwell Rd BS13 22 B5
Flushing Mdw BA21 219 E5
FODDINGTON 174 E8
Foghamshire La BA11 143 D6
Foldhill Cl 25 TA12 185 E6
Foldhill La
Ash BA22 186 A6
Martock TA12 185 F6
Folke La DT9 189 A1
Folleigh Cl BS41 11 B2
Folleigh Dr BS41 11 B2
Folleigh La BS41 11 B2
Folliott Rd BA6 206 E6
Folly Cl
Cannington TA5 135 B2
Midsomer Norton BA3 96 E7
Folly Dr BA4 159 C7
Folly Dro TA19 183 A5
Folly Farm Nature Reserve★ BS39 58 B5
Folly Fields BA21 219 B7
Folly La
Buckland St Mary TA20 182 E1
Kington Magna SP8 177 F2
Nether Compton DT9 187 F4
North Wootton BA4 140 C4
Shipham BS25 70 E7
South Cadbury BA22 175 D4
Weston-Super-Mare BS23 48 E1
Folly Rd TA12 185 B7
Folly The
Cold Ashton SN14 12 F6
Ditcheat BA4 159 C7
Paulton BS39 77 F6
Saltford BS31 25 F2
Fons George TA1 212 F2
Fons George Cl TA1 212 E2
Fons George Rd TA1 212 F2
Fonthill Rd BA1 27 E2
Font La BA22 197 B7
Fontmell Ct BS14 23 D7
Font Villas BA22 197 B8
Football La BA9 216 B4
Footlands Cl TA1 212 F1
Forbes Fraser Hospl BA1 44 B8
Forches Cnr EX15 181 A4
Forche's La TA24 131 D3
FORD
Chewton Mendip 94 E8
Holcombe Rogus 178 F5
Wiveliscombe 210 F6
Forde Abbey & Gardens★ TA20 198 F8
Forde Pk BA21 218 C7
FORDGATE 154 C3
Fordhay BA22 196 E7
Fordhay Terr BA22 196 E7
Ford La
Chewton Mendip BA3 94 D8
Pilton BA4 140 F3
Stawell TA7 137 A1
Yarley BA5 139 B8
Fordmill Cross EX16 164 D1
Ford Orch EX16 178 D1
Ford Rd
Bampton EX16 164 C1
Peasedown St John BA2 79 D8
Wellow BA2 62 F1
Wiveliscombe TA4 210 C4
Ford St TA21 222 F4
FORD STREET 180 D5
Forefield Pl BA2 228 C1
Forefield Rise BA2 45 B4
Forefield Terr BA2 45 A4
Forelands BS23 30 B1
Fore Leaze Dro TA12 184 E7
Fore St
9 Bampton EX16 164 B1
Bridgwater TA6 208 F5
Cannington TA5 135 B2
Castle Cary BA7 214 C5
Chard TA20 223 C4
Dulverton TA22 163 D6
Holcombe Rogus TA21 178 F5
Milverton TA4 167 A4
North Petherton TA6 153 E3
Othery TA7 155 C2
Tatworth TA20 198 D8
Taunton TA1 212 F3
Thorncombe TA20 199 B6
Wellington TA21 222 D6
West Camel BA22 174 D3
Westonzoyland TA7 154 E5
Williton TA4 202 D3
Winsham TA20 194 E1
Forest Dr BS23 31 A1
Forest Dro TA3 182 F5
Forester Ave BA2 45 B8
Forester Ct BA2 228 C4
Forester La BA2 45 B8
Forester Rd
Bath BA2 45 B8
Portishead BS20 2 D4
Foresters Cl TA4 202 E3
Forest Hill BA20 218 E2
Forest La TA20 193 E8
Forest Mill La TA19 183 B1
Forest Rd
Frome BA11 120 B7
Horningsham BA11, BA12 144 B4
Forest Wlk BA13 121 C4
Forge Cnr
Somerton TA11 211 C4
Stogursey TA5 134 B6
Forge End BS20 3 E3
Forge La
East Chinnock BA22 196 E8
Zeals SP8, BA12 161 F2
Fortescue Rd BA3 78 F2
Fortfield Rd BS14 23 B5
Forth Ave BS20 2 F6
Forth Cl BA16 207 A4
Fortnum Pl TA19 221 D3
FORTON 223 F1
Forton La
Chard TA20 223 F1
Tatworth TA20 194 A1
Forton Rd TA20 223 D2
Forts Orch BA22 186 E6
Forum Bldgs BA1 228 C1
Forum La BA4 205 A7
Forum The BA21 218 C6
Forward's La TA3 181 C5
Fosgrove La TA3 181 E7
Fosse Barton BS48 8 D2
Fosse Cl
Nailsea BS48 8 C2
Yeovil BA21 218 D7
Fossedale Ave BS14 23 C6
Fossefield Rd BA3 97 B6
Fosse Gdns BA2 62 D8
Fosse Gn BA3 78 E4
Fosse La
Batheaston BA1 29 A4
Blackford BS28 107 C3
Clandown BA3 78 D3
Nailsea BS48 8 D2
Shepton Mallet BA4 205 D4
Fosse Lane Junc BA4 205 E5
Fosse Lane Trad Est BA4 205 D5
Fosse Rd BA3 115 C3
Fosse The TA3 170 C4
Fosseway
Clandown BA3 78 E4
Clevedon BS21 6 C2
Midsomer Norton BA3 97 A5
Radstock BA3 97 C8
Fosse Way
Nailsea BS48 8 C2
Yeovil BA21 218 D7
Fosseway Cl BA2 79 C7
Fosse Way Cotts BA3 78 D2
Fosseway Ct
Bristol BS8 226 A2
Ilchester BA22 173 E2
Fosse Way Est BA2 44 D1
Fosseway Gdns BA3 78 D1
Fosseway S BA3 97 B7
Fosse Way Sch BA3 97 C8
Fosseway The BS8 226 A3
Foster Cl BA5 112 E1
Foster Rd BA11 120 A3
Fosters 10 DT9 225 E4
Foster's Almshouses 3 BS1 227 A3
Foster's La BA22 175 A7
Foundry Barton 2 BA11 119 F5
Foundry Cotts BA2 60 B4
Foundry Mews
Chard TA20 223 C4
Foundry Mews *continued*
2 Crewkerne TA18 224 C5
Foundry Rd TA1 212 F4
Foundry Sq 1 TA18 224 C5
Foundry The BA1 228 C3
Fountain Bldgs 7 BA1 228 B3
Fountain Ho 8 BA1 228 B3
Fountain La BS25 70 B7
Fountains Cl BA21 218 C7
Four Acre Mdw TA6 208 E6
Four Acre Mead 1 TA4 167 F8
Four Acres
Bristol BS13 21 E4
Shepton Mallet BA4 205 C5
Fouracres Cl TA1 213 B1
Four Acres Cl
Bristol BS13 21 F4
Nailsea BS48 18 E8
Four Acres Prim Sch BS13 21 E4
Four Elms TA21 179 A6
FOUR FORKS 152 F8
Four Forks La TA5 152 F7
Four Lanes TA20 193 F6
Fourth Ave
Bristol BS14 23 B7
Radstock BA3 97 D8
Fourways Cl BA7 214 D6
Fouts Cross TA19 184 F2
Fowey Cl BS48 19 A8
Fowey Rd BS22 32 A4
Fowler St TA2 212 E6
Fownes Rd TA24 201 B5
Foxbury Cl BA11 119 F6
Fox Cl TA21 222 A6
Foxcombe La DT9 176 C1
Foxcombe Rd
Bath BA1 44 B7
Bristol BS14 23 B4
FOXCOTE 79 F4
Foxcote BA20 218 C2
Foxcote Ave BA2 79 E7
Foxcote Gdns BA11 120 C7
Foxdon Hill TA20 223 A7
Foxdown Hill TA21 222 C4
Foxdown Ho TA21 222 C4
Foxdown Terr TA21 222 D4
Foxglove Cl BS22 32 A5
Foxglove Way
Chard TA20 223 F5
Yeovil BA22 218 A5
Foxhanger La TA22 148 A2
FOX HILL 45 A2
Fox Hill BA2 45 A2
Foxhill Ho BA2 45 A1
FOX HILLS 79 A1
Foxhole La TA3 169 E5
Foxholes La BA2, BA11 100 D5
Fox & Hounds La BS31 24 F5
Fox Mdws TA18 224 D7
Fox Rd BA16 207 A5
Fox's Dro BA11 102 C1
Fox Way TA5 134 B2
Foxwell La BA22 196 C7
Foye Ho BS8 11 E6
Frampton Rd TA6 208 F2
Francis Cl TA3 169 D5
Francis Fox Rd 7 BS23 48 E7
Francis Ho BS2 227 A4
Francis Reed Cl TA7 154 F5
Francis Wlk DT9 225 E5
Francombe Ho BS1 227 A1
Frankcom Ho BA2 45 B7
Frank Foley Parkway The TA8 104 D6
Frankford Mans 7 BS23 30 C1
Frankland Cl BA1 27 B1
Frankley Bldgs BA1 28 B1
Frankley Terr 6 BA1 28 B1
Franklin Cl TA2 212 B7
Franklin Ct BS1 227 B1
Franklin's Way BS49 17 F1
Franklyn Terr BS39 77 A4
Frank Webber Rd TA21 222 A5
Fraser Cl
Burnham-on-S TA8 104 C7
Weston-Super-Mare BS22 31 F4
Frederick Ave BA2 79 C7
Frederick Ct BA5 203 C4
Frederick Pl BS8 226 B3
Frederick Rd TA6 209 C6
Fredrick Pl 5 BA20 219 B4
Freedom Ave BA21 218 E6
Free Hill BA5 110 E6
Freeland Pl BS8 11 F6
Freelands BS21 16 C8
Freeling Ho BS1 227 B1
Freemans La BS48 20 B2
Freemantle Ho BS2 227 A4
Free St BA22 173 E1
Freeview Rd BA2 44 A5
Freezinghill La BS30 12 B4
Fremantle Rd TA1 213 B1
Frenchay Rd BS23 48 E4
French Cl
Nailsea BS48 8 F3
Peasedown St John BA2 79 D7
Frenchfield Rd BA2 79 D7
French Weir Ave TA1 212 E5
French Weir Cl TA1 212 E4
FRESHFORD 64 B5
Freshford CE Prim Sch BA3 64 B5
Freshford La BA3 64 A4
Freshford Sta BA3 64 C5
Freshmoor 6 BS21 6 F3
Frethey Rd TA1, TA4 168 B3
Friar Ave BS22 31 E3

FRIARN 133 F1
Friarn Ave TA6 208 F4
Friarn Lawn TA6 208 F4
Friarn St TA6 208 F4
Friars Ave BA21 218 D6
Friars Cl BA22 173 D1
Friars Way TA8 104 B6
Friary BS1 227 C1
Friary Cl
Clevedon BS21 6 C5
Westwood BA15 64 E4
Witham Friary BA11 143 C3
Friary Rd BS20 2 B5
Friday St TA24 200 F7
Friendly Row BS20 4 C5
Friendship Gr 2 BS48 8 F2
Friendship Rd BS48 8 F3
FRIEZE HILL 212 D5
Friggle St BA11 120 D1
Frithfield La BA4 205 C6
Frobisher Ave BS20 2 B5
Frobisher Cl
Burnham-on-S TA8 104 D8
Portishead BS20 2 A5
Weston-Super-Mare BS22 31 E4
Frobisher Way TA2 212 B6
Frog La
Bristol BS1 226 C2
Combe St Nicholas TA20 193 D6
Creech St Michael TA3 169 F6
Dinnington TA17 195 B8
Enmore TA5 153 A6
Felton BS40 37 C8
Galhampton BA22 175 E8
Haselbury Plucknett TA18 196 C6
Holcombe Rogus TA21 178 F5
Ilminster TA19 221 C4
Kingsdon TA11 173 D5
Langport TA10 171 F5
North Curry TA3 170 D5
Shepton Mallet BA4 205 E4
Stoke St Michael BA3 116 A4
Ubley BS40 55 D1
Wanstrow BA4 142 F4
West Camel BA22 174 D3
Winford BS40 37 F5
Froglands La BS27 90 C7
Froglands Way BS27 90 C7
Frogmore St BS1 226 C2
Frogs La TA21 180 F7
Frog St
Bampton EX16 164 B1
East Quantoxhead TA5 133 B6
Lopen TA13 185 A1
Frogwell Cross TA4 164 D6
FROME 119 E4
Frome Com Coll BA11 120 A7
FROMEFIELD 120 A6
Fromefield BA11 120 A6
Fromefield Ho BA11 120 A6
Frome Mus★ BA11 119 F5
Frome Old Rd BA3 79 A2
Frome Rd
Bath BA2 44 D1
Beckington BA11 101 D3
Bruton BA10 215 F7
Maiden Bradley BA12 144 B3
Norton St Philip BA2 81 F3
Nunney BA11 143 B8
Radstock BA3 79 B2
Rode BA11 101 F7
Southwick BA14 83 F3
Wingfield BA14 83 C5
Frome Sta BA11 120 A4
Frome View BA12 144 C2
Front St
Chapel Allerton BS26 88 D1
Chedzoy TA7 154 D8
Churchill BS25 52 E4
Monksilver TA4 150 B8
FROST HILL 34 C6
Frost Hill BS49 34 D7
Frost La TA19 183 F4
Frys House of Mercy 11 BS1 227 B1
Frys La TA7 154 E8
Fry's La BS40 53 F3
Frys Leaze BA1 28 B2
Frys Mews TA1 213 C2
Fry's Well BA3 96 D3
Fry's Wlk BA4 205 A5
Fryth Ho BS48 9 D3
Fryth Way BS48 8 C2
FULFORD 168 C8
Fulford Ct TA24 200 F7
Fulford Rd BS13 22 C5
Fulford Wlk BS13 22 B5
Fullands Ave TA1 168 F1
Fullands Ct TA1 168 F1
Fullands Rd TA1 213 B1
Fullens Cl BS22 49 D7
Fuller Cl BA4 205 D5
Fuller Rd BA1 28 C2
Fullers La BS25 70 A6
Fullers Way BA2 62 D8
Fullwell Cl BA3 80 D1
Fulmar Rd BS22 31 F1
Fulwell La BA3 80 D1
Fulwood Cl TA1 212 D1
Furge Gr BA8 190 A6
Furge La BA8 190 A6
Furland Rd
Crewkerne TA18 224 C5
Weston-Super-Mare BS22 31 C2
Furland Way TA18 224 C5
Furlong Cl BA3 96 F7
Furlong Cotts EX16 179 A4
Furlong Gn TA3 168 D1
Furlong La
Curry Rivel TA10 171 C3
Milborne Port DT9 217 B3
Furlong Pl BS26 70 C1
Furlongs Ave TA6 208 E2
Furlongs The DT9 225 D5
FURNHAM 223 D5
Furnham Cl TA20 223 D5
Furnham Cres TA20 223 D6
Furnham Rd TA20 223 D5
Furnleaze BS39 58 E3
Furpits La TA10 172 B6
Furringdons Cross TA18 195 F6
Furze Cl
Bridgwater TA6 208 D4
Weston-Super-Mare BS22 31 B2
Furzeclose La BA4 142 C7
Furzehill TA20 223 D5
Furzehill La TA24 147 C6
Furzeland Rd TA24 124 A4
Furze Rd BS22 31 A3
Furze The BA20 218 C2
Fylton Croft BS14 23 B3
Fyne Court Nat Res & Visitor Ctr★ TA5 152 E3

G

Gables Cl BS29 51 B3
Gables The TA21 222 C6
Gabriel Cl BA11 120 C6
Gadd's La BS27 90 B8
Gagley La BA5 111 B2
Gainesmarsh La TA10 172 C5
Gainsborough DT9 217 C2
Gainsborough Ct BA1 27 B1
Gainsborough Dr
Sherborne DT9 225 B3
Weston-Super-Mare BS22 31 F3
Gainsborough Gdns BA1 44 C8
Gainsborough Hill DT9 225 E2
Gainsborough Rd BS31 24 F5
Gainsborough Way BA21 219 E8
Galahad Cl BA21 218 D7
Gale's Dro BA6 139 D3
GALHAMPTON 175 D8
Galhampton Hill BA7, BA22 214 C2
Galingale Way BS20 2 F5
Gallagher Ret Pk
TA6 209 A6
Weston-Super-Mare BS23 49 A5
Galleries The BS1 227 B3
Galley Batch BA3 114 F4
Galley Batch La BA3 114 F4
Galloping Bottom La TA23 149 E5
GALMINGTON 212 C2
Galmington Cl TA1 212 C3
Galmington Dr TA1 212 C2
Galmington La TA1 212 C2
Galmington Rd TA1 212 C2
Gamblyn Cross TA4 164 F5
Gammins Cotts TA24 129 E2
Gander Cl BS13 22 B5
Gandstone Cross TA4 150 D2
Ganesfield BA4 141 E6
Ganges Cl TA3 170 F2
Gange's Hill TA3 170 F2
Gannet Rd BS22 31 F1
Gants Mill & Gdn★ BA10 215 C5
Gants Mill La BA10 215 D5
Gaol La BA4 205 C6
Garamond Ct BS1 227 B1
Garden City TA10 172 A6
Garden Cl
Bristol BS9 5 C5
Norton Fitzwarren TA2 168 B4
Weston-Super-Mare BS22 31 E2
Garden Ct BS8 226 A4
Gardeners Cl
Bradford On Tone TA4 167 F1
Cheddar BS27 90 B8
Gardeners Wlk BS41 11 B1
Garden Ground BA4 205 C4
Gardenhurst TA8 85 B1
Garden Hurst Cl TA8 104 B8
Garden Plot Hill TA3 183 E7
Gardens Rd BS21 6 C4
Gardens The
Dulverton TA22 163 D7
East Pennard BA4 158 F8
Sherborne DT9 225 C3
1 Wellington TA21 222 D5
2 Wells BA5 203 D4
Garden Terr TA21 222 B7
Garden Way TA24 200 D7
Garden Wlk TA6 208 E2
Gardiners Bsns Pk TA7 136 F3
Gardiners Orch BS28 108 C4
Gardner Ave BS13 21 F7
Gardner Rd BS20 2 D6
Garfield Terr 1 BA1 28 C2
GARLANDHAYES 180 F2
Garlandhayes La EX15 180 E2
Garland Ho 7 BS21 6 C2
Garner Ct 4 BS22 32 B4
Garonor Way BS20 3 F5
Garre Ho BA2 43 F5
Garrett Rd BA20 218 D3
Garrick Rd BA2 43 F5
Garsdale BA11 120 A4
Garsdale Rd BS22 49 D8
Garston Cotts BS40 54 E3
Garstone La TA16 195 F8
Garston La
Blagdon BS40 54 E3
Garston La *continued*
Frome BA11 120 A4
Marston Magna BA22 174 F1
Garston Lodge 11 BA11 119 F4
Garston Rd BA11 120 A4
Garstons
Bathford BA1 29 D2
7 Clevedon BS21 6 B1
Wrington BS40 35 E1
Garstons Cl
Backwell BS48 18 F6
Wrington BS40 35 E2
Garstons Orch BS40 35 D1
Garston St BA4 205 C6
Garstons The BS20 2 D4
Garth Rd BS13 22 A8
Gartons Mead BA4 141 E1
Gartons Mead Rd BA4 141 E1
Garvins Rd BA6 206 C4
Gasferry Rd BS1 226 B1
Gashay La EX13 199 B3
Gas La TA17 195 D7
Gason La BA22 174 F4
GASPER 161 E4
Gasper St BA12 161 E3
Gass Cl TA9 104 F4
Gasson's La TA11 211 C3
Gaston Ave BS31 24 F6
Gaston Cl BA16 207 C4
Gaston's La TA12 185 D5
Gastons The BS11 5 A8
Gaswell La TA7 155 E8
Gatchell Gn TA3 168 D1
Gatchell Mdw TA3 168 D1
Gatchells La TA4 132 F2
Gatchell's La TA3 181 B5
Gatcombe Farm Ind Est BS40 35 D3
Gatcombe Rd BS13 22 B5
Gate Cl EX13 198 E3
Gatehouse Ave BS13 22 A5
Gatehouse Cl BS13 22 A5
Gatehouse Ct BS13 22 B5
Gatehouse Ctr The BS13 22 B5
Gatehouse Way BS13 22 A5
Gate La BA5 203 D2
Gaunton Cl TA1 212 D2
Gaunts Cl BS20 1 F4
Gaunt's La BS1 226 C2
Gaunts Rd TA6 135 E6
Gay Cl TA21 222 E6
Gay Ct BA1 28 E3
Gay Elms Prim Sch BS13 22 A4
Gay Elms Rd BS13 22 A4
Gaylard's La TA20 194 B5
Gay's Hill BA1 228 C4
Gay St
Bath BA1 228 B3
Mells BA11 118 B7
Wellington TA21 222 E6
Gazelle Rd
Weston-Super-Mare BS24 49 B3
Yeovil BA20 218 D3
Gefle Cl BS1 226 B1
Geldof Dr BA3 78 A2
Gelosia Cl TA7 154 F6
General Higgins Ho TA9 104 E3
Gennes Gr BA9 216 C4
Gentle St
Frome BA11 119 F4
Horningsham BA12 144 E4
Geoffrey Cl BS13 21 E6
George Cl BS48 19 D7
George & Crown Cotts TA17 195 C7
George La
Marshfield SN14 13 E8
South Petherton TA13 220 C4
George Maher Ct TA19 221 C3
Georges Bldgs BA1 28 C3
George's Ground BA11 119 E2
George Sh Ctr The TA18 224 C6
Georges Ho BA2 45 B6
Georges Mews TA1 213 C2
George Smith Way BA22 218 A6
George's Pl BA2 45 B6
George's Rd BA1 28 A1
Georges Sq BS1 227 B2
George St
Bath BA1 228 B3
Bath, Bathwick BA2 45 B6
Bridgwater TA6 208 F5
Burnham-on-S TA8 104 A7
Charlton Adam TA11 173 F7
Glastonbury BA6 206 D5
Portishead BS20 2 C2
Sherborne DT9 225 D4
Taunton TA2 212 F6
Wellington TA21 222 D6
Weston-Super-Mare BS23 48 E7
George Sweetman Cl BA9 216 D4
George William Ct TA6 208 F4
Georgian Ct BA11 119 D3
Georgian Ho BA2 228 C2
Georgian House (Mus)★ BS1 226 C2
Georgian View BA2 44 C2
Gerard Rd BS23 48 F8
Gerbestone La TA21 180 E6
Gerrard Bldgs 5 BA2 45 B7
Gerrard Cl BS4 22 D7
Geys Hill BA12 144 D8
Giant's Grave TA20 193 A7
Giant's Grave Rd TA20 193 A7
Gibbet La BS14 23 D1
Gibbet Rd BA9 176 B6
Gibbsfold Rd BS13 22 C4
Gibbs' La TA19 184 D5
Gibbs Marsh Trad Est DT10 190 D6
Gibraltar Cotts TA24 123 E4
Giddy La BA3 116 A4
Gielgud Cl TA8 104 D6
Gifford Cl TA20 223 D5
Giffords La TA18 196 C5
Giffords Orch TA12 185 A7
Giffords Pl BS13 22 A7
Gigg La SP8 177 C2
Gilbeck Rd BS48 8 C2
Gilberts Cnr BA6 158 A6
Gilbert Scott Ho BA5 113 A1
Gilbert Scott Mews BA5 113 A2
Gilbert Scott Rd BA5 113 A1
Gilberyn Dr BS22 32 A3
Gilda Cl BS14 23 C5
Gilda Cres BS14 23 B6
Gilda Par BS14 23 C5
Gilda Sq W BS14 23 B5
Giles Cl TA10 171 D4
Giles Farm BA5 113 A1
Gillards TA1 212 B4
Gillards Cl TA21 222 B4
Gillards Mead TA3 192 A7
Gill Cres TA1 212 B1
Gillebank Cl BS14 23 D5
Gillingham Ct TA20 223 D5
Gillingham Terr 3 BA1 28 B1
Gill Mews BS22 32 B4
Gillmore Cl BS22 31 D1
Gillmore Rd BS22 31 D1
Gills La BS26 87 B5
Gillson Cl BS24 49 D2
Gimblett Rd BS22 32 B4
Gipsy Cross TA4 166 A2
Gipsy Dro TA20 193 C4
Gipsy La
Burcott BA5 139 E8
Frome BA11 120 B7
Glastonbury BA6 139 D1
Halse TA4 167 B6
Sampford Arundel TA21 179 D5
Staplegrove TA2 212 D7
Street BA16 207 E4
Taunton TA1 212 C3
Wells BA5 203 A4
GIRT 175 C2
Gladstone Ct BA2 45 C2
Gladstone Pl BA2 45 C2
Gladstone Rd
Bath BA2 45 C2
Bristol BS14 23 B6
Gladstone St
Midsomer Norton BA3 78 B3
Taunton TA2 212 E6
Gladstone Terr
Minehead TA24 201 A5
Wellington TA21 222 E6
Gladstone Villas BA3 115 C5
Glanfield Cl TA4 167 E8
Glanfield Terr BA22 173 F1
Glanvill Ave TA20 223 C5
Glanville Dr BS39 75 E6
Glanville Rd BS28 108 C4
Glanvill Rd BA16 207 C3
Glasses Mead TA1 212 B2
Glass House Hill DT9 225 E3
Glass's Cross TA4 149 E1
Glass's Rocks La TA4 149 D1
GLASTONBURY 206 F6
Glastonbury Abbey★ BA6 206 E4
Glastonbury Cl BS48 9 B1
Glastonbury Ct BA21 218 D6
Glastonbury Rd
Meare BA6 138 E4
Wells BA5 203 B2
Glastonbury Tor★ BA6 139 D1
Glastonbury Way BS22 32 A2
Glaston Ho BA16 207 D7
Glaston Rd BA16 207 D7
Glebe Ave BS20 2 E4
Glebe Cl BS41 11 C2
Glebe Cotts TA3 169 E2
Glebe Cres TA24 200 E8
Glebe Ho
Bath BA2 45 B5
Portishead BS20 2 E4
Weston-Super-Mare BS22 31 F3
Glebe Inf Sch The BS49 34 C4
Glebeland Cl TA7 156 B8
Glebelands
7 Merriott TA16 195 F7
Minehead TA24 200 E8
Norton Sub Hamdon TA14 185 F3
Nunney BA11 143 B7
Radstock BA3 78 D1
Glebelands Cl BS27 90 B6
Glebe Paddock BA5 139 E8
Glebe Rd
Bath BA2 44 B4
Clevedon BS21 6 C2
Long Ashton BS41 11 C2
Portishead BS20 2 E4
Weston-Super-Mare BS23 48 E8
Glebe The
Fivehead TA3 170 F1
Freshford BA3 64 B4
Hinton Charterhouse BA2 63 D2
Queen Camel BA22 174 F3
Timberscombe TA24 130 B4
Timsbury BA2 60 B3
Wrington BS40 35 D2
Glebe Way BS27 90 C6
Glebe Wlk BS31 24 C4
Glebe Yd TA10 172 E4
Glen Ave BS8 10 F8
Glenavon Pk BS9 5 C4
Glen Brook BS9 5 D4
Glencairn Ct BA2 45 B6
Glen Cl TA2 168 B5
Glencoe Bsns Pk BS23 49 A7
Glencoe Terr TA3 168 D1
Glencot La BA5 203 A7
Glencot Rd BA5 203 A6
Glencroft Way BS22 31 E3
Glendale 16 BS8 11 F6
Glendevon Rd BS14 23 A3
Glen Dr
Bristol BS9 5 D5
Taunton TA2 168 F6
Gleneagles Cl
Nailsea BS48 9 A1
Weston-Super-Mare BS22 31 F3
Glenmore Rd TA24 201 A7
Glen The
Saltford BS31 25 F1
Weston-Super-Mare BS22 31 B2
Glenthorne Ave BA21 219 B7
Glenthorne Nature Trail Gate★ EX35 122 D5
Glenthorne Rd 9 TA2 212 F6
Glentworth Ct 19 BS23 30 C1
Glentworth Rd BS8 226 B2
Glen View BA3 115 E7
Glenview Ho BA2 79 D8
Glenville Rd BA21 219 D6
Glenwood Gdns TA2 212 F8
Glenwood Mans BS23 30 D1
Glenwood Rise BS20 1 F5
Glen Yeo Terr BS49 34 C4
Globe Orch TA18 196 C6
Gloucester Ho 11 BS2 227 C3
Gloucester La 18 BS2 227 C3
Gloucester Rd
Bath BA1 28 C3
Bridgwater TA6 208 F2
Burnham-on-S TA8 104 C7
Upper Swainswick BA1 28 A7
Gloucester Row 6 BS8 11 F7
Gloucester St
4 Bath BA1 228 B3
5 Bristol BS2 227 B4
8 Bristol, Clifton BS8 11 F7
Taunton TA1 213 A4
Weston-Super-Mare BS23 48 D7
Glovers DT9 225 D5
Glovers Cl
Milborne Port DT9 217 D2
4 Stoke sub Hamdon TA14 185 F4
Glovers Ct BA20 218 F4
Glovers Field BS25 70 F7
Glovers Wlk 18 BA20 219 B4
Glovers Wlk Sh Ctr BA20 219 B5
Glynsmead TA20 198 C8
Glynswood TA20 223 C5
GOAR KNAPP 219 D5
GOATHILL 189 B4
Goathill La BA8 176 C3
Goathill Rd DT9 189 B4
GOATHURST 153 B5
Godhams La TA4 165 A7
Godminster Ct BA10 215 E6
Godminster La BA10 215 E4
GODNEY 139 A5
Godney Dro BA5 139 B6
Godney Rd BA5, BA6 139 A4
Godwin Dr BS48 8 C3
Goeffrey Farrant Wlk TA1 213 A5
Goes La BA7 158 F2
Gogs Orch BS28 108 C3
Gold Corner Dro TA9 137 A6
Goldcrest Way BS20 2 F6
Goldcroft BA21 219 B6
Goldcroft Ct BA21 219 B6
Goldenhaye La TA20 194 D3
Golden Hill
Stourton Caundle DT10 189 F1
Wiveliscombe TA4 210 C5
Golden Lion Ct BS1 227 B2
Golden Valley La BS30 25 E8
Golden Valley Prim Sch BS48 8 F2
Goldfinches La BA6 139 D3
Gold Hill
Batcombe BA4 142 D2
Shepton Mallet BA4 205 B7
Golding Cl BA5 203 C4
Golding's La DT9 217 C1
Goldney Ave BS8 226 A2
Goldney Cl BS39 58 F1
Goldney Rd BS8 226 A2
Goldney Way BS39 58 F1
GOLD'S CROSS 57 E6
Goldsmiths La EX13 198 A4
Goldsmoor Cross EX16 178 E3
Gold St DT10 190 B4
Golf Club La BS31 25 E2
Golf Course Rd BA2 45 D6
Golf Links La BA3 114 E3
Golf Links Rd TA8 85 A2
Golledge Cl BA3 96 C4
GOLSONCOTT 131 D2
Gooch Cl
Bridgwater TA6 209 B4
Frome BA11 120 D6
Gooch Way BS22 32 B3
Goodard Dr BS22 32 B4
Goodeaves Cl BA3 117 A7

Goodeaves Cotts BA3 . . . 117 A7
Goodeve Pk BS9 . . . . 5 D3
Goodeve Rd BS9 . . . . 5 D3
Good Hill BA4 . . . . 142 E2
Goodlands La TA1 . . . . . . 212 F4
Good's La TA5 . . . . 152 C5
Goodwin Dr BS14 . . . . 22 F4
Goodymoor Ave BA5 . . . . 203 B5
Goodymoor La BA5 . . . . . 203 B5
Goold Cl BA2 . . . . 43 A8
Goosander Cl TA24 . . . . . . 201 C4
Goosard La BS39 . . . . 77 E8
Gooseacre Ct BA22 . . . . . . 197 B8
Gooseacre La
East Coker BA22 . . . . 197 B8
Yeovil BA22 . . . . 218 A1
Gooseham La BS28 . . . . . . 108 F4
Gooseham Mead BS49 . . . 34 D4
Goose La
Chilton Polden TA7 . . . . 137 B3
Horton TA19 . . . . 183 C2
Gooselade BA16 . . . . 207 C3
Gooseland Cl BS14 . . . . 22 F3
GOOSENFORD 169 A6
Goose St BA11 . . . . 101 E5
Goosey La BS22 . . . . 32 C2
Gordano Bsns Pk BS20 . . . . . 2 E5
Gordano Gdns BS20 . . . . 4 B4
Gordano Rd BS20 . . . . 3 D7
Gordano Sch BS20 . . . . 2 D3
Gordano View BS20 . . . . 2 C5
Gordano Way BS20 . . . . 3 F5
Gordon Bldgs BA3 . . . . 79 A3
Gordon Rd
Bath BA2 . . . . 45 B5
Bristol BS8 . . . . 226 B3
Peasedown St John BA2 . . . 79 D8
Taunton TA1 . . . . 213 A3
Weston-Super-Mare BS23 . . 48 F7
Yeovil BA21 . . . . 219 C6
Gordon's Cl TA1 . . . . 213 B1
Gordon Terr TA6 . . . . 209 A5
GORE 187 F6
Gorefield TA13 . . . . 220 D2
Gorehedge 14 BA11 . . . . . 119 F4
Gore La
Chapmanslade BA13 . . . . . 121 B4
Pitney TA10 . . . . 172 C7
Gore Rd TA8 . . . . 85 A1
Gores Pk BS39 . . . . 59 B2
Gore Sq TA4 . . . . 167 E8
Gorlangton Cl BS14 . . . . . . 23 A7
Gorlegg TA21 . . . . 179 E5
Gorpit La TA5 . . . . 134 F8
Gorse La
Bristol BS8 . . . . 226 B2
Cold Ashton BS30, SN14 . . . 12 D7
Gort Rd TA2 . . . . 168 B6
Gosford Mans 6 BS23 . . . 30 C1
Goslet Rd BS14 . . . . 23 E5
Goss Barton BS48 . . . . 8 D1
Goss Cl BS48 . . . . 8 C1
Goss Dr BA16 . . . . 207 B3
Goss La BS48 . . . . 8 C1
Goss View BS48 . . . . 8 C1
Goswell Cl BA16 . . . . 207 C5
Goswell Rd BA16 . . . . 207 C5
GOTHELNEY GREEN 153 B8
GOTTON 169 B7
Gough Cl 11 TA16 . . . . 195 F7
Gough Pl BS27 . . . . 90 A8
Gough's Caves★ BS27 . . . . 90 D8
Gould Cl BA9 . . . . 207 E6
Gouldsbrook Terr TA18 . . 224 B6
Gouldsbrook View TA18 . 224 C7
GOULD'S GROUND 119 E5
Gould's Ground 2 BA11 . 119 E5
Gould's La 1 BA11 . . . . . 119 E5
Goulston Rd BS13 . . . . 22 A5
Goulston Wlk BS13 . . . . 22 A5
Gournay Ct BS39 . . . . 77 A3
Governors Ho BA2 . . . . 44 D6
Govier's La TA23 . . . . 202 C7
Grace Cl BS49 . . . . 34 B8
Grace Dr BA3 . . . . 78 A2
Grace Martin's La BA22 . 174 F3
Grace Rd BS22 . . . . 32 B4
Gradwell Cl BS22 . . . . 32 B3
Grafton Cl TA2 . . . . 213 A8
Graham Rd BS23 . . . . 48 E7
Graham Way TA4 . . . . 167 E6
Grainger Ct BS11 . . . . 4 E7
Grain Store The 9 BS1 . . 227 A2
Graitney Cl BS49 . . . . 35 A8
Granary Orch DT9 . . . . 187 F5
Granary The 8 BS1 . . . . . 227 A2
Granary Way TA3 . . . . 181 D8
Granby Hill BS8 . . . . 11 F6
Granby Rd BA22 . . . . 174 A2
Grand Par BA2 . . . . 228 C2
Grand Pier★ BS23 . . . . 48 D7
Grand Western Canal (Country Pk)★ EX16 . . . 178 F2
Granfield Gdns BS40 . . . . . 53 A5
Grange Ave
Highbridge TA9 . . . . 104 E3
Street BA16 . . . . 207 B6
Grange Bsns Pk The BS24 33 A5
Grange Cl
Cannington TA5 . . . . 135 C2
Wellington TA21 . . . . 222 E5
Weston-Super-Mare BS23 . . 48 E1
Grange Cnr DT8 . . . . 199 E7
Grange Dr
Bridgwater TA6 . . . . 208 D4
Grange Dr *continued*
Taunton TA2 . . . . 213 A6
Grange End BA3 . . . . 97 B7
Grange Farm Rd BS49 . . . . 17 A1
Grangefields BA16 . . . . . . 207 D5
Grange Gdns TA2 . . . . 213 A7
Grange Paddock TA9 . . . . 106 E4
Grange Rd
Bristol, Bishopsworth BS13 . . . . 22 A5
Bristol BS8 . . . . 226 A3
Frome BA11 . . . . 120 A7
Huntspill TA9 . . . . 136 A8
Saltford BS31 . . . . 25 C3
Street BA16 . . . . 207 D7
Weston-Super-Mare BS23 . . 48 E1
Grange The
Bath BA1 . . . . 27 C1
Bristol BS9 . . . . 5 D7
Chilton Polden TA7 . . . . . . 137 B2
Flax Bourton BS48 . . . . 19 F7
Kingston St Mary TA2 . . . . 168 E8
Langport TA10 . . . . 171 E5
Grange Way TA6 . . . . 135 F5
Grange Wlk TA2 . . . . 213 A6
Grants Cl BA9 . . . . 216 B4
Grant's Hill EX16, TA22 . . . 163 F2
Grants La BA9 . . . . 216 D4
Grant's La
Wedmore BS28 . . . . 108 D4
Wiveliscombe TA4 . . . . 210 D6
Granville Chapel 5 BS8 . . 11 F5
Granville Rd BA1 . . . . 27 E4
Granville Way DT9 . . . . . . 225 E6
Grasmere TA6 . . . . 208 C5
Grasmere Dr BS23 . . . . 48 F4
Grass Meers Dr BS14 . . . . . 23 A4
Grassmere Rd BS49 . . . . . . 34 B8
Grass Rd TA8 . . . . 65 F4
Grass Royal BA21 . . . . 219 C6
Grass Royal Jun Sch BA21 . . . . 219 C6
Gratton La EX35 . . . . 122 A4
Gravelands La TA3 . . . . . . 169 D3
Gravel Hill BS40 . . . . 56 B7
Gravel La TA3, TA19 . . . . . . 183 F6
Gravel Pit Cross EX36 . . . 145 E6
Gravel Pits DT9 . . . . 225 D3
Gravel Wlk BA1 . . . . 228 B3
Gravenchon Way BA16 . . 207 A6
Graves Cl 7 TA6 . . . . 209 B4
Gray Hollow BS40 . . . . 74 F4
Grayling Ho BS9 . . . . 5 F7
Gray's Almshouses 17 TA1 . . . . 213 A4
Grays Ave TA7 . . . . 154 E6
Grays Hill BA2 . . . . 80 B5
Gray's Hill EX15 . . . . 180 D1
Gray's La EX15 . . . . 180 D1
Grays Rd TA1 . . . . 213 B4
Grays Terr TA1 . . . . 213 B4
Great Ann St BS2 . . . . 227 C3
Great Barton BA4 . . . . 205 D6
Great Bedford St BA1 . . . 228 B4
Great Bow Yd TA10 . . . . . 171 F5
Great Brockeridge BS9 . . . . . 5 F6
Great Cl EX15 . . . . 179 E1
Great Cnr 5 BA21 . . . . . . 218 C6
GREAT ELM 118 F7
Great Field La TA14 . . . . . 185 F4
Great Gardens BA4 . . . . . . 205 C6
Great George St
Bristol, Brandon Hill BS1 . . 226 C2
Bristol, St Pauls BS2 . . . . . 227 C3
Great Hayles Rd BS14 . . . . 23 A6
Great Hill BA9 . . . . 161 D2
Great House Ct BA6 . . . . . 138 D4
Great House St TA24 . . . . 130 B5
Great La
Knole TA10 . . . . 173 A4
Shepton Beauchamp TA19 . 184 E4
Great Mdw TA22 . . . . 163 D6
Great Mead
Taunton TA1 . . . . 212 B3
Yeovil BA21 . . . . 219 F7
Great Orch BA22 . . . . 173 E2
Great Ostry BA4 . . . . 205 B6
Great Pit La BA22, DT9 . . . 188 B7
Great Pulteney St BA2 . . . 228 C3
Great Ringaton La EX36 . 162 B6
Great St TA14 . . . . 185 E2
Great Stanhope St BA1 . . 228 A2
Greatstone La BS40 . . . . . . 37 F5
Great Western La TA11 . . 211 D3
Great Western Rd
Chard TA20 . . . . 223 D5
Clevedon BS21 . . . . 6 D2
Martock TA12 . . . . 185 E7
Great Western Terr BA21 . . . . 219 D5
Great Western Way TA2 . 212 A6
Great Withy Dro BA5 . . . . 206 C8
Greatwood Cl TA6 . . . . . . 209 A2
Great Wood Cl BS13 . . . . . 22 C4
Grebe Cl TA6 . . . . 209 B4
Grebe Ct TA6 . . . . 209 B4
Grebe Rd
Bridgwater TA6 . . . . 209 B4
Taunton TA2 . . . . 213 B6
Greenacre
Wembdon TA6 . . . . 208 D6
Weston-Super-Mare BS22 . . 31 B2
Green Acre Rd BS14 . . . . . . 23 A3
Greenacres
Bath BA1 . . . . 27 B3
Bristol BS9 . . . . 5 E7
Midsomer Norton BA3 . . . . . 77 E1
Greenacres Pk BA21 . . . . 187 A5
Greenaleigh Lower Rd TA24 . . . . 125 C4
Greenaleigh Upper Rd TA24 . . . . 125 C4
Greenbank Gdns BA1 . . . . 27 B1
Greenbrook Terr TA1 . . . 212 E4
Green Cl
Holford TA5 . . . . 133 D4
Paulton BS39 . . . . 77 E6
Sparkford BA22 . . . . 175 A4
Green Cotts BA2 . . . . 45 C2
Greendale TA19 . . . . 221 B3
Greenditch Ave BS13 . . . . . 22 C5
Greenditch Cl BA3 . . . . 96 C3
Green Ditch La BA3 . . . . . . 96 B6
GREEN DOWN 94 B8
Greendown Pl BA2 . . . . 45 A1
Green Dragon Ct 4 TA6 . 208 F4
Green Dro TA11 . . . . 158 A4
Green Farm Ind Est BA13 . . . . 121 C4
Greenfield Cres BS48 . . . . . . 8 E3
Greenfield La TA7 . . . . . . 136 D2
Greenfield Pk BS20 . . . . 2 C3
Greenfield Pl BS23 . . . . . . 48 C8
Greenfield Prim Sch BS4 . 22 C7
Greenfields
Bridgwater TA6 . . . . 208 F3
Crewkerne TA18 . . . . 224 C7
Greenfields Ave BS29 . . . . 51 A3
Greenfield Terr TA20 . . . . 198 D8
Greenfield Wlk BA3 . . . . . . 78 A3
Greenfylde CE First Sch TA19 . . . . 221 C3
Greengage Cl 6 BS22 . . . . 49 E8
GREEN GATE 178 B2
Green Gate EX16 . . . . 178 B2
GREENHAM
Drimpton 199 E7
Wellington 179 B7
Greenham Bsns Pk TA21 179 C5
Greenham La TA18 . . . . . . 199 E7
Greenham's Cross TA14 . 185 F2
Greenham Yd TA18 . . . . . 199 E7
Greenhayes BS27 . . . . 90 B8
Greenhays Foot EX13 . . . 198 B6
GREENHILL 78 A3
Greenhill DT9 . . . . 225 D4
Greenhill Cl
Nailsea BS48 . . . . 8 D2
Weston-Super-Mare BS22 . . 32 A3
Greenhill Croft BS25 . . . . . 52 B4
Greenhill Cross EX36 . . . . 162 B2
Greenhill La
Alston Sutton BS26 . . . . . . 88 E5
Sandford BS25 . . . . 52 B4
Greenhill Pl BA3 . . . . 78 A3
Greenhill Rd
Midsomer Norton BA3 . . . . 78 A3
Sandford BS25 . . . . 52 B4
Yeovil BA21 . . . . 219 D7
Green Knap La TA20 . . . . 193 C2
Green La
Bristol BS11 . . . . 4 B8
Brompton Regis TA22 . . . . 148 B1
Butcombe BS40 . . . . 55 A7
Castle Cary BA7 . . . . 214 F4
Chard Junction TA20 . . . . 198 D7
Chardstock EX13 . . . . 198 B7
Chard TA20 . . . . 193 F1
Charlton Horethorne DT9 . 176 A2
Charlton Horethorne, Sigwells DT9 . . . . 175 F2
Corfe TA3 . . . . 181 E7
Corsley Heath BA12 . . . . . 144 E7
Cricket St Thomas TA20 . . . 194 F3
East Chinnock BA22 . . . . . 196 E8
East Coker BA22 . . . . 197 B8
Failand BS8 . . . . 10 C4
Farrington Gurney BS39 . . . 76 F6
Felton BS40 . . . . 37 C3
Fivehead TA3 . . . . 170 E2
Freshford BA3 . . . . 64 B2
Frome BA11 . . . . 119 D4
Hinton Charterhouse BA2 . . 63 E1
Ilminster TA19 . . . . 183 E2
Kington Magna SP8 . . . . . 177 E2
Leigh u M BA3, BA11 . . . . 117 B2
Marshfield SN14 . . . . 13 E8
Oakhill BA3 . . . . 114 E4
Pitcombe BA7 . . . . 215 A1
Priddy BS40 . . . . 73 B7
Queen Camel BA22 . . . . . . 174 F3
Sampford Arundel TA21 . . . 179 F4
Shepton Beauchamp TA19 . 184 E3
Sherborne DT9 . . . . 188 E1
Southwick BA14 . . . . 83 D2
Stoke St Michael BA3 . . . . 116 B5
Stratton-on-t F BA3 . . . . . . 96 E1
Street BA16 . . . . 207 C4
Tatworth TA20 . . . . 193 D1
Winsley BA15 . . . . 64 F6
Greenland La TA24 . . . . . . 131 B1
Greenland Rd BS22 . . . . . . 31 D1
Greenlands TA1 . . . . 213 B2
Greenlands Rd BA2 . . . . . . 79 C8
Green Lane Ave BA16 . . . 207 C4
Green Lane End TA19 . . . 184 E3
Green Lane Gate BA9 . . . 176 A8
Green Mead BA21 . . . . . . 218 C5
Greenmoor La BA21 . . . . . 187 A5
GREEN ORE 94 C1
Green Ore Est BA5 . . . . 94 B1
Green Park La BA11 . . . . 101 F6
Green Park Mews BA1 . . 228 A2
Green Park Rd BA1 . . . . . 228 B2
Green Parlor Rd BA3 . . . . 79 D1
GREEN PARLOUR 79 D2
Green Pastures Rd BS48 . . . 9 B2
Green Pits La BA11 . . . . . . 143 B7
Green Pk
Bath BA1 . . . . 228 B2
Rode BA11 . . . . 101 E8
Green Quarry BA21 . . . . . . 219 A6
Green Ride BA12 . . . . 161 F7
Greenridge BS39 . . . . 58 F3
Greenridge Cl BS13 . . . . . . 21 E4
GREENSBROOK 58 F3
Green's Dro BA6 . . . . 206 C7
Green's Hill TA4 . . . . 151 C5
Greenslade Gdns BS48 . . . . 8 D3
Greens Pl BA5 . . . . 203 D3
Green St
Bath BA1 . . . . 228 C2
Hinton St George TA17 . . . 195 D7
Shoscombe BA2 . . . . 79 E5
Ston Easton BA3 . . . . 95 E8
Greenstalls Pk BA22 . . . . . 173 F2
Green The
Backwell BS48 . . . . 19 A5
8 Barwick BA22 . . . . 197 F8
Bath BA2 . . . . 44 D1
Bridgwater TA6 . . . . 208 E2
Brushford TA22 . . . . 163 E4
Coleford BA3 . . . . 116 F6
Easton BA5 . . . . 111 A4
Faulkland BA3 . . . . 80 D2
Hinton Charterhouse BA2 . . 63 F1
Ilchester BA22 . . . . 173 E2
Locking BS24 . . . . 50 A4
33 Martock TA12 . . . . 185 E6
Pill BS20 . . . . 4 D4
Pitminster TA3 . . . . 181 E6
1 Sherborne DT9 . . . . 225 D4
Williton TA4 . . . . 202 D3
Winscombe BS25 . . . . 70 A7
Green Tree Rd BA3 . . . . . . 78 B3
GREENVALE 60 B1
Greenvale Cl BA2 . . . . 60 B1
Greenvale Dr BA2 . . . . 60 B1
Greenvale Rd BS39 . . . . 77 D5
GREENWAY 167 D8
Greenway
Bishops Lydeard TA4 . . . . . 167 E8
Faulkland BA3 . . . . 80 C1
Ilminster TA19 . . . . 221 B1
Minehead TA24 . . . . 200 D6
Monkton Heathfield TA2 . . 169 B6
North Curry TA3 . . . . 170 B3
Watchet TA23 . . . . 202 B7
Greenway Ave TA2 . . . . . . 212 E6
Greenway Cl BA9 . . . . 216 D4
Greenway Cotts TA4 . . . . 167 E8
Greenway Cres TA2 . . . . . 212 E7
Greenway Ct BA2 . . . . 44 F4
Greenway La
Barrington TA13 . . . . 184 E5
Bath BA2 . . . . 45 A4
Blagdon Hill TA3 . . . . 181 B5
Cold Ashton SN14 . . . . 12 D5
Combe St Nicholas TA20 . . 193 E6
Stoke St Mary TA3 . . . . 169 D2
Wiveliscombe TA4 . . . . 210 A5
Greenway Pk 3 BS21 . . . . . . 6 F3
Greenway Rd
Castle Cary BA7 . . . . 214 B6
Rockwell Green TA21 . . . . . 222 A5
Taunton TA2 . . . . 212 E6
Greenways BA3 . . . . 96 C2
Greenway Terr TA2 . . . . . 168 D8
Greenwell La BS40 . . . . 53 C7
Greenwood Cl TA9 . . . . . . 136 B8
Greenwood Rd
Weston-Super-Mare BS22 . . 31 E2
Yeovil BA21 . . . . 218 D7
Gregory Mead BS49 . . . . . . 17 A1
Gregorys Gr BA2 . . . . 62 D8
Gregorys Tyning BS39 . . . . 77 F6
GREINTON 155 F7
Greinton BS24 . . . . 49 A2
Grenville Ave BS24 . . . . . . 50 A4
Grenville Cl BA6 . . . . 157 E4
Grenville Ho TA6 . . . . 208 F2
Grenville Pl 7 BS1 . . . . 11 F5
Grenville Rd TA8 . . . . 104 C7
Grenville View TA4 . . . . . . 167 E6
GREYFIELD 59 C2
Greyfield Comm BS39 . . . . 59 C2
Greyfield Rd BS39 . . . . 59 C2
Greyfield View BS39 . . . . . 58 F1
Greyhound Cl BA9 . . . . . . 216 C4
GREYLAKE 155 C4
GREYLAKE FOSSE 155 E6
Greylake Reserve★ TA7 . . 155 D5
Greylands Rd BS13 . . . . 21 F7
Grey's Cnr BA9 . . . . 161 A3
Greys Rd TA16 . . . . 195 F7
Greystoke Bsns Ctr BS20 . . 2 D4
GRIBB 199 B6
Gribb View TA20 . . . . 199 B6
Grib La BS40 . . . . 54 F2
Griffen Cl TA6 . . . . 208 E6
Griffen Rd BS24 . . . . 49 E7
Griffin Cl
Wells BA5 . . . . 203 B6
Weston-Super-Mare BS22 . . 32 B2
Griffin Ct BA1 . . . . 228 B2
Griffin La TA3 . . . . 182 F7
Griffin Rd
Clevedon BS21 . . . . 6 E3
Hatch Beauchamp TA3 . . . . 182 F7
Griggfield Wlk BS14 . . . . . . 23 A7
Grimsey La SP8 . . . . 177 F8
Grinfield Ave BS13 . . . . 22 C4
Grinfield Ct BS13 . . . . 22 C4
Groats 9 TA4 . . . . 167 F8
Grooms Orch TA21 . . . . . . 222 C5
GROSVENOR 28 C1
Grosvenor Bridge Rd BA1 28 C1
Grosvenor Ct BA22 . . . . . . 173 E2
Grosvenor Pk BA1 . . . . 28 C1
Grosvenor Pl BA1 . . . . 28 C1
Grosvenor Rd
Bristol BS2 . . . . 227 C4
Stalbridge DT10 . . . . 190 B4
Grosvenor Terr BA1 . . . . . . 28 C2
Grosvenor Villas 9 BA1 . . 28 B1
Grove Alley BA10 . . . . 215 E6
Grove Ave
Bristol BS1 . . . . 227 A1
Bristol, Coombe Dingle BS9 . . 5 C7
Yeovil BA20 . . . . 218 F5
Grove Cl
Penselwood BA9 . . . . 161 E2
Watchet TA23 . . . . 202 C6
Grove Ct BS9 . . . . 5 E5
Grove Dr
Taunton TA2 . . . . 212 F8
Weston-Super-Mare BS22 . . 31 C1
Grove Hill TA7 . . . . 155 B1
Grove Ho
Bath BA2 . . . . 45 B6
Burnham-on-S TA8 . . . . 104 A8
Grove Jun Sch BS48 . . . . . 18 D8
Grove La
Faulkland BA3 . . . . 80 D2
Frome BA11 . . . . 119 E3
Knole TA10 . . . . 173 A4
North Cheriton BA8 . . . . . . 176 E5
Stalbridge DT10 . . . . 190 B4
West Anstey EX36 . . . . 162 D6
Weston-Super-Mare BS23 . . 48 D8
Grove Lane Cl DT10 . . . . . 190 B4
Grove Leaze BS11 . . . . 4 D6
Grove Mead BA11 . . . . 119 E2
Grove Orch BS40 . . . . 54 E2
Grove Park Ct BS23 . . . . . . 30 D1
Grove Park Rd BS23 . . . . . . 30 D1
Grove Pl TA24 . . . . 201 B4
Grove Rd
Banwell BS29 . . . . 50 E4
Blue Anchor TA24 . . . . 131 B6
Bristol, Coombe Dingle BS9 . . 5 D8
Burnham-on-S TA8 . . . . 104 A8
Huntspill TA9 . . . . 136 A8
Weston-Super-Mare BS23 . . 48 D8
Weston-Super-Mare, Milton BS22 . . . . 31 C1
Groves La TA24 . . . . 131 B6
Grove St BA2 . . . . 228 C3
Groves The BS13 . . . . 22 D4
Grove Terr 8 TA2 . . . . . . 212 F6
Grove The
Bath BA1 . . . . 27 C1
Bristol BS1 . . . . 227 A1
Burnham-on-S TA8 . . . . 85 B1
Frome BA11 . . . . 119 E2
Hallatrow BS39 . . . . 77 B7
Ruishton TA3 . . . . 169 C3
Sherborne DT9 . . . . 225 D3
Winscombe BS25 . . . . 51 F1
Wraxall BS48 . . . . 9 C3
Grove Wood Rd BA3 . . . . . 78 F1
Grughay La TA3 . . . . 182 E5
Grunter's La BA3 . . . . 114 F7
Gryphon Sch The DT9 . . . 225 E6
Guard Ave BA22 . . . . 218 B6
Guard House La 9 BA5 . 203 D4
Gug The BS39 . . . . 59 C2
Guild Ct BS1 . . . . 227 B2
Guildford Pl TA1 . . . . 212 F3
Guildhall La BS28 . . . . 108 C4
Guineagore La DT9 . . . . . . 188 B4
Guinea La BA1 . . . . 228 C3
Guinea St BS1 . . . . 227 A1
Guinevere Cl BA21 . . . . . . 218 D7
Gullen BA2 . . . . 80 A6
Gulliford Cl TA9 . . . . 104 D4
Gulliford's Bank BS21 . . . . . . 6 F2
Gullimores Gdns BS13 . . . . 22 B4
Gullock Tyning BA3 . . . . . . 78 B1
Gullons Cl BS13 . . . . 22 A6
Gullon Wlk BS13 . . . . 21 F5
Gulway Mead TA20 . . . . . . 198 D8
Gumbrells Ct TA6 . . . . 209 A4
Gunners La BA22 . . . . 218 A5
Gunning's La BA4 . . . . 142 F2
Gunville La
Charlton Horethorne DT9 . . . . 176 A2
East Coker BA22 . . . . 197 D8
Gunwyn Cl BA6 . . . . 206 E6
GUPWORTHY 148 C6
GURNEY SLADE 114 F7
Gurney St TA5 . . . . 135 C2
Gurnville Cotts BA11 . . . . 119 F2
Guthrie Rd BS8 . . . . 226 A4
Gwynne La TA1 . . . . 213 A3
Gyffarde Ct 4 TA1 . . . . . . 213 A4
Gyffarde St TA1 . . . . 213 A4
Gypsy La
Cheddar BS28 . . . . 89 D6
Keynsham BS31 . . . . 42 B8
Marshfield SN14 . . . . 13 F7

H

Haberfield Hill BS8 . . . . 4 E2
Haberfield Ho 1 BS8 . . . . 11 F6
Hacketty Way TA24 . . . . . 124 B3
Hack La
Holford TA5 . . . . 133 F2
Nether Stowey TA5 . . . . . . 134 A2

Hack Mead La TA9 105 E1
HACKNESS 136 D8
Hackness Rd TA9 136 E8
Haddon Cl TA22 148 B2
Haddon La
Hartford TA4 164 C7
North Petherton TA6 153 C2
Stalbridge DT10 190 C5
Haddon View TA22 148 B2
Hadley Rd BA2 45 B2
Hadrian Cl BS9 5 C4
HADSPEN 214 F6
Hadspen Garden★ BA7 160 A2
Hadworthy La TA6 153 F4
Hagget Cl TA6 208 F1
Hagleys Gn TA4 151 B7
Haig Cl BS9 5 B7
Haig Rd TA2 168 B6
HAINES HILL 212 E2
Haines Hill TA1 212 E2
Haines La DT8 199 D5
Haines Pk TA1 212 E1
Hains La DT10 190 F7
Halcombe TA20 223 C2
HALCON 213 D5
Halcon Cnr TA1 213 D4
Halcon Com Prim Sch
TA1 213 D4
HALE 177 D6
Hale La BA9 177 C6
Halesleigh Rd TA6 208 E5
Hales Mdw BA21 187 D6
Hale Way TA2 213 D7
Half Acre TA4 202 D2
Half Acre Cl
Bristol BS14 23 A3
Williton TA4 202 D2
Halfacre La BS14 23 B4
Half Acres DT9 225 C3
Half Moon St 6 DT9 225 D3
Halfpenny Row BA11 82 E1
Halfway BA22 186 F6
Half Yd BS40 53 D8
Hallam Ct BS21 6 C4
Hallam Rd BS21 6 C4
Hallards Cl BS11 4 F8
HALLATROW 77 B7
Hallatrow Rd BS39 77 C6
Hallen Dr BS9 5 C7
Hallet Gdns BA20 219 A4
Hallets Orch BA22 186 B6
Hallett Rd BA7 214 B7
Halletts Way
Axminster EX13 198 A1
Portishead BS20 2 D5
Hall Hill EX35 122 B5
Halliwell Rd BS20 1 D4
Hall La BA1 12 B3
Hall Sch The BS25 70 B8
Hall Terr TA8 104 A8
HALSE 167 B6
Halse Cnr TA4 167 D5
Halse La TA24 147 B5
Halse Manor TA4 167 B6
HALSTOCK 197 C3
Halston Dr BS2 227 C4
HALSWAY 151 B8
Halsway TA6 209 C5
Halsway Hill TA4 132 F1
Halsway La
Bicknoller TA4 133 A1
Crowcombe TA4 151 A8
Halswell Cl TA6 208 E4
Halswell Gdns BS13 22 B4
Halswell Rd BS21 6 D1
Halt End BS14 23 C3
Halter Path Dro TA7 137 C7
Halves La BA22 197 C7
Halwyn Cl BS9 5 D5
Halyard Dr TA6 208 E7
Halyard Pl TA24 201 B7
HAM
Creech St Michael 169 E4
Holcombe 116 D6
Paulton 77 F5
Wellington 180 D8
Hamber Lea TA4 167 F8
Hambledon Rd BS22 32 C4
HAMBRIDGE 184 D8
Hambridge Com Prim Sch
TA10 184 D8
Ham Cl BS39 58 F1
Hamdon Cl 12 TA14 185 F4
Hamdon Hill Country Pk★
TA14 185 F3
Hamdon View TA14 185 E3
Hamdown Ct TA10 172 B6
Ham Gn
Hambridge TA10 184 D8
Pill BS20 4 D3
Ham Gr BS39 77 E5
HAM GREEN 4 E4
Ham Hill
Coleford BA3 116 D6
Combe St Nicholas TA20 193 D8
High Ham TA10 156 A2
Langford Budville TA21 166 A1
Radstock BA3 78 F3
Ham Hill Ctry Pk★ TA14 186 A3
Ham Hill Rd
Odcombe BA22 186 C2
Stoke sub Hamdon TA14 185 F4
Hamilton Ct
11 Bristol BS1 227 A4
Taunton TA1 213 C4
Wells BA5 203 B4
Hamilton Ho BA1 27 E3
Hamilton Rd
Bath BA1 27 E2
Taunton TA1 213 C4
8 Weston-Super-Mare
BS23 30 C1
Hamilton Terr BA2 79 F5
Ham La
Bishop Sutton BS39 57 C5
Burnham-on-S TA8 104 B6
Compton Dundon TA11 157 A3
Croscombe BA4, BA5 204 E7
Dundry BS41 21 D3
Farrington Gurney BS39 76 F5
Kingston Seymour BS21 16 B2
Marnhull DT10 190 F6
North End BS49 17 A3
Paulton BS39 77 E5
Pawlett TA6 135 E6
Rodhuish TA23 149 C8
Shepton Mallet BA4 205 A7
Sherborne DT9 188 A5
Trent DT9 187 F5
Wraxall BS48 9 B4
Yatton BS49 17 A3
Ham La E BA4 204 F7
Hamlands La TA21 167 D1
Hamlet The
Nailsea BS48 9 A3
Templecombe BA8 176 E1
Hamley La
Buckland St Mary TA20 193 B8
Combe St Nicholas TA20 182 F1
Ham Link BS40 53 F3
Hamlyn Cl TA1 212 C1
Hamlyn Rd BA6 206 E6
Ham Mdw DT10 190 E6
Hammer La BA2, BA3 100 C8
Hammer St BA10 161 B8
Hammet St
8 North Petherton TA6 153 E3
Taunton TA1 212 F4
Hammets Wharf 1 TA1 212 F4
Hammond Gdns BS9 5 E7
HAMP 208 F2
Hamp Ave TA6 208 F3
Hamp Brook Way TA6 208 E2
Hamp Com Jun Sch TA6 208 F3
Hampden Rd BS22 31 E2
Hamp Green Rise TA6 209 A3
Hamp Ind Est TA6 209 A3
Hamp Inf Sch TA6 208 F3
Hamp St TA6 208 F3
Hampton Cl
5 Barwick BA22 197 F8
Bridgwater TA6 209 D7
Hampton Cnr BS11 4 E6
Hampton H BA2 45 D8
Hampton Ho 10 BA1 28 C1
Hampton La BS8 226 B4
Hampton Rd BS6 226 C4
Hampton Row BA2 45 B8
Hampton View BA1 28 B1
Ham Rd
Brean BS24, TA8 66 B3
Burnham-on-S TA9 85 E4
Creech St Michael TA3 169 D4
Wellington TA21 180 D8
Hamrod La TA7 154 E5
Hams La BS26 68 C3
Ham's La TA11 174 D7
Hams Rd BS31 24 F7
Ham St BA6 158 B5
HAM STREET 158 B5
Ham Wall Wetland★
BA6 138 C2
Hamway La TA20 193 C8
HAMWOOD 68 C7
Hamwood TA1 212 B4
Ham Wood Cl BS24 49 B2
Hamwood Cotts TA1 212 B4
Hamwood La TA3 181 B8
Hamwood Terr TA1 212 B4
Hanbury Ct BS8 226 A4
Hanbury Rd BS8 226 A4
Handel Rd BS31 24 E5
Handlemaker Rd BA11 119 E2
Handy Cross TA4 151 A2
Hanford Ct BS14 23 D7
Hangerland La TA4 150 E6
Hanger's Way TA24 201 D2
Hang Hill BA2 80 A6
Hanging Hill La TA13 184 F4
Hanglands La BA8 176 C2
Hanham La BS39 77 F7
Hanham Way BS48 8 B2
Hankridge Way TA1 213 E5
Hanna Cl BA2 44 B6
Hannah More Cl
Cheddar BS27 90 B7
Wrington BS40 35 E2
Hannah More Inf Sch
BS48 18 D8
Hannah More Prim Sch
BS1 227 C2
Hannah More Rd BS48 18 C8
Hannahs La BA5 110 E6
Hannay Rd BS27 71 B1
Hann Cl BA5 203 B2
Hanning Cl TA19 221 F6
Hanning Pk TA19 183 C1
Hanning Rd TA19 183 C1
Hanny's La BS40 39 C3
Hanover Cl
Shepton Mallet BA4 205 A6
Weston-Super-Mare BS22 32 A4
Hanover Ct
Bath BA1 28 B2
Castle Cary BA7 214 C5
Hanover Ct *continued*
Dulverton TA22 163 D7
Radstock BA3 79 C2
Hanover Gdns BA11 119 D3
Hanover Ho BS20 2 B5
Hanover Pl
Bath BA1 45 B8
Bristol BS1 226 B1
Hanover St
2 Bath BA1 28 B1
2 Bristol BS1 227 A2
Hanover Terr 5 BA1 28 B1
Hansetown Rd TA4 148 F1
Hansford Cl BA2 44 E1
Hansford Mews BA2 44 F1
Hansford Sq BA2 44 E1
Hanson's Way 4 BS21 6 C2
Hans Price Cl 18 BS23 48 E8
Hans Price Ho 13 BS23 48 E8
Hantone Hill BA2 45 F8
Happerton La BS20 4 D2
Hapsburg Cl BS22 32 A4
HAPSFORD 119 B8
Hapsford Hill BA11 119 C8
Harbour BA21 218 C5
Harbour Cres BS20 2 E5
Harbour Ct TA5 135 B5
Harbourne Cl TA8 104 C8
Harbour Rd
Portishead BS20 2 D6
Sherborne DT9 225 E5
Watchet TA23 202 C7
Harbour Road Trad Est
BS20 2 F6
Harbour Terr DT9 225 E5
Harbour View TA5 135 B5
Harbour Wall BS9 5 B4
Harbour Way
Bristol BS1 226 C1
Sherborne DT9 225 E5
Harbour Wlk BS1 226 C1
Harbutts BA2 28 F1
Harcourt Cl BS31 25 E2
Harcourt Gdns BA1 27 B2
Harcourt Mews BA11 120 A4
Harcourt St TA2 212 E6
Harden Rd BS14 23 E5
Harding Ct TA11 211 D3
Harding Pl BS31 25 B5
Hardings Cl 8 TA6 153 F3
Hardings Ct TA13 220 C5
Harding's Hill TA10, TA11 172 F5
Harding's House La DT9 225 A6
Harding's La BA8 176 D4
HARDINGTON 99 E6
Hardington Dr BS31 25 A2
HARDINGTON
MANDEVILLE 197 A6
HARDINGTON MARSH 196 F4
HARDINGTON MOOR 197 A7
Hardington Moor National
Nature Reserve★ BA22 197 A7
Hardmead La BS27 90 E2
Hardwarden Terr BA22 175 A5
HARDWAY 161 A5
Hardwick Rd BS20 4 C5
Hardy Cres DT10 190 B4
Hardy Ct TA18 224 C5
Hardy Mead Dro TA9 136 B7
HARE 182 F2
Hareclive Prim Sch BS13 22 C4
Hareclive Rd BS13 22 C4
Hare La TA20 182 E2
Harepark Terr TA24 201 A5
Hare Path TA24 147 F8
Hare Path Cross TA24 129 D1
Harepits La BA6 157 E3
Hare Pk TA24 124 C4
Harestone Cross EX13 198 B7
Harewell Wlk BA5 203 B3
Harfield Terr 10 BA20 219 B4
Harford Cl BS9 5 C7
Harford Sq BS40 39 B3
Hargrove La DT10 190 C2
Harington Pl 2 BA1 228 B2
Harley Ct 3 BS8 11 F7
Harley La BS21 7 C6
Harley Mews 2 BS8 11 F7
Harley Pl 4 BS8 11 F7
Harley St BA1 228 B4
Harmony Dr BS20 1 F4
Harnell Cl TA1 213 C3
Harnhill Cl BS13 22 B4
Harp Chase TA1 213 B1
Harper Rd TA18 224 C5
Harper's La TA23 131 D1
Harpitts La SP8 177 F2
Harp Rd
Brent Knoll TA9 105 E6
South Petherton TA13 220 C3
Harptree BS24 49 A2
Harptree Cl BS48 18 D8
Harptree Hill BS40 74 B5
Harrier Path 3 BS22 49 E8
Harriets Yd BS31 24 F5
Harrington Ave BS14 23 E6
Harrington Cl BS30 25 E8
Harrington Gr BS14 23 E6
Harrington Rd BS14 23 E6
Harrington Wlk BS14 23 E6
Harris Cl
Frome BA11 120 B4
Westleigh EX16 179 A4
Harris Gr BS13 22 B3
Harris La
Abbots Leigh BS8 10 F8
Curry Mallet TA3 183 C8
Harrison's La TA19 184 E1
Harris Vale BA3 116 F7
Hart Cl BS20 4 E4
HARTCLIFFE 22 C4
Hartcliffe Engineering Com
Coll BS13 22 E4
Hartcliffe Rd BS4 22 E8
Hartcliffe Way BS3, BS4,
BS13 22 C7
Hartcliffe Wlk BS4 22 F8
Harters Cl BA5 139 E6
Harter's Hill La BA5 139 E6
Hartfield Ave BS6 226 C4
HARTFORD 164 C8
Hartgill Cl BS13 22 B3
Hartlake Cl BA6 206 F7
Hartland 14 BS22 32 A2
Hartley Cotts BA4 204 B1
Hartley Ho BA1 228 B3
Hartley Way TA1 213 D2
HARTMOOR 177 F3
Hartmoor Hill SP8 177 E3
Hartrow Cl TA1 212 E1
Harts Cl TA19 221 A4
Hartsfield TA20 223 D2
Hart's La
Hallatrow BS39 77 B7
Huish Champflower TA4 165 D7
Sherborne DT9 188 A3
Harts Paddock BA3 77 F3
HARTSWELL 210 B3
Hartswell TA4 210 C3
Harvesters Dr BA16 207 B4
Harvest La
Charlton Horethorne
DT9 176 A2
Weston-Super-Mare BS22 50 B8
Harvest Way BS22 32 A5
Harvey Cl BS22 32 A4
Harvey's Rd TA13 220 C4
Harvey Way TA19 183 B4
Harwood Cross TA24 130 A4
Harwood Gn BS22 31 E4
Harwood La
Timberscombe TA24 130 A4
Wootton Courtenay TA24 129 F4
Haselbury Gr BS31 25 E2
HASELBURY
PLUCKNETT 196 C6
Haselbury Plucknett CE Fst
Sch TA18 196 C5
Haseley Ct TA1 212 D2
Haslands BS48 18 D8
Hassage Hill BA2 80 E7
Hassock's La BA10 160 E8
HASTINGS 183 B3
Hastings Cross TA19 183 B3
HATCH BEAUCHAMP 183 A7
Hatch Beauchamp CE Prim
Sch TA3 183 A7
Hatch Court★ TA3 183 A8
Hatcher Cl TA8 104 D5
Hatchers Ct TA2 212 F7
Hatchet Hill BA3, BA11 98 E4
HATCH GREEN 183 A6
Hatch Green La TA3 182 F6
Hatch Mews Bsns Pk
TA3 183 A7
Hatfield Bldgs BA2 45 B5
Hatfield Rd
Bath BA2 44 F3
Weston-Super-Mare BS23 49 A8
Hathaway Ho 18 BS2 227 A4
Hathermead Gdns BA21 219 D7
Haunts TA18 196 C8
Havage Cl TA9 104 E5
Havage Dro BS24 51 D8
Haven Cl TA24 201 F3
Haven View BS20 2 E5
Haversham Cl BS22 31 D1
Haviland Gr BA1 27 B3
Haviland Ho 7 BS2 227 C3
Haviland Pk BA1 27 B2
Havory BA1 28 C1
Havyat Rd BS40 53 E8
Havyat Road Trad Est
BS40 35 E1
HAVYATT 157 F8
HAVYATT GREEN 53 F7
Hawarden Terr BA1 28 B1
Hawcombe View TA24 124 A3
Hawcombe Woods National
Nature Reserve★ TA24 123 E2
HAWKCHURCH 198 E3
Hawkchurch CE Prim Sch
EX13 198 E3
Hawkchurch Cross EX13 198 E2
Hawkchurch Rd EX13 198 E3
HAWKCOMBE 124 A3
Hawke Rd BS22 31 E4
Hawkers Cl 9 TA5 135 B2
Hawker's La BA5 112 E1
Hawkfield Bsns Pk BS14 22 D5
Hawkfield Cl BS14 22 D5
Hawkfield Rd BS13 22 D5
Hawkfield Way BS14 22 D5
Hawkins Cl
Burnham-on-S TA8 104 C7
Street BA16 207 E6
Hawkin's La TA4 165 E7
Hawkins St BS2 227 C3
Hawkins Way 2 BA21 218 C6
Hawkmoor Hill DT6, EX13 199 B2
HAWKRIDGE 146 D1
Hawkridge Cross TA22 146 D1
Hawkridge Rd TA6 208 B4
Hawksmoor Cl BS14 23 A6
Hawks Rise BA22 218 B5
Hawk's Worth Cl BA11 120 C7
Hawksworth Dr BS22 32 C4
Hawksworth Rd TA24 201 B6
Hawkwell Cross EX16 162 F4
Hawley Way TA8 104 C7
Hawthorn Cl
Bridgwater TA6 209 D4
High Ham TA10 156 A2
Portishead BS20 1 F5
Hawthorn Coombe BS22 31 E3
Hawthorn Cres
Shepton Mallet BA4 205 A6
Yatton BS49 17 A2
Hawthorne Cl TA18 224 D7
Hawthorne Rd TA21 222 F5
Hawthorn Gdns BS22 31 D2
Hawthorn Gr BA2 45 A1
Hawthorn Hill
Kingsbury Episcopi TA13 185 B6
Weston-Super-Mare BS22 31 E2
Hawthorn Hts BS22 31 D3
Hawthorn Pk BS22 31 E3
Hawthorn Rd
Frome BA11 120 A6
Minehead TA24 200 D7
Radstock BA3 79 B2
Street BA16 207 E6
Taunton TA1 213 C1
Yeovil BA21 219 D7
Hawthorns La BS31 24 E5
Hawthorns The
Clevedon BS21 6 C3
Stalbridge DT10 190 C4
Hawthorn Way BS48 9 A2
Haxen La TA17 195 A8
Hayboro Way BS39 77 E4
HAYBRIDGE 203 A5
Haybridge Villas BA5 203 A5
Haycombe BS14 22 F6
Haycombe Dr BA2 44 A4
Haycombe La BA2 44 A3
Hayden Cl BA2 228 A1
HAYDON
Milborne Port 189 B2
Radstock 97 F8
Taunton 213 E2
Wells 113 D5
Haydon Cl TA1 212 B4
Haydon Dro BA5 113 C6
Haydon Gate BA3 97 F8
Haydon Hill BA3 98 A8
Haydon Hollow DT9 189 B3
Haydon Ind Est BA3 97 F8
Haydon La TA1, TA3 213 E2
Haydon Rd TA1 213 A4
Hayesdown Fst Sch
BA11 120 B5
Hayes End TA13 220 D4
Hayes End Manor TA13 220 D4
Hayesfield Pk BA2 228 B1
Hayesfield School Tech Coll
BA2 228 A1
Hayesfield Sch Tech Coll
BA2 44 D6
Hayes La TA11 156 F2
HAYES PARK 78 A2
Hayes Park Rd BA3 77 F2
Hayes Pl BA2 228 B1
Hayes Rd
Compton Dundon TA11 156 F3
Midsomer Norton BA3 77 F1
Hayes The BS27 90 B8
Hayeswood Farm BA15 46 F5
Hayeswood Rd BA2 59 E3
Hayfield Rd TA24 201 B6
Haygarth Ct BA1 228 B4
Haygrove La TA6 208 C3
Haygrove Pk TA3 168 D1
Haygrove Rd TA6 208 C3
Haygrove Sch TA6 208 C4
Hay Hill
Bath BA1 228 B3
Croscombe BA5 204 B8
Hay La BS40 37 D6
Hayleigh Ho BS13 22 C4
Hayman Rd TA24 200 F7
Haymarket The BS1 227 A3
Haymarket Wlk 9 BS1 227 A4
Haymoor Dro BA5 139 D7
Haymoor La
Coxley BA5 139 E6
Long Sutton TA10 172 D4
Hayne Cross EX16 164 B4
Hayne La TA5 153 B7
Haynes Motor Mus★
BA22 175 A6
Hayne Wlk TA7 137 B2
Hay St BA3 96 A8
Haytor Pk BS9 5 D6
Hayward Ave BS24 50 C8
Hayward Cl BS21 6 C1
Hayward Dr BA6 158 A6
Haywood Cl BS24 49 A1
Haywood Gdns BS24 49 B1
Haywood Rd TA1 213 D2
Hazel Barrow BS40 74 A7
Hazelbury Rd
Bristol BS14 23 C7
Nailsea BS48 8 D1
Hazel Cl TA1 213 C1
Hazel Cote Rd BS14 23 B4
Hazel Ct BA11 120 A3
Hazeldene Rd BS23 49 A8
Hazel Gr
Bath BA2 44 D4
Midsomer Norton BA3 97 B8

Hazelgrove House (Sch) BA22 174 F5
Hazell Cl BS21 6 E1
Hazel Terr BA3 97 C8
Hazel View TA18 224 D7
Hazel Way BA2 62 D8
Hazelwell La TA19 221 A4
Hazelwood Ct BS9 5 D3
Hazelwood Dr TA6 209 E5
Hazelwood Rd BS9 5 D3
Hazleton Gdns BA2 45 F3
Head Croft BS48 20 B8
Head Dro
  Catcott TA7 137 D3
  Othery TA7 155 D3
Headley Ct BS13 22 B6
Headley La BS13 22 B7
HEADLEY PARK 22 B6
Headley Park Ave BS13 22 B7
Headley Park Prim Sch BS13 22 B6
Headley Park Rd BS13 22 A7
Headley Rd BS13 22 A6
Headley Wlk BS13 22 B7
Headon Cross TA24 129 F8
Head St BA22 186 B6
Headstock Cross TA20 198 E6
Headstock Rd TA20 198 E7
Headwell TA3 183 C8
Headwell Cl TA3 183 C8
Headwell Hill TA3 183 C8
Heal Cl TA8 104 D5
HEALE 142 C7
Heale La TA10 171 C4
Healeys TA24 124 A4
Heal's Field EX13 198 A2
Healys Mdw TA4 167 E6
Hearn La BA22 175 D8
Heart Meers BS14 23 B5
Heath Cl BA12 144 D8
Heathcombe Rd TA6 208 B4
Heathcote Rd BA22 174 A2
Heath Dr BA11 119 F6
Heather Cl
  Bridgwater TA6 209 B3
  Minehead TA24 201 C4
  Taunton TA1 169 A1
Heatherdene BS14 22 F7
Heather Dr BA2 62 D8
Heather Rd BA21 219 D7
Heatherton Park Ho TA4 180 E8
Heather Way BA22 218 A5
HEATHFIELD 167 E5
Heathfield TA4 151 E4
Heathfield Cl
  Bath BA1 27 A3
  Creech St Michael TA3 169 D6
  Keynsham BS31 24 C5
  5 North Petherton TA6 153 F4
  West Bagborough TA4 151 E4
Heathfield Com Sch TA2 213 F8
Heathfield Cres BS14 23 B4
Heathfield Dr TA2 213 F8
Heathfield Rd BS48 8 E3
Heathfield Way BS48 8 E2
Heathgate BS49 34 B8
Heathgates BS23 48 D4
HEATH HOUSE 107 F1
Heath Rd BS48 8 F3
Heath Ridge BS41 11 A2
Heathstock Hill TA4 210 D5
Heathway BA12 144 D8
Heathway La BA6 138 B4
HEAVEN'S DOOR 188 A8
Heavitree Way TA2 213 A6
Hebden Rd BA15 64 F3
Heber's La TA19 195 A5
Heckley La BA3 115 B5
Hector Rd TA7 137 D2
Hectors La TA3 170 D8
Hectors Stones TA7 136 E4
Heddon Oak TA4 151 A8
Hedge La BA4 141 B2
Hedgemead Ct BA1 228 C4
Hedges Cl 3 BS21 6 B1
Hedges The BS22 32 C3
Hedgestocks BA4 160 C8
HEDGING 170 A8
Hedging La TA7 170 A8
Heggard Cl BS13 22 A5
Heights The TA19 221 B4
HELE 168 A3
Hele La
  Langport TA10 172 C4
  South Petherton TA13 220 C4
Helena Rd BA20 218 D1
Helens Rd BS25 52 B4
HELLAND 170 C3
Helland Hill TA3 170 C3
Helland La TA3 170 D4
Helliar's La
  Curry Mallet TA3 183 D8
  Fivehead TA3 170 D1
Hellier's Cl TA20 223 B4
Hellier's La BS27 89 E6
Helliers Rd TA20 223 B4
Hellier Wlk BS13 22 C3
Helling's Cross TA4 166 A4
Helmstedt Way TA20 223 D6
Helston Rd BS48 9 A1
Helvier's La TA4 167 A7
Helwell Gn TA23 202 D6
Helyar Cl BA6 206 D5
Hembridge La BA4 158 E7
Hembury La BA5 139 C7
HEMINGTON 99 B7
Hemington Prim Sch BA3 99 B7
Hemming Way BS24 49 E3
Hemp Gdn TA24 200 F8
Hempitts Rd BA16 156 E7
Hemplow Cl BS14 23 D7
Hemstich Hill TA7 138 C1
HEMYOCK 180 B1
Henacre Rd BS11 4 F8
Henbury Hill BS9 5 F8
Henbury Ho BA2 45 E4
Henbury Rd BS9 5 F8
Hencliffe Rd BS14 23 D7
Henderson Cl TA1 212 C2
Henderson Dr TA20 223 D2
Henderson Ho 1 BS2 227 B4
Henderson Pl 5 BA5 203 D4
Hendford BA20 219 A4
Hendford Ct BA20 219 A3
Hendford Gr BA20 219 A4
Hendford Hill BA20 219 A3
Hendon Cl TA9 104 E5
Hendon Cross EX16 178 B8
HENGROVE 23 B6
Hengrove Ave BS14 23 B8
Hengrove Com Arts Coll BS14 23 B7
Hengrove La BS14 23 B8
Hengrove Way BS14 22 E6
Henhayes La TA18 224 C6
Hen La BS40 37 E3
HENLADE 169 D2
HENLEY 156 B3
Henley Cl EX13 198 B7
Henley Gr TA1 212 D4
Henley La
  Butleigh BA6 157 E4
  Wookey BA5 139 E8
  Yatton BS49 34 D7
Henley Lodge BS49 34 D7
Henley Pk BS49 34 C7
Henley Rd
  High Ham TA10 156 B3
  Kingsdon TA11 173 E5
  Taunton TA1 212 D3
Henley Rise BA4 205 D4
Henley View
  Crewkerne TA18 224 C4
  Wellow BA2 62 D1
Henley Way BA11 119 F5
Henmore La BS26 88 E6
Hennessy Cl BS14 22 F3
Henning Way DT9 217 D3
Henrietta Ct BA2 228 C4
Henrietta Gdns BA2 228 C3
Henrietta Mews BA2 228 C3
Henrietta Pl BA2 228 C3
Henrietta Rd BA2 228 C3
Henrietta St
  Bath BA2 228 C3
  Bristol BS2 227 A4
Henry Butt Ho 11 BS23 48 E8
Henry Rogers Ho 2 TA5 135 B2
Henry St BA1 228 C2
Hensley Gdns BA2 44 E4
Hensley Rd BA2 44 E3
Hensman's Hill BS8 226 A2
Henson Pk TA20 223 E5
Hensons Dr EX16 179 A3
HENSTRIDGE 190 A6
HENSTRIDGE ASH 189 F7
HENSTRIDGE BOWDEN 189 D7
HENSTRIDGE MARSH 190 C7
Henstridge Trad Est BA8 190 C7
HENTON 139 B8
Hepburn Rd BS2 227 B4
Herald Cl BS9 5 D5
Herbert Ho TA22 163 D6
Herbert Rd
  Bath BA2 44 D5
  Burnham-on-S TA8 104 A8
  Clevedon BS21 6 D4
Herbert St TA2 212 E6
Herblay Cl BA21 219 E6
Hereford Dr TA2 213 A8
Heritage Cl BA2 79 D8
Heritage Ct BA6 206 D4
Heritage Ctyd BA5 203 D4
Heritage The BA2 78 E8
Herluin Way BS22, BS23 49 B6
Hermes Cl BS31 25 D2
Hermes Pl BA22 173 E2
Hermitage Cl BS11 4 E7
Hermitage Hill TA10 172 D6
Hermitage Rd
  Bath BA1 27 E1
  Langport TA10 172 D6
Hermitage St TA18 224 C5
Herne Rise TA19 221 B2
Hern La BS48 20 E5
Heron Cl
  Minehead TA24 201 C4
  Weston-Super-Mare BS22 49 E8
Heron Ct BS21 6 C2
Heron Dr TA1 212 B4
Heron Gate TA1 213 E6
Heron Gate Office Pk TA1 213 E5
Heron Gdns BS20 2 E4
Heron Ho 2 TA6 209 C4
Heron Pk TA8 84 E8
HERONS GREEN 56 C3
Herons La TA4 167 A4
Heronsmead Wlk BA21 219 D8
Herons Moor Prim Sch BS24 50 A8
Heron Way TA19 221 C2
Herridge Cl BS13 22 B4
Herridge Rd BS13 22 B4
Herschel Museum of Astronomy* BA1 228 B2
Hersey Gdns BS13 21 E3
Hertford Rd BA21 219 E8
Hervey Cl BS28 108 C4
Hervey Rd
  Chard TA20 223 D3
  Wells BA5 112 E1
Hestercombe Cl TA6 208 B4
Hestercombe House Gdns* TA2 169 A7
Hestercombe Rd
  Bristol BS13 22 B6
  Taunton TA2 169 A7
Hetling Ct 7 BA1 228 B2
Hewett Cl TA3 168 D1
HEWISH
  Crewkerne 195 D3
  Weston-super-Mare 33 C5
Hewish Ct BS23 48 E8
Hewish La
  Crewkerne TA18 224 A5
  Hewish TA18 195 D3
Hext Ct TA11 211 D3
Hexton Rd BA6 206 E5
Heyron Wlk BS13 22 B4
Heywood Rd BS20 4 C4
Heywood Terr BS20 4 C4
Hibbs Cl SN14 13 F8
HICKS GATE 24 B8
Hicks's La BA22 214 D1
Hidcote Mews BS24 49 E7
Hide Mkt BS2 227 C3
Hidewood La EX15 180 F1
Higgin's Grave La TA13 220 B1
High Acre BS39 77 F4
Highaton Head Cross EX36 162 C4
High Bank
  Porlock TA24 124 A3
  Watchet TA23 202 C7
High Bannerdown BA1 29 B4
High Bolham EX16 163 C1
HIGHBRIDGE 104 E3
Highbridge TA4 202 F4
Highbridge & Burnham Sta TA9 104 E3
Highbridge Rd TA8 104 B5
Highbrooks Rd TA11 173 B5
Highburn Cl TA8 104 C4
HIGHBURY 117 A7
Highbury Cotts
  8 Bath BA1 28 A1
  Coleford BA3 116 F7
Highbury Ct 15 BS23 30 C1
Highbury Farm Bsns Pk BS39 77 A8
Highbury Par BS23 30 C1
Highbury Pl BA1 28 A1
Highbury Rd
  Hallatrow BS39 77 B7
  Weston-Super-Mare BS23 30 C1
Highbury St BA3 117 A7
Highbury Terr 10 BA1 28 A1
Highbury Villas
  9 Bath BA1 28 A1
  Bristol BS2 226 C4
Highcroft
  Weston-Super-Mare BS23 30 F1
  Woolavington TA7 136 E4
High Cross EX16 164 A1
Highdale Ave BS21 6 E3
Highdale Cl BS14 23 B4
Highdale Rd BS21 6 E3
High Down Jun & Inf Schs BS20 2 A4
Higher Actis BA6 206 E3
HIGHER ALHAM 142 C4
Higher Backway BA10 215 E6
Higher Barton
  Martock TA12 185 D4
  Trent DT9 187 F5
Higher Beacon TA19 221 B4
Higher Beadon TA16 195 E7
Higher Brooks BA16 207 C2
Higher Bullen BA22 197 F8
HIGHER BURROW 184 E7
Higher Burton BA22 197 C8
Higher Cheap St 3 DT9 225 D4
HIGHER CHILLINGTON 194 F5
Higher Coombses TA20 198 D8
Higher Cross EX15 179 C1
HIGHER DURSTON 169 E7
Higher Easthams La TA18 224 F7
Higher Farm La
  Podimore BA22 174 A4
  Sparkford BA22 175 B3
Higher Farm Trad Est BA20 218 C5
Higher Gunville DT9 217 D2
HIGHER HADSPEN 214 E4
HIGHER HALSTOCK LEIGH 197 A2
Higher Heathfield TA4 151 E4
Higher Kingsbury DT9 217 D3
Higher Kingsbury Cl DT9 217 C3
Higher Kingston BA21 219 B5
Higher Mead TA19 221 B3
Higher Millhayes EX15 180 B1
Higher North Town La BA22 175 D7
HIGHER NYLAND 177 C1
HIGHER ODCOMBE 186 C2
Higher Orch
  Martock TA12 185 D4
Higher Orch *continued*
  Minehead TA24 200 C8
Higher Palmerston Rd TA2 212 D6
Higher Park La TA24 129 E2
Higher Pk TA24 200 D6
Higher Rd
  Chedzoy TA7 154 D8
  Horsington BA8 176 D3
  Shepton Beauchamp TA19 184 E3
  Woolavington TA7 136 E4
Higher Ream BA21 218 C6
Higher Rodhuish Rd TA24 131 B3
HIGHER SANDFORD 188 C7
Higher St
  Curry Mallet TA3 183 C8
  Martock TA12 185 D4
  Merriott TA16 195 F8
  Norton Sub Hamdon TA14 185 E2
  West Chinnock TA18 196 B8
Higher Street TA5 133 B5
Higher Tolbury BA10 215 E6
HIGHER TOWN 200 E8
Higher Town EX16 178 C1
HIGHER VEXFORD 150 E6
Higher Westbury DT9 187 E1
Higher West Hatch La TA3 182 D7
Higher Westholme Rd
  North Wootton BA4 140 D4
  Pilton BA4 204 A1
Highfield
  Coleford BA3 116 E8
  Ilminster TA19 221 B4
  Taunton TA1 212 A2
  Taunton TA1 212 C3
  Wells BA5 140 C7
  West Chinnock TA18 196 B8
Highfield Cl
  Bath BA2 44 B5
  Somerton TA11 211 C4
  Taunton TA1 212 A2
Highfield Cres
  Chilcompton BA3 96 C4
  Taunton TA1 212 A2
Highfield Dr BS20 1 E3
Highfield La
  Compton Martin BS40 74 B6
  East Harptree BS40 75 A3
Highfield Rd
  Keynsham BS31 24 F2
  Peasedown St John BA2 79 C8
  Street BA16 207 B5
  Weston-Super-Mare BS24 49 A1
  Yeovil BA21 219 C6
Highfields
  Barrington TA19 184 C5
  Clandown BA3 78 E4
  Midsomer Norton BA3 78 D2
  Stanton Drew BS39 39 F1
Highfield Terr TA12 185 D5
Highfield Trad Est BA21 219 C6
Highfield View BA3 116 E8
Highfield Way TA11 211 C4
High Gn BA5 111 A4
High Gr BS9 5 B7
Highgrove TA1 212 E1
Highgrove Cl TA6 209 A2
Highgrove Wlk BS24 50 A8
HIGH HAM 156 A2
High Ham CE Prim Sch TA10 156 A1
High Kingsdown BS2 226 C4
High La
  Barton St David TA11 158 A2
  Shapwick TA7 155 F8
Highland Cl BS22 31 B2
Highland Ct BA21 219 C6
Highland Rd BA2 44 B5
Highlands TA1 212 E1
Highlands La BS24 50 A8
Highlands Rd
  Long Ashton BS41 11 A2
  Portishead BS20 2 B5
Highland Terr BA2 44 D6
High Lea BA21 219 B8
HIGH LITTLETON 59 C1
High Littleton CE Prim Sch BS39 59 C1
High Mdws BA3 77 F1
Highmead Gdns BS13 21 E4
High Mead Gdns BS39 57 D3
Highmore Rd DT9 225 C5
High Path TA21 222 C7
High Pk BS39 77 D6
High Rd BA22 175 D8
HIGHRIDGE
  Bristol 21 F7
  Dundry 21 D3
Highridge Cres BS13 21 F5
Highridge Gn BS13 21 E6
Highridge Inf Sch BS13 21 F6
Highridge Pk BS13 21 F6
Highridge Rd BS13, BS41 21 E4
Highridge Wlk BS13 21 E7
High St
  Aller TA10 171 E8
  Ashcott TA7 156 B8
  Axbridge BS26 70 B2
  Bampton EX16 164 B1
  Banwell BS29 51 A2
  Bathampton BA2 28 F1
  Bath BA1 228 C2
  Batheaston BA1 28 F3
  Bathford BA1 29 D2
  Bath, Twerton BA2 44 B6
  Bath, Weston BA1 27 B1
High St *continued*
  Bishops Lydeard TA4 167 E8
  Bitton BS30 25 E8
  Blackford BS28 107 E4
  Blagdon BS40 54 E3
  Bourton SP8 161 F2
  Bridgwater TA6 208 F5
  Bristol BS1 227 A2
  Bristol, Shirehampton BS11 4 E6
  Bruton BA10 215 E6
  Buckland Dinham BA11 100 A3
  Burnham-on-S TA8 104 A6
  Butleigh BA6 157 E4
  Cannington TA5 135 B2
  Carhampton TA24 131 A5
  Castle Cary BA7 214 C5
  Chapmanslade BA13 121 C4
  Chard TA20 223 B4
  Charlton Adam TA11 173 F7
  Chew Magna BS40 39 A3
  Chewton Mendip BA3 94 F7
  Claverham BS49 17 F1
  Coleford BA3 116 F6
  Congresbury BS49 34 D4
  Dulverton TA22 163 D6
  Dunster TA24 201 E2
  East Chinnock BA22 196 E8
  East Harptree BS40 74 F5
  Evercreech BA4 141 E1
  Faulkland BA3 80 D1
  Freshford BA3 64 B5
  Frome BA11 119 E5
  Glastonbury BA6 206 E4
  Hardington Mandeville BA22 197 A6
  Henstridge BA8 190 A6
  High Littleton BS39 59 D1
  Hinton Charterhouse BA2 63 E1
  Hinton St George TA17 195 D7
  Ilchester BA22 173 E1
  Ilminster TA19 221 B4
  Keinton Mandeville TA11 158 A1
  Keynsham BS31 24 E6
  Kingweston BA6 157 E1
  Lynford-on-F TA11 158 C2
  Maiden Bradley BA12 144 C2
  Marshfield SN14 13 F8
  Midsomer Norton BA3 78 B1
  Milborne Port DT9 217 D2
  Milton Clevedon BA4 160 A8
  Milverton TA4 166 F5
  Monksilver TA4 150 B8
  Nailsea BS48 8 F3
  North Cadbury BA22 175 D6
  North Petherton TA6 153 E4
  North Wootton BA4 140 C4
  Norton St Philip BA2 81 E4
  Nunney BA11 143 B8
  Oakhill BA3 115 A3
  Othery TA7 155 C2
  Paulton BS39 77 E5
  Paulton, Plummer's Hill BS39 77 E6
  Pensford BS39 40 E4
  Porlock TA24 124 A3
  Portbury BS20 3 E3
  Portishead BS20 2 D5
  Queen Camel BA22 174 F3
  Rimpton BA22 188 A8
  Rode BA11 101 E8
  Saltford BS31 25 F3
  Shepton Mallet BA4 205 B5
  Sparkford BA22 175 A5
  Spaxton TA5 152 E7
  Stalbridge DT10 190 B5
  Stogumber TA4 150 D8
  Stogursey TA5 134 C5
  Stoke sub Hamdon TA14 185 F4
  Ston Easton BA3 95 E8
  Stoney Stratton BA4 141 F2
  Stourton BA12 161 F5
  Stourton Caundle DT10 189 F2
  Street BA16 207 C6
  Taunton TA1 212 F3
  Templecombe BA8 176 E1
  Thorncombe TA20 199 B6
  Timsbury BA2 60 B2
  Wellington TA21 222 E6
  Wellow BA2 62 D1
  Wells BA5 203 D4
  West Coker BA22 197 A8
  Weston-Super-Mare BS23 48 D8
  Weston-Super-Mare, Worle BS22 31 E2
  Williton TA4 202 D2
  Wincanton BA9 216 C4
  Winford BS40 38 A7
  Winsham TA20 194 E1
  Wiveliscombe TA4 210 C4
  Wookey BA5 139 D8
  Wookey Hole BA5 203 A8
  Woolley BA1 27 F6
  Wrington BS40 35 D2
  Yatton BS49 34 C8
  Yenston BA8 189 F8
  Yeovil BA20 219 B4
High View BS20 2 A4
High View Dr TA7 156 B8
Highwall La BS14, BS31 23 F1
HIGHWAY 185 E7
Highwoods Cl TA14 185 F2
Higson Cl BA22 186 D3
Hilary Rd TA1 212 D3
Hildesheim Bridge BS23 48 F7
Hildesheim Cl BS23 48 F6
Hildeshiem Ct 9 BS23 48 E7
Hilhouse BS9 5 C6
Hill Ave BA2 44 F1

Hillborne Gdns BA21 218 C5
Hillbrook Ct DT9 225 D4
Hill Brow DT9 225 B2
Hill Cl BA9 216 D4
Hillclose La TA19 221 F2
HILL CORNER 120 E6
Hillcote Est BS24 67 B8
Hillcrest
Crowcombe TA4 151 B7
Peasedown St John BA2 79 C7
Pensford BS39 40 E3
Hillcrest Cl
Nailsea BS48 8 E1
Yeovil BA21 219 C7
Hillcrest Dr BA2 44 C4
Hillcrest Rd
Nailsea BS48 8 E1
Portishead BS20 1 E4
Templecombe BA8 176 E1
Hill Crest Rd BA21 219 C6
Hillcroft Cl BS22 31 A2
Hill Cross BA22 196 F6
Hill Ct BS39 77 E6
Hilldale Rd BS48 19 B5
Hill Dr BS8 10 C3
HILL END 196 F6
Hillend BS22 31 E3
HILLFARRANCE 167 E3
Hillfield BS27 90 B7
Hill Gay Cl BS20 1 F4
Hill Ground BA11 119 E5
Hillgrove Ave BA20 218 F2
Hillgrove Cl TA6 208 E5
Hillgrove Rd BA5 93 C1
Hillgrove St N BS2 227 A4
Hillgrove St BS2 227 B4
Hillgrove Terr BS23 48 D1
Hill Head BA6 206 D3
Hill Head Cl
Glastonbury BA6 206 D3
Taunton TA1 213 A3
Hillhead Cotts TA2 212 C8
Hillhead Cross TA24 128 D3
Hillhouse EX14 192 D3
Hill House Cl DT9 225 E5
Hillier's La
Churchill BS25 52 D4
Yarley BA5 139 C8
Hillingdon Ct BA21 218 C6
Hill La
Bicknoller, Culverhays TA4 133 A1
Bicknoller TA4 132 F2
Brent Knoll TA9 86 B3
Carhampton TA24 131 A4
Chipstable TA4 165 C6
Clevedon BS21 7 C4
Draycott BS27 90 C2
Portishead BS20 1 F1
Rodney Stoke BS27 91 B2
Rowberrow BS25 53 A1
Shepton Mallet BA4 205 B6
Waterrow TA4 165 E5
West Quantoxhead TA4 132 F4
Hill Lea Gdns BS27 90 B8
Hillmead
Churchill BS40 53 A5
Shepton Mallet BA4 205 B6
Hillmer Rise BS29 50 F3
Hill Moor BS21 6 E2
Hillpath BS29 51 B2
Hill Pk BS49 34 E5
Hill Rd
Allerford TA24 124 E4
Clevedon BS21 6 D4
Dundry BS41 21 D2
Minehead TA24 125 B4
Sandford BS25 52 A3
Weston-Super-Mare BS23 48 F8
Weston-Super-Mare, Worle BS22 31 E2
Hill Rd E BS22 31 E2
Hillsboro TA7 136 E4
Hillsborough BS8 226 A2
Hillsborough Gdns TA8 85 B1
Hillsborough Ho BS23 49 A4
Hills Cl BS31 25 A5
Hills Cotts TA4 167 A7
Hillsdon Rd BS9 5 F8
HILLSIDE
Axbridge 70 C2
Midsomer Norton 96 E8
Hillside
Bristol BS6 226 C4
Chard TA20 223 B4
Horrington BA5 113 A2
Portbury BS20 3 D3
Puriton TA7 136 C4
West Pennard BA6 140 B1
Hillside Ave
Frome BA11 119 F2
Midsomer Norton BA3 96 F8
Hillside Cl
Curry Rivel TA10 171 D4
Paulton BS39 77 F6
Hill Side Cl BA5 203 C5
Hillside Cres
Midsomer Norton BA3 96 E8
Puriton TA7 136 C4
Hillside Dr
Frome BA11 120 B4
Puriton TA7 136 C4
Hillside Fst Sch BS22 31 E2
Hillside Gdns
Bishop Sutton BS39 57 C3
Weston-Super-Mare BS22 31 B1
Hillside Gr TA1 212 C1
Hillside Ho BA11 119 F3
Hillside Rd
Backwell BS48 19 A4
Bath BA2 44 D4
Bleadon BS24 67 B8
Clevedon BS21 6 D3
Long Ashton BS41 11 B2
Midsomer Norton BA3 96 F8
Portishead BS20 1 D4
Hillside Terr BA21 219 C5
Hillside View
1 Barwick BA22 197 F8
Midsomer Norton BA3 78 A3
Peasedown St John BA2 79 C8
Yeovil BA22 219 D1
Hillside W BS24 49 F2
Hill's La 10 TA12 185 E6
Hills Orch 9 TA12 185 E6
Hill St
Bristol BS1 226 C2
Stogumber TA4 150 D8
Hill Terr TA1 212 A4
Hill The
Freshford BA3 64 C5
Langport TA10 172 A5
Hill Top BS20 2 A4
Hilltop La TA5 133 D6
Hilltops TA8 65 F6
Hillview
Midsomer Norton BA3 96 E7
Timsbury BA2 60 B1
Hill View
Brean TA8 65 E2
Bristol BS8 226 B2
Brompton Ralph TA4 150 C3
Farrington Gurney BS39 77 B3
Marksbury BA2 42 B1
Mudford BA21 187 D6
Priston BA2 61 A5
Queen Camel BA22 174 F4
Yeovil BA21 219 C5
Hillview Ave BS21 6 D2
Hillview Cl TA24 200 D7
Hill View Cl
Ilton TA19 183 F4
7 Stoke sub Hamdon TA14 185 F4
West Chinnock TA18 196 B8
Hill View Ct
Evercreech BA4 141 E1
Weston-Super-Mare BS22 49 D8
Hill View Cvn Pk BS40 20 B1
Hillview Gdns BS40 37 C8
Hill View Park Homes BS22 49 D8
Hillview Rd
Loxton BS26 68 C4
Minehead TA24 200 D7
Hill View Rd
Bath BA1 28 B2
Bristol BS13 22 A8
Carhampton TA24 131 A5
Weston-Super-Mare BS23 49 A7
Hillview Terr TA12 185 D5
Hill View Terr
Ilminster TA19 221 B4
Lyng TA3 170 C7
Hill View Trd Est TA4 151 E4
Hillway TA11 173 E7
Hillworth Ho 26 BA4 205 B6
Hillyfield Rd BS13 22 A6
Hillyfields
Taunton TA1 213 C2
Winscombe BS25 70 B8
Hillyfields Way BS25 70 A8
Hilly Head TA21 222 B5
Hilly Pk TA2 168 B5
Hinam Cross TA22 163 B7
Hinckley Cl BS22 32 C4
Hincombe Hill BA4 142 E2
Hindhayes Inf Sch BA16 207 D5
Hindhayes La BA16 207 D6
Hind Pitts BS25 70 F7
Hine Rd TA1 212 B1
Hinkley Point Nature Trail* TA5 134 C8
Hinkley Point Visitor Ctr* TA5 134 C8
HINTON 187 D7
Hinton BS24 49 A2
HINTON BLEWETT 75 F6
HINTON CHARTERHOUSE 63 E1
Hinton Cl
Bath BA2 43 F6
Hinton St George TA17 195 D7
Saltford BS31 25 E3
Hinton Cross BA22 187 D7
Hinton Dr TA1 212 E1
Hinton Hill BA2, BA3 63 A1
Hinton La 12 BS8 11 F6
Hinton Rd TA18 224 B8
HINTON ST GEORGE 195 D7
Hinton St George CE Sch TA17 195 C7
Hinton Villas BA2 63 E1
Hippisley Dr BS26 70 D2
Hippisley Ho BA5 113 A1
Hiscocks Dr BA2 44 E4
Hiscocks La BA8 176 E2
Hitchen TA16 195 F7
Hitchen Cl SN14 13 F8
Hitchen Hill BA4 140 F3
Hitchings La TA3 170 B7
Hitchin La BA4 205 A5
Hither Acre TA19 221 A4
Hither Bath Bridge BS4 23 C8
Hither Gn BS21 6 F2
Hither Green Ind Est BS21 6 F2
Hither Mead TA4 167 F8
Hittsford La EX36 162 A1
Hoare's La BA11 98 B3
Hobart Rd BS23 48 F3
Hobbiton Rd BS22 32 A4
Hobbs Ct 1 BS48 8 F2
Hobbs La BS48 20 E3
Hobb's La BS1 226 C2
Hobbs Mead 7 TA4 167 F8
HOBB'S WALL 59 E5
Hob La TA2 168 E8
Hobwell La BS41 11 C2
Hoccombe Ford TA4 150 F1
Hocken Cl TA20 223 D6
HOCKHOLLER 180 E8
HOCKHOLLER GREEN 180 E8
Hockley Ct BA1 27 D1
Hockley La BA22 175 E5
Hockpitt La TA5 134 A2
HOCKWORTHY 178 D6
Hodder's Cl BA11 119 E5
Hodges Barton TA11 211 C4
Hodshill BA2 62 F6
Hoecroft BA3 96 D2
Hoecroft Gdns BA3 96 D3
Hogarth Mews BS22 32 A3
Hogarth Wlk BS22 32 A3
HOGGINGTON 83 D4
Hoggington La BA14 83 E3
Hogues Wlk BS13 22 B4
Holbeach Way BS14 23 A2
HOLBEAR 223 D2
Holbear TA20 223 D2
Holbrook Cres BS13 22 D4
Holbrook Pk TA13 220 C5
Holburne Museum & Crafts Study Ctr* BA2 45 B7
HOLCOMBE 116 C8
Holcombe BS14 23 A5
Holcombe Cl BA2 28 F1
Holcombe Gn BA1 27 B2
Holcombe Gr BS31 24 D5
Holcombe Hill BA3 116 C7
Holcombe La
Bathampton BA2 28 F1
Doulting BA4 141 E4
HOLCOMBE ROGUS 178 F5
Holcombe Vale BA2 28 F1
Holden's Way TA10 171 C3
Holden's Way TA10 171 D3
Holders Wlk BS41 20 F8
Holdfast La TA14 185 D1
Holditch Court La TA20 198 E5
Holditch La EX13, TA20 198 E5
Holdscroft La DT6 199 B1
Holeground Villas BA5 203 A8
Holemore Cross EX14 191 F5
Holes La BA11 118 B6
Holes Sq TA24 130 B5
HOLFORD 133 D4
Holford Cl BS48 8 E1
Holford Ct BS14 23 B5
Holford La TA4 151 C5
Holford Rd
Bridgwater TA6 208 B4
Taunton TA2 212 E8
Hollam Cross TA22 163 E7
Hollam Dr TA22 163 D6
Hollam La TA22 163 D7
Holland Ct BA16 207 D7
Holland Rd
Bath BA1 28 B1
Clevedon BS21 6 B1
HOLLANDS 219 A7
Holland's La TA4 149 E1
Holland St BS23 49 A8
Holland's Wash Dro TA20 193 C5
Holleys Cl TA20 198 D8
Hollies Cl
Martock TA12 185 D5
Middlezoy TA7 155 B3
Shepton Mallet BA4 205 C6
Hollies La BA1 29 A6
Hollies The
Crewkerne TA18 224 C4
Midsomer Norton BA3 78 A1
Yeovil BA21 219 C7
Hollis Ave BS20 2 C3
Hollis Cl
Halstock BA22 197 D3
Long Ashton BS41 21 A8
Hollis Cres BS20 2 C3
Hollister's Dr BS13 22 D4
Hollis Way
Halstock BA22 197 D3
Southwick BA14 83 F3
Holloway
Bath BA2 228 B1
Lopen TA13 185 A1
Minehead TA24 200 F7
Holloway Rd TA7 155 B2
Holloway St TA24 200 F7
Holloway The TA21 179 E7
HOLLOW BROOK 57 C6
Hollowbrook La BS39, BS40 57 D6
Hollowell Hill
Norton Sub Hamdon TA14, TA18 185 E1
West Chinnock TA18 196 B8
Hollow La
Baltonsborough BA6 158 B8
Dinnington TA17 195 B7
Lopen TA13 185 A1
Montacute TA15 186 B3
Wembdon TA5, TA6 208 C7
Weston-Super-Mare BS22 31 F3
Hollow Marsh La BA3, BS39 76 B4
Hollowmead BS49 34 E8
Hollowmead Cl BS49 34 F8
Hollow Rd
Shepton Beauchamp TA19 184 D3
Shipham BS25 70 F8
Hollow The
Bath BA2 44 B4
Corsley Heath BA12 144 E8
Dunkerton BA2 61 D4
Westbury-sub-Mendip BA5 110 D7
Hollway Cl BS14 23 E5
Hollway Rd BS14 23 E5
HOLLY BROOK 110 F5
Hollybush Cl BA15 64 E7
Hollybush La
Bristol BS9 5 E5
Bristol BS9 5 F4
Leigh u M BA3 117 A2
Holly Cl
Bridgwater TA6 209 E5
Nailsea BS48 9 A3
7 North Petherton TA6 153 F3
Taunton TA1 213 C1
Weston-Super-Mare BS22 32 A1
Holly Ct
Bristol BS2 226 C4
Frome BA11 120 B7
Holly Dr BA2 62 D8
Holly Gr TA18 224 D7
Holly Hill BA4 142 C1
Holly La
Clevedon BS21 6 F6
Drimpton DT8 199 F8
Shepton Mallet BA4 205 C4
Hollyman Wlk 5 BS21 6 F3
Hollymead La BS9 5 E4
Hollyridge BS14 23 C6
Holly Ridge BS20 2 A5
Holly Terr
Chard TA20 223 C4
Odcombe BA22 186 C2
Holly Tree Wlk BA20 218 E3
Holly Wlk
Keynsham BS31 24 D4
Radstock BA3 78 E1
Holman Cl BA6 206 E6
HOLMAN CLAVEL 181 E3
Holman's BA6 157 E4
Holmbury Cl BA11 120 D6
Holmbush TA24 128 E8
Holm Cl TA8 104 B5
Holmlea
Portishead BS20 2 F5
1 Wookey BA5 139 D8
Holmoak Rd BS31 24 C4
Holm Oaks BA6 157 E4
Holm Rd BS24 49 E2
Holms Rd BS23 49 A5
Holsom Cl BS14 23 F6
Holsom Rd BS14 23 F6
Holst Gdns BS4 22 D7
Holt Ball Steep TA24 129 D7
Holten's La BA22 196 E6
Holt Hill DT9 189 C1
Holt La
Halstock BA22 197 F3
South Perrott DT8 196 D1
Stourton Caundle DT9, DT10 189 E1
West Pennard BA6 140 D2
HOLTON 176 C5
Holton Cross BA9 176 C6
Holton St BA9 176 C5
Holt Rd
North Brewham BA11 161 E8
Witham Friary BA11 143 D1
Holtsdown La BA1 28 F7
Holvert La TA20 194 F1
HOLWAY
Sherborne 188 D7
Taunton 213 C2
Thorncombe 199 C6
Holway
North Petherton TA6 153 F4
Tatworth TA20 198 D8
Holway Ave TA1 213 B3
Holway Deane TA1 213 D2
Holway Gn TA1 213 C2
Holway Hill TA1 213 B2
Holway House Pk TA19 183 E2
Holway Park Com Prim Sch TA1 213 C3
Holway Rd TA1 213 B3
HOLWELL 143 B8
Holwell Cl BS39 77 E4
Holwell Hill BA11 143 B7
Holwell La BS27 89 F8
Holworthy La TA22 148 E2
Holy Moor Cross EX36 162 C1
Holy Moor La EX36 162 C1
Holyoake St TA21 222 C7
Holyrood Com Sch (Lower) TA20 223 C4
Holyrood Com Sch (Upper) TA20 223 C5
Holyrood St TA20 223 C3
Holy Tree Cross TA14 185 E3
Holy Trinity CE Prim Sch
Taunton TA1 213 A3
Yeovil BA20 218 E2
HOLYWELL 197 C8
HOLYWELL LAKE 179 E7
Holy Well Rd TA7 137 C2
Homberg Way TA6 208 E6
Homeavon Ho BS31 24 F5
Homecanton Ho BA9 216 C4
Homecastle Ho 2 TA6 208 F5
Homechime Ho BA5 203 D3
Home Cl
Westbury-sub-Mendip BA5 110 E6
West Camel BA22 174 D3
Wrington BS40 35 E3
Homeclose La EX13, TA20 198 A8
Home Cotts TA1 212 D5
Home Dr
Wincanton BA9 216 C3
Yeovil BA21 218 E5
Home Farm Cl BA2 79 B7
Home Farm La BA22 188 A8
Home Farm Pk TA19 183 E2
Home Farm Rd BS8 11 B8
Home Farm Way TA19 183 E2
Homefield
Bishops Lydeard TA4 167 E8
Congresbury BS49 34 E3
Locking BS24 50 A5
Timsbury BA2 60 C2
Wellington TA21 222 E4
Homefield Cl
Beckington BA11 101 E4
Creech St Michael TA3 169 D4
Locking BS24 50 A5
Saltford BS31 25 E3
Winscombe BS25 51 F1
Home Field Cl TA11 157 B4
Homefield Ct BA22 174 F1
Homefield Ind Est BS24 50 A5
Homefield Rd BS31 25 F3
Homefields BA5 110 E6
Home Fields BA4 205 C4
Homeground BS21 6 F2
Home Ground BS11 4 D7
Homelea Pk E BA1 44 A7
Homelea Pk W BA1 44 A7
Home Mdw TA24 200 D7
Homemead BA2 43 A8
Home Mead BS4 22 E7
Home Orch
Chew Stoke BS40 56 D8
Hatch Beauchamp TA3 183 A7
Homestead BS20 1 E3
Homestead Pk BA5 203 A7
Homestead The
Clevedon BS21 6 C3
Keynsham BS31 24 F2
Homestead Way BS25 70 A8
Homeville Ho BA20 219 A4
Home Way Cnr BA6 138 B4
Hone Cross EX16 164 F5
Hone La TA22 147 F4
Honeycombe Rise DT9 225 B2
Honey Crock La TA7 155 E8
Honeygar La BA6 138 B5
Honey Garston Cl BS13 22 B4
Honey Garston Rd BS13 22 B4
HONEY HALL 52 C7
Honeyhall La BS49 52 D7
Honeyhurst La BS27 109 F8
Honeylands
Curry Rivel TA10 171 D4
Portishead BS20 2 C3
Honeymead
Bristol BS14 23 C6
Croscombe BA5 204 B8
Honey Mead La BA6, TA11 158 B4
Honeypot La TA11 158 C1
Honey Pot La BA11 144 A4
Honey Row La TA4 132 E2
Honeysuckle Pl BS24 50 A8
Honeywell La BA3 94 F4
Honiton 9 BS22 32 A2
Honiton Rd
Clevedon BS21 6 E1
Taunton TA3 168 D1
Hood Cl BA6 206 E3
Hood Rd BA21 219 F8
HOOK
Chard 198 B8
Timsbury 60 D2
Hookedmead La BS26 88 A1
Hook Hill BA2 60 D2
Hook La
Hinton Blewett BA3, BS39 75 E4
North Cheriton BA9 176 C5
Hooks Batch BS40 54 C4
Hookway Hill TA24 123 A3
Hooper Ave BA5 112 E1
Hooper Cl
Burnham-on-S TA8 104 D5
Highbridge TA9 104 F4
Hooper Rd
Bristol BS14 23 D5
Street BA16 207 B5
Hoopers Barton 9 BA11 119 E5
Hooper's Cl TA1 212 B2
Hoopers Cross EX16 164 D3
Hooper's La
East Coker BA22 197 F7
Fordgate TA7 154 E3
HOOPERS POOL 83 D1
Hopcott Cl TA24 200 E6
Hopcott Rd TA24 200 F5
Hopcott Terr TA24 201 A5
Hopechapel Hill 10 BS8 11 F6
Hope Cl BA5 203 C4
Hope Corner Cl TA2 212 E8

Hope Corner La TA2 .... 212 F8
Hope Cote Lodge BA2 .... 45 C1
Hope Cotts
Highbridge TA9 ....104 D3
Kingston Seymour BS21 ... 16 B2
Hope Cross SP8.........177 D3
Hope Ct BS1............226 B1
Hope Sq BS8 ....11 F6
Hope Terr BA3...........78 B1
Hopewell Gdns BS11.......4 F7
Hopkins Ct BA9.........216 C2
Hopkins Ho BA22........218 A5
Hopkins St BS23.........48 E8
Hopton Ct BA4..........141 E1
Horesham Gr BS13.......22 C5
Horfield Rd BS2........227 A4
HORN ASH...............199 D7
Hornbeam Cl
Bridgwater TA6.........209 D5
Frome BA11.............120 C6
Taunton TA1............213 D2
Hornbeam Wlk BS31......24 C3
HORNBLOTTON...........158 F5
Horne Cl BA3............96 F1
HORNER 129 B8
Horner Nature Trails★
TA24..................129 B8
Horner Rd TA2..........213 B7
HORNINGSHAM...........144 C4
Horningsham Prim Sch
BA12...................144 D4
Horn La TA20...........194 B2
HORNSBURY.............223 E7
Hornsbury Hill TA20.... 223 E8
Hornsbury Mill Mus★
TA20...................223 E8
Hornsey La TA20........182 B1
Horns La BA9...........160 B2
Horn's La BS26..........70 B2
Horn St BA11...........143 B8
Hornswell DT9..........189 D4
HORRINGTON............113 A1
Horrington Prim Sch
BA5....................113 B3
HORSECASTLE............17 A2
Horsecastle Cl BS49......17 A1
Horsecastle Farm Rd
BS49....................17 A1
Horsecastle La DT9.....225 C3
Horsecastles DT9.......225 D3
Horse Cl BA11..........101 D5
Horsecombe Brow BA2... 45 A1
Horsecombe Gr BA2 .....45 A1
Horsecombe Vale BA2 ... 45 A1
Horsecroft La TA3......170 B4
Horsefair The BS1......227 B3
Horseham La TA5.......134 E8
Horsehill La BA4.......142 D2
Horse La DT9...........176 A2
Horseland La TA24......131 A5
Horseleaze La BS25......52 D1
Horsemans Mews BA6 ... 206 D5
Horse Mill Cross DT6...199 D3
Horse Mill La TA11.....211 E4
Horsepark La TA24......130 A4
Horse Pond La TA6......208 F4
Horsepool Rd BS13.......21 E3
Horse Race La BS8.......10 A6
Horse Rd TA24..........130 F5
Horseshoe Cotts TA12...185 E7
Horseshoe Dr BS9.........5 C4
Horseshoe Rd TA20......199 A6
Horseshoe Wlk BA2.......45 B5
HorseWorld Visitor Ctr★
BS14....................23 D4
HORSEY................136 C2
Horsey La
Horsey TA7.............136 C2
Langport TA10..........172 B4
Yeovil BA20............219 A4
Horsey Rdbt BA20.......219 A3
HORSINGTON............176 D2
Horsington CE Prim Sch
BA8....................176 D3
Horsington Ho BA8 .....176 E2
Horstmann Cl 2 BA1......44 B7
Hortmead La TA19......183 E3
HORTON................183 C1
Horton Cl BA21.........218 D6
HORTON CROSS..........183 D2
Horton Ho BA2..........228 C4
Horton St
Bristol BS2............227 C3
Frome BA11.............119 D5
Horton Way TA7.........136 E4
Horts Rd TA1...........212 C1
Horwood Rd BS48..........8 F1
Hosey Wlk BS13..........22 A5
Hoskins Cl TA10........171 C4
Hospital La
Sherborne DT9..........225 D4
South Petherton TA13...220 D5
Hospital Rdbt BA20.....219 A5
Host St BS1............227 A3
Hot Bath St 6 BA1......228 B2
Hotwell Rd BS8.........226 B1
HOTWELLS...............226 A1
Hotwells Prim Sch BS8... 11 F6
Houlgate Way BS26.......70 B1
Houlton St BS2.........227 C4
Houndsmill BA8.........176 E2
HOUNDSMOOR............167 A4
Houndsmoor La TA4 .....167 A4
Hound St DT9...........225 D4
HOUNDSTONE 218 A6
Houndstone Bsns Pk
BA22...................218 B6
Houndstone Cl BA21 ....218 C5
Houndstone Cnr BA22...218 A5
Houndstone Ct BA22 ....218 A5
Houndstone Pk BA22....218 A5
Houndstone Ret Pk
BA22...................218 B5
Houndwood Cl BA16 ....207 A6
Houndwood Dro BA16...207 A6
HOUNSLEY BATCH.........38 A3
House Gate Rd BA11 ....143 F2
House's La TA20........193 F1
Housman Rd BA16.......207 D5
Houston Way BA11......119 D5
Hoveland Cres TA1.....212 D2
Hoveland Ct TA1.......212 E2
Hoveland Dr TA1.......212 D1
Hoveland La TA1.......212 C2
Howard Cl
Burnham-on-S TA8......104 C7
Saltford BS31...........25 D3
Howard Rd
Wellington TA21........222 D7
Yeovil BA21............219 E6
Howards Row TA20 .....223 C4
Howecroft Ct BS9..........5 E4
Howecroft Gdns BS9.......5 E4
Howell Hill BA22.......174 D4
Howell's La TA2, TA6 ....153 D1
Howgrove Hill La BS40... 37 C2
How Hill BA2............44 A6
Howitt Way 1 BS24.......49 F7
Howleigh La TA3.......181 C5
HOWLEY..................192 F4
Hownel La TA22........147 F2
Hoyles Cl TA21.........222 E4
Hoyles Rd TA21.........222 E4
Hozzard La BS28........107 E2
Huckeymead La BA4.....158 F7
Huddleston Ct 10 BA5...203 D4
Hudson St TA8..........104 B6
Hudson Way TA2........212 C6
Huett Cl TA8............65 F3
Hugdole La TA7.........137 D2
Hughenden Rd BS23......49 A8
Hughes Cl 6 TA6........209 B4
Hughes Ct BA11.........101 E8
Hugh Sexey CE Mid Sch
BS28...................107 E3
Hugo St TA1............213 A4
Huish BA20.............219 A5
Huish Ball Steep TA24...129 D7
HUISH CHAMPFLOWER....165 F8
Huish Cl
Highbridge TA9........104 D4
Taunton TA1...........213 D4
Huish Cleeve TA4.......165 E7
Huish Ct BA3............79 B2
HUISH EPISCOPI........172 B5
Huish Episcopi Prim Sch
TA10...................172 A5
Huish Episcopi Sch
TA10...................172 A5
Huish Gdns 2 BA20.....219 A5
Huish La
Alweston DT9..........189 B2
Washford TA23.........131 E4
Wyke Champflower BA10 .215 C7
Huish Mdw TA23........131 E4
Huish Park (Yeovil Town FC)
BA22...................218 B7
Huish Prim Sch BA20....219 A5
Huish Rd TA11..........173 C7
Huish Row TA24........129 A8
Hukeley Head Cross
EX16...................164 D3
Hulk Moor Dro BA16,
BA16...................207 C8
Hulkshay La TA6.......153 E3
Hull La DT9, BA8.......176 B3
Humber Gr TA1.........213 D3
Humberstan Wlk BS11.....4 E8
Humphreys Rd TA21 ....222 E7
Humphry Davy Way 6
BS8.....................11 F5
Humpy La DT9..........189 A1
Hundredstone Cl BA21 ..219 B8
Hundry La TA10........184 C8
HUNGERFORD...........131 E3
Hungerford Cl BS4.......23 E8
Hungerford Gdns BS4.....23 E8
Hungerford Rd
Bath BA1................44 C7
Bristol BS4.............23 E8
Hungerford Terr BA2.....62 D1
Hung Rd BS11.............4 E5
HUNSTRETE...............41 D2
Hunstrete Rd BA2........59 F7
Huntash La TA4........167 A4
Huntenhull Gn BA13....121 C3
Huntenhull La BA13.....121 D4
Hunter's Hill EX15 .....179 E1
Hunters Moon Touring Pk
EX13...................198 E1
Hunters Rest Miniature
Rlwy★ BS39..............59 A5
Hunter's Way EX15......179 E1
Huntham Cl TA3........170 E6
Huntham La TA3........170 E5
Huntham Rd TA3........170 D4
Huntingham Rd BS13......21 F4
Huntley Cl EX13........198 A2
Huntley Gr BS48...........9 A1
Huntley La
Chardstock EX13........198 A8
Tatworth EX13, TA20.....193 D1
HUNTSCOTT.............129 E6
HUNTSHAM...............178 A7
Hunts La TA5...........133 D5
Hunt's La BS49..........34 E8
Huntsmans Ridge BS27... 90 C7
Hunts Mead DT9........225 B2
HUNTSPILL.............136 B8
Huntspill Rd TA9.......104 D2
Huntspill River National
Nature Reserve★ TA9 ..136 D6
HUNTSTILE.............153 C4
HUNTWORTH..............154 B5
Huntworth Bsns Pk TA6 .154 A5
Huntworth La
Fordgate TA7...........154 C5
North Petherton TA6 .....153 F4
HURCOTT...............173 C8
Hurcott Cross TA19.....184 D3
Hurcott La TA19 ....184 D4
Hurdle Way TA1 ....213 A3
Hurd's Bldgs BA11......119 F4
Hurley La TA4 ....151 B8
Hurlstone Pk TA24......124 B3
Hurmans Cl TA7.........156 B8
Hurn Dro BA5...........139 B6
Hurn La
Berrow TA8..............84 F7
Keynsham BS31...........25 A3
Pitcombe BA7..........215 A1
Shepton Montague BA7...160 A2
Hurn Rd BS21..............6 F2
Hursley Hill
Bristol BS14.............40 D8
Whitchurch BS14.........23 D1
Hursley La BS14 ....23 E1
HURST.................185 D5
Hurst TA12.............185 D5
Hurst Dro
Compton Dundon TA11....157 A3
Hambridge TA10, TA12....184 E8
Hurst Mews TA12 ....185 D5
Hurston Rd BS4..........22 D7
Hurst Pk TA12..........185 D5
Hurst Rd
Bristol BS4.............22 F8
Weston-Super-Mare BS23.. 49 A6
Hurst Wlk BS4...........22 F8
Hussey's DT10..........190 F5
Hutchings's La TA4 .....167 D4
Hutchin's La BA10 ......160 F8
HUTTON..................49 E2
Hutton CE Prim Sch BS24 49 E2
Hutton Cl
Bristol BS9...............5 E7
Keynsham BS31...........25 A2
Hutton Hill BS24.........49 F2
Hutton Moor La BS22,
BS24....................49 C6
Hutton Moor Pk BS24 ....49 C6
Hutton Moor Rd BS22 ....49 C7
Hutton Moor Rdbt BS22 .. 49 C7
Huxham La BA4..........158 F7
Hyacinth Terr TA21.....222 C5
Hyatt Pl BA4...........204 F5
Hyatts Wood Rd BS48 ....19 E1
Hyde Ct BA21...........218 C6
Hyde La
Monkton Heathfield TA2 ..169 C5
Taunton TA2............213 F6
Hyde Lane Cotts TA2....169 C5
Hyde Park Ave 4 TA6....153 E3
Hyde Pk 5 TA6..........153 E3
Hyde Rd
Minehead TA24..........200 E6
Montacute TA15.........186 B4
Hyde's La SN14..........13 A6
Hyde The
Clevedon BS21...........16 C8
Keynsham BS31...........24 F6
Hyland Gr BS9.............5 F8
Hylton Cl TA2..........212 F8
Hynicombe La TA4.......165 D6
Hythe La BS27...........89 E5

I

Iberry La TA3...........183 E8
ICELTON..................32 C8
Idwal Cl BA2.............79 C8
Iford Cl BS31............25 E3
Iford Fields BA15........64 E2
Iford Hill BA15..........64 E2
Iford La BA3, BA15.......64 C3
ILCHESTER...............173 E1
Ilchester Com Prim Sch (Inf)
BA22...................173 E2
Ilchester Com Prim Sch
(Jun) BA22.............173 E2
Ilchester Cres BS13......22 B8
Ilchester La TA10.......172 F4
ILCHESTER MEAD.........173 D1
Ilchester Mead BA22.....173 D1
Ilchester Mus★ BA22.....173 E1
Ilchester Rd
Bristol BS13.............22 B8
Charlton Mackrell TA11...173 F6
Chilthorne Domer BA21,
BA22...................186 F6
Yeovil BA21............218 F8
Ile Ct TA19.............221 C4
Ilex Ave BS21.............6 E2
Ilex Cl
Bristol BS13.............21 F6
Huntspill TA9..........136 B8
Ilex La BS25.............51 F1
ILFORD.................184 A4
Ilford Ct TA1...........212 C2
Illustrious Cres BA22....173 E2
ILMINSTER..............221 C4
Ilminster BS24...........49 A2
Ilminster Ave BS4........22 F8
Ilminster Avenue Prim Sch
BS4......................23 A8
Ilminster Cl
Clevedon BS21............6 E2
Nailsea BS48.............18 D8
Ilminster Rd TA1........213 D4
Ilsyn Gr BS14............23 D7
ILTON...................183 E4
Ilton Bsns Pk TA19......183 F5
Imbercourt Cl BS14.......23 B8
Immenstadt Dr TA21.....222 D4
Imperial Pk BS13.........22 C6
Imperial Rd BS14.........23 C8
Imperial Way BA11.......120 D7
Improvement Pl 5 TA21 222 D5
Inchalloch 19 BA1........28 A1
Incline The TA19........221 B3
Inclosures The 5 BS22... 49 F8
INGLESBATCH..............61 C8
Ingleton Dr BS22.........32 A4
Ingrams Mdw TA23.......202 C6
Inkerman Ct TA1.........213 A3
Inman Ho BA1............228 C4
INMAN'S BATCH............38 A5
Inn Cotts BS11............5 A7
Inner Circ TA1..........213 D5
Inner Elm Terr BA3.......78 C1
Inner Gullands TA1......212 D3
Innicks Cl BS40..........55 D1
Innox Gdns BS13..........22 A5
Innox Gr BA2.............43 F2
INNOX HILL..............119 F6
Innox Hill BA11.........119 E6
Innox La BA1.............28 B5
Innox Rd BA2.............44 B5
Inns Court Ave BS4.......22 D7
Inns Court Dr BS4........22 D6
Inns Court Gn BS4........22 D7
Innsmead La TA7.........137 B1
Instow 7 BS22............32 A2
Instow Rd BS4............22 E8
Instow Wlk BS4...........22 E8
International Coll Sherborne
Sch DT9................225 D5
International Helicopter
Mus★ BS24...............49 E5
Inverness Rd BA2.........44 C6
Inwood Rd TA6..........208 C5
Irene Cl TA6............209 D7
Ireson Cl BA9...........216 D4
Ireson La BA9...........216 D4
Irnham Rd TA24..........201 A7
Iron Dish La TA13.......184 E6
Iron Mill La BA11.......101 A1
Ironmould La BS31........24 A8
Iron Post TA22..........163 B5
Irons Way BS24...........50 C8
Irvine Cl TA2...........212 C6
Irving Cl BS21............6 F3
Irving Ho BS1...........226 C3
Irving Rd TA11..........158 A1
Irwell Gn TA1...........213 D4
Isaacs Cl BA16..........207 B4
Island The BA3...........78 A1
ISLE ABBOTTS............183 F7
ISLE BREWERS............184 A8
Islemoor Dro TA3........184 A8
Islemoor La TA13........220 B6
Islemoor Rd TA3.........183 F8
Isleport Bsns Pk TA9....104 F4
Isleport Rd TA9.........104 F3
Isles La
East Coker, Lyatts BA22...197 C6
East Coker, Sutton Bingham
BA22...................197 D6
Ivel Ct BA21............219 C5
Ivel Gdns BA22..........173 E1
Ivel Sq BA20............219 B5
Ivelway TA18............224 C5
Ivo Peters Rd BA2.......228 A2
Ivors Way TA6...........153 E4
Ivy Ave BA2..............44 C4
Ivy Bank Pk BA2..........44 F2
Ivybridge 8 BS22.........32 A2
Ivy Cl BS48...............8 D1
Ivy Cotts TA3...........181 E3
Ivy Cross TA21..........179 D7
Ivy Ct BS20...............1 F5
Ivy Gn TA20.............223 C3
Ivy Gr BA2...............44 C4
Ivy Grove Cl TA6........209 D7
Ivy Ho
Chard TA20.............223 B4
Wellington TA21........222 C6
Ivy House Cotts BS29.....50 D7
Ivy House Pk TA3.......169 C2
Ivy La BS24..............50 A8
Ivyleaf Rd TA11.........211 C4
Ivy Pl BA2...............44 C4
Ivythorn Cl BA16........207 C4
Ivy Thorn La BA16.......207 A1
Ivythorn Rd BA16........207 C4
Ivywell Rd BS9.............5 E3
Ivy Wlk
Banwell BS29.............50 E4
Midsomer Norton BA3.....97 B8
Yeovil BA20............218 E3
IWOOD....................35 A3
Iwood La BS40............35 A2

J

Jack Price Cl BS13.......22 C3
Jack's Dro BS28.........137 F8
Jack's La
Croscombe BA5..........204 C7
Frome BA11.............119 D7
Jackson's La TA5........134 A2
Jack White's Gibbet BA9 176 B8
Jacobs Cl BA6...........206 E5
Jacob's Ct BS1..........226 C2
Jacobs Mdw BS20............2 F4
Jacob St
Bristol BS2............227 B3
Bristol BS2............227 C3
Jacob's Wells Rd BS8 ...226 B2
Jagaar Ct TA7...........137 D5
Jaguar Ho 3 BA1.........228 B3
Jamaica St BS2..........227 B4
James Cl
Holcombe BA3...........116 C8
Shepton Mallet BA4......205 C4
James La EX14...........192 F2
James Lane Cross EX13 . 193 A1
James St W BA1..........228 B2
James's Hill BA10.......161 A8
James St BS5............227 C4
Jane Austin Centre The★
BA1....................228 B3
Janson Cl TA6...........209 D6
Japonica Cl TA6.........209 D5
Jarman Way TA20........223 D6
Jarmany Hill BA6........157 F3
Jarmyns TA1............212 A3
Jarvis Cl DT10..........190 B4
Jarvis La TA9............86 D4
Jarvis Way DT10.........190 B4
Jasmine Cl
Crewkerne TA18.........224 D7
Highbridge TA9.........104 D4
Weston-Super-Mare BS22.. 32 A1
Yeovil BA22............218 B5
Jasmine Ct 8 BS23........48 E8
Jasmine La BS49..........17 F2
Jasmine Way BS24.........32 A1
Jay Cl BA11.............120 B6
Jaycroft Rd TA8.........104 B6
Jay View BS23............49 A5
Jeffreys' Way TA1.......212 A2
Jeffries Cl TA19........183 C4
Jeffs Way 3 EX13........198 A1
Jellalabad Ct TA1.......212 F3
Jellicoe Ct BS22.........31 E4
Jena Ct BS31.............25 D3
Jenson Ave BA11.........120 D8
Jesmond Rd
Clevedon BS21.............6 C3
Weston-Super-Mare BS22.. 32 C4
Jesse Hughes Ct BA1......28 C2
Jessop Ct BS1...........227 B2
Jessop Underpass BS3 ... 11 F4
Jews La
Bath BA2.................44 C6
Churchill BS25...........52 F4
Wiveliscombe TA4.......210 B5
Jill Dando Memorial
Garden★ 8 BS23..........48 D8
Jill's Cl BA4............142 A6
Jim O'Neil Ho BS11........4 D7
Jocelin Dr BS22..........31 F4
Jocelin Rd BA6..........206 F5
Jocelyn Dr BA5..........203 B3
John Beales Hill BA4....140 F3
John Cabot Ct BS1.......226 A1
John Carr's Terr BS8....226 B2
John Cozens Ho 6 BS2 .227 C3
John Grinter Way TA21..222 D4
John Gunn Cl TA20.......223 C5
John St S TA8...........104 A7
John Slessor Ct BA1 ....228 B4
Johnson Cl
East Brent TA9...........86 D5
Wells BA5...............203 F5
Johnson Flats BA21......219 C7
Johnson's Ctyd DT9......225 D3
John St
Bath BA1...............228 B3
Bristol BS1............227 A3
Burnham-on-S TA8.......104 A7
Highbridge TA9.........104 D3
Johnstone Ct BA16.......207 B3
Johnstone St BA2........228 C2
John Wesleys Chapel★
BS1....................227 B3
Joles La BA11...........120 F1
Jones Cl BS49............17 A1
Joselin Ct DT9..........225 D5
Joyden Ct TA20..........223 D2
Joy Hill BS8.............11 F6
Juan's La SP8...........177 E1
Jubilee Cl
Bridgwater TA6.........209 C4
Castle Cary BA7........214 C6
Chard TA20.............223 C3
Jubilee Cotts 10 BA11 ..119 F4
Jubilee Ct
8 Wellington TA21......222 D5
Weston-Super-Mare BS23.. 48 F8
Jubilee Dr BS8...........10 B4
Jubilee Gdns
Milverton TA4..........167 A4
South Petherton TA13....220 C4
Jubilee La BS40..........53 A6
Jubilee Path BS22........31 C1
Jubilee Pl
Bristol BS1............227 A1
Clevedon BS21.............6 D1

Jubilee Pl *continued*
Yeovil BA21 218 D5
Jubilee Rd
Axbridge BS26 70 C2
Radstock BA3 78 D1
Street BA16 207 C4
Weston-Super-Mare BS23 48 E7
Jubilee St
Bristol BS2 227 C2
Burnham-on-S TA8 104 B6
Taunton TA2 212 E6
Jubilee Terr
Frome BA11 119 E5
Hemington BA3 99 C7
Paulton BS39 77 E6
Jubilee Way BS22 32 C3
Judy's Orch TA7 154 F5
Julian Cl
Bristol BS9 5 E3
Shepton Mallet BA4 205 C4
Julian Ct BS9 5 E3
Julian Rd
Bath BA1 228 B3
Bristol BS9 5 E3
Julian's Acres TA8 84 F4
Julier Ho BA1 228 C4
Jumpers Combe TA23 148 E8
Junction Ave BA2 228 A1
Junction Dro TA3 170 C2
Junction Rd BA2 228 A1
Juniper Cl
Bridgwater TA6 209 E4
Yeovil BA20 218 F3
Juniper Pl BS22 31 F4
Juniper Rd TA1 213 C2
Jurston La
Wellington TA21 222 E6
Wellington TA21 222 F5
Jury Hill TA22 163 E6
Jury Rd TA22 163 E6
Justice Ave BS31 25 E3
Justice La BA11 119 F5

K

Kale St BA4 142 D2
Kale Street Cotts BA4 142 D2
Karen Cl BS48 19 A4
Karen Dr BS48 19 A5
Kaynton Mead BA1 44 B7
Keats Ho 4 BS23 48 F4
Keats Rd
Radstock BA3 97 C8
Taunton TA1 213 C3
Kebby's Farm Cl TA4 202 E3
Keble Ave BS13 21 F5
Keeds La BS41 10 F1
Keedwell Hill BS41 10 F1
Keel Ave BS20 2 F7
Keel's Hill BA2 79 C8
Keene's Way BS21 6 C2
Keens Cl BA16 207 D5
Keen's Elm La BA16 207 E4
Keens La TA7 155 C2
KEENTHORNE 134 D2
Keep St BA22 174 D3
Keep The BS22 32 A3
Keg Store The BS1 227 B2
KEINTON MANDEVILLE 158 B1
Keinton Mandeville Prim Sch
TA11 158 A1
Kellways BS48 19 A4
Kelson's La BS28 108 B3
Kelso Pl BA1 44 D7
Kelso Villas BA1 44 D7
KELSTON 26 C3
Kelston Cl BS31 25 D4
Kelston Gdns BS22 32 B5
Kelston Rd
Bath BA1 26 E1
Keynsham BS31 24 D5
Weston-Super-Mare BS22 32 B5
Kelston View BA2 44 A5
Kelting Gr BS21 6 F2
Keltings TA6 208 C6
Kelway Rd TA21 222 E7
Kember's Hill BA22, DT9 175 C3
Kemble Cl BS48 9 A1
Kemble Gdns BS11 4 F5
Kemm Cl BS27 90 B6
Kempe's Cl BS41 11 A2
Kempe Way BS24 49 E7
Kemps La TA24 147 B7
Kemp's La BA11 120 F7
Kemps Way TA22 163 D6
Ken Cl
Chard TA20 223 D3
Wells BA5 140 C8
Kencot Wlk BS13 22 B3
Kendale Rd TA6 208 E6
Kendall Cl TA3 169 D6
Kendrick Ct 1 BA5 203 D4
Kenilworth Cl BS31 24 D4
Kenilworth Ct BA1 45 B8
Kenmare Rd BS4 22 E8
Kenmeade Cl BS25 70 E8
Kenmore Dr BA21 219 B6
KENN 16 F7
Kennard Cl BA6 206 F3
Kennard Moor Dro
Butleigh BA6 157 E7
Glastonbury BA6 206 F1
Kennaway Rd BS21 6 E2
Kenn Bsns Pk BS21 16 E8
Kenn Cl BS23 49 A5
Kenn Court BS4 22 E7
Kennedy Cl TA9 104 E4
Kennel Batch BA5 111 D4
Kennel La
Compton Bishop BS26 68 E3
East Pennard BA4 158 F8
Langport TA10 172 A6
West Bagborough TA4 151 D4
Kennel Lodge Rd BS3 11 E4
Kenn Est BS21 16 E5
Kennet Gr TA1 213 D4
Kennet Ho 10 BA1 228 B2
Kennet Pk BA2 28 E1
Kennet Rd BS31 25 A4
Kennford 6 BS22 31 F2
Kennington Rd BA1 44 B7
Kennion Cl TA20 223 D3
Kennion Rd BA5 203 C5
Kenn Moor Dr BS21 6 E1
KENN MOOR GATE 17 F4
Kennmoor Rd BS21 17 A6
Kenn Moor Rd BS49 17 B1
Kenn Rd BS21 16 F6
Kenn St BS21 16 F7
KENNY 183 B4
Kensington Ct
Bath BA1 28 B2
Bristol BS8 226 A3
Kensington Fields BA14 83 F7
Kensington Gdns
Bath BA1 28 B1
Bridgwater TA6 209 D6
Kensington Gr TA24 200 E6
Kensington Pl
Bath BA1 28 B1
Bristol BS8 226 A3
Kensington Rd BS23 48 F5
Kent Ave
Bridgwater TA6 209 A2
Weston-Super-Mare BS24 50 C8
Weston-Super-Mare BS24 50 D8
Kentisworth Rd DT10 190 F5
Kent La
Shapwick TA7 137 F1
Shepton Mallet BA4 205 A5
Kent Rd
Congresbury BS49 34 D5
Tatworth TA20 198 D8
Kent's Bglws TA20 198 D8
Kents Cl TA20 198 C8
Kent's Cotts TA20 198 D8
Kentshare La BS40 38 B6
Kents La TA20 198 D8
Kent's Orch TA20 198 D8
Kent St BS27 71 B1
Kent Way BS22 32 B4
Kenwyn Cl TA1 213 D3
Keppel Cl BS31 25 D2
Kerry Croft BA11 143 C3
Kersey Ct BA11 119 C5
Kersham La TA24 130 A1
Kestrel Cl TA6 209 C3
Kestrel Dr BS22 31 E1
KEWARD 203 C2
Keward Ave BA5 203 B3
Keward Cl BA5 203 B3
Keward Mill Trad Est
BA5 203 B2
Keward Wlk BA5 203 C3
Kew Rd BS23 30 E1
Kewside BS22 31 B4
KEWSTOKE 31 B4
Kewstoke Prim Sch BS22 31 B3
Kewstoke Rd
Bath BA2 45 A2
Bristol BS9 5 E4
Weston-Super-Mare BS22 31 C3
Kew Wlk BS4 23 C8
Keyes Path BS22 31 F4
KEYFORD 119 F3
Keyford BA11 119 F3
Keyford Cotts 15 BA11 119 F4
Keyford Ct BA11 119 F2
KEYFORD FIELD 119 F2
Keyford Field Cotts
BA11 119 F2
Keyford Gdns BA11 119 F3
Keyford Pl BA11 119 F4
Keyford Rdbt BA22 197 E8
Keyford Terr BA11 119 F4
Keyhaven Bglws BS22 31 B4
Key Hill BA22 197 E8
KEYNSHAM 24 E3
Keynsham By-Pass BS31 24 E7
Keynsham Hospl BS31 24 F4
Keynsham Prim Sch BS31 24 D5
Keynsham Rd BS30, BS31 25 A8
Keynsham Sta BS31 24 F6
Keyton Hill BS28 107 E2
Kicks Hill TA7 155 B4
Kicks Hill La TA7 155 B4
Kidder Bank BA5 203 F5
Kiddles BA21 219 C5
Kidd's La BA4 205 D6
Kid Gate Dro TA9, BS28 137 D8
Kidner Cl TA7 136 E4
Kidsbury Rd TA6 208 E5
Kielder Dr BS22 31 F3
Kilbirnie Rd BS14 23 A3
Kilburn Dr TA6 209 D6
Kildare BA2 45 B7
Kildare Gdns TA24 200 F6
Kildare Rd BS13 22 D8
Kilkenny Ave 5 TA2 212 F6
Kilkenny Ct TA2 212 F6
Kilkenny La
Bath BA2 62 B8
Wraxall BA4 159 A6
Kilkenny Pl BS20 2 C6
Killams Ave
Staplehay TA3 181 F8
Taunton TA1 168 F1
Killams Cl TA1 168 F1
Killams Cres TA1 168 F1
Killams Dr TA1 168 F1
Killams Gn TA1 168 F1
Killams La TA1 168 F1
Killarney Ave TA8 104 C6
Killick Way TA4 202 D3
KILLING'S KNAP 97 B4
KILMERSDON 98 B5
Kilmersdon CE Prim Sch
BA3 98 A6
Kilmersdon Hill BA3 98 A5
Kilmersdon Rd
Bristol BS13 22 B4
Radstock BA3 97 E8
KILMINGTON 161 F7
KILMINGTON COMMON 161 F6
Kilminster Rd BS11 4 D7
Kilmorie Cl TA1 212 C2
Kiln Cl TA5 135 B5
Kiln Dr
Evercreech BA4 141 E1
Highbridge TA9 104 D3
Kiln Pk BS23 49 A6
KILTON 133 E6
Kilton Cross TA5 133 E5
KILVE 133 C6
Kilve BS24 49 A2
Kilve Cl TA2 212 F7
Kilve Cres TA2 212 F7
Kilve Ct TA5 133 C5
Kilver St BA4 205 D6
Kilver Street Hill BA4 205 D7
Kimber Cl TA9 104 D3
Kimberley Rd BS21 6 C2
Kimberley Terr TA6 209 B7
Kinber Cl BA1 27 A3
Kinforde TA20 223 C5
King Alfred Cl 3 TA6 153 F4
King Alfred Dr TA20 223 C2
King Alfred Sch The TA9 104 C5
King Alfreds Ctyd 7
BA5 203 D4
King Alfreds Way BS28 108 B4
King Alfred Way BA15 64 D7
King Arthur Dr BA21 218 D7
King Arthurs Com Sch
BA9 216 A4
King Athelstan Dr TA20 223 D2
King Ceol Cl TA20 223 D2
King Cerdic Cl TA20 223 D2
Kingcott Mill Farm Cvns
BS48 20 B8
King Cuthred Cl TA20 223 C2
King Cuthred Dr TA20 223 C2
Kingdom BA5 113 A4
Kingdom La TA2 168 B4
Kingdon Mead TA3 169 D4
KINGDOWN 37 D5
Kingdown Rd BS40 37 C5
King Edward Cl BS14 23 A6
King Edward Rd
Bath BA2 44 D5
Minehead TA24 201 A6
King Edward's Jun Sch
BA2 45 C7
King Edward's Pre-Prep Sch
BA1 44 C8
King Edward's Sch BA2 45 C7
Kingfisher Cl TA6 209 C3
Kingfisher Cl BA20 218 D3
Kingfisher Ct BA3 64 C6
Kingfisher Dr BA3 97 B8
Kingfisher Rd
Portishead BS20 3 A7
Weston-Super-Mare BS22 49 F8
King George Ave TA6 208 F2
King George Cl TA6 209 A2
King George Rd TA24 201 A6
King George's Rd
Bath BA2 44 C6
Bristol BS13 21 F5
King George St 2 BA20 219 B4
King George V Pl 7
BS1 227 A2
King Ina Rd TA11 211 D4
King Ine Cl N TA20 223 C2
King Ine Cl S TA20 223 C2
King La BS39 58 F4
Kinglake Villas TA6 209 A2
King Rd BS49 52 E6
Kingsacre BA7 214 B5
Kings Acre TA4 151 B5
KINGSBRIDGE 148 E8
KINGSBURY EPISCOPI 185 A8
Kingsbury Episcopi Prim Sch
TA12 185 A6
KINGSBURY REGIS 217 D3
Kings Castle Bsns Est
TA6 209 A6
King's Castle Rd BA5 112 E1
Kings Cl
Shepton Mallet BA4 205 B5
Taunton TA1 213 A2
Kingscliffe Terr TA6 209 A2
King's Cnr TA22 163 D6
King's Coll TA1 213 B2
Kingscombe BA3 114 E6
Kingscourt Cl BS14 23 A4
Kings Cres DT9 225 D5
Kings Croft BS41 10 E1
Kings Ct
Bath BA1 228 B2
Bristol BS1 227 A2
Bristol, St Pauls BS1 227 B4
Kings Ct *continued*
2 Bristol, Withywood BS13 21 F4
Sherborne DT9 225 D6
Yeovil BA21 219 C6
KINGSDON 173 E4
Kingsdon CE Prim Sch
TA11 173 D5
Kingsdon Hill TA11 173 D5
Kingsdon Manor Sch
TA11 173 D4
KINGSDOWN
Box 29 F3
Bristol 227 A4
Kingsdown Cl TA6 209 D6
Kingsdown Gr SN13 29 F3
Kingsdown Par BS6 227 A4
Kingsdown View 16 BA1 28 A1
Kings Dr TA7 154 E6
Kingsettle Hill BA10 161 B5
Kingsfield BA2 44 C3
Kingsford Gate Cross
TA24 145 B7
Kingsford Hill TA24 145 C7
King's Hall Sch TA2 168 E6
Kingshams BA22 173 E1
King's Head La BS13 21 F7
Kingshill BS48 8 C2
Kings Hill BA22 186 E6
King's Hill BA3 94 F7
Kingshill CE Prim Sch
BS48 8 D3
Kingshill Gdns BS48 8 C1
Kingshill La BS40 56 C4
Kingsholme Ct BS23 30 E1
Kings La TA7 156 B8
King's La
Binegar BA3 95 E1
Clevedon BS21 6 D5
6 Weston-Super-Mare
BS23 48 E8
Kingsland TA23 202 D7
Kingsland Grange 1
BA21 218 C6
Kingsland La TA24 148 D5
Kingsland Rd BA4 205 B5
Kingsland Trad Est BS2 227 C3
Kings Lear TA19 183 F4
Kingsley Cl TA1 212 C1
Kingsley Ho BS2 227 C2
Kingsley Rd
Clevedon BS21 6 D2
Radstock BA3 78 C1
Weston-Super-Mare BS23 48 F3
KINGSMEAD 228 A2
Kingsmead BS48 8 C2
Kingsmead Cl
Holcombe BA3 116 C8
Wiveliscombe TA4 210 C3
Kingsmead Com Sch
TA4 210 C3
Kingsmead Ct 8 BA1 228 B2
Kingsmead N BA1 228 B2
Kingsmead Sq BA1 228 B2
Kingsmead St BA1 228 B2
Kingsmead W BA1 228 B2
Kingsmill BS9 5 D5
King's Mill Rd DT10 190 D3
Kingsmoor Prim Sch
TA7 136 E2
Kings Oak Mdw BS39 58 E2
Kings of Wessex Com Sch
The BS27 90 B7
King's Pl TA6 208 F5
King Sq
Bridgwater TA6 208 F5
Bristol BS2 227 A4
King Square Ave BS2 227 A4
Kings Rd
Sherborne DT9 225 D5
Stoke sub Hamdon TA14 185 F5
Wells BA5 140 C8
Wrington BS40 35 D1
King's Rd
Bristol BS8 226 A3
Clevedon BS21 6 D5
Doulting BA4 141 E7
Portishead BS20 1 F4
Kings Ride TA20 223 B6
King's Sch BA10 215 E6
Kings Sq BS30 25 D8
King St
Bridgwater TA6 209 A5
Bristol BS1 227 A2
Frome BA11 119 F5
Glastonbury BA6 206 D5
Highbridge TA9 104 D3
Yeovil BA21 219 B6
Kingston BA20 219 A5
Kingston Ave
Clevedon BS21 6 E3
Saltford BS31 25 C3
Kingston Bldgs 5 BA1 228 C2
Kingston Cl
Street BA16 207 D6
Taunton TA2 212 E7
Kingston Dr BS48 18 C8
KINGSTONE 221 E2
Kingstone Cross TA19 221 F2
Kingstone Hill TA19 221 F2
Kingston La
Felton BS40 37 F8
Maiden Bradley BA12 144 C1
Kingston Mead BS40 37 F7
Kingston Mews 3 TA2 212 F6
Kingston Rd
Bath BA1 228 C2
Nailsea BS48 18 C8
Taunton TA2 212 E7
KINGSTON ST MARY 168 E8
Kingston St Mary CE Prim
Sch TA2 168 D8
KINGSTON SEYMOUR 16 C2
Kingston View BA21 219 B6
Kingston Way BS48 18 C8
Kingston Well La TA20 194 C2
KINGSWAY 44 C3
Kingsway
Bath BA2 44 C3
Holcombe BA3 116 C8
Mark BS26, TA9 87 D3
Portishead BS20 1 F4
Taunton TA1 168 F1
Kingsway Ctr BA11 119 F4
Kingsway Rd TA8 104 B7
Kingswear 3 BS22 32 A2
Kings Weston Ave BS11 4 E8
Kings Weston La BS11 5 A8
Kings Weston Rd BS9 5 B8
Kingsweston Sch BS11 5 A8
Kings Wlk BS13 21 E7
KINGSWOOD 150 E8
Kingswood Chase BA14 83 F6
Kingswood Prep Sch BA1 27 E1
Kingswood Rd TA18 224 C4
Kingswood Sch BA1 27 E2
KINGTON MAGNA 177 E2
Kington View BA8 176 E1
Kingwell View BS39 59 D2
KINGWESTON 157 E2
Kingweston Rd
Butleigh BA6 157 E3
Charlton Mackrell TA11 173 E8
King William Ave BS1 227 A2
King William Rd TA7 137 D2
Kinsale Rd BS14 23 C7
Kinvara Rd BS4 22 E8
Kinver Terr TA8 104 A7
Kipling Ave BA2 44 F4
Kipling Rd
Radstock BA3 78 C1
Weston-Super-Mare BS23 49 A3
Kippax Ave BA5 203 F5
Kipscombe Cross EX35 122 A6
Kirk Dr TA7 154 E6
Kirke Gr TA2 213 B8
Kirkham St TA11 211 E4
Kirlegate BA6 138 C4
Kissing Batch BA11 119 C6
KITBRIDGE 198 A6
Kitchener Rd TA2 168 A6
Kitchens La TA13 185 A1
Kite La BA4 159 C6
Kites Croft BA5 110 E7
Kite's Nest La SP8 161 F1
Kite Wlk 2 BS22 49 E8
Kithill TA18 224 D4
Kitley Hill BA3 78 C4
Kitridge La TA24 146 B7
Kitrow La TA24 131 A6
Kit's La TA4 166 A6
Kitswall La TA24 130 D5
Kitt Hill DT9 225 C4
KITTISFORD 166 B1
Kitton La DT9 188 A4
Kitts TA21 222 D4
KITTWHISTLE 199 D6
Knacker's Hole La
Churchinford TA3 192 A6
Thorncombe DT6, TA20 199 C4
Knap Hill BA3 117 B2
KNAPP 169 F4
Knapp TA16 195 F7
Knapp Cotts TA4 151 E1
Knapp Hill Cl BA5 113 A2
Knapp La
Bishops Lydeard TA4 151 E1
North Curry TA3 170 B4
Knapp Rd
Creech St Michael TA3 169 F4
North Curry TA3 170 A4
Knapps Cl BS25 69 F8
Knapps Dr BS25 69 F8
Knapps La
Chard TA20 194 C4
Langport TA10 172 B5
Knapp The TA24 130 B4
Knap The BA8 176 E1
Knaptons Hill BA11 118 C6
Kneller Cl BS11 5 A8
Knight Cl BS22 32 A5
KNIGHTCOTT 50 F3
Knightcott BS29 50 F3
Knightcott Gdns BS29 50 F3
Knightcott Ind Est BS29 50 E3
Knightcott Pk BS29 51 A3
Knightcott Rd
Abbots Leigh BS8 10 F8
Banwell BS29 50 F3
Knightlands La TA10 172 F4
KNIGHTON 184 D7
Knighton TA5 134 B7
Knighton Dro TA10 184 D7
Knightsbridge Pk BS13 22 E4
Knightsbridge Way TA6 209 D6
Knight's Cross TA21 181 A5
Knight's Ct BA11 119 F4
Knight Shute La TA20 193 D6
Knight's La
Axminster EX13 198 A4
Higher Chillington TA19 194 E5
Knights Rd TA21 180 D8
Knights Templar CE Meth
Com Sch TA23 202 D6

Knightstone TA3 169 D3
Knightstone Cl
Axbridge BS26 70 C1
Kingsbury Episcopi TA12 185 B8
Peasedown St John BA2 79 B8
Knightstone Cswy BS23 48 C8
Knightstone Ct
Burnham-on-S TA8 104 B6
Clevedon BS21 6 D1
Stalbridge DT10 190 B4
Taunton TA2 213 A6
Weston-Super-Mare BS23 30 D1
Knightstone Gn BS23 48 E6
Knightstone Ho
[1] Bristol BS2 227 A4
Weston-Super-Mare BS23 48 D8
Knightstone Hts BA11 119 F3
Knightstone Mead TA22 148 A2
Knightstone Pk [4] BS23 48 E5
Knightstone Pl
Bath BA1 27 B1
[7] Weston-Super-Mare BS22 31 F2
Knightstone Rd BS23 48 C8
Knightstone Sq BS14 23 C5
Knightstone Wlk BS2 226 C4
Knights Yd BA7 214 C5
Knobsbury Hill BA3 98 D6
Knobsbury La BA3 98 C7
KNOLE 173 A4
Knole Cswy
Knole TA10 173 A4
Long Sutton TA10 172 F4
Knole Pit La TA10 173 A4
Knoll Ct BS9 5 D3
Knoll Green La TA5 134 F2
Knoll Hill BS9 5 D3
Knoll Hill View BA11 143 C6
Knoll Ho [5] BA11 119 F4
Knoll La BA4 142 E3
Knoll Pk TA8 65 F2
Knoll The BS20 2 D7
Knoll View
Burnham-on-S TA8 104 C8
[4] Frome BA11 119 F4
Knotcroft La TA2 153 D1
Knotts Paddock DT9 225 E4
KNOWLE 136 D2
Knowle Cross DT8 199 F6
Knowle Dro
Middlezoy TA7 155 A4
Westonzoyland TA7 154 F5
Knowle End TA7 136 E3
Knowle La
Chard TA20 194 B6
Dunster TA24 201 B1
Misterton DT8, TA18 224 E2
Shepton Mallet BA4 204 E5
Wookey BA5 110 E1
Knowle Moor Dro BA5 110 C2
Knowle Rd TA6 209 C6
KNOWLE ST GILES 194 B6
Knowles Rd BS21 6 C2
Knowleyards Rd TA7 155 B4
KNOWSTONE 162 A2
Kuching Rd BA22 174 A2
Kylross Ave BS14 23 B5
Kyrle Gdns BA1 28 F3
Kyte Rd BA4 205 C5

L

Labbott The BS31 24 E5
Labourham Dro BS27 90 B5
Labourham Way BS27 90 B6
Laburnum Cl
Bridgwater TA6 209 D4
Frome BA11 120 B7
Midsomer Norton BA3 96 F8
Somerton TA11 211 D4
Laburnum Cotts [7] TA21 222 D5
Laburnum Cres TA18 224 D7
Laburnum Ct
[7] Taunton TA1 213 A4
Weston-Super-Mare BS23 49 B7
Laburnum Dr TA11 211 D4
Laburnum Gr BA3 96 F8
Laburnum Lodges TA9 136 A8
Laburnum Rd
Wellington TA21 222 E5
Weston-Super-Mare BS23 49 B7
Laburnum St TA1 213 A4
Laburnum Terr
Batheaston BA1 28 F3
Creech St Michael TA3 169 D4
Laburnum Way BA20 218 D2
Laburnum Wlk BS31 24 C3
Lacey Rd BS14 23 F6
La Ciotat Ho TA6 209 A4
Ladd Cl TA9 104 D3
Ladies Mile BS8 5 E1
Ladman Gr BS14 23 E6
Ladman Rd BS14 23 E5
Ladycroft [5] BS21 6 B1
Ladye Bay BS21 6 D7
Ladye Wake BS22 31 F4
Lady Harriet Acland's Dr TA22 164 A8
Lady Lawn TA3 168 D1
Ladymead BS20 2 F5
Ladymead Cl TA6 208 B4
Ladymead Com Sch TA2 168 E6
Ladymeade
Backwell BS48 19 A7
Ladymeade *continued*
Ilminster TA19 221 B3
Ladymead Ho BA1 228 C3
Ladymead La BS40 52 F5
Ladymead Rd TA2 168 F6
Lady St TA22 163 D7
Lady Victoria's Dr TA22 163 E6
Ladywell BS40 35 D2
Laggan Gdns BA1 27 E1
Laggan Ho BA1 27 E1
Lagger Hill TA5 133 C5
Lahs Pl BA11 101 E4
Lakefields BA22 197 B8
Lakemead Gdns [3] BS13 21 F4
Lakemead Gr BS13 21 F6
Lake Mews BA22 219 B1
Lake Rd BS20 2 D7
Lakeside TA9 104 E4
Lakeside Cl BS40 55 D5
Lakeside Ct BS24 32 B1
Lakeside Pk
Bridgwater TA6 209 A3
Vobster BA11 117 E8
Lakeview Cres TA9 104 E3
Lake Wall TA7 154 E4
Lambert Cl DT9 217 C2
Lambert Ct DT9 217 D2
Lambert La TA19 194 F5
Lambert Pl BS4 22 D6
Lambert's Hill BA4 204 F3
Lamberts Marsh BA14 83 E2
Lamb La TA6 208 F4
Lambourne Ct TA18 224 D7
Lambourne Way BS20 2 F5
Lambourn Rd BS31 25 A4
Lambpark Ct TA3 191 F6
LAMBRIDGE 28 C2
Lambridge [6] BA1 28 C1
Lambridge Bldgs [1] BA1 28 C1
Lambridge Grange [6] BA1 28 C2
Lambridge Mews [5] BA1 28 C1
Lambridge Pl BA1 28 C2
Lambridge St BA1 28 C1
Lambrok Cl BA14 83 F6
Lambrok Rd BA14 83 F6
Lambrook Cl TA1 213 B4
Lambrook Gate TA13 184 F5
Lambrook Ho BA9 216 C4
Lambrook Rd
Shepton Beauchamp TA19 184 E4
Taunton TA1 213 B4
Lambrook St BA6 206 E4
Lambrook Way TA1 213 C4
Lambs Field DT9 225 E5
Lamb St BS2 227 C3
Lamington Cl BS13 21 F6
Lamont Ho [7] BA1 28 C1
Lampard's Bldgs BA1 228 B4
Lamparts Way TA19 183 C2
Lampeter Rd BS9 5 F7
Lampley Rd BS21 16 D2
Lampreys La TA13 220 C3
Lampton Ave BS13 22 E3
Lampton Gr BS13 22 E3
Lampton Rd BS41 10 F1
LAMYATT 159 F6
Lancaster House Sch BS23 48 F8
Lancer Ct TA21 222 D6
Lanch La SP8 177 F5
Lancock St TA21 222 A5
Lancombe La BA10 215 C3
Landacre La TA24 146 A7
Landemann Cir BS23 30 E1
Landemann Path [2] BS23 48 E8
Landlord's Hill TA21 179 E7
Landmark Ct BS1 226 C1
Landmead BA6 206 D5
Landmoor La TA10 172 D4
Landsdown Mews BA11 119 D5
Landseer BA8 176 D4
Landseer Cl BS22 31 F3
Landseer Rd BA2 44 B6
Landshire La
Charlton Horethorne DT9 176 A1
Chilton Polden TA7 137 A3
Henstridge BA8 190 C6
Odcombe BA22 186 C1
LANE END 144 D8
Lane End BA12 144 D8
Lane Foot TA24 129 D7
Lane Head TA24 123 E4
Lanesborough Rise BS14 23 D7
Lanes End Hill BA11, BA12 144 D8
Laneys Dro BS24 49 E5
LANGALLER 169 C6
Langaller Hill TA22 163 D4
Langdon Cl TA20 223 D6
Langdon Rd BA2 44 B4
Langdons DT9 225 E5
Langdons Way TA20 198 C8
Langdown Ct BS14 23 E5
Langer's La TA19 194 E5
LANGFORD 212 A8
LANGFORD BUDVILLE 166 E2
Langford Budville CE Prim Sch TA21 166 F1
Langford Cl TA3 170 F1
Langford Ct [14] TA1 213 A4
Langford Ct Cotts BS40 53 E5
Langford Gate TA4 166 F2
Langford La
Fivehead TA3 170 F2
Lower Langford BS40 53 E5
Langford La *continued*
Norton Fitzwarren TA2 168 C6
Langford Rd
Bristol BS13 21 F8
Lower Langford BS40 53 C6
Weston-Super-Mare BS23 49 A6
Langfords La BS39 77 C8
Langford's La BS39 59 D1
LANGHAM
Chard 223 C7
Gillingham 177 F4
Langham Dr TA1 212 C1
Langham Gdns TA1 212 C1
Langham La SP8 177 F5
Langham Pl BA11 82 F1
Langhill Ave BS4 22 D7
Langland La TA7 137 D2
Langlands [8] TA14 185 F4
Langlands La TA3 169 F2
Langland's La TA9 104 B1
LANGLEY 210 C6
Langley Cres BS3 11 E1
Langley Cross TA4 210 B6
LANGLEY MARSH 210 A7
Langleys Cotts BA3 96 B8
Langley's La BA3, BS39 77 C1
Langmead Dro
Middlezoy TA7 155 A4
Westonzoyland TA7 154 F5
Langmead La TA7 155 A4
Langmead Pl TA18 224 C4
Langmead Rd TA18 224 C4
Langmead Sq TA18 224 C4
Langmoor La EX13 198 D2
LANGPORT 172 B5
Langport Gdns BS48 18 E8
Langport Rd
Long Sutton TA10 172 E5
Middlezoy TA7 155 B4
Somerton TA11 211 B4
Weston-Super-Mare BS23 48 E5
Lang Rd TA18 224 C4
LANGRIDGE 27 E7
Langridge La BA1 27 D8
Lang's Cnr TA19 183 B1
Langton Ho [9] BS2 227 C3
Langworthy Orch TA19 183 C1
LANSDOWN
Bath 27 E1
Langridge 27 B6
Lansdown Cres
[2] Bath BA1 27 F1
Timsbury BA2 60 C2
Lansdown Ct BS23 48 F8
Lansdowne Pl BA9 216 C4
Lansdowne Rd TA2 213 A6
Lansdown Gdns BS22 32 B5
Lansdown Gr BA1 228 B4
Lansdown Grove Ct BA1 228 B4
Lansdown Grove Lodge BA1 228 B4
Lansdown Ho BA1 27 F1
Lansdown Hts BA1 27 F1
Lansdown La
Bath BA1 27 B4
Upton Cheyney BS30 26 D8
Lansdown Mans BA1 228 B4
Lansdown Pk BA1 27 E3
Lansdown Pl
Bristol BS8 226 A3
Frome BA11 119 D5
High Littleton BS39 59 D1
Lansdown Pl E BA1 228 B4
Lansdown Pl W [1] BA1 27 F1
Lansdown Rd
Bath BA1 27 E2
Bristol BS8 226 A3
Saltford BS31 25 E3
Lansdown View
Bath BA2 44 C5
Faulkland BA3 80 D1
Timsbury BA2 60 C2
Tunley BA2 61 B4
Lanthony Cl BS24 50 A8
Lapwing Cl
Minehead TA24 201 C5
Portishead BS20 2 F6
Lapwing Gdns BS22 31 F1
Larch Ave TA20 223 B5
Larch Cl
Bridgwater TA6 209 D6
Churchill BS40 53 A5
Nailsea BS48 9 A2
Taunton TA1 213 D2
Larch Ct BA3 97 D8
Larches The BS22 32 A3
Larchfield Cl BA11 120 B7
Larchfield Trad Est TA19 221 B1
Larchgrove Cres BS22 31 F1
Larchgrove Wlk BS22 31 F1
Larchwood Ct BA3 79 A3
Lark Cl BA3 97 B8
LARKHALL 28 C2
Larkhall Pl BA1 28 C2
Larkhall Terr BA1 28 C2
Larkhill Rd
Locking BS24 50 B6
Yeovil BA21 218 D7
Lark Pl BA1 44 D7
Lark Rd BS22 31 F1
Larks Mdw DT10 190 C4
Larkspur Cl TA1 213 C1
Larkspur Cres BA21 218 D7
Larkspur Ct TA2 212 D7
Larspur Rd TA6 208 E1
Larviscombe Cl TA4 202 D4
Larviscombe Rd TA4 202 D4
Lasbury Gr BS13 22 C5
Lascot Hill BS28 108 C5
LATCHAM 108 F4
Latcham Dro BS27, BS28 109 A4
Latches La BS27 90 D3
Latchmoor Ho BS13 22 A8
Late Broads BA15 64 D7
LATTIFORD 176 D5
Lauder Ct DT9 217 D2
LAUNCHERLEY 140 B5
Launcherley Cross BA5 140 A6
Launcherley Rd BA4, BA5 140 B5
Launder Cl BA6 206 E4
Laura Pl BA2 228 C3
Laurel Ave TA9 86 A2
Laurel Cl
East Coker BA22 197 B8
Frome BA11 120 B7
Taunton TA1 213 C1
Laurel Dr
Nailsea BS48 8 F2
Paulton BS39 77 E5
Weston-Super-Mare BS23 48 E2
Laurel Gdns
Chard TA20 223 B5
Timsbury BA2 60 B1
Yatton BS49 17 B1
Laurel La BA22 174 F3
Laurel St BA6 140 A1
Laurels The
Churchill BS25 52 F4
Crewkerne TA18 224 D7
Wembdon TA6 208 C6
Weston-Super-Mare BS23 48 E2
Westwood BA15 64 F3
Laurel Terr BS49 17 B1
Lavender Cl BS22 32 A5
Lavender Ct
Frome BA11 120 B7
Street BA16 207 B4
Lavender Gr TA1 212 C3
LAVERLEY 140 C2
Laverley Cotts BA6 140 C2
Laverock Ct TA1 212 E5
Lavers Ct TA12 186 A7
Laver's La TA20 198 F5
Lavers Oak TA12 185 E7
LAVERTON 100 F7
Lavington Cl BS21 6 B1
LAWFORD 151 B7
Lawfords Gate BS2 227 C3
Lawfords Gate Ho [17] BS2 227 C3
Lawford St BS2 227 C3
Law La
Drayton TA10 171 F3
Langport TA10 172 A3
Lawn La
Galhampton BA22 175 D8
Shapwick TA7 137 F1
Lawn Mdw TA3 169 C3
Lawnmoor La TA10 184 C6
Lawn Rd TA2 212 C8
Lawnside BS48 19 B5
Lawns The
Bristol BS11 4 E7
Combe St Nicholas TA20 193 D6
Weston-Super-Mare BS22 32 B3
Yatton BS49 17 A1
Lawn The [1] TA21 222 D6
Lawpool Ct [12] BA5 203 D4
Lawrence Cl
Burnham-on-S TA8 104 D5
Highbridge TA9 104 F4
Somerton TA11 211 D3
Weston-Super-Mare BS22 31 E2
Lawrence Hayes BA9 216 D3
Lawrence Hill BA9 216 A2
Lawrence Hill Bsns Ctr BA9 216 B3
Lawrence Mews BS22 31 E2
Lawrence Rd
Coleford BA3 116 F7
Weston-Super-Mare BS22 31 E2
Wrington BS40 35 E2
Laws Dr BS24 49 F7
Lawson Cl
[5] Martock TA12 185 E6
Saltford BS31 25 C2
Lawyer's Hill TA5 152 C7
Lax Ct BA5 203 B4
Laxton Cl TA1 213 D5
Laxton Rd TA1 213 E5
Laxton Way BA2 79 D7
Laycock Hill DT9 217 D7
Layfield La TA3 170 C3
LAYMORE 199 C7
Layne Terr TA18 196 B8
Lays Bsns Ctr BS31 24 C4
Lays Dro BS31 24 C5
Lays La BS40 54 D4
Lays The BA11 101 E5
Leach Cl BS21 6 D1
Leaches Cl BA22 186 B6
Leach Rd TA20 223 D7
Leach's Field TA2 168 D8
Lea Cl BA21 219 B8
Lea Croft BS13 22 A4
Leading Edge The BS8 226 B2
Leadon Gr TA1 213 D4
Leafield Cl TA2 168 B5
Leafy Way BS24 50 B4
Lea Grove Rd BS21 6 C4
Leaholme Gdns BS14 23 A3
Lear's La BA9 177 C6
Leat The [8] TA4 167 F8
Leawood Ct [3] BS23 30 C1
Leaze Cl BA11 119 D5
Leaze Dro BA5 139 A7
Leaze Ho BA11 119 D5
Leaze House Mews BA11 119 D5
Leaze La
Blagdon BS40 72 E8
West Chinnock TA18 196 B8
Yeovil BA21 219 F4
Leazemoor La TA10 172 B8
Leaze Rd BA11 119 D5
Leaze The
Radstock BA3 97 D8
Rode BA2 82 C1
Leazeway Dro TA7 155 C1
Lecher La DT8, TA18 196 B1
Leda Ave BS14 23 A7
Leedham Rd BS24 50 C5
LEEFORD 122 B5
Leeford La EX35 122 B5
Leeming Way BS11 4 C8
Lee Pk TA21 180 F7
Leeside BS20 2 C5
Leet Ct DT9 225 B2
Leeward Cl TA6 209 C4
Leewood Rd BS23 30 F1
Leffman Ct TA11 211 C4
Leggar The TA6 209 A6
Legion Rd BA21 218 F6
Leg La BS40 54 B3
Leg Of Mutton Rd BA6 206 E6
Leg Sq BA4 205 C6
Leg Square Ct BA4 205 C6
Leigh Cl BA1 28 A2
Leigh Court Bsns Ctr BS8 5 A2
Leigh Furlong Rd BA16 207 B4
Leigh La
Cold Ashton BA1 13 B3
Crowcombe TA4 151 A7
Halstock BA22 197 C3
Winsford TA22 147 C2
Winsham TA20 199 A8
LEIGHLAND CHAPEL 149 C7
Leigh Rd
Bristol BS8 226 B4
Leigh u M BA11 117 C2
Street BA16 207 C5
Taunton TA2 213 B8
Leigh St BA3 116 F3
LEIGHTON 142 E6
Leighton Cl BA4 141 E1
Leighton Cres BS24 67 A8
Leighton La BA4 141 E1
Leighton Lane Ind Est BA4 141 E1
Leighton Rd BA1 27 A3
LEIGH UPON MENDIP 116 F3
Leigh upon Mendip Fst Sch BA3 117 A3
Leigh View Rd BS20 2 E7
Leighwood Dr BS48 8 B1
LEIGH WOODS 11 D6
Leigh Woods Forest Walks★ BS8 5 C1
Leigh Woods National Nature Reserve★ BS8 11 D8
Leinster Ave BS4 22 D8
Lemon La BS2 227 C4
Lenover Gdns BS13 22 B4
Lenthay Cl DT9 225 C2
Lenthay Ct DT9 225 C3
Lenthay Rd DT9 225 B2
Leonard Houlden Ct [7] TA2 213 A8
Leonard La BS1 227 A3
Leonard's Barton BA11 119 E6
Leopold Bldgs BA1 228 C4
Lerburne The BS28 108 D4
Leslie Ave TA2 212 E6
Leslie Rise BA15 64 F3
Les Rosiers Gdns BA9 216 C4
Lester Dr BS22 32 A3
Lester La DT9 176 A2
Letham Ct TA19 221 B4
Lethbridge Pk TA4 151 D1
Lethbridge Rd BA5 203 C4
Level La DT9 176 A2
Level View TA10 172 C5
Leversedge Rd BA11 120 A7
LEWCOMBE 197 E2
Lewins Mead BS1 227 A3
Lewis Cres BA11 119 F6
Lewisham Gr BS23 49 A8
Lewis Rd
Bristol BS13 22 A8
Taunton TA2 212 E7
Lewis's Dro BA5 138 E7
Lewmond Ave BA5 203 F5
Leycroft Cl TA1 213 B4
Leycroft Gr TA1 213 B4
Leycroft Rd TA1 213 B4
Leyland Wlk BS13 21 F4
Leys Hill BA11 120 A6
Leys La BA11 119 F7
Leys The BS21 6 B1
Leystone Cl BA11 120 A6
Leyton Dr TA6 209 D6
Lias Rd BA16 207 B4
Liberty Gdns BS1 226 C1
Liberty La BS40 54 E2
Liberty Pl TA6 209 B4
Liberty The BA5 203 E5
Liddon Hill TA18 195 C5
Liddymore La
Watchet TA23 202 D5
Williton TA4, TA23 202 E4
Liddymore Rd TA23 202 C6
Lightermans Cl TA24 201 B7
Lightgate TA13 220 D5
Lightgate La TA13 220 D4

Lightgate Rd TA13 220 D4
Lilac Cl TA1 213 C2
Lilac Ct BS31 24 C4
Lilac Terr BA3 78 C2
Lilac Way BS22 32 A5
Lilian Terr BS39 77 E5
Lillebonne Cl TA21 222 F6
Lillesdon Terr TA3 170 A2
Lillington Cl BA3 79 B2
Lillington Rd BA3 79 B2
Lillington Way TA20 223 C5
Lilly Batch BA11 119 F7
Lillycombe La TA3, EX15 191 B8
Lillypool Cheese & Cider Farm★ BS25 70 F6
LILSTOCK 133 F7
Lily La BA8 176 E1
Limber Rd BA22 218 A6
Limbers La BA5 139 B8
Limbury 2 TA12 185 E6
Limbury Cotts 3 TA12 185 E6
Limebreach Wood BS48 8 D3
Limeburn Hill BS40 38 E5
Lime Cl
Frome BA11 120 B7
Locking BS24 50 B4
Minehead TA24 200 D7
Street BA16 207 C5
Weston-Super-Mare BS22 32 A1
Lime Cres TA1 213 C2
Lime Ct BS31 24 C4
Lime Gr
Bath BA2 45 B6
Shepton Mallet BA4 205 A6
Lime Grove Gdns BA2 45 B6
Lime Kiln BA21 218 C5
Limekiln La
Bath BA2 45 F4
Chard, Forton TA20 223 D1
Chard, Lydmarsh TA20 194 C3
Cricket St Thomas TA20 194 E2
Leigh u M BA11 117 C3
Oakhill BA3 114 E5
Stoke St Michael BA3 115 F4
Tatworth TA20 193 F1
Lime Kiln La
Castle Cary BA7 214 E4
Clevedon BS21 6 D3
Henstridge BA8 190 A6
Wookey Hole BA5 203 B7
Lime Kiln Rd BS1 226 B2
Limekilns Cl BS31 24 F5
Limepits La TA10 172 D5
Limerick Cl DT9 217 D2
Limerick La BA11 101 F2
Limes Cl TA4 202 E3
Lime St
Nether Stowey TA5 134 B2
Stogursey TA5 134 C6
Limestone Hill TA5 135 C1
Lime Terr BA3 78 D1
Lime Tree Ave BA20 218 E2
Lime Tree Cl TA6 209 D4
Lime Tree Gr BS20 4 D3
LIMINGTON 174 A1
Limington Rd BA22 173 E1
Limousin Way TA6 209 A1
Limpetshell La TA4 202 E3
LIMPLEY STOKE 64 A6
Limpley Stoke Rd BA15 64 D6
Linch La BA4 142 D2
Lincolm Hill TA19 184 E4
Lincoln Cl BS31 24 C4
Lincombe Rd BA3 97 D8
Lincott View BA2 79 C8
Linden Ave BS23 49 B8
Linden Cl
Bridgwater TA6 209 C4
Bristol BS14 23 E6
Frome BA11 119 D5
Radstock BA3 97 E8
Linden Ct BS21 6 D4
Linden Gdns BA1 44 D8
Linden Gr TA1 212 E5
Linden Hill TA21 222 A6
Linden Rd
Clevedon BS21 6 D4
Yeovil BA20 218 F5
Lindens The BS22 31 E4
Lindisfarne Cl BA15 64 E6
Lindsey Cl BS20 1 F4
Lindsey Cres 1 TA6 153 F3
Linemere Cl BS48 19 D6
Lines Way BS14 23 C3
Liney Rd TA7 154 F6
Lingfield Ave BA21 219 D7
Linham Rd TA6 208 F6
Linhay Cl EX15 179 E1
Linkhay TA20 198 D8
Linkhay Cl TA20 198 D8
Link La
Burrington BS40 53 F3
Monkton Farleigh BA15 46 F8
Linkmead BA3 96 F2
Link Rd
Nailsea BS48 8 F2
Portishead BS20 2 C5
Links Ct BS23 48 D4
Links Gdns TA8 84 F3
Linkside BS21 6 E6
Links Rd BS23 48 C2
Link The BS27 90 B8
Linley Cl
Bath BA2 44 A5
Bridgwater TA6 209 D7
Linleys The BA1 44 C7
Linne Ho BA2 44 A5
Linnet Cl
Taunton TA1 212 B4
Weston-Super-Mare BS22 31 E1
Linnet Gdns 5 BS20 2 F6
Linnet Way
Frome BA11 120 B6
Midsomer Norton BA3 97 B8
Linsvale Cl BA11 120 C5
Linsvale Dr BA11 120 C5
Lintern Cl BA4 159 C7
Linton's Wlk BS14 23 A7
Lion Cl BS48 8 D2
Lion D'angers TA4 210 D4
Lion Ho 20 BA4 205 B6
Lion Mews TA11 211 E4
Lipe Hill La TA3, TA4 168 B1
Lipe La TA3 169 C3
Lipgate Pl BS20 2 D3
Lippetts Way TA7 137 D1
Lippiat Hill BA3 80 C3
Lippiatt La
Cheddar BS27 90 C7
Shipham BS25 70 F8
Timsbury BA2 60 B3
Lippiatt The BS27 90 C8
LIPYEATE 97 E1
Lisieux Ct TA1 213 D2
Lisieux Way TA1 213 C3
Lisle Rd BS22 32 B4
Listercombe Cl TA19 221 C2
Lister Gr BA15 64 F3
Lister's Hill TA19 221 C2
LISTOCK 170 C2
Litfield Pl BS8 11 F7
Litfield Rd BS8 11 F8
Litt Hill BA3 75 F2
Little Ann St BS2, BS5 227 C4
Little Birch Croft BS14 23 A3
Little Bishop St BS2 227 B4
Littlebrook BS39 77 E6
Little Brooks La BA4 205 C4
Little Burrow Dro TA7 155 A1
Little Caroline Pl 4 BS8 11 F5
Little Cl TA2 212 C8
Little Elm Rd TA7 155 C4
Little England TA7 155 C2
Little Entry BA5 203 F5
Littlefield DT9 225 B3
Littlefield Cl BA16 156 E7
Littlefield La TA10 172 E4
Little Field La BA5 110 F7
Littlefields Ave BS29 51 B3
Littlefields La TA19 184 F3
Littlefields Rd BS29 51 B3
Littlefields Rise BS29 51 B3
Little George St
Bristol BS2 227 C4
Weston-Super-Mare BS23 48 E7
Little Gn BA5 111 A4
LITTLE GREEN 118 B6
Little Halt BS20 1 E4
Little Ham BS21 16 C8
Littleham Cotts TA3 181 E6
Little Headley Cl BS13 22 B7
LITTLE HILL 192 F8
LITTLE KEYFORD 119 E1
Little Keyford La BA11 119 E1
Little King St BS1 227 A2
Little La
Farmborough BA2 60 A6
Kingsbury Episcopi TA12 185 A7
Little Leaze La TA7 137 D2
Little Lester TA19 221 C2
LITTLE LONDON 114 F3
Little Marston Rd BA22 174 F1
Little Mdw
6 Bishops Lydeard TA4 167 F8
Ilchester BA22 173 E2
Little Mead TA14 185 F2
Little Mead Cl BS24 49 E3
Little Meadow End BS48 18 E8
Little Moor Rd TA9 106 F3
Littlemore Dro TA7 154 C3
LITTLE NORTON 186 A2
Little Orch
Cheddar BS27 90 C8
Street BA16 207 D7
Weston-Super-Mare BS23 48 D1
Little Orchard 34 TA12 185 E6
Little Paul St BS2 226 C4
Little Pen TA8 84 F5
Little Plover Cl TA24 201 C5
Little Sammons BA22 186 E5
Little Silver Ct TA23 202 C7
Little Silver La TA21 222 D2
Little St TA14 185 E2
Little Stanhope St BA1 228 A2
Little Stoke Rd BS9 5 E4
LITTLETON 38 D4
Littleton Hill TA11 211 E6
Littleton La
Wellow BA2 80 C7
Winford BS40 38 D5
Little Trumps BA22 186 B7
LITTLE WESTON 175 B4
Little Withey Mead BS9 5 F5
Little Wiveliscombe La TA4 165 D6
Littlewood BA11 143 C4
Littlewood Cl BS14 23 B3
Littlewood La BS49 18 C2
LITTON 75 F2
Litton BS24 49 A2
Liver Moor Dro TA11 156 E2
Livingstone Rd BA2 44 D5
Livingstone Terr BA2 228 A1
Livingstone Way TA2 212 B6
Llewellyns Almshouses 6 BA5 203 D4
Llewellyn Way BS22 32 B3
Lloyd Cl TA1 212 B1
Load La TA7 154 E5
Load Pool TA7 155 C2
Lobelia Cl TA9 104 D5
Lockemor Rd BS13 22 F4
Locketts Barton TA3 170 D7
Lockey Rd BA4 205 B4
Lock Gdns BS13 21 E7
LOCKING 50 A4
Locking Farm Ind Est BS24 50 A5
Locking Head Dro
Locking BS24 49 F5
Weston-Super-Mare BS24 50 A6
Locking Moor Rd
Locking BS24 50 B5
Weston-Super-Mare BS22 49 D8
Locking Prim Sch BS24 50 B4
Locking Rd BS22, BS23 49 B7
Lockingwell Rd BS31 24 D5
LOCKSBROOK 44 B6
Locksbrook Ct 8 BA1 44 B6
Locksbrook Rd
Bath BA1 44 C6
Weston-Super-Mare BS22 32 B5
Locksbrook Trad Est 7 BA1 44 B6
Lock's Hill BA11 119 F3
Lockside BS20 2 E7
Lockside Sq BS20 2 E7
Lock's La BA9 216 C4
Locks Way TA7 136 F3
Lockswell TA7 136 E4
Lockswell Cotts BA4 141 B1
Lockwood Ct 4 BA21 218 F7
Lockyer Dro TA7 156 A5
Lodes La TA2 168 E8
Lodge Cl
Taunton TA1 212 A2
Wellington TA21 222 D6
Yatton BS49 34 B8
Lodge Cotts TA3 181 D6
Lodge Ct
Bristol BS9 5 E4
Castle Cary BA7 214 B4
Lodge Dr
Long Ashton BS41 11 B2
Weston-Super-Mare BS23 31 A1
Lodge Gdns BA2 44 D1
Lodge Hill
Berkley BA11, BA13 120 F5
Bratton Seymour BA9 176 A7
Somerton TA11 211 F4
Westbury-sub-Mendip BA5 110 D5
Yarlington BA9 175 F7
Lodge Hill Ind Pk BA5 110 D5
Lodge La
Axminster EX13 198 B2
Wraxall BS48 9 B2
Lodge Pl BS1 226 C3
Lodge Rd
Horningsham BA12 144 D4
Kingsdon TA11 173 D4
Lodge Rocks TA24 131 D3
Lodge St BS1 226 C3
Lodges The BA3 96 D1
LODWAY 4 B5
Lodway BS20 4 C4
Lodway Cl BS20 4 C5
Lodway Gdns BS20 4 C4
Lodwells Orch TA3 170 B4
Lombardy Cl 5 BS22 49 E8
London Cross TA4 151 E4
London Dro BA6, BS28 138 D7
London Ho TA4 210 C4
London Rd
Bath BA1 228 C4
Milborne Port DT9 217 E1
London Rd E BA1 29 A3
London Rd W BA1 28 E2
London Sq
28 Martock TA12 185 E6
Portishead BS20 2 E7
London St BA1 228 C4
Longacre BS21 16 B8
Long Acre BA4 205 C4
Longacre Cl TA2 212 E7
Longacre Dro TA7 154 D7
Long Acre Ho BA1 228 C4
Longacre La TA19 194 F6
Long Acre Rd BS14 23 A3
Long Acres Cl BS9 5 D7
LONGALLER 168 B4
LONG ASHTON 11 A1
Long Ashton Bsns Pk BS41 11 B1
Long Ashton Rd BS41 11 B2
Long Ave BS21 6 B2
Long Barnaby BA3 78 A2
Longbottom BS25 71 A6
Longbridge 16 BA4 205 B6
Longbrook Trad Est BS3 11 E3
Long Cl
Ilminster TA19 221 C2
Yeovil BA21 218 C5
Longcombe Dr BA12 144 F6
LONGCROFT 219 A8
Longcroft Rd BA21 219 C6
LONG CROSS 37 D7
Long Cross
Bristol BS11 4 F8
Doulting BA4 141 F8
Felton BS40 37 D7
Nether Stowey TA5 134 A3
Long Cross Bottom
Doulting BA3 142 A8
Stoke St Michael BA3 116 A1
Longdown Dr BS22 32 B4
Long Dro
Broadway TA19, TA20 183 A2
Buckland St Mary TA20 182 F2
Glastonbury BA5 139 E4
Westbury-sub-Mendip BS27 110 A4
Long Eaton Dr BS14 23 B7
Longfellow Ave BA2 44 F4
Longfellow Rd BA3 97 C8
Longfield BA11 118 A7
Longfield Cl TA4 202 E2
Longforth Rd TA21 222 D6
Longforward Hill
Dinnington TA17 195 A8
Seavington St Mary TA19 184 D1
Longforward La
Dinnington TA17 195 B8
Seavington St Mary TA19 184 D1
Long Furlong La
East Coker BA22 197 C8
Long Sutton TA10 172 E5
Long Ground BA11 119 F3
Long Hay Cl BA2 44 B5
LONGHEDGE 144 E7
Long Hill
Clewer BS28 89 D2
Shepton Mallet BA4 141 C8
Long Holcombe Cross EX36 145 E6
LONGHOUSE 61 D5
Long La
Backwell BS48 19 C2
Bourton SP8 161 D1
Cucklington BA9 177 D5
Dinder BA5 140 D7
Felton BS40 37 B5
Fishpond Bottom DT6 199 B1
Walton BA16 156 D7
Wanstrow BA4 142 F5
West Chinnock TA18 196 B7
Wheddon Cross TA24 129 C2
Wootton Courtenay TA24 129 E8
Wrington BS40 36 B2
Long Lakes TA4 202 E4
Longlands La
East Coker BA22 197 C8
Westbury-sub-Mendip BA5 110 E7
Longleat Cl BA11 119 F3
Longleat Ct BA11 119 E4
Longleat Forest Holiday Village★ BA12 144 F5
Longleat House★ BA12 144 D6
Longleat La BA3 116 C8
Longleat Rd BA3 116 B8
Longleat Rly★ BA12 144 C6
Longleat Safari & Adventure Park★ BA12 144 D6
Longleaze Gdns BS24 49 F3
LONG LOAD 172 E2
Long Load Rd TA12 185 E8
Longman's Lea BA4 159 C7
Longmarsh La TA10 172 E6
Longmead TA4 165 E8
Long Mead BA21 218 C5
Longmead Cl
Norton St Philip BA2 81 F4
Taunton TA1 212 D2
Wellington TA21 222 B8
Longmead Cotts TA21 222 B8
Longmead Croft BS13 21 F4
Longmeadow Rd BS31 24 C4
Longmead Way TA1 212 D2
Long Moor Dro TA7, TA9 137 A7
Long Orchard Hill TA19 221 E3
Longreach Gr BS14 23 D6
Long Ride Dro BA6 157 F3
Longridge Way BS24 49 F7
Long Row BS1 227 B2
Long Run BA22 186 C2
Longrun La TA1 212 D4
Longs Field TA3 170 C4
Long St
Croscombe BA5 204 B7
Galhampton BA22 175 E8
High Ham TA10 156 A1
Sherborne DT9 225 E4
Williton TA4 202 E3
Longstone Ave TA6 209 C5
Longstone Cl TA5 134 B2
Longstrings La TA18 224 C8
LONG SUTTON 172 F4
Long Sutton CE Prim Sch TA10 172 E4
Long-Thorn BS48 18 F6
Longthorne Pl BA2 44 F2
Long Thorn La BS40 55 E7
Longton Grove Rd 3 BS23 48 E8
Longton Ind Est BS23 48 F6
Long Valley Rd BA2 43 F5
Longvernal BA3 77 F1
Longvernal Prim Sch BA3 77 F1
Longway Ave BS13, BS14 22 F4
Longwood Ho BS8 10 D4
Longwood La
Burlescombe TA21 179 C4
Long Ashton BS8, BS41 10 F4
Lonsdale Ave BS23 48 F4
Lonsdale Rd TA5 135 C2
Look's La BA6 157 C6
Looseall La TA22 163 D8
LOPEN 185 A1
Lopen Head TA13 220 A1
Lopen La TA13 220 C1
Lopen Rd TA13, TA17 195 D8
Lordsleaze La TA20 223 D3
Lords Meadow La 5 EX16 164 B1
Lords Way TA6 208 E6
Loretto Gdns 5 EX13 198 A1
Loretto Rd EX13 198 A1
Lorne Pl BA5 203 E5
Lorne Rd BA2 44 D6
Lotment Hill TA11 173 D5
LOTTISHAM 158 D5
Lottisham La BA4, BA6 158 D6
Lottisham Rd BA6 158 C6
Lotts' Ave BS48 19 B5
Lotus Ct BS22 31 C1
Louisa Gate TA22 163 F7
Louisa St BS2 227 C2
Loundshay La TA4 167 A4
Louvigne Cl TA8 104 C7
Love La
Burnham-on-S TA8 104 C7
Ilminster TA19 221 C3
Marnhull DT10 190 F6
Shepton Beauchamp TA19 184 E4
Wincanton BA9 216 F5
Lovelands DT2 197 A1
Lovelinch Gdns BS41 10 F1
Lovell Dr BS39 57 C4
Lovells Mead DT10 190 F6
Lovells Mill BS39 57 D4
Lovells The BS20 4 B4
Loveridge La TA20 198 D8
Lovers La BA3, BS39 78 A5
Lovers Wlk BA5 203 D5
Lovers' Wlk
4 Cannington TA5 135 B2
Weston-Super-Mare BS23 48 D8
Loves Hill BA2 60 A1
Loves La BA14 83 C7
Love's La BA2 59 F6
LOVINGTON 158 F1
Lovington CE Prim Sch BA7 158 F2
Lowbourne BS14 22 F6
Lower Acreman St 3 DT9 225 D3
Lower Actis BA6 206 E3
LOWER AISHOLT 152 C6
Lower Ansford BA7 214 B7
Lower Backway BA10 215 E6
Lower Batch BS40 39 B3
Lower Bath Rd TA6 209 B6
Lower Beadon TA16 195 F7
Lower Borough Walls BA1 228 C2
Lowerbourne Terr TA24 124 A3
Lower Boyston La DT9 188 F5
Lower Bristol Rd
Bath BA2 44 B6
Clutton BS39 58 F4
Lower Burlington Rd BS20 2 E7
LOWER BURROW 184 F7
Lower Camden Pl BA1 228 C4
LOWER CANADA 49 F2
Lower Castle St BS1 227 B3
Lower Chapel Ct BA5 113 A1
Lower Cheriton La BA8 176 D4
LOWER CHILTON CANTELO 187 C8
Lower Church La BS2 227 A3
Lower Church Rd BS23 48 D8
LOWER CLAVERHAM 17 F2
Lower Claverham BS49 17 F3
Lower Clifton Hill BS8 226 B2
Lower College St BS1 226 C2
Lower Coombses TA20 198 D8
Lower Cross EX15 179 C1
Lower Down Rd BS20 2 B5
LOWER DOWNSIDE 205 C7
LOWER DURSTON 169 F7
Lower East Coker Rd BA20 218 F1
Lower East Hayes BA1 45 B8
LOWER FAILAND 10 A8
Lower Fairfield TA4 166 F5
Lower Fairmead Rd BA21 219 D8
Lower Fallow Cl BS14 22 F3
Lower Farm DT9 187 E4
Lower Farm La BA2 43 B7
Lowerfield La TA19 184 E1
Lower Foxmoor Rd TA21 222 B5
Lower Gay St BS2 227 A4
LOWER GODNEY 138 F5
Lower Guinea St BS1 227 A1
Lower Gully Dro BS28 89 F3
Lower Gunville DT9 217 D2
LOWER HALSTOCK LEIGH 197 B2
LOWER HARMSWELL 12 C3
Lower Hedgemead Rd BA1 228 C4
Lower High St BS11 4 D7
LOWER HOLDITCH 198 D5
Lower Holway Cl TA1 213 D2
Lower Hyde Rd TA15 186 B4
Lower Innox BA11 119 E6
LOWER KEYFORD 119 F3
Lower Keyford BA11 119 F3
Lower Kingsbury DT9 217 D3
Lower Kingsdown Rd SN13 29 F3
Lower Knowles Rd BS21 6 C2
Lower La
Shepton Mallet BA4 205 C6

Lower La *continued*
Weston Town BA4 142 E5
Lower Lamb St BS1 226 C2
LOWER LANGFORD 53 C5
LOWER LEIGH 207 C6
Lower Linden Rd BS21 6 D3
Lower Lodfin EX16 164 B2
Lower Marshfield Rd
TA24 201 B6
LOWER MARSTON 143 E7
Lower Maudlin St BS1 227 A3
Lower Mdw TA19 221 A4
Lower Meadow Rd TA24 201 B5
LOWER MERRIDGE 152 C5
Lower Middle St TA1 212 F4
LOWER MILTON 203 B8
Lower New Rd BS27 90 A7
Lower Northend BA1 28 F5
Lower North St BS27 90 B8
Lower North Town La
BA22 175 D7
Lower Norton La
Weston-Super-Mare BS22 31 E4
Weston-Super-Mare, Norton
BS22 31 C4
Lower Notlake Dro BS28 89 E4
LOWER ODCOMBE 186 D2
Lower Odcombe BA22 186 C2
Lower Oldfield Pk BA2 228 A1
Lower Orch TA19 184 C5
Lower Parade Ground Rd
BS24 50 C5
Lower Park La TA24 129 E1
Lower Park Row BS1 227 A3
LOWER PEASEDOWN 79 B8
Lower Pk TA24 200 E7
Lower Queen's BS21 6 D3
Lower Rd
Hinton Blewett BS39 75 E6
Horsington BA8 176 D3
Kingsdon TA11 173 D5
Stalbridge DT10 190 C4
Woolavington TA7 136 E4
Lower Ream BA21 218 C5
LOWER ROADWATER 131 D1
Lower Rocke's Cotts
BA6 157 D4
LOWER RUDGE 102 D4
Lower Severalls Gdn★
TA18 196 A6
Lowerside La BA6 206 D7
Lowerside Rd BA6 206 E6
Lower Silk Mill BA4 204 F6
LOWER SOMERTON 211 E3
Lower Somerton TA11 211 F3
Lower St
Buckland Dinham BA11 100 A2
Carhampton TA24 131 B4
Chewton Mendip BA3 94 F7
Curry Mallet TA3 183 C8
Merriott TA16 195 F7
Pilton BA4 140 F3
Rode BA11 101 E8
Upton Noble BA4 142 F2
West Chinnock TA18 196 B8
Lower Stoke BA2, BA3 64 A8
LOWER STRATTON 220 E1
LOWER STRODE 56 A8
Lower Strode BS40 56 A7
Lower Strode Rd BS21 16 A7
LOWER SWAINSWICK 28 C3
LOWER TIPPACOTT 122 A4
Lower Touches TA20 223 E5
Lower Town
Montacute TA15 186 B4
Sampford Peverell EX16 178 D1
Lower Turners Barn La
BA20 218 F2
LOWER VELLOW 132 D1
Lower Vellow TA4 132 D2
LOWER VEXFORD 150 F6
LOWER WEACOMBE 132 E3
LOWER WEARE 88 D8
LOWER WESTFORD 222 A6
LOWER WESTHOLME 140 C3
Lower Westholme Rd
BA4 140 D3
LOWER WESTON 44 C7
LOWER WHATLEY 118 D3
Lower Whitelands BA3 79 B3
Lower Woodcock St
BA7 214 C5
LOWER WOOLSTON 175 F6
Lower Wraxhill Rd BA20 218 F1
LOWER WRITHLINGTON 79 C3
LOW HAM 172 B8
Low Ham Rd TA10 172 B8
Lowlands Terr TA1 212 B4
Lowman Cross EX16 178 B2
Lowmoor Ind Est TA21 222 B8
Low's Hill La DT9 188 B3
Lowsome La DT9 188 A5
Lowther Rd BA21 219 E7
LOWTON 181 B5
Lowtrow Cross TA4 165 A8
LOW WATER 119 E6
Loxhams TA10 156 B2
Loxleigh Ave TA6 209 B4
Loxleigh Gdns TA6 209 B4
Loxley Batch TA7 156 A8
Loxley Gdns BA2 44 C4
Loxley Terr TA6 208 F7
LOXTON 68 C4
Loxton Dr BA2 44 B6
Loxton Rd BS23 48 F2
Loxton Sq BS14 23 A6
Lubborn La BA6 158 B5
LUCCOMBE 129 D7
Lucerne Cres TA6 208 D1
Luckes La TA4 132 E3
Luckington Cross BA11 98 B2
Lucklands Rd BA1 27 C1
Luckley Ave BS13 22 C5
LUCKWELL BRIDGE 129 C1
Luckwells La TA24 129 E2
Lucott Cross TA24 128 C6
Ludbourne Rd DT9 225 E3
Ludlow Ave TA2 213 A8
Ludlow Cl
Bridgwater TA6 209 A2
Frome BA11 120 C6
Keynsham BS31 24 D5
LUDNEY 194 F7
Ludney Cross TA19 194 F7
Ludney La
Dinnington TA17 195 A8
Ilminster TA19 194 F7
Ludwells Orch BS39 77 E5
LUFTON 186 D3
Lufton Coll of FE BA22 186 D4
Lufton Heights Commerce Pk
BA22 218 A7
Lufton Trad Est BA22 218 A7
Lufton Way BA22 218 A6
Luggard's Cross BS21 8 C4
Lugshorn La TA11 211 C8
Luke's Cl BA3 78 F3
Lukes Gdn TA24 131 B4
Luke St EX16 161 B1
LULLINGTON 101 A4
Lullington La BA11 101 B3
LULSGATE BOTTOM 37 A8
Lulsgate Rd BS13 22 A8
Lulworth Rd BS31 24 E4
Lundy Dr TA8 104 B5
Luns Hill BA6 157 F1
Lunty Mead BS48 18 F6
Lupin Way BA22 218 B5
LUPPITT 191 B1
Lush Path DT9 225 E4
Lusty Gdns BA10 215 E5
Luttrell Cl TA2 213 B8
Luttrell Gdns TA24 200 F6
Luvers La BS40 54 D1
LUXBOROUGH 148 E8
Luxborough Rd TA6 208 B4
Lux Furlong BS9 5 B7
Luxhay Cl TA2 213 B8
LUXTON 192 A6
Luxton's La BA3, BA4 116 F1
Lyatt La BA5 140 E8
LYATTS 197 B6
Lyatts Hill BA22 197 B6
Lychgate Pk BS24 50 A4
Lyddieth Ct BA15 64 E7
Lyddon Cl TA21 222 D4
Lyddon Rd BS22 32 B3
Lyddon's Hill TA22 148 A1
Lyddons Mead TA20 223 E4
Lydeard Cross TA5 152 E3
Lydeard Down Hill TA4 151 B4
Lydeard Mead TA4 167 E8
LYDEARD ST
LAWRENCE 151 B3
Lydeard St Lawrence Com
Prim Sch TA4 151 A3
Lyde Ct BA21 219 E6
Lyde Gn BA2 81 E5
Lyde La BA21 219 F6
Lyde Rd BA21 219 E7
LYDFORD FAIR PLACE 158 C3
LYDMARSH 194 C3
Lydon La TA4 165 D5
LYE CROSS 36 C1
Lye Cross Rd BS40 36 C1
Lyefield Rd BS22 31 E4
LYE HOLE 36 E2
Lye Hole La BS40 36 D2
Lye La BA4 158 F6
Lye Mead BS40 38 A6
LYE'S GREEN 121 B1
Lyes The BS49 34 D3
Lyewater TA18 224 B6
Lyme Gdns BA1 44 B7
Lyme Rd
Axminster EX13 198 A1
Bath BA1 44 B7
Crewkerne TA18 224 B4
Lymore Ave BA2 44 C5
Lymore Gdns BA2 44 C5
Lymore Terr BA2 44 C4
LYMPSHAM 67 B1
Lympsham CE Fst Sch
BS24 67 B1
Lympsham Gn BA2 62 D8
Lympsham Rd BS24 67 B1
Lynbrook BS41 10 F1
Lynbrook La BA2 44 F3
Lynch Cl BS22 31 F3
Lynchcombe La BA5 110 F6
Lynch Cres BS25 69 F7
Lynch Hill BA3 96 A3
Lynch La
Cheddar BS27 90 C8
Hardington Mandeville
BA22 197 A6
Westbury-sub-Mendip
BA5 110 D8
Lynchmead BS25 70 A7
Lynch The BS25 69 F7
Lyncombe Hall BA2 45 A4
LYNCOMBE HILL 45 A4
Lyncombe Hill BA2 228 C1
LYNCOMBE VALE 45 A3
Lyncombe Vale BA2 45 B4
Lyncombe Vale Rd BA2 45 A4
Lyndale Ave
Bridgwater TA6 208 E5
Bristol BS9 5 D5
Lynde Cl BS13 22 B4
Lyndhurst Cres TA6 208 C5
Lyndhurst Gr TA12 185 D7
Lyndhurst Rd
Bath BA2 44 C6
Bristol BS9 5 F7
Keynsham BS31 24 F3
Midsomer Norton BA3 97 B8
Weston-Super-Mare BS23 48 E4
Lyndhurst Terr BA1 228 C4
Lynfield Pk BA1 27 C1
Lynfield Rd BA11 119 D5
Lynford La TA11 158 C1
LYNFORD-ON-FOSSE 158 C2
LYNG 170 C7
LYNGFORD 213 A7
Lyngford Cres TA2 213 A7
Lyngford La TA2 168 F6
Lyngford Park Prim Sch
TA2 213 B8
Lyngford Pl TA2 213 A7
Lyngford Rd TA2 213 A7
Lyngford Sq TA2 213 A7
Lynmouth Cl BS22 32 A2
Lynor Cl TA1 213 D3
Lynton Cl BS20 2 E4
Lynton Rd
Burnham-on-S TA8 104 B6
Midsomer Norton BA3 97 B8
Lynwood Cl
Frome BA11 119 D4
Midsomer Norton BA3 97 A8
Lynx Cres BS24 49 B2
Lynx Trad Est BA20 218 D3
Lynx West Trad Est
BA20 218 C3
Lyons Court Rd BS14 23 D7
Lyons Ct BS23 48 F7
Lype La TA22 147 E4
Lypstone Cl BS24 50 A8
Lypyatt La BA6 206 F4
Lysander Rd BA20 218 E3
Lysander Ret Pk BA20 219 A3
Lysander Road Rdbt
BA20 218 C3
Lyster Cl BA22 173 E1
Lyster Gdns BA22 173 E1
Lyte's Cary★ TA11 173 F5
Lytes Cary Rd BS31 25 A3
Lytton Gdns BA2 44 B4
Lytton Gr BS31 25 A5
Lyveden Gdns BS13 22 B5
Lyvedon Way BS41 11 B1

M

McAdam Way BS1 11 F5
MacAulay Bldgs BA2 45 C4
McCrae Rd BS24 50 B5
McCreath Cl [3] TA6 153 F3
Mc Creery Rd DT9 225 D6
Macey's Rd BS13 22 D3
Macfarlane Chase BS23 49 A5
Machine Cross TA22 163 F6
Macies The BA1 27 B3
MACKHAM 191 A4
McKinley Terr TA23 131 E4
Mackley La BA2 81 E3
MacLeod Cl BS21 6 A2
Macquarie Farm Cl BS49 17 A1
Macrae Rd BS20 4 E4
Madam La
Weston-Super-Mare BS22 31 F2
Weston-Super-Mare BS22 32 A3
Weston-Super-Mare BS22 32 A4
Madam's Paddock BS40 39 B3
Madden Cl TA8 104 C7
Maddocks Pk BA9 216 C3
Maddocks Slade TA8 104 A8
Madeira Ct BS23 48 C8
Madeira Rd
Clevedon BS21 6 D3
Weston-Super-Mare BS23 30 C1
Madgeon La TA20 192 E8
Madison Ct [5] TA18 224 C6
Madwoman's La BS28 108 B2
Maesbury Rd BS31 25 A2
Maesdown Cl BA4 141 E2
Maesdown Cotts BA4 141 E2
Maesdown Hill BA4 141 E3
Maes Down Ho [10] BA4 205 B6
Maesdown Rd
Doulting BA4 141 E4
Evercreech BA4 141 E2
Maesknoll La BS14, BS39 40 B8
Magdalana Ct BS1 227 B1
Magdalen Ave BA2 228 B1
Magdalene Cl BA6 206 D4
Magdalene Ct [9] TA1 212 F4
Magdalene La [10] TA1 212 F4
Magdalene Rd BA3 79 C2
Magdalene St
Glastonbury BA6 206 D4
Taunton TA1 212 F4
Magdalen La BA14 83 B7
Magdalen Rd BA2 228 B1
Magdalen Way BS22 32 A3
Magellan Cl BS22 31 F4
Maggs Folly BS39 59 D2
Maggs Hill BA2 60 B2
Maggs La
Castle Cary BA7 214 C7
Whitchurch BS14 23 C4
Maglands Rd TA23 202 D6
Magna Cl BA21 219 D8
Magnolia Ave BS22 32 A1
Magnolia Cl
Frome BA11 120 C7
Weston-Super-Mare BS22 49 E7
Magnolia Rd BA3 78 E1
Magnolia Tree Rd TA6 209 E5
Magpie Cl
Burnham-on-S TA8 85 B1
Weston-Super-Mare BS22 49 E8
Maiden Beech Mid Sch
TA18 224 B4
MAIDEN BRADLEY 144 C1
MAIDENBROOK 213 D7
Maidenbrook La TA2 169 A6
Maiden Croft La BA6 139 D2
MAIDEN HEAD 21 F1
Maidenhead Cross EX16 179 C2
Maidenhead Rd BS13 22 D3
Maiden Way BS11 4 C8
Maidstone Gr BS24 49 A1
Maincombe Cl TA18 224 C4
MAINES BATCH 35 E3
Main Rd
Brockley BS49 18 D2
Burrowbridge TA7 154 F1
Cannington TA5 135 C1
Coxley BA5 139 E6
Flax Bourton BS48 19 F7
Huntspill TA9 136 B8
Hutton BS24 49 E2
Kilve TA5 133 C5
Lyng TA3, TA7 170 C7
Middlezoy TA7 155 B3
Othery TA7 155 B2
Shapwick TA7 155 F8
Westhay BA6 138 B5
Westonzoyland TA7 154 F5
Main St
Babcary TA11 174 C7
Barton St David TA11 158 A3
Chilthorne Domer BA22 186 E6
Farrington Gurney BS39 77 A4
Martock TA12 185 F7
Walton BA16 156 D7
Malago Wlk BS13 21 E4
Malden Mead BS14 23 A5
Malherbie Ct TA20 194 B6
Malin Par BS20 2 F6
Mallard Pl TA9 104 C4
Mallard Rd TA24 201 C5
Mallard Way TA6 209 B4
Mallard Wlk [7] BS22 49 E8
Mallory Cl TA2 212 C6
Mallow Cl BS21 6 E2
Mall The
Bath BA1 228 C2
Bristol, Clifton BS8 11 F7
Malmesbury Ct [6] BA21 218 C6
Malmesbury Way BA21 218 C6
MALMSMEAD 122 C4
Mal's Mead La TA20 194 C3
Malta Way BA22 174 A2
Malt Ho The TA4 210 C4
Malthouse Cl BA9 216 C4
Malthouse Ct
Frome BA11 119 E3
Taunton TA1 212 A4
Malthouse La DT9 187 F5
Malthouses TA21 167 A1
Maltings Ind Est The BA1 44 B6
Maltings The
Chard TA20 223 C3
Frome BA11 119 F4
Midford BA2 63 C5
Sherborne DT9 225 E4
Weston-Super-Mare BS22 31 F2
Maltlands BS22 49 D8
Malvern Bldgs BA1 28 A2
Malvern Cl TA6 209 D6
Malvern Ct BA21 218 D6
Malvern Rd BS23 48 E5
Malvern Terr
[4] Bath BA1 28 A1
Taunton TA2 212 F6
Malvern Villas [3] BA1 28 A1
Mamsey La TA4 202 C3
Manchester Cotts BS22 31 E3
Mancroft Ave BS11 4 F7
Mandarin Cl TA6 209 B4
Mandy Mdws BA3 77 F1
Mangle Cave Hill TA18 195 C5
Manilla Cres BS23 30 C1
Manilla Pl BS23 30 C1
Manilla Rd BS8 226 A3
Manleaze Cvn Pk BA4 205 D3
Manleys Cotts TA2 168 C6
Manmoor La BS21 7 A1
Manning Cl BA5 203 F5
Manning Rd TA4 167 E6
Manning's La BA3 94 F3
Manor Barton TA14 185 E2
Manor Bldgs TA18 196 C4
Manor Cl
Berrow TA8 84 F6
Bradford Abbas DT9 187 E1
Chard TA20 223 C2
Charlton Horethorne DT9 176 A2
Cossington TA7 136 F3
Ditcheat BA4 159 C7
East Brent TA9 86 D5
Easton-in-G BS20 4 A4
Farrington Gurney BS39 77 A3
Glastonbury BA6 206 D5
Manor Cl *continued*
Kingsdon TA11 173 D5
Portishead BS20 2 A5
South Perrott DT8 196 C1
Sparkford BA22 175 A4
Taunton TA1 212 E3
Templecombe BA8 189 E8
Wellow BA2 62 D1
Manor Cl The BS8 11 A8
Manor Copse Rd BA3 79 C2
Manor Court Prim Sch
TA20 223 C3
Manor Ct
Backwell BS48 19 A5
Burnham-on-S TA8 104 B7
Cossington TA7 136 F3
Easton BA5 111 A4
Horsington BA8 176 D2
Locking BS24 50 B4
Sherborne DT9 225 D5
Stawell TA7 137 A1
Weston-Super-Mare BS23 49 A8
Manor Dr
Bathford BA1 29 C2
Berrow TA8 84 F6
Chedzoy TA7 154 D8
East Coker BA22 197 B8
[10] Merriott TA16 195 F7
Staplegrove TA2 212 C7
Taunton TA1 212 E3
Manor Farm
Chard TA20 223 C3
East Coker BA22 197 B8
Manor Farm Barns TA7 169 E8
Manor Farm Cl
Tatworth TA20 198 C8
Weston-Super-Mare BS24 49 B2
Manor Farm Cres BS24 49 B2
Manor Furlong BA11 119 E2
Manor Gdns
Farmborough BA2 59 F6
Farrington Gurney BS39 77 A3
Ilchester BA22 173 E1
Locking BS24 50 A4
Weston-Super-Mare BS22 31 B4
Manor Gn EX14 191 F2
Manor Grange BS24 67 B7
Manor Ho BS2 226 C3
Manor House Gdns BA6 206 D5
Manor House Rd BA6 206 D5
Manor La
Abbots Leigh BS8 10 F8
Wedmore BS28 108 D5
Manor Mews TA2 212 D8
Manor Orch TA1 212 D2
Manor Park Cl BA3 79 C2
Manor Pk
Bath BA1 44 B8
Keinton Mandeville TA11 158 B1
Norton Fitzwarren TA2 168 B4
Pawlett TA6 135 F6
Radstock BA3 79 C2
Weston-Super-Mare BS23 48 E1
Manor Pl TA11 158 B1
Manor Rd
Abbots Leigh BS8 10 F7
Bath BA1 27 C1
Bridgwater TA6 209 C6
Bristol, Bishopsworth BS13 22 A6
Burnham-on-S TA8 104 B7
Chedzoy TA7 154 D8
Cossington TA7 136 F3
Edington TA7 137 D2
Frome BA11 119 E2
Isle Abbotts TA3 183 F7
Kingsdon TA11 173 D5
Milborne Port DT9 217 C3
Minehead TA24 201 B4
Pawlett TA6 135 F6
Radstock BA3 79 C2
Saltford BS31 25 C2
Staplegrove TA2 212 C8
Taunton TA1 212 D3
Weston-Super-Mare BS23 49 A8
Yeovil BA20 219 A4
Manor Ride TA9 86 B2
Manor St BA22 197 A8
Manor Terr BA3 79 C2
Manor Valley BS23 31 A1
Manor View
Crewkerne TA18 224 C4
Golsoncott TA23 131 D1
Manor Villas BA1 27 C1
Manor Way
Berrow TA8 84 F6
Failand BS8 10 C4
Frome BA11 119 E2
Manse La TA7 136 C4
Mansel Cl BS31 25 C3
Mansfield Ave BS23 49 B8
Mansfield Rd TA1 213 A3
Manshay La DT6 199 D1
Manship Gn BA4 205 B4
Manston Cl BS14 23 C7
Mantle St TA21 222 C5
Mantle VC Rd BA22 174 A2
Manvers St BA1 228 C1
Manworthy Cross TA4 166 C4
MAPERTON 176 B5
Maperton Rd DT9 176 A2
Maple Cl
Bristol BS14 23 D5
Evercreech BA4 141 F1
North Petherton TA6 153 F3
Puriton TA7 136 C4
Street BA16 207 C5
Taunton TA2 213 A7
Weston-Super-Mare BS23 49 A8

Maple Cl *continued*
Wincanton BA9 216 C2
Maple Ct
Bridgwater TA6 209 D6
Bristol BS9 5 F8
Frome BA11 120 A7
9 Weston-Super-Mare BS23 30 C1
Maple Dr
Burnham-on-S TA8 104 B5
Crewkerne TA18 224 D7
Radstock BA3 78 E1
Yeovil BA20 218 F3
Maple Gdns BA2 44 E4
Maple Gr BA2 44 E4
Maple Ho BS2 227 A4
Maple Leaf Ct BS8 226 A3
Maple Rd
Curry Rivel TA10 171 D4
Langport TA10 172 A6
Maple Rise BA3 79 B2
Maples The
Nailsea BS48 8 C1
Shepton Mallet BA4 205 C6
Maplestone Rd BS14 23 A3
Maple Tree Ct TA7 136 F3
Maple Wlk BS31 24 D4
Mapstone Cl BA6 206 E3
Marchant-Holliday Sch BA8 176 C5
Marchant's Hill BA3 95 F2
Marchants Pass BA1 228 C1
Marchfields Way BS23 49 A5
March La BA22 175 D8
Marconi Cl BS23 49 B7
Marconi Dr TA9 104 D5
Marconi Rd BS20 1 F5
Marden Gr TA1 213 D3
Marden Rd BS31 25 A4
Mardi's La TA11 158 C2
Mardyke Ferry Rd BS1 226 B1
Mare La TA13 220 C5
Mares La BA5 110 E7
Margaret Cres TA8 104 A5
Margaret Rd 4 BS13 21 F4
Margaret's Bldgs BA1 228 B3
Margaret's Hill BA1 228 C4
Margery Fish Gdns* TA13 220 C8
Marguerite Rd BS13 21 F7
Marina Row TA6 209 B4
Marindin Dr BS22 32 B4
Marine Ct BA21 219 D5
Marine Dr TA8 104 B5
Marine Hill BS21 6 C5
Marine Par
Clevedon BS21 6 C4
Pill BS20 4 C5
Weston-Super-Mare BS23 30 B1
Weston-Super-Mare BS23 48 D6
Mariners Cl
Backwell BS48 19 A6
Bridgwater TA6 209 A5
Minehead TA24 201 B7
Mariner's Cl BS22 31 D1
Mariners Ct TA6 209 A5
Mariners Dr
Backwell BS48 19 A6
Bristol BS9 5 D4
Mariners' Path BS9 5 E3
Mariners Way TA23 202 D6
Mariner's Way BS20 4 C5
Marino Way 7 TA6 154 A5
Maritime Heritage Ctr* BS1 226 B1
Marjoram Way BS20 2 F5
MARK 106 D4
MARK CAUSEWAY 106 A3
Mark CE Fst Sch TA9 106 A4
Mark Coll TA9 106 E4
Mark Cswy TA9 106 B4
Market Ave BS22 32 C3
Market Cl
4 Bampton EX16 164 B1
Brushford TA22 163 E4
Market Ct
8 Bridgwater TA6 208 F5
2 Crewkerne TA18 224 C6
Market Gate BS2 227 C3
Market House La TA24 200 F7
Market House Mus The* TA23 202 C7
Market Ind Est BS49 17 B1
Market La BS23 48 D8
Market Pl
Burlescombe EX16 179 B4
Castle Cary BA7 214 C5
Frome BA11 119 F5
Glastonbury BA6 206 D4
Ilchester BA22 173 E1
Radstock BA3 78 F2
23 Shepton Mallet BA4 205 B6
Somerton TA11 211 E4
Wells BA5 203 E4
Wincanton BA9 216 C4
Winford BS40 37 F7
Wiveliscombe TA4 210 C4
Market Pl The BA11 143 B8
Market Sq
Crewkerne TA18 224 C6
South Petherton TA13 220 C4
Market St
Bridgwater TA6 208 F5
Crewkerne TA18 224 C6
Highbridge TA9 104 E3
Watchet TA23 202 C7
Wells BA5 203 D4
Yeovil BA20 219 B5
Market Terr TA9 104 E3
Mark La BS1 226 C2
Marklands BS9 5 E3
Mark Rd
Burtle TA7 137 D6
Highbridge TA9 105 A2
MARKSBURY 42 B1
Marksbury CE Prim Sch BA2 42 B2
Marks Cl TA3 169 C4
Marksmead DT8 199 F8
Marksview Bsns Ctr BA21 219 F7
Marlborough Ave TA6 209 A2
Marlborough Bldgs
Bath BA1 228 A3
Langport TA10 171 F5
Marlborough Cl TA6 209 A2
Marlborough Ct TA8 85 B1
Marlborough Dr BS22 32 B2
Marlborough Flats 8 BS2 227 A4
Marlborough Hill BS2 227 A4
Marlborough Hill Pl BS2 227 A4
Marlborough La BA1 228 A3
Marlborough Rd BA21 219 E6
Marlborough St
Bath BA1 228 A4
Bristol BS2 227 A4
Marl Cl BA21 218 E7
Marle Ground TA19 184 E2
Marlepit Gr BS13 21 F6
Marley Cl TA24 201 A5
Marley's Row TA24 124 A3
Marleys Way BA11 119 C5
Marlfield Wlk BS13 21 E7
Marling Ho TA24 201 B7
Marl La DT9 187 E3
Marlowe Ho 3 BS23 48 F4
Marl Pits 1 BS48 19 A6
Marl Pits La BA11 143 C7
Marne Cl BS14 23 D5
MARNHULL 190 F5
Marnhull Cl DT10 190 F6
Marriage La DT10 190 F3
Marron Cl BS26 70 C2
Marsden Rd BA2 44 B3
MARSH 192 E5
MARSHALL'S ELM 207 D2
Marshall Way BA11 120 D8
Marshall Wlk BS4 22 D7
MARSHALSEA 199 C3
Marshalsea Est DT6 199 C3
Marshbridge Cross TA22 163 C7
Marshclose Hill TA22 146 E2
Marsh Cross TA24 200 D1
MARSHFIELD 13 E8
Marshfield Rd TA24 201 B5
Marshfield Way BA1 28 A1
Marsh Hill TA22 163 C8
Marsh La
Barrington TA19 184 E5
Barton St David TA11 158 A3
Bridgwater TA6 209 B1
Buckhorn Weston BA9 177 C4
Cannington TA5 135 C2
Dunster TA24 201 E3
Easton-in-G BS20 4 A4
Farrington Gurney BS39 77 A3
Henstridge BA8 190 B7
Holcombe BA3 116 C5
Penselwood BA9 161 D2
Pitney TA10 172 D7
Portbury BS20 3 F6
South Cheriton BA8 176 E4
Temple Cloud BS39 59 A1
Tintinhull BA22 186 A5
Yeovil BA21 218 F8
Yeovil Marsh BA21 187 A5
Marsh Lane Ind Est BS20 3 F7
Marsh Pottinson Ho 16 BA20 219 B4
Marsh Rd
Bristol BS3 11 F3
Rode BA11 82 F1
Standerwick BA11 102 D1
Yatton BS49 34 B8
Marsh St
Avonmouth BS11 4 C8
4 Bristol BS1 227 A2
Dunster TA24 201 E3
MARSH STREET 201 F3
Marshway TA3 170 D1
MARSHWOOD 199 C2
Marshwood CE Prim Sch DT6 199 C2
Marshwood Cross DT6 199 E1
Marson Rd BS21 6 D3
MARSTON BIGOT 143 D7
Marston Cl
Frome BA11 119 D2
Taunton TA1 212 E1
MARSTON GATE 119 C1
Marston La BA11 119 D2
MARSTON MAGNA 174 F1
Marston Mead BA11 119 D2
Marston Rd
Frome BA11 119 D1
Nunney BA11 143 D8
Sherborne DT9 225 B5
Marston Trad Est BA11 119 E2
Martcombe Rd BS20 4 C2
Martha's Orch BS13 21 E7
Martindale Ct BS22 49 D8
Martindale Rd BS22 49 D8
Martins TA3 169 C4
Martins Bldgs 4 TA21 222 D5
Martins Cl
Evercreech BA4 141 E1
Wellington TA21 222 D5
Wells BA5 203 B3
Martin's Cl TA8 85 A3
Martins Gr BS22 31 E2
Martins La BA4 205 E5
Martins Paddock BA4 142 A6
Martin St BA6 158 A5
Martins The BS20 3 A6
Martland Cl TA7 136 E3
Martlet Rd TA24 200 F7
MARTOCK 185 D6
Martock BS24 48 F2
Martock Bsns Pk TA12 185 D7
Martock CE Prim Sch TA12 185 D6
Martock La TA12 185 F7
Martock Rd
Keynsham BS31 25 A3
Long Sutton TA10 172 E4
Mart Rd TA24 201 B7
Mart The 6 BS23 48 E7
Martyn Cl TA5 135 B5
Marwin Cl TA12 185 E7
Marwood Cl TA8 104 C8
Marwood Rd BS4 22 E8
Mary Brown Davis La 6 BA5 139 D8
Marybush La BS2 227 B3
Mary Elton Prim Sch BS21 6 B1
Mary Hart Cl BA16 207 B7
Mary La 10 EX16 164 B1
Mary Rd BA5 203 C5
Mary St
Taunton TA1 212 F3
Yeovil BA21 219 B5
Masefield Ho BS23 49 A4
Mason La TA15 186 B4
Masons Way BA11 119 D1
Mason's Way BS27 90 C7
Mason Way BA4 205 A4
Massingham Pk TA2 213 B6
Materman Rd BS14 23 E5
Matfurlong Cl TA12 185 D5
Matthews Cl BS14 23 F6
Matthews Rd
Taunton TA1 212 B1
Yeovil BA21 219 C5
Mattock's Tree Hill TA3 169 E1
Matt's La TA14 185 F4
Mattys Cross EX14 191 D3
MAUDLIN 199 C8
Maudlin Cross TA20 199 C8
Maudlin La TA20 199 C8
Maudslay Field BA22 197 C8
MAUNDOWN 165 F7
Maunsell Rd BS24 49 E7
Maunsel Rd TA7 153 F1
Max Mill La BS25 69 C8
Maxwell Rd BA4 205 B4
Maxwell St TA2 212 E6
Maybrick Rd BA2 44 D5
Mayfair Ave BS48 8 F1
Mayfield Ave BS22 31 E1
Mayfield Cl BA22 175 D8
Mayfield Dr TA6 208 B4
Mayfield Rd
Bath BA2 44 D5
Yeovil BA21 219 D6
Mayfields BS31 24 E5
Mayfield Terr TA4 210 C4
Mayflower Cl TA6 209 D5
Mayflower Ct TA9 104 E4
Mayflower Gdns BS48 9 A2
Maynard Cl
Bristol BS13 22 C5
4 Clevedon BS21 6 F3
Maynard Rd BS13 22 C5
Maynard Terr BS39 58 F3
Maypole Cl BS39 58 E3
MAY POLE KNAP 211 C4
May Pole Knap TA11 211 C4
Maysfield Cl BS20 2 D3
Maysgreen La BS24 33 B3
May's La BS24 33 C3
Maysmead La BS40 53 C6
May Terr TA23 131 E3
Maytree Ave BS13 22 B7
Maytree Cl
Bristol BS13 22 B7
Frome BA11 120 B7
May Tree Cl BS48 8 C1
May Tree Rd BA3 78 E1
May Tree Wlk BS31 24 C3
Mead Ave BA22 218 B6
Mead Cl
Bath BA2 44 E3
Bristol BS11 4 E6
Cheddar BS27 90 B6
East Huntspill TA9 136 E8
Stoke St Michael BA3 116 B2
Meade Cl TA6 153 F3
Meade Ho BA2 44 A5
Meade La TA19 184 E1
MEADGATE EAST 60 E2
MEADGATE WEST 60 D2
Mead La
Blagdon BS40 54 E3
Lydford Fair Place TA11 158 C3
Saltford BS31 25 F4
Sandford BS25 51 E4
Stocklinch TA19 184 C4
Wanstrow BA4 142 F4
West Pennard BA6 140 C2
Meadlands BA2 43 B7
Meadowbank BS22 31 F3
Meadow Cl
Backwell BS48 19 B6
Chilton Trinity TA5 135 F2
Farrington Gurney BS39 77 A3
Henstridge BA8 190 A7
Highbridge TA9 104 D4
Kingston St Mary TA2 168 E8
Langport TA10 172 A6
Nailsea BS48 8 E3
Nether Stowey TA5 134 A2
Stalbridge DT10 190 B4
Street BA16 207 B4
Wincanton BA9 216 D3
Meadow Cotts TA24 131 B4
Meadow Croft BS24 49 B2
Meadowcroft Dr TA8 104 C8
Meadow Ct BA1 44 A7
Meadow Dr
Bath BA2 62 D8
Locking BS24 50 B4
Portishead BS20 1 F1
Meadow Gdns
Bath BA1 27 A1
Stogursey TA5 134 C6
Meadow Gr BS11 4 D7
Meadow La
Bathampton BA2 28 D1
Walton BA16 156 E7
Meadowland BS49 17 A1
Meadowlands BS22 32 C2
Meadowlands Ave TA6 208 E6
Meadow Pk
Bathford BA1 29 B3
Wembdon TA6 208 C5
Meadow Pl BS22 32 D3
Meadow Rd
Clevedon BS21 6 E3
Frome BA11 119 F7
Paulton BS39 77 F4
Yeovil BA21 219 E7
Meadow Rise BA4 205 B7
Meadow Sch The BA10 215 E6
Meadows Cl BS20 1 F5
Meadows End BS25 52 D4
Meadowside
Carhampton TA24 131 A5
Rockwell Green TA21 222 B5
Meadowside Cl TA1 212 B4
Meadowside Dr BS14 23 A3
Meadows Prim Sch The BS30 25 D8
Meadow St
Axbridge BS26 70 C2
Weston-Super-Mare BS23 48 E7
Meadows The
2 Bourton SP8 161 F1
Drayton TA10 171 E3
Porlock TA24 124 A3
Meadow Terr TA24 201 A5
Meadow View
2 Bampton EX16 164 B1
4 Barwick BA22 197 F8
East Coker BA22 197 C8
Glastonbury BA6 206 E3
Long Sutton TA10 172 E1
Radstock BA3 79 A1
Timberscombe TA24 130 B5
Meadow View Cl BA1 44 A8
Meadow Villas 14 BS23 48 E8
Mead Rd BS20 2 C2
Meads Ct TA6 208 E3
Meads Droveway TA3 169 D5
Mead St BS3 227 C1
Meads The DT9 217 D2
Mead Terr BS40 54 E2
Mead The
Clutton BS39 58 E3
Dundry BS41 21 D2
East Brent TA9 86 E5
Farmborough BA2 60 A6
Henstridge BA8 190 A6
Holcombe BA3 116 C8
Ilchester BA22 173 D1
Ilminster TA19 221 B3
Paulton BS39 77 D5
Rode BA11 101 E8
14 Shepton Mallet BA4 205 B6
Shipham BS25 70 E8
Stoke St Michael BA3 116 B2
Stratton-on-t F BA3 96 F2
Street BA16 207 D7
Timsbury BA2 60 C3
Winsley BA15 64 E7
Mead Vale BS22 49 E8
Mead Vale Com Prim Sch BS22 31 E1
Meadway
Bristol BS9 5 C6
Farmborough BA2 60 A6
Temple Cloud BS39 58 E1
Woolavington TA7 136 E4
Mead Way TA2 169 B6
Meadway Ave BS48 8 D2
Mearcombe La BS24 67 F6
Meardon Rd BS14 23 E6
MEARE 138 D4
Meare BS24 48 F2
MEARE GREEN
Hatch Beauchamp 169 F1
Stoke St Gregory 170 D5
Meare Rd
Bath BA2 45 A2
Glastonbury BA6 206 B6
Meare Village Prim Sch BA6 138 D4
Meareway BA6 138 C5
MEARNS 59 E2
Mearn's Cross BA3 94 B6
Mede Cl BS1 227 B1
Medical Ave BS2, BS8 226 C3
Medway Cl
Keynsham BS31 25 A3
Taunton TA1 213 D4
Medway Dr BS31 25 A3
Meetinghouse La BS49 18 A1
Melbourne House Mews BA5 203 D4
Melbourne Pl TA6 209 B6
Melbourne Terr 2 BS21 6 D2
Melcombe Ct BA2 44 D4
Melcombe La TA6 153 E3
Melcombe Rd BA2 44 D4
Mellanby Cl BA16 207 D5
Mellent Ave BS13 22 C3
MELLS 118 B7
Mells CE Fst Sch BA11 118 A6
Mells Cl BS31 25 A2
MELLS GREEN 118 A6
Mells La BA3 79 B1
Melrose Ave
Bristol BS8 226 B4
Wells BA5 203 C4
Melrose Ct 3 BA5 203 C4
Melrose Gr BA2 44 B3
Melrose Pl BS8 226 B4
Melrose Rd BA21 219 B6
Melrose Terr BA1 28 A2
Melsbury La BA5 139 E6
Memorial Ave TA18 224 C5
Memorial Rd
Wrington BS40 35 E2
Yeovil BA22 218 B6
Mendip Ave
Shepton Mallet BA4 205 E4
Weston-Super-Mare BS22 31 F2
Mendip Cl
Axbridge BS26 70 D2
Frome BA11 120 A7
Keynsham BS31 24 D5
3 Nailsea BS48 8 E1
Paulton BS39 77 E4
Yatton BS49 34 B7
Mendip Dr BA11 120 A7
Mendip Edge BS24 66 F8
Mendip Fields BA3 96 C2
Mendip Gdns
Bath BA2 62 D8
Frome BA11 120 B7
Yatton BS49 34 B7
Mendip Green Fst Sch BS22 31 E1
Mendip Ho TA1 212 F3
Mendip Lea Cl BS27 90 F2
Mendip Lodge BS25 70 A8
Mendip Rd
Bridgwater TA6 209 C4
Locking BS24 50 D4
Portishead BS20 2 B5
Rooks Bridge BS26 87 A6
Stoke St Michael BA3 116 A2
Weston-Super-Mare BS23 49 A7
Yatton BS49 34 B7
Mendip Rise BS24 50 B4
Mendip Vale BA3 116 E7
Mendip Vale Sta* BA4 205 F3
Mendip Vale Trad Est BS27 90 A7
Mendip View
Coleford BA3 116 F7
Street BA16 207 B7
Mendip Villas
Cheddar BS27 71 A1
Compton Martin BS40 73 F7
Emborough BA3 95 E3
Mendip Way
Burnham-on-S TA8 104 B7
Radstock BA3 78 F3
Menlea BS40 54 D3
Mercer Ct BS14 23 B8
Merchants Almshouses 6 BS1 227 A2
Merchants' Barton 3 BA11 119 F4
Merchants Barton Ind Est BA11 119 F4
Merchants Ct BS8 226 A1
Merchants Quay BS1 227 A1
Merchants Rd
Bristol BS8 226 A3
Bristol, Hotwells BS8 226 A1
Merchants Row BS1 226 C1
Merchant St BS1 227 B3
Meredith Cl BA22 197 C3
Meredith Ct BS1 226 A1
Merevale Way BA21 218 C7
Meriden BA1 44 D8
Meridian Pl BS8 226 B3
Meridian Vale BS8 226 B3
Meriet Ave BS13 22 B4
Merle Cl TA6 209 B4
Merlin Cl
Bristol BS9 5 F8
1 Weston-Super-Mare BS22 49 E8
Merlin Dr BA5 203 B5
Merlin Ind Pk TA2 213 B6
Merlin Pk BS20 2 A4
Merrick Ct BS1 227 A1
Merrick Rd BA6 206 E7
MERRIDGE 152 D5
Merridge Cl TA6 208 A4
Merridge Hill TA5 152 D6
Merrifields TA4 167 E6

Merriman Gdns BA16 207 C5
Merriman Rd BA16 207 C5
Merrimans Rd BS11 4 D8
MERRIOTT 195 E7
Merriott Fst Sch TA16 195 F7
Merriott Rd
Hinton St George TA17 195 D7
Merriott TA16 195 F6
MERRIOTTSFORD 195 F7
Merry-field BA3 116 E8
Merryfield La
Doulting BA4 141 F5
Ilton TA19 183 E4
Merryfield Lane Halt★
BA4 141 F5
Merryfield Rd BS24 50 B6
Merryfields TA9 106 D5
Merry La TA9 136 F8
Merthyr Guest Cl BA8 176 E1
Merton Dr BS24 50 A8
Mervyn Ball Cl TA20 223 C5
Methwyn Cl BS22 49 C7
Metropole Ct TA24 201 A7
Metropolitan The BS1 227 B1
Mews The
Bath BA1 44 A8
5 Bridgwater TA6 209 B4
East Coker BA22 197 C7
Minehead TA24 201 A7
Wiveliscombe TA4 210 C4
Mewswell Dr BS27 71 B1
Mezellion Pl 14 BA1 28 B1
Mianda Terr TA19 221 C3
Michaels Mead BA1 27 B2
Midas Ct TA11 211 D3
Middle Ave BS1 227 A2
Middle Brooks BA16 207 C3
MIDDLE BURNHAM 104 D8
MIDDLE CHINNOCK 196 C8
Middlecombe Cross
TA24 200 C6
Middle Dro
Baltonsborough BA6 158 B4
Compton Dundon TA11 156 F3
Glastonbury BA6 206 B5
Hambridge TA10, TA12 184 F8
Lydford Fair Place TA11 158 C3
Rodney Stoke BS27 109 C6
Street BA6 157 C7
Middlefield La
Barrington TA10 184 D6
Norton Sub Hamdon TA13,
TA16 185 D1
West Chinnock TA16 196 A8
Middle Field La DT9 188 B7
Middlefield Rd TA10 172 C7
Middleford Ho BS13 22 C4
Middle Gate TA10 172 D8
Middlegate Rd TA10 172 C7
MIDDLE GREEN 222 D3
Middle Green Rd TA21 222 E3
Middle La
Bath BA1 28 B1
Kingston Seymour BS21 15 F4
Middle Leaze Dro TA12 185 F7
MIDDLE LEIGH 207 C4
Middle Leigh BA16 207 C5
MIDDLE LUXTON 191 F5
Middlemead BA3 96 F3
Middle Moor Drove TA5 134 D7
Middle Moor La BS27 89 E7
Middlemoor Water Pk★
TA7 136 F5
Middle Path TA18 224 B5
Middlepiece La BA2, BS31 42 B7
Middle Rd TA7 137 A3
Middle Ridge La DT9 175 D1
Middleroom Dro TA3 182 E4
Middle's La BA4 140 C4
Middle St
Ashcott TA7 156 B7
Burnham-on-S TA9 85 E5
East Harptree BS40 74 F4
East Lambrook TA13 220 C8
Galhampton BA22 175 D8
Kingsdon TA11 173 D5
Martock TA12 185 D4
Minehead TA24 200 F8
Misterton TA18 224 F3
Montacute TA15 186 B3
North Perrott TA18 196 C4
Puriton TA7 136 C4
Rimpton BA22 188 A8
Shepton Beauchamp TA19 184 E3
Taunton TA1 212 F4
Yeovil BA20 219 B4
Middle Stoke BA3 64 A6
MIDDLE STOUGHTON 108 A8
Middle Stream Cl TA6 208 D2
Middleton La
Clatworthy TA4 149 C2
Shepton Mallet BA4 205 B4
Middleton Rd BS11 4 F8
Middle Touches TA20 223 E5
Middleway TA1 212 E2
Middle Way TA11 157 B4
Middleway Ct TA1 212 E2
Middleway Rd BA4 158 E8
Middlewood Cl BA2 44 C2
Middle Yeo Gn BS48 8 D3
MIDDLEZOY 155 B3
Middlezoy Prim Sch TA7 155 B3
Midelney Rd TA10 171 E2
MIDFORD 63 C6
Midford BS24 48 F2
Midford Hill BA2, BA3 63 C5
Midford La BA2, BA3 63 E7
Midford Rd
Southstoke BA2 63 B7
Taunton TA1 213 B4
Midhaven Rise BS22 31 E4
Midland Bridge Rd BA1,
BA2 228 A2
Midland Mews BS2 227 C3
Midland Rd
Bath BA1 44 D7
Bristol BS2 227 C3
Midland St BS2 227 C2
Midleaze DT9 225 A3
Midney La BA9 177 D8
Midsomer Ent Pk BA3 78 C2
MIDSOMER NORTON 78 B3
Midsomer Norton Prim Sch
BA3 78 B1
Midsomer Norton South★
BA3 97 A8
Midsummer Bldgs BA1 28 B2
MIDWAY 115 E2
MILBORNE PORT 217 E2
Milborne Port Bsns Ctr
DT9 217 D2
Milborne Port Prim Sch
DT9 217 D2
MILBORNE WICK 217 B6
Milburn Rd BS23 48 F7
Milbury Gdns BS22 31 C2
Mildmay Dr BA22 174 F3
Mildmay's Rd TA10 155 F1
Mildred Rd BA16 156 E7
Miles Cl BS20 4 E3
Miles's Bldgs BA1 228 B3
Miles St BA2 228 C1
Milestone Cl TA6 153 F4
Milestone Ct BS22 32 D2
Mile Wlk BS14 23 A6
Milford Inf Sch BA21 219 B7
Milford Jun Sch BA21 219 B7
Milford Pk BA21 219 C7
Milford Pl 3 TA1 213 A4
Milford Rd BA21 219 C7
Milking La BS27 90 E2
Milk St
Bath BA1 228 B2
Frome BA11 119 E5
Millands La TA5 133 C6
Millands The TA11 211 E4
Millards Ct BA3 78 B3
Millards Hill BA3 78 B3
Millard's Hill
Batcombe BA4 142 D2
Midsomer Norton BA3 78 C3
Mill Ave BS1 227 A2
Millbatch BA6 138 C4
Mill Batch Farm Ind Est
TA9 86 F4
Mill Bay TA6 153 E4
Millbourn Cl BA15 64 D7
Millbourne Rd BS27 90 C7
Millbridge Gdns TA24 200 F7
Millbridge Rd TA24 200 E7
MILLBROOK 198 A1
Millbrook BA20 219 A4
Millbrook Cross 1 EX13 198 A1
Millbrook Ct BA2 228 C1
Millbrook Dale EX13 198 A1
Millbrook Gdns BA7 214 B5
Millbrook Pl BA2 228 C1
Mill Cl
Cannington TA5 135 B2
East Coker BA22 197 C8
Frome BA11 119 F6
Nether Stowey TA5 134 A2
Portbury BS20 3 D2
Mill Cotts
Creech St Michael TA3 169 D4
Saltford BS31 25 F2
Millcross BS21 16 C8
Mill Cross
Halstock BA22 197 C3
Kingston St Mary TA2 168 E7
Mill Ct
Midsomer Norton BA3 78 A1
Watchet TA23 202 B7
Millennium Cl BA3 116 A3
Millennium Sq BS1 226 C2
Miller Cl BS23 48 F8
Miller Ho BS8 226 A2
Millers Cl
Bourton SP8 161 F1
Pill BS20 4 C4
Millers Ct BS21 16 E8
Millers Gdns BA5 203 E5
Miller's Hill DT9 217 A5
Millers Orch TA3 170 F1
Millers Rise BS22 32 A4
Millers Way 11 TA4 167 F8
Miller Way DT9 225 E5
Miller Wlk BA2 28 F1
Milletts Cl 2 TA24 131 A5
Mill Farm Hill TA5 134 F1
Millfield
Chard TA20 223 D3
Ilchester BA22 173 E2
Midsomer Norton BA3 96 F8
Millfield Cl TA20 223 D3
Millfield Ind Est TA20 223 E3
Millfield Prep Sch BA6 139 D1
Millfield Sch BA16 207 E5
Millford La BA4 159 C6
Mill Gdns TA24 201 D1
Millgreen Cl TA9 136 B8
Millground Rd BS13 21 F5
Millham La TA22 163 D6
MILLHAYES 180 C1
Mill Hill BA2 62 E1
Mill Ho BS1 227 A2
Mill House Ct BA11 119 F5
Millier Rd BS49 35 B8
Milliman Cl BS13 22 C5
Milliner Ct BA4 205 B5
Mill La
Alhampton BA4 159 C5
Axminster EX13 198 F3
Batcombe BA4 142 C1
Bathampton BA2 28 F2
3 Bath BA2 44 B6
Beckington BA11 101 D5
Bishops Lydeard TA4 167 F8
Bitton BS30 25 E8
Bourton SP8 161 F1
Bradford Abbas DT9 187 E1
Bruton BA10 215 E6
Butcombe BS40 55 A8
Cannington TA5 135 B2
Chard TA20 223 C3
Chard, Wambrook TA20 193 C2
Charlton Mackrell TA11 173 E7
Chew Stoke BS40 56 D8
Clatworthy TA4 149 E2
Compton Martin BS40 74 A7
Congresbury BS49 34 D4
Corfe TA3 181 F6
Corsley Heath BA11, BA12 144 C8
Creech St Michael TA3 169 D4
Crewkerne, Misterton
TA18 196 B3
Crewkerne TA18 224 D5
Dinnington TA17 195 B8
Dowlish Wake TA19 194 E7
Dunster TA24 201 D1
East Coker BA22 197 C7
East Coker, Holywell BA22 197 B8
East Huntspill TA9 136 D8
Exford TA24 128 C2
Halstock BA22 197 C3
Higher Chillington TA19 194 E5
Ilchester BA22 173 F1
Ilminster TA19 221 B7
Kingstone TA19 221 F1
Lopen TA13 185 A1
Lynford-on-F TA11 158 C2
Maiden Bradley BA12 144 B3
Marnhull DT10 190 F6
Milverton TA4 167 A5
Monkton Combe BA2 63 E8
Nether Stowey TA5 134 A2
North Wootton BA4 140 D5
Othery TA7 155 C2
Pitcombe BA10 215 C3
Porlock TA24 124 A3
Portbury BS20 3 E3
Priston BA2 61 A7
Shapwick TA7 155 F8
Shepton Mallet BA4 204 E4
Somerton TA11 211 D2
South Petherton TA13 220 E6
Stoke St Michael BA3 116 B3
Stone Allerton BS26 88 D4
Taunton TA3 168 D1
Thurloxton TA2 153 D1
Timsbury BA2 60 B1
Trent DT9 187 F5
Watchet TA23 202 C7
Wedmore BS28 108 E3
Wells BA5 203 A1
West Monkton TA2 169 D8
Wiveliscombe TA4 210 C4
Wrington BS40 53 F8
Yeovil BA20 219 B4
Mill Lane Cl TA3 168 D1
Mill La Trad Est BA20 219 C4
Mill Leat BA6 157 F5
Mill Leg BS49 34 D4
Millmead Ho BS13 22 C4
Millmead Rd BA2 44 C5
MILLMOOR 179 E1
Millmoot La TA7 136 F3
Mill on the Brue★ BA10 215 D5
Millpill Cl BS9 5 D5
Mill Rd
Barton St David TA11 158 A3
Radstock BA3 79 B2
Mill Rise
Bourton SP8 161 F1
Staplegrove TA2 212 B7
Mill Road Ind Est BA3 79 B3
Mill St
Carhampton TA24 131 B4
North Petherton TA6 153 F3
Rimpton BA22 188 A8
Watchet TA23 202 C7
Wells BA5 203 D4
Wincanton BA9 216 C4
Millstream Cl TA24 200 F6
Mill Stream Cl BS26 70 C1
Mill Stream Gdns TA21 222 B7
Mill Street Cl BA9 216 C4
Millthorn Ho 2 BA16 207 C5
Millward Terr BS39 77 E6
Millway
Chard TA20 193 C2
Rodney Stoke BS27 110 B8
Millway Rise Ind Est
EX13 198 A2
Millwey Ave EX13 198 A2
MILLWEY RISE 198 A2
Mill Wlk TA7 136 E3
Millwood Cl TA6 208 E2
Milne Cl TA6 208 F2
Milsom Pl TA4 167 F6
Milsom St BA1 228 B3
MILTON
Martock 185 E8
Weston-Super-Mare 31 C2
Milton Ave
Bath BA2 44 F4
Weston-Super-Mare BS23 49 A8
Milton Brow BS22 31 B2
Milton Cl
Nailsea BS48 8 E3
Taunton TA1 213 C3
Yeovil BA21 218 C6
MILTON CLEVEDON 160 A8
Milton Ct BA4 205 B7
Milton Gn BS22 31 C1
Milton Hill
Monkton Heathfield TA2 213 E7
Weston-Super-Mare BS22 31 B2
Milton Ho BA21 187 D6
Milton Jun & Inf Schs
BS22 31 C1
Milton La
Martock TA12 185 E8
Wells BA5 203 D5
Wookey Hole BA5 203 B8
Milton Leaze TA10 172 E2
Milton Lodge Gdns★
BA5 203 D7
Milton Park Rd BS22 31 C1
Milton Pl TA6 208 E4
Milton Rd
Radstock BA3 78 C1
Taunton TA1 213 C3
Weston-Super-Mare BS22,
BS23 49 B8
Milton Rise BS22 31 C1
Miltons Cl BS13 22 D4
Milton Terr BA5 203 A8
MILVERTON 166 F4
Milverton BS24 48 F2
Milverton Com Prim Sch
TA4 166 F4
Milverton Rd TA21 222 B8
Milward Rd BS31 24 E6
Minchington's Cl TA14 185 F2
MINEHEAD 201 A8
Minehead First Sch
TA24 200 F6
Minehead Hospl TA24 200 F7
Minehead La TA22 164 A7
Minehead Mid Sch TA24 201 A6
Minehead Rd
Bishops Lydeard TA4 167 E8
Bristol BS4 23 A8
Minehead Sta★ TA24 201 B7
Miners Cl BS41 10 F2
Minerva Ct BA2 228 C3
Minerva Gdns BA2 44 C4
Minnows The TA20 223 C3
Minsmere Rd BS31 25 A4
Minster Cl TA1 212 C1
Minster Ct TA1 212 C1
Minster Way BA2 45 C8
Minton Cl BS14 23 B5
Mintons TA20 223 B3
Mintons Orch TA20 223 B3
Mint The BA11 119 E5
Misburg Cl BA4 204 F6
MISTERTON 224 E3
Misterton CE Fst Sch
TA18 224 F3
Mistletoe La BA4 205 D3
Mitchell Gdns TA20 223 B3
Mitchell La BS1 227 B2
Mitchell's Pool TA21 222 E6
Mitchell's Row BA22 175 D6
Mitchell St TA21 222 C7
Mitchell Terr BA5 112 E1
Mitchelmore Rd BA21 219 B5
Mitford-Slade Ct BS49 34 C7
Mitre Ct TA1 213 B4
Mizzymead Cl 1 BS48 8 D1
Mizzymead Rd BS48 8 E1
Mizzymead Rise BS48 8 E1
Moffats Dr BA5 113 A2
Molesworth Cl BS13 22 A4
Molesworth Dr BS13 22 A4
Molly Cl BS39 76 E8
Monarch Ctr TA2 213 C6
Monday's Court La TA10 172 E5
Money Pit La EX13 193 A1
Monger Cotts BS39 77 F4
Monger La
Midsomer Norton BA3 78 A3
Paulton BS39 78 A4
Monington Rd BA6 206 E6
Monk Barton Cl BA21 218 C7
Monk Cross TA24 128 D1
Monkley La BA11 83 C1
Monks Cl
Rooks Bridge BS26 87 B5
Taunton TA1 213 B5
Monks Dale BA21 218 D6
Monksdale Rd BA2 44 D4
Monks Dr TA7 137 F1
Monks Ford BA5 139 D8
Monksford La BA5 139 C8
Monks Hill BS22 31 B3
MONKSILVER 150 A8
Monks' Path TA23, TA24 131 E4
Monkstone Dr TA8 84 F5
Monkstone Gdns 6
EX13 198 A1
Monksway TA23 131 E4
Monks Way TA8 104 B6
Monkton Ave BS24 49 A2
MONKTON COMBE 45 F1
Monkton Combe Jun Sch
BA2 45 C1
Monkton Combe Jun Sch
(Pre-Prep) BA2 45 C1
Monkton Combe Sch BA2 45 E1
MONKTON FARLEIGH 46 F7
MONKTON
HEATHFIELD 213 E8
Monkton La TA5 134 D5
Monmouth Cl
Chard TA20 223 E4
Glastonbury BA6 206 D5
Portishead BS20 1 F4
Westonzoyland TA7 154 F6
Monmouth Ct
Bath BA1 228 A2
Chard TA20 223 E4
Pill BS20 4 C5
Monmouth Dr BA11 120 B6
Monmouth Farm Cl TA6 135 F5
Monmouth Paddock BA2 81 E5
Monmouth Pl BA1 228 B2
Monmouth Rd
Keynsham BS31 24 D5
Pill BS20 4 C5
Shepton Mallet BA4 205 A5
Taunton TA1 213 B5
Westonzoyland TA7 154 F6
Yeovil BA21 219 D7
Monmouth St
Bath BA1 228 B2
Bridgwater TA6 209 A5
MONTACUTE 186 B3
Montacute Cir 4 BS22 49 F8
Montacute House★
TA15 186 B4
Montacute Rd
Montacute TA14, TA15 186 B4
Tintinhull BA22 186 B6
Montacute TV, Radio & Toy
Mus★ TA15 186 C4
Montague Ct 4 BS2 227 A4
Montague Flats 6 BS2 227 A4
Montague Gdns BA7 214 B5
Montague Hill BS2 227 A4
Montague Hill S 5 BS2 227 A4
Montague Ho 8 BA1 28 C1
Montague Pl BS6 227 A4
Montague Rd
Saltford BS31 25 D2
Shoscombe BA2 79 E5
Montague St BS1 227 A4
Montague Way TA20 223 C3
Monteclefe CE Jun Sch
TA11 211 E3
Montepelier BS23 48 F8
Montgomery Ct BA11 120 A4
Montpelier E BS23 30 F1
Montrose Cotts BA1 27 C1
Montrose Rd BA21 219 E7
Montrose Villas BS27 90 C7
Montsurs Cl BA3 96 D3
Montys La TA2 168 A6
Monument Cl TA21 222 E4
Monument Rd TA21 222 E3
MOOLHAM 221 C1
Moolham La
Ilminster TA19 194 D7
Kingstone TA19 221 D1
Moondown La TA13 220 B2
Moonhayes Cross EX14 191 F4
Moon La TA7 153 E1
Moonraker Cl 8 TA6 209 B4
Moon's Dro TA7 155 A1
Moons Hill BA3 116 B4
Moonshill Cl BA3 116 A3
Moonshill Cotts BA3 116 A3
Moonshill Rd BA3 116 A3
Moon St BS2 227 B4
MOOR 220 C3
Moor Cl
Compton Dundon TA11 156 F2
Langport TA10 172 A6
Wincanton BA9 216 C3
Moorclose Dro TA7 137 C3
Moorclose La BA4 158 E6
Moor Croft Rd BS24 49 E3
Moor Dro TA7 155 F6
Moorend Gdns BS11 4 F7
Moor End Spout BS48 8 D2
Moore's La TA5, TA6 208 C7
Moores Yd BA14 83 C6
Moorfield Gdn TA24 146 C6
Moorfield Rd BS48 19 A6
Moorfields Cl BA2 44 D3
Moorfields Ct BS48 8 D2
Moorfields Dr BA2 44 D4
Moorfields Ho BS48 8 D2
Moorfields Rd
Bath BA2 44 D4
Nailsea BS48 8 D2
Moor Gate BS20 2 F4
Moor Gn BS26 70 C1
Moor Gr BS11 5 A8
Moorgrove Ho BS9 5 C7
Moorham Rd BS25 52 A1
MOORHAYNE 192 D2
Moorhouse La TA4 165 A8
Moor House La TA5 133 E4
Moorings The
Bath BA2 45 B6
Pill BS20 4 C4
Moor La
Alhampton BA4 159 C5
Backwell BS48 18 F6
Batcombe BA4 142 D1
Brushford TA22 163 F4
Churchinford TA3 192 A7

Moor La *continued*
Clapton in G BS20 2 E1
Clevedon BS21 6 E2
Clevedon BS21 7 A2
Cucklington SP8 177 E5
Draycott BS27 90 F1
East Coker BA22 197 D7
Hardington Mandeville BA22 197 A7
Higher Chillington TA20 194 F5
Hutton BS24 49 D3
North Curry TA3 170 B4
South Petherton TA13 220 B3
Tickenham BS21 7 F4
Walton in G BS21 7 C6
Westbury-sub-Mendip BA5 110 C5
Weston-Super-Mare BS24 49 F7
Wincanton BA9 216 C2
Moorland Cl TA1 213 C5
Moorland Cotts BS26 69 F2
Moorland Pk BS24 33 E5
Moorland Pl TA1 213 C5
Moorland Rd
Bath BA2 44 D5
Bridgwater TA6 209 D4
Street BA16 207 B7
Taunton TA1 213 C5
Weston-Super-Mare BS23 48 E4
MOORLANDS 44 D3
Moorlands TA4 167 F8
Moorlands Cl
16 Martock TA12 185 E6
Nailsea BS48 8 D2
Moorlands Ct TA16 195 F7
Moorlands Inf Sch BA2 44 D4
Moorlands Jun Sch BA2 44 D3
Moorlands Pk 18 TA12 185 E6
Moorlands Pk Sh Ctr 19 TA12 185 E6
Moorlands Rd TA16 195 E6
Moorland St BS26 70 C1
Moorlands The BA2 44 D3
Moorland Way TA6 209 D5
Moor Lane Cl TA3 170 B4
Moorlay Cres BS40 37 F8
MOORLEDGE 39 E1
Moorledge La BS39, BS40 57 F7
Moorledge Rd BS40 39 B1
MOORLINCH 155 E7
Moorlinch Right Dro TA7 155 D6
Moor Park Rd TA10 171 F5
Moor Pk
Clevedon BS21 6 E2
Langport TA10 171 F5
Moor Rd
Banwell BS29 51 B5
Middlezoy TA7 155 B4
Minehead TA24 200 E8
Moorlinch TA7 155 D7
Sutton Mallet TA7 155 B8
Yatton BS49 17 B2
Moorsfield BS39 58 F3
Moor Sherd BS28 110 C1
Moorside BS49 17 B1
Moorside Ct BS21 6 E2
Moorside Villas BS21 6 E2
Moortown La TA10 171 B2
Moorview Cl BA6 138 C4
Moor Villas TA13 220 B3
Moorway La DT9 188 C6
Moots La TA6 209 D4
Morangis Way TA20 223 B6
Moravia Cl TA6 208 E6
Morden Wlk BS14 23 D7
MOREBATH 164 B3
Moreton Cl BS14 23 A4
Moreton La BS40 56 E2
Moreton Mans 5 BS23 30 C1
Morford St BA1 228 B4
Morgan Cl
Saltford BS31 25 D2
Weston-Super-Mare BS22 50 B8
Morgan Pl BS48 20 B8
Morgans Bldgs BS20 8 F8
Morgans Hill Cl BS48 18 D8
Morgan's La
East Harptree BS40 74 F2
8 Frome BA11 119 E5
Morgans Rise TA1 212 A3
Morgan Way BA2 79 E7
Morland Rd TA9 104 D4
Morlands Ind Pk TA9 104 D4
Morley Terr
Bath BA2 44 D6
Radstock BA3 79 A3
Mornington Pk TA21 222 E5
Morpeth Rd BS4 22 D8
Morrell's Cross EX16 164 B4
Morrell's La EX16 178 B6
Morris Cl
Barrington TA19 184 C5
Bathford BA1 29 B3
Morris La BA1 29 B3
Morston Ct BS22 49 C7
Mortimer Cl
Bath BA1 27 B2
Woolavington TA7 136 E4
Mortimer Rd BS8 226 A3
Morton's La TA10 156 C1
Moseley Gr BS23 48 E2
Moss Cl TA6 209 C6
Moss La TA3 169 C3
Mosterton Down La DT8 196 A1
Moulton Cl BA4 205 A4
Mound The BA6 206 C4
Mounsdon Cl BA6 157 E4
Mountain Ash BA1 27 D1
Mountain's La BA2 59 E6
Mountain Wood BA1 29 C2
Mountbatten Cl
Burnham-on-S TA8 85 A1
Weston-Super-Mare BS22 31 E4
Mountbatten Ho TA6 209 C5
Mount Beacon BA1 28 A1
Mount Beacon Pl 3 BA1 27 F1
Mount Beacon Row 1 BA1 28 A1
Mounters Cl DT10 190 F5
Mounter's Hill EX13, TA20 193 B2
Mountery Cl BA5 203 D5
Mountery Rd BA5 203 D5
Mountfields Ave TA1 213 B1
Mountfields Pk TA1 213 B1
Mountfields Rd TA1 213 B1
Mount Gr BA2 44 B3
Mount Hey TA11 211 E3
Mount Hindrance Cl TA20 223 D6
Mount Hindrance La TA20 223 D6
Mount Ho TA1 212 F3
Mount La
Charlton Horethorne DT9 176 A1
Golsoncott TA23, TA24 131 C1
Mount Nebo TA1 212 E2
Mount Pleasant
Bath BA2 45 D1
Castle Cary BA7 214 C5
Crewkerne TA18 224 D6
Frome BA11 119 F2
Kilmington BA12 161 F6
Pill BS20 4 D4
Pilton BA4 140 F3
Radstock BA3 79 B2
Yeovil BA21 219 C5
Mount Pleasant Ave BA5 203 B5
MOUNT RADFORD 208 C6
Mount Rd
Bath BA1 228 B4
Bath, Southdown BA2 44 B3
Nether Stowey TA5 134 A2
Mountsfield BA11 120 A2
Mount St
Bishops Lydeard TA4 167 E8
Bridgwater TA6 208 F5
Taunton TA1 212 F3
Mount Terr TA1 213 A3
Mount The
Frome BA11 119 F2
Taunton TA1 212 F3
Yatton BS49 34 C8
Mount View
Bath, Beacon Hill BA1 28 A1
Bath, Southdown BA2 44 B3
Woolavington TA7 136 E4
Mount View Terr TA6 135 F6
Mountway TA1 213 A3
Mountway Cl TA1 212 C4
Mountway La TA1 212 C4
Mountway Rd TA1 212 C4
Movey La BA22 173 F1
Mow Barton
Bristol BS13 21 F6
8 Martock TA12 185 E6
Mow Barton Rd TA11 173 D5
Mowbray Rd BS14 23 C7
Mowcroft Rd BS13 22 D4
Mowes La DT10 190 F4
Mowground La TA7 137 A3
Mowleaze 11 BA22 197 F8
Mowries Ct TA11 211 D4
Moxham Dr BS13 22 C4
M Shed★ BS1 227 A1
MUCHELNEY 172 B3
Muchelney Abbey★ TA10 172 A3
MUCHELNEY HAM 172 B2
Muchelney Hill BA6 158 B5
Muchelney Ho TA19 221 B3
Muchelney Pottery & The John Leach Gall★ TA10 172 B2
Muchelney Way BA21 218 C7
Muckleditch La TA19 184 D3
Muddicombe Cross TA24 128 B2
Muddicombe La TA24 128 B2
Muddyford La TA4 151 A3
Muddy La BS22 32 A8
MUDFORD 187 D6
Mudford Hill BA21 187 C5
Mudford Rd BA21 219 B8
MUDFORD SOCK 187 B6
MUDGLEY 138 D8
Mudgley Cross Roads BS28 108 F1
Mudgley Hill BS28 108 E1
Mudgley Rd
Rooks Bridge BS26 87 A4
Wedmore BS28 108 E3
Mud La BS49 17 D2
Mulberry Ave BS20 2 E5
Mulberry Cl
Backwell BS48 19 A6
Portishead BS20 2 F5
Taunton TA1 213 C2
Weston-Super-Mare BS22 32 A1
Mulberry Ct BA11 120 B7
Mulberry Farm BA6 140 B1
Mulberry Gdns
4 Crewkerne TA18 224 C5
Sherborne DT9 225 C5
Mulberry La
Bleadon BS24 67 C6
Stoke Sub Hamdon TA14 186 A4
Mulberry Rd BS49 34 E3
Mulberry Tree Cl TA6 209 D5
Mulberry Wlk BS9 5 C8
Mulholland Way TA9 104 D5
Mullins Cl BA5 203 B3
Mullins Way BA7 214 B6
Mundays Mead BA9 216 D3
Munden's La DT9 189 A1
Murford Ave BS13 22 B4
Murford Wlk BS13 22 B4
Murhill BA3 64 C6
Muriel Terr BA5 203 D3
Murray-Smith Dr BA22 218 A6
Murray Way BA9 216 B3
Murtry Hill La BA11 100 C2
Musbury Cl DT10 190 F6
Musbury La DT10 190 F6
Muscovy Dr 1 TA6 154 A5
Museum of Somerset★ TA1 212 F4
Museum of South Somerset★ BA20 219 B4
Musgraves TA22 163 E6
Musgrove Rd TA1 212 C3
Musmoor La BA22 174 F7
Mus of Bath at Work★ BA1 228 B4
Mus of East Asian Art★ BA1 228 B3
Mutton La BS28 108 D4
Mutton St DT6 199 D1
Mux's La TA4 151 B3
Myrtleberry Mead BS22 32 A5
Myrtle Cl TA6 209 D5
Myrtle Dr
Bristol BS11 4 E5
Burnham-on-S TA8 104 A7
Myrtle Gdns BS49 34 C8
Myrtle Hill BS20 4 C5
Myrtle La TA21 179 E7
Myrtle Rd
Bristol BS2 226 C4
22 Martock TA12 185 E6
Myrtles The BS24 49 D2
Myrtle Tree Cres BS22 31 A6
Myrtlle Cotts TA3 182 D7

N

Nag's La TA18 195 B1
NAILSBOURNE 168 D7
NAILSEA 8 E3
Nailsea and Backwell Station BS48 18 F7
Nailsea Cl BS13 22 A7
Nailsea Com Sch BS48 8 E1
Nailsea Moor La BS48 17 F7
Nailsea Park Cl BS48 8 F2
Nailsea Pk BS48 8 F2
Nailsea Wall BS21 17 C8
Nailsea Wall La BS48 17 E7
NAILWELL 61 D6
Naishes Ave BA2 79 D7
Naish Farm BA3 96 D3
Naish Hill BS20 2 F1
Naish Ho BA2 44 A6
Naish La BS48 20 D3
Naisholt Rd BA4 204 F6
Naish Rd TA8 85 A3
Naish's Cross BA3 96 D3
Naish's St BA11 119 E5
Nanga-gat Rd BA22 174 A2
Nanny Hurn's La BS39 58 A1
Napier Ct
Bristol BS1 226 B1
Sherborne DT9 225 B2
Napier Miles Rd BS11 5 A8
Napier Rd BA1 27 A3
Naples View TA6 208 E7
NARFORD'S 193 C1
Narfords La TA20 193 C1
Narrow Plain BS2 227 B2
Narrow Quay BS1 227 A2
NASH 197 C8
Nash Barton BA22 197 C8
Nash Cl BS31 25 A5
Nash Gn TA2 212 B7
Nash La
Dinnington TA17, TA19 195 A6
East Coker BA22 197 C8
Marshwood DT6 199 B2
Yeovil BA20 218 D1
Nates La BS40 35 F1
Nathan Cl BA20 218 D2
Naunton Way BS22 31 B2
Neale's Way BA4 141 E2
Neathem Rd BA21 219 C7
Neat La BA4 204 D1
Nedge Cnr BA3 94 D4
Nedge Hill BA3 94 D3
Nedge La BA3 94 C4
Needhams Patch TA4 167 E6
NEIGHBOURNE 115 C5
Nelson Bldgs BA1 228 C4
Nelson Ct
Bridgwater TA6 208 F5
Weston-Super-Mare BS22 31 E4
Nelson Ho
Bath BA1 228 A3
5 Bristol BS1 227 A3
Nelson Pl BA1 228 C4
Nelson Pl E BA1 228 C4
Nelson Pl W BA1 228 A2
Nelson St BS1 227 A3
Nelson Terr BA1 228 C4
Nelson Villas BA1 228 A2
Nempnett St BS40 55 D5
NEMPNETT THRUBWELL 55 D5
Neroche Prim Sch TA19 183 C2
Neroche View TA3 183 A7
Nerrols Dr TA2 213 C7
Neston Wlk BS4 22 F8
NETHERCLAY 182 B7
Netherclay TA1 212 A4
Netherclay La TA3 182 B7
NETHER COMPTON 187 F4
Nethercoombe La DT9 225 C5
NETHERCOTT 151 C3
Nethercott La TA4 151 C3
Nethercott Way TA4 151 A3
NETHERHAY 199 F8
Netherhay La DT8 199 F8
Nethermoor Rd TA7 155 B3
NETHERSTOKE 197 D3
Netherstoke La BA22 197 C3
NETHER STOWEY 134 B3
Nether Stowey CE Prim Sch TA5 134 A2
Netherton Cross BA22 197 E6
Netherton La
East Coker BA22 197 F6
Marston Magna BA22 175 A1
Netherton Rd BA21 219 D7
Netherton Wood La BS48 18 A6
Netherways BS21 6 B1
Netley BA21 218 D6
NETTLEBRIDGE 115 D6
Nettlebridge Hill BA3 115 D5
NETTLECOMBE 149 F8
Nettlecombe Hill
Castle Cary BA7 214 F6
Pitcombe BA7 215 A2
Nettlecombe Ho BA5 113 A1
Nettlecombe Park Rd
Monksilver TA4 132 A1
Sticklepath TA4 149 F7
Nettle Combe View BA5 113 A2
Neva Rd BS23 48 E6
Neville Cl 1 TA11 173 F7
Neville Pk BA6 158 A5
Nevys La TA4 150 E8
Newark St BA1 228 C1
Newbarn Park Rd TA1 212 B1
Newberrys Patch TA3 192 A7
Newbery Cl 4 EX13 198 A1
Newbery La TA18 224 F3
New Bldgs
3 Bampton EX16 164 C1
Dunwear TA7 209 D1
Frome BA11 119 F3
Ilminster TA19 221 B1
North Perrott TA18 196 C4
Oake TA4 167 C4
Peasedown St John BA2 79 B8
New Bond St BA1 228 C2
New Bond Street Pl BA1 228 C2
Newbourne Rd BS22 49 C8
NEWBRIDGE 44 B8
Newbridge Ct BA1 44 B7
Newbridge Dro TA9 105 A1
Newbridge Gdns BA1 44 A8
Newbridge Hill BA1 44 B7
Newbridge Ho BS9 5 C4
Newbridge La TA9 104 F1
New Bridge Prim Sch BA1 44 B7
Newbridge Rd BA1, BA2 44 B7
New Bristol Rd BS22 31 E1
New Buildings La BA11 119 F3
New Bungalows TA20 223 C3
NEWBURY
Coleford 98 B1
Horningsham 144 E4
Newbury BA12 144 E4
Newbury Cotts BA3 117 A8
Newbury Terr 3 BA21 218 F7
Newchester Cross TA16 195 E7
New Church Rd BS23 48 D2
New Cl
Bourton SP8 161 F1
Haselbury Plucknett TA18 196 B5
Horrington BA5 113 A4
Street BA16 207 B4
Newclose La BS40 56 D1
Newclose Terr TA14 185 E4
Newcombe Cvn Pk TA8 104 B8
Newcombe Dr BS9 5 C4
Newcombe La BS25 70 B7
Newcombe Rd BS9 5 F7
Newcot Cross EX15 191 A5
NEWCOTT 192 C3
New Cotts
Milton Clevedon BA4 160 A8
West Chinnock TA18 196 B8
NEW CROSS 184 F6
New Cross TA11 211 C3
New Cross Hill
Barrington TA12, TA13 184 F6
Kingsbury Episcopi TA12 185 A6
New Cut BA5 203 D7
New Cut Bow BS21 16 A6
Newditch La BS40 20 C1
Newell DT9 225 C4
Newfield TA4 166 F4
Newfields BS40 72 C8
New Fosseway Rd BS14 23 B6
New Fosseway Sch BS14 23 B6
Newfoundland Rd BS2 227 C4
Newfoundland St BS2 227 C4
Newfoundland Way
Bristol BS2 227 C4
Portishead BS20 2 E6
New Friary Cotts BA11 143 C3
Newgate BS1 227 B3
Newgate Cross TA22 163 D7
Newgate La TA4 210 C5
Newhaven Pl BS20 1 E4
Newhaven Rd BS20 1 D4
New Hill TA11 211 E4
Newhouse La TA4 165 E6
Newington Cl BA11 119 E3
Newington Terr BA11 119 E4
New Kingsley Rd BS2 227 C2
New King St BA1 228 B2
New La
Bampton EX16 163 F2
Charlton Horethorne DT9 176 A1
Creech St Michael TA3 169 D5
Cricket St Thomas TA20 194 E4
Haselbury Plucknett TA18 196 C6
Tatworth TA20 198 C8
Witham Friary BA11 143 C4
Newland DT9 225 E4
Newland Cross TA24 128 B1
Newland Dr BS13 22 A4
Newland Flats 5 DT9 225 E4
Newland Gdn 8 DT9 225 E4
Newland Ho BA1 27 F1
Newland Rd
Bristol BS13 22 A3
Weston-Super-Mare BS23 48 F6
Newlands Cl BS20 2 C5
Newlands Cres TA3 169 C3
Newlands Gn BS21 6 E1
Newlands Gr TA3 169 C3
Newlands Hill BS20 2 C4
Newlands Rd
Keynsham BS31 24 D4
Ruishton TA3 169 C3
Newland Wlk BS13 22 A3
Newlyn Ave BS9 5 D5
Newlyn Cres TA7 136 B4
Newman Cl BA6 206 E6
Newmans La
East Huntspill TA9 105 C1
Timsbury BA2 60 B2
Newmarket Ave 9 BS1 227 A3
New Mdws BS14 23 A6
Newnham Cl BS14 23 D7
New Oak Prim Sch BS14 23 B7
New Orchard St BA1 228 C2
New Park Ho BS21 6 D5
New Pit Cotts BA2 60 F1
New Pk EX16 162 E4
NEWPORT 170 B2
Newport Cl
Clevedon BS21 6 C2
Portishead BS20 1 F4
Newport Hill TA3 170 B2
Newport Rd BS20 4 C5
Newquay Rd BS4 22 F8
New Rd
Banwell BS29 50 E4
Barwick BA22 197 F8
Bathford BA1 29 D2
Bawdrip TA7 136 D2
Bridgwater TA6 209 A5
Burrowbridge TA3, TA7 170 E8
Cannington TA5 135 C1
Carhampton TA24 131 A5
Chapel Allerton BS26 88 C2
Chard Junction TA20 198 F8
Churchill BS25 52 F4
Clevedon BS21 6 D2
Combe St Nicholas TA20 193 D6
Crewkerne TA18 195 B4
Crickham BS28 108 D8
Draycott BS27 91 C3
East Huntspill TA9 136 D8
Freshford BA3 64 B5
Frome BA11 120 B4
Hambridge TA12 184 E7
Haselbury Plucknett TA18 196 E6
High Littleton BS39 59 C3
Hinton St George TA17 195 C7
Ilminster TA19 221 B4
Kilmersdon BA3 98 E4
Kilmington BA12 161 E7
Lyng TA3 170 B6
North Wootton BA4 140 A4
Norton Sub Hamdon, Chiselborough TA14 185 F1
Norton Sub Hamdon TA14 185 E3
Oare EX35 122 D4
Odcombe BA22 186 D3
Othery TA7 155 C2
Pensford BS39 40 D3
Pill BS20 4 C4
Porlock TA24 123 E3
Rawridge EX14 191 E1
Redhill BS40 37 A4
Seavington St Mary TA19 184 E1
Sherborne DT9 225 E3
Shipham BS25 52 E1
South Cadbury BA22 175 E4
Stalbridge DT10 190 B4
Staple Fitzpaine TA3 182 D5
Taunton TA3 168 D1
West Bagborough TA4 151 E4
Weston Town BA4 142 D5
Wiveliscombe TA4 166 A6
Yeovil BA22 218 A5
New Road Gate EX35 122 D5
New Rock Ind Est BA3 96 D2
Newsome Ave BS20 4 C4
New Sq BA5 113 A2

New St
Bath BA1 228 B2
Bristol BS2 227 C3
Long Sutton TA10 172 E4
Marnhull DT10 190 F5
Mells BA11 118 B7
North Perrott TA18 196 C4
Somerton TA11 211 E4
Wells BA5 203 D5
New Street Flats 4 BS2 227 C3
New Thomas St BS2 227 C2
NEWTON
Combe St Nicholas 193 A7
Watchet 132 E1
Newton Cl
Burnham-on-S TA8 85 A2
West Harptree BS40 74 E6
Newton Ct 14 EX16 164 B1
Newton Gn BS48 18 C8
Newton La
Bicknoller TA4 132 E1
Corfe TA3 181 F6
Newton Rd
Barwick BA22 197 F8
Bath BA2 43 F6
North Petherton TA6 153 F3
Taunton TA1 213 E4
Weston-Super-Mare BS23 48 E6
Yeovil BA20 219 D3
NEWTON ST LOE 43 D6
Newton Sq 8 EX16 164 B1
Newton's Rd
Weston-Super-Mare BS22 31 E3
Weston-Super-Mare BS22 31 E4
NEWTOWN
Axbridge 69 D2
Bridgwater 208 E6
NEW TOWN
Bishop Sutton 57 D7
Freshford 81 F8
Hatch Beauchamp 182 E4
Kington Magna 177 E1
Milborne Port 217 B2
Paulton 77 D6
Wedmore 138 E8
Yeovil 219 C6
Newtown TA12 185 E7
Newtown La BA6 140 A1
Newtown Pk TA10 172 A6
Newtown Rd
Highbridge TA9 104 D3
Langport TA10 172 A6
New Way TA10 172 B7
Nibley Rd BS11 4 E5
Nicholas Cl TA22 163 E4
Nicholls Cl TA6 208 D4
Nichol Pl TA4 167 F6
Nichol's Rd BS20 1 F5
Nick Reed's La EX15 180 D1
Nidon La TA7 137 D3
Nigel Pk BS11 4 E7
Nightingale Acre TA3 183 A7
Nightingale Ave BA11 120 B6
Nightingale Cl
1 Bridgwater TA6 209 C4
Burnham-on-S TA8 85 B1
Wells BA5 203 B3
Weston-Super-Mare BS22 31 E1
Nightingale Ct
16 Taunton TA1 213 A4
Weston-Super-Mare BS22 31 E1
Nightingale Gdns BS48 8 D2
Nightingale Gr BA4 205 C5
Nightingale La BA22 174 F6
Nightingale Rise BS20 1 F3
Nightingales TA4 167 E6
Nightingale Way BA3 97 B8
Nile St BA1 228 A2
NIMMER 223 C8
Nine Acre Dro TA7 138 B2
Nine Acre La TA3 170 C4
Nine Barrows La BA5 92 E4
Nippors Way BS25 69 F8
Nithsdale Rd BS23 48 E4
Nixon Trad Units BS24 49 A3
No 1 Royal Cres Mus★ BA1 228 B3
Noah's Ark Zoo Farm★ BS48 9 B7
Noah's Hill TA2 169 B7
Noake Rd DT9 225 B3
Noble St TA1 213 B4
Noel Coward Cl TA8 104 C6
Nomis Pk BS49 34 E2
No Place La TA5 152 E5
Norbins Rd BA6 206 D5
Nordens Mdw TA4 210 D4
Nordrach La BS40 73 D5
Nore Gdns BS20 2 C6
Nore Park Dr BS20 1 F5
Nore Rd BS20 2 A6
Norfolk Ave BS2 227 B4
Norfolk Bldgs BA1 228 A2
Norfolk Cl TA6 209 C3
Norfolk Cres BA1 228 A2
Norfolk Gr BS31 24 C4
Norfolk Hts 10 BS2 227 B4
Norfolk Rd
Portishead BS20 2 E4
Weston-Super-Mare BS23 48 F5
Norland Rd BS8 11 F8
Norlet Ct BA6 206 D5
Normandy Ave TA23 202 E6
Normandy Dr TA1 213 C3
Normandy Ho BA16 207 B6
Norman La TA7 156 B7
Norman Rd BS31 25 E3
Normans The BA2 28 F1
Normans Way BS20 3 E7
Norrington Way TA20 223 D2
Northam Farm Cvn Pk & Camp Site TA8 65 F4
Northampton Bldgs BA1 228 B4
Northampton Ho BS48 9 D3
Northampton St BA1 228 B4
Northanger Ct 5 BA2 228 C3
North Ave TA9 104 C4
NORTHAY
Combe St Nicholas 193 B6
Hawkchurch 199 A3
Northay Cross EX13 199 B3
Northay La
Axminster EX13 199 A3
Combe St Nicholas TA20 193 B6
North Bank BA5 203 A8
NORTH BARROW 175 A8
NORTH BREWHAM 161 A7
Northbrook Dr TA7 137 F1
Northbrook Rd
Cannington TA5 135 C2
Shapwick TA7 138 A1
Yeovil BA21 219 D7
NORTH CADBURY 175 D6
North Cadbury CE Prim Sch BA22 175 D6
NORTH CHERITON 176 C4
North Chew Terr BS40 39 B3
North Chine Dro BA5 138 D8
North Cl BS27 90 F3
NORTH COKER 197 D8
Northcombe La TA22 163 E7
Northcote Cres BA11 120 A7
Northcote Rd BS8 5 F1
North Cres DT9 217 D3
North Croft TA4 202 D3
NORTH CURRY 170 C4
North Curry CE Prim Sch TA3 170 B3
North Down Cl BS25 70 F8
North Down La BS25 70 F8
Northdown Rd BA3 78 E5
North Dro BS48 8 A2
NORTHEND 28 F5
NORTH END
Clutton 58 E5
Millmoor 179 E3
Taunton 169 D5
Yatton 16 F3
North End
Charlton Horethorne DT9 176 A2
Creech St Michael TA3 169 D5
Midsomer Norton BA3 78 B2
North End Rd BS49 16 F3
Northern Path BS21 6 F3
Northern Way BS21 6 F3
NORTHFIELD
Bridgwater 208 C4
Radstock 79 B1
Somerton 211 C5
Northfield
Bridgwater TA6 208 E4
Radstock BA3 79 A3
Somerton TA11 211 C4
Timsbury BA2 60 C3
Winsley BA15 64 F7
Northfield Ave TA1 212 E4
Northfield Cl TA5 134 C6
Northfield Gdns TA1 212 E5
Northfield Ho
Bath BA1 27 F1
Glastonbury BA6 206 E4
Northfield La
Dinnington TA17 195 B8
South Petherton TA13 220 C2
Northfield Rd
Minehead TA24 201 A8
Portishead BS20 1 E3
Taunton TA1 212 E4
Northfields
Bath BA1 27 F1
Taunton TA1 212 B3
Northfields Cl BA1 27 F1
Northfield Way TA11 211 C5
NORTHGATE 210 C5
Northgate
Bridgwater TA6 208 F5
Wiveliscombe TA4 210 C5
Northgate St BA1 228 C2
North Gr
Pill BS20 4 C4
Wells BA5 203 E5
North Green St 11 BS8 11 F6
North Hill House BA11 120 A6
North Hill Mews BA11 119 F5
North Hill Rd TA24 200 F8
North Hills Cl BS24 49 B2
North Hill Woodland Trail★ TA24 125 B4
North La
Bath BA2 45 D5
Berrow TA8 65 F1
Challacombe EX31, TA24 126 B4
East Coker BA22 197 A7
Nailsea BS48 8 B1
Othery TA7 155 C2
Stogursey TA5 134 C7
2 Weston-Super-Mare BS23 48 E7
Yeovil BA20 219 B5
Northleach Wlk BS11 4 F5
North Leaze BS41 11 B2
Northleaze CE Prim Sch BS41 11 B2
Northleaze Ho BA16 207 C6
North Leaze La BA22 175 C7
Northleigh Ave BS22 31 C1
Northleigh Rd TA1 213 B3
Northload Bridge BA6 206 C5
Northload Bridge Rdbt BA6 206 D5
Northload Dro BS28 109 E2
Northload La BS28 109 D1
Northload St BA6 206 D5
Northload Terr BA6 206 D5
North Mdws BA2 79 E8
Northmead Ave BA3 77 F2
Northmead Cl BA3 77 F2
Northmead Dro TA3 170 A1
Northmead Rd BA3 77 F2
North Mills La TA13 220 C5
Northmoor La TA3 170 C7
Northmoor Rd
Dulverton TA22 163 D7
Othery TA10 155 D1
NORTH NEWTON 153 F2
NORTHOVER
Glastonbury 206 B3
Ilchester 173 E2
Northover Bldgs BA6 206 B3
Northover Dr TA20 223 B5
Northover Farmhouse BA6 207 D8
North Par
Bath BA2 228 C2
Frome BA11 119 F5
North Parade Bldgs 8 BA1 228 C2
North Parade Pas 7 BA1 228 C2
North Parade Rd BA2 45 B6
NORTH PERROTT 196 C4
North Perrott Rd TA18 196 C5
NORTH PETHERTON 153 F4
North Petherton Com Jun Sch TA6 153 F3
North Petherton Inf Sch TA6 153 F3
North Rd
Banwell BS29 51 A3
Bath, Bathwick BA2 45 C6
Bath, Combe Down BA2 45 B2
Charlton Horethorne DT9 176 A2
Eastertown BS24 67 D2
Leigh Woods BS8 11 D7
Midsomer Norton BA3 78 A1
Minehead TA24 201 A7
Sherborne DT9 225 E5
Timsbury BA2 60 C2
Wells BA5 203 E5
Williton TA4 202 D4
Northside
Castle Cary BA7 214 C6
Rockwell Green TA21 222 B5
North Side Rd BS48 36 F8
North Somerset Mus★ BS23 48 E8
North St
Babcary TA11 174 C7
Bradford Abbas DT9 187 E1
Bridgwater TA6 208 E4
Bristol BS1 227 B4
Castle Cary BA7 214 C5
Crewkerne TA18 224 C7
Drayton TA10 171 E3
Haselbury Plucknett TA18 196 C6
Ilminster TA19 221 C4
Langport TA10 172 A5
Martock TA12 185 E6
Milborne Port DT9 217 D2
Milverton TA4 167 A4
Nailsea BS48 8 B1
North Petherton TA6 153 E4
Norton St Philip BA2 81 E4
Norton Sub Hamdon TA14 185 E1
Shepton Beauchamp TA19 184 E4
Somerton TA11 211 E4
South Petherton TA13 220 C5
Stoke sub Hamdon TA14 185 F4
Taunton TA1 212 F4
Wellington TA21 222 D6
Weston-Super-Mare BS23 48 E8
Williton TA4 202 D3
Wincanton BA9 216 C4
Wiveliscombe TA4 210 B4
NORTH STOKE 26 C6
North Stoke La BS30 26 B8
North Terr BA21 219 C6
NORTH TOWN
North Cadbury 175 C7
North Wootton 140 D5
Taunton 212 E5
North Town TA11 173 D5
North Town Com Prim Sch TA1 212 E4
Northtown La
North Wootton BA4 140 C4
Taunton TA1 212 E4
North Town Mews TA1 212 E5
Northumberland Bldgs 1 BA1 228 B2
Northumberland Pl 1 BA1 228 C2
North View BA3 79 B2
North View Cl BA2 44 B5
North View Dr BS29 51 A2
North Villas TA4 167 F6
North Way
Bath BA2 44 A5
Midsomer Norton BA3 78 A1
NORTH WESTON 2 C2
NORTHWICK 105 F6
NORTH WICK 39 D8
Northwick Gdns BS39 57 D4
Northwick Rd
Chew Magna BS39, BS41 39 D7
Mark TA9 106 B5
NORTH WIDCOMBE 57 B1
Northwood Cl TA2 168 B4
Northwood Dro BA6 158 A6
NORTH WOOTTON
Sherborne 188 F1
Wells 140 C4
NORTON 31 D4
Norton Cl
Chew Magna BS40 39 B3
Shepton Mallet BA4 205 A5
Norton Dro TA12 185 B8
NORTON FITZWARREN 168 B4
Norton Fitzwarren CE Com Prim Sch TA2 168 B5
Norton Grange BA2 81 E5
NORTON HAWKFIELD 39 F6
NORTON HILL 97 B7
Norton Hill Sch BA3 97 B8
Norton Ho 7 BS1 227 B1
Norton La
Chew Magna BS39, BS40 39 D5
Wellow BA2 81 B7
Weston-Super-Mare BS22 31 C4
Whitchurch BS14 23 C2
NORTON MALREWARD 40 B7
Norton Radstock Coll BA3 78 F2
Norton Rd TA14 185 E3
NORTON ST PHILIP 81 F4
Norton St Philip CE Fst Sch BA2 81 E4
NORTON SUB HAMDON 185 F3
Norton sub Hamdon CE Prim Sch TA14 185 F3
NORTON'S WOOD 7 C5
Nortons Wood La BS21 7 A5
Norville Cl BS27 90 B8
Norville La BS27 90 B8
Norwich Cl TA1 212 C1
Norwich Ct TA1 212 D2
Norwood Ave BA2 45 E5
Norwood Gr BS20 1 F5
Notgrove Cl BS22 31 B2
Notlake Dro BS27 89 E4
Notting Hill Way BS26 88 D6
Nova Scotia Pl BS1 226 A1
Novers Cres BS4 22 C8
Novers Hill BS4 22 C8
Novers La BS4 22 D7
NOVERS PARK 22 D8
Novers Park Dr BS4 22 C8
Novers Park Rd BS4 22 D8
Novers Rd BS4 22 C8
Nowers La TA21 222 C3
Nowhere La BS48 9 A1
Number 15 BA21 219 F7
NUNNEY 143 C8
Nunney Barton BA11 119 D4
Nunney Castle★ BA11 143 B8
NUNNEY CATCH 143 B7
Nunney Catch Rbt BA11 143 B7
Nunney Cl
Burnham-on-S TA8 85 C1
Keynsham BS31 25 A2
Nunney Fst Sch BA11 143 B8
Nunney Rd BA11 119 D4
Nurcott La TA24 147 C7
Nursery Cl TA5 135 B5
Nursery Gdns TA20 223 E4
Nursery La BA9 216 C4
Nursery Rd BA20 219 A3
Nursery Rise BA3 96 E4
Nursery Terr TA6 208 E5
Nursery Villas TA20 223 E4
Nutgrove La BS40 39 A4
Nutshole La TA20 194 B2
Nut Tree Cl TA9 136 E8
Nut Tree La TA18 224 D7
Nutts La BA11 101 F8
Nutwell Rd BS22 31 E2
Nutwell Sq BS22 31 E2
Nydon The TA7 137 D3
NYE 51 E8
Nye Cl BS27 90 C7
Nye Dro BS24 51 E8
Nye Rd BS25 51 F5
NYLAND 90 C1
Nyland Dro BS27 90 B1
Nyland La BA8 190 C8
Nyland View BS27 90 F3
NYNEHEAD 167 C1
Nynehead Hollow TA21 167 C1
Nynehead Prim Sch TA21 167 B1
Nynehead Rd
Nynehead TA21 167 C1
Wellington TA21 222 F8
Nythe Rd TA7 156 A5

O

Oak Apple Dr TA6 208 D6
Oak Ave BA2 44 C3
Oak Cl TA24 200 D7
Oak Ct
Bristol BS14 23 A5
Weston-Super-Mare BS22 32 C3
Oakdale Gdns BS22 31 F2
Oakdale Rd BS14 23 A8
Oak Dr
Crewkerne TA18 224 D7
Oak Dr *continued*
Portishead BS20 2 B4
OAKE 167 D4
Oake Acres TA4 167 D4
Oake & Bradford Com Prim Sch TA4 167 D4
Oake Cl TA4 167 D4
Oake Gn TA4 167 D4
Oak End Way TA20 223 C5
Oaken Ground TA21 222 B5
Oakfield Cl
Bath BA1 44 D8
Frome BA11 119 D5
Oakfield Gr BS8 226 B4
Oakfield Pk TA21 222 E4
Oakfield Pl BS8 226 B4
Oakfield Rd
Bridgwater TA6 208 C4
Bristol BS8 226 B4
Frome BA11 119 D4
Keynsham BS31 24 F2
Street BA16 207 B4
Oakfield Sch BA11 119 D4
Oakford Ave BS23 48 F8
Oakford La BA1 29 A8
Oak Gr BS20 4 C5
Oakgrove Way TA6 209 D6
OAKHILL 115 A3
Oakhill BS24 49 A2
Oakhill CE Prim Sch BA3 115 B3
Oakhill Cl BS48 9 B1
Oakhill Ct BA3 116 E3
Oakhill Rd BA2 44 F2
Oak Ho
Brean TA8 65 E2
Bristol BS13 22 D4
Oakhurst Rd BS9 5 F5
Oak La
East Anstey TA22 162 E6
Rodhuish TA24 131 A3
Taunton TA2 212 F6
Oakland Ct TA12 185 E7
Oakland Dr
Hutton BS24 49 E3
Martock TA12 185 E7
Oakland Rd TA12 185 E7
Oaklands
Cheddar BS27 90 A8
Clevedon BS21 6 C4
Paulton BS39 77 E4
Temple Cloud BS39 58 E1
Oaklands Ave TA20 223 F4
Oaklands Rd BA21 219 D7
Oakleigh BA20 218 D2
Oakleigh Cl BS48 19 B5
Oakley
Bath BA2 45 E5
Clevedon BS21 16 B8
Oakley Cl TA7 154 F5
Oakley La BA22 186 F6
Oak Lodge Cres TA24 200 F7
Oak Rd
Nether Stowey TA5 134 B2
Winscombe BS25 70 A8
Oakridge Cl BS25 70 B7
Oakridge La BS25 70 C6
Oakridge Pk BA21 219 A6
Oak's Dro BA5 138 E8
Oaksey Gr BS48 9 A1
Oak St BA2 228 B1
Oaks The
Nailsea BS48 9 A2
Taunton TA1 213 C1
Wembdon TA6 208 C6
Winford BS40 37 F7
Oak Terr BA3 78 D1
Oak Tree Cl EX14 191 F2
Oaktree Ct BS11 4 E7
Oaktree Gdns BS13 21 E5
Oak Tree Ho 13 TA14 185 F4
Oaktree Pk BS24 49 E5
Oaktree Pl BS22 32 C3
Oak Tree Pl TA8 85 A3
Oak Tree Way TA5 135 B2
Oak Tree Wlk BS31 24 D3
Oak Vale La BA8 190 A6
Oak Way BA22 218 A7
OARE 122 E4
OAREFORD 122 F3
Oare Post TA24 123 B3
Oatfield BS48 19 F1
OATHILL 199 E8
Oathill Cotts BA4 140 F3
Oathill La
Clapton TA18 195 C1
Winsham TA18 199 E8
Oatlands Ave BS14 23 A6
Oatley La TA5 134 F2
Oborne Rd DT9 225 F5
OBRIDGE 213 A6
Obridge Cl TA2 213 A6
Obridge Cres TA2 213 A6
Obridge La TA2 213 A6
Obridge Rd TA2 213 A6
Obridge Viaduct TA2 213 B6
Observatory Field BS25 70 B8
Observatory The BS22 31 D3
Ocean Way BA22 174 B3
Octagon The 5 TA1 212 F4
ODCOMBE 186 D2
Odcombe Hollow BA22 196 E8
ODD DOWN 44 D2
Odeon Bldgs BS23 48 E7
Odins Rd BA2 44 D1
Olands Rd TA21 222 D6
Old Acre Rd BS14 23 A3

Old Airfield Cvn Pk The
TA7 155 A4
Old Ansford Inn BA7 214 C6
Old App BA7 159 A3
Old Banwell Rd BS24 50 B4
Oldbarn La
Bampton EX16 163 E1
Compton Martin BS40 56 D1
Old Barn La
Felton BS40 37 A5
Hatch Beauchamp TA3 182 F6
Old Barn Way BA20 218 E3
Old Barrow Hill BS11 4 D7
Old Basin TA6 209 B2
Oldberry La TA22 163 D6
Old Bond St 4 BA1 228 B2
Old Bowden Way DT9 217 D4
Old Bread St BS2 227 C2
Old Brewery Ind Est The
TA4 210 C4
Old Brewery Rd TA4 210 C4
Old Brewery The
6 Frome BA11 119 F4
Rode BA11 101 E8
Old Brewhouse The BA1 27 B2
Old Bridge Cl BA6 206 D5
Oldbridge Rd BS14 23 C3
Old Bristol Rd
East Brent TA9 86 E4
Oakhill BA3, BA4 114 E1
Priddy BA5, BS40 93 A6
Shepton Mallet BA4 141 C8
Wells BA5 112 B5
Weston-Super-Mare BS22 32 A2
Oldbroach La TA3 213 F2
Old Bull La BA4 141 F7
Old Burnham Rd TA9 104 D4
Old Chapel BA1 228 C4
Old Chapel Ct TA10 172 A6
Old Chapel Rd TA7 155 B3
Old Chelsea La BS8 10 C4
Old Church Rd
Axbridge BS26 70 C1
Clevedon BS21 6 C3
Nailsea BS48 18 D8
Weston-Super-Mare BS23 48 D2
OLD CLEEVE 131 E5
Old Cleeve CE Sch TA23 131 E4
Old Coach Rd BS26 69 E2
Old Combe Hill TA3 181 F5
Old Co-op Cotts BA3 117 A7
Old Dairy Ct BS21 6 E3
Old Dairy The BA2 44 D4
OLD DITCH 110 E7
Old Ditch BA5 110 E7
Old Ditch La TA7 155 E7
OLD DOWN 95 F3
Old Down La BA4 142 A6
Old Drill Hall The BS2 227 C3
Old England Way BA2 79 E8
Old Farm DT9 225 C4
Old Farm Cl TA24 200 E6
Old Farm Ct
Blackford BS28 107 E4
Queen Camel BA22 174 F3
Old Farm Pl TA17 195 C7
Old Farm Rd
Minehead TA24 200 E6
Nether Stowey TA5 134 B2
Old Ferry Rd BA2 44 C6
Oldfield BS21 6 E1
Oldfield Girls Sch BA1 26 F1
Oldfield La BA2 44 E4
OLDFIELD PARK 44 E4
Oldfield Park Inf Sch BA2 44 D6
Oldfield Park Jun Sch
BA2 44 C4
Oldfield Park Sta BA2 44 D6
Oldfield Pl BS8 11 F5
Oldfield Rd
Bath BA2 228 A1
Bristol BS8 226 A1
OLDFORD 101 B1
Oldford Hill BA11 101 B1
Oldford Residential Pk
BA11 101 B1
Old Forge The BA2 61 B4
Old Forge Way BA2 79 E8
Old Fosse Rd
Bath BA2 44 C1
Clandown BA3 78 E4
Old Frome Rd
Bath BA2 62 E8
Doulting BA4 141 E8
Horrington BA5 113 D3
Oakhill BA3, BA4 115 B1
Old Glove Factory The
BA22 186 B6
Old Gore La BA3 95 E3
Old Green The 2 DT9 225 D4
Old Ham TA5 133 D6
Old Hill
Wincanton BA9 216 C5
Winford BS40 37 D6
Wrington BS40 35 F3
Old Hitchen 5 TA16 195 F7
Old Ho The BA3 64 C5
Old Junction Rd BS23 49 B5
Old King St BA1 228 B3
Old King Street Ct BS1 227 B3
Old La
Farmborough BA2 60 A6
Nailsea BS21 8 C4
Porlock TA24 124 B3
Old Main Rd TA6 135 F5
Old Malt Ho BS2 227 C4
Old Maltings The BA3 115 A3
Old Manor Est BA3 116 C8
Old Market 6 TA12 185 E6
Old Market Ct BA6 206 D5
Old Market Mews DT10 190 B4
Old Market Rd BA4 205 B6
Old Market Rdbt BS2 227 C3
Old Market St BS2 227 C3
Oldmead La BS26 87 C5
Oldmead Wlk BS13 21 E7
Old Midford Rd BA2 63 B7
Old Millard's Hill BA3 78 B3
Old Mill Rd
Portishead BS20 2 D5
Woolavington TA7 136 E4
OLD MILLS 77 D3
Old Mills Ind Est BS39 77 E2
Old Mills La BS39 77 D3
Old Mill Way
Wells BA5 203 B2
Weston-Super-Mare BS24 50 A8
OLDMIXON 49 B1
Oldmixon Cres BS24 49 A3
Oldmixon Prim Sch BS24 49 A2
Oldmixon Rd BS24 49 B1
Old Mixon Rd BS24 49 C2
Old Newbridge Hill BA1 44 A8
Old Oaks Cl TA6 208 D5
Old Orch TA20 223 F1
Old Orchard BA1 228 C3
Old Orchard Cl TA19 183 F4
Old Orchards TA20 223 E4
Old Orchard St BA1 228 C2
Old Orchard The TA19 221 A5
Old Orch The TA13 220 D4
Old Park Hill BS2 226 C3
Old Park Rd
Bristol BS11 4 D7
Clevedon BS21 6 E4
Old Pawlett Rd TA9 136 A7
Old Pit Rd BA3 97 C8
Old Pit Terr BA3 78 E4
Old Pk BS2 226 C3
Old Police Station The
BA9 216 C4
Old Post Office Cotts
TA7 153 F2
Old Post Office La BS23 48 D8
Old Pound Ct SP8 161 E1
Old Print Works 6 BA11 119 E5
Old Priory Rd BS20 4 B4
Old Quarry BA2 44 D2
Old Quarry Rd BS11 4 E7
Old Quarry Rise BS11 4 E7
Old Rd
North Petherton TA6 153 F4
Odcombe BA22 186 C2
Pensford BS39 40 E3
Radstock BA3 79 C1
South Cadbury BA22 175 E4
Old Rd The BA8 189 D6
Old Rectory The TA9 86 C4
Oldrey La TA24 147 C8
Old Saw Mills The BA3 117 A3
Old Sawmill The BA12 161 F6
Old School Cl
Alweston DT9 189 A1
Ashcott TA7 156 B8
Churchill BS25 52 F4
Yeovil BA21 218 C5
Old School Hill BA2 62 F7
Old School Ho BA21 219 C5
Old School Ho The
Bath BA1 228 B4
Whatley BA11 118 A3
Old School La
Bleadon BS24 67 C6
Catcott TA7 137 D2
Lynford-on-F TA11 158 C2
Old School Pl
Sherborne DT9 225 D3
Wells BA5 203 E5
Old School The BA11 119 E4
Oldshute La TA22 163 C7
Old Sneed Ave BS9 5 D4
Old Sneed Cotts BS9 5 E4
Old Sneed Pk BS9 5 D4
Old Sneed Rd BS9 5 D4
Old St BS21 6 E3
Old Station Cl
Cheddar BS27 90 A7
Wrington BS40 35 D1
Old Station Ct TA20 223 D5
Old Station Gdns BA8 190 A7
Old Station La BA10 215 C4
Old Station Rd BA20 219 C4
Old Station Way BA20 219 C4
Old Stream Farm TA10 171 E3
Old Street La BA5 204 B7
Old Tannery The 20 BS2 227 C3
Old Tarnwell BS39 40 B2
Old Taunton Rd TA6 209 A4
Old Threshing Mill The
BA4 141 B2
Old Tiverton Rd EX16 164 C1
Old Tk BA2 63 F7
Old Town TA20 223 C3
Old Vicarage Cl TA7 137 B2
Old Vicarage Ct BS14 23 C4
Old Vicarage Gdns TA13 220 C4
Old Vicarage Gn BS31 24 E6
Old Vicarage La TA4 167 E8
Old Vicarage The TA21 222 E6
Oldville Ave BS21 6 D2
Old Walcot Sch The BA1 228 B3
Old Wall BS24 66 D5
Old Water Gdns The BS40 54 E2
OLD WAY 184 A4
Old Way
Chipstable TA4 165 D6
Old Way *continued*
Stogumber TA4 150 D8
Oldway Ho TA21 222 F4
Oldway La TA3 183 A8
Oldway Pk TA21 222 F4
Oldway Pl TA9 104 D4
Oldway Rd
East Anstey TA22 162 F5
Wellington TA21 222 E4
OLDWAYS END 162 E3
Old Wells Rd
Bath BA2 44 F3
Croscombe BA5 204 D6
Doulting BA4 142 A8
Glastonbury BA6 206 F6
Leigh u M BA3, BA4, BA11 117 B2
Shepton Mallet BA4 205 A5
Old Weston Rd
Congresbury BS49 34 B5
Flax Bourton BS48 20 B8
Old Yarn Mills The DT9 225 D2
Oliver Brooks Rd BA3 96 E7
Oliver's La TA19 183 B2
Olivier Cl TA8 104 C6
One Elm TA10 172 B7
Onega Ctr BA1 228 A3
Onega Terr BA1 228 A3
Oolite Gr BA2 44 D1
Oolite Rd BA2 44 D1
Orange Gr BA1 228 C2
Orange St BS2 227 C4
Orchard Ave
Bristol BS1 226 C2
Midsomer Norton BA3 77 F1
Portishead BS21 7 E4
Orchard Cl
Banwell BS29 51 B3
Bishop Sutton BS39 57 C3
Bradford On Tone TA4 167 F1
Bristol, Westbury on T BS9 5 F5
Carhampton TA24 131 B5
Castle Cary BA7 214 B7
Cheddar BS27 90 B8
Coleford BA3 117 A7
Congresbury BS49 34 D4
Cossington TA7 137 A3
Coxley BA5 139 E6
Drimpton DT8 199 F8
East Brent TA9 86 E4
East Chinnock BA22 196 E8
East Huntspill TA9 136 E8
Felton BS40 37 C8
Flax Bourton BS48 20 A8
Frome BA11 119 D4
Highbridge TA9 104 E4
Keynsham BS31 24 D6
Long Sutton TA10 172 E4
3 North Petherton TA6 153 E3
Odcombe BA22 186 C2
Portishead BS20 2 D5
Queen Camel BA22 174 F3
Rockwell Green TA21 222 A5
South Petherton TA13 220 C5
Sparkford BA22 175 A5
Taunton TA3 168 D1
Wedmore BS28 108 C4
West Coker BA22 197 A8
Weston-Super-Mare, Kewstoke
BS22 31 B3
Weston-Super-Mare, Worle
BS22 31 F2
Westwood BA15 64 F3
Wincanton BA9 216 D3
Wrington BS40 35 E2
Yeovil Marsh BA21 187 A5
Orchard Cl The BS24 49 F4
ORCHARD COMMON 182 A8
Orchard Cotts
Croscombe BA5 204 B7
Timsbury BA2 60 F1
Orchard Cres BS11 4 D7
Orchard Ct
Claverham BS49 17 F1
Highbridge TA9 104 E3
Minehead TA24 201 B4
Street BA16 207 C6
Wellington TA21 222 E6
Orchard Dr
Bristol BS13 22 A6
Sandford BS25 52 A4
Southwick BA14 83 E3
Taunton TA1 212 A3
Orchard End BS40 74 F4
Orchard Gdns
Paulton BS39 77 E6
West Buckland TA21 180 F7
Orchard Gn TA2 212 F8
Orchard Ho
Weston-Super-Mare BS22 31 F2
Yeovil BA21 219 A6
Orchard La
Allerford TA24 124 B4
Bristol BS1 226 C2
Chewton Mendip BA3 94 F6
Crewkerne TA18 224 C6
Evercreech BA4 141 E1
Kingsbury Episcopi TA12 185 B8
Thorncombe TA20 199 B6
Wembdon TA6 208 D5
Orchard Lea
Coxley BA5 139 E7
Pill BS20 4 D4
Wells BA5 203 C5
Orchardleigh BA22 196 E8
Orchardleigh View BA11 119 D6
Orchard Lodge BA2 45 F8
Orchard Mead TA19 183 C1
Orchard Paddock BA5 203 A7
Orchard Pk
Bristol BS14 23 D4
West Camel BA22 174 D3
Orchard Pl
Aller TA10 171 D8
1 Weston-Super-Mare
BS23 48 E7
Orchard Rd
Axbridge BS26 70 C1
Backwell BS48 19 A6
Carhampton TA24 131 B5
Clevedon BS21 6 D2
Hutton BS24 49 E2
Long Ashton BS41 10 F1
Milborne Port DT9 217 C2
Minehead TA24 200 F8
Nailsea BS48 8 D1
Paulton BS39 77 E6
Somerton TA11 211 B4
Street BA16 207 C6
Orchard Rise
Crewkerne TA18 224 C5
Fivehead TA3 170 F2
Porlock TA24 124 A3
Ruishton TA3 169 C4
Orchards Sh Ctr TA1 212 F3
Orchard St
Bristol BS1 226 C2
Frome BA11 119 E5
Weston-Super-Mare BS23 48 E8
Yeovil BA20 219 A4
Orchards The
Bristol, Shirehampton BS11 4 E6
Horrington BA5 113 A2
Stocklinch TA19 184 C4
Orchard Terr
5 Bath BA2 44 B6
Glastonbury BA6 206 D5
Orchard The
Banwell BS29 51 A3
Bath, Combe Down BA2 45 B1
Bath, Newbridge BA1 44 A7
Chard TA20 223 D2
Corston BA2 43 B8
Freshford BA3 64 C5
Holywell Lake TA21 179 E7
Locking BS24 50 A5
Meare BA6 138 D4
Pensford BS39 40 E4
Pill BS20 4 C4
Ruishton TA3 169 C2
Upper Stanton Drew BS39 40 A2
Orchard Vale
Ilminster TA19 221 B3
Langport TA10 172 A5
Midsomer Norton BA3 77 F1
Orchard View
Baltonsborough BA6 158 B6
Haselbury Plucknett TA18 196 C6
Orchard Way
Charlton Horethorne
DT9 176 A2
Cheddar BS27 90 B8
Keinton Mandeville TA11 158 A1
Misterton TA18 224 F3
Peasedown St John BA2 79 D7
Shapwick TA7 137 F1
Taunton TA1 213 D5
Timberscombe TA24 130 B5
Williton TA4 202 E4
Woolavington TA7 136 E3
Orchard Wlk
Churchill BS25 52 E4
Milborne Port DT9 217 C2
Orchard Wyndham*
TA4 132 B2
Orchid Cl TA1 169 A1
Orchid Dr BA2 44 C2
Orchids The TA8 85 A2
Oriel Dr BA6 206 D4
Oriel Gdns BA1 28 C2
Oriel Gr BA2 44 B4
Oriel Rd BA16 207 C5
Orme Dr BS21 6 D5
Ormerod Rd BS9 5 E5
Orneage Cl BA11 101 E8
Orwell Dr BS31 25 A4
Osborne Ave BS23 48 F7
Osborne Gr TA1 212 E3
Osborne Pl TA16 195 F7
Osborne Rd
Bath BA1 44 B7
Bridgwater TA6 208 F6
Bristol BS3 226 C1
Weston-Super-Mare BS23 48 F7
Yeovil BA20 219 A5
Osborne Villas BS2 226 C4
Osborne Wallis Ho BS8 226 A1
Osborne Way TA1 212 E3
Osborne Wlk TA8 104 C6
Osmond Dr BA5 203 B3
Osmond Rd 2 BS24 49 F7
Osprey Ct BS14 22 D5
Osprey Gdns BS22 31 F1
Ostlings La BA1 29 B2
Ostrey Mead BS27 90 B7
Otago Terr 5 BA1 28 C2
OTHERY 155 B2
Othery Village Prim Sch
TA7 155 C2
Ottawa Rd BS23 48 F3
OTTERFORD 181 E1
Otterford Cl BS14 23 B5
Otterford Gypsy Pk TA3 181 D2
Otterford Lakes Nature
Trail* TA3 181 E1
Otterham La TA3 183 F8
OTTERHAMPTON 135 A6
Otterhampton Prim Sch
TA5 135 B5
Otter Rd 1 BS21 6 E1
Otter Vale Cl EX14 191 F1
Ottery La DT9 225 C3
Our Lady of Mount Carmel
RC Prim Sch BA9 216 C3
Our Lady of the Rosary RC
Prim Sch BS11 5 A8
Outer Circ TA1 213 D5
Outer Gullands TA1 212 D2
Oval The BA2 44 C4
Overbrook Bsns Ctr
BS28 107 D4
Overcombe BA8 189 E8
OVER COMPTON 187 F4
Overdale
Clandown BA3 78 E5
Peasedown St John BA2 60 F3
Overhill BS20 4 D4
Over Innox BA11 119 F6
Overland La TA3 170 C3
Overlands
North Curry TA3 170 C4
Ruishton TA3 169 C4
OVERLEIGH 207 C3
Overleigh
Street BA16 207 C3
Street BA16 207 C4
Overstables La BS21 6 D3
OVER STOWEY 134 A1
OVER STRATTON 220 D1
OVERTON 169 C7
Overton BA9 216 D4
Owen Dr BS8 10 B4
Owen St TA21 222 C6
Owlaborough La EX36 162 B2
Owl St
South Petherton TA13 220 B8
Stocklinch TA19 184 C3
Owsley Cotts TA19 184 E4
Oxendale BA16 207 B5
Oxen La TA3 170 B3
OXENPILL 138 C4
Oxenpill BA6 138 C4
Oxen Rd TA18 224 C6
Oxford Pl
Bath BA2 45 C2
19 Bristol, Clifton BS8 11 F6
10 Taunton TA2 213 A8
Weston-Super-Mare BS23 48 D7
Oxford Rd BA21 219 E7
Oxford Row BA1 228 B3
Oxford Sq BS24 50 B6
Oxford St
Bristol BS2 227 C2
Bristol, Tyndall's Park BS2 226 C4
Burnham-on-S TA8 104 B6
Evercreech BA4 141 E1
Weston-Super-Mare BS23 48 D7
Oxford Terr 4 TA6 209 B4
Oxhayes DT8 199 F8
Oxhouse La
Failand BS8 10 B6
Winford BS40 37 D6
Oxleaze
5 Bishops Lydeard TA4 167 F8
Bristol BS13 22 D4
Oxleaze La BS41 21 E3
Oxley Cotts DT9 225 C4
Ozenhay BS39 75 E6

P

Packers' Way TA18 196 B3
Pack Horse La BA2 62 F7
PACKSADDLE 119 F7
Packsaddle Way BA11 119 F7
Pacquet Ho BS20 4 D5
Paddles La BA11 119 D1
Paddock Cl TA3 169 D5
Paddock Dr TA9 104 D4
Paddock Gdn BS14 22 F4
Paddock Park BS22 32 B2
Paddocks Cvn Pk The
BS26 87 A7
Paddocks The
Bath BA2 45 B1
Ilchester BA22 173 E1
Sandford BS25 52 C4
Wellington TA21 222 E5
Weston-Super-Mare BS23 48 D2
Paddock The
Banwell BS29 51 A3
Clevedon BS21 6 D2
Corston BA2 43 B7
Dulverton TA22 163 D6
Galhampton BA22 175 D8
Portishead BS20 2 D4
Taunton, Dowsland TA1 168 F1
Taunton, Trull TA3 168 D1
Paddock Wlk DT9 217 C2
Paddock Woods BA2 45 D2
Paddons Farm TA5 134 C6
Padfield Cl BA2 44 B5
Padfield Gn BA4 141 E6
Padleigh Hill BA2 44 B2
Padstow Rd BS4 22 F8
Paganel Cl TA24 200 F6
Paganel Rd TA24 200 F6
Paganel Rise TA24 200 E6
Paganel Way TA24 200 E6
Pagans Hill BS40 38 D2
Pageant Dr DT9 225 D3

Page La BA6 140 A2
Page's Ct BS49 34 C8
Page's Hill BA16 207 C1
Pages Mead BS11 4 C8
PAINTMOOR 194 B4
Paintmoor La TA20 194 B4
Palace Ct BA5 203 D3
Palace Gdns TA4 210 C4
Palace Yard Mews BA1 228 B2
Palfrey's La TA20 193 D3
Palmer Cl TA6 208 F2
Palmer Row 7 BS23 48 E8
Palmers Cl TA8 104 D8
Palmer's Elm BS24 33 B4
Palmer's End La TA12 184 F7
Palmers La BA2 61 B3
Palmers Rd BA6 206 D4
Palmer St
Frome BA11 119 F4
South Petherton TA13 220 C4
Weston-Super-Mare BS23 48 E8
Palmerston Rd TA1 212 D5
Palmer's Way BS24 49 D2
Palm Tree Cl TA6 209 E5
PANBOROUGH 138 F8
Panborough Dro BA5 138 F8
Panoramic The BS1 226 C3
Parade Nurseries TA24 200 F7
Parade The
1 Bath BA2 44 B6
Bristol, Bishopsworth BS13 22 A6
Bristol, Shirehampton BS11 4 E6
Chardstock EX13 198 A7
Minehead TA24 200 F7
Paradise Cres BA4 141 E2
Paradise La
Croscombe BA5 204 B7
Glastonbury BA6 139 D2
Langport TA10 172 A7
Tatworth TA20 193 F1
Paradise Rd BA6 206 D5
Paradise Row BS39 41 A6
Paragon Ct 13 BS23 30 C1
Paragon Rd BS23 30 C1
Paragon Sch The BA2 45 A3
Paragon The
Bath BA1 228 C3
Bristol BS8 11 F6
Paray Dr BA5 203 F5
PARBROOK 158 D7
Parbrook Ct BS14 23 B5
Parbrook La BA6 158 D7
Parcroft Com Jun Sch
BA20 218 F5
Parcroft Gdns BA20 218 F5
PARDLESTONE 133 C5
Pardlestone La TA5 133 C5
Parfields BA20 218 F5
Parish Brook Rd BS48 8 B2
Parish Hill BA22 175 D5
Parish Land La TA5 152 D5
Parish Mews BA20 218 C5
PARK 156 D1
Park Ave
Bath BA2 228 B1
Bridgwater TA6 208 D4
Castle Cary BA7 214 B4
Yatton BS49 17 B1
Park Barn La TA19 183 C4
Park Batch BS40 54 F3
Park Bglws EX16 179 B3
Park Cl
Barton St David TA11 158 A3
Cossington TA7 136 F3
Keynsham BS31 24 D5
Paulton BS39 77 D5
Staplehay TA3 181 D8
Street BA16 207 C5
Park Cnr
Hambridge TA3 184 B7
Leigh u M BA11 117 D3
PARK CORNER 64 A4
Park Cotts TA20 223 B5
Park Cres
Chard TA20 223 B5
Cossington TA7 136 F3
Park Ct 5 BS23 48 E5
Park End BS29 50 E4
Parker Cl TA21 222 E6
Parkes Rd BS24 50 C5
Park Farm BA6 206 C4
Park Farm Rd BA6 206 C4
Parkfield Cl TA6 153 F4
Parkfield Cres TA1 212 D2
Parkfield Dr TA1 212 D3
Parkfield Gdns BS39 57 D3
Parkfield Prim Sch TA1 212 D3
Parkfield Rd
Axbridge BS26 70 D1
Taunton TA1 212 D3
Parkfields Orch BA6 157 E4
Parkfields Residential Home
BA6 157 E4
Park Gate TA2 168 F7
Parkgate La BA11 101 E7
Park Gdns
Bath BA1 44 D8
Yeovil BA20 219 A5
Park Gr DT10 190 B4
Park Hayes BA3 116 F3
Park Hill
Bristol BS11 4 F6
Mells BA11 118 C7
Pilton BA4 140 E3
Park Hill Dr BA11 119 F6
Park Ho BA2 44 E4
Parkhouse La BS31 24 C2
Parkhouse Rd TA24 200 E7
Parkhurst Rd BS23 49 A7
Park La
Barton St David TA11 158 A3
Bath BA1 44 D7
Blagdon BS40 54 F3
Bristol BS2 226 C3
Cannington TA5 135 B3
Carhampton TA24 131 A5
Castle Cary BA7 214 D7
Clapton TA18 195 B1
Combe St Nicholas TA20 193 C6
Downhead BA4 117 A1
Faulkland BA3 80 B1
Goathurst TA5 153 C4
Henstridge BA8 190 A8
High Ham TA10 156 D1
Ilminster TA19 183 E1
Kingsdon TA11 173 E5
Kingston St Mary TA2 168 C8
Langport TA10 171 E4
Montacute BA22, TA15 186 B3
North Newton TA7 154 A3
North Petherton TA6 153 F4
Seavington St Mary TA19 184 C1
Thorncombe TA20 199 A7
Wellington TA21 222 C1
West Buckland TA21 180 E7
Yenston BA8 189 F8
Parklands BS39 59 D2
Parklands Ave BS22 32 A4
Parklands Rd
Bristol BS3 11 E4
Wellington TA21 222 D7
Parklands Rise TA24 200 D7
Parklands Way TA11 211 B4
Parkland Wlk TA18 224 C4
Park Lane Cl TA24 131 A5
Park Lodge BA20 219 A5
Parkmead TA2 213 E8
Park Pl
Bath BA1 228 A4
Bristol BS2 226 C3
Bristol BS8 226 B3
Castle Cary BA7 214 C5
Weston-Super-Mare BS23 48 D8
Park Rd
Bath BA1 44 B7
Bridgwater TA6 208 D4
Bristol BS3 226 B1
Bristol, Shirehampton BS11 4 F6
Bruton BA10 215 E5
Chard TA20 223 C4
Clevedon BS21 6 D4
Congresbury BS49 34 E3
Frome BA11 119 E4
Henstridge BA8 190 A6
Keynsham BS31 24 E4
Paulton BS39 77 D5
Shepton Mallet BA4 205 B5
Stalbridge DT10 190 B4
Street BA16 207 C5
Yeovil BA20 219 B5
Park Row BS1 226 C3
Park Sch The BA20 219 A5
Parks Cotts TA2 168 D8
Parkside Ct 1 TA6 209 B4
Parkside Inf Sch BA1 228 B3
Parks La
Brompton Ralph TA4 150 C3
Minehead TA24 200 F7
Park St
Bath BA1 228 A4
Bristol BS1 226 C3
Castle Cary BA7 214 C5
Dunster TA24 201 D1
Exford TA24 128 D1
Minehead TA24 200 F7
Taunton TA1 212 E3
Yeovil BA20 219 B4
Parks The
Bridgwater TA6 208 D4
Minehead TA24 200 E7
Parkstone Ave TA6 209 A2
Park Street Ave BS1 226 C3
Park Street Mews BA1 228 A4
Parks View TA24 124 A4
Parksway Ct TA24 200 E7
Park Terr
Chard TA20 223 B6
Glastonbury BA6 206 D4
Minehead TA24 200 F7
Park The
Castle Cary BA7 214 B4
Keynsham BS31 24 E6
Portishead BS20 2 F5
Yatton BS49 17 B1
Yeovil BA20 219 A5
Park View
Axminster EX13 198 A3
Bath BA2 44 D6
Cotford St Luke TA4 167 F6
Crewkerne, Misterton
TA18 196 B3
Crewkerne TA18 224 C4
Montacute TA15 186 B3
Stogursey TA5 134 C5
Park Villas BS23 48 D8
Park Wall BA10 215 F5
Park Wall Dro TA7 209 F4
Park Water La DT8 199 F5
Parkway
Bridgwater TA6 209 C5
Timsbury BA2 60 E2
Park Way
Bruton BA10 215 E5
Park Way *continued*
Midsomer Norton BA3 97 A8
Ruishton TA3 169 C3
Park Way BS22 32 B1
Parkway La BA2 60 D3
Park Wlk BS20 4 D4
Park Wood Cl BS14 22 F4
Parlour Ho TA1 213 B5
Parmin Cl TA1 213 C3
Parmin Way TA1 213 C3
Parnell Rd BS21 6 D3
Parnell Way TA8 104 B8
Parrett Cl TA10 171 F5
Parrett Mead
South Perrott DT8 196 C1
Taunton TA1 213 D3
Parrett Way TA6 209 B3
Parrett Works Cotts
TA12 220 F8
Parricks La EX13 198 D3
Parrocks La TA20 198 C8
Parry Cl BA2 44 B4
Parry's Cl BS9 5 E5
Parrys Gr BS9 5 E5
Parry's La BS9 5 F5
Parsonage Cl
Langport TA10 172 A5
Somerton TA11 211 E3
West Harptree BS40 74 E6
Winford BS40 37 F6
Parsonage Cotts
Kingston St Mary TA2 168 D8
West Camel BA22 174 D3
Parsonage Cres BA7 214 B6
Parsonage Ct
Puriton TA7 136 B4
Taunton TA1 212 A4
Parsonage Hill TA11 211 E3
Parsonage La
Ashill TA19 183 C4
Axbridge BS26 70 E2
Bath BA1 228 B2
Charlton Musgrove BA9 161 B1
Chilcompton BA3 96 C4
Kingston St Mary TA2 168 D8
Milverton TA4 167 A4
Pensford BS39 40 D6
Staple Fitzpaine TA3 182 C4
Winford BS40 37 F6
Parsonage Pl TA10 171 D4
Parsonage Rd
Berrow TA8 84 F5
Long Ashton BS41 11 C2
West Camel BA22 174 D3
Parson's Batch BA4 140 E3
Parsons Cl
Bicknoller TA4 132 F2
Long Sutton TA10 172 F4
Nether Stowey TA5 134 A3
Parson's Dro BS28 138 C7
Parsons Gate BA7 214 B7
Parsons Gn
Clevedon BS21 16 C8
Weston-Super-Mare BS22 32 A3
Parson's La TA11 173 D5
Parsons' La TA5 152 A7
Parsons Mead BS48 19 F7
Parsons Paddock BS14 23 A7
Parsons Pen BS27 90 B7
Parsons Rd TA9 104 C4
Parson's St TA24 124 A3
Parsons Way
Wells BA5 203 B4
Winscombe BS25 69 E6
Partis Coll BA1 44 A8
Partis Way BA1 44 A8
Partition St BS1 226 C2
Partman's Hill BA3 116 B3
Partridge Cl
Moorlinch TA7 155 F7
Weston-Super-Mare BS22 31 F1
Partway La
Chard Junction TA20 198 F6
East Chinnock BA22 196 F7
Passage Leaze BS11 4 D6
Passage St BS2 227 B2
Pastures Ave BS22 32 C3
Pastures The BA15 64 E3
Patch Croft BS21 16 C8
Pathe Rd TA7 155 B1
Pathfinder Terr 3 TA6 209 B4
Patrick's Way TA3 181 D8
Patrum Cl TA1 212 B1
Patson Hill La DT9 188 B5
Patterson Ho 8 BS1 227 B1
Pattinson Cl BA21 219 D6
Pattons TA3 169 C1
Patwell La BA10 215 E6
Patwell St BA10 215 E6
Paullet EX16 178 C1
Paulls Cl TA10 172 A6
Paull's La TA19 183 B2
Paulman Gdns BS41 20 F8
Paulmont Rise BS39 58 E1
Paul's Cswy BS49 34 D4
Pauls Rd TA11 211 C3
Paul St
Bristol BS2 226 C4
Frome BA11 119 F5
Shepton Mallet BA4 205 B6
Taunton TA1 212 F3
Paulto' Hill BA3, BS39 78 B6
PAULTON 77 F5
Paulton Inf Sch BS39 77 E5
Paulton Jun Sch BS39 77 E5
Paulton La BA2, BA3 78 D7
Paulton Memorial Hospl
BS39 77 F4
Paulton Rd
Farrington Gurney BS39 77 B4
Hallatrow BS39 77 B7
Midsomer Norton BA3 77 F1
Paulwood Rd BS39 58 E1
Pavement The TA3 170 B4
Pavey Cl BS13 22 C4
Pavey Rd BS13 22 C4
Pavyotts La BA22 197 E8
Pawelski Cl BA4 142 B7
PAWLETT 136 A5
Pawlett BS24 49 A2
Pawlett Mead Dro TA6 136 A5
Pawlett Prim Sch TA6 135 F5
Pawlett Rd
Bristol BS13 22 C3
Walpole TA6 136 B4
West Huntspill TA6, TA9 136 A7
Pawletts Almshouses
TA5 134 C5
Pawlett Wlk BS13 22 C3
Paybridge Rd BS13 21 F4
Payne Rd BS24 49 D2
Paynes Ho 17 BS23 48 E8
Paynes La TA7 155 C2
Payne's La TA12 185 E8
PAYTON 179 F7
Payton Rd
Holywell Lake TA21 179 F7
Rockwell Green TA21 222 A5
Peace Cl TA6 209 D6
Peacehay La TA21 179 E4
Peach Tree Cl TA6 209 E5
Peacocks Cl TA21 180 F7
Peacocks Hill TA11 158 A2
Peadon La TA5 134 C4
Peak La
Compton Dundon TA11 157 A2
Shepton Beauchamp TA19 184 D3
PEAR ASH 161 E2
Pear Ash La BA9 161 E2
Pearce Dr TA9 104 D4
Pearmain Rd BA16 207 B4
Pearse Cl BS22 32 B5
Pearson Ho BA21 219 A6
Peart Cl BS13 21 E5
Peart Dr BS13 21 E4
Peartree Cl BS13 22 B4
Pear Tree Cl
Bridgwater TA6 209 D4
Westleigh EX16 179 A4
Peartree Field BS20 2 F5
Peartree Gdns BS24 67 C6
Pear Tree Ind Est BS40 53 C4
Pear Tree Way TA21 222 F7
Peartwater Hill TA5 152 D8
Peartwater Rd TA5 152 D7
PEASEDOWN ST JOHN 79 C8
Peasedown St John Prim Sch
BA2 79 C7
PEASMARSH 194 B7
Pebbles Orch TA19 184 E4
PECKING MILL 159 D8
Pecking Mill Rd BA4 141 E1
Pedder Rd BS21 6 D1
Peddles Cl TA10 171 D8
Peddles La TA11 173 E8
Pedlars Gr
Chapmanslade BA13 121 C4
Frome BA11 119 E7
PEDWELL 156 A7
Pedwell Cvn Pk TA7 156 A7
Pedwell Hill TA7 156 A7
Pedwell La TA7 156 A7
Peel Ct TA23 202 C7
Peel St BS5 227 C4
Peerage Ct TA24 201 A6
Pegasus Ct 17 BA20 219 B4
Peggy's La TA18 196 C5
Peile Dr TA2 212 E7
Peir Cl BS20 2 E7
Pelham Ct TA6 209 D7
Pelican Cl BS22 49 F8
Pelting Dro BA5 92 D1
Pembroke Ave BS11 4 E6
Pembroke Cl
Burnham-on-S TA8 85 B1
Taunton TA1 212 C1
Yeovil BA21 219 E7
Pembroke Ct BS21 6 C4
Pembroke Gr BS8 226 A3
Pembroke Ho 1 BS23 30 C1
Pembroke Mans BS8 226 A4
Pembroke Pl BS8 226 A1
Pembroke Rd
Bridgwater TA6 209 C3
Bristol BS8 226 A4
Bristol, Shirehampton BS11 4 E6
Portishead BS20 1 E4
Weston-Super-Mare BS23 48 F4
Pembroke St BS2 227 B4
Pembroke Vale BS8 226 A4
Pemswell Rd TA24 200 F8
Penarth Dr BS24 49 A1
Penarth Rd TA6 208 D4
Pen Cross BA22 197 B6
Pendle Cl BS25 70 A7
Pendlesham Gdns BS23 31 A1
PENDOMER 197 B5
Pendomer Rd BA22 197 B5
Pendragon Pk BA6 206 D5
Pen Elm Cotts TA2 168 B5
Pen Elm Hill TA2 168 B6
Penel Orlieu TA6 208 F4
Penfield BA21 219 C5
Pen Hill BA9 161 C4
Penlea Ave TA6 208 E2
Penlea Cl TA6 208 E2
Penlea Ct BS11 4 D7
Pen Mill Hill SP8, BA12 161 F2
Pen Mill Inf Sch BA21 219 D6
Pen Mill Trad Est BA21 219 F6
Penmoor Pl TA8 84 F5
Penmoor Rd TA8 84 F5
Penmore Rd BA22, DT9 188 B7
Pennant Pl BS20 2 F7
Pennard BS24 49 A2
Pennard Ct
Bath BA2 44 A6
Bristol BS14 23 B5
Pennard Gn BA2 44 A6
Pennard La BA6 140 A2
Penn Cl
Cheddar BS27 90 C7
Wells BA5 112 E2
Penn Ct BS26 70 C1
Penneys Piece BA11 120 C6
Penn Gdns BA1 44 A8
Penn Hill BA20 219 B4
Penn Hill Pk BA20 219 B4
Penn Hill Rd BA1 27 A1
Pennine Gdns BS23 31 A1
Penn La BA22 197 A6
Pennlea BS13 22 C7
Penn Lea Ct BA1 44 B8
Penn Lea Rd BA1 44 B8
PENN MILL 219 E6
Pennon Rise BS1 226 C1
Penn Rd BS27 90 C7
Penn St BS1 227 B3
Penns The BS21 6 E2
PENNSYLVANIA 12 F7
Penn View BA9 216 D4
Penn Way BS26 70 C1
Penny Batch La BA5 139 E8
Penny Cl TA21 222 D7
Pennycress BS22 49 D7
Penny Lea TA23 202 C6
Pennyquick BA2 43 D6
Pennyquick View BA2 43 F6
Penny's Meade TA19 183 F4
Pennywell Est 3 BS21 6 D2
Pennywell Rd BS2 227 C4
Penpole Ave BS11 4 E6
Penpole Cl BS11 4 D7
Penpole La BS11 4 E7
Penpole Pk BS11 4 E7
Penpole Pl BS11 4 E6
Penrice Cl BS22 31 C2
Penrose BS14 22 F7
Penrose Sch TA6 208 E4
PENSELWOOD 161 C2
PENSFORD 40 E4
Pensford Ct BS14 23 D5
Pensford Hill BS39 40 D5
Pensford La BS39 40 A3
Pensford Old Rd BS39 40 E3
Pensford Prim Sch BS39 40 D4
Pensford Way BA11 120 D7
Pentagon The BS9 5 B5
Penthouse Hill BA1 28 F3
Pentire Ave BS13 22 A6
Pentridge La DT10 190 E2
Penzoy Ave TA6 209 B4
Pepperall Rd TA9 104 D4
Peppershells La BS39 41 C6
Pepys Cl BS31 25 D2
Pera Pl BA1 228 C4
Pera Rd BA1 228 C4
Perch Hill BA5 110 E6
Percivale Rd BA21 218 D7
Percival Rd BS8 11 F8
Percy Pl 13 BA1 28 B1
Percy Rd BA21 219 D6
Peregrine Cl BS22 31 F1
Perfect View BA1 28 A1
PERITON 200 D6
Periton Cross TA24 200 D6
Periton Ct TA24 200 D6
Periton La TA24 200 D7
Periton Mead Sch TA24 200 D6
Periton Rd TA24 200 D6
Periton Rise TA24 200 D6
Periton Way TA24 200 D6
Perkins Ct BA5 203 B4
Perley La TA23 148 D8
Perrett Ho 22 BS2 227 C3
Perretts Ct BS1 226 C1
Perrett Way BS20 4 E4
Perridge Hill BA4 140 D4
Perrin Cl BS39 76 E8
Perrings The BS48 18 E8
Perrott Hill Sch TA18 196 B4
Perrow La BS28 89 C2
Perry Court Inf Sch BS14 23 A6
Perry Court Jun Sch
BS14 23 A6
Perrycroft Ave BS13 22 A6
Perrycroft Rd BS13 22 A6
PERRY GREEN 208 B8
Perry Hill TA11 174 D8
Perry Hill Rd TA11 211 D2
Perry La TA9 106 F5
Perry Lake La BA5 139 B7
Perrymans Cl BS30 12 A8
PERRYMEAD 45 B3
Perrymead
Bath BA2 45 B3
Weston-Super-Mare BS22 32 B5
Perrymead Ct BA2 45 B4
Perrymead Pl BA2 45 B4
Perry New Rd TA22 163 F4
Perry Pl BA21 219 C5
Perry Rd
Blackford TA9 107 A6
Bristol BS1 227 A3

Perry's Cider Mills★
TA19 . . . . 194 E7
Perry's Cl BS27 . . . . 90 A7
Perry St TA20 . . . . 198 D8
PERRY STREET 198 E8
Pesley Cl BS13 . . . . 22 A4
Pesters La TA11 . . . . 211 E3
Pestlefield La TA3 . . . . . . 170 C1
Petercole Dr BS13 . . . . . . 22 A6
Peter's Gore DT6 . . . . . . 199 B1
Peterside BS39 . . . . 76 E8
Peterson Sq BS13 . . . . . . 22 C3
Peter St
Shepton Mallet BA4 . . . . . . 205 B6
Taunton TA2 . . . . 212 F6
Yeovil BA20 . . . . 219 B4
Petherton Gdns BS14 . . . . 23 B7
Petherton Rd
Bristol BS14 . . . . 23 B7
North Newton TA7 . . . . . . 153 F2
Pethick Ho BS4 . . . . 22 F8
Peto Garden at Iford Manor The★ BA15 . . . . 64 E3
Peto Gr BA15 . . . . 64 F3
Petrel Cl TA6 . . . . 209 D7
Petter's Way BA20 . . . . . . 219 B4
Petticoat La BA4 . . . . . . 205 B6
Pettitts Cl DT9 . . . . 187 E1
PETTON 165 A3
Petton Cross EX16 . . . . . . 165 A3
Petvin Cl BA16 . . . . 207 D4
Petvins Ct TA18 . . . . 196 C5
Pevensey Wlk BS4 . . . . . . 22 D7
Pharmacy Flats The
DT10 . . . . 190 F6
Pheasant The TA19 . . . . . . 184 E1
Phelps Cl TA20 . . . . 223 D6
Philippa Cl BS14 . . . . 23 A7
Philips Ho 2 BS2 . . . . . . 227 B4
Phillip Ho TA6 . . . . 208 F2
Phillips Cl TA6 . . . . 208 D4
Phillip's Dro TA3 . . . . . . 170 D7
Phillips Rd BS23 . . . . 49 A6
Phillis Hill BS39 . . . . 77 F4
Phippen St 1 BS1 . . . . . . 227 B1
Phoenix Ct
Frome BA11 . . . . 119 D4
Taunton TA1 . . . . 212 F3
Phoenix Ho
Bath BA1 . . . . 228 B4
Frome BA11 . . . . 119 D4
Phoenix Rd TA6 . . . . 209 B3
Phoenix Terr TA8 . . . . . . 104 B6
Phoenix Way BS20 . . . . 2 F6
PIBSBURY 172 C5
Piccadilly Pl BA1 . . . . 45 B8
Piccadilly Ho 13 BA4 . . . . 205 B6
Pickeridge Cl TA2 . . . . . . 213 B7
Picket La DT8 . . . . 196 C1
Pickett La BA21 . . . . 219 A7
PICKNEY 168 B8
Pickney La TA2 . . . . 168 B7
Pickpurse La TA4 . . . . . . 150 E8
Pickwick Rd BA1 . . . . 28 A2
PICT'S HILL 172 B6
Piece TA19 . . . . 184 E4
Piece La TA19 . . . . 184 E4
Piece Rd DT9 . . . . 217 C3
Piece The 2 TA16 . . . . . . 195 F7
Pier Rd BS20 . . . . 2 E7
Pierrepont Pl 9 BA1 . . . . 228 C2
Pierrepont St BA1 . . . . . . 228 C2
Piers Rd BA4 . . . . 142 A6
Pier St TA8 . . . . 104 A6
Piffin La TA4 . . . . 167 E8
Pigeon House Dr BS13 . . . . 22 D4
Pigeon La BS40 . . . . 36 E1
Pig Hill BA22 . . . . 197 A7
Pightley La TA5 . . . . 152 F6
Pightley Rd TA5 . . . . 152 E7
Pig La TA7 . . . . 154 D8
Pig Market La TA1 . . . . . . 212 F3
Pigott Ave BS13 . . . . 22 A4
Pigs Hill La TA5 . . . . 134 D1
Pike Cl BA6 . . . . 206 C5
Pike Hill BA4 . . . . 205 A7
Pike La BA4 . . . . 205 B6
Pikes Cres
Dunster TA24 . . . . 201 D2
Taunton TA1 . . . . 212 E1
Pilcorn St BS28 . . . . 108 C4
Pile La
Curry Mallet TA3 . . . . . . 183 C8
Stourton Caundle DT10 . . . 189 F3
Piley La TA21 . . . . 179 D8
Pilgrims Way
Bristol BS11 . . . . 4 C7
Chew Stoke BS40 . . . . . . 56 D8
Lovington BA7 . . . . 158 E2
Weston-Super-Mare BS22 . . 31 E3
Pilgrim's Way TA6 . . . . . . 135 F5
PILL 4 C4
Pillar La BA11 . . . . 99 D4
Pill Bridge La BA22 . . . . . 173 D1
Pill Head La TA18 . . . . . . 196 C4
Pill Mdw SP8 . . . . 177 E2
Pillmead La BS28 . . . . . . 108 D5
Pillmoor Dro BA5 . . . . . . 139 F6
Pillmoor La BA5 . . . . 139 F6
Pillmore La
Highbridge TA9 . . . . 105 A4
Watchfield TA9 . . . . 105 C4
Pill Rd
Abbots Leigh BS8 . . . . 4 F1
Pill BS20 . . . . 4 E2
Rooks Bridge BS26, TA9 . . . 87 C2
Pill St BS20 . . . . 4 D4
Pill Way BS21 . . . . 6 B2
Pilots Helm TA6 . . . . 153 E4
PILSDON 199 F2
Pilsdon La DT6 . . . . 199 F3
PILTON 140 F3
Pilton Hill BA4 . . . . 140 C4
Pilton Manor Vineyard★
BA4 . . . . 140 E3
Pimms La BS22 . . . . 31 B3
Pimm's La BS22 . . . . 31 B2
Pimpernel Cl BA16 . . . . . . 207 B7
Pince's Knap TA20 . . . . . . 198 F5
Pinchay La BS40 . . . . 38 A4
Pinckney Gn BA15 . . . . 46 E5
Pincushion Cnr BA22 . . . . 197 E6
Pine Ave TA20 . . . . 223 C5
Pine Cl
Street BA16 . . . . 207 B3
Taunton TA1 . . . . 213 D2
Weston-Super-Mare BS22 . . 31 D2
Pinecroft
Bristol BS14 . . . . 22 F7
Portishead BS20 . . . . 1 F6
Pine Ct
Chew Magna BS40 . . . . 39 B3
Frome BA11 . . . . 120 B7
Keynsham BS31 . . . . 24 C4
Radstock BA3 . . . . 79 A2
Pine Hill BS22 . . . . 31 D2
Pine Lea BS24 . . . . 67 B6
Pine Ridge Cl BS9 . . . . 5 C4
Pines Cl
Chilcompton BA3 . . . . 96 D3
Wincanton BA9 . . . . 216 C3
Pines Residential Site The
BA11 . . . . 120 D8
Pines Way
Bath BA2 . . . . 228 A2
Radstock BA3 . . . . 79 A2
Pines Way Ind Est BA2 . . 228 A2
Pine Tree Ave BA20 . . . . . 218 F3
Pine Tree Cl TA6 . . . . 209 D4
Pinetree Rd BS24 . . . . 50 D4
Pine Wlk BA3 . . . . 78 E1
Pinewood TA11 . . . . 211 D4
Pinewood Ave BA3 . . . . 77 F1
Pinewood Dr TA11 . . . . . . 211 D4
Pinewood Gr BA3 . . . . 77 F1
Pinewood Rd BA3 . . . . 77 F1
Pinewood Way TA8 . . . . . . 65 F3
Pinford La DT9 . . . . 188 F3
Pinhay Rd BS13 . . . . 22 B6
Pinkham Hill TA20 . . . . . . 194 B6
Pinkhams Twist BS14 . . . . 23 A5
Pink Knoll Hollow DT9 . . 188 C8
Pinksmoor La TA21 . . . . . 179 E7
Pinkwood La BA10 . . . . . . 160 E7
Pinmore BA11 . . . . 119 E2
Pinney Cl TA1 . . . . 212 B1
Pinnockscroft TA8 . . . . 84 F5
Pintail Rd TA24 . . . . 201 C5
Pinter Cl TA8 . . . . 104 C6
Pioneer Ave BA2 . . . . 44 F1
Pipehouse BA2 . . . . 63 E4
Pipehouse La BA2 . . . . 63 F4
Pipe La BS1 . . . . 226 C2
Piper's Alley TA19 . . . . . . 221 B4
Pipers Cl BS26 . . . . 88 E6
Pipers Pl EX14 . . . . 191 F2
Pippard Cl BA16 . . . . 207 E5
Pippin Cl BA2 . . . . 79 D7
Pippins The
Portishead BS20 . . . . 2 F5
Wembdon TA6 . . . . 208 D6
Pipplepen La DT8, TA18 . . 196 B2
Pitchcombe Gdns BS9 . . . . . . 5 D7
Pitcher's Hill TA2 . . . . . . 168 F7
Pitching The
Castle Cary BA7 . . . . 214 C5
Chilcompton BA3 . . . . 96 D5
Pitch & Pay La BS9 . . . . 5 E3
Pitch & Pay Pk BS9 . . . . 5 E3
PITCOMBE 215 D3
Pitcombe Hill BA10 . . . . . 215 B2
Pitcombe La TA4 . . . . 165 B5
Pitcombe Rock BA10 . . . . . 215 C3
PITCOT 115 F7
Pitcot La BA3 . . . . 115 F7
Pitfield Cnr BA22 . . . . . . 188 A7
Pitfour Terr BA2 . . . . 60 B2
Pithay Ct BS1 . . . . 227 A3
Pithay The
Bristol BS1 . . . . 227 A3
Paulton BS39 . . . . 77 E6
Pit Hill TA17 . . . . 195 B7
Pit Hill La TA7 . . . . 155 C7
Pit La
Sticklepath TA23 . . . . . . 149 D7
Sutton Mallet TA7 . . . . . . 155 C7
Ubley BS40 . . . . 55 F5
Pitman Ct BA1 . . . . 28 C2
Pitman Ho BA2 . . . . 44 D4
Pitman Rd BS23 . . . . 48 E6
PITMINSTER 181 E6
PITNEY 172 C7
Pitney Hill TA10 . . . . 172 C6
Pit Rd
Dinnington TA17 . . . . 195 C7
Midsomer Norton BA3 . . . . . 78 B1
PITSFORD HILL 150 E1
Pitsham La TA4 . . . . 164 E6
Pitt Ct TA10 . . . . 171 B3
Pitten St BA3 . . . . 116 E3
Pitt La
Huish Champflower TA4 . . . 165 E8
Porlock Weir TA24 . . . . . . 123 C3
Waterrow TA4 . . . . 165 F5
Pitts Cl TA1 . . . . 212 C1
Pitts La TA3 . . . . 183 F7
Pitt's La BS40 . . . . 39 B1
Pitway TA13 . . . . 220 D5
Pitway Cl BS39 . . . . 76 F4
Pitway Hill TA13 . . . . 220 D6
Pitway La BS39 . . . . 76 E4
Pixash Bsns Ctr BS31 . . . . 25 B5
Pixash La BS31 . . . . 25 C5
Pix La TA4 . . . . 167 B4
Pixton Way TA22 . . . . 163 E6
Pizey Ave
Burnham-on-S TA8 . . . . 85 A1
Clevedon BS21 . . . . 6 B2
Pizey Ave Ind Est BS21 . . . . 6 C2
Pizey Cl BS21 . . . . 6 B2
Place Dro TA7 . . . . 154 F4
Placket La BA20 . . . . 218 D1
Plain Pond TA4 . . . . 210 C5
PLAINSFIELD 152 B7
Plain The BA2 . . . . 81 E4
Plais St TA2 . . . . 212 F6
Plantaganet Chase BA20 218 D2
Plantagenet Pk BA20 . . . . 218 E3
Platterwell La (East Town La) BA4 . . . . 141 B3
Players La TA8 . . . . 85 A1
Playfield Cl 2 BA8 . . . . . . 190 A6
Playford Gdns BS11 . . . . 4 E8
Playses Gn TA10 . . . . 184 D8
PLEAMORE CROSS 222 A2
Pleasant Pl BA1 . . . . 29 D2
Pleshey Cl BS22 . . . . 31 D2
Plimsoll Ho 3 BS1 . . . . . . 227 B1
Plot La DT9 . . . . 187 F5
Plott La BA8 . . . . 190 B7
Plough Cl BA16 . . . . 207 A4
Ploughed Paddock BS48 . . 8 D1
Plover Cl
Milborne Port DT9 . . . . 217 C2
Minehead TA24 . . . . 201 C5
Weston-Super-Mare BS22 . . 31 F1
Plover Ct BA21 . . . . 218 D6
Plover Rd DT9 . . . . 217 C2
Plovers Rise BA3 . . . . 79 A3
Plowage La BA22 . . . . 174 D3
Plox BA10 . . . . 215 E6
Plox Gn BA10 . . . . 215 E6
Plucknett Row BA20 . . . . . 218 D5
Plud St BS28 . . . . 108 B3
Plumber's Barton 9
BA11 . . . . 119 F4
Plumers Cl 4 BS21 . . . . 6 C1
Plum La TA6 . . . . 209 C2
Plumley Cres BS24 . . . . 50 A4
Plumley Ct BS23 . . . . 48 D4
PLUMMER'S HILL 77 E6
Plummer's La BA5 . . . . 92 D5
Plum Orch DT9 . . . . 187 F4
Plumptre Ave BA5 . . . . 203 F5
Plumptre Cl BS39 . . . . 77 E5
Plumptre Rd BS39 . . . . 77 E5
Plumtree Cl BS25 . . . . 52 A1
Plum Tree Cl TA6 . . . . 209 E5
Plum Tree Rd BS22 . . . . 49 E8
Plunder St BS49 . . . . 35 B7
Plunging Dr BA6 . . . . 206 F1
Plymor Rd TA9 . . . . 136 A8
Poachers End TA24 . . . . . . 201 C4
Pococks Yd TA10 . . . . 171 F5
Podgers Dr BA1 . . . . 27 B2
Podger's La TA19 . . . . 183 F4
PODIMORE 174 A3
Podium Sh Ctr The BA2 . 228 C2
Poets Cnr BA3 . . . . 97 C8
Polden Bsns Ctr The
TA6 . . . . 136 B2
Polden Cl BS48 . . . . 8 E1
Polden Ct TA6 . . . . 209 B5
Polden Rd
Portishead BS20 . . . . 2 B5
Weston-Super-Mare BS23 . . 48 F8
Polden St TA6 . . . . 209 B5
Polden View BA6 . . . . 206 E3
Polden Wlk TA7 . . . . 136 E3
Pole Rue La TA20 . . . . 193 C6
POLESHILL 166 C1
Polestar Way BS24 . . . . 50 A8
Polham La TA11 . . . . 211 D3
Polkes Field TA3 . . . . 170 F6
Pollard Rd
Bridgwater TA6 . . . . 209 D6
Weston-Super-Mare BS22 . . 49 F8
Pollards Ct TA24 . . . . 124 A3
Pollard's La TA21 . . . . 180 F7
Pollards Way TA1 . . . . 212 E4
POLSHAM 139 D5
Polygon Rd BS8 . . . . 226 A2
Polygon The 15 BS8 . . . . 11 F6
Pomeroy La BA14 . . . . 83 B6
Pomfrett Gdns BS14 . . . . . . 23 E5
Pond Cl 5 BA8 . . . . 190 A6
Pond Cotts BA3 . . . . 80 D2
Pond Head BS20 . . . . 4 D4
Pondhead Cross TA4 . . . . 202 E3
Pond La TA21 . . . . 179 D3
Pond Orch TA4 . . . . 150 B8
Pondpool La TA3 . . . . 170 C3
Pond Wlk DT10 . . . . 190 B4
Ponsford Rd
Bristol BS14 . . . . 23 B8
Minehead TA24 . . . . 201 A6
Pookfield Cl BA11 . . . . . . 143 B7
Poolbridge Rd BS28 . . . . . 107 C4
Pool Cl TA7 . . . . 136 C4
POOLE 222 F8
Poole Hill TA22 . . . . 163 B5
Poole Ho BA2 . . . . 43 F5
Poolemead Rd BA2 . . . . . . 43 F5
Pooles Cl TA5 . . . . 134 A2
Pooles La TA20 . . . . 194 E1
Poole St BS11 . . . . 4 B8
Pooles Wharf BS8 . . . . . . 226 A1
Pooles Wharf Ct BS8 . . . . 226 A1
Pool Hill TA21 . . . . 165 E1
Pool La BS40 . . . . 38 A2
POOLTOWN 148 E8
Poop Hill TA18 . . . . 196 C8
Poop Hill La TA18 . . . . . . 196 C8
Poor Hill BA2 . . . . 59 F6
Poorhouse La DT6 . . . . . . 199 E1
Pope Cl TA1 . . . . 168 D1
Popery La TA24 . . . . 129 E1
Pope's La
Milborne Port DT9 . . . . 217 D2
Rockwell Green TA21 . . . . . 222 B4
Pope's Wlk BA2 . . . . 45 B3
Popham Cl
Bridgwater TA6 . . . . 209 D5
East Brent TA9 . . . . 86 D5
Popham Flats TA21 . . . . . 222 D6
Pop La EX13, TA20 . . . . . . 198 B8
Poplar Ave BS9 . . . . 5 D6
Poplar Cl
Bath BA2 . . . . 44 D4
Frome BA11 . . . . 120 B7
Poplar Dr BA21 . . . . 218 C7
Poplar Est TA9 . . . . 104 D3
Poplar Farm BA5 . . . . 111 A4
Poplar La
Catcott TA7 . . . . 137 D1
Mark TA9 . . . . 105 E3
Poplar Pl 16 BS23 . . . . 48 E8
Poplar Rd
Bath BA2 . . . . 62 D8
Bridgwater TA6 . . . . 209 D7
Bristol, Highridge BS13 . . . . 21 F7
Burnham-on-S TA8 . . . . 104 A8
Street BA16 . . . . 207 C3
Taunton TA1 . . . . 213 D2
Poplars Cl BA21 . . . . 187 A5
Poplars The
Easton-in-G BS20 . . . . 4 B4
Porlock TA24 . . . . 124 A3
Weston-Super-Mare BS22 . . 32 A1
Poplar Tree La BA14 . . . . . . 83 C2
Poplar Wlk BS24 . . . . 49 E5
Poples Bow TA9 . . . . 104 E5
Pople's La BA11 . . . . 117 F8
Pople's Well TA18 . . . . . . 224 B6
Poppy Cl
Weston-Super-Mare BS22 . . 32 A5
Yeovil BA22 . . . . 218 B5
Porch EX13 . . . . 198 A3
Porch Cl BA6 . . . . 206 E3
Porchestall Dro BA6 . . . . . 206 B4
PORLOCK 124 A4
Porlock Cl
3 Clevedon BS21 . . . . 6 E1
Weston-Super-Mare BS23 . . 48 F2
Porlock Dr TA1 . . . . 212 E1
PORLOCKFORD 123 F4
Porlock Gdns BS48 . . . . 8 E1
Porlock Hill TA24 . . . . 123 F3
Porlock Rd
Bath BA2 . . . . 45 A1
Minehead TA24 . . . . 200 C7
Porlock Visitor Ctr★
TA24 . . . . 124 A3
PORLOCK WEIR 123 D4
Portal Rd BS24 . . . . 50 D4
PORTBURY 3 D3
Portbury Comm BS20 . . . . . 2 E4
Portbury Gr BS11 . . . . 4 D6
Portbury Hundred The
BS20 . . . . 3 C4
Portbury La BS20 . . . . 9 E7
Portbury Way BS20 . . . . 3 E5
Portbury Wlk BS11 . . . . 4 D6
Portcullis Rd TA10 . . . . . . 172 A6
Porter's Hatch BA6 . . . . . . 138 D4
PORTFIELD 171 E5
Portfield La TA10 . . . . 171 F5
PORTISHEAD 2 B4
Portishead Bsns Pk BS20 . . . 2 E5
Portishead Lodge BS20 . . . . 2 D6
Portishead Prim Sch
Portishead BS20 . . . . 2 C5
Portishead BS20 . . . . 2 E6
Portishead Rd BS22 . . . . . . 32 B4
Portishead Way BS3 . . . . . 11 E3
Port La TA22 . . . . 164 A5
PORTLAND 207 A6
Portland Cl
Cannington TA5 . . . . 135 B2
Nailsea BS48 . . . . 8 D1
Portland Ct BS1 . . . . 226 B1
Portland Dr BS20 . . . . 2 E4
Portland Grange 6 TA1 . 212 E3
Portland Lofts 8 BS2 . . . 227 B4
Portland Mans 9 BS2 . . . 227 B4
Portland Pl
Bath BA1 . . . . 228 B4
Brent Knoll TA9 . . . . 86 B1
Bridgwater TA6 . . . . 208 D5
Frome BA11 . . . . 119 D5
Portland Rd
Bath BA1 . . . . 228 B4
Frome BA11 . . . . 119 D5
Langport TA10 . . . . 172 B5
Street BA16 . . . . 207 A6
Portland Sq BS2 . . . . 227 B4
Portland St
Bristol, Clifton BS8 . . . . 11 F7
Taunton TA1 . . . . 212 E4
Portland Terr
Bath BA1 . . . . 228 B4
Watchet TA23 . . . . 202 C7
Portman Cres 9 TA6 . . . . 153 F3
Portman Ct BA22 . . . . 196 E8
Portman Dr TA6 . . . . 153 E3
Portman Rd TA6 . . . . 153 E3
Portmans TA3 . . . . 170 B3
Portman St TA2 . . . . 212 F6
Portmeade Dro BS26 . . . . . 70 C1
Portmeirion Cl BS14 . . . . . 23 B5
Portnell's La BA12 . . . . . . 161 F2
Portobello Bldgs TA20 . . 223 B4
Portreeve Dr BA21 . . . . . . 219 B6
Port View BS20 . . . . 4 C5
Portview Rd BS11 . . . . 4 B8
Portwall Dro TA7 . . . . 209 F5
Portwall La BS1 . . . . 227 B1
Portwall La E 10 BS1 . . . . 227 B1
PORTWAY 207 D4
Portway
Bristol, Shirehampton BS11 . 4 C6
Bristol, Sneyd Park BS8 . . . . . 5 C3
Frome BA11 . . . . 120 A4
Holford TA5 . . . . 133 D4
Street BA16 . . . . 207 D4
Wells BA5 . . . . 203 C4
Port Way BA2 . . . . 100 D7
Portway Ave BA5 . . . . 203 D4
Portway Com Sch BS11 . . . . 4 E7
Portway Hill
Batcombe BA4 . . . . 142 C1
Bruton BA4 . . . . 159 F6
Portway La
Binegar BA3 . . . . 95 E1
Holford TA5 . . . . 133 E4
Portway Lodge 1 BA5 . . 203 C4
Portway Rdbt BS11 . . . . 4 C8
Portway Villas BA11 . . . . . 120 A4
Positano Ct 2 TA6 . . . . . . 208 E7
Poskitt Ho TA6 . . . . 208 F6
Post Cl TA21 . . . . 222 E4
Post La
Malmsmead EX35 . . . . 122 C4
Skilgate TA4 . . . . 164 E7
Post Office La
Blagdon BS40 . . . . 54 D3
Flax Bourton BS48 . . . . 19 F7
Minehead TA24 . . . . 200 F7
Tatworth TA20 . . . . 198 C8
Post Office Rd BS24 . . . . . . 50 C5
Post Office Yd DT8 . . . . . . 199 F7
Poston Way BA15 . . . . 64 E7
Pot La BA11 . . . . 120 F8
Potter's Cross TA4 . . . . . . 165 C7
POTTERS HILL 20 B1
Potters Ho 1 BA4 . . . . . . 205 B6
Potterton Cl TA6 . . . . 208 F1
Pottery Cl BS23 . . . . 49 A6
Pottery Rd TA19 . . . . 183 C1
Pottery View TA19 . . . . . . 183 C1
Pottle St BA12 . . . . 144 D3
Potts Cl BA1 . . . . 28 F3
Poulett Cotts TA17 . . . . . . 195 D7
POUND 220 F2
Pound Cl
Glastonbury BA6 . . . . 206 D5
Stalbridge DT10 . . . . 190 B4
Yeovil BA21 . . . . 218 C5
Pound Farm Cl TA6 . . . . . 208 D3
Poundfield Rd TA24 . . . . . 200 E6
Pound Fold BA5 . . . . 204 C7
Pound Hill TA21 . . . . 179 A5
Poundisford Cl TA1 . . . . . . 212 D1
Pound La
Bishops Lydeard TA4 . . . . . 151 F1
Buckland St Mary TA20 . . . 193 A8
Downhead BA4 . . . . 117 A1
Easton BA5 . . . . 111 A4
Lydford Fair Place TA11 . . . 158 C3
Martock TA12 . . . . 185 D6
Nailsea BS48 . . . . 8 D3
Oakhill BA3 . . . . 115 B5
Rawridge EX14 . . . . 191 F1
Yarcombe EX14 . . . . 192 E2
Yarlington BA9 . . . . 175 F8
Yeovil BA22 . . . . 218 A2
Pound Mead BS40 . . . . 37 C8
Pound Orch TA4 . . . . 151 C7
Pound Pool TA11 . . . . 211 C4
Pound Rd
Axminster EX13 . . . . 198 F2
Broadway TA19 . . . . 183 B2
Pawlett TA6 . . . . 135 F5
Poundsclose TA22 . . . . 163 E4
Pound Terr 3 TA21 . . . . . 222 D5
Pound The BS40 . . . . 36 D3
Pound Way TA10 . . . . 172 B3
Pounsell La TA10 . . . . 172 B5
Powell Cl TA3 . . . . 169 D4
Powell Ct BA5 . . . . 203 B4
Powells Acres BS21 . . . . 6 E3
Powis Cl BS22 . . . . 31 C2
Powlett Ct BA2 . . . . 45 B7
Powlett Rd BA2 . . . . 45 B8
Pow's Hill BA3 . . . . 78 D5
Pow's Orch BA3 . . . . 78 A1
Powy's Gn DT9 . . . . 225 C4
Powy's La DT9 . . . . 225 C4
POYNTINGTON 188 E6
Poyntz Rd BS4 . . . . 22 F8
Prankerds Rd DT9 . . . . . . 217 C2
Preachers Vale BA3 . . . . . 116 F7
Preanes Gn BS22 . . . . 32 A2
Precinct The BS20 . . . . 2 D5
Prescot Cl BS22 . . . . 31 B2
PRESCOTT 179 C1
Prescott Rd EX15 . . . . 179 D1

PRESTLEIGH 141 D3
Prestleigh La BA4 141 E4
Prestleigh Rd BA4 141 E2
PRESTON 150 E6
PRESTON BOWYER 167 B5
Preston CE Prim Sch BA21 218 C7
Preston Cross TA4 150 E6
Preston Gr BA20 218 F5
Preston La TA4 150 E6
PRESTON PLUCKNETT 218 D4
Preston Rd
  Yeovil BA20 218 E5
  Yeovil, Houndstone BA22 218 B5
Preston Road Rdbt BA21 218 C5
Preston Sch BA21 218 D5
Prestor 9 EX13 198 A1
Pretwood Cl TA19 221 C3
Prewett St BS1 227 B1
Prey La TA3 182 D7
Preywater Rd BA5 139 D8
Prices Bldgs TA6 209 A4
Priddles La TA20 193 C8
PRIDDY 92 D3
Priddy Cl
  Bath BA2 44 B5
  Frome BA11 120 C7
Priddy Ct BS14 23 B5
Priddy Dr BS14 23 B5
Priddy Nine Barrows★ BA5 92 F4
Priddy Prim Sch BA5 92 D3
Priddy Rd BA5 112 E8
Priddy Veal La BA5 111 A5
Priestlands DT9 225 D5
Priestlands La DT9 225 D5
Priestley Way TA8 104 C5
Priest Row BA5 203 D4
Priest's House★ TA10 172 A3
Priest St TA4 202 C2
Priests Way BS22 31 D2
Prigg La TA13 220 C4
Primmerfield La BA3 94 C8
PRIMROSE HILL 27 D1
Primrose Hill
  Bath BA1 27 D1
  Charlton Mackrell TA11 173 F7
  East Coker BA22 197 B7
  Nunney BA11 143 B8
Primrose Hill Pk Homes TA11 173 F7
Primrose La
  Midsomer Norton BA3 78 B1
  Yeovil BA21 187 D5
Prince Philip Cl TA20 223 B3
Princes Bldgs BA1 228 B3
Prince's Bldgs 17 BS8 11 F6
Prince's Cl 11 TA14 185 F4
Princes' La BS8 11 F6
Princes Rd BA5 203 D4
Prince's Rd
  Clevedon BS21 6 D3
  Shepton Mallet BA4 205 C6
  Street BA16 207 B5
Princess Anne Rd BA11 120 A7
Princess Cl
  Keynsham BS31 24 E4
  12 North Petherton TA6 153 F4
Princess Rd TA1 212 D2
Princess Row BS2 227 A4
Princess St TA8 104 B7
Princes St
  Bath BA1 228 B2
  Taunton TA1 213 B4
  Yeovil BA20 219 B5
Prince's St
  Bristol BS2 227 C4
  Clandown BA3 78 E5
Princess Victoria St BS8 11 F6
Prince St BS1 227 A1
Prince Street Rdbt BS1 227 A2
Printers Ct 32 TA12 185 E6
Prior Park Bldgs BA2 45 B5
Prior Park Coll BA2 45 C2
Prior Park Cotts BA2 228 C1
Prior Park Gdns BA2 45 B5
Prior Park Landscape Gdn★ BA2 45 C3
Prior Park Rd BA2 45 B4
Priors Hill BA2 60 A2
Prior's Wlk TA1 212 F4
PRIORSWOOD 213 B7
Priorswood Ind Est TA2 213 B6
Priorswood Pl 8 TA2 213 A8
Priorswood Prim Sch TA2 212 F6
Priorswood Rd TA2 213 A6
Priory TA21 222 E6
Priory Ave TA1 213 A4
Priory Bridge Rd TA1 213 A5
Priory Cl
  Bath BA2 45 B2
  Cannington TA5 135 C2
  Castle Cary BA7 214 B5
  Chilton Polden TA7 137 B2
  Ilchester BA22 173 E1
  Midsomer Norton BA3 78 A1
  Yeovil BA20 218 D1
Priory Com Sch BS22 32 B3
Priory Ct
  Bridgwater TA6 208 F4
  9 Stoke sub Hamdon TA14 185 F4
  5 Taunton TA1 213 A4
  Wellington TA21 222 E7
Priory Farm Trad Est BS20 3 D3
Priory Fields TA1 213 A5
Priory Fields Ret Pk TA1 213 A5
Priorygate Ct BA7 214 B6
Priory Gdns
  Bristol, Shirehampton BS11 4 D7
  Burnham-on-S TA8 104 B6
  Easton-in-G BS20 4 B4
  Wellington TA21 222 E6
Priory Glade BA21 218 C6
Priory Gn TA24 201 E2
Priory Hill TA5 134 C5
Priory Hospl BA5 203 C3
Priory Mead BA10 215 F8
Priory Mews BS23 49 B7
Priory Path BA7 214 C5
Priory Pl BA5 203 D3
Priory Rd
  Bristol BS8 226 C4
  Bristol, Shirehampton BS11 4 D6
  Chilton Polden TA7 137 B2
  Easton-in-G BS20 4 B4
  Ilchester BA22 173 E1
  Keynsham BS31 24 E7
  Portbury BS20 3 D3
  Wells BA5 203 D3
  Weston-Super-Mare BS23 49 A7
Priory Sch The TA2 213 B7
Priory View BA7 214 B6
Priory Villas BA9 216 C3
Priory Way TA1 213 B5
Priory Way Ind Est TA1 213 B5
Priory Wlk
  Portbury BS20 3 D3
  Taunton TA1 213 A5
PRISTON 61 B5
Priston Cl BS22 32 B5
Priston La BA2, BA3 61 A5
Priston Rd BA2 61 D6
Pritchard St BS2 227 B4
Private Rd
  North Brewham BA11 161 E8
  Staplegrove TA2 212 D7
Privet Dr BS13 22 C5
Proctor Ho BS1 227 B1
Prophet's La TA14 185 E3
Prospect Cl
  East Brent TA9 86 E5
  Shepton Mallet BA4 205 A6
Prospect Gdns BA1 28 F5
Prospect Ho BS22 31 E3
Prospect Pl
  Bath, Beacon Hill BA1 28 A1
  Bathford BA1 29 D2
  Bath, Weston BA1 27 C2
  9 Weston-Super-Mare BS23 48 E8
Prospect Rd BA2 45 C4
Prospect Row TA18 224 F3
Prospect Terr TA1 212 F5
Prospect Villas BA4 159 C7
Protheroes Ho BS1 226 C2
Proud Cross BS40 74 E4
Providence La BS41 10 F2
Providence Pl
  Bristol BS2 227 C2
  Bruton BA10 215 D6
PROVIDENCE PLACE 77 F1
Providence Rise BS41 10 F2
Providence View BS41 11 A1
Provident Pl TA6 208 E5
Prowle's Cross BA22 197 F5
Prowse La TA9 106 C7
Prowse's La BS26 70 A1
Prowses Mdw TA2 168 B4
PUBLOW 40 F5
Publow La BS39 40 E5
PUCKINGTON 184 B5
Pud Brook DT9 217 D1
Pudding Pie Cl BS40 53 A5
Pudding Pie La BS40 53 A6
Puddle Town TA18 196 B5
Puddy's La TA9 105 D4
PUDLEIGH 223 B8
Pudleigh La TA20 223 B8
Puffin Cl
  Minehead TA24 201 C5
  Weston-Super-Mare BS22 49 F8
Pullen Ct BA4 205 B4
Pulmans La TA18 224 C5
Pulpitsway Dro TA12 185 A8
Pulteney Ave BA2 45 B6
Pulteney Bridge BA2 228 C2
Pulteney Gdns BA2 45 B6
Pulteney Gr BA2 45 B6
Pulteney Mews 4 BA2 45 B7
Pulteney Rd BA2 45 B6
Pulteney Terr BA2 45 B6
Pump La
  Bathford BA1 29 B2
  Bristol BS1 227 B1
  Redhill BS40 36 D2
Pump Sq BS20 4 D5
Punnet Cl BS27 90 B7
Puppy Cross Ways BA3 94 F5
Puppy La BA3 94 F5
Purcell Wlk BS4 22 D7
Purdue Cl BS22 32 B3
Purewell TA7 136 C4
PURITON 136 C4
Puriton Hill TA7 136 C3
Puriton Manor TA7 136 C4
Puriton Pk TA7 136 C4
Puriton Prim Sch TA7 136 C4
Puriton Rd
  Pawlett TA6 136 A5
  West Huntspill TA9 136 B7
Purlewent Dr BA1 27 C1
Purley Dr TA6 209 D6
PURN 67 A7
Purn La BS24 67 A8
Purn Rd BS24 66 F8
Purn Way BS24 67 B7
PURSE CAUNDLE 189 D4
Purse Caundle Manor House★ DT9 189 D4
Pursey Ave BA16 207 E5
PURTINGTON 195 A4
Purving Row BS24 67 C1
Purving Row La BS24 67 C1
Putham La TA24 129 F1
Putsham Hill TA5 133 D5
Putsham Mead TA5 133 D5
Puttingthorpe Dr BS22 49 C7
Putts La DT9 175 D1
Putt's La DT9 188 D8
Puxley Cl BS14 23 E6
PUXTON 33 D3
Puxton La BS24 33 D3
Puxton Moor La BS24 33 E2
Puxton Rd BS24 33 C2
Pyde La TA10 184 D6
Pye Cnr
  Churchill BS25 52 D4
  Merriott TA16 195 F6
  Somerton TA11 211 D4
Pye La TA20 198 E8
PYLEIGH 151 B1
Pyleigh La TA4 151 A1
Pyle La BA22 174 A2
Pyles Thorne TA21 222 F4
Pyles Thorne Cl TA21 222 E5
Pyles Thorne Rd TA21 222 E4
Pylewell La BS25 52 D1
Pyle Well La TA11 174 E8
PYLLE 141 B1
Pylle Hill BA4 141 A1
Pylle La BA4 141 B1
Pylle Rd BA4 141 A2
Pyncombe La TA4 210 B3
Pyne Point BS21 6 C3
Pynne Cl BS14 23 F5
Pynne Rd BS14 23 F5
Pyracantha Wlk BS14 23 A6
PYRLAND 213 A8
Pyrland Ave TA2 212 F8
Pyrland Pl TA2 213 A8
Pyrland Wlk TA6 208 B4

Q

Quab La
  Alston Sutton BS26 88 F3
  Wedmore BS28 108 B5
Quab Lane Cl BS28 108 B4
Quaish La BA4 140 C4
Quakers' Friars BS1 227 B3
Quaker's La TA4 210 C3
Quakinghouse La TA4 166 E5
Quantick Gdns TA24 201 B5
Quantock Ave TA6 208 D5
Quantock Cl
  Burnham-on-S TA8 104 B7
  North Petherton TA6 153 E4
Quantock Ct
  Burnham-on-S TA8 104 A5
  Ilminster TA19 221 C4
  Street BA16 207 B5
  Williton TA4 202 D2
Quantock Gr TA4 202 E2
Quantock Ho TA6 153 E4
Quantock Mdw TA6 208 C5
Quantock Par TA6 153 E4
Quantock Rd
  Bridgwater TA5, TA6 208 B5
  Cannington TA5 135 C1
  Portishead BS20 2 B5
  Taunton TA2 212 E8
  Watchet TA23 202 C6
  Wellington TA21 222 D7
  Weston-Super-Mare BS23 48 E4
Quantock Rise
  Kingston St Mary TA2 168 E8
  Pawlett TA6 135 F5
Quantocks BA2 45 A1
Quantock Terr TA6 209 A6
Quantock View
  Bishops Lydeard TA4 167 F8
  Highbridge TA9 104 D3
  Kilve TA5 133 C6
Quantock Way
  Bridgwater TA6 208 C5
  Kingston St Mary TA2 168 D8
Quaperlake St BA10 215 F7
Quarme La TA24 147 E7
QUARR 177 E5
Quarr BA4 205 C6
Quarr Cross SP8 177 E4
Quarr Dr DT9 225 D6
Quarr La DT9 225 D6
Quarr Lane Pk DT9 225 D6
Quarry Batch
  Street BA16 207 A5
  Walton BA16 156 E7
Quarry Cl
  Bath BA2 44 F1
  Limpley Stoke BA3 64 D6
  Minehead TA24 201 B5
Quarry Cotts BA22 197 F8
Quarry Hay BS40 56 D8
Quarry Hill BA22 175 F4
Quarry La
  Blagdon Hill TA3 181 D4
  Bradford Abbas DT9 187 E1
  Butleigh BA6 157 D3
Quarry La *continued*
  Combe St Nicholas TA20 193 D6
  Kingston St Mary TA2 168 F7
Quarrylands La BS26 88 B4
Quarrymans Ct BA2 45 B1
Quarry Rd
  Bath BA2 45 D6
  Kingsdon TA11 173 D5
  Portishead BS20 2 C4
  Sandford BS25 52 A2
  Street BA16 207 B4
  Washford TA23 131 F4
Quarry Rise BS24 66 F8
Quarry Rock Gdns BA2 45 D4
Quarry Vale Cotts BA2 45 B1
Quarry Way BS48 8 D2
Quartley Hill EX16 164 E4
Quay La TA24 201 A8
Quays Ave BS20 2 E5
Quayside TA6 208 F5
Quay St
  Bristol BS1 227 A3
  Minehead TA24 201 A8
Quays The BS1 226 C1
Quay W TA24 125 D4
Quebec BA2 44 A6
Quedam Sh Ctr 6 BA21 219 B5
Queen Anne Ct TA24 200 F7
QUEEN CAMEL 174 F3
Queen Charlotte St BS1 227 A2
QUEEN CHARLTON 24 B3
Queen Charlton La BS14 23 E2
Queen Elizabeth Ct
  Bridgwater TA6 209 A5
  Street BA16 207 C6
Queen Elizabeth's Hospital Sch BS8 226 B3
Queen Quay BS1 227 A2
Queen's Ave
  Bristol BS8 226 B3
  Portishead BS20 2 C5
Queens Cl TA20 223 B2
Queen's Coll TA1 212 D1
Queen's Coll Jun Sch TA1 212 D1
Queenscote BS20 2 F5
Queens Cres TA14 185 F5
Queen's Ct BS8 226 B3
Queen's Down TA3 169 C4
Queens Dr TA1 168 D1
Queen's Dr BA2 45 A2
Queens Gate BS9 5 D5
Queens Gate Terr TA1 213 A3
Queens Gr BA9 161 E2
Queens Par BS1 226 C2
Queen's Par BA1 228 B3
Queen's Parade Pl BA1 228 B3
Queens Pl BA2 45 B5
Queen Sq
  Bath BA1 228 B2
  Bristol BS1 227 A2
  North Curry TA3 170 B4
  Saltford BS31 25 F3
Queen Square Ave 10 BS1 227 A2
Queen Square Pl BA1 228 B3
Queens Rd
  Banwell BS29 51 A3
  Bradford Abbas DT9 187 E1
  Frome BA11 119 D4
  Keynsham BS31 24 D4
  Minehead TA24 201 A6
  Nailsea BS48 8 D1
  Portishead BS20 1 E4
  Somerton TA11 211 D4
  Street BA16 207 B5
  Wellington TA21 222 E4
Queen's Rd
  Bridgwater TA6 208 F2
  Bristol, Bishopsworth BS13, BS41 21 F4
  Bristol BS8 226 B3
  Clevedon BS21 6 D3
  Evercreech BA4 141 E2
  Radstock BA3 79 B2
  Shepton Mallet BA4 205 A5
  Weston-Super-Mare BS23 30 D1
Queens Row BS27 90 C8
Queens Sq TA9 104 C4
Queen St
  Bath BA1 228 B2
  Bridgwater TA6 208 F5
  Bristol BS2 227 B3
  Keinton Mandeville TA11 158 A1
  North Petherton TA6 153 F4
  Taunton TA1 213 B4
  Tintinhull BA22 186 B7
  11 Wells BA5 203 D4
  Yarlington BA9 175 F8
Queens Terr TA1 213 A3
Queen's Terr
  Sherborne DT9 225 D6
  Wiveliscombe TA4 210 C4
Queensway
  Taunton TA1 212 B1
  Yeovil BA20 219 A4
Queens Way BS20 1 E4
Queen's Way BS22 31 F4
Queensway Cl TA9 106 E5
Queensway Ctr BS22 32 B2
Queensway Pl BA20 219 A4
Queenswood Rd TA6 208 C4
Queenwood Ave BA1 28 A1
Quicksilver Rdbt BA20 218 F2
Quickthorn Cl BS14 23 A6
Quiet St BA1 228 B2
Quilter Gr BS4 22 D7
Quirke St TA24 200 F7

R

Raby Mews BA2 45 B7
Raby Pl BA2 45 B7
Rackclose Gdns TA20 223 A4
Rackclose Ho TA20 223 A4
Rackclose Pk TA20 223 B4
Rackfield TA21 222 A5
Rackfield Pl BA2 44 B6
Rackhay BS1 227 A2
Rackley La
  Buckland St Mary TA20 182 B1
  Compton Bishop BS26 69 B2
Rackstile TA20 223 A7
Rackvernal Ct BA3 78 B1
Rackvernal Rd BA3 78 B1
RADDINGTON 165 B4
Raddon Cl BA4 205 B6
RADFORD 78 C8
Radford Hill
  Camerton BA2, BA3 78 C7
  Timsbury BA2 60 C1
Radigan La TA3, TA19 183 C5
RADLET 134 C1
Radlet Cl TA2 213 B7
Radnidge La EX16 162 D4
RADSTOCK 78 E1
Radstock & District Mus★ BA3 78 F2
Radstock Rd BA3 78 C2
Ragged Dro BA6 158 A7
Rag Hill BA3 79 D5
Rag La
  Babcary BA22 174 B6
  Yarcombe EX14 192 D2
Raglan Cl
  Bridgwater TA6 209 D7
  Chilcompton BA3 96 C4
Raglan Ct 4 TA2 212 F6
Ragland La BA1 28 A2
Ragland St BA1 28 A2
Raglan La BS40 37 E7
Raglan Pl 20 BS23 30 C1
Raglan's Cross TA4 202 F2
Raglan Terr
  Bath BA1 28 A2
  Yeovil BA21 218 F7
Raglan Wlk BS31 24 D4
Railford Hill BA11 118 B3
Railway Arches BS2 227 C2
Railway Cotts BA11 143 C3
Railway La BA2 62 D1
Railway Pl BA1 228 C1
Railway St
  Bath BA1 228 C1
  Taunton TA2 212 F6
Railway Terr BA2 79 E4
Railway View Pl BA3 78 B2
Rainbow La TA3 191 C7
Rainham Ct 2 BS23 30 C1
Rains Batch BS40 72 E6
Raisey La TA20 193 C7
Raleigh Cl
  Bridgwater TA6 209 C5
  Saltford BS31 25 D2
Raleigh Ct
  Sherborne DT9 225 E4
  3 Weston-Super-Mare BS23 48 E5
Raleigh Ho TA6 209 C5
Raleigh Rd DT10 190 B4
Raleigh Rise BS20 2 B5
Raliegh Pl DT9 225 D2
Ralph Allen Dr BA2 45 B3
Ralph Allen Sch BA2 45 E2
Ralston Ct BA9 216 C4
Rambler Way TA6 208 E6
Ramon Ave TA23 202 D7
Ramsay Cl BS22 31 E4
Ramsay Way TA8 104 C8
Ramscombe Forest Wlks★ TA5 151 E8
Ramscombe La BA1 28 F6
Ramsey La TA21 179 F8
Ramshorn Cl TA1 212 C2
Ramshorn Gn TA1 212 D2
Ramshorn Pl TA1 212 D3
Ranchways BS20 1 F4
Randall Rd BS8 226 B2
Randolph Ave BS13 22 B5
Randolph Cl BS13 22 B5
Randolph Rd BA11 119 F4
Ranger Rd BA6 206 C3
Rangoon Rd TA23 202 E6
Rankers La BS39 41 C5
Rank The
  Coxley BA5 139 F6
  Maiden Bradley BA12 144 C2
  Vobster BA3 117 D6
Ranscombe Ave BS22 31 D2
Ransford BS21 6 B1
Raphael Ct BS1 227 B1
RAPPS 183 D3
Raps Cl TA1 213 E5
Raps Gn TA1 213 E5
Rashwood La BA11 118 B6
Ratleigh La DT9 188 A3
Rattigan Cl TA8 104 C6
Rattle Row TA24 131 B4
Raven Cl BS22 31 E1
Raven Ct BS9 5 F8
Ravenhead Dr BS14 23 B8
Ravensmead TA20 223 C5
Ravenswood Special Sch BS48 8 D3
Ravensworth Terr TA8 104 B7
Rawle's Bldgs TA24 124 A3

Rawlings La BS26 . . . . 88 E2
Rawlins Ave BS22 . . . . 32 A5
RAWRIDGE 191 F1
Rayens Cl BS41 . . . . 10 F1
Rayens Cross Rd BS41 . . . . 10 F1
Rayleigh Rd BS9 . . . . 5 E7
Raymar Flats TA19 . . . . . . 221 A4
Raymond St TA2 . . . . 212 E6
Raymore Rise BS41 . . . . . . 10 F1
Rayneswood BS23 . . . . 48 F8
Read Mead BA6 . . . . 206 E3
Reakes Cl BA5 . . . . 203 C4
Rebels Way BA6 . . . . 206 D5
Reckleford BA20, BA21 . . . 219 B5
Reckleford Inf Sch BA21 219 C5
Rector's Cl TA8 . . . . 65 F3
Rector's Way BS23 . . . . 48 F6
Rectory Cl
Farmborough BA2 . . . . 60 A6
6 North Petherton TA6 . . 153 E3
Staplegrove TA2 . . . . 212 C8
Wraxall BS48 . . . . 9 A2
Rectory Ct TA20 . . . . 193 D6
Rectory Dr
Burnham-on-S TA8 . . . . 104 B8
Staplegrove TA2 . . . . 212 C7
Yatton BS49 . . . . 34 C7
Rectory Farm Cl BA22 . . . 174 F3
Rectory Gdns TA20 . . . . . 193 D6
Rectory Hill
Chapel Allerton BS26 . . . . . . 88 D2
Pitney TA10 . . . . 172 C7
South Cadbury BA22 . . . . . 175 C3
Rectory La
Bleadon BS24 . . . . 67 C6
Compton Martin BS40 . . . . . 74 B6
Hardington Mandeville BA22 . . . . 197 A6
Horsington BA8 . . . . 176 E2
Norton Sub Hamdon TA14 . 185 F2
Shalford BA9 . . . . 216 E6
Sparkford BA22 . . . . 175 A3
Timsbury BA2 . . . . 60 B2
Rectory Lawn TA8 . . . . . . 104 B8
Rectory Pl TA8 . . . . 104 C8
Rectory Rd
Ashbrittle TA21 . . . . 178 F8
Burnham-on-S TA8 . . . . 104 B8
Easton-in-G BS20 . . . . 4 B3
Norton Fitzwarren TA2 . . . . 168 B5
Shepton Mallet BA4 . . . . . . 205 B6
Staplegrove TA2 . . . . 212 C8
Rectory Way
Lympsham BS24 . . . . 66 F2
Yatton BS49 . . . . 34 C7
Recurium Lodge BS26 . . . . 70 B2
Redacre BS40 . . . . 36 D3
RED BALL 179 C4
Red Barn La TA20 . . . . 193 D4
Redcliff Backs BS1 . . . . . . 227 B2
REDCLIFFE BAY 1 E4
Redcliffe Cl BS20 . . . . 1 E3
Redcliffe Par E BS1 . . . . . 227 A1
Redcliffe Par W BS1 . . . . 227 A1
Redcliffe St BS27 . . . . 90 C7
Redcliffe Way BS1 . . . . . . 227 B1
Redcliff Hill BS1 . . . . 227 B1
Redcliff Mead La BS1 . . . 227 B1
Redcliff St BS1 . . . . 227 B2
Red Cotts
Blagdon BS40 . . . . 54 D6
Corsley Heath BA12 . . . . . 144 E8
Redcroft BS40 . . . . 36 D3
Redcross Mews 14 BS2 . . 227 C3
Redcross St BS2 . . . . 227 C3
Redding Pit La BS40 . . . . . 37 E4
Reddings The BS40 . . . . . . 74 B7
Redfield Gr BA3 . . . . 97 A8
Redfield Rd BA3 . . . . 97 A8
Redford Cres BS13 . . . . 21 F3
Redford Wlk BS13 . . . . 21 F3
Redgate Pk TA18 . . . . 224 C8
Redgates Rd TA24 . . . . . . 200 E7
Redgate St TA6 . . . . 209 B4
REDHILL 36 D3
Red Hill
Peasedown St John BA2 . . . 60 E1
Redhill BS40 . . . . 36 D2
West Monkton TA2 . . . . 169 B7
Redhill La BA3 . . . . 95 A2
Red Hill La TA7 . . . . 155 E7
Redhole La DT9 . . . . 225 D8
Red House La BS9 . . . . 5 E6
Red House Rd TA9 . . . . 86 D5
Red La
Churchinford TA3 . . . . 191 F7
Hemyock EX15 . . . . 180 E3
Seaborough DT8 . . . . 195 E1
Staplehay TA3 . . . . 181 E8
Redlake Dr TA1 . . . . 213 D3
Redland Ave BS20 . . . . 3 F6
Redland La TA3 . . . . 183 C8
Redland Pk BA2 . . . . 43 F6
Redlands La TA7 . . . . 137 C2
Redlands Terr BA3 . . . . 96 F8
Redland Terr BA11 . . . . . . 119 F3
REDLANE 191 F7
Red Lion Ct
3 Crewkerne TA18 . . . . . . 224 C6
Somerton TA11 . . . . 211 E4
Red Lodge Bsns Pk BS24 . 32 D1
REDLYNCH 160 D4
Redlynch Cross BA10 . . . . 160 E4
Redlynch La BS31 . . . . 24 D2
Redmans Hill BS28 . . . . . . 107 E4
Redpoll Dr BS20 . . . . 3 A6
RED POST 79 B7

Red Post
Chard TA20 . . . . 193 D3
Isle Abbotts TA3 . . . . 183 E7
Porlock TA24 . . . . 124 B3
Red Post Cross TA11 . . . . 173 D4
Red Post Ct BA2 . . . . 79 B7
Red Rd
Berrow TA8 . . . . 85 A7
Brean TA8 . . . . 66 A2
Redshard La BS40 . . . . 53 B7
Redstart Prim Sch The TA20 . . . . 223 C5
Redstart Rd TA20 . . . . 223 C6
Redway TA24 . . . . 124 A3
Red Way The BA12 . . . . . . 144 F6
Redwing Dr BS22 . . . . 31 F1
Red Wing Rd DT9 . . . . 217 C2
Redwood Cl
Nailsea BS48 . . . . 9 A2
Radstock BA3 . . . . 97 E8
Redwood Ho BS13 . . . . 22 D3
Redwood La BS48 . . . . 20 C7
Redwood Rd BA21 . . . . . . 219 E8
Reed Cl
Bridgwater TA6 . . . . 208 F2
Chard TA20 . . . . 223 D6
Watchet TA23 . . . . 202 D6
Reedley Rd BS9 . . . . 5 F5
Reedmoor Gdns TA6 . . . . 208 E7
Reeds Dr TA7 . . . . 136 F4
Reed Way BS22 . . . . 32 C3
Rees Way BS26 . . . . 87 E7
Reeves Cl BS27 . . . . 90 F2
Regal Rd BA4 . . . . 205 B6
Regal Way 24 BA4 . . . . 205 B6
Regency Cl TA8 . . . . 85 A2
Regency Ct BA5 . . . . 203 C4
Regency Wlk BA11 . . . . 119 E4
Regent Ct BA22 . . . . 173 E2
Regent Gn TA4 . . . . 167 F1
Regent Mews TA20 . . . . . . 223 C3
Regent St
Bradford On Tone TA4 . . . . 167 F1
Bristol BS8 . . . . 226 A2
Burnham-on-S TA8 . . . . 104 A7
Weston-Super-Mare BS23 . . 48 E7
Regents The
Cotford St Luke TA4 . . . . . . 167 E6
Keynsham BS31 . . . . 24 F6
4 Yeovil BA21 . . . . 218 C6
Regents Way TA24 . . . . . . 200 E6
Regent Way TA6 . . . . 209 A2
REGIL 37 F2
Regil La BS40 . . . . 38 A6
Regil Rd BS40 . . . . 37 F3
Regina The BA1 . . . . 228 B3
Reid Ct BA5 . . . . 203 B4
Remalard Ct BA7 . . . . 214 B5
Rendcomb Cl BS22 . . . . 31 B2
Rennison Ct BS23 . . . . 48 E4
Reservoir La BA5 . . . . 203 C6
Retford Ho BA2 . . . . 45 E5
Retreat Cvn Pk The TA8 . . 85 A2
Retreat The
Foxcote BA3 . . . . 79 E3
Frome BA11 . . . . 120 B4
Taunton TA2 . . . . 168 F6
Weston-Super-Mare BS23 . . 30 C1
Reubens Ct BS22 . . . . 31 F3
Rex Rd BA22 . . . . 186 C2
Rex's La
Barwick BA22 . . . . 197 F8
Yeovil BA22 . . . . 219 C1
Rexton La TA4 . . . . 150 F5
Reynald's Way
Butleigh BA6 . . . . 157 C4
Street BA16 . . . . 207 D1
Reynolds TA21 . . . . 166 F2
Reynolds Cl BS31 . . . . 25 A5
RHODE 153 D5
Rhode Cl BS31 . . . . 25 A3
Rhode La TA6 . . . . 208 E2
Rhodes Cl TA2 . . . . 212 C7
Rhodyate BS40 . . . . 54 D2
Rhodyate Hill BS49 . . . . . . 34 F6
Rhodyate La BS49 . . . . 35 A7
Rhodyate The BS29 . . . . . . 51 C1
Rhydderch Way TA18 . . . . 224 C5
Rhyll Gate Cross TA22 . . . 162 E7
Rhyne Terr BS23 . . . . 48 D2
Rhyne View BS48 . . . . 8 B1
Richard Beadon Cl TA4 . . 210 B4
Richard Huish Coll TA1 . . 213 A2
Richards Cl
Wellington TA21 . . . . 222 C8
Weston-Super-Mare BS22 . . 32 B4
Richards Cres TA2 . . . . . . 169 B6
Richmond Cl
Bath BA1 . . . . 27 F1
Bridgwater TA6 . . . . 208 F7
Keynsham BS31 . . . . 24 D4
Minehead TA24 . . . . 200 E6
Portishead BS20 . . . . 2 E5
Sampford Peverell EX16 . . 178 D1
Sherborne DT9 . . . . 225 C3
Richmond Ct BA22 . . . . . . 173 E2
Richmond Gn
Nailsea BS48 . . . . 8 F1
Sherborne DT9 . . . . 225 C4
Taunton TA1 . . . . 212 D5
Richmond Hill
Bath BA1 . . . . 27 F1
Bristol BS8 . . . . 226 B3
Richmond Hill Ave BS8 . . 226 B3
Richmond Ho
Crewkerne TA18 . . . . 224 C6
9 Shepton Mallet BA4 . . . 205 B6
Yeovil BA20 . . . . 219 A4

Richmond Hts
Bath BA1 . . . . 27 F2
Bristol BS8 . . . . 226 B3
Richmond La
Bath BA1 . . . . 27 F1
Bristol BS8 . . . . 226 B3
Richmond Mews BS8 . . . 226 A3
Richmond Park Rd BS8 . . 226 A3
Richmond Pk TA1 . . . . 212 C4
Richmond Pl BA1 . . . . 27 F1
Richmond Rd
Bath BA1 . . . . 27 F1
2 Frome BA11 . . . . 119 E3
Sherborne DT9 . . . . 225 C3
Taunton TA1 . . . . 212 D5
Yeovil BA20 . . . . 219 A4
Richmond St BS23 . . . . 48 D7
Richmond Terr BS8 . . . . . 226 A3
Richmond Villas BA6 . . . . 206 E4
Richmond Way BA21 . . . . 218 C6
Rich's Farmhouse Cider Farm★ TA9 . . . . 105 D3
RICH'S HOLFORD 151 C4
Ricketts La BS22 . . . . 32 A2
RICKFORD 54 B3
Rickford La BS40 . . . . 54 A3
Rickford Rd BS48 . . . . 8 F1
Rickford Rise BS40 . . . . . . 54 A3
Rickhayes BA9 . . . . 216 B4
Rickhay Rise TA18 . . . . . . 196 B8
Ricklands The BS40 . . . . . . 38 A6
Ricksey Cl TA11 . . . . 211 B3
Ricksey La TA11 . . . . 211 B3
Ricksmead Dro TA7 . . . . . 155 B2
Rickyard Rd BS40 . . . . 35 E2
RIDGE 74 C5
Ridge Cl BS20 . . . . 2 A4
Ridge Cres BS40 . . . . 74 E6
Ridge Green Cl BA2 . . . . . . 62 D8
Ridge Highway TA4 . . . . . 166 A3
Ridge Hill TA4 . . . . 210 D5
Ridge La
Corton Denham DT9 . . . . . 175 D1
East Chinnock BA22 . . . . . 196 F8
East Coker BA22 . . . . 197 A7
Pitcombe BA7, BA10 . . . . . 215 A2
Ridge BS40 . . . . 74 D5
Shepton Mallet BA4 . . . . . . 205 B3
Ridgemead BA20 . . . . 218 D2
Ridgemeade BS14 . . . . 23 B4
Ridgemount Gdns BS14 . . 23 B5
Ridge Rd
Croscombe BA4, BA5 . . . . . 204 D5
West Anstey TA22 . . . . 162 D7
Ridge The
Bristol BS11 . . . . 4 E7
Porlock TA24 . . . . 124 B3
Poyntington DT9 . . . . 188 F7
Yatton BS49 . . . . 34 B8
Ridgeview BS41 . . . . 11 B2
Ridgeview Ho BS20 . . . . 2 E3
RIDGEWAY 143 C7
Ridgeway
Ashcott TA7 . . . . 156 B8
Nailsea BS48 . . . . 8 C1
Nunney BA11 . . . . 143 C8
Sherborne DT9 . . . . 225 B3
Ridgeway Ave BS23 . . . . . . 48 E6
Ridgeway Cl BS40 . . . . 74 E6
Ridgeway Ct BS14 . . . . 23 C5
Ridgeway Gdns
Bristol BS14 . . . . 23 C5
Glastonbury BA6 . . . . 206 F5
Ridgeway La
Bristol BS14 . . . . 23 B5
Moorlinch TA7 . . . . 155 F7
North Cadbury BA22 . . . . . 175 D6
Nunney BA11 . . . . 143 C8
Shillingford EX16 . . . . 164 D2
Stolford TA5 . . . . 134 E8
Ridgeway Rd BS41 . . . . 11 A2
Ridgeway The BS22 . . . . . . 31 B2
Ridgewood BS9 . . . . 5 D3
Ridgewood Cross EX15 . . 191 B8
Ridgewood La EX15 . . . . . 191 A8
Ridgway TA18 . . . . 196 B8
Ridgway Cross EX36 . . . . 145 K1
RIDING GATE 177 B8
Ridings The BS13 . . . . 21 E4
Ridley Cnr TA10 . . . . 171 C5
Ridley Hill TA10 . . . . 171 E8
Riec-Sur-Belon Way TA19 . . . . 221 A4
Rigg La DT9 . . . . 187 F5
Rigg Lane Cotts DT9 . . . . 187 F5
Riggles Cross EX14 . . . . . 191 D3
RIMPTON 188 A8
Rimpton Hill BA22 . . . . . . 188 A7
Rimpton Rd BA22 . . . . 174 F1
Ringdown La EX15 . . . . . . 180 F2
Ringolds Way BA16 . . . . . 207 B4
Ringspit La BS14, BS39 . . . 40 E8
Ring St DT10 . . . . 190 B4
Ringstone TA9 . . . . 136 B8
Ringswell Gdns BA1 . . . . . 28 B1
Ringwell BA2 . . . . 81 E4
Ringwell Hill TA12 . . . . . . 185 D4
Ringwell La BA2 . . . . 81 E4
Ringwood Gr BS23 . . . . 31 A1
Ringwood Rd
Bath BA2 . . . . 44 C5
Bridgwater TA6 . . . . 209 A2
Riphay Cross TA22 . . . . . . 163 E3
Rippleside BS20 . . . . 2 C5
Rippleside Rd BS21 . . . . 6 E5
Ripple The BS21 . . . . 8 D4
Risdale Rd BS3 . . . . 11 F1
Risdon Rd TA23 . . . . 202 C6

Risedale Cl TA6 . . . . 208 C5
Risedale Rd BS25 . . . . 70 A8
Risemoor Rd TA6 . . . . 208 E2
Ritchie Rd BA22 . . . . 218 A5
Rivendell BS22 . . . . 32 A4
Riverbed Ho TA9 . . . . 104 D3
River Dro TA7 . . . . 155 E4
River La TA7 . . . . 209 E1
Riverland Dr BS13 . . . . 21 F5
Riverleaze
Bristol BS9 . . . . 5 C5
Portishead BS20 . . . . 1 F6
River Mead BS21 . . . . 16 D8
River Pl BA2 . . . . 44 B6
River Rd
East Huntspill TA7 . . . . 137 B8
Mark TA9 . . . . 106 D1
Pawlett TA6 . . . . 135 F5
Portbury BS20 . . . . 3 F8
Riversgate BS1 . . . . 227 C2
RIVERSIDE
Midsomer Norton 96 F7
Wellington 222 B6
Riverside
Banwell BS24, BS29 . . . . . . 51 B5
Bridgwater TA6 . . . . 208 F6
Burrowbridge TA7 . . . . 154 F1
Combwich TA5 . . . . 135 C5
Dinder BA5 . . . . 140 D7
Horton TA19 . . . . 183 C2
Meare BA5 . . . . 138 F5
Taunton TA1 . . . . 212 E4
Wellington TA21 . . . . 222 B7
Riverside Cl
Bridgwater TA6 . . . . 208 F7
Bristol BS11 . . . . 4 F5
Clevedon BS21 . . . . 6 B1
Midsomer Norton BA3 . . . . . 96 F7
Weston-Super-Mare BS22 . . 32 C3
Riverside Cotts BA3 . . . . . . 79 A2
Riverside Ct BA2 . . . . 228 B1
Riverside Gdns
Bath BA1 . . . . 228 B2
Dunster TA24 . . . . 201 E3
Midsomer Norton BA3 . . . . . 96 F7
Riverside Pl 2 TA1 . . . . . 212 F4
Riverside Rd
Bath BA2 . . . . 228 B2
Midsomer Norton BA3 . . . . . 96 F7
Riverside Row TA24 . . . . . 124 A3
Riverside Terr BA11 . . . . . 119 F5
Riverside Wlk BA3 . . . . 96 F7
Rivers Rd
Bath BA1 . . . . 228 C4
Yeovil BA21 . . . . 219 D8
Rivers Reach BA11 . . . . . . 120 A5
Rivers St BA1 . . . . 228 B3
Rivers Street Mews BA1 . 228 B3
River St BS2 . . . . 227 C3
River Street Pl 5 BA1 . . . 228 B3
River Terr BS31 . . . . 24 F5
Riverton Rd TA7 . . . . 136 B4
River View
Bridgwater TA6 . . . . 208 F6
Combwich TA5 . . . . 135 B5
Exebridge TA22 . . . . 163 F3
Riverway BS48 . . . . 8 F3
River Wlk BS22 . . . . 32 D2
Roachill Cross EX36 . . . . . 162 C1
Road Hill
Alcombe SN13 . . . . 29 E8
Langford Budville TA4 . . . . 166 B3
ROADWATER 131 C1
Roath Rd BS20 . . . . 2 D5
Robbins Cl SN14 . . . . 13 F8
Robert Blake Science Coll TA6 . . . . 208 F3
Robert Ct BS8 . . . . 11 D7
Roberts Dr TA6 . . . . 209 A2
Roberts Rd TA2 . . . . 168 A6
Robert St TA4 . . . . 202 D2
Robin Cl
Bristol BS14 . . . . 23 D6
Midsomer Norton BA3 . . . . . 97 B8
Taunton TA1 . . . . 212 B4
Weston-Super-Mare BS22 . . 49 E8
Robin Dr BS24 . . . . 49 E2
Robinia Wlk BS14 . . . . 23 A7
Robin La BS21 . . . . 6 D5
Robin Pl BS20 . . . . 3 A6
Robins Ct
Chard TA20 . . . . 223 C5
Frome BA11 . . . . 119 D5
Robins Dr
Bridgwater TA6 . . . . 209 A6
Burtle TA7 . . . . 137 D6
Robins La
Burtle TA7 . . . . 137 C6
Frome BA11 . . . . 119 D5
Shepton Beauchamp TA19 . 184 E4
Robinson Cl BS48 . . . . 19 A5
Robinson Hts DT10 . . . . . . 190 B4
Robinson Way BS48 . . . . . . 19 A5
Rob-Lynne Ct BS25 . . . . . . 69 F8
Roche Cl BA21 . . . . 218 C7
Rochester Cl BS24 . . . . 49 A1
Rochester Rd TA2 . . . . 213 A8
Rochfort Ct BA1 . . . . 45 B8
Rock Ave BS48 . . . . 8 C2
Rock Cotts BS20 . . . . 4 E4
Rockeries Dr BS25 . . . . 69 F8
Rockeries The BS25 . . . . . . 69 F8
Rocketts Cl TA3 . . . . 169 D4
Rocketts Cotts TA3 . . . . . . 169 C4
Rockfield Cotts TA21 . . . . 179 F7
Rock Hall Cotts BA2 . . . . . . 45 B1
Rockhall Ho 10 BS23 . . . . . 30 C1
Rock Hall Ho BA2 . . . . 45 B1

Rock Hall La BA2 . . . . 45 B1
Rock Hill TA3 . . . . 170 C1
Rockhill Est BS31 . . . . 24 F4
Rockingham Gdns BS11 . . . 5 A8
Rockingham Gr BS23 . . . . . 31 A1
Rock La
Bath BA2 . . . . 45 B1
Exford TA24 . . . . 128 D1
West Bagborough TA4 . . . . 151 E5
Rockleaze
Bristol BS9 . . . . 5 E2
Evercreech BA4 . . . . 141 E2
Rockleaze Ave BS9 . . . . 5 E3
Rockleaze Ct BS9 . . . . 5 E3
Rockleaze Mans 12 BS23 . 30 C1
Rockleaze Rd BS9 . . . . 5 E3
Rockliffe Ave BA2 . . . . 45 B8
Rockliffe Rd BA2 . . . . 45 B8
Rock Rd
Chilcompton BA3 . . . . 96 D2
Keynsham BS31 . . . . 24 E5
Midsomer Norton BA3 . . . . . 78 B2
Yatton BS49 . . . . 34 C7
Rock's Dro BA16 . . . . 138 F3
Rocks La BS40 . . . . 20 E1
Rocks St BA5 . . . . 204 C7
Rocks The BA4 . . . . 142 B7
Rock Terr BA3 . . . . 116 F6
Rockway TA3 . . . . 170 C1
Rockwell Gate TA21 . . . . . 222 B5
ROCKWELL GREEN 222 B5
Rockwell Green CE Prim Sch TA21 . . . . 222 B5
Rocky Hill TA11 . . . . 173 D5
Rocky La TA23 . . . . 131 E2
Rodber Cl BA9 . . . . 216 B4
Rodber Gdns BA9 . . . . 216 B4
Roddenbury Cl BA11 . . . . 120 B5
Roddenbury View BA12 . 144 D8
Rodden Rd BA11 . . . . 120 A5
RODE 101 F8
Rode Hill
Rode BA11 . . . . 82 E1
Southwick BA11 . . . . 83 A1
Rode Methodist Fst Sch BA11 . . . . 101 E8
Rodfords Mead BS14 . . . . . 23 A7
RODGROVE 177 C3
RODHUISH 131 B2
Rodhuish Cross TA24 . . . . 131 B3
Rodhuish Hill La TA24 . . . 131 A3
Rod La TA19 . . . . 183 F4
Rodmead La BA5 . . . . 110 E4
Rodmead Wlk BS13 . . . . . . 22 A4
Rodmoor Rd BS20 . . . . 2 D6
Rodmore Cres BA4 . . . . . . 141 E1
Rodmore Rd BA4 . . . . 141 E1
Rodney BS24 . . . . 49 A2
Rodney Ct BA22 . . . . 218 A5
Rodney Ho BA2 . . . . 44 A6
Rodney Pl BS8 . . . . 226 A3
Rodney Rd
Backwell BS48 . . . . 19 A6
Saltford BS31 . . . . 25 E2
RODNEY STOKE 91 A1
Rodney Stoke National Nature Reserve★ BS27 . . 91 B2
RODWAY 135 B3
Rodway TA5 . . . . 135 B3
Rodwell La TA13 . . . . 184 E5
Roe Ave BA22 . . . . 218 A5
Roebuck Cl BS22 . . . . 32 B4
Roebuck Gate La TA4 . . . . 151 B6
Roe Cl TA6 . . . . 209 D4
Roe La BA22 . . . . 188 B8
Roemead La BA3 . . . . 114 C5
Roemead Rd BA3 . . . . 114 C4
Rogers Cl
Buckland Dinham BA11 . . . 100 A3
Clutton BS39 . . . . 58 E3
North Petherton TA6 . . . . . 153 F3
Rogers Wlk TA4 . . . . 167 E6
Roland Cl TA1 . . . . 212 C2
ROLSTONE 32 F2
Roman Baths The★ BA1 . 228 C2
Roman Ct BA21 . . . . 219 D6
Roman Farm Rd BS4 . . . . . 22 E7
Roman Ho BA1 . . . . 228 C4
Roman La TA6 . . . . 208 C3
Roman Rd
Bath BA1 . . . . 228 C3
Bleadon BS24 . . . . 67 C8
Sandford BS25 . . . . 51 F4
Taunton TA1 . . . . 213 C5
Roman Villas BA4 . . . . 205 E4
Roman Way
Bristol BS9 . . . . 5 C4
Coleford BA3 . . . . 116 F7
Paulton BS39 . . . . 77 C6
Peasedown St John BA2 . . . 79 E7
Watchet TA23 . . . . 202 C7
Roman Way The BA6 . . . . 206 C3
Romney Mead TA1 . . . . . . 213 D4
Romney Rd 2 TA6 . . . . . . 154 A5
Romsey Rd BA21 . . . . 219 E8
Ron Jones Ho 3 BS1 . . . . 227 B4
Rookery Cl
Puriton TA7 . . . . 136 C4
Rooks Bridge BS26 . . . . 87 A6
Weston-Super-Mare BS22 . . 31 E3
Rookery La
Croscombe BA5 . . . . 204 B7
Drimpton DT8 . . . . 199 F6
Rookery Terr TA21 . . . . . . 222 C5
Rookery The BA5 . . . . 140 D7

Rookery Way BS14 22 F4
ROOKHAM 112 B5
Rook La BA11 119 F4
ROOKS BRIDGE 87 C5
Rooksbridge Rd BS24, BS26 87 B6
Rooksbridge Wlk BA2 44 B5
Rooks La BA11 120 E7
Rook's Meade La TA19 184 E1
ROOK'S NEST 150 C4
Room Hill Rd TA24 146 D7
Roper's La BS40 35 E3
Rope Walk Ho 23 BS2 227 C3
Ropewalk The TA20 223 B5
Rope Wk TA24 201 B7
Rope Wlk
Backwell BS48 19 A5
Bridgwater TA6 209 A5
Coleford BA3 116 E8
Evercreech BA4 141 E1
14 Martock TA12 185 E6
Wellington TA21 222 C4
Rope Wlk The TA23 202 C7
Roping Rd BA21 219 B6
Rosary Dr TA6 208 B4
Rosebank Rd TA4 167 A4
Roseberry Cotts BA3 117 A7
Roseberry Pl BA2 44 C6
Roseberry Rd BA2 44 C6
Roseberry Terr TA1 212 D5
Rosebery Ave
Bridgwater TA6 209 B5
Yeovil BA21 219 D6
Rosebery St TA2 212 E7
Rosebery Terr BS8 226 B2
Rose Cotts
Taunton TA1 213 B3
Weston-Super-Mare BS22 32 C2
Rose & Crown Cotts BA3 116 F6
Rose Ct
Keinton Mandeville TA11 158 A1
Shepton Mallet BA4 205 B6
Rosedale Ave BS23 49 A7
Rose Dale Wlk BA11 119 F6
Rose Gdns BS22 32 B4
Rose Hill
Bath BA1 28 C3
Spaxton TA5 152 F2
Rose La
Crewkerne, Misterton TA18 196 B3
Crewkerne TA18 224 B6
Purtington TA20 195 A3
Roseland Cl BA1 28 C3
Roselyn Cres DT9 189 A1
Rosemary Cres BS20 2 F5
Rosemary La
Dulverton TA22 163 D6
Freshford BA3 64 B4
ROSEMARY LANE 180 D1
Rosemarylane Cross EX15 180 D1
Rosemary St DT9 217 C2
Rose Meare Gdns BS13 21 E7
Rose Mills Ind Est TA19 183 E2
Rosemont Terr BS8 226 A2
Rosemount La BA2 45 B4
Rosemount Rd BS48 20 B8
Roseneath Ave TA8 84 F4
Rose Terr
Bath BA2 45 C2
Bristol BS8 226 B3
Rose Tree Paddock TA8 84 F4
Rosette Cotts TA12 185 B7
Rosevean Cl TA6 209 D7
Rose Villas TA5 135 B2
Rosewarn Cl BA2 44 A4
Rosewell Ct BA1 228 B2
Rosewood Ave TA8 104 C6
Rosewood Cl TA8 104 C7
Rosewood Dr TA8 104 C6
Roslyn Ave BS22 31 C1
Rossendale Cl BS22 31 F3
Rosshayne La EX14 192 C2
Rossiter Grange 5 BS13 21 F4
Rossiter Rd BA2 228 C1
Rossiter's Hill BA11 119 F3
Rossiter's Rd BA11 119 E3
Rosslyn Cl 1 BA1 44 B7
Rosslyn Rd BA1 44 B7
ROTCOMBE 59 D2
Rotcombe La BS39 59 D2
Rotcombe Vale BS39 59 D2
Rotton Row TA4 210 C4
Roughmoor TA4 202 E4
Roughmoor Cl TA1 212 D5
Roughmoor Cotts TA1 212 D5
Roughmoor Cres TA1 212 D5
Roughmoor La BA5 110 C7
ROUNDHAM 195 D4
Roundhill Gr BA2 44 B3
Roundhill Pk BA2 44 A4
Roundmoor Cl BS31 25 D3
Roundmoor Gdns BS14 23 D7
Roundoak Gdns TA21 167 C2
Round Oak Gr BS27 90 A8
Round Oak Rd BS27 90 A8
Round Pool La TA4 151 B7
Roundwell Cl BA4 204 F6
Roundwell St TA13 220 C4
Rowacres
Bath BA2 44 B3
Bristol BS14 22 F6
Rowan Cl
Nailsea BS48 9 A2
Rowan Cl *continued*
Puriton TA7 136 C4
Wincanton BA9 216 D2
Rowan Ct
Frome BA11 120 B7
Radstock BA3 78 E1
Rowan Dr
Berrow TA8 84 F5
Taunton TA1 213 D1
Rowan Ho BS13 22 D4
Rowan Pl BS24 32 B1
Rowans Cl TA6 209 C6
Rowans The BS20 2 B4
Rowan Way
Churchill BS40 53 A5
Yeovil BA20 218 F3
Rowan Wlk BS31 24 C4
Rowbarrow Hill
Rimpton DT9 188 A7
Trent DT9 187 F6
ROWBARTON 212 E7
Rowbarton Cl TA2 212 F7
ROWBERROW 53 A1
Rowberrow BS14 22 F7
Rowberrow La BS25 70 F8
Rowberrow Way BS48 8 E1
Rowcliffe Cotts TA21 178 F8
Rowdells Orch TA19 184 D1
Rowden Mill La DT10 189 F1
Rowdens Rd BA5 203 D3
Rowditch La TA5 133 D5
Rowe Cl TA21 222 A4
Rowe's Hill BA12 144 E4
ROWFORD 168 F6
Row La
Keinton Mandeville TA11 158 A1
Laverton BA2 100 D8
Rowlands Cl BA1 29 B2
Rowlands Rise TA7 136 C4
Rowley Rd BA6 206 E5
Rowls La BA9 177 E6
Rowmarsh La TA10 172 D5
Rownham Cl BS3 11 E4
Rownham Ct BS8 226 A1
Rownham Hill BS8 11 E6
Rownham Mead BS8 226 A1
Row Of Ashes La BS40 36 F4
Rows La EX16 164 A1
Rows The BS22 31 E2
Row The
Hambridge TA10 184 D8
Langport TA10 172 B3
Royal Ave BA1 228 B3
Royal Cl BA21 219 C6
Royal Cres* BA1 228 A3
Royal Cres BS23 48 D8
Royal Ct BS23 48 D4
Royal Fort Rd BS2, BS8 226 C3
Royal High Sch The BA1 228 B4
Royal Ho 4 BA4 205 B6
Royal Hospl for Sick Children BS2 226 C3
Royal National Hospl for Rheumatic Diseases BA1 228 B2
Royal Par
Bristol BS8 226 B3
Weston-Super-Mare BS23 48 D8
Royal Park Mews BS8 226 A3
Royal Pk BS8 226 A3
Royal Portbury Dock Rd BS20 3 E5
Royal Prom BS8 226 B3
Royal Sands BS23 48 D4
Royal Sch The BA1 27 F2
Royal United Hospl BA1 44 B8
Royal West of England Acad BS8 226 B3
Royal York Cres BS8 11 F6
Royal York Ho 7 BS8 226 A2
Royal York Mews 6 BS8 226 A2
Royal York Villas BS8 226 A2
Royces La TA19 184 C5
Roynon Way BS27 90 B7
Royston Lodge BS23 48 D6
Royston Rd TA3 192 A7
ROYSTON WATER 192 B7
Rozel Ho 14 BS23 30 C1
Rubbery La TA11 158 D1
Rubens Cl BS31 25 A5
Ruborough Rd TA6 209 C4
Ruckley Ford BA3 80 A2
Ruddock Cl BA22 197 B8
Ruddock Way BA22 197 B8
Ruddymead BS21 6 D2
RUDGE 102 D5
Rudge Hill BA11 102 D5
Rudge La
Beckington BA11 102 B6
Standerwick BA11 102 D3
Rudge Rd BA11 102 B2
Rudgeway Rd BS39 77 E4
Rudgewood Cl BS13 22 D4
Rudgleigh Ave BS20 4 C4
Rudgleigh Rd BS20 4 C4
Rudhall Gn BS22 32 B3
Rudmore Pk BA1 44 A7
Rue La
Alweston DT9 189 C2
Hambridge TA3 184 B7
Ruett La BS39 77 B4
Rugg's Dro
Chedzoy TA7 154 D7
West Huntspill TA9 136 B7
Rugg's Hill TA22 148 E2
Rughill BS28 108 D8
Rugosa Dr TA8 84 F4
RUISHTON 169 C3
Ruishton CE Prim Sch TA3 169 C3
Ruishton La TA3 169 C3
Ruishton Lane Cotts TA3 169 C3
RUMWELL 168 B2
RUNNINGTON 179 F8
Runnymede Rd BA21 219 D8
Rupert St
Bristol BS1 227 A3
Taunton TA2 212 E6
Rusham BS13 21 F4
Rush Ash La BA3 116 E8
Rushgrove Gdns BS39 57 C4
RUSH HILL 44 B2
Rush Hill
Bath BA2 44 C2
Farrington Gurney BS39 76 F3
Rush Hill La BS28 107 F3
Rushmoor BS21 6 A1
Rushmoor Gr BS48 19 A5
Rushmoor La BS48 19 A5
Rushway BS40 53 F4
Ruskin Cl TA1 213 C4
Ruskin Rd BA3 78 C1
Ruskway La TA10 184 C6
Russell Cl BS40 38 A6
Russell Pl
Bridgwater TA6 208 F6
Milborne Port DT9 217 C3
Russell Pope Ave TA20 223 D2
Russell Rd
Clevedon BS21 6 C3
Locking BS24 50 C6
Russell's TA4 210 C4
Russell's Barton BA11 143 B8
Russell St BA1 228 B3
Russet Cl TA21 222 F7
Russets The BS20 2 F4
Russett Cl BS48 19 B6
Russett Gr BS48 18 C8
Russett Rd
Street BA16 207 C4
Taunton TA1 213 E5
Russet Way
Peasedown St John BA2 79 D7
Yeovil BA20 218 D2
Russ La BS21 16 E4
Russ St BS2 227 C2
Rusty Well BA20 218 F3
Rusty Well Pk BA20 218 F3
Ruthven Rd BS4 22 E8
Rutland Cl BS22 49 C8
Rutter's La TA19 221 B4
Ryalls Ct BA21 219 C5
Ryburn Cl TA1 213 D3
Rydal Ave BS24 50 A4
Rydal Rd BS23 48 F4
RYDON 169 E8
Rydon Cres TA5 135 C2
Rydon La
Lopen TA13 185 A1
South Petherton TA13 220 A5
Taunton TA2 212 F8
Rye TA7 136 C4
Rye Cl BS13 21 E6
Ryecroft Ave BS22 31 E2
Ryecroft Rise BS41 11 B1
Ryefields Cl BA22 197 B8
Rye Gdns BA20 218 D2
Rye La TA7 155 C2
Ryelands Farm Ind Est TA21 222 B3
Ryepool TA4 167 F8
Ryesland Way TA3 169 D4
Rye Water La DT2 197 A1
Rylands BA11 101 E4
Rylands Cl TA4 202 D2
Rylestone Gr BS9 5 F5
Rysdale Rd BS9 5 F6

S

Sabrina Way BS9 5 C4
Sackmore Gn DT10 190 F6
Sackmore La DT10 190 F5
Saco Ho BS1 227 B2
Sacred Heart Prep Sch BS40 39 A3
Sadborow La TA20 199 B4
Sadborow Pound TA20 199 B5
Sadbury Cl BS22 32 B4
Sadler St BA5 203 D4
Sadlier Cl BS11 5 A8
Saffron Cl TA1 168 F1
Saffron Ct
Bath BA1 228 C4
Sherborne DT9 225 E4
Saffron Ho 10 BS23 48 E8
Saffrons The 7 BS22 32 B4
Sage Cl BS20 1 E4
Sage's La BA3 94 D6
Sainsbury Cl TA24 200 D7
Sainsbury Rd TA24 200 D7
St Agnes Cl BS48 9 A1
St Albans Pl TA2 212 F8
St Aldhelm's CE Prim Sch BA4 141 E6
St Aldhelm's Cl BA11 119 D4
St Aldhelms Ct BA11 119 D4
St Aldhelm's Rd DT9 225 D6
St Algars Yd BA11 144 A4
St Andrew's CE Jun Sch TA8 104 B7
St Andrew's CE Jun Sch BS49 34 C4
St Andrew's CE Prim Sch
Bath BA1 228 B4
Taunton TA2 212 F6
St Andrew's CE Sch EX13 198 A7
St Andrews Cl
Castle Cary BA7 214 B7
Nailsea BS48 9 A1
Weston-Super-Mare BS22 31 F3
St Andrew's Cl
Congresbury BS49 34 C4
Curry Rivel TA10 171 D4
High Ham TA10 156 A2
St Andrews Ct TA24 200 F7
St Andrew's Ct BA5 203 F5
St Andrews Dr EX13 198 A2
St Andrew's Dr BS21 6 A2
St Andrews La TA24 200 F7
St Andrews Mews 4 BA5 203 C3
St Andrew's Par 1 BS23 48 F4
St Andrews Pk BA5 203 D3
St Andrews Rd
Backwell BS48 19 B5
Cheddar BS27 90 C7
Yeovil BA20 218 F5
St Andrew's Rd
Burnham-on-S TA8 104 B7
Stogursey TA5 134 C5
6 Taunton TA2 212 F6
St Andrew St BA5 203 E4
St Andrew's Terr BA1 228 B3
St Andrews View TA2 212 F6
St Andrews Wlk 5 BA5 203 C3
St Anne's Ave BS31 24 D6
St Anne's CE Prim Sch BS24 33 B5
St Anne's Cl BA6 158 A5
St Anne's Ct BS31 24 D6
St Anne's Gdns BA21 218 E6
St Ann's Cl TA2 212 E7
St Ann's Dr TA8 85 A1
St Ann's Pl BA1 228 B2
St Ann's Way BA2 45 C6
St Anthony's Cl BA3 78 A2
St Antonys Sq 1 DT9 225 D3
St Aubyn's Ave BS23 48 D2
St Audries Cl TA5 134 C6
St Audries Ct TA23 202 B7
St Augustine of Canterbury Sch The TA2 213 A7
St Augustines Ct 1 TA1 213 A4
St Augustine's Par BS1 227 A2
St Augustine's Pl 1 BS1 227 A2
St Augustine St TA1 213 A4
St Austell Cl BS48 19 A8
St Austell Rd BS22 49 B8
St Barnabas CE Prim Sch BS20 2 B5
St Barnabas Cl BA3 78 B3
St Bartholomew's CE Fst Sch TA18 224 D5
St Benedict's CE Jun Sch BA6 206 D4
St Benedict's Cl BA6 206 D4
St Benedict's RC Prim Sch BA3 97 C7
St Bernadette RC Prim Sch BS14 23 B6
St Bernadette RC Sch BS14 23 B6
St Bernard's RC Prim Sch BS11 4 E6
St Bernard's Rd BS11 4 E6
St Brandon's Sch BS21 6 B3
St Brides Cl BA6 206 D5
St Bridges Cl BS22 31 A6
St Bridges Ct BS22 31 A6
St Bridget's Cl TA8 65 F5
St Cadoc Ho BS31 24 F5
ST CATHERINE 13 F1
St Catherine's Cl BA2 45 C6
St Catherine's Cres DT9 225 B3
St Catherine's Ct 10 BA11 119 E5
St Catherines Hill BA10 215 E6
St Catherine's Mead BS20 4 D3
St Catherine's Way DT9 225 B3
St Chad's Ave BA3 78 A1
St Chad's Gn BA3 97 A8
St Charles Cl BA3 78 A2
St Christopher's Cl BA2 45 C8
St Christopher's Ct BS21 6 C5
St Christopher's Way TA8 85 A2
ST CLEERS 211 C3
St Cleers TA11 211 C3
St Cleer's Orch TA11 211 C3
St Cleers Way TA11 211 C3
St Clements Ct
Bath BA1 27 C1
Bristol BS2 227 C4
Clevedon BS21 6 C4
Keynsham BS31 24 E4
2 Weston-Super-Mare BS22 32 A2
St Clements Rd BS31 24 F4
St Cuthbert Ave BA5 203 B5
St Cuthbert's CE Inf Sch BA5 203 C3
St Cuthbert's Lodge 3 BA5 203 D4
St Cuthbert St BA5 203 D4
St Cuthbert's Villas BA5 203 A5
St Cuthbert Way BA5 203 B5
St Davids Cl EX13 198 A2
St David's Cl BA6 206 E4
St David's Cl
Taunton TA2 213 A8
St David's Cl *continued*
Weston-Super-Mare BS22 31 B2
St David's Cres BA21 219 B7
St Davids Ct TA6 209 D3
St David's Ct BS21 16 E8
St David's Dr EX13 198 A2
St David's Gdns TA2 212 F8
St Davids Mews BS1 226 C2
St Davids Pl BA10 215 E7
ST DECUMANS 202 B6
St Decuman's Rd TA23 202 C7
St Dubricius CE Sch TA24 124 A3
St Dunstans Cl
Glastonbury BA6 206 D5
Keynsham BS31 24 E6
St Dunstan's Com Sch BA6 206 D5
St Dunstan's Pk BA6 158 A5
St Edmund's Rd BA6 206 D5
St Edmunds's Rd BA6 206 E5
St Edmund's Terr BA3 117 C7
St Edward's Cl TA7 137 B2
St Edward's Rd BS8 226 B2
St Edyth's Rd BS9 5 C6
St Elizabeth's Way TA13 220 C4
SS Peter & Paul RC Cath* BS8 226 A4
SS Peter & Paul RC Prim Sch BS8 226 C4
St Francis Prim Sch BS48 8 F1
St Francis Rd BS31 24 D6
St George CE Prim Sch BS1 226 B2
ST GEORGES 32 D3
St Georges Ave EX13 198 A2
St George's Ave
Taunton TA2 212 F8
Yeovil BA21 219 B7
St Georges Bldgs BA1 228 A3
St George's CE Sch, Bourton SP8 161 E1
St George's Cl TA24 201 D2
St George's Cross BA11 101 E1
St Georges Ct BA6 206 E5
St George's Hill
Bath BA2 45 D8
Easton-in-G BS20 4 A3
St George's Ho BS8 226 B2
St Georges Mews TA1 212 F3
St Georges Pl BA1 228 A3
St George's Pl TA1 212 F3
St Georges Prim Sch BS22 32 C3
St George's RC Prim Sch TA1 213 A3
St Georges Rd BS1 226 C2
St George's Rd
Keynsham BS31 24 D6
Portbury BS20 3 E7
St Georges Sq TA1 212 F3
St George's St TA24 201 D2
St Georges Way TA1 212 E2
St Gildas TA20 223 D4
St Gilda's Cl TA10 172 A5
St Gildas Ct TA10 172 A5
St Gildas RC Prim Sch BA21 219 B5
St Gilda's Way BA6 206 D4
St Gregory's CE Prim Sch DT10 190 F5
St Gregory's RC Sch BA2 62 D8
St Helens BA22 175 D8
St Hilary Cl BS9 5 D5
St Ives Cl BS48 9 A1
St Ives Rd BS23 49 A5
St James' Barton BS1 227 B4
St James Cl TA1 212 F4
St James Ct
Bridgwater TA6 209 D3
4 Taunton TA1 212 F4
St James Mews TA13 220 C4
St James's Cl BA21 218 D5
St James's Par BA1 228 B2
St James's Pk
Bath BA1 228 B4
Yeovil BA20 218 C5
St James' Sq BA6 157 D4
St James's Sq BA1 228 A4
St James's St
Bath BA1 228 B4
South Petherton TA13 220 C4
St James St
Taunton TA1 212 F4
Weston-Super-Mare BS23 48 D7
St James Terr BA22 197 A7
St John's BA1 44 B8
St John & St Francis CE Prim Sch TA6 209 D4
St John's Ave BS21 6 D3
St John's Bridge 4 BS1 227 A3
St John's CE Fst Sch BA11 119 F4
St John's CE Inf Sch BA6 206 E5
St John's CE Jun Sch TA9 104 D4
St John's CE Prim Sch BS31 24 E5
St John's CE Prim Sch
Midsomer Norton BA3 78 A1
Wellington TA21 222 E6
St Johns Cl TA21 222 E6
St John's Cl
Peasedown St John BA2 79 B7
Skilgate TA4 164 E6
Weston-Super-Mare BS23 30 D1
St John's Cres
Midsomer Norton BA3 78 A2

St John's Cres *continued*
Trowbridge BA14 ... 83 F6
St Johns Ct
Axbridge BS26 ... 70 B2
Bath BA2 ... 228 C3
Keynsham BS31 ... 24 E6
Wells BA5 ... 203 D3
St Johns Ho 3 BA20 ... 219 B5
St John's Pl BA1 ... 228 B2
St John's RC Prim Sch BA2 ... 45 B6
St John's RC Prim Sch (Annexe) BA2 ... 44 D4
St Johns Rd BA2 ... 60 B1
St John's Rd
Backwell BS48 ... 19 B5
Bath BA2 ... 228 C3
Bath, Lower Weston BA1 ... 44 C7
Burnham-on-S TA8 ... 104 B7
Clevedon BS21 ... 6 D3
Frome BA11 ... 120 B5
Taunton TA1 ... 212 E3
Yeovil BA21 ... 219 D7
St Johns Ret Pk TA1 ... 213 B5
St John's Sq BA6 ... 206 D5
St John St
Bridgwater TA6 ... 209 B4
Wells BA5 ... 203 D4
St John's Terr BA11 ... 119 E3
St Johns Wlk BA6 ... 206 D5
St John the Evangelist CE Prim Sch BS21 ... 6 C1
St Joseph & St Teresa RC Prim Sch BA5 ... 203 D4
St Josephs Field TA1 ... 213 A3
St Joseph's RC Prim Sch
Bridgwater TA6 ... 208 D4
Burnham-on-S TA8 ... 104 B6
St Joseph's RC Prim Sch BS20 ... 2 D3
St Joseph's Rd BS23 ... 30 E1
St Judes Ho 21 BS2 ... 227 C3
St Jude's Terr BS22 ... 31 C1
St Julian's CE Prim Sch BA2 ... 62 E1
St Julian's Cl BS39 ... 77 E4
St Julian's Rd BA2 ... 79 F5
St Juthware Cl BA22 ... 197 C3
St Katherine's CE Prim Sch BS40 ... 37 A7
St Katherine's Sch BS20 ... 4 E3
St Kenya Ct BS31 ... 24 F5
St Keyna Rd BS31 ... 24 E5
St Kilda's Rd BA2 ... 44 D5
St Ladoc Rd BS31 ... 24 D6
St Laud Cl BS9 ... 5 D5
St Lawrence's CE Prim Sch BA5 ... 110 E6
St Leonards Ct BA20 ... 219 A4
St Loe Cl BS14 ... 22 F3
St Louis RC Prim Sch BA11 ... 119 E5
St Luke's Cl TA8 ... 104 B7
St Lukes Mews TA4 ... 167 E6
St Lukes Rd BA11 ... 101 E5
St Luke's Rd
Bath BA2 ... 44 F3
Midsomer Norton BA3 ... 77 F2
St Margarets Cl BS48 ... 19 A5
St Margaret's Cl BS31 ... 24 D6
St Margarets Ct TA1 ... 213 B4
St Margarets La TA20 ... 198 C8
St Margaret's La BS48 ... 19 A5
St Margaret's Rd BA22 ... 186 B6
St Margaret's Sch BA22 ... 186 C6
St Margaret's Terr BS23 ... 48 D8
St Mark's CE Sch BA1 ... 28 B2
St Marks Cl
Chedzoy TA7 ... 154 E8
Keynsham BS31 ... 24 E6
St Marks Ct TA6 ... 209 D3
St Mark's Ecumenical CE/ Methodist Prim Sch BS22 ... 31 F4
St Marks Gdns BA2 ... 228 C1
St Mark's Rd
Bath BA2 ... 228 C1
Burnham-on-S TA8 ... 104 B8
Midsomer Norton BA3 ... 78 A2
Weston-Super-Mare BS22 ... 32 A3
St Martins BS21 ... 6 C5
St Martin's CE Jun Sch BS22 ... 31 D2
St Martin's Cl
Fivehead TA3 ... 170 F1
Zeals BA12 ... 161 F3
St Martins Ct BS22 ... 31 E3
St Martin's Ct BA2 ... 44 E1
St Martin's Garden Prim Sch BA2 ... 44 D1
St Martins Hospl BA2 ... 44 E1
St Martin's La SN14 ... 13 F8
St Martin's Pk SN14 ... 13 F8
St Martin's Sch TA18 ... 224 B6
St Martins Way BA20 ... 218 D2
St Mary CE Prim Sch BA2 ... 45 C8
St Mary Redcliffe & Temple CE Sch BS1 ... 227 B1
St Mary & St Peter's CE Fst Sch
Barrington TA19 ... 184 D5
Ilton TA19 ... 183 E4
St Mary's Bldgs BA2 ... 228 B1
St Mary's CE Prim Sch
Bradford Abbas DT9 ... 187 E1
Bridgwater TA6 ... 208 C4
St Mary's CE Prim Sch BA3 ... 79 C1
St Mary's CE Prim Sch
Thorncombe TA20 ... 199 B6
Timsbury BA2 ... 60 C3
St Marys Cl
Hutton BS24 ... 49 D2
Seavington St Mary TA19 ... 184 D1
Wedmore BS28 ... 108 C4
St Mary's Cl
10 Axminster EX13 ... 198 A1
Bath BA2 ... 45 B6
Chard TA20 ... 223 C2
Cossington TA7 ... 136 F3
Timsbury BA2 ... 60 B2
St Mary's Cres
Chard TA20 ... 223 C3
13 North Petherton TA6 ... 153 F4
Yeovil BA21 ... 219 C8
St Marys Ct TA6 ... 153 E4
St Mary's Ct 1 TA6 ... 208 F4
St Mary's Ct BS24 ... 49 A1
St Mary's Gdns BS40 ... 53 B5
St Mary's Gr BS48 ... 18 C8
St Mary's Hospl BS8 ... 226 B3
St Mary's La BA4 ... 140 E3
St Mary's Park Rd BS20 ... 2 C4
St Mary's Pk
Langport TA10 ... 172 A5
Nailsea BS48 ... 18 C8
St Marys Pl BA4 ... 142 F4
St Mary's Prim Sch BS20 ... 3 E3
St Mary's RC Prim Sch
Axminster EX13 ... 198 A1
Bath BA1 ... 27 B1
St Mary's Rd
Bristol BS11 ... 4 D7
Burnham-on-S TA8 ... 104 B7
Frome BA11 ... 120 B5
Hutton BS24 ... 49 D2
Leigh Woods BS8 ... 11 D6
Meare BA6 ... 138 D4
Oxenpill BA6 ... 138 C4
Portishead BS20 ... 2 D4
Sherborne DT9 ... 225 B3
Westonzoyland TA7 ... 154 F5
St Marys Rise BA3 ... 79 C2
St Mary's St BS26 ... 70 C2
St Mary St
Bridgwater TA6 ... 208 F4
Nether Stowey TA5 ... 134 B2
St Mary's View BA22 ... 196 F7
St Mary's Wlk BS11 ... 4 D6
St Mathew's Pl BA2 ... 45 B5
St Mathias Ho BS2 ... 227 C3
St Matthew's Cl BS23 ... 30 D1
St Matthew's Field TA6 ... 208 E4
St Matthews Gn TA6 ... 208 E4
St Matthew's Rd BS6 ... 227 A4
St Matthias Pk BS2 ... 227 C3
St Medard Rd BS28 ... 108 C4
St Michael Cl TA3 ... 169 D4
St Michael on the Mount CE Prim Sch BS2 ... 226 C3
St Michael Rd TA3 ... 169 D4
St Michael's Ave
Clevedon BS21 ... 6 D1
Weston-Super-Mare BS22 ... 32 A3
Yeovil BA21 ... 219 C7
St Michael's CE First Sch TA24 ... 200 F7
St Michael's CE Jun Sch BA2 ... 44 A6
St Michaels Cl
Nether Compton DT9 ... 187 F3
Stoke St Michael BA3 ... 116 B3
St Michael's Cl
Buckland Dinham BA11 ... 100 A3
Glastonbury BA6 ... 206 E3
Nether Stowey TA5 ... 134 A2
St Michael's Cres TA2 ... 213 A8
St Michaels Ct
Bawdrip TA7 ... 136 E2
Walton BA16 ... 156 D7
Yeovil BA21 ... 219 C8
St Michael's Ct BA2 ... 63 E8
St Michael's Gdns TA13 ... 220 D5
St Michael's Hill
Bristol BS2 ... 226 C4
Milverton TA4 ... 167 A4
St Michael's Hospl BS2 ... 226 C4
St Michael's Pk BS2 ... 226 C4
St Michael's Pl BA1 ... 228 B2
St Michaels Rd BA2 ... 44 A5
St Michael's Rd
Bath BA1 ... 44 D7
Burnham-on-S TA8 ... 104 B7
Minehead TA24 ... 200 F8
Yeovil BA21 ... 219 D6
St Michael's View TA15 ... 186 B4
St Nicholas Almshouses 5 BS1 ... 227 A2
St Nicholas CE Prim Sch
Combe St Nicholas TA20 ... 193 D6
Henstridge BA8 ... 190 A7
St Nicholas' CE Prim Sch BA3 ... 79 A2
St Nicholas Chantry CE Prim Sch BS21 ... 6 E3
St Nicholas Cl
4 Henstridge BA8 ... 190 A6
Winsley BA15 ... 64 D7
Yeovil BA20 ... 219 B4
St Nicholas Ct BA2 ... 28 F1
St Nicholas Pk BA20 ... 219 B4
St Nicholas Rd
Bristol BS2 ... 227 C4
Weston-Super-Mare BS23 ... 48 D2
Whitchurch BS14 ... 23 C4
St Nicholas St BS1 ... 227 A2
St Nicholas Way BS48 ... 18 D2
St Oswald's Ct BS13 ... 22 A8
St Patricks Ct 3 TA2 ... 213 A8
St Patricks Ct BS31 ... 24 E5
St Patrick's Ct BA2 ... 45 B6
St Patrick's Rd
Taunton TA2 ... 213 A8
Yeovil BA21 ... 218 D7
ST PAULS ... 227 C4
St Paul's CE Jun Sch BA4 ... 205 B5
St Pauls Cl TA13 ... 220 D4
St Paul's Cl DT9 ... 225 E6
St Pauls Ct TA6 ... 209 D3
St Paul's Flats DT9 ... 225 E6
St Paul's Gn DT9 ... 225 E6
St Pauls Pl
Bath BA1 ... 228 B2
Midsomer Norton BA3 ... 78 A2
St Paul's Rd
Bristol BS8 ... 226 B4
Burnham-on-S TA8 ... 104 B7
Weston-Super-Mare BS23 ... 48 E5
St Paul St BS2 ... 227 B4
St Paul's Terr BA5 ... 111 A4
St Peter's Ave BS23 ... 30 D1
St Peters CE Fst Sch TA4 ... 202 D4
St Peters CE Prim Sch BS20 ... 2 D4
St Peters Cl
Ilton TA19 ... 183 F4
Staple Fitzpaine TA3 ... 182 C5
Williton TA4 ... 202 D2
St Peter's Cl
Horton TA19 ... 183 C1
Taunton TA2 ... 213 B7
St Peters Ct TA6 ... 209 D3
St Peter's Ho BS8 ... 226 B2
St Peters Lodge BS20 ... 2 D4
St Peters Rd
Portishead BS20 ... 2 D4
Shepton Mallet BA4 ... 205 A6
St Peter's Rd
Burnham-on-S TA8 ... 104 B7
Radstock BA3 ... 97 C8
St Peter's Rise
Bristol BS13 ... 22 B7
South Petherton TA13 ... 220 D4
St Peters Terr 21 BA4 ... 205 B6
St Peter's Terr BA2 ... 44 D6
St Philip's CE Prim Sch BA2 ... 44 D2
St Philips Rd BS2 ... 227 C3
St Pias X RC Prim Sch BS13 ... 22 A5
St Quintin Pk TA2 ... 213 E6
St Rayn Hill TA17 ... 195 B4
St Saviour's Ave TA6 ... 209 A4
St Saviour's CE Inf Sch BA1 ... 28 B2
St Saviour's CE Jun Sch BA1 ... 28 B2
St Saviour's Rd BA1 ... 28 C2
St Saviour's Terr 10 BA1 ... 28 B1
St Saviours Way 4 BA1 ... 28 C1
St Stephen's Ave 3 BS1 ... 227 A2
St Stephen's CE Prim Sch BA1 ... 27 F1
St Stephen's Cl BA1 ... 27 F1
St Stephen's Ct BA1 ... 228 B4
St Stephen's Pl BA1 ... 228 B4
St Stephen's Rd BA1 ... 228 B4
St Stephen's St BS1 ... 227 A2
St Swithins Cl DT9 ... 225 E4
St Swithin's Pl BA1 ... 228 C4
St Swithin's Rd DT9 ... 225 E4
St Swithin's Yd BA2 ... 228 C3
St Thomas Cross BA21 ... 219 C5
St Thomas Ct TA6 ... 209 D3
St Thomas' Ct BA5 ... 203 F5
St Thomas Mews BA5 ... 203 F5
St Thomas Pl BS1 ... 227 B2
St Thomas Rd BA3 ... 78 B2
St Thomas St E BS1 ... 227 B2
St Thomas St
Bristol BS1 ... 227 B2
Dunster TA24 ... 201 E2
Wells BA5 ... 203 E5
St Thomas Terr BA5 ... 203 F5
St Vigor & St John CE Prim Sch BA3 ... 96 E3
St Vincent's Rd BS8 ... 226 A2
St Whytes Rd BS4 ... 22 D8
St Winifreds Dr BA2 ... 45 D2
Salcombe Gdns BS22 ... 32 A2
Salcombe Rd BS4 ... 23 A8
Salerno Cl BA22 ... 173 E2
Sales Ho 15 BA4 ... 205 B6
Salisbury Rd
Bath BA1 ... 28 B2
Burnham-on-S TA8 ... 104 C7
Paulton BS39 ... 77 F4
Weston-Super-Mare BS22 ... 31 C1
Salisbury St TA2 ... 212 E6
Salisbury Terr
Castle Cary BA7 ... 214 B5
4 Frome BA11 ... 119 E3
Gurney Slade BA3 ... 114 E8
Weston-Super-Mare BS23 ... 48 D7
Sally Hill BS20 ... 2 E7
Sally In The Wood BA1, BA15 ... 46 D6
Sally Lovell's La BA8 ... 189 F8
Sally Lunn's Kitchen Mus★ BA1 ... 228 C2
Sallysmead Cl BS13 ... 22 B4
Salmon Par TA6 ... 209 A4
SALTFORD ... 25 D2
Saltford CE Prim Sch BS31 ... 25 E2
Saltford Ct BS31 ... 25 E3
Salthouse Ct BS21 ... 6 B2
Salthouse La BA20 ... 219 A4
Salthouse Rd BS21 ... 6 B2
Saltings Cl BS21 ... 6 B2
Saltlands TA6 ... 208 F7
Saltlands Ave TA6 ... 208 F7
Saltlands Ho TA6 ... 208 F7
Saltry La TA24 ... 131 A6
Saltwell Ave BS14 ... 23 C5
Salway Cl BS40 ... 38 E1
Salway Gdns 11 EX13 ... 198 A1
Samarate Way BA20 ... 218 D4
Sambourne La BS20 ... 4 C4
SAMPFORD ARUNDEL ... 179 E5
Sampford Arundel Com Prim Sch TA21 ... 179 E5
SAMPFORD BRETT ... 202 E1
SAMPFORD MOOR ... 179 F5
SAMPFORD PEVERELL ... 178 E1
Sampford Peverell CE Prim Sch EX16 ... 178 C1
Sampford Rocks TA4 ... 202 F1
Sampsons Rd BS13 ... 22 D4
Samuel Ct BA8 ... 176 F1
Samuels Ct TA2 ... 212 E6
Samways Cl BA22 ... 218 B5
Sanctuary Gdns BS9 ... 5 D3
Sanctuary La TA22 ... 148 A2
SAND ... 108 C2
Sandalwood Ride TA6 ... 153 F5
Sandbrook La BA22 ... 175 D7
Sandburrows Rd BS13 ... 21 F6
Sandburrows Wlk BS13 ... 21 F6
Sandcroft BS14 ... 22 F6
Sandcroft Ave BS23 ... 48 D2
Sandene Cl TA2 ... 212 C8
Sanderling BS20 ... 2 F6
Sand Farm La BS22 ... 31 A6
SANDFORD ... 52 A3
SANDFORD BATCH ... 51 F2
Sandford Cl 2 BS21 ... 6 B1
Sandford Hill TA5, TA6 ... 208 A6
SANDFORD ORCAS ... 188 C7
Sandford Orcas Manor Ho★ DT9 ... 188 C8
Sandford Orcas Rd DT9 ... 225 B7
Sandford Pk BA14 ... 83 F7
Sandford Prim Sch BS25 ... 52 B4
Sandford Rd
Bristol BS8 ... 226 A1
Weston-Super-Mare BS23 ... 49 A7
Winscombe BS25 ... 51 F1
Sandhill La TA24 ... 131 C4
Sandhills Dr TA8 ... 84 F4
Sandhurst Rd BA20 ... 218 F1
Sanding's La
Chapel Leigh TA4 ... 167 A8
Fitzhead TA4 ... 166 F8
Lydeard St Lawrence TA4 ... 151 A1
Sandlewood Cl BA21 ... 219 E8
Sandmead Rd BS25 ... 52 A4
Sandown Cl
Bridgwater TA6 ... 209 A2
3 Yeovil BA20 ... 219 A5
Sandpiper Cl
Bridgwater TA6 ... 209 A4
Minehead TA24 ... 201 C5
Sandpiper Dr BS22 ... 31 F1
Sandpiper Rd TA6 ... 209 A4
Sandpits Rd BA6 ... 206 F5
Sand Rd
Wedmore BS28 ... 108 C3
Weston-Super-Mare BS22 ... 31 B5
Sandringham Cl TA6 ... 209 C7
Sandringham Ct 2 BS23 ... 48 F5
Sandringham Rd
1 Weston-Super-Mare BS23 ... 48 F5
Yeovil BA21 ... 219 E6
Sandrocks La TA24 ... 131 B3
Sandscross La BA11 ... 100 A3
Sand St TA4 ... 166 F4
Sandy Cl TA9 ... 104 D4
Sandy Hole TA16 ... 195 F7
Sandy La
Beckington BA11 ... 101 E4
Cannington TA5 ... 135 A3
Easton-in-G BS8 ... 10 A8
Failand BS8 ... 10 C7
Stanton Drew BS39, BS40 ... 39 E3
Wiveliscombe TA4 ... 210 C7
Sandyleaze BS9 ... 5 E7
Sandy's Hill La BA11 ... 119 E1
Sandy's La EX14 ... 191 F2
Sandys Moor TA4 ... 210 D4
Sandy View BA11 ... 101 E4
Sandyway Cross EX36 ... 145 H4
Sansome's Hill DT9 ... 217 D2
Sansom's Cross DT6 ... 199 F1
Sarabeth Dr BA2 ... 61 A4
Saracen St BA1 ... 228 C3
Saunder's Piece La TA18 ... 224 A7
Saunters Cl BA9 ... 216 B4
Saunton Wlk BS4 ... 22 E8
Savannah Dr 3 TA6 ... 154 A5
Savernake Rd BS22 ... 31 F3
Savery or Cottage Row TA1 ... 213 B3
Saviano Way TA6 ... 208 E7
Saville Cres BS22 ... 49 C8
Saville Gate Cl BS9 ... 5 F4
Saville Mews BS6 ... 227 A4
Saville Pl BS8 ... 226 A2
Saville Rd
Bristol BS9 ... 5 F3
Weston-Super-Mare BS22 ... 49 C8
Saville Row BA1 ... 228 B3
Savoy The BS11 ... 4 E6
Saw Cl BA1 ... 228 B2
Sawmill Cotts BA11 ... 143 B8
Sawmill Gdns BA3 ... 96 D3
Sawpit La BA6 ... 140 C2
Sawpits Cl TA4 ... 150 D8
Sawyers Cl
Chilcompton BA3 ... 96 D3
Wraxall BS48 ... 9 A2
Sawyers Ct BS21 ... 6 E3
SAWYER'S HILL ... 180 E7
Sawyers Leigh TA2 ... 168 D8
Sawyers Mill EX16 ... 164 E2
Saxby Cl
Clevedon BS21 ... 6 B1
Weston-Super-Mare BS22 ... 32 B4
Saxon Cl
Oake TA4 ... 167 D4
Watchet TA23 ... 202 B7
Saxon Ct
Ilminster TA19 ... 221 B4
Weston-Super-Mare BS22 ... 32 D3
Saxondale Ave TA8 ... 85 A3
Saxon Gn TA6 ... 209 C4
Saxon Pl BS27 ... 90 B7
Saxon Rd
Bridgwater TA6 ... 209 C4
Weston-Super-Mare BS22 ... 49 C8
Saxon Ridge TA23 ... 202 B7
Saxon St BS40 ... 53 D6
Saxonvale BA11 ... 119 F4
Saxon Way
Cheddar BS27 ... 90 B6
Peasedown St John BA2 ... 79 E8
Wedmore BS28 ... 108 C4
Wincanton BA9 ... 216 B3
Winsley BA15 ... 64 F7
Saxony Pl 3 TA6 ... 209 A1
Says La BS40 ... 53 B4
Scadden's La BS27 ... 91 B1
Scafell Cl
Taunton TA1 ... 212 C1
Weston-Super-Mare BS23 ... 31 A1
Scamel Ho 11 BA4 ... 205 B6
Scaurs The BS22 ... 31 F2
School Cl
Bampton EX16 ... 164 B1
Banwell BS29 ... 51 B3
Bristol, Whitchurch BS14 ... 22 F4
Tintinhull BA22 ... 186 C6
Watchet TA23 ... 202 C7
School Cotts
13 East Coker BA22 ... 197 F8
Enmore TA5 ... 153 A5
Taunton TA2 ... 168 F6
School Dr DT9 ... 225 E5
School Fields
Cannington TA5 ... 135 C2
2 North Petherton TA6 ... 153 F3
School Hill
Ashcott TA7 ... 156 B8
Cucklington BA9 ... 177 D6
Misterton TA18 ... 224 F3
South Perrott DT8 ... 196 C1
Westbury-sub-Mendip BA5 ... 110 E6
Wookey Hole BA5 ... 203 A8
SCHOOL HOUSE ... 199 A5
School La
Barrow Gurney BS48 ... 20 D5
Batheaston BA1 ... 28 F4
Blackford BS28 ... 107 D4
Burrowbridge TA7 ... 154 F1
Chew Stoke BS40 ... 56 D8
Combwich TA5 ... 135 B5
Compton Dundon TA11 ... 157 A3
Doulting BA4 ... 141 E6
Draycott BS27 ... 90 F3
Drimpton DT8 ... 199 E6
Farrington Gurney BS39 ... 77 A4
Horrington BA5 ... 113 A1
Kilmersdon BA3 ... 98 A6
Lopen TA13 ... 185 A1
7 North Petherton TA6 ... 153 F4
Rowberrow BS25 ... 53 A1
Seavington St Michael TA19 ... 184 E2
Shapwick TA7 ... 137 F1
Sherborne DT9 ... 225 D3
Somerton TA11 ... 211 E3
Tatworth TA20 ... 198 C8
Templecombe BA8 ... 176 E1
Wick St Lawrence BS22 ... 32 B7
Woolavington TA7 ... 136 E4
School of Christ the King RC Prim BS4 ... 22 E8
School Rd
Kingsdon TA11 ... 173 D5
Monkton Heathfield TA2 ... 213 F8
Parbrook BA6 ... 158 C7
Westonzoyland TA7 ... 154 E5
Wrington BS40 ... 35 E2
School St
Curry Rivel TA10 ... 171 D4
Drayton TA10 ... 171 E3
School View BS48 ... 9 B1
Schooner Pl TA24 ... 201 B7
Scimitar Rd BA22 ... 218 B6
Scobell Rise BS39 ... 59 C2
Score La BS40 ... 54 E2
Score The BS40 ... 54 E2
Scornfield La BS40 ... 56 D7

Scotch Horn Cl BS48 . . . . 8 F2
Scotch Horn Way 5 BS48 . . 8 F2
Scot Cl TA6 . . . . 135 F5
Scot Elm Dr BS24 . . . . 32 D1
Scot La BS40 . . . . 38 D1
Scotland La
Axbridge BS26 . . . . 107 D8
Chapel Allerton BS26 . . . . . 107 D8
Rudge BA11 . . . . 102 C4
Scots Pine Ave 3 BS48 . . . . 8 F2
Scott Cl TA2 . . . . 212 C6
Scott Rd
Frome BA11 . . . . 119 F5
Highbridge TA9 . . . . 104 D3
Weston-Super-Mare BS23 . . 49 A4
Scotts Cl BA3 . . . . 116 C8
Scott's Hill
Huish Champflower TA4 . . . 165 E8
Seavington St Mary TA19 . . 184 D1
Scotts La TA7 . . . . 137 D1
Scott's La
Baltonsborough BA6 . . . . . 158 A8
Wellington TA21 . . . . 222 E6
Scotts Way TA18 . . . . 196 B8
Scouse Cross EX13 . . . . . . 198 E2
Scouse La EX13 . . . . 198 E2
Scrapton La TA20 . . . . 193 D5
Scruibbitts La TA7 . . . . . . 137 B2
Scumbrum La BS39 . . . . . . 59 C2
SEABOROUGH 195 E1
Seaborough View TA18 . . 224 C4
Seabrook Rd BS22 . . . . 31 D1
Sea King Rd BA20 . . . . 218 D3
Sea La
Carhampton TA24 . . . . 131 A7
Dunster TA24 . . . . 201 F4
Kilve TA5 . . . . 133 C6
Watchet TA23 . . . . 132 D5
Sealey Cl BS27 . . . . 90 F3
Sealey Cres BA5 . . . . 112 E1
Sealeys Cl TA9 . . . . 136 A8
SEA MILLS 5 B6
Sea Mills Inf Sch BS9 . . . . . 5 C7
Sea Mills Jun Sch BS9 . . . . . 5 B5
Sea Mills La BS9 . . . . 5 C5
Sea Mills Sta BS9 . . . . 5 B4
SeaQuarium★ BS23 . . . . . . 48 D6
Searle Cres BS23 . . . . 49 A6
Searle Ct
Clevedon BS21 . . . . 6 E2
Somerton TA11 . . . . 211 D3
Seat La BA4 . . . . 142 D1
Seaton Ct BA20 . . . . 219 A4
Seaton Rd BA20 . . . . 218 F4
Seavale Mews BS21 . . . . 6 C4
Seavale Rd BS21 . . . . 6 C4
Seaview Rd
Portishead, Redcliffe Bay
BS20 . . . . 1 F4
Portishead, West Hill BS20 . . 1 F6
Sea View Rd TA8 . . . . 104 A8
SEAVINGTON ST MARY . . . 184 D1
SEAVINGTON ST
MICHAEL 184 F2
Seawalls BS9 . . . . 5 D2
Seawalls Rd BS9 . . . . 5 D2
Seaward Dr TA6 . . . . 208 F6
Seaward Way TA24 . . . . . . 201 C6
Second Ave
Axminster EX13 . . . . 198 A2
Bath BA2 . . . . 44 D5
Bristol BS14 . . . . 23 B7
Radstock BA3 . . . . 97 C7
Second Dro TA7 . . . . 155 D3
Secret World Wildlife
Rescue★ TA9 . . . . 136 C8
SECTOR 198 B1
Sector Hill EX13 . . . . 198 B1
Sector La EX13 . . . . 198 A1
Sedge Cl TA6 . . . . 208 F2
Sedge Dro TA7 . . . . 137 C3
Sedge Mead BA11 . . . . 119 F7
Sedgemoor Cl
Nailsea BS48 . . . . 18 E8
Yeovil BA21 . . . . 219 D7
Sedgemoor Coll TA3 . . . . 170 A2
Sedgemoor Dro
Sutton Mallet TA7 . . . . 155 A6
Wrantage TA3 . . . . 170 B2
Sedgemoor Hill Dr TA7 . . 155 B7
Sedgemoor Manor Com Jun
Sch TA6 . . . . 209 C6
Sedgemoor Manor Inf Sch
TA6 . . . . 209 D5
Sedgemoor Rd
Bath BA2 . . . . 44 F2
Bridgwater TA6 . . . . 209 C3
Weston-Super-Mare BS23 . . 30 F1
Woolavington TA7 . . . . 136 E3
Sedgemoor Way
Glastonbury BA6 . . . . 206 D5
Woolavington TA7 . . . . 136 E3
Sedgemount Ind Pk TA6 136 A2
Sedgewick Ho BS11 . . . . 4 E7
Seeley Cres BA16 . . . . 207 B3
Sefton Sq BS24 . . . . 50 A8
Selbourne Cl BA1 . . . . 44 A8
Selbourne Pl TA24 . . . . . . 200 F6
Selbourne Rd BS23 . . . . . . 48 E4
Selden Rd BS14 . . . . 23 E5
Sellbed Cross TA24 . . . . . 146 A8
Selley Wlk BS13 . . . . 22 A5
Selway Ct BA2 . . . . 45 B2
Selwood TA20 . . . . 223 C5
Selwood Cl BS22 . . . . 49 C7
Selwood Cres BA11 . . . . . 120 A7
Selwood Mid Sch BA11 . . 120 B6
Selwood Rd
Frome BA11 . . . . 119 E5
Glastonbury BA6 . . . . 206 F6
Selwood St BA11 . . . . 118 B7
SELWORTHY 124 D3
Selworthy Cl
Bridgwater TA6 . . . . 208 F1
Keynsham BS31 . . . . 24 D5
Selworthy Gdns 4 BS48 . . . 8 E1
Selworthy Ho BA2 . . . . 44 F2
Selworthy Rd
Taunton TA2 . . . . 213 B8
Weston-Super-Mare BS23 . . 49 A4
Selworthy Specl Sch
TA2 . . . . 213 A8
Selworthy Terr BA2 . . . . . . 44 F2
Semington Cl TA1 . . . . 213 D4
Septimus Bldgs BS14 . . . . 22 D5
Serbert Cl BS20 . . . . 2 E5
Serbert Rd BS20 . . . . 2 E5
Serbert Way BS20 . . . . 2 E5
Sercombe Pk BS21 . . . . 6 E1
Serel Dr BA5 . . . . 203 B3
Serlo Ct BS22 . . . . 32 A4
Serotines The TA10 . . . . . 171 D8
Sevenacres TA11 . . . . 211 C3
Seven Acres La BA1 . . . . . . 28 F5
Seven Acres The 3 BS24 . 49 F7
SEVEN ASH 151 D4
Seven Dials BA1 . . . . 228 B2
Seventh Ave BS14 . . . . 23 A7
Seven Thorns EX35 . . . . . 122 D5
Severalls Park Ave TA18 . 224 C5
Severn Ave BS23 . . . . 48 E5
Severn Cl TA6 . . . . 209 D7
Severn Dr TA1 . . . . 213 C4
Severn Gr TA8 . . . . 104 B5
Severnleigh Gdns BS9 . . . . . 5 F3
Severnmeade BS20 . . . . 1 F5
Severn Rd
Bristol BS11 . . . . 4 D6
Pill BS20 . . . . 4 C5
Portishead BS20 . . . . 2 C5
Weston-Super-Mare BS23 . . 48 E5
Severn Terr TA23 . . . . 202 C7
Severn Way BS31 . . . . 25 A5
Sevier Rd BS26 . . . . 68 C3
Seville Ct
Portishead BS20 . . . . 2 E7
Taunton TA1 . . . . 212 D2
Seville Rd BS20 . . . . 2 E7
Seward Terr BA3 . . . . 79 C2
Sewell Ho BS25 . . . . 70 A8
Sexey's Hospl BA10 . . . . . 215 E6
Sexey's Hospl (Almshouses)
BA10 . . . . 215 E6
Sexey's Rd BS28 . . . . 107 E4
Sexey's Sch BA10 . . . . 215 D5
Seymour Cl
Clevedon BS21 . . . . 6 E3
Wells BA5 . . . . 203 C5
Weston-Super-Mare BS22 . . 31 F4
Seymour Rd
5 Bath BA1 . . . . 28 A1
Bridgwater TA6 . . . . 209 D5
Street BA16 . . . . 207 D4
Seymour St TA21 . . . . 222 C6
Shackel Cross EX15 . . . . . 191 B8
Shadow Wlk BS24 . . . . 50 C3
Shadwell Ct BA9 . . . . 216 C4
Shadwell La BA9 . . . . 216 C4
Shaftesbury Ave 2 BA1 . . 44 C7
Shaftesbury Cl BS48 . . . . . 18 D8
Shaftesbury La BA9 . . . . . 177 B6
Shaftesbury Mews 7
BA2 . . . . 44 D5
Shaftesbury Rd
Bath BA2 . . . . 44 D5
Henstridge BA8 . . . . 190 C8
Weston-Super-Mare BS23 . . 49 B8
Shaftesbury Terr BA3 . . . . 79 A3
Shaftgate Ave BA4 . . . . . . 205 A6
Shaft Rd BA2 . . . . 45 E1
Shakespeare Ave
Bath BA2 . . . . 44 F4
Taunton TA1 . . . . 213 C3
Shakespeare Ct BS23 . . . . 48 F2
Shakespeare Rd BA3 . . . . . 78 C1
Shaking Dro TA9 . . . . 137 B6
SHALFORD 216 D8
Shalford La
Charlton Musgrove BA9 . . . 161 A2
Shalford BA9 . . . . 216 C8
Shallows The BS31 . . . . 25 F3
Shambles The TA3 . . . . . . 170 B4
Sham Castle La BA2 . . . . . . 45 C7
Shannon Wlk BS20 . . . . 2 F6
Shapcott La EX36 . . . . 162 C2
Shapcott Wood Hill
EX36 . . . . 162 A2
Shaplands BS9 . . . . 5 F4
Shapway TA19 . . . . 184 F3
Shapway Cross TA19 . . . . 184 F3
Shapway La BA4 . . . . 141 F2
Shapway Rd BA4 . . . . 141 E2
SHAPWICK 137 F1
Shapwick Heath National
Nature Reserve★ TA7 . . 137 F4
Shapwick Hill TA7 . . . . . . 155 F8
Shapwick Rd BA6 . . . . 138 A4
Shapwick Right Dro TA7 155 C6
Sharland Cl BS9 . . . . 5 E3
Sharland Gr BS13 . . . . 22 C4
Sharlands TA19 . . . . 184 C5
Sharpenton La TA7 . . . . . . 155 D6
Sharpham Dro BA16 . . . . 138 E1
Sharpham La
Glastonbury BA16 . . . . 138 D1
Stoke St Gregory TA3 . . . . . 170 E5
Sharpham Rd
Cheddar BS27 . . . . 89 F7
Glastonbury BA6 . . . . 206 F7
SHARPSTONE 64 A4
Shatterwell Cotts BA9 . . 216 C4
Shatt La TA5 . . . . 152 F3
Shatwell La
Castle Cary BA9 . . . . 214 F1
Yarlington BA9 . . . . 175 F8
Shaulders The TA2 . . . . . . 213 C7
Shave Cross DT6 . . . . 199 F1
Shave Hill SP8 . . . . 177 D4
Shave La
Crewkerne TA18 . . . . 224 A3
Donyatt TA19 . . . . 183 D1
Horton TA19 . . . . 183 C1
South Brewham BA10 . . . . 161 A6
SHAWFORD 101 D7
Shawford La BA11 . . . . . . 101 D7
Shaw Gdns BS14 . . . . 23 A8
Shaw Path TA8 . . . . 104 C6
Shaws Way BA2 . . . . 43 F5
Sheafhayne Cross EX14 . 192 E4
Shearing Cross TA20 . . . . 199 A5
Shearn La TA8 . . . . 104 B7
Shearwater Cl TA6 . . . . . . 209 D3
Shedrick Hill TA20 . . . . . . 199 B8
Sheepfair La SN14 . . . . 13 F8
Sheephouse Cvn Pk BS20 . . 3 E7
Sheeplands La DT9 . . . . . 225 B5
Sheeplands The DT9 . . . . 225 B5
Sheeps Croft BS13 . . . . 22 A5
Sheepstealing La TA4 . . . 150 E5
SHEEPWAY 3 B5
Sheepway BS20 . . . . 3 B5
Sheep Way TA19 . . . . 184 E3
Sheepway La BS20 . . . . 3 C5
Sheldon Cl BS21 . . . . 6 F2
Sheldon Ct TA1 . . . . 212 E4
Sheldon Dr BA5 . . . . 203 C3
Sheldon Mill 3 BA5 . . . . . 203 C3
Sheldon's La TA22 . . . . . . 163 A7
Shelduck Cl TA24 . . . . 201 C5
Shelley Ave BS21 . . . . 6 D2
Shelley Cl
Burnham-on-S TA8 . . . . 85 A2
Yeovil BA21 . . . . 218 D6
Shelley Dr TA8 . . . . 85 B2
Shelley Gr TA1 . . . . 213 B3
Shelley Rd
Bath BA2 . . . . 44 F4
Radstock BA3 . . . . 78 C1
Weston-Super-Mare BS23 . . 49 A4
Shell's La
Chard TA20 . . . . 193 A3
Shepton Beauchamp TA19 . 184 E4
Shellthorn Gr TA6 . . . . 208 F2
Shelthorn Hill TA5 . . . . . . 152 F3
Shelway La TA19 . . . . 184 C4
Shepherds Cl TA6 . . . . 208 D6
Shepherd's Cl TA11 . . . . . 157 A4
Shepherd's Cnr TA23 . . . . 131 E4
Shepherds Cross BA8 . . . 176 C5
Shepherd's Dro TA7 . . . . . 155 A3
Shepherd's Hay TA1 . . . . 212 C2
Shepherd's Hill SP8 . . . . . 177 E4
Shepherd's La
Chard TA20 . . . . 223 B4
Frome BA11 . . . . 144 B7
Hemyock EX15 . . . . 180 F1
Shepherds Way BS22 . . . . . 32 C2
Sheppard's Barton 11
BA11 . . . . 119 E5
Sheppard's Cnr TA5 . . . . 153 B5
Sheppards Gdns BA1 . . . . . 27 B1
Sheppards Wlk BA3 . . . . . . 96 D3
Sheppy's Cider Farm
Centre★ TA4 . . . . 167 F1
Sheppy's Mill BS49 . . . . . . 34 D5
Shepton BS24 . . . . 49 A2
SHEPTON BEAUCHAMP . . 184 E3
Shepton Beauchamp CE Fst
Sch TA19 . . . . 184 E4
SHEPTON MALLET 205 D6
Shepton Mallet Com Hospl
BA4 . . . . 204 F6
Shepton Mallet Inf Sch
BA4 . . . . 205 C6
SHEPTON MONTAGUE . . . 160 B2
Shepton Old Rd
Croscombe BA5 . . . . 204 A6
Dinder BA5 . . . . 140 D7
Shepton Rd BA4, BA5 . . . 204 D7
SHERBORNE
Litton 75 D3
Milborne Port 225 C6
Sherborne Abbey★ DT9 . 225 D3
Sherborne Abbey CE Prim
Sch DT9 . . . . 225 B2
Sherborne Castle★ DT9 . 225 F3
Sherborne Hill DT9 . . . . . 225 E1
Sherborne Mus★ DT9 . . 225 D4
Sherborne Old Castle★
DT9 . . . . 225 F4
Sherborne Prep Sch
DT9 . . . . 225 D3
Sherborne Prim Sch
DT9 . . . . 225 E5
Sherborne Rd
Milborne Port DT9 . . . . . . 217 C2
Yenston BA8 . . . . 189 E6
Yeovil BA21 . . . . 219 D5
Sherborne Sch DT9 . . . . . 225 D4
Sherborne Sch for Girls
DT9 . . . . 225 C4
SHERFORD 212 E1
Sherford Rd TA1 . . . . 212 E1
Sherford Terr TA1 . . . . . . 212 E1
Sheridan Cl TA6 . . . . 209 D3
Sheridan Gdns BA14 . . . . . 83 F6
Sheridan Rd
Bath BA2 . . . . 43 F5
Burnham-on-S TA8 . . . . 104 C6
Sherlands 4 TA16 . . . . . . 195 F7
Sherlands Gdns 3 TA16 . 195 F7
Sherring Rd BA4 . . . . 205 D4
Sherrin Way BS13 . . . . 21 E3
Sherston Cl BS48 . . . . 9 A1
Shervage Ct TA6 . . . . 209 C5
Sherwood Cl BS31 . . . . 24 E5
Sherwood Cres BS22 . . . . . 31 F3
Sherwood Rd BS31 . . . . 24 E5
Shetland Way BS48 . . . . 9 A1
Shickle Gr BA2 . . . . 44 D1
Shiller's La DT9 . . . . 188 C7
SHILLINGFORD 164 E2
Shiners Elms BS49 . . . . 34 B8
SHIPHAM 70 F7
Shipham CE Fst Sch BS25 70 E8
Shipham Cl
Bristol BS14 . . . . 23 B5
Nailsea BS48 . . . . 18 F8
Shipham La BS25 . . . . 52 B1
Shipham Rd BS27 . . . . 71 A3
Ship La
Bristol BS1 . . . . 227 B1
Combwich TA5 . . . . 135 B5
SHIPLATE 67 F6
Shiplate Rd BS24 . . . . 67 E6
Shipney La DT10 . . . . 190 C5
Shircombe La TA22 . . . . . 147 F2
Shire Gdns BS11 . . . . 4 D8
SHIREHAMPTON 4 E7
Shirehampton Prim Sch
BS11 . . . . 4 D6
Shirehampton Rd BS9 . . . . 5 C6
Shirehampton Sta BS11 . . . 4 D5
Shiremoor Hill TA16 . . . . 195 F7
Shire St TA6 . . . . 209 A1
Shires The TA24 . . . . 201 C5
Shires Yd BA1 . . . . 228 B3
SHOCKERWICK 29 F5
Shockerwick La BA1 . . . . . 29 D4
Shoe La TA7 . . . . 209 E7
Shoot Hill TA17 . . . . 195 C8
Shophouse Rd BA2 . . . . . . 44 B5
Shop La
Pilton BA4 . . . . 140 E3
Wingfield BA14 . . . . 83 C6
Shopland Ho 8 BS21 . . . . . 6 C2
SHOPNOLLER 151 E3
SHOREDITCH 169 A1
Shoreditch BS40 . . . . 56 C7
Shoreditch Rd
Stoke St Mary TA3 . . . . 169 A1
Taunton TA1 . . . . 213 B1
Shoredown La DT9, BA8 . . 217 E6
Short Dro
Mudgley BS28 . . . . 138 C7
Westbury-sub-Mendip BA5,
BS27 . . . . 110 B4
Short La
Draycott BS27 . . . . 90 E3
Litton BA3 . . . . 75 F2
Long Ashton BS41 . . . . 11 A2
Stone Allerton BS26 . . . . . . 88 C2
Shortland La BS28 . . . . . . 108 C3
Shortmarsh La BA22 . . . . 196 F4
SHORT STREET 121 F6
Short Way BS8 . . . . 10 B4
Shortwood Rd BS13 . . . . . . 22 E3
Shortwood Wlk BS13 . . . . . 22 E3
SHOSCOMBE 79 E6
Shoscombe CE Prim Sch
BA2 . . . . 79 F5
Shoscombe Gdns BA11 . . 120 C7
SHOSCOMBE VALE 79 E5
Shovel La TA6 . . . . 153 E3
Showell Pk TA2 . . . . 212 B7
Showering Cl BS14 . . . . . . 23 D5
Showering Rd BS14 . . . . . . 23 D5
Showground Rd TA6 . . . . 209 B1
Shrewsbury Bow BS24 . . . 50 A8
Shrewsbury Rd BA22 . . . . 218 B7
Shrubbery Ave BS23 . . . . . 30 D1
Shrubbery Cl TA8 . . . . 84 E8
Shrubbery Rd BS23 . . . . . . 30 D1
Shrubbery Terr 11 BS23 . . 30 C1
Shrubbery Wlk BS23 . . . . . 30 D1
Shrubbery Wlk W BS23 . . . 30 D1
Shudrick La TA19 . . . . 221 C3
Shums Ct 3 BA1 . . . . 228 C2
Shurtland La TA4 . . . . 150 C3
SHURTON 134 C7
Shurton La TA5 . . . . 134 C6
Shute La
Bruton BA10 . . . . 215 D6
Huish Champflower TA4 . . . 165 C8
Long Sutton TA10 . . . . 172 E4
Shute Lake La TA18 . . . . . 224 D5
Shuteleigh TA21 . . . . 222 E5
Shutemead TA1 . . . . 212 A4
Shute Row TA21 . . . . 222 E5
Shuter Rd BS13 . . . . 21 E5
Shute's La SP8 . . . . 177 E4
Shutewater Cl TA1 . . . . . . 212 A4
Shutewater Hill TA1 . . . . 212 A4
Shutgate Mdw TA4 . . . . . . 202 D3
Shuttern 2 TA1 . . . . 212 E3
Shuttern Bridge 3 TA1 . . 212 E3
Shutwell La BA4 . . . . 140 E3
Shyners Terr 8 TA16 . . . . 195 F7
SIDBROOK 169 B6
SIDCOT 70 C7
Sidcot Dr BS25 . . . . 70 A7
Sidcot La BS25 . . . . 70 A7
Sidcot Sch BS25 . . . . 70 B7
Sideland Cl BS14 . . . . 23 E6
Sidelings The BS40 . . . . . . 73 D8
Side Wood La EX36 . . . . . 162 A1
Sidings The DT10 . . . . 190 C4
Sidmouth Cl TA8 . . . . 104 C8
Sidney Hill Cottage Homes
BS25 . . . . 52 E4
SIGWELLS 175 E2
Silbury Rd BS3 . . . . 11 E2
Silbury Rise BS31 . . . . 25 A2
Silcox Rd BS13 . . . . 22 C4
Silk Cl BA4 . . . . 205 B7
Silk House Barton DT10 . 190 B4
Silklands Gr BS9 . . . . 5 C6
Silk Mills La TA2 . . . . 212 B6
Silk Mills Rd TA1 . . . . 212 B4
Silton Rd 1 SP8 . . . . 161 F1
Silverberry Rd BS22 . . . . . 32 A1
Silvercombe 1 BS23 . . . . . 48 E5
Silver Ct BS48 . . . . 8 C2
Silverdale Cl
Brushford TA22 . . . . 163 E4
Wembdon TA6 . . . . 208 C5
Silverdown Hill TA4 . . . . 150 C7
Silver La BA11 . . . . 144 B7
Silverlake Cotts DT9 . . . . 188 B2
Silverlow Rd BS48 . . . . 8 D2
Silvermead TA24 . . . . 201 B5
Silver Mead BS49 . . . . 34 D2
Silvermead Ct TA24 . . . . . 201 B5
Silver Moor La BS29 . . . . . 50 F7
Silver Rd BA16 . . . . 207 C5
Silver Springs TA19 . . . . . 184 E3
Silver St
11 Bampton EX16 . . . . 164 B1
Barrington TA19 . . . . 184 D5
Barton St David TA11 . . . . . 158 A3
Barwick BA22 . . . . 197 F8
Bridgwater TA6 . . . . 208 F4
Bristol BS1 . . . . 227 A3
Bruton BA10 . . . . 215 E6
Chard TA20 . . . . 223 C3
Cheddar BS27 . . . . 90 B8
Chew Magna BS40 . . . . 39 B3
Congresbury BS49 . . . . 34 D2
Crewkerne TA18 . . . . 196 B3
Curry Mallet TA3 . . . . 183 C8
Ditcheat BA4 . . . . 159 C7
East Lambrook TA13 . . . . . 220 C8
Fivehead TA3 . . . . 170 F1
Glastonbury BA6 . . . . 206 E4
Holcombe BA3 . . . . 97 C1
Huntspill TA9 . . . . 136 A8
Ilminster TA19 . . . . 221 B4
Kilmersdon BA3 . . . . 98 B5
Kingsbury Episcopi TA12 . . 185 B8
Kingsdon TA11 . . . . 173 D5
Langport TA10 . . . . 172 A3
Midsomer Norton BA3 . . . . . 97 A7
Milverton TA4 . . . . 167 A4
Nailsea BS48 . . . . 8 D2
Portishead BS20 . . . . 1 F1
Shepton Beauchamp TA19 . 184 E3
South Petherton TA13 . . . . 220 D5
Taunton TA1 . . . . 213 A3
Wells BA5 . . . . 203 E3
West Buckland TA21 . . . . . 180 F7
Wincanton BA9 . . . . 216 C4
Wiveliscombe TA4 . . . . 210 C4
Wrington BS40 . . . . 35 E2
Yeovil BA20 . . . . 219 B5
Silverstone Way BS49 . . . . 34 D3
SILVER STREET 180 F8
Simbriss Rd BA3 . . . . 114 F5
Simmental St TA6 . . . . . . 209 A1
Simmons Cl BA16 . . . . 207 D5
SIMONSBATH 127 B2
SIMONSBURROW 180 C3
Simons Cl BS22 . . . . 32 A2
Simon's Cl BS39 . . . . 77 F5
Simons Mews
Chard TA20 . . . . 223 E4
3 Weston-Super-Mare
BS23 . . . . 48 F7
Simons Rd DT9 . . . . 225 D5
Sinclair Ho BS8 . . . . 226 A2
Singapore Rd BS23 . . . . . . 48 E3
Singer Ct BA11 . . . . 119 F5
Singer's Knoll BA11 . . . . . 119 F4
SINGLE HILL 80 A5
Single Hill BA2 . . . . 79 F5
Singleton Ct BA5 . . . . 203 C5
SION HILL 27 E1
Sion Hill
Bath BA1 . . . . 27 E1
Bristol BS8 . . . . 11 F7
Sion Hill Pl BA1 . . . . 27 E1
Sion La BS8 . . . . 11 F7
Sion Pl
Bath BA2 . . . . 45 B6
Bristol BS8 . . . . 11 F7
Sion Rd BA1 . . . . 27 E1
Sir Bevil Grenville's Mon★
BA1 . . . . 12 A1
Sir Gilbert Scott Ct TA4 . 202 E3
Sirius Wood BA2 . . . . 44 B2
Siskin Wlk BS22 . . . . 49 F8
Sisters The BA4 . . . . 205 A6
Six Acres Cl TA1 . . . . 213 C5
Sixpence BS39 . . . . 59 D2
Six Streams BA1 . . . . 27 B2
Sixteen Acre La TA20 . . . 193 D8
Sixth Ave BS14 . . . . 23 A7
Sixty Acres Cl BS8 . . . . 10 B4

Six Ways BS21 6 C4
SKILGATE 164 E6
Skillgate La TA14 185 E1
Skimmerton La TA5, TA6 208 A5
Skinner's Hill BA2 78 F7
Skinners La BS25 52 F4
Skinner's La TA14 185 F2
Skitmoor Dro BS28 109 C2
Skylark Ave BS21 1 B1
Slab Dro TA7 155 A1
Sladacre La BS40 54 E2
Sladebrook Ave BA2 44 C3
Sladebrook Ct BA2 44 C3
Sladebrook Rd BA2 44 B4
Slade Cl TA4 150 E8
Slade La
Barrow Gurney BS48 20 C4
Golsoncott TA23 131 E1
Hawkridge TA22 146 D1
Lympsham BS24 67 B1
Rimpton BA22 188 A7
Rooks Bridge BS26 87 E4
West Anstey EX36 162 B6
Slade Rd BS20 2 D5
Slade's Cross TA20 193 D7
Slades Ct [2] BS48 19 A6
Slades Hill BA8 176 E1
Slades Orch TA19 183 C1
Slade Way TA4 202 E4
Slait Hill BA4 142 C7
Slait La BA9 216 C7
SLAPE CROSS 209 F6
Slapes Cl TA2 168 F6
Slate La BS14, BS31 41 B7
Sleep La BS14 23 D3
Sleight Cl BA21 218 C6
Sleight La BA5 140 E8
Slippery Batch TA11 211 A6
Sloe Cl BS22 49 D8
Slopers La BA9 176 D5
SLOUGH GREEN 182 D7
Slough Green Cvn Pk
TA3 182 D8
Slough Hill TA3 182 D6
Slough La
Cold Ashton SN14 12 F5
Crowcombe TA4 151 A8
North Wootton BA4 140 B3
Stoke St Gregory TA3 170 F6
Upottery EX14 191 F5
Sloway La TA6, TA9 136 A8
Slow Court La BA22 174 D3
Slowland La BA5 110 D8
Slugg Hill BA16 207 C3
Smallacombe Hill EX16,
EX36 162 D4
Smallbrook La BS39 41 B6
Smallcombe Cl BA3 78 E5
Smallcombe Rd BA3 78 E4
Small Down End BS25 51 F2
Small Down La BA4 142 B2
Small La EX16 179 B2
Small Mead Dro BA6 157 F4
Smallmoor Chase BA16 156 E7
Smallmoor Dro TA7 155 C3
Small Moor La BA16 156 E7
Smallridge Rd EX13 198 A4
Smalls Mead [2] TA11 173 F7
Small St BS1 227 A3
SMALL WAY 214 B2
Smallway BS49 34 D5
Small Way La BA22 214 C1
Smallways La TA7 137 B3
Smallwood View BA3 96 E7
SMEATHARPE 191 E5
Smeathy La EX15 180 F3
Smeaton Rd BS1 11 F5
Sminhays Cnr TA23 149 B5
SMITHAM HILL 74 D2
Smithfield Rd BA16 207 B4
Smithick's La BA11 143 E6
Smithmead BS13 22 B5
Smiths Cl BS27 91 A1
Smith's Forge Ind Est
BS49 16 F3
Smith's Hill TA18 196 C8
Smith's La BA4 159 C6
Smith's Row TA15 186 B4
Smith's Terr BA21 219 C6
Smith Way TA9 104 D3
Smithy TA1 212 B3
Smithyard La TA4, TA23 202 A3
Smithy La BA11 119 E4
Smokeham La TA4 151 D5
Smoky Hole La TA18 185 F1
Smurl La TA9 104 C1
Smythe Croft BS14 23 A3
Smythes Cross EX15 191 C7
Snagg La BA4 159 D5
Snag La BA9 216 E3
Snake La BS28 109 C1
Snakelake Hill BA10 160 C7
Snap Hill TA11 173 D8
Snathe Lea [4] TA4 167 F8
Snedden Gr TA1 213 B5
SNEYD PK 5 D3
Snipefield La BS28 108 A6
Snowberry Cl BS22 32 A1
Snowberry Ct TA1 213 C2
Snowdon Cottage La
TA20 223 B4
Snowdon Hts TA20 223 B4
Snowdon Vale BS23 31 A1
Snowdrop Cl BS22 32 A5
Snow Hill BA1 28 A1
Snow Hill Ho BA1 228 C4
Society Rd BA4 205 A6
SOCKETY 196 D1
Sock Hill BA21 187 C6
Sock La BA21 187 C6
Sock's La BA10 160 F8
SOHO 117 A5
Soho BA2 81 E5
Solomon's Hollow TA3 169 F2
Solon Ct BS13 21 F5
Solsbury Ct BA1 28 F3
Solsbury La BA1 28 F4
Solsbury View [17] BA1 28 A1
Solsbury Way BA1 28 A2
Somer Ave BA3 77 F2
Somer Ct BA3 78 B1
SOMERDALE 24 E7
Somerdale Ave
Bath BA2 44 D2
Bristol BS4 22 F8
Weston-Super-Mare BS22 49 C8
Somerdale Cl BS22 49 C8
Somerdale Rd BS31 24 F7
Somerdale Rd N BS30,
BS31 24 F8
Somerdale View BA2 44 C2
Somer Ho BA3 78 A1
Somerhouse Orch BA6 206 E5
Somer Lea BA3 96 D5
Somerleaze Cl BA5 203 B3
Somer Rd BA3 77 F2
Somerset Ave
Taunton TA1 212 B2
Weston-Super-Mare BS22,
BS24 50 A8
Somerset Brick & Tile Mus★
TA6 209 A6
Somerset Bridge Prim Sch
TA6 209 A1
Somerset Cl
Martock TA12 185 E7
Shepton Mallet BA4 205 C5
Somerset Coll of Arts & Tech
TA1 212 D4
Somerset Coll of Arts & Tech
(Annexe) TA1 212 E5
Somerset Coll of Arts & Tech
(Bishops Hull Annexe)
TA1 212 C3
Somerset Ct BA21 219 A6
Somerset Cty Cricket Gd★
TA1 212 F4
Somerset Distillery The★
TA12 184 F7
Somerset & Dorset Joint
Rly★ BA3 97 A8
Somerset & Dorset Rlwy
Trust Mus★ TA23 131 E4
Somerset Fire HQ TA2 169 A7
Somerset Folly BA2 60 B2
Somerset Gdns TA6 209 C3
Somerset Ho
Bath BA2 44 D3
[12] Bristol BS2 227 C3
Somerset La BA1 27 E1
Somerset Levels National
Nature Reserve★ TA7 155 C6
Somerset Mews BS23 48 F6
Somerset Nuffield Hospl
TA2 212 B7
Somerset Pl
Bath BA1 27 E1
Taunton TA1 213 B4
Yeovil BA20 219 A3
Somerset Rd
Bridgwater TA6 209 C3
Clevedon BS21 6 E3
Frome BA11 119 E4
Portishead BS20 1 F5
Somerset Rural Life Mus★
BA6 206 E4
Somerset Shire Horses★
TA7 156 C6
Somerset Sq
Bristol BS1 227 B1
[3] Nailsea BS48 8 E2
Somerset St
Bath BA1 228 C1
Bristol BS1 227 B1
Bristol, Kingsdown BS2 227 A4
Somerset Way
Highbridge TA9 104 E3
Paulton BS39 77 E6
Somer's Hill BA11 117 D3
SOMERTON 211 D3
Somerton BS24 49 A2
Somerton Bsns Pk TA11 211 B5
Somerton Cl TA6 209 D4
Somerton Door Dro
Compton Dundon TA11 156 E1
Somerton TA11 211 A7
Somerton Dro TA11 156 E1
Somertonfield Rd TA11 172 E7
Somerton Gdns BA11 120 C7
Somerton Hill
Langport TA10 172 E7
Somerton TA11 211 A3
Somerton Inf Sch TA11 211 C4
SOMERTON RANDLE 173 C7
Somerton Rd
Clevedon BS21 6 E1
Langport TA10 172 A6
Street BA16 207 D4
Somervale Rd BA3 78 E2
Somervale Sch BA3 78 A1
Somerville Cl
Saltford BS31 25 E2
Shepton Mallet BA4 205 D4
Somerville Cotts BA5 204 B8
Somerville Rd
Sandford BS25 52 A4
Somerville Rd *continued*
Wells BA5 203 C5
Somerville Way TA6 209 D3
Soper Gdns BS4 22 D7
Sopers Field TA20 223 D2
Sophia Gdns BS22 32 B4
Sorrel Gdns BS20 2 F5
Southampton Row [5]
TA2 213 A8
South Ave
Bath BA2 44 D5
Highbridge TA9 104 C4
Portishead BS20 2 D6
Sherborne DT9 225 B2
SOUTHAY 185 B6
Southay Cross TA20 193 A4
Southay La TA20 192 F4
South Bank
Castle Cary BA7 214 B3
Wookey Hole BA5 203 A8
SOUTH BARROW 175 A6
Southbourne Gdns BA1 28 B1
Southbourne Ho TA6 208 E4
Southbourne Mans BA2 228 C2
South Brent Cl TA9 85 F3
SOUTH BREWHAM 161 A6
South Bristol Bsns Pk
BS4 22 E7
South Bristol Trad Pk BS3 11 F3
Southbrook TA5 135 C2
Southbrook Cl TA5 135 C2
Southbrook Cotts BA9 216 F4
SOUTH CADBURY 175 C4
South Cary La BA7 214 A5
SOUTH CHARD 198 C8
SOUTH CHERITON 176 D3
South Cl
Draycott BS27 90 E2
Lympsham BS24 86 B8
Walton BA16 156 E7
South Combe BS24 67 B6
Southcombe House (Queens
Coll) TA3 168 D1
Southcombe Way BA22 186 B6
SOUTH COMMON 198 A4
South Common La EX13 198 A5
Southcot Pl BA2 228 C1
South Croft BS25 51 F2
Southcroft Dr BA13 121 D4
South Ct DT9 225 B3
South Dene BS9 5 E6
SOUTHDOWN 44 B4
SOUTH DOWN 191 F6
Southdown
Charlton Horethorne
DT9 176 A1
Weston-Super-Mare BS22 31 F4
Southdown Ave BA2 44 B3
Southdown Com Inf Sch
BA2 44 B3
Southdown Cross EX16 179 B2
Southdown Jun Sch BA2 44 B3
Southdown Rd
Bath BA2 44 B4
Bristol BS9 5 F8
South Dro
Curry Rivel TA10 171 B4
North Curry TA3 170 D2
Southend Gdns TA9 104 E5
Southend Rd BS23 48 E4
Southernhay BS8 226 B2
Southernhay Ave BS8 226 B2
Southernhay Cres BS8 226 B2
Southern Lea Rd TA8 104 C8
Southern Ring Path [4]
BS21 6 B1
Southern Way BS21 6 C1
South Espl TA8 104 A5
Southey Rd BS21 6 D2
SOUTHFIELD 79 A2
Southfield
Cheddar BS27 90 B8
Norton St Philip BA2 81 F4
Radstock BA3 79 A2
Southwick BA14 83 F2
Wiveliscombe TA4 210 C3
Southfield Cl
Nailsea BS48 8 E3
Taunton TA2 168 F6
Weston-Super-Mare BS23 48 D2
Woolavington TA7 136 E3
Southfield Farm Cvn Pk &
Camp Site TA8 65 F4
Southfield Hill BA3 99 A6
Southfield Rd
Nailsea BS48 8 F3
Shepton Mallet BA4 205 A5
Southfield Rd Trad Est
BS48 8 F3
Southfields
Frome BA11 120 A2
Ilminster TA19 183 E2
South Fields BA6 206 E3
Southgate
Bath BA1 228 C2
Frome BA11 120 D7
Wiveliscombe TA4 210 C3
Southgate Ave TA6 209 A3
Southgate Dr BA9 216 C3
Southgate Rd BA9 216 C3
Southgate Sh Ctr BA1 228 C2
South Gr BS20 4 C4
South Green St [8] BS8 11 F6
South Harp TA13 220 E1
South Hele Cross EX16 165 C1
SOUTH HILL 211 A1
South Hill BS25 51 F2
South La
Challacombe EX31 126 A3
Nether Stowey TA5 134 B2
Southlands
Bath BA1 27 B1
Carhampton TA24 131 B5
Southlands Dr BA2 60 B2
Southlands Way BS49 34 E5
South Lawn BS24 49 F4
South Lawn Cl BS24 49 F4
South Lea Rd BA1 44 A8
Southleaze BS25 70 A6
Southleaze Orch BA16 207 C6
Southleaze Rd BA16 207 B6
Southleigh BS25 69 F8
Southleigh Rd
Bristol BS8 226 B4
Taunton TA1 213 B3
SOUTHMARSH 161 B1
South Mdw BA5 113 A1
South Mdws BS40 35 E2
Southmead
West Camel BA22 174 D3
Winscombe BS25 70 A8
Southmead Cres TA18 224 C5
Southmead La BA8 190 A6
Southmead Rd BS22 49 B7
Southmead Terr TA18 224 C5
South Molton Rd EX16 164 B1
South Moors La TA7 137 B2
Southover BA5 203 D3
Southover Rd BS39 59 D1
South Par
Bath BA2 228 C2
Chew Magna BS40 39 B3
Frome BA11 119 E4
Weston-Super-Mare BS23 48 D8
South Parade Cotts BA2 45 C1
SOUTH PERROTT 196 C1
SOUTH PETHERTON 220 C4
South Petherton Hospl
TA13 220 D5
South Petherton Inf Sch
TA13 220 C4
South Petherton Jun Sch
TA13 220 D3
South Pk TA24 200 D6
South Rd
Brean TA8 65 F3
Lympsham BS24 67 B1
Midsomer Norton BA3 78 B1
Portishead BS20 2 D7
Taunton TA1 213 A2
Timsbury BA2 60 B2
Watchet TA23 202 C6
Weston-Super-Mare BS23 30 C1
Southridge Hts BS24 67 A8
South Road Villas BA9 216 C3
South Rock Ind Est BA3 96 D1
Southside BS23 48 E8
South Side BS49 34 E5
Southside Cl BS9 5 B8
Southside Cres BS22 31 A4
South St
Burnham-on-S TA8 104 A6
Castle Cary BA7 214 B4
Crewkerne TA18 224 D5
Hinton St George TA17 195 D7
Holcombe Rogus TA21 178 F5
Kington Magna SP8 177 E1
Milborne Port DT9 217 D2
Montacute TA15 186 B3
Sherborne DT9 225 E3
South Petherton TA13 220 D4
Stratton-on-t F BA3 96 F2
Taunton TA1 213 A3
Walton BA16 156 E7
Wellington TA21 222 E5
Wells BA5 203 D4
West Camel BA22 174 D3
Wincanton BA9 216 C3
Wiveliscombe TA4 210 C4
Yeovil BA20 219 B4
SOUTHSTOKE 62 E7
Southstoke La BA2 62 F8
Southstoke Rd BA2 44 F1
South Terr
Burnham-on-S TA8 104 B6
Weston-Super-Mare BS23 48 D8
SOUTHTOWN 183 C3
Southtown La BA6 158 B8
SOUTH TWERTON 44 C5
Southview TA3 168 D1
South View
[12] Barwick BA22 197 F8
Bawdrip TA7 136 E2
Bradford Abbas DT9 187 E1
Broadway TA19 183 C2
Clandown BA3 78 E5
Ditcheat BA4 159 C6
Horrington BA5 113 A1
Lynford-on-F TA11 158 C1
Monkton Combe BA2 45 E1
Paulton BS39 77 E6
Portishead BS20 2 D7
Queen Camel BA22 174 F3
Timsbury BA2 60 B2
Westleigh EX16 179 A3
Southview Cl
Hutton BS24 49 E2
Westonzoyland TA7 154 F5
South View Pl BA3 78 B2
Southview Rd TA7 154 F5
South View Rd
Bath BA2 44 D6
Milborne Port DT9 217 C3
South View Terr
Taunton TA3 168 D1
South View Terr *continued*
Yatton BS49 17 B1
South Villas TA4 167 F6
Southville BA21 219 C5
Southville Rd BS23 48 E4
Southville Terr BA2 45 B4
SOUTHWAY 139 D5
Southway Cl BA21 218 F6
Southway Cres BA21 218 F6
Southway Ct BS21 6 D1
Southway Dr BA21 218 F6
Southwell TA3 168 D1
Southwell Cl TA3 168 D1
Southwell Cres TA9 104 E3
Southwell Ct TA9 104 E3
Southwell St BS2 226 C4
South Western Bsns Pk
DT9 225 D3
South Western Terr
BA20 219 C4
SOUTHWICK
Trowbridge 83 F2
Watchfield 105 E2
Southwick CE Prim Sch
BA14 83 F3
Southwick Ctry Pk★ BA14 83 F5
Southwick Rd TA9 106 C1
SOUTH WIDCOMBE 75 C6
Southwood BA4 159 D8
Southwood Ave BS9 5 C8
Southwood Dr BS9 5 B8
Southwood Dr E BS9 5 C8
Southwood Gr TA1 212 C2
Southwoods BA20 219 A3
Southwood Way TA3 181 C5
Sovereign Rd TA6 209 D7
Sovereign Sh Ctr BS23 48 D8
Sowden Hill TA5 134 D4
Spanish Hill TA6 153 F2
Spargrove La BA4 142 B1
SPARKFORD 175 A5
Sparkford Hill La BA22 175 A4
Sparkford Rd BA22 175 A6
Sparkhayes La TA24 124 A3
Sparks Way TA9 104 D3
Sparrow Hill Way BS26 88 E6
Sparrow La TA24 146 C7
Sparrow Rd BA21 219 B6
Spartley Dr BS13 21 F6
Spartley Wlk BS13 21 F6
SPAXTON 152 E8
Spaxton CE Prim Sch
TA5 152 E7
Spaxton Cl TA8 104 C8
Spaxton Rd TA5 153 C7
Spearcey Cl TA3 181 D8
Spearcey La TA3 181 D8
Spearhay La TA20 198 F5
Spear Mead DT8 199 F7
Spears La TA4 166 A4
Specket La DT8 199 E5
SPECKINGTON 174 C2
Speckington La BA22 174 B2
Specklemead BS39 77 D5
Speedwell Ind Est [1] BS21 6 C2
Speke Cl
Ilminster TA19 221 B4
Merriott TA16 195 F7
Staplegrove TA2 212 B6
Speke Ct TA19 221 B4
Spencer Ave TA2 212 E6
Spencer Cl TA6 209 D3
Spencer Dr
Midsomer Norton BA3 78 A2
Weston-Super-Mare BS22 32 B3
Spencer Ho [6] BS1 227 B1
Spencers Belle Vue BA1 228 B4
Sperring Ct BA3 96 F8
Sperry Cross TA4 149 B1
Spicer Way TA20 223 D2
SPIKE ISLAND 226 B1
Spillers Cl TA6 208 E2
Spindleberry Gr BS48 9 A2
Spiningmill Cotts [3]
BA11 119 E5
Spinners End BS22 32 B4
Spinners Ho [5] BA4 205 B6
Spinney Croft BS13 21 F5
Spinneyfield TA4 167 F7
Spinney Rd BS24 50 D4
Spinney The
Ashcott TA7 156 A8
Portishead BS20 2 C4
Taunton TA1 212 D2
Weston-Super-Mare BS24 48 F1
Yeovil BA20 218 D2
Spire Cross TA24 147 A4
SPLATT 152 E8
Splatt La TA5 152 E8
Splott BS26 88 F6
Spoonbill Rd TA6 209 B4
Spratts Bridge BS40 39 A3
Sprigg Dr BS20 1 F1
Springbok Cl BA16 207 D7
Spring Cres BA2 228 C2
Springer's Hill BA3 116 E6
Springfield
Ilminster TA19 221 B2
Norton St Philip BA2 81 E4
Peasedown St John BA2 79 C7
Street BA16 207 B5
Springfield Ave
Bridgwater TA6 208 C3
Bristol, Shirehampton BS11 4 D6
Weston-Super-Mare BS22 31 D1

Springfield Bldgs
Midsomer Norton BS39 77 D2
Radstock BA3 79 A3
Springfield Cl
Bath BA2 44 B5
Cheddar BS27 90 A8
Cross BS26 69 F2
Springfield Cotts
Upton Cheyney BS30 26 A8
Winsford TA24 147 A6
Springfield Cres BA3 79 A3
Spring Field Cres DT9 225 C3
Springfield Ct BA4 205 A5
Springfield Dr BS28 108 C3
Springfield Flats TA20 223 C4
Springfield Gdns BS29 51 A3
Springfield Ho
Bristol BS6 226 C4
Portishead BS20 2 C4
Springfield Hts BA3 78 E4
Springfield Lawn BS11 4 D6
Springfield Pl
Bath BA1 27 F1
Clandown BA3 78 E4
Yeovil BA21 218 E7
Springfield Rd
Cheddar BS27 90 A8
Highbridge TA9 104 E4
Milborne Port DT9 217 D3
Pill BS20 4 C4
Portishead BS20 2 B5
Wellington TA21 222 C7
Wincanton BA9 216 B4
Yeovil BA21 218 E7
Springfields
East Chinnock BA22 196 E8
Stalbridge DT10 190 C4
Springfield Terr
Street BA16 207 B5
Tatworth TA20 198 D8
SPRING GARDENS 119 D8
Spring Gardens Rd BA2 228 C2
Spring Gdns
Minehead TA24 201 B5
Wiveliscombe TA4 210 C5
Spring Ground Rd BS39 77 E5
Spring Hill
Bristol BS2 227 A4
Weston-Super-Mare BS22 31 D2
Springhill Cl BS39 77 C6
Spring Hill Dr BS22 31 E1
Spring La
Bath BA1 28 B2
Dundry BS41 22 A1
Sandford Orcas DT9 188 C7
Springley Rd TA6 209 D6
Springmead TA20 223 B3
Springmead Sch BA11 101 E4
Spring Rd BA11 119 F6
Spring Rise
Portishead BS20 2 C3
Puriton TA7 136 C4
Wells BA5 203 C3
Spring Terr
Frome BA11 119 D2
Weston-Super-Mare BS22 31 C2
Spring Vale BA1 28 B2
Spring Valley BS22 31 C2
Springway Ind Est TA7 155 A5
Spring Wood Gdns BS24 49 E3
Spruce Way
Bath BA2 62 E8
Weston-Super-Mare BS22 49 E8
Spurwells TA19 183 F4
Squares Rd TA5 135 F2
Square The
Axbridge BS26 70 C2
Banwell BS29 51 B3
Bath BA2 228 B1
Edington TA7 137 C2
Maiden Bradley BA12 144 C2
Shipham BS25 70 E7
Taunton TA1 213 C2
Temple Cloud BS39 58 E1
Wellow BA2 62 D1
Westbury-sub-Mendip BA5 110 E6
Winscombe BS25 69 E6
Wiveliscombe TA4 210 C4
Woolavington TA7 136 E4
Squibbs Cl TA6 209 D5
Squibbs Ho TA6 208 F5
Squire La BS40 55 C1
Squirrel Ct TA21 222 D5
Stabbins Cl BS22 32 B5
Stables The BA3 98 B5
Stable Yd BA2 44 D6
Stacey's Ct TA10 171 F5
Staddlestones BA3 96 F7
Staddonhill Rd TA24 146 F8
Stafford Pl BS23 48 E8
Stafford Rd
Bridgwater TA6 209 C3
Portishead BS20 2 E4
Weston-Super-Mare BS23 48 F7
STAFFORD'S GREEN 188 D8
Stagman La TA7, BA16 156 C8
Stag Mill Cross EX16 178 B3
Stag Way BA6 206 C4
Stainer Cl BS4 22 D7
Staker's Cross TA20 195 B2
Staker's Cross La TA18, TA20 195 B2
STALBRIDGE 190 C4
Stalbridge Cl DT10 190 B4
Stalbridge La
Marnhull DT10 190 F2
Sturminster Newton DT10 190 F1
Stalbridge Pk DT10 190 A4
Stalbridge Prim Sch DT10 190 B5
Stalbridge Rd
Henstridge BA8 190 A6
Stalbridge Weston DT10 190 A3
Stourton Caundle DT10 189 F2
STALBRIDGE WESTON 190 A3
Stalcombe La BA2 42 B4
Staling Way BA4 205 C4
Stallards TA21 222 C3
STALLEN 188 A3
Stallgrove La BA16 207 D3
Stall St BA1 228 C2
Stalls The BA12 144 D7
Stambrook Pk BA1 29 A5
Stammery Hill EX13 198 C1
Stanchester Com Sch TA14 186 A4
Stanchester Way TA10 171 D4
Stancombe La
Flax Bourton BS48 19 E7
Westbury-sub-Mendip BA5 110 F8
Standards Rd TA7 154 E5
Standards The TA7 137 D2
STANDERWICK 102 C2
Standerwick Cross BA11 102 B2
Standerwick Orch TA19 183 C2
Standfast Pl TA2 213 C8
Standhill Rd TA10 155 F2
Standish Ct TA1 212 F4
Standish St TA6 208 F7
Stane Way BS11 4 C7
Stanford Pl BS4 22 D7
Stanhope Pl BA1 228 A2
Stanhope Rd BS23 48 E3
Stanier Cl BA11 120 D6
Stanier Rd BA2 228 A2
Stankley View TA19 184 F4
Stanley Cl
Bridgwater TA6 208 F2
Staplegrove TA2 212 C6
Stanley Ct BA3 78 B2
Stanley Gr BS23 48 F7
Stanley Rd 2 BS23 48 F7
Stanley Rd W BA2 44 D5
Stanley Terr BA3 79 A3
Stanley Villas 12 BA1 28 A1
Stanmoor Rd TA7 170 F8
Stanshalls Cl BS40 37 C8
Stanshalls Dr BS40 37 C8
Stanshalls La BS40 37 C8
STANTON DREW 39 F2
Stanton Drew Prim Sch BS39 40 A2
Stanton Drew Stone Circles★ BS39 40 A3
Stanton La BS39 40 D4
STANTON PRIOR 42 E2
Stanton Rd BS40 39 B3
STANTON WICK 58 D8
Stanton Wick La BS39 40 B1
Stant Way TA20 193 C6
Stanway Cl
Bath BA2 44 D1
Taunton TA2 212 D7
Staple Cl TA4 132 E4
Staplecombe Vineyard★ TA2 168 C6
STAPLE FITZPAINE 182 C5
Staplegate EX16 178 A3
Staple Gr BS31 24 D5
STAPLEGROVE 212 C8
Staplegrove CE Prim Sch TA2 212 C7
Staplegrove Manor TA2 212 D8
Staplegrove Rd
Staplegrove TA2 212 C7
Taunton TA1, TA2 212 E5
STAPLEHAY 181 D8
Staple Hill TA3 182 C5
Staple La TA4 132 E4
STAPLE LAWNS 182 B5
Staples Cl BS21 6 E1
Staples Gn BS22 32 B3
Staples Hill BA3 64 C4
Staples Mdw TA20 198 D8
STAPLETON 185 E8
Stapleton Cl TA12 185 E7
Stapleton Cross TA12 185 E7
Stapleton Rd TA12 185 F7
STAPLEY 191 D8
Stapley Cross TA3 181 B1
Stapling La TA24 130 F3
STAR 52 D1
Starcross Rd BS22 32 A2
Star La BS20 4 D4
Starling Cl BS22 49 E8
Starrs Cl BS26 70 B2
Stars La BA20 219 C4
Statham Cl
Cheddar BS27 90 B7
Taunton TA1 212 C2
Statham Gr TA1 212 C2
STATHE 171 B8
Stathe Cotts TA7 171 B7
Stathe Rd TA7 171 A8
Station App
Bristol BS1 227 C1
Frome BA11 120 A4
Ilminster TA19 183 E1
Pensford BS39 40 D5
Weston-Super-Mare BS23 48 E7
Station Cl
Backwell BS48 18 F7
Station Cl *continued*
Congresbury BS49 34 C4
Station Lodge 8 BS23 48 E7
Station Mead BA3 96 D3
Station Path TA11 211 D3
Station Rd
Ashcott TA7 156 B8
Axbridge BS26 70 C2
Backwell BS48 19 A6
Bampton EX16 164 B1
Bath BA1 44 C7
Binegar BA3 114 D7
Bishops Lydeard TA4 167 E8
Blagdon BS40 54 E3
Bristol, Shirehampton BS11 4 D5
Bristol, Shirehampton BS11 4 E6
Bruton BA10 215 F6
Burlescombe EX16 179 B3
Burnham-on-S TA9 85 F3
Burtle TA7 137 D6
Castle Cary BA7 214 B6
Chard Junction TA20 198 D8
Cheddar BS27 90 B7
Clevedon BS21 6 D3
Clutton BS39 58 E3
Congresbury BS49 34 C4
Cossington TA7 136 F3
Draycott BS27 90 E2
Dunster TA24 201 E4
Flax Bourton BS48 20 A8
Freshford BA3 64 C5
Hatch Beauchamp TA3 183 A7
Ilminster TA19 221 A4
Keynsham BS31 24 E6
Meare TA7 138 C1
Midsomer Norton BA3 78 B2
Milborne Port DT9 217 D4
Milverton TA4 167 A5
Misterton TA18 224 E4
Nailsea BS48 8 F2
Norton Fitzwarren TA2 168 B4
Pill BS20 4 C4
Portbury BS20 3 D3
Portishead BS20 2 D6
Sandford BS25 51 F4
Shapwick TA7 137 F2
Shepton Mallet BA4 205 B5
Sherborne DT9 225 E3
Stalbridge DT10 190 B4
Stogumber TA4 150 D8
Taunton TA1 212 F5
Templecombe BA8 176 E1
Walpole TA6 136 B3
Wanstrow BA4 142 F4
Washford TA23 131 E4
Wellington TA21 222 C7
Wellow BA2 62 D1
Westbury-sub-Mendip BA5 110 E5
Weston-Super-Mare BS23 48 E7
Weston-Super-Mare, St Georges BS22 32 D2
Weston-Super-Mare, Worle BS22 31 F2
Williton TA4 202 E3
Wincanton BA9 216 C3
Wiveliscombe TA4 210 C4
Wrington BS40 35 D2
Yatton BS49 17 B1
Station Rd (Blackmoor La) BA8 190 A7
Station Rd Ind Est BA10 215 F6
Station Road Bsns Pk DT10 190 B5
Station Terr TA24 201 A7
Station Way BA4 141 E1
Station Wlk TA9 104 E3
Staundle La TA3 183 B8
Staunton Fields BS14 23 C4
Staunton La
Minehead TA24 201 A4
Whitchurch BS14 23 D3
Staunton Rd TA24 201 A5
Staunton Rise TA24 201 A5
Staunton Way BS14 23 D4
Stavordale Gr BS14 23 B6
STAWELL 137 A1
Stawell Rd TA7 137 B1
STAWLEY 166 A1
Stawley Prim Sch TA21 179 B8
Steamalong TA3 183 E7
Steam Mills BA3 96 F8
Steam Packet Terr 2 TA6 209 B4
STEANBOW 140 D2
Steanbow Cotts BA4 140 D3
STEART
Babcary 174 C6
Combwich 135 D8
Steart Ave TA8 104 B6
Steart Cl TA8 104 B6
Steart Cotts TA3 169 C3
Steart Ct TA8 104 A7
Steart Dr TA8 104 A6
Steart Dro TA10 156 D1
Steart Gdns TA8 104 B6
Steart Hill BA22 174 D5
Steart La
Babcary TA11 174 B6
Wheddon Cross TA24 129 F3
Stedhams Cl TA21 222 D7
Steeds Terr BA3 115 D6
Steel La TA7 137 D2
Steel Mills BS31 24 F4
Steel's La BA9 161 D2
Steel Well La BA8 190 A6
Steep La TA22 164 C8
Steeple View BA3 116 A3
Steep The TA24 147 C5
Steevens Ho (Almshouses) 13 BS2 227 C3
STEMBRIDGE 185 A7
Stembridge Rd TA10 156 B1
Stembridge Tower Mill★ TA10 156 B1
Stembridge Way TA2 168 B4
Stephen's Hill TA10 172 E4
Stephenson Dr BA11 120 D6
Stephenson Rd TA24 201 B6
Stephen St TA1 213 A4
Stephen Way 6 TA1 213 A4
Steppes Cres 13 TA12 185 E6
Steppes Mdw TA12 185 E6
Steps La BA2 100 E7
Stert Dro TA5 135 B7
Steven's Cl BA4 205 A5
Stevens La
Frome BA11 119 F3
Lympsham BS24 67 C3
Stewart Ct EX13 198 A2
Steway La BA1 29 B6
STEWLEY 183 B5
Stibbear La TA19 194 A8
Stiby Ct BA21 218 F7
Stiby Rd BA21 218 E7
Stickland BS21 6 C1
Stickleball La BA4, BA6 140 D1
Stickle Hill TA4 151 B7
STICKLEPATH
Combe St Nicholas 193 D7
Monksilver 149 E7
Stickle Path EX16 165 C1
STICKLINCH 140 C1
Sticklinch Rd BA6 140 C2
Stilemead La BS40 55 D1
Stiles Ct BA5 203 B4
STILEWAY 138 E3
Stileway BA6 138 E4
Stileway Bsns Pk BS21 16 B8
Stiling Cl TA9 104 D4
Stillingfleet Rd BS13 22 C5
Stillington Cl BA5 203 B3
Stillman Cl BS13 21 E4
Stirling Way
Frome BA11 120 C6
Keynsham BS31 24 E4
Stirtingale Ave BA2 44 C3
Stirtingale Rd BA2 44 C3
Stitching La BS28 138 C8
Stitchings La BA2 61 D7
Stitchings Shord La BS39 57 C4
Stoate Cl TA23 202 C5
Stoberry Ave BA5 203 E5
Stoberry Cres BA5 203 E5
Stoberry Park Sch BA5 203 E5
STOCK 53 B8
Stockbridge TA17 195 D7
Stockbridge La BA6 140 B2
Stockditch Rd TA12 185 B7
Stockers Cl TA4 210 B4
Stockham Cross TA4 151 D5
Stockham Hill TA22 163 E8
Stock Hill BA3 115 B8
Stockhill Cl BA3 96 C3
Stock Hill Ct BA3 117 B7
Stockhill Rd BA3 96 C2
Stockholm Dr 10 TA6 154 A5
Stock La
Buckhorn Weston SP8 177 F5
Lower Langford BS40 53 A7
STOCKLAND BRISTOL 135 A6
Stockland Hill EX14 192 A1
Stockland Manor TA5 134 F6
STOCKLINCH 184 B4
STOCKLINCH OTTERSEY 184 C4
STOCKLINCH ST MAGDALEN 184 C4
Stockman La TA20 198 C7
Stockmead BS40 53 B5
Stockmoor Cl TA6 209 A2
Stockmoor Dr TA6 209 A1
Stock Moor Dro TA6 209 A1
Stock's La
Hatch Beauchamp TA3, TA19 183 B6
Leigh u M BA3 116 E3
North Wootton BA4 140 C4
Stockstyle La EX13 198 A8
Stockton Cl BS14 22 F4
Stock Way N BS48 8 F2
Stock Way S BS48 8 E2
Stockwitch Cross BA22 174 B3
STOCKWOOD 23 E5
Stockwood Green Prim Sch BS14 23 E4
Stockwood Hill BS31 24 C7
Stockwood La BS14 23 E5
Stockwood Rd BS4, BS14 24 A7
STOCKWOOD VALE 24 C6
Stockwood Vale BS31 24 C6
Stodden's La TA8 104 E8
Stodden's Rd TA8 85 C1
Stodden's Wlk TA8 104 B8
Stodeleigh Cl BS22 32 B3
STOFORD 197 F8
Stoford La
Broadway TA19 183 C2
West Buckland TA21 181 A7
Stoford Pl TA19 183 C2
STOGUMBER 150 D8
Stogumber CE Fst Sch TA4 150 D8
Stogumber Sta★ TA4 150 E8
STOGURSEY 134 C5
Stogursey CE Prim Sch TA5 134 B5
Stogursey La TA5 134 A3
STOKE BISHOP 5 E5
Stoke Bishop CE Prim Sch BS9 5 D5
Stoke Cotts BS9 5 E4
Stoke Cres BA3 116 A2
Stoke Cross 10 TA14 185 F4
Stoke Gr BS9 5 E6
Stoke Hamlet BS9 5 F6
Stoke Hill
Bristol BS9 5 E3
Chew Stoke BS40 56 D7
Stoke St Mary TA3 169 D1
Stoke St Michael BA3 116 A2
Stoney Stoke BA9 160 E3
Stoke La
Bristol, Westbury on T BS9 5 F6
Stoke St Mary TA3 169 A1
Wincanton BA9 216 F5
Yarlington BA9 175 E7
Stokeleigh Wlk BS9 5 C5
Stoke Mead BA2 63 F7
Stoke Moor Dro BS27 109 D6
Stoke Paddock Rd BS9 5 D6
Stoke Park Rd BS9 5 F4
Stoke Park Rd S BS9 5 E3
STOKE PERO 128 F6
Stoke Rd
Bristol BS9 5 F3
Martock TA12 185 E5
North Curry TA3 170 C4
Portishead BS20 2 D5
Ruishton TA3 169 C2
Stoke St Mary TA3 169 B1
Street BA16 207 E6
Taunton TA1 213 B1
Westbury-sub-Mendip BA5 110 D6
STOKE ST GREGORY 170 E6
Stoke St Gregory CE Prim Sch TA3 170 E6
STOKE ST MARY 169 C1
STOKE ST MICHAEL 116 B2
Stoke St Michael Prim Sch BA3 116 A3
Stokes Croft BS1 227 B4
Stokes La DT10 189 F2
Stoke St BS27 110 B8
STOKE SUB HAMDON 185 F5
Stoke sub Hamdon Castle Prim Sch TA14 185 F4
Stoke sub Hamdon Priory★ TA14 185 F4
STOKE TRISTER 177 B7
STOLFORD 134 F8
Stolford Hill TA22 148 A4
Stonage La TA18 196 C5
Stoneable Rd BA3 79 A3
Stoneage La BA2 61 B1
STONE ALLERTON 88 C3
Stone Allerton Dro BS26 88 B2
STON EASTON 95 E8
Stonebarrow La EX13 198 F2
Stoneberry Rd BS14 23 B3
STONEBRIDGE
Banwell 51 A4
Frome 120 A7
Stonebridge BS21 6 D1
Stonebridge Dr BA11 120 B7
Stonebridge Rd BS23 48 F4
Stonechat Green BS20 3 A6
Stone Cl TA1 168 D1
Stone Cross TA24 128 E1
Stonedene DT9 225 D6
Stone Down La BA6 139 D1
STONE-EDGE BATCH 8 D4
Stonegallows TA1 212 A3
Stonehenge La BS48 8 E4
STONE HILL 207 A4
Stonehill
South Cadbury BA22 175 C3
Stoke Sub Hamdon TA14 186 A4
Street BA16 207 B5
Stone Hill Ct TA24 200 F7
Stone Hill La TA4 166 D3
Stonehouse Cl BA2 45 B2
Stonehouse La BA2 45 B2
Stone La
East Pennard BA4 158 E6
Exford TA24 128 E1
Winsford TA24 147 E6
Yeovil BA21 187 B5
Stoneleigh
Chew Magna BS40 39 B3
Wellington TA21 222 B8
Stoneleigh Cl
Burnham-on-S TA8 104 C8
Staplegrove TA2 212 C8
Stoneleigh Ct
Bath BA1 27 E3
Taunton TA1 212 C1
Stoneleigh Mews BA21 218 C7
Stoneleigh Rise BA11 120 A6
Stone Mead La TA10 173 A4
Stone Rd TA8 104 D5
Stoneridge La TA4 165 D5
Stones Cross BA3 78 B2
Stonesfield TA18 196 B5
Stones Paddock BA3 116 C7
Stonewall Terr BA11 119 F2
Stonewell Dr BS49 34 D3
Stonewell Gr BS49 34 D3
Stonewell La BS49 34 D3
Stonewell Park Rd BS49 34 D3
Stoneyard La BA3 75 D2
Stoney Cl TA24 129 F6
Stoneyfield Cl BS20 4 B5
Stoneyfields BS20 4 B4
Stoney Furlong TA2 213 B8

Stoney Head Cvn Pk TA3 169 F1
Stoneyhurst Dr TA10 171 C3
Stoney La
Bishops Lydeard TA4 167 E8
Curry Rivel TA10 171 C3
East Coker BA22 197 D6
Stocklinch TA19 184 C4
Stoney Lane Cross EX16 178 B3
Stoney Littleton Long Barrow★ BA2 80 C7
Stoney St TA24 129 C7
Stoney Steep BS48 9 A5
STONEY STOKE 160 F3
STONEY STRATTON 141 F2
STONY HEAD 169 F1
Stonyhead Hill TA3 169 F1
STONY KNAPS 199 D7
Stony La
Axminster EX13 198 A1
Hawkridge TA22 146 E3
Whatley BA11 118 A2
STONY LITTLETON 80 B6
Stony St BA11 119 F5
STOODHAM 220 D6
Stoodham TA13 220 D5
Stoodly La
North Wootton BA4 140 D4
Pilton BA4 204 A2
Stooper's Hill TA20 193 C6
STOPGATE 192 C4
Stopgate Cross EX14 192 C4
Stoppard Rd TA8 104 C6
Stopper's La BA5 139 F6
Stormont Cl BS23 48 F3
Stormore BA13 121 F8
Storridge La
Axminster EX13 198 B6
Brompton Regis TA22 148 A1
Storridge View TA22 148 A2
STOUGHTON CROSS 108 B8
Stourhead Gardens★ BA12 161 F5
Stourhead House★ BA12 161 F5
Stour Hill SP8 177 E1
Stour Hill Pk SP8 177 F1
STOURTON 161 F5
STOURTON CAUNDLE 189 F2
Stourton Cl BA11 119 E3
Stourton Gdns [1] BA11 119 E3
Stourton La BA12 161 F6
Stourton View BA11 119 E3
Stourton Way BA21 218 D6
STOUT 156 B2
Stout Cross EX14 192 C5
Stout's Way La
Luxborough TA23 148 F8
Rodhuish TA24 131 A1
Stowborough Cotts BA2 79 C7
STOWELL 176 C1
Stowell Hill DT9 176 C1
Stowell La TA20 198 D8
Stowers Row [31] TA12 185 E6
STOWEY 57 F4
Stowey Bottom BS39 57 E5
Stowey Cross Rds BS39 57 F5
Stowey La
Curry Mallet TA3 183 E8
Fivehead TA3 170 E1
Stowey Pk BS49 34 D7
Stowey Rd
Pitney TA10 172 D7
Taunton TA2 212 E8
Yatton BS49 34 C8
Stow Ho BS11 4 E5
Stradling Ave BS23 48 F5
Stradling Cl TA7 137 B2
Stradling's Hill TA5 135 B3
Stradlings Yd BS2 226 C4
Straight Dro
Burrowbridge TA7 155 B1
Chilton Trinity TA5 135 F2
West Huntspill TA9 136 B7
Woolavington TA9 137 A6
Straight La BA11 101 D7
Straightmead BA3 75 F1
Straight St BS2 227 C2
Strap La
Ston Easton BA3 95 F7
Upton Noble BA4, BA10 143 A1
Stratford Cl BS14 22 F3
Stratford Ct BS9 5 F8
Stratford La BS40 56 E1
Stratford Rd BA21 218 D5
Stratheden BS8 226 A4
Stratton Cl TA6 209 D3
STRATTON-ON-THE FOSSE 96 F1
Stratton Rd
Holcombe BA3 116 B8
Saltford BS31 25 E3
Strawberry Bank TA19 221 C4
Strawberry Cl BS48 8 D1
Strawberry Field BS26 70 D2
Strawberry Gdns BS48 18 D8
Strawberry Hill
Clevedon BS21 6 F4
Street BA16 207 B7
Strawberry La BS13, BS41 21 E3
Strawberry Way BA5 203 C4
Strawberry Way Rdbt
BA5 203 D3
Streaked La TA3 170 C6
STREAM 132 A2
Streamcombe La TA22 163 B5
Streamcross BS49 17 D1
Streamleaze BS40 39 B3
Streamside
Chew Magna BS40 39 B3
Streamside *continued*
[1] Clevedon BS21 6 F3
Taunton TA1 213 C2
STREET
Chard 194 C2
Glastonbury 207 C7
STREET ASH 193 C8
Street Ash La TA20 193 C8
Street Dro
Street BA16 207 E7
Street, Marshall's Elm BA16 207 B1
STREET END 54 D3
Street End BS40 54 D2
Street End La BS40 54 D2
Street Ho TA19 221 B3
Street La
Odcombe BA22 186 C2
South Brewham BA10 161 A7
STREET ON THE FOSSE 141 C2
Street Rd
Compton Dundon TA11 157 A4
Glastonbury BA6 206 D3
Street BA6 207 D8
Street Rdbt BA16 207 D7
Street Shoe Mus★ BA16 207 C6
Street The
Bishop Sutton BS39 57 D4
Chew Stoke BS40 56 D8
Chilcompton BA3 96 D5
Compton Martin BS40 74 B7
Draycott BS27 90 F2
Farmborough BA2 59 F6
Kilmington BA12 161 F6
Radstock BA3 78 F2
Stowey BS39 57 F4
Ubley BS40 55 D1
Wanstrow BA4 142 F4
West Monkton TA2 169 C7
Winford BS40 37 F1
Stretcholt La TA6 135 F6
Stretford La TA19 194 F7
Stringfellow Cres TA20 223 D5
Stringfellow Mews TA20 223 C3
Stringland's La TA24 131 B2
STRINGSTON 133 F5
STRODE 55 E7
Strode Coll BA16 207 D6
Strode Ho [7] BA4 205 B6
Strode Rd
Clevedon BS21 6 C2
Street BA16 207 D6
Strode Way
Clevedon BS21 6 B1
Shepton Mallet BA4 205 A5
Stroud Rd BS11 4 E5
Stroud Way BS24 49 E7
Strowland La BS24 86 F6
Strowlands BS24, TA9 86 E6
Struthers Cl BA16 207 B7
Strutter's Hill BA10 215 D2
Stuart Ho BS23 30 D1
Stuart Pl BA2 44 D6
Stuart Rd BS23 49 A5
Stuarts Cl BA5 203 D3
Stubb's La BA11 101 D4
STUDLEY GREEN 83 F6
Studley La BA4 142 F4
Studley Mdws BA4 142 F4
Stump Cross
Pitcombe BA7 215 A1
Shepton Mallet BA4 204 D5
STURFORD 144 F7
Sturford La BA12 144 E7
Sturmey Way BS20 4 E3
Sturminster Cl BS14 23 D6
Sturminster Lodge BS14 23 D5
Sturminster Rd BS14 23 D7
Stutts End TA4 167 E6
Style Flats TA4 210 C5
Style Rd TA4 210 C5
Styles Ave BA11 120 C4
Styles Cl BA11 120 B4
Styles Hill BA11 120 B4
Styles Mdw BA11 120 C5
Styles Pk BA11 120 B4
Sub Rd BA6 157 D4
Suffolk Cl TA6 209 C3
Suffolk Cres TA1 212 C1
Suffolk Ct TA1 212 C1
Suffolk Ho BA1 44 C8
Sugg's La TA19 183 C2
Sulis Manor Rd BA2 62 D8
Sullivan Cl BS4 22 D6
Sully Cl TA6 209 D6
Sumerleaze Cres TA2 213 C8
Sumerlin Dr BS21 6 F3
Summer Ct BS8 226 B3
Summerfield BS22 32 A3
Summerfield Ave TA21 180 D8
Summerfield Cl TA7 154 F5
Summerfield Ct TA1 212 E4
Summerfield Rd BA1 28 A1
Summerfields BA8 190 A7
Summerfields Rd TA20 223 C3
Summerfield Terr BA1 28 A1
Summerfield Way TA21 180 D8
Summerhedge Cres TA7 155 C2
Summerhedge Rd TA7 155 C1
Summer Hill
Frome BA11 119 F3
Hinton St George TA17 195 D7
Summerhill Rd BA1 27 D1
Summerhouse BS21 8 D4
Summer House Terr
BA20 219 B4
Summerhouse View
BA21 219 C6
Summer La
Banwell BS29 50 E5
Chard TA20 194 C4
Hinton St George TA13, TA17 195 C8
Monkton Combe BA2 63 D8
Weston-Super-Mare BS22, BS24 32 B1
Weston-Super-Mare BS29 50 B8
Weston-Super-Mare BS29 50 D7
Summer La N BS22 32 A2
Summerland Ave TA24 201 A7
Summerland Pl TA24 200 F7
Summerland Rd TA24 200 F7
SUMMERLANDS 218 F6
Summerlands
Backwell BS48 19 B5
Yeovil BA21 218 E6
Summerlands Hospl BA21 218 F6
Summerlands Park Ave
TA19 221 B4
Summerlands Park Cl
TA19 221 B4
Summerlands Park Dr
TA19 221 B4
Summerlands Rd BS23 49 B8
Summer Lane Cvn Pk
BS29 50 E3
Summer Lane Park Homes
BS29 50 E4
Summerlays Ct BA2 45 B6
Summerlays Pl BA2 45 B6
Summerlea BA2 61 A5
Summerleaze BS31 24 E7
Summerleaze Cres TA2 213 C7
Summerleaze Pk BA20 218 F5
Summer Shard TA13 220 C4
Summers Hill La BA4 204 C2
Summerville Terr TA8 104 B6
Summerway TA24 129 E1
Summerway Dro TA7 209 E4
Summerwood Rd BA16 207 B4
Sun Batch BS27 91 A3
Sunderland Pl BS8 226 B3
Sunderland St [2] BA2 228 C3
Sundew Cl TA1 213 C1
Sunfield Rd BS24 49 E3
Sunningdale BS8 226 B4
Sunningdale Cl BS48 9 A1
Sunningdale Rd
Weston-Super-Mare BS22 31 F3
Yeovil BA21 219 C6
Sunnybank BA2 45 B4
Sunny Bank TA4 150 B8
Sunnybank Ct BS24 32 B1
Sunnybank Rd TA6 208 E2
Sunnybank Way BS24 32 B1
Sunnybrow Cl [10] TA6 153 F4
Sunny Cl TA9 136 B8
Sunny Hill
Bristol BS9 5 C7
Pitcombe BA10 215 C4
Sunnyhill Dr BS11 4 E6
Sunnyhill Ho E BS11 4 E6
Sunnyhill Ho W BS11 4 E6
Sunny La BA10 215 C4
Sunnymead
Bridgwater TA6 208 E2
Keynsham BS31 24 F3
Midsomer Norton BA3 77 F2
Oakhill BA3 114 F3
Stratton-on-t F BA3 96 F2
Sunnymeade BA6 138 C4
Sunnymede Rd BS48 8 D3
Sunnyside
Barrington TA19 184 C5
Bristol BS9 5 E5
Burlescombe EX16 179 C2
Clatworthy TA4 149 F1
Clutton BS39 59 B4
Farrington Gurney BS39 77 B3
Frome BA11 119 F3
Sunnyside Cotts TA24 129 A8
Sunnyside Cres BS21 6 D3
Sunnyside Farm Trad Est BS20 4 C2
Sunnyside Gdns BA2 60 B2
Sunnyside Pl BA11 119 F3
Sunnyside Rd
Clevedon BS21 6 D3
Weston-Super-Mare BS23 48 E5
Sunnyside Rd N BS23 48 E6
Sunnyside Terr [6] DT9 225 E4
Sunnyside View BA2 79 C7
Sunnyvale
Camerton BA2 78 E8
Clevedon BS21 6 B1
Sunridge Cl BA3 96 F8
Sunridge Pk BA3 96 F8
Sunset Cl BA2 79 C7
Sun St BA11 119 E5
Suprema Ave TA7 137 C2
Suprema Est TA7 137 D2
Surrey St BS2 227 B4
Susanna's Cross BA3 116 B2
Susanna's La BA3 116 C2
Sussex Ave TA6 209 B3
Sussex Cl TA6 209 B3
Sussex Lodge TA1 212 F5
Sussex Pl BA2 228 C1
Sutherland Ave TA8 104 B6
Sutherland Cl TA1 212 C1
Sutherland Ct TA1 212 C1
Sutherland Dr BS24 49 D2
SUTTON 159 B4
SUTTON BINGHAM 197 D6
Sutton Cl
Frome BA11 120 B7
Weston-Super-Mare BS22 49 E8
Sutton Cross TA10 172 F4
Sutton Grange BA21 218 C6
Sutton Hill
East Coker BA22 197 D6
Long Sutton TA10 172 E3
Sutton Hill Rd BS39 57 D4
Sutton La
Redhill BS40 36 F1
Walton BA16 156 D6
SUTTON MALLET 155 B7
SUTTON MONTIS 175 C3
Sutton Pk BS39 57 D4
Sutton Rd TA11 211 C2
Sutton St BA2 45 B7
Sutton View TA10 172 E2
SUTTON WICK 57 B2
Swains TA21 222 D4
Swains La TA21 222 D4
Swain St TA23 202 C7
Swainswick BS14 22 F6
Swainswick CE Prim Sch BA1 28 B5
Swainswick Gdns BA1 28 C2
Swainswick La BA1 28 D4
Swallow Cl BA3 97 B8
Swallowcliffe Ct [5]
BA20 219 A5
Swallowcliffe Gdns
BA20 219 A5
Swallow Ct BS14 23 F6
Swallow Ct EX16 178 F1
Swallow Dr BA11 120 B6
Swallow Gdns BS22 49 E8
Swallow Hill TA10 172 A6
Swallow St BA1 228 C2
Swallows The BS22 49 D7
Swan Cl BS22 49 E8
Swancombe
Blagdon BS40 54 E2
Clapton in G BS20 8 E8
Swan Down TA20 194 E4
Swane Rd BS14 23 F6
Swan Hill TA18 196 C5
Swan Ho [3] BA4 205 B6
Swanmead Com Sch TA19 221 C3
Swan Prec TA19 221 C3
Swanshard La BA5 139 D6
Swans La BS27 90 F2
Swan Yd DT9 225 D4
Swedish Hos TA13 220 D1
Sweetgrass Rd BS24 50 A8
Sweethay Cl TA3 181 D8
Sweethay Cross TA3 181 C8
Sweethay La TA3 181 C8
Sweetleaze BA3 116 A2
SWELL 171 A2
Swell Cl TA9 136 B8
Swell La TA3 171 A2
Swiddacombe La EX36 162 C7
Swift Cl BS22 31 F1
Swift Lodge BA20 219 A4
Swifts TA21 166 F1
Swillbridge Cvn Pk TA23 202 F6
SWINEFORD 26 A7
Swingbridge TA2 213 E7
Swiss Dr BS3 11 F2
Swiss Rd
Bristol BS3 11 F1
Weston-Super-Mare BS23 48 F7
Sycamore Cl
Bridgwater TA6 209 D5
Burnham-on-S TA8 104 A5
Nailsea BS48 8 E2
Shipham BS25 70 E8
Taunton TA1 213 C2
Weston-Super-Mare BS23 49 A8
Weston-Super-Mare, Locking BS24 49 E5
Westonzoyland TA7 154 E5
Sycamore Ct TA20 223 C5
Sycamore Dr
Crewkerne TA18 224 D7
Frome BA11 120 B7
Langport TA10 172 A6
Yeovil BA20 218 F2
Sycamore Rd
Minehead TA24 200 D7
Radstock BA3 79 B2
Sycamores BS23 30 E1
Sycamore Sq TA20 223 C5
Sycamore Wlk TA3 169 D4
SYDENHAM 209 C5
Sydenham Bldgs BA2 228 A2
Sydenham Cl
Bridgwater TA6 209 C6
Porlock TA24 124 B4
Sydenham Rd
Bath BA2 228 A2
Bridgwater TA6 209 C6
Sydenham Terr BA2 45 C1
Sydling Rd BA21 219 D6
Sydnalls La BA12 144 E8
Sydney Bldgs BA2 45 B6
Sydney Ho BA2 45 B7
Sydney Mews BA2 45 B7
Sydney Pl BA2 45 B7
Sydney Rd BA2 45 B7
Sydney Row BS1 226 B1
Sydney Wharf BA2 45 B7
Sylvan Rd TA21 222 E5
Sylvan Way
Bristol BS9 5 B7
Monkton Heathfield TA2 213 E8
Symes Ave BS13 22 C4
Symes Cl
Chard TA20 223 C4
North Perrott TA18 196 C4
Symes Pk BA1 27 A2
Symons Way
Bridgwater TA6 209 A6
Cheddar BS27 90 C7
Syndercombe La TA4, TA23 149 D2
SYNDERFORD 199 C6

T

Tabernacle La [4] BA20 219 B4
TACKER STREET 149 C8
TADHILL 116 F2
Tadhill La BA3 116 D2
TADWICK 12 E1
Tadwick La BA1 28 A6
Tail Mill TA16 195 F7
Tailor's Ct [7] BS1 227 A3
Talbot Cl TA9 104 D3
Tallis Gr BS4 22 D6
Tallowood BA4 205 D5
Tamar Ave TA1 213 B1
Tamar Dr BS31 25 A4
Tamar Rd BS22 32 A2
Tamblyn Cl BA3 79 A3
Tamsin Ct BS31 24 F5
Tamworth Rd BS31 24 E4
Tancred St TA1 213 A4
TANGIER 212 E4
Tangier TA1 212 E4
Tankard's Cl BS8 226 C3
Tankey's Cl BA11 120 A7
Tan La SP8 161 F1
Tanner Cl BA3 97 C8
Tanner's Hill TA4 165 E7
Tanners La SN14 13 F8
Tanners Wlk
Bath BA2 43 F5
Marshfield SN14 13 F8
Tannery Cl BA16 207 C5
Tannery Ct TA18 224 C7
Tanorth Cl BS14 23 A3
Tanorth Rd BS14 22 F3
Tansee Hill TA20 199 B6
Tansey BA4 142 A6
Tansy La BS20 2 F5
Tanyard
Broadway TA19 183 C2
Nether Stowey TA5 134 B2
Tanyard Cotts TA24 131 A5
Tanyard La
Langport TA10 172 A5
North Wootton BA4 140 C4
North Wootton, Lower Westholme BA4 140 D3
Tan Yard La TA13 184 F5
Tanyards BA10 215 F7
Tanyard The BA16 207 C5
Tape La BA3 114 F7
Taphouse La DT6 199 E1
Tapmoor Rd TA7 155 C8
Tappers La [2] TA6 153 E3
Tapps La TA7 136 E4
Tapstone Rd TA20 223 D4
Taranto Hill BA22 173 E2
Taranto Way BA22 174 A2
Target La TA12 185 D4
TARNOCK 87 D6
Tarnock Ave BS14 23 A7
Tarnwell BS39 40 A2
Tarragon Pl BS20 2 F5
Tarrant La BA20 218 F1
Tarratt La
East Coker BA22 197 E8
Yeovil BA20, BA22 219 A1
Tarratt Rd BA20 218 F1
Tarr Post TA22 146 C1
Tarr Steps★ TA22 146 E3
Tarr Steps National Nature Reserve★ TA22 146 E3
Tarr Water Cotts TA23 148 E8
Tatham Ct TA1 212 D4
TATWORTH 198 C8
Tatworth Prim Sch TA20 198 C8
Tatworth Rd TA20 223 C2
Tatworth St TA20 198 C8
Tauntfield Cl TA1 213 A3
TAUNTON 212 D5
Taunton Rd
Ashcott TA7 156 B7
Bishops Lydeard TA4 167 F7
Bridgwater TA6 209 A3
North Petherton TA6 153 F4
Thurloxton TA6 153 E2
Wellington TA21 222 E7
Weston-Super-Mare BS22 32 B4
Wiveliscombe TA4 210 D4
Taunton Sch TA2 212 D6
Taunton & Somerset Hospl (Musgrove Pk) TA1 212 C3
Taunton Sta TA1 212 F5
Taunton Third Way TA1 212 F4
Taunton Trad Est TA2 212 A7
Taunton Vale Pk TA2 213 F8
Taunusstein Way [12]
BA20 219 B4
Taveners Wlk BS48 8 F3
Taverner Cl BS4 22 D7
Taverners Cl [6] BS23 48 F4
TAVERN SCOTT 38 D1
Tavistock Rd BS22 32 A2

Tawny Way BS22 49 F8
Taylor Cl TA2 168 B5
Taylor Ct
Bridgwater TA6 209 A5
Weston-Super-Mare BS22 32 B4
Taylor Gdns BS13 21 F4
Taylor Ho TA19 221 B3
Taylor's Meade TA20 193 D6
Taylor's Orch TA14 185 E1
Tayman Ridge BS30 25 D8
Teagle Cl BA5 203 F5
Teak Cl TA6 209 D6
Teal Cl
Bridgwater TA6 209 A4
Weston-Super-Mare BS22 31 F1
Tealham Moor Dro BS28 137 E8
Teal Rd TA24 201 C5
Teals Acre 8 TA5 135 B2
Teal Way BS20 2 F6
Teapot Lane (Worms Lane)
BA6 158 B6
Teasel Wlk BS22 49 D7
Technical St TA8 104 B6
Teck Hill TA6 153 E2
Teckhill La TA6 153 E2
Teddington Cl BA2 44 C4
Teesdale Cl BS22 49 D8
Teeside BA14 83 F4
Teeswater Way 9 TA6 154 A5
Teign Ct BA16 156 D7
Teignmouth Rd BS21 6 E3
Telephone Ave BS1 227 A2
Telford Ho
Bath BA2 44 D3
Leigh Woods BS8 11 E7
Tellis Cross BA22 197 D8
TELLISFORD 82 E4
Tellisford La BA2 81 F4
Tellis La BA3 114 D8
Temblett Gn TA6 208 C5
Templars Barton BA8 176 E1
Templars Ct
Long Sutton TA10 172 E1
1 Weston-Super-Mare
BS22 49 D7
Templars Pl BA8 176 E1
Templars Way BS25 70 E7
TEMPLE 144 E7
Temple Back BS1 227 B2
Temple Back East BS1 227 C2
Temple Bridge Bsns Pk
BS39 76 F7
Temple Circus Giratory
BS1 227 C1
TEMPLE CLOUD 58 E1
TEMPLECOMBE 176 E1
Templecombe La SP8 177 C3
Templecombe Sta BA8 176 E1
Temple Ct BS31 24 E5
Temple Field TA23 202 C6
Temple Gate BS1 227 B1
Temple Inf Sch BS31 24 F5
Temple Inn La BS39 58 E1
Temple La BA8 176 F1
Templeland Rd BS13 21 F5
Temple of Harmony★
TA5 153 B5
Temple Prim Sch BS31 24 F6
Temple Rose St BS1 227 B2
Temple St
Bristol BS1 227 B2
Keynsham BS31 24 F5
Temple Way BS2 227 B2
Temple Way Underpass
BS2 227 C3
Tenby Rd BS31 24 D4
Tengore La TA10 172 C6
Tennis Corner Dro BA11 102 D2
Tennis Court Ave BS39 77 D5
Tennis Court Rd BS39 77 D5
Tennyson Ave BS21 6 B2
Tennyson Cl BS31 24 F6
Tennyson Rd
Bath BA1 44 D7
Weston-Super-Mare BS23 49 A3
Tenterk Cl BS24 67 B6
Tents Hill BA11 118 B6
TERHILL 151 F3
Terhill La TA4 151 F3
Termare Cl BA22 218 B6
Terrace The
Minehead TA24 201 A5
Shipham BS25 70 E7
Terrace View DT9 225 E5
Terrace Wlk BA1 228 C2
Terrell St BS2 227 A4
Terry Hill BA3 98 D8
Terry Ho BS1 226 C3
Tetbury Gdns BS48 9 A1
Tetton Cl TA6 208 B4
Teviot Rd BS31 25 A4
Tewkesbury BA21 218 D6
Tewther Rd BS13 22 D3
Teyfant Com Sch BS13 22 E4
Teyfant Rd BS13 22 E4
Teyfant Wlk BS13 22 E4
Thackeray Ave BS21 6 E4
Thackeray Ho BS23 49 A5
Thackeray Rd BS21 6 E4
Thames Dr TA1 213 D4
Thatcham Cl 2 BA21 218 F7
Thatcham Ct 1 BA21 218 F7
Thatcham Pk BA21 218 F7
Thatch Cotts TA20 194 E1
Thatcher Cl BS20 2 D4
Thatch The TA11 211 C4
Theaks Mews TA1 213 A3
THEALE 109 C1
Theatre Royal BS1 227 A2
THE BUTTS 119 E3
THE FOLLY 94 F6
Theillay Cl TA5 134 A3
THE MOUNT 119 F2
THE OVAL 44 C4
There-and-Back-Again La
BS1 226 C3
THE WRANGLE 74 A5
Theynes Croft BS41 11 B1
THICKET MEAD 77 F3
Thicket Mead BA3 78 A2
Thickthorn Cross TA19 183 C3
Thimble La DT9 217 D2
Third Ave
Bath BA2 44 D5
Bristol BS14 23 B7
Radstock BA3 97 D7
Thirlmere Rd BS23 49 A4
Thistledoo Vine TA7 136 F2
Thistle Pk TA6 209 B1
Thomas Cl BS29 51 A3
Thomas Ct BS1 227 B2
Thomas La BS1 227 B2
Thomas Lane Appartments
BS1 227 B2
Thomas St
Bath BA1 228 C4
Bristol BS2 227 B4
Taunton TA2 212 F6
Thomas Way BA6 206 B4
Thomas Way Ind Est
BA6 206 B4
Thompson Cl TA6 209 D6
Thompson Rd BS14 23 E6
Thompson Way BS24 50 C8
Thomson Dr TA18 224 D5
Thong La TA10 184 D6
Thornash Cl TA2 213 F8
Thornbank Ct DT9 225 E4
Thornbank Pl BA2 228 A1
Thornbury Dr BS23 48 D2
Thornbury Rd BS23 48 C2
Thornbush Cross TA4 150 F3
Thorn Cl BS22 32 B2
THORNCOMBE 199 B6
Thorncombe Cres TA6 209 C5
Thorncombe Thorn
TA20 199 B5
Thorndale BS8 226 A4
Thorndale Cl BS22 49 D8
Thorndale Mews BS8 226 A4
Thorndun Park Dr TA20 223 D6
THORNE COFFIN 218 A8
Thorne Cross BA22 218 B7
Thorne Cross Way TA21 178 D8
Thorne Gdns BA21 218 C7
Thorne La
Wheddon Cross TA24 147 C8
Winsford TA24 147 C8
Yeovil BA21 218 C8
Thorne Pk TA8 104 B5
THORNE ST
MARGARET 179 D8
THORNEY 172 A1
Thorneymoor La TA10 172 A3
Thorney Rd TA12 185 B8
THORNFALCON 169 E2
Thornhill Dro TA12 173 A1
Thornhill Rd DT10 190 B4
Thorn La TA3 169 D2
Thornton Rd BA21 218 D7
Thornwell La BA9 216 D3
Thornwell Way BA9 216 C3
Thorny La BA21 187 E8
Thornymarsh La BA7 175 B8
THOULSTONE 121 F4
THREE ASHES
North Cadbury 175 C7
Oakhill 115 E1
Three Ashes DT8 199 D7
Three Ashes La TA11 157 B4
Three Corner Mead
BA21 218 C5
Three Gates Cross TA22 163 C6
Three Hill View BA6 206 E5
Three Horse Shoes Hill
TA5 152 C4
Three Oaks Cross TA19 183 C4
Three Queens' La BS1 227 B2
Three Ways Sch Lime Grove
Site BA2 45 B6
Threeways Sch Summerfield
Site BA1 27 D1
Three Wells Rd BS13 21 F4
Thrift Cl DT10 190 C4
Throgmorton Rd BS4 22 F8
Throop Rd BA8 176 F1
Thrubwell La BS40 37 B4
Thrupe La BA5 114 A2
Thrush Cl 4 BS22 49 E8
Thumb La BA4 158 E7
THURLBEAR 182 C8
Thurlbear CE Prim Sch
TA3 182 C8
Thurlestone BS14 23 A6
Thurlocks BA22 186 B6
THURLOXTON 153 D1
Thyme Cl BS20 2 F5
Thynne Cl BS27 90 B6
Tibbott Rd BS14 23 D5
Tibbott Wlk BS14 23 D5
Tichborne Rd BS23 30 E1
TICKENHAM 7 F4
Tickenham CE Prim Sch
BS21 7 F4
Tickenham Hill BS48 8 E4
Tickenham Rd BS21 7 A4
Tide Gr BS11 5 A8
Tides Reach TA24 125 C4
Tiffany Ct BS1 227 B1
Tiledown BS39 58 E1
Tiledown Cl BS39 58 F1
Tile Hill BA10 161 A7
Tile House Rd
East Huntspill TA7 137 B8
Mark TA9 106 C1
Tilery EX14 192 D3
Tilham St BA6 158 B6
Tilley Cl
Farmborough BA2 60 A5
Keynsham BS31 25 A2
Tilley La BA2 60 A5
Tilleys Dro BA5 138 F7
TILLWORTH 198 D3
Tilsey La TA4 150 C5
Tilton Ct 5 DT9 225 D3
TIMBERSCOMBE 130 C4
Timberscombe CE First Sch
TA24 130 B5
Timberscombe Way TA6 208 B4
Timberscombe Wlk BS14 23 C5
Timbers The BA3 97 B7
Timberyard TA7 137 F1
Timewell Hill EX16 164 C4
TIMSBURY 60 B1
TIMSBURY BOTTOM 60 A1
Timsbury Rd
Farmborough BA2 60 B5
High Littleton BS39 59 D1
Timsbury Village Workshops
BA2 59 F3
Tin Bridge Rdbt BA6 139 D3
Tinker's La
Compton Martin BS40 74 B7
Cucklington BA9 177 D7
Halse TA4 167 C6
Kilmersdon BA11 98 B1
Tinneys La DT9 225 E4
Tintagel Cl BS31 24 D4
Tintagel Rd BA21 218 D7
Tintern BA21 218 C6
TINTINHULL 186 C6
Tintinhull Gdn★ BA22 186 C6
Tintinhull Rd BA21 186 F5
Tipcote Hill 17 BA4 205 B6
Tipnoller Hill TA4 210 F7
Tippacott La EX35 122 A4
Tiptoft 3 TA14 185 F4
Tirley Way BS22 31 B2
Titan Barrow BA1 29 C2
Tithe Barn Cross EX15 179 D2
Tithe Ct BA20 218 D5
Tithe Mdw TA4 167 A7
Tithill La TA4 167 F7
Titlands La BA5 203 A7
Tiverton Gdns BS22 32 A2
Tiverton Rd
Bampton EX16 164 C1
2 Clevedon BS21 6 E1
TIVINGTON 129 F8
Tivington Cross TA24 129 F8
Tivoli Ho BS23 48 E8
Tivoli La BS23 48 E8
Toghill La BS30 12 A8
Tolbury La BA10 215 D6
Tolbury Mill BA10 215 E6
TOLLAND 150 E3
Tolland BS24 49 A2
Tolland Cross TA4 150 E3
Toll Bridge Rd BA1 28 E3
Tolley's La TA20 194 C3
Toll Gate TA4 210 C4
Toll House Rd 1 TA5 135 B2
Toll Rd
Porlock TA24 124 A3
Weston-Super-Mare BS23 66 F8
Toms Cl TA20 223 B3
Tomtit's La TA11 211 C3
TONE 222 A8
TONEDALE 222 B7
Tonedale Bsns Pk TA21 222 B7
Tonedale Ind Est TA21 222 B8
Tone Dr TA6 209 B3
Tone Gn TA4 167 E2
Tone Hill TA21 222 B8
Tone Rd BS21 6 D1
Toneway TA2 213 C6
Toose The BA21 218 C6
Top Hill BA4 142 F2
Top La
Gasper BA12 161 E4
Mells BA11 118 B6
Top Rd
Charlton Adam TA11 173 F7
Cheddar BS27 90 E5
Shipham BS25 70 F7
Westbury-sub-Mendip BA5 110 E6
Top St
Kingsdon TA11 173 D5
Pilton BA4 140 F3
Top Wood BA3 116 B7
Torbay Cl BA7 214 B5
Torbay Rd BA7 214 A5
Torbay Road Ind Est
BA7 214 A5
Torbay Villas BA7 214 A5
Tor Cl BS22 32 A2
Torhill La BA5 203 F4
Torhole Bottom BA3 94 A4
Tori Green 2 TA6 209 A1
Tormynton Rd BS22 31 E3
Torre Cider Farm★
TA23 131 E3
Torre Rocks TA23 131 E2
Torres Vedras Dr TA21 222 F7
Torre The BA21 218 C6
Torridge Mead TA1 213 D4
Torridge Rd BS31 25 A4
Torrington Ave BS4 22 F8
Torrington Cres BS22 32 A3
Tor St BA5 203 E4
Tor View
Cheddar BS27 90 C7
Woolavington TA7 136 E4
Tor View Ave BA6 206 D3
Tor Wood View BA5 203 E5
T'OTHER SIDE THE HILL 115 B7
Totnes Cl BS22 32 A2
Totney Dro BS28 137 E8
Totshill Dr BS13 22 E4
Totshill Gr BS13 22 E4
Tottenham Pl BS8 226 B3
Totterdown La
Pilton BA4 204 B1
Weston-Super-Mare BS24 49 A1
Totterdown Rd BS23 48 F4
Touches La TA20 223 E5
Touches Mdw TA20 223 E5
Touching End La SN14 13 F8
Touch La TA10 156 C1
Touchstone Cl TA20 223 B4
Touchstone La TA20 223 B4
Toulouse Rd 5 TA6 209 A1
TOULTON 152 A2
Tout Hill BA9 216 C3
Tout La BA22.TA11 174 A6
Tovey Cl BS22 31 E4
Tower Cl
Cheddar BS27 90 B6
Stoke St Michael BA3 116 A3
TOWERHEAD 51 D4
Towerhead Rd BS29 51 D3
Tower Hill
Bristol BS2 227 B3
Bruton BA10 215 D6
Holcombe Rogus TA21 178 D5
Horsington BA8 176 E2
Locking BS24 50 D4
Stogursey TA5 134 B5
Stoke St Michael BA3 116 A3
Williton TA4 202 E2
Tower Hill Rd TA18 224 B5
Tower House La BS48 9 A4
Tower La
Bristol BS1 227 A3
Taunton TA1 212 E4
Towerleaze BS9 5 D3
Tower Rd
Kilmington BA12 161 D6
Portishead BS20 2 A4
Stawell TA7 137 B1
Yeovil BA21 219 C8
Tower St
Bristol BS1 227 B2
Taunton TA1 212 E4
Tower The BS1 227 B2
Tower View
Frome BA11 119 F2
South Cheriton BA8 176 D3
Wanstrow BA4 142 E4
Tower Wlk BS23 30 D1
Town Barton BA2 81 F4
Town Cl
North Curry TA3 170 B4
Stogursey TA5 134 B6
Town End BA2 81 F4
Townend Villas TA14 185 F2
Town Farm TA3 170 B4
Townhall Bldgs BA5 203 E4
Town Hill EX36 162 C6
Town La BA4 205 C6
Town Marsh TA22 163 D7
Townrise 15 BA20 219 B4
TOWNSEND 92 D4
TOWNS END 77 E4
TOWN'S END 116 E3
Townsend
East Harptree BS40 75 A5
Ilminster TA19 221 D3
Marston Magna BA22 174 F1
Middlezoy TA7 155 C3
Montacute TA15 186 B3
Shepton Mallet BA4 205 B5
Westonzoyland TA7 154 F5
Williton TA4 202 E3
Townsend Cl
Bristol BS14 23 F5
Bruton BA10 215 F7
Townsend Cotts TA24 147 C5
Townsend Gn 10 BA8 190 A6
Townsend La
Chilton Polden TA7 137 B2
Emborough BA3 95 B2
Theale BS28 109 A2
Townsend Orch
Merriott TA16 195 F8
Street BA16 207 B5
Townsend Pk BA10 215 F7
Townsend Rd
Bristol BS14 23 F5
Minehead TA24 201 A6
Townsend Rise BA10 215 F7
Townsend Sh Pk BA4 205 B5
Townshend Rd BS22 32 B5
Town St BA4 205 B6
Town Tree Farm Nature
Trail★ TA12 185 C8
Town Tree La TA10, TA12 185 D8
TRACEBRIDGE 179 A8
Tracey Cl TA7 209 E8
Trackfordmoor Cross
TA22 163 B3
Tracy Cl BS14 22 F7
Trafalgar Rd BA1 27 B1
Traits La BA22 174 E4
Trajan's Way BA4 205 E5
Tramshed The BA1 228 C3
Transform Ind Est TA6 209 A6
Transom Ho BS1 227 B2
Transom Pl TA24 201 B7
Travers Cl BS4 22 D6
Trawden Cl BS23 31 A1
Treasure Ct TA8 85 A1
Treasurer's Ho★ TA12 185 E6
TREBLE'S HOLFORD 151 C4
TREBOROUGH 149 A7
Treborough Cl TA2 213 B8
Treefield Rd BS21 6 D2
Tregarth Rd BS3 11 F1
Tregelles Cl TA9 104 C4
Tregonwell Rd TA24 201 A7
Trelawn Cl BS22 32 D2
Trelissick Gdns 3 BS22 49 F8
Trellech Ct 3 BA21 218 C6
Tremes Cl SN14 13 F8
Tremlett Mews 3 BS22 32 B4
Trenchard Rd
Locking BS24 50 D4
Saltford BS31 25 D3
Trenchard St BS1 226 C3
Trendle La
Bicknoller TA4 132 F2
Stoney Stoke BA9 160 E3
Trendle Rd TA1 212 B1
Trendle St DT9 225 D3
Trendlewood Way BS48 9 A1
Trenleigh Dr BS22 32 A2
TRENT 187 F5
Trent Cl BA21 219 E8
Trent Ct TA1 213 D4
Trent Gr BS31 25 A4
Trent Mdw TA1 213 E4
Trent Path La DT9 225 A5
Trent Youngs CE Prim Sch
DT9 187 F5
Tresco Spinney BA21 218 C6
Trescothick Cl BS31 24 E6
Trevanna Rd BS3 11 F1
Trevelyan Rd BS23 48 F7
Trevett Rd TA1 212 C2
Trevithick Cl BA11 120 C6
Trevor Rd TA6 209 C6
Trevor Smith Pl TA1 213 A3
Trewartha Cl BS23 48 F8
Trewartha Pk BS23 48 F8
Trewint Gdns BS4 22 F8
Triangle Ct 2 BA2 44 D5
Triangle Ctr The BS21 6 D3
Triangle E BA2 44 D5
Triangle N BA2 44 D5
Triangle S BS8 226 B3
Triangle The
Castle Cary BA7 214 C5
Clevedon BS21 6 D3
North Curry TA3 170 A4
Paulton BS39 77 E6
Portishead BS20 2 B5
Somerton TA11 211 D4
Wrington BS40 35 D2
Triangle Villas 1 BA2 44 D5
Triangle W
Bath BA2 44 D5
Bristol BS8 226 B3
Tribunal & Lake Village
Mus★ BA6 206 D4
Trickey Warren La TA3 181 C1
Trim Bridge 3 BA1 228 B2
Trim St BA1 228 B2
Trinder Rd BS20 4 B4
Trindlewell La TA18 196 C4
TRINITY 119 E5
Trinity Bsns Ctr TA1 213 A3
Trinity CE Fst Sch BA11 119 C4
Trinity Cl
Bath BA1 228 B2
Blackford BS28 107 D4
Burnham-on-S TA8 85 A1
Wellington TA21 222 C5
Trinity Coll BS9 5 E4
Trinity Ct
Bridgwater TA6 208 F6
Nailsea BS48 8 C1
13 Yeovil BA20 219 B4
Trinity Gate TA1 213 A3
Trinity Mews 15 BS2 227 C3
Trinity Pl
3 Bristol BS8 226 A2
4 Weston-Super-Mare
BS23 30 C1
Trinity Prim Sch BS20 2 F5
Trinity Rd
Bath BA2 45 B2
Nailsea BS48 8 D1
Taunton TA1 213 B3
Weston-Super-Mare BS23 30 C1
Trinity Rise TA8 85 A1
Trinity Row
Frome BA11 119 E5
Wellington TA21 222 C5
Trinity St
Bath BA1 228 B2
Frome BA11 119 E5
Taunton TA1 213 B3
Trinity Way
Bridgwater TA6 208 E6
Minehead TA24 201 B7

Trinity Wlk
Bristol BS2 227 C3
Frome BA11 119 E5
Trin Mills BS1 227 A1
Tripps Cnr BS49 34 D7
Tripps Dro BA5 139 A6
Tripps Row BS41 11 A1
TRISCOMBE 151 D6
Triscombe Ave TA6 208 D4
Triscombe Gate TA24 147 D8
Triscombe Ho TA4 151 D5
Triscombe Rd TA2 212 E8
Tristram Dr TA3 169 D4
Tropical Bird Garden★ TA8 47 F2
Tropiquaria Zoo★ TA23 131 F4
Trossachs Dr BA2 45 D8
Trotts La TA19 183 B2
Trottsway Cross TA24 129 C2
TROWBRIDGE 83 F7
Trowbridge Cl TA9 104 D4
Trowell La TA4 165 E4
Trow La BA12 144 C2
Truckwell La TA4 150 D4
TRUDOXHILL 143 C6
TRULL 168 D1
Trull CE Prim Sch TA3 168 D1
Trull Green Dr TA3 168 D1
Trull Rd TA1 212 E2
Trumps Cross EX16 178 E3
Truro Cl TA8 104 C7
Truro Rd BS48 9 A1
Trym Bank BS9 5 D7
Trym Cross Rd BS9 5 C5
Trymleaze BS9 5 C5
Trym Side BS9 5 C5
Trymwood Par BS9 5 D6
Tucker's Cross DT9 188 A4
Tuckers La BA7 214 B7
Tucker's La
Baltonsborough BA6 157 F6
Ubley BS40 73 E8
Tucker's Moor Cross EX16 162 F3
Tucker St BA5 203 C4
TUCKERTON 169 F8
Tuckerton La TA7 153 F1
TUCKING MILL 63 C8
Tuckingmill La BS39 41 E5
Tuckmarsh La BA11 143 E7
Tuckmill BS21 6 B1
Tudballs TA24 128 D1
Tuddington Gdns BA5 203 B4
TUDHAY 198 C3
Tudor Ct
Chard TA20 223 C6
Yeovil BA20 219 A4
Tudor Rd
Portishead BS20 2 E4
Weston-Super-Mare BS22 32 A4
Tudor Way TA6 209 A1
Tudway Cl BA5 203 C4
Tufton Ave BS11 5 A8
Tugela Rd BS13 21 F7
Tuggy's La BA2 63 E1
Tulip Tree Rd TA6 209 E5
Tulse Hill BA12 161 F2
Tunbridge Cl BS40 39 B2
Tunbridge Rd BS40 39 B2
Tuncombe La TA18 195 D4
Tundra Walk 5 TA6 154 A5
TUNLEY 61 B3
Tunley Hill BA2 60 E2
Tunley Rd BA2, BA3 61 D5
Tunnel La BA3 96 F5
Tunnell La 14 TA14 185 F4
Tunnel The TA24 128 B2
Tunscombe La BA4 142 D8
Tunstall Cl BS9 5 E4
Turin Path 4 TA6 208 E7
Turkey Ct 5 TA1 212 E3
TURLEIGH 64 F6
Turnbury Ave BS48 9 A1
Turnbury Cl BS22 31 F3
Turner Cl
Bridgwater TA6 209 A4
Keynsham BS31 25 A5
Turner Ct
Wells BA5 203 D3
Weston-Super-Mare BS22 31 F3
Turner Rd TA2 212 E7
Turner's Barn La BA20 218 F2
Turner's Court La BA3 114 D8
Turner's La DT6 199 B2
Turner's Twr BA3 80 A1
Turner Way BS21 6 B1
Turn Hill TA10 155 F2
Turnhill Rd TA10 156 A2
Turnock Gdns BS24 50 D8
Turnpike
Milverton TA4 167 A4
Sampford Peverell EX16 178 C1
Turnpike Cl TA18 196 B3
Turnpike Cnr BA3 95 B8
Turnpike Cross TA14 185 E2
Turnpike Cvn Pk TA20 193 A4
Turnpike Gn TA18 196 B3
Turnpike La BA4 142 B6
Turnpike Rd
Cross BS26 69 E1
Shipham BS25 70 E8
Turnstone 3 BS20 2 F6
Turstin Rd BA6 206 F6
Turtlegate Ave BS13 21 E4
Turtlegate Wlk BS13 21 E4
Tut Hill DT9 189 C1
Tutton Way BS21 6 D1
Tuttors Hill BS27 71 C1
Tuxwell La TA5 152 C8
Tweed Rd BS21 6 C1
Tweed Rd Ind Est 2 BS21 6 C1
Tweentown BS27 90 B8
Twelve Acre Post TA22 163 A4
TWERTON 44 A5
Twerton Farm Cl 2 BA2 44 B6
Twerton Inf Sch BA2 44 A5
Twinell La TA5 152 D7
Twines Cl BA22 175 A5
Twinhoe La BA2 62 E2
Twistgates La EX14 192 A4
Twitchen Ball Cnr EX36 145 G3
Twitchens La BS27 90 F2
Two Acres Cvn Pk BS21 1 B1
Two Acres Rd BS14 23 A7
Two Ash Hill TA20 193 F1
Two Ash La TA20 194 A1
Two Elms BA21 187 E8
Two Tower La BA22 219 B2
Two Trees BS40 72 E8
Twyford Pl TA21 222 D5
Tydeman Rd BS20 2 F5
Tyler Gn 2 BS22 32 B4
Tylers End TA9 104 F3
Tyler's La TA4 167 A7
Tyler Way TA9 104 D3
Tyndall Ave BS8 226 C4
Tyndall Ho 5 BS2 227 C3
TYNDALL'S PARK 226 C4
Tyndalls Park Mews BS2 226 C4
Tyndall's Park Rd BS8 226 C4
Tyne Gr BS20 2 F6
Tyne Pk TA1 213 D3
TYNING
Radstock 79 B3
Timsbury 60 A2
Tyning Cl BS14 23 A7
Tyning Cotts BA3 116 C7
Tyning End BA2 45 B5
Tyning Hill
Hemington BA3 99 C8
Radstock BA3 79 B3
Tyning La BA1 28 B1
Tyning Pl BA2 45 C2
Tyning Rd
Bathampton BA2 28 F2
Bath BA2 45 C2
Peasedown St John BA2 79 D7
Saltford BS31 25 E2
Winsley BA15 64 E7
Tynings BS39 58 D3
Tynings La BA5 203 C8
Tynings Mews BS23 48 E4
Tynings Rd BA16 207 B4
Tynings The
Clevedon BS21 6 A1
Portishead BS20 1 F1
Tynings Way
Clutton BS39 58 E3
Westwood BA15 64 F3
Tyning Terr 15 BA1 28 A1
Tyning The
Bath BA2 45 B5
Freshford BA3 64 B4
Tynte Ave BS13 22 E3
Tynte Rd TA6 209 D6
Tyntesfield Rd BS13 22 A8
Tyrone Wlk BS4 22 E8
TYTHERINGTON 143 E8
Tytherington La BA11 143 E8
TYTHERLEIGH 198 C6
Tythe St BA6 206 E3
Tythings Com Ctr The BA9 216 C3
Tythings Ct TA24 200 F7
Tything Way BA9 216 D3

U

UBLEY 55 E1
Ubley CE Prim Sch BS40 55 D1
Ubley Dro BS40 73 B7
UBLEY SIDELING 73 D8
UDLEY 35 C4
ULLCOMBE 192 A4
Ullcombe La EX14 191 F4
Ullswater Cl BS23 49 A4
Ullswater Dr BA1 28 A2
Uncombe Cl BS48 19 D7
Underbanks BS20 4 D4
Underdown BA21 219 F5
Underdown Ho BS1 227 A1
Underdown Hollow
Bradford Abbas DT9 187 E2
Yeovil BA21 219 F4
Underdown La DT9 225 F6
Underhill
Gurney Slade BA3 114 E7
Hambridge TA10 184 D8
Penselwood BA9 161 D1
Underhill Ave BA3 77 F2
Underhill Cl BA16 207 B5
Underhill Dr BS23 48 D1
Underhill La
Midsomer Norton BA3 77 F2
Staple Fitzpaine TA3 182 B4
Underhill Rd BA16 207 B5
Under Knoll BA2 79 E8
Under La BS40 36 D1
Underleaf Way BA2 79 D7
Undertown BS40 74 A7
Undertown La BS40 74 A7
Under Way TA20 193 D6
Underwood Ave BS22 31 B1
Underwood Bsns Pk BA5 203 B6
Underwood End BS25 52 A4
Underwood La TA10 172 C8
Underwood Rd
Glastonbury BA6 206 D6
Kingsdon TA11 173 D5
Portishead BS20 2 C3
Union Dro TA10 172 B6
Union La TA4 202 E4
Union Pas BA1 228 C2
Union Pl BS23 48 D7
Union St
Bath BA1 228 C2
Bridgwater TA6 209 B6
Bristol BS1 227 B3
Cheddar BS27 90 B7
Dulverton TA22 163 D6
Nailsea BS48 8 C1
Wells BA5 203 D4
Weston-Super-Mare BS23 48 D7
Yeovil BA20 219 B4
Unite Ho BS1 226 C2
Unity Ct BS31 25 A5
Unity Rd BS31 25 A6
Unity St BS1 226 C2
University Cl BS9 5 F4
University of Bristol Dorothy Hodgkin Bldg BS1 227 A4
University Rd BS8 226 C3
University Wlk BS8 226 C3
Univ of Bath BA2 45 E5
Univ of Bristol BS8 226 C3
Univ of Bristol Dept of Ed BS8 226 C3
Univ of Bristol Langford House Sch of Veterinary Science BS40 53 B6
Univ of Bristol Sch of Veterinary Science BS2 226 C4
Univ of the West of England BS3 11 E4
Upcot Cres TA1 212 B2
UPCOTT 168 B3
Upcott La
Bicknoller TA4 132 F1
Winsford TA24 147 D7
Upcott Rd TA1, TA4 168 B3
UPHILL 48 C2
Uphill Ct BS23 48 D2
Uphill Dr BA1 28 B1
Uphill Farm Cvn Pk BS23 48 E1
Uphill Prim Sch BS23 48 D2
Uphill Rd N BS23 48 D4
Uphill Rd S BS23 48 D2
Uphills BA10 215 E7
Uphill Way BS23 48 D1
Upjohn Cres BS13 22 D3
Uplands
Bratton Seymour BA9 176 B8
Mark TA9 106 E4
Uplands Cl BA2 63 F7
Uplands Dr BS31 25 F2
Uplands Rd BS31 25 F2
Uplands Terr BA22 197 B8
Uplands The BS48 18 C8
UPLOWMAN 178 B2
Uplowman CE Prim Sch EX16 178 B2
UP MUDFORD 187 D5
UPOTTERY 191 F2
Upottery Prim Sch EX14 191 F2
Upper Belgrave Rd BS8 5 F1
UPPER BENTER 115 C7
Upper Berkeley Pl BS8 226 B3
Upper Bloomfield Rd BA2 44 D1
Upper Borough Walls BA1 228 C2
Upper Breach BA5 113 A2
Upper Bristol Rd
Bath BA1 44 D7
Clutton BS39 58 D3
Weston-Super-Mare BS22 31 B1
Upper Byron Pl BS8 226 B3
Upper Camden Pl BA1 228 C4
UPPER CHEDDON 168 F7
Upper Church La
Bristol BS2 226 C3
Hutton BS24 49 D2
Upper Church Rd BS23 30 D1
Upper Church St BA1 228 B3
UPPER COXLEY 139 F6
Upper Crannel Dro BA6 139 C4
Upper Ct BA3 97 C8
Upper East Hayes BA1 28 B1
Upper Farm Cl BA2 81 F4
Upper Flowerfield BA11 143 B7
Upper Furlong BA2 60 B3
UPPER GODNEY 139 A6
Upper Green La BS40 55 B7
Upper Hedgemead Rd BA1 228 B4
Upper High St
Castle Cary BA7 214 C5
Taunton TA1 212 F3
Upper Holway Rd TA1 213 C2
Upper Kewstoke Rd BS23 30 B1
Upper Lambridge St BA1 28 C2
UPPER LANGFORD 53 C3
UPPER LANGRIDGE 27 B7
Upper Lansdown Mews BA1 27 F1
UPPER LITTLETON 38 B6
Upper Maudlin St BS2 227 A3
Upper Merrifield BA3 116 E8
Upper Merryfield BA3 97 E1
UPPER MILTON 203 D7
Upper Mount Pleasant BA3 64 A4
Upper Myrtle Hill BS20 4 C4
Upper New Rd BS27 90 A8
Upper North St BS27 90 B8
Upper Oldfield Pk BA2 228 A1
Upper Pitching BA3 96 D5
UPPER RADFORD 78 B8
Upper Rd BS39 75 E6
Upper Stanton BS39 40 A2
UPPER STANTON DREW 40 B2
Upper Strode BS40 55 F7
UPPER SWAINSWICK 28 B5
Upper Town La BS40 37 C8
UPPER VOBSTER 117 D8
Upper Wells St BS1 226 C2
UPPER WESTHOLME 140 D4
UPPER WESTON 27 A3
UPPER WESTWOOD 64 E4
Upper Whatcombe BA11 119 E6
Upper Wood St TA1 212 E4
Upper York St BS2 227 B4
UPPOTERY 191 F2
UPTON
Langport 172 D5
Skilgate 164 F8
Upton BS24 49 A2
UPTON CHEYNEY 26 B8
Upton Cotts BS41 38 F8
Upton La
Dundry BS41 39 A8
Seavington St Michael TA19 184 E2
UPTON NOBLE 142 F2
Upton Noble CE Prim Sch BA4 142 F2
Urchinwood La BS49 34 F4
URGASHAY 174 C3

V

VAGG 186 F5
Vagg Hill BA22 186 E5
Vagg La BA22 186 F5
Vagg Pk BA22 186 F5
Valda Rd BS22 31 C2
Vale Cl TA18 224 C4
Vale Cres BS22 32 C2
Vale Ct BS8 226 A4
Vale End BS48 8 D1
Vale La BS3 22 C8
Vale Mill Way BS24 49 F8
Valentine Cl BS14 23 B5
Valentines TA22 163 E6
Vale Rd
Stalbridge DT10 190 B4
Yeovil BA21 219 E6
Valerian Cl BS11 4 F6
Vale St BA8 190 A6
Valetta Cl BS23 48 F3
Valetta Pl TA6 208 F5
Vale View
Aller TA10 171 E8
Henstridge BA8 190 A7
Radstock BA3 79 A2
Wincanton BA9 216 F5
Vale View Cotts TA4 151 E4
Vale View Gdns BA9 216 C2
Vale View Pl 16 BA1 28 B1
Vale View Terr BA1 28 F3
Valley Cl
6 Nailsea BS48 8 E2
Wells BA5 203 C4
Yeovil BA21 219 B6
Valley Ct BS20 1 E3
Valley Gdns BS48 8 E2
Valley Line Ind Pk BS27 90 A7
Valley Rd
Bristol, Bedminster Down BS13 22 A8
Clevedon BS21 6 F5
Crewkerne TA18 224 C4
Leigh Woods BS8 11 C7
Portishead BS20 2 A2
Taunton TA1 213 C5
Valley View
8 Axminster EX13 198 A1
Chilcompton BA3 96 D3
Clutton BS39 58 E3
Frome BA11 119 D6
Millmoor EX15 179 E1
Morebath EX16 164 B3
Valley View Cl BA1 28 B3
Valley View Rd
Bath BA1 28 C3
Paulton BS39 77 E6
Valley Way Rd BS48 8 E3
Valley Wlk BA3 78 B2
Vallis Ct 7 BA11 119 E5
Vallis Fst Sch BA11 119 E5
Vallis Rd BA11 119 D5
Vallis Trad Est BA11 119 D5
Vallis Way BA11 119 E5
Van Diemen's La BA1 27 F2
Vandyck Ave BS31 24 F6
Vane St 7 BA2 45 B7
Vanguard Ct BA22 218 A5
Varsity Way BS24 50 B6
Vaughan Ct BA5 203 B4
Veales DT10 189 F2
Veale The BS24 67 C6
Veal La
Horrington BA5 113 B2
Walton BA16 156 E6
Vedal Dro TA10 172 D4
Vee La BS40 37 D8
Vellore La BA2 45 C7
Vellow Rd TA4 150 D8
Vellow Wood La TA4 132 D1
Vemplett's Cross TA23 131 E1
Venford Hill
East Anstey TA22 162 E8
Hawkridge TA22 146 D1
Venland Bsns Pk TA24 201 B6
Venland Ind Pk TA24 201 A6
Venn Cl TA4 167 E6
Venn Cross TA4 165 D3
Venn Hill DT6, TA20 199 C6
Venniford Cross TA24 129 F8
Vennland Way TA24 201 A6
Venns Cl BS27 90 B7
Venns Gate BS27 71 A1
Venture 7 BA20 218 C3
Venture 20 BA20 218 C3
Venture Eleven The TA2 213 B6
Venture Way TA2 213 B6
Venus La BS39 58 E3
Venus St BS49 34 E2
Vera St TA2 212 F7
Verbena Way BS22 32 A1
Verdun Terr TA23 131 E4
Vereland Rd BS24 49 E3
Verlands BS49 34 E5
Vernal La BA11 119 D6
Vernalls Rd DT9 225 D5
Vernham Gr BA2 44 C1
Vernhamwood Cl BA2 44 C1
Vernon Cl BS31 25 D3
Vernon La BS26 69 B3
Vernon Pk BA2 44 C6
Vernon Terr BA2 44 C6
Vernslade BA1 27 A2
Verriers 10 TA6 153 E3
VERRINGTON 216 A5
Verrington Hospl BA9 216 B4
Verrington La BA9 216 B5
Verrington Park Rd BA9 216 B4
Vesey's Hole Hill SP8 177 E4
Vestry Cl BA16 207 C5
Vestry Ct 1 BA16 207 C5
Vestry Rd BA16 207 C5
Vian End BS22 31 F4
Vicarage Cl
Chard TA20 223 C3
Coxley BA5 139 E6
Creech St Michael TA3 169 D4
8 Frome BA11 119 F4
Stogursey TA5 134 C6
Weston-Super-Mare BS22 32 A3
Westonzoyland TA7 154 F5
Vicarage Ct
Burnham-on-S TA8 104 A7
Timberscombe TA24 130 B5
Vicarage Gdns BA2 79 B7
Vicarage Hill
Combe St Nicholas TA20 193 D6
Dulverton TA22 163 D6
Vicarage La
Barrow Gurney BS48 20 C6
Compton Bishop BS26 69 B3
Compton Dando BS39 41 D6
Creech St Michael TA3 169 D4
Draycott BS27 90 F3
Mark TA9 106 E5
Norton St Philip BA2 81 E4
Pawlett TA6 135 F5
Shapwick TA7 137 F1
7 Wookey BA5 139 D8
Vicarage Lawns TA3 169 D4
Vicarage Rd
Bristol, Bishopsworth BS13 22 A6
Carhampton TA24 131 B5
Leigh Woods BS8 11 D6
Minehead TA24 200 F8
Stogursey TA5 134 C6
Wookey BA5 139 E8
Woolavington TA7 136 E4
Vicarage St
Burnham-on-S TA8 104 A7
Frome BA11 119 F4
Tintinhull BA22 186 C6
6 Yeovil BA20 219 B4
Vicarage Wlk BA20 219 B5
Vicar's Cl BA5 203 E5
Vicars La TA6 208 D5
Vicar's La TA12 184 F7
Vickery Cl
Bridgwater TA6 208 D3
Curry Rivel TA10 171 D4
Victoria Art Gall The★ BA2 228 C2
Victoria Ave TA20 223 D4
Victoria Bldgs
Bath BA2 44 D6
Glastonbury BA6 206 E4
Victoria Bridge Ct BA1 228 A3
Victoria Bridge Rd BA1, BA2 228 A2
Victoria Bsns Pk TA20 223 D4
Victoria Cl
Bath BA2 44 C5
Portishead BS20 2 D5
Yeovil BA21 219 D6
Victoria Cotts BA2 62 F7
Victoria Ct
Castle Cary BA7 214 B5
Chard TA20 223 D4
Frome BA11 120 A4
Ilminster TA19 221 C4
Portishead BS20 2 D5
Victoria Gate TA1 213 B4
Victoria Gdns
Batheaston BA1 28 F3
Castle Cary BA7 214 B6

Victoria Gdns *continued*
15 Henstridge BA8 190 A6
Victoria Gr BA4 205 D5
Victoria Ho
Bath BA1 44 D8
Keynsham BS31 24 F4
Victoria Hospl BA11 119 E4
Victoria Jubilee Homes
BS40 53 C6
Victoria La BA4 141 E1
Victoria Lodge BS22 31 E2
Victoria Mews BA7 214 B5
VICTORIA PARK 226 B3
Victoria Park Bsns Ctr
BA1 44 D7
Victoria Pk
Castle Cary BA7 214 B5
Weston-Super-Mare BS23 30 D1
Victoria Pl
Bath, Combe Down BA2 45 C1
2 Bath, Lambridge BA1 28 C1
Chardstock EX13 198 A7
Highbridge TA9 104 D3
Paulton BS39 77 D5
Weston-Super-Mare BS23 48 D8
Victoria Quadrant BS23 48 E8
Victoria Rd
Avonmouth BS11 4 B7
Bath BA2 44 D6
Bridgwater TA6 208 E5
Castle Cary BA7 214 B5
Clevedon BS21 6 C3
Frome BA11 120 A4
Minehead TA24 201 A5
Saltford BS31 25 D3
Yeovil BA21 219 D6
Victoria Sh Mews TA18 224 C6
Victoria Sq
Bristol BS8 226 A3
Crewkerne TA18 224 B6
Evercreech BA4 141 E1
Portishead BS20 2 D5
Weston-Super-Mare BS23 48 D7
Victoria St
Bristol BS1 227 B2
Burnham-on-S TA8 104 A7
Taunton TA1 213 B4
Wellington TA21 222 D6
Victoria Terr
Bath BA2 44 D6
11 Bristol, Clifton BS8 11 F6
14 Henstridge BA8 190 A6
Paulton BS39 77 E6
Victoria Way TA5 152 E7
Victory Rd TA2 213 A7
Vienna Way 4 TA6 154 A5
Vigor Rd BS13 22 B5
Viking Cl TA23 202 D7
Vilberie Cl TA2 212 A7
Village Rd TA3 182 F6
Villa Rosa 16 BS23 30 C1
Villes La TA24 124 A4
Villice La BS40 74 A7
Vincent Cl TA8 104 C7
Vincent Pl BA20 219 B5
Vincents Cl DT9 189 A1
Vincent St 5 BA20 219 B5
Vine Gdns
Frome BA11 119 F6
Weston-Super-Mare BS22 32 A2
Vine Gr BA8 176 E1
Vine House Gdns TA20 223 C3
Vinery The BS25 70 A7
Vine St BA8 176 E1
Vineyards BA1 228 C3
Viney La EX14 191 F1
Viney St TA1 213 B3
Viney's Yd BA10 215 F6
Vining's Hill BA4 142 D1
Vinney La BA11 143 F8
Violet La DT9 176 A2
Virginia Cl 1 BA8 190 A6
Virginia Orch TA3 169 C3
Viscount Sq TA6 208 E7
Vivary Ct TA1 212 E3
Vivary Gate TA1 212 F3
Vivary Hts TA1 212 E2
Vivary Rd TA1 212 E3
Vivien Ave BA3 78 A2
Vixen Cl BA22 174 A3
VOBSTER 117 C7
Vobster Cross BA3 117 D7
Vobster Hill BA3 117 D7
VOLE 106 B8
Vole Rd
Brent Knoll TA9 86 D1
Mark TA9 106 B7
Volis Cross TA5 152 F1
Volis Hill TA2 168 F8
Vowell Cl BS13 22 B4
Vowles Cl BS48 9 A3
VOXMOOR 222 F1
Vulcan Ho BA2 228 C3
Vulcan Rd TA24 201 B6
Vynes Cl BS48 9 A1
Vynes Ind Est BS48 9 A3
Vynes Way BS48 9 A1
Vyvyan Rd BS8 226 A3
Vyvyan Terr BS8 226 A3

W

WADBROOK 198 C4
Wadbrook Cross EX13 198 C4
WADBURY 118 D7
WADDICOMBE 162 E6
Wade Cl TA7 154 E6
WADEFORD 193 D5
Wadeford Hill TA20 193 D5
Wade St BS2 227 C3
Wadham Cl
Bridgwater TA6 209 D6
Ilminster TA19 221 A4
Wadham Cross
Knowstone EX36 162 A2
West Anstey EX36 162 A4
Wadham Hill EX36 162 A2
Wadham's Almshouses
TA19 183 E4
Wadham Sch TA18 224 D7
Wadham St BS23 48 D8
WAGG 172 B5
Wagg Dro TA10 172 B5
WAGGS PLOT 198 B4
Waggs Plot EX13 198 B4
Wagon And Horses Hill
BA4 141 E8
Wagtail Cres BS20 3 A6
Wagtail Gdns BS22 49 E8
Wains Cl 3 BS21 6 C2
Wainwright Cl 5 BS22 32 B4
Wainwright Ct BA4 205 B4
Wainwright Dr BA11 120 C7
Waits Cl BS29 50 F3
Wakedean Gdns BS49 17 A1
WALCOMBE 203 E7
Walcombe La BA5 203 E6
Walcot Bldgs
Bath BA1 45 B8
Bath BA1 228 C4
Walcot CE Inf Sch BA1 228 C4
Walcot Ct BA1 228 C4
Walcot Gate BA1 228 C4
Walcot Ho BA1 228 C4
Walcot Par BA1 228 C4
Walcot St BA1 228 C3
Walcot Terr BA1 228 C4
Waldegrave Rd BA1 27 E1
Waldegrave Terr BA3 79 A3
Walden Rd BS31 25 A4
Waldock Barton TA13 220 D4
Waldron's Cross TA21 165 E1
WALES 174 E3
Wales La BA22 174 E3
WALFORD 169 D7
Walford Ave BS22 32 C3
Walford Cross Roads
TA2 169 D7
Walker Rd BA11 120 A3
Walkers Dr BS24 49 F7
Walkers Gate TA21 222 D5
Walker St BS2 226 C4
Walk La TA13 184 F1
WALLACE 74 E3
Wallace La BS40 74 E3
Wallace Rd BA1 28 B1
Wallace Wells Rd TA8 104 D5
Wallbridge BA11 120 B4
Wallbridge Ave BA11 120 A4
Wallbridge Gdns BA11 120 A4
Wallbridge Ho BA11 120 A4
Wallbridge Ind Est BA11 120 B4
Wall Ditch La TA16 196 A8
Wallenge Cl BS39 77 F6
Wallenge Dr BS39 77 F6
Walley La BS40 57 B7
Wall Gn BS26 70 C1
Wallingford Rd BS4 22 D7
Wallington Way BA11 119 D6
Walliscote Grove Rd 11
BS23 48 E7
Walliscote Prim Sch BS23 48 E7
Walliscote Rd BS23 48 D6
Walliscote Rd S BS23 48 D4
WALL MEAD 60 C4
Walls La BS28 108 B8
Walls The TA7 137 C2
Wall The TA9 106 D5
Wally Court Rd BS40 56 E8
Walmsley Terr 4 BA1 28 B1
Walnut Bldgs BA3 79 A3
Walnut Cl
Axbridge BS26 70 B1
Cheddar BS27 90 B7
Easton-in-G BS20 4 A3
Keynsham BS31 24 C4
Nailsea BS48 18 E8
Puriton TA7 136 C4
Rode BA11 101 E8
Taunton TA1 212 B4
Weston-Super-Mare BS24 49 B2
Walnut Dr
Bath BA2 44 E4
Bridgwater TA6 209 D3
Somerton TA11 211 D4
Walnut Gr BA4 205 C4
Walnut La TA7 136 F3
Walnut Rd TA10 172 A6
Walnuts The TA7 137 B2
Walnut Tree Cl
Ubley BS40 55 D1
Wells BA5 203 C5
Walnut Tree Cnr TA23 131 F4
Walnut Tree Ct BS49 34 D4
Walnut Tree Dr TA24 131 A5
Walnut Wlk
Bristol BS13 22 A6
Walnut Wlk *continued*
Frome BA11 120 B7
Keynsham BS31 24 C4
WALPOLE 136 B4
Walridge Cross TA4 166 A4
Walrond Ct TA19 221 B3
Walrond's Pk TA3 184 B7
WALROW 105 C2
Walrow TA9 104 E3
Walrow Ind Est TA9 104 F2
Walrow Terr TA9 104 E3
Walscombe Cl 1 TA14 185 F4
Walsh Ave BS14 23 A7
Walsh Cl BS24 49 B2
Waltham End BS24 50 A8
WALTON 156 E7
Walton BS24 49 A2
Walton Bay House Park
Homes BS21 1 B1
Walton CE Prim Sch
BA16 156 E7
Walton Cl
Bridgwater TA6 209 D5
Keynsham BS31 24 D4
Walton Cres BS40 37 F8
Walton Cross BS21 7 B7
Walton Ct TA24 201 A7
Walton Dro BA16 156 D5
WALTON IN GORDANO 7 B7
Walton Rd
Bristol BS11 4 D6
Clevedon BS21 6 F4
WALTON ST MARY 6 E5
Walton St
Portishead BS21 1 A1
Walton in G BS21 7 A8
Walwyn Cl BA2 44 A6
Walwyn Gdns BS13 22 C3
WAMBROOK 193 C3
Wambrook Cl TA1 212 E1
Wansbeck Gn TA1 213 D3
Wansbeck Rd BS31 25 A4
Wansbrough Rd BS22 32 B4
Wansdyke Bsns Ctr BA2 44 D4
Wansdyke Ct BS14 23 B5
Wansdyke Prim Sch BS14 22 F4
Wansdyke Rd BA2 44 D1
Wansdyke Sch BA2 62 E8
Wansdyke Workshops
Keynsham BS31 25 A6
Peasedown St John BA2 79 D6
WANSTROW 142 F4
Wapping Rd BS1 227 A1
Warden Rd TA24 200 F6
Ward La TA7 154 E8
Wardleworth Way TA21 222 C7
Wardour Rd BS4 22 D8
Wareham Cl BS48 8 D1
Wareham Cross EX13 198 E1
Wareham Rd EX13 198 E2
Wares La TA6 208 D6
Waring Ho BS1 227 A1
WARLEIGH 46 C6
Warleigh Cl BA11 119 D4
Warleigh Dr BA1 29 A3
Warleigh La BA1 46 C5
Warleys La BS24 32 C1
Warman Cl BS14 23 F6
Warman Rd BS14 23 F6
War Memorial Hospl
TA8 104 B7
Warmington Rd BS14 23 C8
Warminster Rd
Beckington BA11 101 E4
Claverton BA2, BA3 46 B5
Frome BA11 120 B4
Warne Pk BS23 49 A6
Warner Cl BS49 35 A7
Warne Rd BS23 49 A6
Warren Cl
Bridgwater TA6 208 F6
Bruton BA10 215 E6
Charlton Horethorne DT9 176 A2
Hutton BS24 49 D2
Warren Farm Cvn Pk & Camp
Site TA8 65 F5
Warren Gdns BS14 23 F5
Warren La BS41 20 E8
Warren Rd
Brean TA8 65 F6
Minehead TA24 201 B7
Warren's Cl BS27 71 B1
Warrens Hill BS27 71 B1
Warrens Hill Rd BS27 71 D4
Warren St TA21 222 A4
Warrens Way BA5 113 A1
Warren The BA16 207 A5
Warres Rd TA2 213 C8
Warrilow Cl BS22 32 B5
Warrior Ave BA22 218 B6
Warry Cl BS48 9 B2
Warth La BS22 32 A8
Warwick Ave TA6 209 C3
Warwick Cl BS22 49 C8
Warwick Gdns
Burnham-on-S TA8 85 B1
Clutton BS39 58 D3
Taunton TA1 213 C2
Warwick Rd
3 Bath BA1 44 B7
Keynsham BS31 24 D4
Taunton TA2 213 A8
WASHBROOK 89 A1
Washcross La TA19 184 E3
WASHFORD 131 F4
Washford Cross TA23 131 F3
Washford Hill TA23 202 A5
Washford Sta TA23 131 E4
Washingpool DT9 188 E7
Washing Pound La
Bristol BS14 23 B4
Nailsea BS48 8 B4
Washington Gdns TA6 208 E5
Washington Terr TA20 223 B5
Wash La TA15 186 B4
Washpool La BA2 43 F2
Wassail Cl 5 TA24 131 A5
Wassail View TA2 168 B4
WATCHET 202 B6
Watchet Boat Mus*
TA23 202 C7
Watchet Sta TA23 202 C7
WATCHFIELD 105 D2
Watch House Pl BS20 2 E7
Watch House Rd BS20 4 D4
Watchill Ave BS13 21 F6
Watchill Cl BS13 21 F6
Watchwell Dro BA6 157 D7
Waterbridge Rd BS13 21 F4
Watercombe Hts BA20 218 D2
Watercombe La
Yeovil BA20 218 C2
Yeovil, Preston Plucknett
BA20 218 D5
Watercombe Pk BA20 218 D3
Watercress Cl BS48 9 B2
Waterfield Cl TA1 212 B3
Waterfield Dr TA1 212 B3
Waterford Beck BA14 83 F6
Waterford Cl TA6 209 A2
Waterford Pk BA3 78 E1
Waterfront Ho BA2 228 B1
WATERGORE 220 B2
Water Hill TA4 150 F7
Waterhouse La BA2 63 F8
Water La
Bristol BS1 227 B2
Butleigh BA6 157 E4
Charlton Horethorne DT9 176 A2
Crowcombe TA4 151 A7
Frome BA11 119 E3
Horningsham BA12 144 D4
Keenthorne TA5 134 C1
Lopen TA13 185 A1
Nether Stowey TA5 134 A1
Paulton BA3, BS39 78 A4
Pill BS20 4 C4
Somerton TA11 211 C3
Stogumber TA4 150 F7
Waterlake DT10 190 B4
Waterlake Rd TA20 198 C8
Waterlands La TA18 224 C8
Waterleaze TA2 213 D7
WATERLIP 142 A7
Waterlip BA4 141 F7
Waterloo
Frome BA11 119 F5
Puriton TA7 136 C4
Waterloo Bldgs 4 BA2 44 B6
Waterloo Cl TA7 136 C4
Waterloo Cotts TA1 212 B4
Waterloo Cres DT9 176 A1
Waterloo Ho BS20 4 D5
Waterloo La
Stalbridge DT10 190 A1
Yeovil BA20 219 A4
Waterloo Pl 19 BS2 227 C3
Waterloo Rd
Bristol BS2 227 C3
Radstock BA3 79 A2
Shepton Mallet BA4 205 B7
Wellington TA21 222 C6
Waterloo St
Bristol BS2 227 C3
9 Bristol, Clifton BS8 11 F7
Weston-Super-Mare BS23 48 E8
Waterloo Terr DT9 225 F4
Watermans Mdw TA6 208 E6
Watermead TA20 198 D8
Watermead Cl 9 BA1 228 B2
Water Path TA21 222 A5
WATERROW 165 F4
Waters Edge BS20 2 E7
WATERSIDE 78 E1
Waterside Cres BA3 78 D1
Waterside La BA3 98 A6
Waterside Pk BS20 1 D4
Waterside Rd
Radstock BA3 78 D1
Wincanton BA9 216 C4
Waterside Way BA3 97 D8
Waters La BS27 90 C8
Watersmeet Cl
Golsoncott TA23 131 D1
Rooks Bridge BS26 87 B5
Water St
Barrington TA19 184 D5
Curry Rivel TA10 171 C4
East Harptree BS40 74 F4
East Lambrook TA13 220 C8
Hambridge TA10 171 D1
Lopen TA13 185 A1
Martock TA12 185 D5
Seavington St Michael
TA19 184 E1
Watery Combe BA3 94 E7
Watery La
Axminster EX13 198 A3
Bath BA2 44 A6
Broadway TA19 194 B8
Charlton Horethorne DT9 176 C1
Clatworthy TA4 149 C2
Coultings TA5 134 E3
Doynton BS30 12 A8
Halstock BA22 197 D3
Hewish TA18 195 D3
Watery La *continued*
Langford Budville TA4,
TA21 166 C2
Minehead TA24 200 F7
Nailsea BS48 8 B2
North Petherton TA6 153 E4
Spaxton TA5 152 F4
Stogursey TA5 134 C5
Stratton-on-t F BA3 97 A3
Williton TA4 202 E4
Winford BS40 38 B4
Wiveliscombe TA4 210 C6
Watling St BA21 218 D7
Watling Way BS11 4 D7
Watsons La TA6 209 A5
Watts Corner BA6 206 F7
Watts La TA4 151 E1
Watts's Quarry La TA10,
TA11 173 A5
Watt's Rd TA7 137 D8
Waveney Rd BS31 25 A3
Wavering Down Rise
BS26 70 A3
Waverley TA11 211 C4
Waverley Cl
Frome BA11 120 C6
Somerton TA11 211 C4
Waverley Rd
Backwell BS48 19 A7
Bridgwater TA6 208 F6
Bristol, Shirehampton BS11 4 E6
Weston-Super-Mare BS23 48 F4
Waverly Ct BS49 34 D3
Waverney Cl TA1 213 D3
Wayacre Dro BS24 66 E6
Wayclose La BA9 177 D5
Waycroft Prim Sch BS14 23 E5
Waydown Cross TA24 130 A4
Waydown La TA24 130 A4
Wayfield Gdns BA1 28 F4
WAYFORD 195 B1
Wayford Cl BS31 25 A3
Wayford Hill TA18 195 C1
Wayland Rd BS22 31 E3
Waysdown La TA4 149 D1
Wayside
Staplehay TA3 181 D8
Weston-Super-Mare BS22 31 D2
Wayside Cl BA11 120 C6
Wayside Dr BS21 6 E5
WAY WICK 32 E1
WCA Ho BS1 227 A2
WEACOMBE 132 F3
Weacombe Rd
Bridgwater TA6 209 C5
Taunton TA2 212 F7
Weal Terr BA1 27 B2
Weal The BA1 27 C2
WEARE 88 E6
Weare CE Fst Sch BS26 88 D7
Weare Ct BS1 226 A1
Weares La TA7 137 D2
WEARNE 172 A7
Weatherley Dr BS20 1 F3
Weatherly Ave BA2 44 D2
Weavers Cl
Crewkerne TA18 224 D5
Shepton Mallet BA4 205 D4
Weavers Ct BA11 119 E3
Weavers Orch BA2 62 D1
Weaver's Reach TA21 222 B7
Weavers The BA11 101 E4
Webber Rd BA4 205 D4
Webbers TA4 167 F7
Webbers CE Prim Sch
TA21 178 F5
Webbers Cl TA21 222 E4
Webbers Way TA7 136 B4
WEBBINGTON 68 E4
Webbington Rd BS26 69 C3
Webb's Cl BA5 203 D3
Webb's Hill BA11 119 B5
Webbs Mead
Beckington BA11 101 E4
Chew Stoke BS40 56 D8
Wedgwood Cl BS14 23 B5
Wedgwood Rd BA2 44 A5
Wedlakes TA23 202 C6
Wedlands TA2 212 F7
Wedlock Way BS3 11 F3
WEDMORE 108 D3
Wedmore Cl
Bath BA2 44 A3
Burnham-on-S TA8 104 C8
Frome BA11 120 C7
Weston-Super-Mare BS23 48 F2
Wedmore Fst Sch BS28 108 B4
Wedmore Pk BA2 44 A3
Wedmore Rd
Cheddar BS27 90 A7
Clevedon BS21 6 B1
Nailsea BS48 18 E8
Saltford BS31 25 D4
Weekesley La BA2 60 D1
Weekes Mdw TA21 179 E6
Week La TA22 147 D4
WEEKMOOR 167 B3
Weetwood Rd BS49 34 E5
Weind The BS22 31 D2
Weirfield Gn TA1 212 D5
Weirfield Rd TA24 201 A8
Weir Head Cotts TA22 163 D7
Weir La
Abbots Leigh BS8 10 F5
Marshfield SN14 13 F8
Pilton BA4 140 E3
Yeovilton BA22 174 A1
Weir Rd BS49 34 E3

Welbeck Rd BA21 219 E7
WELHAM 160 A2
Welland Cl TA1 213 D4
Welland Rd
Keynsham BS31 24 F4
Yeovil BA21 219 D7
Wellard Cl 1 BS22 32 B4
Well Cl
Long Ashton BS41 11 B1
Weston-Super-Mare BS24 49 B2
Winscombe BS25 70 A8
Wellesley Ct TA1 212 C1
Wellesley Gn BA10 215 E6
Wellesley Park Prim Sch
TA21 222 E4
Wellesley Pk TA21 222 D4
Wellesley St TA2 212 F6
Wellesley Way TA3 192 A7
Wellfield Hill DT6, EX13 199 B2
Well House Cl BS9 5 E3
Wellhouse La BA6 206 F4
Wellings Cl TA20 198 C8
WELLINGTON 222 D7
Wellington Bldgs BA1 27 B2
Wellington Cottage Hospl
TA21 222 D5
Wellington Ct BS21 6 C5
Wellington Flats BA20 219 A4
Wellington Hill TA21 222 F2
Wellington Jun Sch
TA21 222 E5
Wellington Mews BS11 4 D5
Wellington Monument*
TA21 180 B4
Wellington Mus TA21 222 D6
Wellington New Rd TA1 212 B3
Wellington Pl
Cheddar BS27 90 B7
Weston-Super-Mare BS23 48 D7
Wellington Rd
Bridgwater TA6 209 B5
Bristol BS2 227 C4
Taunton TA1 212 D4
Wellington Sch TA21 222 E5
Wellington Sq TA24 200 F7
Wellington Terr
18 Bristol BS8 11 F6
Clevedon BS21 6 D5
Wiveliscombe TA4 210 C5
WELLISFORD 179 D8
Well La
Banwell BS29 50 E3
Purse Caundle DT9 189 D4
Timberscombe TA24 130 A5
Yatton BS49 34 C8
WELLOW 62 D1
Wellow Brook Ct BA3 78 B3
Wellow Brook Mdw BA3 78 B2
Wellow Dr BA11 120 C7
Wellow La
Hinton Charterhouse BA2 63 D1
Norton St Philip BA2 81 D5
Peasedown St John BA2 79 C6
Shoscombe BA2 79 E6
Wellow Mead BA2 79 B7
Wellow Rd BA2 80 B8
Wellow Tyning BA2 79 D7
Well Pk BS49 34 E4
WELLS 203 E4
Wells Cathedral* BA5 203 E4
Wells Cathedral Jun Sch
BA5 203 E5
Wells Cathedral Sch
BA5 203 E5
Wells Central CE Jun Sch
BA5 203 C3
Wells Cl
Bristol BS14 23 C5
Burnham-on-S TA8 104 C7
Nailsea BS48 9 B1
Taunton TA2 213 A8
Wells & District Hospl
BA5 203 F5
Wellsea Gr BS23 49 B7
Wellshead La TA24 128 A3
Wells & Mendip Mus*
BA5 203 E4
WELLSPRINGS 212 F8
Wellsprings Prim Sch
TA2 212 F8
Wellsprings Rd TA2 212 F7
Wells Rd
Bath BA2 228 B1
Bristol BS14 23 C7
Chilcompton BA3 96 F4
Clevedon BS21 6 D1
Corston BA2 43 B7
Dundry BS40, BS41 38 F7
Glastonbury BA6 206 E6
Glastonbury, Southway BA5,
BA6 139 D4
Hallatrow BS39 77 B7
Norton St Philip BA2, BA3 81 C3
Priddy BA5 92 E2
Radstock BA3 78 E2
Rodney Stoke BS27 91 B1
Shepton Mallet BA4 204 E6
Theale BS28 109 B1
Westbury-sub-Mendip BA5 110 E6
Wookey Hole BA5 203 A7
Yarley BA5 139 C8
Wells Road Trad Est BA6 206 F7
Wells Sq BA3 78 D1
Wellsway
Bath BA2 44 F3
Keynsham BS31 24 F3
Wells Way BS28 107 F3
Wellsway Pk BA2 62 D8
Wellsway Sec Sch BS31 25 A5
Well The TA21 222 B5
Welsford Ave BA5 203 C5
Welsford Cl BA5 203 B5
Welsh Back BS1 227 A2
Welsh Ct BA5 203 B4
WELSHMILL 119 F6
Welshmill La BA11 119 F5
Welshmill Rd BA11 119 F5
WELTON 78 B2
Welton Gr BA3 78 B3
WELTON HOLLOW 78 D2
Welton Prim Sch BA3 78 C2
Welton Rd BA3 78 E2
Welton Vale BA3 78 B2
WEMBDON 208 C6
Wembdon Ct TA6 208 E4
Wembdon Hill TA6 208 C6
Wembdon Orch TA6 208 C6
Wembdon Rd TA6 208 E4
Wembdon Rise TA6 208 D5
Wembdon St George's CE
Prim Sch TA6 208 C6
Wemberham Cres BS49 17 A1
Wemberham La BS49 33 E8
Wendick Dro TA10 171 E3
Wentwood Dr BS24 49 A1
Wentworth Cl BS22 32 A3
Wentworth Rd BA21 219 E7
Werren Cl TA23 202 B7
Wesley Ave BA3 78 C1
Wesley Cl
Brean TA8 65 F3
Frome BA11 119 F4
Southwick BA14 83 E2
Taunton TA1 212 C1
Wanstrow BA4 142 F4
Wesley Ct BS23 48 F8
Wesley Dr BS22 32 A3
Wesley La BA14 83 E2
Wesley Mews BS27 90 B7
Wesley Rd BA3 78 D1
Wesley Slope 13 BA11 119 F4
Wesley Villas
Coleford BA3 116 F6
12 Frome BA11 119 F4
Wessex Bldgs TA11 211 B5
Wessex Bsns Ctr BS27 90 A7
Wessex Cl
Bridgwater TA6 209 C4
Chard TA20 223 C2
Street BA16 207 D6
Wessex Ct 4 DT9 225 D3
Wessex Dr DT9 187 E1
Wessex Fields BA11 119 D2
Wessex Fields Ret Pk
BA11 119 D2
Wessex Ho 10 BS2 227 C3
Wessex Pk TA11 211 B5
Wessex Rd
Stalbridge DT10 190 C4
Taunton TA1 168 E1
Weston-Super-Mare BS24 49 B2
Yeovil BA21 218 D8
Wessex Rise TA11 211 E3
Wessex Way BA9 216 B3
Westacre BA16 207 A4
Westacre Cl BS27 90 B8
Westacre Rd BS27 90 B8
WEST ANSTEY 162 C6
West Anstey School Cross
EX36 162 C5
West Approach Rd TA7 136 D4
West Ave
Bath BA2 44 C5
Highbridge TA9 104 C4
Westaway Cl BS49 34 C7
Westaway Pk BS49 34 D7
WEST BAGBOROUGH 151 F4
West Bank BA5 203 A8
Westbourne Ave
Clevedon BS21 6 B2
Keynsham BS31 24 E5
Westbourne Cl BA20 218 E5
Westbourne Cres BS21 6 B2
Westbourne Gr BA20 218 E5
Westbourne Ho BA2 228 C2
Westbourne Pl BS8 226 B3
WEST BOURTON 177 E8
West Bourton Rd SP8 177 E8
West Bower La TA5 153 C7
West Bow Ho TA6 208 E4
WEST BRADLEY 158 C7
Westbridge Pk DT9 225 B2
West Brook BA21 218 D6
Westbrook Ct BA4 141 E1
Westbrooke Ct BS1 226 A1
Westbrook Pk BA1 27 A2
Westbrook Rd
Bristol BS4 23 D8
Evercreech BA4 141 E1
Weston-Super-Mare BS22 31 D1
Westbrook Vale BA4 141 E1
WEST BUCKLAND 180 F7
West Buckland Com Prim
Sch TA21 180 F7
West Buckland Rd TA21 180 D7
Westbury
Bradford Abbas DT9 187 E1
Sherborne DT9 225 D3
Westbury Court Rd BS9 5 F7
Westbury Cres BS23 48 F2
Westbury Gdns BA22 186 C2
Westbury La BS9 5 C7
WESTBURY ON TRYM 5 F7
WESTBURY-SUB-
MENDIP 110 D6
Westbury Terr
Dunkerton BA2 61 E5
2 Sherborne DT9 225 D3
Westbury View BA2 79 E8
WEST CAMEL 174 D3
West Camel Farm BA22 174 E3
West Camel Rd BA22 174 E3
West Charlton TA11 173 E7
WEST CHINNOCK 196 B8
West Chinnock CE Prim Sch
TA18 196 B8
West Cl
Bath BA2 44 A5
Dunster TA24 201 D2
WEST COKER 197 A8
West Coker CE Prim Sch
BA22 197 A8
West Coker Rd BA20 218 E2
WESTCOMBE
Batcombe 142 B2
Somerton 172 E7
Westcombe BA8 176 E1
Westcombe Hill BA4 142 C2
Westcombe Rd
Evercreech BA4 141 F2
Westcombe BA4 142 A2
Westcombes EX13 198 B7
Westcombe Trad Est
TA19 183 E1
WEST COMPTON 204 C3
West Compton La BA4 204 E3
West Coombe
Bristol BS9 5 D6
Yeovil BA21 218 D6
West Coombe La TA4 165 D8
West Cornmoor Dro
TA9 136 D7
Westcott Cl BA11 120 C6
Westcott Cross TA23 130 D1
Westcott La TA4 148 F2
West Cotts TA24 127 A2
West Cres TA19 221 B2
West Croft
Blagdon BS40 54 E2
Clevedon BS21 6 B2
West Ct
Horrington BA5 112 F1
Portishead BS20 2 D4
Templecombe BA8 176 E1
West Dene BS9 5 E6
West Dro TA7 137 D4
West Dundry La BS41 21 E2
WEST END
Blagdon 54 E3
Chewton Mendip 93 F6
Clevedon 6 B2
Frome 119 F5
Nailsea 17 F7
Somerton 211 C3
West End
Bristol BS3 226 C1
Bristol, Kingsdown BS2 227 A4
Frome BA11 119 F5
Lower Weare BS26 88 D8
Marston Magna BA22 174 E1
Somerton TA11 211 C4
Street BA16 207 B5
Wedmore BS28 108 C3
West End Cl
Somerton TA11 211 C4
South Petherton TA13 220 B4
West End Ct
Chedzoy TA7 136 D1
South Petherton TA13 220 B4
West End Farm Cvn Pk
BS24 49 E4
Westend La BA11 143 C6
West End La BS48 18 A8
West End Trad Est BS48 8 B1
West End View
Barrington TA19 184 C5
South Petherton TA13 220 B4
West End Way TA13 220 B4
Westerkirk Gate TA2 212 C7
Westerleigh Rd
Bath BA2 45 B1
Clevedon BS21 6 B2
Westerly Ct TA19 221 B4
Western Approaches
BA22 174 A2
Western Ave BA21 218 B6
Western Ct
Clevedon BS21 6 D3
Shepton Mallet BA4 205 B6
Western Dr BS14 22 E6
Western Gate TA10 172 C7
Western La
Minehead TA24 200 F7
Ridge BS40 74 C3
Western Retreat BA5 203 B5
Western St DT9 187 E4
Western Way
Bridgwater TA6 208 F7
Winsham TA20 194 E1
Westex Ho BS23 49 B5
WESTFIELD 97 C8
Westfield
Bruton BA10 215 D5
Clevedon BS21 16 D8
Curry Rivel TA10 171 C3
Shepton Mallet BA4 205 A6
Sherborne DT9 225 B2
Westfield Ave BA21 218 E6
Westfield Cl
Backwell BS48 19 A6
Bath BA2 44 E3
Bridgwater TA6 208 E4
Burnham-on-S TA8 104 B8
Westfield Cl *continued*
Keynsham BS31 24 C5
Weston-Super-Mare BS23 48 D2
West Field Cl TA1 212 A2
Westfield Com Sch BA21 218 E6
Westfield Cres
Banwell BS29 51 A3
Yeovil BA21 218 F6
Westfield Ct TA8 104 B8
Westfield Dr
Backwell BS48 19 A6
Burnham-on-S TA8 104 B8
Westfield Est BA12 161 F2
Westfield Gr BA21 218 F6
Westfield Ho
Bath BA2 44 E3
Bridgwater TA6 208 E4
Westfield Ind & Trad Est
BA3 97 C7
Westfield Inf Com Sch
BA21 218 E6
Westfield La
Curry Rivel TA10 171 C3
Draycott BS27 90 E3
North Curry TA3 170 C3
Rodney Stoke BS27 110 C8
Street BA6, BA16 207 E2
West Field Lawn TA8 104 B8
Westfield Pk BA1 44 A7
Westfield Pk S BA1 44 A7
Westfield Pl
Bristol BS8 11 F7
Yeovil BA21 218 E6
Westfield Prim Sch BA3 97 C8
Westfield Rd
Backwell BS48 19 A6
Banwell BS29 51 A3
Burnham-on-S TA8 104 B8
Frome BA11 119 D3
Wells BA5 203 C4
Weston-Super-Mare BS23 48 D2
Yeovil BA21 218 F6
Westfields TA19 184 C5
Westfield Terr BA3 78 D1
WESTFORD 179 F7
Westford Cl TA21 222 A5
Westford Ct TA21 222 A5
Westford Dr TA21 222 A5
West Garston BS29 51 A3
Westgate BS1 226 B1
Westgate Bldgs BA1 228 B2
Westgate St
Bath BA1 228 B2
4 Taunton TA1 212 E3
Westhall Rd BA1 44 D7
WESTHAM 107 C2
WEST HARPTREE 74 E6
West Harptree Rd BS40 74 F5
WEST HATCH 182 E7
West Hatch La TA3 182 F8
Westhaven Cl BS48 19 A6
Westhaven Sch BS23 48 D2
WESTHAY 138 A5
Westhay Broad Dro TA7 137 E6
Westhay Cross EX13 198 F3
Westhay Moor Dro BA5,
BA6 138 D6
Westhay Rd BA6 138 C4
West Hay Rd BS40 35 C3
West Hendford BA20 218 F3
WEST HEWISH 33 A5
WEST HILL
Nailsea 9 A5
Portishead 2 A5
Wincanton 216 B4
West Hill
Milborne Port DT9 217 D2
Nailsea BS48 9 A5
Portishead BS20 2 B5
Wincanton BA9 216 B4
West Hill Ct BS20 2 C6
WEST HILL GARDENS 78 E1
Westhill Gdns BS20 2 C5
West Hill Gdns
Radstock BA3 78 D1
Radstock BA3 78 E1
Westhill La TA9 105 C2
West Hill Rd BA3 78 D1
Westholm Rd TA11 211 B4
West Howetown La
TA24 147 D5
WEST HUNTSPILL 136 A7
West Huntspill Com Prim
Sch TA9 104 C1
West La
Alhampton BA4 159 C5
Alweston DT9 189 A2
Barrington TA13 184 F5
Croscombe BA5 140 F8
Felton BS40 37 C8
Lynford-on-F TA11 158 D2
Sherborne DT9 188 F1
Westlake Cl TA7 155 C2
WEST LAMBROOK 184 F5
Westland Rd BA20 218 F4
West Lea Rd BA1 27 A1
West Leaze BA16 207 B6
WESTLEIGH 179 A4
WEST LEIGH 150 F1
Westleigh Gdns BA4 205 A6
West Leigh Inf Sch BS48 19 A6
Westleigh Pk BS14 23 B8
Westleigh Rd TA1 213 B3
West Links BS23 48 D2
West Links Cl BS22 31 B3
West Littleton Rd SN14 13 F8
West Lodge BA4 205 A5
WEST LUCCOMBE 124 C3
WEST LYDFORD 158 C2
WEST LYNG 170 B7
West Lynne BS27 90 B8
West Mall BS8 11 F7
Westmans Est TA8 104 C7
Westmarch Way BS22 32 A4
Westmead BA3 96 D3
Westmead Gdns BA1 27 A2
West Mendip Com Hospl
BA6 139 D3
Westmere Cres TA8 104 C8
West Mill La
Marnhull DT10 190 D6
Sherborne DT9 225 C2
Westminster BA21 218 C7
Westminster Bldgs DT10 190 B4
Westminster Cotts DT10 190 B4
Westminster St BA20 219 A4
WEST MONKTON 169 C7
West Monkton CE Prim Sch
TA2 213 F8
Westmoor Dro TA10,
TA12 184 E7
Westmoor La TA10 184 D8
Westmoreland Dr BA2 228 A2
Westmoreland Rd BA2 228 A1
Westmoreland St BA2 228 A2
Westmoreland Station Rd
BA2 228 A1
WEST MUDFORD 187 C7
WEST NEWTON 169 F8
WESTON 27 B1
Weston All Saints CE Prim
Sch BA1 27 A2
WESTON BAMPFYLDE 175 B3
Weston Bsns Pk BS24 49 E5
Weston Cl
Bristol BS9 5 C7
East Chinnock BA22 196 E8
Weston Coll BS48 8 E2
Weston College BS23 48 D8
Weston Coll (Westcliff)
BS23 30 B1
Weston Ct BS24 49 B3
Weston Dro BS20 7 F8
Weston Euro Pk BS24 49 B4
Weston Express Bsns Pk
BS22 49 C6
Weston Farm La BA1 27 C2
Weston Gateway Tourist Pk
BS24 32 C1
Weston General Hospl
BS23 48 E2
Weston Hill SP8 177 D3
Westonia BS22 31 E2
Westonian Ct BS9 5 C4
Weston Ind Est BS24 49 B2
WESTON IN GORDANO 1 F1
Weston La
Bath BA1 44 C8
Christon BS26 68 C7
East Coker BA22 197 E5
Halstock DT2 196 F1
Weston Lock Ret BA2 44 C6
Weston Lodge BS23 48 D8
Weston Milton Sta BS22 49 C7
Weston Miniature Rly*
BS23 48 D5
WESTON PARK 27 C1
Weston Park Ct BA1 27 D1
Weston Park Prim Sch
BS11 4 F8
Weston Pk BA1 27 C1
Weston Pk E BA1 27 D1
Weston Pk W BA1 27 C1
Weston Rd
Bath BA1 44 D8
Brean TA8 66 A5
Congresbury BS49 34 B5
East Brent BS24, TA9 86 D6
Failand BS8 10 C3
Long Ashton BS41 20 D8
Weston Ret Pk BS23 49 A6
Weston Sixth Form Coll
BS23 48 F2
Weston St
Buckhorn Weston SP8 177 D3
East Chinnock BA22 196 E8
WESTON-SUPER-MARE 48 B7
Weston-Super-Mare Sta
BS23 48 E7
WESTON TOWN 142 E5
Weston Town BA4 141 E1
Weston Way BS24 49 F2
Weston Wlk BA11 119 C6
Weston Wood Rd BS20 2 C3
WESTONZOYLAND 154 E5
Westonzoyland Prim Sch
TA7 154 F5
Westonzoyland Pumping
Sta* TA7 154 D3
Westonzoyland Rd TA6,
TA7 209 E4
Westover
Frome BA11 119 D4
Nunney BA11 143 B7
Westover Ct BA11 119 D4
Westover Gdns BS9 5 F8
Westover Gn TA6 208 E4
Westover Green Com Sch
TA6 208 E4
Westover La
Crewkerne TA18 224 B7
Martock TA12 185 F8
Westover Rd BS9 5 F8

Westover's Cnr BS28 108 B4
Westover Trad Est TA10 171 F5
Westover View TA18 224 C7
WESTOWE 151 A3
Westowe Hill TA4 151 A3
West Par BS9 5 C7
Westpark TA21 180 D7
West Park Cl TA24 200 E7
WEST PENNARD 140 B1
West Pennard CE Prim Sch BA6 140 B1
West Pk
  Bristol BS8 226 B4
  Butleigh BA6 157 E4
  Castle Cary BA7 214 B6
  Minehead TA24 200 E7
  Yeovil BA20 218 F5
WEST PORLOCK 123 F4
WESTPORT 184 C7
Westport La TA3, TA10 184 B7
WEST QUANTOXHEAD 132 E4
West Quay TA6 208 F5
West Rd
  East Brent BS24, TA9 86 B7
  Lympsham BS24 67 B1
  Midsomer Norton BA3 78 A3
  Wiveliscombe TA4 210 B4
  Yatton BS49 34 B7
Westridge DT9 225 C3
Westridge Way TA4 167 E7
West Rocke Ave BS9 5 D6
West Rolstone Rd BS24 33 A1
West Sedgemoor Nature Reserve★ TA3 170 F3
West Sedgemoor Rd TA3 170 D3
WEST SHEPTON 205 A4
West Shepton BA4 205 A5
West Somerset Com Coll The TA24 201 B5
West Somerset Railway★ TA4 150 F7
West Somerset Rly★ TA4 151 C4
West Somerset Rural Life Mus★ TA24 124 C4
West St
  Ashcott TA7 156 B8
  Axbridge BS26 70 B2
  Bampton EX16 164 B1
  Banwell BS29 51 A3
  Banwell BS29 51 B3
  Bishops Lydeard TA4 167 E8
  Bridgwater TA6 208 E4
  Bristol BS2 227 C3
  Carhampton TA24 131 B4
  Crewkerne TA18 224 B6
  Dunster TA24 201 D1
  Hinton St George TA17 195 C7
  Ilchester BA22 173 E1
  Ilminster TA19 221 B4
  Kington Magna SP8 177 E1
  Martock TA12 185 E8
  Minehead TA24 200 E6
  Seavington St Mary TA19 184 D1
  Somerton TA11 211 D4
  South Petherton TA13 220 B4
  Stoke sub Hamdon TA14 185 E3
  Templecombe BA8 189 E8
  Watchet TA23 202 B7
  Wells BA5 203 C3
  Weston-Super-Mare BS23 48 D8
  Wiveliscombe TA4 210 C4
  Yarlington BA9 175 F7
  Yeovil BA20 218 F4
WEST STOKE 185 E4
WEST STOUGHTON 107 E6
West Terr BA2 82 C1
WEST TOWN
  Backwell 18 F5
  Baltonsborough 157 F6
  Ubley 55 B6
West Town Gr BS4 23 D8
West Town La
  Baltonsborough BA6 157 F5
  Bristol BS4, BS14 23 C8
West Town Pk BS4 23 D8
West Town Rd
  Backwell BS48 19 A5
  Bristol BS11 4 C7
West Tyning BA2 42 B1
Westview BS39 77 C5
West View
  Creech St Michael TA3 169 D5
  Long Sutton TA10 172 E4
  Milborne Port DT9 217 D3
  Queen Camel BA22 174 F4
  South Cadbury BA22 175 D4
  West Monkton TA2 169 D8
West View Cl TA7 155 B4
Westview Orch BA3 64 B5
West View Rd
  Batheaston BA1 29 A3
  Keynsham BS31 24 E5
West Villas TA4 167 F6
Westville BA21 219 C5
Westward BS41 11 B2
Westward Cl BS40 35 D2
Westward Dr BS20 4 C4
Westward Gdns BS41 11 B2
Westward Rd BS13 21 F7
Westway
  Nailsea BS48 8 E2
  Street BA16 207 B6
West Way BS21 6 C3
Westway Ctr BA11 119 F5
Westway La BA4 205 B4
West Ways BA22 196 E8
West Well La BS28 109 C1
WEST WICK 32 C1
West Wick BS24 32 C1
West Wick Rdbt BS22, BS24 50 B8
WESTWOOD 64 E3
Westwood BA2 45 E6
Westwood Ave BS39 59 C2
Westwood Cl 2 BS22 31 F2
Westwood Cotts BA8 176 E1
Westwood Dr BA11 119 C4
Westwood Dro TA11 158 C3
WEST WOODLANDS 143 F6
Westwood Rd
  Bridgwater TA6 209 D7
  Bristol BS4 23 D8
Westwoods BA1 29 B3
Westwood with Iford Prim Sch BA15 64 F3
Wetherell Pl BS8 226 B3
Wet La BS27 90 F2
Wetlands La BS20 2 C3
Wetlands & Willows Visitor Ctr★ TA3 170 D5
Wetmoor La
  Langport TA10 172 C2
  Westbury-sub-Mendip BA5 110 E1
Wexford Rd BS4 22 D8
WEYCROFT 198 B2
Weycroft Ave EX13 198 A2
Weylands BA11 119 E6
Weymont Cl TA7 155 B3
Weymouth Ct BA1 45 B8
Weymouth Rd
  Evercreech BA4 141 E1
  Frome BA11 119 E4
Weymouth St BA1 45 B8
Whaddon Hill BA10 160 C7
Wharf Cotts TA21 222 B8
Wharf Ho TA19 221 B4
Wharf La
  Ilminster TA19 221 B3
  Portbury BS20 3 B5
Wharfside BS24 66 E3
Wharnecliffe Cl BS14 23 B5
Wharnecliffe Gdns BS14 23 B5
Whatcombe Rd BA11 119 E6
Whatcombe Terr BA11 119 E6
WHATLEY
  Frome 118 D4
  Winsham 194 C1
Whatley TA10 171 F5
Whatley Cross TA20 194 C1
Whatley La
  Buckland St Mary TA20 192 D7
  Langport TA10 172 A5
  Tatworth TA20 194 C1
  Winsham TA20 199 A8
Whatley Mews TA10 171 F5
Whatley Vineyard & Herb Gdn★ BA11 118 D4
Wheatfield Dr BS22 32 A5
Wheatfield La BA3 95 A6
Wheathill Cl
  Keynsham BS31 24 D5
  Milborne Port DT9 217 D2
Wheathill La DT9 217 E3
Wheathill Way DT9 217 D2
Wheatleigh Cl TA1 212 E2
Wheatley Cres TA1 213 B5
Wheatstones 10 TA4 167 F8
WHEDDON CROSS 129 E1
Wheeler Gr BA5 203 B4
Wheelers Cl BA3 78 D2
Wheelers Dr BA3 78 C2
WHEELER'S HILL 78 C2
Wheelers Rd BA3 78 D2
Wheel House La TA20 199 B7
Wheelwright & Gypsy Mus★ BS26 68 D4
Whellers Mdw TA12 185 E7
Whetham Mill Cross DT8 199 F5
Whetham Mill La DT8 199 F6
Whetstones Almshouses TA19 183 F4
Whimbrel Ave 2 BS20 2 F6
WHIPCOTT 179 B5
Whippington Ct BS1 227 B3
Whirligg La 15 TA14 185 F4
Whirligig La TA1 212 F4
Whirligig Pl 7 TA1 212 F4
Whistley La BS40 74 F6
Whitbourne Moor BA12 144 E8
WHITBOURNE SPRINGS 144 F7
Whitbourne Springs BA12 144 F7
Whitchey Dro TA9 137 A5
WHITCHURCH 23 D4
Whitchurch District Ctr BS14 23 A5
Whitchurch La
  Bristol, Bishopsworth BS13 22 B5
  Bristol, Hartcliffe BS13 22 C5
  Bristol, Whitchurch BS14 22 C5
  Dundry BS41 22 C1
  Henstridge BA8 190 A7
  Yenston BA8 189 F8
Whitchurch Prim Sch BS14 23 C4
Whitchurch Rd BS13 22 A6
WHITCOMBE 175 D2
Whitcombe Farm La DT9 175 D2
Whitcross 10 BA22 197 F8
White Ash La TA20 193 A5
WHITE BALL 179 D6
Whitebeam Cl TA6 209 D5
Whitebrook La BA2 79 A8
Whitebrook Terr TA21 178 F5
White Cats Cotts BA8 176 E3
Whitechapel La BA11 101 C1
Whitecroft TA4 202 E4
WHITECROSS 171 E3
WHITE CROSS
  Bishop Sutton 57 E1
  Burnham-on-Sea 105 B8
  Hallatrow 76 F6
  Zeals 161 F3
White Cross
  Brent Knoll TA9 105 C8
  Exford TA24 128 B1
Whitecross Ave BS14 23 C6
White Cross Gate BS39 76 F6
Whitecross La
  Banwell BS29 51 A4
  Minehead TA24 200 E7
Whitecross Rd
  East Harptree BS40 74 F4
  Weston-Super-Mare BS23 48 E6
Whitecross Way TA24 200 E7
Whitedown Cross EX15 191 B4
WHITEFIELD 210 B8
Whitefield Cl BA1 29 B4
White field Cross EX36 162 D3
Whitefield La TA19 184 D4
Whitefield Rocks TA4 150 B1
WHITE GATE 194 B1
Whitegate Cl
  Bleadon BS24 67 B6
  Minehead TA24 201 A6
Whitegate Rd TA24 201 A6
Whitegates Gdns TA24 200 F6
WHITEHALL 180 A1
Whitehall
  Taunton TA1 212 F5
  Watchet TA23 202 B7
Whitehall Cl TA13 220 D4
Whitehall Ct TA18 224 C7
White Hart La TA21 222 D6
WHITE HILL 79 F6
White Hill
  Langport TA10 172 A7
  Shoscombe BA2 79 F6
White Hill Dro TA20 193 C5
Whitehole Hill BA3 116 E4
White Horse Dr BA11 120 C6
White Horse La BS28 138 D8
White Horse Rd BA15 64 E7
Whitehouse Ctr (PRU) BS13 22 C5
Whitehouse La
  Litton BA3 75 D3
  Wraxall BS48 9 A6
White House La
  East Huntspill TA9 136 E7
  Loxton BS26 68 A3
Whitehouse Rd BS49 34 F8
White House Rd TA5, TA6 135 D5
WHITELACKINGTON 184 C2
Whiteladies Rd BS8 226 B4
Whitelands Hill BA3 79 B3
Whiteleaze La
  Thurloxton TA2 153 C1
  West Monkton TA2 169 D8
White Lodge Pk BS20 2 D6
White Mead BA21 218 D6
Whitemill La BA11 119 C3
Whitemoor Hill TA20 194 C4
Whitemoor La TA4 150 F3
Whitemore Ct BA1 29 A4
Whiteoak Way BS48 18 D8
White Oxmead La BA2 61 E1
White Ox Mead La BA2 61 F1
White Post
  Midsomer Norton BA3 97 B6
  Twitchen EX36 145 K2
Whitepost Gate DT9 188 D6
Whites Cl TA6 208 E2
White's Dro BA5 138 F7
Whitesfield Ct BS48 8 D2
Whitesfield Rd BS48 8 D1
White's La TA4 133 A1
Whitesome's Dro BS27 109 C6
White St
  Bristol BS5 227 C4
  Creech St Michael TA3 169 E4
  Horningsham BA12 144 E4
  North Curry TA3 170 C4
WHITESTAUNTON 193 B5
Whitestaunton Cross TA20 193 B5
Whitestone Rd BA11 120 B6
Whitewall Cnr TA3 181 D2
WHITEWAY 44 A4
Whiteway TA20 193 E6
Whiteway Rd BA2 44 A3
Whitewell Pl BA11 119 E3
Whitewell Rd BA11 119 E3
Whitewells Rd BA1 28 A2
Whitewick La TA5 134 F8
Whitfield Rd TA6 209 D6
Whitford Hill
  Corfe TA3 182 A4
  Pitminster TA3 181 F5
Whitford La TA3 182 A4
Whithys The BA16 207 C7
Whiting Cl BA4 205 C4
Whiting La 1 TA6 153 E3
Whiting Rd
  Bristol BS13 22 A4
Whiting Rd *continued*
  Glastonbury BA6 206 F5
Whiting Way BA5 203 D4
Whitland Ave BS13 22 B5
Whitland Rd BS13 22 B5
WHITLEY BATTS 40 F2
Whitley La BA16 156 D7
Whitley Rd TA7, BA16 156 C8
Whitling St BS40 38 A2
Whitmead Gdns BS13 22 C4
Whitmore La TA2 212 D8
Whitmore Rd TA2 212 E8
WHITNAGE 178 C2
Whitnage La EX16 178 C2
WHITNELL 134 D2
Whitnell Cnr BA5 113 F6
Whitnell La
  Binegar BA3 114 B8
  Keenthorne TA5 134 D2
Whitney Hill TA19 193 F8
Whitson Ho 1 BS2 227 C3
Whitson St BS1 227 A4
Whitstone BA4 205 C5
Whitstone Cl BA4 205 C6
Whitstone Cnr BA4 205 D1
Whitstone Ct BA4 205 D5
Whitstone Hill BA4 204 C1
Whitstone La BA4 205 E1
Whitstone Rd BA4 205 D4
Whitstone Rise BA4 205 D4
Whitswood Steep TA24 130 D4
Whittakers Ho 6 BA4 205 B6
Whitting Rd BS23 48 E4
Whittington Dr BS22 31 D2
Whittock Rd BS14 23 D6
Whittock Sq BS14 23 D7
Whittox La BA11 119 E5
Whitwell Rd BS14 23 B8
Whitworth Rd
  Frome BA11 119 F2
  Minehead TA24 200 D7
WICK
  Burnham-on-Sea 85 E8
  Glastonbury 139 E2
  Stogursey 134 D7
Wicketsbeer Rd BA22 197 C6
Wickfield BS21 6 C1
Wickham Ct BS21 6 C3
Wickham Rise BA11 119 F6
Wickham's Cross or Beggar's Grave BA6 157 C3
Wickham Way
  East Brent TA9 86 D4
  Shepton Mallet BA4 205 A6
Wick Hill
  Charlton Horethorne DT9 176 A1
  Milborne Port DT9 217 B6
Wickhill Rd TA10 171 D5
Wick Hollow BA6 206 F5
Wick House Cl BS31 25 D3
Wick La
  Burnham-on-S TA9 85 E6
  Glastonbury BA6 139 E2
  Lympsham BS24 66 E1
  Peasedown St John BA2, BA3 60 F1
  Pensford BS39 40 D3
  Upton Cheyney BS30 26 A8
WICKLANE 61 A1
Wicklow Rd BS4 22 E8
Wick Moor Dro TA5 134 C7
Wick Rd
  Bishop Sutton BS39 57 C3
  Lympsham BS24 66 D2
  Milborne Port DT9 217 C4
  Wick St Lawrence BS22 32 B7
WICK ST LAWRENCE 32 B7
WIDCOMBE 45 C4
Widcombe BS14 23 A6
Widcombe CE Jun Sch BA2 45 B5
Widcombe Cres BA2 45 B5
Widcombe Hill BA2 45 C4
Widcombe Inf Sch BA2 45 B5
Widcombe Par BA2 228 C1
Widcombe Rise BA2 45 B5
Widcombe Terr BA2 45 B5
Wideatts Rd BS27 90 A7
Widmore Gr BS13 22 B5
WIGBOROUGH 220 F1
Wigeon Cl TA24 201 C5
Wight Row BS20 2 F6
Wigmore Gdns BS22 31 D2
Wiindsor Cres TA20 223 B3
Wilbye Gr BS4 22 D7
Wildcountry La BS48 20 E6
Wilde Cl TA8 104 C6
Wilder Ct BS2 227 B4
Wilderness Dro BA16 138 E2
Wilderness The 9 DT9 225 E4
Wilder St BS2 227 B4
Wildmoor La TA21 180 F6
Wild Oak Ho TA3 168 D1
Wild Oak La TA3 168 D1
Wilfred Rd TA1 213 A4
Wilfrid Rd BA16 207 D6
Wilkins Cl TA20 223 E4
Wilkins Rd TA6 209 D5
WILKINTHROOP 176 C2
WILLAND 191 E8
Willcocks Cl 6 TA21 222 D5
Willcox Cl BA6 206 E5
Willet Cl TA9 104 D3
Willet's La BA3 94 D6
WILLETT 150 E4
Willett Hill Cross TA4 150 D5
Willey Rd TA3 170 E6
WILLHAYNE 223 A8
William Daw Cl BS29 50 F3
William Reynolds Ho BA16 207 D7
William St
  Bath BA2 228 C3
  Taunton TA2 212 F6
Williamstowe BA2 45 C1
Willie Gill Ct TA1 212 E4
Willinton Rd BS4 22 F8
Willis Hay DT9 225 D3
Willis's La TA18 196 C4
WILLITON 202 D3
Williton Cres BS23 48 F3
Williton & District Hospl TA4 202 D3
Williton Sta TA4 202 F4
Will La TA4 151 A3
Willmott Cl BS14 22 F3
Willmotts Cl TA7 137 B2
Willoughby Cl BS13 22 B7
Willoughby Pl TA20 223 D3
Willoughby Rd TA6 208 C4
Willowbank TA24 130 B4
Willow Cl
  Bath BA2 62 E8
  Clevedon BS21 6 E3
  East Huntspill TA9 136 E7
  Langport TA10 172 A6
  Long Ashton BS41 10 F1
  Portishead BS20 2 C4
  Radstock BA3 78 E2
  Taunton TA1 213 D1
  Weston-Super-Mare, St Georges BS22 32 D2
  Weston-Super-Mare, Uphill BS23 48 E2
  Westonzoyland TA7 154 E5
  Williton TA4 202 E3
Willow Ct TA6 209 D5
Willowdown BS22 31 E4
Willow Dr
  Bleadon BS24 67 C6
  Hutton BS24 49 E2
  Shepton Mallet BA4 205 A6
  Weston-Super-Mare BS24 49 E5
Willowfalls The BA1 28 E3
Willow Gdns BS22 32 D2
Willow Gn
  Bath BA2 44 D4
  Chedzoy TA7 154 D8
Willow Gr TA23 131 E4
Willow Ho BS13 22 D4
Willow La EX15 180 F2
Willow Rd
  Street BA16 207 B3
  Yeovil BA21 218 F6
Willows The
  Brent Knoll TA9 86 A2
  Nailsea BS48 8 F3
Willow The BA3 96 F2
Willow Tree Cl BA22 174 A4
Willow Vale BA11 119 F5
Willow Way TA18 224 D7
Willow Wlk
  Bridgwater TA6 209 C4
  Keynsham BS31 24 D4
Wills Ind Est TA6 209 A4
Wills Rd TA6 208 F1
Wills Way BS4 22 D6
Willway St BS2 227 C3
WILMINGTON 43 A1
Wilmots Way BS20 4 D4
Wilsham Cross EX35 122 A5
Wilsham La EX35 122 A5
Wilson Pl BS2 227 C4
Wilsons Cl TA5 134 B2
Wilson St BS2 227 C4
WILSTOCK VILLAGE TA6 153 F5
WILTON 212 F2
Wilton Cl
  Burnham-on-S TA8 104 C8
  Street BA16 207 D5
  Taunton TA1 212 E3
Wilton Ct BS23 48 D7
Wilton Gdns BS23 48 D7
Wilton Gr TA1 212 E3
Wilton Orch
  Street BA16 207 D5
  Taunton TA1 212 E2
Wilton Rd BA21 219 E8
Wiltons BS40 35 D2
Wilton St TA1 212 E3
WILTOWN
  Curry Rivel 171 C3
  Wellington 180 F3
Wiltown TA10 171 D3
Wiltown La EX15 180 F3
Wiltshire Cl TA1 212 C2
Wiltshire Ct TA1 212 C2
Wiltshires Barton 4 BA11 119 E5
Wiltshire Way BA1 28 A2
Wilway La TA22 163 C6
Wimblestone Rd BS25 51 F2
Wimborne Cl TA1 213 D3
Wimborough La BA22 196 F6
Winash Cl BS14 23 D7
WINCANTON 216 B3
Wincanton Bsns Pk BA9 216 B3
Wincanton Cl BS48 9 B1
Wincanton Mus★ BA9 216 C4
Wincanton Prim Sch BA9 216 C3
Winchcombe Cl BS48 19 A8
Winchcombe Gr BS11 4 F5
Winchester Cotts TA19 184 E1
Winchester Gdns BA21 219 C7

Winchester Ho 2 TA1 ... 213 A4
Winchester Rd
5 Bath BA2 ... 44 D5
Burnham-on-S TA8 ... 104 C7
Winchester St TA1 ... 213 A4
Winchball Hill TA22 ... 163 B7
Windcliff Cres BS11 ... 4 E7
Wind Down Cl TA6 ... 208 C4
Windermere Ave BS23 ... 48 F4
Windermere Cl BA20 ... 218 F2
Windmill TA3 ... 170 F5
Windmill Bsns Pk BS21 ... 16 E8
Windmill Cl TA9 ... 105 B7
Windmill Cotts TA15 ... 186 C4
Windmill Cres TA7 ... 136 E3
WINDMILL HILL ... 183 B3
Windmill Hill
Hutton BS24 ... 50 A2
Wrantage TA3 ... 170 A2
Windmill Hill La
Ashill TA19 ... 183 B3
Westbury-sub-Mendip BA5 ... 110 D4
Windmill Hill Rd BA6 ... 206 E5
Windmill La
Langport TA10 ... 172 C5
Montacute TA15 ... 186 C4
West Pennard BA6 ... 140 C1
Windmill Rd
Clevedon BS21 ... 16 E8
High Ham TA10 ... 156 A1
Windmill Rise TA18 ... 224 C7
Windrush Cl BA2 ... 43 F4
Windrush Gn BS31 ... 25 A4
Windrush Rd BS31 ... 25 A4
Windsbatch Hill BA11 ... 101 C1
Windsbatch La BA11 ... 101 B1
Windsor Ave BS31 ... 24 E4
Windsor Bridge Rd BA1, BA2 ... 44 D7
Windsor Castle BA1 ... 44 D7
Windsor Cl
Burnham-on-S TA8 ... 85 B1
Clevedon BS21 ... 6 D2
Minehead TA24 ... 200 E6
Taunton TA1 ... 212 C1
Windsor Cres BA11 ... 120 A5
Windsor Ct
4 Bath BA1 ... 44 C7
13 Bristol, Clifton BS8 ... 11 F6
Windsor Dr
Bridgwater TA6 ... 209 D7
Nailsea BS48 ... 8 E2
Windsor Hill La BA4 ... 141 B8
Windsor Ho TA6 ... 209 C5
Windsor La TA14 ... 186 A4
Windsor Pl
5 Bath BA1 ... 44 C7
Bristol, Clifton BS8 ... 11 F6
Windsor Rd
Bridgwater TA6 ... 209 D7
Weston-Super-Mare BS22 ... 31 C2
Windsor Terr
Bristol, Clifton BS8 ... 11 F6
17 Henstridge BA8 ... 190 A6
Paulton BS39 ... 77 E5
Windsor Villas 3 BA1 ... 44 C7
Windway Hill TA4 ... 164 D6
Windwhistle Circ BS23 ... 48 F4
Windwhistle La
Sticklepath TA4 ... 149 F6
Weston-Super-Mare BS23 ... 48 E3
Windwhistle Prim Sch BS23 ... 48 F3
Windwhistle Rd BS23 ... 48 D3
Windy Ridge TA17 ... 195 D7
Windyridge La TA11 ... 211 B1
Wine St
Bath BA1 ... 228 C2
Bristol BS1 ... 227 A3
Frome BA11 ... 119 E4
Yeovil BA20 ... 219 B4
WINFORD ... 37 F7
Winford CE Prim Sch BS40 ... 37 F7
Winford Cl BS20 ... 2 E4
Winford Gr BS13 ... 22 A8
Winford La BS41 ... 21 C1
Winford Rd BS40 ... 38 F3
Winford Rural Workshops BA22 ... 197 A2
Winford Terr
Bridgwater TA6 ... 209 B6
Bristol BS41 ... 21 C5
Wingard Cl BS23 ... 48 D2
Wingard Ct 6 BS23 ... 48 E5
Wingate Ave BA21 ... 219 C7
WINGFIELD ... 83 C6
Wingfield CE Prim Sch BA14 ... 83 C6
Wingfield Rd DT9 ... 225 C3
Winifred Cliff Ct 1 EX16 ... 164 B1
Winifred's La BA1 ... 27 E1
Winkworth Way TA1, TA2 ... 213 A5
Winnibrook La TA24 ... 131 A5
Winnowing End BS25 ... 52 A3
Winpenny La TA2 ... 168 E8
Winsbeer La
Rockwell Green TA21 ... 222 A6
Runnington TA21 ... 179 F8
Winsbury View BA2 ... 42 B1
WINSCOMBE ... 69 F7
Winscombe Cl BS31 ... 24 D6
Winscombe Ct BA11 ... 120 B5
Winscombe Dro
Shipham BS25 ... 70 D6
Winscombe BS25 ... 70 A5
Winscombe Hill BS25 ... 69 F5
Winscombe Rd BS23 ... 49 A7
Winscombe Woodborough Prim Sch BS25 ... 70 A8
WINSFORD ... 147 C5
WINSHAM ... 194 D1
Winsham Cl BS14 ... 23 B5
Winsham Prim Sch TA20 ... 194 E1
Winslade Cl TA2 ... 213 B7
WINSLEY ... 64 D7
Winsley CE Prim Sch BA15 ... 64 E7
Winsley Hill BA3 ... 64 B6
Winsley Rd BA15 ... 64 F7
Winsors La TA24 ... 131 A5
Winstitchen Cross TA24 ... 127 C2
Winstitchen La TA24 ... 127 C2
Winston Cl TA2 ... 212 E6
Winston Dr BA21 ... 218 F8
Winstone Ct BS2 ... 226 C3
Winterfield TA18 ... 196 B5
Winterfield Pk BS39 ... 77 E4
Winterfield Rd BS39 ... 77 E5
WINTERHAY GREEN ... 221 A5
Winterhay La TA19 ... 221 A5
WINTERHEAD ... 70 D8
Winter La DT9 ... 188 C8
Winters Cross TA4 ... 165 C8
Winters Field TA1 ... 213 A5
Winters Hill La BA4 ... 204 C3
Winters La BS40 ... 36 D6
Winter's La TA4 ... 150 C3
Winters Orch TA3 ... 169 C1
Winterstoke Commercial Ctr BS23 ... 49 A6
Winterstoke Rd
Bristol BS3 ... 11 F3
Weston-Super-Mare BS23, BS24 ... 49 B4
Winterstoke Underpass BS3 ... 11 F4
WINTER WELL ... 182 C7
Winterwell La BA4 ... 141 F4
Wint Hill BS29 ... 51 B2
WINYARD'S GAP ... 196 E1
Winyards View TA18 ... 224 D4
Wireworks Est The TA6 ... 136 A2
Wirral Park Rd BA6 ... 206 C3
Wirral Park Rdbt BA6 ... 206 C3
Wishford Mews BA3 ... 78 C2
Wisley Wlk BS22 ... 49 F7
Wisteria Ave BS24 ... 49 D2
Wisteria Cl BA22 ... 218 B5
Wiston Cross EX36 ... 162 D2
Witches Wlk TA6 ... 208 E2
Witch Hazel Rd BS13 ... 22 E3
WITCOMBE ... 185 F8
Witcombe Dro TA12 ... 172 F1
Witcombe La TA12 ... 185 F8
Witham Cl TA1 ... 213 D3
WITHAM FRIARY ... 143 C3
Witham Rd BS31 ... 25 A3
Withey Cl E BS9 ... 5 F6
Withey Cl W BS9 ... 5 F5
Witheys The BS14 ... 23 C4
Withial Hill BA4 ... 158 D8
Withiel Dr TA5 ... 135 B2
WITHIEL FLOREY ... 148 E4
Withiel Hill TA24 ... 148 F6
Withies La BA3 ... 97 A8
Withies Pk BA3 ... 96 F8
Withmoor Dro TA10 ... 172 E4
Withybed La BA9 ... 177 E6
WITHYBROOK ... 115 E3
Withy Cl BS48 ... 8 F3
WITHYCOMBE ... 131 B4
Withycombe Cross TA24 ... 131 C4
Withycombe Hill TA5 ... 135 A5
Withycombe Hill Gate TA24 ... 130 F4
Withycombe La TA24 ... 131 B5
Withy Cotts BA3 ... 115 C5
WITHYDITCH ... 61 C3
Withyditch La BA2 ... 61 C4
Withy Gr TA9 ... 136 C7
Withy Grove Cl TA6 ... 209 D7
Withy Hays Rd 3 TA11 ... 173 F7
Withy La
Barton St David TA11 ... 158 A3
Clatworthy TA4 ... 149 B2
Hemyock EX15 ... 180 B1
Oakhill BA3 ... 115 C5
WITHY MILLS ... 78 A7
WITHYPOOL ... 146 C6
Withypool Cross
Hawkridge TA22 ... 146 C2
Twitchen EX36 ... 145 J4
Withypool Gdns BS14 ... 23 B5
Withy Rd TA9 ... 136 C7
Withys The BS20 ... 4 D4
Withywine La TA22 ... 164 C5
WITHYWOOD ... 22 A4
Withywood Com Sch BS13 ... 22 A5
Withywood Gdns 1 BS13 ... 21 F4
Withy Wood La BA4 ... 142 C5
Withywood Rd BS13 ... 21 F4
Witney Cl BS31 ... 25 D3
Witney La
Chard TA20 ... 223 B8
Tatworth TA20 ... 193 F1
Wittey's La TA20 ... 199 B6
WIVELISCOMBE ... 210 B4
Wiveliscombe Prim Sch TA4 ... 210 B5
Wivenhoe Ct BA11 ... 120 C6
Woburn Rd BA21 ... 219 E7
Wolfester Terr BA22 ... 174 F4
Wollens Cl BA6 ... 206 C4
Wolmer Cl TA6 ... 208 E2
Wolsey Cl BA5 ... 203 B3
Wolverlands BA22 ... 175 A6
Wolvershill Ind Units BS29 ... 50 C6
Wolvershill Pk BS29 ... 51 A3
Wolvershill Rd
Banwell BS29 ... 50 E6
Weston-Super-Mare BS24 ... 50 C8
WONDERSTONE ... 67 D6
Wonhouse Dro BS28 ... 138 B6
Woodacre BS20 ... 2 E7
Woodadvent La TA23 ... 131 E1
Woodbarton TA4 ... 166 F4
Woodbirds Hill La TA10 ... 172 C8
WOODBOROUGH ... 70 B8
Woodborough Cres BS25 ... 70 A7
Woodborough Ct BS25 ... 70 A8
Woodborough Dr BS25 ... 70 A8
Woodborough Hill Cotts BA2 ... 79 C4
Woodborough La BA3 ... 79 A4
Woodborough Rd
Radstock BA3 ... 79 A3
Winscombe BS25 ... 69 F8
Woodburn Cross EX16 ... 162 F2
Woodburn Hill EX16 ... 162 F2
Woodburn Water Cross EX16 ... 162 F1
Woodbury Ave BA5 ... 203 F5
Woodbury Cl BA5 ... 203 F5
Woodbury Rd TA6 ... 208 D4
Wood Cl BA5 ... 203 B4
Woodcliff Ave BS22 ... 31 C1
Woodcliff Rd BS22 ... 31 C1
Wood Close La TA17 ... 195 A8
Woodcock St BA7 ... 214 C5
Woodcock Way EX13 ... 198 B7
WOODCOMBE ... 200 C8
Woodcombe Brake TA24 ... 200 D7
Woodcombe Cotts TA24 ... 200 C8
Woodcombe La TA24 ... 200 C8
Woodcote BA20 ... 218 D2
Woodcroft BS39 ... 57 C3
Woodcroft Mdws TA20 ... 192 E7
Wooddene BS25 ... 70 A8
Wood Dro TA10 ... 171 E8
Wood End TA4 ... 167 D6
Wood End Wlk BS9 ... 5 C6
Wood Farm Cotts TA5 ... 134 E4
Woodfield Cl TA8 ... 104 C5
WOODFORD
Watchet ... 132 A1
Wells ... 140 A6
Woodford Cl BS48 ... 9 A1
Woodford Cotts TA4 ... 132 A1
Woodford Ct 2 BS23 ... 48 E5
Woodford La
Coxley BA5 ... 139 F6
Wells BA5 ... 203 B1
Woodford Rd BA5 ... 140 A6
Woodfords Gn BA7 ... 214 B6
WOODGATE ... 179 E2
Woodhayes BA8 ... 190 A6
Woodhayes Ct 19 BA8 ... 190 A6
Woodhayes Ho 12 BA8 ... 190 A6
Woodhayes Rd BA11 ... 120 C6
Woodhenge BA22 ... 218 B5
WOODHILL
Portishead ... 2 D7
Stoke St Gregory ... 170 F6
Woodhill BS49 ... 34 E6
Woodhill Ave BS20 ... 2 D6
Woodhill Ct BS20 ... 2 D6
Wood Hill Pk BS20 ... 2 D7
Woodhill Rd BS20 ... 2 D6
Woodhill Terr TA3 ... 170 F6
Woodhill Views BS48 ... 8 F3
Woodhouse Cross SP8 ... 177 F6
Woodhouse La
Axminster EX13 ... 198 D1
Chard TA20 ... 194 B6
Marston Magna BA22 ... 175 B1
Montacute TA15 ... 186 C3
Woodhouse Rd
Axminster EX13 ... 198 D1
Bath BA2 ... 44 A6
Woodhurst Rd BS23 ... 49 A7
Woodington Rd BS21 ... 6 C1
Wood Kilns The BS49 ... 17 A1
Wood La
Axbridge BS26 ... 70 D2
Blue Anchor TA24 ... 131 C6
Butleigh BA6 ... 157 C4
Carhampton TA24 ... 131 B4
Chapmanslade BA13 ... 121 D4
Clapton in G BS20 ... 8 E8
Crowcombe TA4 ... 151 C7
Drimpton DT8 ... 199 E7
High Ham TA10 ... 155 E1
Marnhull DT10 ... 190 F2
Moorlinch TA7 ... 155 E8
Rodney Stoke BS27 ... 91 B1
South Cheriton BA8 ... 176 C4
Stalbridge DT10 ... 190 B4
Stawell TA7 ... 137 A1
Stogumber TA4 ... 150 D7
Weston-Super-Mare BS23 ... 30 F1
Woodland Ave TA7 ... 154 F5
Woodland Cl
6 Carhampton TA24 ... 131 A5
Failand BS8 ... 10 B4
Woodland Cotts BA3 ... 64 D6
Woodland Ct BS9 ... 5 C3
Woodland Glade BS21 ... 6 E5
Woodland Gr
Bath, Bushey Norwood BA2 ... 45 E5
Bath, Weston Park BA1 ... 27 C1
Bristol BS9 ... 5 D6
Yeovil BA20 ... 219 B4
Woodland Pl BA2 ... 45 D5
Woodland Rd
Bristol BS8 ... 226 C4
Frome BA11 ... 119 F4
Nailsea BS48 ... 8 E3
Taunton TA2 ... 213 A7
Watchet TA23 ... 202 C6
Weston-Super-Mare BS23 ... 48 D4
WOODLANDS ... 183 E6
Woodlands
Axbridge BS26 ... 70 D2
Wellington TA21 ... 222 F3
Weston-Super-Mare BS23 ... 30 D1
Woodlands Bsns Pk EX16 ... 179 C3
Woodlands Ct BS11 ... 4 E5
Woodlands Dr
Ruishton TA3 ... 169 C3
Winsley BA3 ... 64 B6
Woodlands La
Holcombe BA3 ... 116 B7
Isle Abbotts TA3 ... 183 E6
Woodlands Mead DT10 ... 190 F6
Woodlands Pk BA1 ... 28 C2
Woodlands Rd
Baltonsborough BA6 ... 158 A8
Clevedon BS21 ... 6 C4
Portishead BS20 ... 2 D8
Woodlands The
Peasedown St John BA2 ... 60 F3
Shepton Mallet BA4 ... 205 D5
Woodland Way
Failand BS8 ... 10 B4
Frome BA11 ... 120 D7
Woodleaze BS9 ... 5 B6
Woodleigh Gdns BS14 ... 23 C6
Woodmarsh Cl BS14 ... 23 A4
Woodmead Gdns BS13 ... 22 C4
Woodmill BS49 ... 17 A1
Woodmill Cl DT10 ... 190 B5
Woodpecker Ave BA3 ... 97 B8
Woodpecker Dr BS22 ... 49 E8
Woodram La TA3 ... 181 E5
Wood Rd
Ashill TA19 ... 183 B4
High Ham TA10 ... 172 A8
Woodridge Mead TA4 ... 167 F8
Wood Rock EX36 ... 162 C5
Woodrush Cl TA1 ... 213 C1
Woods Batch BA16 ... 207 B6
Woods Cnr TA11 ... 173 E8
Wood's Cross EX36 ... 162 C5
Woods Hill BA3 ... 64 A6
Woodside
Bristol BS9 ... 5 D3
Midsomer Norton BA3 ... 77 E1
Woodside Ave BS24 ... 49 B2
Woodside Cl TA24 ... 200 D7
Woodside Ct BS23 ... 49 A8
Woodside Gdns BS20 ... 1 E5
Woodside Rd BS21 ... 6 E5
Woodspring Ave BS22 ... 31 B3
Woodspring Cres BS22 ... 31 A3
Woodspring Mus★ BS23 ... 48 E8
Woodspring Priory★ BS22 ... 14 C1
Woods Rd BA16 ... 207 A6
Wood St
Bath BA1 ... 228 B2
Bath, Beechen Cliff BA2 ... 228 B1
Milverton TA4 ... 166 F5
Taunton TA1 ... 212 E4
Woodstock Rd
Taunton TA1 ... 212 E5
Weston-Super-Mare BS22 ... 49 B8
Yeovil BA21 ... 219 C7
Woodview
Chilcompton BA3 ... 96 E5
2 Clevedon BS21 ... 6 F3
Paulton BS39 ... 77 C5
Wells BA5 ... 203 E5
Woodview Cl BS11 ... 4 E7
Woodview Dr BS49 ... 35 B8
Woodview Rd BS27 ... 90 C7
Woodview Terr
Nailsea BS48 ... 8 F2
Weston-Super-Mare BS23 ... 49 A6
Wood Way EX35 ... 122 D4
Woodwell Rd BS11 ... 4 E5
WOOKEY ... 139 E8
Wookey Cl BS48 ... 18 F8
WOOKEY HOLE ... 203 A7
Wookey Hole Cave★ BA5 ... 111 E5
Wookey Hole Papermill & Mus★ BA5 ... 203 A8
Wookey Hole Rd BA5 ... 203 B5
Wookey Prim Sch BA5 ... 139 D8
WOOLAVINGTON ... 136 F4
Woolavington Hill TA7 ... 136 E3
Woolavington Rd TA7 ... 136 D4
Woolavington Right Dro TA7 ... 154 D6
Woolavington Village Prim Sch TA7 ... 136 E4
Woolcott La SP8 ... 161 E1
Wooler Rd BS23 ... 48 E8
Wooley La TA19, TA20 ... 194 C6
Woolhayes La TA20 ... 223 A8
WOOLLARD ... 41 A6
Woollard La
Bristol BS14, BS39 ... 41 A7
Woollard La *continued*
Whitchurch BS14 ... 23 E1
Woollen La BA22 ... 174 F1
WOOLLEY ... 27 F5
Woolley La BA1 ... 28 A4
Woolley Rd BS14 ... 23 E5
WOOLMINSTONE ... 195 B3
Woolpit La TA24 ... 146 B7
Woolshed Cl TA24 ... 129 E1
WOOLSTON
North Cadbury ... 175 E6
Watchet ... 132 D2
Woolstone La TA5 ... 134 F7
Woolston Rd BA22 ... 175 E6
Woolvers Way BS24 ... 50 B6
WOOLVERTON ... 82 C1
Wooton Hill BA6 ... 157 C5
WOOTTON COURTENAY ... 129 F6
Wootton Cross EX13 ... 198 F1
Wootton Gr DT9 ... 225 E5
Wootton St BA6 ... 157 C6
Wootton Vineyard★ BA4 ... 140 C5
Worberry La BA3 ... 95 B7
Worcester Bldgs BA1 ... 28 B2
Worcester Cl BA2 ... 79 D7
Worcester Cres BS8 ... 226 A4
Worcester Ct BS8 ... 226 A4
Worcester Gdns BS48 ... 18 C8
Worcester Pk BA1 ... 28 B2
Worcester Pl BA1 ... 28 B2
Worcester Rd BS8 ... 226 A4
Worcester Terr
Bath BA1 ... 28 B2
Bristol BS8 ... 226 A4
Wordsworth Ave TA6 ... 208 E6
Wordsworth Cl TA8 ... 85 B2
Wordsworth Dr TA1 ... 213 B3
Wordsworth Rd
Clevedon BS21 ... 6 C2
Weston-Super-Mare BS23 ... 49 A3
World's End La BS31 ... 25 C5
WORLE ... 31 F2
WORLEBURY ... 31 A2
Worlebury CE Fst Sch BS22 ... 31 B3
Worlebury Cl BS22 ... 31 B3
Worlebury Hill Rd BS22, BS23 ... 31 B2
Worlebury Park Rd BS22 ... 31 A2
Worle Com Sch BS22 ... 31 E1
Worle Ct BS22 ... 31 F3
Worle Ind Est BS22 ... 32 B2
Worle Moor Rd BS24 ... 49 E7
Worle Sta BS22 ... 32 B1
Wormcliff La SN13 ... 29 F3
WORMINSTER ... 140 C5
Worminster Batch BA4 ... 140 D5
Worston La TA8 ... 104 C5
Worston Orch TA9 ... 104 E4
Worston Rd TA9 ... 104 E5
WORTH ... 139 D8
Worthings The BS24 ... 67 B1
Worthington Cl BS28 ... 108 D5
Worth La TA22, TA24 ... 146 C4
WORTHY ... 123 E5
Worthy Cres BS24 ... 67 B1
Worthy La
Creech St Michael TA3 ... 169 D5
Pilton BA4 ... 140 F3
5 Weston-Super-Mare BS23 ... 48 E8
West Pennard BA4, BA6 ... 140 D1
Worthy Pl 4 BS23 ... 48 E8
Worthy Toll Rd TA24 ... 123 D4
Wouldham Rd TA23 ... 202 D6
Wrangcombe La TA21 ... 180 A4
Wrangcombe Rd TA21 ... 180 A4
Wrangle Farm Gn BS21 ... 6 E2
Wrangle The 5 BS24 ... 49 F7
WRANGWAY ... 180 A4
Wrangway Rd EX15 ... 180 A3
WRANTAGE ... 170 A1
WRAXALL
Ditcheat ... 159 A7
Nailsea ... 9 C3
Wraxall CE Prim Sch BS48 ... 9 B4
Wraxall Cross Rds BA4 ... 159 A7
Wraxall Gr BS13 ... 22 A8
Wraxall Hill
Ditcheat BA4 ... 159 A8
Wraxall BS48 ... 9 C5
Wraxall Rd BA4 ... 159 B7
Wraxall Vineyard★ BA4 ... 159 A7
Wraxhill Cl BA16 ... 207 D5
Wraxhill Rd
Street BA16 ... 207 C5
Yeovil BA20 ... 218 E1
WREATH ... 194 C3
Wreath La TA20 ... 194 B3
Wren Cl
Frome BA11 ... 120 B6
Taunton TA1 ... 212 C4
Weston-Super-Mare BS22 ... 49 D8
Wren Gdns BS20 ... 3 A7
Wrenmoor Cl TA6 ... 209 C3
WRINGTON ... 35 E1
Wrington CE Prim Sch BS40 ... 35 E2
Wrington Cres BS13 ... 22 A7
Wrington Hill BS40 ... 35 F5
Wrington La BS49 ... 34 E5
Wrington Mead BS49 ... 34 E5
Wrington Rd BS49 ... 34 F4
Wristland Rd TA23 ... 202 D7
WRITHLINGTON ... 79 C2

Writhlington Ct BA3...... 79 C2
Writhlington Sch BA3.... 79 C1
Writh Rd DT9........... 189 B1
Wroughton Dr BS13...... 22 D4
Wroughton Gdns BS13 ... 22 D4
Wry La TA4............. 149 F2
Wyatt Ave BS13.......... 21 F5
Wyatt Cl BS13 .... 21 F5
Wyatt's Cl BS48........... 8 D2
Wyatts Ct TA17 .... 195 C7
Wyatts Field TA3........ 168 D1
Wyatts Way TA19 .... 183 C4
Wych Ct EX13........... 198 E3
Wych Elm Rd BA11...... 120 C6
Wydford Cl DT9......... 225 B3
Wydon La TA24 .... 124 F3
Wye Ave TA6 .... 209 D3
Wyedale Ave BS9 .... 5 C7
WYKE CHAMPFLOWER ... 215 A6
Wyke La
Wyke Champflower BA10................ 215 A5
Wyke Champflower BA10 . 215 A6
Wyke Rd
Castle Cary BA7, BA10 ... 214 E7
Wyke Champflower BA10 . 215 C6
Wylds Rd TA6........... 209 A7
Wyllie Ct BS22........... 32 A5
Wymbush Cres BS13 ..... 22 C5
Wymbush Gdns BS13..... 22 C5
Wyndam Ct BS2......... 227 B4
Wyndeats La TA5 .... 134 B5
Wyndham Cres BS20 .... 4 B4
Wyndham Ct BA21 ...... 219 C5
Wyndham Rd
Bridgwater TA6 .... 209 C6
Taunton TA2............. 212 E7
Watchet TA23............ 202 C6
Wyndham's TA4 .... 210 C4
Wyndham St BA20 ...... 219 C5
Wyndham View BA21.... 219 D5
Wyndham Way BS20 .... 2 E5
Wyndham Way Ret Pk BS20..................... 2 D5
Wynford Rd BA11 .... 120 B5
Wynnes Cl DT9 .... 225 C3
Wynnes Rise DT9 .... 225 C3
Wynsome St BA14........ 83 F3
Wynter Cl BS22.......... 32 A3
Wyrral Cl BA6 .... 206 D3
Wytch Gn EX13 .... 198 E3
Wythburn Rd BA11...... 120 C5
Wyvern Cl
Bruton BA10 .... 215 F7
Weston-Super-Mare BS23.. 48 F7
Yeovil BA20............ 218 C1
Wyvern Com Sch BS23 ... 48 F5
Wyvern Ct TA18......... 224 C6
Wyvern Mews [5] BS23 ... 48 F7
Wyvern Rd TA1 .... 168 E1
Wyville Rd BA11 .... 120 C6

Y

Yadley Cl BS25........... 70 A7
Yadley La BS25 .... 70 A6
Yadley Way BS25 .... 70 A7
Yallands Hill TA2 .... 213 E8
YALWAY 153 A1
Yanel La BS25 .... 52 B5
Yanhey Hill EX16........ 162 E4
Yanleigh Cl BS13......... 21 D6
YANLEY 21 C8
Yanley La BS41, BS13 ..... 21 C7
Yarbury Way BS24 .... 32 B1
YARCOMBE............. 192 D3
YARDE................. 132 A2
Yarde Pl TA1 .... 212 F4
Yard La
Marshwood DT6 .... 199 F3
Wiveliscombe TA4 .... 210 C6
Yardleigh Cross EX13 ... 198 D4
Yard The BA11.......... 143 C4
Yardwall Rd TA9........ 106 A3
YARFORD 168 C8
YARLEY 139 C8
Yarley Cross BA5 .... 139 C8
Yarley Field La BA5 ..... 139 B7
Yarley Hill BA5 .... 139 C7
YARLINGTON 175 F8
Yarlington Cl TA2....... 168 B4
Yarnbarton BA8......... 176 E1
Yarn Barton BA20....... 219 A4
YARROW 106 E3
Yarrow Ct BS22.......... 32 A5
Yarrow Rd TA9 .... 106 D3
YATTON................. 34 C8
Yatton Cl BS13........... 21 F8
Yatton Jun & Inf Schs BS49.................... 34 C8
Yatton Station BS49...... 17 A1
YEABRIDGE............. 220 E2
Yeabsleys Way BA7 ..... 214 C6
Yealscombe La TA24 .... 128 B2
Yeamen's Ho BS1........ 227 B1
Yeap's Dro BA5......... 139 A7
Yearmoor La TA5 .... 134 F8
Yearnor Mill La
Oare TA24 .... 122 F5
Porlock Weir TA24 .... 123 B5
Yeates Ct BS21 .... 6 E3
Yeatman Cl BS39 .... 57 D4
Yeatman Hospl DT9..... 225 D4
Yellingmill La BA4 ...... 141 C8
Yellowcombe La TA24... 147 C5
Yellow Rose Cvn Pk TA20 .... 193 D6
Yellow Way Rd
Maiden Bradley BA11, BA12................ 144 A3
Witham Friary BA11 ..... 143 F3
Yellow Wood Cross TA4 132 D2
YENSTON 189 F8
Yenston Hill BA8........ 189 F8
Yeo Bank La BS21........ 15 F1
Yeo Cl
Cheddar BS27 .... 90 B6
Weston-Super-Mare BS23.. 49 A5
Yeo Ct
Clevedon BS21............ 6 C2
Congresbury BS49........ 34 D4
Yeo La
Bridgwater TA6 .... 209 B2
Long Ashton BS41 .... 10 F1
Yeolands Dr BS21.......... 6 B1
Yeo Leisure Pk★ BA20 .. 219 C4
Yeomanry Way BA4 ..... 205 D5
Yeomans Cl BS9 .... 5 D5
Yeomanside Cl BS14 ..... 23 C5
Yeomans Lodge BA11 ... 119 C4
Yeomans Orch BS40 ..... 35 E3
Yeomead BS48............. 8 F3
Yeomeads BS41.......... 10 F1
Yeo Mill Cross EX36..... 162 C5
Yeo Moor BS21 .... 6 E2
Yeo Moor Dro BS27, BS28 .... 109 D3
Yeo Moor Inf Sch BS21..... 6 E2
Yeo Moor Jun Sch BS21.... 6 E2
Yeo Rd TA6............. 209 B2
Yeo Valley [2] BA22...... 197 F8
Yeo Valley Way BS48....... 9 B2
YEOVIL................. 218 E4
Yeovil Bsns Ctr BA21.... 219 F7
Yeovil Coll BA21 .... 219 A6
Yeovil District Hospl BA21.................. 219 B5
Yeovil Junction Sta BA22.................. 219 E1
YEOVIL MARSH 187 A6
Yeovil Marsh Pk BA21... 187 A5
Yeovil Pen Mill Sta BA21 219 E5
Yeovil Railway Ctr★ BA22.................. 219 D1
Yeovil Rd
Crewkerne TA18......... 224 E7
Halstock BA22.......... 197 D3
Montacute TA15......... 186 B3
Sherborne DT9 .... 225 C4
Tintinhull BA22 .... 186 C6
Yeovil BA22 .... 218 F1
Yeovil Small Bsns Ctr BA22.................. 218 B6
YEOVILTON............ 174 A1
Yeovil Trinity Foyer [7] BA20 .... 219 B4
Yeoward Rd BS21.......... 6 E1
Yeo Way BS21 .... 6 B2
Yet Mead La BS27....... 110 B7
Yewcroft Cl BS14 .... 23 A4
Yewtree Batch BS40 ..... 37 A1
Yew Tree Cl
Bishop Sutton BS39....... 57 D4
Lower Langford BS40 ..... 53 E6
Nailsea BS48............. 8 C1
Yeovil BA20............ 218 E2
Yew Tree Cotts BS40..... 54 E3
Yew Tree Ct BS14........ 23 B5
Yew Tree Dr BS22........ 50 B8
Yew Tree Gdns
Nailsea BS48............. 8 C1
Pill BS20 .... 4 C4
Sandford BS25........... 52 A4
Yew Tree La
Compton Martin BS40..... 74 A7
Kingston Seymour BS21 ... 16 B1
Taunton TA2............ 213 E6
Yew Tree Pk BS49 .... 34 D3
Yomede Pk BA1 .... 44 A7
Yonder Dro TA10 .... 184 E8
Yonder Hill Cotts TA20 .. 198 E7
Yonder Mead TA4....... 167 F7
York Bldgs TA6 .... 208 F5
York Cl
Axminster EX13......... 198 A1
Weston-Super-Mare BS22.. 32 A4
York Ct BS2 .... 227 B4
York Gdns BS8........... 11 F6
York Lodge [4] BA20..... 219 A5
York Pl
Bath BA1 .... 45 B8
Bristol, Brandon Hill BS1.. 226 C2
Bristol, Victoria Park BS8 . 226 B3
Yeovil BA20............ 219 A5
York Rd
Bridgwater TA6 .... 208 F2
Bristol BS2............. 227 C1
Taunton TA1............ 213 C5
York's La BA3........... 94 B6
York St
Bath BA1 .... 228 C2
Bristol BS2............. 227 B4
[5] Frome BA11 .... 119 E5
Weston-Super-Mare BS23.. 48 D7
Youngwood La BS48 ..... 18 D7

Z

ZEALS 161 F2
Zeals Rise BA12......... 161 F2
Zembard La TA20 .... 223 C4
Zeta Cl TA7............. 209 E8
Zig Zag BS21 .... 6 D4
Zion Hill
Midsomer Norton BA3..... 96 B7
Oakhill BA3 .... 115 A3
[18] Shepton Mallet BA4 ... 205 B6

Notes

Notes